Great news!
MyEconLab can help you improve your grades!

With your purchase of a new copy of this textbook, you received a Student Access Kit for **MyEconLab** for Bade/Parkin. Your Student Access Kit looks like this:

DON'T THROW IT AWAY!

What is **MyEconLab** and how will it help you? **MyEconLab** is an extensive online learning environment with a variety of tools to help raise your test scores and increase your understanding of economics. **MyEconLab** includes the following resources:

- ***Foundations eText:*** Your textbook in an online interactive format, with animated graphs and audio narrations
- ***Foundations eStudy Guide:*** The Study Guide online, integrated with the eText
- ***Foundations Interactive:*** An online tutorial that allows you to manipulate variables, draw graphs, review concepts, and self-test
- ***Diagnostic Quizzes:*** Four levels of quizzes with instant grading and feedback
- ***Office Hours:*** A link that allows you to ask the textbook authors economics-related questions
- ***MathXL for Economics:*** A basic math skills tutorial with help on creating and interpreting graphs, solving applied problems using graphs, calculating ratios and percentages, and calculating average, median and mode
- Many other text-specific Web resources!

If you did not purchase a new textbook or cannot locate the Student Access Kit and would like to access the resources in **MyEconLab** for Bade / Parkin, you may purchase a subscription online with a major credit card at www.myeconlab.com/bade.

To activate your prepaid subscription:

1. Locate the **MyEconLab** Student Access Kit that came bundled with your textbook.
2. Ask your instructor for your **MyEconLab** course ID.*
3. Go to www.myeconlab.com/bade. Follow the instructions on the screen and use the access code in your **MyEconLab** Student Access Kit to register as a new user.

* If your instructor does not provide you with a Course ID, you can still access most of the online resources listed above. Go to www.myeconlab.com/bade to register.

		NATIONAL INCOME AND PRODUCT ACCOUNTS	1968	1969	1970	1971	1972	1973	1974	1975	1976	1977
		EXPENDITURES APPROACH										
the sum of	1	Personal consumption expenditures	558.7	605.5	648.9	702.4	770.7	852.5	932.4	1,030.3	1,149.8	1,278.4
	2	Gross private domestic investment	141.2	156.4	152.4	178.2	207.6	244.5	249.4	230.2	292.0	361.3
	3	Government purchases	212.8	224.6	237.1	251.0	270.1	287.9	322.4	361.1	384.5	415.3
	4	Exports	45.3	49.3	57.0	59.3	66.2	91.8	124.3	136.3	148.9	158.8
less	5	Imports	46.6	50.5	55.8	62.3	74.2	91.2	127.5	122.7	151.1	182.4
equals	6	Gross domestic product	911.5	985.3	1,039.7	1,128.6	1,240.4	1,385.5	1,501.0	1,635.2	1,823.9	2,031.4
		INCOMES APPROACH										
the sum of	7	Compensation of employees	524.3	577.6	617.2	658.8	725.1	811.2	890.2	949.0	1,059.3	1,180.4
	8	Proprietors' income	75.4	78.9	79.8	86.1	97.7	115.2	115.5	121.6	134.3	148.3
	9	Rental income of persons	20.2	20.3	20.3	21.2	21.6	23.1	23.0	22.0	21.5	20.4
	10	Corporate profits	96.5	93.7	81.6	95.1	109.8	123.9	114.5	133.0	160.6	190.9
	11	Net interest	27.2	32.2	38.4	42.6	46.2	53.9	68.8	76.6	80.8	95.7
equals	12	National income	743.6	802.7	837.5	903.9	1,000.4	1,127.4	1,211.9	1,302.2	1,456.4	1,635.8
plus	13	Indirect business tax minus subsidies	70.8	76.7	86.7	98.1	100.4	102.5	108.6	128.8	141.3	143.3
	14	Consumption of fixed capital	90.9	99.8	109.1	118.9	130.9	142.9	164.8	190.9	209.0	231.6
	15	Net factor incomes from rest of world	6.2	6.1	6.4	7.7	8.7	12.7	15.7	13.3	17.2	20.7
equals	16	Gross domestic product	911.5	985.3	1,039.7	1,128.6	1,240.4	1,385.5	1,501.0	1,635.2	1,823.9	2,031.4
	17	Real GDP (billions of 1996 dollars)	3,466.1	3,571.4	3,578.0	3,697.7	3,898.4	4,123.4	4,099.0	4,084.4	4,311.7	4,511.8
	18	Real GDP growth (percent per year)	4.8	3.0	0.2	3.3	5.4	5.8	−0.6	−0.4	5.6	4.6
		OTHER DATA										
	19	Population (millions)	200.7	202.7	205.1	207.7	209.9	211.9	213.9	216.0	218.0	220.2
	20	Labor force (millions)	78.7	80.7	82.8	84.4	87.0	89.4	91.9	93.8	96.2	99.0
	21	Employment (millions)	75.9	77.9	78.7	79.4	82.2	85.1	86.8	85.8	88.8	92.0
	22	Unemployment (millions)	2.8	2.8	4.1	5.0	4.9	4.4	5.2	7.9	7.4	7.0
	23	Labor force participation rate (percent)	59.6	60.1	60.4	60.2	60.4	60.8	61.3	61.2	61.6	62.3
	24	Unemployment rate (percent of labor force)	3.6	3.5	4.9	5.9	5.6	4.9	5.6	8.5	7.7	7.1
	25	Real GDP per person (1996 dollars per year)	17,270	17,621	17,449	17,806	18,573	19,458	19,167	18,912	19,775	20,486
	26	Growth rate of real GDP per person (percent per year)	3.7	2.0	−1.0	2.0	4.3	4.8	−1.5	−1.3	4.6	3.6
	27	Quantity of money (M2, billions of dollars)	566.8	587.9	626.4	710.1	802.1	855.2	901.9	1,015.9	1,151.7	1,269.9
	28	GDP deflator (1996 = 100)	26.3	27.6	29.1	30.5	31.8	33.6	36.6	40.0	42.3	45.0
	29	GDP deflator inflation rate (percent per year)	4.3	4.9	5.3	5.0	4.2	5.6	9.0	9.3	5.7	6.4
	30	Consumer price index (1982–1984 = 100)	34.8	36.7	38.8	40.5	41.8	44.4	49.3	53.8	56.9	60.6
	31	CPI inflation rate (percent per year)	4.3	5.5	5.8	4.3	3.3	6.2	11.1	9.1	5.7	6.5
	32	Current account balance (billions of dollars)	0.6	0.4	2.3	−1.4	−5.8	7.1	2.0	18.1	4.3	−14.3

ESSENTIAL FOUNDATIONS *of* ECONOMICS

The challenge and thrill of learning a new subject is like the task of the explorers who first charted America's lakes and rivers. When we set out, we are unsure of the direction to take. Along the way, we often feel lost. But as we progress forward, we see ever more clearly the path we're taking, even the parts where we felt lost, and we see how our path fits into a bigger and broader picture.

Students, like explorers, benefit enormously from the experience of those who have traveled before them and from the maps that these earlier explorers have made. They also benefit from retracing their path. And they gain perspective by pausing and looking back at where they've been.

Our aims in *Essential Foundations of Economics* are to travel with you on a journey of discovery, to support you every step of the way so that you are never disoriented or lost, and to help you understand and appreciate the economic landscape that surrounds you.

The cover of this text symbolizes our aims. The lake is the terrain of economics that we're going to cover, understand, and appreciate. The rising sun and *Foundations* icon are our light sources—the clearest and most sharply focused explanations and illustrations of economic principles and ideas. The icon also emphasizes the idea of building blocks that fit one on top of another but that stand on a firm foundation. Each block is a small and easily handled object that can be understood on its own and then more keenly appreciated as part of a larger picture.

ESSENTIAL FOUNDATIONS *of* ECONOMICS

Second Edition

Robin Bade

Michael Parkin

University of Western Ontario

Boston San Francisco New York
London Toronto Sydney Tokyo Singapore Madrid
Mexico City Munich Paris Cape Town Hong Kong Montreal

Editor-in-Chief	Denise Clinton
Senior Editor	Victoria Warneck
Editorial Assistant	Catherine Bernstock
Executive Development Manager	Sylvia Mallory
Senior Project Manager	Mary Clare McEwing
Supplements Editor	Jason Miranda
Senior Administrative Assistant	Dottie Dennis
Senior Media Producer	Melissa Honig
Senior Marketing Manager	Stephen Frail
Online Marketing Specialist	Katherine Kwack
Managing Editor	James Rigney
Senior Production Supervisor	Nancy Fenton
Senior Design Manager	Regina Kolenda
Technical Illustrator	Richard Parkin
Electronic Publisher	Sally Simpson
Electronic Publishing Specialist	Laura Wiegleb
Senior Manufacturing Buyer	Hugh Crawford
Copy Editor	Barbara Willette
Indexer	Robin Bade

Library of Congress Cataloging-in-Publication Data

Bade, Robin.
Essential foundations of economics / Robin Bade, Michael Parkin.-- 2nd ed.
p. cm.
Includes bibliographical references and index.
ISBN 0-201-74880-0
1. Economics. I. Parkin, Michael, 1939– II. Title

HB171.5.B154 2004
330—dc21 2003050234

Printed in the United States of America.

1 2 3 4 5 6 7 8 9 10—WCT—07 06 05 04 03

Text and photo credits appear on page C–1, which constitutes a continuation of the copyright page.

To Erin, Tessa, Jack,
and Abby

About the Authors

Robin Bade was an undergraduate at the University of Queensland, Australia, where she earned degrees in mathematics and economics. After a spell teaching high school math and physics, she enrolled in the Ph.D. program at the Australian National University, from which she graduated in 1970. She has held faculty appointments at the University of Edinburgh in Scotland, at Bond University in Australia, and at the Universities of Manitoba, Toronto, and Western Ontario in Canada. Her research on international capital flows appears in the *International Economic Review* and the *Economic Record*.

Robin first taught the principles of economics course in 1970 and has taught it (alongside intermediate macroeconomics and international trade and finance) most years since then. She developed many of the ideas found in this text while conducting tutorials with her students at the University of Western Ontario.

Michael Parkin studied economics in England and began his university teaching career immediately after graduating with a B.A. from the University of Leicester. He learned the subject on the job at the University of Essex, England's most exciting new university of the 1960s, and at the age of 30 became one of the youngest full professors. He is a past president of the Canadian Economics Association and has served on the editorial boards of the *American Economic Review* and the *Journal of Monetary Economics*. His research on macroeconomics, monetary economics, and international economics has resulted in more than 160 publications in journals and edited volumes, including the *American Economic Review*, the *Journal of Political Economy*, the *Review of Economic Studies*, the *Journal of Monetary Economics*, and the *Journal of Money, Credit, and Banking*. He is author of the best-selling textbook, *Economics* (Addison-Wesley), now in its Sixth Edition.

Robin and Michael are a wife-and-husband duo. Their most notable joint research created the Bade-Parkin Index of central bank independence and spawned a vast amount of research on that topic. They don't claim credit for the independence of the new European Central Bank, but its constitution and the movement toward greater independence of central banks around the world were aided by their pioneering work. Their joint textbooks include *Macroeconomics* (Prentice-Hall), *Modern Macroeconomics* (Pearson Education Canada), and *Economics: Canada in the Global Environment*, the Canadian adaptation of Parkin, *Economics* (Addison-Wesley). They are dedicated to the challenge of explaining economics ever more clearly to an ever-growing body of students.

Music, the theater, art, walking on the beach, and four fast-growing grandchildren provide their relaxation and fun.

Economics

Brief Contents

Contents

PART 2 A CLOSER LOOK AT MARKETS 117

Preface

We began the preface to our first edition of *Foundations of Economics* by attempting to answer a question that we thought would be on many people's minds: *Why*? With Michael's book, *Economics*, Sixth Edition, an established, best-selling text, why on earth would we write a new book?

In retrospect, as we publish the Second Edition of *Foundations of Economics* and its companion volume, *Essential Foundations of Economics*, we find ourselves wondering more and more why we didn't write *Foundations* sooner. The response from the economics community has been tremendous. Clearly, many of you agree with our view that

- Most introductory economics textbooks try to do too much;
- Students too frequently get lost in a sea of detail; and
- Economics is a subject that can be learned only by doing it.

We have encountered this view from our own students, and we have heard it echoed by literally hundreds of colleagues across the United States and throughout the world. But creating a teaching and learning system that takes this view seriously is no easy task. *Foundations of Economics* is the result of our best effort to do so and to help students and teachers meet the challenges we all face.

LOWERING THE BARRIERS TO ENTRY

Most economics professors want to teach a serious, analytical course that explains the core principles of our subject and helps students apply these principles in their lives and jobs. We are not content to teach "dumbed-down" economics. But most students drown rather than learn to swim when thrown into the deep end of the pool. In this book and its accompanying learning tools, we make painstaking efforts to lower the barriers to learning and to reach out to the beginning student.

We focus on core concepts. We steer a steady path between an overload of detail that swamps the students and a minimalist approach that leaves the student dangling with too much unsaid. We explain tough concepts with the simplest, most straightforward language possible, and we reinforce them with clear, fully explained graphs. And we offer students a rich array of active learning tools that provide alternative ways of accessing and mastering the material.

■ FOCUS ON CORE CONCEPTS

Each chapter of *Essential Foundations* concentrates on a manageable number of main ideas (most commonly three or four) and reinforces each idea several times throughout the chapter. This patient, confidence-building approach guides students through unfamiliar terrain and helps them to focus their efforts on the most important tools and concepts of our discipline.

■ DIAGRAMS THAT TELL THE WHOLE STORY

We developed the style of our diagrams with extensive feedback from faculty focus group participants and student reviewers. All figures make consistent use of color to show the direction of shifts and contain detailed, numbered captions designed to direct students' attention step by step through the action. Because beginning students of economics are often apprehensive about working with graphs, we have made a special effort to present material in as many as three ways—with graphs, words, and tables—in the same figure. And in an innovation that seems necessary but is to our knowledge unmatched, nearly all of the information supporting a figure appears on the same page as the figure itself. No more flipping pages back and forth!

■ MANY LEARNING TOOLS FOR MANY LEARNING STYLES

Our text and its integrated print and electronic learning package recognize that students have a variety of learning styles. Some learn easily by reading the textbook; others benefit from audio and visual reinforcement. All students can profit from an active learning approach. Your students' textbooks come with access to a suite of innovative learning tools, including tutorial software, an eText featuring animated graphs with audio voiceovers, interactive quizzes, and more.

PRACTICE MAKES PERFECT

Everyone agrees that the only way to learn economics is to do it! Reading and remembering doesn't work. Active involvement, working problems, repeated self-testing: These are the ingredients to success in this subject. We have structured this text and its accompanying electronic and print tools to encourage learning by doing. The central device that accomplishes this goal is a tightly knit learning system based on our innovative *Checklist-Checkpoints* structure.

■ CHECKLISTS

Each chapter opens with a *Chapter Checklist*—a list of (usually) three or four tasks the student will be able to perform after completing the chapter. Each Checklist item corresponds to a section of the chapter that engages the student with a conversational writing style, well-chosen examples, and carefully designed illustrations.

■ CHECKPOINTS

A full-page *Checkpoint*—containing a Practice Problem with solution and a parallel Exercise—immediately follows each chapter section. The Checkpoints serve as stopping points and encourage students to review the concept and to practice using it before moving on to new ideas. Diagrams and tables bring added clarity to the Checkpoint problems and solutions.

Each Checkpoint also contains a page reference to the corresponding material in the Study Guide as well as a reference to the corresponding section of our online learning environment. We describe these learning tools more fully below.

■ CHAPTER CHECKPOINTS

At the end of each chapter, a *Chapter Checkpoint* summarizes what the student has just learned with a set of key points and a list of key terms. It also contains a further set of questions divided into three groups: exercises, critical thinking, and Web exercises.

■ CONVEYING THE EXCITEMENT

Students learn best when they can see the point of what they are studying. We show the point in a series of *Eye On...* features. Current and recent events appear in *Eye on the U.S. Economy* boxes. We place our present experience in global and historical perspectives with *Eye on the Global Economy* and *Eye on the Past* boxes. All of our *Eye On...* boxes connect theory with reality.

ORGANIZATION

Our text focuses on core topics with maximum flexibility. We cover all the standard topics of the one-term principles of economics curriculum. And we do so in the order that is increasingly finding favor in the principles course. We believe that a powerful case can be made for teaching the subject in the order in which we present it here.

We introduce and explain the core ideas about efficiency and fairness early and then cover major policy issues using only the tools of demand and supply and the ideas of marginal benefit, marginal cost, and consumer and producer surplus. Topics such as cost curves, which are more technical, are covered later.

Deciding the order in which to teach the components of microeconomics involves a tradeoff between building all the foundations and getting to policy issues early in the course. There is little disagreement that the place to begin is with production possibilities and demand and supply. We provide a carefully paced and thoroughly modern treatment of these topics.

Following the order of this text, the course quickly gets to interesting policy issues. Two further chapters lay the foundation: elasticity in Chapter 5 and a discussion of the efficiency and fairness of markets in Chapter 6. Introducing students to both efficiency and fairness (equity) issues early in the course enables a more complete and engaging discussion of topics such as taxes, price floors, price ceilings, and externalities, all of which we cover in Chapters 7 and 8. Teaching this material early in the course maintains student interest, directly serves the role of the principles course as a foundation for citizenship, and provides an immediate payoff from learning the demand-supply and related tools. Only when these policy issues have been covered do we dig more deeply behind the consumption and production decisions.

Teachers who prefer to cover policy issues later in the course can skip Chapters 6 through 8 and move straight from elasticity to the economics of the firm. The policy-related chapters can be covered at any chosen point later in the course.

Our coverage of macroeconomics is organized in two parts: Monitoring the Macroeconomy and Understanding the Macroeconomy. We provide three solid chapters that deal respectively with measuring real GDP and the standard of living (Chapter 13); measuring the CPI and the cost of living (Chapter 14); and measuring the state of the labor market and fluctuations around full employment (Chapter 15).

The chapters that explain macroeconomic performance exploit the idea that at full employment, the real economy is influenced by only real variables and the price level is proportional to the quantity of money. So Chapter 16 explains economic growth and Chapters 17–19 explain the monetary system and long-term inflation trends. Away from full employment, real variables and nominal variables interact to bring the business cycle. Chapter 20 explains the cycle using the *AS-AD* model and Chapter 21 studies the use of monetary and fiscal policy to stabilize the business cycle.

By providing a firm understanding of the forces that determine potential GDP and long-term growth, the student better appreciates the more complex interactions of real and monetary factors that bring economic fluctuations. Further, the student sees that the long-term trends in our economy play a larger role in determining our standard of living and cost of living than do the fluctuations around those trends.

Extensive reviewing suggests that most teachers agree with our view on how to organize the course. But we recognize that there is a range of opinion about sequencing, and we have structured our text so that it works equally well if other sequences are preferred. Some teachers want to follow the measurement material with aggregate supply and aggregate demand, then money and the price level and finally economic growth. Our text supports this sequence. After Chapter 14, it is possible to jump to Chapter 20 (*AS-AD* and the Business Cycle). The money chapters (17, 18, and 19) can be covered next, followed by stabilization policy (Chapter 21).

A RICH ARRAY OF SUPPORT MATERIALS FOR THE STUDENT

Essential Foundations of Economics is accompanied by the most comprehensive set of learning tools ever assembled. All the components of our package are organized by Checkpoint topic so that the student may move easily between the textbook, the Study Guide, eText, interactive tutorial, and online diagnostic quizzes, while mastering a single core concept.

The variety of tools that we provide enables students to select the path through the material that best suits their individual learning styles. The package is technology-enabled, not technology-dependent. Active learners will make extensive use of the *Foundations Interactive* tutorial and the animated graphics of eText, our online version of the textbook. Reflective learners may follow a print-only path if they prefer.

STUDY GUIDE

Tom Meyer of Patrick Henry Community College, Neil Garston and Tom Larson of California State University, Los Angeles, and Mark Rush of the University of Florida have prepared a Study Guide that is available in both print and electronic formats. The Study Guide provides an expanded Chapter Checklist that enables the student to break the learning tasks down into smaller, bite-sized pieces; self-test materials; expanded explanations of the solutions to the practice problems in the text; and additional practice problems. To ensure consistency across the entire package, the authors who wrote the questions for the Test Bank also wrote the self-test questions for the Study Guide.

FOUNDATIONS INTERACTIVE

A Java and JavaScript tutorial software program that runs in a Web browser, *Foundations Interactive* contains electronic interactive versions of most of the textbook figures. The student manipulates the figures by changing the conditions that lie behind them and observes how the economy responds to events. Quizzes that use five question types (fill-in-the-blank, true-or-false, multiple-choice, complete-the-graph, and numeric) can be worked with, or optionally without, detailed feedback. *Foundations Interactive* is available through the Foundations Web site, within the MyEconLab course, and on CD-ROM.

FOUNDATIONS WEB SITE

The Foundations Web site is a powerful and tightly integrated online learning environment. For students, the site includes

- eText—the entire textbook in PDF format with hyperlinks to all the other components of the Web site with video clips and animated figures accompanied by audio explanations prepared by us
- eStudy Guide—the entire Study Guide online
- *Foundations Interactive*—tutorials, quizzes, and graph tools that with a click of the mouse make curves shift and graphs come to life
- Diagnostic quizzes for every Checkpoint with feedback that includes hyperlinks to the e-text, e-Study Guide, and *Foundations Interactive*
- Economics in the News updated daily during the school year
- Online "Office Hours"—ask a question via email and one of us will respond within 24 hours!
- Economic links—links to sites that keep students up to date with what's going on in the economy and that enable them to work end-of-chapter Web exercises

MyEconLab COURSE

MyEconLab delivers the entire content of the Foundations Web site in a course management system. Students whose instructors use MyEconLab gain access not only to the resources of the Foundations Web site, but also to

- MathXL for Economics—a powerful tutorial to refresh students on the basics of creating and interpreting graphs, solving applied problems using graphs, calculating ratios and percentages, performing calculations, calculating average, median and mode, and finding areas.

- Research Navigator™—a one-stop research tool, with extensive help on the entire research process, including evaluating sources, drafting, and documentation, and access to a variety of scholarly journals and publications, a complete year of search for full-text articles from the *New York Times*, and a "Best of the Web" Link Library of peer-reviewed Web sites.
- eThemes of the Times—thematically related articles from the *New York Times* accompanied by critical thinking questions.

The Student Access Kit that arrives bundled with all new books walks students step-by-step through the registration process.

THE ECON TUTOR CENTER

Staffed by qualified, experienced college economics instructors, the Econ Tutor Center is open five days a week, seven hours a day. Tutors can be reached by phone, fax, and e-mail. The Econ Tutor Center hours are designed to meet your students' study schedules, with evening hours Sunday through Thursday. Students receive one-on-one tutoring on examples, related exercises, and problems. Please contact your Addison-Wesley representative for information on how to make this service available to your students.

ECONOMIST.COM EDITION

The premier online source of economic news analysis, economist.com provides your students with insight and opinion on current economic events. Through an agreement between Addison-Wesley and *The Economist*, your students can receive a low-cost subscription to this premium Web site for 3 months, including the complete text of the current issue of *The Economist* and access to *The Economist's* searchable archives. Other features include web-only weekly articles, news feeds with current world and business news, and stock market and currency data. Professors who adopt this special edition will receive a complimentary one-year subscription to economist.com.

THE WALL STREET JOURNAL EDITION

Addison-Wesley is also pleased to provide your students with access to *The Wall Street Journal*, the most respected and trusted daily source for information on business and economics. For a small additional charge, Addison-Wesley offers your students a 10-week subscription to *The Wall Street Journal* print edition and *The Wall Street Journal Interactive Edition*. Adopting professors will receive a complimentary one-year subscription of both the print and interactive versions.

FINANCIAL TIMES EDITION

Featuring international news and analysis from FT journalists in more than 50 countries, the *Financial Times* will provide your students with insights and perspectives on economic developments around the world. The *Financial Times Edition* provides your students with a 15-week subscription to one of the world's leading business publications. Adopting professors will receive a complimentary one-year subscription to the *Financial Times* as well as access to the Online Edition at FT.com.

A QUALITY-ASSURED SUPPORT SYSTEM FOR THE INSTRUCTOR

Our instructor resource tools are the most comprehensive, carefully developed, and accurate materials ever made available. *Foundations Interactive*, the Study Guide, the diagnostic quizzes on the Foundations Web site, the PowerPoint lecture notes, the Instructor's Manual, and the Test Banks, all key off the Checkpoints in the textbook. The entire package has a tight integrity. We are the authors of *Foundations Interactive*, the diagnostic quizzes, and PowerPoint notes. We have paid close attention to the design, structure, and organization of the Web site. And we have helped in the reviewing and the revising of the Study Guide, Instructor's Manual, and Test Banks to ensure that every element of the package achieves the consistency that students and teachers need.

INSTRUCTOR'S MANUAL

The Instructor's Manual contains chapter outlines and road maps, answers to in-text exercises, additional exercises with solutions, and a virtual encyclopedia of suggestions on how to enrich class presentation and use class time efficiently. The micro portion has been written by Carol Dole (State University of West Georgia) and Mark Rush, and the macro portion has been written by Richard Gosselin (Houston Community College) and Mark Rush.

THREE TEST BANKS

Three separate Test Banks are available for *Essential Foundations of Economics*, with more than 5,000 multiple-choice, true-false, numerical, fill-in-the-blank, short-answer, and essay questions. New to this edition, integrative questions build on material from more than one Checkpoint or more than one chapter. Mark Rush reviewed and edited questions from seven dedicated principles instructors for microeconomics and six for macroeconomics to form one of the most comprehensive testing systems on the market. Our questions authors on the micro side are Seemi Ahmad (Dutchess Community College), Sue Bartlett (University of South Florida), Jack Chambless (Valencia Community College), Carol Dole (State University of West Georgia), Paul Harris (Camden County Community College), William Mosher (Assumption College), and Terry Sutton (Southeast Missouri State University). Our questions authors on the macro side are Ali Ataiifar (Delaware County Community College), Diego Mendez-Carbajo (Illinois Wesleyan University), William Mosher (Assumption College), Terry Sutton (Southeast Missouri State University), Cindy Tori (Valdosta State University), and Nora Underwood (University of California-Davis). These Test Bank authors also wrote questions for the Study Guide to ensure consistency.

POWERPOINT RESOURCES

We have created the PowerPoint resources based on our 10 years of experience using this tool in our own classrooms. Every figure and table—every single one, even those used in Checkpoint questions and solutions—is included in the PowerPoint lecture notes, many of them animated so that you can build them gradually in the classroom. Key figures can be expanded to full screen size or shrunk to make space for text explanations at a single mouse click during a lecture. We have determined the optimal build sequence for the animated figures and produced them with the same degree of clarity and precision as the figures in the text.

The speaking notes sections of the PowerPoint files provide material from the Instructor's Manual on teaching tips and suggestions.

MyEconLab

Custom built for *Essential Foundations*, MyEconLab delivers all of the interactive resources available on the Foundations Web site in a comprehensive online course. With MyEconLab, instructors can customize existing content and add their own. They can manage, create, and assign tests to students, choosing from our extensive test bank, or upload tests they've written themselves. MyEconLab also includes advanced tracking features that record students' usage and performance, and a Gradebook feature to see students' test results. In addition, the instructor will find short video clips for each chapter—ideal for sparking classroom discussion or motivating lectures. Please refer to the Instructor Quick Start Guide or contact your Addison-Wesley sales representative to set up your course.

VIDEOS

In addition to the short video clips mentioned above, a comprehensive series of lecture videos accompanies the text. The videos follow the same Checklist-Checkpoint format as the book itself, and feature presentations by Robin Bade, Michael Parkin, Kaya Ford (Northern Virginia Community College), Gary Latanich (Arkansas State University), Kirk Gifford (Brigham Young University, Idaho), and Carol Dole (State University of West Georgia). The videos are available on VHS tapes and on CD-ROM.

OVERHEAD TRANSPARENCIES

Full-color overhead transparencies of *all* figures from the text will improve the clarity of your lectures. They are available to qualified adopters of the text (contact your Addison-Wesley sales representative).

INSTRUCTOR'S RESOURCE DISK WITH COMPUTERIZED TEST BANKS

This CD-ROM contains Computerized Test Bank files, Test Bank and Instructor's Manual files in Microsoft Word, and PowerPoint files. All three Test Banks are available in Test Generator Software (TestGen-EQ with QuizMaster-EQ). Fully networkable, it is available for Windows and Macintosh. TestGen-EQ's graphical interface enables instructors to view, edit, and add questions, transfer questions to tests, and print different forms of tests. Tests can be formatted by varying fonts and styles, margins, and headers and footers, as in any word-processing document. Search and sort features let the instructor quickly locate questions and arrange them in a preferred order. QuizMaster-EQ, working with your school's computer network, automatically grades the exams, stores the results on disk, and allows the instructor to view and print a variety of reports.

FASTFAX TESTING

FastFax Testing is designed for instructors who do not have access to a computer or an assistant who can help prepare tests for students. Simply choose from a large pool of questions in the print test bank and include custom headers, if you like. Fill out the test information sheet that lists instructor-selected questions and test preferences that describe how the test should be generated. You may even request multiple forms of a test and receive answer keys for each one.

Turnaround time is usually 48 hours or less and test pages can be mailed or faxed back to you by the date the test is needed. FastFax Testing is fast, reliable, and free to qualified adopters of this text.

ACKNOWLEDGMENTS

Working on a project such as this generates many debts that can never be repaid. But they can be acknowledged, and it is a special pleasure to be able to do so here and to express our heartfelt thanks to each and every one of the following long list, without whose contributions we could not have produced *Essential Foundations*.

Mark Rush is our Study Guide, Instructor's Manual, and Test Bank coordinator and manager. He assembled, polished, wrote, and rewrote these materials to ensure their close consistency with the text. He and we were in constant contact as all the elements of our text and package came together. Mark also made many valuable suggestions for improving the text and the Checkpoints. His contribution went well beyond that of a reviewer. And his effervescent sense of humor kept us all in good spirits along the way. Working closely with Mark, Tom Meyer, Neil Garston, and Tom Larson wrote content for the Study Guide and Carol Dole and Richard Gosselin wrote content for the Instructor's Manual. Seemi Ahmad, Ali Ataiifar, Sue Bartlett, Jack Chambless, Carol Dole, Paul Harris, Diego Mendez-Carbajo, William Mosher, Terry Sutton, Cindy Tori, and Nora Underwood provided questions for the Study Guide and Test Banks.

The ideas that ultimately became *Foundations* began to form over dinner at the Andover Inn in Andover, Massachusetts, with Denise Clinton and Sylvia Mallory. We gratefully acknowledge Sylvia's role not only at the birth of this project but also in managing the entire development team. Denise has been our ongoing inspiration for almost ten years. She is the most knowledgeable economics editor in the business, and we are privileged to have the benefit of her enormous experience.

The success of *Foundations* owes much to Victoria Richardson Warneck, our outstanding sponsoring editor. We are in awe of Victoria's extraordinary editorial craft. It has been, and we hope it will for many future editions remain, a joy to work with her.

Mary Clare McEwing has been our indomitable development editor, ably assisted by Dottie Dennis. We said in the preface to the first edition that Mary Clare had rounded up the best group of reviewers we'd ever worked with. We are astounded to report that for this edition, she has surpassed even the high standards she previously achieved. Mary Clare has steered the revision along through several redrafts and polishes. And she began the design process with focus groups that told us what teachers and students look for in the design of a textbook.

Gina Kolenda converted the raw ideas into this outstandingly designed text. Meredith Nightingale provided the detailed figure designs.

Jason Miranda did an incredible job as editor of our print supplements and coordinated the work of our large team of coauthors.

Michelle Neil, Executive Media Producer, and Melissa Honig, our technology gurus, have brought much to this project. Michelle spearheaded the effort to set up MyEconLab, worked creatively to improve our technology systems, and worked with our editors and us to develop our media strategy. Melissa built our Web site and worked tirelessly to help develop the engine that drives *Foundations Interactive*. They have both been sources of high energy, good sense, and level-headed advice, and have quickly found creative solutions to all our technology problems.

Nancy Fenton, our ever cheerful, never stressed production supervisor, ensured that all the elements eventually came together to bring our text out on schedule. Sally Simpson, our electronic publisher, and Laura Wiegleb, electronic production specialist, performed their magic to make our pages look beautiful. And Hugh Crawford oversaw the manufacturing process and worked with the printers and binders to produce beautiful, on-time books.

Our marketing manager, Adrienne D'Ambrosio, added enormous value, not only by being acutely intelligent and having a sensitive understanding of the market, but also by sharpening our vision of our text and package. As this book was in progress, Adrienne moved on to become an economics acquisitions editor and Stephen Frail joined us as marketing manager. Jit Teo and Catherine Bernstock stayed late many nights fielding requests from the sales force, and Kathy Kwack managed our online marketing efforts.

Our copy editor, Barbara Willette, and supplements copy editor, Sheryl Nelson, gave our work a thorough review and helpful polish.

Richard Parkin, our technical illustrator, created the figures in the text, the dynamic figures in the online version of the text, the illustrations in *Foundations Interactive*, and the animated versions of the figures in the PowerPoint presentations and contributed many ideas to improve the clarity of our illustrations. Laurel Davies created and edited the *Foundations Interactive* database and acted as its accuracy checker and reviewer.

Jeannie Gillmore, our personal assistant, worked closely with us in creating *Foundations Interactive* and the diagnostic Web quizzes and served as a meticulous accuracy checker on the text, Study Guide, and Instructor's Manual. John Graham of Rutgers University, Stephen McCafferty of Ohio State University, Harry Ellis of the University of North Texas, Paul Poast of Ohio State University, and Kate Krause of the University of New Mexico also provided careful accuracy reviews.

Jane McAndrew, economics librarian at the University of Western Ontario, went the extra mile on many occasions to help us track down the data and references we needed.

Finally, our reviewers, whose names appear on the following pages, have made an enormous contribution to this text. In the many texts that we've now written, we've never seen reviewing of the quality that we enjoyed on this project. It has been a pleasure (if at times a challenge) to respond constructively to their many excellent suggestions.

Robin Bade
Michael Parkin
London, Ontario, Canada
robin@econ100.com
michael.parkin@uwo.ca

Reviewers

Charles Aguilar, El Paso Community College
Seemi Ahmad, Dutchess Community College
William Aldridge, Shelton State Community College
Ali Ataiifar, Delaware County Community College
John Baffoe-Bonnie, Pennsylvania State University, Delaware County Campus
Kenneth Baker, University of Tennessee, Knoxville
A. Paul Ballantyne, University of Colorado
Sue Bartlett, University of South Florida
Klaus Becker, Texas Tech University
Daniel Bernhofen, Clark University
John Bethune, Barton College
David Bivin, Indiana University–Purdue University at Indianapolis
Geoffrey Black, Boise State University
Barbara Brogan, Northern Virginia Community College
Christopher Brown, Arkansas State University
Donna Bueckman, University of Tennessee, Knoxville
Nancy Burnett, University of Wisconsin at Oshkosh
Barbara Caldwell, University of South Florida
Bruce Caldwell, University of North Carolina, Greensboro
Robert Carlsson, University of South Carolina
Shawn Carter, Jacksonville State University
Jack Chambless, Valencia Community College
Joni Charles, Southwest Texas State University
Robert Cherry, Brooklyn College
Paul Cichello, Xavier University
Quentin Ciolfi, Brevard Community College
Jim Cobbe, Florida State University
John Cochran, Metropolitan State College
Ludovic Comeau, De Paul University
Carol Conrad, Cerro Coso Community College
Christopher Cornell, Fordham University
Richard Cornwall, University of California, Davis
Kevin Cotter, Wayne State University
Tom Creahan, Morehead State University
Elizabeth Crowell, University of Michigan at Dearborn
Susan Dadres, Southern Methodist University
Jeffrey Davis, ITT Technical Institute (Utah)
Dennis Debrecht, Carroll College
Al DeCooke, Broward Community College
Vince DiMartino, University of Texas at San Antonio
Carol Dole, State University of West Georgia
John Dorsey, University of Maryland, College Park
Marie Duggan, Keene State College

David Eaton, Murray State University
Harry Ellis, University of North Texas
Stephen Ellis, North Central Texas College
Carl Enomoto, New Mexico State University
Gary Ferrier, University of Arkansas
Rudy Fichtenbaum, Wright State University
Kaya Ford, Northern Virginia Community College
Robert Francis, Shoreline Community College
Roger Frantz, San Diego State University
Arthur Friedberg, Mohawk Valley Community College
Todd Gabe, University of Maine
James Gale, Michigan Technological University
Julie Gallaway, Southwest Missouri State University
Neil Garston, California State University at Los Angeles
Lisa Geib-Gunderson, University of Maryland
Linda Ghent, Eastern Illinois University
Kirk Gifford, Ricks College
Maria Giuili, Diablo Valley Community College
Mark Gius, Quinnipiac College
Randall Glover, Brevard Community College
Stephan Gohmann, University of Louisville
Richard Gosselin, Houston Community College
John Graham, Rutgers University
Warren Graham, Tulsa Community College
Jang-Ting Guo, University of California, Riverside
Dennis Hammett, University of Texas at El Paso
Leo Hardwick, Macomb Community College
Mehdi Haririan, Bloomsburg University
Paul Harris, Camden County Community College
Gus Herring, Brookhaven College
Michael Heslop, Northern Virginia Community College
Steven Hickerson, Mankato State University
Andy Howard, Rio Hondo College
Yu Hsing, Southeastern Louisiana University
Matthew Hyle, Winona State University
Harvey James, University of Hartford
Russell Janis, University of Massachusetts at Amherst
Philip N. Jefferson, Swarthmore College
Ted Joyce, City University of New York, Baruch College
Arthur Kartman, San Diego State University
Chris Kauffman, University of Tennessee
Diane Keenan, Cerritos College
Brian Kench, University of Tampa
John Keith, Utah State University
Douglas Kinnear, Colorado State University
Morris Knapp, Miami-Dade Community College
Steven Koch, Georgia Southern University
Kate Krause, University of New Mexico

Stephan Kroll, St. Lawrence University
Charles Krusekopf, Austin College
Joyce Lapping, University of Southern Maine
Tom Larson, California State University, Los Angeles
Robert Lemke, Florida International University
Tony Lima, California State University at Hayward
Kenneth Long, New River Community College
Marty Ludlum, Oklahoma City Community College
Zachary B. Machunda, Minnesota State University, Moorhead
Roger Mack, De Anza College
Michael Magura, University of Toledo
Mark Maier, Glendale College
Paula Manns, Atlantic Cape Community College
Kathryn Marshall, Ohio State University
Drew E. Mattson, Anoka-Ramsey Community College
Stephen McCafferty, Ohio State University
Thomas McCaleb, Florida State University
Diego Mendez-Carbajo, Illinois Wesleyan University
Thomas Meyer, Patrick Henry Community College
Meghan Millea, Mississippi State University
Michael Milligan, Front Range Community College
Jenny Minier, University of Miami
David Mitchell, Valdosta State University
William Mosher, Assumption College
Ronald Nate, Brigham Young University, Idaho
Michael Nelson, Texas A&M University
Charles Newton, Houston Community College Southwest
Melinda Nish, Salt Lake Community College
Lee Nordgren, Indiana University at Bloomington
William C. O'Connor, Western Montana College–University of Montana
Charles Okeke, College of Southern Nevada
Kathy Parkison, Indiana University, Kokomo
Sanjay Paul, Elizabethtown College
Ken Peterson, Furman University
Tim Petry, North Dakota State University
Charles Pflanz, Scottsdale Community College
Paul Poast, Ohio State University
Greg Pratt, Mesa Community College
Fernando Quijano, Dickinson State University
Karen Reid, University of Wisconsin, Parkside
Mary Rigdon, University of Texas, Austin
Helen Roberts, University of Illinois, Chicago
Barbara Ross-Pfeiffer, Kapiolani Community College
Jeffrey Rous, University of North Texas
Udayan Roy, Long Island University
Mark Rush, University of Florida
Joseph Santos, South Dakota State University
Roland Santos, Lakeland Community College

Ted Scheinman, Mount Hood Community College
Jerry Schwartz, Broward Community College
Sharmistha Self, College of St. Benedict/St. John's University
Gautam Sethi, Bard College
Martin Spechler, Indiana University
John Stiver, University of Connecticut
Terry Sutton, Southeast Missouri State University
Vera Tabakova, Louisiana State University
Donna Thompson, Brookdale Community College
James Thorson, Southern Connecticut State University
Marc Tomljanovich, Colgate University
Cynthia Royal Tori, Valdosta State University
Ngoc-Bich Tran, San Jacinto College South
Nora Underwood, University of California, Davis
Christian Weber, Seattle University
Jack Wegman, Santa Rosa Junior College
Jason White, Northwest Missouri State University
Benjamin Widner, Colorado State University
Barbara Wiens-Tuers, Pennsylvania State University, Altoona
William Wood, James Madison University
Ben Young, University of Missouri, Kansas City
Michael Youngblood, Rock Valley College
Joachim Zietz, Middle Tennessee State University
Armand Zottola, Central Connecticut State University

CHAPTER 1

Getting Started

CHAPTER CHECKLIST

When you have completed your study of this chapter, you will be able to

1. **Define economics, distinguish between microeconomics and macroeconomics, and explain the questions economics tries to answer.**
2. **Describe the work of economists as social scientists.**
3. **Explain five core ideas that define the economic way of thinking.**
4. **Explain why economics is worth studying.**

You are studying economics at a time of enormous change. After a decade of technological change that brought MP3 music, DVD movies, cell phones, Palm Pilots, and a host of other gadgets and toys that have transformed the way we work and play, our lives were changed by the terrorist attacks of September 11, 2001. The shock waves from that day will pulsate through our economy for many years. They have shrunk our airlines, expanded our security and defense industries, and created huge uncertainty about the future.

Outside the United States, more than 1 billion of the world's 6.3 billion people survive on $1 a day or less. Disturbed by the combination of increasing wealth and persistent poverty, some people are pointing to globalization as the source of growing economic inequality.

Your course in economics will help you to understand the powerful forces that are shaping our economic world and help you to navigate it in your everyday life and work.

1.1 DEFINITIONS AND QUESTIONS

All economic questions and problems arise because human wants exceed the resources available to satisfy them. We want good health and long lives. We want spacious and comfortable homes. We want a huge range of sports and recreational equipment from running shoes to jet skis. We want the time to enjoy our favorite sports, video games, novels, music, and movies; to travel to exotic places; and just to hang out with friends.

In the world of politics, it is easy to get carried away with the idea that we can have it all. Politicians tell us they will provide all the extra public services that we want, and at the same time, they will cut our taxes so that we can spend more on the things that we enjoy.

Despite the promises of politicians, we cannot have it all. The ability of each of us to satisfy our wants is limited by time and by the incomes we earn and the prices we pay for the things we buy. These limits mean that everyone has unsatisfied wants. Our ability as a society to satisfy our wants is limited by the productive resources that exist. These resources include the gifts of nature, our own labor and ingenuity, and tools and equipment that we have produced.

Scarcity
The condition that arises because the available resources are insufficient to satisfy wants.

Our inability to satisfy all our wants is called **scarcity**. The poor and the rich alike face scarcity. A child wants a $1.00 can of soda and two 50¢ packs of gum but has only $1.00 in his pocket. He faces scarcity. A millionaire wants to spend the weekend playing golf *and* spend the same weekend at the office attending a business strategy meeting. She faces scarcity. A society wants to provide vastly improved health care, install an Internet connection in every classroom, explore space, clean polluted lakes and rivers, and so on. Society also faces scarcity.

Faced with scarcity, we must make choices. We must *choose* among the available alternatives. The child must *choose* the soda *or* the gum. The millionaire must *choose* the golf game *or* the meeting. As a society, we must *choose* among health care, computers, space exploration, the environment, and so on.

Incentive
A reward or a penalty—a "carrot" or a "stick"—that encourages or discourages an action.

The choices we make depend on the incentives we face. An **incentive** is a reward or a penalty—a "carrot" or a "stick"—that encourages or discourages an action. If the price of gum rises and the price of soda falls, the child has an *incentive*

Even parrots face scarcity!

Not only do I want a cracker—we all want a cracker!

to choose less gum and more soda. If a profit of $10 million is at stake, the millionaire has an *incentive* to attend the meeting and skip the golf game. As computer prices tumble, school boards have a stronger *incentive* to connect more classrooms to the Internet.

Economics is the social science that studies the choices that we make as we cope with *scarcity* and the *incentives* that influence and reconcile our choices. The subject divides into two main parts:

- Microeconomics
- Macroeconomics

Economics
The social science that studies the choices that we make as we cope with *scarcity* and the *incentives* that influence and reconcile our choices.

Microeconomics

Microeconomics is the study of the choices that individuals and businesses make and the way these choices respond to incentives, interact, and are influenced by governments. Some examples of microeconomic questions are: Why are more people buying SUVs and fewer people buying minivans? How will a cut in the price of the Sony PlayStation and Microsoft Xbox affect the quantities of these items that people buy?

Microeconomics
The study of the choices that individuals and businesses make and the way these choices respond to incentives, interact, and are influenced by governments.

Macroeconomics

Macroeconomics is the study of the aggregate (or total) effects on the national economy and the global economy of the choices that individuals, businesses, and governments make. Some examples of macroeconomic questions are: Why did production and jobs expand so rapidly in the United States during the 1990s? Why has Japan been in a long period of economic stagnation? Why did the Federal Reserve cut interest rates during 2001 and keep them low through 2002?

Macroeconomics
The study of the aggregate (or total) effects on the national economy and the global economy of the choices that individuals, businesses, and governments make.

Microeconomic Questions

The economic choices that individuals, businesses, and governments make and the interactions of those choices answer the three major questions:

- What?
- How?
- For whom?

The distinction between microeconomics and macroeconomics is similar to the distinction between two views of a display of national flags in an Olympic stadium. The micro view (left) is of a single participant and the actions he or she is taking. The macro view (right) is the patterns formed by the joint actions of all the people participating in the entire display.

What?

Goods and services
The objects that people value and produce to satisfy human wants. Goods are physical objects and services are tasks performed for people.

What goods and services get produced and in what quantities? **Goods and services** are the objects that people value and produce to satisfy human wants. Goods are physical objects such as golf balls. Services are tasks performed for people such as haircuts. The nation's farms, factories, construction sites, shops, and offices produce a dazzling array of goods and services that range from necessities such as food, houses, and apartments to leisure items such ocean cruises, SUVs, and DVD players.

What determines the quantities of corn we grow, homes we build, and DVD players we produce? How do these quantities change over time? And how are they affected by the ongoing changes in technology that make an ever-wider array of goods and services available to us?

In a California vineyard a machine and a few workers do the same job as a hundred French grape pickers.

How?

How are goods and services produced? In a vineyard in France, basket-carrying workers pick the annual grape crop by hand. In a vineyard in California, a huge machine and a few workers do the same job that a hundred French grape pickers do. Look around you and you will see many examples of this phenomenon—the same job being done in different ways. In some supermarkets, checkout clerks key in prices. In others, they use a laser scanner. One farmer keeps track of his livestock feeding schedules and inventories by using paper-and-pencil records, while another uses a personal computer. GM hires workers to weld auto bodies in some of its plants and uses robots to do the job in others.

Why do we use machines in some cases and people in others? Do mechanization and technological change destroy more jobs than they create? Do they make us better off or worse off?

For Whom?

For whom are goods and services produced? The answer to this question depends on the incomes that people earn and the prices they pay for the goods and services they buy. At given prices, a person who has a high income is able to buy more goods and services than a person who has a low income. Doctors earn much higher incomes than do nurses and medical assistants. So doctors get more of the goods and services produced than nurses and medical assistants get.

You probably know about many other persistent differences in incomes. Men, on the average, earn more than women. Whites, on the average, earn more than minorities. College graduates, on the average, earn more than high school graduates. Americans, on the average, earn more than Europeans, who in turn earn more, on the average, than Asians and Africans earn. But there are some significant exceptions. The people of Japan and Hong Kong now earn an average income similar to that of Americans. And there is a lot of income inequality throughout the world.

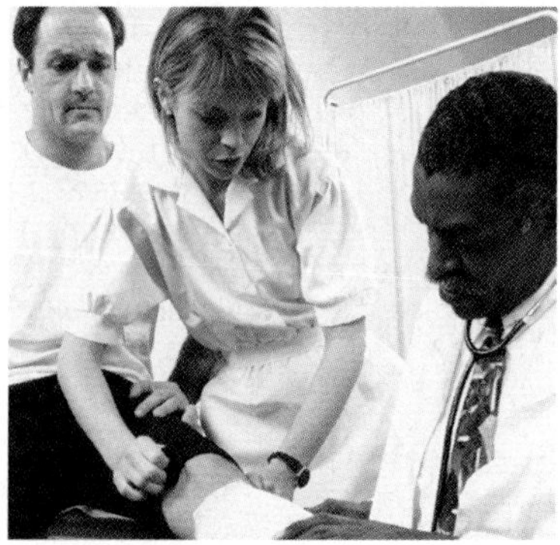

A doctor gets more of the goods and services produced than a nurse or a medical assistant gets.

What determines the incomes we earn? Why do doctors earn larger incomes than nurses? Why do white male college graduates earn more than minority female high school graduates? Why do Americans earn more, on the average, than Africans?

Microeconomics explains how the economic choices that individuals, businesses, and governments make and the interactions of those choices end up determining *what*, *how*, and *for whom* goods and services get produced.

Standard of living
The level of consumption of goods and services that people enjoy, on the average; it is measured by average income per person.

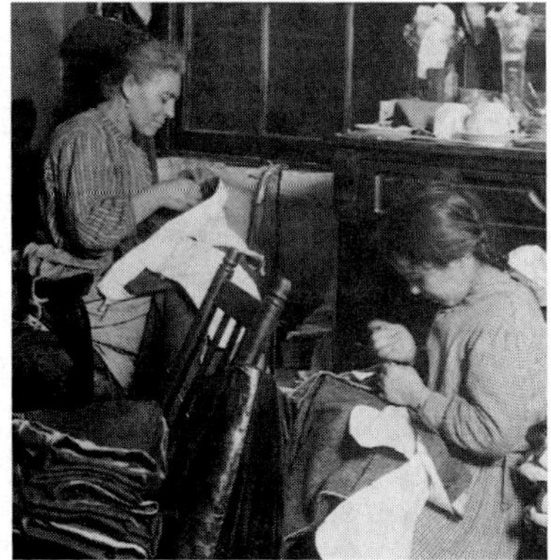

Rising living standards have transformed working in the home from drudgery to a form of leisure.

Unemployment
The state of being available and willing to work but unable to find an acceptable job.

Cost of living
The number of dollars it takes to buy the goods and services that achieve a given standard of living.

Inflation
A situation in which the cost of living is rising and the value of money is shrinking.

Deflation
A situation in which the cost of living is falling and the value of money is rising.

Macroeconomic Questions

The three big issues that macroeconomics tries to understand are

- The standard of living
- The cost of living
- Economic fluctuations—recessions and expansions

The Standard of Living

The **standard of living** is the level of consumption of goods and services that people enjoy, on the average, and is measured by average income per person. In 2003, the quantity of goods and services produced by the nation's farms, factories, shops, and offices, measured by their value in today's prices, was 20 times greater than that in 1903. But over that same 100 years, the population of the United States has increased to not quite four times its 1903 level. Because we now produce more goods and services per person, we have a much higher standard of living than our grandparents had.

For most of us, achieving a high standard of living means finding a good job. And if we lose our job, it means spending some time being unemployed while we search for the right new job. **Unemployment** is the state of being available and willing to work but unable to find an acceptable job. In the United States in 2003, employment was high and unemployment low. In January 2003, 63 percent of adults had jobs and 6 percent of people who think of themselves as being in the labor force were looking for jobs but unable to find them. Some other countries—for example, Canada, France, and Germany—experience higher unemployment rates than does the United States.

Will our standard of living continue rise? Will your world and the world of your children be more prosperous than today's? Your study of macroeconomics will help you to understand the progress that economists have made in seeking answers to these questions.

The Cost of Living

The **cost of living** is the number of dollars it takes to buy the goods and services that achieve a given standard of living. A rising cost of living, which is called **inflation**, means a shrinking value of the dollar. A falling cost of living, which is called **deflation**, means a rising value of the dollar.

Has the cost of living increased or decreased? If we look back over the past 100 years, we see that it has increased and the value of the dollar has shrunk. In your great-grandparents' youth, when the electric light bulb was the latest big thing, the average American earned a wage of $1 a day. But your great-grandparents' dime would buy what you need a dollar to buy today. So the dollar of 2003 is worth only one tenth of the dollar of 1903. If the value of the dollar continues to shrink at its average rate of loss since 1903, by the time you retire (sure, that's a long time in the future), you'll need $3.30 to buy what $1 buys today. The dollar of 2053 will be worth about one third of the value of the dollar of 2003. But during the past few years, the cost of living has increased slowly and some people even talk about the possibility of deflation. Can we avoid the extremes of deflation and rapid inflation and keep our cost of living stable? Your study of macroeconomics will answer questions like these.

Economic Fluctuations: Recessions and Expansions

Business cycle
A periodic but irregular up-and-down movement in production and jobs.

Over long periods, both the standard of living and the cost of living have increased. But these increases have not been smooth and continuous. Our economy fluctuates in a **business cycle**, a periodic but irregular up-and-down movement in production and jobs.

When production and jobs increase the economy is in a business cycle *expansion*. When production and jobs shrink, the economy is in a *recession*.

Figure 1.1 illustrates the phases and turning points of a business cycle. The economy in this figure has a recession from year 2 to year 4, then an expansion through year 8, followed by another recession through year 10. An expansion ends at a peak, and a recession ends at a trough.

The last recession in the United States occurred in 2001. The U.S. economy had an unusually long expansion that ran from the trough of the 1991 recession until early 2001.

Great Depression
A period during the 1930s in which the economy experienced its worst-ever recession.

The worst recession ever experienced occurred during the 1930s in an episode called the **Great Depression**. During this period, production shrank by more than 20 percent.

Jobs also fluctuate over the business cycle. During the Great Depression, a quarter of the U.S. labor force was unable to find jobs. During the early 1980s, a recession saw the U.S. unemployment rate climb to 10 percent of the labor force. But in the 2001 recession, the U.S. unemployment rate peaked at only 6 percent.

What kind of job market will you find when you graduate? Will you have lots of choices, or will you face a labor market with a high level of unemployment in which jobs are hard to find? Macroeconomics helps to answer these questions.

FIGURE 1.1
Business Cycle Phases and Turning Points

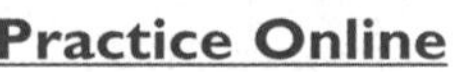

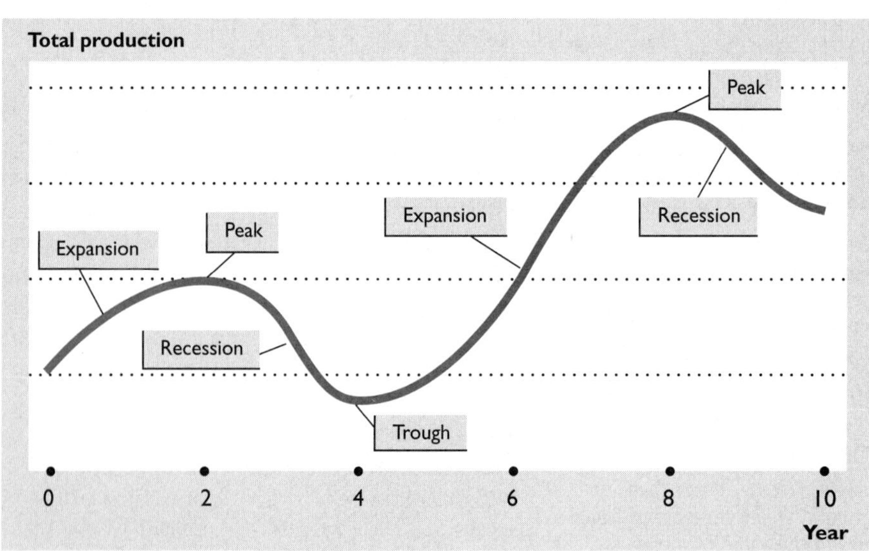

In a business cycle expansion, production increases, construction booms, and jobs are plentiful. In a recession, production and jobs shrink and unemployment lines lengthen. An expansion ends at a peak, and a recession ends at a trough.

CHECKPOINT 1.1

1 **Define economics, distinguish between microeconomics and macroeconomics, and explain the questions economics tries to answer.**

Study Guide **pp. 2–5**

Practice Online 1.1

Practice Problems 1.1

1. Economics studies choices that arise from one fact. What is that fact?
2. Provide three examples of wants in the United States today that are especially pressing but not satisfied.
3. Provide an example of an incentive that is like a carrot and one that is like a stick.
4. Match the following headlines with the What, How, and For whom questions:
   a. With more research, we will cure cancer.
   b. A good education is the right of every child.
   c. What will the government do with its budget surplus?
5. Sort the following headlines into those that deal with (i) the standard of living, (ii) the cost of living, and (iii) the business cycle:
   a. Production per worker has grown for the tenth straight year.
   b. Firms lay off more workers as orders decline.
   c. New robots boost production across a wide range of industries.
   d. Money doesn't buy what it used to.

Exercise 1.1

1. Every day, we make many choices. Why can't we avoid having to make choices?
2. Look at today's newspaper and find an example of a want that is not satisfied.
3. What is the incentive that Venus Williams and Tiger Woods face each day?
4. Check your local media for headlines that concern three microeconomic issues and three macroeconomic issues.

Solution to Practice Problems 1.1

1. The fact is scarcity—human wants exceed the resources available.

2. Security from international terrorism, cleaner air in our cities, better public schools. (You can perhaps think of some more.)

3. If your economics instructor offers you an opportunity to earn 5 bonus points by completing an assignment on time, your incentive is a carrot. If your economics instructor warns you that there is a 5-point penalty for a late assignment, your incentive is a stick.

4a. More research is a How question, and a cure for cancer is a What question.
4b. Good education is a What question, and every child is a For whom question.
4c. Who will get the budget surplus is a For whom question.

5a. Deals with the standard of living because when production per worker grows, income per person, which measures the standard of living, increases.
5b. Deals with unemployment and the business cycle because as orders decline, production decreases and more workers become unemployed.
5c. Deals with the standard of living because robots that increase production across a wide range of industries increases production per worker.
5d. Deals with the cost of living because the value of money has fallen.

1.2 ECONOMICS: A SOCIAL SCIENCE

We've defined economics as the *social science* that studies the choices that individuals and societies make as they cope with scarcity. We're now going to look at the way economists go about their work as social scientists and at some of the problems they encounter.

The major goal of economists is to discover how the economic world works. In pursuit of this goal, economists (like all scientists) distinguish between two types of statements:

- What *is*
- What *ought to be*

Statements about what *is* are called *positive* statements. They say what is currently understood about the way the world operates. A positive statement might be right or wrong. And we can test a positive statement by checking it against the data. When a chemist does an experiment in her laboratory, she is attempting to check a positive statement against the facts.

Statements about what *ought to be* are called *normative* statements. These statements depend on values and cannot be tested. When Congress debates a motion, it is ultimately trying to decide what ought to be. It is making a normative statement.

To see the distinction between positive and normative statements, consider the controversy about global warming. Some scientists believe that 200 years of industrial activity and the large quantities of coal and oil that we burn are increasing the carbon dioxide content of the earth's atmosphere with devastating consequences for life on this planet. Other scientists disagree. The statement "Our planet is warming because of an increased carbon dioxide buildup in the atmosphere" is a positive statement. It can (in principle and with sufficient data) be tested. The statement "We should cut back on our use of carbon-based fuels such as coal and oil" is a normative statement. You may agree with or disagree with this statement, but you can't test it. It is based on values. Health-care reform provides another economic example of the distinction. "Universal health care will cut the amount of work time lost to illness" is a positive statement. "Every American should have equal access to health care" is a normative statement.

The task of economic science is to discover and catalog positive statements that are consistent with what we observe in the world and that enable us to understand how the economic world works. This task is a large one that can be broken into three steps:

- Observing and measuring
- Model building
- Testing

Observing and Measuring

The first step toward understanding how the economic world works is to observe and measure it. Economists keep track of huge amounts of economic data. Some examples are the amounts and locations of natural and human resources; wages and work hours; the prices and quantities of the different goods and services produced; taxes and government spending; and the volume of international trade.

Model Building

The second step is to build models. An **economic model** is a description of some aspect of the economic world that includes only those features of the world that are needed for the purpose at hand. A model is simpler than the reality it describes. What a model includes and what it leaves out result from *assumptions* about what are essential and what are inessential details.

Economic model
A description of some aspect of the economic world that includes only those features of the world that are needed for the purpose at hand.

You can see how ignoring details is useful—even essential—to our understanding by thinking about a model that you see every day: the TV weather map. The weather map is a model that helps to predict the temperature, wind speed and direction, and precipitation over a future period. The weather map shows lines called isobars—lines of equal barometric pressure. It doesn't show the interstate highways. The reason is that we think the location of the highways has no influence on the weather but the air pressure patterns do have an influence.

An economic model is similar to a weather map. It tells us how a number of variables are determined by a number of other variables. For example, an economic model of Boston's "Big Dig"—a $15 billion project to place the city's major highways underground—might tell us the impact of the project on house prices, apartment rents, jobs, and commuting times.

Economists use a variety of methods to describe their economic models. Most commonly, the method is mathematical. And if you plan on a career in economics, you will study a good deal of math. But the basic ideas of all economic models can be described using words and pictures or diagrams. That is how economic models are described in this text.

A rare exception is a model called the Phillips Economic Hydraulic Computer, shown here. Bill Phillips, a New Zealand-born engineer-turned-economist, created this model using plastic tubes and Plexiglas tanks at the London School of Economics in 1949. The model still works today in a London museum.

The Phillips Economic Hydraulic Computer: Colored water in plastic tubes and Plexiglas tanks illustrates the effects of government actions on incomes and expenditures. This model economy is in a London museum.

Testing

The third step is testing models. A model's predictions might correspond to or conflict with the data. If there is a conflict, the model needs to be modified or rejected. A model that has repeatedly passed the test of corresponding well with real-world data is the basis of an economic theory. An **economic theory** is a generalization that summarizes what we understand about the economic choices that people make and the economic performance of industries and nations.

Economic theory
A generalization that summarizes what we understand about the economic choices that people make and the economic performance of industries and nations based on models that have repeatedly passed the test of corresponding well with real-world data.

The process of building and testing models creates theories. For example, meteorologists have a theory that if the isobars form a particular pattern at a particular time of the year (a model), then it will snow (reality). They have developed this theory by repeated observation and by carefully recording the weather that follows specific patterns of isobars.

Economics is a young science. Although philosophers have written about economic issues since the time of the ancient Greeks, it is generally agreed that as a modern social science, economics was born in 1776 with the publication of Adam Smith's *The Wealth of Nations*. Over the years since then, economists have discovered many useful theories. But in many areas, economists are still looking for answers. The gradual accumulation of economic knowledge gives most economists some faith that their methods will eventually provide usable answers.

But progress in economics comes slowly. A major reason is that it is difficult in economics to unscramble cause and effect.

Eye on the Past

Adam Smith and the Birth of Economics as a Modern Social Science

Many people had written about economics before Adam Smith, but he made economics a social science.

Born in 1723 in Kirkcaldy, a small fishing town near Edinburgh, Scotland, Smith was the only child of the town's customs officer. Lured from his professorship (he was a full professor at 28) by a wealthy Scottish duke who gave him a pension of £300 a year—ten times the average income at that time—he devoted ten years to writing his masterpiece, *An Inquiry into the Nature and Causes of the Wealth of Nations*, published in 1776.

Why, Adam Smith asked in that book, are some nations wealthy while others are poor? He was pondering these questions at the height of the Industrial Revolution. During these years, new technologies were applied to the manufacture of textiles, iron, transportation, and agriculture.

Adam Smith answered his questions by emphasizing the role of the division of labor and free markets. To illustrate his argument, he used the example of a pin factory. He guessed that one person, using the hand tools available in the 1770s, might make 20 pins a day. Yet, he observed, by using those same hand tools but breaking the process into a number of individually small operations in which people specialize—by the division of labor—ten people could make a staggering 48,000 pins a day. One draws out the wire, another straightens it, a third cuts it, a fourth points it, a fifth grinds it. Three specialists make the head, and a fourth attaches it. Finally, the pin is polished and packaged.

But a large market is needed to support the division of labor: One factory employing ten workers would need to sell more than 15 million pins a year to stay in business!

Unscrambling Cause and Effect

Are computers getting cheaper because people are buying them in greater quantities? Or are people buying computers in greater quantities because they are getting cheaper? Or is some third factor causing both the price of a computer to fall and the quantity of computers to increase? Economists want to answer questions like these, but doing so is often difficult. The central idea that economists (and all scientists) use to unscramble cause and effect is *ceteris paribus*.

Ceteris Paribus

Ceteris paribus Other things remaining the same (often abbreviated as *cet. par.*).

Ceteris paribus is a Latin term (often abbreviated as *cet. par.*) that means "other things being equal" or "if all other relevant things remain the same." Ensuring that other things are equal is crucial in many activities and all successful attempts to make scientific progress use this device. By changing one factor at a time and holding all the other relevant factors constant, we isolate the factor of interest and are able to investigate its effects in the clearest possible way.

Economic models, like the models in all other sciences, enable the influence of one factor at a time to be isolated in the imaginary world of the model. When we use a model, we are able to imagine what would happen if only one factor changed. But *ceteris paribus* can be a problem in economics when we try to test a model.

Laboratory scientists, such as chemists and physicists, perform controlled experiments by holding all the relevant factors constant except for the one under investigation. In economics, we observe the outcomes of the *simultaneous* operation of many factors. Consequently, it is hard to sort out the effects of each individual factor and to compare the effects with what a model predicts. To cope with this problem, economists take three complementary approaches:

- Natural experiments
- Statistical investigations
- Economic experiments

Natural Experiments

A natural experiment is a situation that arises in the ordinary course of economic life in which the one factor of interest is different and other things are equal (or similar). For example, Canada has higher unemployment benefits than the United States, but the people in the two nations are similar. So to study the effects of unemployment benefits on the unemployment rate, economists might compare the United States with Canada.

Statistical Investigations

Statistical investigations look for correlations. **Correlation** is the tendency for the values of two variables to move in a predictable and related way. For example, there is a correlation between the amount of cigarette smoking and the incidence of lung cancer. There is also a correlation between the size of a city's police force and the city's crime rate. Two economic examples are the correlation between household income and spending and the correlation between the price of a telephone call and the number of calls made. We must be careful to interpret a correlation correctly. Sometimes a correlation shows the strength of a *causal* influence of one variable on the other. For example, smoking causes lung cancer, and higher incomes cause higher spending. Sometimes the direction of causation is hard to determine. For example, does a larger police force *detect* more crimes or does a higher crime rate cause a larger police force to be hired? And sometimes a third factor causes both correlated variables. For example, advances in communication technology have caused both a fall in the price of phone calls and an increase in the quantity of calls. So the correlation between the price and quantity of phone calls has a deeper cause.

Correlation
The tendency for the values of two variables to move in a predictable and related way.

Sometimes, the direction of cause and effect can be determined by looking at the timing of events. But this method must be handled with care because of a problem known as the *post hoc* fallacy.

Post Hoc *Fallacy* Another Latin phrase—*post hoc ergo propter hoc*—means "after this, therefore because of this." The ***post hoc* fallacy** is the error of reasoning that a first event *causes* a second event because the first occurred before the second. Suppose you are a visitor from a far-off world. You observe lots of people shopping in early December, and then you see them opening gifts and celebrating on Christmas Day. Does the shopping cause Christmas, you wonder? After a deeper study, you discover that Christmas causes the shopping. A later event causes an earlier event.

***Post hoc* fallacy**
The error of reasoning that a first event *causes* a second event because the first occurred before the second.

Just looking at the timing of events often doesn't help to unravel cause and effect in economics. For example, the stock market booms, and some months later the economy expands—jobs and incomes grow. Did the stock market boom cause the economy to expand? Possibly, but perhaps businesses started to plan the expansion of production because a new technology that lowered costs had become available. As knowledge of the plans spread, the stock market reacted to *anticipate* the economic expansion.

To disentangle cause and effect, economists use economic models to interpret correlations. And when they can do so, economists perform experiments.

Economic Experiments

Economic experiments put real subjects in a decision-making situation and vary the influence of interest to discover how the subjects respond to one factor at a time. Most economic experiments are done using students as the subjects. But some use the actual people whose behavior economists want to understand and predict. An example of an economic experiment on actual subjects is one designed to discover the effects of changing the way welfare benefits are paid in New Jersey. Another experiment was conducted to discover how telecommunications companies would bid in different types of auctions for the airwave frequencies they use to transmit cellular telephone messages. Governments have made billions of dollars using the results of this experiment.

CHECKPOINT 1.2

Study Guide pp. 5–7

Practice Online 1.2

2 Describe the work of economists as social scientists.

Practice Problems 1.2

1. Classify each of the following statements as positive or normative:
   a. There is too much poverty in the United States.
   b. An increase in the gas tax will cut pollution.
   c. Cuts to social security in the United States have been too deep.
2. Provide two examples of the *post hoc* fallacy.

Exercises 1.2

1. Classify each of the following statements as positive or normative:
   a. More scholarships to students from poor families will reduce U.S. poverty.
   b. Free trade will harm developing countries.
   c. Cuts to public education in the United States have been too high.
2. How might an economist test one of the positive statements in exercise 1?

Solutions to Practice Problems 1.2

1a. A normative statement. It cannot be tested.
1b. A positive statement. An experiment will test it.
1c. A normative statement. It cannot be tested.

2. Examples are: New Year celebrations cause January sales. A booming stock market causes a Republican president to be elected.

1.3 THE ECONOMIC WAY OF THINKING

You've seen that to understand what, how, and for whom goods and services are produced, economists build and test models of peoples' choices and the interactions of those choices. Five core ideas summarize the economic way of thinking about people's choices, and these ideas form the basis of all microeconomic models. The ideas are

- People make *rational choices* by comparing *costs* and *benefits*.
- *Cost* is what you *must give up* to get something.
- *Benefit* is what you gain when you get something and is measured by what you *are willing to give up* to get it.
- A rational choice is made on the *margin*.
- People respond to *incentives*.

Rational Choice

The most basic idea of economics is that in making choices, people act rationally. A **rational choice** is one that uses the available resources to most effectively satisfy the wants of the person making the choice.

Rational choice
A choice that uses the available resources to most effectively satisfy the wants of the person making the choice.

Only the wants and preferences of the person making the choice are relevant to determine its rationality. For example, you might like chocolate ice cream more than vanilla ice cream, but your friend prefers vanilla. So it is rational for you to choose chocolate and for your friend to choose vanilla.

A rational choice might turn out to have been not the best choice after the event. A farmer might decide to plant wheat rather than soybeans. Then, when the crop comes to market, the price of soybeans might be much higher than the price of wheat. The farmer's choice was rational when it was made, but subsequent events made it less profitable than a different choice.

The idea of rational choice provides an answer to the first question: What goods and services will get produced and in what quantities? The answer is: Those that people rationally choose to produce!

But how do people choose rationally? Why have we chosen to build an interstate highway system and not an interstate high-speed railroad system? Why have most people chosen to use Microsoft's Windows operating system rather than another? Why do more people today choose to drink bottled water and sports energy drinks than in the past?

We make rational choices by comparing *costs* and *benefits*. But economists think about costs and benefits in a special and revealing way. Let's look at the economic concepts of cost and benefit.

Cost: What You *Must Give Up*

Whatever you choose to do, you could have done something else instead. You could have done lots of things other than what you actually did. But one of these other things is the *best* alternative given up. This alternative that you *must* give up to get something is the **opportunity cost** of the thing that you get. The thing that you could have chosen—the highest-valued alternative forgone—is the cost of the thing that you did choose.

Opportunity cost
The opportunity cost of something is the best thing you *must* give up to get it.

"There's no such thing as a free lunch" is not a clever but empty saying. It expresses the central idea of economics: that every choice involves a cost.

We use the term *opportunity cost* to emphasize that when we make a choice in the face of scarcity, we give up an opportunity to do something else. You can quit school right now, or you can remain in school. Suppose that if you quit school, the best job you can get is at McDonald's, where you can earn $10,000 during the year. The opportunity cost of remaining in school includes the things that you could have bought with this $10,000. The opportunity cost also includes the value of the leisure time that you must forgo to study.

Opportunity cost is *only* the alternative forgone. It does not include all the expenditures that you make. For example, when you contemplate whether to remain in school, your expenditure on tuition is part of the opportunity cost of remaining in school. But the cost of your school meal voucher is *not* part of the opportunity cost of remaining in school. You must buy food whether you remain in school or not.

Also, past expenditures that cannot be reversed are not part of opportunity cost. Suppose you've paid your term's tuition and it is nonrefundable. If you now contemplate quitting school, the paid tuition is irrelevant. It is called a sunk cost. A **sunk cost** is a previously incurred and irreversible cost. Whether you remain in school or quit school, having paid the tuition, the tuition is not part of the opportunity cost of remaining in school.

Sunk cost
A previously incurred and irreversible cost.

Benefit: Gain Measured by What You Are *Willing to Give Up*

Benefit
The benefit of something is the gain or pleasure that it brings.

The **benefit** of something is the gain or pleasure that it brings. Benefit is how a person *feels* about something. You might be extremely anxious to get the latest version of a video game. It will bring you a large benefit. And you might have almost no interest in the latest Yo Yo Ma cello concerto CD. It will bring you a small benefit.

Economists measure the benefit of something by what a person is *willing to give up* to get it. You can buy CDs, sodas, or magazines. The sodas or magazines that you are *willing to give up* to get a CD measure the benefit you get from a CD.

For these students, the opportunity cost of being in school is worth bearing.

For the fast-food worker, the opportunity cost of remaining in school is too high.

On the Margin

A choice on the **margin** is a choice that is made by comparing *all* the relevant alternatives systematically and incrementally. For example, you must choose how to divide the next hour between studying and e-mailing your friends. To make this choice, you must evaluate the costs and benefits of the alternative possible allocations of your next hour. You choose on the margin by considering whether you will be better off or worse off if you spend an extra few minutes studying or an extra few minutes e-mailing.

Margin
A choice on the margin is a choice that is made by comparing *all* the relevant alternatives systematically and incrementally.

The margin might involve a small change, as it does when you're deciding how to divide an hour between studying and e-mailing friends. Or it might involve a large change, as it does, for example, when you're deciding whether to remain in school for another year. Attending school for part of the year is no better (and might be worse) than not attending at all—it is not a *relevant* alternative. So you likely will want to commit the entire year to school or to something else. But you still choose on the margin. It is just that the marginal change is now a change for one year rather than a change for a few minutes.

Marginal Cost

The opportunity cost of a one-unit increase in an activity is called **marginal cost**. Marginal cost is what you *must* give up to get *one more* unit of something. Think about your marginal cost of going to the movies for a third time in a week. Your marginal cost is what you must give up to see that one additional movie. It is *not* what you give up to see all three movies. The reason is that you've already given up something for two movies, so you don't count this cost as resulting from the decision to see the third movie.

Marginal cost
The opportunity cost that arises from a one-unit increase in an activity. The marginal cost of something is what you *must* give up to get *one more* unit of it.

The marginal cost of any activity usually increases as you do more of it. You know that going to the movies decreases your study time and lowers your grade. Suppose that seeing a second movie in a week lowers your grade by five percentage points. Seeing a third movie will lower your grade by more than five additional percentage points. Your marginal cost of moviegoing is increasing.

Marginal Benefit

The benefit of a one-unit increase in an activity is called marginal benefit. **Marginal benefit** is what you gain when you get *one more* unit of something. Think about your marginal benefit from the movies. You've been to the movies twice this week, and you're contemplating going for a third time. Your marginal benefit is the benefit you will get from the one additional movie. It is *not* the benefit you get from all three movies. The reason is that you already have had the benefit from two movies, so you don't count this benefit as resulting from the third movie.

Marginal benefit
The benefit that arises from a one-unit increase in an activity. The marginal benefit of something is *measured* by what you *are willing to* give up to get *one more* unit of it.

Marginal benefit is *measured by* the most you *are willing to* give up to get *one more* unit of something. And a fundamental feature of marginal benefit is that it usually diminishes. The benefit from seeing the first movie in the week is greater than the benefit from seeing the second movie in the week. Because the marginal benefit decreases as you see more movies in the week, *you are willing to give up less* to see one more movie. You know that going to the movies decreases your study time and lowers your grade. Suppose that you were willing to give up ten percentage points to see your second movie. You won't be willing to take such a big hit on your grades to see the third movie in a week. Your marginal benefit of moviegoing is decreasing.

Making a Rational Choice

So will you go to the movies for that third time in a week? If the marginal cost is less than the marginal benefit, your rational choice will be to see the third movie. If the marginal cost exceeds the marginal benefit, your rational choice will be to spend the evening studying. We make a rational choice and use our scarce resources in the way that makes us as well off as possible when we take those actions for which marginal cost is less than or equal to marginal benefit.

Responding to Incentives

In making our choices, we respond to incentives—we respond to "carrots" and "sticks." The carrots that we face are marginal benefits. The sticks are marginal costs. A change in marginal benefit or a change in marginal cost brings a change in the incentives that we face and leads us to change our actions.

Most students believe that the payoff from studying just before a test is greater than the payoff from studying a month before a test. In other words, as a test date approaches, the marginal benefit of studying increases and the *incentive* to study becomes stronger. For this reason, we observe an increase in study time and a decrease in leisure pursuits during the last few days before a test. And the more important the test, the greater is this effect.

A change in marginal cost also changes incentives. For example, suppose that last week, you found your course work easy. You scored 100 percent on all your practice quizzes. The marginal cost of taking off an evening to enjoy a movie was low. Your grade on this week's test will not suffer. So you have an incentive to enjoy a movie feast. But this week, suddenly, the going has gotten tough. You are just not getting it. Your practice test scores are low, and you know that if you take off even one evening, your grade on next week's test will suffer. The marginal cost of seeing a movie is higher this week than last week. So you now have an incentive to give the movies a miss and study.

The central idea of economics is that we can measure changes in incentives, and these measurements enable us to predict the choices that people make as their circumstances change.

Changes in marginal benefit and marginal cost change the incentive to study or to enjoy a movie.

CHECKPOINT 1.3

3 **Explain five core ideas that define the economic way of thinking.**

Study Guide pp. 7–9

Practice Online 1.3

Practice Problem 1.3

Kate usually plays tennis for two hours a week, and her grade on each math test is usually 70 percent. Last week, after playing two hours of tennis, Kate thought long and hard about playing for another hour. She decided to play another hour of tennis and cut her study time by one additional hour. But the grade on last week's math test was 60 percent.

a. What was Kate's opportunity cost of the third hour of tennis?

b. Given that Kate made the decision to play the third hour of tennis, what can you conclude about the comparison of her marginal benefit and marginal cost of the second hour of tennis?

c. Was Kate's decision to play the third hour of tennis rational?

d. Did Kate make her decision on the margin?

Exercises 1.3

1. Bill Gates gives away a lot of money: $200 million to put computers in libraries that can't afford them and $135 million to universities, cancer research, a children's hospital, and the Seattle Symphony. Doesn't Bill Gates experience scarcity? Are his donations rational? In making these donations, might Bill Gates have responded to any incentive?

2. Steve Fossett spent a lot of money trying to be the first person to circumnavigate the world in a hot-air balloon. Anheuser-Busch offered a prize of $1 million for the first balloonist to do so in 15 days nonstop. What was the opportunity cost of Steve Fossett's adventure? But Steve Fossett was not the first person to circumnavigate the world in a balloon, so did he get any benefits? Why did Anheuser-Busch offer the prize?

3. Tony is an engineering student, and he is considering taking an extra course in history. List the things that might be part of his costs and benefits of the history course. Think of an incentive that might encourage him to take the course.

Solution to Practice Problem 1.3

a. Kate's opportunity cost of the third hour of tennis was the ten percentage point drop in her grade. If Kate had not played tennis for the third hour, she would have studied and her grade would not have dropped. The best alternative forgone is her opportunity cost of the third hour of tennis.

b. The marginal benefit from the second hour of tennis must have exceeded the marginal cost of the second hour because Kate chose to play tennis for the third hour. If the marginal benefit did not exceed the marginal cost, she would have chosen to study and not play tennis for the third hour.

c. If for Kate marginal benefit exceeded marginal cost, her decision was rational.

d. Kate made her decision on the margin because she considered the benefit and cost of *one additional hour*.

1.4 WHY ECONOMICS IS WORTH STUDYING

In 1961, Mick Jagger, then the 19-year-old lead singer with a group that would become the Rolling Stones, enrolled in an economics degree program at the London School of Economics. During the day, he was learning about opportunity cost, and each night, his rock group was earning today's equivalent of $120. Mick soon realized that his opportunity cost of remaining in school was too high, and so he dropped out. (A faculty advisor is reputed to have told Mick that he would not make much money in a rock band. But within a few months, the Rolling Stones, along with the Beatles, shot to international stardom and multimillion-dollar recording contracts!)

Mick Jagger used one of the big ideas of economics to make his own rational decision. And you can do the same. Let's look at the benefits and costs of studying economics and check that the benefits outweigh the costs.

Two main benefits from studying economics are

- Understanding
- Expanded career opportunities

Understanding

George Bernard Shaw, the great Irish dramatist and thinker, wrote, "Economy is the art of making the most of life." Life is certainly full of economic problems, some global or national in scope and some personal.

Every day, on television, on the Internet, and in newspapers and magazines, we hear and read about global or national economic issues: Should Nike pay higher wages to its workers in Asia? Is there too much economic inequality in the world today? How can we improve health care, welfare, and education? Are taxes too high or too low? Will the Federal Reserve increase interest rates next week?

And every day in your own life, you're confronted with personal economic choices: Will you buy pizza or pasta? Will you skip class today? Will you put your summer earnings in the bank or the stock market?

Studying economics equips you with tools and insights that help you to understand the world's problems, to participate in the political debate that surrounds them, and to understand and solve your personal economic problems.

John Maynard Keynes, a famous British economist of the twentieth century, wrote, "The ideas of economists . . . , both when they are right and when they are wrong, are more powerful than is commonly understood. Indeed the world is ruled by little else. Practical men [and women, he would have written today], who believe themselves to be quite exempt from any intellectual influences, are usually the slaves of some defunct economist."

Keynes was correct. You can't ignore economic ideas. They are all around you. You use them every day in your personal life and in your work. You use them when you vote and when you argue with your friends. But you don't need to be the slave of some defunct economist. By studying economics, you will learn how to develop your own ideas and to test them against the ideas of others. As you progress with your study of economics, you will start to listen to the news and read your newspaper with a deeper understanding of what's going on. You will also find yourself increasingly using the economics that you are learning when you make your own economic choices.

Expanded Career Opportunities

Robert Reich, a former U.S. Secretary of Labor, predicts that the three big jobs of the twenty-first century will be what he calls *problem identifying, problem solving,* and *strategic brokering*. The people who are good at these tasks command soaring incomes. And there is no better way to train yourself in these skills than to study economics. You can think of economics as a workout regimen for your brain. Almost everything that you study in economics is practice at thinking abstractly and rigorously about concrete things. You will constantly be asking, "What if?" Although students of economics learn many useful economic concepts, it is the training and practice in abstract thinking that really pays off.

Most students of economics don't go on to major in the subject. And even those who do major in economics don't usually go on to become economists. Rather, they work in fields such as banking, business, management, finance, insurance, real estate, marketing, law, government, journalism, health care, and the arts. A course in economics is a very good choice for a pre-med, pre-law, or pre-MBA student.

Economics graduates are not the highest-paid professionals. But they are close to the top, as you can see in Figure 1.2. Engineers and computer scientists, for example, earn up to 20 percent more than economics graduates. Economics graduates earn more than most others, and significantly, they earn more than business graduates.

FIGURE 1.2
Average Incomes

Practice Online

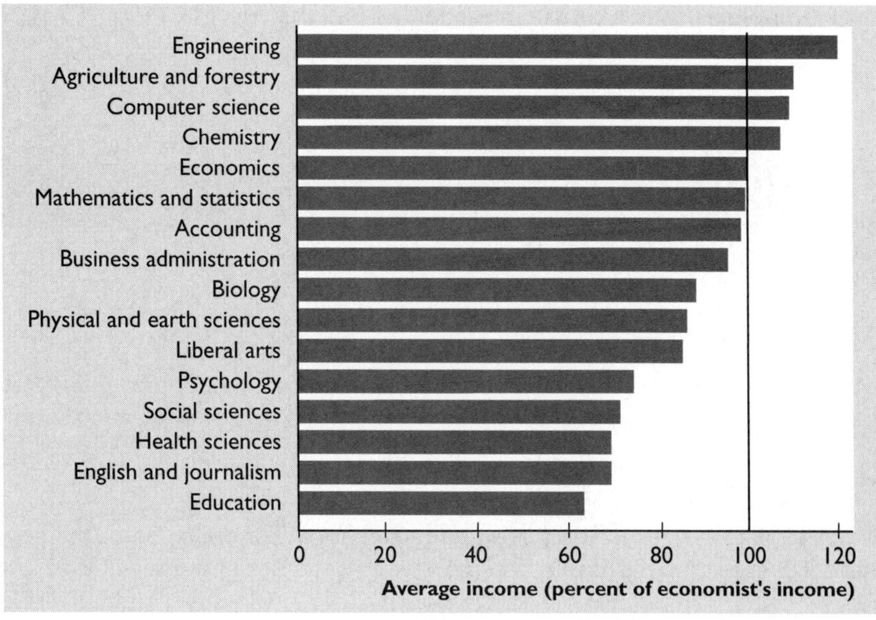

Graduates in disciplines that teach *problem identifying, problem solving*, and *strategic brokering* (engineering, computer science, and economics) are at the top of the earnings distribution.

SOURCES: U.S. Department of Commerce, Bureau of the Census, *Educational Background and Economic Status: Spring 1990*, Current Population Reports, Series P-70, No. 32, and *Statistical Abstract of the United States*, 1994, Table 246, and authors' calculations.

The Costs of Studying Economics

Regardless of what you study, you must buy textbooks and supplies and pay tuition. So these expenses are *not* part of the opportunity cost of studying economics.

One cost of studying economics is forgone knowledge of some other subject. If you work hard at studying economics, you must forgo learning some other subject. You can't study everything.

Another cost, and the main cost of studying economics, is forgone leisure time. Economics is a demanding subject, and it takes time to master. Most students say that they find it difficult. They often complain that they understand the subject when they read the textbook or listen to their instructor but then, when they take an exam, they just can't figure out the correct answers.

The trick is practice, or learning-by-doing. Economics is not a subject that you learn by memorizing things. You must memorize definitions and technical terms. But beyond that, memory is not your main mental tool. Working problems and learning how to analyze and solve problems are the key. And this activity is time consuming.

Benefits Versus Costs

So which is larger: the benefit or the cost? Economics says that only you can decide. You are the judge of value or benefit to yourself. So you must weigh the benefits and the costs that we've identified (and consider any others that are important to *you*).

If you're clear that the benefits outweigh the costs, you're well on your way to having a good time in your economics course. If the costs outweigh the benefits, don't waste your time. Life is too short.

If you're on the fence, try to get more information. But if you remain on the fence, complete this one course in economics and then decide.

CHECKPOINT 1.4

Study Guide pp. 9–10

Practice Online 1.4

4 Explain why economics is worth studying.

Practice Problem 1.4

A student is choosing between an economics course and a popular music course. List two opportunity costs and two benefits from taking a course in economics.

Exercise 1.4

Why did Mick Jagger quit his economics course? What are some of the benefits that Mick Jagger might have given up?

Solution to Practice Problem 1.4

Opportunity costs include the leisure forgone and forgone appreciation of popular music. Benefits include expanded career opportunities, better understanding of the world, and better problem-solving skills.

CHAPTER CHECKPOINT

Key Points

1 Define economics, distinguish between microeconomics and macroeconomics, and explain the questions economics tries to answer.

- Economics is the social science that studies the choices that we make as we cope with scarcity and the incentives that influence and reconcile our choices.
- Microeconomics explains how choices end up determining *what* goods and services get produced, *how* they get produced, and *for whom* they get produced.
- Macroeconomics explains how choices influence the standard of living, the cost of living, and economic fluctuations.

2 Describe the work of economists as social scientists.

- Positive statements are about what is, and they can be tested. Normative statements are about what ought to be, and they cannot be tested.
- To explain the economic world, economists build and test economic models.
- Economists use the *ceteris paribus* assumption to try to disentangle cause and effect, and they use natural experiments, statistical investigations, and economic experiments.

3 Explain five core ideas that define the economic way of thinking.

- People make rational choices by comparing costs and benefits.
- Cost is what you *must* give up to get something.
- Benefit is what you gain when you get something and is measured by what you *are willing to* give up to get it.
- A rational choice is made on the margin.
- People respond to incentives.

4 Explain why economics is worth studying.

- The benefits of studying economics are understanding of the economic world and expanded career opportunities.
- The costs of studying economics are forgone knowledge of some other subject and leisure time.

Key Terms

Exercises

1. Provide three examples of scarcity that illustrate why even the wealthiest people who live in the most lavish luxury still face scarcity.

2. Provide two examples of incentives, one a carrot and the other a stick, that have influenced major government decisions during the past few years.

3. Think about the following news items and label each as involving a microeconomic or a macroeconomic issue:
   a. An increase in the tax on cigarettes will decrease teenage smoking.
   b. It would be better if the United States spent more on cleaning up the environment and less on space exploration.
   c. A government scheme called "work for welfare" will reduce the number of people unemployed.
   d. An increase in the number of police on inner-city streets will reduce the crime rate.

4. Think about the following news items and label each as involving a What, How, or For Whom question:
   a. Today most stores use computers to keep their inventory records, whereas 20 years ago most stores used paper records.
   b. Health care professionals and drug companies say that Medicaid drug rebates should be available to everyone in need.
   c. A doubling of the gas tax might lead to a better public transit system.

5. Think about the following news items and label each as a positive or a normative statement. In the United States,
   a. The poor pay too much for housing.
   b. The number of farms has decreased over the last 50 years.
   c. The population in rural areas has remained constant over the past decade.

6. Explain how economists try to unscramble cause and effect. Explain why economists use the *ceteris paribus* assumption.

7. What is correlation? What approaches do economists use to try to sort out the cause-and-effect relationship that a correlation might indicate? Describe each of these approaches.

8. What is the *post hoc* fallacy? Provide two examples of the *post hoc* fallacy.

9. Pam, Pru, and Pat are deciding how they will celebrate the New Year. Pam prefers to go on a cruise, is happy to go to Hawaii, but does not want to go skiing. Pru prefers to go skiing, is happy to go to Hawaii, but does not want to go on a cruise. Pat prefers to go to Hawaii or to take a cruise but does not want to go skiing. Their decision is to go to Hawaii. Is this decision rational? What is the opportunity cost of the trip to Hawaii for each of them? What is the benefit each gets?

10. Your school has decided to increase the intake of new students next year. What economic concepts would your school consider in reaching its decision? Would the school make its decision at the margin?

11. In California, most vineyards use machines and a few workers to pick grapes, while some vineyards use no machines and many workers. Which vineyards have made a rational choice? Explain your answer.

Critical Thinking

12. The largest lottery jackpot prizes in U. S. history were $363 million and $331 million, both won in the Big Game Jackpot.
    a. Do the people who buy lottery tickets face scarcity?
    b. Do the winners of big prizes face scarcity after receiving their winners' checks?
    c. Do you think lotteries have both microeconomic effects and macroeconomic effects or only microeconomic effects? Explain.
    d. How do you think lotteries change what and for whom goods and services are produced?
    e. Think about the statement "Lotteries create more problems than they solve and should be banned." Which part of this statement is positive and how might it be tested? Which part of this statement is normative?
    f. Do people face a marginal cost and a marginal benefit when they decide to buy a lottery ticket?
    g. Does a person who buys a lottery ticket make a rational choice?
    h. Do the people who buy lottery tickets respond to incentives?
    i. How do you think the size of the jackpot affects the number of lottery tickets sold? What role do incentives play in this response?

13. "Spider-Man" was the most successful movie of 2002, with box office receipts of more than $400 million. Creating a successful movie brings pleasure to millions, generates work for thousands, and makes a few people rich.
    a. What contribution does a movie like "Spider-Man" make to coping with scarcity?
    b. Does the decision to make a blockbuster movie mean that some other more desirable activities get fewer resources than they deserve?
    c. Was your answer to part **b** a positive or a normative answer? Explain.
    d. Who decides whether a movie is going to be a blockbuster?
    e. How do you think the creation of a blockbuster movie influences what, how, and for whom goods and services are produced?
    f. What do you think are some of the marginal costs and marginal benefits that the producer of a movie faces?
    g. Suppose that Tobey Maguire had been offered a bigger and better part in another movie and that to hire him for "Spider-Man," the producer had to double Tobey's pay. What incentives were changed? How might the changed incentives have changed the choices that people made?

14. Think about each of the following situations and explain how they affect incentives and might change the choices that people make.
    a. Drought hits the Midwest.
    b. The World Series begins tonight, and there is a thunderstorm warning in effect for the stadium.
    c. The price of a personal computer falls to $50.
    d. Political instability in the Middle East cuts world oil production and sends the price of gasoline to $2 a gallon.
    e. Your school builds a new parking garage that increases the number of parking places available but doubles the price of parking on campus.
    f. A math professor awards grades based on the percentage of questions answered correctly and an economics professor awards grades based on rank in class—the top 10 percent get As, the bottom 10 percent get Cs, and the rest of the class get Bs regardless of the percentage of questions answered correctly.

Practice Online

Web Exercises

If you haven't already done so, take a few minutes to visit your Foundations Web site, sign in, and obtain your username and password. Browse the site and become familiar with its structure and content. You'll soon appreciate that this Web site is a very useful and powerful learning tool. For each chapter, you will find quizzes, e-text, e-study guide, interactive tutorials and graphics, and animations of your textbook figures. You will also find the links you need to work the Web exercises.

Use the links on your Foundations Web site to work the following exercises.

15. Visit some news Web sites and review today's economic news. Summarize a news article that deals with an economic issue that interests you. Say whether the story deals with a microeconomic or a macroeconomic issue.
16. Visit the Campaign for Tobacco-Free Kids. Obtain data on changes in state tobacco taxes and changes in state tobacco consumption.
    a. Calculate the percentage change in tobacco taxes in each of the states for which you have data.
    b. Make a graph that plots the percentage change in the tobacco tax on the x-axis and the percentage change in state tobacco consumption on the y-axis.
    c. Describe the relationship between these two variables. (Look at pages 25, 26, and 27 if you need help with making and interpreting your graph.)
    d. How would you expect a rise in the tobacco tax to influence the incentive for a young person to smoke cigarettes?
    e. Do the data that you've obtained confirm what you expected or were you surprised by the data? Explain your answer.
    f. What can you infer about cause and effect in the data on tobacco taxes and tobacco consumption?
    g. What is the main obstacle to drawing a strong conclusion about the effect of tobacco taxes on tobacco consumption?
17. Visit the *Statistical Abstract of the United States* and obtain data on the levels of average annual pay and the percentage of persons with a bachelor's degree in each of the states.
    a. Which state has the highest average pay and which has the lowest?
    b. Where in the ranking of average pay does your state stand?
    c. Which state has the highest percentage of people with a bachelor's degree and which has the lowest?
    d. Where in the ranking of people with a bachelor's degree does your state stand?
    e. What do you think these numbers tell us about what, how, or for whom goods and services are produced?
    f. What is the difficulty in using these numbers to determine whether education levels influence pay levels?
18. Visit the Inflation Calculator. Then make this choice: You can have $11 and pay the prices of 1800, or you can have $100 and pay the prices of 2000. Which do you prefer and why?
19. Visit the Federal Reserve and view the latest edition of the Beige Book. What are the recent changes in the standard of living and the cost of living in the United States and of your region?

APPENDIX: MAKING AND USING GRAPHS

When you have completed your study of this appendix, you will be able to

1. **Interpret a scatter diagram, a time-series graph, and a cross-section graph.**
2. **Interpret the graphs used in economic models.**
3. **Define and calculate slope.**
4. **Graph relationships among more than two variables.**

Basic Idea

A graph represents a quantity as a distance and enables us to visualize the relationship between two variables. To make a graph, we set two lines called *axes* perpendicular to each other, like those in Figure A1.1. The vertical line is called the y-axis, and the horizontal line is called the x-axis. The common zero point is called the *origin*. In Figure A1.1, the x-axis measures temperature in degrees Fahrenheit. A movement to the right shows an increase in temperature, and a movement to the left shows a decrease in temperature. The y-axis represents ice cream consumption, measured in gallons per day. To make a graph, we need a value of the variable on the x-axis and a corresponding value of the variable on the y-axis. For example, if the temperature is 40°F, ice cream consumption is 5 gallons a day at point A in the graph. If the temperature is 80°F, ice cream consumption is 20 gallons a day at point B in the graph. Graphs like that in Figure A1.1 can be used to show any type of quantitative data on two variables.

FIGURE A1.1
Making a Graph

Practice Online

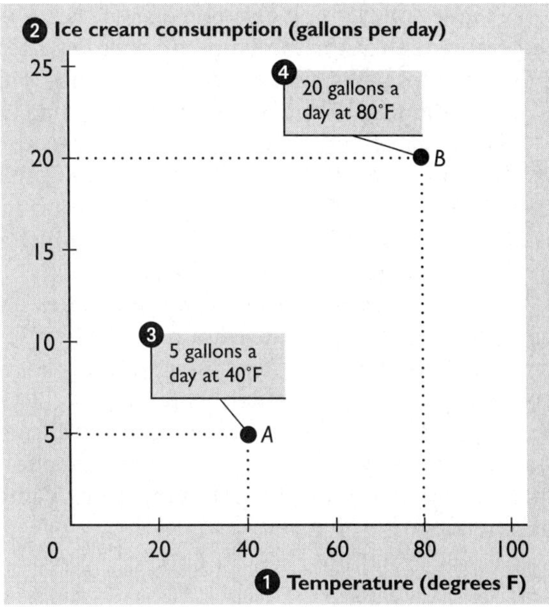

All graphs have axes that measure quantities as distances.

1. The horizontal axis (x-axis) measures temperature in degrees Fahrenheit. A movement to the right shows an increase in temperature.
2. The vertical axis (y-axis) measures ice cream consumption in gallons per day. A movement upward shows an increase in ice cream consumption.
3. Point A shows that 5 gallons of ice cream are consumed on a day when the temperature is 40°F.
4. Point B shows that 20 gallons of ice cream are consumed on a day when the temperature is 80°F.

Interpreting Data Graphs

Scatter diagram
A graph of the value of one variable against the value of another variable.

A **scatter diagram** is a graph of the value of one variable against the value of another variable. It is used to reveal whether a relationship exists between two variables and to describe the relationship. Figure A1.2 shows two examples.

Figure A1.2(a) shows the relationship between expenditure and income. Each point shows expenditure per person and income per person in the United States in a given year from 1992 to 2002. The points are "scattered" within the graph. The label on each point shows its year. The point marked 96 shows that in 1996, income per person was $21,100 and expenditure per person was $20,100. This scatter diagram reveals that as income increases, expenditure also increases.

Figure A1.2(b) shows the relationship between the number of minutes of international phone calls made from the United States and the average price per minute. This scatter diagram reveals that as the price per minute falls, the number of minutes called increases.

Time-series graph
A graph that measures time on the *x*-axis and the variable or variables in which we are interested on the *y*-axis.

A **time-series graph** measures time (for example, months or years) on the *x*-axis and the variable or variables in which we are interested on the *y*-axis. Figure A1.2(c) shows an example. In this graph, time (on the *x*-axis) is measured in years, which run from 1972 to 2002. The variable that we are interested in is the price of coffee, and it is measured on the *y*-axis.

A time-series graph conveys an enormous amount of information quickly and easily, as this example illustrates. It shows when the value is

1. High or low. When the line is a long way from the *x*-axis, the price is high, as it was in 1977. When the line is close to the *x*-axis, the price is low, as it was in 2002.
2. Rising or falling. When the line slopes upward, as in 1976, the price is rising. When the line slopes downward, as in 1978, the price is falling.
3. Rising or falling quickly and slowly. If the line is steep, then the price is rising or falling quickly. If the line is not steep, the price is rising or falling slowly. For example, the price rose quickly in 1976 and slowly in 1993. The price fell quickly in 1978 and slowly in 1982.

Trend
A general tendency for the value of a variable to rise or fall.

A time-series graph also reveals whether the variable has a trend. A **trend** is a general tendency for the value of a variable to rise or fall. You can see that the price of coffee had a general tendency to fall from the mid-1970s to the early 1990s. That is, although the price rose and fell, it had a general tendency to fall.

With a time-series graph, we can compare different periods quickly. Figure A1.2(c) shows that the 1990s were different from the 1970s. The price of coffee fluctuated more violently in the 1970s than it did in the 1990s. This graph conveys a wealth of information, and it does so in much less space than we have used to describe only some of its features.

Cross-section graph
A graph that shows the values of an economic variable for different groups in a population at a point in time.

A **cross-section graph** shows the values of an economic variable for different groups in a population at a point in time. Figure A1.2(d) is an example of a cross-section graph. It shows the percentage of people who participate in selected sports activities in the United States in 2000. This graph uses bars rather than dots and lines, and the length of each bar indicates the participation rate. Figure A1.2(d) enables you to compare the participation rates in these ten sporting activities. And you can do so much more quickly and clearly than by looking at a list of numbers.

FIGURE A1.2
Data Graphs

Practice Online

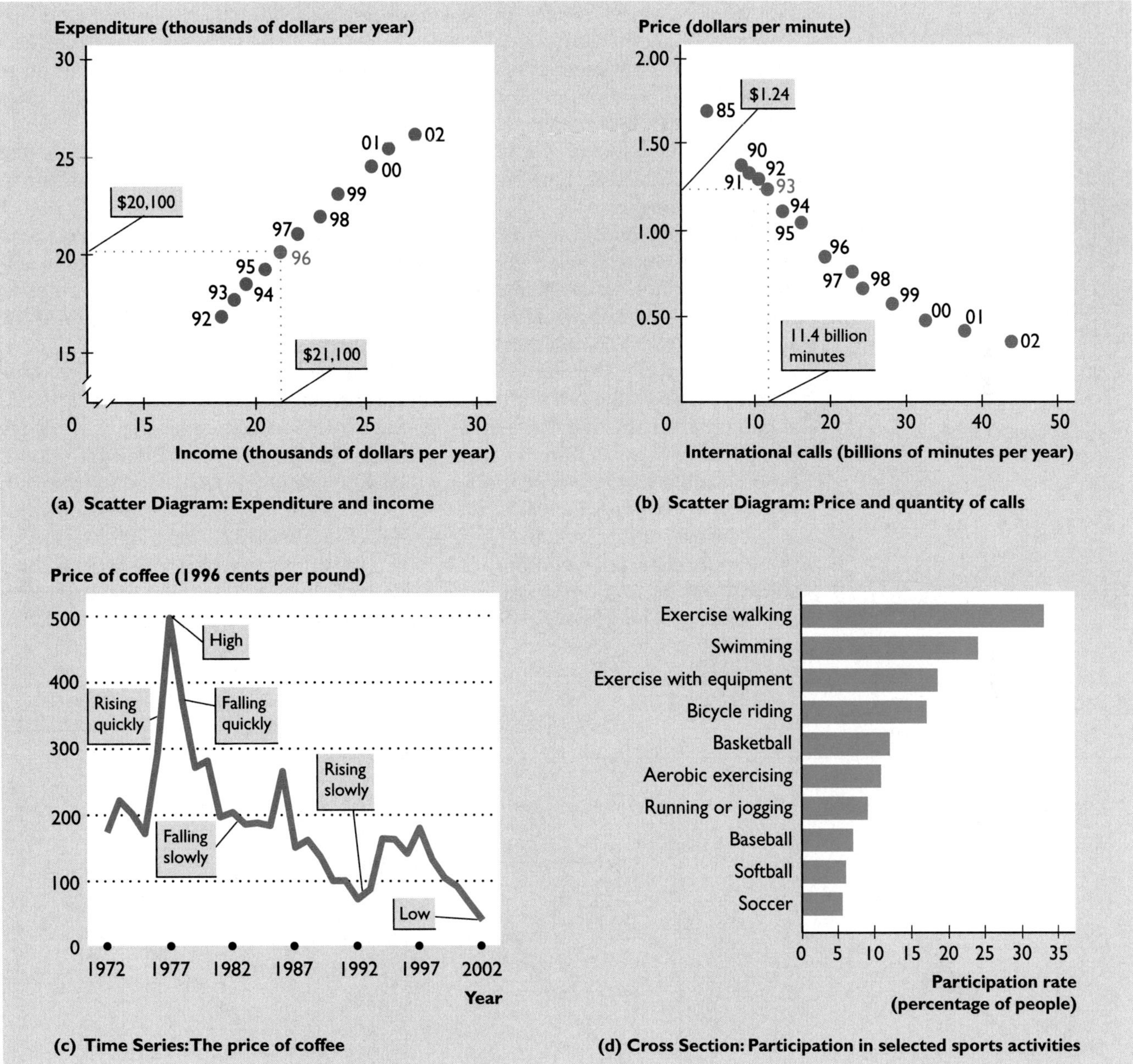

(a) Scatter Diagram: Expenditure and income

(b) Scatter Diagram: Price and quantity of calls

(c) Time Series: The price of coffee

(d) Cross Section: Participation in selected sports activities

A scatter diagram reveals the relationship between two variables. In part (a), as income increases, expenditure increases. In part (b), as the price per minute falls, the number of minutes called increases.

A time-series graph plots the value of a variable on the *y*-axis against time on the *x*-axis. Part (c) plots the price of coffee each year from 1972 to 2002. The graph shows when the price of coffee was high and low, when it increased and decreased, and when it changed quickly and slowly.

A cross-section graph shows the value of a variable across the members of a population. Part (d) shows the participation rate in the United States in each of ten sporting activites in 2000.

Interpreting Graphs Used in Economic Models

We use graphs to show the relationships among the variables in an economic model. An *economic model* is a simplified description of the economy or of a component of the economy such as a business or a household. It consists of statements about economic behavior that can be expressed as equations or as curves in a graph. Economists use models to explore the effects of different policies or other influences on the economy in ways similar to those used to test model airplanes in wind tunnels and models of the climate.

Positive relationship or direct relationship
A relationship between two variables that move in the same direction.

Linear relationship
A relationship that graphs as a straight line.

Figure A1.3 shows graphs of the relationships between two variables that move in the same direction. Such a relationship is called a **positive relationship** or **direct relationship**.

Part (a) shows a straight-line relationship, which is called a **linear relationship**. The distance traveled in 5 hours increases as the speed increases. For example, point *A* shows that 200 miles are traveled in 5 hours at a speed of 40 miles an hour. And point *B* shows that the distance traveled increases to 300 miles if the speed increases to 60 miles an hour.

Part (b) shows the relationship between distance sprinted and recovery time (the time it takes the heart rate to return to its normal resting rate). An upward-sloping curved line that starts out quite flat but then becomes steeper as we move along the curve away from the origin describes this relationship. The curve slopes upward and becomes steeper because the extra recovery time needed from sprinting another 100 yards increases. It takes less than 5 minutes to recover from sprinting 100 yards but more than 10 minutes to recover from sprinting 200 yards.

Part (c) shows the relationship between the number of problems worked by a student and the amount of study time. An upward-sloping curved line that starts out quite steep and becomes flatter as we move away from the origin shows this

FIGURE A1.3
Positive (Direct) Relationships

Practice Online

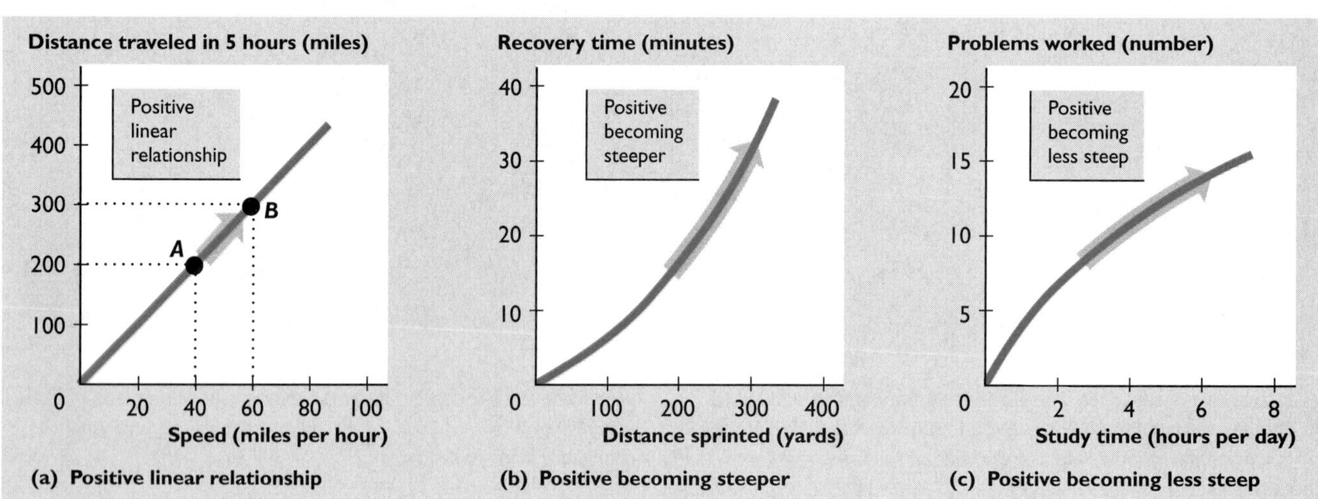

Part (a) shows that as speed increases, the distance traveled increases along a straight line.

Part (b) shows that as the distance sprinted increases, recovery time increases along a curve that becomes steeper.

Part (c) shows that as study time increases, the number of problems worked increases along a curve that becomes less steep.

relationship. Study time becomes less effective as you increase the hours worked and become more tired.

Figure A1.4 shows relationships between two variables that move in opposite directions. Such a relationship is called a **negative relationship** or **inverse relationship**.

Negative relationship or inverse relationship
A relationship between two variables that move in opposite directions.

Part (a) shows the relationship between the number of hours for playing squash and the number of hours for playing tennis when the total number of hours available is five. One extra hour spent playing tennis means one hour less playing squash and vice versa. This relationship is negative and linear.

Part (b) shows the relationship between the cost per mile traveled and the length of a journey. The longer the journey, the lower is the cost per mile. But as the journey length increases, the cost per mile decreases, and the fall in the cost gets smaller. This feature of the relationship is shown by the fact that the curve slopes downward, starting out steep at a short journey length and then becoming flatter as the journey length increases. This relationship arises because some of the costs are fixed, such as auto insurance, and the fixed costs are spread over a longer journey.

Part (c) shows the relationship between the amount of leisure time and the number of problems worked by a student. Increasing leisure time produces an increasingly large reduction in the number of problems worked. This relationship is a negative one that starts out with a gentle slope at a small number of leisure hours and becomes steeper as the number of leisure hours increases. This relationship is a different view of the idea shown in Figure A1.3(c).

Many relationships in economic models have a maximum or a minimum. For example, firms try to make the largest possible profit and to produce at the lowest possible cost. Figure A1.5 shows relationships that have a maximum or a minimum.

FIGURE A1.4
Negative (Inverse) Relationships

Practice Online

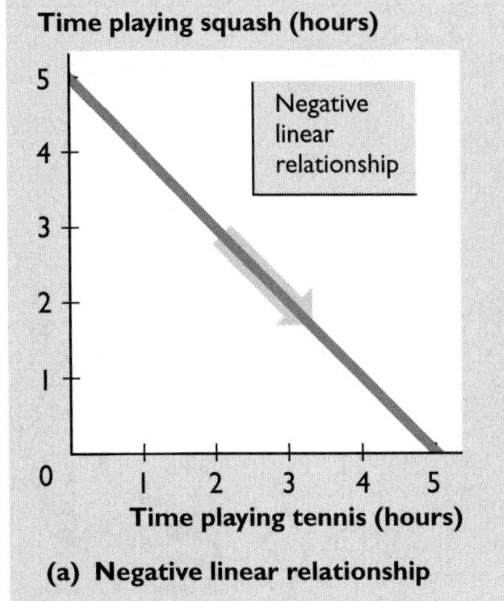

(a) Negative linear relationship

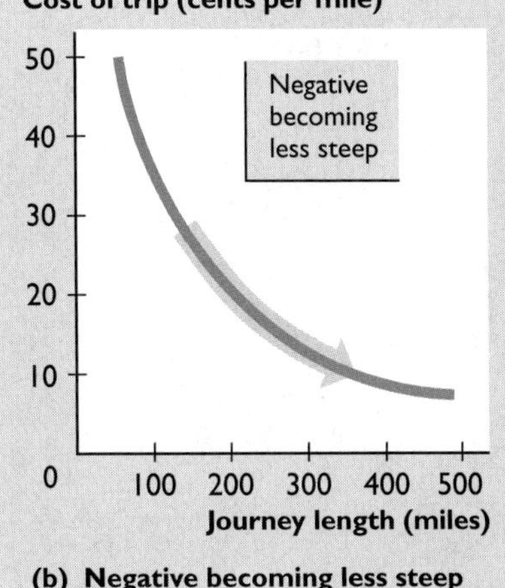

(b) Negative becoming less steep

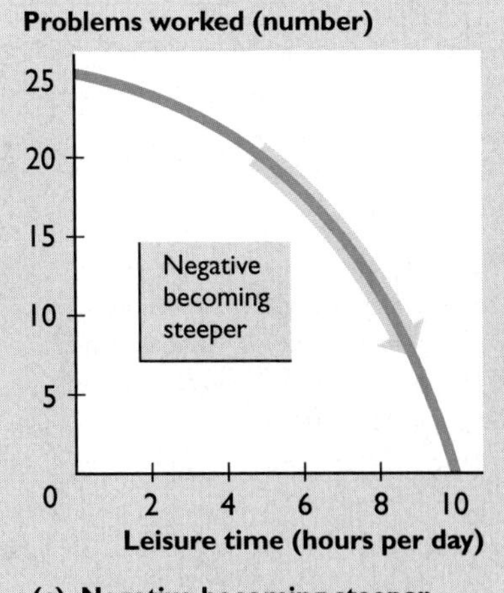

(c) Negative becoming steeper

Part (a) shows that as the time playing tennis increases, the time playing squash decreases along a straight line.

Part (b) shows that as the journey length increases, the cost of the trip falls along a curve that becomes less steep.

Part (c) shows that as leisure time increases, the number of problems worked decreases along a curve that becomes steeper.

FIGURE A1.5
Maximum and Minimum Points

Practice Online

In part (a), as the rainfall increases, the curve ❶ slopes upward as the yield per acre rises, ❷ is flat at point *A*, the maximum yield, and then ❸ slopes downward as the yield per acre falls.

In part (b), as the speed increases, the curve ❶ slopes downward as the cost per mile falls, ❷ is flat at the minimum point *B*, and then ❸ slopes upward as the cost per mile rises.

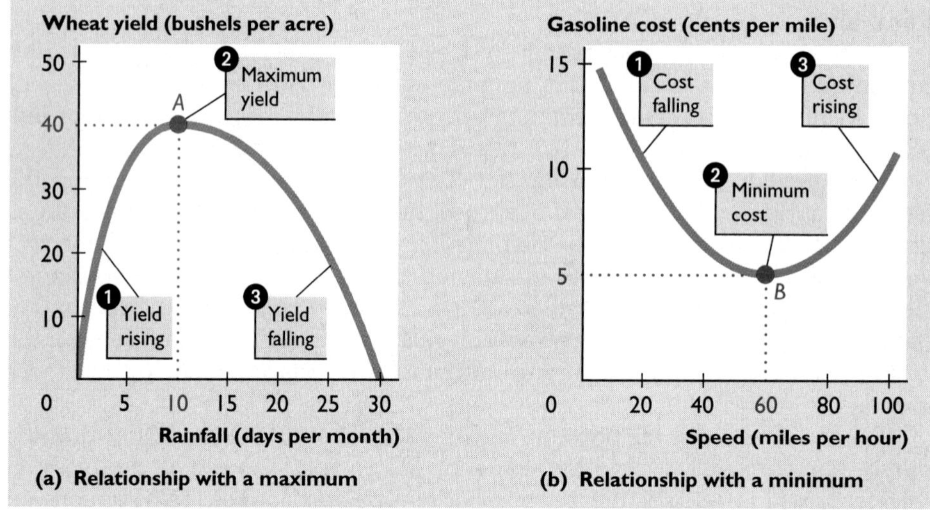

Part (a) shows the relationship that starts out sloping upward, reaches a maximum, and then slopes downward. Part (b) shows a relationship that begins sloping downward, falls to a minimum, and then slopes upward.

Finally, there are many situations in which, no matter what happens to the value of one variable, the other variable remains constant. Sometimes we want to show two variables that are unrelated in a graph. Figure A1.6 shows two graphs in which the variables are independent.

FIGURE A1.6
Variables That Are Unrelated

Practice Online

In part (a), as the price of bananas increases, the student's grade in economics remains at 75 percent. These variables are unrelated, and the curve is horizontal.

In part (b), the vineyards of France produce 3 billion gallons of wine no matter what the rainfall in California is. These variables are unrelated, and the curve is vertical.

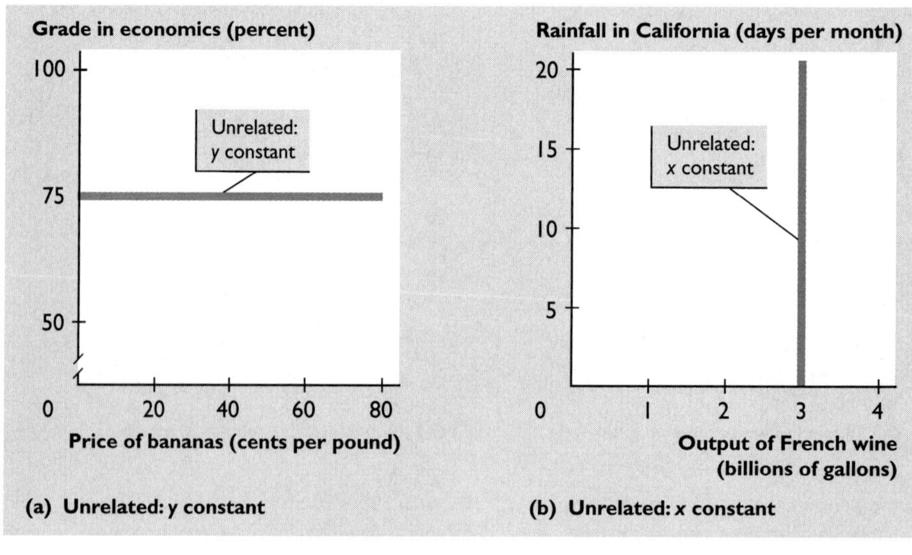

The Slope of a Relationship

We can measure the influence of one variable on another by the slope of the relationship. The **slope** of a relationship is the change in the value of the variable measured on the y-axis divided by the change in the value of the variable measured on the x-axis. We use the Greek letter Δ (delta) to represent "change in." So Δy means the change in the value of y, and Δx means the change in the value of x, and the slope of the relationship is

$$\Delta y \div \Delta x.$$

Slope
The change in the value of the variable measured on the y-axis divided by the change in the value of the variable measured on the x-axis.

If a large change in y is associated with a small change in x, the slope is large and the curve is steep. If a small change in y is associated with a large change in x, the slope is small and the curve is flat.

Figure A1.7 shows you how to calculate slope. The slope of a straight line is the same regardless of where on the line you calculate it—the slope is constant. In part (a), when x increases from 2 to 6, y increases from 3 to 6. The change in x is +4—that is, Δx is 4. The change in y is +3—that is, Δy is 3. The slope of that line is 3/4. In part (b), when x increases from 2 to 6, y *decreases* from 6 to 3. The change in y is *minus* 3—that is, Δy is –3. The change in x is plus 4—that is, Δx is 4. The slope of the curve is –3/4. In part (c), we calculate the slope at a point on a curve. To do so, place a ruler on the graph so that it touches point A and no other point on the curve, then draw a straight line along the edge of the ruler. The slope of this straight line is the slope of the curve at point A. This slope is 3/4.

FIGURE A1.7
Calculating Slope

Practice Online

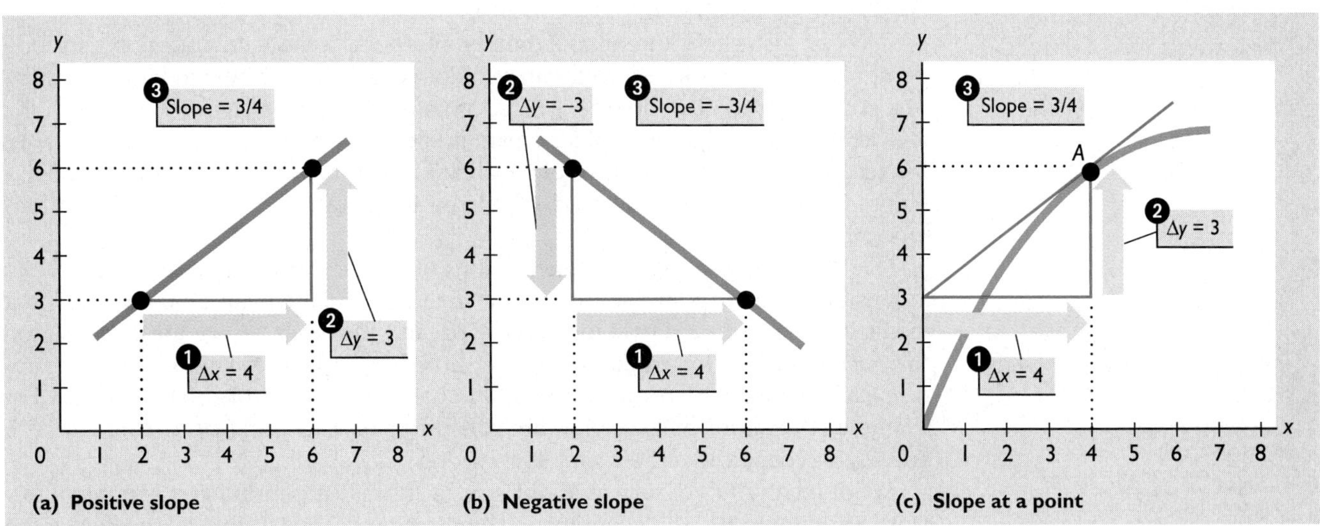

In part (a), ❶ when Δx is 4, ❷ Δy is 3, so ❸ the slope ($\Delta y/\Delta x$) is 3/4.

In part (b), ❶ when Δx is 4, ❷ Δy is –3, so ❸ the slope ($\Delta y/\Delta x$) is –3/4.

In part (c), the slope of the curve at point A equals the slope of the red line. ❶ When Δx is 4, ❷ Δy is 3, so ❸ the slope ($\Delta y/\Delta x$) is 3/4.

Relationships Among More Than Two Variables

We have seen that we can graph the relationship between two variables as a point formed by the x and y values. But most of the relationships in economics involve relationships among many variables, not just two. For example, the amount of ice cream consumed depends on the price of ice cream and the temperature. If ice cream is expensive and the temperature is low, people eat much less ice cream than when ice cream is inexpensive and the temperature is high. For any given price of ice cream, the quantity consumed varies with the temperature; and for any given temperature, the quantity of ice cream consumed varies with its price.

Figure A1.8 shows a relationship among three variables. The table shows the number of gallons of ice cream consumed per day at various temperatures and ice cream prices. How can we graph these numbers?

To graph a relationship that involves more than two variables, we use the *ceteris paribus* assumption.

Ceteris Paribus

The Latin phrase *ceteris paribus* means "other things remaining the same." Every laboratory experiment is an attempt to create *ceteris paribus* and isolate the relationship of interest. We use the same method to make a graph.

Figure A1.8(a) shows an example. This graph shows what happens to the quantity of ice cream consumed when the price of ice cream varies while the temperature remains the same. The curve labeled 70°F shows the relationship between ice cream consumption and the price of ice cream if the temperature is 70°F. The numbers used to plot that curve are those in the first and fourth columns of the table in Figure A1.8. For example, if the temperature is 70°F, 10 gallons are consumed when the price is 60¢ a scoop and 18 gallons are consumed when the price is 30¢ a scoop. The curve labeled 90°F shows consumption as the price varies if the temperature is 90°F.

We can also show the relationship between ice cream consumption and temperature while the price of ice cream remains constant, as shown in Figure A1.8(b). The curve labeled 60¢ shows how the consumption of ice cream varies with the temperature when the price of ice cream is 60¢ a scoop, and a second curve shows the relationship when the price of ice cream is 15¢ a scoop. For example, at 60¢ a scoop, 10 gallons are consumed when the temperature is 70°F and 20 gallons when the temperature is 90°F.

Figure A1.8(c) shows the combinations of temperature and price that result in a constant consumption of ice cream. One curve shows the combination that results in 10 gallons a day being consumed, and the other shows the combination that results in 7 gallons a day being consumed. A high price and a high temperature lead to the same consumption as a lower price and a lower temperature. For example, 10 gallons of ice cream are consumed at 90°F and 90¢ a scoop, at 70°F and 60¢ a scoop, and at 50°F and 45¢ a scoop.

With what you've learned about graphs in this Appendix, you can move forward with your study of economics. There are no graphs in this textbook that are more complicated than the ones you've studied here.

FIGURE A1.8

Graphing a Relationship Among Three Variables

Practice Online

Price (cents per scoop)	Ice cream consumption (gallons per day)			
	30°F	50°F	70°F	90°F
15	12	18	25	50
30	10	12	18	37
45	7	10	13	27
60	5	7	10	20
75	3	5	7	14
90	2	3	5	10
105	1	2	3	6

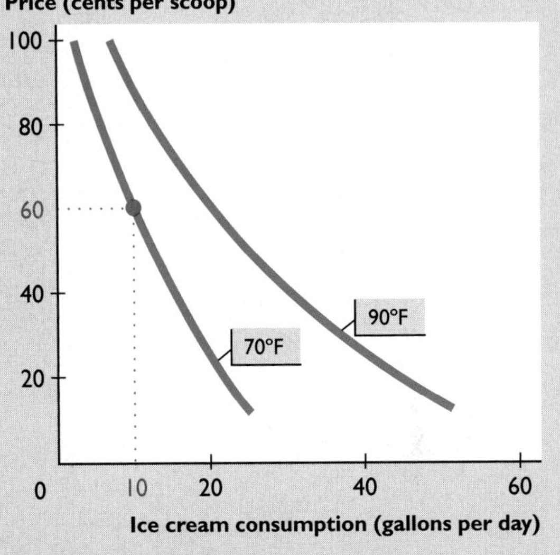

(a) Price and consumption at a given temperature

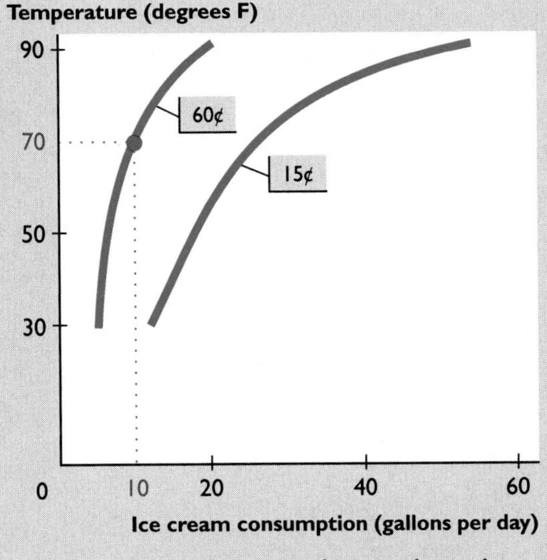

(b) Temperature and consumption at a given price

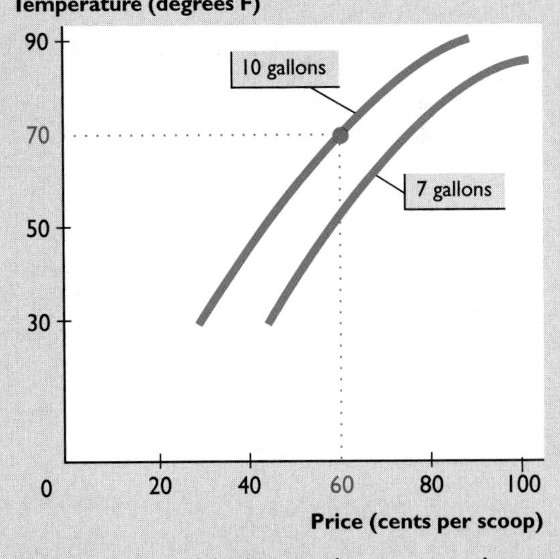

(c) Temperature and price at a given consumption

The table tells us how many gallons of ice cream are consumed each day at different prices and different temperatures. For example, if the price is 60¢ a scoop and the temperature is 70°F, 10 gallons of ice cream are consumed. This set of values is highlighted in the table and each part of the figure.

Part (a) shows the relationship between price and consumption when temperature is held constant. One curve holds temperature at 90°F, and the other at 70°F.

Part (b) shows the relationship between temperature and consumption when price is held constant. One curve holds the price at 60¢ a scoop, and the other at 15¢ a scoop.

Part (c) shows the relationship between temperature and price when consumption is held constant. One curve holds consumption at 10 gallons, and the other at 7 gallons.

APPENDIX CHECKPOINT

Study Guide pp. 14–19

Practice Online A1.1

Exercises

The spreadsheet provides data on the U.S. economy: Column A is the year; the other columns are actual and projected expenditures per person in dollars per year on recorded music (column B), Internet services (column C), and movies in theaters (column D). Use this spreadsheet to answer exercises 1, 2, 3, 4, and 5.

	A	B	C	D
1	1992	43	4	23
2	1993	47	5	24
3	1994	56	6	25
4	1995	57	11	25
5	1996	57	17	27
6	1997	55	26	29
7	1998	56	32	30
8	1999	58	37	31
9	2000	62	43	32
10	2001	66	48	33
11	2002	69	53	34

1. Draw a scatter diagram to show the relationship between expenditure on recorded music and expenditure on Internet services. Describe the relationship.
2. Draw a scatter diagram to show the relationship between expenditure on Internet services and expenditure on movies in theaters. Describe the relationship.
3. Draw a scatter diagram to show the relationship between expenditure on recorded music and expenditure on movies in theaters. Describe the relationship.
4. Draw a time-series graph of expenditure on Internet services. Say in which year or years (a) expenditure was highest, (b) expenditure was lowest, (c) expenditure increased the most, and (d) expenditure increased the least. Also, say whether the data show a trend and describe its direction.
5. Draw a time-series graph of expenditure on recorded music. Say in which year or years (a) expenditure was highest, (b) expenditure was lowest, (c) expenditure increased the most, and (d) expenditure increased the least. Also, say whether the data show a trend and describe its direction.
6. Draw a graph to show the relationship between the two variables x and y:

x	0	1	2	3	4	5	6	7	8
y	0	1	4	9	16	25	36	49	64

   a. Is the relationship positive or negative?
   b. Calculate the slope of the relationship between x and y when x equals 2 and when x equals 4.
   c. How does the slope of the relationship change as the value of x increases?
   d. Think of some economic relationships that might be similar to this one.

7. Draw a graph to show the relationship between the two variables x and y:

x	0	1	2	3	4	5	6	7	8
y	60	49	39	30	22	15	9	4	0

   a. Is the relationship positive or negative?
   b. Calculate the slope of the relationship between x and y when x equals 2 and when x equals 4.
   c. How does the slope of the relationship change as the value of x increases?
   d. Think of some economic relationships that might be similar to this one.

8. The table provides data on the price of a balloon ride, the temperature, and the number of rides a day. Draw graphs to show the relationship between:
   a. The price and the number of rides, holding the temperature constant.
   b. The number of rides and the temperature, holding the price constant.
   c. The temperature and the price, holding the number of rides constant.

Price (dollars per ride)	Balloon rides (number per day)		
	50°F	70°F	90°F
5	32	50	40
10	27	40	32
15	18	32	27
20	10	27	18

The U.S. and Global Economies

CHAPTER **2**

CHAPTER CHECKLIST

When you have completed your study of this chapter, you will be able to

1. **Describe what, how, and for whom goods and services are produced in the United States.**
2. **Use the circular flow model to provide a picture of how households, firms, and governments interact.**
3. **Describe the macroeconomic performance—standard of living, cost of living, and economic fluctuations—of the United States and other economies.**

You've learned that economics is the social science that studies the choices that people, businesses, and governments make to cope with *scarcity* and the *incentives* that influence and reconcile our choices. These choices and the interactions among them determine *what*, *how*, and *for whom* goods and services are produced. These choices also determine the standard of living and the cost of living and bring economic fluctuations—recessions and expansions.

Most of your economics course explains the principles and theories that *explain* and in some cases enable economists to *predict* choices and their consequences. But before we turn to this task, we are going to *describe* the main features of the U.S. and global economies. In this chapter, you will learn *what*, *how*, and *for whom* goods and services are produced; about the resources available and how they are used; and about the standard of living, the cost of living, and economic fluctuations around the world.

2.1 WHAT, HOW, AND FOR WHOM?

Walk around a shopping mall and pay close attention to the range of goods and services that are being offered for sale. Go inside some of the shops and look at the labels to see where various items are manufactured. The next time you travel on an interstate highway, look at the large trucks and pay attention to the names and products printed on their sides and the places in which the trucks are registered. Open the Yellow Pages and flip through a few sections. Notice the huge range of goods and services that businesses are offering.

You've just done a sampling of *what* goods and services are produced and consumed in the United States today.

What Do We Produce?

We divide the vast array of goods and services produced into four large groups:

- Consumption goods and services
- Investment goods
- Government goods and services
- Export goods and services

Consumption goods and services
Goods and services that are bought by individuals and used to provide personal enjoyment and contribute to a person's standard of living.

Investment goods
Goods that are bought by businesses to increase their productive resources.

Government goods and services
Goods and services that are bought by governments.

Export goods and services
Goods and services produced in one country and sold in other countries.

Consumption goods and services are items that are bought by individuals and used to provide personal enjoyment and contribute to a person's standard of living. They include items such as housing, SUVs, popcorn and soda, movies and chocolate bars, microwave ovens and inline skates, and dental and dry cleaning services.

Investment goods are goods that are bought by businesses to increase their productive resources. They include items such as auto assembly lines and shopping malls, airplanes, and oil tankers.

Government goods and services are items that are bought by governments. Governments purchase missiles and weapons systems, travel services, Internet services, police protection, roads, and paper and paper clips.

Export goods and services are items produced in one country and sold in other countries. U.S. export goods and services include the airplanes produced by Boeing that Singapore Airlines buys, the computers produced by Dell that Europeans buy, and licenses sold by U.S. film companies to show U.S. movies in European movie theaters.

Figure 2.1(a) provides a snapshot of the division of total production in the United States in 2002 into these four groups. You can see that consumption goods and services have the largest share at 61 percent of the total. Investment goods accounts for 13 percent of total production. Goods and services bought by governments take 17 percent of the total, and 9 percent is exported.

Figure 2.1(b) shows the production of the largest five services and goods. Real estate services are the largest item and represent 11 percent of the value of total production. The main component of this item is the services of rental and owner-occupied housing. Retail and wholesale trades are the next two largest categories. Health services and education complete the largest five services.

The largest categories of goods—construction, electronic equipment such as computers, food, industrial equipment, and chemicals—each account for less than 4 percent of the value of total production.

FIGURE 2.1
What We Produce

Practice Online

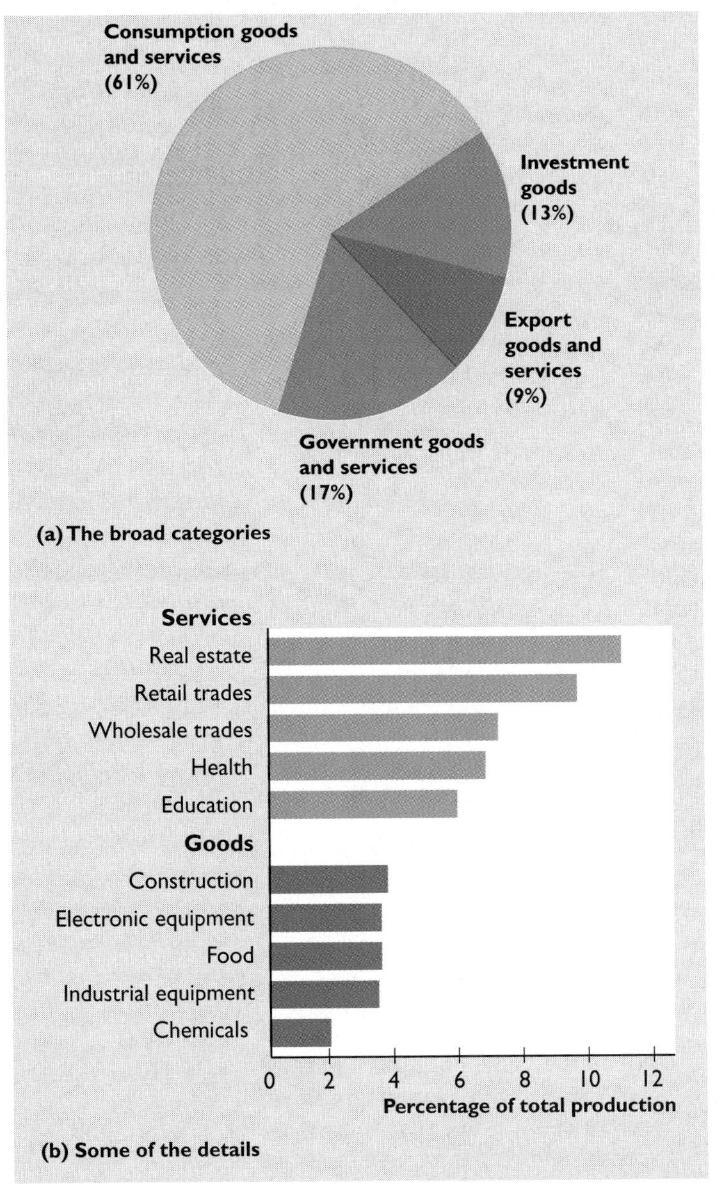

SOURCE: Bureau of Economic Analysis.

In 2002, consumption goods and services accounted for 61 percent of total production. Investment goods accounted for 13 percent, government goods and services accounted for 17 percent, and export goods and services accounted for 9 percent of total production.

Real estate services, retail and wholesale trades, health, and education are the largest five services produced. Construction, electronic equipment, food, industrial equipment, and chemicals are the largest five goods produced. Services production exceeds goods production and is growing faster.

Eye on the Past

Changes in What We Produce

Sixty years ago, one American in four worked on a farm. That number has shrunk to one in thirty-five. The number of people who produce goods—in mining, construction, and manufacturing—has also shrunk from one person in three to one in five. In contrast, the number of people who produce services has expanded from one in two to almost four out of five. These changes in employment reflect changes in what we produce—services.

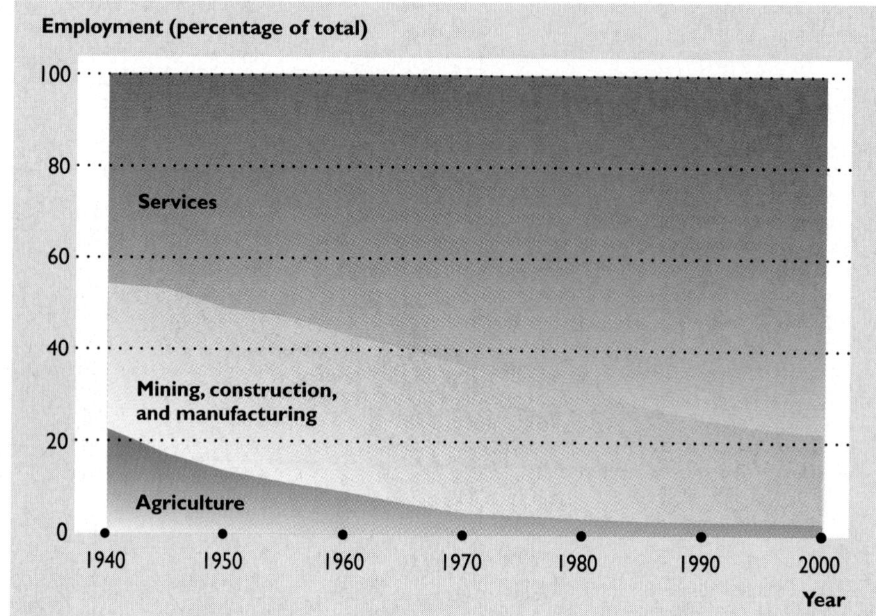

SOURCE: U.S. Census Bureau, *Statistical Abstract of the United States*, 2000.

How Do We Produce?

Factors of production
The productive resources used to produce goods and services—land, labor, capital, and entrepreneurship.

Goods and services are produced by using productive resources. Economists call the productive resources **factors of production**. Factors of production are grouped into four categories:

- Land
- Labor
- Capital
- Entrepreneurship

Land

Land
The "gifts of nature," or *natural resources*, that we use to produce goods and services.

In economics, **land** includes all the "gifts of nature" that we use to produce goods and services. Land is what, in everyday language, we call *natural resources*. It includes land in the everyday sense, minerals, energy, water, and air, and wild plants, animals, birds, and fish. Some of these resources are renewable, and some are nonrenewable. The U.S. Geological Survey maintains a national inventory of the quantity and quality of natural resources and monitors changes to that inventory.

The United States covers almost 2 billion acres. About 45 percent of the land is forest, lakes, and national parks. In 2000, almost 50 percent of the land was used for agriculture and 5 percent was urban, but urban land use is growing and agricultural land use is shrinking.

Our land surface and water resources are renewable, and some of our mineral resources can be recycled. But many mineral resources, and all those that we use to create energy, can be used only once. They are nonrenewable resources. Of these, the United States has vast known coal reserves but much smaller known reserves of oil and natural gas.

Labor

Labor is the work time and work effort that people devote to producing goods and services. It includes the physical and mental efforts of all the people who work on farms and construction sites and in factories, shops, and offices. The Census Bureau and Bureau of Labor Statistics measure the nation's labor force every month.

Labor
The work time and work effort that people devote to producing goods and services.

In the United States in 2002, 144 million people had jobs or were available for work. Some worked full time, some part time, and some were unemployed but looking for an acceptable job. The total amount of time worked during 2002 was about 234 billion hours.

The quantity of labor increases as the adult population increases. The quantity of labor also increases if a larger percentage of the population takes jobs. During the past 50 years, a larger proportion of women have taken paid work and this trend has increased the quantity of labor.

The quality of labor depends on how skilled people are. Economists use a special name for human skill: human capital. **Human capital** is the knowledge and skill that people obtain from education, on-the-job training, and work experience. You are building your own human capital right now as you work on your economics course and other subjects. And your human capital will continue to grow when you get a full-time job and become better at it. Human capital improves the *quality* of labor. Figure 2.2 shows that today more than 80 percent of the U.S. population has completed high school and 25 percent has a college or university degree.

Human capital
The knowledge and skill that people obtain from education, on-the-job training, and work experience.

FIGURE 2.2
Measures of Human Capital

Practice Online

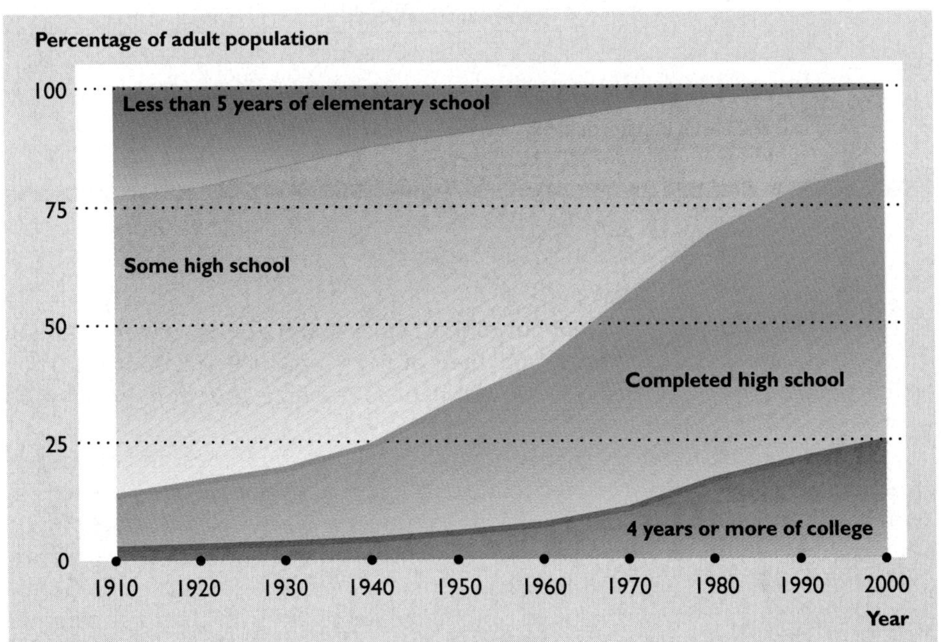

In 2000, 25 percent of the population had 4 years or more of college, up from 3 percent in 1910. An additional 58 percent had completed high school, up from 11 percent in 1910.

SOURCE: U.S. Census Bureau, *Statistical Abstract of the United States*, 2002.

Eye on the U.S. Economy

How We Produce in the New Economy

The new economy consists of the jobs and businesses that produce Internet services, e-commerce, database and other information services, and other computer-driven services. The new economy also consists of the biotechnology industries.

These new economy sectors are indeed growing rapidly. But they are not really the heart of tomorrow's economy.

Tomorrow's economy, like today's economy, will be an increasingly service-oriented economy.

In 1996, some 15 million people worked in general clerical and sales jobs. By 2006, their number will be swelled by another 2 million workers, an increase of 14 percent since 1996. Clerical work and retail selling are the core of tomorrow's economy.

Health care and personal care make up a second large and fast-growing area. The 6 million workers in these jobs will grow to almost 8 million by 2006.

Food preparation and serving will grow by 1 million workers to more than 7 million by 2006. This increase continues the trend toward people buying an ever-increasing proportion of their meals away from home.

The education sector will also expand quickly with close to a million more teachers by 2006, an increase of 33 percent since 1996.

The computer-driven economy will expand rapidly too. In fact, it will grow more quickly than any of the areas we've just reviewed. In 1996, about 1 million people worked in this sector. By 2006, this number will have more than doubled.

These projections through 2006 reinforce the strong sense that our economy is increasingly a service economy.

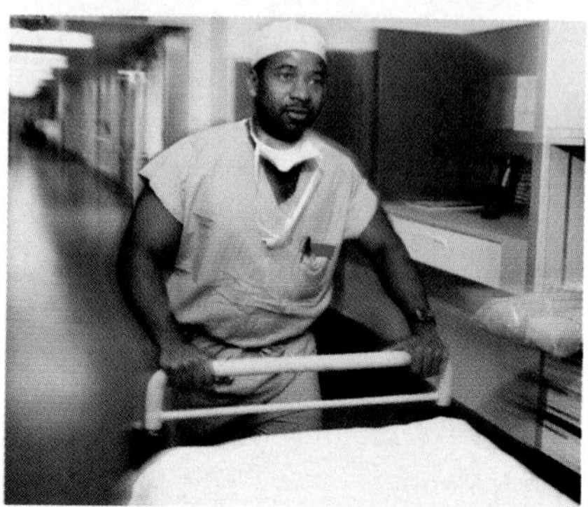

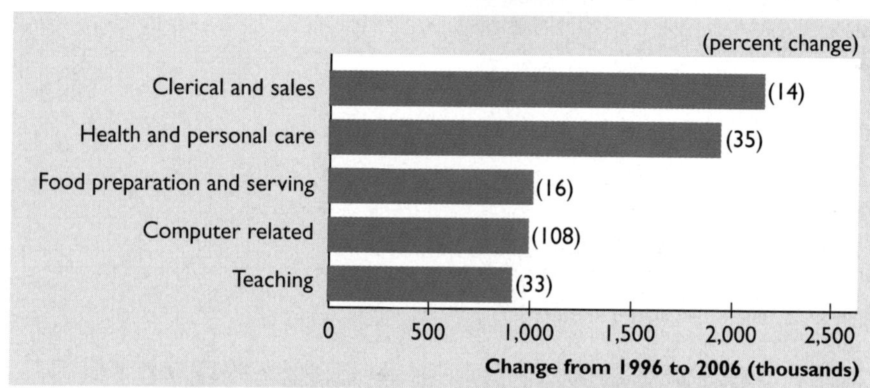

SOURCE: U.S. Census Bureau, *Statistical Abstract of the United States*, 2000.

Capital

In everyday language, we talk about money, stocks, and bonds as being capital. These items are *financial capital*, and they are not productive resources. They enable people to provide businesses with financial resources, but they are *not* used to produce goods and services. They are not capital.

Capital
Tools, instruments, machines, buildings, and other constructions that have been produced in the past and that businesses now use to produce goods and services.

Capital consists of the tools, instruments, machines, buildings, and other constructions that have been produced in the past and that businesses now use to produce goods and services. Capital includes hammers and screwdrivers, computers, auto assembly lines, office towers and warehouses, dams and power plants, airports and airplanes, shirt factories, and cookie shops. The Bureau of Economic Analysis in the U.S. Department of Commerce keeps track of the total value of capital, which grows over time. In the United States today, it is around $20 trillion. The global value of capital exceeds $130 trillion.

Entrepreneurship

Entrepreneurship is the human resource that organizes labor, land, and capital. Entrepreneurs come up with new ideas about what and how to produce, make business decisions, and bear the risks that arise from these decisions.

Entrepreneurship
The human resource that organizes labor, land, and capital.

The quantity of entrepreneurship is hard to describe or measure. At some periods, there appears to be a great deal of imaginative entrepreneurship around. People such as Sam Walton, who created Wal-Mart, one of the world's largest retailers; Bill Gates, who founded the Microsoft empire; and Michael Dell, who established Dell Computers, are examples of extraordinary entrepreneurial talent. But these highly visible entrepreneurs are just the tip of an iceberg that consists of hundreds of thousands of people who run businesses, large and small.

For Whom Do We Produce?

Who gets the goods and services that are produced depends on the incomes that people earn and the goods and services that they choose to buy. A large income enables a person to buy large quantities of goods and services. A small income leaves a person with few options and small quantities of goods and services.

People earn their incomes by selling the services of the factors of production they own. **Rent** is paid for the use of land, **wages** are paid for the services of labor, **interest** is paid for the use of capital, and entrepreneurs receive a **profit** (or incur a **loss**) for running their businesses.

Which factor of production in the United States earns more income: labor or capital? Figure 2.3(a) provides the answer.

Rent
Income paid for the use of land.

Wages
Income paid for the services of labor.

Interest
Income paid for the use of capital.

Profit (or loss)
Income earned by an entrepreneur for running a business.

FIGURE 2.3
For Whom?

Practice Online

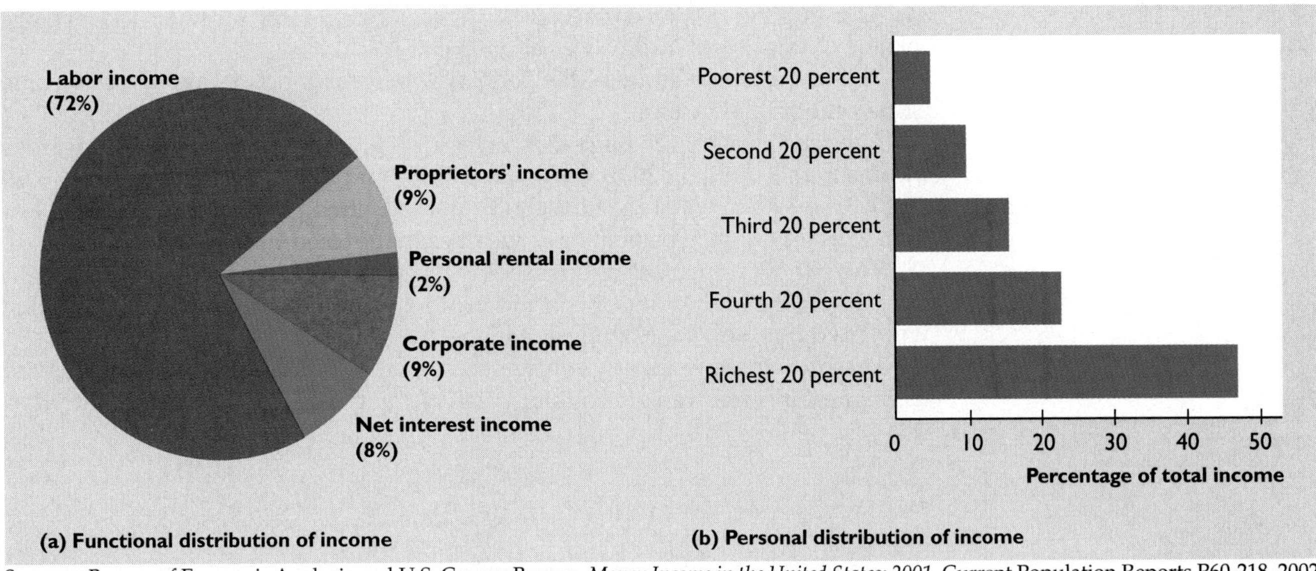

SOURCES: Bureau of Economic Analysis and U.S. Census Bureau, *Money Income in the United States: 2001*, Current Population Reports P60-218, 2002.

Incomes determine who consumes the goods and services produced. In 2002, labor income was 72 percent of total income, capital income (corporate income and net interest income) was 17 percent, and proprietors' income, which includes both wages and rent, was almost 9 percent. Personal rental income was 2 percent of the total. More than 70 percent of total income is from labor. The richest 20 percent of the population receives almost 50 percent of total income. The poorest 20 percent receives only 5 percent of total income.

Functional distribution of income
The distribution of income among the factors of production.

The figure shows the **functional distribution of income**, which is the distribution of income among the factors of production. Labor earns most of the income: 72 percent of total income in 2002. Capital income—corporate income and net interest income—was 17 percent in 2002. The proprietors of businesses, whose earnings are a mixture of labor and capital income, earned 9 percent of total income in 2002. Personal rental income was 2 percent in 2002. These percentages remain remarkably constant over time.

The data in Figure 2.3(a) tell us how income is distributed among the factors of production. But the data don't tell us how income is distributed among individuals.

You know of lots of people who earn very large incomes. Tiger Woods wins several million dollars a year in prize money and earns substantially more than this amount in endorsements. The average salary of major league baseball players in 2002 was $2.4 million, and some stars, such as Barry Bonds, Sammy Sosa, Manny Ramirez, Kevin Brown, Carlos Delgado, and Alex Rodriguez received between $15 million and $22 million a year.

You know of even more people who earn very small incomes. Servers at McDonald's average around $6.50 an hour; checkout clerks, gas station attendants, and textile and leather workers earn less than $10 an hour.

Personal distribution of income
The distribution of income among households.

Figure 2.3(b) shows the **personal distribution of income** after households have paid their income taxes and received benefits from governments. Households are divided into five groups, each of which represents 20 percent of all households. If incomes were equal, each 20 percent group would earn 20 percent of total income. You know that incomes are unequal, and the figure provides a measure of just how unequal they are.

The poorest 20 percent of households receives only 5 percent of total income. The average income of this group in 2001 was about $10,000.

The second poorest 20 percent receives 10 percent of total income. The average income of this group in 2001 was about $25,000.

The middle 20 percent receives 16 percent of total income. The average income of this group in 2001 was about $43,000.

All three of these groups—the poorest 60 percent of households—receive only 31 percent of total income.

The second richest 20 percent receives 23 percent of total income. The average income in this group in 2001 was about $67,000 and the highest income was about $85,000. So 80 percent of the households in the United States have incomes of less than $85,000. Only 20 percent have incomes that exceed this amount.

The richest 20 percent of households receives 47 percent of total income. We don't know the highest income in this group, but some of the famous names that we started out with are examples of high earners.

Based on these numbers, you can see that the 20 percent of households with the highest incomes can afford to buy half of the goods and services produced.

CHECKPOINT 2.1

1 Describe what, how, and for whom goods and services are produced in the United States.

Study Guide pp. 24–26

Practice Online 2.1

Practice Problems 2.1

1. Name the four broad categories of goods and services that we use in economics, provide an example of each (different from those in the chapter), and say what percentage of total production each accounted for in 2002.
2. Name the four factors of production and the incomes they earn.
3. Distinguish between the functional distribution of income and the personal distribution of income.
4. In the United States, which factor of production earns the largest share of income and what percentage does it earn?

Exercises 2.1

1. What is the distinction between consumption goods and services and investment goods? Which one of them brings an increase in productive resources?
2. Describe the changes that have occurred in the education levels of the U.S. labor force during the last few decades.
3. If everyone were to consume an equal quantity of goods and services, what percentage of total income would the poorest 20 percent of individuals have to receive from higher-income groups? What percentage would the second poorest 20 percent have to receive?
4. Compare the percentage of total U. S. income that labor earns with the percentage earned by all the other factors of production combined.

Solutions to Practice Problems 2.1

1. The four categories are consumption goods and services, investment goods, government goods and services, and export goods and services. An example of a consumption service is a haircut, of an investment good is an oil rig, of a government service is police protection, and of an export good is a computer chip sold to Ireland. Of total production, consumption goods and services are 61 percent; investment goods are 13 percent; government goods and services are 17 percent; and export goods and services are 9 percent.
2. The factors of production are land, labor, capital, and entrepreneurship. Land earns rent; labor earns wages; capital earns interest; and entrepreneurship earns profit or incurs a loss.
3. The functional distribution of income shows the percentage of total income received by each factor of production. The personal distribution of income shows the percentage of total income received by households.
4. Labor is the factor of production that earns the largest share of income in the United States. In 2002, labor earned 72 percent of total income.

2.2 CIRCULAR FLOWS

Circular flow model
A model of the economy that shows the circular flow of expenditures and incomes that result from decision makers' choices, and the way those choices interact to determine what, how, and for whom goods and services are produced.

We can organize the data you've just studied using the **circular flow model**—a model of the economy that shows the circular flow of expenditures and incomes that result from decision makers' choices and the way those choices interact to determine what, how, and for whom goods and services are produced. Figure 2.4 shows the circular flow model.

Households and Firms

Households
Individuals or groups of people living together.

Firms
The institutions that organize the production of goods and services.

Households are individuals or groups of people living together. The 109 million households in the United States own the factors of production—land, labor, capital, and entrepreneurship—and choose the quantities of these resources to provide to firms. Households also choose the quantities of goods and services to buy.

Firms are the institutions that organize the production of goods and services. The 20 million firms in the United States choose the quantities of the factors of production to hire and the quantities of goods and services to produce.

Markets

Households choose the quantities of the factors of production to provide to firms, and firms choose the quantities of the services of the factors of production to hire. Households choose the quantities of goods and services to buy, and firms choose the quantities of goods and services to produce. How are these choices coordinated and made compatible? The answer is: by markets.

Market
Any arrangement that brings buyers and sellers together and enables them to get information and do business with each other.

A **market** is any arrangement that brings buyers and sellers together and enables them to get information and do business with each other. An example is the market in which oil is bought and sold—the world oil market. The world oil market is not a place. It is the network of oil producers, oil users, wholesalers, and brokers who buy and sell oil. In the world oil market, decision makers do not meet physically. They make deals by telephone, fax, and the Internet.

Goods markets
Markets in which goods and services are bought and sold.

Factor markets
Markets in which factors of production are bought and sold.

Figure 2.4 identifies two types of markets: goods markets and factor markets. **Goods markets** are markets in which goods and services are bought and sold. **Factor markets** are markets in which factors of production are bought and sold.

Real Flows and Money Flows

When households choose the quantities of land, labor, capital, and entrepreneurship to offer in factor markets, they respond to the incomes they receive—rent for land, wages for labor, interest for capital, and profit for entrepreneurship. When firms choose the quantities of factors to hire, they respond to the rent, wages, interest, and profits they must pay to households.

Similarly, when firms choose the quantities of goods and services to produce and offer for sale in goods markets, they respond to the amounts that they receive from the expenditures that households make. And when households choose the quantities of goods and services to buy, they respond to the amounts they must pay to firms.

Figure 2.4 shows the flows that result from these choices made by households and firms. The real flows are shown in orange. These are the flows of the factors of production that go from households through factor markets to firms and the goods and services that go from firms through goods markets to households. The money flows go in the opposite direction. These flows are the payments made in exchange for factors of production (blue flow) and expenditures on goods and services (red flow).

Lying behind these real flows and money flows are millions of individual choices about what to consume, what to produce, and how to produce. These choices result in buying plans by households and selling plans by firms in goods markets. And the choices result in selling plans by households and buying plans by firms in factor markets. When these buying plans and selling plans are carried out, they determine the prices that people pay and the incomes they earn and so determine for whom goods and services are produced. You'll learn in Chapter 4 how markets coordinate the buying plans and selling plans of households and firms and make them compatible.

Firms produce most of the goods and services that we consume. But governments provide some of the services that we enjoy. And governments play a big role in modifying for whom goods and services are produced by changing the distribution of income. So we're now going to look at the role of governments in the U.S. economy and add them to the circular flow model.

FIGURE 2.4
The Circular Flow Model

Practice Online

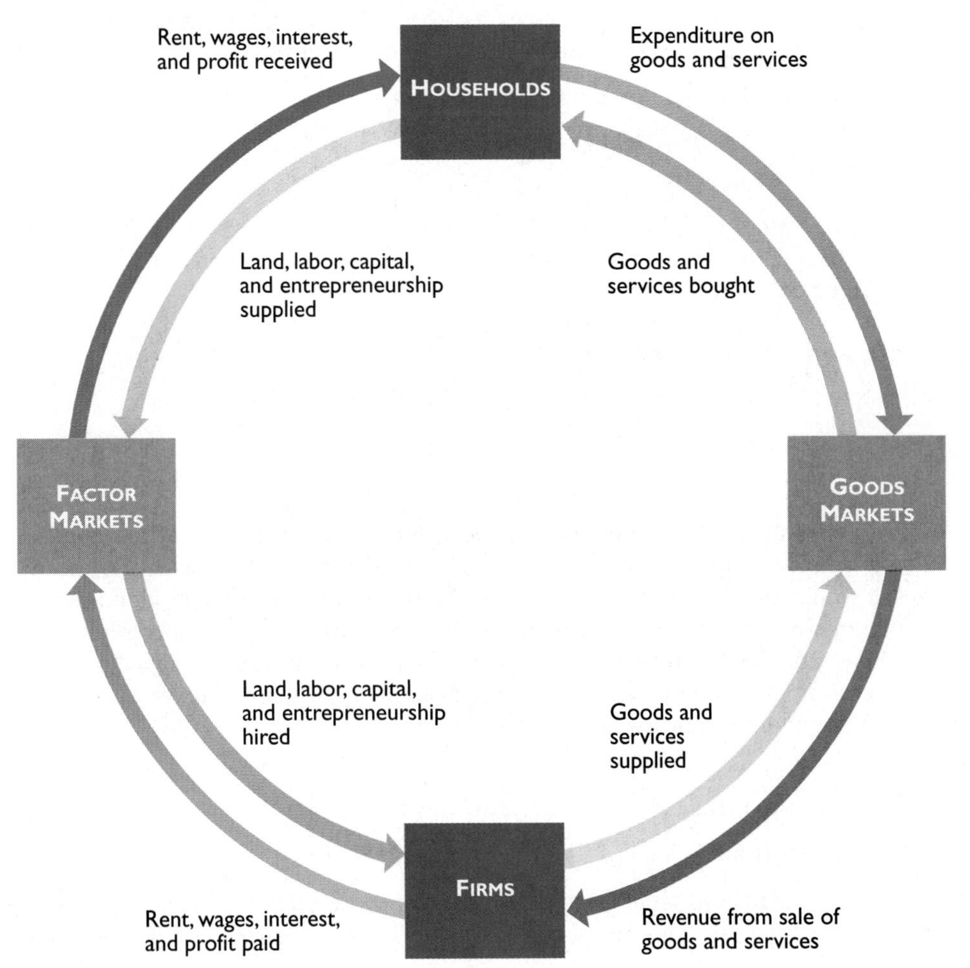

The orange flows are the factors of production that go from households through factor markets to firms and the goods and services that go from firms through goods markets to households.

The blue flow is the incomes earned by the factors of production and the red flow is the expenditures on goods and services.

The choices that generate these flows determine what, how, and for whom goods and services are produced.

Governments

More than 86,000 organizations operate as governments in the United States. Some are tiny like the Yuma, Arizona, school district and some are enormous like the U.S. federal government. We divide governments into two levels:

- Federal government
- State and local government

Federal Government

The federal government's major expenditures are to provide

1. Goods and services
2. Social security and welfare payments
3. Transfers to state and local governments

The goods and services provided by the federal government include the legal system, which defines property rights and enforces contracts, and national defense. Social security and welfare benefits, which include income for retired seniors and programs such as Medicare and Medicaid, are transfers from the federal government to households. Transfers to state and local governments are payments designed to provide more equality across the states and regions.

The federal government finances its expenditures by collecting a variety of taxes. The main taxes paid to the federal government are

1. Personal income taxes
2. Corporate (business) income taxes
3. Social security taxes

In 2002, the federal government spent and raised in taxes more than $2 trillion—about 20 percent of the total value of all the goods and services produced in the United States in that year.

State and Local Government

The state and local governments' major expenditures are to provide

1. Goods and services
2. Welfare benefits

The goods and services provided by state and local governments include the state courts and law enforcement authorities, schools, roads, garbage collection and disposal, water supplies, and sewage management. Welfare benefits provided by state governments include unemployment benefits and other aid to low-income families.

State and local governments finance these expenditures by collecting taxes and receiving transfers from the federal government. The main taxes paid to state and local governments are

1. Sales taxes
2. Property taxes
3. State income taxes

In 2002, state and local governments spent more than $1.3 trillion—about 13 percent of the total value of all the goods and services produced in the United States in that year.

Governments in the Circular Flow

Figure 2.5 adds governments to the circular flow model. As you study this figure, first notice that the outer circle is the same as Figure 2.4. In addition to these flows, governments buy goods and services from firms. The red arrows that run from governments through the goods markets to firms show this expenditure.

Households and firms pay taxes to governments. The green arrows running directly from households and firms to governments show these flows. Also, the governments make money payments to households and firms. The green arrows running directly from governments to households and firms show these flows. Taxes and transfers are direct transactions with governments and do not go through the goods markets and factor markets.

Not part of the circular flow and not visible in Figure 2.5, governments provide the legal framework within which all transactions occur. For example, they operate the courts and legal system that enable contracts to be written and enforced.

FIGURE 2.5
Governments in the Circular Flow

Practice Online

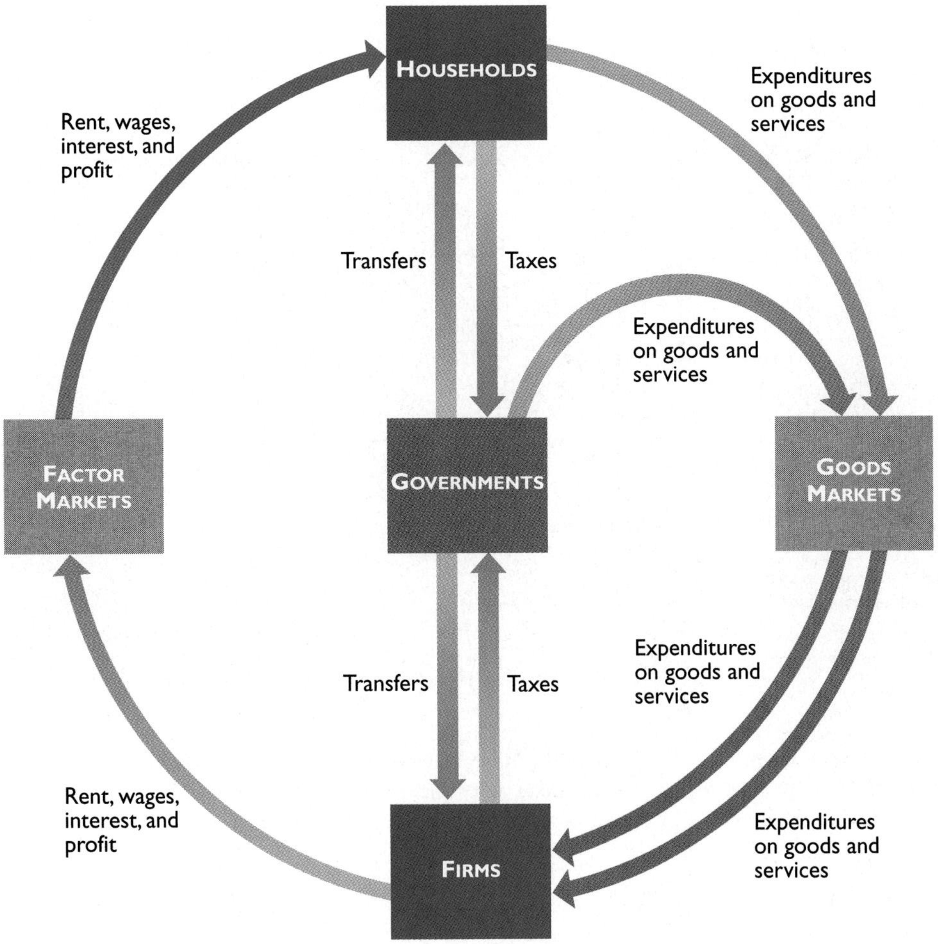

The green flows from households and firms to governments are taxes, and the green flows from governments to households and firms are money transfers.

The red flow from governments through goods markets to firms is the expenditures on goods and services by governments.

Federal Government Expenditures and Revenue

What are the main items of expenditures by the federal government on goods and services and transfers? And what are its main sources of tax revenue? Figure 2.6 answers these questions.

You can see that by far the largest part of what the federal government spends is on social security benefits and other transfers to persons. National defense also takes a big slice of the federal government's expenditures. The interest payment on the national debt is another large item. The **national debt** is the total amount that the federal government has borrowed to make expenditures that exceed tax revenue—to run a government budget deficit. The national debt is a bit like a large credit card balance. And paying the interest on the national debt is like paying the minimum required monthly payment.

National debt
The total amount that the federal government has borrowed to make expenditures that exceed tax revenue—to run a government budget deficit.

Transfers to other levels of government also use up a large part of the federal government's expenditures. Purchases of goods and services (other than national defense) are relatively small, and subsidies and aid to other countries take a tiny slice of expenditures.

Most of the tax revenue of the federal government—almost a half of it—comes from personal income taxes. And two thirds of the rest comes from social security taxes. Corporate income taxes are a small part of the federal government's revenue.

FIGURE 2.6
Federal Government Expenditures and Revenue

Practice Online

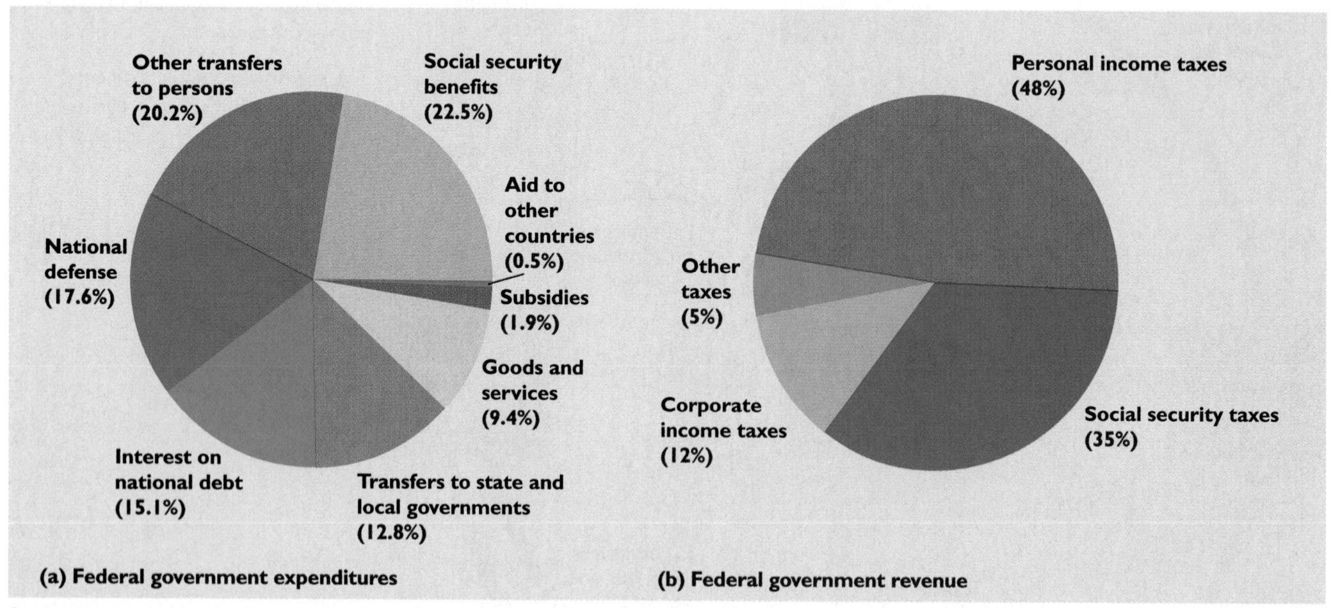

SOURCE: Bureau of Economic Analysis.

Social security benefits and other transfers to persons are the largest slice of federal government expenditures. National defense, interest on the national debt, and transfers to state and local governments also are a large share.

Most of the federal government's revenue comes from personal income taxes and social security taxes. Corporate income taxes are only a small part of total revenue.

State and Local Government Expenditures and Revenue

What are the main items of expenditures by the state and local governments on goods and services and transfers? And what are their main sources of revenue? Figure 2.7 answers these questions.

You can see that education is by far the largest part of the expenditures of state and local governments. This item covers the cost of public schools, colleges, and universities. It absorbs 40 percent of total expenditures—approximately $520 billion, or $1,870 per person.

Welfare benefits are the second largest item, and it takes 20 percent of total expenditures. Highways are the next largest item, and they account for 8 percent of total expenditures. The remaining 32 percent is spent on other local public goods and services such as police services, garbage collection and disposal, sewage management, and water supplies.

Sales taxes and transfers from the federal government bring in similar amounts—about 25 percent of total revenue. Property taxes account for 21 percent of total revenue. Individual income taxes account for 15 percent, and corporate income taxes account for 3 percent. The remaining 13 percent comes from other taxes such as estate taxes.

FIGURE 2.7

State and Local Government Expenditures and Revenue

Practice Online

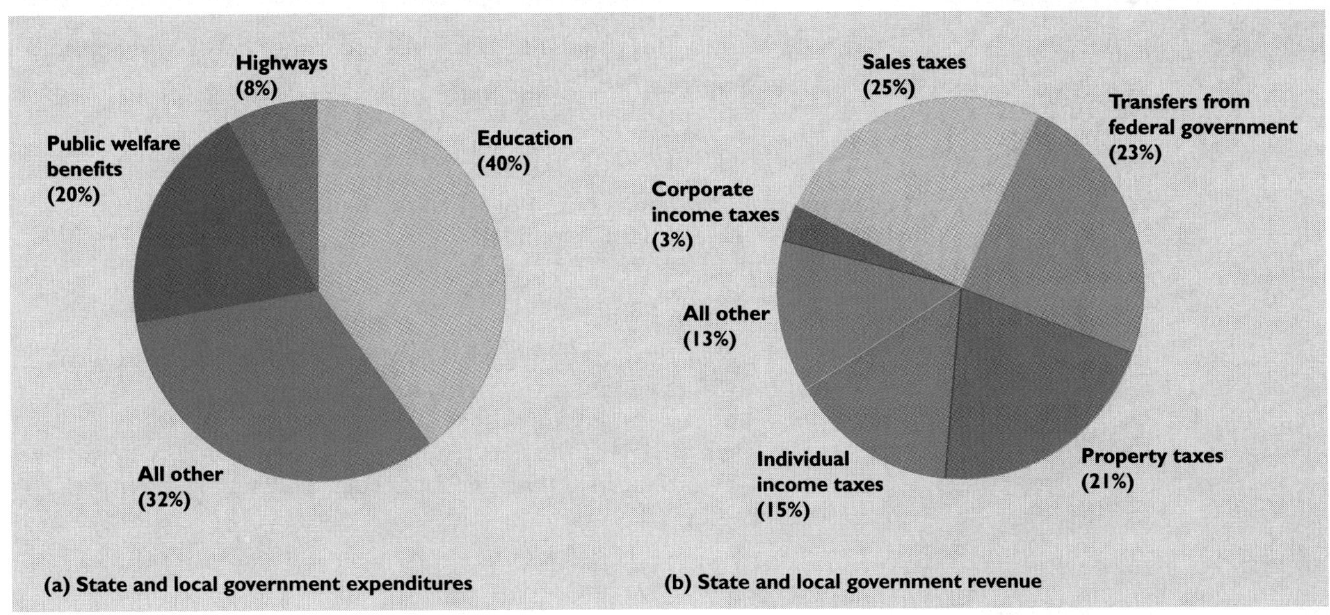

SOURCE: Bureau of Economic Analysis.

Education, highways, and public welfare benefits are the largest slice of state and local government expenditures.

Most of the state and local government revenue comes from sales taxes, property taxes, and transfers from the federal government.

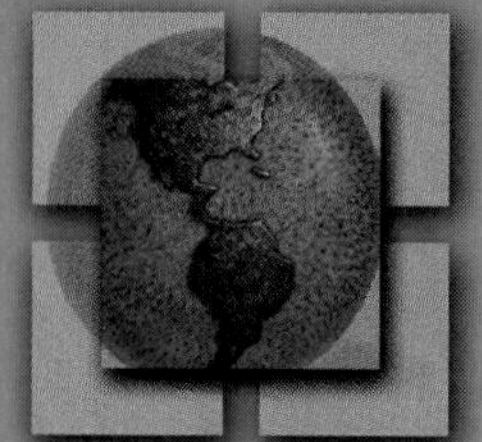

Eye on the Global Economy

Production and People in the World Today

In the United States, 5 percent of the world's people produce 22 percent of the value of the world's output. The figure shows the percentages of population and production for other nations and regions.

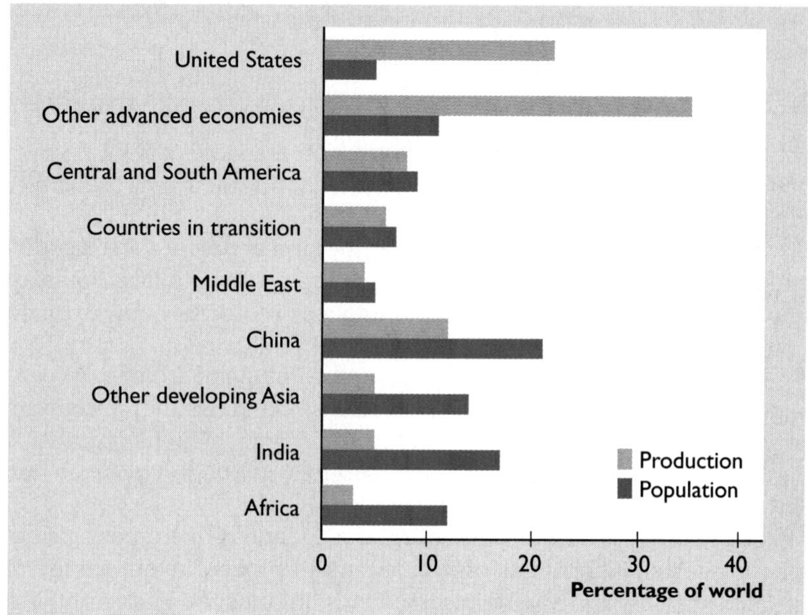

SOURCE: International Monetary Fund, *World Economic Outlook* database.

CHECKPOINT 2.2

Study Guide **pp. 27–29**

Practice Online 2.2

2 **Use the circular flow model to provide a picture of how households, firms, and governments interact.**

Practice Problem 2.2

What are the real flows and money flows that run between households, firms, and governments in the circular flow model?

Exercises 2.2

1. What are the choices made by households and firms that determine what, how, and for whom goods and services are produced? Where, in the circular flow model, do those choices appear?
2. How do the actions of governments modify what, how, and for whom goods and services are produced? Where, in the circular flow model, do those choices appear?

Solution to Practice Problem 2.2

The real flows are the services of factors of production from households to firms and the goods and services from firms to households and from firms to governments. The money flows are factor incomes, household and government expenditures on goods and services, taxes, and transfers.

2.3 MACROECONOMIC PERFORMANCE

Macroeconomic performance has three dimensions:

- Standard of living
- Cost of living
- Economic fluctuations

Standard of Living

The standard of living depends on the quantities of goods and services produced and the number of people among whom those goods and services are shared. The greater the value of production per person, the higher is the standard of living, other things remaining the same. For the world as a whole, the average value of goods and services produced is $21 per person per day. But there is an enormous range around that average. Let's begin our exploration of global living standards by looking at the size and distribution of the population.

World Population

Visit the Web site of the U.S. Census Bureau and find the population clocks. On September 8, 2002, the U.S. clock recorded a population of 287,991,639. The world clock recorded a global population of 6,248,847,500. The U.S. clock ticks along showing a population increase of one person every 14 seconds. The world clock spins much faster, adding 34 people in the same 14 seconds.

Classification of Countries

The world's 6.25 billion (and rising) population lives in 184 economies classified by the International Monetary Fund into three broad groups:

- Advanced economies
- Developing economies
- Transition economies

Advanced Economies Advanced economies are the 28 countries (or areas) that have the highest standards of living. The United States, Japan, Italy, Germany, France, the United Kingdom, and Canada belong to this group. So do four new industrial Asian economies: Hong Kong, South Korea, Singapore, and Taiwan. The other advanced economies include Australia, New Zealand, and most of the rest of Western Europe. Almost 1 billion people live in the advanced economies.

Developing Economies Developing economies are the 128 countries in Africa, Asia, the Middle East, Europe, and Central and South America that have not yet achieved a high standard of living for their people. The standard of living in these economies varies a great deal, but in all cases, it is much lower than that in the advanced economies, and in some cases, it is extremely low. Almost 5 billion people live in the developing economies.

Transition Economies Transition economies are the 28 countries in Europe and Asia that were, until the early 1990s, part of the Soviet Union or its satellites. These countries include Russia, Hungary, Poland, and the Czech Republic.

The economies in this group are small—only 200 million people in total—but are important because they are in transition (hence the name) from a system of state-owned production, central economic planning, and heavily regulated markets to a system of free enterprise and unregulated markets.

Living Standards Around the World

Figure 2.8 shows the distribution of living standards around the world in 2002, measured in dollars per day. You can see that in the United States, the average income is $100 a day. This number tells you that an average person in the United States can buy goods and services that cost $100, which is close to five times the world average. Canada has an average income close to 90 percent of that in the United States. Japan, Germany, France, Italy, the United Kingdom, and the other advanced economies have average incomes around two thirds that of the United States. Living standards fall off quickly as we move farther down the table, with India and the African continent achieving average incomes of only $5 a day.

Most people live in the countries that have incomes below the world average. You can see this fact by looking at the population numbers shown in the figure. The poorest five countries or regions—China, Central Asia, Other Asia, India, and Africa—have a total population of 4 billion.

FIGURE 2.8
The Standard of Living Around the World

Practice Online

Average income per person ranges from $5 a day in Africa to $100 a day in the United States. The world average is $21 a day. Russia and Central and South America have incomes that are close to the world average.

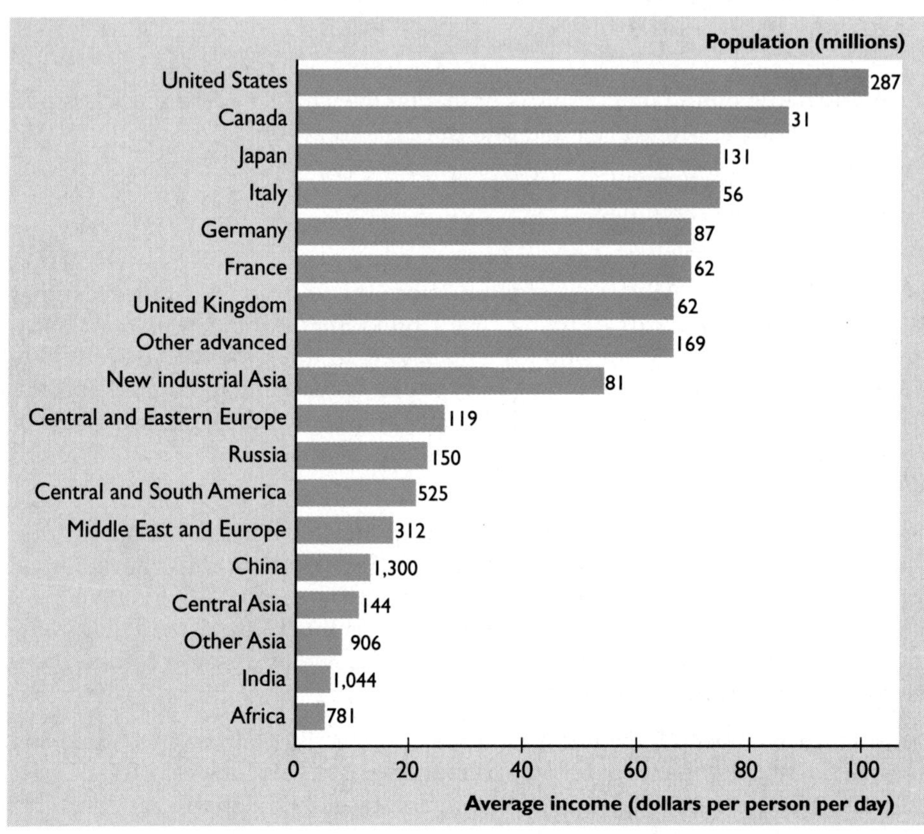

SOURCE: International Monetary Fund, *World Economic Outlook*, April 2002, Washington, D.C.

Unemployment and Living Standards

Unemployment is another factor that influences the standard of living. If jobs are easy to find, then when people lose their jobs they will find new ones after only a short period of unemployment. But if jobs are hard to find, then when people lose their jobs they will find new ones only after a long period of unemployment.

Unemployment rates vary enormously around the world. In the United States, the average unemployment rate during the past 20 years has been 6 percent. That is, for every 100 people in the labor force, 94 have jobs and 6 are looking for jobs but can't find them. At this average unemployment rate, it takes an unemployed person an average of about 15 weeks to find an acceptable job.

Figure 2.9 shows the distribution of unemployment rates among developed countries, on the average for the 1980s and 1990s. (Note that the European Union average includes some of the other countries shown separately.)

The United States has one of the world's lowest unemployment rates. Only Japan and the new industrial economies of Asia (Hong Kong, Korea, Singapore, and Taiwan) have lower rates. Canada, the European Union, and other advanced economies have higher rates. And two members of the European Union—Spain and Ireland—have extremely high unemployment rates.

Figure 2.9 does *not* show the unemployment rates of the developing and transition economies. Why not? No one knows what they are. Data on unemployment is expensive to collect, and only the rich advanced economies devote resources to its measurement. Even though developing and transition economies do not measure unemployment rates, they are likely to be substantially higher than those in the advanced economies and might even exceed the high rate of Spain.

Why unemployment rates differ across economies is a difficult question to answer and is one of the challenges of macroeconomics.

FIGURE 2.9

Unemployment Rates Around the World

Practice Online

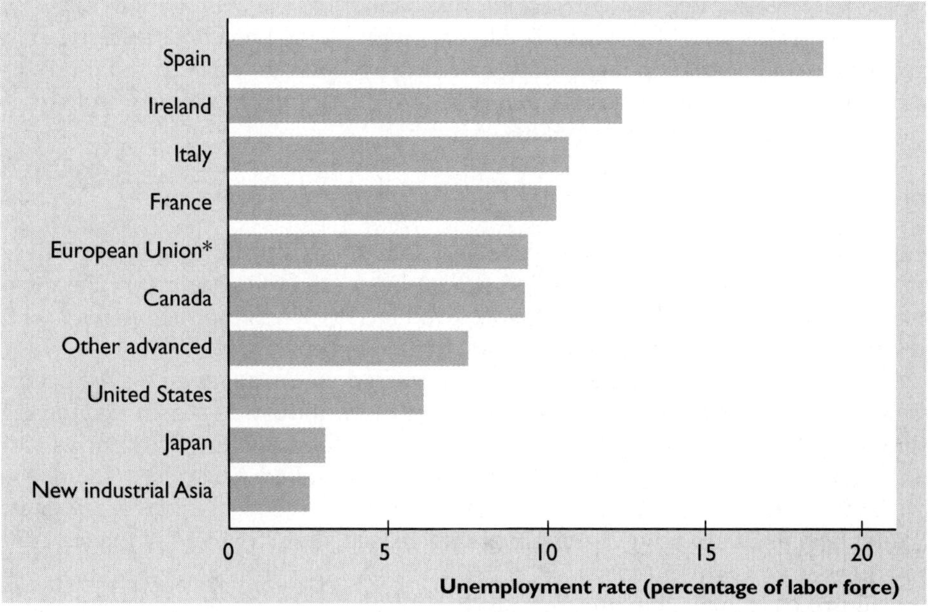

SOURCE: International Monetary Fund, *World Economic Outlook*, April 2002, Washington, D.C.

During the 1980s and 1990s, the average unemployment rate in Spain was much higher than in most advanced economies. The unemployment rate in the United States is among the lowest, but it is not as low as in Japan and in the new industrial Asian economies.

* The European Union average is the average for all 15 member countries, including Spain, Ireland, Italy, and France.

Cost of Living

The cost of living is the amount of money it takes to buy the goods and services that achieve a given standard of living. In the United States, we measure money in dollars. So the cost of living in the United States is the number of dollars it takes to buy the goods and services that achieve a given standard of living. In the United Kingdom, it is the number of pounds; in Japan, the number of yen; in Russia, the number of rubles; and in Indonesia, the number of rupiahs.

Prices in Different Currencies

TABLE 2.1 THE PRICE OF A BIG MAC IN TEN CURRENCIES

Country or Region	Name of currency	Price of a Big Mac
United Kingdom	Pound	2.00
United States	Dollar	2.50
Euro area	Euro	2.67
Brazil	Real	3.60
South Africa	Rand	9.70
Israel	Shekel	13.90
Russia	Ruble	35.00
Japan	Yen	294
South Korea	Won	3,000
Indonesia	Rupiah	14,700

To make this idea concrete, think about the price of a Big Mac. Table 2.1 shows some prices in 10 currencies. The average price of a Big Mac in the United States is $2.50. In the United Kingdom, it is £2.00, and in Japan, it is ¥294. So in the United Kingdom, it costs a smaller number of money units to buy a Big Mac than it does in United States, and in Japan, it costs a larger number of money units. But the price of a Big Mac is actually *more* in the United Kingdom than in either the United States or Japan. The reason is that a pound is worth $1.55, so £2.00 is equivalent to $3.10. And a pound is worth 182 yen, so £2.00 is equivalent to ¥364.

Inflation

The number of money units that something costs is not very important, but the rate at which the number of money units is changing is important. A rising cost of living, called inflation (see p. 5), is measured by the percentage change in the cost of living. Most countries experience inflation, but its rate varies enormously. In the United States, the inflation rate during the 1980s and 1990s was 3 percent a year. To put this number in perspective, a Big Mac that cost $2.50 in 2002 cost $1.80 in 1992 and $1.30 in 1982. Inflation at this rate is not generally regarded as a big problem. But it is a problem that we need to understand.

Most of the advanced economies have low inflation rates, as you can see in Figure 2.10. But the developing economies have higher inflation rates, some of them spectacularly so. In Central and South America, the average inflation rate during the 1980s and 1990s was 107 percent a year. A 100 percent change means a doubling. At this inflation rate, prices are rising by 6 percent a *month*. Inflation this rapid poses huge problems as people try to avoid holding onto money and struggle to cope with an ever-falling value of money.

Economic Fluctuations

Economies expand at an uneven pace and sometimes shrink for a while. These ebbs and flows of economic activity are the business cycle (see p. 6). The most recent recessions in the United States occurred in 1991 when production fell by 1.3 percent and in 2001 when production fell by 0.6 percent.

The most serious recent recessions occurred in Asia. Japan's production shrank by 1 percent and production in the new industrial Asian economies shrank by 2.4 percent in 1998 amidst a crisis of confidence in their currencies and financial systems. Many firms failed during this so-called Asia crisis. The deepest and lengthiest recession of the 1990s was in the transition economies. Production in Russia and its neighbors decreased by 33 percent between 1990 and 1994.

Figure 2.11 shows the recessions and expansions that we've just described.

FIGURE 2.10
Inflation Rates Around the World

Practice Online

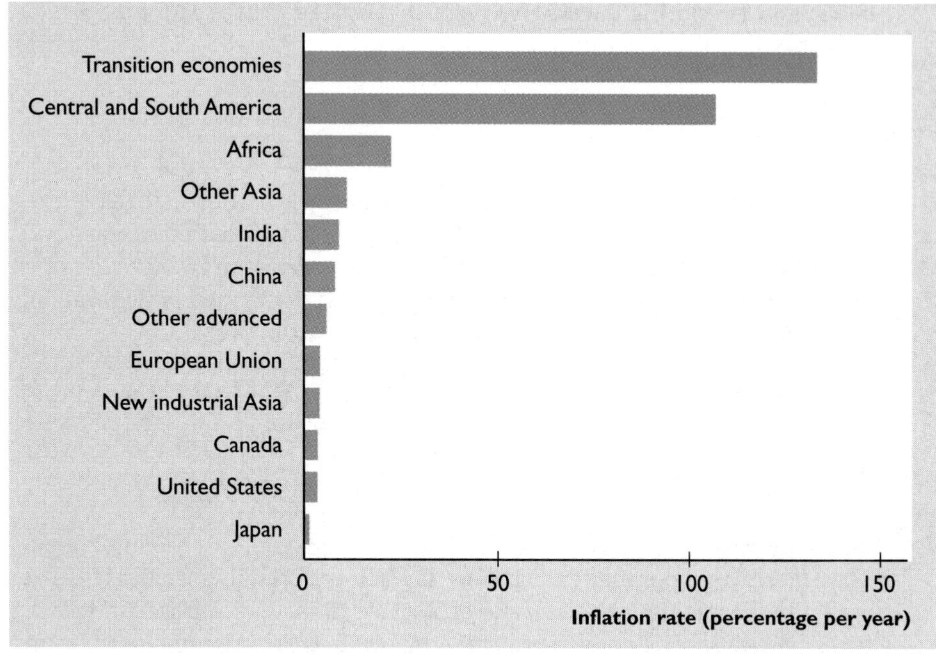

SOURCE: International Monetary Fund, *World Economic Outlook*, April 2002, Washington, D.C.

The most severe inflation has occurred in the transition economies (Russia and its neighbors) and Central and South America. In the United States and the other advanced economies, inflation rates were very low during the 1990s.

FIGURE 2.11
Business Cycles in the Global Economy

Practice Online

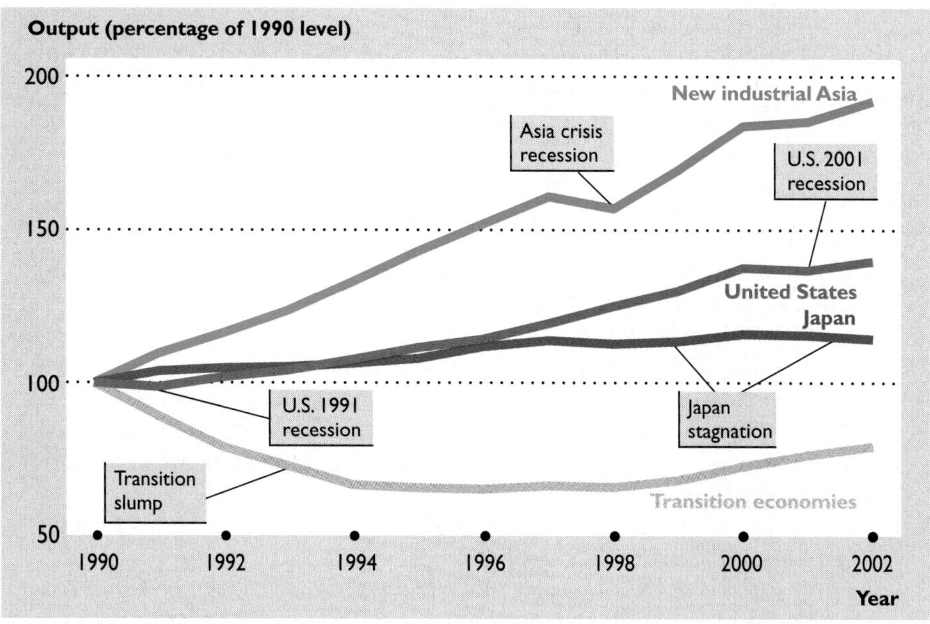

SOURCE: International Monetary Fund, *World Economic Outlook*, April 2002, Washington, D.C.

The United States had recessions in 1991 and 2001. Japan and the new industrial countries of Asia had a sharp recession in 1998. The transition economies had a long and deep recession for most of the 1990s.

CHECKPOINT 2.3

Study Guide pp. 29–31

Practice Online 2.3

3 Describe the macroeconomic performance—standard of living, cost of living, and economic fluctuations—of the United States and other economies.

Practice Problems 2.3

1. What percentage of the world's population live in developing economies and what was the range of incomes that these people earned in 2002?
2. What percentage of the world's population live in advanced economies and what was the range of incomes that these people earned in 2002?
3. What percentage of the world's population live in the United States and what was the average income that Americans earned in 2002?
4. Which countries or regions experienced high inflation during the 1990s?
5. Which countries or regions experienced recession during the 1990s and the early 2000s?

Exercises 2.3

1. What is the current world population and how rapidly is it growing? What is the current U.S. population and how rapidly is it growing? Is the U.S. population becoming larger or smaller relative to the world population?
2. Classify the following countries as (a) advanced, (b) developing, or (c) transition: Canada, Bolivia, Brazil, China, Colombia, Germany, Ghana, India, Japan, Korea, New Zealand, Russia, Singapore, the United States, Vietnam.
3. What was the average income in the world as a whole in 2002? Which regions or nations were closest to that world average, which were the farthest above it, and which were the farthest below it?
4. What was the average U.S. inflation rate during the 1990s? Is inflation at this rate considered to be a serious problem? Why or why not?
5. Compare and contrast the most recent U.S. recession with the most recent recessions in Asia and the transition economies. Which was the deepest? Which lasted the longest?

Solutions to Practice Problems 2.3

1. Approximately 80 percent of the world's population lives in developing economies. In 2002, their average daily incomes ranged from $5 in Africa to $21 in Central and South America.
2. Approximately 16 percent of the world's population lives in advanced economies. In 2002, their average daily incomes ranged from about $55 in the new industrial economies of Asia to $100 in the United States.
3. In 2002, the population of the United States was 287 million—about 5 percent of the world's 6.25 billion population. The average income in the United States was $100 a day.
4. The transition economies and parts of Central and South America experienced high inflation during the 1990s.
5. The transition economies, Japan, and the new industrial economies of Asia experienced recession during the 1990s. The United States was in recession in 1991 and 2001, but for the rest of the 1990s it experienced expansion.

Key Points

1 Describe what, how, and for whom goods and services are produced in the United States.

- Consumption goods and services represent 61 percent of total production; investment goods represent 13 percent.
- Goods and services are produced by using the four factors of production: land, labor, capital, and entrepreneurship.
- The incomes people earn—rent for land, wages for labor, interest for capital, and profit for entrepreneurship—and the taxes they pay and benefits they receive from government determine who gets what is produced.

2 Use the circular flow model to provide a picture of how households, firms, and governments interact.

- The circular flow model shows the real flows of factors and goods and the corresponding money flows of incomes and expenditures.
- Governments in the circular flow receive taxes, make transfers, and buy goods and services.
- Social security, other transfers to persons, national defense, interest on the national debt, and transfers to other levels of government make up most of the federal government's expenditures, and personal income taxes pay the largest share of these expenditures.
- Education, welfare benefits, and highways account for most of the expenditures of the state and local governments, and sales taxes, transfers from the federal government, and property taxes pay for these expenditures.

3 Describe the macroeconomic performance—standard of living, cost of living, and economic fluctuations—of the United States and other economies.

- The standard of living, measured by income per person per day, ranges from an average of $5 in Africa to $100 in the United States.
- Inflation is low in most of the world but has been rapid in the transition economies (Russia and others) and in Central and South America.
- The United States had recessions in 1991 and 2001. Japan, the new industrial economies of Asia, and the transition economies had recessions during the 1990s.

Key Terms

Capital, 40
Circular flow model, 44
Consumption goods and services, 36
Entrepreneurship, 41
Export goods and services, 36
Factor markets, 44
Factors of production, 38
Firms, 44
Functional distribution of income, 42
Goods markets, 44
Government goods and services, 36
Households, 44
Human capital, 39
Interest, 41
Investment goods, 36
Labor, 39
Land, 38
Market, 44
National debt, 48
Personal distribution of income, 42
Profit (or loss), 41
Rent, 41
Wages, 41

Exercises

1. Which of the following items are not consumption goods and services and why?
   a. A chocolate bar
   b. A ski lift
   c. A gold ball
   d. An interstate highway
   e. An airplane
   f. A stealth bomber
2. Which of the following items are not investment goods and why?
   a. An auto assembly line
   b. A shopping mall
   c. A golf ball
   d. An interstate highway
   e. An oil tanker
   f. A construction worker
3. Which of the following items are not factors of production and why?
   a. Vans used by a baker to deliver bread
   b. 1,000 shares of Amazon.com stock
   c. Undiscovered oil
   d. A garbage truck
   e. A pack of bubble gum
   f. The President of the United States
   g. Disneyland
4. Think about the trends in what and how goods and services are produced:
   a. Which jobs will grow fastest during the next decade? Explain your answer.
   b. What types of jobs will most people most likely be doing 50 years from now? Explain your answer.
   c. What do you think will happen to the quantity of human capital over the next decade? Explain your answer.
   d. Do you think that at some future time, there will be no jobs? Why or why not?
5. You've seen that the distribution of income is unequal. Why do you think it is unequal?
6. The government grew larger through the mid-1980s and shrank slightly after that time. Why do you think the government grew until the mid-1980s and then began to shrink slightly?
7. Review the sources of government revenue and determine who pays most of the taxes: workers, businesses, or consumers. Do the same groups that pay most of the federal taxes also pay most of the state and local taxes?
8. On a graph of the circular flow model, label the flows in which the following items occur:
   a. Capital owned by households and used by firms
   b. Computers sold by firms to governments and households
   c. Labor hired by firms
   d. Land rented to businesses
   e. Taxes paid by households and firms
   f. Unemployment benefits
   g. Wages paid by firms
   h. Dividends paid by businesses
   i. Profit paid to entrepreneurs

Critical Thinking

9. You've seen in this chapter that the United States is increasingly becoming a service-producing economy. The production of food and manufactured goods is a shrinking proportion of total production. We continue to consume large quantities of food and manufactures, but these items increasingly are produced in other parts of the world and imported into the United States.

   Reflecting on these facts do you think that we should be concerned that much of our food and most of our clothing, electronic goods, and other manufactured goods come from abroad? Organize your answer around the following five points:

   a. In what ways should we be concerned?
   b. Who in the United States do you think benefits from the availability of cheap foreign-produced food, clothing, electronic goods, and other manufactured goods?
   c. Who in the United States do you think bears the cost of cheap foreign-produced food, clothing, electronic goods, and other manufactured goods?
   d. Who in the rest of the world do you think benefits from the United States buying foreign-produced food, clothing, electronic goods, and other manufactured goods?
   e. Who in the rest of the world do you think bears the cost of the United States buying cheap foreign-produced food, clothing, electronic goods, and other manufactured goods?

10. Although our urban areas use only a bit more than 100 million acres of our 1,944 million acres of land, urban use has increased by 35 million acres in just 20 years. In light of this change, do you think that we should be concerned that too much of our land is becoming urban? Organize your answer around the following five points:
   a. What type of land gets transferred to urban use?
   b. Who benefits from the transfer of an acre of farmland to an acre of suburban housing?
   c. Who bears the cost of the transfer of an acre of farmland to an acre of suburban housing?
   d. What steps could be taken to slow the transfer of farmland to urban use?
   e. Is there a case for not just slowing the transfer of farmland to urban use but either stopping it completely or even trying to reverse the trend?

11. "If the trends in schooling continue, at some point in the future, everyone will have a college degree and no one will be available to work as a janitor or garbage collector." Critically evaluate this statement.

12. "Income is unequally distributed, but because wages account for more than 70 percent of total income, so any redistribution from the rich to the poor means taking from wage earners to give to others." What is wrong with the reasoning in this statement?

13. You've seen that the government grew larger through the mid-1980s and shrank slightly after that time. Do you think the government is too big or too small? Provide your reasons.

14. You've seen that all levels of government get only a small part of their revenues from taxing businesses. Why do you think businesses pay a small share of taxes? Wouldn't it be better if businesses paid more taxes and individuals paid less? Explain your answer.

Practice Online

Web Exercises

Use the links on your Foundations Web site to work the following exercises.

15. Review the special "20th Century Statistics" section of the 1999 *Statistical Abstract of the United States* and find the table that describes the trends in food consumption.
   a. Describe the trends in the consumption of the eight categories of food and drink shown in the table since 1970. Which item has increased most? Which item has increased least?
   b. Can you think of reasons for the trends that you've found?

16. Review the special "20th Century Statistics" section of the 1999 *Statistical Abstract of the United States* and find the table that describes trends in the characteristics of housing and the items that people own.
   a. Describe the trend in the ownership of homes. Do more people own or rent their homes today than the proportions in 1940?
   b. Describe the trend in the ownership of mobile homes and trailers.
   c. Describe the trend in plumbing facilities.
   d. Describe the trend in vehicle ownership.
   e. Describe the trend in telephone ownership.
   f. Can you explain the trends that you've found?

17. Review the special "20th Century Statistics" section of the 1999 *Statistical Abstract of the United States* and find the table that describes trends in transportation.
   a. Describe the trend in air travel.
   b. Describe the trend in the price of air travel.
   c. Can you explain the trends that you've found?
   d. How might these trends be influenced by the events of September 11, 2001?

18. Review the special "20th Century Statistics" section of the 1999 *Statistical Abstract of the United States* and find the table that describes trends in transportation.
   a. Describe the trend in road travel.
   b. Can you explain the trend that you've found?
   c. How might this trend be influenced by the events of September 11, 2001?

19. Visit the regional income pages of the Bureau of Economic Analysis at the U.S. Department of Commerce.
   a. Obtain data on per capita personal income for the states as a percentage of U.S. per capita personal income.
   b. Which state has the highest per capita income and which has the lowest?
   c. Where in the ranking does your state stand?
   d. Can you think of reasons for the ranking that you've found?
   e. Does the ranking change much from year to year? Why or why not?

20. Visit the University of Michigan's Statistical Resources on the Web.
   a. Find data that interest you and that provide information about what, how, and for whom goods and services are produced.
   b. Find data that tell you about the size and the growth of government.
   c. Find data that tell you about the scale and trends in international trade.

CHAPTER 3

The Economic Problem

CHAPTER CHECKLIST

When you have completed your study of this chapter, you will be able to

1. **Use the production possibilities frontier to illustrate the economic problem.**
2. **Calculate opportunity cost.**
3. **Define efficiency and describe an efficient use of resources.**
4. **Explain how people gain from specialization and trade.**
5. **Explain how technological change and increases in capital and human capital expand production possiblities.**

You learned in Chapter 1 that all economic problems arise from scarcity, that scarcity forces us to make choices, and that in making choices, we try to get the most value out of our scarce resources by comparing marginal costs and marginal benefits. You learned in Chapter 2 what, how, and for whom goods and services are produced in the U.S. economy. And you used your first economic model, the circular flow model, to illustrate the choices and interactions that determine what, how, and for whom goods and services are produced.

In this chapter, you will study another economic model: one that illustrates scarcity, choice, and cost and that helps us to understand the choices that people and societies actually make. You will also learn about the central idea of economics—*efficiency*. And you will discover how we gain by specializing and trading with each other and how economic growth expands our production possibilities.

3.1 PRODUCTION POSSIBILITIES

Every working day in the mines, factories, shops, and offices and on the farms and construction sites across the United States, we produce a vast array of goods and services. In the United States in 2002, 234 billion hours of labor equipped with $20 trillion worth of capital produced $10 trillion worth of goods and services. Globally, 6 trillion hours of labor and $100 trillion of capital produced $47 trillion worth of goods and services.

Although our production capability is enormous, it is limited by our available resources and by technology. At any given time, we have fixed quantities of the factors of production and a fixed state of technology. Because our wants exceed our resources, we must make choices. We must rank our wants and decide which wants to satisfy and which to leave unsatisfied. In using our scarce resources, we make rational choices.

To make a rational choice, we must determine the costs and benefits of the alternatives. In the rest of this chapter, we're going to study an economic model that makes the ideas of scarcity, costs and benefits, and rational choice more concrete. We're also going to learn about the economic concept of efficiency.

To illustrate the limits to production, we focus our attention on two goods only and hold the quantities produced of all the other goods and services constant. That is, we use the *ceteris paribus* assumption. We look at a *model* of the economy in which everything remains the same except for the production of the two goods we are currently considering.

Production Possibilities Frontier

Production possibilities frontier
The boundary between the combinations of goods and services that can be produced and the combinations that cannot be produced, given the available factors of production and the state of technology.

The **production possibilities frontier** is the boundary between the combinations of goods and services that can be produced and the combinations that cannot be produced, given the available factors of production—land, labor, capital, and entrepreneurship—and the state of technology. Let's look at the production possibilities frontier for bottled water and CDs.

Land can be used for either water-bottling plants or CD factories. Labor can be trained to work as water bottlers or as CD makers. Capital can be devoted to tapping springs and making water filtration plants or to the computers and lasers that make CDs. And entrepreneurs can devote their creative talents to managing water resources and bottling factories or to running electronics businesses that make CDs. In every case, the more resources that get used to produce bottled water, the fewer are left for producing CDs.

We can illustrate the production possibilities frontier by using either a table or a graph. The table in Figure 3.1 describes six production possibilities for bottled water and CDs—alternative combinations of quantities of these two goods that we can produce.

One possibility, in column *A*, is to devote no factors of production to making bottled water, so bottled water production is zero. In this case, we can devote all the factors of production to making CDs and produce 15 million a year. Another possibility, in column *B*, is to devote resources to bottled water production that are sufficient to produce 1 million bottles a year. But the resources that are being used in water-bottling plants must be taken from CD factories. So we can now produce only 14 million CDs a year. Columns *C*, *D*, *E*, and *F* show other possible combinations of the quantities of these two goods that we can produce. In column *F*, we use all our resources to produce 5 million bottles of water a year and have no resources to devote to producing CDs.

The graph in Figure 3.1 illustrates the production possibilities frontier, *PPF*, for bottled water and CDs. It is a graph of the production possibilities in the table. The *x*-axis shows the production of bottled water, and the *y*-axis shows the production of CDs. Each point on the graph labeled *A* through *F* represents the corresponding column in the table. For example, point *B* represents the production of 1 million bottles of water and 14 million CDs. These quantities also appear in column *B* of the table.

The *PPF* is a valuable tool for illustrating the effects of scarcity and its consequences. It puts three features of production possibilities in sharp focus. They are the distinctions between

- Attainable and unattainable combinations
- Full employment and unemployment
- Tradeoffs and free lunches

FIGURE 3.1
The Production Possibilities Frontier

Practice Online

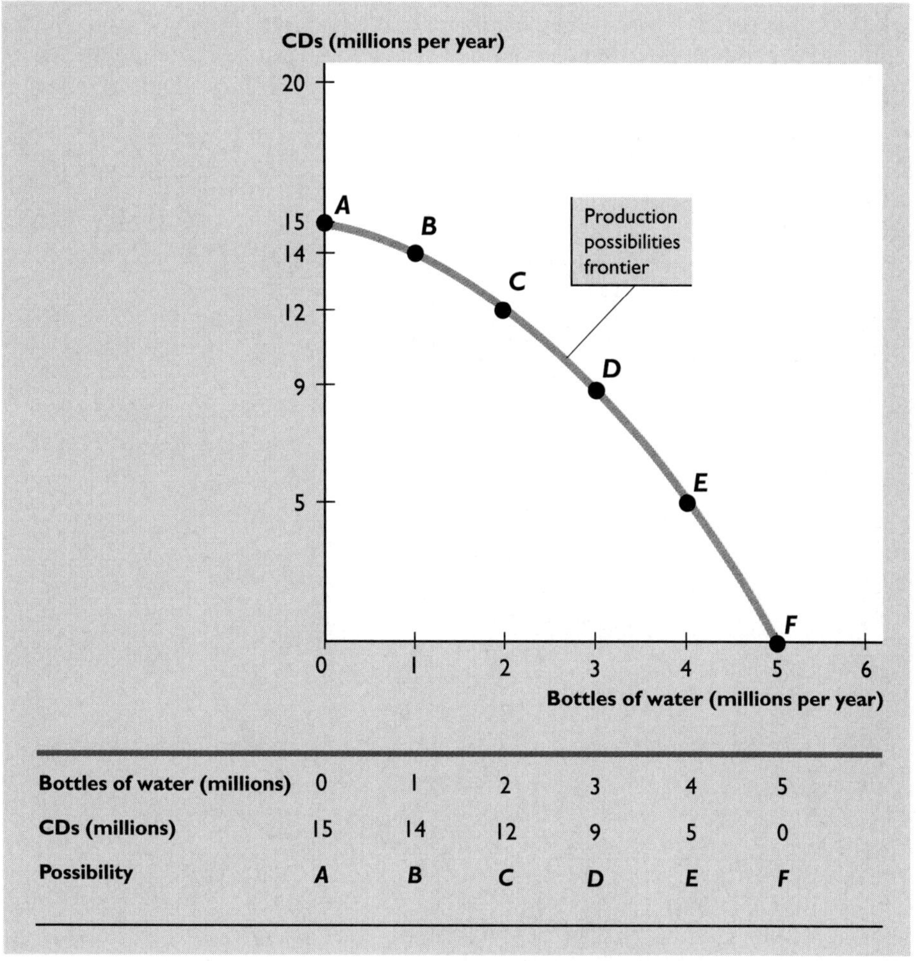

Bottles of water (millions)	0	1	2	3	4	5
CDs (millions)	15	14	12	9	5	0
Possibility	*A*	*B*	*C*	*D*	*E*	*F*

The table and the graph show the production possibilities frontier for bottled water and CDs. Point *A* tells us that if we produce no bottled water, the maximum quantity of CDs we can produce is 15 million a year. Points *A*, *B*, *C*, *D*, *E*, and *F* in the figure represent the columns of the table. The line passing through these points is the production possibilities frontier.

Attainable and Unattainable Combinations

Because the *PPF* shows the *limits* to production, it separates attainable combinations from unattainable ones. We can produce combinations of bottled water and CDs that are smaller than those on the *PPF*, and we can produce any of the combinations *on* the *PPF*. These combinations of bottled water and CDs are attainable. But we cannot produce combinations that are larger than those on the *PPF*. These combinations are unattainable.

Figure 3.2 emphasizes the attainable and unattainable combinations. Only the points on the *PPF* and inside it (in the orange area) are attainable. The combinations of bottled water and CDs beyond the *PPF* (in the white area), such as the combination at point *G*, are unattainable. These points illustrate combinations that cannot be produced with our current resources and technology. The *PPF* tells us that we can produce 4 million bottles of water and 5 million CDs at point *E* or 2 million bottles of water and 12 million CDs at point *C*. But we cannot produce 4 million bottles of water and 12 million CDs at point *G*.

Full Employment and Unemployment

Full employment occurs when all the available factors of production are being used. Unemployment occurs when some factors of production are not used.

The most noticed unemployment affects labor. There is always some unemployed labor, and in a recession, the amount of unemployment can be large. But land and capital can also be unemployed. Land is often unemployed while its owner is trying to work out the land's most valuable use. Look around where you live and

FIGURE 3.2
Attainable and Unattainable Combinations

Practice Online

The production possibilities frontier, *PPF*, separates attainable combinations from unattainable ones. We can produce at any point inside the *PPF* (the orange area) or *on* the frontier. Points outside the production possibilities frontier such as point *G* are unattainable.

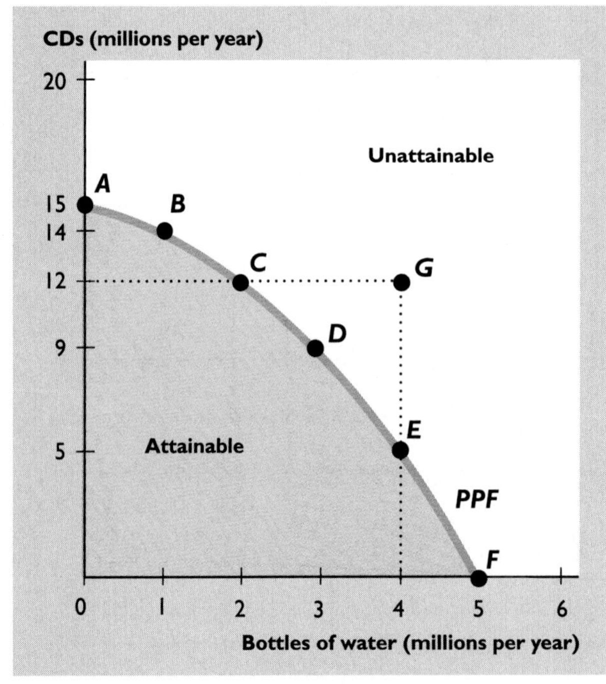

you'll probably be able to find at least one or two city blocks that are currently unemployed. Capital often lies idle. For example, thousands of automobiles are unemployed in parking lots; and restaurant tables and kitchens are often unemployed.

Figure 3.3 illustrates the effects of unemployment. With unemployed resources, the economy might produce at point *H*. Here, with some resources *employed*, it is possible to produce 3 million bottles of water and 5 million CDs. But with full employment, it is possible to move to points such as *D* or *E*. At point *D*, there are more CDs and the same quantity of bottled water as at point *H*. And at point *E*, there are more bottles of water and the same quantity of CDs as at point *H*.

Tradeoffs and Free Lunches

A **tradeoff** is a constraint or limit to what is possible that forces an exchange or a substitution of one thing for something else. If the federal government devotes more resources to finding a cure for AIDS and cuts its transfers to state and local governments, a move that forces state and local governments to increase class sizes and cut back on school libraries and computer facilities, we face a tradeoff between health care and education. If the federal government devotes more resources to national defense and fewer resources to NASA's space exploration program, we face a tradeoff between defense and the space program.

Tradeoff
A constraint or limit to what is possible that forces an exchange or a substitution of one thing for something else.

If lumber producers cut down fewer trees to conserve spotted owls, we face a tradeoff between paper products and wildlife. If Ford Motor Company decreases the production of trucks to produce more SUVs, we face a tradeoff between two types of vehicle. If a student decides to take an extra course and cut back on her weekend job, she faces a tradeoff between course credits and income.

FIGURE 3.3
Full Employment and Unemployment

Practice Online

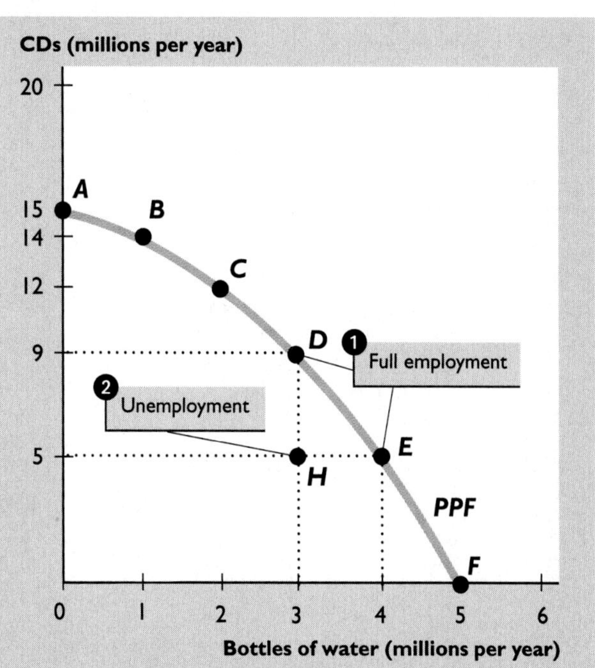

1. When resources are fully employed, production occurs at points on the *PPF* such as *D* and *E*.
2. When resources are unemployed, production occurs at a point inside the frontier such as point *H*.

The *PPF* in Figure 3.4 illustrates the idea of a tradeoff. If we produce at point *E* and would like to produce more CDs, we must forgo some bottled water. For example, we might move from point *E* to point *D*. We exchange some bottles of water for some CDs.

Economists often express the central idea of economics—that every choice involves an opportunity cost—with the saying "There is no such thing as a free lunch." (See Chapter 1, p. 13.) But suppose some resources are not being used or are not being used in their most productive way. Isn't it then possible to avoid opportunity cost and get a free lunch?

The answer is yes. You can see this answer in Figure 3.4. If production is taking place *inside* the *PPF* at point *H*, then it is possible to move to point *D* and increase the production of CDs by using currently unused resources or by using resources in their most productive way. There is a free lunch.

So when production takes place at a point on the *PPF*, we face a tradeoff. But we don't face a tradeoff if we produce inside the *PPF*. More of some goods and services can be produced without producing less of some others.

Because of scarcity and the attempt to get the most out of our scarce resources, we do not leave factors of production idle or use them unproductively if we can avoid it. And if such a situation arises, people seek ways of putting their resources to productive employment. It is for these reasons that economists emphasize the tradeoff idea and deny the existence of free lunches. We might *occasionally* get a free lunch, but we *persistently* face tradeoffs.

FIGURE 3.4
Tradeoffs and Free Lunches

Practice Online

1. When production is *on* the *PPF*, we face a tradeoff. If we are producing 5 million CDs a year at point *E*, to produce 9 million CDs at point *D*, we must trade some bottled water for CDs and move along the *PPF*.

2. When production is *inside* the *PPF*, there is a free lunch. If we are producing 5 million CDs a year at point *H*, to produce 9 million CDs at point *D*, we move to the *PPF* and get a free lunch.

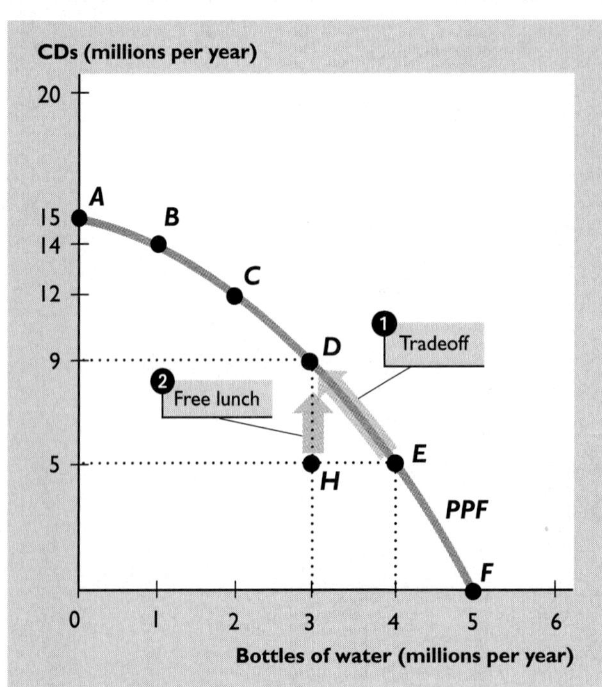

CHECKPOINT 3.1

1 Use the production possibilities frontier to illustrate the economic problem.

Study Guide pp. 36–39

Practice Online 3.1

Practice Problems 3.1

1. Robinson Crusoe, the forerunner of the television program *Survivor*, lived alone on a deserted island. He spent his day fishing and picking fruit. He varied the time spent on these two activities and kept a record of his production. Table 1 shows the numbers that Crusoe wrote in the sand. Use these numbers to make Crusoe's *PPF* if he can work only 8 hours a day.
2. Which combinations (pounds of each) are attainable and which are unattainable: (i) 10 fish and 30 fruit, (ii) 13 fish and 26 fruit, (iii) 20 fish and 21 fruit?
3. Which combinations (pounds of each) use all of Crusoe's available 8 hours a day: (i) 15 fish and 21 fruit, (ii) 7 fish and 30 fruit, (iii) 18 fish and 0 fruit?
4. Which combinations (pounds of each) provide Crusoe with a free lunch and which confront him with a tradeoff when he increases fruit by 1 pound: (i) 0 fish and 36 fruit, (ii) 15 fish and 15 fruit, (iii) 13 fish and 26 fruit?

TABLE 1

Hours	Fish (pounds)		Fruit (pounds)
0	0		0
1	4.0	or	8
2	7.5	or	15
3	10.5	or	21
4	13.0	or	26
5	15.0	or	30
6	16.5	or	33
7	17.5	or	35
8	18.0	or	36

Exercises 3.1

1. In the winter, both fish and fruit are harder to find and Robinson Crusoe can work only 5 hours a day. Table 2 shows the quantities that Crusoe can produce in winter. Use these numbers to make Crusoe's *PPF* in winter.
2. Which combinations (pounds of each) are attainable and which are unattainable: (i) 7.5 fish and 11 fruit, (ii) 9 fish and 11 fruit, (iii) 5.5 fish and 14 fruit?
3. Which combinations (pounds of each) use all Crusoe's available 5 hours a day, which provide Crusoe with a free lunch, and which confront him with a tradeoff: (i) 10 fish and 0 fruit, (ii) 9 fish and 6 fruit, (iii) 3 fish and 16 fruit?

TABLE 2

Hours	Fish (pounds)		Fruit (pounds)
0	0		0
1	3.0	or	6
2	5.5	or	11
3	7.5	or	15
4	9.0	or	18
5	10.0	or	20

Solutions to Practice Problems 3.1

1. Table 3 sets out Crusoe's *PPF*. He has 8 hours a day for fishing and fruit picking. He can produce the combinations of fish and fruit that lie on his *PPF* if he uses a total of 8 hours a day. If he picks fruit for 8 hours, he picks 36 pounds and catches no fish—row *A*. If he picks fruit for 7 hours, he picks 35 pounds and has 1 hour for fishing in which he catches 4 pounds—row *B*. Check that you can construct the other rows of Table 3.
2. (i) 10 fish and 30 fruit is attainable because row *D* tells us that Crusoe can produce 10.5 fish and 30 fruit. (ii) 13 fish and 26 fruit is attainable—row *E*. (iii) 20 fish and 21 fruit is unattainable because when Crusoe picks 21 pounds of fruit, he can catch only 15 pounds of fish (row *F*).
3. (i) 15 fish and 21 fruit uses all 8 hours—it is on his *PPF* (row *F*). (ii) 7 fish and 30 fruit does not use all 8 hours—it is inside his *PPF* (row *C*). (iii) 18 fish and 0 fruit uses all 8 hours—it is on his *PPF* (row *I*).
4. (i) 0 fish and 36 fruit involves a tradeoff because it is on his *PPF*. (ii) 15 fish and 15 fruit provides a free lunch because it is inside his *PPF*. (iii) 13 fish and 26 fruit involves a tradeoff because it is on his *PPF*.

TABLE 3

Possibility	Fish (pounds)		Fruit (pounds)
A	0	and	36
B	4.0	and	35
C	7.5	and	33
D	10.5	and	30
E	13.0	and	26
F	15.0	and	21
G	16.5	and	15
H	17.5	and	8
I	18.0	and	0

3.2 OPPORTUNITY COST

You've just seen that along the *PPF*, all choices involve a tradeoff. But what are the terms of the tradeoff? How much of one item must be forgone to obtain an additional unit of another item—a large amount or a small amount? The answer is given by opportunity cost—the best thing you must give up to get something (see p. 13). The *PPF* enables us to calculate opportunity cost.

The Opportunity Cost of a Bottle of Water

The opportunity cost of a bottle of water is the decrease in the quantity of CDs divided by the increase in the number of bottles of water as we move down along the *PPF* in Figure 3.5.

At point *A*, we produce no bottles of water and 15 million CDs. At point *B*, we produce 1 million bottles of water and 14 million CDs. If we move from point *A* to point *B*, the quantity of water increases by 1 million bottles and the quantity of CDs decreases by 1 million. So the opportunity cost of 1 bottle of water is 1 CD.

At point *C*, we produce 2 million bottles of water and 12 million CDs. If we move from point *B* to point *C*, the quantity of water increases by 1 million bottles and the quantity of CDs decreases by 2 million. So the opportunity cost of 1 bottle of water is now 2 CDs.

Repeat these calculations, moving from *C* to *D*, from *D* to *E*, and from *E* to *F*, and check that you can obtain the opportunity costs shown in the table and graph.

FIGURE 3.5
Calculating the Opportunity Cost of a Bottle of Water

Practice Online

Movement along *PPF*	Decrease in quantity of CDs	Increase in quantity of bottled water	Decrease in CDs divided by increase in bottled water
A to *B*	1 million	1 million	1 CD per bottle
B to *C*	2 million	1 million	2 CDs per bottle
C to *D*	3 million	1 million	3 CDs per bottle
D to *E*	4 million	1 million	4 CDs per bottle
E to *F*	5 million	1 million	5 CDs per bottle

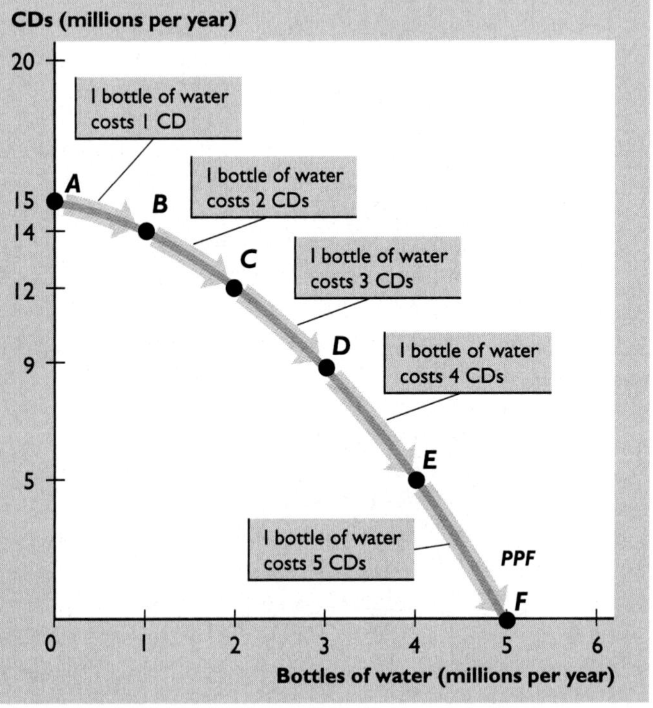

Moving down the *PPF* from *A* to *F*, the opportunity cost of a bottle of water increases as the quantity of bottled water produced increases.

The Opportunity Cost of a CD

The opportunity cost of a CD is the decrease in the quantity of water divided by the increase in the quantity of CDs as we move up along the *PPF* in Figure 3.6.

At point *F*, we produce no CDs and 5 million bottles of water. At point *E*, we produce 5 million CDs and 4 million bottles of water. If we move from point *F* to point *E*, the quantity of CDs increases by 5 million and the quantity of water decreases by 1 million bottles. So the opportunity cost of 1 CD is 1/5 of a bottle of water.

At point *D*, we produce 9 million CDs and 3 million bottles of water. If we move from point *E* to point *D*, the quantity of CDs increases by 4 million and the quantity of water decreases by 1 million bottles. So the opportunity cost of a CD is now 1/4 of a bottle of water.

At point *C*, we produce 12 million CDs and 2 million bottles of water. If we move from point *D* to point *C*, the quantity of CDs increases by 3 million and the quantity of water decreases by 1 million bottles. So the opportunity cost of a CD is now 1/3 of a bottle of water.

Again, repeat these calculations, moving from *C* to *B* and from *B* to *A*, and check that you can obtain the opportunity costs shown in the figure.

Opportunity Cost Is a Ratio

You've seen that to calculate the opportunity cost of a bottle of water, we divide the quantity of CDs forgone by the increase in the quantity of water. And to calculate the opportunity cost of a CD, we divide the quantity of bottled water

FIGURE 3.6
Calculating the Opportunity Cost of a CD

Practice Online

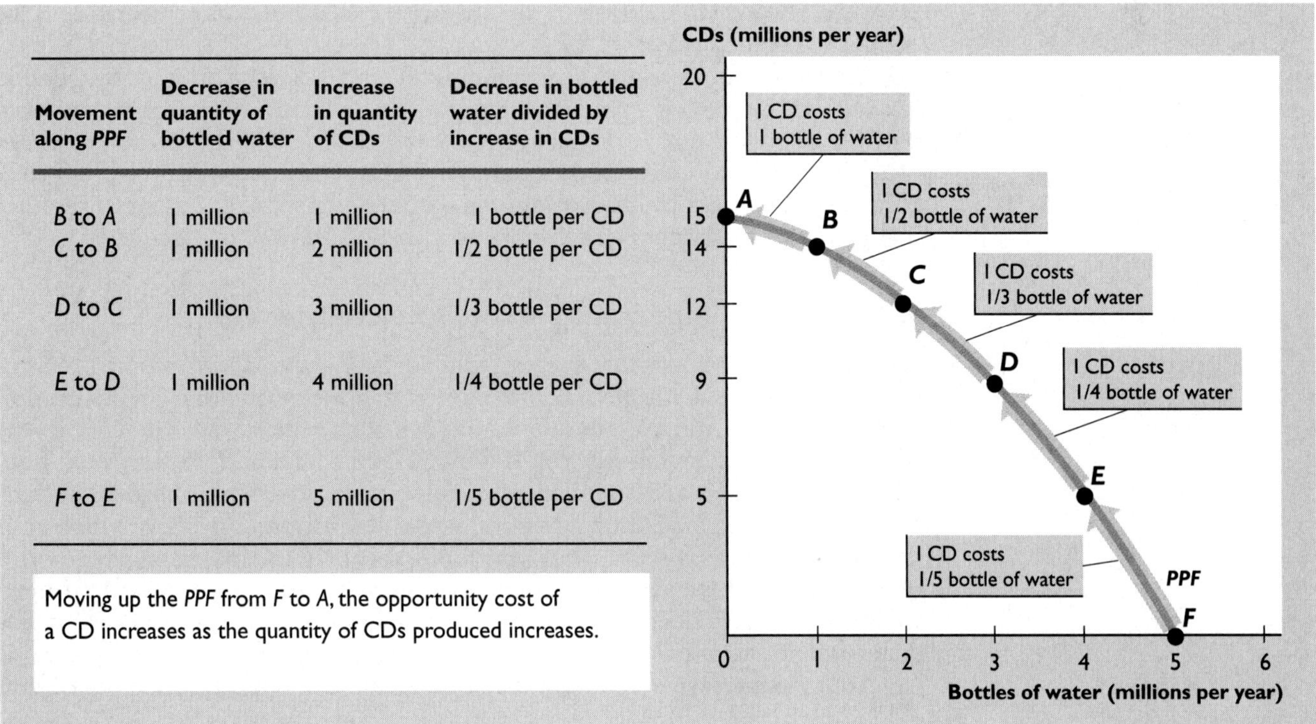

Movement along *PPF*	Decrease in quantity of bottled water	Increase in quantity of CDs	Decrease in bottled water divided by increase in CDs
B to *A*	1 million	1 million	1 bottle per CD
C to *B*	1 million	2 million	1/2 bottle per CD
D to *C*	1 million	3 million	1/3 bottle per CD
E to *D*	1 million	4 million	1/4 bottle per CD
F to *E*	1 million	5 million	1/5 bottle per CD

Moving up the *PPF* from *F* to *A*, the opportunity cost of a CD increases as the quantity of CDs produced increases.

forgone by the increase in the quantity of CDs. So opportunity cost is a ratio—the change in the quantity of one good divided by the change in the quantity of the other good. The opportunity cost of producing water is equal to the inverse of the opportunity cost of producing CDs. Check this proposition by returning to the calculations we've just worked through. When we move along the *PPF* from point *C* to point *D*, the opportunity cost of a bottle of water is 3 CDs. The inverse of 3 is ⅓, so if we increase the production of CDs and decrease the production of water by moving from *D* to *C*, the opportunity cost of a CD must be ⅓ of a bottle of water. This number is correct—it is the number we've just calculated.

Increasing Opportunity Cost

The opportunity cost of a bottle of water increases as the quantity of bottled water produced increases. The opportunity cost of a CD increases as the quantity of CDs produced increases. The phenomenon of increasing opportunity cost is reflected in the shape of the *PPF*. It is bowed outward. When a large quantity of CDs and a small quantity of water are produced—between points *A* and *B* in Figure 3.5—the frontier has a gentle slope. A given increase in the quantity of bottled water costs a small decrease in the quantity of CDs, so the opportunity cost of a bottle of water is a small quantity of CDs.

When a large quantity of bottled water and a small quantity of CDs are produced—between points *E* and *F* in Figure 3.5—the frontier is steep. A given increase in the quantity of bottled water costs a large decrease in the quantity of CDs, so the opportunity cost of a bottle of water is a large quantity of CDs.

The production possibilities frontier is bowed outward because resources are not equally productive in all activities. Production workers with many years of experience working for Aqua Springs are very good at bottling water but not very good at making CDs. So if we move some of these people from Aqua Springs to Sony, we get a small increase in the quantity of CDs but a large decrease in the quantity of bottled water.

Similarly, engineers and production workers who work at Sony are good at making CDs but not very good at bottling water. So if we move some of these people from Sony to Aqua Springs, we get a small increase in the quantity of bottled water but a large decrease in the quantity of CDs. The more we try to produce of either good, the less productive are the additional resources we use to produce that good and the larger is the opportunity cost of a unit of that good.

Increasing Opportunity Costs Are Everywhere

Just about every activity that you can think of is one with an increasing opportunity cost. We allocate the most skillful farmers and the most fertile land to the production of food. And we allocate the best doctors and least fertile land to the production of health-care services. If we shift fertile land and tractors away from farming to hospitals and ambulances and ask farmers to become hospital porters, the production of food drops drastically and the increase in the production of health-care services is small. The opportunity cost of a unit of health-care services rises. Similarly, if we shift our resources away from health care toward farming, we must use more doctors and nurses as farmers and more hospitals as hydroponic tomato factories. The decrease in the production of health-care services is large, but the increase in food production is small. The opportunity cost of a unit of food rises.

CHECKPOINT 3.2

2 Calculate opportunity cost.

Study Guide pp. 39–41

Practice Online 3.2

Practice Problems 3.2

1. Use Robinson Crusoe's production possibilities shown in Table 1 to calculate his opportunity cost of a pound of fish. Make a table that shows Crusoe's opportunity cost of a pound of fish as he increases the time he spends fishing and decreases the time that he spends picking fruit.
2. If Crusoe increases his production of fruit from 21 pounds to 26 pounds and decreases his production of fish from 15 pounds to 13 pounds, what is his opportunity cost of a pound of fruit? Explain your answer.
3. If Crusoe is producing 10 pounds of fish and 20 pounds of fruit, what is his opportunity cost of a pound of fruit and a pound of fish? Explain your answer.

TABLE 1

Possibility	Fish (pounds)	Fruit (pounds)
A	0	36
B	4.0	35
C	7.5	33
D	10.5	30
E	13.0	26
F	15.0	21
G	16.5	15
H	17.5	8
I	18.0	0

Exercises 3.2

1. Use Robinson Crusoe's production possibilities in winter shown in Table 2 to calculate his opportunity cost of a pound of fruit. Make a table that shows Crusoe's opportunity cost of a pound of fruit as he increases the time he spends picking fruit and decreases the time he spends fishing.
2. If Crusoe currently catches 5.5 pounds of fish and picks 11 pounds of fruit a day, calculate his opportunity cost of a pound of fruit and of a pound of fish. Explain your answer.
3. If Crusoe increases the amount of fish caught from 5.5 to 7.5 pounds and decreases the amount of fruit picked from 15 to 11 pounds, what is his opportunity cost of a pound of fish? Explain your answer.
4. Does Crusoe's opportunity cost of a pound of fruit increase as he spends more time picking fruit? Explain why or why not.

TABLE 2

Possibility	Fish (pounds)	Fruit (pounds)
A	0	20
B	3.0	18
C	5.5	15
D	7.5	11
E	9.0	6
F	10.0	0

Solutions to Practice Problems 3.2

1. Crusoe's opportunity cost of a pound of fish is the decrease in fruit divided by the increase in fish as he moves along his *PPF*, increasing the time he spends fishing and decreasing the time he spends picking fruit. For example, when Crusoe spends no time fishing, he produces the quantities in row *A* in Table 1. When he spends more time fishing and moves to row *B* in Table 1, the increase in fish is 4 pounds and the decrease in fruit picked is 1 pound. So the opportunity cost of a pound of fish is ¼ pound of fruit. Check that you can derive the other rows of Table 3.
2. The opportunity cost of a pound of fruit is ⅖ pound of fish. When fruit increases by 5 pounds, fish decreases by 2 pounds. The opportunity cost of a pound of fruit is 2 pounds of fish divided by 5 pounds of fruit. This opportunity cost is the inverse of the opportunity cost of fish (Table 3, move from *E* to *F*).
3. If Crusoe is producing 10 pounds of fish and 20 pounds of fruit, his opportunity cost of fruit and of fish is zero because he can increase the production of both without decreasing the production of either. He is producing a combination inside his *PPF*.

TABLE 3

Move from	Increase in fish (pounds)	Decrease in fruit (pounds)	Opportunity cost of fish (pounds of fruit)
A to *B*	4.0	1	0.25
B to *C*	3.5	2	0.57
C to *D*	3.0	3	1.00
D to *E*	2.5	4	1.60
E to *F*	2.0	5	2.50
F to *G*	1.5	6	4.00
G to *H*	1.0	7	7.00
H to *I*	0.5	8	16.00

3.3 USING RESOURCES EFFICIENTLY

Ralph Nader says that we should expand the use of clean solar technologies and burn less oil and coal. He also says that we should create clean mass transit systems and decrease our reliance on the automobile. Political leaders of all parties say that we should hire more teachers to reduce class size and improve education. They also want to spend more on prescription drug plans for seniors and improve health care for the uninsured. Some political leaders want to enter into a new phase of defense spending and create an effective antimissile defense system. All of these policy proposals and the political debates that surround them are about efficiency.

Efficiency
A situation in which the quantities of goods and services produced are those that people value most highly—in which we cannot produce more of a good or service without giving up some of another good or service that people value more highly.

Economists use the idea of efficiency in a broad way that cuts to the heart of these debates. In economics, **efficiency** occurs when we produce the quantities of goods and services that people value most highly. To put it another way, resource use is *efficient* when we cannot produce more of a good or service without giving up some of another good or service that people value more highly.

If people value a pollution-free environment more highly than they value cheap electric power, it is efficient to use high-cost clean technologies to produce electricity. In this case, Ralph Nader's proposal to limit the use of coal and oil and expand the use of solar energy sources could be efficient. If people value the flexibility of being able to choose when and where to travel more highly than they value low-cost, low-pollution, safe transportation, it is efficient to use high-cost, polluting, accident-prone automobiles.

So just what is the efficient energy policy: one that favors clean energy technologies or one that burns oil and coal? What is the efficient method of urban transportation: one that uses a clean mass transit system or a system of freeways and private automobiles? And what are the efficient quantities of education, health care, and national defense?

These are questions that have enormous consequences for human welfare, and they are difficult questions. But you can see the essence of the answers by thinking about the simpler question: What is the efficient quantity of bottled water to produce? The answer to this question provides the principles that underlie the answers to all questions about how to use our scarce resources.

Two Conditions for Efficiency

Efficiency is achieved when two conditions are met. They are

- Production efficiency
- Allocative efficiency

Production Efficiency

Production efficiency
A situation in which we cannot produce more of one good or service without producing less of some other good or service—production is at a point *on* the *PPF*.

We achieve **production efficiency** if we cannot produce more of one good or service without producing less of some other good or service. When production is efficient, we are at a point *on* the *PPF*. If we are at a point *inside* the *PPF*, production is *inefficient* because we have some *unemployed* resources or resources are not being used most productively. Bringing those resources into their most productive use enables more of both goods to be produced.

You've seen that when resources are unemployed, it is possible to produce more of a good without incurring a cost. So production is not efficient. Only when all resources are fully employed and the economy is operating on the *PPF* is it impossible to produce more of one good or service without producing less of another good or service.

Allocative Efficiency

We achieve **allocative efficiency** when we produce the combination of goods and services on the *PPF* that we value most highly. All the combinations of goods and services on the *PPF* achieve *production efficiency*. Each of these combinations is such that, to produce more of one good or service, we must produce less of the other. But only one of these combinations achieves allocative efficiency. That is, only one combination is the most highly valued. To find this combination, we need some additional information that is not contained in the *PPF*. We need to know the value of each available combination. We express value in terms of the marginal benefit people receive.

Allocative efficiency
The combination of goods and services on the *PPF* that we value most highly.

Marginal Benefit

You learned in Chapter 1 (pp. 14–15) that the *benefit* of something is the gain or pleasure that it brings. Benefit is how a person *feels* about something. We defined *marginal benefit* as the benefit that a person receives from consuming one more unit of a good or service.

You also learned in Chapter 1 that economists measure the benefit of something by what a person *is willing to* give up to get it. So a person's *marginal* benefit of a good or service is what that person *is willing to* give up to get *one more* unit of it.

It is a general principle that the more we have of any good or service, the smaller is our marginal benefit from it—the principle of decreasing marginal benefit. To understand the principle of decreasing marginal benefit, think about your own marginal benefit from bottled water. If bottled water is very hard to come by and you can buy only one or two bottles a year, you will be very pleased to get one more bottle. The marginal benefit of that bottle of water is high. In this situation, you are willing to give up quite a lot of some other good or service to get one more bottle of water. But if there is plenty of bottled water around and you have as much as you can drink, you will get almost no benefit from one more bottle. So you are willing to give up almost nothing for that bottle of water.

The principle of diminishing marginal benefit applies to all goods and services. You get a lot of pleasure from one slice of pizza. A second slice is fine, too, but not quite as satisfying as the first one. But eat three, four, five, six, and more slices, and each additional slice is less enjoyable than the previous one. You get diminishing marginal benefit from pizza. So the more pizza you have, the less of some other good or service you would be willing to give up to get one more slice.

Although marginal benefit expresses a person's *feeling* toward a good or service, it is nonetheless a real, objective phenomenon. It is as real as the physical limits to production that we express in the *PPF*. The *PPF* shows what is *feasible*. Marginal benefit is an expression of what is *desirable*. And we need a way of describing marginal benefit that is as concrete as the *PPF*.

Let's see how economists describe marginal benefit.

Marginal Benefit Schedule and Curve

We describe marginal benefit by using either a marginal benefit schedule or a marginal benefit curve. Figure 3.7 illustrates these concepts, and we continue to use the same two goods as before: bottled water and CDs. The marginal benefit from a bottle of water can be expressed as the number of CDs that a person is willing to forgo to get one more bottle. This amount decreases as the quantity of bottled water available increases.

Begin by looking at the table below the graph. In column *A*, 1 million bottles of water are available, and at that quantity, people are willing to give up 4.5 CDs for a bottle of water. As the quantity of bottled water available increases, the amount that people are willing to give up for an additional bottle falls—3.5 CDs per bottle when 2 million bottles are available in column *B*, 2.5 CDs per bottle when 3 million bottles are available in column *C*, and 1.5 CDs per bottle when 4 million bottles are available in column *D*.

The marginal benefit curve is a graph of the marginal benefit schedule. The points *A*, *B*, *C*, and *D* on the marginal benefit curve correspond to the columns *A*, *B*, *C*, and *D* of the marginal benefit schedule.

The marginal benefit from a bottle of water and the opportunity cost of a bottle of water that you studied on p. 68 are both measured in CDs per bottle. But they are *not* the same concept. The opportunity cost of a bottle of water is the quantity of CDs that people *must forgo* to get another bottle. The marginal benefit from a bottle of water is the quantity of CDs that people are *willing to forgo* to get another bottle.

FIGURE 3.7
Marginal Benefit of a Bottle of Water

Practice Online

The table and the graph show the marginal benefit of a bottle of water. Point *A* tells us that if we produce 1 million bottles of water a year, the maximum quantity of CDs that people are willing to give up for an additional bottle of water is 4.5 CDs. Points *A*, *B*, *C*, and *D* in the graph represent the columns of the table. The line passing through these points is the marginal benefit curve. The marginal benefit of a bottle of water decreases as the quantity of bottled water available increases.

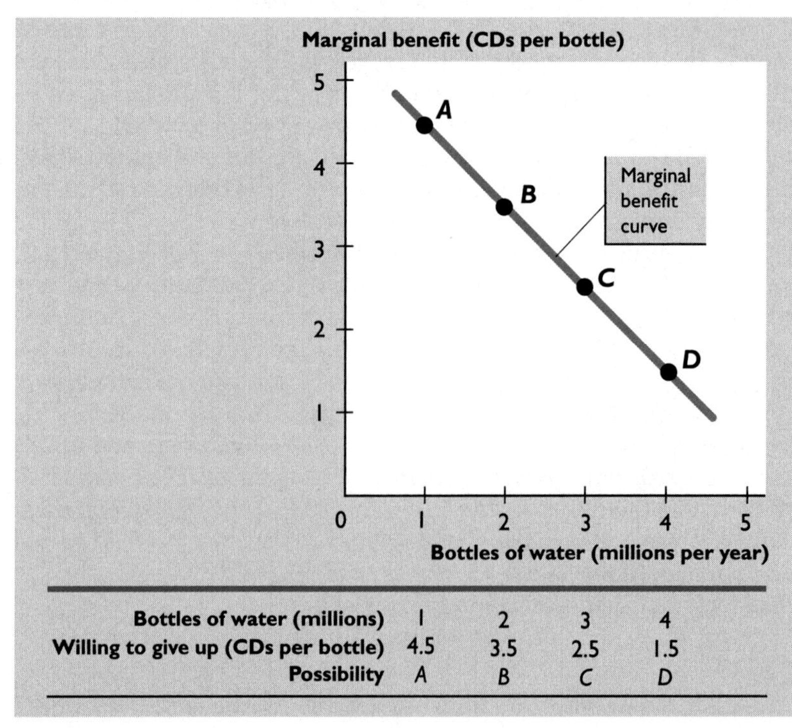

Bottles of water (millions)	1	2	3	4
Willing to give up (CDs per bottle)	4.5	3.5	2.5	1.5
Possibility	*A*	*B*	*C*	*D*

Marginal Cost

To achieve allocative efficiency, we must compare the marginal benefit of a bottle of water with its marginal cost. We defined *marginal cost* in Chapter 1 (p. 15) as the opportunity cost of producing one more unit of a good or service. You've seen how we can calculate opportunity cost as we move along the production possibilities frontier. We can calculate marginal cost in a similar way. The marginal cost of a bottle of water is the opportunity cost of one additional bottle—the quantity of CDs that must be given up to get one more bottle of water—as we move along the *PPF*.

Figure 3.8 illustrates the marginal cost of a bottle of water. It is based on the opportunity cost numbers that you've already calculated. Recall that the opportunity cost of the first 1 million bottles of water is 1 million CDs. So on the average, 1 bottle of water costs 1 CD. We graph this cost midway between zero and 1 million on the graph. The opportunity cost of the second 1 million bottles of water is 2 million CDs. So on the average, 1 bottle of water costs 2 CDs over this range. We graph this cost midway between 1 million and 2 million on the graph.

Figure 3.8 shows that the marginal cost curve of bottled water slopes upward. That is, as the quantity of bottled water produced increases, the marginal cost of bottled water increases. This increasing marginal cost occurs for the same reason the opportunity cost increases.

Let's use the concepts of marginal benefit and marginal cost to discover the efficient quantity of bottled water to produce.

FIGURE 3.8
Marginal Cost of a Bottle of Water

Practice Online

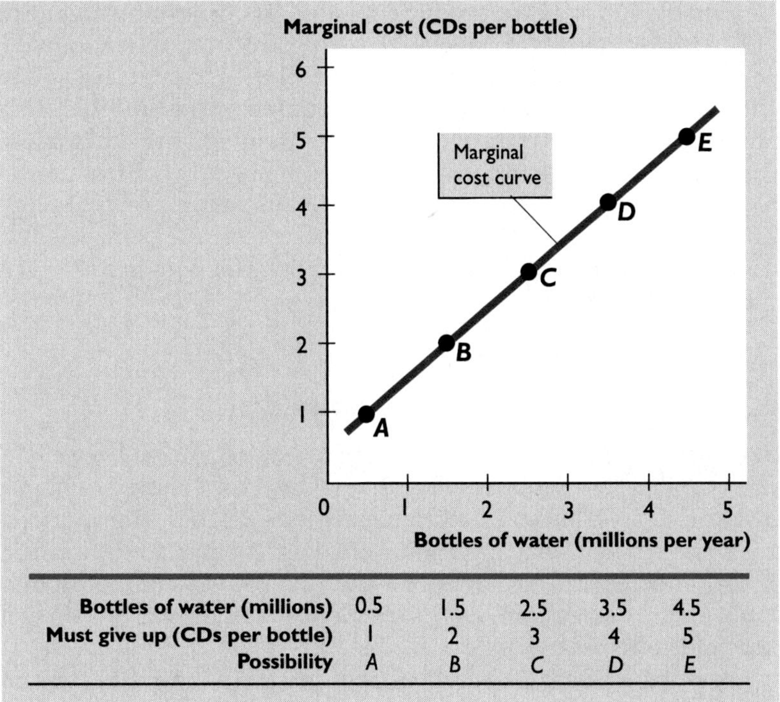

Bottles of water (millions)	0.5	1.5	2.5	3.5	4.5
Must give up (CDs per bottle)	1	2	3	4	5
Possibility	*A*	*B*	*C*	*D*	*E*

The table and the graph show the marginal cost of a bottle of water. Marginal cost is the opportunity cost of producing one more unit and is derived from the *PPF*. Points *A*, *B*, *C*, *D*, and *E* in the graph represent the columns of the table. The marginal cost curve shows that the marginal cost of a bottle of water increases as the quantity of bottled water produced increases.

Efficient Use of Resources

Resource use is efficient when we produce the goods and services that we value most highly. That is, when we are using our resources efficiently, we cannot produce more of any good without producing less of something else that we value even more highly.

We can illustrate an efficient use of resources by continuing to use the example of bottled water and CDs. Figure 3.9(a) shows the production possibilities frontier (the same as in Figure 3.1 on p. 63). And Figure 3.9(b) shows the marginal cost (*MC*) and marginal benefit (*MB*) of a bottle of water.

Suppose we produce 1.5 million bottles of water a year at point *A* on the *PPF* in Figure 3.9(a). This combination of water and CDs meets the conditions for production efficiency because it is on the *PPF*. But does it meet the conditions for allocative efficiency? To answer this question, we need to compare marginal benefit and marginal cost in Figure 3.9(b). The marginal benefit of a bottle of water is 4 CDs, but the marginal cost of a bottle of water is only 2 CDs. Because people value an additional bottle of water more highly than it costs to produce, we are producing too many CDs and not enough bottled water. We can get more value from our resources by moving some of them out of CD production and into bottled water production.

Now suppose that we produce 3.5 million bottles of water a year at point *C* on the *PPF*. Again, this point meets the conditions for production efficiency because it is on the *PPF*. To check whether it meets the conditions for allocative efficiency, we again need to compare marginal benefit and marginal cost. The marginal benefit of a bottle of water is now 2 CDs, but the marginal cost of a bottle of water is 4 CDs. People now value an additional bottle of water less highly than it costs to produce. So we are producing too much bottled water and too few CDs. We can get more value from our resources by moving some of them out of bottled water production and into CD production.

Finally, suppose we produce 2.5 million bottles of water at point *B* on the *PPF*. At this quantity of bottled water production, the marginal cost of a bottle of water equals the marginal benefit. Both marginal cost and marginal benefit are 3 CDs. This combination of bottled water and CDs is efficient. We cannot produce more bottled water without giving up some CDs that we value more highly than the additional water. And we can't produce more CDs without giving up some water that we value more highly than the additional CDs.

So point *B* on the *PPF* meets the conditions for both production efficiency and allocative efficiency.

Efficiency in the U.S. Economy

Does our economy achieve an efficient use of resources? Do we have an efficient energy policy, or would a policy that favors clean-energy technologies be more efficient? Do we have an efficient method of urban transportation, or would more mass transit systems be more efficient? Do we have the efficient quantities of education and health care, or would an increase in the production of these items and a decrease in the production of some other goods and services be more efficient?

You will study these questions and their answers in Chapters 6 through 10.

FIGURE 3.9

The Efficient Quantity of Bottled Water

Practice Online

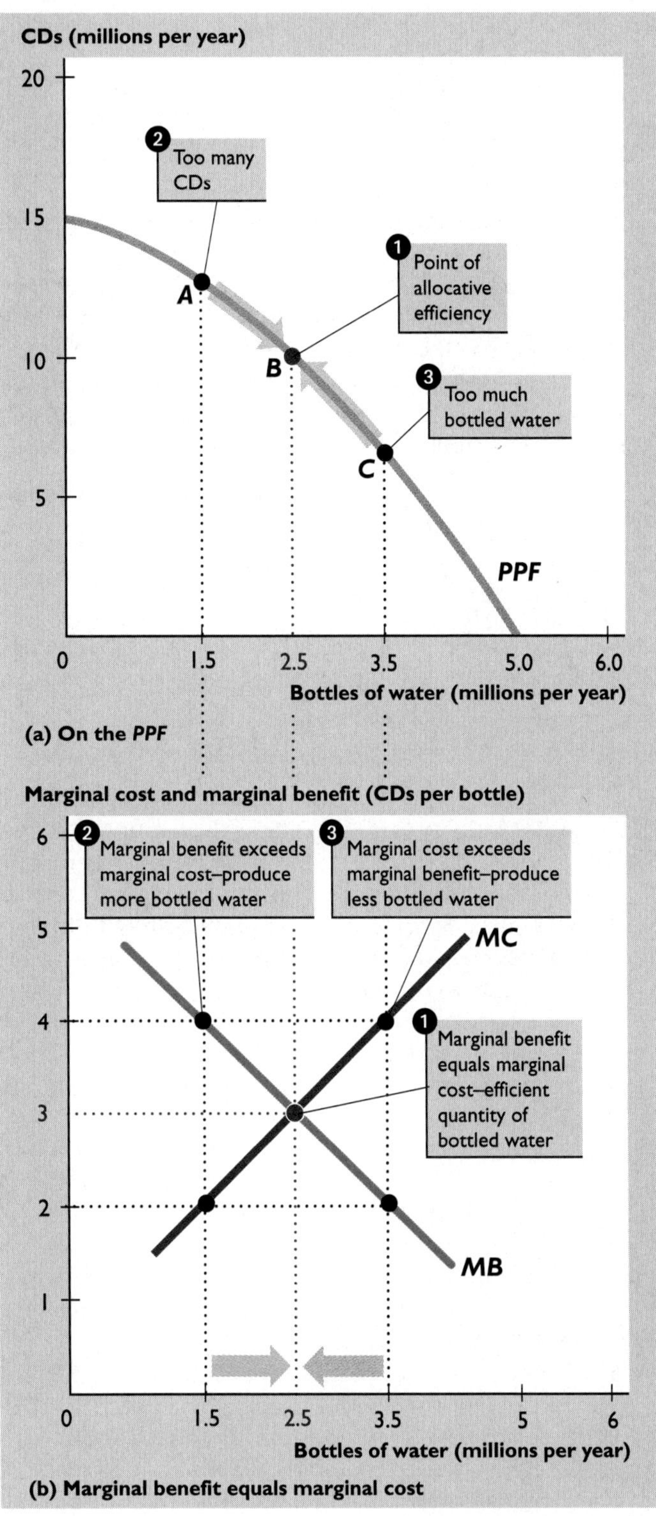

1. Production efficiency occurs at all points on the *PPF* in part (a). But only point *B* meets the condition for allocative efficiency, which occurs where the marginal benefit of a bottle of water (*MB*) equals the marginal cost of a bottle of water (*MC*) in part (b).

2. At point *A*, too many CDs are being produced and too little bottled water is being produced. The marginal benefit of a bottle of water exceeds the marginal cost.

3. At point *C*, too much bottled water is being produced and too few CDs are being produced. The marginal cost of a bottle of water exceeds the marginal benefit.

CHECKPOINT 3.3

Study Guide pp. 41–44

Practice Online 3.3

3 **Define efficiency and describe an efficient use of resources.**

Practice Problems 3.3

TABLE 1

Possibility	Bananas (bunches)	Coffee (pounds)
A	70	40
B	50	100
C	30	140
D	10	160

1. Table 1 shows a nation's production possibilities of bananas and coffee. Use the table to calculate the nation's marginal cost of a bunch of bananas. Draw the marginal cost curve.
2. Use the following data to draw the nation's marginal benefit curve for a bunch of bananas:
   i. When 20 bunches of bananas are available, people are willing to give up 3 pounds of coffee to get an additional bunch of bananas.
   ii. When 40 bunches of bananas are available, people are willing to give up 2 pounds of coffee to get an additional bunch of bananas.
   iii. When 60 bunches of bananas are available, people are willing to give up 1 pound of coffee to get an additional bunch of bananas.
3. Use the data in Practice Problems 1 and 2 to calculate the efficient use of the nation's resources.

Exercise 3.3

Use the *PPF* shown in Figure 1(a) and the marginal benefit curve shown in Figure 1(b) to find the efficient quantities of yogurt and ice cream.

FIGURE 1

(a) *PPF*

(b) Marginal benefit

Solutions to Practice Problems 3.3

1. Figure 2 shows the marginal cost curve. When the quantity of bananas increases from 10 to 30 bunches, the quantity of coffee decreases from 160 to 140 pounds. Bananas increase by 20 bunches and coffee decreases by 20 pounds. So the opportunity cost of 1 bunch of bananas is 1 pound of coffee. In the figure, marginal cost is 1 pound of coffee at the midpoint between 10 and 30 bunches, which is 20 bunches of bananas. When the quantity of bananas increases from 30 to 50 bunches, coffee decreases from 140 to 100 pounds. Bananas increase by 20 bunches, and coffee decreases by 40 pounds. So the opportunity cost of 1 bunch of bananas is 2 pounds of coffee. In the figure, marginal cost is 2 pounds of coffee at the midpoint between 30 and 50 bunches, which is 40 bunches of bananas.
2. Figure 2 shows the marginal benefit curve, which plots the data given. The marginal benefit curve slopes downward because as more bananas are available, the marginal benefit from an additional bunch of bananas decreases.
3. The nation uses its resources efficiently when it produces 40 bunches of bananas and (approximately) 120 pounds of coffee. When the nation produces 40 bunches of bananas and 120 pounds of coffee, it produces on the *PPF* (production efficiency), and it is the highest-valued combination because marginal benefit equals marginal cost (allocative efficiency).

FIGURE 2

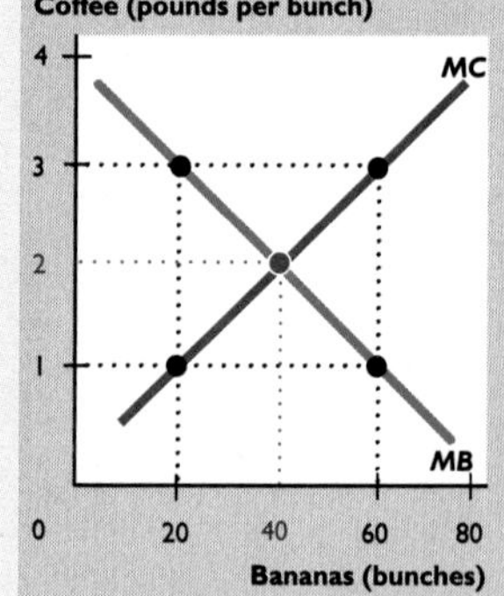

3.4 SPECIALIZATION AND TRADE

People can produce several goods, or they can concentrate on producing one good and then trading some of their own goods for those produced by others. Concentrating on the production of only one good is called *specialization*. We are going to discover how people gain by specializing in the production of the good in which they have a *comparative advantage*.

Comparative Advantage

A person has a **comparative advantage** in an activity if that person can perform the activity at a lower opportunity cost than someone else. Let's explore the idea of comparative advantage by looking at two water-bottling plants, one operated by Tom and the other operated by Nancy.

Comparative advantage
The ability of a person to perform an activity or produce a good or service at a lower opportunity cost than someone else.

Tom produces both water and bottles, and Figure 3.10 shows his production possibilities frontier. If Tom uses all his resources to produce water, he can produce 1,333 gallons an hour, and if he uses all his resources to make bottles, he can produce 4,000 bottles an hour. For each additional 1,000 gallons of water produced, Tom must decrease his production of bottles by 3,000.

Tom's opportunity cost of producing 1 gallon of water is 3 bottles.

Similarly, if Tom wants to increase his production of bottles, he must decrease his production of water. For each 1,000 bottles produced, he must decrease his production of water by 333 gallons. So

Tom's opportunity cost of producing 1 bottle is 0.333 gallon of water.

FIGURE 3.10
Production Possibilities at Tom's Water-Bottling Plant

Practice Online

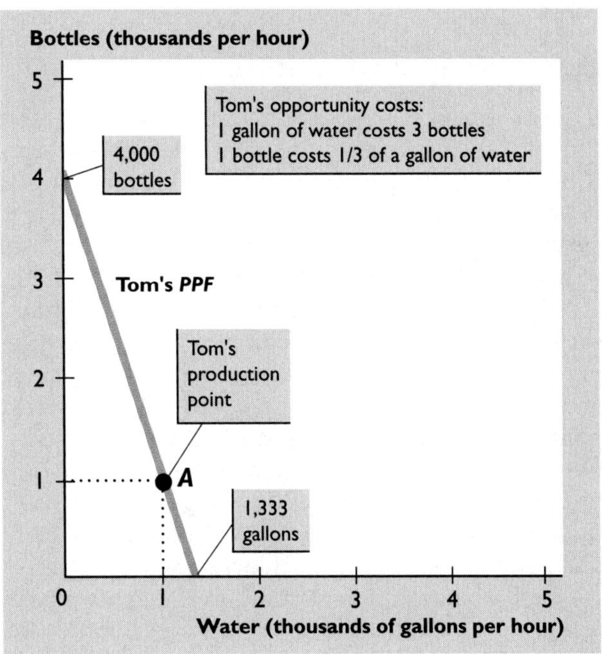

Tom can produce bottles and water along the production possibility frontier *PPF*. For Tom, the opportunity cost of 1 gallon of water is 3 bottles and the opportunity cost of 1 bottle is ⅓ of a gallon of water. If Tom produces at point *A*, he can produce 1,000 gallons of water and 1,000 bottles an hour.

Tom's *PPF* is linear because his workers have similar skills. So if he reallocates them from one activity to another, he faces a constant opportunity cost.

Nancy also produces water and bottles. But Nancy owns a much better spring than Tom. At the same time, her bottle-making equipment is less productive than is Tom's. These differences between the two plants mean that Nancy's production possibilities frontier—shown along with Tom's *PPF* in Figure 3.11—is different from Tom's. If Nancy uses all her resources to produce water, she can produce 4,000 gallons an hour. If she uses all her resources to make bottles, she can produce 1,333 an hour. Nancy's *PPF* is linear, like Tom's, so she faces a constant opportunity cost. For each 1,000 additional bottles produced, she must decrease her production of water by 3,000 gallons.

Nancy's opportunity cost of producing 1 bottle is 3 gallons of water.

Similarly, if Nancy wants to increase her production of water, she must decrease her production of bottles. For each additional 1,000 gallons of water produced, she must decrease her production of bottles by 333. So

Nancy's opportunity cost of producing 1 gallon of water is 0.333 bottle.

Suppose that Tom and Nancy produce both bottles and water and that each produces 1,000 bottles and 1,000 gallons of water—1,000 gallons of bottled water—an hour. That is, each produces at point *A* on their production possibilities frontiers. Total production is 2,000 gallons of bottled water an hour.

In which of the two activities does Nancy have a comparative advantage? Recall that comparative advantage is a situation in which one person's opportunity cost of producing a good is lower than another person's opportunity cost of producing that same good. Nancy has a comparative advantage in producing water. Nancy's opportunity cost of a gallon of water is 0.333 bottle, whereas Tom's opportunity cost of a gallon of water is 3 bottles.

Because Nancy has a comparative advantage in water and Tom has a comparative advantage in bottles, they can both gain from specialization and trade.

Achieving the Gains from Trade

If Tom specializes in bottles, he can produce 4,000 bottles an hour—point *B* on his *PPF*. If Nancy specializes in water, she can produce 4,000 gallons an hour—point *B*' on her *PPF*. By specializing, Tom and Nancy together can produce 4,000 gallons of water and 4,000 bottles an hour—double their total production without specialization. By specialization and trade, Tom and Nancy can get *outside* their individual production possibilities frontiers.

To achieve the gains from specialization, Tom and Nancy must trade with each other. Suppose that each hour, Nancy produces 4,000 gallons of water, Tom produces 4,000 bottles, and Nancy supplies Tom with 2,000 gallons of water in exchange for 2,000 bottles. Tom and Nancy move along the red "Trade line" to point *C*. At this point, each produces 2,000 gallons of bottled water an hour—double their previous production rate.

By specializing and trading with each other, both Tom and Nancy can double their production from 1,000 to 2,000 bottles of water an hour. The increases in production that each of them achieves are the gains from specialization and trade.

Both Nancy and Tom share in the gains. Nancy gets bottles for 1 gallon of water per bottle instead of 3 gallons per bottle. Tom gets water for 1 bottle per

FIGURE 3.11
The Gains from Specialization

Practice Online

1. Tom and Nancy each produce at point *A* on their respective *PPFs*. Tom has a comparative advantage in bottles and Nancy has a comparative advantage in water.

2. If Tom specializes in bottles, he produces at point *B* on his *PPF*.

3. If Nancy specializes in water, she produces at point *B'* on her *PPF*.

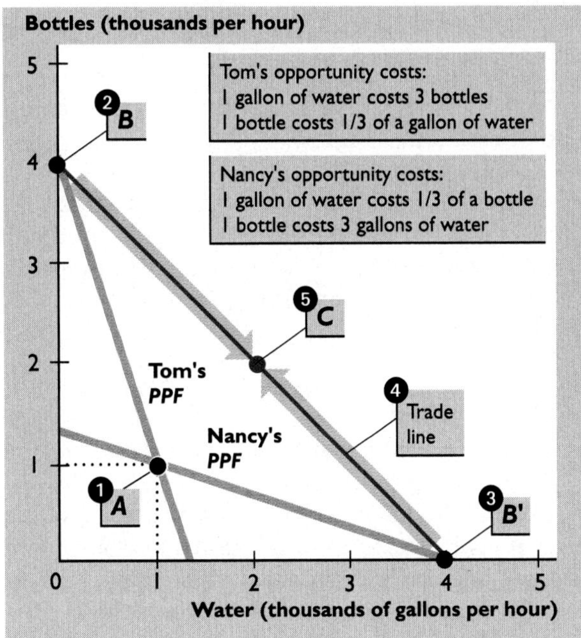

4. They exchange water and bottles along the red "Trade line." Nancy buys bottles from Tom for less than her opportunity cost of producing them, and Tom buys water from Nancy for less than his opportunity cost of producing it.

5. Each goes to point *C*—a point outside his or her individual *PPF*—where each has 2,000 bottles of water an hour. Tom and Nancy increase production with no change in resources.

gallon instead of 3 bottles per gallon. Nancy gets her bottles more cheaply and Tom gets his water more cheaply than when they produced both water and bottles.

Absolute Advantage

Suppose that Nancy invents a production process that makes her four times as productive as she was before in the production of both water and bottles. With her new technology, Nancy now has an **absolute advantage**—she is more productive than Tom in both activities.

Absolute advantage
When one person is more productive than another person in several or even all activities.

But Nancy does not have a *comparative* advantage in both goods. She can produce four times as much of *both* goods as before, but her *opportunity cost* of 1 bottle is still 3 gallons of water. Her opportunity cost is higher than Tom's. So Nancy can still get bottles at a lower cost by trading water for bottles with Tom.

The key point to recognize is that it is *not* possible for *anyone* to have a comparative advantage in everything, even though they might have an absolute advantage in everything. So gains from specialization and trade are always available when opportunity costs diverge.

The principle of comparative advantage and the gains from specialization and trade explain why each individual specializes in a small range of economic activities. It is also the driving force behind international trade. Mexico and the United States, like Tom and Nancy, can *both* gain by specializing in the activities in which they have a comparative advantage and trading with each other. The absolute advantage of the United States is no obstacle to reaping mutual gains from trade.

CHECKPOINT 3.4

Study Guide **pp. 44–46**

Practice Online 3.4

4 **Explain how people gain from specialization and trade.**

FIGURE 1

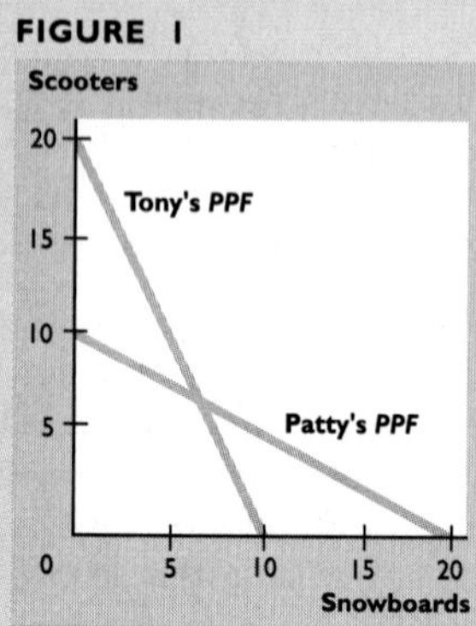

FIGURE 2

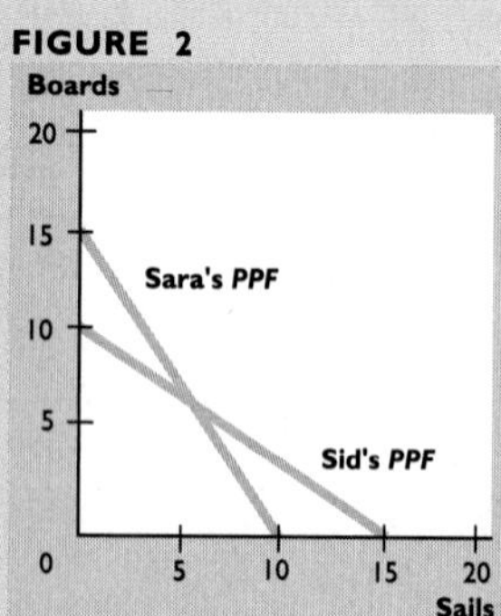

Practice Problem 3.4

Tony and Patty produce scooters and snowboards. Figure 1 shows their production possibilities per day.

a. Calculate Tony's opportunity cost of a snowboard.
b. Calculate Patty's opportunity cost of a snowboard.
c. Who has a comparative advantage in producing snowboards?
d. Who has a comparative advantage in producing scooters?
e. If they specialize and trade, how many snowboards and scooters will they produce?

Exercises 3.4

1. Sara and Sid produce boards and sails for windsurfing. Figure 2 shows their production possibilities per day.
   a. Calculate Sara's opportunity cost of a board.
   b. Calculate Sid's opportunity cost of a board.
   c. Who has a comparative advantage in producing boards?
   d. Who has a comparative advantage in producing sails?
   e. If they specialize and trade, how many boards and sails will they produce?
2. Sid in exercise 1 installs a new machine that doubles his production possibilities.
   a. Who now has a comparative advantage in producing boards?
   b. Are there any gains for Sara and Sid if they specialize and trade? Explain why or why not.

Solution to Practice Problem 3.4

a. Tony's opportunity cost of a snowboard is 2 scooters. If Tony uses all his resources to make scooters, he can make 20 a day. If he uses all his resources to make snowboards, he can make 10 a day. For each snowboard made, Tony forgoes making 2 scooters.

b. Patty's opportunity cost of a snowboard is ½ of a scooter. If Patty uses all her resources to make scooters, she can make 10 a day. If she uses all her resources to make snowboards, she can make 20 a day. For each snowboard made, Patty forgoes making ½ of a scooter.

c. Patty has a comparative advantage in producing snowboards because her opportunity cost of a snowboard is less than Tony's.

d. Tony has a comparative advantage in producing scooters. For each scooter made, Tony forgoes making ½ of a snowboard. His opportunity cost of a scooter is ½ of a snowboard. For each scooter made, Patty forgoes making 2 snowboards. Her opportunity cost of a scooter is 2 snowboards. Tony's opportunity cost is lower than Patty's.

e. Patty specializes in snowboards, and Tony specializes in scooters. Together, they produce 20 snowboards and 20 scooters.

3.5 ECONOMIC GROWTH

Economic growth is the sustained expansion of production possibilities. Our economy grows when we develop better technologies for producing goods and services; improve the quality of labor by education, on-the-job training, and work experience; and get more machines to help us produce.

Economic growth
The sustained expansion of production possibilities.

Economic Growth in an Industry

Figure 3.12 shows the *PPF* for bottled water and water-bottling plants as the curve *JKL*. The amount by which production possibilities expand depends on the number of new bottling plants installed. If we install no new plants (point *L*), the *PPF* remains at *JKL*—the light orange curve. If we decrease the current production of bottled water and build 2 new bottling plants (point *K*), then in the future our *PPF* rotates outward to the new *PPF*. The more resources we devote to producing bottling plants now, the greater is the expansion of our production possibilities in the future.

But economic growth is not free. To make it happen, we must decrease consumption. In Figure 3.12, we move from *L* to *K* and forgo 2 million bottles of water for consumption now. The opportunity cost of more bottling plants is fewer bottles of water today. Also, economic growth is no magic formula for abolishing scarcity. Economic growth rotates the *PPF* outward, but on the new *PPF*, we continue to face opportunity costs.

Economic Growth of Nations

The United States and Hong Kong provide a striking example of the effects of choices on economic growth. Because Hong Kong has devoted more of its

FIGURE 3.12
Expanding Production Possibilities

Practice Online

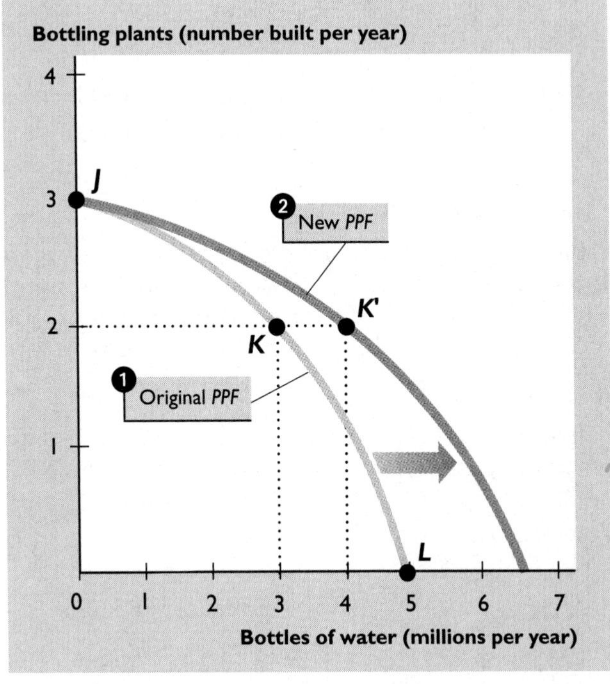

1. The original *PPF* shows the limits to the production of bottled water and water-bottling plants, with the production of all other goods and services remaining the same. If we devote no resources to producing water-bottling plants and produce 5 million bottles of water a month, we remain stuck at point *L*. But if we decrease water production to 3 million bottles a year and produce 2 water-bottling plants, at point *K*, our production possibilities will expand.

2. After a year, the production possibilities frontier shifts outward to the new *PPF* and we can produce at point *K'*, a point outside the original *PPF*. We can shift the *PPF* outward, but we cannot avoid opportunity cost. The opportunity cost of producing more bottled water in the future is less bottled water in the present.

FIGURE 3.13

Economic Growth in the United States and Hong Kong

Practice Online

In 1960, Hong Kong's production possibilities were 25 percent of U.S. production possibilities (per person). By 2000, they had grown to become 80 percent of U.S. production possibilities. Hong Kong grew faster than the United States because it devoted more of its resources to accumulating capital and less to consumption than the United States. In 1960, the United States and Hong Kong operated at point *A* on their respective *PPFs*. In 2000, Hong Kong was at point *B* and the United States was at point *C*. If Hong Kong continues operate at a point like *B*, it will grow more rapidly than the United States and its *PPF* will eventually move out beyond our own. But if Hong Kong increases consumption and decreases capital accumulation, moving to point *D* on its 2000 *PPF*, its rate of economic growth will slow.

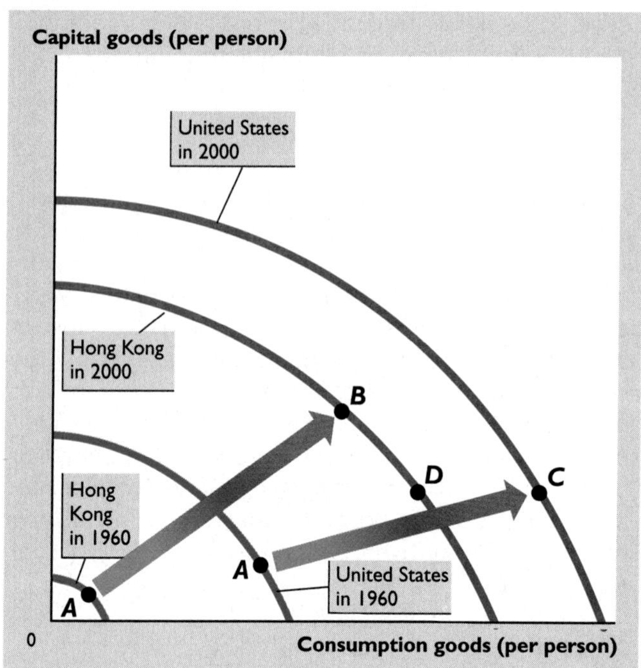

resources to capital accumulation than has the United States, Hong Kong's production possibilities have grown from 25 percent to 80 percent of U.S. production possibilities (per person) between 1960 and 2000.

CHECKPOINT 3.5

Study Guide pp. 46–48

Practice Online 3.5

5 **Explain how technological change and increases in capital and human capital expand production possibilities.**

Practice Problem 3.5

Table 1 shows a nation that produces education services and consumption goods. If the nation currently produces 500 graduates a year and 2,000 units of consumption goods, what is the opportunity cost of growth?

Possibility	Education services (graduates)	Consumption goods (units)
A	1,000	0
B	750	1,000
C	500	2,000
D	0	3,000

Exercise 3.5

If the nation shown in the table uses all its resources to produce consumption goods, at what rate will the economy grow? If the nation increases the number of graduates from 0 to 750, will the nation experience economic growth? Explain your answer.

Solution to Practice Problem 3.5

The opportunity cost is 1,000 units (3,000 minus 2,000) of consumption goods forgone.

CHAPTER CHECKPOINT

Key Points

1 Use the production possibilities frontier to illustrate the economic problem.

- The production possibilities frontier, *PPF*, describes the limits to what we can produce by fully and efficiently using all our available resources.
- Points inside and on the *PPF* are attainable. Points outside the *PPF* are unattainable.
- If production is at a point on the *PPF*, resources are fully employed. If production is at a point inside the *PPF*, resources are unemployed.
- If production is at a point on the *PPF*, we face a tradeoff. If production is at a point inside the *PPF*, there is a free lunch.

2 Calculate opportunity cost.

- Along the *PPF*, the opportunity cost of *X* (the item on the *x*-axis) is the decrease in *Y* (the item on the *y*-axis) divided by the increase in *X*.
- The opportunity cost of *Y* is the inverse of the opportunity cost of *X*.
- The opportunity cost of producing a good increases as the quantity of the good produced increases.

3 Define efficiency and describe an efficient use of resources.

- Resource use is efficient when there is production efficiency and allocative efficiency.
- Production efficiency occurs at *all* points *on* the *PPF*. Points *inside* the *PPF* are inefficient.
- The point on the *PPF* that achieves allocative efficiency is the one at which marginal cost equals marginal benefit.

4 Explain how people gain from specialization and trade.

- A person has a comparative advantage in an activity if he or she can perform that activity at a lower opportunity cost than someone else.
- We gain by specializing in the activity in which we have a comparative advantage and trading.

5 Explain how technological change and increases in capital and human capital expand production possibilities.

- Technological change and increases in capital and human capital expand production possibilities.
- The opportunity cost of economic growth is the decrease in current consumption.

Key Terms

TABLE 1

Corn (bushels per year)		Beef (pounds per year)
1,000	and	0
800	and	900
600	and	1,200
400	and	1,400
200	and	1,450
0	and	1,500

TABLE 2

Entertainment (units)		Good food (units)
100	and	0
80	and	30
60	and	50
40	and	60
20	and	65
0	and	67

TABLE 3

Movies (per week)	Marginal cost (CDs per movie)	Marginal benefit (CDs per movie)
1	2	8
2	4	6
3	6	4
4	8	2
5	10	0

Exercises

1. Table 1 shows the quantities of corn and beef that a farm can produce.
   a. Draw a graph of the farm's production possibilities frontier.
   b. Can the farm produce 500 bushels of corn and 500 pounds of beef?
   c. Can the farm produce 800 bushels of corn and 1,200 pounds of beef?
   d. What is the opportunity cost of the farm expanding beef production from 900 pounds to 1,200 pounds per year?
   e. If the farm produces 400 bushels of corn and 1,400 pounds of beef a year, is the farm using its resources efficiently? Explain your answer.
2. On Survivor Island, the only resources are 5 units of capital and 10 hours of labor a day. Table 2 shows the maximum quantities of entertainment and good food that Survivor Island can produce.
   a. Draw Survivor Island's production possibilities frontier.
   b. The people on Survivor Island want to produce 50 units of entertainment and 50 units of good food. Is this output attainable? If they do, does this output fully employ all the resources? What would be the opportunity cost of producing an additional unit of entertainment?
   c. The people on Survivor Island want to produce 40 units of entertainment and 60 units of good food. Is this output attainable? If they do, do they face a tradeoff? What would be the opportunity cost of producing an additional unit of entertainment?
   d. What can you say about the opportunity cost of a unit of good food as the people on Survivor Island allocate more resources to producing good food?
   e. What is the marginal cost of a unit of entertainment when Survivor Island produces 60 units of entertainment and 50 units of good food?
   f. If the efficient quantity of entertainment is 40 units, what is the marginal benefit from entertainment?
3. Table 3 gives Taylor's marginal cost of and marginal benefit from a movie.
   a. If Taylor sees 3 movies per week, what must she give up to see the third movie?
   b. If Taylor sees 3 movies per week, what is she willing to give up to see the third movie?
   c. What is Taylor's efficient number of movies per week?
4. Tommy spends 5 hours per night playing Chess Online. He really enjoys playing chess but over the past few weeks his economics grade has dropped. Tommy makes a rational decision to spend only 2 hours per night playing Chess Online. When Tommy spent 5 hours per night playing chess, did his marginal cost exceed his marginal benefit or did his marginal benefit exceed his marginal cost? Explain.
5. Tom can produce either 5 kites and 3 jigsaw puzzles an hour or 3 kites and 4 jigsaw puzzles an hour. Tessa can produce either 6 kites and 2 jigsaw puzzles an hour or 2 kites and 5 jigsaw puzzles an hour.
   a. Calculate Tom's opportunity cost of a kite.
   b. Calculate Tessa's opportunity cost of a kite.
   c. Who has a comparative advantage in producing kites?
   d. Who has a comparative advantage in jigsaw puzzles?
6. Tom and Tessa in exercise 5 specialize in producing the good in which they have a comparative advantage.
   a. What are the quantities of jigsaw puzzles and kites produced?
   b. Would Tom and Tessa get any gains from specializing production and trading with each other?

7. Table 4 shows the quantities of robots and consumption goods that the country Alpha can produce along its production possibilities frontier.
   a. If, in a year, Alpha produces 2,000 units of consumption goods, will Alpha experience economic growth? Explain.
   b. If, in a year, Alpha produces 1,100 units of consumption goods, will Alpha experience economic growth? Explain.
   c. If Alpha currently produces no robots and now decides to produce 1 robot, what is the cost of its economic growth?

TABLE 4

Robot services (units)		Consumption goods (units)
0	and	2,000
1	and	1,900
2	and	1,700
3	and	1,400
4	and	1,000
5	and	500

8. People can now obtain music from Web sites such as emusic and MP3.com.
   a. Have these Web sites changed the *PPF* for recorded music and other goods and services? If so, how has it changed?
   b. Is there still a tradeoff between recorded music and other goods and services, or is the opportunity cost of recorded music now zero?

9. AIDS has become an acute problem in Africa.
   a. How has the spread of AIDS influenced the *PPF* of the economies of Africa?
   b. Has the spread of AIDS increased the opportunity cost of some goods and services? Has it decreased the opportunity cost of anything?

10. A farm grows wheat and produces pigs. The marginal cost of producing each of these products increases as more of it is produced.
   a. Make a graph that illustrates the farm's *PPF*.
   b. The farm adopts a new technology, which allows the farm to use fewer resources to fatten pigs. Use your graph to illustrate the impact of the new technology on the farm's *PPF*.
   c. With the farm using the new technology in part **b**, has the opportunity cost of producing a ton of wheat changed? If so, how? If not, why not?

11. Explain how each of the following items might change the U.S. production possibilities frontier. In each case, is an opportunity cost incurred? If so, what is it? If not, why not?
   a. A larger percentage of the government budget is spent on education.
   b. The government spends more on Medicare and less on building the space station.
   c. Wild brush fires sweep through large parts of California and Arizona.

12. Each worker in Canada can produce 10 cars per year, while each worker in Mexico can produce 3 cars per year. But each worker in Mexico can produce 3 tons of steel per year, while each worker in Canada can produce 6 tons of steel per year. Mexico has 100 million workers, and Canada has 25 million workers. Suppose that each country produces only cars and steel.
   a. Draw a graph of Canada's production possibilities frontier.
   b. Draw a graph of Mexico's production possibilities frontier.
   c. Calculate the opportunity cost of producing 1 ton of steel in each country.
   d. Calculate the opportunity cost of producing 1 car in each country.
   e. Does either country have an absolute advantage? Which one?
   f. In which country is the marginal cost of producing a car lower?

Critical Thinking

13. After the terrorist attacks on the United States on September 11, 2001, Congress allocated increased resources to national defense, homeland security, and intelligence gathering. At the same time, Congress voted for lower taxes. Think about the effects of these decisions in terms of the production possibilities frontier for two groups of goods and services: "national security" and "other goods and services."
    - **a.** Show on the *PPF* the changes that have occurred since September 11, 2001.
    - **b.** Do you think that the opportunity cost of a unit of national security has increased or decreased? Explain your answer.
    - **c.** Do you think that the opportunity cost of a unit of other goods and services has increased or decreased? Explain your answer.
14. You have chosen to bear the opportunity cost of remaining in school to obtain a degree. Explain, using the concepts of rational choice, marginal cost, and marginal benefit,
    - **a.** Why have you made this choice?
    - **b.** Why did Bill Gates quit school before completing his degree?
    - **c.** Why do so many people quit school at the end of grade 12?
    - **d.** What can the government do to encourage more people to attend college?
15. The Kyoto agreement requires countries to achieve greenhouse gas reduction targets over the next ten years. The Canadian government has signed the Kyoto agreement but the U.S. government will not sign it.
    - **a.** As the Canadian government allocates more resources over the next ten years to reducing pollution, how will the Canadian *PPF* change?
    - **b.** Do you think that Canadian economic growth will change by more than U.S. economic growth changes? Or will growth in neither country be affected? Explain your answer.
    - **c.** Do you think that Canada will gain or lose some of its comparative advantage relative to the United States? Explain you answer.

<u>**Practice Online**</u>

Web Exercises

Use the links on your Foundations Web site to work the following exercises.

16. Visit the U.S. Census Bureau population clocks.
    - **a.** What is the estimated population of the United States?
    - **b.** What is the estimated population of the world?
    - **c.** How fast is the U. S. population increasing? (Use the second timer on your computer clock to determine the pace of increase.)
    - **d.** How fast is the world population increasing?
    - **e.** What do the population increases that you've found imply about the U.S. *PPF* and the world *PPF*? Which is moving faster?
17. Review the article *What's an MBA Really Worth*?
    - **a.** Is it rational for a person to enroll in an MBA program?
    - **b.** Why don't more people or fewer people enroll in MBA programs?
    - **c.** If an MBA can be completed part time and online, do these options lower the cost of obtaining an MBA or do they increase it?
    - **d.** Would you expect more people to enroll in a part-time or full-time MBA course? Explain why. Is there any conflict between your answers to parts **c** and **d**? Explain why or not.

CHAPTER 4

Demand and Supply

CHAPTER CHECKLIST

When you have completed your study of this chapter, you will be able to:

1. **Distinguish between quantity demanded and demand and explain what determines demand.**
2. **Distinguish between quantity supplied and supply and explain what determines supply.**
3. **Explain how demand and supply determine price and quantity in a market and explain the effects of changes in demand and supply.**

Because we face scarcity, we must make choices. One of these choices is to specialize in the activity in which we have a comparative advantage. Because we specialize, we sell the services of our factors of production in factor markets and we buy the goods and services that we consume in goods markets.

In this chapter, you study the tools of demand and supply that explain how markets work. You will learn how the choices people make about what to buy and sell determine the quantities and prices of the goods and services produced and consumed and the quantities of the factors of production employed.

Throughout your course in economics, you will use these demand and supply tools to understand the forces that allocate scarce resources. Soon, you will find yourself using the tools of demand and supply in your everyday life whenever you need to think about a price or a quantity.

COMPETITIVE MARKETS

When you need a new pair of running shoes, want a bagel and a latte, plan to upgrade your entertainment system, or need to fly home for Thanksgiving, you must find a place where people sell those items or offer those services. The place in which you find them is a *market*. You learned in Chapter 2 that a market is any arrangement that brings buyers and sellers together. A market has two sides: buyers (demanders) and sellers (suppliers). There are markets for *goods* such as apples and hiking boots, for *services* such as haircuts and tennis lessons, for *resources* such as computer programmers and earthmovers, and for other manufactured *inputs* such as memory chips and auto parts. There are also markets for money such as Japanese yen and for financial securities such as Yahoo! stock. Only imagination limits what can be traded in markets.

Some markets are physical places where the buyers and sellers meet and where an auctioneer or a broker helps to determine the prices. Examples of this type of market are the New York Stock Exchange and wholesale fish, meat, and produce markets.

Some markets are groups of people spread around the world who never meet and know little about each other but are connected through the Internet or by telephone. Examples of this type of market are the e-commerce markets and currency markets.

But most markets are unorganized collections of buyers and sellers. You do most of your trading in this type of market. An example is the market for basketball shoes. The buyers in this $3 billion-a-year market are the 45 million Americans who play basketball (or those who want to make a fashion statement) and are looking for a new pair of shoes. The sellers are the tens of thousands of retail sports equipment and footwear stores. Each buyer can visit several different stores, and each seller knows that the buyer has a choice of stores.

Markets vary in the intensity of competition that buyers and sellers face. In this chapter, we're going to study a *competitive market* that has so many buyers and so many sellers that no one can influence the price.

Markets for stocks...

currency...

and running shoes.

4.1 DEMAND

First, we'll study the behavior of buyers in a competitive market. The **quantity demanded** of any good, service, or resource is the amount that people are willing and able to buy during a specified period at a specified price. For example, when spring water costs $1 a bottle, you decide to buy 2 bottles a day. The 2 bottles a day is your quantity demanded of spring water.

Quantity demanded
The amount of any good, service, or resource that people are willing and able to buy during a specified period at a specified price.

The quantity demanded is measured as an amount *per unit of time*. For example, your quantity demanded of water is 2 bottles *per day*. We could express this quantity as 14 bottles per week or some other number per month or per year. But without a time dimension, a particular number of bottles has no meaning.

Many things influence buying plans, and one of them is price. We look first at the relationship between quantity demanded and price. To study this relationship, we keep all other influences on buying plans the same and we ask: How, other things remaining the same, does the quantity demanded of a good change as its price varies? The law of demand provides the answer.

The Law of Demand

The **law of demand** states

> **Other things remaining the same, if the price of a good rises, the quantity demanded of that good decreases; and if the price of a good falls, the quantity demanded of that good increases.**

So the law of demand states that when all else remains the same, if the price of a Palm Pilot falls, people will buy more Palm Pilots; or if the price of a baseball ticket rises, people will buy fewer tickets.

Why does the quantity demanded increase if the price falls, all other things remaining the same?

The answer is that, faced with a limited budget, people always have an incentive to find the best deals they can. If the price of one item falls and the prices of all other items remain the same, the item with the lower price is a better deal than it was before. So people buy more of this item. Suppose, for example, that the price of bottled water fell from $1 a bottle to 25 cents a bottle while the price of Gatorade remained at $1 a bottle. Wouldn't some people switch from Gatorade to water? By doing so, they save 75 cents a bottle, which they can spend on other things they previously couldn't afford.

Think about the things that you buy and ask yourself: Which of these items does *not* obey the law of demand? If the price of a new textbook were lower, other things remaining the same (including the price of a used textbook), would you buy more new textbooks? Then think about all the things that you do not now buy but would if you could afford them. How cheap would a PC have to be for you to buy *both* a desktop and a laptop? There is a price that is low enough to entice you!

Demand Schedule and Demand Curve

Demand is the relationship between the quantity demanded and the price of a good when all other influences on buying plans remain the same. The quantity demanded is *one* quantity at *one* price. *Demand* is a *list of quantities at different prices* illustrated by a demand schedule and a demand curve.

Demand
The relationship between the quantity demanded and the price of a good when all other influences on buying plans remain the same.

Demand schedule
A list of the quantities demanded at each different price when all the other influences on buying plans remain the same.

Demand curve
A graph of the relationship between the quantity demanded of a good and its price when all the other influences on buying plans remain the same.

A **demand schedule** is a list of the quantities demanded at each different price when all the other influences on buying plans remain the same. The table in Figure 4.1 is one person's (Tina's) demand schedule for bottled water. It tells us that if the price of water is $2 a bottle, Tina buys no water. Her quantity demanded is 0 bottles a day. If the price of water is $1.50 a bottle, her quantity demanded is 1 bottle a day. Tina's quantity demanded increases to 2 bottles a day at a price of $1.00 a bottle and to 3 bottles a day at a price of 50 cents a bottle.

A **demand curve** is a graph of the relationship between the quantity demanded of a good and its price when all the other influences on buying plans remain the same. The points on the demand curve labeled *A* through *D* represent the rows *A* through *D* of the demand schedule. For example, point *B* on the graph represents row *B* of the demand schedule and shows that the quantity demanded is 1 bottle a day when the price is $1.50 a bottle. Point C on the demand curve represents row C of the demand schedule and shows that the quantity demanded is 2 bottles a day when the price is $1.00 a bottle.

The downward slope of the demand curve illustrates the law of demand. Along the demand curve, when the price of the good *falls*, the quantity demanded *increases*. For example, in Figure 4.1, when the price of a bottle of water falls from $1.00 to 50 cents, the quantity demanded increases from 2 bottles a day to 3 bottles a day. And when the price *rises*, the quantity demanded *decreases*. For example, when the price rises from $1.00 to $1.50 a bottle, the quantity demanded decreases from 2 bottles a day to 1 bottle a day.

FIGURE 4.1
Demand Schedule and Demand Curve

Practice Online

The table shows a demand schedule, which lists the quantity of water demanded at each price if all other influences on buying plans remain the same. At a price of $1.50 a bottle, the quantity demanded is 1 bottle a day.

The demand curve shows the relationship between the quantity demanded and price, everything else remaining the same. The downward-sloping demand curve illustrates the law of demand. When the price falls, the quantity demanded increases; and when the price rises, the quantity demanded decreases.

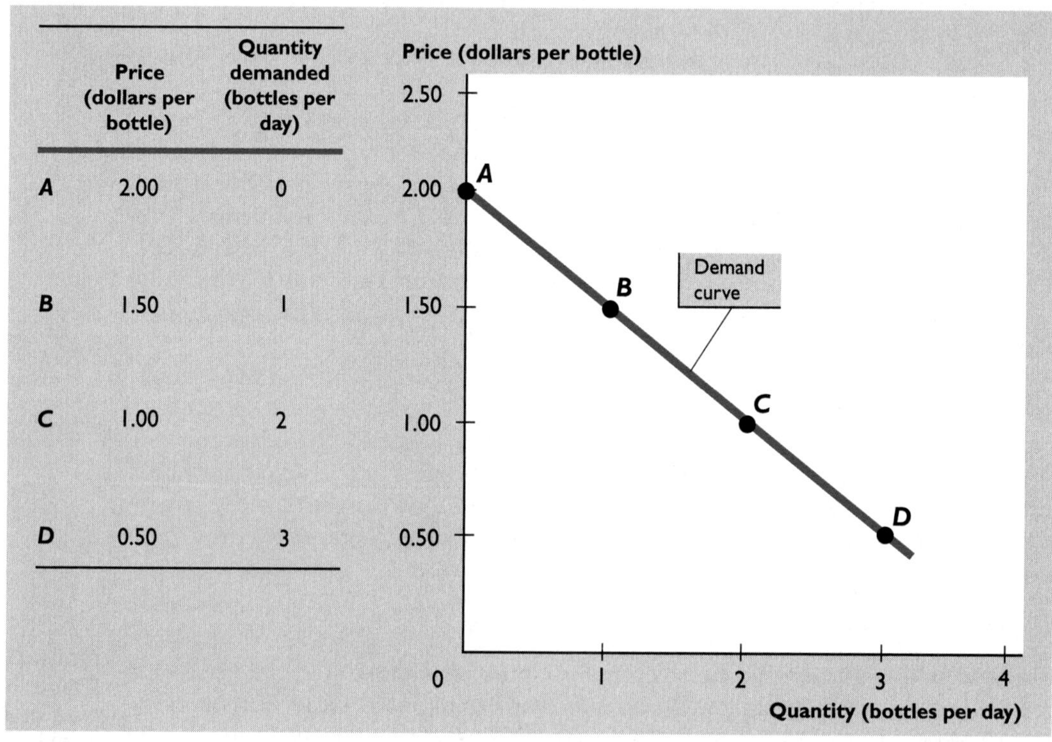

	Price (dollars per bottle)	Quantity demanded (bottles per day)
A	2.00	0
B	1.50	1
C	1.00	2
D	0.50	3

Individual Demand and Market Demand

The demand schedule and the demand curve that you've just studied are for one person. To study a market, we must determine the market demand.

Market demand is the sum of the demands of all the buyers in a market. To find the market demand, imagine a market in which there are only two buyers: Tina and Tim. The table in Figure 4.2 shows three demand schedules: Tina's, Tim's, and the market demand schedule. Tina's demand schedule is the same as before. It shows the quantity of water demanded by Tina at each different price. Tim's demand schedule tells us the quantity of water demanded by Tim at each price. To find the quantity of water demanded in the market, we sum the quantities demanded by Tina and Tim. For example, at a price of $1.00 a bottle, the quantity demanded by Tina is 2 bottles a day, the quantity demanded by Tim is 1 bottle a day, and so the quantity demanded in the market is 3 bottles a day.

Market demand
The sum of the demands of all the buyers in the market.

Tina's demand curve in part (a) and Tim's demand curve in part (b) are graphs of the two individual demand schedules. The market demand curve in part (c) is a graph of the market demand schedule. At a given price, the quantity demanded on the market demand curve equals the horizontal sum of the quantities demanded on the individual demand curves.

FIGURE 4.2
Individual Demand and Market Demand

Practice Online

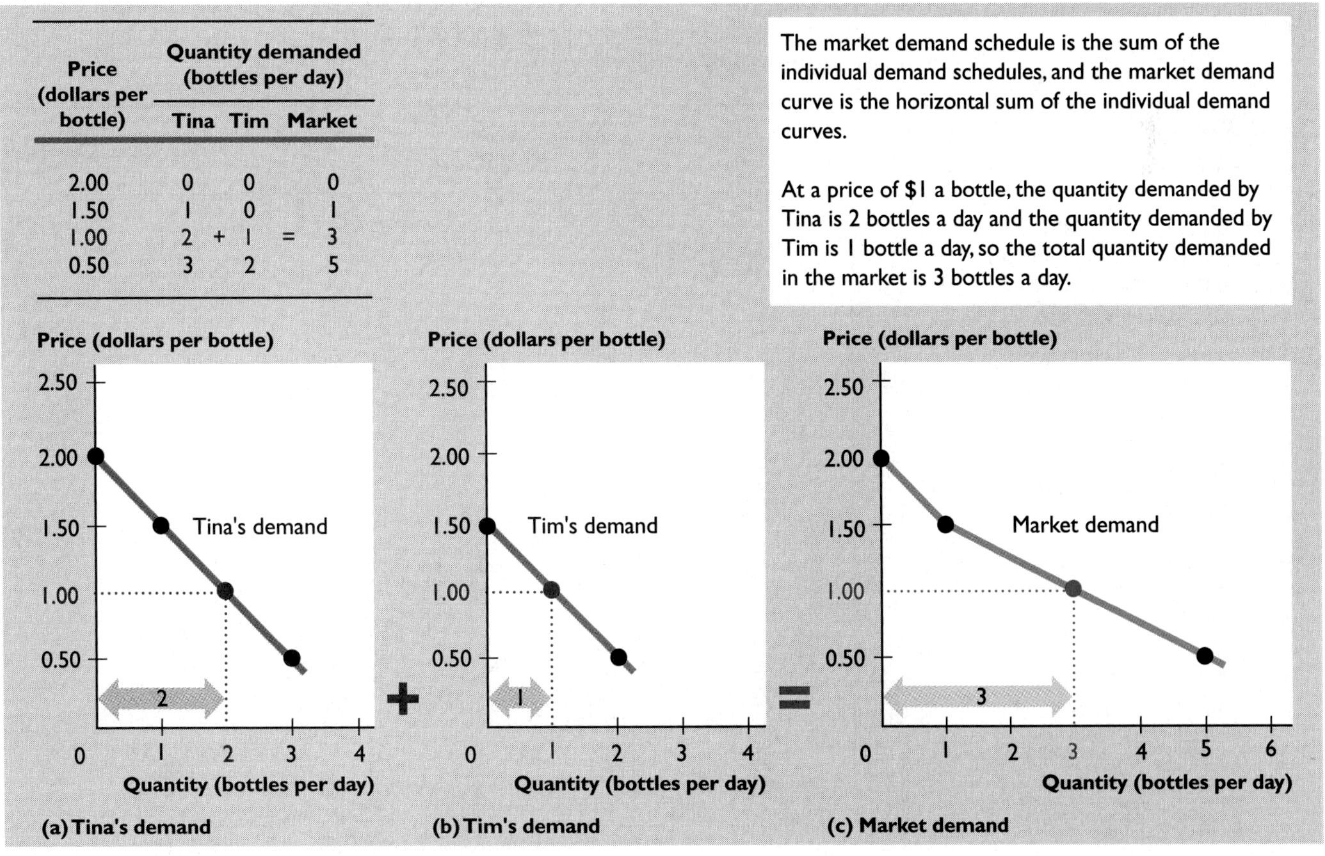

Price (dollars per bottle)	Quantity demanded (bottles per day)		
	Tina	Tim	Market
2.00	0	0	0
1.50	1	0	1
1.00	2 +	1 =	3
0.50	3	2	5

Changes in Demand

Change in the quantity demanded
A change in the quantity of a good that people plan to buy that results from a change in the price of the good.

Change in demand
A change in the quantity that people plan to buy when any influence on buying plans other than the price of the good changes.

The demand curve shows how the quantity demanded changes when the price changes but *all other influences on buying plans remain the same.* When the price changes, we call the resulting change in buying plans a **change in the quantity demanded**, and we illustrate this change by a movement along the demand curve.

When any influence on buying plans other than the price of the good changes, there is a **change in demand**. When demand changes, *the demand curve shifts.* Figure 4.3 illustrates two changes in demand. Initially, the demand curve is D_0. When the demand for bottled water decreases, the demand curve shifts leftward to D_1. On demand curve D_1, the quantity demanded is smaller at each price. And when the demand for bottled water increases, the demand curve shifts rightward to D_2. On demand curve D_2, the quantity demanded is greater at each price.

The main influences on buying plans that change demand are

- Prices of related goods
- Income
- Expectations
- Number of buyers
- Preferences

Prices of Related Goods

Substitute
A good that can be consumed in place of another good.

A change in the price of one good can bring a change in the demand for a related good. Related goods are either substitutes or complements. A **substitute** for a good is another good that can be consumed in its place. Chocolate cake is a substitute for cheesecake, a taxi ride is a substitute for a subway ride, and bottled water is a substitute for Gatorade.

FIGURE 4.3
Changes in Demand

A change in any influence on buyers' plans, other than a change in the price of the good itself, changes demand and shifts the demand curve.

1. When demand decreases, the demand curve shifts leftward from D_0 to D_1.
2. When demand increases, the demand curve shifts rightward from D_0 to D_2.

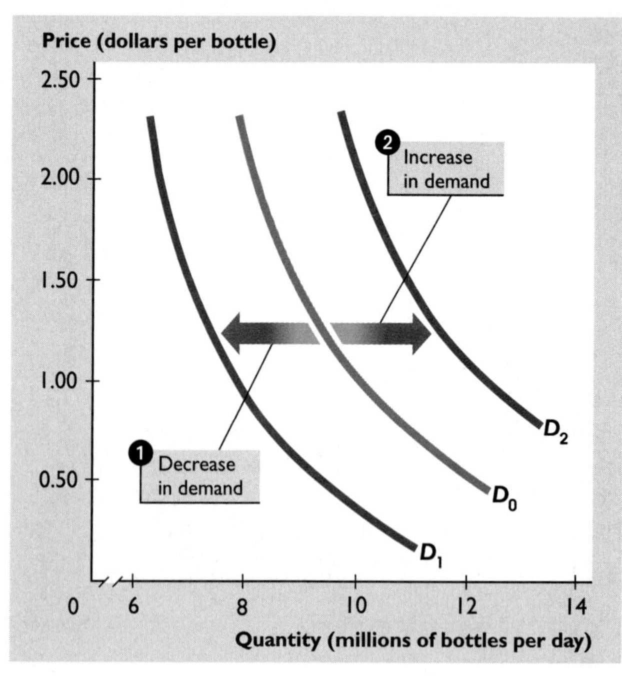

A **complement** of a good is another good that is consumed with it. Salsa is a complement of tortilla chips, wrist guards are a complement of in-line skates, and bottled water is a complement of fitness center services.

Complement
A good that is consumed with another good.

A Change in the Price of a Substitute The demand for a good *increases* if the price of one of its substitutes *rises*; and the demand for a good *decreases* if the price of one of its substitutes *falls*. That is, the demand for a good and the price of one of its substitutes move in the *same direction*. For example, cheesecake and chocolate cake are substitutes, so the demand for cheesecake increases when the price of chocolate cake rises.

A Change in the Price of a Complement The demand for a good *decreases* if the price of one of its complements *rises*; and the demand for a good *increases* if the price of one of its complements *falls*. That is, the demand for a good and the price of one of its complements move in *opposite directions*. For example, salsa and tortilla chips are complements, so the demand for salsa decreases when the price of tortilla chips rises.

Income

A good is a **normal good** if a rise in income brings an increase in demand and a fall in income brings a decrease in demand. For example, if you buy more bottled water when your income increases, then bottled water is a normal good. Most goods are normal goods (hence the name). A good is an **inferior good** if a rise in income brings a *decrease* in demand and a fall in income brings an *increase* in demand. For example, if when your income increases, you buy fewer plastic milk crates and more bookcases, then a plastic milk crate is an inferior good.

Normal good
A good for which demand increases when income increases.

Inferior good
A good for which demand decreases when income increases.

Expectations

Expected future income and prices influence demand. For example, you are offered a well-paid summer job, so you go to Cancun during spring break. Your demand for vacation travel has increased. Or if you expect the price of ramen noodles to rise next week, you buy a big enough stockpile of it now to get you through the rest of the school year. Your demand for ramen noodles today has increased.

Number of Buyers

The greater the number of buyers in a market, the larger is demand. For example, the demand for parking spaces, movies, bottled water, or just about anything is greater in New York City than it is in Boise, Idaho.

Preferences

Tastes or, as economists call them, *preferences* influence demand. When preferences change, the demand for one item increases and the demand for another item (or items) decreases. For example, preferences have changed as people have become better informed about the health hazards of tobacco. This change in preferences has decreased the demand for cigarettes and increased the demand for nicotine patches.

Preferences also change when new goods become available. For example, the development of MP3 technology has decreased the demand for CDs and increased the demand for Internet services and personal computers.

Demand: A Summary

Let's now summarize what you've learned about demand. A change in any influence on buyers' plans causes either a *change in the quantity demanded* or a *change in demand*. When you are thinking about the influences on demand, it is a good idea to get into the habit of asking yourself: Does this influence change the quantity demanded or does it change demand?

The distinction is crucial for figuring out how a market responds to the forces that hit it. The test for which of these two changes is occurring is simple. If the price of the good changes, other things remaining the same, there is a change in the quantity demanded and a movement along the demand curve. If any influence other than the price of the good changes, there is a change in demand and a shift of the demand curve.

Figure 4.4 illustrates and summarizes these distinctions:

- If the price of bottled water *rises* when everything else remains the same, the quantity demanded of bottled water *decreases* and there is a *movement up* along the demand curve D_0. If the price *falls* when everything else remains the same, the quantity demanded *increases* and there is a *movement down* along the demand curve D_0.
- If some other influence on buyers' plans changes, there is a change in demand. When the demand for bottled water *decreases*, the demand curve *shifts leftward* (to the red demand curve D_1). When the demand for bottled water *increases*, the demand curve *shifts rightward* (to the red demand curve D_2).

FIGURE 4.4

Change in Quantity Demanded Versus Change in Demand

Practice Online

1 A decrease in the quantity demanded

If the price of a good rises, *cet. par.*, the quantity demanded decreases. There is a movement up along the demand curve D_0.

2 A decrease in demand

Demand decreases and the demand curve shifts leftward (from D_0 to D_1) if

- The price of a substitute falls.
- The price of a complement rises.
- The price of the good is expected to fall or income is expected to fall in the future.
- Income decreases.*
- The number of buyers decreases.

* Bottled water is a normal good

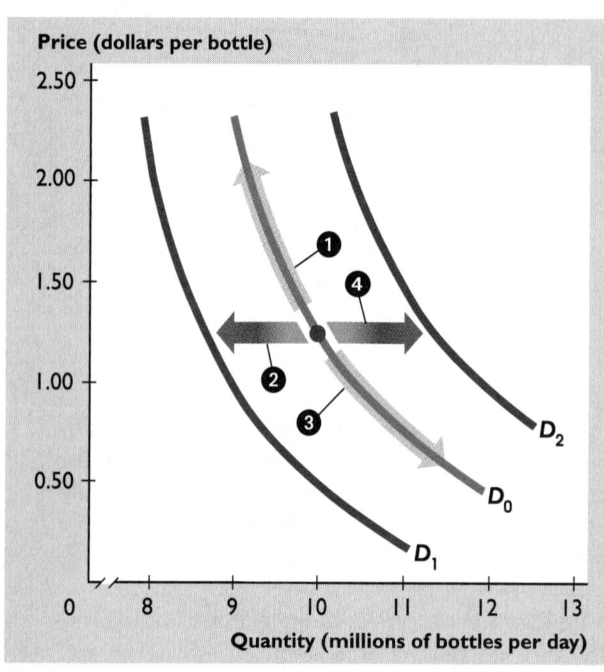

3 An increase in the quantity demanded

If the price of a good falls, *cet. par.*, the quantity demanded increases. There is a movement down along the demand curve D_0.

4 An increase in demand

Demand increases and the demand curve shifts rightward (from D_0 to D_2) if

- The price of a substitute rises.
- The price of a complement falls.
- The price of the good is expected to rise or income is expected to rise in the future.
- Income increases.*
- The number of buyers increases.

CHECKPOINT 4.1

1 **Distinguish between quantity demanded and demand and explain what determines demand.**

Study Guide pp. 55–58

Practice Online 4.1

Practice Problem 4.1

In the market for scooters, several events occur, one at a time. Explain the influence of each event on the quantity demanded of scooters and on the demand for scooters. Illustrate the effects of each event by either a movement along the demand curve or a shift in the demand curve for scooters, and say which event (or events) illustrates the law of demand in action. These events are

a. The price of a scooter falls.
b. The price of a bicycle falls.
c. Citing rising injury rates, cities and towns ban scooters from sidewalks.
d. Income increases.
e. Rumor has it that the price of a scooter will rise next month.
f. Scooters become unfashionable and the number of buyers decreases.

Exercise 4.1

The cell phone was invented in 1973, and during the first 20 years of its life, few people used one, except as a car phone. But during the 1990s, the use of cell phones increased dramatically and the price of cell phone service fell.

a. Are there any substitutes for cell phones? If so, provide an example.
b. Do cell phones have any complements? If so, provide an example.
c. What are the main developments that brought about the dramatic increase in cell phone use during the 1990s?
d. Which of the developments that you have identified increased the demand for cell phones? Illustrate these effects by using the demand curve for cell phones.
e. Which of the developments that you have identified increased the quantity demanded of cell phones? Illustrate these effects by using the demand curve for cell phones.

Solution to Practice Problem 4.1

a. A fall in the price of a scooter increases the quantity demanded of scooters, shown by a movement down along the demand curve for scooters (Figure 1) and is an example of the law of demand in action.
b. A bicycle is a substitute for a scooter. So when the price of a bicycle falls, the demand for scooters decreases. The demand curve shifts leftward (Figure 2).
c. The ban on scooters on sidewalks changes preferences and decreases the demand for scooters. The demand curve shifts leftward (Figure 2).
d. A scooter is (likely) a normal good. So when income increases, the demand for scooters increases. The demand curve for scooters shifts rightward (Figure 2).
e. A rise in the expected price of a scooter increases the demand for scooters now. The demand curve for scooters shifts rightward (Figure 2).
f. A decrease in the number of buyers decreases the demand for scooters. The demand curve shifts leftward (Figure 2).

FIGURE 1

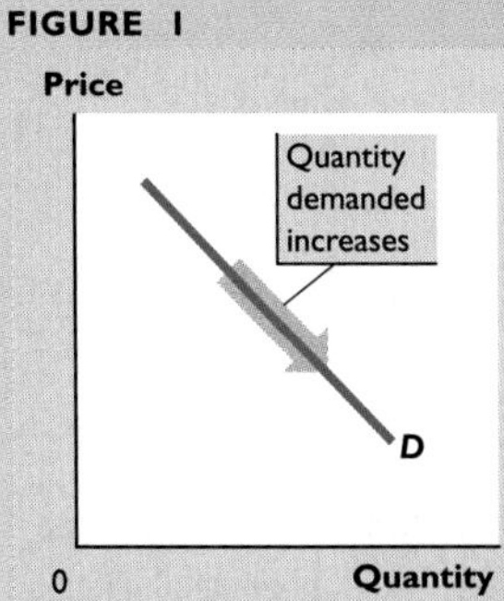

FIGURE 2

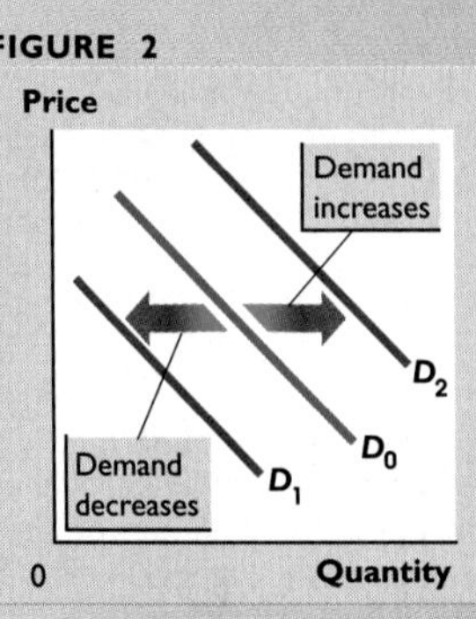

4.2 SUPPLY

A market has two sides. On one side are the buyers, or demanders, that we've just studied. On the other side of the market are the sellers, or suppliers. We now study the forces that determine suppliers' plans.

Quantity supplied
The amount of any good, service, or resource that people are willing and able to sell during a specified period at a specified price.

The **quantity supplied** of a good, service, or resource is the amount that people are willing and able to sell during a specified period at a specified price. For example, when the price of spring water is $1.50 a bottle, a spring owner decides to sell 2,000 bottles a day. The 2,000 bottles a day is the quantity supplied of spring water by this individual producer. (As in the case of demand, the quantity supplied is measured as an amount *per unit of time*.)

Many things influence selling plans, and one of them is the price. We look first at the relationship between quantity supplied of a good and its price. To study this relationship, we keep all other influences on selling plans the same. And we ask: How, other things remaining the same, does the quantity supplied of a good change as its price varies? The law of supply provides the answer.

The Law of Supply

The **law of supply** states

> **Other things remaining the same, if the price of a good rises, the quantity supplied of that good increases; and if the price of a good falls, the quantity supplied of that good decreases.**

So the law of supply states that when all else remains the same, if the price of bottled water rises, spring owners will offer more water for sale; if the price of a CD falls, Sony Corp. will offer fewer CDs for sale.

Why, other things remaining the same, does the quantity supplied increase if the price rises and decrease if the price falls?

The basic answer is that, faced with scarce resources, suppliers have an incentive to use their resources in the way that brings the biggest return. If the price of what they sell rises and the prices of all other items remain the same, the item with the higher price brings a greater return than it did before. So suppliers will want to sell more of this item. Suppose, for example, that the price of bottled water rose from $1 a bottle to $2 a bottle while the prices of everything else, including wages and other costs, remained the same. Wouldn't the spring owners offer more water for sale? By doing so, they receive an extra $1 a bottle.

Think about the resources that you own and can offer for sale to others and ask yourself: Which of these items does *not* obey the law of supply? If the wage rate for summer jobs increased, wouldn't you be encouraged to work longer hours? If the bank offered a higher interest rate on deposits, wouldn't you be inclined to make a greater deposit in the bank? If the used book dealer offered a higher price for last year's textbooks, wouldn't you think about selling that handy math text?

Supply Schedule and Supply Curve

Supply
The relationship between the quantity supplied and the price of a good when all other influences on selling plans remain the same.

Supply is the relationship between the quantity supplied and the price of a good when all other influences on selling plans remain the same. The quantity supplied is *one* quantity at *one* price. *Supply* is a *list of quantities at different prices* illustrated by a supply schedule and a supply curve.

A **supply schedule** lists the quantities supplied at each different price when all the other influences on selling plans remain the same. The table in Figure 4.5 is one firm's (Agua's) supply schedule for bottled water. It tells us that if the price of water is 50 cents a bottle, Agua plans to sell no water. Its quantity supplied is 0 bottles a day. If the price of water is $1.00 a bottle, Agua's quantity supplied is 1,000 bottles a day. Agua's quantity supplied increases to 2,000 bottles a day at a price of $1.50 a bottle and to 3,000 bottles a day at a price of $2.00 a bottle.

Supply schedule
A list of the quantities supplied at each different price when all the other influences on selling plans remain the same.

A **supply curve** is a graph of the relationship between the quantity supplied of a good and its price when all the other influences on selling plans remain the same. The points on the supply curve labeled *A* through *D* represent the rows *A* through *D* of the supply schedule. For example, point *C* on the supply curve represents row C of the supply schedule and shows that the quantity supplied is 1,000 bottles a day when the price is $1.00 a bottle. Point *B* on the supply curve represents row *B* of the supply schedule and shows that the quantity supplied is 2,000 bottles a day when the price is $1.50 a bottle.

Supply curve
A graph of the relationship between the quantity supplied of a good and its price when all the other influences on selling plans remain the same.

The upward slope of the supply curve illustrates the law of supply. Along the supply curve, when the price of the good *rises*, the quantity supplied *increases*. For example, in Figure 4.5, when the price of a bottle of water rises from $1.50 to $2.00, the quantity supplied increases from 2,000 bottles a day to 3,000 bottles a day. And when the price *falls*, the quantity supplied *decreases*. For example, when the price falls from $1.50 to $1.00 a bottle, the quantity supplied decreases from 2,000 bottles a day to 1,000 bottles a day.

FIGURE 4.5
Supply Schedule and Supply Curve

Practice Online

	Price (dollars per bottle)	Quantity supplied (thousands of bottles per day)
A	2.00	3
B	1.50	2
C	1.00	1
D	0.50	0

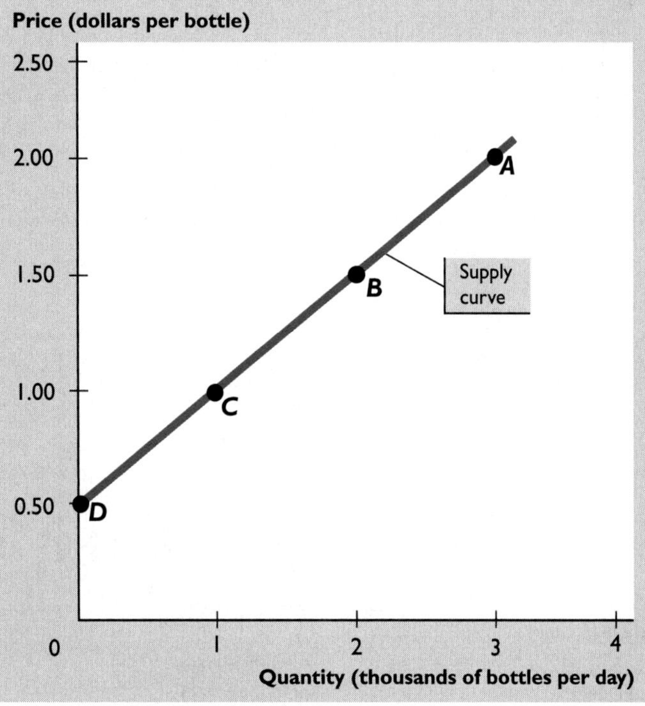

The table shows a supply schedule, which lists the quantity of water supplied at each price if all other influences on selling plans remain the same. At a price of $1.50 a bottle, the quantity supplied is 2,000 bottles a day.

The supply curve shows the relationship between the quantity supplied and price, everything else remaining the same. The upward-sloping supply curve illustrates the law of supply. When the price rises, the quantity supplied increases; and when the price falls, the quantity supplied decreases.

Individual Supply and Market Supply

Market supply
The sum of the supplies of all the sellers in the market.

The supply schedule and the supply curve that you've just studied are for one seller. To study a market, we must determine the market supply.

Market supply is the sum of the supplies of all the sellers in the market. To find the market supply of water, imagine a market in which there are only two sellers: Agua and Prima. The table in Figure 4.6 shows three supply schedules: Agua's, Prima's, and the market supply schedule. Agua's supply schedule is the same as before. Prima's supply schedule tells us the quantity of water that Prima plans to sell at each price. To find the quantity of water supplied in the market, we sum the quantities supplied by Agua and Prima. For example, at a price of $1.00 a bottle, the quantity supplied by Agua is 1,000 bottles a day, the quantity supplied by Prima is 2,000 bottles a day, and the quantity supplied in the market is 3,000 bottles a day.

Agua's supply curve in part (a) and Prima's supply curve in part (b) are graphs of the two individual supply schedules. The market supply curve in part (c) is a graph of the market supply schedule. At a given price, the quantity supplied on the market supply curve equals the horizontal sum of the quantities supplied on the individual supply curves.

FIGURE 4.6
Individual Supply and Market Supply

Practice Online

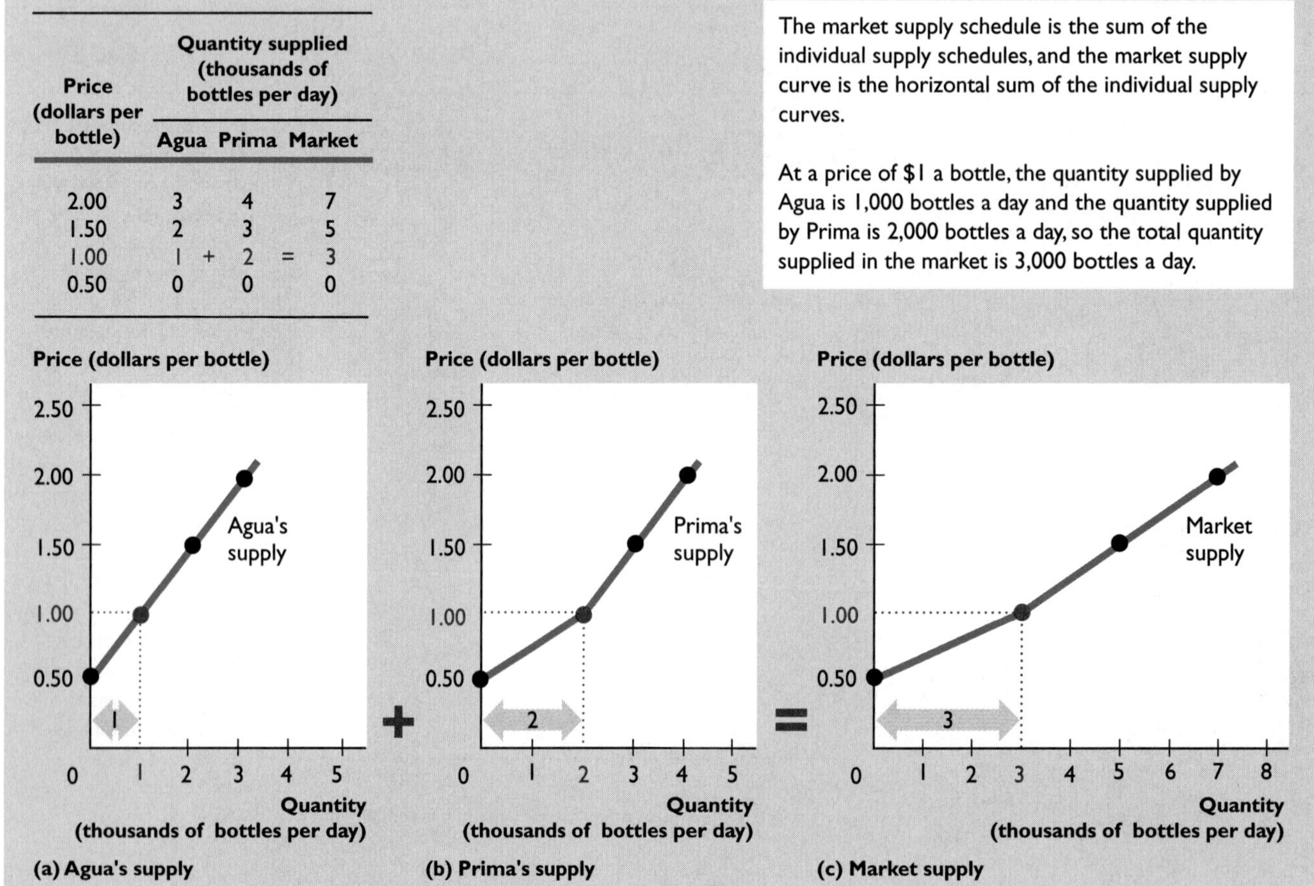

Price (dollars per bottle)	Quantity supplied (thousands of bottles per day)		
	Agua	Prima	Market
2.00	3	4	7
1.50	2	3	5
1.00	1 +	2 =	3
0.50	0	0	0

The market supply schedule is the sum of the individual supply schedules, and the market supply curve is the horizontal sum of the individual supply curves.

At a price of $1 a bottle, the quantity supplied by Agua is 1,000 bottles a day and the quantity supplied by Prima is 2,000 bottles a day, so the total quantity supplied in the market is 3,000 bottles a day.

(a) Agua's supply (b) Prima's supply (c) Market supply

Changes in Supply

The supply curve shows how the quantity supplied changes when the price changes but *all other influences on selling plans remain the same.* When the price changes, we call the resulting influence on selling plans the **change in the quantity supplied**, and we illustrate this change by a movement along the supply curve.

Change in the quantity supplied
A change in the quantity of a good that suppliers plan to sell that results from a change in the price of the good.

When any influence on selling plans other than the price of the good changes, there is a **change in supply**. When supply changes, *the supply curve shifts*. Figure 4.7 illustrates two changes in supply. Initially, the supply curve is S_0. When the supply of bottled water decreases, the supply curve shifts leftward to S_1. On supply curve S_1, the quantity supplied is smaller at each price. And when the supply of bottled water increases, the supply curve shifts rightward to S_2. On supply curve S_2, the quantity supplied is greater at each price.

Change in supply
A change in the quantity that suppliers plan to sell when any influence on selling plans other than the price of the good changes.

The main influences on selling plans that change supply are

- Prices of related goods
- Prices of resources and other inputs
- Expectations
- Number of sellers
- Productivity

Prices of Related Goods

A change in the price of one good can bring a change in the supply of a related good. Related goods are either substitutes in production or complements in production. A **substitute in production** for a good is another good that can be produced in its place. Button-fly jeans are substitutes in production for cargo pants in a clothing factory, and cookie dough ice cream is a substitute in production for chocolate chip ice cream in an ice cream factory.

Substitute in production
A good that can be produced in place of another good.

FIGURE 4.7
Changes in Supply

Practice Online

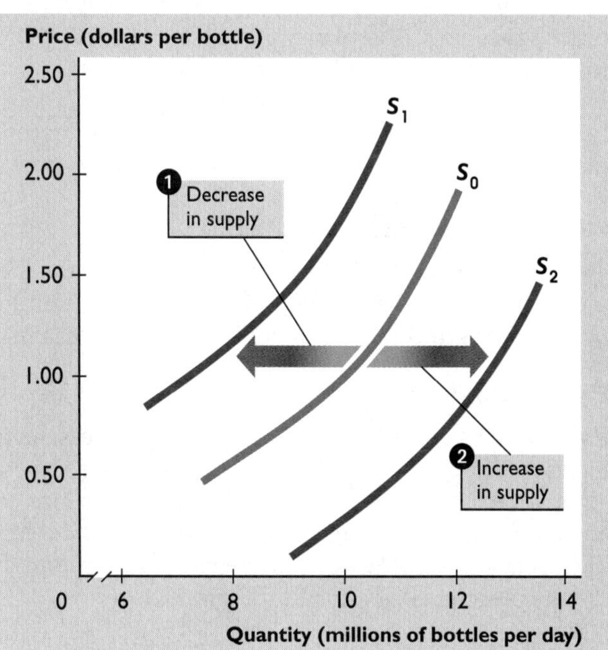

A change in any influence on sellers' plans other than a change in the price of the good itself changes supply and shifts the supply curve.

1. When supply decreases, the supply curve shifts leftward from S_0 to S_1.
2. When supply increases, the supply curve shifts rightward from S_0 to S_2.

Complement in production
A good that is produced along with another good.

A **complement in production** of a good is another good that is produced along with it. Cowhide is a complement in production of beef. And straw is a complement in production of wheat.

A Change in the Price of a Substitute in Production The supply of a good *decreases* if the price of one of its substitutes in production *rises;* and the supply of a good *increases* if the price of one of its substitutes in production *falls.* That is, the supply of a good and the price of one of its substitutes in production move in *opposite directions.* For example, a clothing factory can produce cargo pants or button-fly jeans, so these goods are substitutes in production. The supply of cargo pants decreases when the price of button-fly jeans rises.

A Change in the Price of a Complement in Production The supply of a good *increases* if the price of one of its complements in production *rises;* and the supply of a good *decreases* if the price of one of its complements in production *falls.* That is, the supply of a good and the price of one of its complements in production move in the *same direction.* For example, when a slaughterhouse produces beef, it also produces cowhide, so these goods are complements in production. The supply of cowhide increases when the price of beef rises.

Prices of Resources and Other Inputs

Supply changes when the price of a resource or other input used to produce the good changes. The reason is that resource and input prices influence the cost of production. And the more it costs to produce a good, the smaller is the quantity supplied of that good at each price (other things remaining the same). For example, if the wage rate of bottling-plant workers rises, it costs more to produce a bottle of water. So the supply of bottled water decreases.

Expectations

Expectations about future prices influence supply. For example, Boston's Big Dig is placing its freeways underground. A real estate developer expects the price of office space to rise when the Big Dig is completed. So instead of building new office space now, she plans to build it later when the price is higher. This action makes the supply of office space today less than it otherwise would have been. Expectations of future input prices also influence supply. If the developer expects builders' wages to rise next year, she might build new office space now before the wage rise occurs. This action increases the supply of office space today.

Number of Sellers

The greater the number of sellers in a market, the larger is the supply. For example, many new sellers have developed springs and water-bottling plants in the United States and the supply of bottled water has increased.

Productivity

Productivity is output per unit of input. An increase in productivity lowers costs and increases supply. A decrease in productivity has the opposite effect and decreases supply. Technological change is the main influence on productivity. For example, advances in electronic technology have lowered the cost of computers and increased their supply. Natural events such as weather patterns change farm productivity and change the supply of agricultural products.

Supply: A Summary

Let's now summarize what you've learned about supply. Changes in influences on sellers' plans cause either a *change in the quantity supplied* or a *change in supply*. Just as in the case of demand, when you are thinking about the influences on supply, try to develop the habit of asking yourself: Does this influence change the quantity supplied or does it change supply?

The test for which of these two changes is occurring is simple. If the price of the good changes, other things remaining the same, there is a change in the quantity supplied and a movement along the supply curve. If any influence other than the price of the good changes, there is a change in supply and a shift of the supply curve.

Figure 4.8 illustrates and summarizes these distinctions:

- If the price of bottled water *falls* when other things remain the same, the quantity supplied of bottled water *decreases* and there is a *movement down* along the supply curve S_0. If the price *rises* when other things remain the same, the quantity supplied *increases* and there is a *movement up* along the supply curve S_0.
- If any other influence on water bottlers' plans changes, there is a change in the supply of bottled water. When the supply of bottled water *decreases*, the supply curve *shifts leftward* (to the red supply curve S_1). When the supply of bottled water *increases*, the supply curve *shifts rightward* (to the red supply curve S_2).

FIGURE 4.8

Change in Quantity Supplied Versus Change in Supply

Practice Online

1 A decrease in the quantity supplied

If the price of a good falls, *cet. par.*, the quantity supplied decreases. There is a movement down along the demand curve S_0.

2 A decrease in supply

Supply decreases and the supply curve shifts leftward (from S_0 to S_1) if

- The price of a substitute in production rises.
- The price of a complement in production falls.
- A resource price or other input price rises.
- The price of the good is expected to rise.
- The number of sellers decreases.
- Productivity decreases.

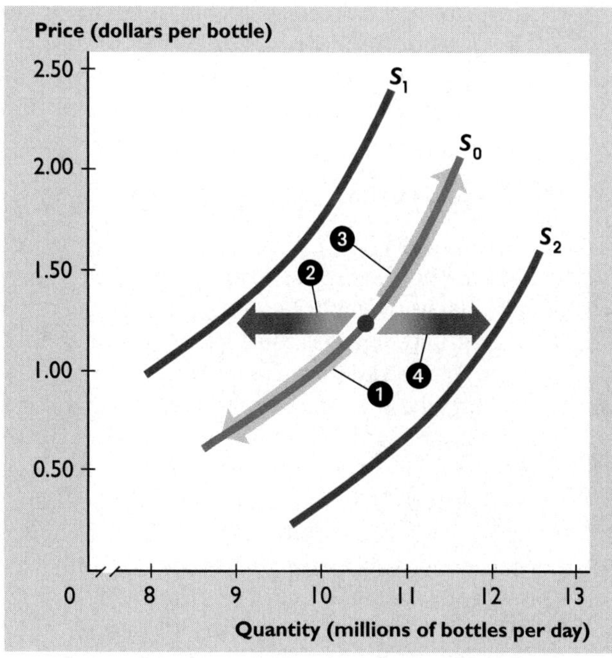

3 An increase in the quantity supplied

If the price of a good rises, *cet. par.*, the quantity supplied increases. There is a movement up along the supply curve S_0.

4 An increase in supply

Supply increases and the supply curve shifts rightward (from S_0 to S_2) if

- The price of a substitute in production falls.
- The price of a complement in production rises.
- A resource price or other input price falls.
- The price of the good is expected to fall.
- The number of sellers increases.
- Productivity increases.

CHECKPOINT 4.2

Study Guide pp. 58–62

Practice Online 4.2

2 Distinguish between quantity supplied and supply and explain what determines supply.

Practice Problem 4.2

In the market for timber beams, several events occur one at a time. Explain the influence of each event on the quantity supplied of timber beams and the supply of timber beams. Illustrate the effects of each event by either a movement along the supply curve or a shift of the supply curve of timber beams, and say which event (or events) illustrates the law of supply in action. These events are

a. The wage rate of sawmill workers rises.
b. The price of sawdust rises.
c. The price of a timber beam rises.
d. The price of a timber beam is expected to rise next year.
e. Environmentalists convince Congress to introduce a new law that reduces the amount of forest that can be cut for timber products.
f. A new technology lowers the cost of producing timber beams.

Exercise 4.2

In the market for DVDs, several events occur one at a time. Explain the influence of each event on the quantity supplied of DVDs and the supply of DVDs. Illustrate the effects of each event by either a movement along the supply curve or a shift of the supply curve of DVDs, and say which event (or events) illustrates the law of supply in action. These events are

a. The price of a CD falls.
b. The price of a DVD falls.
c. The price of a DVD is expected to fall next year.
d. The number of producers of DVDs increases.
e. The wage rate paid to DVD factory workers increases.
f. A new robot technology lowers the cost of producing DVDs.

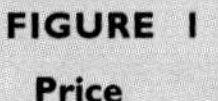

FIGURE 1

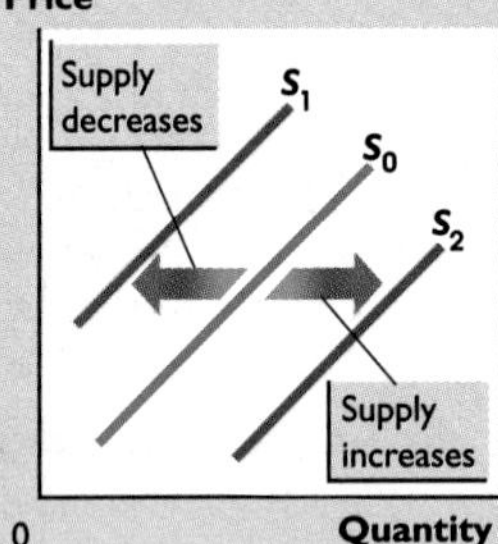

FIGURE 2

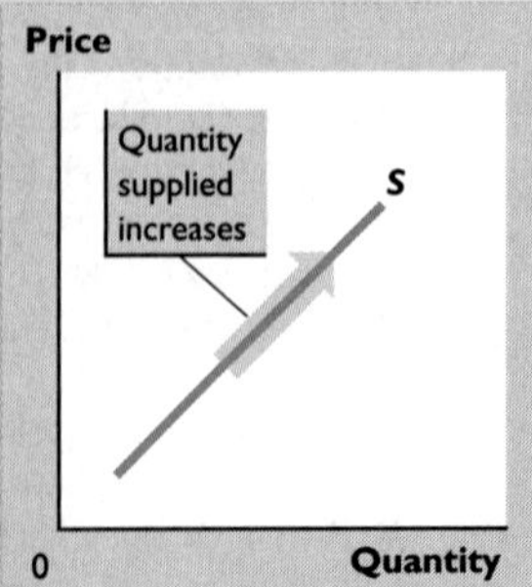

Solution to Practice Problem 4.2

a. A rise in the wage rate of sawmill workers decreases the supply of timber beams. The supply curve of timber beams shifts leftward (Figure 1).
b. Sawdust and timber beams are complements in production. A rise in the price of sawdust increases the supply of timber beams. The supply curve of timber beams shifts rightward (Figure 1).
c. A rise in the price of a timber beam increases the quantity supplied of timber beams, which is shown as a movement up along the supply curve of timber beams and is an example of the law of supply in action (Figure 2).
d. The expected rise in the price of a timber beam decreases the supply of timber beams now. The supply curve of timber beams shifts leftward (Figure 1).
e. The new law decreases the supply of timber beams. The supply curve of timber beams shifts leftward (Figure 1).
f. The new technology increases the supply of timber beams and shifts the supply curve rightward (Figure 1).

4.3 MARKET EQUILIBRIUM

In everyday language, "equilibrium" means "opposing forces are in balance." In a market, the opposing forces are those of demand and supply. Buyers want the lowest possible price, and the lower the price, the greater is the quantity that they plan to buy. Sellers want the highest possible price, and the higher the price, the greater is the quantity that they plan to sell.

Market equilibrium occurs when the quantity demanded equals the quantity supplied—when buyers' and sellers' plans are consistent. The **equilibrium price** is the price at which the quantity demanded equals the quantity supplied. The **equilibrium quantity** is the quantity bought and sold at the equilibrium price.

Market equilibrium
When the quantity demanded equals the quantity supplied—when buyers' and sellers' plans are consistent.

Equilibrium price
The price at which the quantity demanded equals the quantity supplied.

Equilibrium quantity
The quantity bought and sold at the equilibrium price.

Figure 4.9 shows the market for bottled water. The market equilibrium occurs where the demand curve and the supply curve intersect. The equilibrium price is $1 a bottle, and the equilibrium quantity is 10 million bottles a day.

At the equilibrium price, buying plans and selling plans are balanced. People would buy more water at a lower price, and bottlers would sell more water at a higher price. But at a price of $1 a bottle, the quantity that people plan to buy equals the quantity that bottlers plan to sell. The opposing forces of buying plans and selling plans are exactly balanced at a price of $1 a bottle.

An equilibrium might be stable or unstable. Balance an egg on its pointed end (if you can!) and then give it a nudge. The egg rolls over onto its side. The equilibrium was unstable. Now balance an egg on its side and give it a nudge. The egg rocks for a moment but soon settles down in its equilibrium again. Market equilibrium is like an egg balanced on its side. The market is constantly pulled toward a stable equilibrium in which neither buyers nor sellers can improve their positions by changing either the price or the quantity.

FIGURE 4.9
Equilibrium Price and Equilibrium Quantity

Practice Online

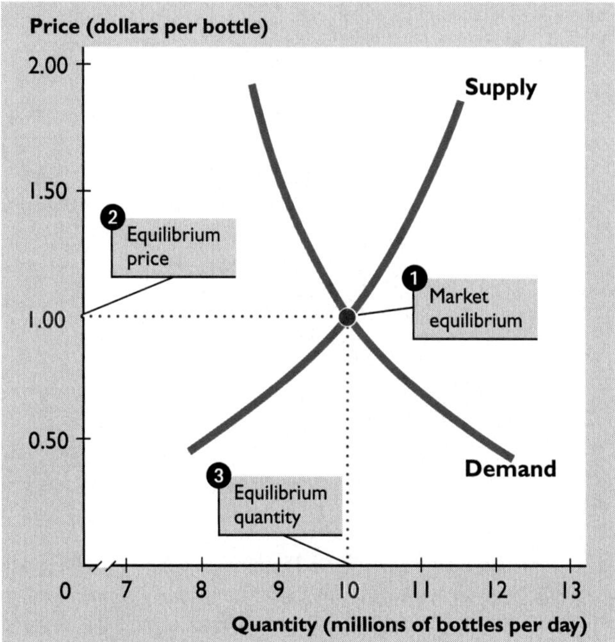

1. Market equilibrium occurs at the intersection of the demand curve and the supply curve.
2. The equilibrium price is $1 a bottle.
3. At the equilibrium price, the quantity demanded and the quantity supplied are 10 million bottles a day, which is the equilibrium quantity.

Price: A Market's Automatic Regulator

When equilibrium is disturbed, market forces restore it. The **law of market forces** states

> **When there is a shortage, the price rises; and when there is a surplus, the price falls.**

Surplus or excess supply
A situation in which the quantity supplied exceeds the quantity demanded.

Shortage or excess demand
A situation in which the quantity demanded exceeds the quantity supplied.

Price is the regulator that pulls the market toward its equilibrium. If the price is above the equilibrium price, there is a **surplus** or **excess supply**—the quantity supplied exceeds the quantity demanded—and the price falls. If the price is below the equilibrium price, there is a **shortage** or **excess demand**—the quantity demanded exceeds the quantity supplied—and the price rises.

In Figure 4.10(a), at \$1.50 a bottle, suppliers plan to sell 11 million bottles but demanders buy only 9 million bottles. There is a surplus of 2 million bottles, and the price begins to fall. As the price falls, the quantity demanded increases, the quantity supplied decreases, and the surplus decreases. The price falls until there is no surplus and comes to rest at \$1 a bottle.

In Figure 4.10(b), at 75 cents a bottle, demanders plan to buy 11 million bottles but suppliers sell only 9 million bottles. There is a shortage of 2 million bottles, and the price begins to rise. As the price rises, the quantity supplied increases, the quantity demanded decreases, and the shortage decreases. The price rises until there is no shortage and comes to rest at \$1 a bottle.

FIGURE 4.10
The Forces That Achieve Equilibrium

Practice Online

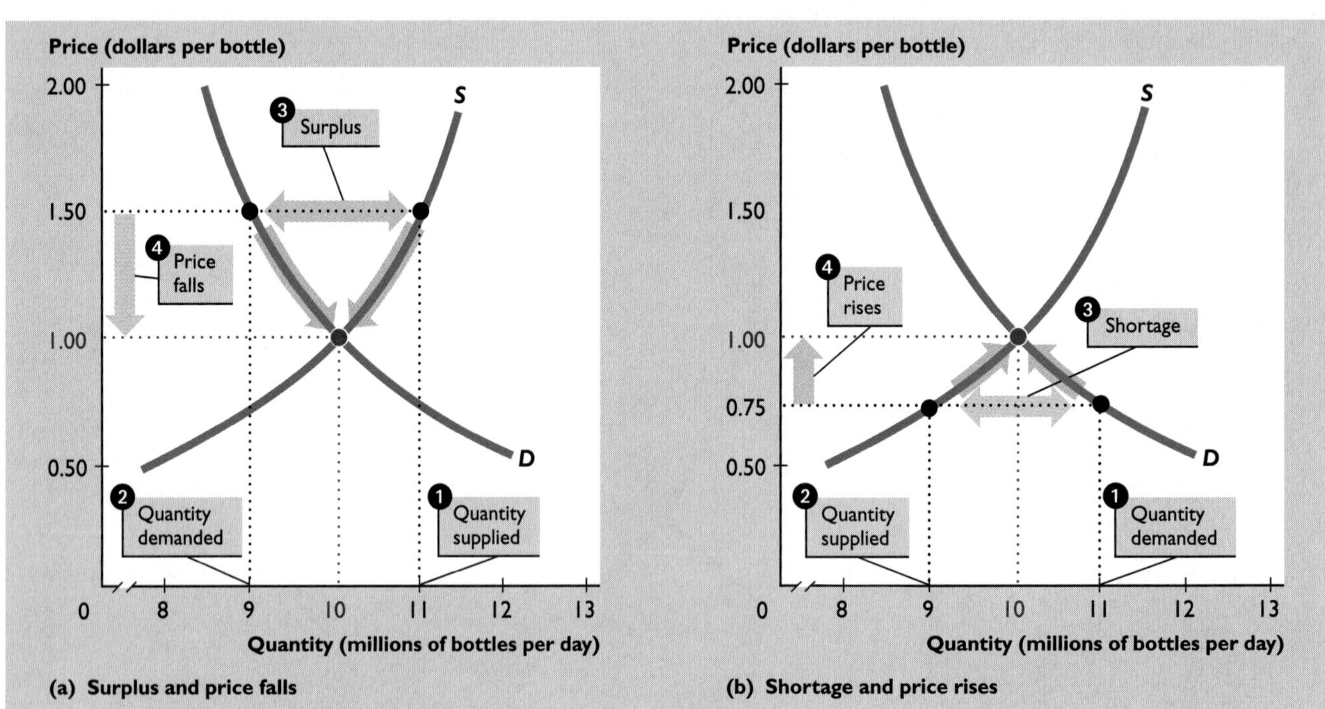

At \$1.50 a bottle, (1) the quantity supplied is 11 million bottles, (2) the quantity demanded is 9 million bottles, (3) the surplus is 2 million bottles, and (4) the price falls.

At 75 cents a bottle, (1) the quantity demanded is 11 million bottles, (2) the quantity supplied is 9 million bottles, (3) the shortage is 2 million bottles, and (4) the price rises.

Effects of Changes in Demand

Markets are constantly hit by events that change demand and supply and bring changes in price and quantity. Some events change demand, and some events change supply. And sometimes these events occur together. We'll look at all the possible cases. But we'll look first at the effects of changes in demand.

In Figure 4.11, the supply curve is S and, initially, the demand curve is D_0. The equilibrium price is \$1 a bottle, and the equilibrium quantity is 10 million bottles.

Suppose that a new study is published that raises concerns about the safety of the public water supply. The demand for bottled water increases. In Figure 4.11(a), the demand curve *shifts rightward* to D_1. At \$1 a bottle, there is now a shortage, so the price rises and the quantity supplied increases. The price rises to \$1.50 a bottle, and the quantity increases to 11 million bottles a day.

Next, suppose that a new zero-calorie sports drink is invented and the demand for bottled water decreases. In Figure 4.11(b), the demand curve *shifts leftward* to D_2. At the initial price of \$1 a bottle, there is now a surplus, so the price falls and the quantity supplied decreases. The price falls to 75 cents a bottle, and the quantity decreases to 9 million bottles a day.

In both cases, when demand changes, there is *no change in supply*. But there is a *change in the quantity supplied*—a movement along the supply curve.

FIGURE 4.11
The Effects of a Change in Demand

Practice Online

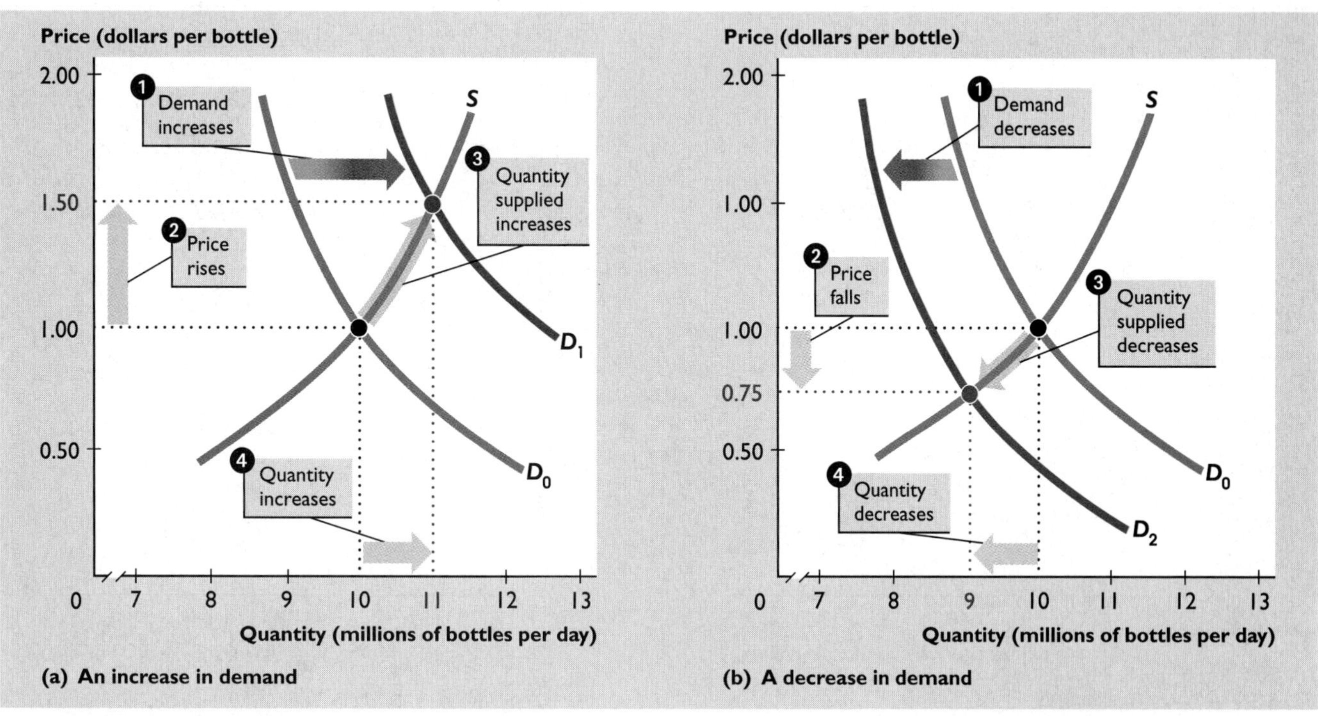

An increase in demand ❶ shifts the demand curve rightward to D_1, ❷ raises the price, ❸ increases the quantity supplied, and ❹ increases the equilibrium quantity.

A decrease in demand ❶ shifts the demand curve leftward to D_2, ❷ lowers the price, ❸ decreases the quantity supplied, and ❹ decreases the equilibrium quantity.

Effects of Changes in Supply

Let's now work out what happens when supply changes.

In Figure 4.12, the demand curve is *D* and, initially, the supply curve is S_0. The equilibrium price is $1 a bottle, and the equilibrium quantity is 10 million bottles.

Suppose that European water bottlers buy springs and open up bottling plants in the United States. The supply of bottled water increases. In Figure 4.12(a), the supply curve shifts rightward to S_1. At the initial price of $1 a bottle, there is now a surplus, so the price falls and the quantity demanded increases. The price falls to 75 cents a bottle, and the quantity increases to 11 million bottles a day.

When supply changes, there is *no change in demand*. But there is a *change in the quantity demanded*—a movement along the demand curve.

Next, suppose that a drought dries up some springs and the supply of bottled water decreases. In Figure 4.12(b), the supply curve shifts leftward to S_2. At the initial price of $1 a bottle, there is now a shortage, so the price rises and the quantity demanded decreases. The price rises to $1.50 a bottle, and the quantity decreases to 9 million bottles a day.

The new equilibrium price is $1.50 a bottle. Again, there is *no change in demand*. There is a *decrease in the quantity demanded*—a movement along the demand curve. The equilibrium quantity decreases to 9 million bottles a day.

FIGURE 4.12
The Effects of a Change in Supply

Practice Online

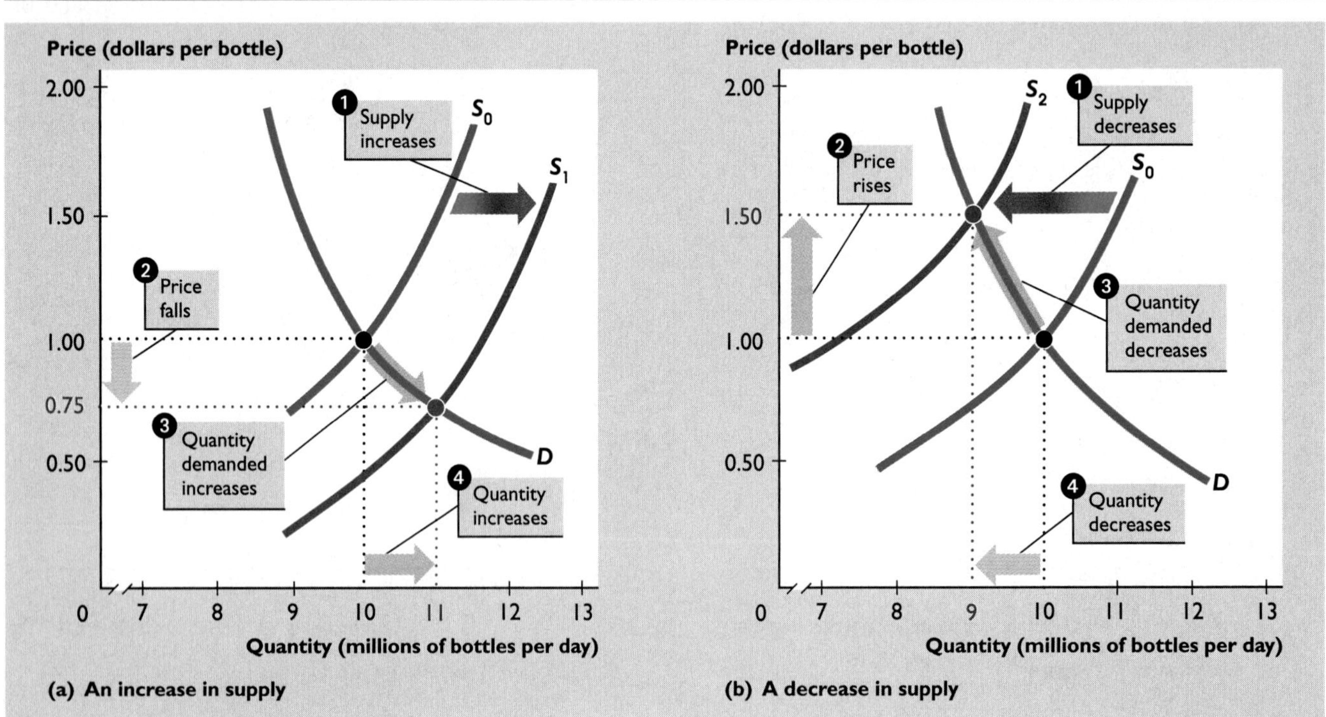

An increase in supply ❶ shifts the supply curve rightward to S_1, ❷ lowers the price, ❸ increases the quantity demanded, and ❹ increases the equilibrium quantity.

A decrease in supply ❶ shifts the supply curve leftward to S_2, ❷ raises the price, ❸ decreases the quantity demanded, and ❹ decreases the equilibrium quantity.

Eye on the Global Economy

A Change in the Demand for Roses

Colombia and Ecuador grow most of the world's roses. On the average, the quantity of roses sold worldwide is around 6 million bunches a month. And the average price that consumers pay is around $40 a bunch.

But one month, February, is not a normal month. Each year, in February, the quantity of roses bought increases to four times that of any other month. The reason: Valentine's Day. And on Valentine's Day, the price of a bunch of roses doubles.

The demand-supply model explains these facts. The figure shows the supply curve of roses and two demand curves. The blue demand curve is the demand for roses in a normal month. This demand curve intersects the supply curve at an equilibrium price of $40 a bunch and an equilibrium quantity of 6 million bunches.

In February, the demand curve shifts rightward to the red curve. The February demand curve for roses intersects the supply curve at an equilibrium price of $80 a bunch and an equilibrium quantity of 24 million bunches.

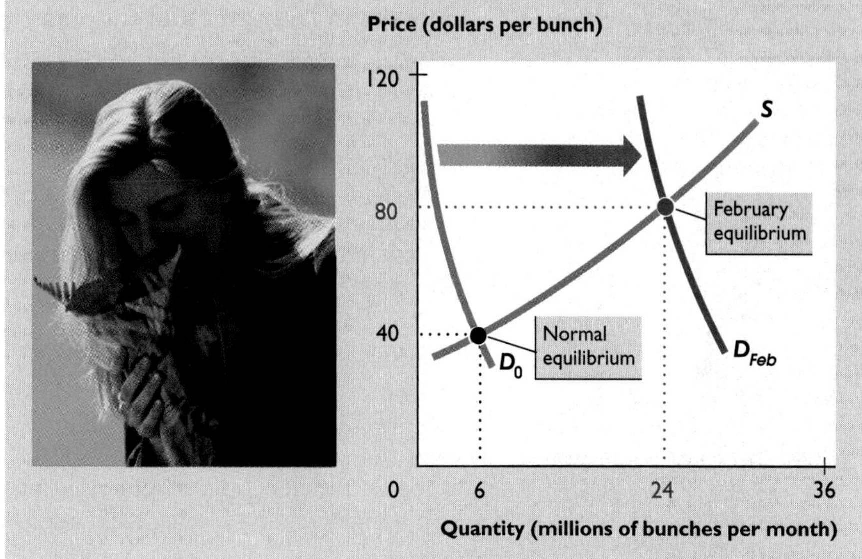

A Change in the Supply of Wheat

During 2002, the price of wheat soared from around $130 per metric ton to $190. The price increase was the consequence of a widespread global drought that decreased production and decreased the supply of wheat.

According to USDA estimates, wheat production fell from about 107 million metric tons in 2001 to about 100 million in 2002. Production was worst hit in the United States, Canada, Argentina, Australia, and the EU—the five largest wheat exporters. Production was up in Russia, Ukraine, and Kazakstan, allowing these countries to gain market share.

The figure shows the effect of the decrease in production. The supply of wheat decreased and the supply curve shifted leftward. The price of wheat increased and the quantity of wheat demanded decreased. (The figure assumes there was no change in the demand for wheat in 2002.)

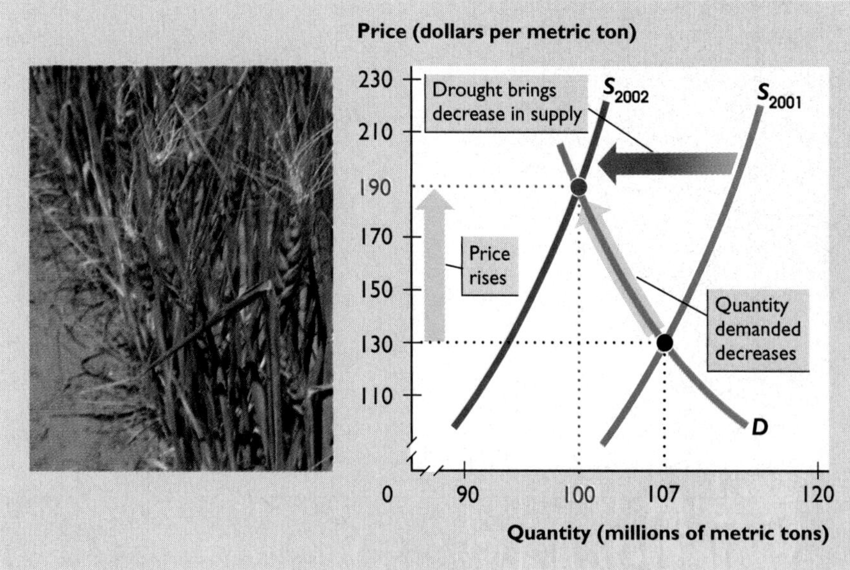

SOURCES: www.fas.usda.gov/grain/circular/2002/06-02/wht_txt.htm and www.uswheat.org/

Changes in Both Demand and Supply

What happens to the price and quantity in the market for bottled water when an event that changes demand occurs at the same time as an event that changes supply? Let's find out by studying the four possible combinations of simultaneous changes in demand and supply.

Increase in Demand and Increase in Supply

Either an increase in demand or an increase in supply increases the equilibrium quantity. But an increase in demand raises the price, and an increase in supply lowers the price. So when demand and supply increase together, the quantity increases and the price might rise, fall, or stay the same. Figure 4.13(a) shows what happens in the market for bottled water when concern about the safety of tap water increases demand and the opening of new bottling plants increases supply. The quantity increases and, because the increase in demand is greater than the increase in supply, the price rises.

Decrease in Demand and Decrease in Supply

Either a decrease in demand or a decrease in supply decreases the equilibrium quantity. But a decrease in demand lowers the price, and a decrease in supply raises the price. So when demand and supply decrease together, the quantity decreases and the price might rise, fall, or stay the same. Figure 4.13(b) shows what happens in the market for bottled water when the invention of a new sports

FIGURE 4.13
Demand and Supply Change in the Same Direction

Practice Online

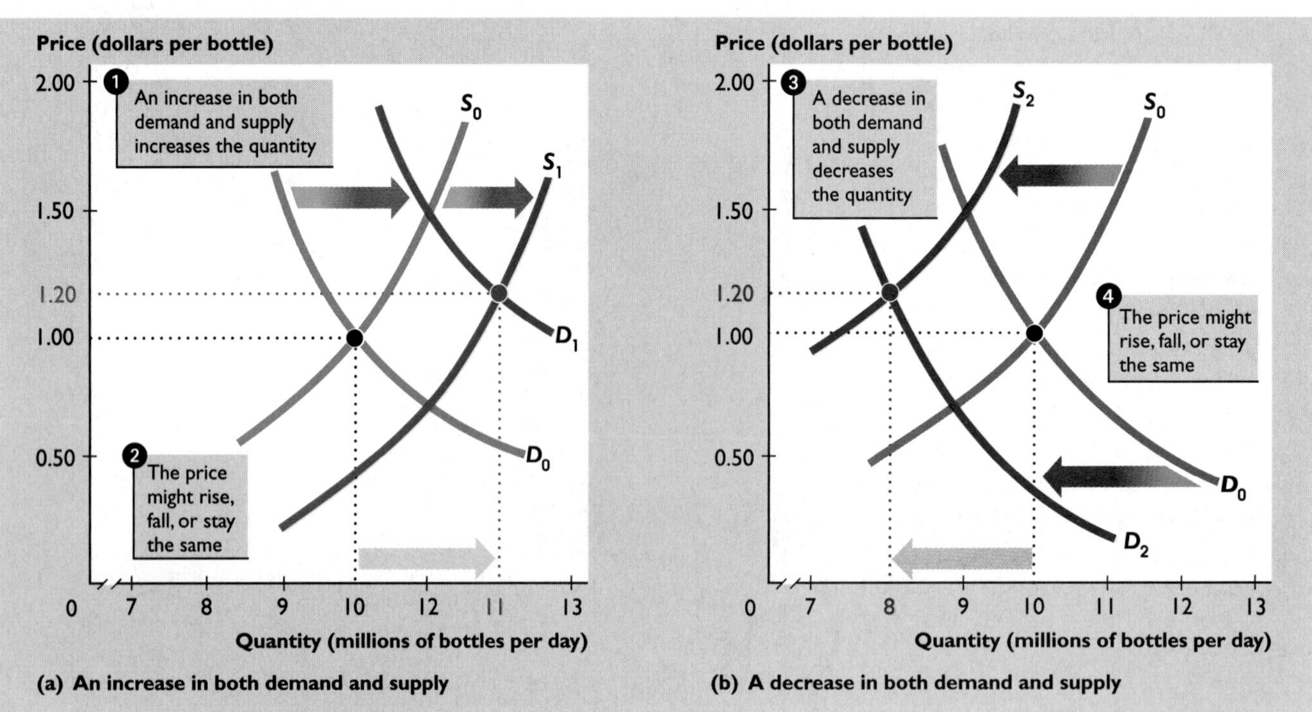

(a) An increase in both demand and supply

(b) A decrease in both demand and supply

drink decreases demand and a drought decreases supply. The quantity decreases and, because the decrease in supply is greater than the decrease in demand, the price rises.

Increase in Demand and Decrease in Supply

Either an increase in demand or a decrease in supply raises the equilibrium price. But an increase in demand increases the quantity, and a decrease in supply decreases the quantity. So when an increase in demand and a decrease in supply occur together, the price rises and the quantity might increase, decrease, or stay the same. Figure 4.14(a) shows what happens in the market for bottled water when concern about the safety of tap water increases demand and a drought decreases supply. The price rises and, because the increase in demand equals the decrease in supply, the quantity remains constant.

Decrease in Demand and Increase in Supply

Either a decrease in demand or an increase in supply lowers the price. But a decrease in demand decreases the quantity, and an increase in supply increases the quantity. So when a decrease in demand and an increase in supply occur together, the price falls and the quantity might increase, decrease, or stay the same. Figure 4.14(b) shows what happens in the market for bottled water when the invention of a new sports drink decreases demand and the opening of new bottling plants increases supply. The price falls and, because the decrease in demand equals the increase in supply, the quantity remains constant.

FIGURE 4.14
Demand and Supply Change in Opposite Directions

Practice Online

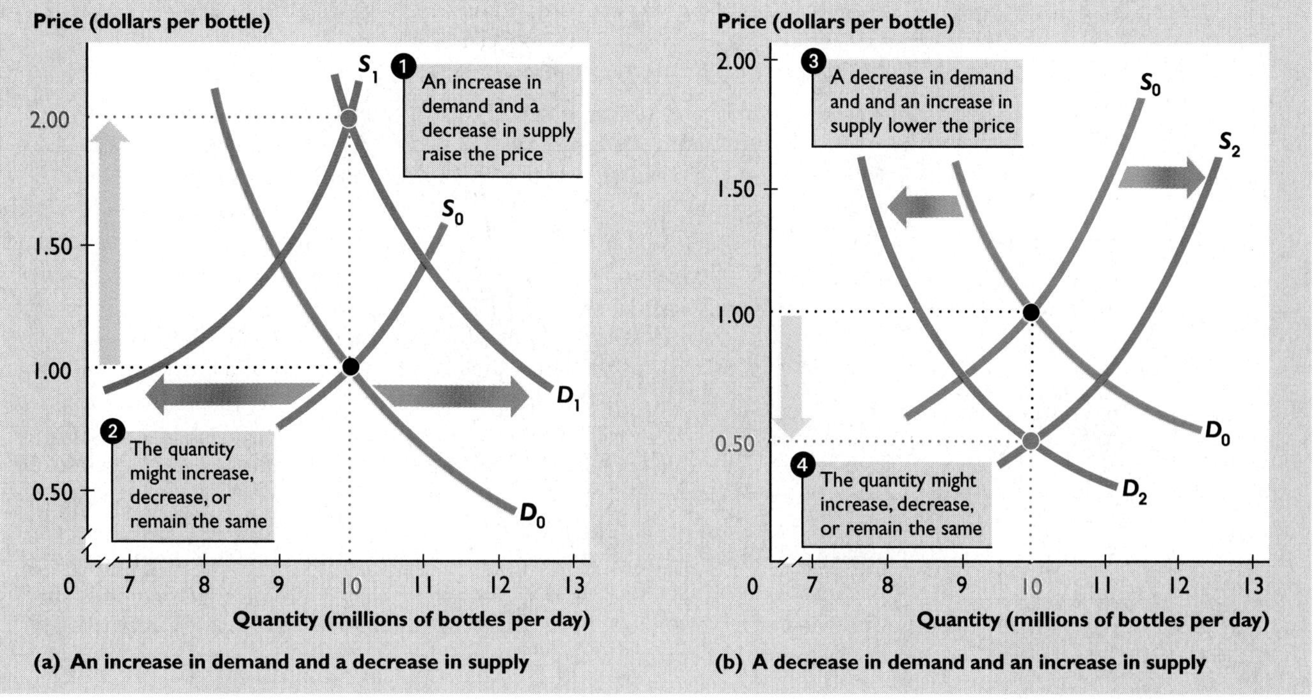

(a) An increase in demand and a decrease in supply

(b) A decrease in demand and an increase in supply

CHECKPOINT 4.3

Study Guide pp. 62–65

Practice Online 4.3

3 **Explain how demand and supply determine price and quantity in a market and explain the effects of changes in demand and supply.**

Price (dollars per carton)	Quantity demanded (cartons per day)	Quantity supplied (cartons per day)
1.00	200	110
1.25	175	130
1.50	150	150
1.75	125	170
2.00	100	190

Practice Problem 4.3

The table shows the demand and supply schedules for milk.

a. What is the market equilibrium in the milk market?

b. Describe the situation in the milk market if the price were $1.75 a carton.

c. If the price is $1.75 a carton, explain how the market reaches equilibrium.

d. A drought decreases the quantity supplied by 45 cartons a day at each price. What is the new equilibrium and how does the market adjust to it?

e. Milk becomes more popular and the quantity demanded increases by 5 cartons a day at each price. Better feeds increase the quantity of milk supplied by 50 cartons a day at each price. If there is no drought, what is the new equilibrium, and how does the market adjust to it?

Price (dollars per roll)	Quantity demanded (rolls per week)	Quantity supplied (rolls per week)
2.00	3,000	1,000
3.00	2,500	1,500
4.00	2,000	2,000
5.00	1,500	2,500
6.00	1,000	3,000

Exercise 4.3

The table shows the demand and supply schedules for rolls of film.

a. What is the market equilibrium?

b. If the price of film is $3 a roll, describe the situation in the film market. Explain how market equilibrium is restored.

c. A rise in income increases the quantity demanded of film by 1,000 rolls a week at each price. Explain how the film market adjusts to its new equilibrium.

d. The number of film production lines increases the quantity supplied of film by 750 rolls a week at each price. People switch to digital cameras and the quantity demanded of film decreases by 250 rolls a week at each price. With no rise in income, explain how the film market adjusts to its new equilibrium.

FIGURE 1

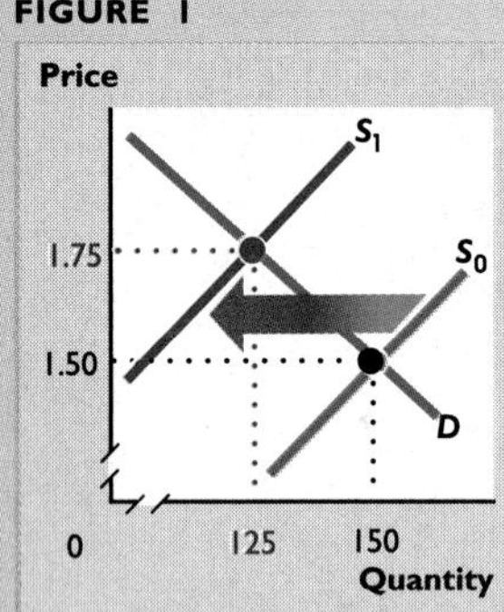

FIGURE 2

Solution to Practice Problem 4.3

a. Market equilibrium occurs at $1.50 a carton and 150 cartons a day.

b. At $1.75 a carton, the quantity demanded (125 cartons) is less than the quantity supplied (170 cartons), so there is a surplus of 45 cartons a day.

c. At $1.75 a carton, there is a surplus of 45 cartons a day. As suppliers lower the price, the quantity demanded increases, the quantity supplied decreases, and the surplus decreases. The price falls until the surplus disappears. The price falls to $1.50 a carton.

d. The supply curve *shifts leftward* by 45 cartons a day. At $1.50, the quantity demanded (150 cartons) exceeds the quantity supplied (105 cartons) and there is a shortage of milk and the price begins to rise. As the price rises, the quantity demanded decreases, the quantity supplied increases, and the shortage decreases. The price rises to $1.75 a carton, and the quantity decreases to 125 cartons a day (Figure 1).

e. The demand curve *shifts rightward* by 5 cartons a day. The supply curve *shifts rightward* by 50 cartons a day. At $1.50 a carton, the quantity demanded (155 cartons) is less than the quantity supplied (200 cartons). There is a surplus and the price begins to fall. As the price falls to $1.25 a carton, the quantity increases to 180 cartons a day (Figure 2).

CHAPTER CHECKPOINT

Key Points

1 Distinguish between quantity demanded and demand and explain what determines demand.

- Other things remaining the same, the quantity demanded increases as the price falls and decreases as the price rises—the law of demand.
- The demand for a good is influenced by the prices of related goods, income, expectations about income and future prices, the number of buyers, and preferences. A change in any of these influences changes the demand for the good.

2 Distinguish between quantity supplied and supply and explain what determines supply.

- Other things remaining the same, the quantity supplied increases as the price rises and decreases as the price falls—the law of supply.
- The supply of a good is influenced by the prices of related goods, prices of resources and other inputs, expectations about future prices and input prices, the number of sellers, and productivity. A change in any of these influences changes the supply of the good.

3 Explain how demand and supply determine price and quantity in a market and explain the effects of changes in demand and supply.

- The law of market forces brings market equilibrium—the equilibrium price and equilibrium quantity at which buyers and sellers trade.
- The price adjusts to maintain market equilibrium—to keep the quantity demanded equal to the quantity supplied. A surplus brings a fall in the price to restore market equilibrium; a shortage brings a rise in the price to restore market equilibrium.
- Market equilibrium responds to changes in demand and supply. An increase in demand increases both the price and the quantity; a decrease in demand decreases both the price and the quantity. An increase in supply increases the quantity but decreases the price; and a decrease in supply decreases the quantity but increases the price.

Key Terms

Exercises

1. Explain how each of the following situations changes the demand or supply of air travel.
   a. Airfares tumble, while long-distance bus fares don't change.
   b. The price of jet fuel rises.
   c. Airlines reduce the number of flights each day.
   d. People expect airfares to increase next summer.
   e. As the winter in the Northeast turns very cold, many people decide to take a mid-winter break in Florida.
   f. With deep snow in the Rockies, many people flock to the ski slopes.
   g. The price of train travel falls.
   h. The price of a pound of air cargo increases.

2. Explain how each of the following items influences the demand for and supply of jeans.
   a. A new technology becomes available that cuts the time it takes to manufacture a pair of jeans by 50 percent.
   b. The price of the cloth (denim) used to make jeans falls.
   c. Jeans go out of fashion.
   d. The price of a pair of jeans falls.
   e. The wage rate paid to garment workers increases.
   f. Disney, CNN, and most baseball clubs start to produce jeans.
   g. The price of a denim skirt doubles.
   h. People's incomes increase.

3. Use the laws of demand and supply to explain whether the following statements are true or false. In your explanation, distinguish between a change in demand and a change in the quantity demanded and between a change in supply and a change in the quantity supplied.
   a. The United States does not allow oranges from Brazil (the world's largest producer of oranges) to be sold in the United States. If Brazilian oranges were sold in the United States, oranges and orange juice would be cheaper.
   b. If soccer becomes more popular in the United States and basketball becomes less popular, the price of a pair of basketball shoes will rise.
   c. It is more expensive to ski in Aspen in the winter than in the spring.
   d. If the price of frozen yogurt falls, the quantity of ice cream consumed will decrease and the price of ice cream will rise.

4. What is the effect on the equilibrium price and quantity of orange juice of the following events if they occur one at a time?
   a. The price of apple juice decreases.
   b. The price of apple juice decreases and the wage rate paid to orange grove workers increases.
   c. Orange juice becomes more popular and a cheaper machine for picking oranges is used.
   d. Joggers switch from bottled water to orange juice.

5. Gasoline producers invent a new fuel that is cheaper and cleaner than gasoline. All new cars use the new fuel. Use a demand-supply graph to explain the effect of this new fuel on
   a. The price of gasoline and the quantity of gasoline bought.
   b. The price of a used car.

Price (dollars per pad)	Quantity demanded	Quantity supplied
	(mouse pads per week)	
3.00	160	120
4.00	150	130
5.00	140	140
6.00	130	150
7.00	120	160
8.00	110	170

6. The table shows the demand and supply schedules for mouse pads.
   a. What is the market equilibrium?
   b. If the price of a mouse pad is $7.00, describe the situation in the market. Explain how market equilibrium is restored.
   c. Explain what happens to the market equilibrium and how the market adjusts to its new equilibrium if a fall in the price of a computer changes the quantity demanded of mouse pads by 20 a week at each price.
   d. Explain what happens to the market equilibrium in part **a** and how the market adjusts if new voice-recognition software changes the quantity demanded by 10 mouse pads a week at each price and at the same time the cost of producing a mouse pad falls and changes the quantity supplied by 30 a week at each price.
7. "As more people buy computers, the demand for Internet service will increase and the price of an Internet service will decrease. The decrease in the price of an Internet service will decrease the supply of Internet services." Is this statement true or false? Explain your answer.
8. "With oil $30 a barrel, war drums beating, and world economic recovery hanging in the balance, expectations are that the Organization of the Petroleum Exporting Countries (OPEC) will increase production at their September 21 meeting," according to a news item on September 15, 2002.
   a. Draw a demand-supply graph to illustrate the situation in the world oil market on September 15, 2002. The price is $30 a barrel, and output is 76.7 million barrels a day.
   b. OPEC was expected to increase its production in October by 1 million barrels a day. Show the effect of this expected increase on your graph. How will the price of oil change? Explain your answer.
   c. If war breaks out in the Middle East, what changes will occur in the world oil market? Use a demand-supply graph to illustrate your answer.
   d. If a Middle East war does not occur but average income in the world falls, what changes do you think will occur in the world oil market? Use a demand-supply graph to illustrate your answer.
   e. The price of oil increased 50 percent from January 2002 to September 2002. The Qatari oil minister said, "There is no shortage—on the contrary, the market is saturated with more than enough oil supplies." Why would the price have increased 50 percent since January if the market were saturated with oil?
9. During 2002, wheat growers in Canada and Australia experienced drought. As a result, the amount of wheat harvested in Canada and Australia was expected to be smaller than usual.
   a. Draw a demand-supply graph to show the equilibrium in the world wheat market in a normal year.
   b. Use your graph to illustrate the effect of the smaller harvests in Canada and Australia, assuming that other wheat-growing countries have experienced normal growing conditions.
   c. What do you predict will happen to the price of wheat and the quantity bought and sold in 2002?
   d. What do you predict will happen to the price of bread in 2002?

Critical Thinking

10. In 1995, 90 salmon farms operated in British Columbia. In 1995, the Canadian government banned the creation of any new salmon farms because the farms create pollution and might introduce disease into the wild salmon population. In September 2002, the Canadian government lifted this ban. The Heart and Stroke Foundation tells us that "salmon is one of the healthiest foods we can eat. There's no shortage of it. We're eating three times as much of it as we did just a few years ago."
    - **a.** What do you predict happened to the price of farm-raised salmon and the quantity of farm-raised salmon grown from 1996 through 2001?
    - **b.** What effect do you think the lifting of the ban will have on the price of farm-raised salmon and the quantity of farm-raised salmon bought?
    - **c.** If disease breaks out in the salmon farms of British Columbia, describe what effects it will have on the market for wild Pacific salmon.
11. The Andean Trade Preferences Act, signed in 1988, was designed to encourage South American farmers to switch from growing drug crops such as coca to growing flowers. U.S. restrictions on flower imports from these South American countries were removed.
    - **a.** What incentives do you think were needed to encourage Andean farmers to switch from growing drug crops to growing roses?
    - **b.** As Andean farmers started to grow roses, what happened to the world price of roses?
    - **c.** How did U.S. rose growers respond as Andean roses entered the U.S. rose market?

Practice Online

Web Exercises

Use the links on your Foundations Web site to work the following exercises.

12. Obtain information about the history of the price of crude oil.
    - **a.** What are the major changes that have occurred in the market for crude oil?
    - **b.** On what two occasions did the price of oil rise by the largest amount?
    - **c.** What events occurred to trigger the price hikes that you've just described?
    - **d.** Did the events that you've just described change the demand for crude oil, the supply, both, or neither? Explain your answer.
    - **e.** Use the law of market forces and demand-supply graphs to explain the changes in the price and quantity of crude oil on the two occasions you identified in part **b**.
    - **f.** How do you think the price of crude oil influences the markets for coal and natural gas?
    - **g.** How do you think the advances in technology that increased fuel efficiency in automobiles, airplanes, and home heating furnaces have influenced the world market for crude oil?
13. Visit eBay.
    - **a.** What is eBay? Describe how eBay works.
    - **b.** Do you think the prices of the items traded on eBay are determined by demand and supply or in some other way? Explain your answer.

CHAPTER 5

Elasticities of Demand and Supply

CHAPTER CHECKLIST

When you have completed your study of this chapter, you will be able to

1. **Define, explain the factors that influence, and calculate the price elasticity of demand.**
2. **Define, explain the factors that influence, and calculate the price elasticity of supply.**
3. **Define and explain the factors that influence the cross elasticity of demand and the income elasticity of demand.**

The equilibrium quantities and prices in the markets for goods, services, and factors of production determine *what, how,* and *for whom* goods and services are produced.

Changes in demand and supply bring changes in equilibrium quantities and prices. But by how much do prices and quantities change when demand and supply change? Does a frost in Florida bring a massive or a modest rise in the price of oranges? And does a smaller orange crop mean good news or bad news for orange growers? To answer these questions, we need to know more about demand and supply.

You are now going to learn about the *elasticity of demand* and the *elasticity of supply*—powerful ways of describing demand and supply that enable us to predict the magnitudes of price and quantity changes when either demand or supply changes.

We'll learn first about the price elasticity of demand, then about the price elasticity of supply, and finally about two other elasticities of demand.

5.1 THE PRICE ELASTICITY OF DEMAND

Price elasticity of demand
A measure of the extent to which the quantity demanded of a good changes when the price of the good changes and all other influences on buyers' plans remain the same.

The **price elasticity of demand** is a measure of the extent to which the quantity demanded of a good* changes when the price of the good changes and all other influences on buyers' plans remain the same. To determine the price elasticity of demand, we compare the percentage change in the quantity demanded with the percentage change in price.

Percentage Change in Price

Suppose that Starbucks raises the price of a latte from \$3 to \$5 a cup. What is the percentage change in price? The change in price is the new price minus the initial price. And the percentage change is calculated as the change in price divided by the initial price, all multiplied by 100. The formula for the percentage change is

$$\text{Percentage change in price} = \left(\frac{\text{New price} - \text{Initial price}}{\text{Initial price}}\right) \times 100.$$

In this example, the initial price is \$3 and the new price is \$5, so

$$\text{Percentage change in price} = \left(\frac{\$5 - \$3}{\$3}\right) \times 100 = \left(\frac{\$2}{\$3}\right) \times 100 = 66.67 \text{ percent}.$$

Now suppose that Starbucks cuts the price of a latte from \$5 to \$3 a cup. What now is the percentage change in price? The initial price is now \$5 and the new price is \$3, so the percentage change in price is calculated as

$$\text{Percentage change in price} = \left(\frac{\$3 - \$5}{\$5}\right) \times 100 = \left(\frac{-\$2}{\$5}\right) \times 100 = -40 \text{ percent}.$$

The same price change, \$2, over the same interval, \$3 to \$5, is a different percentage change depending on whether the price rises or falls.

Because elasticity compares the percentage change in quantity demanded with the percentage change in price, we need a measure of percentage change that does not depend on the direction of the price change. The measure that economists use is called the *midpoint method.*

The Midpoint Method

To calculate the percentage change in price using the midpoint method, we divide the change in the price by the *average price*—the *average* of the initial price and the new price—and then multiply by 100. The average price is at the midpoint between the initial and new price, hence the name *midpoint method.*

The formula for the percentage change using the midpoint method is

$$\text{Percentage change in price} = \left(\frac{\text{New price} - \text{Initial price}}{(\text{New price} + \text{Initial price}) \div 2}\right) \times 100.$$

* What you learn in this chapter also applies to services and factors of production.

In this formula, the numerator, (New price – Initial price), is the same as before. The denominator, (New price + Initial price) ÷ 2, is the average of the new price and the initial price.

To calculate the percentage change in the price of a Starbucks latte using the midpoint method, put $5 for new price and $3 for initial price in the formula:

$$\text{Percentage change in price} = \left(\frac{\$5 - \$3}{(\$5 + \$3) \div 2}\right) \times 100$$

$$= \left(\frac{\$2}{\$8 \div 2}\right) \times 100$$

$$= \left(\frac{\$2}{\$4}\right) \times 100 = 50 \text{ percent.}$$

Because the average price is the same regardless of whether the price rises or falls, the percentage change in price calculated by the midpoint method is the same for a price rise and a price fall.

Percentage Change in Quantity Demanded

If Starbucks raises the price of a latte, the quantity of latte demanded decreases. We calculate the percentage change in quantity demanded using the midpoint method. Suppose that when the price of a latte rises from $3 to $5 a cup, the quantity demanded decreases from 15 cups to 5 cups an hour. The percentage change in the quantity demanded using the midpoint method is

$$\begin{array}{c}\text{Percentage change}\\ \text{in quantity}\end{array} = \left(\frac{\text{New quantity} - \text{Initial quantity}}{(\text{New quantity} + \text{Initial quantity}) \div 2}\right) \times 100$$

$$= \left(\frac{5 - 15}{(5 + 15) \div 2}\right) \times 100$$

$$= \left(\frac{-10}{20 \div 2}\right) \times 100$$

$$= \left(\frac{-10}{10}\right) \times 100 = -100 \text{ percent.}$$

Minus Sign

When the price of a good *rises*, the quantity demanded of it *decreases*—a *positive* change in price brings a *negative* change in the quantity demanded. To compare the percentage change in the price and the percentage change in the quantity demanded, we use the absolute values or magnitudes and ignore the minus sign.

Elastic and Inelastic Demand

In the Starbucks latte example, the percentage change in the quantity demanded exceeds the percentage change in price. But for other goods, the percentage change in the quantity demanded might exceed the percentage change in price, equal the percentage change in price, or be less than the percentage change in price. These three possibilities give three cases for the price elasticity of demand.

Elastic demand
When the percentage change in the quantity demanded exceeds the percentage change in price.

Unit elastic demand
When the percentage change in the quantity demanded equals the percentage change in price.

Inelastic demand
When the percentage change in the quantity demanded is less than the percentage change in price.

Perfectly elastic demand
When the quantity demanded changes by a very large percentage in response to an almost zero percentage change in price.

Perfectly inelastic demand
When the quantity demanded remains constant as the price changes.

- Demand is **elastic** if the percentage change in the quantity demanded exceeds the percentage change in price.
- Demand is **unit elastic** if the percentage change in the quantity demanded equals the percentage change in price.
- Demand is **inelastic** if the percentage change in the quantity demanded is less than the percentage change in price.

Figure 5.1 shows the different types of demand curves that illustrate the range of possible price elasticities of demand. Part (a) shows an extreme case of an elastic demand called a **perfectly elastic demand**—an almost zero percentage change in the price brings a very large percentage change in the quantity demanded. Consumers are willing to buy any quantity of the good at a given price but none at a higher price. Part (b) shows an elastic demand—the percentage change in the quantity demanded exceeds the percentage change in price. Part (c) shows a unit elastic demand—the percentage change in the quantity demanded equals the percentage change in price. Part (d) shows an inelastic demand—the percentage change in the quantity demanded is less than the percentage change in price. Finally, part (e) shows an extreme case of an inelastic demand called a **perfectly inelastic demand**—the percentage change in the quantity demanded is zero for any percentage change in price.

Influences on the Price Elasticity of Demand

What makes the demand for some things elastic and the demand for others inelastic? The influences on the price elasticity of demand fall into two groups:

- Substitution effects
- Income effects

Substitution Effects

The demand for a good is elastic if a substitute for it is easy to find. Pepsi containers can be made of either aluminum or plastic and it doesn't matter which, so the demand for aluminum is elastic.

The demand for a good is inelastic if a substitute for it is hard to find. Oil has poor substitutes (imagine a coal-fueled car), so the demand for oil is inelastic.

Three main factors influence the ability to find a substitute for a good: whether the good is a luxury or a necessity, how narrowly it is defined, and the amount of time available to find a substitute for it.

Luxury Versus Necessity We call goods such as food and housing *necessities* and goods such as exotic vacations *luxuries*. A necessity has poor substitutes—you must eat—so the demand for a necessity is inelastic. A luxury has many substitutes—you don't absolutely have to go to Galapagos this summer—so the demand for a luxury is elastic.

FIGURE 5.1
The Range of Price Elasticities of Demand

Practice Online

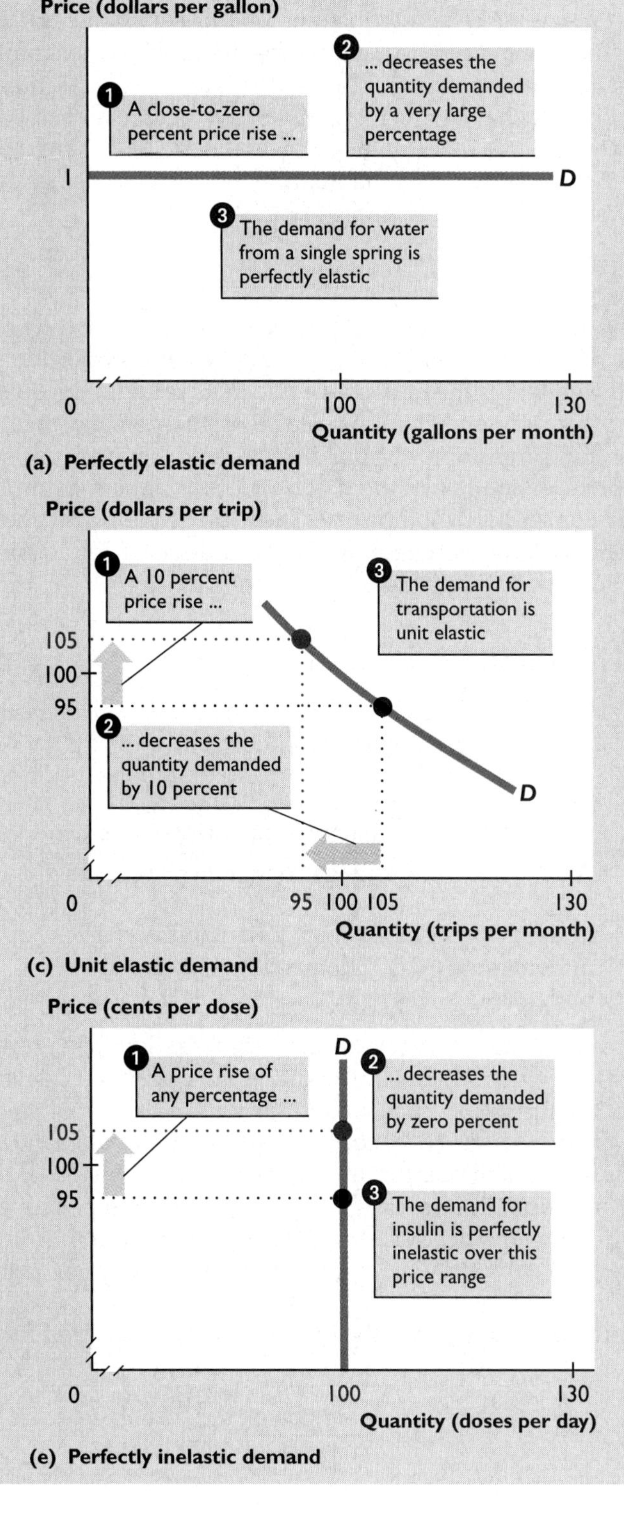

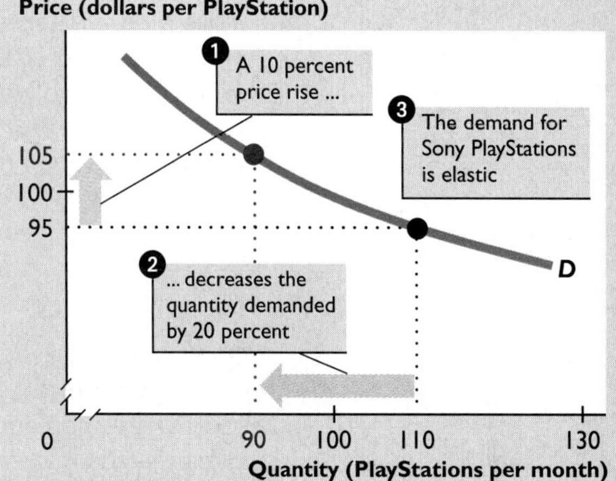

(b) Elastic demand

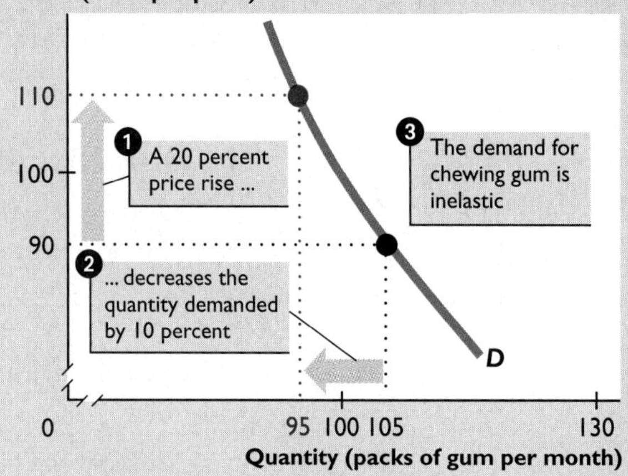

(d) Inelastic demand

❶ A price rise brings ❷ a decrease in the quantity demanded. The relationship between the percentage change in the quantity demanded and the percentage change in price determines ❸ the price elasticity of demand, which ranges from perfectly elastic (part a) to perfectly inelastic (part e).

Narrowness of Definition The demand for a narrowly defined good is elastic. For example, the demand for a Starbucks latte is elastic because a New World latte is a good substitute for it. The demand for a broadly defined good is inelastic. For example, the demand for coffee is inelastic because tea is a poor substitute for it.

Time Elapsed Since Price Change The longer the time that has elapsed since the price of a good changed, the more elastic is demand for the good. For example, when the price of gasoline increased steeply during the 1970s and 1980s, the quantity of gasoline demanded didn't change much because many people owned gas-guzzling automobiles—the demand for gasoline was inelastic. But eventually, fuel-efficient cars replaced gas guzzlers and the quantity of gasoline demanded decreased—the demand for gasoline became more elastic.

Income Effects

A price rise, like a decrease in income, means that people cannot afford to buy the same quantities of goods and services as before. The greater the proportion of income spent on a good, the greater is the impact of a rise in its price on the quantities that people can afford to buy and the more elastic is the demand for the good. Toothpaste takes a tiny proportion of your budget, and housing takes a large proportion. If the price of toothpaste doubles, you buy almost as much toothpaste as before. Your demand for toothpaste is inelastic. If your apartment rent doubles, you shriek and look for more roommates. Your demand for housing is more elastic than your demand for toothpaste.

Computing the Price Elasticity of Demand

To determine whether the demand for a good is elastic, unit elastic, or inelastic, we compute a numerical value for the price elasticity of demand by using the following formula:

$$\text{Price elasticity of demand} = \frac{\text{Percentage change in quantity demanded}}{\text{Percentage change in price}}.$$

- If the price elasticity of demand is greater than 1, demand is elastic.
- If the price elasticity of demand equals 1, demand is unit elastic.
- If the price elasticity of demand is less than 1, demand is inelastic.

Let's calculate the price elasticity of demand for a Starbucks latte, given the numbers we assumed above. Figure 5.2 illustrates and summarizes the calculation. Initially, the price is $3 a cup and 15 cups an hour are sold—the initial point in the figure. Then the price rises to $5 a cup and the quantity demanded decreases to 5 cups an hour—the new point in the figure. The price increases by $2 a cup and the average, or midpoint, price is $4 a cup, so the percentage change in price is 50. The quantity demanded decreases by 10 cups an hour and the average, or midpoint, quantity is 10 cups an hour, so the percentage change in quantity demanded is 100.

Using the above formula, you can see that the price elasticity of demand for a Starbucks latte is

$$\text{Price elasticity of demand} = \frac{100 \text{ percent}}{50 \text{ percent}} = 2.$$

FIGURE 5.2
Price Elasticity of Demand Calculation

Practice Online

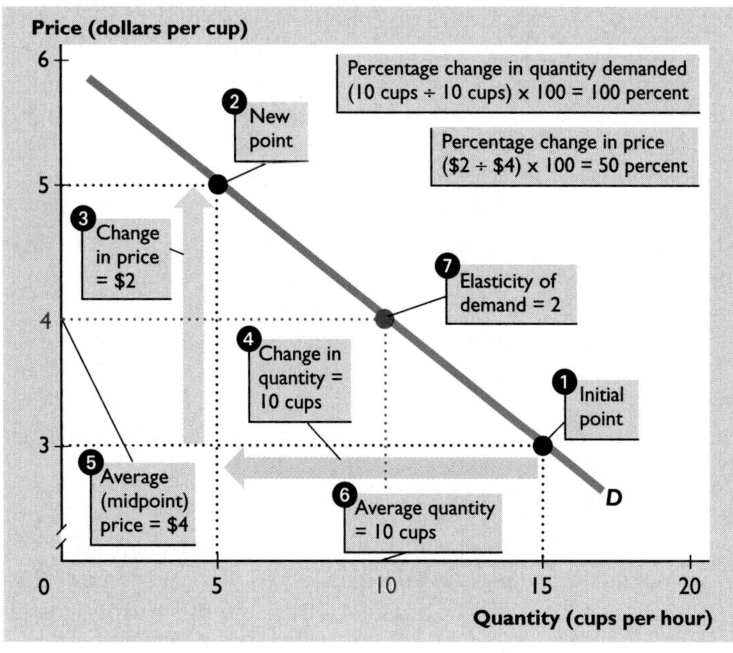

❶ At the initial point, the price is $3 and the quantity demanded is 15 cups an hour.

❷ At the new point, the price is $5 and the quantity demanded is 5 cups an hour.

❸ The change in price is $2 a cup, and ❹ the change in the quantity demanded is 10 cups an hour.

❺ The average price is $4, and the ❻ average quantity demanded is 10 cups an hour.

The percentage change in quantity demanded is 100, the percentage change in price is 50, and ❼ the price elasticity of demand is 2.

The price elasticity of demand is 2 at the midpoint between the initial point and the new point on the demand curve. In this example, over this price range, the demand for a Starbucks latte is elastic.

Slope and Elasticity

The price elasticity of demand measures how the quantity demanded changes when the price changes along a demand curve. The *slope* of the demand curve also measures how the quantity demanded changes when the price changes (see p. 31). The slope of a relationship depends on the units of measurement. In the current example, the slope of the demand curve is in dollars per cup. In the case of the demand for coffee beans, the slope is in dollars per pound. Because the slope of the demand curve depends on the units of measurement of the good, we cannot use slope to compare the demand curves of different goods. But we *can* use elasticity.

A Units-Free Measure

Elasticity is a *units-free* measure. The percentage change in price is independent of the units in which the price is measured. It is the ratio of dollars to dollars (or cents to cents). The percentage change in quantity is also independent of the units in which the quantity is measured. For a latte, the percentage change in quantity is the ratio of cups to cups; and for coffee beans, it is the ratio of pounds to pounds. In each case, the units of measurement cancel. Better yet, when we calculate elasticity, we get a number that is the ratio of one percentage change to another percentage change—a number without units. So we can compare the demand for a latte with the demand for coffee beans.

Elasticity Along a Linear Demand Curve

Along a linear (straight-line) demand curve, the slope is constant but the elasticity varies. Figure 5.3 shows the same demand curve for a Starbucks latte as that in Figure 5.2 but with the axes extended to show some lower prices and larger quantities demanded.

Let's calculate the elasticity of demand at point *A*. If the price rises from $3 to $5 a cup, the quantity demanded decreases from 15 cups to 5 cups an hour. The average price is $4, and the average quantity is 10 cups—point *A*. The elasticity of demand at point *A* is 2, and demand is elastic.

Let's calculate the elasticity of demand at point *C*. If the price falls from $3 to $1 a cup, the quantity demanded increases from 15 cups to 25 cups an hour. The average price is $2, and the average quantity is 20 cups—point *C*. The elasticity of demand at point *C* is 0.5, and demand is inelastic.

Finally, let's calculate the elasticity of demand at point *B*, which is the midpoint of the demand curve. If the price rises from $2 to $4 a cup, the quantity demanded decreases from 20 cups to 10 cups an hour. The average price is $3, and the average quantity is 15 cups—point *B*. The elasticity of demand at point *B* is 1, and demand is unit elastic.

Along a linear demand curve,

- Demand is unit elastic at the midpoint of the curve.
- Demand is elastic at all points above the midpoint of the curve.
- Demand is inelastic at all points below the midpoint of the curve.

FIGURE 5.3
Elasticity Along a Linear Demand Curve

Practice Online

On a linear demand curve, the slope is constant but the elasticity decreases as the price falls and the quantity demanded increases.

1. At point *A*, demand is elastic.
2. At point *B*, which is the midpoint of the demand curve, demand is unit elastic.
3. At point *C*, demand is inelastic.

Demand is elastic at all points above the midpoint of the demand curve and inelastic at all points below the midpoint of the demand curve.

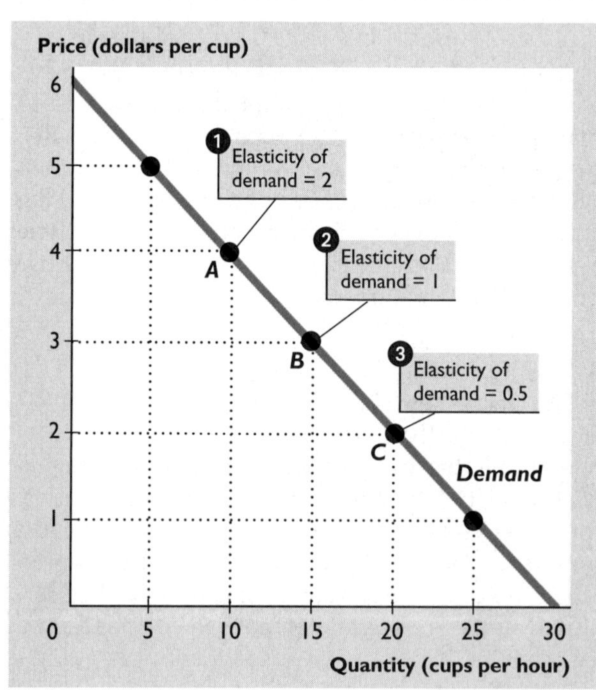

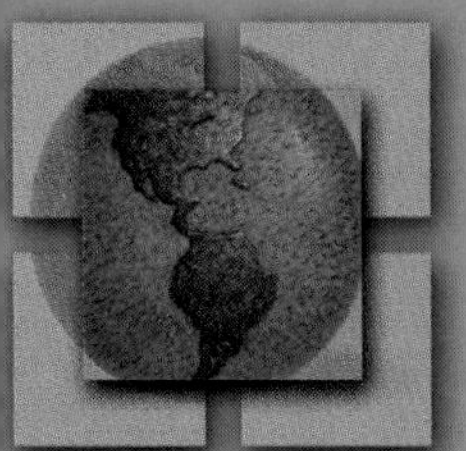

Eye on the Global Economy

Price Elasticities of Demand

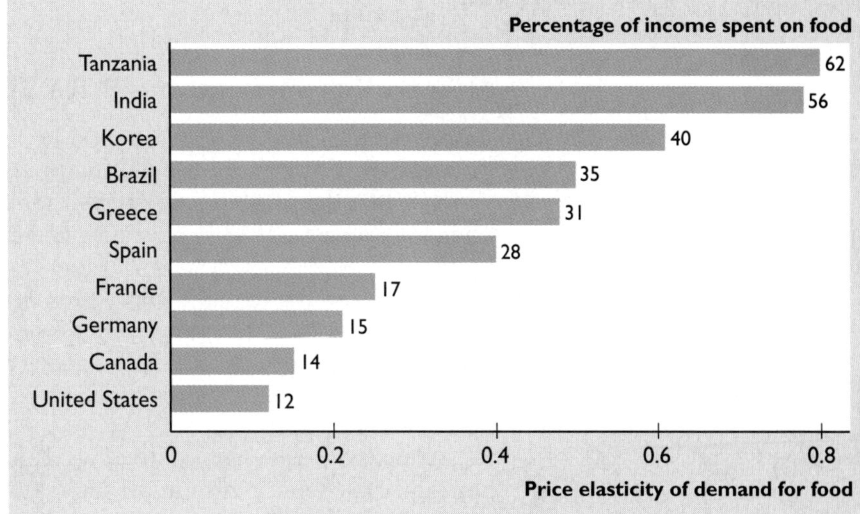

The real-world elasticities of demand in the table range from 1.52 for metals to 0.12 for food. Metals have good substitutes, such as plastics, while food has virtually no substitutes.

As we move down the list of items, they have fewer good substitutes and are more likely to be in the category of necessities.

The figure shows the percentage of income spent on food and the price elasticity of demand for food in ten countries. This figure confirms a general rule: The larger the proportion of income spent on an item, the larger is the price elasticity of demand for it. For example, in Tanzania, a low-income nation where 62 percent of income is spent on food, the price elasticity of demand for food is 0.77. In contrast, in the United States, where 12 percent of income is spent on food, the price elasticity of demand for food is 0.12.

Some Price Elasticities of Demand

Good or Service	Elasticity
Elastic Demand	
Metals	1.52
Electrical engineering products	1.39
Mechanical engineering products	1.30
Furniture	1.26
Motor vehicles	1.14
Instrument engineering products	1.10
Professional services	1.09
Transportation services	1.03
Inelastic Demand	
Gas, electricity, and water	0.92
Oil	0.91
Chemicals	0.89
Beverages (all types)	0.78
Clothing	0.64
Tobacco	0.61
Banking and insurance services	0.56
Housing services	0.55
Agricultural and fish products	0.42
Books, magazines, and newspapers	0.34
Food	0.12

SOURCES: Ahsan Mansur and John Whalley, "Numerical Specification of Applied General Equilibrium Models: Estimation, Calibration, and Data," in Applied General Equilibrium Analysis, eds. Herbert E. Scarf and John B. Shoven (New York: Cambridge University Press, 1984), 109; and Henri Theil, Ching-Fan Chung, and James L. Seale, Jr., *Advances in Econometrics, Supplement I, 1989, International Evidence on Consumption Patterns* (Greenwich, Conn.: JAI Press Inc., 1989). Reprinted with permission.

Total Revenue and the Price Elasticity of Demand

Total revenue
The total revenue from the sale of a good equals the price of the good multiplied by the quantity sold.

Total revenue is the amount spent on a good and received by its sellers and equals the price of the good multiplied by the quantity of the good sold. For example, suppose that the price of a Starbucks latte is $3 and that 15 cups an hour are sold. Then total revenue is $3 a cup multiplied by 15 cups an hour, which equals $45 an hour.

We can use the demand curve for a Starbucks latte to illustrate total revenue. Figure 5.4(a) shows the total revenue from the sale of latte when the price is $3 a cup and the quantity of latte demanded is 15 cups an hour. Total revenue is shown by the blue rectangle, the area of which equals $3, its height, multiplied by 15, its length, which equals $45.

When the price changes, total revenue can change in the same direction, the opposite direction, or remain constant. Which of these outcomes occurs depends on the price elasticity of demand. By observing the change in total revenue that results from a price change (other things remaining the same), we can estimate the price elasticity of demand. This method of estimating the price elasticity of demand is called the **total revenue test**.

Total revenue test
A method of estimating the price elasticity of demand by observing the change in total revenue that results from a price change (with all other influences on the quantity sold remaining unchanged).

If demand is elastic, a given percentage rise in price brings a larger percentage decrease in the quantity demanded, so total revenue—price multiplied by quantity—decreases. Figure 5.4(a) shows this outcome. When the price of a latte is $3, the quantity demanded is 15 an hour and total revenue is $45 ($3 × 15). If the price of a latte rises to $5, the quantity demanded decreases to 5 an hour and total revenue *decreases* to $25 ($5 × 5).

If demand is inelastic, a given percentage rise in price brings a smaller percentage decrease in the quantity demanded, so total revenue increases. Figure 5.4(b) shows this outcome. When the price of a textbook is $50, the quantity demanded is 5 million a year and total revenue is $250 million ($50 × 5 million). If the price of a textbook rises to $75, the quantity demanded decreases to 4 million a year and total revenue *increases* to $300 million ($75 × 4 million).

The relationship between the price elasticity of demand and total revenue is

- If price and total revenue change in opposite directions, demand is elastic.
- If a price change leaves total revenue unchanged, demand is unit elastic.
- If price and total revenue change in the same direction, demand is inelastic.

Your Expenditure and *Your* Elasticity of Demand

Your expenditure on a good is its price multiplied by the quantity that you buy. So expenditure for the buyer is like total revenue for the seller. When the price of a good changes, the change in your expenditure on it depends on *your* elasticity of demand. When the price of a good *rises*, your demand for that good is

- Elastic if your expenditure on it decreases.
- Unit elastic if your expenditure on it remains constant.
- Inelastic if your expenditure on it increases.

Pay attention the next time you are confronted with a price change. Note how your expenditure on the item changes and check whether your demand for it is elastic or inelastic. Think about why it is elastic or inelastic by checking back with the list of influences on the price elasticity of demand.

FIGURE 5.4

Total Revenue and the Price Elasticity of Demand

Practice Online

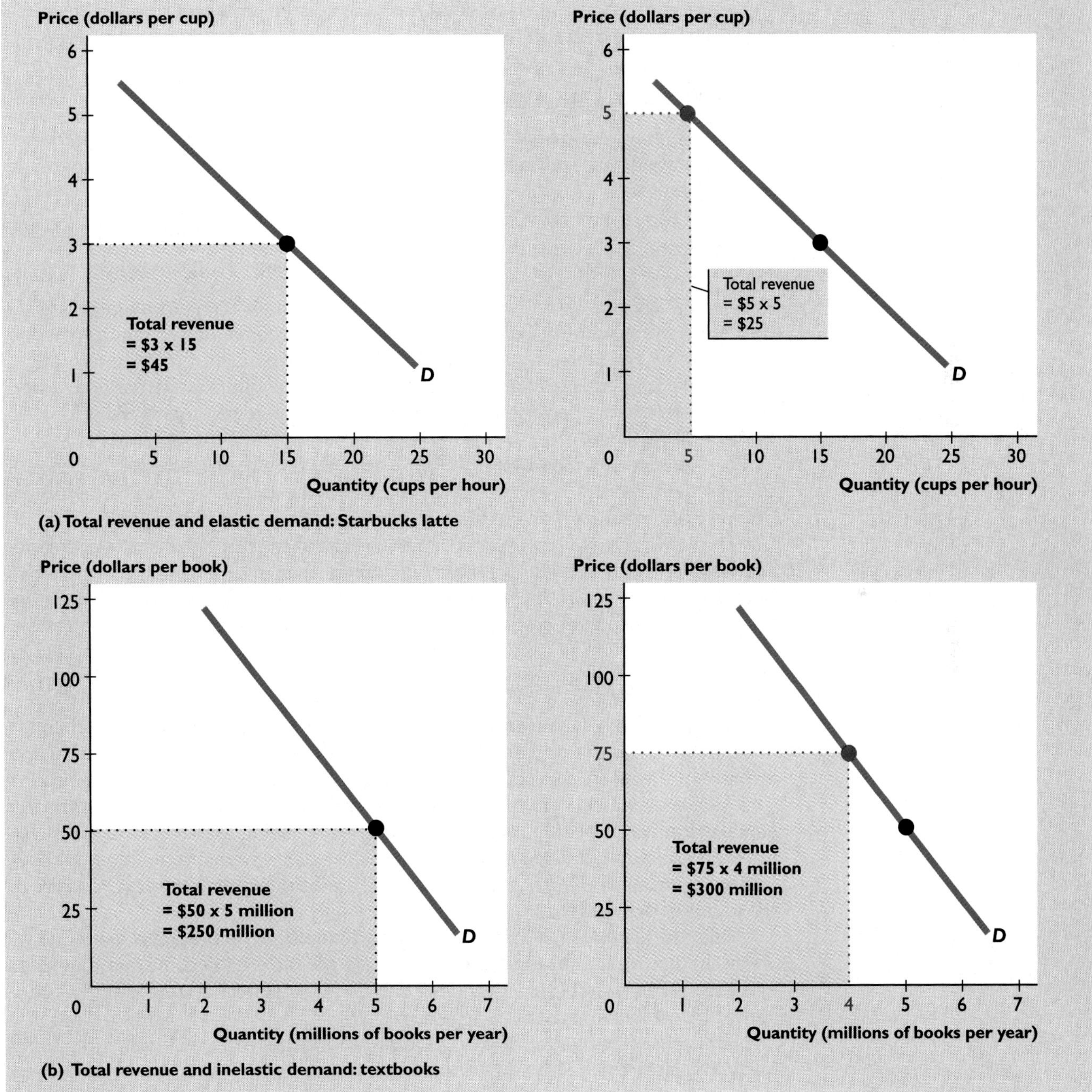

Total revenue equals price multiplied by quantity. In part (a), when the price is $3 a cup, the quantity demanded is 15 cups an hour and total revenue equals $45 an hour. When the price rises to $5 a cup, the quantity demanded decreases to 5 cups an hour and total revenue decreases to $25 an hour. Demand is elastic.

In part (b), when the price is $50 a book, the quantity demanded is 5 million books a year and total revenue equals $250 million a year. When the price rises to $75 a book, the quantity demanded decreases to 4 million books a year and total revenue increases to $300 million a year. Demand is inelastic.

Applications of the Price Elasticity of Demand

At the beginning of this chapter, we asked two questions: Does a frost in Florida bring a massive or a modest rise in the price of oranges? And does a smaller orange crop mean bad news or good news for orange growers? Knowledge of the price elasticity of demand for oranges enables us to answer these questions.

Farm Prices and Total Revenue

Economists have estimated the price elasticity of demand for agricultural products to be about 0.4—an inelastic demand. If this number applies to the demand for oranges, then

$$\text{Price elasticity of demand} = 0.4 = \frac{\text{Percentage change in quantity demanded}}{\text{Percentage change in price}}.$$

The percentage change in the quantity demanded equals the percentage change in the equilibrium quantity. So if a frost in Florida decreases the orange harvest and decreases the equilibrium quantity of oranges by 1 percent, the price of oranges will rise by 2.5 percent. The percentage change in the quantity demanded (1 percent) divided by the percentage change in price (2.5 percent) equals the price elasticity of demand (0.4).

So the answer to the first question is that when the frost strikes, the price of oranges will rise by a larger percentage than the decrease in the quantity of oranges. But what happens to the total revenue of the orange growers?

The answer is again provided by knowledge of the price elasticity of demand. Because the price rises by a larger percentage than the percentage decrease in quantity, total revenue increases. A frost is bad news for consumers and those growers who lose their crops but good news for growers who escape the frost.

Addiction and Elasticity

We can gain important insights that might help to design potentially effective policies for dealing with addiction to drugs, whether legal (such as tobacco and alcohol) or illegal (such as crack cocaine or heroin). Nonusers' demand for addictive substances is elastic. A moderately higher price leads to a substantially smaller number of people trying a drug and so exposing themselves to the possibility of becoming addicted to it. But the existing users' demand for addictive substances is inelastic. Even a substantial price rise brings only a modest decrease in the quantity demanded.

These facts about the price elasticity of demand mean that high taxes on cigarettes and alcohol limit the number of young people who become habitual users of these products, but high taxes have only a modest effect on the quantities consumed by established users.

Similarly, effective policing of imports of an illegal drug that limits its supply leads to a large price rise and a substantial decrease in the number of new users but only a small decrease in the quantity consumed by addicts. Expenditure on the drug by addicts increases. Further, because many drug addicts finance their purchases with crime, the amount of theft and burglary increases.

Because the price elasticity of demand for drugs is low for addicts, any successful policy to decrease drug use will be one that focuses on the demand for drugs and attempts to change preferences through rehabilitation programs.

CHECKPOINT 5.1

1 Define, explain the factors that influence, and calculate the price elasticity of demand.

Study Guide pp. 70–74

Practice Online 5.1

Practice Problem 5.1

A 10 percent increase in the price of a good has led to a 2 percent decrease in the quantity demanded of that good.

a. How would you describe the demand for this good?
b. Are substitutes for this good easy to find or does it have poor substitutes?
c. Is this good more likely to be a necessity or a luxury? Why?
d. Is the good more likely to be narrowly or broadly defined? Why?
e. Calculate the price elasticity of demand for this good.
f. Has the total revenue from the sale of the good changed? Explain your answer.
g. This good might be which of the following goods: orange juice, bread, toothpaste, theater tickets, clothing, blue jeans, Super Bowl tickets? Why?

Exercise 5.1

The price of Internet service rises from \$24 to \$26 a month, and the quantity demanded decreases from 204 million to 196 million subscribers.

a. Calculate the percentage change in the price of Internet service.
b. Calculate the percentage change in the quantity demanded of Internet services.
c. Is the demand for Internet services elastic or inelastic?
d. Would the demand for AOL service be more elastic or less elastic than the demand for Internet service? Why?
e. Calculate the price elasticity of demand for Internet service.
f. At what price is the price elasticity of demand for Internet service equal to your answer in part **e**?
g. What is the change in the total revenue of Internet service providers?
h. If the demand curve for Internet service is a straight-line demand curve, is the price at which the demand for Internet service is unit elastic a higher price or a lower price than your answer to part **f**? Why?

Solution to Practice Problem 5.1

Figure 1 illustrates a 10 percent increase in the price of a good that has led to a 2 percent decrease in the quantity demanded of it.

a. The percentage change in the quantity demanded is less than the percentage change in the price, so the demand for the good is inelastic.
b. A good with an inelastic demand usually has poor substitutes.
c. A good with an inelastic demand is likely to be a necessity.
d. A good with an inelastic demand is likely to be broadly defined.
e. Price elasticity of demand equals the percentage change in the quantity demanded divided by the percentage change in price, which equals 2/10, or 0.2.
f. When demand is inelastic, a price rise increases total revenue.
g. The good might be a necessity (bread), have poor substitutes (toothpaste), or be broadly defined (clothing).

FIGURE 1

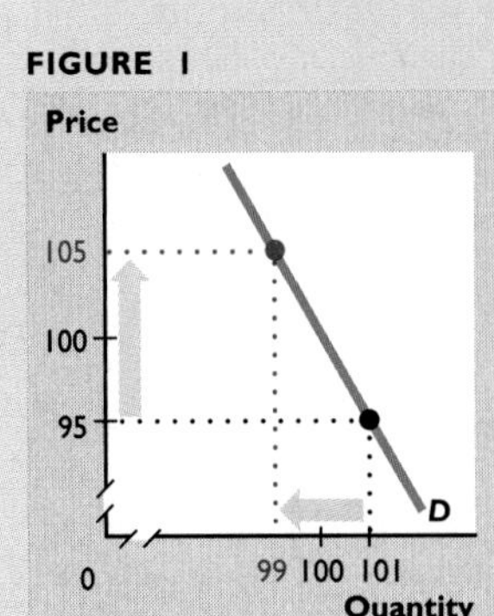

5.2 THE PRICE ELASTICITY OF SUPPLY

You know that when demand increases, the equilibrium price rises and the equilibrium quantity increases. But does the price rise by a large amount and the quantity increase by a little? Or does the price barely rise and the quantity increase by a large amount? To answer this question, we need to know the price elasticity of supply.

Price elasticity of supply
A measure of the extent to which the quantity supplied of a good changes when the price of the good changes and all other influences on sellers' plans remain the same.

The **price elasticity of supply** is a measure of the extent to which the quantity supplied of a good changes when the price of the good changes and all other influences on sellers' plans remain the same. We determine the price elasticity of supply by comparing the percentage change in the quantity supplied with the percentage change in price.

Elastic and Inelastic Supply

Supply might be

- Elastic
- Unit elastic
- Inelastic

Perfectly elastic supply
When the quantity supplied changes by a very large percentage in response to an almost zero percentage change in price.

Elastic supply
When the percentage change in the quantity supplied exceeds the percentage change in price.

Unit elastic supply
When the percentage change in the quantity supplied equals the percentage change in price.

Inelastic supply
When the percentage change in the quantity supplied is less than the percentage change in price.

Perfectly inelastic supply
When the quantity supplied remains the same as the price changes.

Figure 5.5 illustrates the range of supply elasticities. Figure 5.5(a) shows the extreme case of a **perfectly elastic supply**—an almost zero percentage change in price brings a very large percentage change in the quantity supplied. Figure 5.5(b) shows an **elastic supply**—the percentage change in the quantity supplied exceeds the percentage change in price. Figure 5.5(c) shows a **unit elastic supply**—the percentage change in the quantity supplied equals the percentage change in price. Figure 5.5(d) shows an **inelastic supply**—the percentage change in the quantity supplied is less than the percentage change in price. And Figure 5.5(e) shows the extreme case of a **perfectly inelastic supply**—the percentage change in the quantity supplied is zero when the price changes.

Influences on the Price Elasticity of Supply

What makes the supply of some things elastic and the supply of others inelastic? The two main influences on the price elasticity of supply are

- Production possibilities
- Storage possibilities

Production Possibilities

Some goods can be produced at a constant (or very gently rising) opportunity cost. These goods have an elastic supply. The silicon in your computer chips is an example of such a good. Silicon is extracted from sand at a tiny and almost constant opportunity cost. So the supply of silicon is perfectly elastic.

Some goods can be produced in only a fixed quantity. These goods have a perfectly inelastic supply. A beachfront home in Santa Monica can be built only on a unique beachfront lot. So the supply of these homes is perfectly inelastic.

Hotel rooms in New York City can't easily be used as office accommodation and office space cannot easily be converted into hotel rooms, so the supply of hotel rooms in New York City is inelastic. Paper and printing presses can be used to produce textbooks or magazines, and the supplies of these goods are elastic.

FIGURE 5.5
The Range of Price Elasticities of Supply

Practice Online

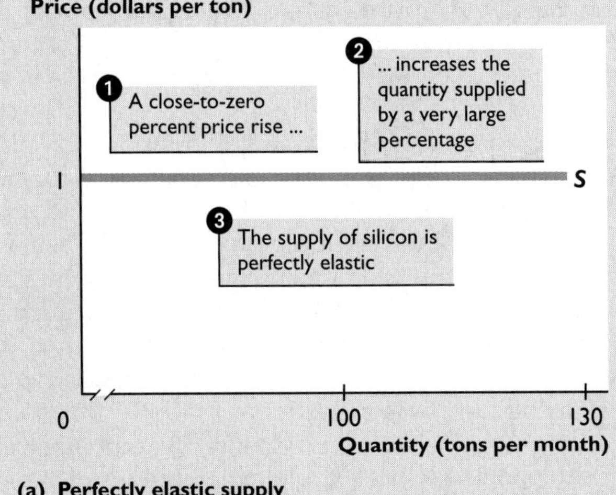

(a) Perfectly elastic supply

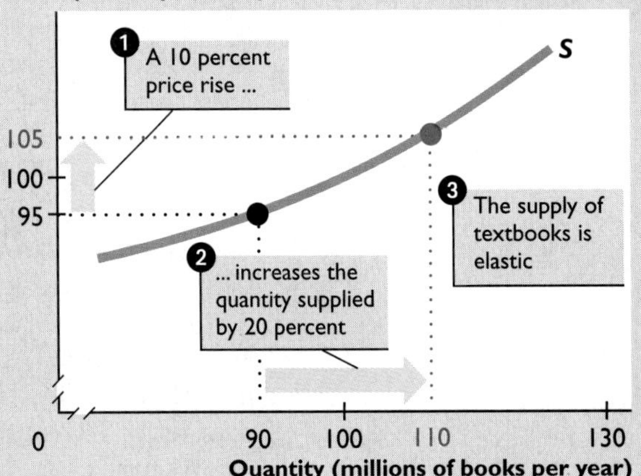

(b) Elastic supply

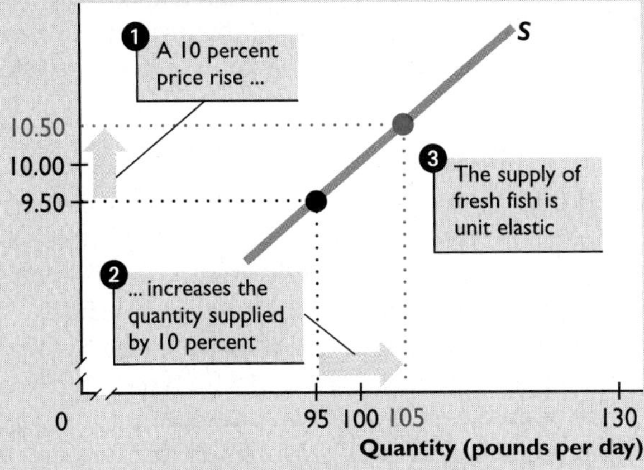

(c) Unit elastic supply

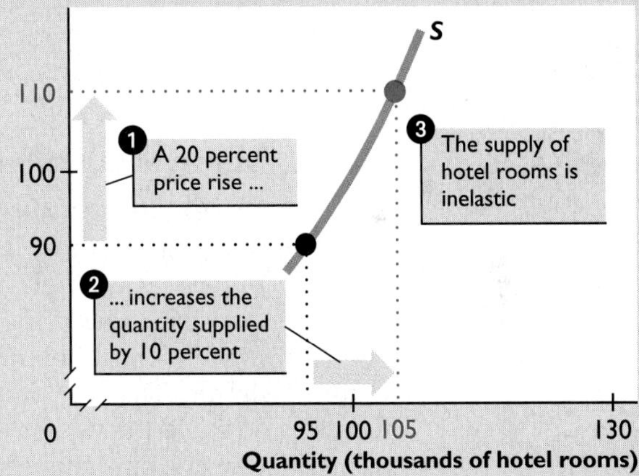

(d) Inelastic supply

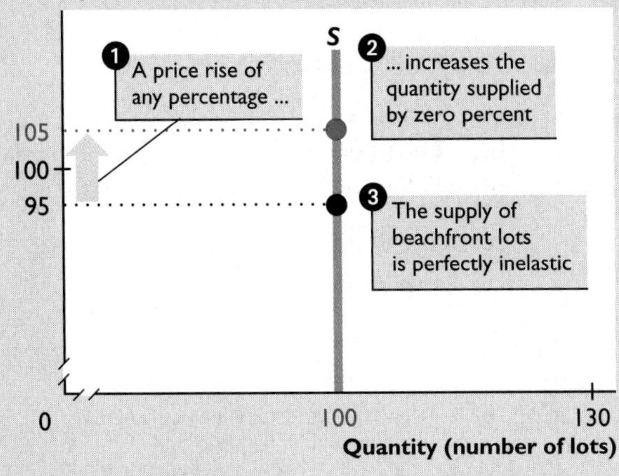

(e) Perfectly inelastic supply

❶ A price rise brings ❷ an increase in the quantity supplied. The relationship between the percentage change in the quantity supplied and the percentage change in price determines ❸ the price elasticity of supply, which ranges from perfectly elastic (part a) to perfectly inelastic (part e).

Time Elapsed Since Price Change As time passes after a price change, it becomes easier to change production plans and supply becomes more elastic. For some items—fruits and vegetables are examples—it is difficult or perhaps impossible to change the quantity supplied immediately after a price change. These goods have a perfectly inelastic supply on the day of a price change. The quantities supplied depend on crop-planting decisions that were made earlier. In the case of oranges, for example, planting decisions have to be made many years in advance of the crop being available.

Many manufactured goods also have an inelastic supply if production plans have had only a short period in which to change. For example, before it launched the PlayStation 2 in 2000, Sony made a forecast of demand, set a price, and made a production plan to supply the United States with the quantity that it believed people would be willing to buy. It turned out that demand outstripped Sony's earlier forecast. The price increased on eBay, an Internet auction market, to bring market equilibrium. At the high price that emerged, Sony would have liked to ship more PlayStations. But it could do nothing to increase the quantity supplied in the near term. The supply of the PlayStation 2 was inelastic.

As time passes, the elasticity of supply increases. After all the technologically possible ways of adjusting production have been exploited, supply is extremely elastic—perhaps perfectly elastic—for most manufactured items. By early 2001, Sony was able to step up the production rate of the PlayStation 2 and the price on eBay fell to the price at which Sony initially planned to sell the product. Over this longer time frame, the supply of the PlayStation 2 had become perfectly elastic.

Storage Possibilities

The elasticity of supply of a good that cannot be stored (for example, a perishable item such as fresh strawberries) or a service depends only on production possibilities. But the elasticity of supply of a good that can be stored depends on the decision to keep the good in storage or offer it for sale. A small price change can make a big difference to this decision, so the supply of a storable good is highly elastic. The cost of storage is the main influence on the elasticity of supply of a storable good. For example, rose growers in Colombia, anticipating a surge in demand on Valentine's Day in February, hold back supplies in late January and early February and increase their inventories of roses. They then release roses from inventory for Valentine's Day.

Computing the Price Elasticity of Supply

To determine whether the supply of a good is elastic, unit elastic, or inelastic, we compute a numerical value for the price elasticity of supply in a way similar to that used to calculate the price elasticity of demand. We use the formula:

$$\text{Price elasticity of supply} = \frac{\text{Percentage change in quantity supplied}}{\text{Percentage change in price}}.$$

- If the price elasticity of supply is greater than 1, supply is elastic.
- If the price elasticity of supply equals 1, supply is unit elastic.
- If the price elasticity of supply is less than 1, supply is inelastic.

Let's calculate the price elasticity of supply of roses. We'll use the numbers that you saw in Chapter 4 on p. 109. Figure 5.6 illustrates and summarizes the calculation. In a normal month, the price of roses is \$40 a bunch and 6 million bunches are supplied—the initial point in the figure. In February, the price rises to \$80 a bunch and the quantity supplied increases to 24 million bunches—the new point in the figure. The price increases by \$40 a bunch and the average, or midpoint, price is \$60 a bunch, so the percentage change in the price is 66.67. The quantity supplied increases by 18 million bunches and the average, or midpoint, quantity is 15 million bunches, so the percentage change in the quantity supplied is 120.

Using the above formula, you can see that the price elasticity of supply of roses is

$$\text{Price elasticity of supply} = \frac{120 \text{ percent}}{66.67 \text{ percent}} = 1.8.$$

The price elasticity of supply is 1.8 at the midpoint between the initial point and the new point on the supply curve. In this example, over this price range, the supply of roses is elastic.

FIGURE 5.6
Price Elasticity of Supply Calculation

Practice Online

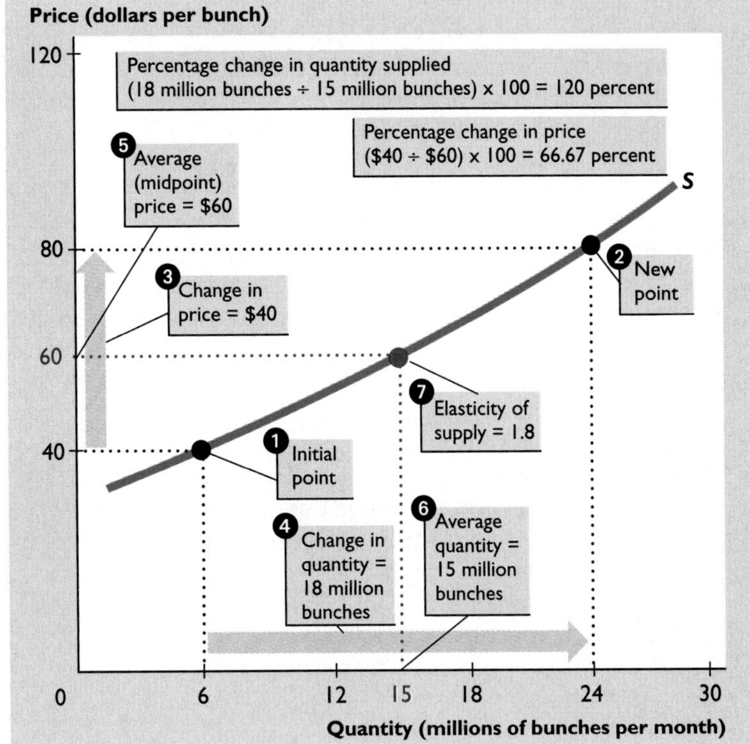

1 At the initial point, the price is \$40 and the quantity supplied is 6 million bunches a month.

2 At the new point, the price is \$80 and the quantity supplied is 24 million bunches a month.

3 The change in price is \$40 a bunch, and 4 the change in the quantity supplied is 18 million bunches a month.

5 The average price is \$60, and the 6 average quantity supplied is 15 million bunches a month.

The percentage change in quantity supplied is 120, the percentage change in price is 66.67, and 7 the price elasticity of supply is 1.8.

CHECKPOINT 5.2

Study Guide pp. 74–76

Practice Online 5.2

2 Define, explain the factors that influence, and calculate the price elasticity of supply.

Practice Problem 5.2

You are told that a 10 percent increase in the price of a good has led to a 1 percent increase in the quantity supplied of the good after one month. Use this information to answer the following questions:

a. How would you describe the supply of this good?
b. What can you say about the production possibilities of this good?
c. Calculate the price elasticity of supply.
d. If after one year, the quantity supplied has increased by 25 percent, describe how the supply has changed over the year.
e. Calculate the elasticity of supply after one year.

Exercise 5.2

The price of asparagus crashed from $45 a crate to $15 a crate in 2002. A typical California asparagus farmer would have supplied 2,000 crates a day at $45 a crate but at $15 a crate would plow the crop into the ground and supply nothing.

a. How would you describe the California supply of asparagus?
b. How do you think production possibilities and storage possibilities influence the price elasticity of supply of asparagus?
c. Calculate the price elasticity of supply of California asparagus.
d. If the price of asparagus remains at $15 a crate, do you think the elasticity of supply will change over the coming years? Explain your answer.

Solution to Practice Problem 5.2

FIGURE 1

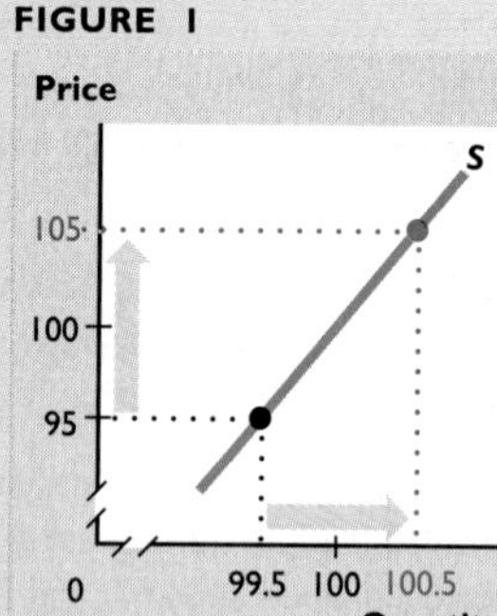

Figure 1 illustrates a 10 percent increase in the price of a good that has led to a 1 percent increase in the quantity supplied of it.

a. The percentage change in the quantity supplied is less than the percentage change in the price of the good, so the supply of the good is inelastic.
b. Because the quantity supplied increases by such a small percentage after one month, the factors of production that are used to produce this good are more likely to be unique or rare.
c. The elasticity of supply equals the percentage change in the quantity supplied divided by the percentage change in the price, which is 1 ÷ 10 or 0.1.
d. The supply of the good has become more elastic over the year since the price rise because other producers will have gradually started producing the good.
e. The elasticity of supply equals the percentage change in the quantity supplied divided by the percentage change in the price. After one year, the elasticity of supply is 25 ÷ 10, which equals 2.5.

5.3 CROSS ELASTICITY AND INCOME ELASTICITY

Domino's Pizza in Chula Vista has a problem. Burger King has just cut its prices. Domino's manager, Pat, knows that pizzas and burgers are substitutes. He also knows that when the price of a substitute for pizza falls, the demand for pizza decreases. But by how much will the quantity of pizza bought decrease if Pat maintains his current price?

Pat also knows that pizza and soda are complements. He knows that if the price of a complement of pizza falls, the demand for pizza increases. So he wonders whether he might keep his customers by cutting the price he charges for soda. But he wants to know by how much he must cut the price of soda to keep selling the same quantity of pizza with cheaper burgers all around him.

To answer these questions, Pat needs to calculate the cross elasticity of demand. Let's examine this elasticity measure.

Cross Elasticity of Demand

The **cross elasticity of demand** is a measure of the extent to which the demand for a good changes when the price of a substitute or complement changes, other things remaining the same. It is calculated by using the formula:

Cross elasticity of demand
A measure of the extent to which the demand for a good changes when the price of a substitute or complement changes, other things remaining the same.

$$\text{Cross elasticity of demand} = \frac{\text{Percentage change in quantity demanded of a good}}{\text{Percentage change in price of one of its substitutes or complements}}.$$

Suppose that when the price of a burger falls by 10 percent, the quantity of pizza demanded decreases by 5 percent.* The cross elasticity of demand for pizza with respect to the price of a burger is

$$\text{Cross elasticity of demand} = \frac{-5 \text{ percent}}{-10 \text{ percent}} = 0.5.$$

The cross elasticity of demand for a substitute is positive. A *fall* in the price of a substitute brings a *decrease* in the quantity demanded of the good. The quantity demanded of a good and the price of one of its substitutes change in the same direction.

Suppose that when the price of soda falls by 10 percent, the quantity of pizza demanded increases by 2 percent. The cross elasticity of demand for pizza with respect to the price of soda is

$$\text{Cross elasticity of demand} = \frac{+\,2 \text{ percent}}{-10 \text{ percent}} = -0.2.$$

The cross elasticity of demand for a complement is negative. A *fall* in the price of a complement brings an *increase* in the quantity demanded of the good. The quantity demanded of a good and the price of one of its complements change in opposite directions.

*As before, these percentage changes are calculated by using the midpoint method.

FIGURE 5.7
Cross Elasticity of Demand

Practice Online

1 A burger is a *substitute* for pizza. When the price of a burger falls, the demand curve for pizza shifts leftward from D_0 to D_1. At the fixed price of pizza, the quantity demanded of pizza decreases. The cross elasticity of the demand for pizza with respect to the price of a burger is *positive*.

2 Soda is a *complement* of pizza. When the price of soda falls, the demand curve for pizza shifts rightward from D_0 to D_2. At the fixed price of pizza, the quantity demanded of pizza increases. The cross elasticity of the demand for pizza with respect to the price of soda is *negative*.

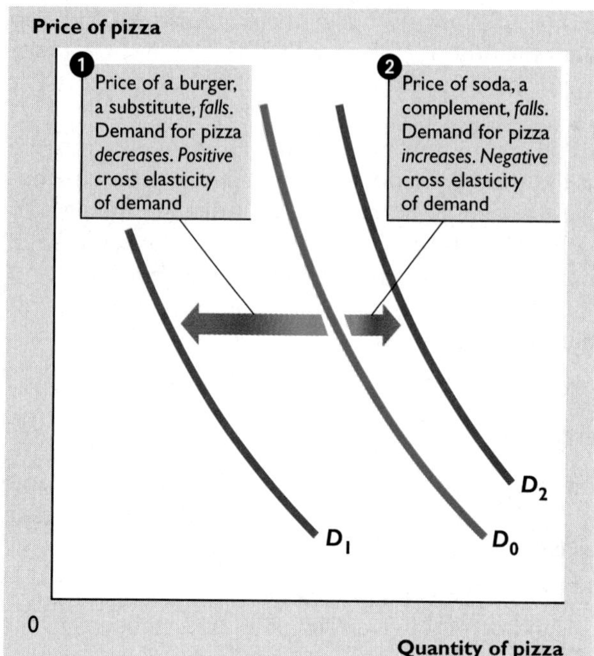

Figure 5.7 illustrates these two cross elasticities of demand for pizza. When the price of a burger falls, the demand for pizza decreases and the demand curve for pizza shifts leftward from D_0 to D_1. When the price of soda falls, the demand for pizza increases and the demand curve for pizza shifts rightward from D_0 to D_2. The magnitude of the cross elasticity determines how far the demand curve shifts.

Income Elasticity of Demand

The economy is expanding, and people are enjoying rising incomes. This prosperity is bringing an increase in the demand for all types of goods. But by how much will the demand for pizza increase?

Income elasticity of demand
A measure of the extent to which the demand for a good changes when income changes, other things remaining the same.

The answer depends on the income elasticity of demand for the good. The **income elasticity of demand** is a measure of the extent to which the demand for a good changes when income changes, other things remaining the same. It is calculated by using the following formula:

$$\text{Income elasticity of demand} = \frac{\text{Percentage change in quantity demanded}}{\text{Percentage change in income}}.$$

The income elasticity of demand falls into three ranges:

- Greater than 1 (*normal* good, income elastic)
- Between zero and 1 (*normal* good, income inelastic)
- Less than zero (*inferior* good)

In Figure 5.8(a), the quantity demanded increases more quickly than income increases. Demand is income elastic. Airline travel and jewelry are examples. In Figure 5.8(b), the quantity demanded increases less quickly than income increases.

FIGURE 5.8
Income Elasticity of Demand

Practice Online

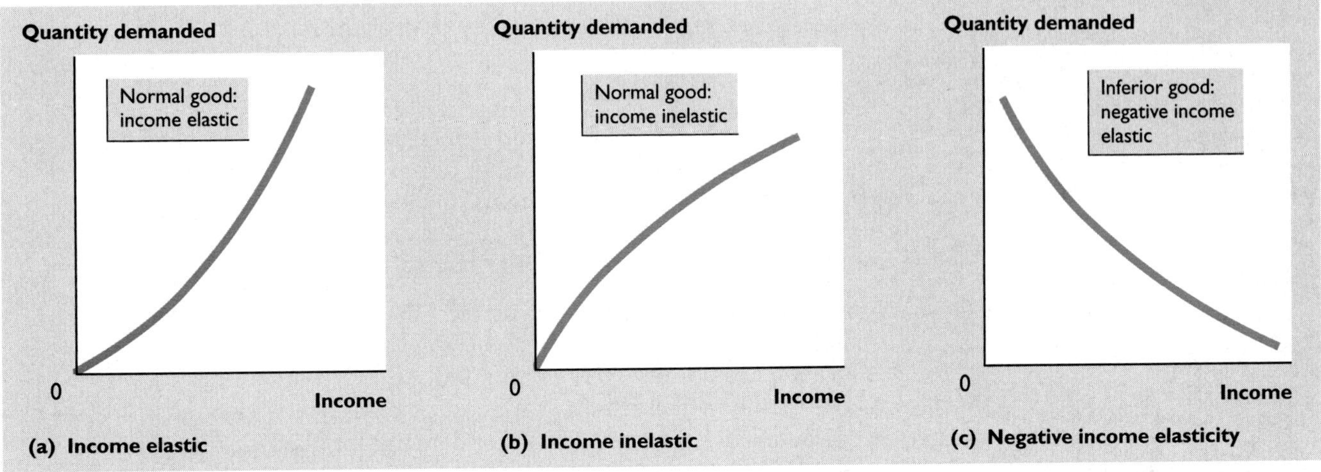

Demand is income inelastic. Food and clothing are examples. In Figure 5.8(c), the quantity demanded *decreases* as income *increases*. Demand is negative income elastic. Milk crates used as bookshelves are an example.

Income Elasticities of Demand

In the United States, necessities such as food and clothing are income inelastic; luxuries such as airline and foreign travel are income elastic.

The *level* of income has a big effect on income elasticities of demand. Using data for ten countries, the figure shows that the lower the income level, the more income elastic is the demand for food.

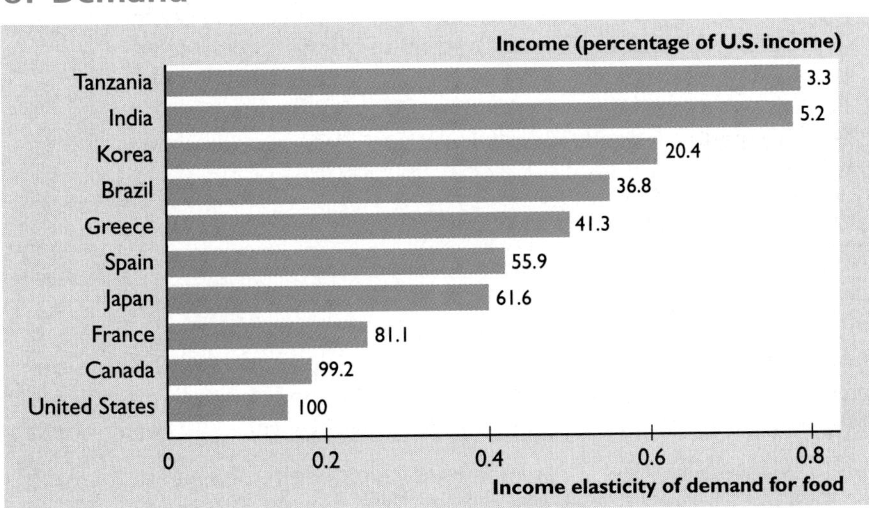

SOURCES: See page. 125.

Some Income Elasticities of Demand

Good or Service	Elasticity
Income Elastic	
Airline travel	5.82
Movies	3.41
Foreign travel	3.08
Electricity	1.94
Restaurant meals	1.61
Local buses and trains	1.38
Haircuts	1.36
Cars	1.07
Income Inelastic	
Tobacco	0.86
Alcoholic beverages	0.62
Furniture	0.53
Clothing	0.51
Newspapers	0.38
Telephone	0.32
Food	0.14

CHECKPOINT 5.3

Study Guide pp. 77–79

Practice Online 5.3

3 **Define and explain the factors that influence the cross elasticity of demand and the income elasticity of demand.**

Practice Problems 5.3

1. If the quantity demanded of good *A* increases by 5 percent when the price of good *B* rises by 10 percent and other things remain the same:
   - **a.** Are goods *A* and *B* complements or substitutes? Why?
   - **b.** Describe how the demand for good *A* changes.
   - **c.** Calculate the cross elasticity of demand of good *A* with respect to good *B*.
2. If, when income rises by 5 percent and other things remain the same, the quantity demanded of good *C* increases by 1 percent:
   - **a.** Is good *C* a normal good or an inferior good? Why?
   - **b.** Describe how the demand for good *C* changes when income increases.
   - **c.** Calculate the income elasticity of demand for good *C*.

Exercises 5.3

1. Suppose that when the price of a pizza decreases from $9 to $7 and other things remain the same, the quantity demanded of pizza increases from 100 an hour to 200 an hour and the quantity demanded of burgers decreases from 200 an hour to 100 an hour. At the same time, the quantity demanded of cola increases from 150 an hour to 250 an hour.
   - **a.** Calculate the cross elasticity of demand for cola with respect to pizza.
   - **b.** Are cola and pizza substitutes or complements? Why?
   - **c.** Calculate the cross elasticity of demand for burgers with respect to pizza.
   - **d.** Are burgers and pizza substitutes or complements? Why?
   - **e.** Describe how the demand for cola and the demand for burgers have changed.
2. When Larry's income rises by 10 percent and other things remain the same, Larry decreases the quantity demanded of frozen fish cakes by 5 percent and increases the quantity demanded of fresh fish by 15 percent.
   - **a.** Calculate the income elasticity of demand for frozen fish cakes.
   - **b.** Are frozen fish cakes a normal good or an inferior good? Why?
   - **c.** Calculate the income elasticity of demand for fresh fish.
   - **d.** Is fresh fish a normal good or an inferior good? Why?
   - **e.** Is the demand for fresh fish income elastic or income inelastic?

FIGURE 1

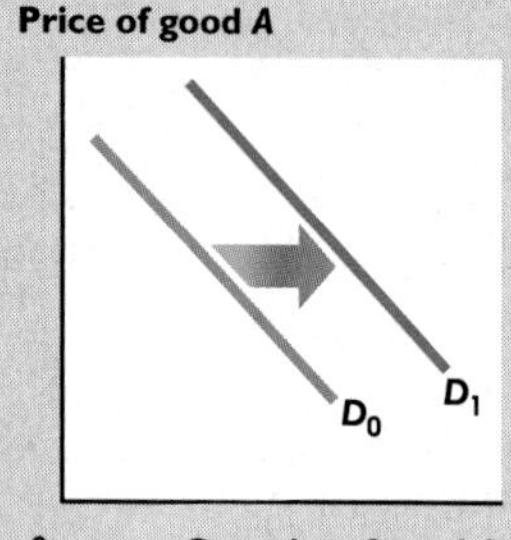

FIGURE 2

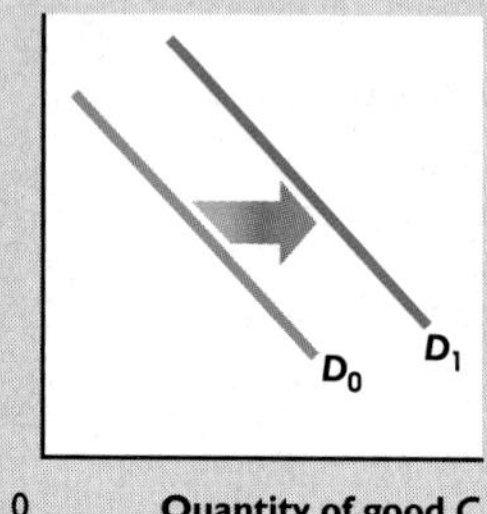

Solutions to Practice Problems 5.3

1a. Goods *A* and *B* are substitutes because when the price of good *B* rises, the quantity demanded of good *A* increases. People switch from good *B* to good *A*.

1b. The demand for good *A* increases (Figure 1).

1c. The cross elasticity of demand of good *A* with respect to good *B* equals the percentage change in the quantity demanded of good *A* divided by the percentage increase in the price of good *B*, which is 5 percent ÷ 10 percent or 0.5.

2a. Good *C* is a normal good; as income rises, the quantity demanded increases.

2b. The demand for good *C* increases (Figure 2).

2c. The income elasticity of demand of good *C* is 1 percent ÷ 5 percent = 0.2.

CHAPTER CHECKPOINT

Key Points

1 Define, explain the factors that influence, and calculate the price elasticity of demand.

- The demand for a good is elastic if when its price changes, the percentage change in the quantity demanded exceeds the percentage change in price.
- The demand for a good is inelastic if when its price changes, the percentage change in the quantity demanded is less than the percentage change in price.
- The price elasticity of demand for a good depends on how easy it is to find substitutes for the good and on the proportion of income spent on it.
- Price elasticity of demand equals the percentage change in the quantity demanded divided by the percentage change in price.
- If demand is elastic, a rise in price leads to a decrease in total revenue. If demand is unit elastic, a rise in price leaves total revenue unchanged. And if demand is inelastic, a rise in price leads to an increase in total revenue.

2 Define, explain the factors that influence, and calculate the price elasticity of supply.

- The supply of a good is elastic if when its price changes, the percentage change in the quantity supplied exceeds the percentage change in price.
- The supply of a good is inelastic if when its price changes, the percentage change in the quantity supplied is less than the percentage change in price.
- The main influences on the price elasticity of supply are the flexibility of production possibilities and storage possibilities.

3 Define and explain the factors that influence the cross elasticity of demand and the income elasticity of demand.

- Cross elasticity of demand shows how the demand for a good changes when the price of one of its substitutes or complements changes.
- Cross elasticity is positive for substitutes and negative for complements.
- Income elasticity of demand shows how the demand for a good changes when income changes. For a normal good, the income elasticity of demand is positive. For an inferior good, the income elasticity of demand is negative.

Key Terms

Cross elasticity of demand, 135
Elastic demand, 120
Elastic supply, 130
Income elasticity of demand, 136
Inelastic demand, 120
Inelastic supply, 130
Perfectly elastic demand, 120
Perfectly elastic supply, 130
Perfectly inelastic demand, 120
Perfectly inelastic supply, 130
Price elasticity of demand, 118
Price elasticity of supply, 130
Total revenue, 126
Total revenue test, 126
Unit elastic demand, 120
Unit elastic supply, 130

Exercises

1. One winter recently, the price of home heating oil increased by 20 percent and the quantity demanded decreased by 2 percent and with no change in the price of wool sweaters, the quantity demanded of wool sweaters increased by 10 percent. Use this information to answer the following questions:
   a. How would you describe the demand for home heating oil?
   b. Calculate the price elasticity of demand for home heating oil.
   c. Is home heating oil more likely to be a necessity or a luxury good? Why?
   d. How did the total revenue from the sale of home heating oil change? Why?
   e. Calculate the cross elasticity of demand of wool sweaters with respect to the price of home heating oil.
   f. Are home heating oil and wool sweaters substitutes or complements? Why?

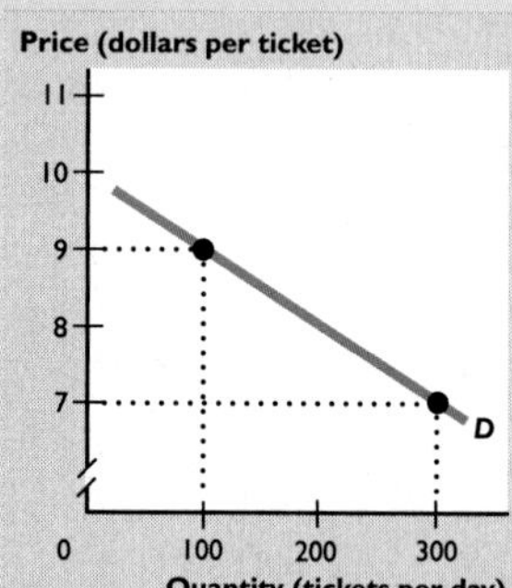

2. The figure shows the demand for movie tickets. If the price of a movie ticket falls from $9 to $7,
   a. Calculate the price elasticity of demand for movie tickets.
   b. Is demand for movie tickets elastic or inelastic?
   c. What is the change in the total revenue from the sale of movie tickets?

3. The price elasticity of demand for Pete's chocolate chip cookies is 1.5. Pete wants to increase his total revenue. Would you recommend that Pete raise his price or lower his price of cookies? Explain your answer.

4. When heavy rain ruined the banana crop in Central America, the price of bananas rose from $1 a pound to $2 a pound. Banana sellers sold fewer bananas but their total revenue remained unchanged.
   a. By how much did the quantity demanded of bananas change?
   b. Is the demand for bananas from Central America elastic or inelastic?

5. The price elasticity of demand for plane rides is 0.5. The price elasticity of demand for train rides is 0.2. The cross elasticity of demand for train rides with respect to the price of a plane ride is 0.4.
   a. If the price of a plane ride rises by 10 percent, what is the percentage change in the quantity demanded of plane rides?
   b. If the price of a plane ride rises by 10 percent, what is the percentage change in the quantity demanded of train rides?
   c. If the price of a train ride rises by 10 percent, what is the percentage change in the quantity demanded of train rides?
   d. When the price of a plane ride rises by 10 percent, what is the percentage change in the price of a train ride that will lead to no change in the quantity demanded of train rides?
   e. In part **d**, there is a movement along the demand curve for which ride and a shift of the demand curve for which ride?

6. When income increased by 10 percent, the quantity of memberships of athletic clubs increased by 15 percent, the quantity demanded of spring water increased by 5 percent, and the quantity demanded of soft drinks decreased by 2 percent. Use the information to answer the following questions:
   a. Describe the demand for memberships of athletic clubs.

b. Describe the demand for spring water.
c. Describe the demand for soft drinks.
d. The demand for which good is income elastic? Which is income inelastic?
e. Which of the three goods are normal goods? Is any good an inferior good?

7. In Pioneer Ville, the price elasticity of demand for bus rides is 0.5, the income elasticity of demand for bus rides is –0.1, and the cross elasticity of demand for bus rides with respect to gasoline is 0.2.
   a. Is the demand for bus rides elastic or inelastic with respect to the price of a bus ride? Why?
   b. Would an increase in bus fares increase the bus company's total revenue? Explain your answer.
   c. Describe the relationship between bus rides and gasoline. Explain.
   d. If the price of gasoline increases by 10 percent with no change in the price of a bus ride, how will the number of bus rides change?
   e. If incomes in Pioneer Ville increase by 5 percent with no change in the price of a bus ride, how will the number of bus rides change?
   f. In Pioneer Ville, is a bus ride a normal good or an inferior good? Why?
   g. In Pioneer Ville, are bus rides and gasoline substitutes or complements? Why?

8. The income elasticity of demand for haircuts is 1.5 and the income elasticity of demand for food is 1.4. You take a weekend job, and the income you have to spend on food and haircuts doubles. If the prices of food and haircuts remain the same, will you double your expenditure on haircuts and double your expenditure on food? Explain why or why not.

9. Drought in many wheat-growing areas cut the quantity supplied of wheat in 2002 by 2 percent. The price elasticity of demand for wheat is 0.5, and the cross elasticity of the demand for pasta with respect to the price of wheat is 2.
   a. By how much will the price of wheat rise?
   b. By how much will the quantity demanded of pasta change?
   c. Pasta makers estimate that the change in the price of wheat in part **a** will increase the price of pasta by 25 percent. What is the pasta makers' estimate of the price elasticity of demand for pasta?

10. How might the owners of the Houston Galleria shopping mall use the concept of cross elasticity of demand to determine the best combination of stores to operate in the Galleria?

11. "In a market in which demand is price inelastic, producers can gouge consumers and the government must set high standards of conduct for producers to ensure that consumers gets a fair deal." Do you agree or disagree with each part of this statement? Explain how you might go about testing the parts of the statement that are positive and lay bare the normative parts.

12. If textbooks became more expensive, but no other prices changed and your income remained the same, do you think you would spend more, less, or the same as you spend now on textbooks? What does your answer tell you about *your* price elasticity of demand for textbooks?

Critical Thinking

13. Ron Gettelfinger, president of the United Autoworkers (UAW), wants your help. He's noticed that when he negotiates a pay increase for UAW members, the number of jobs available for them doesn't change at first, but then, over the next year or so, the number of jobs decreases. He's noticed that on the average, after a year, for every 1 percent rise in the wage rate, the number of jobs decreases by 1.5 percent.
    a. Describe the demand for UAW members' labor services.
    b. Calculate the price elasticity of demand for UAW members' labor services.
    c. How does the total wage bill of the employers of UAW members change immediately after a pay increase? Why?
    d. How does the total wage bill of the employers of UAW members change a year after a pay increase? Why?
    e. Can you think of any ways in which the UAW can make the demand for its members' labor services less elastic?
    f. Can you think of any ways in which the employers of UAW members can make the demand for labor services more elastic?

14. The Organization of the Petroleum Exporting Countries, OPEC, produces about 40 percent of the world's output of crude oil. OPEC knows that it can raise the world price of oil by cutting the total production of its member countries. OPEC also knows that the demand for crude oil is inelastic.
    a. Explain to the OPEC ministers, who are not economists, why it is not possible to conclude from these facts that OPEC's total revenue would increase if it were to cut its production.
    b. Does the elasticity of non-OPEC supply have any influence on how the price of crude oil changes when OPEC cuts production? Again, explain your answer in simple language that the OPEC ministers can understand.

<u>Practice Online</u>

Web Exercises

Use the links on your Foundations Web site to work the following exercises.

15. Visit the California Farm Bureau Federation. Use the information provided in the Ag Alert article to answer the following questions:
    a. Why did the price of asparagus fall?
    b. Do you think the demand for asparagus is likely to be elastic or inelastic?
    c. Do you think the supply of asparagus is likely to be elastic or inelastic?
    d. Is the demand for California asparagus likely to be elastic or inelastic?
    e. Is the supply of California asparagus likely to be elastic or inelastic?
    f. What does Marc Marchini's decision tell you about the elasticity of supply of asparagus from his farm?
    g. In the long run, do you think that California farmers will grow asparagus?

16. Visit 3M and McDonald's. Think about the range of items each firm produces.
    a. Which firm do you think produces goods that have elastic demands? Why?
    b. If the demand for burgers is inelastic, does that mean that McDonald's can keep raising the price of a burger? Why or why not?
    c. If the demand for Post-it Notes is elastic, does that mean that 3M can be relied upon to keep the price of Post-it Notes low? Why or why not?

Efficiency and Fairness of Markets

CHAPTER 6

CHAPTER CHECKLIST

When you have completed your study of this chapter, you will be able to

1. **Distinguish between value and price and define consumer surplus.**
2. **Distinguish between cost and price and define producer surplus.**
3. **Explain the conditions in which markets are efficient and inefficient.**
4. **Explain the main ideas about fairness and evaluate claims that competitive markets result in unfair outcomes.**

We try to get the greatest value out of our scarce resources by comparing marginal costs and marginal benefits. You learned in Chapter 3 that when production is at a point on the *PPF* and when marginal benefit equals marginal cost, resources are being used *efficiently*.

You learned in Chapter 4 how the equilibrium quantities and prices in the market for goods, services, and factors of production determine *what*, *how*, and *for whom* goods and services are produced.

The first question that we study in this chapter brings these two sets of ideas together and asks: Are the equilibrium quantities of goods, services and factors of production the efficient quantities? In other words, are markets efficient?

The second question that we study asks: Are markets fair? Do they deliver a distribution of gains from trade that benefit both buyers and sellers in a fair way? Or do they create injustices?

6.1 VALUE, PRICE, AND CONSUMER SURPLUS

To investigate whether a market is efficient, we need to understand the connection between demand and marginal benefit and between supply and marginal cost.

Demand and Marginal Benefit

In everyday life, when we talk about "getting value for money," we're distinguishing between *value* and *price*. Value is what we get, and price is what we pay. In economics, the everyday idea of value is *marginal benefit*, which we measure as the maximum price that people are willing to pay for another unit of the good or service. The demand curve tells us this price. In Figure 6.1(a), the demand curve shows the quantity demanded at a given price—when the price is $10, the quantity demanded is 10,000 pizzas a day. In Figure 6.1(b), the demand curve shows the maximum price that people are willing to pay when there is a given quantity—when 10,000 pizzas a day are available, the most that people are willing to pay for the 10,000th pizza is $10. The marginal benefit from the 10,000th pizza is $10.

A demand curve is a marginal benefit curve. The demand curve for pizza tells us the dollars' worth of other goods and services that people are willing to forgo to consume one more pizza.

FIGURE 6.1
Demand, Willingness to Pay, and Marginal Benefit

Practice Online

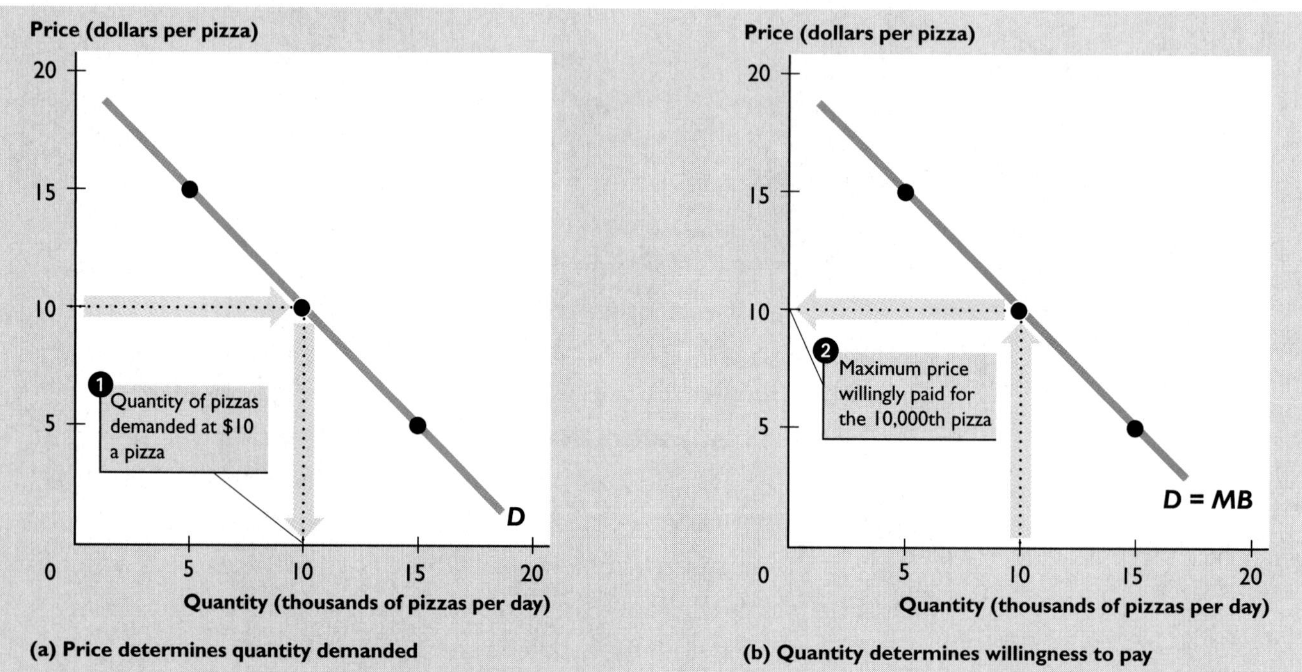

❶ The demand curve for pizza, *D*, shows the quantity of pizza demanded at each price, other things remaining the same. At $10 a pizza, the quantity demanded is 10,000 pizzas a day.

❷ The demand curve shows the maximum price willingly paid if there is a given quantity. If 10,000 pizzas are available, the maximum price willingly paid for the 10,000th pizza is $10.

Consumer Surplus

We don't always have to pay as much as we're willing to pay. When people buy something for less than it is worth to them, they receive a consumer surplus. **Consumer surplus** is the marginal benefit from a good minus the price paid for it, summed over the quantity consumed.

Consumer surplus
The marginal benefit from a good or service minus the price paid for it, summed over the quantity consumed.

Figure 6.2 illustrates consumer surplus. Lisa's demand curve for pizza tells us the quantities of pizza she plans to buy at each price and her marginal benefit from pizza at each quantity. If the price of pizza is $1.00 a slice, Lisa buys 20 slices a week. She spends $20 on pizza, which is shown by the area of the blue rectangle.

To calculate Lisa's consumer surplus, we must find her consumer surplus on each slice and add these consumer surpluses together. For the 20th slice, her marginal benefit equals $1 and she pays $1, so her consumer surplus on this slice is zero. For the 10th slice (highlighted in the figure), her marginal benefit is $1.50. So on this slice, she receives a consumer surplus of $1.50 minus $1.00, which is 50¢. For the first slice, Lisa's marginal benefit is almost $2, so on this slice she receives a consumer surplus of almost $1.

Lisa's consumer surplus—the sum of the consumer surpluses on the 20 slices she buys—is $10 a week, which is shown by the area of the green triangle. (The base of the triangle is 20 slices a week and its height is $1, so its area is 20 × $1 ÷ 2 = $10.)

Lisa's *total benefit* is the amount she pays, $20 (blue rectangle), plus her consumer surplus, $10 (green triangle), and is $30. Because Lisa must pay $20 for the pizza she consumes, her net benefit is equal to her total benefit minus what she pays. Consumer surplus is the net benefit to the consumer.

FIGURE 6.2
A Consumer's Demand and Consumer Surplus

Practice Online

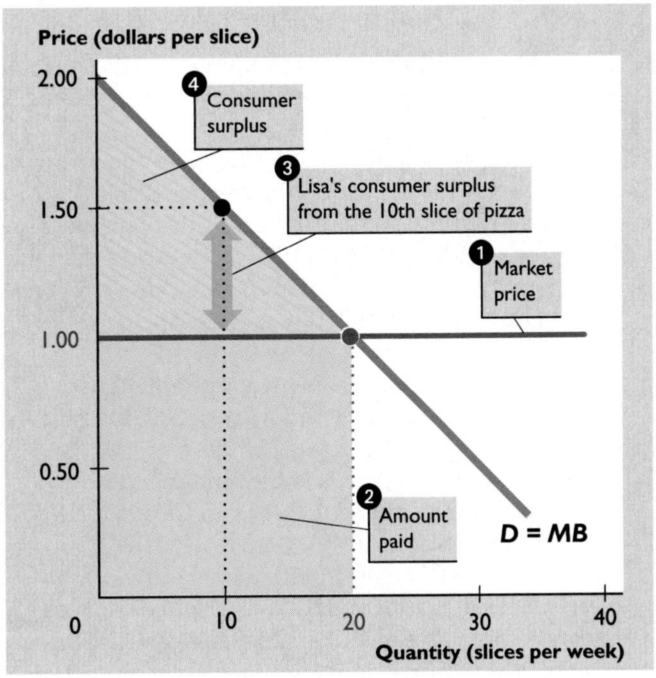

1. The market price of pizza is $1.00 a slice.
2. At the market price, Lisa buys 20 slices a week and spends $20 on pizza—the blue rectangle.
3. Lisa's demand curve tells us that she is willing to pay $1.50 for the 10th slice, so she receives a consumer surplus of 50¢ on the 10th slice.
4. Lisa's consumer surplus from the 20 slices she buys is $10—the area of the green triangle. Lisa's total benefit from pizza is the $20 she pays for it plus the $10 consumer surplus she receives, or $30.

CHECKPOINT 6.1

Study Guide pp. 84–87

Practice Online 6.1

1 Distinguish between value and price and define consumer surplus.

Practice Problem 6.1

Figure 1 shows the demand curve for CDs and the market price of a CD. Use the figure to answer the following questions.

a. What is the value of the 10th CD?
b. What is the willingness to pay for the 20th CD?
c. What is the consumer surplus on the 10th CD?
d. What are the quantity of CDs bought and the consumer surplus?
e. What is the amount paid for the CDs in part **d**?
f. What is the total benefit from the CDs bought in part **d**?
g. If the price of a CD rises to $20, what is the change in the consumer surplus?

FIGURE 1

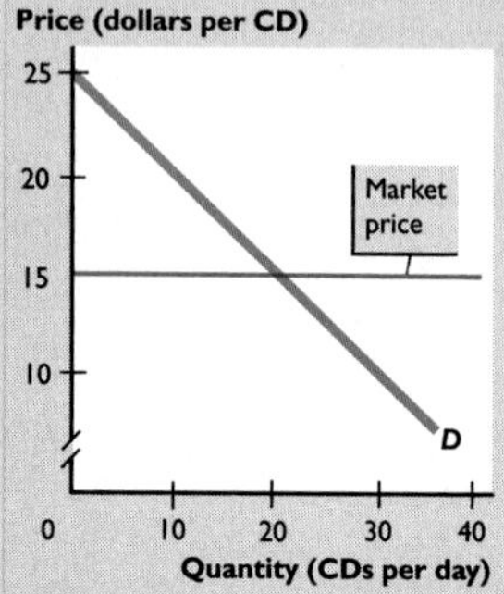

Exercise 6.1

Figure 2 shows the demand curve for ice cream cones and the market price of an ice cream cone. Use the figure to answer the following questions.

a. What is the value of the 15th cone?
b. What is the willingness to pay for the 5th cone?
c. What is the consumer surplus on the 5th cone?
d. What are the quantity of ice cream cones bought and the consumer surplus?
e. What is the total expenditure on ice cream cones?
f. What is the total benefit from ice cream cones?
g. If the price of an ice cream cone rises to $3.00 a cone, what is the change in the consumer surplus?

FIGURE 2

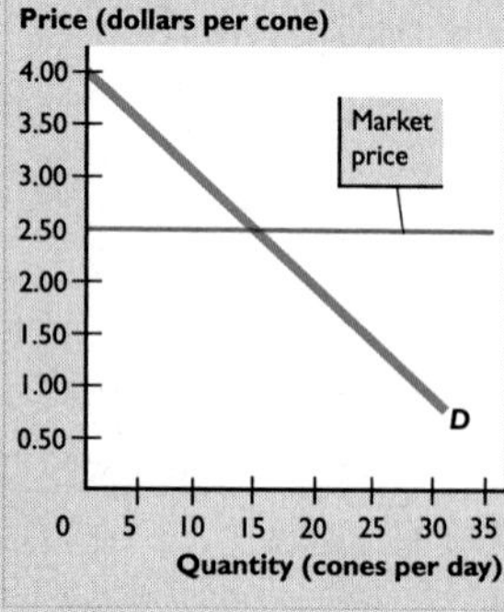

Solution to Practice Problem 6.1

a. The value of the 10th CD is the marginal benefit from the 10th CD. Value is equal to the maximum price that someone is willing to pay for the 10th CD, which is $20 (Figure 3).
b. The willingness to pay for the 20th CD is the maximum price that someone is willing to pay for the 20th CD, which is $15 (Figure 3).
c. Consumer surplus on the 10th CD is its marginal benefit minus the price of a CD, which is $20 – $15 = $5 (the green arrow in Figure 3).
d. The quantity of CDs bought is 20 a day, and the consumer surplus is ($25 – $15) × 20 ÷ 2 = $100 (the green triangle in Figure 3).
e. The amount paid for CDs is price multiplied by quantity bought, which is $15 × 20 = $300 (the blue rectangle in Figure 3).
f. The total benefit from CDs is the amount paid for CDs plus the consumer surplus from CDs, which is $300 + $100 = $400.
g. If the price of a CD rises to $20, the quantity of CDs bought decreases to 10 a day. The consumer surplus from CDs decreases to ($25 – $20) × 10 ÷ 2 = $25 (the smaller green triangle in Figure 4).

FIGURE 3

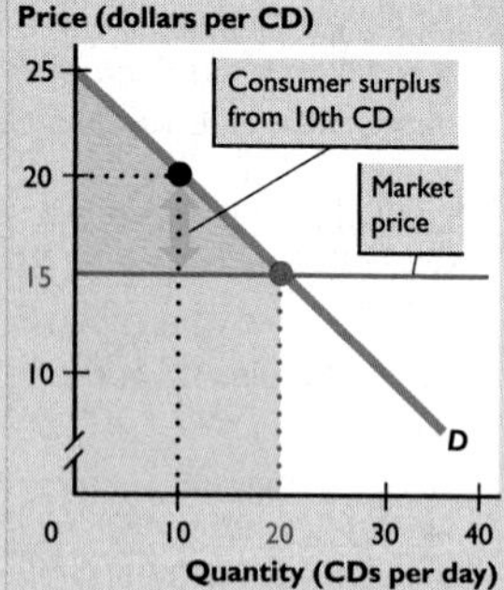

FIGURE 4

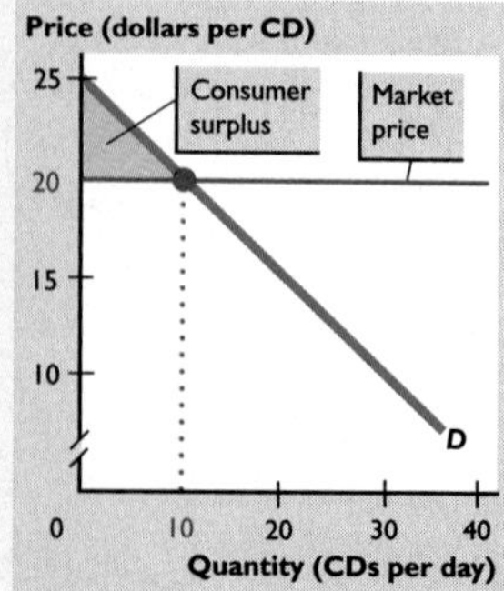

6.2 COST, PRICE, AND PRODUCER SURPLUS

What you are now going to learn about cost, price, and producer surplus parallels what you've learned about value, price, and consumer surplus.

Supply and Marginal Cost

Just as buyers distinguish between *value* and *price*, so sellers distinguish between *cost* and *price*. Cost is what a seller must give up to produce the good, and price is what a seller receives when the good is sold. The cost of producing one more unit of a good or service is its *marginal cost*. It is just worth producing one more unit of a good or service if the price for which it can be sold equals marginal cost. But the supply curve tells us this price. In Figure 6.3(a), the supply curve shows the quantity supplied at a given price—when the price of a pizza is $10, the quantity supplied is 10,000 pizzas a day. In Figure 6.3(b), the supply curve shows the minimum price that producers must receive to supply a given quantity—to supply 10,000 pizzas a day, producers must be able to get at least $10 for the 10,000th pizza. The marginal cost of the 10,000th pizza is $10. So:

> **A supply curve is a marginal cost curve. The supply curve of pizza tells us the dollars' worth of other goods and services that people must forgo if firms produce one more pizza.**

FIGURE 6.3

Supply, Minimum Supply Price, and Marginal Cost

Practice Online

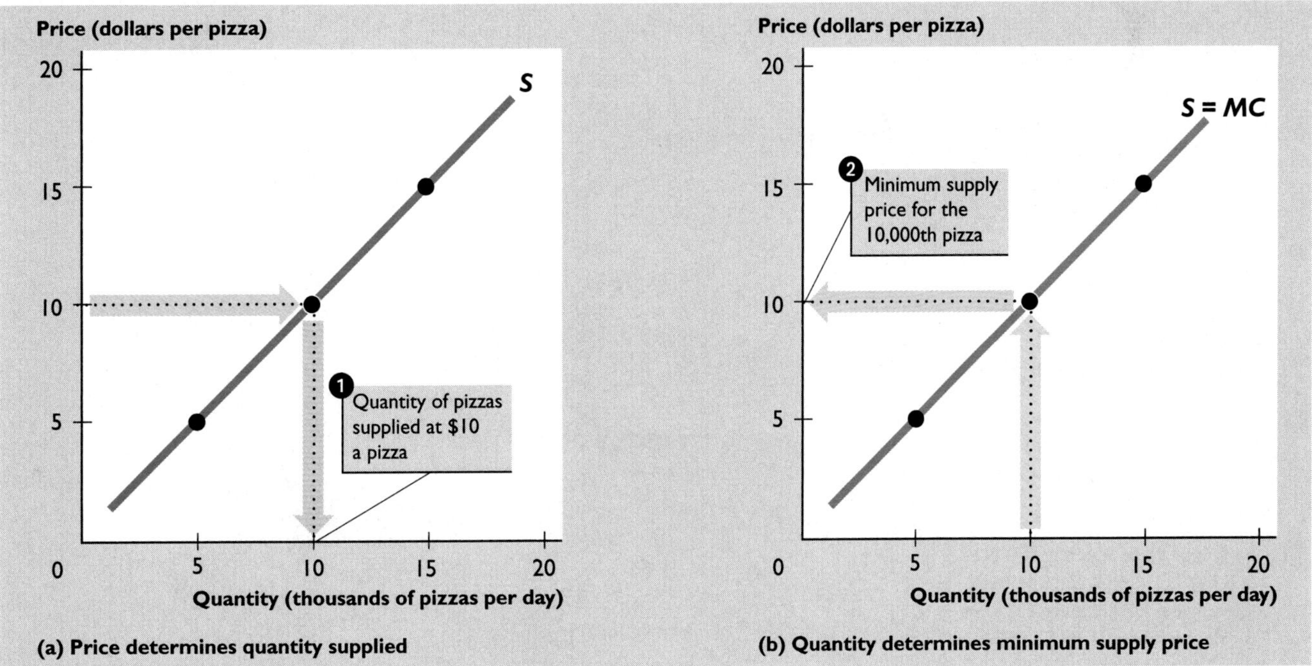

1 The supply curve of pizza, *S*, shows the quantity of pizza supplied at each price, other things remaining the same. At $10 a pizza, the quantity supplied is 10,000 pizzas a day.

2 The supply curve shows the minimum price that firms must be offered to supply a given quantity. The minimum supply price for the 10,000th pizza is $10.

Producer Surplus

Producer surplus
The price of a good minus the marginal cost of producing it, summed over the quantity produced.

When the price exceeds marginal cost, the firm obtains a producer surplus. **Producer surplus** is the price of a good minus the marginal cost of producing it, summed over the quantity produced.

Figure 6.4 illustrates producer surplus. Max can produce pizza or bake bread. The more pizza he bakes, the less bread he can bake. His marginal cost (opportunity cost) of pizza is the value of the bread he must forgo. The marginal cost of pizza increases as Max produces more pizza.

Max's supply curve of pizza tells us the quantities of pizza that Max plans to sell at each price and his marginal cost of producing at each quantity. If the price of a pizza is $10, Max produces 100 a day. Max's total revenue is $1,000 a day ($10 × 100 = $1,000).

To calculate Max's producer surplus, we must find the producer surplus on each pizza and add these producer surpluses together. The marginal cost of the 100th pizza is $10 and equals the $10 he can sell it for, so his producer surplus on this pizza is zero. For the 50th pizza (highlighted in the figure), his marginal cost is $6. So on this pizza, he receives a producer surplus of $10 minus $6, which is $4. For the first pizza produced, Max's marginal cost is a bit more than $2, so on this pizza, he receives a producer surplus of almost $8.

Max's producer surplus—the sum of the producer surpluses on the 100 pizzas he sells—is $400 a day, which is shown by the blue triangle. (The base of the triangle is 100 pizzas a day and its height is $8, so its area is 100 × $8 ÷ 2 = $400.)

The red area shows Max's cost of producing 100 pizzas a day, which is $600. This amount equals Max's total revenue of $1,000 a day minus his producer surplus of $400 a day.

FIGURE 6.4
A Producer's Supply and Producer Surplus

Practice Online

1. The market price of a pizza is $10. At this price, Max sells 100 pizzas a day and receives a total revenue of $1,000 a day.
2. Max's supply curve shows that the minimum that he must be offered for the 50th pizza a day is $6, so he receives a producer surplus of $4 on the 50th pizza.
3. Max's producer surplus from the 100 pizzas he sells is $400 a day—the area of the blue triangle.
4. Max's cost of producing 100 pizzas a day is the red area beneath the marginal cost curve. It equals Max's total revenue of $1,000 minus his producer surplus of $400 and is $600 a day.

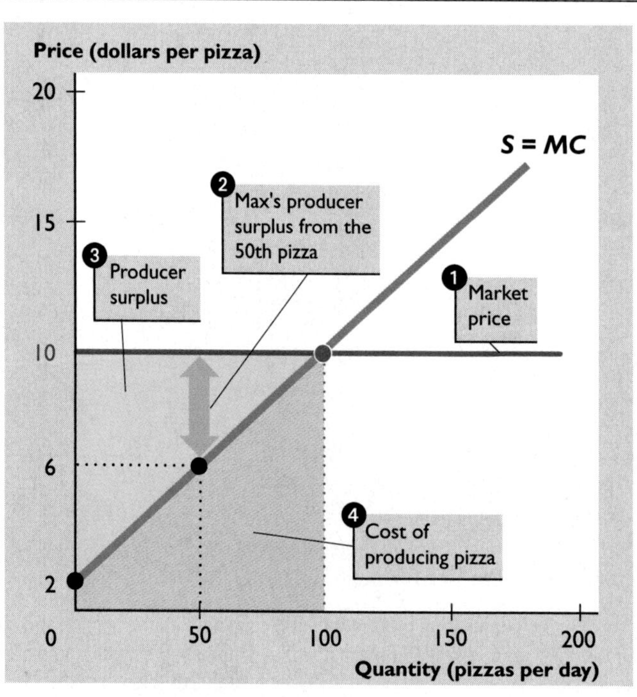

CHECKPOINT 6.2

2 **Distinguish between cost and price and define producer surplus.**

Study Guide pp. 87–90

Practice Online 6.2

Practice Problem 6.2

Figure 1 shows the supply curve of CDs and the market price of a CD. Use the figure to answer the following questions.

a. What is the marginal cost of the 10th CD?
b. What is the minimum supply price of the 20th CD?
c. What is the producer surplus on the 10th CD?
d. What are the quantity of CDs sold and the producer surplus?
e. What is the total revenue from the CDs sold in part **d**?
f. What is the cost of producing the CDs sold in part **d**?
g. If the price of a CD falls to $10, what is the change in the producer surplus?

FIGURE 1

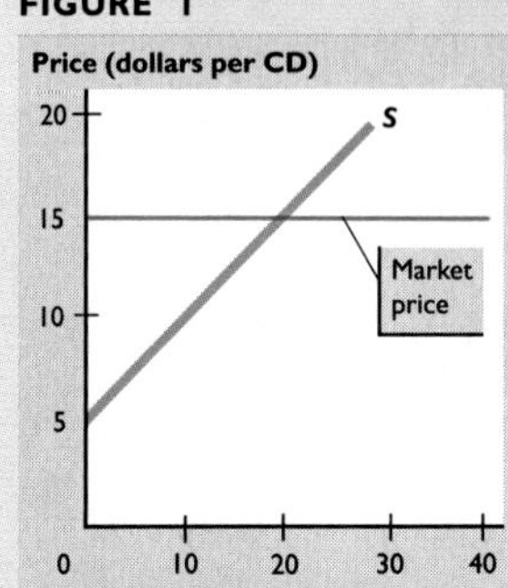

Exercise 6.2

Figure 2 shows the supply curve of ice cream cones and the market price of an ice cream cone. Use the figure to answer the following questions.

a. What is the opportunity cost of the 15th cone?
b. What is the minimum supply price of the 5th cone?
c. What is the producer surplus on the 5th cone?
d. What are the quantity of ice cream cones sold and the producer surplus?
e. What is the total revenue from ice cream cones ?
f. What is the total cost of producing ice cream cones?
g. If the price of an ice cream cone falls to $2.00 a cone, what is the change in the producer surplus?

FIGURE 2

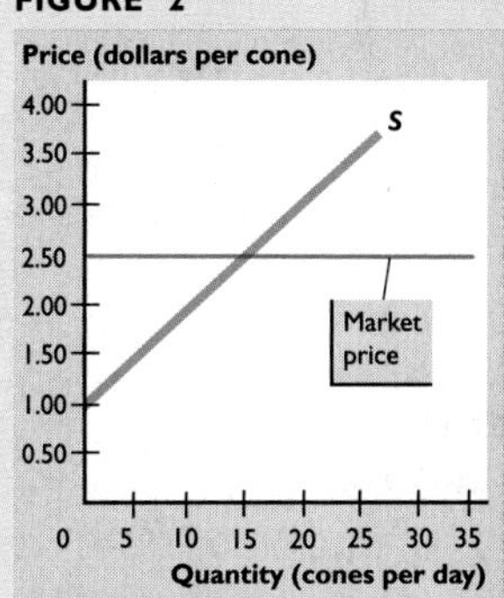

Solution to Practice Problem 6.2

a. The marginal cost of the 10th CD is equal to the minimum supply price for the 10th CD, which is $10 (Figure 3).
b. The minimum supply price of the 20th CD is the marginal cost of the 20th CD, which is $15 (Figure 3).
c. Producer surplus on the 10th CD is its market price minus its marginal cost, which is $15 – $10 = $5 (the blue arrow in Figure 3).
d. The quantity of CDs sold is 20 a day, and the producer surplus is ($15 – $5) × 20 ÷ 2 = $100 (the blue triangle in Figure 3).
e. The total revenue from CDs is the total expenditure on them, which is price multiplied by quantity sold. Total revenue is $15 × 20 = $300.
f. The cost of producing CDs equals total revenue minus producer surplus, which is $300 – $100 = $200 (the red area in Figure 3).
g. If the price of a CD falls to $10, the quantity of CDs sold decreases to 10 a day. The producer surplus on CDs decreases to ($10 – $5) × 10 ÷ 2 = $25 (the smaller blue triangle in Figure 4). The change in the producer surplus = $100 – $25, which is $75.

FIGURE 3

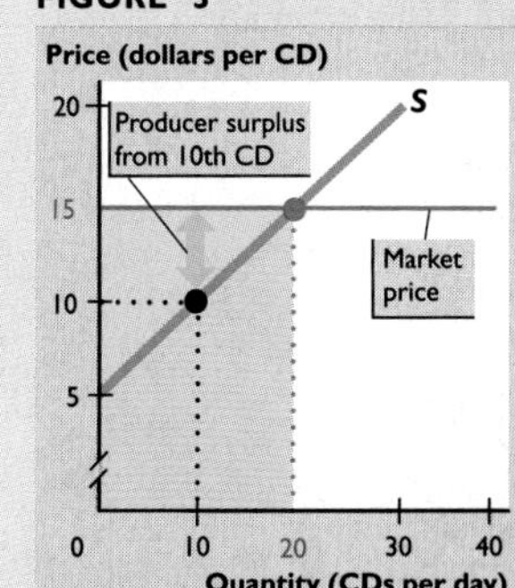

FIGURE 4

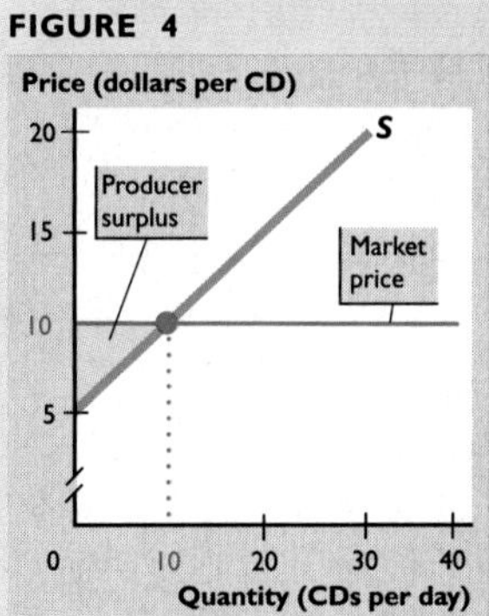

6.3 ARE MARKETS EFFICIENT?

Figure 6.5 shows the market for pizza. The demand curve, *D*, shows the demand for pizza. The supply curve, *S*, shows the supply of pizza. The equilibrium price is $10 a pizza, and the equilibrium quantity is 10,000 pizzas a day.

The market forces that you studied in Chapter 4 (pp. 105–106) will pull the pizza market to its equilibrium. If the price exceeds $10 a pizza, a surplus of pizza will force the price down. If the price is less than $10 a pizza, a shortage of pizza will force the price up. Only if the price is $10 a pizza is there neither a surplus nor a shortage of pizza and no forces operate to change its price.

So the market price and quantity are pulled toward their equilibrium values. But is this competitive equilibrium efficient? Does it produce the efficient quantity of pizza?

Efficiency of Competitive Equilibrium

The equilibrium in Figure 6.5 is efficient. Resources are being used to produce the quantity of pizza that people value most highly. It is not possible to produce more pizza without giving up some of another good or service that is valued more highly. And if a smaller quantity of pizza is produced, resources are used to produce some other good that is not valued as highly as the pizza forgone.

FIGURE 6.5
An Efficient Market for Pizza

Practice Online

❶ Market equilibrium occurs at a price of $10 a pizza and a quantity of 10,000 pizzas a day.

❷ The supply curve is also the marginal cost curve.

❸ The demand curve is also the marginal benefit curve.

Because at the market equilibrium, marginal benefit equals marginal cost, the ❹ efficient quantity of pizza is produced. The sum of the ❺ consumer surplus and ❻ producer surplus is maximized.

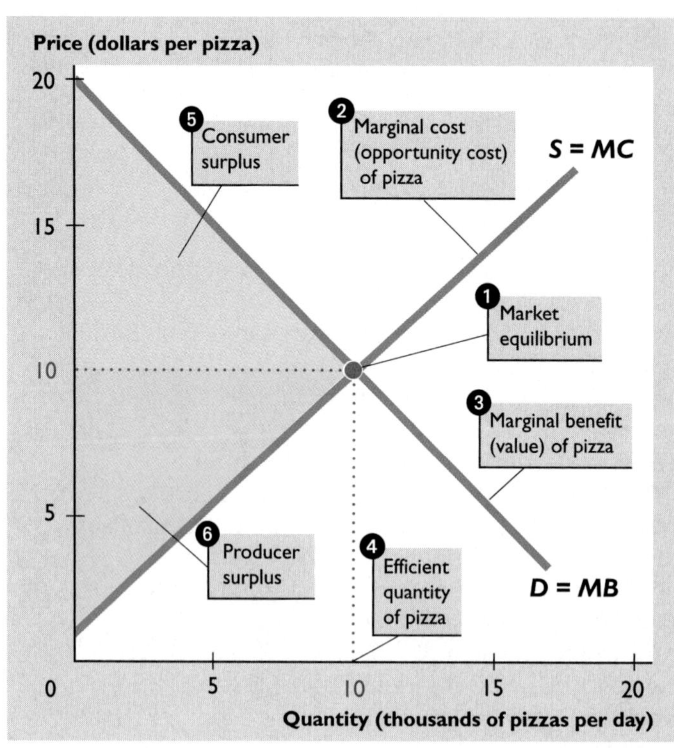

To see why the equilibrium in Figure 6.5 is efficient, think about the interpretation of the demand curve as a marginal benefit curve and the supply curve as a marginal cost curve. The demand curve tells us the marginal benefit from pizza. The supply curve tells us the marginal cost of pizza. So where the demand curve and the supply curve intersect, marginal benefit equals marginal cost.

But this condition—marginal benefit equals marginal cost—is the condition that delivers an efficient use of resources. It allocates resources to the activities that create the greatest possible value. So a competitive equilibrium is efficient.

If production is less than 10,000 pizzas a day, someone is willing to buy a pizza for more than it costs to produce. So buyers and sellers will gain if production increases. If production exceeds 10,000 pizzas a day, it costs more to produce a pizza than anyone is willing to pay for it. So buyers and sellers will gain if production decreases. Only when 10,000 pizzas a day are produced is there no unexploited gain from changing the quantity of pizza produced.

The competitive market pushes the quantity of pizza produced to its efficient level of 10,000 a day. If production is less than 10,000 pizzas a day, a shortage raises the price, which stimulates an increase in production. If production exceeds 10,000 pizzas a day, a surplus lowers the price, which decreases production.

In a competitive equilibrium, resources are used efficiently to produce the goods and services that people value most highly. And when the competitive market uses resources efficiently, the sum of consumer surplus and producer surplus is maximized.

Buyers and sellers each attempt to do the best they can for themselves, and no one plans for an efficient outcome for society as a whole. Buyers seek the lowest possible price, and sellers seek the highest possible price.

The Invisible Hand

Writing in his *Wealth of Nations* in 1776, Adam Smith was the first to suggest that competitive markets send resources to the uses in which they have the highest value. Smith believed that each participant in a competitive market is "led by an invisible hand to promote an end [the efficient use of resources] which was no part of his intention."

You can see the effects of the invisible hand at work every day. Your campus bookstore is stuffed with texts at the start of each term. It has the quantities that it predicts students will buy. The coffee shop has the variety and quantities of drinks and snacks that people plan to buy. Your local clothing shop has the sweatpants and socks and other items you plan to buy. Truckloads of textbooks, coffee and cookies, and sweatpants and socks roll along our highways and bring these items to where you and your friends want to buy them. Firms that don't know you anticipate your wants and work hard to help you satisfy them.

No government organizes all this production, and no government auditor monitors producers to ensure that they serve the public interest. The allocation of scarce resources is not planned. It happens because prices adjust to make buying plans and selling plans compatible. And it happens in a way that sends resources to the uses in which they have the highest value.

Adam Smith explained why all this amazing activity occurs. "It is not from the benevolence of the butcher, the brewer, or the baker that we expect our dinner," he wrote, "but from their regard to their own interest."

Publishing companies, coffee growers, garment manufacturers, and a host of other producers are led by their regard for their own interest to serve *your* interest.

Eye on the U.S. Economy

The Invisible Hand and e-Commerce

You can see the influence of the invisible hand at work in the cartoon and in today's information economy.

The cold drinks vendor has both cold drinks and shade. He has an opportunity cost and a minimum supply price of each item. The park bench reader has a marginal benefit from a cold drink and from shade. The transaction that occurs tells us that the reader's marginal benefit from shade exceeds the vendor's marginal cost, but the vendor's marginal cost of a cold drink exceeds the reader's marginal benefit. The transaction creates consumer surplus and producer surplus. The vendor obtains a producer surplus from selling the shade for more than its opportunity cost, and the reader obtains a consumer surplus from buying the shade for less than its marginal benefit. In the third frame of the cartoon, both the consumer and the producer are better off than they were in the first frame. The umbrella has moved to its highest value use.

The market economy relentlessly performs the activity illustrated in the cartoon to achieve an efficient allocation of resources. And rarely has the market been working as hard as it is today. Think about a few of the changes taking place in our economy and notice how the market is guiding resources toward their efficient use.

New technologies have cut the cost of producing computers. As these advances have occurred, the supply of computers has increased and the price of a computer has fallen. Lower prices have encouraged an increase in the quantity demanded of this now less costly tool. The marginal benefit from computers is brought to equality with their marginal cost.

During the past few years, hundreds of Web sites have been established that are dedicated to facilitating trading in all types of goods, services, and factors of production. One of these sites is Freeshop.com (http://www.freeshop.com/), which organizes access to hundreds of other sites that among them offer more than 1,000 "free and trial offers."

Another notable online market maker is the electronic auction site eBay (http://www.ebay.com/), where you can offer to buy or sell any of a huge variety of items.

These e-commerce innovations are increasing consumer surplus, increasing producer surplus, and achieving yet greater allocative efficiency.

Obstacles to Efficiency

Although markets generally do a good job at sending resources to where they are most highly valued, they do not always produce the efficient quantities. Sometimes markets over-produce a good or service, and sometimes they under-produce. The most significant obstacles to achieving an efficient allocation of resources in the market economy are

- Price ceilings and price floors
- Taxes, subsidies, and quotas
- Externalities
- Public goods and common resources
- Monopoly

Price Ceilings and Price Floors

A *price ceiling* is a regulation that makes it illegal to charge a price higher than a specified level. An example is a price ceiling on apartment rents, which some cities impose. A *price floor* is a regulation that makes it illegal to pay a lower price than a specified level. An example is the minimum wage. (We study both of these restrictions on buyers and sellers in Chapter 7.)

The presence of a price ceiling or a price floor blocks the forces of demand and supply and results in a quantity produced that might exceed or fall short of the quantity determined in an unregulated market.

Taxes, Subsidies, and Quotas

Taxes increase the prices paid by buyers and lower the prices received by sellers. So they decrease the quantity produced to less than the efficient quantity (for reasons that are explained in Chapter 7). All kinds of goods and services are taxed, but the highest taxes are on gasoline, alcohol, and tobacco.

Subsidies, which are payments by the government to producers, decrease the prices paid by buyers and increase the prices received by sellers. Subsidies increase the quantity produced to more than the efficient quantity.

A quota is a limit to the quantity that a firm is permitted to produce. Farms are sometimes subject to quotas—for example tobacco farmers face quotas.

Externalities

An *externality* is a cost or a benefit that arises from a production activity that falls on someone other than the producer; or a cost or a benefit that arises from a consumption activity that falls on someone other than the consumer. A *spillover effect* is another name for an externality. When an electric power utility burns coal to generate electricity, it puts sulfur dioxide into the atmosphere, which falls as acid rain and damages crops. This is an example of an *external cost* of production. The utility does not consider the cost of pollution when it decides the quantity of power to produce. Its supply curve is based on its own costs, not on the costs that it inflicts on others. So too much electric power is produced.

When a homeowner maintains a beautifully landscaped yard, she benefits all the people who live around her. This is an example of an *external benefit* of consumption. The homeowner does not consider her neighbor's marginal benefit when she decides the quantity of landscaping services to buy. Her demand curve for landscaping services is based on her own marginal benefit. In this case, the quantity falls short of the efficient quantity. (We study externalities in Chapter 8.)

Public Goods and Common Resources

A *public good* is a good or service that is consumed simultaneously by everyone even if they don't pay for it. Examples are national defense and law enforcement. Competitive markets would produce too small a quantity of a public good because of a *free-rider problem*—the fact that it is in each person's interest to free ride on everyone else and avoid paying for her or his share of a public good. So a competitive market produces less of a public good than the efficient quantity.

Monopoly

A *monopoly* is a firm that has sole control of a market. For example, local water supply and cable television are produced by monopolies. Although it might earn a large profit, a monopoly prevents the market from achieving an efficient use of resources. The goal of a monopoly is to maximize profit. To achieve this goal, a monopoly produces less than the efficient quantity and raises its price. (We study monopoly in Chapter 11.)

Underproduction and Overproduction

The impediments to efficiency that we've just reviewed and that you will study in greater detail in later chapters result in two possible outcomes:

- Underproduction
- Overproduction

Underproduction

Suppose that in the pizza market in Figure 6.5, the quantity of pizza produced is only 5,000 a day. Figure 6.6(a) shows that at this quantity, consumers are willing to pay $15 for a pizza that costs only $6 to produce. The quantity produced is inefficient.

The sum of consumer surplus and producer surplus is decreased by the amount of the gray triangle in Figure 6.6(a). This triangle is called deadweight loss. **Deadweight loss** is the decrease in consumer surplus and producer surplus that results from an inefficient level of production. The deadweight loss is borne by the entire society. It is not a loss for the consumers and a gain for the producer. It is a *social* loss.

Deadweight loss
The decrease in consumer surplus and producer surplus that results from an inefficient level of production.

Overproduction

Now suppose that in the pizza market in Figure 6.5, the quantity of pizza produced is 15,000 a day. Figure 6.6(b) shows that at this quantity, consumers are willing to pay only $5 for that marginal pizza but the opportunity cost of that pizza is $14. It now costs more to produce a pizza than consumers are willing to pay for it. If we produce the 15,000th pizza, we lose $9.

Again, deadweight loss is shown by the gray triangle. The sum of consumer surplus and producer surplus is smaller than its maximum by the amount of deadweight loss.

FIGURE 6.6
Underproduction and Overproduction

Practice Online

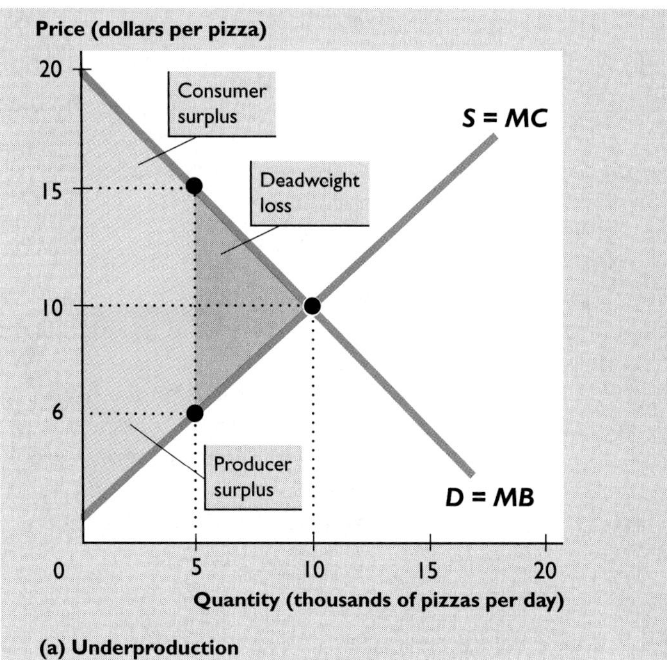

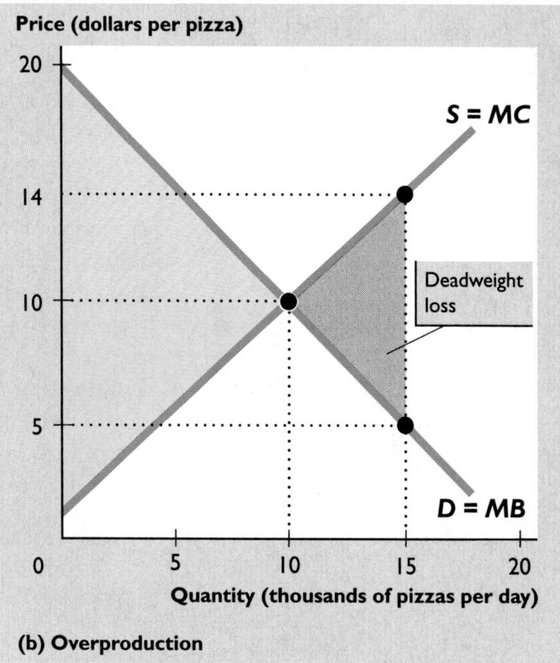

If pizza production is restricted to 5,000 a day, a deadweight loss (the gray triangle) arises. The sum of the consumer surplus (the green area) and producer surplus (the blue area) is reduced.

If production increases to 15,000, a deadweight loss arises. Consumer surplus plus producer surplus equals the sum of the green and blue areas minus the gray deadweight loss triangle.

Eye on the Global Economy

Are Mega-Mergers Efficient or Inefficient?

AOL Time Warner was created by merging the resources of America Online and media giant Time Warner. Time Warner itself came from a merger of Time Inc., the producer of *Time* magazine, and Warner Brothers, the moviemaker. Time-Warner also bought CNN from Ted Turner.

These mergers in the media industry are just the tip of a huge iceberg of merger activity in the U.S. and global economies. Mergers of automakers keep reducing the number of independent firms in that industry. For example, Germany's Daimler has bought Chrysler. Ford has bought Sweden's Volvo and Britain's Jaguar. Mercedes-Benz has bought Volkswagen. In the oil industry, Exxon and Mobil have become one firm.

Mergers enable firms to avoid duplication of activities and bring resources into one organization so that they can be used more efficiently. But do mergers result in a more efficient allocation of resources? Do the bigger firms impose external costs? Do they restrict output and produce less than the efficient quantity? Do mergers need to be scrutinized by the government and sometimes blocked?

These are controversial questions that often don't have definite answers. But you can think about these questions by using what you've learned in this chapter.

Mergers are efficient if they cut costs or if they bring marginal benefit closer to marginal cost. Mergers are inefficient if they raise costs or if they widen the gap between marginal benefit and marginal cost.

CHECKPOINT 6.3

Study Guide pp. 90–93

Practice Online 6.3

3 Explain the conditions in which markets are efficient and inefficient.

Practice Problem 6.3

Figure 1 shows the market for paper. Use the figure to answer the following questions.

a. What are the equilibrium price and the equilibrium quantity of paper?
b. In market equilibrium, what is the consumer surplus?
c. In market equilibrium, what is the producer surplus?
d. Is the market for paper efficient? Why or why not?
e. If a news magazine lobby group persuaded the government to pass a law requiring paper producers to sell 50 tons of paper a day, would the market for paper be efficient? Why or why not?
f. In the situation described in part **e**, shade the deadweight loss on the figure.
g. If an environmental lobby group persuaded the government to pass a law restricting producers of paper to sell only 20 tons of paper a day, would the market for paper be efficient? Why or why not?
h. In the situation described in part **g**, shade the deadweight loss on the figure.

FIGURE 1

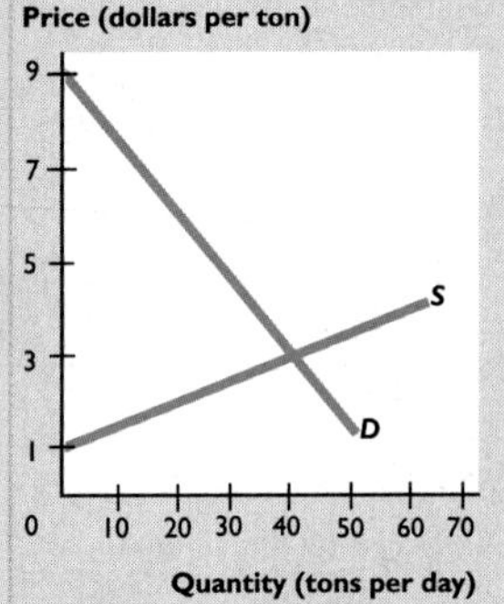

Exercise 6.3

Figure 2 shows the market for ice cream cones. Use the figure to answer the following questions.

a. What are the equilibrium price and equilibrium quantity of ice cream cones?
b. In market equilibrium, what is the consumer surplus?
c. In market equilibrium, what is the producer surplus?
d. Is the market for ice cream cones efficient? Why or why not?
e. If the government restricted producers to 10 ice cream cones per day, would the market for ice cream cones be efficient? Why or why not?
f. In the situation described in part **e**, what is the deadweight loss?
g. If the government passed a law requiring producers of ice cream cones to sell 20 cones a day, would the market for ice cream cones be efficient? Why or why not?
h. In the situation described in part **g**, what is the deadweight loss?

FIGURE 2

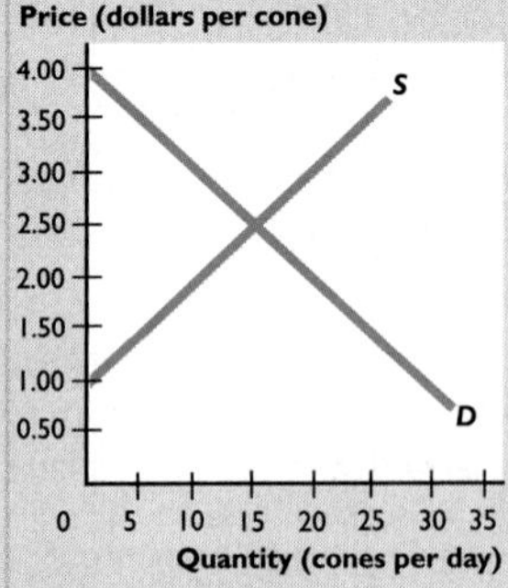

Solution to Practice Problem 6.3

a. Market equilibrium is 40 tons a day at a price of \$3 a ton (Figure 3).
b. Consumer surplus is (\$9 – \$3) × 40 ÷ 2 = \$120 (the green triangle in Figure 3).
c. Producer surplus is (\$3 – \$1) × 40 ÷ 2 = \$40 (the blue triangle in Figure 3).
d. The market equilibrium is efficient because marginal benefit equals marginal cost and the sum of consumer surplus and producer surplus is a maximum.
e. If the quantity produced is 50 tons a day, the market for paper is inefficient because marginal cost exceeds marginal benefit.
f. With 50 tons produced, the deadweight loss is the gray triangle labeled 1 in Figure 4.
g. If the quantity produced is 20 tons a day, the market for paper is inefficient because marginal benefit exceeds marginal cost.
h. With 20 tons produced, the deadweight loss is the gray triangle labeled 2 in Figure 4.

FIGURE 3

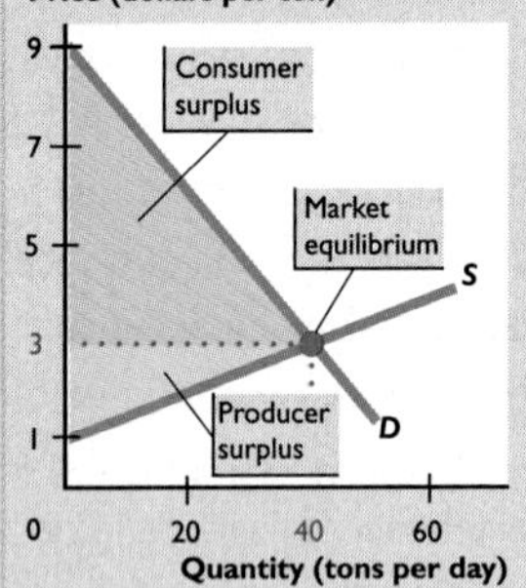

FIGURE 4

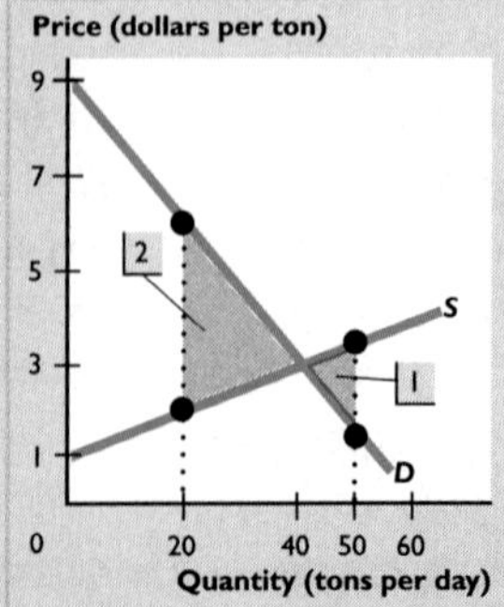

6.4 ARE MARKETS FAIR?

Is an efficient allocation of resources fair? Does the competitive market provide people with fair incomes for their work? And do people always pay a fair price for the things they buy? Do we need the government to step into some competitive markets to prevent the price from rising too high or falling too low?

When a natural disaster strikes, such as a severe winter storm or a hurricane, the prices of many essential items jump. The reason the prices jump is that some people have a greater demand and greater willingness to pay while at the same time, the items are in limited supply. So the higher prices achieve an efficient allocation of scarce resources. News reports of these price hikes almost never talk about efficiency. Instead, they complain about their unfairness. In Florida, there are even laws that prevent large price increases once a hurricane watch is in effect and the state has set up an Anti-Gouging Hot Line.

Similarly, when low-skilled people work for a wage that is below what most would regard as a living wage, the media and politicians talk of employers taking unfair advantage of their workers.

How do we decide whether something is fair or unfair? You know when *you* think something is unfair. But how do you know? What are the *principles* of fairness?

Economists agree about efficiency. They agree that we should make the economic pie as large as possible and bake it at the lowest possible cost. But they do not agree about what are fair shares of the economic pie for all the people who make it. The reason is that ideas about fairness are not exclusively economic ideas. They involve politics and ethics. Here we can only provide a selective sketch of the huge literature on this subject.

All ideas about fairness are based on a fundamental principle that seems to be hard-wired into the human brain called the symmetry principle. The **symmetry principle** is the requirement that people in similar situations be treated similarly. It is the principle that lies at the center of all the main moral codes that tell us, in some form or other, to behave toward other people in the way we expect them to behave toward us.

Symmetry principle
The requirement that people in similar situations be treated similarly.

Unfortunately, the symmetry principle does not deliver universally accepted prescriptions for fair arrangements and leaves a big question unanswered. To see what this unanswered question is, think of economic life as a game—a serious game. A game has an outcome or result, and it has rules. Does obeying the symmetry principle and treating people in similar situations similarly require that all the players face the same rules, or does it require that they get the same score? This question lies at the heart of disagreement about fairness in economics. Two broad and generally conflicting views of fairness are

- It's not fair if the *result* isn't fair.
- It's not fair if the *rules* aren't fair.

It's Not Fair If the *Result* Isn't Fair

The earliest efforts to establish a principle of fairness were based on the view that the result is what matters. And the general idea was that it is unfair if people's incomes are too unequal. It is unfair that bank presidents earn millions of dollars a year while bank tellers earn only thousands of dollars a year. It is unfair that a store owner enjoys a larger profit and her customers pay higher prices in the aftermath of a winter storm.

There was a lot of excitement during the nineteenth century when economists thought they had made the incredible discovery that efficiency requires equality of incomes. To make the economic pie as large as possible, they thought, it must be cut into equal pieces, one for each person. This idea turns out to be wrong, but there is a lesson in the reason that it is wrong. So this idea is worth a closer look.

Utilitarianism

Utilitarianism
A principle that states that we should strive to achieve "the greatest happiness for the greatest number."

The nineteenth century idea that only equality brings efficiency is an extreme version of utilitarianism. **Utilitarianism** is a principle that states that we should strive to achieve "the greatest happiness for the greatest number." The people who developed this idea were known as utilitarians. They included the most eminent minds such as Jeremy Bentham and John Stuart Mill.

Some utilitarians argued that to achieve "the greatest happiness for the greatest number," income must be transferred from the rich to the poor up to the point of complete equality—to the point at which there are no rich and no poor.

They reasoned in the following way: First, everyone has the same basic wants and is similar in the capacity to enjoy life. In the technical language of economics that you've now learned to use, everyone has the same marginal benefit schedule or curve. Second, the greater a person's income, the smaller is the marginal benefit of a dollar's worth of goods and services. The millionth dollar spent by a rich person brings a smaller marginal benefit to that person than the marginal benefit of the thousandth dollar spent by a poorer person. So by transferring a dollar from the millionaire to the poorer person, more is gained than is lost, and the two people added together are better off.

But the same is true for every dollar transferred until there is no poor or rich person. Only when everyone's share of the economic pie is the same as everyone else's are we sharing resources in the most efficient way and bringing the greatest attainable total benefit. So complete equality is the only fair outcome.

The Big Tradeoff

Big tradeoff
A tradeoff between efficiency and fairness that recognizes the cost of making income transfers.

One big problem with the utilitarian idea of complete equality is that it ignores the costs of making income transfers. Recognizing the costs of making income transfers leads to what is called the **big tradeoff**, which is a tradeoff between efficiency and fairness.

The big tradeoff is based on the following facts. Income can be transferred from people with high incomes to people with low incomes only by taxing incomes. Taxing people's income from employment discourages work. It results in the quantity of labor being less than the efficient quantity. Taxing people's income from capital discourages saving. It results in the quantity of capital being less than the efficient quantity. With smaller quantities of both labor and capital, the quantity of goods and services produced is less than the efficient quantity. The economic pie shrinks.

The tradeoff is between the size of the economic pie and the degree of equality with which it is shared. The greater the amount of income redistribution through income taxes, the greater is the inefficiency—the smaller is the economic pie.

There is a second source of inefficiency. A dollar taken from a rich person does not end up as a dollar in the hands of a poorer person. Some of it is spent on administration of the tax and transfer system. The cost of tax-collecting agencies, such as the IRS, and welfare-administering agencies, such as the Health Care Financing Administration, which administers Medicaid and Medicare, must be paid with some of the taxes collected. Also, taxpayers hire accountants, auditors, and lawyers to help them ensure that they pay the correct amount of tax. These activities use skilled labor and capital resources that could otherwise be used to produce other goods and services that people value.

You can see that when all these costs are taken into account, transferring a dollar from a rich person does not give a dollar to a poor person. It is even possible that with high taxes, those with low incomes end up being worse off. Suppose, for example, that highly taxed entrepreneurs decide to work less hard and shut down some of their businesses. Low-income workers get fired and must seek other, perhaps even lower-paid work.

Because of the big tradeoff, those who say that fairness is equality propose a modified version of utilitarianism.

Make the Poorest as Well Off as Possible

A Harvard philosopher, John Rawls, proposed a modified version of utilitarianism in a classic book entitled *A Theory of Justice*, published in 1971. Rawls said that, taking all the costs of income transfers into account, the fair distribution of the economic pie is the one that makes the poorest person as well off as possible. The incomes of rich people should be taxed, and after paying the costs of administering the tax and transfer system, what is left should be transferred to the poor. But the taxes must not be so high that they make the economic pie shrink by so much that the poorest person ends up with a smaller piece. A bigger share of a smaller pie can be a smaller piece than a smaller share of a bigger pie. The goal is to make the piece enjoyed by the poorest person as big as possible. Most likely, this piece will not be an equal share.

The "fair results" ideas require a change in the results after the game is over. Some economists say that these changes are themselves unfair, and they propose a different way of thinking about fairness.

It's Not Fair If the *Rules* Aren't Fair

The idea that it's not fair if the rules aren't fair translates into *equality of opportunity*. But equality of opportunity to do what? Another Harvard philosopher, Robert Nozick, answered this question in a book entitled *Anarchy, State, and Utopia*, published in 1974.

Nozick argued that the rules must be fair and must respect two principles:

- The state must enforce laws that establish and protect private property.
- Private property may be transferred from one person to another only by voluntary exchange.

The first rule says that everything that is valuable must be owned by individuals and that the state must ensure that theft is prevented. The second rule says that the only legitimate way a person can acquire property is to buy it in exchange for something else that the person owns. If these rules—which Nozick said are the only fair rules—are followed, the result is fair. It doesn't matter how unequally the economic pie is shared, provided that it is baked by people each one of whom voluntarily provides services in exchange for the share of the pie offered in compensation.

These rules satisfy the symmetry principle. And if these rules are not followed, the symmetry principle is broken. You can see these facts by imagining a world in which the laws are not followed.

First, suppose that some resources or goods are not owned. They are common property. Then everyone is free to participate in a grab to use these resources or goods. The strongest will prevail. But when the strongest prevails, the strongest effectively *owns* the resources or goods in question and prevents others from enjoying them.

Second, suppose that we do not insist on voluntary exchange for transferring ownership of resources from one person to another. The alternative is *involuntary* transfer. In simple language, the alternative is theft.

Both of these situations violate the symmetry principle. Only the strong get to acquire what they want. The weak end up with only the resources and goods that the strong don't want.

In contrast, if the two rules of fairness are followed, everyone—strong and weak—is treated in a similar way. Everyone is free to use their resources and human skills to create things that are valued by themselves and others and to exchange the fruits of their efforts with each other. This is the only set of arrangements that obeys the symmetry principle.

If private property rights are enforced and if voluntary exchange takes place in a competitive market, then resources will be allocated efficiently if there are no external costs and external benefits, public goods, monopolies, price ceilings and price floors, taxes, subsidies, or quotas.

According to the Nozick rules, the resulting distribution of income and wealth will be fair. Let's study a concrete example to examine the claim that if resources are allocated efficiently, they are also allocated fairly.

A Price Hike in a Natural Disaster

An earthquake has broken the pipes that deliver drinking water to a city. The price of bottled water jumps from $1 to $8 a bottle in the 30 or so shops that have water for sale.

First, let's agree that the water is being used *efficiently*. There is a fixed amount of bottled water in the city, and given the quantity available, some people are willing to pay $8 to get a bottle. The water goes to the people who value it most highly. Marginal benefit equals marginal cost, and consumer surplus plus producer surplus is maximized.

So the water resources are being used efficiently. But are they being used fairly? Shouldn't people who can't afford to pay $8 a bottle get some of the available water for a lower price that they can afford? Isn't the fair solution for the shops to sell water for a lower price that people can afford? Or perhaps it might be fairer if the government bought the water and then made it available to people through a government store at a "reasonable" price. Let's think about these alternative solutions to the water problem of this city.

The first answer that jumps into your mind is that the water should somehow be made available at a more reasonable price. But is this the correct answer?

Shop Offers Water for $5 Suppose that Chip, a shop owner, offers water at $5 a bottle. Who will buy it? There are two types of buyers. Larry is an example of one type. He values water at $8—is willing to pay $8 a bottle. Recall that given the quantity of water available, the equilibrium price is $8 a bottle. If Larry buys the water, he consumes it. Larry ends up with a consumer surplus of $3 on the bottle, and Chip receives $3 *less* of producer surplus.

Mitch is an example of the second type of buyer. Mitch would not pay $8 for a bottle. In fact, he wouldn't even pay $5 to consume a bottle of water. But he buys a bottle for $5. Why? Because he plans to sell the water to someone who is willing to pay $8 to consume it. When Mitch buys the water, Chip again receives a producer surplus of $3 less than he would receive if he charged the going market price. Mitch now becomes a water dealer. He sells the water to Larry for the going price of $8 and earns a producer surplus of $3.

So by being public-spirited and offering water for less than the market price, Chip ends up $3 a bottle worse off and the people who buy from him end up $3 a bottle better off. Larry consumes the water in both situations because he values the water at $8 a bottle. But the distribution of consumer surplus and producer surplus is different in the two cases. When Chip offers the water for $5 a bottle, he ends up with a smaller producer surplus and either Larry gets a larger consumer surplus or Mitch gets a larger producer surplus.

So which is the fair arrangement: the one that favors Chip or the one that favors Larry or Mitch? The fair-rules view is that both arrangements are fair. Chip voluntarily sells the water for $5, so in effect, he is helping the community to cope with its water problem. It is fair that he should help. But the choice is his. He owns the water. It is not fair that he should be compelled to help.

Government Buys Water Now suppose instead that the government buys all the water. The going price is $8 a bottle, so that's what the government pays. Now the government offers the water for sale for $1 a bottle, its "normal" price.

The quantity of water supplied is exactly the same as before. But now, at $1 a bottle, the quantity demanded is much larger than the quantity supplied. There is a shortage of water.

Because there is a water shortage, the government must use some mechanism to ration the available quantity. We'll assume that the government allocates everyone a lottery ticket. But only 50 percent of the tickets are winners and entitle the holder to one bottle of water. Suppose that Mitch is a winner and Larry is a loser. So Mitch, who is willing to pay less than $5, gets a bottle for $1, and Larry, who is willing to pay $8 a bottle, misses out.

What does Mitch do? Does he drink his bottle? He does not. He sells it to Larry, who values the water at $8. And Mitch enjoys a $7 producer surplus from his temporary water trading business.

The main difference between the government scheme and Chip's private charitable contributions lies in the fact that to buy the water for $8 and sell it for $1, the government must tax someone $7 for each bottle sold. So whether this arrangement is fair depends on whether the taxes are fair.

Taxes are an involuntary transfer of private property, so, according to the fair-rules view, they are unfair. But most economists, and most people, think that there is such a thing as a fair tax. So it seems that the fair-rules view needs to be weakened a bit. Agreeing that there is such a thing as a fair tax is the easy part. Agreeing on what is a fair tax brings endless disagreement and debate.

CHECKPOINT 6.4

Study Guide pp. 93–95

Practice Online 6.4

4 Explain the main ideas about fairness and evaluate claims that competitive markets result in unfair outcomes.

Practice Problem 6.4

A winter storm cuts the power supply and isolates a small town in the mountains. The people rush to buy candles from the town store, which is the only source of candles. The store owner decides to ration the candles to one per family but keep the price of a candle unchanged.

a. Who gets to consume the candles?
b. Who receives the consumer surplus on candles?
c. Who receives the producer surplus on candles?
d. Is the outcome efficient?
e. Is the outcome fair according to the utilitarian principle?
f. Is the process fair according to the symmetry principle?
g. If the town government declares a state of emergency and gives every family $100 to cope with the crisis, does this produce a more efficient and fairer outcome?

Exercise 6.4

An earthquake destroys the homes of a quarter of a city's population. People who are lucky enough to own one of the remaining homes offer rooms for rent at the highest amount that people are willing to pay.

a. Who gets to occupy the available rooms?
b. Who receives the consumer surplus on rooms?
c. Who receives the producer surplus on rooms?
d. Is the outcome efficient?
e. Is this outcome fair or unfair?
f. By what principle of fairness is the outcome fair or unfair?

Solution to Practice Problem 6.4

a. The people who buy candles from the town store are not necessarily the people who consume the candles. A buyer from the town store can sell a candle and will do so if the price exceeds her or his marginal benefit. The people who value them most—who are willing to pay the most—will consume the candles.
b. Only the consumers—the people who are willing to pay the most for candles—receive the consumer surplus on candles.
c. The town store owner receives the same producer surplus as normal. People who sell the candles they buy from the store receive additional producer surplus.
d. The outcome is efficient.
e. The outcome is unfair according to the utilitarian principle because candles are shared unequally.
f. The process is fair according to the symmetry principle because only voluntary transactions occur.
g. Providing every family with $100 increases the equilibrium price of candles. But it doesn't change the quantity of candles available. And to pay the $100, the town government must raise taxes, which might be fair or unfair.

CHAPTER CHECKPOINT

Key Points

1 Distinguish between value and price and define consumer surplus.

- Marginal benefit is measured by the maximum price that consumers are willing to pay for another unit of a good or service.
- A demand curve is a marginal benefit curve.
- Value is what people are *willing to* pay; price is what people *must* pay.
- Consumer surplus equals marginal benefit minus price, summed over the quantity consumed.

2 Distinguish between cost and price and define producer surplus.

- Marginal cost is measured by the minimum price producers must be offered to increase production by one unit.
- A supply curve is a marginal cost curve.
- Opportunity cost is what producers pay; price is what producers receive.
- Producer surplus equals price minus marginal cost, summed over the quantity produced.

3 Explain the conditions in which markets are efficient and inefficient.

- In a competitive equilibrium, marginal benefit equals marginal cost and resource allocation is efficient.
- Effective price ceilings decrease the quantity produced to less than the efficient quantity and effective price floors increase the quantity produced to more than the efficient quantity.
- Taxes and quotas decrease the quantity produced to less than the efficient quantity, and subsidies increase the quantity produced to more than the efficient quantity.
- The market provides more than the efficient quantity of goods and services that have external costs and less than the efficient quantity of goods and services that have external benefits.
- The market provides less than the efficient quantity of public goods because of the free-rider problem.
- A monopoly produces less than the efficient quantity.
- Both underproduction and overproduction create a deadweight loss.

4 Explain the main ideas about fairness and evaluate claims that competitive markets result in unfair outcomes.

- Ideas about fairness divide into two groups: fair *results* and fair *rules*.
- Fair-results ideas require income transfers from the rich to the poor.
- Fair-rules ideas require property rights and voluntary exchange.

Key Terms

Exercises

TABLE 1

Price (dollars per sandwich)	Quantity demanded (sandwiches per hour)	Quantity supplied (sandwiches per hour)
0	400	0
1	350	50
2	300	100
3	250	150
4	200	200
5	150	250
6	100	300
7	50	350
8	0	400

1. Table 1 shows the demand and supply schedules for sandwiches. Use the table to answer the following questions:
   a. What is the efficient quantity of sandwiches?
   b. What is the consumer surplus if the efficient quantity of sandwiches is produced?
   c. What is the producer surplus if the efficient quantity of sandwiches is produced?
   d. If Sandwiches To Go, Inc. buys all the sandwich producers and cuts production to 100 sandwiches an hour, what is the deadweight loss that is created?
   e. If in part **d**, Sandwiches To Go, Inc. rations sandwiches to two per person, is this distribution of sandwiches fair? By what principle of fairness would the distribution be unfair?

TABLE 2

Price (dollars per bag)	Quantity demanded before flood (thousands of bags)	Quantity demanded during flood (thousands of bags)	Quantity supplied (thousands of bags)
0	40	70	0
1	35	65	5
2	30	60	10
3	25	55	15
4	20	50	20
5	15	45	25
6	10	40	30
7	5	35	35
8	0	30	40

2. Table 2 shows the demand and supply schedules for sandbags before and during a major flood. Use the table to answer the following questions:
   a. What happens to consumer surplus and producer surplus during the flood?
   b. Is the allocation of resources efficient (i) before the flood and (ii) during the flood?
   c. If, during the flood, the government rationed sandbags and gave all families an equal quantity of them, what would happen to the consumer surplus, producer surplus, quantity, and price of sandbags?
   d. Is the outcome described in part **c** more efficient than it would be if the government took no action?
   e. Is the outcome described in part **c** fairer than it would be if the government took no action?

3. In California, farmers pay a lower price for water than do city residents. If farmers were charged the same price as city residents pay,
   a. Explain how the price of agricultural produce, the quantity of produce grown, consumer surplus, and producer surplus would change.
   b. Would the use of water be more efficient? Why or why not?
   c. Would the use of water be fairer? Why or why not?

4. Students can visit many museums at a discount. Is this arrangement efficient? Is it fair? Explain.

TABLE 3

Price (dollars per haircut)	Quantity supplied: Dan (haircuts per day)	Quantity supplied: Zoe (haircuts per day)
0	0	0
5	0	0
10	2	0
15	4	40
20	6	60
25	8	80
30	10	100

5. Dan operates a one-person barbershop, and Zoe runs a large hairdressing salon. Table 3 shows the quantities of haircuts supplied by Dan and Zoe at various prices per haircut. Use the table to answer the following questions.
   a. If the price of a haircut is $15, who makes the larger producer surplus?
   b. If the price of a haircut is $10, who makes the larger producer surplus?
   c. Are both outcomes in parts **a** and **b** fair according to the utilitarian view of fairness? Explain why or why not.
   d. Are both outcomes in parts **a** and **b** fair according to John Rawls's view of fairness? Explain why or why not.
   e. Are both outcomes in parts **a** and **b** fair according to Robert Nozick's view of fairness? Explain why or why not.

6. The winner of the men's tennis singles at the U.S. Open is paid much more than the runner-up, but it takes two to have a singles final. Is this compensa-

tion arrangement efficient? Is it fair? Explain why it might illustrate the big tradeoff.

7. In tennis, men play the best of five sets and women play the best of three sets, but the winner of the men's tennis singles at the U.S. Open is paid the same as the winner of the women's singles. In contrast, in golf, men and women play the same number of holes and rounds, but the winners of men's golf tournaments are paid much more than the winners of women's golf tournaments. Are these compensation arrangements efficient? Are they fair? Explain.

8. Is it fair that Tiger Woods wins so many golf competitions? Would it be fair if the rule that after three wins in a season, a golfer was not permitted to compete for the rest of the season were adopted? Explain.

Critical Thinking

9. In the weeks after September 11, 2001, some people received envelopes containing deadly anthrax through the mail. The drug that is used to treat anthrax is called Cipro, which is produced by Bayer, a multinational drug company that holds the patent on this drug. The retail price of Cipro is about $4 a pill. But the U.S. government struck a deal with Bayer to obtain the drug for 95¢ a pill. And Bayer sells Cipro under a special deal with hospitals that treat poor people for 43¢ a pill.
   a. Although we don't know the marginal cost of producing Cipro, what do you suspect is the maximum probable marginal cost and why?
   b. Does the market for Cipro operate efficiently or inefficiently?
   c. If you think the market for Cipro is inefficient, is it the consumer, the producer, or both who bear the deadweight loss? If you think the Cipro market operates efficiently, how does it avoid deadweight loss?
   d. Is it fair that Cipro is sold to some buyers at a higher price than others pay?
   e. Taking everything that is relevant into account, do you think that Bayer is doing a good job and coping appropriately with balancing the goals of efficiency and equity—with facing the big tradeoff?

10. Poor countries that join the World Trade Organization (the WTO) must agree to prevent the illegal production of generic drugs that violate the patents of multinational drug companies and the illegal copying of music CDs, software, and textbooks that violate copyrights.
    a. Do you think that it is efficient or inefficient if people in poor countries create cheap copies of drugs, music, software, and textbooks? Explain using the concepts of marginal benefit, marginal cost, consumer surplus, producer surplus, and deadweight loss.
    b. Do you think that it is fair or unfair if people in poor countries create cheap copies of drugs, music, software, and textbooks? Which concept of fairness do you think is relevant for deciding this issue and why?
    c. Would it be efficient or inefficient, fair or unfair, to impose a large fine on a poor country that failed to prevent the illegal production of generic drugs or the illegal copying of music CDs, software, and textbooks? Explain using the concepts of marginal benefit, marginal cost, consumer surplus, producer surplus, and deadweight loss and explain the concept of fairness that you are using.

Practice Online

Web Exercises

Use the links on your Foundations Web site to work the following exercises.

11. Visit the California Farm Bureau Federation and read the information provided in the Ag Alert article.
    a. Is it efficient to buy asparagus from Mexico at $15 a crate when the effect is to shut down asparagus growers in California?
    b. Use a graph to show the change in consumer surplus that occurs when the price of asparagus falls from $45 to $15.
    c. What is the change in producer surplus that occurs when the price of asparagus falls from $45 to $15 a crate? Show on a graph the change for a California producer like Marc Marchini and for a Mexican producer.
    d. Suppose the government prohibited the importing of asparagus from Mexico. How would a ban affect the producer surplus of Californian asparagus growers? How would it affect consumer surplus?
    e. Do you think it is fair that cheap Mexican asparagus is giving Marc Marchini a hard time? What concept of fairness are you using and why?
    f. Do you think the big tradeoff applies to the California asparagus industry? Explain why or why not.

12. Visit Hershey Foods, Cadbury-Schweppes, Mars, Nestlé, and Hoover's sugar and confectionery page. In 2002, Hershey announced that it was for sale, and Cadbury-Schweppes and Nestlé expressed an interest in buying the firm. But a few weeks later (see the news report on CNN), Hershey announced that it was not for sale.
    a. Do you think it is efficient or inefficient for the number of competing producers of chocolate and candy to be large?
    b. Under what circumstances do you think it would be more efficient for Cadbury-Schweppes and Nestlé to operate Hershey? Use the concepts of marginal cost, marginal benefit, producer surplus, consumer surplus, and deadweight loss to answer this question.
    c. Would it be fair or unfair if Cadbury-Schweppes and Nestlé operated Hershey? Which concept of fairness is relevant to make your decision?

13. Read the article about wage negotiations at the huge Los Angeles–Long Beach docks. At most of the world's big docks, containers pass through quickly as electronic scanners keep track of their origin, content, and destination. At Long Beach, containers creep through the docks as clerks copy down numbers by hand and other clerks key the numbers into computer databases. Also, most of the world's docks operate 24 hours a day and 7 days a week. The Long Beach docks operate for only 8 hours a day.
    a. Do you think the Long Beach docks are efficient or inefficient?
    b. If Long Beach operated like one of the world's other big ports, would there be a gain in consumer surplus, producer surplus, neither, or both?
    c. Who do you think gains from the arrangements at Long Beach and why do you think those arrangements persist?
    d. Do you think the arrangements at Long Beach are fair? What is the concept of fairness that you think is relevant in this case and why?

Government Influences on Markets

CHAPTER 7

CHAPTER CHECKLIST

When you have completed your study of this chapter, you will be able to

1. **Explain the effects of taxes on goods and labor and determine who pays the taxes.**
2. **Explain how a rent ceiling creates a housing shortage, inefficiency, and unfairness.**
3. **Explain how the minimum wage creates unemployment, inefficiency, and unfairness.**

Governments influence markets when they collect the tax revenues that finance public expenditures on such items as national defense, education, welfare, police, and fire protection. Governments also influence markets when they control prices in an attempt to redistribute income toward those who are at the lower end of the economic ladder.

Can Congress target taxes at businesses so that workers pay the least tax? And can governments help low-income people by holding down their cost of housing or by boosting their wages and employment benefits?

This chapter studies these questions. It expands your study of demand, supply, and market equilibrium in Chapter 4, elasticity in Chapter 5, and efficiency and fairness in Chapter 6.

First, we look at the effects of taxes. We then look at rent ceilings. And finally, we study minimum wage laws.

7.1 TAXES

Almost everything you buy, from a new futon frame to a plane ticket home to a late-night order of chow mein, is taxed. But who really pays the tax? Because the sales tax is added to the price of a good or service when it is sold, isn't it obvious that *you* pay the tax? Isn't the price higher than it otherwise would be by an amount equal to the tax? It can be, but usually it isn't. And it is even possible that you actually pay none of the tax!

When you work, you pay income tax on your wage income. And you and your employer each pay a half of a tax called FICA (Federal Insurance Contribution Act). Who really pays these taxes? Again, isn't it obvious that you pay the income tax and you and your employer split the FICA tax equally? The answer again is no!

To see how we can make sense of these apparently absurd statements, we first define the concept of *tax incidence*.

Tax Incidence

Tax incidence
The division of the burden of a tax between the buyer and the seller.

Tax incidence is the division of the burden of a tax between the buyer and the seller. When the government imposes a tax on the sale of a good, the price of the good might rise by the full amount of the tax, by some lesser amount, or not at all. If the price rises by the full amount of the tax, then the burden of the tax falls entirely on the buyer. If the price rises by a lesser amount than the tax, then the burden of the tax falls partly on the buyer and partly on the seller. And if the price doesn't change, then the burden of the tax falls entirely on the seller.

To see the determinants of tax incidence, suppose the government puts a $10 tax on CD players. What are the effects of this tax on the price and quantity of CD players? To answer this question, we need to work out what happens to demand and supply in the market for CD players.

Figure 7.1 shows this market. With no tax on CD players, the equilibrium price of a CD player is $100 and 5,000 players are bought and sold each week.

When a good is taxed, it has two prices: a price that excludes the tax and a price that includes the tax. Buyers respond only to the price that includes the tax, because that is the price they pay. Sellers respond only to the price that excludes the tax, because that is the price they receive. The tax is like a wedge between these two prices.

Let's make the price on the vertical axis of Figure 7.1 the price paid by the buyer—the price that *includes* the tax. When a tax is imposed and the price changes, there is a change in the quantity demanded but no change in demand. That is, there is a movement along the demand curve and no shift of the demand curve.

But the supply changes and the supply curve shifts. The tax is like an increase in the suppliers' cost, so supply decreases and the supply curve shifts leftward to the curve labeled *S* + *tax*. To determine the position of this new supply curve, we add the tax to the minimum price that sellers are willing to accept for each quantity. For example, with no tax, sellers are willing to offer 5,000 CD players a week for $100 each. So with a $10 tax, sellers would be willing to offer 5,000 CD players a week for $110 each—a price that includes the tax. The *S* + *tax* curve describes the terms on which sellers are willing to offer CD players for sale now that there is a $10 tax.

FIGURE 7.1
A Tax on CD Players

Practice Online

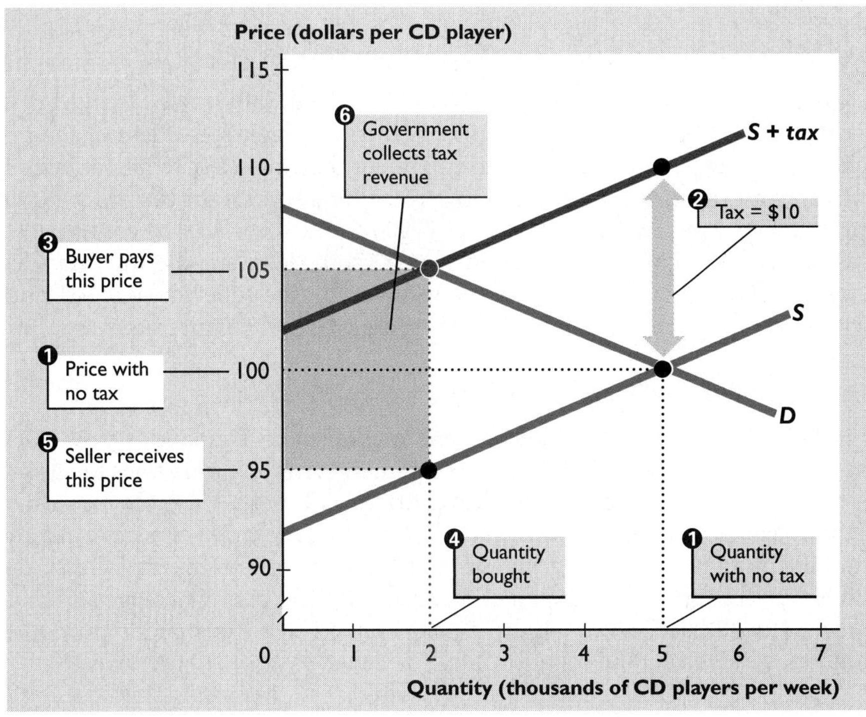

1. With no tax, the price of a CD player is $100 and 5,000 CD players a week are bought.
2. A $10 tax on CD players shifts the supply curve to S + *tax*.
3. The price rises to $105—an increase of $5 a CD player.
4. The quantity decreases to 2,000 CD players a week.
5. Sellers receive $95—a decrease of $5 a CD player.
6. The government collects tax revenue of $20,000 a week—the purple rectangle.

The burden of the tax is split equally between the buyer and the seller—each pays $5 per CD player.

Equilibrium occurs where the new supply curve intersects the demand curve—at a price of $105 and a quantity of 2,000 CD players a week. The $10 tax increases the price paid by the buyer by $5—from $100 to $105 a player. And it decreases the price received by the seller by $5—from $100 to $95 a player. The buyer and the seller share the $10 tax equally.

This tax brings in tax revenue to the government equal to the tax per CD player ($10) multiplied by the number of CD players sold (2,000 a week), which is $20,000 a week. The purple rectangle in Figure 7.1 illustrates the tax revenue.

Tax Incidence and Elasticities of Demand and Supply

In the example that you've just studied, the buyer and the seller split the tax equally. This equal sharing of the tax is a special case and does not usually occur. But some sharing of the tax between the buyer and seller is usual. Also, there are other special cases in which either the buyer or the seller pays the entire tax.

The division of the burden of the tax between the buyer and the seller depends on the elasticities of demand and supply:

- For a given elasticity of supply, the buyer pays a larger share of the tax the more inelastic is the demand for the good.
- For a given elasticity of demand, the seller pays a larger share of the tax the more inelastic is the supply of the good.

Tax Incidence and Elasticity of Demand

To see how the division of a tax between the buyer and the seller depends on the elasticity of demand, we'll look at two extreme cases.

Perfectly Inelastic Demand: Buyer Pays Entire Tax

Figure 7.2(a) shows the market for insulin, a vital daily medication of diabetics. Demand is perfectly inelastic at 100,000 doses a week regardless of the price, as shown by the vertical demand curve. (Demand is not likely to be perfectly inelastic at every price, but over some low price range, it might be.) With no tax, the price is $2 a dose and the quantity is 100,000 doses a week. If the government taxes insulin at 20¢ a dose, the price rises to $2.20 a dose but the quantity does not change. The 20¢ tax leaves the price received by the seller unchanged but raises the price paid by the buyer by 20¢. The buyer pays the entire tax.

Perfectly Elastic Demand: Seller Pays Entire Tax

Figure 7.2(b) shows the market for pink marker pens. Demand is perfectly elastic at $1 a pen, as shown by the horizontal demand curve. If pink pens are less expensive than other pens, everyone uses pink. If pink pens are more expensive than other pens, no one uses a pink pen. With no tax, the price of a pink marker is $1 and the quantity is 4,000 pens a week. If the government taxes pink marker pens at 10¢ a pen, the price remains at $1 a pen and the quantity decreases to 1,000 a week. The 10¢ tax leaves the price paid by the buyer unchanged but lowers the amount received by the seller by 10¢. The seller pays the entire tax.

Tax Incidence and Elasticity of Supply

To see how the division of a tax between the buyer and the seller depends on the elasticity of supply, we'll again look at two extreme cases.

Perfectly Inelastic Supply: Seller Pays Entire Tax

Figure 7.2(c) shows the market for water from a mineral spring that flows at a constant rate that can't be controlled. Supply is perfectly inelastic at 100,000 bottles a week, as shown by the vertical supply curve. With no tax, the price is 50¢ a bottle and the 100,000 bottles that flow from the spring are bought. If the government taxes spring water at 5¢ a bottle, the supply curve does not change. Spring owners still produce 100,000 bottles a week regardless of the price they receive. But buyers are willing to buy the 100,000 bottles only if the price is 50¢ a bottle. So the price remains at 50¢ a bottle. The tax lowers the price received by the seller by 5¢ a bottle. The seller pays the entire tax.

Perfectly Elastic Supply: Buyer Pays Entire Tax

Figure 7.2(d) shows the market for sand from which computer-chip makers extract silicon. Supply of this sand is perfectly elastic at a price of 10¢ a pound as shown by the horizontal supply curve. With no tax, the price is 10¢ a pound and 5,000 pounds a week are bought. If the government taxes sand at 1¢ a pound, the price rises to 11¢ a pound and the quantity decreases to 3,000 pounds a week. The tax increases the price paid by the buyer by 1¢ a pound. The buyer pays the entire tax.

FIGURE 7.2

Tax Incidence and the Elasticities of Demand and Supply

Practice Online

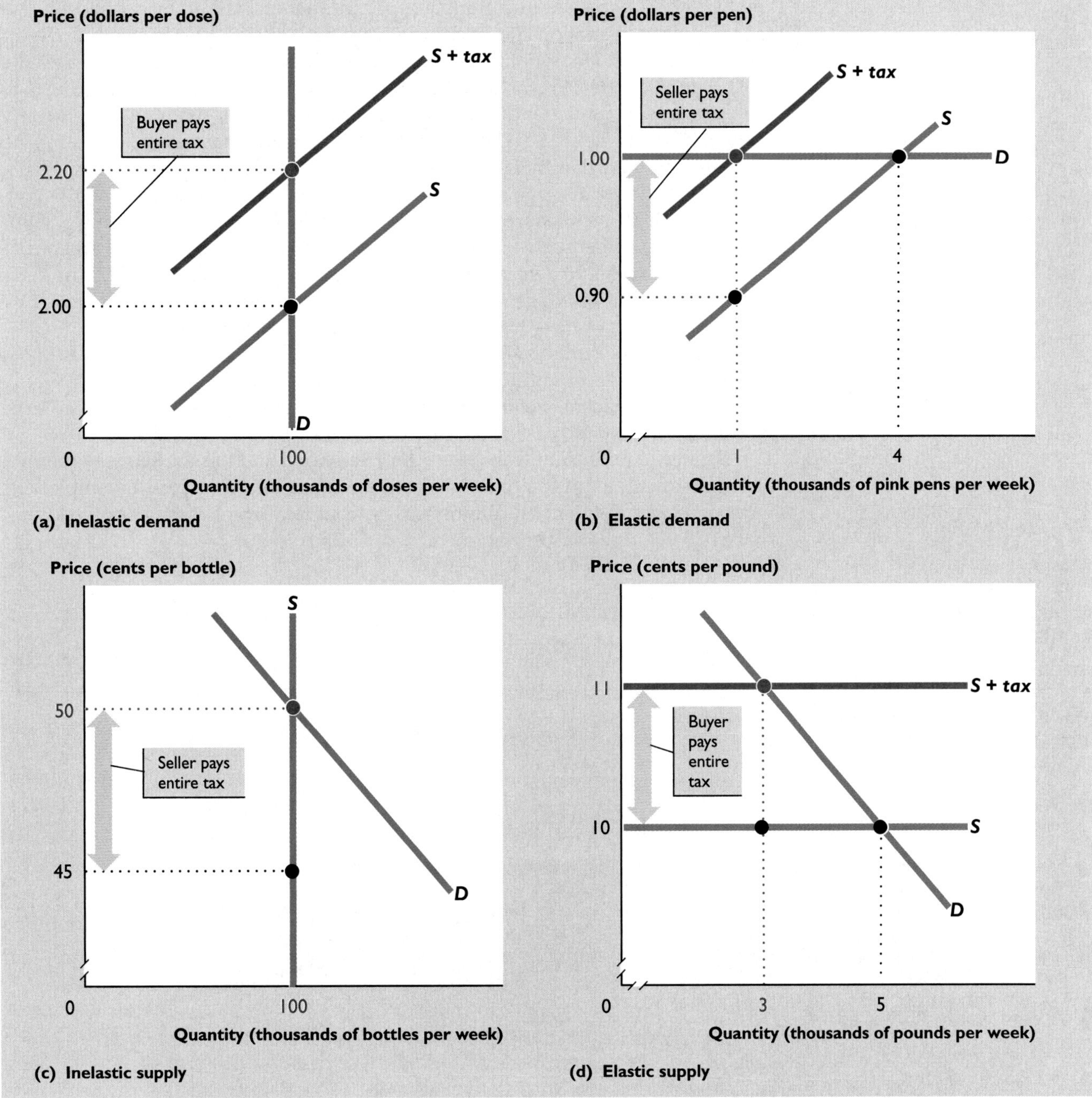

In part (a), the demand for insulin is perfectly inelastic. A tax of 20¢ a dose raises the price by 20¢, and the buyer pays all the tax.

In part (b), the demand for pink marker pens is perfectly elastic. A tax of 10¢ a pen lowers the price received by the seller by 10¢, and the seller pays all the tax.

In part (c), the supply of mineral spring water is perfectly inelastic. A tax of 5¢ a bottle lowers the price received by the seller by 5¢, and the seller pays all the tax.

In part (d), the supply of sand is perfectly elastic. A tax of 1¢ a pound increases the price by 1¢ a pound, and the buyer pays all the tax.

Taxes on Income and Employment

The principles that you've just learned apply to all types of taxes. Let's see how they apply to the income tax and the payroll tax.

Figure 7.3 shows demand and supply in a labor market. Firms decide how much labor to demand. The lower the wage rate, the greater is the quantity of labor demanded. Households decide how much labor to supply. The higher the wage rate, the greater is the quantity of labor supplied. The wage rate adjusts to make the quantity of labor demanded equal to the quantity supplied. Without any taxes, the wage rate is $6 an hour and 4,000 people are employed.

Now suppose that the government introduces a 20 percent income tax. That is, for every dollar of wage income earned, people must pay 20 cents to the government. If 4,000 people were willing to work for $6 an hour, this quantity of labor will now be supplied only if people can earn an after-tax income of $6 an hour.

If the tax rate is 20 percent, the pre-tax wage rate will need to be $7.50 an hour to deliver an after-tax wage rate of $6 an hour. (Check that if the pre-tax wage rate is $7.50 and the tax rate is 20 percent, the amount of tax paid out of $7.50 is $1.50—20 percent or one fifth of $7.50—so the wage rate after tax is $7.50 minus $1.50, which equals $6.)

With a 20 percent income tax, the supply of labor curve shifts to the curve labeled *S* + *tax*—a decrease in supply.

The new equilibrium wage rate is $6.25 an hour, and the equilibrium quantity of employment is 3,000. With a wage rate of $6.25 an hour paid by employers, workers *receive* that amount minus a 20 percent tax, which is $5 an hour. (Check that $1.25 equals 20 percent or one fifth of $6.25.)

FIGURE 7.3
The Income Tax

Practice Online

With no income tax, the wage rate is $6.00 an hour and 4,000 people are employed.

1. An income tax of 20 percent shifts the supply curve to *S* + *tax*.
2. The wage rate paid by employers rises to $6.25 an hour—an increase of 25 cents an hour.
3. The number of people employed decreases to 3,000.
4. Workers receive $5.00 an hour—a decrease of $1 an hour.
5. The government collects tax revenue shown by the purple rectangle.

Workers pay most of the tax because the supply of labor is more inelastic than the demand for labor.

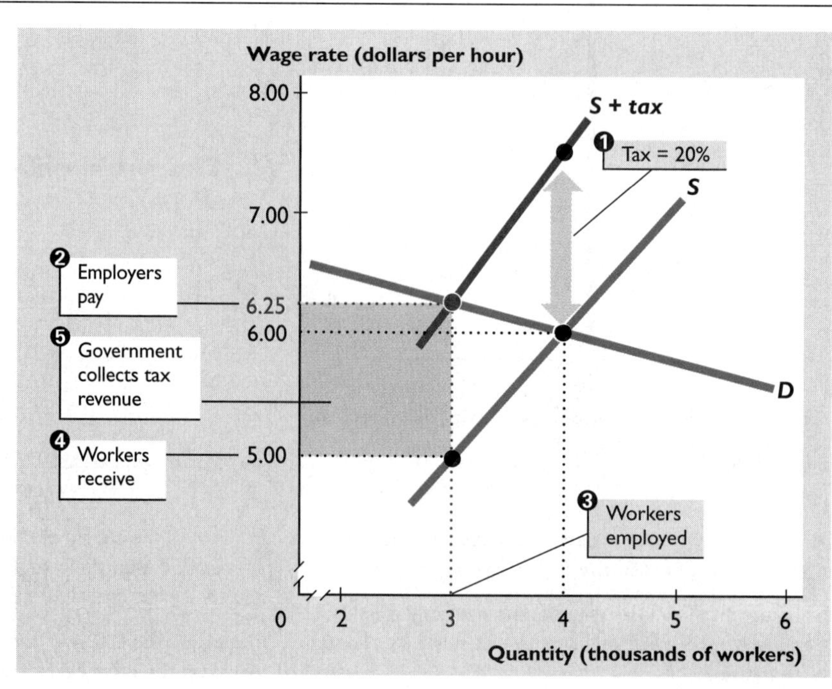

So with the income tax, the tax paid is $1.25 an hour. Of this amount, the employer pays 25 cents and the worker pays $1. This division of the burden arises because the demand for labor is more elastic than the supply of labor.

Suppose that people are annoyed because workers pay $1 and firms pay only 25 cents of the income tax. And suppose that Congress decides to make the employers pay more. Congress abolishes the income tax and replaces it with a payroll tax. A **payroll tax** is a tax on employers based on the wages they pay their workers.

Payroll tax
A tax on employers based on the wages they pay their workers.

To make it easy to compare the payroll tax and the income tax, suppose that the new payroll tax is set at $1.25 an hour, which is equivalent to the 20 percent income tax paid in previous example.

Figure 7.4 shows the effects of this new tax. As before, with no taxes, the equilibrium wage rate is $6 an hour and 4,000 people are employed. With a $1.25 an hour payroll tax, firms are no longer willing to hire 4,000 people at a $6 an hour wage rate. Because firms must pay $1.25 an hour to the government, they will hire 4,000 people at a wage rate of $6 minus $1.25, which is $4.75 an hour. The demand for labor decreases, and the demand for labor curve shifts to *D* – *tax*. The equilibrium wage rate falls to $5 an hour, and 3,000 people are employed.

The total cost of labor to the firm is $6.25 an hour, the $5 an hour wage rate plus the $1.25 an hour tax. The purple rectangle shows the tax paid.

Notice that the payroll tax delivers the same outcome as the income tax. Workers receive the same take-home wage, and firms pay the same total wage. Congress has tried to get employers to pay the tax that workers were previously paying, but the law has failed. When the laws of Congress come into conflict with the laws of economics, economics wins. This fact is not surprising. No one thinks that Congress can repeal the law of gravity. And Congress can't repeal the laws of supply and demand either.

FIGURE 7.4
A Payroll Tax

Practice Online

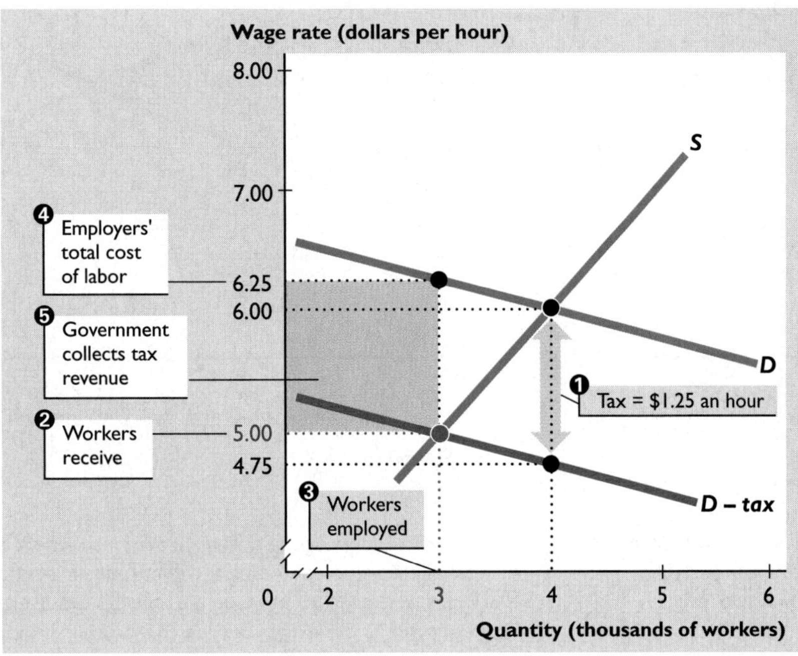

With no taxes, the wage rate is $6.00 an hour and 4,000 people are employed.

1. A payroll tax of $1.25 an hour shifts the demand curve to *D – tax*.
2. The wage rate falls to $5 an hour—a decrease of $1.00 an hour.
3. The number of workers employed decreases to 3,000.
4. Employers' total cost of labor rises to $6.25 an hour—the $5.00 wage rate plus the $1.25 payroll tax.
5. The government collects tax revenue shown by the purple rectangle.

Taxes and Efficiency

You've seen that a tax places a wedge between the price paid by buyers and the price received by sellers. The price paid by buyers equals marginal benefit, and the price received by sellers equals marginal cost. Because a tax places a wedge between the buyers' price and the sellers' price, it also puts a wedge between marginal benefit and marginal cost. The equilibrium quantity is less than the efficient quantity and a deadweight loss arises.

Figure 7.5 shows the inefficiency of taxes. In part (a), with no tax, marginal benefit equals marginal cost and the market is efficient. In part (b), with a tax, marginal benefit exceeds marginal cost. Consumer surplus and producer surplus shrink. Part of each surplus goes to the government as tax revenue—the purple area—and part of each surplus becomes a deadweight loss—the gray area.

Because a tax creates a deadweight loss, the burden of the tax exceeds the tax revenue. To remind us of this fact, we call the deadweight loss that arises from a tax the **excess burden** of the tax. But because the government uses the tax revenue to provide goods and services that people value, only the excess burden is the cost of the tax. And even this excess burden might be worth bearing to obtain the benefits of government-provided services. We'll examine this issue further when we study public goods and the tax system in Chapter 9.

Excess burden
The deadweight loss from a tax—the amount by which the burden of a tax exceeds the tax revenue received by the government.

FIGURE 7.5
Taxes and Efficiency

Practice Online

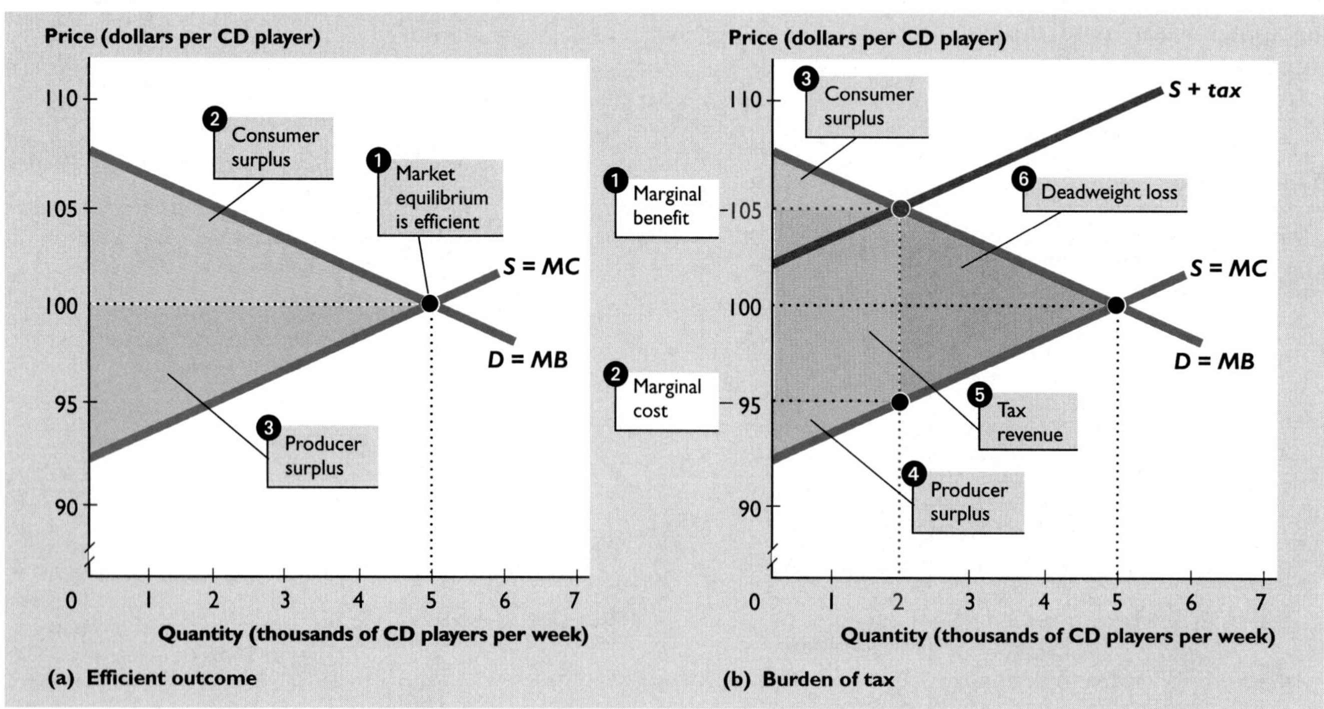

❶ The market is efficient with marginal benefit equal to marginal cost. The sum of ❷ consumer surplus (green area) and ❸ producer surplus (blue area) is at its maximum possible level.

A $10 tax drives a wedge between ❶ marginal benefit and ❷ marginal cost. ❸ Consumer surplus and ❹ producer surplus shrink by the amount of the ❺ tax revenue plus the ❻ deadweight loss. The deadweight loss is the excess burden of the tax.

CHECKPOINT 7.1

1 Explain the effects of taxes on goods and labor and determine who pays the taxes.

Study Guide pp. 102–107

Practice Online 7.1

Practice Problems 7.1

1. Figure 1 shows the market for golf balls. If the government imposes a sales tax on golf balls at 60 cents a ball:
   a. What is the increase in the price that buyers pay for golf balls?
   b. What is the decrease in the price that sellers receive?
   c. What is the decrease in the quantity of golf balls?
   d. What is the tax revenue from golf ball sales?
   e. Which is the more inelastic: the demand for golf balls or the supply of golf balls? How can you tell?
   f. What is the excess burden of the sales tax on golf balls?
2. The supply of labor in Hawaii is elastic, and the demand for labor is inelastic.
   a. Does the employer or the worker pay more of the tax on labor income?
   b. If a payroll tax replaces the income tax in (a), does the employer or the worker pay more of the tax?

FIGURE 1

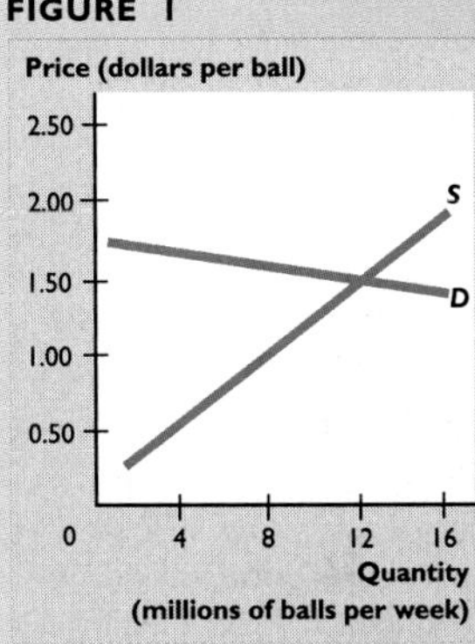

Exercises 7.1

1. With the growth in telephone calls in recent years, the government decides to tax calls at 20 cents each. If the supply of telephone calls is perfectly elastic and the demand for telephone calls is elastic:
   a. How much of the tax would the buyer pay on a call?
   b. Would the tax reduce the number of calls?
   c. Would the market for telephone calls be efficient?
   d. What is the excess burden of the tax?
2. Under what circumstances would the buyer pay all of a sales tax?
3. Under what circumstances would the employer pay all of a payroll tax? In this case, would the labor market be efficient?

Solutions to Practice Problems 7.1

Figure 2 illustrates the solutions to Practice Problem 1.

1a. When golf balls are taxed at 60 cents each, the price rises from \$1.50 to \$1.60.
1b. The price that sellers receive falls from \$1.50 to \$1.00.
1c. The quantity of golf balls decreases from 12 million to 8 million a week.
1d. The tax revenue from golf ball sales is \$0.60 multiplied by 8 million, which equals \$4.8 million a week.
1e. Supply is the more inelastic because the seller pays more of the tax.
1f. The excess burden of the sales tax on golf balls is \$1.2 million. Excess burden equals the deadweight loss, which is (\$4 million balls × 60 cents) ÷ 2 (the gray triangle in Figure 2).
2a. The employer pays more of the income tax.
2b. It makes no difference.

FIGURE 2

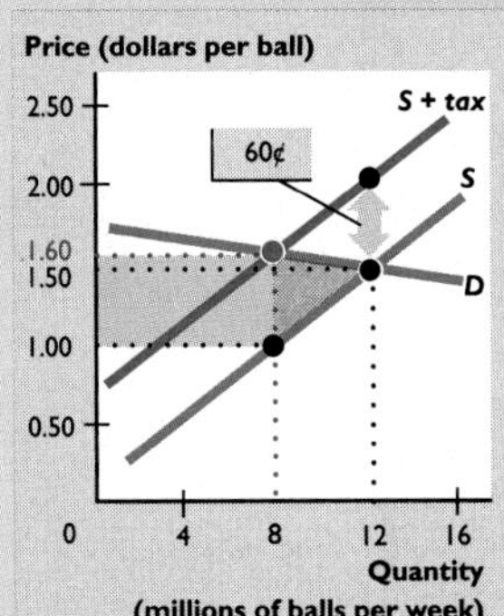

7.2 PRICE CEILINGS

People with low incomes would be able to buy more goods and services if prices were lower. One price that looms large in everyone's budget is that of housing. The price of housing is the rent that people pay for a house or apartment. This rent is determined by demand and supply in the housing market.

Figure 7.6 shows the apartment rental market in Biloxi, Mississippi. The rent is $550 a month, and 4,000 apartments are rented.

A Rent Ceiling

Rent ceiling
A government regulation that makes it illegal to charge more than a specified rent for housing.

Price ceiling
The highest price at which it is legal to trade a particular good, service, or factor of production. A rent ceiling is an example of a price ceiling.

Biloxi apartment rents have increased by $100 a month in just two years. Suppose that concerned citizens ask the mayor to impose a **rent ceiling**—a government regulation that makes it illegal to charge more than a specified rent for housing. A rent ceiling is an example of a **price ceiling**, which is the highest price at which it is legal to trade a particular good, service, or factor of production. How would a rent ceiling affect the Biloxi housing market?

The effect of a rent ceiling depends on whether it is imposed at a level above or below the equilibrium rent. In Figure 7.6, the equilibrium rent is $550 a month. If Biloxi introduced a rent ceiling above $550 a month, nothing would change. The reason is that people are already paying $550 a month, and because this rent is below the rent ceiling, the rent paid doesn't change.

But a rent ceiling that is set *below* the equilibrium rent has powerful effects on the market. The reason is that it attempts to prevent the rent from rising high enough to regulate the quantities demanded and supplied. The law and the market are in conflict, and one (or both) of them must yield.

FIGURE 7.6
A Housing Market

Practice Online

The demand for and supply of housing determine the equilibrium rent of $550 a month and the equilibrium quantity of 4,000 units of housing.

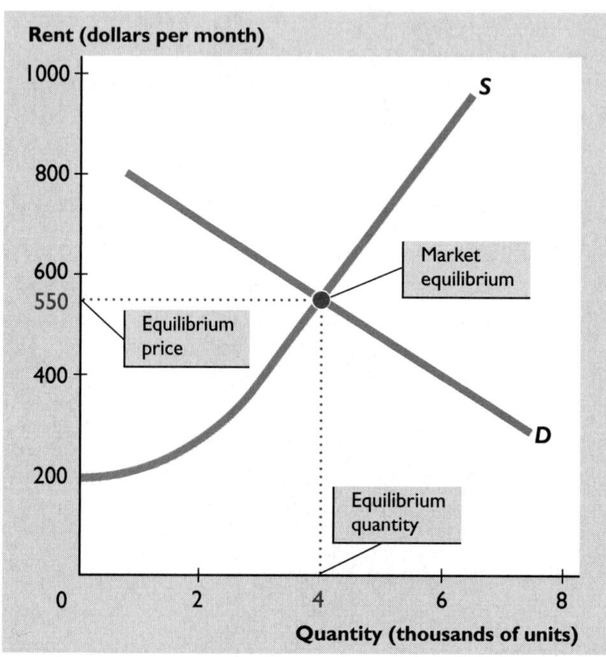

Figure 7.7 shows one effect of a rent ceiling that is set below the equilibrium rent. The rent ceiling is $400 a month. We've shaded the area *above* the rent ceiling because a rent in this region is illegal. At a rent of $400 a month, the quantity of housing supplied is 3,000 units and the quantity demanded is 6,000 units. So there is a shortage of 3,000 units of housing.

The first effect, then, of a rent ceiling is a housing shortage. People are seeking a larger amount of housing than builders and the owners of existing buildings have an incentive to make available.

But the story does not end here. Somehow the 3,000 units of housing that owners are willing to make available must be allocated among people who are seeking 6,000 units. How is this allocation achieved? When a rent ceiling creates a housing shortage, two developments occur:

- A black market
- Increased search activity

A Black Market

A **black market** is an illegal market that operates alongside a government-regulated market. A rent ceiling sometimes creates a black market in housing as frustrated renters and landlords try to find ways of raising the rent above the legally imposed ceiling. Landlords want higher rents because they know that renters are willing to pay more for the existing quantity of housing. Renters are willing to pay more to jump to the head of the queue.

Black market
An illegal market that operates alongside a government-regulated market.

Because raising the rent is illegal, landlords and renters use creative tricks for getting around the law. One of these tricks is for a new tenant to pay a high price

FIGURE 7.7
A Rent Ceiling Creates a Shortage

Practice Online

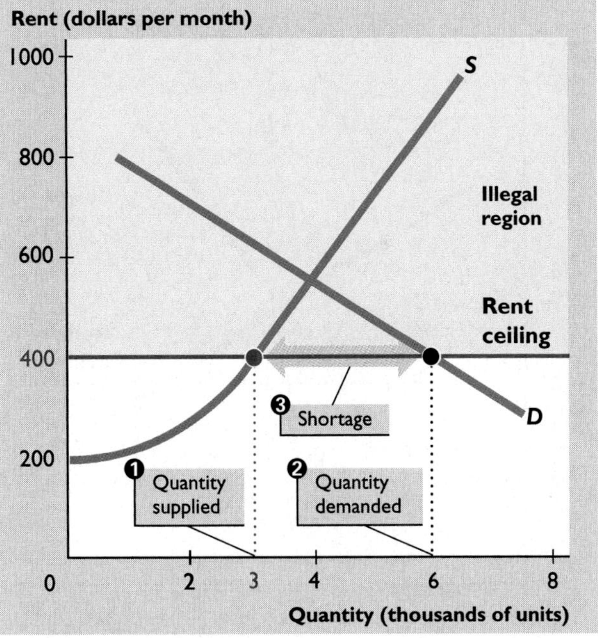

A rent ceiling is imposed below the equilibrium rent. In this example, the rent ceiling is $400 a month.

❶ The quantity of housing supplied decreases to 3,000 units.

❷ The quantity of housing demanded increases to 6,000 units.

❸ A shortage of 3,000 units arises.

for worthless fittings—perhaps paying $2,000 for threadbare drapes. Another is for the tenant to pay a high price for new locks and keys—called "key money."

Figure 7.8 shows how high the black market rent might go in Biloxi. With strict enforcement of the rent ceiling, the quantity of housing available is 3,000 units. But at this quantity, renters are willing to offer as much as $625 a month—the amount determined on the demand curve.

So a small number of landlords illegally offer housing for rents up to $625 a month. The black market rent might be at any level between the rent ceiling of $400 and the maximum that a renter is willing to pay of $625.

Increased Search Activity

Search activity
The time spent looking for someone with whom to do business.

The time spent looking for someone with whom to do business is called **search activity**. We spend some time in search activity almost every time we buy something. You want the latest hot CD, and you know 4 stores that stock it. But which store has the best deal? You need to spend a few minutes on the telephone finding out. In some markets, we spend a lot of time searching. An example is the used car market. People spend a lot of time checking out alternative dealers and cars.

But when a price ceiling creates a shortage of housing, search activity *increases*. In a rent-controlled housing market, frustrated would-be renters scan the newspapers, not only for housing ads but also for death notices! Any information about newly available housing is useful. And they race to be first on the scene when news of a possible apartment breaks.

The *opportunity cost* of a good is equal to its price *plus* the value of the search time spent finding the good. So the opportunity cost of housing is equal to the rent plus the value of the search time spent looking for an apartment. Search activity is costly. It uses time and other resources, such as telephones, automobiles, and

FIGURE 7.8
A Rent Ceiling Creates a Black Market and Housing Search

Practice Online

With a rent ceiling of $400 a month,

1. 3,000 units of housing are available.
2. Someone is willing to pay $625 a month for the 3,000th unit of housing.
3. Black market rents might be as high as $625 a month and resources get used up in costly search activity.

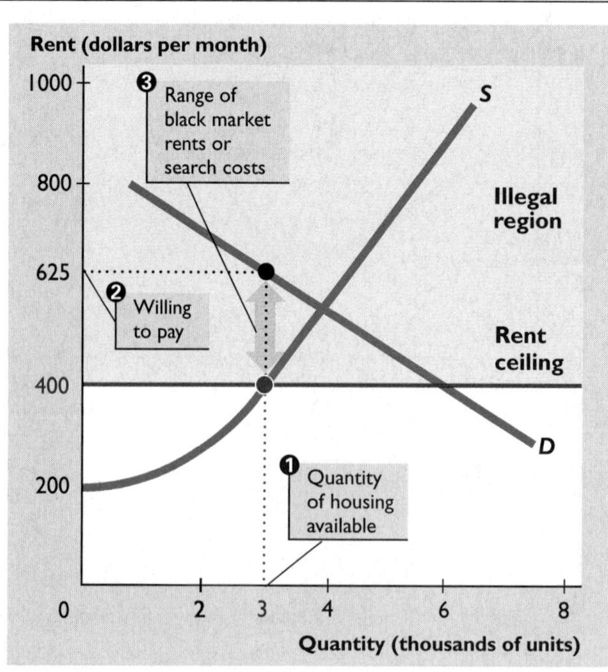

gasoline that could have been used in other productive ways. In Figure 7.8, to find accommodation at $400 a month, someone who is willing to pay a rent of $625 a month would be willing to spend on search an amount that is equivalent to adding $225 a month to the rent. For a one-year lease, this amount is enormous.

A rent ceiling controls the rent portion of the cost of housing, but it does not control the search cost. So when the search cost is added to the rent, some people end up paying a higher opportunity cost for housing than they would if there were no rent ceiling.

Eye on the Past

An Earthquake and a Rent Ceiling: A Tale of Two Eras in One City

Let's transport ourselves to San Francisco in April 1906, as the city is suffering from a massive earthquake and

fire. You can sense the enormity of San Francisco's problems from a headline in the *New York Times* on April 19, 1906 describing the first days of the crisis:

Over 500 Dead, $200,000,000 Lost in San Francisco Earthquake: Nearly Half the City Is in Ruins and 50,000 Are Homeless

The commander of federal troops in charge of the emergency described the magnitude of the problem:

> Not a hotel of note or importance was left standing. The great apartment houses had vanished ... two-hundred-and-twenty-five thousand people were ... homeless.[1]

In a single day, more than half the people in a city of 400,000 had lost their homes. Temporary shelters and camps alleviated some of the problem, but the apartment buildings and houses left standing had to accommodate 40 percent more people than they had before the earthquake.

The *San Francisco Chronicle* was not published for more than a month after the earthquake. When it reappeared on May 24, 1906, the city's housing shortage—what would seem to be a major news item that would still be of grave importance—was not even mentioned. Milton Friedman and George Stigler describe the situation:

> *There is not a single mention of a housing shortage*! The classified advertisements listed sixty-four offers of flats and houses for rent, and nineteen of houses for sale, against five advertisements of flats or houses wanted. Then and thereafter a considerable number of all types of accommodation ... were offered for rent.[2]

How did San Francisco cope with such a devastating decrease in the supply of housing? The answer is that a free market brought a rise in the rent and an increase in the intensity of use of the buildings that remained. People rented out rooms that they had previously used themselves. The high rents were an incentive for owners to rebuild as quickly as possible.

At the end of World War II (in 1945), the population of San Francisco grew by 30 percent. At the same time, a large-scale building program increased the number of houses and apartments by 20 percent. So each dwelling unit had to accommodate 10 percent more people. San Francisco had a housing "problem" about a quarter of the magnitude of that following the 1906 earthquake. Yet in 1946, the city's housing shortage was a huge political problem. Newspaper advertisements seeking apartments outnumbered those offering apartments by more than seven to one. Why? San Francisco had rent ceilings in 1946. It had a free housing market in 1906.

[1] Milton Friedman and George J. Stigler, "Roofs or Ceilings? The Current Housing Problem," in *Popular Essays on Current Problems*, Vol. 1, No. 2 (New York: Foundation for Economic Education, 1946), 3–159.

[2] Friedman and Stigler, p. 3.

Are Rent Ceilings Efficient?

A housing market with no rent ceiling determines the rent at which the quantity demanded equals the quantity supplied. In this situation, scarce housing resources are allocated efficiently because the marginal cost of housing equals the marginal benefit. Figure 7.9(a) shows this efficient outcome in the Biloxi apartment rental market. In this efficient market, the sum of *consumer surplus* (the green area) and *producer surplus* (the blue area) is maximized at the equilibrium rent and quantity of housing (see Chapter 6, pp. 150–151).

Figure 7.9(b) shows that with a rent ceiling, the outcome is inefficient. Marginal benefit exceeds marginal cost. Producer surplus and consumer surplus shrink, and a deadweight loss (the gray area) arises. This loss is borne by the people who can't find housing and by landlords who can't offer housing at the lower rent ceiling.

But the total loss exceeds the deadweight loss. Resources get used in costly search activity and in evading the law in the black market. The value of these resources might be as large as the red rectangle. There is yet a further loss: the cost of enforcing the rent ceiling law. This loss, which is borne by taxpayers, is not visible in the figure.

FIGURE 7.9
The Inefficiency of a Rent Ceiling

Practice Online

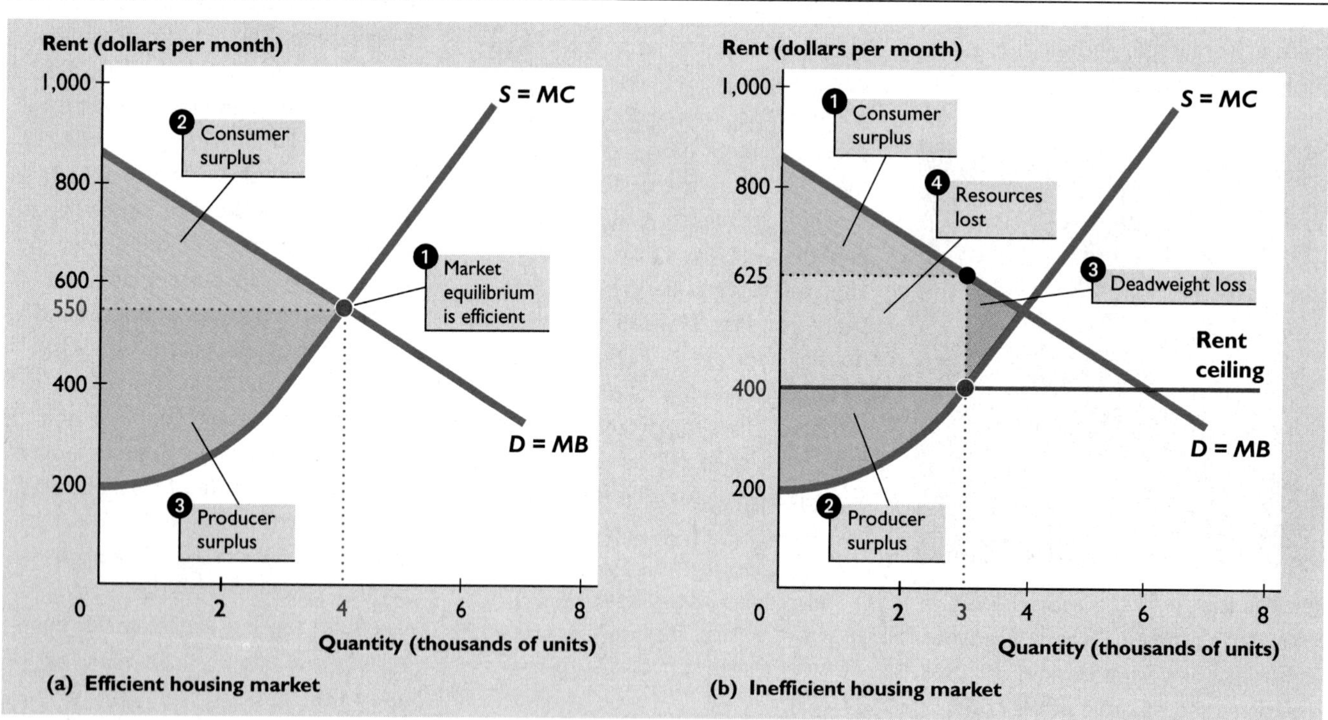

❶ The market equilibrium is efficient with marginal benefit equal to marginal cost. The sum of ❷ consumer surplus (green area) and ❸ producer surplus (blue area) is maximized.

A rent ceiling is inefficient. ❶ Consumer surplus and ❷ producer surplus shrink, a ❸ deadweight loss arises, and ❹ resources are lost in search activity and evading the rent ceiling law.

While a rent ceiling causes inefficiency, not everyone loses. Those people who live in apartments at the rent ceiling get an increase in consumer surplus. And landlords who charge a black market rent get an increase in producer surplus.

The costs of a rent ceiling that we've just considered are only the initial costs. With the rent below the market rent, landlords have no incentive to maintain their buildings in a good state of repair. So over time, the quality and quantity of housing supplied *decrease* and the loss arising from a rent ceiling increases.

The size of the loss from a rent ceiling depends on the elasticities of supply and demand. If supply is inelastic, a rent ceiling brings a small decrease in the quantity of housing supplied. And if demand is inelastic, a rent ceiling brings a small increase in the quantity of housing demanded. So the more inelastic the supply or the demand, the smaller is the shortage of housing and the smaller is the deadweight loss.

Are Rent Ceilings Fair?

We've seen that rent ceilings prevent scarce resources from being allocated efficiently—resources do not flow to their highest-valued use. But don't they ensure that scarce housing resources are allocated more fairly?

You learned in Chapter 6 (pp. 157–161) that fairness is a complex idea about which there are two broad views: fair *results* versus fair *rules*. Rent controls violate the fair rules view of fairness because they block voluntary exchange. But do they deliver a fair result? Do rent ceilings ensure that scarce housing goes to the poor people whose need is greatest?

Blocking rent adjustments that bring the quantity of housing demanded into equality with the quantity supplied doesn't end scarcity. So when the law prevents the rent from adjusting and blocks the price mechanism from allocating scarce housing, some other allocation mechanism must be used. If that mechanism were one that provided the housing to the poorest, then the allocation might be regarded as fair.

But the mechanisms that get used do not usually achieve such an outcome. First-come-first-served is one allocation mechanism. Discrimination based on race, ethnicity, or sex is another. And discrimination against young newcomers and in favor of old established families is yet another. None of these mechanisms delivers a fair outcome.

Rent ceilings in New York City provide examples of these mechanisms at work. The main beneficiaries of rent ceilings in New York City are families that have lived in the city for a long time—including some rich and famous ones. These families enjoy low rents while newcomers pay high rents for hard-to-find apartments.

If Rent Ceilings Are So Bad, Why Do We Have Them?

The economic case against rent ceilings is now widely accepted, so *new* rent ceiling laws are rare. But when governments try to repeal rent control laws, as the New York City government did in 1999, current renters lobby politicians to maintain the ceilings. Also, people who are prevented from finding housing would be happy if they got lucky and managed to find a rent-controlled apartment. So there is plenty of political support for rent ceilings.

Apartment owners who oppose rent ceilings are a minority, so their views are not a powerful influence on politicians. Because more people support rent ceilings than oppose them, politicians are sometimes willing to support them too.

CHECKPOINT 7.2

Study Guide pp. 107–110

Practice Online 7.2

2 **Explain how a rent ceiling creates a housing shortage, inefficiency, and unfairness.**

Practice Problem 7.2

FIGURE 1

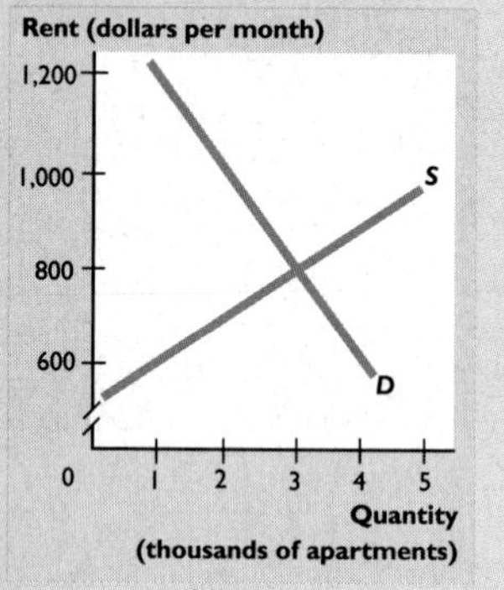

Rent (dollars per month)

1,200 1,000 800 600 S D 0 1 2 3 4 5

Quantity (thousands of apartments)

Figure 1 shows the rental market for apartments in a Chicago suburb:

a. What is the rent in this suburb and how many apartments are rented?
b. If the city of Chicago imposes a rent ceiling of $900 a month, what is the rent in this suburb and how many apartments are rented?
c. If the city of Chicago imposes a rent ceiling of $600 a month, what is the rent in this suburb and how many apartments are rented?
d. With a strictly enforced $600 rent ceiling, is the housing market efficient? Explain why or why not.
e. If the city strictly enforces the rent ceiling, is the housing market fair? Explain why or why not.
f. If a black market develops, how high could the black market rent be? Explain your answer.

Exercise 7.2

FIGURE 2

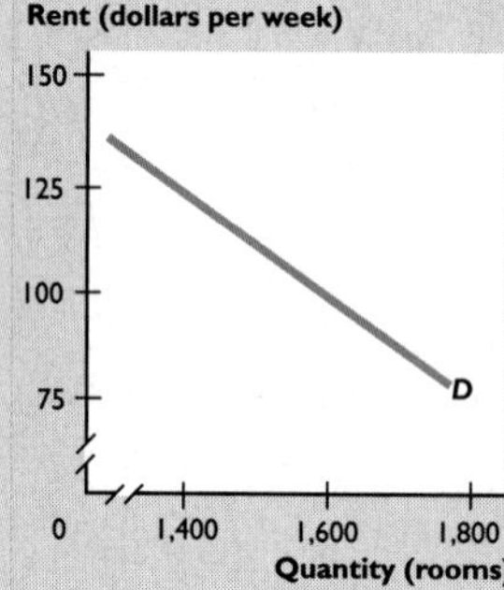

Figure 2 shows the demand for on-campus student housing at Fort Lewis College, Durango. The college has 1,400 rooms for rent.

a. What are the equilibrium rent and the equilibrium quantity of rooms rented?
b. If the city imposed a rent ceiling on on-campus housing of $100 a week, how would you describe the on-campus housing market? Would the allocation of housing be efficient? Would it be fair?
c. If the rent ceiling of $100 a week were strictly enforced and there were no black market, who would gain and who would lose?
d. If with the $100 a week rent ceiling a black market developed, what rent would be offered for a room? Would the allocation of housing be efficient? Would it be fair?

Solution to Practice Problem 7.2

FIGURE 3

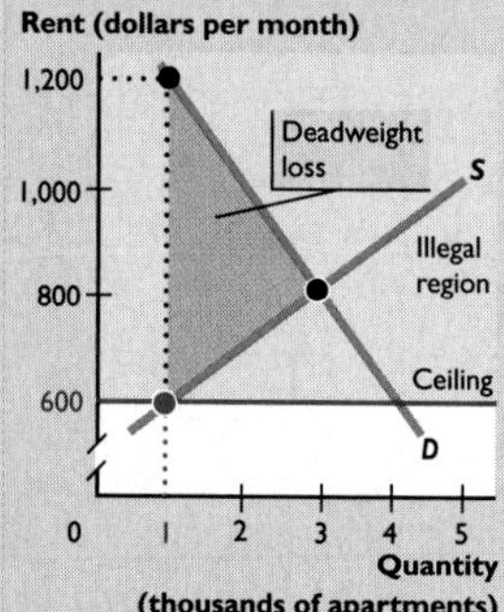

a. The equilibrium rent is $800 a month, and 3,000 apartments are rented.
b. A rent ceiling of $900 a month is above the equilibrium rent, so the outcome is the market equilibrium rent of $800 a month with 3,000 apartments rented.
c. With the rent ceiling at $600 a month, the number of apartments rented is 1,000 and the rent is $600 a month (Figure 3).
d. The housing market is not efficient. With 1,000 apartments rented, marginal benefit exceeds marginal cost and a deadweight loss arises (Figure 3).
e. The rent ceiling makes the allocation of housing less fair in both views of fairness: It blocks voluntary transactions, and it does not provide more housing to those in most need.
f. In a black market, some people will be willing to rent an apartment for more than the rent ceiling. The highest rent that someone would offer is $1,200 a month. This rent equals the willingness of someone to pay for the 1,000th apartment (Figure 3).

7.3 PRICE FLOORS

The labor market influences the jobs we get and the wages we earn. Firms hire labor, so they decide how much labor to demand. The lower the wage rate, the greater is the quantity of labor that firms demand. Households decide how much labor to supply. The higher the wage rate, the greater is the quantity of labor households are willing to supply. The wage rate adjusts to make the quantity of labor demanded equal to the quantity supplied.

The equilibrium wage rate might be high or low. Figure 7.10 shows a market in which the equilibrium wage rate is low. It is the market for fast-food servers in Yuma.

In this market, the demand for labor curve is *D*. On this demand curve, at a wage rate of $10 an hour, the quantity of fast-food servers demanded is zero. If A&W, Burger King, Taco Bell, McDonald's, Wendy's, and the other fast-food places had to pay servers $10 an hour, they wouldn't hire any. They would replace them with vending machines! But at wage rates below $10 an hour, they would hire servers. At a wage rate of $5 an hour, they would hire 5,000 servers.

On the supply side of the market, no one is willing to work for $2 an hour. To attract servers, the firms must pay more than $2 an hour.

Equilibrium in this market occurs at a wage rate of $5 an hour with 5,000 people employed as servers.

Suppose that the government thinks that no one should have to work for a wage rate as low as $5 an hour and decides it wants to increase the wage rate. Can the government improve conditions for these workers by passing a minimum wage law? Let's find out.

FIGURE 7.10
A Market for Fast-Food Servers

Practice Online

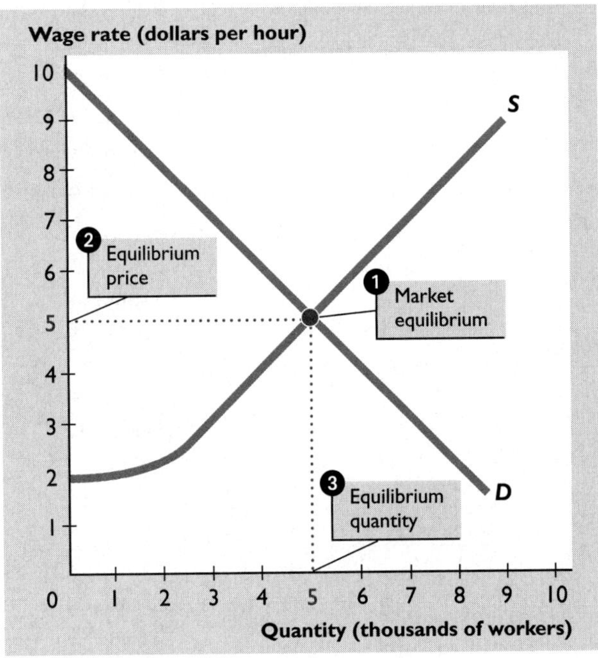

The figure shows the demand curve, *D*, and the supply curve, *S*, for fast-food servers.

1. The market is in equilibrium when the quantity demanded equals the quantity supplied.
2. The equilibrium price (wage rate) is $5 an hour.
3. The equilibrium quantity is 5,000 servers.

The Minimum Wage

Minimum wage law
A government regulation that makes hiring labor for less than a specified wage illegal.

Price floor
The lowest price at which it is legal to trade a particular good, service, or factor of production. The minimum wage is an example of a price floor.

A **minimum wage law** is a government regulation that makes hiring labor for less than a specified wage illegal. Firms are free to pay a wage rate that exceeds the minimum wage but may not pay less than the minimum. A minimum wage is an example of a **price floor**, which is the lowest price at which it is legal to trade a particular good, service, or factor of production.

The effect of a price floor depends on whether it is set below or above the equilibrium price. In Figure 7.10, the equilibrium wage rate is $5 an hour and at this wage rate, firms hire 5,000 workers. If the government introduced a minimum wage below $5 an hour, nothing would change. The reason is that firms are already paying $5 an hour, and because this wage exceeds the minimum wage, the wage rate paid doesn't change. Firms continue to hire 5,000 workers.

But the aim of a minimum wage is to boost the incomes of low-wage earners. So in the markets for the lowest-paid labor, the minimum wage will exceed the equilibrium wage.

Suppose that the government introduces a minimum wage of $7 an hour. Figure 7.11 shows the effects of this law. Wage rates below $7 an hour are illegal, so we've shaded the illegal region *below* the minimum wage. Firms and workers are no longer permitted to operate at the equilibrium point in this market because it is in the illegal region. Market forces and political forces are in conflict.

The government can set a minimum wage. But it can't tell employers how many workers to hire. If firms must pay $7 an hour for labor, they will hire only 3,000 workers. At the equilibrium wage rate of $5 an hour, they hired 5,000 workers. So when the minimum wage is introduced, firms fire 2,000 workers.

FIGURE 7.11
A Minimum Wage Creates Unemployment

Practice Online

A minimum wage is introduced above the equilibrium wage rate. In this example, the minimum wage rate is $7 an hour.

1. The quantity of labor demanded decreases to 3,000 workers.
2. The quantity of labor supplied increases to 7,000 people.
3. 4,000 people are unemployed.

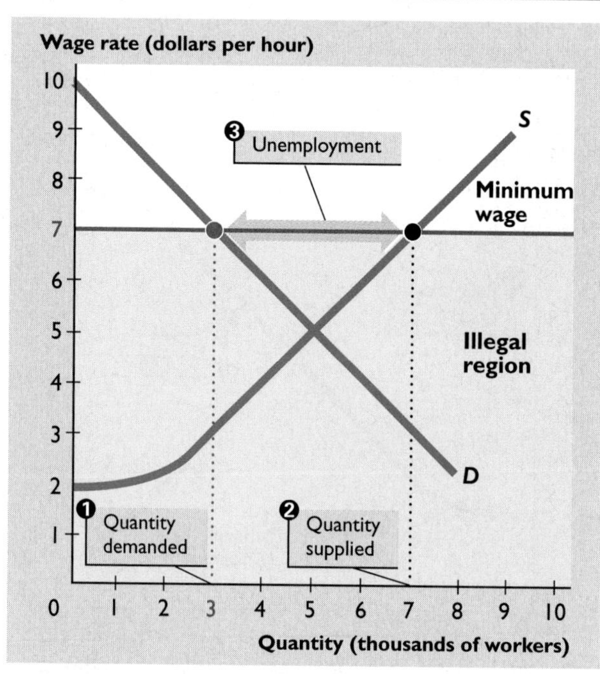

But at a wage rate of $7 an hour, another 2,000 people who didn't want to work for $5 an hour now try to find work as servers—at $7 an hour, the quantity supplied is 7,000 workers. With 2,000 workers fired and another 2,000 looking for work at the higher wage rate, 4,000 people who would like to work as servers are unemployed.

Somehow, the 3,000 jobs available must be allocated among the 7,000 people who are available for and willing to work. How is this allocation achieved? The answer is by increased job–search activity and illegal hiring.

Increased Job Search Activity

People spend a good deal of time and resources finding a good job. But with a minimum wage, more people are looking for jobs than the number of jobs available. Frustrated unemployed workers spend time and other resources searching for hard-to-find jobs. In Figure 7.12, to find a job at $7 an hour, someone who is willing to work for $3 an hour would be willing to spend on search an amount that is equivalent to subtracting $4 an hour from the wage rate. For a job that might last a year or more, this amount is large.

Illegal Hiring

With more people looking for work than the number of jobs available, some firms and workers might agree to do business at an illegal wage rate below the minimum wage—a black market in which the illegal wage is below the minimum wage.

FIGURE 7.12
A Minimum Wage Increases Job Search

Practice Online

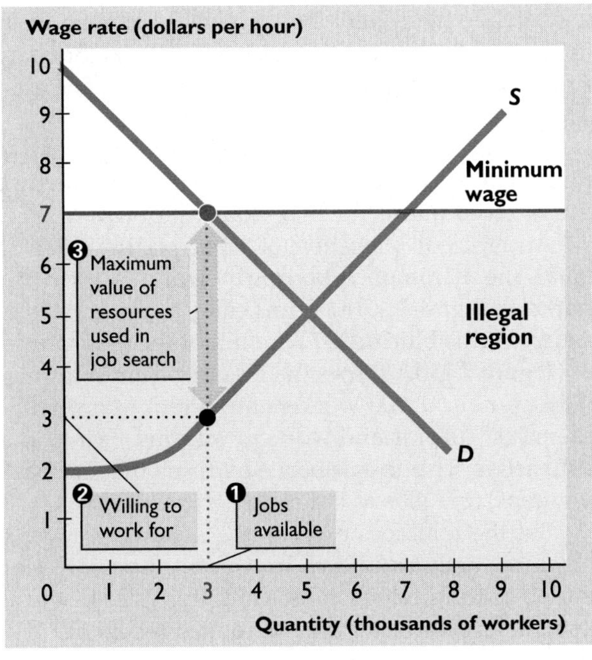

The minimum wage rate is set at $7 an hour:

1. 3,000 jobs are available.
2. The lowest wage rate for which someone is willing to work is $3 an hour.
3. Illegal wage rates might range from just below the legal minimum of $7 an hour to the lowest that someone is willing to accept of $3 an hour.

The maximum people are willing to spend on job search is an amount equivalent to subtracting $4 an hour—the $7 they would receive if they found a job minus the $3 they are willing to work for—from the wage rate.

Eye on the U.S. Economy

The Federal Minimum Wage

The federal government's *Fair Labor Standards Act* sets the minimum wage, which was last changed in 1997 when it was raised to $5.15 an hour.

The minimum wage creates unemployment. But how much unemployment does it create? Until recently, most economists believed that a 10 percent increase in the minimum wage rate decreased teenage employment by between 1 and 3 percent.

David Card of the University of California at Berkeley and Alan Krueger of Princeton University, have challenged this view. They claim that following a rise in the minimum wage in California, New Jersey, and Texas, the *employment* rate of low-income workers *increased*. They suggest three reasons why a rise in the wage rate might increase employment:

(1) Workers become more conscientious and productive.

(2) Workers are less likely to quit, so costly labor turnover is reduced.

(3) Managers make a firm's operations more efficient.

Most economists are skeptical about these ideas. They say that if higher wages make workers more productive and reduces labor turnover, firms will freely pay workers a higher wage. And they argue that there are other explanations for the employment increase that Card and Krueger found.

Daniel Hamermesh of the University of Texas at Austin says that they got the timing wrong. Firms *anticipated* the minimum wage rise and so cut employment *before* it occurred. Looking at employment changes *after* the minimum wage increased missed its main effect. Finis Welch of Texas A&M University and Kevin Murphy of the University of Chicago say the employment effects that Card and Krueger found are caused by regional differences in economic growth, not changes in the minimum wage.

Also, looking only at employment misses the supply-side effect of the minimum wage. It brings an increase in the number of people who drop out of high school to look for work.

Is the Minimum Wage Efficient?

The efficient allocation of a factor of production is similar to that of a good or service, which you studied in Chapter 6. The demand for labor tells us about the marginal benefit of labor to the firms that hire it. Firms benefit because the labor they hire produces the goods or services that they sell. Firms are willing to pay a wage rate equal to the benefit they receive from an additional hour of labor. So in Figure 7.13(a), the demand curve for labor tells us the marginal benefit that the firms in Yuma receive from hiring fast-food servers. The marginal benefit minus the wage rate is a surplus for the firms.

The supply of labor tells us about the marginal cost of working. To work, people must forgo leisure or working in the home, activities that they value. The wage rate received minus the marginal cost of working is a surplus for workers.

An efficient allocation of labor occurs when the marginal benefit to firms equals the marginal cost borne by workers. Such an allocation occurs in the labor market in Figure 7.13(a). Firms enjoy a surplus (the green area), and workers enjoy a surplus (the blue area). The sum of these surpluses is maximized.

Figure 7.13(b) shows the loss from a minimum wage. With a minimum wage of $5 an hour, 3,000 workers are hired. Marginal benefit exceeds marginal cost. The firms' surplus and workers' surplus shrink, and a deadweight loss (the gray area) arises. This loss is borne by firms that cut back employment and by people who can't find jobs at the higher wage rate.

But the total loss exceeds the deadweight loss. Resources get used in costly job-search activity as each unemployed person keeps looking for a job—writing letters, making phone calls, going for interviews, and so on. The value of these resources might be as large as the red rectangle.

FIGURE 7.13
Inefficiency of the Minimum Wage

Practice Online

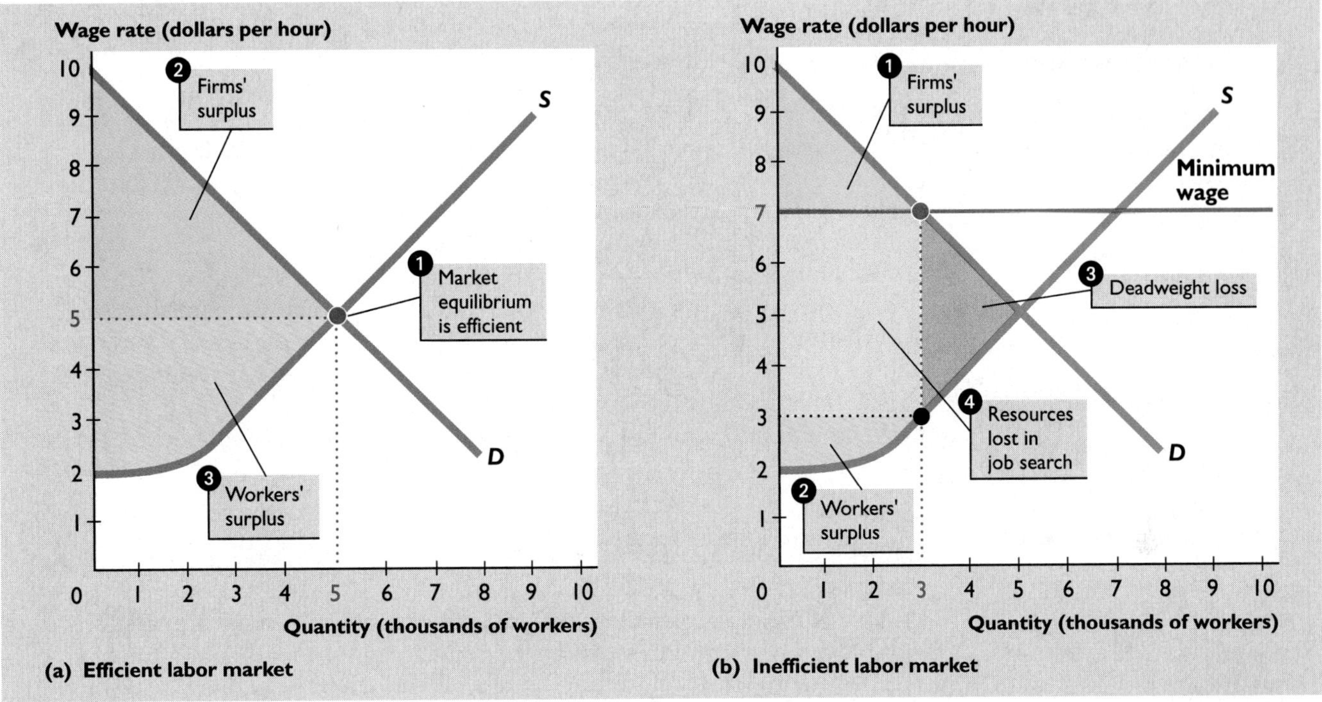

❶ The market equilibrium is efficient with marginal benefit equal to marginal cost. The sum of ❷ the firms' surplus (blue area) and ❸ workers' surplus (green area) is maximized.

A minimum wage is inefficient. ❶ The firms' surplus and ❷ workers' surplus shrinks, a ❸ deadweight loss arises, and ❹ the resources are lost in job search.

Is the Minimum Wage Fair?

The minimum wage is unfair on both views of fairness—it delivers an unfair *result* and imposes unfair *rules*. The *result* is unfair because only those people who find jobs benefit. The unemployed end up worse off than with no minimum wage. And those who get jobs are probably not the least well off. When the wage rate doesn't allocate jobs, discrimination, another source of unfairness, increases. The minimum wage imposes unfair *rules* because it blocks voluntary exchange. Firms are willing to hire more labor and people are willing to work more. But they are not permitted by the minimum wage law to do so.

If the Minimum Wage Is So Bad, Why Do We Have It?

Although the minimum wage is inefficient, not everyone loses from it. The people who find jobs at the minimum wage rate are better off. Other supporters of the minimum wage believe that the elasticities of demand and supply in the labor market are low, so not much unemployment results. Labor unions support the minimum wage because it puts upward pressure on all wage rates including those of union workers. Nonunion labor is a substitute for union labor, so when the minimum wage rises, the demand for union labor increases.

CHECKPOINT 7.3

Study Guide pp. 110–113

Practice Online 7.3

3 **Explain how the minimum wage creates unemployment, inefficiency, and unfairness.**

FIGURE 1

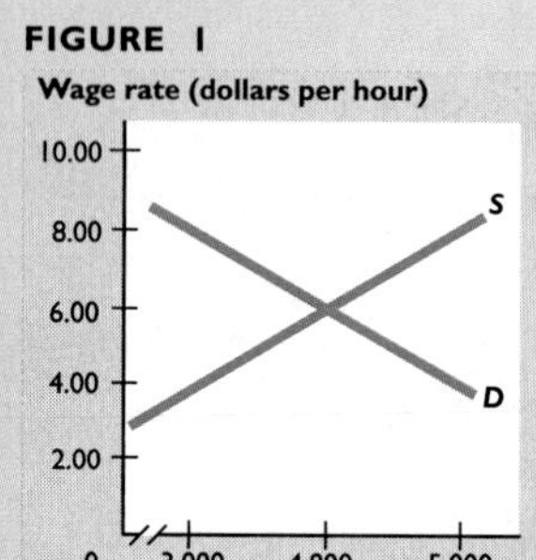

Practice Problem 7.3

Figure 1 shows the market for tomato pickers in southern California.

a. What is the equilibrium wage rate of tomato pickers and what is the equilibrium quantity of tomato pickers employed?
b. Is the market for tomato pickers efficient?
c. If California introduces a minimum wage for tomato pickers of $4 an hour, how many tomato pickers are employed and how many are unemployed?
d. If California introduces a minimum wage for tomato pickers of $8 an hour, how many tomato pickers are employed and how many are unemployed?
e. Is the minimum wage of $8 an hour efficient? Is it fair?
f. Who gains and who loses from the minimum wage of $8 an hour?

FIGURE 2

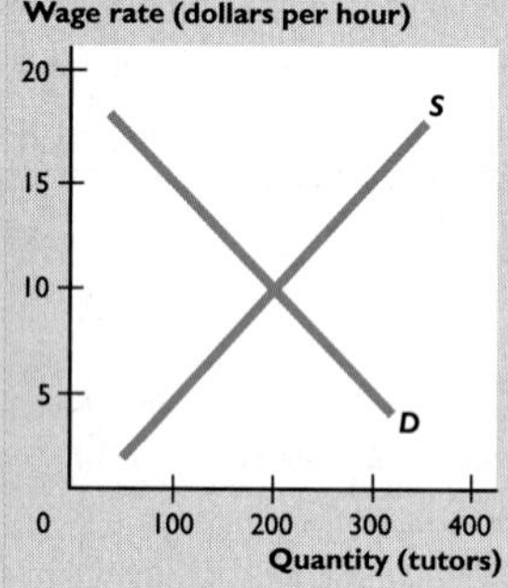

Exercise 7.3

Figure 2 shows a market for private math tutors in Madison organized by the Students' Union.

a. What is the wage rate that math tutors earn and how many are hired?
b. If the Students' Union sets the minimum wage for private math tutors at $8 an hour, how many tutors are employed and what wage rate do they earn?
c. If the Students' Union sets the minimum wage for private math tutors at $15 an hour, how many tutors are employed and what wage rate do they earn?
d. Is the minimum wage of $15 an hour efficient? Is it fair?
e. If a black market gets going and the Students' Union cannot enforce the minimum wage, what wage rate might some unscrupulous tutors earn?

Solution to Practice Problem 7.3

a. The equilibrium wage rate is $6 an hour, and 4,000 pickers are employed.
b. The market for tomato pickers is efficient because the marginal benefit to tomato growers equals the marginal cost borne by the pickers.
c. The minimum wage of $4 an hour is below the equilibrium wage rate, so 4,000 tomato pickers are employed and none are unemployed.
d. The minimum wage of $8 an hour is above the equilibrium wage rate, so 3,000 pickers are employed (determined by the demand for tomato pickers) and 5,000 people would like to work as pickers for $8 an hour (determined by the supply curve), so 2,000 are unemployed (Figure 3).
e. The minimum wage of $8 an hour is not efficient because it creates a deadweight loss—the marginal benefit to growers (on the demand curve) exceeds the marginal cost to pickers (on the supply curve). An additional loss arises as unemployed tomato pickers search for jobs. The minimum wage is unfair by both of the fairness criteria.
f. Tomato pickers who find work at $8 an hour gain. Tomato growers and unemployed pickers lose.

FIGURE 3

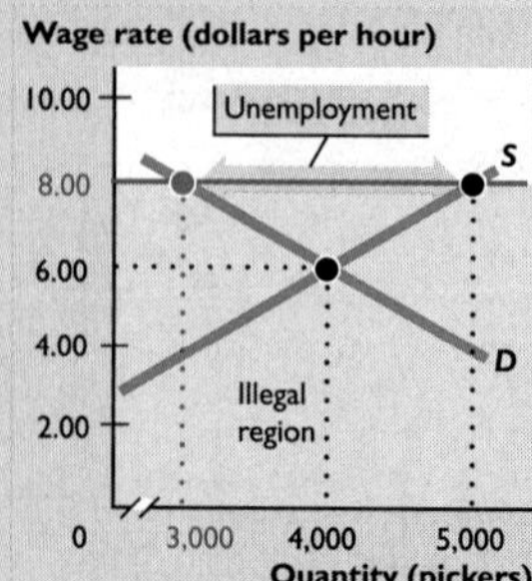

CHAPTER CHECKPOINT

Key Points

1 Explain the effects of taxes on goods and labor and determine who pays the taxes.

- A tax on a good raises the price of the good but usually by less than the tax.
- The shares of a tax paid by the buyer and by the seller depend on the elasticity of demand and the elasticity of supply.
- The less elastic the demand and the more elastic the supply, the greater is the price increase, the smaller is the quantity decrease, and the larger is the share of the tax paid by the buyer.
- If demand is perfectly elastic or supply is perfectly inelastic, the seller pays all the tax. And if demand is perfectly inelastic or supply is perfectly elastic, the buyer pays all the tax.
- The elasticities of demand and supply, not Congress, determine who pays the income tax and who pays a payroll tax.
- Taxes create inefficiency by driving a wedge between marginal benefit and marginal cost and creating a deadweight loss.

2 Explain how a rent ceiling creates a housing shortage, inefficiency, and unfairness.

- A price ceiling set above the equilibrium price has no effects.
- A price ceiling set below the equilibrium price creates a shortage, costly search, and a black market.
- A price ceiling is inefficient and unfair.
- A rent ceiling is an example of a price ceiling.

3 Explain how the minimum wage creates unemployment, inefficiency, and unfairness.

- A price floor set below the equilibrium price has no effects.
- A price floor set above the equilibrium price creates a surplus, costly search, and illegal trading.
- A price floor is inefficient and unfair.
- The minimum wage is an example of a price floor.

Key Terms

Exercises

1. In Florida, sunscreen and sunglasses are vital items. If the sales tax on them is doubled, who will pay most of the sales tax increase: buyers or sellers? Will the tax increase halve the quantity of sunscreen and sunglasses bought?

TABLE 1

Price (dollars per month)	Quantity demanded (units per month)	Quantity supplied (units per month)
0	30	0
10	25	10
20	20	20
30	15	30
40	10	40
50	5	50
60	0	60

2. Table 1 illustrates the market for Internet services. Use a demand-supply graph to answer the following questions.
   a. What is the market price of an Internet service?
   b. If the government put a tax of $15 a month on Internet service, what price would the buyer of an Internet service pay?
   c. What price would the seller of the Internet service receive?
   d. Does the buyer or the seller pay more of the tax?
   e. What is the tax revenue collected by the government?
   f. What is the deadweight loss created by the tax?
3. The supply of luxury boats is perfectly elastic, and the demand for luxury boats is unit elastic. The government decides to put a tax of 20 percent on luxury boats. Before the tax is introduced, the price of a luxury boat is $1 million and 240 luxury boats a week are bought.
   a. What is the price paid by a buyer of a luxury boat after the tax is imposed?
   b. How much of the tax is paid by the buyers of luxury boats and how much by the sellers?
   c. How much tax revenue will the government raise?
   d. Show in a graph the excess burden of this tax.
   e. Will this tax be efficient? Explain your answer.
   f. Will it be fair? Explain your answer.

TABLE 2

Price (dollars per tube)	Quantity demanded (thousands of tubes per week)	Quantity supplied (thousands of tubes per week)
0.00	11	6.5
0.50	10	7.0
1.00	9	7.5
1.50	8	8.0
2.00	7	8.5
2.50	6	9.0
3.00	5	9.5
3.50	4	10.0
4.00	3	10.5
4.50	2	11.0
5.00	1	11.5

4. Table 2 shows the demand schedule and the supply schedule of toothpaste. If the government put a $1.50 a tube tax on toothpaste
   a. What price would the buyer pay for toothpaste?
   b. What price would the seller receive?
   c. How much tax revenue would the government collect?
   d. What is the deadweight loss created by the tax?
5. To encourage inner-city youths to spend more time playing sports, the government introduces a super income tax of 10 percent on professional basketball players and plans to use the revenue to improve inner-city sports facilities.
   a. Will the super income tax raise much revenue for the government?
   b. Who will pay most of the tax: the players or the team owners?
   c. Will the tax create a large or a small excess burden?
6. In exercise 5, suppose that a payroll tax of 10 percent replaces the super income tax.
   a. Will the revenue for the government be the same as with the super income tax?
   b. Who would pay the payroll tax: the players or the team owners?
7. Table 3 shows the demand and supply schedules for on-campus housing.
   a. What are the equilibrium rent and number of rooms?

b. If the college puts a rent ceiling on rooms of $650 a month, what is the rent and how many rooms are rented?
c. If the college puts a rent ceiling of $550 a month, what is the rent and how many rooms are rented?
d. If the college strictly enforced the rent ceiling of $550 a month, is the on-campus housing market efficient? Explain why or why not.
e. If a black market develops, how high could the black market rent be? Explain.
f. If a black market develops, is the housing market fair? Explain.

TABLE 3

Rent (dollars per month)	Quantity demanded (rooms)	Quantity supplied (rooms)
500	2,500	2,000
550	2,250	2,000
600	2,000	2,000
650	1,750	2,000
700	1,500	2,000
750	1,250	2,000

8. During the 1996 Olympic Games, many residents of Atlanta left the city and rented out their homes. Despite the increase in the quantity of housing available, rents soared. If at the same time, the city of Atlanta had imposed a rent ceiling, describe how the housing market would have functioned.

9. Concerned about the political fallout from rising gas prices, the government decides to impose a price ceiling on gasoline of $1.00 a gallon.
   a. Explain how the market for gasoline would react to this price ceiling if
      (i) The oil-producing nations increased production and drove the equilibrium price of gasoline to 90 cents a gallon.
      (ii) A global shortage of oil sent the equilibrium price of gasoline to $2.00 a gallon.
   b. Which of the situations in part **a** would result in an efficient use of resources? Explain why.

10. Suppose the government introduced a ceiling on the fees that lawyers are permitted to charge.
    a. Explain the effects of such a ceiling on
       (i) The amount of work done by lawyers.
       (ii) The consumer surplus of people who hire lawyers.
       (iii) The producer surplus of law firms.
    b. Would this fee ceiling result in an efficient use of resources? Why or why not?

11. Table 4 shows the demand and supply schedules for student workers at on-campus venues.
    a. What is the equilibrium wage rate of student workers, and what is the equilibrium number of students employed?
    b. Is the market for student workers at on-campus venues efficient?
    c. If the college introduces a minimum wage of $5.50 an hour, how many student workers are employed and how many are unemployed?
    d. If the college introduces a minimum wage of $6.50 an hour, how many student workers are employed and how many are unemployed?
    e. Is the minimum wage of $6.50 an hour efficient? Is it fair?
    f. Who gains and who loses from the minimum wage of $6.50 an hour?

TABLE 4

Wage rate (dollars per hour)	Quantity demanded (student workers)	Quantity supplied (student workers)
5.00	600	300
5.50	500	350
6.00	400	400
6.50	300	450
7.00	200	500
7.50	100	550

12. Bakers earn $15 an hour, gas pump attendants earn $6 an hour, and copy shop workers earn $7 an hour. If the government introduces a minimum wage of $7 an hour, explain how the markets for bakers, gas pump attendants, and copy shop workers will respond initially to the minimum wage.

Critical Thinking

13. The government of the U.S. Virgin Islands seeks your help to evaluate two sales tax schemes. In scheme A, food is not taxed, luxury goods are taxed at 10 percent, and all other goods are taxed at 5 percent. In scheme B, there is a flat 3 percent tax on all goods and services. The government asks you to explain what research must be undertaken and what features of the markets for food, luxury goods, and other goods will influence.
    - **a.** How the prices and the quantities of food, luxury goods, and all other goods will differ under the two schemes.
    - **b.** The excess burden of the taxes under the two schemes. Which tax would be more efficient if both schemes generated the same amount of tax revenue?
14. The New York City Rent Guidelines Board is mandated to establish rent adjustments for the nearly one million apartments and houses that are subject to the city's Rent Stabilization Law. The board holds public hearings to consider testimony from owners, tenants, advocacy groups, and housing industry experts. Write a brief report to the New York City Rent Guidelines Board that explains why it is not possible to improve on permitting the market forces of supply and demand to determine rents at the levels that make the quantity demanded and quantity supplied equal.
15. "Market prices might be fine in a rich country, but in a poor developing African nation where there are shortages of most items, without government control of prices everything would be too expensive." Do you agree or disagree with this statement? Use the concepts of efficiency and fairness to explain why.

Web Exercises

Use the links on your Foundations Web site to work the following exercises.

Practice Online

16. Obtain data on the sales tax rates in each state.
    - **a.** Which state has the highest sales tax rate and which states have the lowest?
    - **b.** Which states have the most exemptions?
    - **c.** Compare California and its neighbors, Nevada and Washington. In which state do you think consumer surplus and producer surplus (per person) is greatest? Why?
17. Visit the Web site of the Harvard Living Wage Campaign.
    - **a.** What is the campaign for a living wage?
    - **b.** How would you distinguish the minimum wage from a living wage?
    - **c.** If the Living Wage Campaign succeeds in getting wages increased above their equilibrium levels, what do you predict its effect would be?
    - **d.** Would a living wage above the equilibrium wage be efficient?
    - **e.** Who would gain and who would lose from a living wage above the equilibrium wage?
    - **f.** Would a living wage above the equilibrium wage be fair?

CHAPTER 8

Externalities

CHAPTER CHECKLIST

When you have completed your study of this chapter, you will be able to

1. **Explain why negative externalities lead to inefficient overproduction and how property rights, pollution charges, and taxes can achieve a more efficient outcome.**

2. **Explain why positive externalities lead to inefficient underproduction and how public provision, subsidies, vouchers, and patents can achieve a more efficient outcome.**

You learned in Chapter 6 that markets are not always efficient. And you saw in Chapter 7 some government actions that create inefficiency. In this chapter, we study markets in which governments can help to achieve a more efficient outcome. In these markets, the actions of buyers and sellers affect other people, for ill or good, in ways that are ignored by the market participants.

We burn huge quantities of coal and oil that bring acid rain and global warming, and we dump toxic waste into rivers, lakes, and oceans. These environmental issues are simultaneously everybody's problem and nobody's problem. How can we create incentives that make us consider the damage that we inflict on others every time we turn on our heating or air conditioning?

Almost every day, we hear about a new discovery in medicine, engineering, chemistry, physics, and even economics. Advances in knowledge bring benefits to all, not just to the scientists who make the advances. How much should we spend on the education and research that make these advances possible?

EXTERNALITIES IN OUR DAILY LIVES

Externality
A cost or a benefit that arises from production that falls on someone other than the producer; or a cost or benefit that arises from consumption that falls on someone other than the consumer.

Negative externality
A production or consumption activity that creates an external cost.

Positive externality
A production or consumption activity that creates an external benefit.

An **externality** is a cost or a benefit that arises from production that falls on someone other than the producer; or a cost or a benefit that arises from consumption that falls on someone other than the consumer. Before we embark on the two main tasks of this chapter, we're going to review the range of externalities, classify them, and give some everyday examples.

First, an externality can arise from either a production activity or a consumption activity. Second, it can be either a **negative externality**, which imposes an external cost, or a **positive externality**, which provides an external benefit. So there are four types of externalities:

- Negative production externalities
- Positive production externalities
- Negative consumption externalities
- Positive consumption externalities

Negative Production Externalities

When the U.S. Open tennis tournament is being played at Flushing Meadows, players, spectators, and television viewers around the world share a negative production externality that many New Yorkers experience every day—the noise of airplanes taking off from Kennedy Airport. Aircraft noise imposes a large cost on millions of people who live under the flight paths to airports in every major city.

Logging and the clearing of forests is the source of another negative production externality. These activities destroy the habitat of wildlife and influence the amount of carbon dioxide in the atmosphere, which has a long-term effect on temperature. So these external costs are borne by everyone and by future generations.

Pollution, which we examine in more detail in the next section, is a major example of this type of externality.

Positive Production Externalities

To produce orange blossom honey, Honey Run Honey of Chico, California, locates beehives next to an orange orchard. The honeybees collect pollen and nectar from the orange blossoms to make the honey. At the same time, they transfer pollen between the blossoms, which helps to fertilize them. Two positive production

Negative production externality.

Positive production externality.

externalities are present in this example. Honey Run Honey gets a positive production externality from the owner of the orange orchard. And the orange grower gets a positive production externality from Honey Run.

Negative Consumption Externalities

Negative consumption externalities are a source of irritation for most of us. Smoking tobacco in a confined space creates fumes that many people find unpleasant and that pose a health risk. So smoking in restaurants and on airplanes generates a negative externality. To avoid this negative externality, many restaurants and all airlines ban smoking. But while a smoking ban avoids a negative consumption externality for most people, it imposes a negative consumption externality on smokers. The majority, for whom the ban is in place, impose a cost on the minority—the smokers who would prefer to enjoy the consumption of tobacco while dining or taking a plane trip.

Noisy parties and outdoor rock concerts are other examples of negative consumption externalities. And they are also examples of the fact that a simple ban on an activity is not a solution. Banning noisy parties avoids the external cost on sleep-seeking neighbors, but it results in the sleepers imposing an external cost on the fun-seeking partygoers.

Permitting dandelions to grow in lawns, not picking up leaves in the fall, allowing a dog to bark loudly or to foul a neighbor's lawn, and letting your cell phone ring in class are other examples of negative consumption externalities.

Positive Consumption Externalities

When you get a flu vaccination, you lower your risk of being infected during the winter. But if you avoid the flu, your neighbor, who didn't get vaccinated, has a better chance of remaining healthy. Flu vaccinations generate positive consumption externalities.

When its owner restores a historic building, everyone who sees the building gets pleasure from it. Similarly, when someone erects a spectacular home—such as those built by Frank Lloyd Wright during the 1920s and 1930s—or other exciting building—such as the Chrysler and Empire State Buildings in New York or the Wrigley Building in Chicago—an external consumption benefit flows to everyone who has an opportunity to view it.

Education, which we examine in more detail in this chapter, is another and a major example of this type of externality.

Negative consumption externality.

Positive consumption externality.

8.1 NEGATIVE EXTERNALITIES: POLLUTION

You've just seen that pollution is an example of a negative externality. Both production and consumption activities create pollution. But here, we'll focus on pollution as a negative production externality. When a chemical factory dumps waste into a river, the people who live by the river and use it for fishing and boating bear the cost of the pollution. The chemical factory does not consider the cost of pollution when it decides the quantity of chemicals to produce. Its supply curve is based on its own costs, not on the costs that it inflicts on others. You're going to discover that when external costs are present, we produce more output than the efficient quantity and we get more pollution than the efficient quantity.

Pollution and other environmental problems are not new. Preindustrial towns and cities in Europe had severe sewage disposal problems that created cholera epidemics and plagues that killed millions. Nor is the desire to find solutions to environmental problems new. The development in the fourteenth century of a pure water supply and the hygienic disposal of garbage and sewage are examples of early contributions to improving the quality of the environment.

Popular discussions about pollution and the environment often pay little attention to economics. They focus on physical aspects of the environment, not on costs and benefits. A common assumption is that activities that damage the environment are morally wrong and must cease. In contrast, an economic study of the environment emphasizes costs and benefits. Economists talk about the efficient amount of pollution or environmental damage. This emphasis on costs and benefits does not mean that economists, as citizens, don't share the same goals as others and value a healthy environment. Nor does it mean that economists have the right answers and everyone else has the wrong ones. Rather, economics provides a set of tools and principles that help to clarify the issues.

The starting point for an economic analysis of the environment is the distinction between private costs and social costs.

Private Costs and Social Costs

A *private cost* of production is a cost that is borne by the producer of a good or service. *Marginal cost* is the cost of producing an *additional unit* of a good or service. So **marginal private cost** (*MC*) is the cost of producing an additional unit of a good or service that is borne by the producer of that good or service.

Marginal private cost
The cost of producing an additional unit of a good or service that is borne by the producer of that good or service.

Marginal external cost
The cost of producing an additional unit of a good or service that falls on people other than the producer.

Marginal social cost
The marginal cost incurred by the entire society—by the producer and by everyone else on whom the cost falls. It is the sum of marginal private cost and marginal external cost.

You've seen that an *external cost* is a cost of producing a good or service that is *not* borne by the producer but borne by other people. A **marginal external cost** is the cost of producing an additional unit of a good or service that falls on people other than the producer.

Marginal social cost (*MSC*) is the marginal cost incurred by the entire society—by the producer and by everyone else on whom the cost falls—and is the sum of marginal private cost and marginal external cost. That is,

$$MSC = MC + \text{Marginal external cost.}$$

We express costs in dollars. But we must always remember that a cost is an opportunity cost—the best thing we give up to get something. A marginal external cost is what someone other than the producer of a good or service must give up when the producer makes one more unit of the item. Something real that people value, such as a clean river or clean air, is given up.

Valuing an External Cost

Economists use market prices to put a dollar value on the cost of pollution. For example, suppose that there are two similar rivers, one polluted and the other clean. Five hundred identical homes are built along the side of each river. The homes on the clean river rent for $2,500 a month, and those on the polluted river rent for $1,500 a month. If the pollution is the only detectable difference between the two rivers and the two locations, the rent decrease of $1,000 per month is the cost of the pollution. For the 500 homes, the external cost is $500,000 a month.

External Cost and Output

Figure 8.1 shows an example of the relationship between output and cost in a chemical industry that pollutes. The marginal cost curve, *MC*, describes the private marginal cost borne by the firms that produce the chemical. Marginal cost increases as the quantity of the chemical produced increases. If the firms dump waste into a river, they impose an external cost that increases with the amount of the chemical produced. The marginal social cost curve, *MSC*, is the sum of marginal private cost and marginal external cost. For example, when output is 4,000 tons a month, marginal private cost is $100 a ton, marginal external cost is $125 a ton, and marginal social cost is $225 a ton.

In Figure 8.1, as the quantity of the chemical produced increases, the amount of pollution increases and the external cost of pollution increases. The quantity of the chemical produced and the pollution created depend on how the market for the chemical operates. First, we'll see what happens when the industry is free to pollute.

FIGURE 8.1
An External Cost

Practice Online

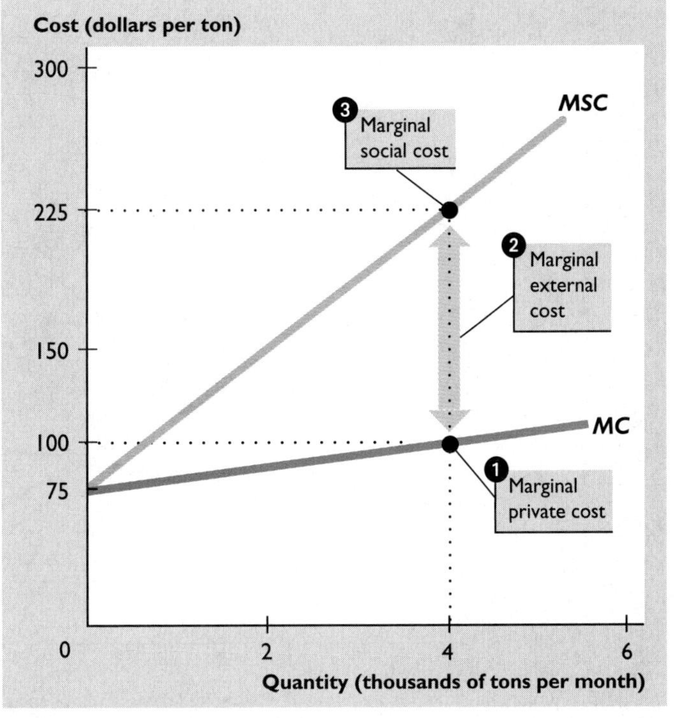

The *MC* curve shows the private marginal cost borne by the factories that produce a chemical. The *MSC* curve shows the sum of marginal private cost and marginal external cost. When output is 4,000 tons of chemicals a month, (1) marginal private cost is $100 a ton, (2) marginal external cost is $125 a ton, and (3) marginal social cost is $225 a ton.

Production and Pollution: How Much?

When an industry is unregulated, the amount of pollution it creates depends on the market equilibrium price and quantity of the good produced. Figure 8.2 illustrates the outcome in the market for a pollution-creating chemical.

The demand curve for the chemical is *D*. This curve also measures the marginal benefit, *MB*, to the buyers of the chemical (see Chapter 6, p. 144). The supply curve is *S*. This curve also measures the marginal private cost, *MC*, of the producers (see Chapter 6, p. 147). The supply curve is the marginal private cost curve because when firms make their production and supply decisions, they consider only the costs that they will bear. Market equilibrium occurs at a price of $100 a ton and a quantity of 4,000 tons a month.

This equilibrium is inefficient. You learned in Chapter 6 that the allocation of resources is efficient when marginal benefit equals marginal cost. But we must count all the costs—private and external—when we compare marginal benefit and marginal cost. So with an external cost, the allocation is efficient when marginal benefit equals marginal *social* cost. This outcome occurs when the quantity of the chemical produced is 2,000 tons a month. The market equilibrium overproduces by 2,000 tons a month and creates a deadweight loss, the gray triangle.

How can the people who live by the polluted river get the chemical factories to decrease their output of the chemical and create less pollution? If some method can be found to achieve this outcome, everyone—the owners of the factories and the residents of the riverside homes—can gain. Let's explore some solutions.

FIGURE 8.2
Inefficiency with an External Cost

Practice Online

The market supply curve is the marginal private cost curve, *S* = *MC*. The demand curve is the marginal benefit curve, *D* = *MB*.

1. Market equilibrium at a price of $100 a ton and 4,000 tons a month is inefficient because
2. marginal social cost exceeds
3. marginal benefit.
4. The efficient quantity is 2,000 tons a month.
5. The gray triangle shows the deadweight loss created by the pollution externality.

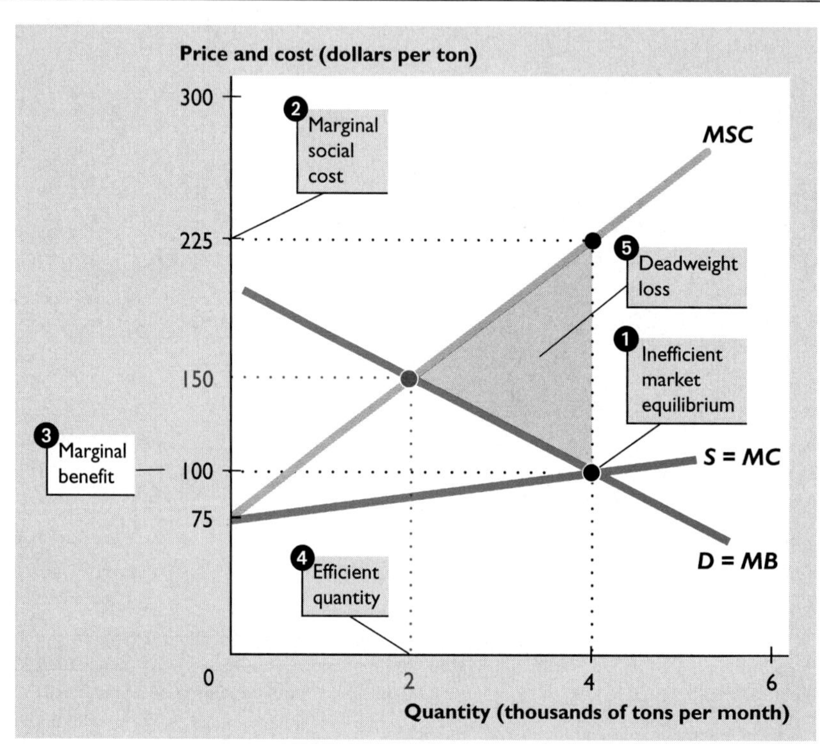

Property Rights

Sometimes it is possible to reduce the inefficiency arising from an externality by establishing a property right where one does not currently exist. **Property rights** are legally established titles to the ownership, use, and disposal of factors of production and goods and services that are enforceable in the courts.

Property rights
Legally established titles to the ownership, use, and disposal of factors of production and goods and services that are enforceable in the courts.

Suppose that the chemical factories own the river and the 500 homes alongside it. The rent that people are willing to pay depends on the amount of pollution. Using the earlier example, people are willing to pay $2,500 a month to live alongside a pollution-free river but only $1,500 a month to live with the pollution created by 4,000 tons of chemical a month. If the factories produce this quantity, they lose $1,000 a month for each home and a total of $500,000 a month.

The chemical factories are now confronted with the cost of their pollution decision. They might still decide to pollute, but if they do, they face the opportunity cost of their actions—forgone rent from the people who live by the river.

Figure 8.3 illustrates the outcome by using the same example as in Figure 8.2. With property rights in place, the original marginal cost curve no longer measures all the costs that the factories face in producing the chemical. It excludes the pollution cost that they must now bear. The former *MSC* curve now becomes the marginal private cost curve *MC*. All the costs fall on the factories, so the market supply curve is based on all the marginal costs and is the curve labeled *S* = *MC*.

Market equilibrium now occurs at a price of $150 a ton and a quantity of 2,000 tons a month. This outcome is efficient. The factories still produce some pollution, but it is the efficient quantity.

FIGURE 8.3
Property Rights Achieve an Efficient Outcome

Practice Online

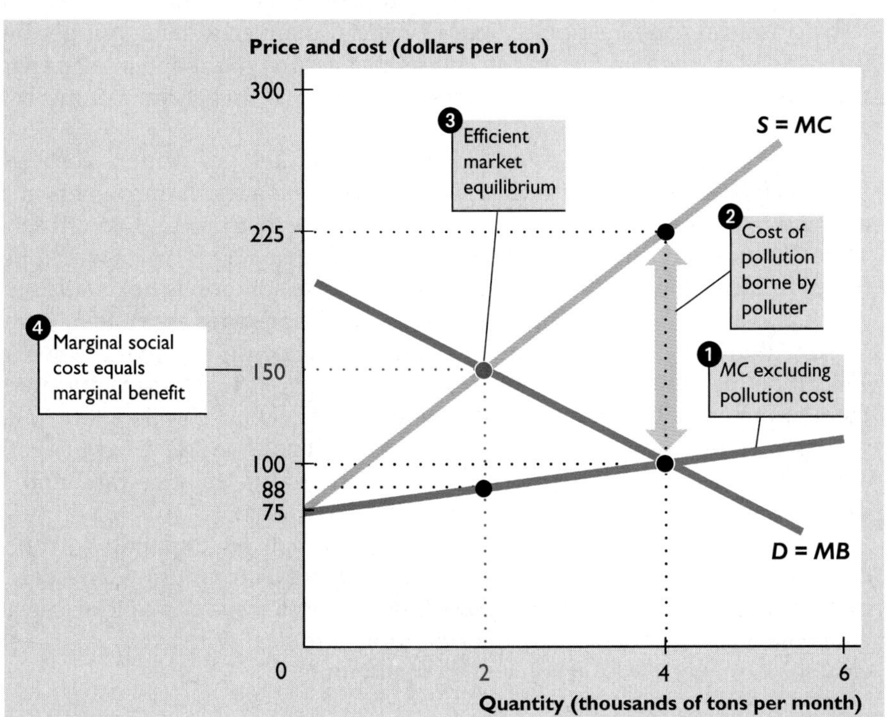

1. With property rights, the marginal cost curve that excludes the cost of pollution shows only part of the producers' marginal cost.

The marginal private cost curve includes 2 the cost of pollution, so the supply curve is *S* = *MC*.

3. Market equilibrium is at a price of $150 a ton and a quantity of 2,000 tons a month and is efficient because 4 marginal social cost equals marginal benefit.

The Coase Theorem

Does it matter how property rights are assigned? Does it matter whether the polluter or the victim of the pollution owns the resource that might be polluted? Until 1960, everyone—including economists who had thought long and hard about the problem—thought that it did matter. But in 1960, Ronald Coase had a remarkable insight, now called the Coase theorem.

Coase theorem
The proposition that if property rights exist, only a small number of parties are involved, and transactions costs are low, then private transactions are efficient and the outcome is not affected by who is assigned the property right.

The **Coase theorem** is the proposition that if property rights exist, only a small number of parties are involved, and transactions costs are low, then private transactions are efficient. There are no externalities because the transacting parties take all the costs and benefits into account. Furthermore, it doesn't matter who has the property rights.

Application of the Coase Theorem

Let's apply the Coase theorem to the polluted river. In the example that we've just studied, the factories own both the river and the homes. Suppose that instead, the residents own both their homes and the river. Now the factories must pay a fee to the homeowners for the right to dump their waste. The greater the quantity of waste dumped into the river, the more the factories must pay. So again, the factories face the opportunity cost of the pollution they create. The quantity of chemicals produced and the amount of waste dumped are the same whoever owns the homes and the river. If the factories own them, they bear the cost of pollution because they receive a lower income from home rents. And if the residents own the homes and the river, the factories bear the cost of pollution because they must pay a fee to the homeowners. In both cases, the factories bear the cost of their pollution and dump the efficient amount of waste into the river.

Transactions costs
The opportunity costs of conducting a transaction.

The Coase solution works only when transactions costs are low. **Transactions costs** are the opportunity costs of conducting a transaction. For example, when you buy a house, you incur a series of transactions costs. You might pay a realtor to help you find the best place and a financial planner to help you get the best loan, and you pay a lawyer to run checks that assure you that the seller owns the property and that after you've paid for it, the ownership has been properly transferred to you.

In the example of the homes alongside a river, the transactions costs that are incurred by a small number of chemical factories and a few homeowners might be low enough to enable them to negotiate the deals that produce an efficient outcome. But in many situations, transactions costs are so high that it would be inefficient to incur them. In these situations, the Coase solution is not available.

Suppose, for example, that everyone owns the airspace above their homes up to, say, 10 miles. If someone pollutes your airspace, you can charge a fee. But to collect the fee, you must identify who is polluting your airspace and persuade them to pay you. Imagine the cost to you and the 50 million people who live in your part of the United States (and perhaps in Canada or Mexico) of negotiating and enforcing agreements with the several thousand factories that emit sulfur dioxide and create acid rain that falls on your property!

In this situation, we use public choices through governments to cope with externalities. But the transactions costs that prevent us from using the Coase solution are opportunity costs, and governments can't wave a magician's wand to eliminate them. So attempts by the government to deal with externalities offer no easy solution. Let's look at some of these attempts.

Government Actions in the Face of External Costs

The three main methods that governments use to cope with externalities are

- Emission charges
- Marketable permits
- Taxes

Emission Charges

Emission charges confront a polluter with the external cost of pollution and provide an incentive to seek new technologies that are less polluting. In the United States, the Environmental Protection Agency (EPA) sets emission charges, which are, in effect, a price per unit of pollution. The more pollution a firm creates, the more it pays in emission charges. This method of dealing with environmental externalities has been used only modestly in the United States, but it is common in Europe. For example, in France, Germany, and the Netherlands, water polluters pay a waste disposal charge.

To work out the emission charge that achieves efficiency, the regulator must determine the marginal external cost of pollution at different levels of output and levy a charge on polluters that equals that cost. The polluter then incurs a marginal cost that includes both private and external costs. But to achieve the efficient outcome, the regulator needs a lot of information about the polluting industry that, in practice, is not available.

Another way of overcoming excess pollution is to issue firms with pollution quotas that they can buy and sell—with marketable permits. Let's look at this alternative.

Marketable Permits

An alternative to an emission charge is to assign each polluter an emission limit. Provided that the marginal benefit and marginal cost are assessed correctly, the same efficient outcome can be achieved with emission limits as with emission charges. But in the case of emission limits, a cap must be set for each polluter.

Marketable permits are a clever way of overcoming the need for the regulator to know every firm's marginal cost schedule. The government issues each firm an emissions permit, and firms can buy and sell these permits. Firms with a low marginal cost of reducing pollution sell permits and firms with a high marginal cost of reducing pollution buy permits. The market in permits determines the price at which firms trade permits. And firms buy or sell permits until their marginal cost of pollution equals the market price.

The 1990 Clear Air Act and the 1994 Regional Clean Air Incentives Market (RECLAIM) in the Los Angeles basin successfully use this method of dealing with pollution. The method provides an even stronger incentive than do emission charges to find technologies that pollute less because the price of a permit to pollute rises as the demand for permits increases.

Taxes

The government can use taxes as an incentive for producers to cut back on an activity that creates an external cost. By setting the tax rate equal to the marginal external cost, firms can be made to behave in the same way as they would if they bore the cost of the externality directly.

Eye on the U.S. Economy

Pollution Trends

Air quality in the United States is getting better. Lead has been almost eliminated, and sulfur dioxide, carbon monoxide, and suspended particulates have been reduced substantially. But nitrogen dioxide and ozone have persisted at close to their 1975 levels.

The earth's average temperature has increased over the past 100 years, and most of the increase occurred before 1940. No one knows why this temperature increase has occurred, but some scientists believe the cause to be carbon dioxide emissions from road transportation and electric utilities, methane created by cows and other livestock, nitrous oxide emissions of electric utilities and from fertilizers, and chlorofluorocarbons (CFCs) from refrigeration equipment and (in the past) aerosols.

The ozone layer in the earth's atmosphere protects us from cancer-causing ultraviolet rays from the sun. A hole in the ozone layer over Antarctica is getting bigger. How our industrial activity influences the ozone layer is not well understood, but some scien-

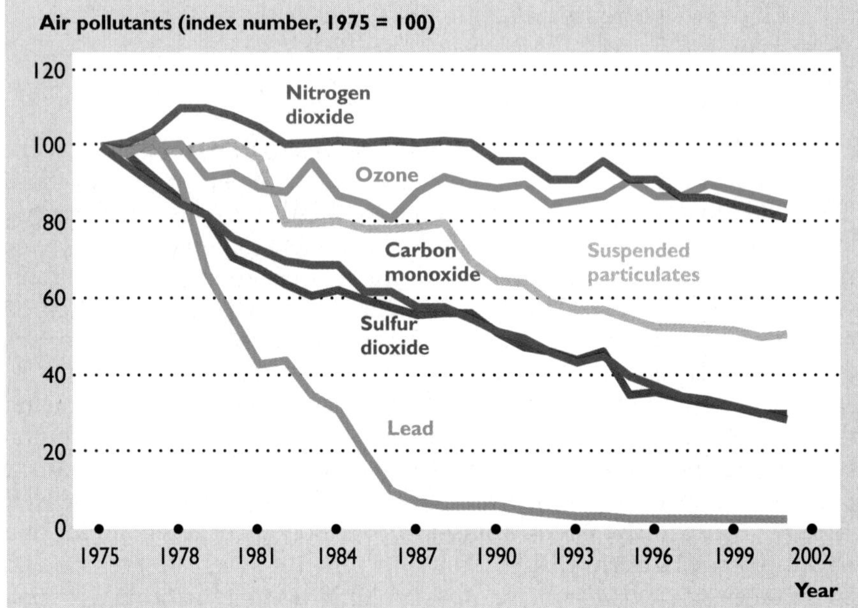

SOURCE: Environmental Protection Agency, *National Air Quality: 2001 Status and Trends*, 1999.

Effects of Government Actions

To see how government actions can change market outcomes in the face of externalities, let's return to the example of the chemical factories and the river.

Assume that the government has assessed the marginal external cost accurately and imposes a tax on the factories that exactly equals this cost.

Figure 8.4 illustrates the effects of this tax. The demand curve and marginal benefit curve *D* = *MB* and the firms' marginal cost curve *MC* are the same as in Figure 8.2. The pollution tax equals the marginal external cost of the pollution. We add this tax to marginal cost to find the market supply curve. This curve is the one labeled *S* = *MC* + *tax* = *MSC*. This curve is the market supply curve because it tells us the quantities supplied at each price given the firms' marginal cost and the tax they must pay. This curve is also the marginal social cost curve because the pollution tax has been set equal to the marginal external cost.

Demand and supply now determine the market equilibrium price at $150 a ton and the equilibrium quantity at 2,000 tons a month. At this scale of chemical production, the marginal social cost is $150 and the marginal benefit is $150, so the outcome is efficient. The firms incur a marginal cost of $88 a ton and pay a tax of $62 a ton. The government collects tax revenue of $124,000 a month.

tists think that CFCs are one source of ozone layer depletion.

The largest sources of water pollution are the dumping of industrial waste and treated sewage in lakes and rivers and the runoff from fertilizers. A more dramatic source is the accidental spilling of crude oil into the oceans such as the *Exxon Valdez* spill in Alaska in 1989 and an even larger spill from the *Prestige* off Spain in 2002. The most frightening is the dumping of nuclear waste into the ocean by the former Soviet Union.

Land pollution arises from dumping toxic waste products. Ordinary household garbage does not pose a pollution problem unless dumped garbage seeps into the water supply. This possibility increases as less suitable landfill sites are used. It is estimated that 80 percent of existing landfills in the United States will be full by 2010.

Some densely populated regions (such as New York and New Jersey) and densely populated countries (such as Japan and the Netherlands), where land costs are high, are seeking less costly alternatives to landfill, such as recycling and incineration. Recycling is an apparently attractive alternative, but it requires an investment in new technologies to be effective. Incineration is a high-cost alternative to landfill, and it produces air pollution. These alternatives become efficient only when the cost of using landfills is high, as it is in densely populated regions and countries.

FIGURE 8.4
A Pollution Tax

Practice Online

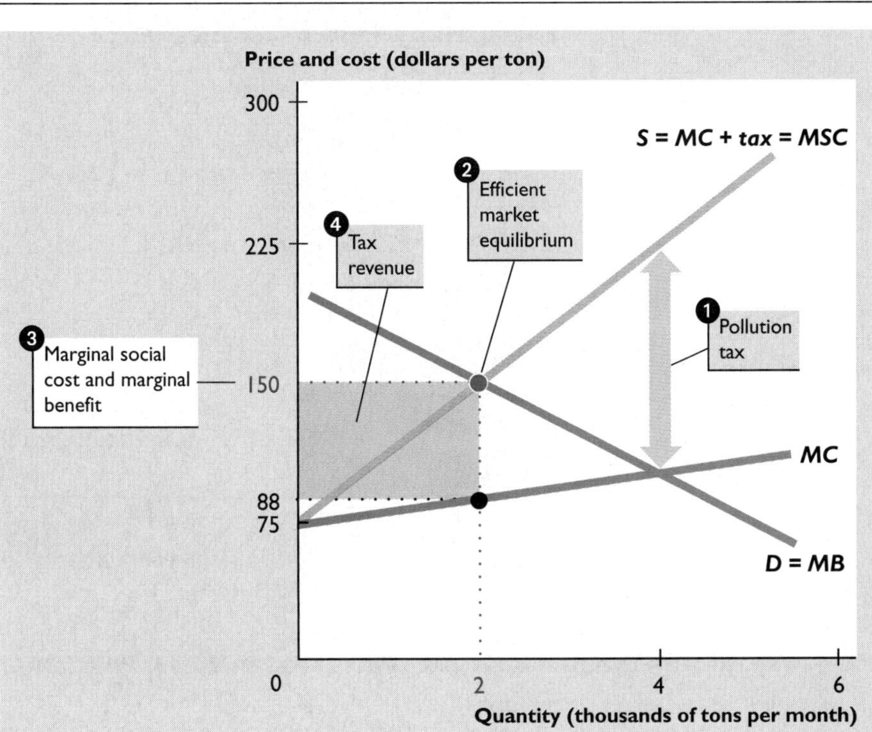

1. A pollution tax is imposed that is equal to the marginal external cost of pollution. The supply curve becomes the marginal private cost curve, *MC*, plus the tax—the curve labeled *S* = *MC* + *tax*.
2. Market equilibrium is at a price of $150 a ton and a quantity of 2,000 tons a month and is efficient because 3 marginal social cost equals marginal benefit.
4. The government collects tax revenue shown by the purple rectangle.

Eye on the Global Economy

A Carbon Fuel Tax?

Most countries tax gasoline at a much higher rate than does the United States. Why don't we have a higher gas tax to encourage a large reduction in emissions?

The question becomes even more pressing when we consider not only the current levels of greenhouse gases but also their projected future levels. In 1990, annual carbon emissions worldwide were a staggering 6 billion tons. By 2050, with current policies, that annual total is predicted to be 24 billion tons.

Part of the reason we do not have a higher gas tax is that many people do not accept the scientific evidence that emissions produce global warming. Climatologists are uncertain about how carbon emissions translate into atmospheric concentrations—about how the flow of emissions translates into a stock of pollution. The main uncertainty arises because carbon drains from the atmosphere into the oceans and vegetation at a rate that is not well understood. Climatologists are also uncertain about the connection between carbon concentration and temperature. And economists are uncertain about how a temperature increase translates into economic costs and benefits. Some economists believe that the costs and benefits are almost zero, while others believe that a temperature increase of 5.4 degrees Fahrenheit by 2090 will reduce the total output of goods and services by 20 percent.

Another factor weighing against a large change in fuel use is that the costs would be borne now, while the benefits, if any, would come many years in the future. To compare future benefits with current costs, we must use an interest rate. If the interest rate is 1 percent a year, a dollar today becomes \$2.70 in 100 years. If the interest rate is 5 percent a year, a dollar today becomes more than \$131.50 in 100 years. So at an interest rate of 1 percent a year, it is worth spending \$1 million in 2000 on pollution control to avoid \$2.7 million in environmental damage in 2100. At an interest rate of 5 percent a year, it is worth spending \$1 million today only if this expenditure avoids \$131.5 million in environmental damage 100 years from now.

Because large uncertain future benefits are needed to justify small current costs, a general tax on carbon fuels is not a high priority on the political agenda.

A final factor working against a large change in fuel use is the international pattern of the use of carbon fuels. Right now, carbon pollution comes in even doses from the industrial countries and the developing countries. But by 2050, three quarters of the carbon pollution will come from the developing countries (if the trends persist).

One reason for the high pollution rate in some developing countries (notably China, Russia, and other Eastern European countries) is that their governments subsidize the use of coal or oil. These subsidies lower producers' marginal costs and encourage the greater use of these fuels. The result is that the quantity of carbon fuels used exceeds the efficient quantity—and by a large amount. It is estimated that by 2050, these subsidies will induce annual global carbon emissions of some 10 billion tons—about two fifths of total emissions. If the subsidies were removed, global emissions in 2050 would be 10 billion tons a year less.

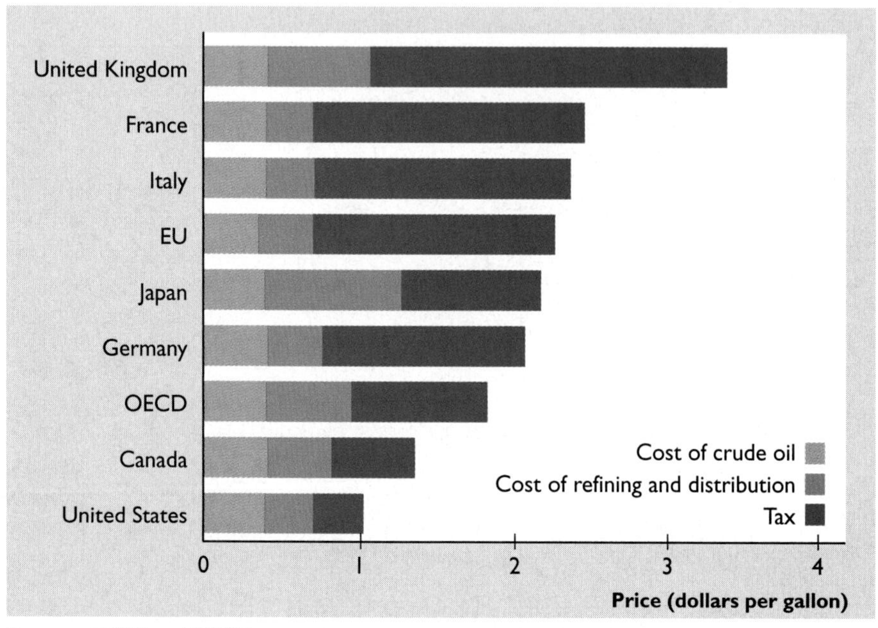

SOURCES: OPEC and OECD.

CHECKPOINT 8.1

1 Explain why negative externalities lead to inefficient overproduction and how property rights, pollution charges, and taxes can achieve a more efficient outcome.

Study Guide pp. 118–122

Practice Online 8.1

Practice Problem 8.1

Figure 1 illustrates the unregulated market for pesticide. When the factories produce pesticide, they also create waste, which they dump into a lake on the outskirts of the town. If the marginal external cost of the dumped waste is equal to the marginal private cost of producing the pesticide, then the marginal social cost of producing the pesticide is double the marginal private cost.

a. What is the quantity of pesticide produced if no one owns the lake?
b. What is the efficient quantity of pesticide?
c. If the residents of the town own the lake, what is the quantity of pesticide produced and how much do the pesticide factories pay to residents of the town?
d. If the pesticide factories own the lake, how much pesticide is produced?
e. Suppose that no one owns the lake but that the government levies a pollution tax. What is the tax per ton of pesticide that will achieve the efficient outcome?

FIGURE 1

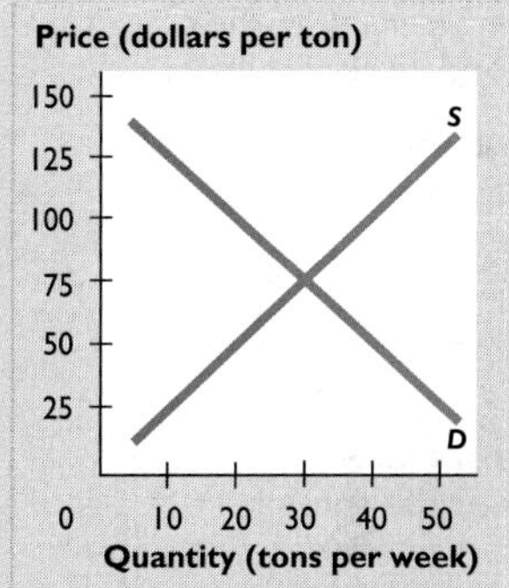

Price (dollars per ton)
150
125
100
75
50
25
0
S
D
10 20 30 40 50
Quantity (tons per week)

Exercise 8.1

Suppose that, in Practice Problem 8.1, the marginal external cost increases to twice the marginal private cost, so the marginal social cost of producing the pesticide is 3 times the marginal private cost. With no property rights, the government issues enough marketable permits to the town's residents to enable the factory to produce the efficient output of pesticide.

a. How much pesticide gets produced?
b. What is the price of a permit?
c. How, if at all, would the outcome change if the government allocated the permits to the factories instead of to the town's residents?

Solution to Practice Problem 8.1

a. The quantity of pesticide produced is 30 tons a week (Figure 2).
b. The efficient quantity of pesticide is 20 tons a week. At the efficient quantity, the marginal benefit to the factories equals the marginal social cost, which is the sum of the marginal private cost and the marginal external cost. When the factories produce 20 tons a week, the marginal social cost is $100 a ton and the marginal benefit is $100 a ton.
c. The quantity of pesticide produced is the efficient quantity, 20 tons a week, and the factories pay the townspeople the marginal external cost of $50 a ton.
d. The factories produce the efficient quantity—20 tons a week.
e. A tax of $50 a ton will achieve the efficient quantity of pesticide produced.

FIGURE 2

Price and cost (dollars per ton)
150
125
100
75
50
25
0
MSC
MC
D = MB
10 20 30 40 50
Quantity (tons per week)

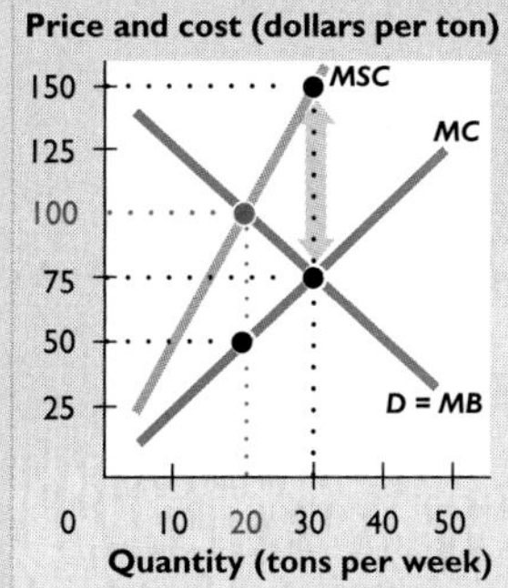

8.2 POSITIVE EXTERNALITIES: KNOWLEDGE

Knowledge comes from education and research. To study the economics of knowledge, we must distinguish between private benefits and social benefits.

Private Benefits and Social Benefits

Marginal private benefit
The benefit from an additional unit of a good or service that the consumer of that good or service receives.

Marginal external benefit
The benefit from an additional unit of a good or service that people other than the consumer of the good or service enjoy.

Marginal social benefit
The marginal benefit enjoyed by society—by the consumers of a good or service and by everyone else who benefits from it. It is the sum of marginal private benefit and marginal external benefit.

A *private benefit* is a benefit that the consumer of a good or service receives. *Marginal benefit* is the benefit from an *additional unit* of a good or service. So **marginal private benefit** (*MB*) is the benefit from an additional unit of a good or service that the consumer of that good or service receives.

You've seen that an *external benefit* is a benefit from a good or service that someone other than the consumer receives. A **marginal external benefit** is the benefit from an additional unit of a good or service that people other than the consumer enjoy.

Marginal social benefit (*MSB*) is the marginal benefit enjoyed by society—by the consumers of a good or service (marginal private benefit) plus the marginal benefit enjoyed by others (the marginal external benefit). That is,

$$MSB = MB + \text{Marginal external benefit.}$$

Figure 8.5 shows an example of the relationship between marginal private benefit, marginal external benefit, and marginal social benefit. The marginal benefit curve, *MB*, describes the marginal private benefit—such as expanded job opportunities and higher incomes—enjoyed by college graduates. Marginal private benefit decreases as the quantity of education increases.

FIGURE 8.5
An External Benefit

Practice Online

The *MB* curve shows the private marginal benefit enjoyed by the people who receive a college education. The *MSB* curve shows the sum of marginal private benefit and marginal external benefit. When 15 million students attend college, ❶ marginal private benefit is $10,000 per student, ❷ marginal external benefit is $15,000 per student, and ❸ marginal social benefit is $25,000 per student.

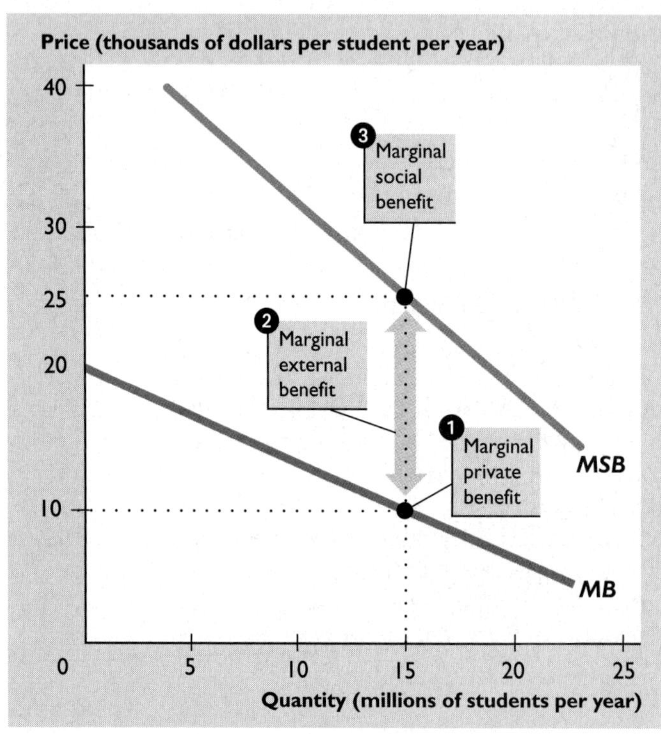

But college graduates generate external benefits. On the average, college graduates communicate more effectively with others and tend to be better citizens. Their crime rates are lower, and they are more tolerant of the views of others. And a society with a large number of college graduates can support activities such as high-quality newspapers and television channels, music, theater, and other organized social activities.

In the example in Figure 8.5, the marginal external benefit is $15,000 per student per year when 15 million students enroll in college. The marginal social benefit curve, *MSB*, is the sum of marginal private benefit and marginal external benefit. For example, when 15 million students a year enroll in college, the marginal private benefit is $10,000 per student and the marginal external benefit is $15,000 per student, so the marginal social benefit is $25,000 per student.

When people make decisions about how much schooling to undertake, they ignore its external benefits and consider only its private benefits. The result is that if education were provided by private schools that charged full-cost tuition, we would produce too few college graduates.

Figure 8.6 illustrates the underproduction if the government left education to the private market. The supply curve is the marginal cost curve of the private schools, *S* = *MC*. The demand curve is the marginal private benefit curve, *D* = *MB*. Market equilibrium is at a tuition of $15,000 per student per year and 7.5 million students per year. At this equilibrium, marginal social benefit is $38,000 per student, which exceeds marginal cost by $23,000. There are too few students in college. The efficient number is 15 million, where marginal social benefit equals marginal cost. The gray triangle shows the deadweight loss created by the underproduction.

FIGURE 8.6
Inefficiency with an External Benefit

Practice Online

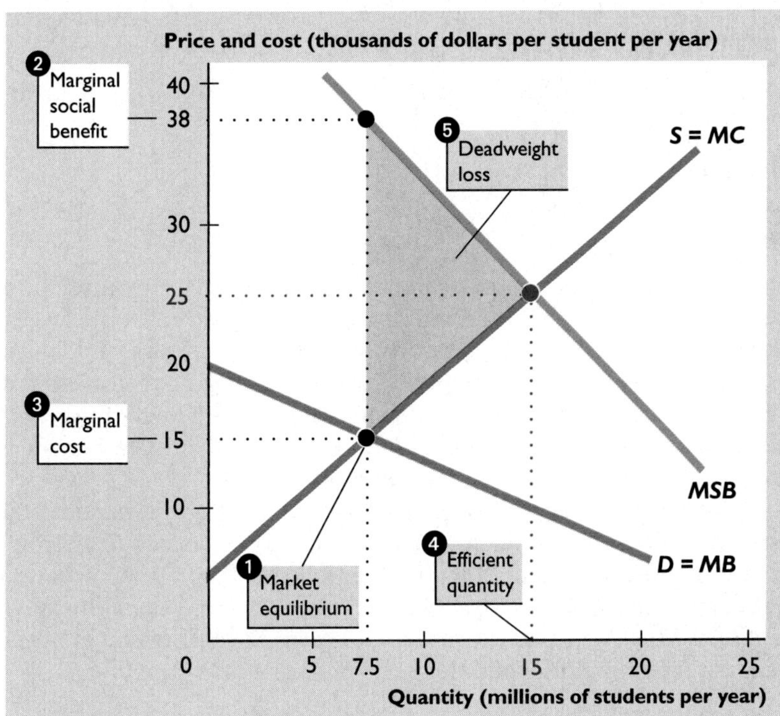

The market demand curve is the marginal private benefit curve, *D* = *MB*. The supply curve is the marginal cost curve, *S* = *MC*.

1. Market equilibrium is at a tuition of $15,000 a year and 7.5 million students and is inefficient because 2 marginal social benefit exceeds 3 marginal cost.
4. The efficient quantity is 15 million students.
5. The gray triangle shows the deadweight loss created because too few students enroll in college.

Underproduction similar to that in Figure 8.6 would occur at other levels of education—grade school and high school—if an unregulated market produced it. When children learn basic reading, writing, and number skills, they receive the private benefit of increased earning power. But even these basic skills bring the external benefit of developing better citizens.

External benefits also arise from research that leads to the discovery of new knowledge. When Isaac Newton worked out the formulas for calculating the rate of response of one variable to another—calculus—everyone was free to use his method. When a spreadsheet program called VisiCalc was invented, Lotus Corporation and Microsoft were free to copy the basic idea and create 1-2-3 and Excel. When the first shopping mall was built and found to be a successful way of arranging retailing, everyone was free to copy the idea, and malls spread like mushrooms.

Once someone has discovered how to do something, others can copy the basic idea. They do have to work to copy an idea, so they face an opportunity cost. But they do not usually have to pay the person who made the discovery to use it. When people make decisions about how much research to undertake, they ignore its external benefits and consider only its private benefits.

When people make decisions about the quantity of education or the amount of research to undertake, they balance the marginal private cost against the marginal private benefit. They ignore the external benefit. As a result, if we left education and research to unregulated market forces, we would get too little of these activities.

To get closer to producing the efficient quantity of a good or service that generates an external benefit, we make public choices, through governments, to modify the market outcome.

Government Actions in the Face of External Benefits

Four devices that governments can use to achieve a more efficient allocation of resources in the presence of external benefits, such as those that arise from education and research, are

- Public provision
- Private subsidies
- Vouchers
- Patents and copyrights

Public Provision

Public provision
The production of a good or service by a public authority that receives most of its revenue from the government.

Public provision is the production of a good or service by a public authority that receives most of its revenue from government. The education services produced by the public universities, colleges, and schools are examples of public provision.

Figure 8.7(a) shows how public provision might overcome the underproduction that arises in Figure 8.6. Public provision cannot lower the cost of production, so marginal cost is the same as before. Marginal private benefit and marginal external benefit are also the same as before.

The efficient quantity occurs where marginal social benefit equals marginal cost. In Figure 8.7(a), this quantity is 15 million students. Tuition is set to ensure that the efficient number of students enrolls. That is, tuition is set at the level that equals the marginal private benefit at the efficient quantity. In Figure 8.7(a), tuition is $10,000 a year. The rest of the cost of the public university is borne by the taxpayers and, in this example, is $15,000 per student per year.

Private Subsidies

A **subsidy** is a payment that the government makes to private producers. By making the subsidy depend on the level of output, the government can induce private decision makers to consider external benefits when they make their choices.

Subsidy
A payment that the government makes to private producers that depends on the level of output.

Figure 8.7(b) shows how a subsidy to private colleges works. In the absence of a subsidy, the marginal cost curve is the market supply curve of private college education, $S = MC$. The marginal benefit is the demand curve, $D = MB$. In this example, the government provides a subsidy to colleges of $15,000 per student per year. We must subtract the subsidy from the marginal cost of education to find the colleges' supply curve. That curve is $S = MC - subsidy$ in the figure. The equilibrium tuition (market price) is $10,000 a year, and the equilibrium quantity is 15 million students. To educate 15 million students, colleges incur a marginal cost of $25,000 a year. The marginal social benefit is also $25,000 a year. So with marginal cost equal to marginal social benefit, the subsidy has achieved an efficient outcome. The tuition and the subsidy just cover the colleges' marginal cost.

Whether a public school operating on government-provided funds or a private school receiving a subsidy does a better job is a difficult question to resolve.

FIGURE 8.7
Public Provision or Private Subsidy to Achieve an Efficient Outcome

Practice Online

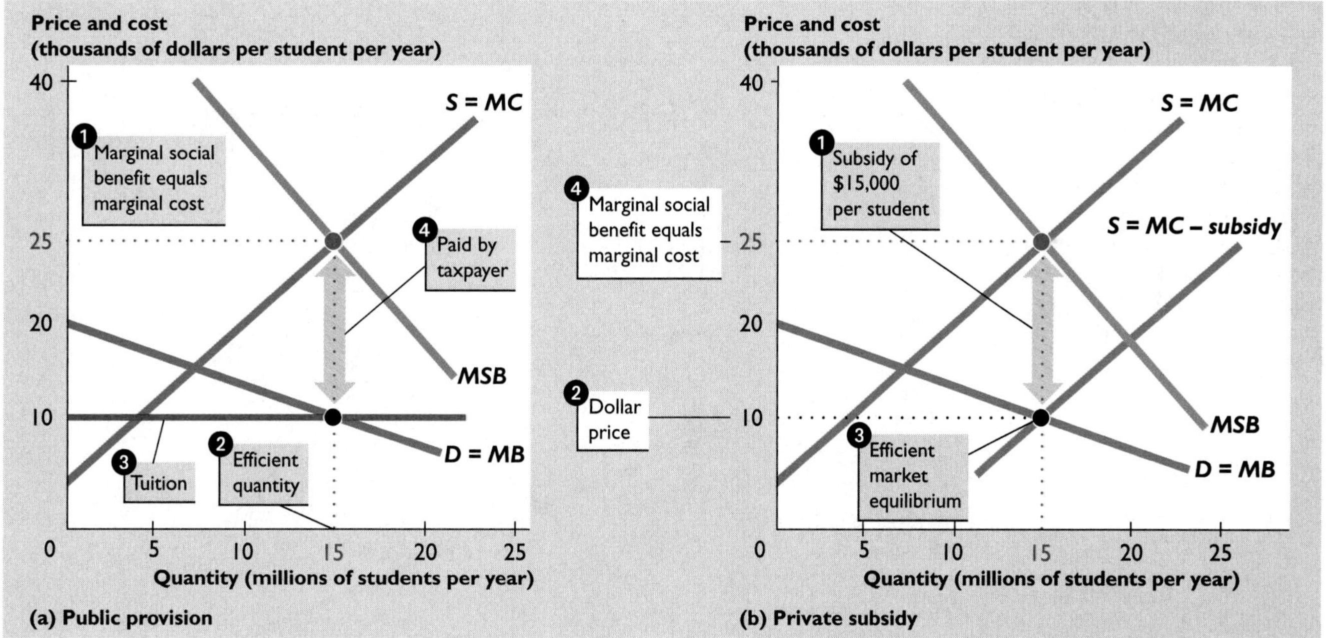

❶ Marginal social benefit equals marginal cost with 15 million students enrolled in college, the ❷ efficient quantity.

❸ Tuition is set at $10,000 per year, and ❹ the taxpayers cover the remaining $15,000 of marginal cost per student.

With a ❶ subsidy of $15,000 per student, the supply curve is $S = MC - subsidy$. ❷ The equilibrium price is $10,000, and ❸ the market equilibrium is efficient with 15 million students enrolled in college. ❹ Marginal social benefit equals marginal cost.

It turns on the efficiency of alternative mechanisms for monitoring school performance and on the strength of the incentives that school boards and private school operators have to deliver a high-quality service.

Vouchers

Voucher
A token that the government provides to households that can be used to buy specified goods or services.

A **voucher** is a token that the government provides to households, which they can use to buy specified goods or services. Food stamps that the U.S. Department of Agriculture provides under a federal Food Stamp Program are examples of vouchers. The vouchers (stamps) can be spent only on food and are designed to improve the diet and health of extremely poor families.

School vouchers have been advocated as a means of improving the quality of education and have been used in Cleveland and Milwaukee, though a proposition to introduce school vouchers in Michigan was defeated in the 2000 election.

A school voucher allows parents to choose the school their children will attend and to use the voucher to pay part of the cost. The school cashes the vouchers to pay its bills. A voucher could be provided to a college student in a similar way, and although technically not a voucher, a federal Pell Grant has a similar effect.

Because vouchers can be spent only on a specified item, they increase the willingness to pay for that item and so increase the demand for it. Figure 8.8 shows how a voucher system works. The government provides vouchers worth $15,000 per student per year. Parents (or students) use these vouchers to supplement the dollars they pay for college education. The market equilibrium occurs at a price of

FIGURE 8.8
Vouchers Achieve an Efficient Outcome

Practice Online

With vouchers, buyers are willing to pay *MB* plus the value of the voucher. 1 With a voucher worth $15,000, I market equilibrium is efficient. With 15 million students enrolled in college, 2 marginal social benefit equals marginal cost. The tuition, 3 the dollar price, is $10,000 and the school collects $15,000 from the government.

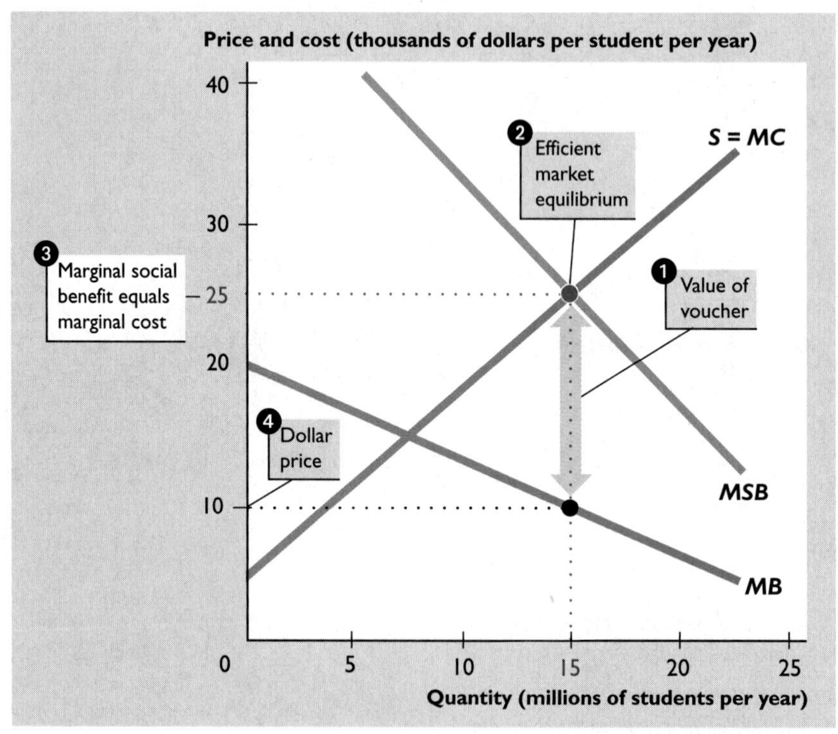

$25,000 per student per year and 15 million students attend college. Each student pays $10,000 tuition, and schools collect an additional $15,000 per student from the voucher.

If the government estimates the value of the external benefit correctly and makes the value of the voucher equal the marginal external benefit, the outcome from the voucher scheme is efficient. Marginal cost equals marginal social benefit, and the deadweight loss is eliminated.

Vouchers are similar to subsidies, but they provide the consumer rather than the producer with the financial resources. Advocates of vouchers say that they offer a more efficient outcome than subsidies do because the consumer can monitor school performance more effectively than the government can.

Patents and Copyrights

Every inventor benefits from previous inventions. Some inventions are so fundamental that they benefit many subsequent inventors. Some examples are calculus, invented by Newton and Leibniz, and the structure of DNA discovered by Crick and Watson. *Basic research* is the activity that leads to the development of these fundamental tools.

Research and development efforts build on the fruits of basic research to refine and improve on earlier advances. For example, each advance in knowledge about how to design and manufacture a processor chip for a PC has brought ever-larger increments in performance and productivity. Similarly, each advance in knowledge about how to design and build an airplane has brought ever larger increments in performance: Orville and Wilbur Wright's "Flyer 1" was a one-seat plane that could hop a farmer's field. The Lockheed Constellation could fly 120 passengers from New York to London, with two refueling stops, not much space, and a lot of noise and vibration. The latest Boeing 747 can carry 450 people nonstop from Los Angeles to Sydney or New York to Tokyo (flights of 7,500 miles that take 14 hours). Examples of the cumulative fruits of research and development efforts such as these can be found in fields as diverse as agriculture, biogenetics, communications, entertainment, medicine, and publishing.

Because discoveries build on previous discoveries, research generates external benefits. So it is necessary to use public policies to ensure that those who develop new ideas have incentives to encourage an efficient level of effort. The main way of providing the right incentives uses the central idea of the Coase theorem and assigns property rights—called **intellectual property rights**—to creators. The legal device for establishing intellectual property rights is the patent or copyright. A **patent** or **copyright** is a government-sanctioned exclusive right granted to the inventor of a good, service, or productive process to produce, use, and sell the invention for a given number of years. A patent enables the developer of a new idea to prevent others from benefiting freely from an invention for a limited number of years. But to obtain the protection of the law, an inventor must make knowledge of the invention public.

Intellectual property rights
The property rights of the creators of knowledge and other discoveries.

Patent or copyright
A government-sanctioned exclusive right granted to the inventor of a good, service, or productive process to produce, use, and sell the invention for a given number of years.

Although patents encourage invention and innovation, they do so at an economic cost. While a patent is in place, its holder has a monopoly. And monopoly is another source of inefficiency (which is explained in Chapter 11). But without a patent, the effort to develop new goods, services, or processes is diminished and the flow of new inventions is slowed. So the efficient outcome is a compromise that balances the benefits of more inventions against the cost of temporary monopoly in newly invented activities.

CHECKPOINT 8.2

Study Guide pp. 122–126

Practice Online 8.2

2 **Explain why positive externalities lead to inefficient underproduction and how public provision, subsidies, vouchers, and patents can achieve a more efficient outcome.**

Practice Problem 8.2

FIGURE 1

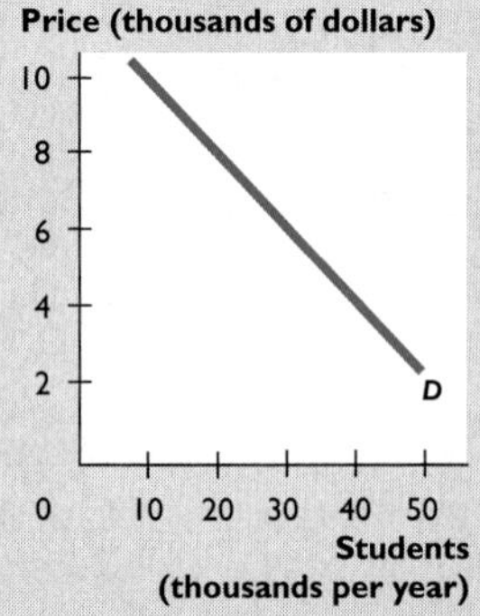

Figure 1 shows the marginal private benefit from college education. The marginal cost of a college education is a constant $6,000 a year. The marginal external benefit from a college education is $4,000 per student per year.

a. If colleges are private and government has no involvement in college education, how many people will undertake a college education and what will be the tuition?

b. What is the efficient number of students?

c. If the government decides to provide public colleges, what tuition will these colleges charge to achieve the efficient number of students? How much will taxpayers have to pay?

d. If the government decides to subsidize private colleges, what subsidy will achieve the efficient number of college students?

e. If the government offers vouchers to those who enroll at a college and no subsidy, what is the value of the voucher that will achieve the efficient number of students?

Exercise 8.2

FIGURE 2

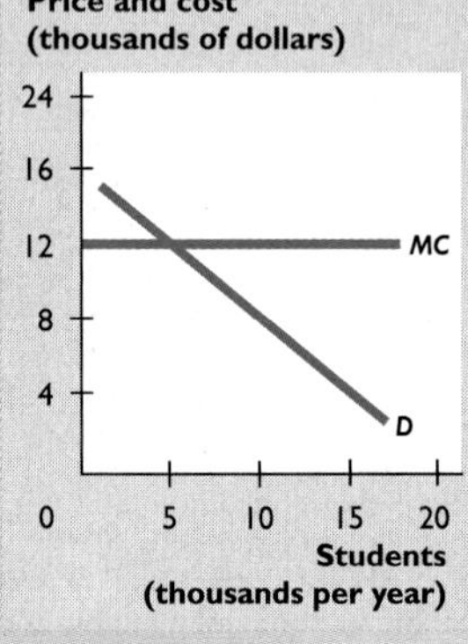

Figure 2 shows the marginal private benefit from a law degree and the marginal cost of obtaining a law degree. The marginal external benefit is $8,000 per law graduate per year.

a. If colleges are private and there is no government involvement in educating lawyers, how many people enroll in law school and what is the tuition?

b. What is the efficient number of law students?

c. If the government decides to provide public law schools, what tuition will the public schools charge to achieve the efficient number of students?

d. If the government decides to subsidize private law schools, what subsidy will achieve the efficient number of students?

e. If the government offers vouchers to law students, what is the value of the voucher that will achieve the efficient number of students?

Solution to Practice Problem 8.2

FIGURE 3

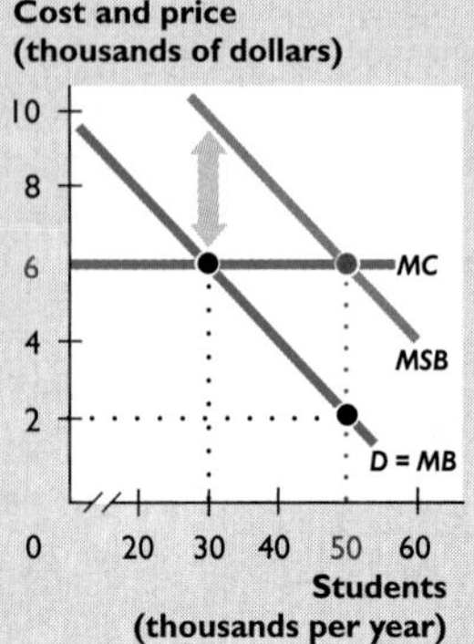

a. The tuition will be $6,000 a year, and 30,000 students will enroll—the intersection of the *MB* and *MC* curves (Figure 3).

b. The efficient number of students is 50,000 a year—the intersection of the *MSB* and *MC* curves (Figure 3).

c. To enroll 50,000 students, public colleges would charge $2,000 per student and taxpayers would pay $4,000 per student (Figure 3).

d. The subsidy would be $4,000 per student, which is equal to the marginal external benefit.

e. The value of the voucher will be $4,000 per student. The enrollment will be 50,000 if the tuition is $2,000. But the private college tuition is $6,000, so to get 50,000 students to enroll, the value of the voucher will have to be $4,000.

CHAPTER CHECKPOINT

Key Points

1 Explain why negative externalities lead to inefficient overproduction and how property rights, pollution charges, and taxes can achieve a more efficient outcome.

- External costs are costs of production that fall on people other than the producer of a good or service. Marginal social cost equals marginal private cost plus marginal external cost.
- Producers take account only of marginal private cost and produce more than the efficient quantity when there is a marginal external cost.
- Sometimes it is possible to overcome a negative externality by assigning a property right.
- When property rights cannot be assigned, governments might overcome a negative externality by using emission charges, marketable permits, or taxes.

2 Explain why positive externalities lead to inefficient underproduction and how public provision, subsidies, vouchers, and patents can achieve a more efficient outcome.

- External benefits are benefits that are received by people other than the consumer of a good or service. Marginal social benefit equals marginal private benefit plus marginal external benefit.
- External benefits from education arise because better-educated people are better citizens, commit fewer crimes, and support social activities.
- External benefits from research arise because once someone has worked out a basic idea, others can copy.
- Vouchers or subsidies to private schools or the provision of public education below cost can achieve a more efficient provision of education.
- Patents and copyrights create intellectual property rights and an incentive to innovate. But they do so by creating a temporary monopoly, the cost of which must be balanced against the benefit of more inventive activity.

Key Terms

Exercises

1. A city borders on a polluting steel mill. Table 1 shows the cost of cutting the pollution and the property taxes that people are willing to pay at different levels of pollution. Assume that the property taxes willingly paid measure the total benefit from cleaner air that results from the percentage cut in pollution.
   a. With no pollution control, how much pollution will there be?
   b. What is the efficient percentage decrease in pollution?
   c. If the city owns the steel mill, how much pollution will there be?
   d. If the city is a company town owned by the steel mill, how much pollution will there be?

TABLE 1

Pollution cut (percentage)	Property taxes willingly paid (dollars per day)	Total cost of pollution cut (dollars per day)
0	0	0
10	150	10
20	285	25
30	405	45
40	510	70
50	600	100
60	675	135
70	735	175
80	780	220
90	810	270

2. Tom and Larry are working on a project that makes it necessary for them to spend a day together. Tom likes to smoke, and his marginal benefit from one cigar a day is $20. The price of a cigar is $2. Larry dislikes cigar smoke, and his marginal benefit from a smoke-free environment is $25 a day. What is the outcome if they
   a. Meet at Tom's home?
   b. Meet at Larry's home?

3. If in exercise 2, Tom's marginal benefit from one cigar a day is $25 and Larry's marginal benefit from a smoke-free environment is $20 a day, what is the outcome if they:
   a. Meet at Tom's home?
   b. Meet at Larry's home?

4. The marginal cost of educating a college student is $5,000 a year. Table 2 shows the marginal private benefit schedule from a college education. The marginal external benefit for college education is $2,000 per student per year.
   a. With no public colleges and no government involvement in college education, how many students will enroll and what is the tuition?
   b. If the government subsidizes private colleges and sets the subsidy so that the efficient number of students will enroll in college, what is the subsidy per student? How many students will enroll?
   c. If the government offers vouchers to students (but no subsidy to private colleges) and values the vouchers so that the efficient number of students will enroll in college, what is the value of the voucher? How many students will enroll?

TABLE 2

Students (millions per year)	Marginal private benefit (dollars per student per year)
1	5,000
2	3,000
3	2,000
4	1,500
5	1,200
6	1,000
7	800
8	500

5. For many people, distance education has cut the cost of a college education. If in exercise 4, an Internet course cuts the cost to $3,500 a year and increases the marginal external benefit to $3,000 per student per year, what now are your answers to exercise 4?

6. Suppose that researchers could not obtain patents for their discoveries.
   a. What do you think would happen to the pace of technological change?
   b. Would consumers' or producers' interests be damaged by a lack of patent protection?
   c. Would anyone gain?

7. Suppose that popular singers could not obtain copyrights for their recordings.
   a. What do you think would happen to the quantity and quality of recorded music?
   b. Would consumers be better off because they could buy cheaper CDs? Explain why or why not.

Critical Thinking

8. The Kyoto Protocol on greenhouse gas emissions was adopted at the United Nations Framework Convention on Climate Change in 1997. The major provision of the protocol is a set of national targets, with dates, for the reduction of greenhouse gas emissions. Countries with large amounts of emissions (of which the United States is one) have the most severe targets. The United States has steadfastly refused to ratify the Kyoto Protocol, but the European Union has ratified it.
   - **a.** Why do you think the United States might be reluctant to ratify the Kyoto Protocol?
   - **b.** Why do you think the European Union was willing to ratify it?
   - **c.** In light of the principles you've learned in this chapter, what types of data would you need to collect if you were to determine whether the emission target for the United States laid out in the Kyoto Protocol is efficient?
   - **d.** What is your own view on whether the United States should ratify the Kyoto Protocol and why?

9. The price of gasoline in Europe is much higher than that in the United States, and the reason is that the gas tax is much higher there than here.
   - **a.** What is the range of externalities that arise from automobiles?
   - **b.** In light of the principles you've learned in this chapter, what is the case *for* increasing the gas tax in the United States to the European level?
   - **c.** In light of the principles you've learned in this chapter, what is the case *against* increasing the gas tax in the United States to the European level?
   - **d.** What is your view on whether the United States should raise the gas tax to the European level and why?

10. The debate over school vouchers often creates more heat than light.
    - **a.** Why do you think that school vouchers are controversial?
    - **b.** In light of the principles you've learned in this chapter, what is the case *for* replacing the existing school funding arrangements with vouchers?
    - **c.** In light of the principles you've learned in this chapter, what is the case *against* replacing the existing school funding arrangements with vouchers?

11. It has been estimated that developing new technologies and figuring out how to use them accounts for more than half of economic growth—the expansion of production possibilities. In light of this fact:
    - **a.** Do you think that the government should subsidize research and development?
    - **b.** Do you think that the government should subsidize basic research?
    - **c.** Do you think it would be a good idea to award prizes to firms for the successful development of a new technology?
    - **d.** Do you think that firms should be given tax breaks for the successful development of a new technology?
    - **e.** Do you think the patent laws should be strengthened so that the inventor of a new technology can be protected from competition for longer than is currently the case?
    - **f.** Provide your own ranking of the alternatives in parts **a** through **e** along with the further alternative of leaving research and development to unregulated market forces. Explain your ranking, being explicit about your assumptions about the efficiency of each approach.

Practice Online

Web Exercises

Use the links on your Foundations Web site to work the following exercises.

12. Visit the EPA "Search Your Community" page. Enter your zip code in the box provided and press the "Submit" button.
   a. Obtain information about a negative production externality in your neighborhood.
   b. Explain which, if any, of the tools reviewed in this chapter the government is using to address the externality.
   c. Explain how the government's action will work or why you think it will not work. Use the concepts of marginal private cost, marginal external cost, marginal social cost, and efficiency in your explanation.
   d. If you think the current measures for dealing with this externality are not working or are not working well enough, what do you think needs to be done? Again, use the concepts of marginal private cost, marginal external cost, marginal social cost, and efficiency in your analysis.

13. Visit the EPA "Ground Water and Drinking Water" page.
   a. What types of externalities arise in the production of safe drinking water?
   b. Review and summarize the elements of the cost-benefit analysis that the EPA is undertaking on this issue.
   c. What do you think are the main outstanding issues to be resolved in ensuring the provision of safe drinking water in the United States? Use the concepts of marginal private cost, marginal external cost, marginal social cost, and efficiency in your analysis.

14. Visit the Cape Cod Times and read the article about wind farms off the New England coast.
   a. What types of externalities arise in the production of electricity using wind technologies?
   b. Comparing the externalities from wind technologies with those from burning coal and oil, which do you think are the more widespread and affect more people?
   c. How do you think the external costs of using wind technologies should be dealt with? Compare all the alternative methods suggested by the range of solutions considered in this chapter.
   d. Can you think of reasons why, despite the lower external costs, a campaign against the use of wind technology might be more successful than a campaign against the use of coal or oil?

15. Learn about the destruction of the habitat of the northern spotted owl.
   a. What production activity is creating problems for the northern spotted owl?
   b. What type of externalities arise from this production activity?
   c. How would you set about designing a method for dealing with this externality?

16. Visit the Global Policy site and read about the idea of introducing a carbon tax. Explain how a carbon tax might work. Would it increase or decrease the quantity of electricity consumed? How would it change the ways in which electricity is generated? Who would bear the costs of the tax and who would enjoy the benefits? Do you think such a tax is likely to be introduced? Why or why not?

CHAPTER 9

Production and Cost

CHAPTER CHECKLIST

When you have completed your study of this chapter, you will be able to

1. **Explain how economists measure a firm's cost of production and profit.**
2. **Explain the relationship between a firm's output and labor employed in the short run.**
3. **Explain the relationship between a firm's output and costs in the short run.**
4. **Derive and explain a firm's long-run average cost curve.**

In this chapter, you're going to lay the foundation for understanding how firms' decisions in competitive markets lead to the law of supply. We continue to use the big ideas that define the economic way of thinking. But we now apply these ideas to the decisions of firms. Firms face scarcity and make *rational* choices; the *cost* of something is what a firm *must give up* to produce it; and firms respond to *incentives*.

You're now going to see how these principles lead firms to make decisions that minimize the cost of producing a given output. In this chapter, you'll learn how a firm's costs are determined and how they vary as the firm varies its output.

What you learn in this chapter you will use again and again in the other three chapters of this part, so it is very important that you thoroughly understand the content of this chapter before moving forward to Chapter 10.

9.1 ECONOMIC COST AND PROFIT

The 20 million firms in the United States differ in size and in what they produce. But they all perform the same basic economic function: They hire factors of production and organize them to produce and sell goods and services. To understand the behavior of a firm, we need to know its goals.

The Firm's Goal

If you asked a group of entrepreneurs what they are trying to achieve, you would get many different answers. Some would talk about making a high-quality product, others about business growth, others about market share, and others about work force job satisfaction. All of these goals might be pursued, but they are not the fundamental goal. They are a means to a deeper goal.

The firm's goal is to *maximize profit*. A firm that does not seek to maximize profit is either eliminated or bought by firms that *do* seek that goal. To calculate a firm's profit, we must determine its total revenue and total cost. Economists have a special way of defining and measuring cost and profit, which we'll explain and illustrate by looking at Sam's Smoothies, a firm that is owned and operated by Samantha.

Accounting Cost and Profit

In 2002, Sam's Smoothies' total revenue from the sale of smoothies was $150,000. The firm paid $20,000 for fruit, yogurt, and honey; $22,000 in wages for the labor it hired; and $3,000 in interest to the bank. These expenses totaled $45,000.

Sam's accountant said that the depreciation of the firm's blenders, refrigerators, and shop during 2002 was $10,000. Depreciation is the fall in the value of the firm's capital, and accountants calculate it by using the Internal Revenue Service's rules, which are based on standards set by the Financial Accounting Standards Board. So the accountant reported Sam's Smoothies' total cost for 2002 as $55,000 and the firm's profit as $95,000—$150,000 of total revenue minus $55,000 of total costs.

Sam's accountant measures cost and profit to ensure that the firm pays the correct amount of income tax and to show the bank how Sam's has used its bank loan. Economists have a different purpose: to predict the decisions that a firm makes to maximize its profit. These decisions respond to *opportunity cost* and *economic profit*.

Opportunity Cost

To produce its output, a firm employs factors of production: land, labor, capital, and entrepreneurship. Another firm could have used these same resources to produce alternative goods or services. In Chapter 3 (pp. 68–70), resources can be used to produce either bottled water or CDs, so the opportunity cost of producing a bottle of water is the number of CDs forgone. Pilots who fly passengers for United Airlines can't at the same time fly freight for Federal Express. Construction workers who are building an office tower can't simultaneously build apartments. A communications satellite operating at peak capacity can carry television signals or e-mail messages but not both at the same time. A journalist writing for the *New*

York Times can't at the same time create Web news reports for CNN. And Samantha can't simultaneously run her smoothies business and a flower shop.

The highest-valued alternative forgone is the opportunity cost of a firm's production. From the viewpoint of the firm, this opportunity cost is the amount that the firm must pay the owners of the factors of production it employs to attract them from their best alternative use. So a firm's opportunity cost of production is the cost of the factors of production it employs.

To determine these costs, let's return to Sam's and look at the opportunity cost of producing smoothies.

Explicit Costs and Implicit Costs

The amount that a firm pays to attract resources from their best alternative use is either an explicit cost or an implicit cost. A cost paid in money is an **explicit cost**. Because the amount spent could have been spent on something else, an explicit cost is an opportunity cost. The wages that Samantha pays labor, the interest she pays the bank, and her expenditure on fruit, yogurt, and honey are explicit costs.

Explicit cost
A cost paid in money.

A firm incurs an **implicit cost** when it uses a factor of production but does not make a direct money payment for its use. The two categories of implicit cost are economic depreciation and the cost of the firm owner's resources.

Implicit cost
An opportunity cost incurred by a firm when it uses a factor of production for which it does not make a direct money payment.

Economic depreciation is the opportunity cost of the firm using capital that it owns. It is measured as the change in the *market value* of capital—the market price of the capital at the beginning of a period minus its market price at the end of a period. Suppose that Samantha could have sold her blenders, refrigerators, and shop on December 31, 2001, for $250,000. If she can sell the same capital on December 31, 2002, for $246,000, her economic depreciation during 2002 is $4,000. This is the opportunity cost of using her capital during 2002, not the $10,000 depreciation calculated by Sam's accountant.

Economic depreciation
An opportunity cost of a firm using capital that it owns—measured as the change in the *market value* of capital over a given period.

Interest is another cost of capital. When the firm's owner provides the funds used to buy capital, the opportunity cost of those funds is the interest income forgone by not using them in the best alternative way. If Sam loaned her firm funds that could have earned her $1,000 in interest, this amount is an implicit cost of producing smoothies.

When a firm's owner supplies labor, the opportunity cost of the owner's time spent working for the firm is the wage income forgone by not working in the best alternative job. For example, instead of working at her next best job that pays $34,000 a year, Sam supplies labor to her smoothies business. This implicit cost of $34,000 is part of the opportunity cost of producing smoothies.

Finally, a firm's owner often supplies entrepreneurship, the factor of production that organizes the business and bears the risk of running it. The return to entrepreneurship is **normal profit**. Normal profit is part of a firm's opportunity cost because it is the cost of a forgone alternative—running another firm. Instead of running Sam's Smoothies, Sam could earn $16,000 a year running a flower shop. This amount is an implicit cost of production at Sam's Smoothies.

Normal profit
The return to entrepreneurship. Normal profit is part of a firm's opportunity cost because it is the cost of not running another firm.

Economic Profit

A firm's **economic profit** equals total revenue minus total cost. Total revenue is the amount received from the sale of the product. It is the price of the output multiplied by the quantity sold. Total cost is the sum of the explicit costs and implicit costs and is the opportunity cost of production.

Economic profit
A firm's total revenue minus total cost.

TABLE 9.1
Economic Accounting

Practice Online

Item		
Total Revenue		**$150,000**
Explicit Costs		
Cost of fruit, yogurt, and honey	$20,000	
Wages	$22,000	
Interest	$3,000	
Implicit Costs		
Samantha's forgone wages	$34,000	
Samantha's forgone interest	$1,000	
Economic depreciation	$4,000	
Normal profit	$16,000	
Opportunity Cost		**$100,000**
Economic Profit		**$50,000**

Because one of the firm's implicit costs is *normal profit*, the return to the entrepreneur equals normal profit plus economic profit. If a firm incurs an economic loss, the entrepreneur receives less than normal profit.

Table 9.1 summarizes the economic cost concepts, and Figure 9.1 compares the economic view and the accounting view of cost and profit. The total revenue received by Sam's Smoothies is $150,000; the opportunity cost of the resources that Sam uses is $100,000; and Sam's economic profit is $50,000.

FIGURE 9.1
Two Views of Cost and Profit

Practice Online

Economists measure economic profit as total revenue minus opportunity cost. Opportunity cost includes explicit costs and implicit costs. Normal profit is an implicit cost. Accountants measure profit as total revenue minus explicit costs—costs paid in money—and depreciation.

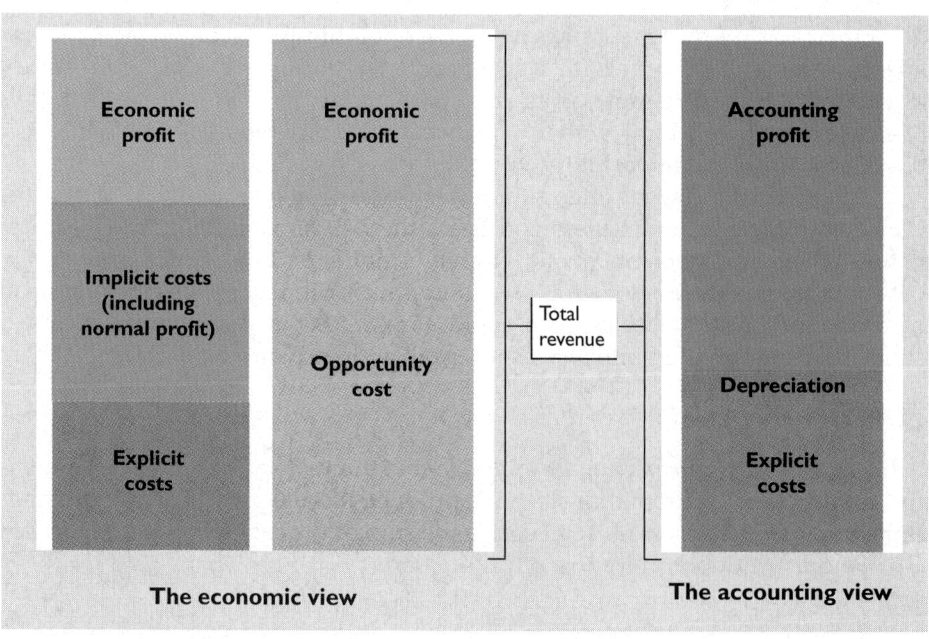

CHECKPOINT 9.1

1 **Explain how economists measure a firm's cost of production and profit.**

Study Guide pp. 132–135

Practice Online 9.1

Practice Problem 9.1

Lee is a computer programmer who earned $35,000 in 2001. But Lee loves water sports and in 2002 he opened a body board manufacturing business. At the end of the first year of operation, he submitted the following information to his accountant:

- **i.** He stopped renting out his seaside cottage for $3,500 a year and used it as his factory. The market value of the cottage increased from $70,000 to $71,000.
- **ii.** He spent $50,000 on materials, phone, utilities etc.
- **iii.** He leased machines for $10,000 a year.
- **iv.** He paid $15,000 in wages.
- **v.** He used $10,000 from his savings account at the bank, which pays 5 percent a year interest.
- **vi.** He borrowed $40,000 at 10 percent a year from the bank.
- **vii.** He sold $160,000 worth of body boards.
- **viii.** Normal profit is $25,000 a year.

a. Calculate Lee's explicit costs and implicit costs.
b. Calculate Lee's economic profit.
c. Lee's accountant recorded the depreciation on Lee's cottage during 2002 as $7,000. What did the accountant say Lee's profit or loss was for the year?

Exercise 9.1

In 2002, Toni taught music and earned $20,000. She also earned $4,000 by renting out her basement. On January 1, 2003, she quit teaching, stopped renting out her basement, and began to use it as the office for her new Web site design business. She took $2,000 from her savings account to buy a new computer. During 2003, she paid $1,500 for the lease of a Web server and $1,750 for high-speed Internet service. She received a total revenue from Web site designing of $45,000 and earned interest at 5 percent a year on her savings account balance. The normal profit of a Web site design firm is $55,000 a year. At the end of 2003, Toni could have sold her computer for $500. For 2003, calculate Toni's

a. Explicit costs.
b. Implicit costs.
c. Economic profit.

Solution to Practice Problem 9.1

a. Explicit costs are costs paid with money. Explicit costs are items (ii), (iii), (iv), and (vi). Explicit costs are $50,000 + $10,000 + $15,000 + $4,000, or $79,000. Implicit costs are the wages forgone and items (i), (v), and (viii) minus the increase in the market value of the cottage. That is, implicit costs are $35,000 + $3,500 + $500 + $25,000 – $1,000, or $63,000.

b. Economic profit equals total revenue minus total costs. Total cost is the sum of explicit costs plus implicit costs. Total costs are $79,000 + $63,000, or $142,000. So Lee's economic profit is $160,000 – $142,000, or $18,000.

c. The accountant measures Lee's profit as total revenue minus explicit costs minus depreciation. That is, profit is $160,000 – $79,000 – $7,000, or $74,000.

SHORT RUN AND LONG RUN

The main goal of this chapter is to explore the influences on a firm's cost. The key influence on cost is the quantity of output that the firm produces per period. The greater the output rate, the higher is the total cost of production. But the effect of a change in production on cost depends on how soon the firm wants to act. A firm that plans to change its output rate tomorrow has fewer options than a firm that plans ahead and intends to change its production six months from now.

To study the relationship between a firm's output decision and its costs, we distinguish between two decision time frames:

- The short run
- The long run

The Short Run: Fixed Plant

Short run
The time frame in which the quantities of some resources are fixed. In the short run, a firm can usually change the quantity of labor it uses but not its technology and quantity of capital.

The **short run** is the time frame in which the quantities of some resources are fixed. For most firms, the fixed resources are the firm's technology and capital—its equipment and buildings. The management organization is also fixed in the short run. The fixed resources that a firm uses are its *fixed factors of production* and the resources that it can vary are its *variable factors of production*. The collection of fixed resources is the firm's *plant*. So in the short run, a firm's plant is fixed.

Sam's Smoothies' plant is its blenders, refrigerators, and shop. Sam's cannot change these inputs in the short run. An electric power utility can't change the number of generators it uses in the short run. An airport can't change the number of runways, terminal buildings, and traffic control facilities in the short run.

To increase output in the short run, a firm must increase the quantity of variable factors it uses. Labor is usually the variable factor of production. To produce more smoothies, Sam must hire more labor. Similarly, to increase the production of electricity, a utility must hire more engineers and run its generators for longer hours. To increase the volume of traffic it handles, an airport must hire more check-in clerks, cargo handlers, and air-traffic controllers.

Short-run decisions are easily reversed. A firm can increase or decrease output in the short run by increasing or decreasing the labor hours it hires.

The Long Run: Variable Plant

Long run
The time frame in which the quantities of *all* resources can be varied.

The **long run** is the time frame in which the quantities of *all* resources can be varied. That is, the long run is a period in which the firm can change its *plant*.

To increase output in the long run, a firm can increase the size of its plant. Sam's Smoothies can install more blenders and refrigerators and increase the size of its shop. An electric power utility can install more generators. And an airport can build more runways, terminals, and traffic-control facilities.

Long-run decisions are *not* easily reversed. Once a firm buys a new plant, its resale value is usually much less than the amount the firm paid for it. The difference between the cost of the plant and its resale value is a *sunk cost*. A sunk cost is irrelevant to the firm's decisions (see Chapter 1, p. 14). The only costs that influence the firm's decisions are the short-run cost of changing its labor inputs and the long-run cost of changing its plant.

We're going to study costs in the short run and the long run. We begin with the short run and describe the limits to the firm's production possibilities.

9.2 SHORT-RUN PRODUCTION

To increase the output of a fixed plant, a firm must increase the quantity of labor it employs. We describe the relationship between output and the quantity of labor employed by using three related concepts:

- Total product
- Marginal product
- Average product

Total Product

Total product (*TP*) is the total quantity of a good produced in a given period. Total product is an output *rate*—the number of units produced per unit of time (for example, per hour, day, or week). Total product increases as the quantity of labor employed increases, and we illustrate this relationship as a total product schedule and total product curve like those in Figure 9.2. The total product schedule (the table below the graph) lists the maximum quantities of smoothies per hour that Sam can produce with her existing plant at each quantity of labor. Points *A* through *H* on the *TP* curve correspond to the columns in the table.

Total product
The total quantity of a good produced in a given period.

FIGURE 9.2
Total Product Schedule and Total Product Curve

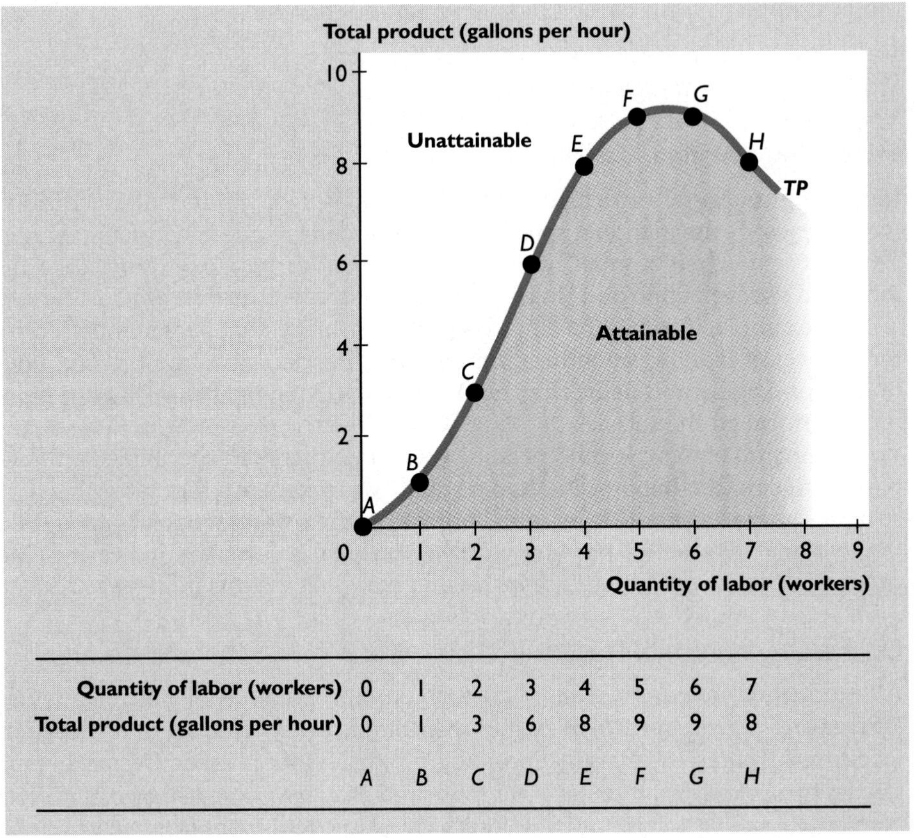

Quantity of labor (workers)	0	1	2	3	4	5	6	7
Total product (gallons per hour)	0	1	3	6	8	9	9	8
	A	*B*	*C*	*D*	*E*	*F*	*G*	*H*

The total product schedule shows how the quantity of smoothies that Sam's can produce changes as the quantity of labor employed changes. In column *C*, Sam's employs 2 workers and can produce 3 gallons of smoothies an hour.

The total product curve, *TP*, graphs the data in the table. Points *A* through *H* on the curve correspond to the columns of the table. The total product curve separates attainable outputs from unattainable outputs. Points below the *TP* curve are inefficient. Points on the *TP* curve are efficient.

Like the *production possibilities frontier* (see Chapter 3, p. 62), the total product curve separates attainable outputs from unattainable outputs. All the points that lie above the curve are unattainable. Points that lie below the curve, in the orange area, are attainable. But they are inefficient: They use more labor than is necessary to produce a given output. Only the points *on* the total product curve are efficient.

Marginal Product

Marginal product
The change in total product that results from a one-unit increase in the quantity of labor employed.

Marginal product (*MP*) is the change in total product that results from a one-unit increase in the quantity of labor employed. It tells us the contribution to total product of adding one additional worker. When the quantity of labor increases by more (or less) than one worker, we calculate marginal product as

Marginal product = Change in total product ÷ Change in quantity of labor.

Figure 9.3 shows Sam's Smoothies' marginal product curve, *MP*, and its relationship with the total product curve. You can see that as the quantity of labor increases from 1 to 3 workers, marginal product increases. But as yet more workers are employed, marginal product decreases. When the 7th worker is employed, marginal product is negative.

Notice that the steeper the slope of the total product curve in part (a), the greater is marginal product in part (b). And when the total product curve turns downward in part (a), marginal product is negative in part (b).

The total product curve and marginal product curve in Figure 9.3 incorporate a feature that is shared by all production processes in firms as different as the Ford Motor Company, Jim's Barber Shop, and Sam's Smoothies:

- Increasing marginal returns initially
- Decreasing marginal returns eventually

Increasing Marginal Returns

Increasing marginal returns
When the marginal product of an additional worker exceeds the marginal product of the previous worker.

Increasing marginal returns occur when the marginal product of an additional worker exceeds the marginal product of the previous worker. Increasing marginal returns occur when a small number of workers are employed and arise from increased specialization and division of labor in the production process.

For example, if Samantha employs just one worker, that person must learn all the aspects of making smoothies: running the blender, cleaning it, fixing breakdowns, packaging and delivering, buying and checking the fruit. That one person must perform all these tasks.

If Samantha hires a second person, the two workers can specialize in different parts of the production process. As a result, two workers produce more than twice as much as one worker. The marginal product of the second worker is greater than the marginal product of the first worker. Marginal returns are increasing. Most production processes experience increasing marginal returns initially.

Decreasing Marginal Returns

Decreasing marginal returns
When the marginal product of an additional worker is less than the marginal product of the previous worker.

All production processes eventually reach a point of *decreasing* marginal returns. **Decreasing marginal returns** occur when the marginal product of an additional worker is less than the marginal product of the previous worker. Decreasing marginal returns arise from the fact that more and more workers use the same equipment and work space. As more workers are employed, there is less and less that is productive for the additional worker to do. For example, if Samantha hires a

FIGURE 9.3

Total Product and Marginal Product

Practice Online

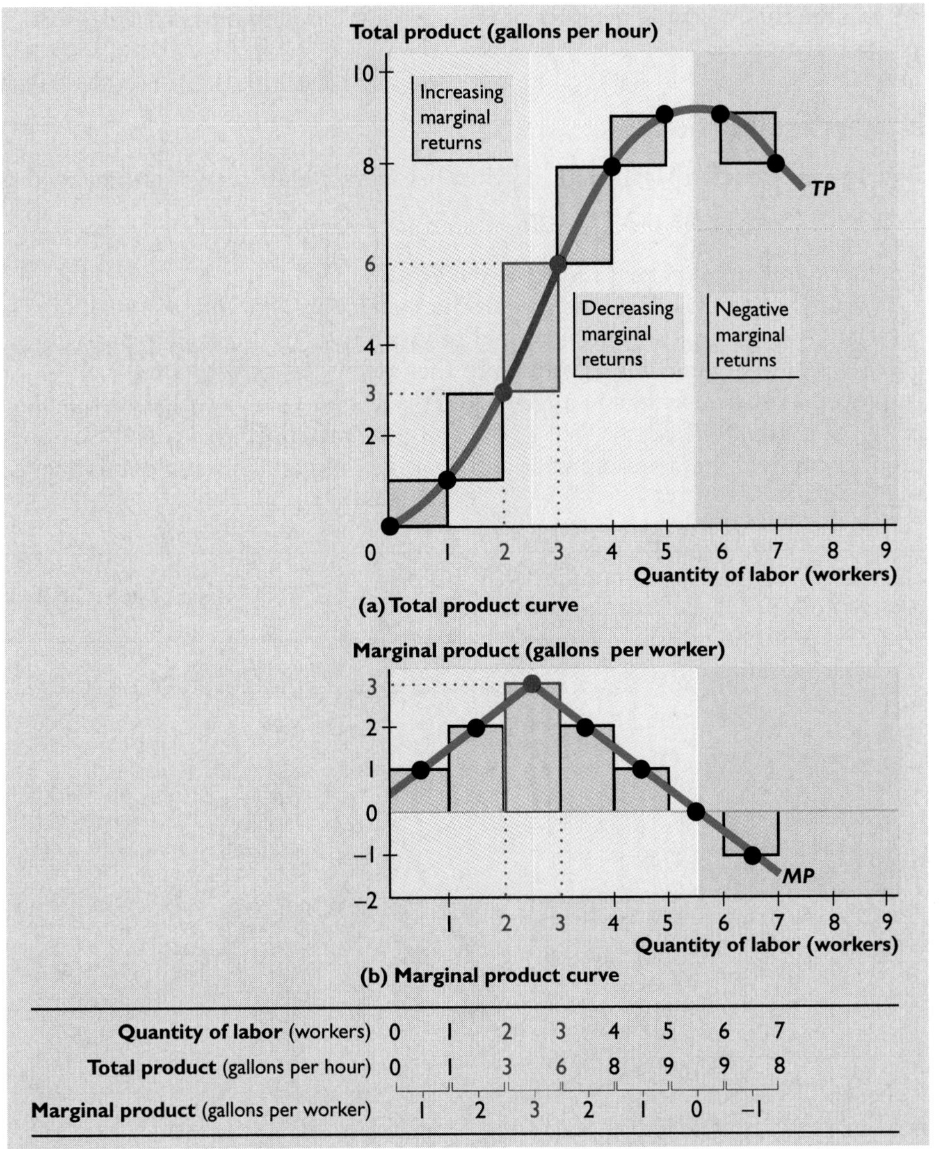

Quantity of labor (workers)	0	1	2	3	4	5	6	7
Total product (gallons per hour)	0	1	3	6	8	9	9	8
Marginal product (gallons per worker)		1	2	3	2	1	0	–1

The table calculates marginal product and the orange bars illustrate it. When labor increases from 2 to 3 workers, total product increases from 3 gallons to 6 gallons an hour. So marginal product is the orange bar whose height is 3 gallons (in both parts of the figure).

In part (b), marginal product is graphed midway between the labor inputs to emphasize that it is the result of *changing* inputs. Marginal product increases to a maximum (when 3 workers are employed in this example) and then declines—diminishing marginal product.

fourth worker, output increases but not by as much as it did when she hired the third worker. In this case, three workers exhaust all the possible gains from specialization and the division of labor. By hiring a fourth worker, Sam's produces more smoothies per hour, but the equipment is being operated closer to its limits. Sometimes the fourth worker has nothing to do because the machines are running without the need for further attention.

Hiring yet more workers continues to increase output but by successively smaller amounts until Samantha hires the sixth worker, at which point total product stops rising. Add a seventh worker and the workplace is so congested that the workers get in each other's way and total product falls.

Decreasing marginal returns are so pervasive that they qualify for the status of a law: the **law of decreasing returns**, which states that

> **As a firm uses more of a variable input, with a given quantity of fixed inputs, the marginal product of the variable input eventually decreases.**

Average Product

Average product
Total product divided by the quantity of an input. The average product of labor is total product divided by the quantity of labor employed.

Average product (*AP*) is the total product per worker employed. It is calculated as

Average product = Total product ÷ Quantity of labor.

Another name for average product is *productivity*.

Figure 9.4 shows the average product of labor, *AP*, and the relationship between average product and marginal product. Average product increases from 1 to 3 workers (its maximum value) but then decreases as yet more workers are employed. Notice also that average product is largest when average product and marginal product are equal. That is, the marginal product curve cuts the average product curve at the point of maximum average product. For employment levels

FIGURE 9.4
Average Product and Marginal Product

Practice Online

The table calculates average product. For example, when the quantity of labor is 3 workers, total product is 6 gallons an hour, so average product is 6 ÷ 3 = 2 gallons a worker.

The average product curve is *AP*. When marginal product exceeds average product, average product is increasing. When marginal product is less than average product, average product is decreasing.

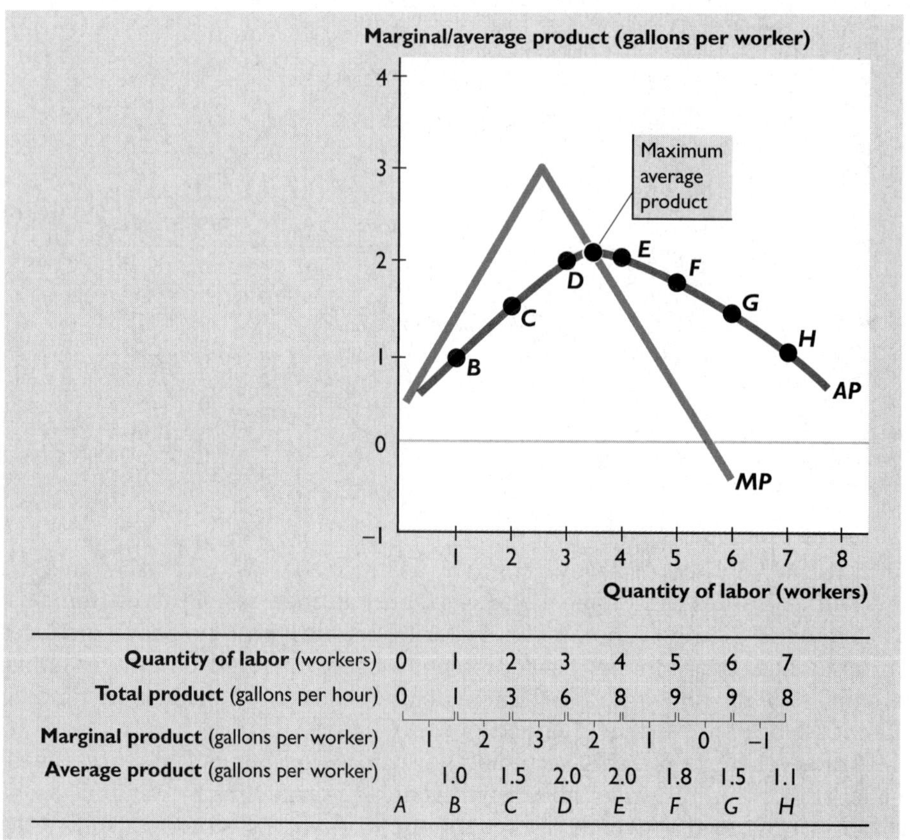

Quantity of labor (workers)	0	1	2	3	4	5	6	7
Total product (gallons per hour)	0	1	3	6	8	9	9	8
Marginal product (gallons per worker)		1	2	3	2	1	0	–1
Average product (gallons per worker)		1.0	1.5	2.0	2.0	1.8	1.5	1.1
	A	B	C	D	E	F	G	H

at which marginal product exceeds average product, the average product curve slopes upward and average product increases as more labor is employed. For employment levels at which marginal product is less than average product, the average product curve is downward sloping and average product decreases as more labor is employed.

The relationship between average product and marginal product is a general feature of the relationship between the average value and the marginal value of any variable. Let's look at a familiar example.

Marginal Grade and Grade Point Average Samantha is a part-time student who takes just one course each semester. To understand the relationship between average product and marginal product, think about the relationship between Sam's average grade and her marginal grade over five semesters, shown in Figure 9.5. In the first semester, Samantha takes French and her grade is a C (2). This grade is her marginal grade—the grade on the last course taken. It is also her average grade—her GPA. In the next semester, Samantha takes calculus and gets a B (3). Calculus is Sam's marginal course, and her marginal grade is 3. Her GPA rises to 2.5. Because her marginal grade exceeds her average grade, it pulls her average up. In the third semester, Samantha takes economics and gets an A (4)—her new marginal grade. Because her marginal grade exceeds her GPA, it again pulls her average up. Sam's GPA is now 3, the average of 2, 3, and 4. The fourth semester, she takes history and gets a B (3). Because her marginal grade is equal to her average, her GPA does not change. In the fifth semester, Samantha takes English and gets a D (1). Because her marginal grade of 1 is below her GPA of 3, her GPA falls.

This everyday relationship between average and marginal values is similar to the relationship between average and marginal product. Sam's GPA increases when her marginal grade exceeds her GPA. Her GPA falls when her marginal grade is below her GPA. And her GPA is constant when her marginal grade equals her GPA. The relationship between marginal product and average product is exactly the same as that between Sam's marginal and average grades.

FIGURE 9.5
Marginal Grade and Grade Point Average

Practice Online

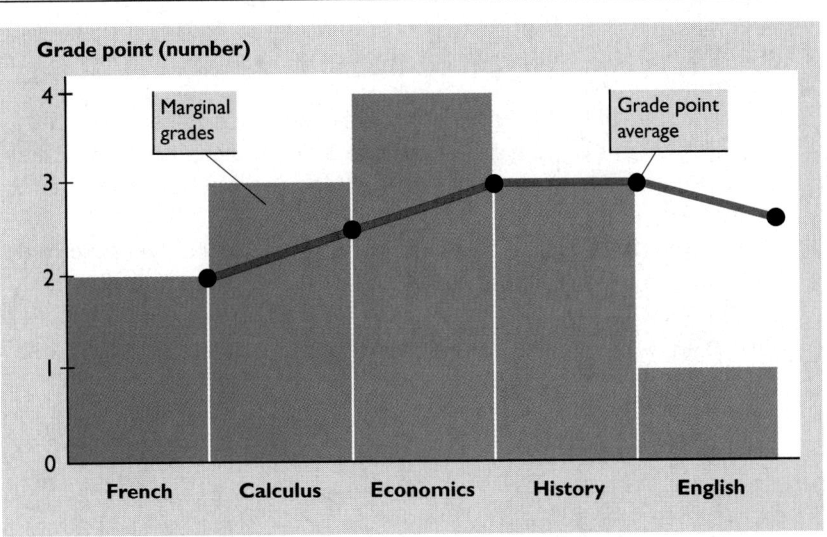

Sam's first course is French, for which she gets a C (2). Her marginal grade is 2, and her GPA is 2. She then gets a B (3) in calculus, which pulls her average up to 2.5. Next, she gets an A (4) in economics, which pulls her GPA up to 3. In her next course, history, she gets a B (3), which maintains her GPA. In her final course, English, she gets a D (1), which pulls her GPA down.

CHECKPOINT 9.2

Study Guide pp. 135–137

Practice Online 9.2

2 **Explain the relationship between a firm's output and labor employed in the short run.**

Practice Problem 9.2

Tom leases a farmer's field and grows pineapples. Tom hires students to pick and pack the pineapples. Table 1 sets out Tom's total product schedule.

a. Calculate the marginal product of the third student.
b. Calculate the average product of three students.
c. Over what numbers of students does marginal product increase?
d. When marginal product increases, compare average product and marginal product.

TABLE 1

Labor (students)	Total product (pineapples per day)
0	0
1	100
2	220
3	300
4	360
5	400
6	420
7	430

Exercise 9.2

Lizzie hires students in the summer to paint houses. Table 2 sets out her total product schedule.

a. Calculate the marginal product of the fourth student.
b. Calculate the average product of four students.
c. Over what numbers of students does marginal product decrease?
d. When marginal product decreases, compare average product and marginal product.

TABLE 2

Labor (students)	Total product (houses painted per week)
0	0
1	2
2	5
3	9
4	12
5	14
6	15

Solution to Practice Problem 9.2

a. Marginal product of the third student is the change in total product that results from hiring the third student. When Tom hires 2 students, total product is 220 pineapples a day. When Tom hires 3 students, total product is 300 pineapples a day. Marginal product of the third worker is the total product of 3 workers minus the total product of 2 workers, which is 300 pineapples a day minus 220 pineapples a day, or 80 pineapples a day.

b. Average product equals total product divided by the number of students. When Tom hires 3 students, total product is 300 pineapples a day, so average product is 300 pineapples a day divided by 3 students, which equals 100 pineapples a day.

c. Marginal product of the first student is 100 pineapples a day, that of the second student is 120 pineapples a day, and that of the third student is 80 pineapples a day. So marginal product increases when Tom hires the first and second students.

d. When Tom hires 1 student, marginal product is 100 pineapples a day and average product is 100 pineapples a day. When Tom hires 2 students, marginal product is 120 pineapples a day and average product is 110 pineapples a day. That is, when Tom hires the second student, marginal product exceeds average product.

9.3 SHORT-RUN COST

To produce more output (total product) in the short run, a firm must employ more labor, which means that it must increase its costs. We describe the relationship between output and cost using three cost concepts:

- Total cost
- Marginal cost
- Average cost

Total Cost

A firm's **total cost** (*TC*) is the cost of all the factors of production used by the firm. Total cost divides into two parts: total fixed cost and total variable cost. **Total fixed cost** (*TFC*) is the cost of a firm's fixed factors of production: land, capital, and entrepreneurship. Because in the short run, the quantities of these inputs don't change as output changes, total fixed cost doesn't change as output changes. **Total variable cost** (*TVC*) is the cost of a firm's variable factor of production—labor. To change its output in the short run, a firm must change the quantity of labor it employs, so total variable cost changes as output changes.

Total cost
The cost of all the factors of production used by a firm.

Total fixed cost
The cost of the fixed factors of production used by a firm—the cost of land, capital, and entrepreneurship.

Total variable cost
The cost of the variable factor of production used by a firm—the cost of labor.

Total cost is the sum of total fixed cost and total variable cost. That is,

$$TC = TFC + TVC.$$

Table 9.2 shows Sam's Smoothies' total costs. Sam's fixed costs are $10 an hour regardless of whether it operates or not—*TFC* is $10 an hour. To produce smoothies, Samantha hires labor, which costs $6 an hour. *TVC*, which increases as output increases, equals the number of workers per hour multiplied by $6. For example, to produce 6 gallons an hour, Samantha hires 3 workers, so *TVC* is $18 an hour. *TC* is the sum of *TFC* and *TVC*. So to produce 6 gallons an hour, *TC* is $28. Check the calculation in each row and note that to produce some quantities—2 gallons an hour, for example—Sam hires a worker for only part of the hour.

TABLE 9.2
Sam's Smoothies' Total Costs

Practice Online

Labor (workers per hour)	Output (gallons per hour)	Total fixed cost (dollars per hour)	Total variable cost (dollars per hour)	Total cost (dollars per hour)
0	0	10	0.00	10.00
1.00	1	10	6.00	16.00
1.60	2	10	9.60	19.60
2.00	3	10	12.00	22.00
2.35	4	10	14.10	24.10
2.70	5	10	16.20	26.20
3.00	6	10	18.00	28.00
3.40	7	10	20.40	30.40
4.00	8	10	24.00	34.00
5.00	9	10	30.00	40.00

Figure 9.6 illustrates Sam's total cost curves. The green total fixed cost curve (*TFC*) is horizontal because total fixed cost does not change when output changes. It is a constant at $10 an hour. The purple total variable cost curve (*TVC*) and the blue total cost curve (*TC*) both slope upward because variable cost increases as output increases. The arrows highlight total fixed cost as the vertical distance between the *TVC* and *TC* curve.

Let's now look at Sam's Smoothies' marginal cost.

Marginal Cost

In Figure 9.6, total variable cost and total cost increase at a decreasing rate at small levels of output and then begin to increase at an increasing rate as output increases. To understand these patterns in the changes in total cost, we need to use the concept of *marginal cost*.

Marginal cost
The change in total cost that results from a one-unit increase in output.

A firm's **marginal cost** is the change in total cost that results from a one-unit increase in output. Table 9.3 calculates the marginal cost for Sam's Smoothies. When, for example, output increases from 5 gallons to 6 gallons an hour, total cost increases from $26.20 to $28. So the marginal cost of this gallon of smoothies is $1.80 ($28 – $26.20).

Marginal cost tells us how total cost changes as output changes. The final cost concept tells us what it costs, on the average, to produce a unit of output. Let's now look at Sam's average costs.

FIGURE 9.6
Total Cost Curves at Sam's Smoothies

Practice Online

Total fixed cost (*TFC*) is constant—it graphs as a horizontal line—and total variable cost (*TVC*) increases as output increases. Total cost (*TC*) also increases as output increases. The vertical distance between the total cost curve and the total variable cost curve is total fixed cost, as illustrated by the two arrows.

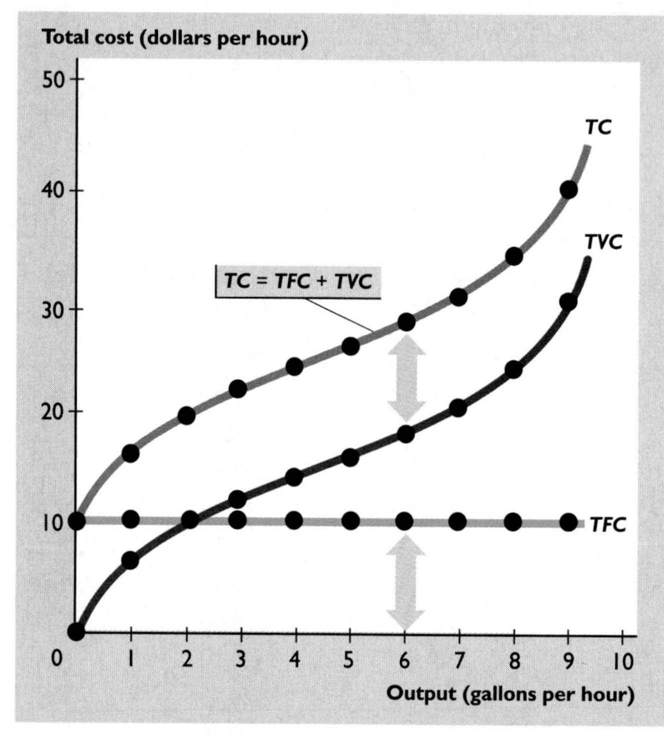

Average Cost

There are three average cost concepts:

- Average fixed cost
- Average variable cost
- Average total cost

Average fixed cost (AFC) is total fixed cost per unit of output. **Average variable cost** (AVC) is total variable cost per unit of output. **Average total cost** (ATC) is total cost per unit of output. The average cost concepts are calculated from the total cost concepts as follows:

$$TC = TFC + TVC.$$

Divide each total cost term by the quantity produced, Q, to give

$$\frac{TC}{Q} = \frac{TFC}{Q} + \frac{TVC}{Q},$$

or

$$ATC = AFC + AVC.$$

Table 9.3 shows these average costs. For example, when output is 3 gallons an hour, average fixed cost is ($10 ÷ 3), which equals $3.33; average variable cost is ($12 ÷ 3), which equals $4.00; and average total cost is ($22 ÷ 3), which equals $7.33. Note that average total cost ($7.33) equals average fixed cost ($3.33) plus average variable cost ($4.00).

Average fixed cost
Total fixed cost per unit of output.

Average variable cost
Total variable cost per unit of output.

Average total cost
Total cost per unit of output, which equals average fixed cost plus average variable cost.

TABLE 9.3
Sam's Smoothies' Marginal Cost and Average Cost

Practice Online

Output (gallons per hour)	Total cost (dollars per hour)	Marginal cost (dollars per gallon)	Average fixed cost (dollars per gallon)	Average variable cost (dollars per gallon)	Average total cost (dollars per gallon)
0	10.00		–	–	–
		6.00			
1	16.00		10.00	6.00	16.00
		3.60			
2	19.60		5.00	4.80	9.80
		2.40			
3	22.00		3.33	4.00	7.33
		2.10			
4	24.10		2.50	3.53	6.03
		2.10			
5	26.20		2.00	3.24	5.24
		1.80			
6	28.00		1.67	3.00	4.67
		2.40			
7	30.40		1.43	2.91	4.34
		3.60			
8	34.00		1.25	3.00	4.25
		6.00			
9	40.00		1.11	3.33	4.44

Figure 9.7 graphs the marginal cost and average cost data in Table 9.3. The red marginal cost curve (*MC*) is U-shaped because of the way in which marginal product changes. Recall that when Samantha hires a second or a third worker, marginal product increases. Over this range, output increases and marginal cost decreases. But when Samantha hires a fourth or more workers, marginal product decreases. Over this range, output increases and marginal cost increases.

The green average fixed cost curve (*AFC*) slopes downward. As output increases, the same constant total fixed cost is spread over a larger output. The blue average total cost curve (*ATC*) and the purple average variable cost curve (*AVC*) are U-shaped. The vertical distance between the average total cost and average variable cost curves is equal to average fixed cost—as indicated by the two arrows. That distance shrinks as output increases because average fixed cost decreases with increasing output.

The marginal cost curve intersects the average variable cost curve and the average total cost curve at their minimum points. That is, when marginal cost is less than average cost, average cost is decreasing; and when marginal cost exceeds average cost, average cost is increasing. This relationship holds for both the *ATC* curve and the *AVC* curve and is another example of the relationship you saw in Figure 9.4 for average product and marginal product and in Sam's course grades.

FIGURE 9.7

Average Cost Curves and Marginal Cost Curve at Sam's Smoothies

Practice Online

Average fixed cost (*AFC*) decreases as output increases. The average total cost curve (*ATC*) and average variable cost curve (*AVC*) are U-shaped. The vertical distance between these two curves is equal to average fixed cost, as illustrated by the two arrows.

Marginal cost is the change in total cost when output increases by one unit. The marginal cost curve (*MC*) is U-shaped and intersects the average variable cost curve and the average total cost curve at their minimum points.

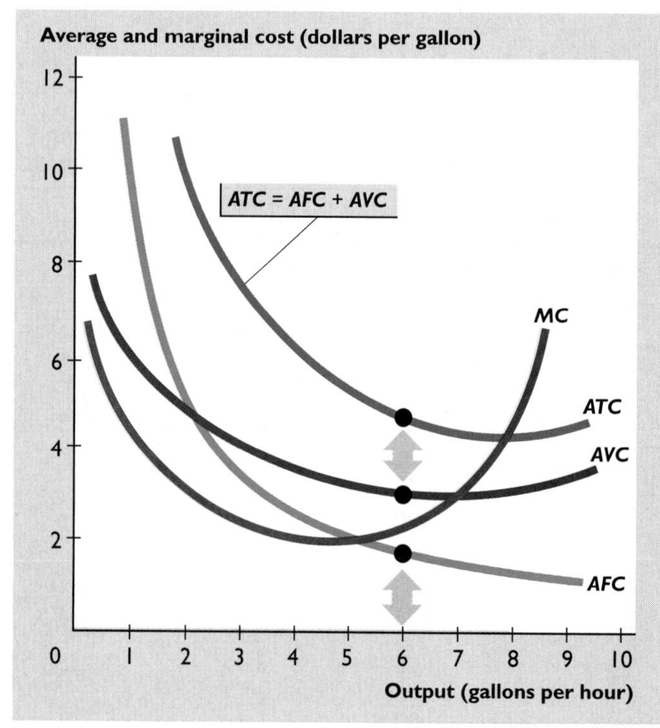

Why the Average Total Cost Curve Is U-Shaped

Average total cost, *ATC*, is the sum of average fixed cost, *AFC*, and average variable cost, *AVC*. So the shape of the *ATC* curve combines the shapes of the *AFC* and *AVC* curves. The U-shape of the average total cost curve arises from the influence of two opposing forces:

- Spreading total fixed cost over a larger output
- Decreasing marginal returns

When output increases, the firm spreads its total fixed costs over a larger output and its average fixed cost decreases—its average fixed cost curve slopes downward.

Decreasing marginal returns means that as output increases, ever larger amounts of labor are needed to produce an additional unit of output. So average variable cost eventually increases, and the *AVC* curve eventually slopes upward.

The shape of the average total cost curve combines these two effects. Initially, as output increases, both average fixed cost and average variable cost decrease, so average total cost decreases and the *ATC* curve slopes downward. But as output increases further and decreasing marginal returns set in, average variable cost begins to increase. Eventually, average variable cost increases more quickly than average fixed cost decreases, so average total cost increases and the *ATC* curve slopes upward.

All the short-run cost concepts that you've met are summarized in Table 9.4.

TABLE 9.4
A Compact Glossary of Costs

Practice Online

Term	Symbol	Definition	Equation
Fixed cost		The cost of a fixed factor of production that is independent of the quantity produced	
Variable cost		The cost of a variable factor of production that varies with the quantity produced	
Total fixed cost	*TFC*	Cost of the fixed factors of production	
Total variable cost	*TVC*	Cost of the variable factor of production	
Total cost	*TC*	Cost of all factors of production	$TC = TFC + TVC$
Marginal cost	*MC*	Change in total cost resulting from a one-unit increase in output (Q)	$MC = \Delta TC \div \Delta Q$*
Average fixed cost	*AFC*	Total fixed cost per unit of output	$AFC = TFC \div Q$
Average variable cost	*AVC*	Total variable cost per unit of output	$AVC = TVC \div Q$
Average total cost	*ATC*	Total cost per unit of output	$ATC = AFC + AVC$

*In this equation, the Greek letter delta (Δ) stands for "change in."

Cost Curves and Product Curves

A firm's cost curves and product curves are linked, and Figure 9.8 shows how. The top figure shows the average product curve and the marginal product curve—like those in Figure 9.4. The bottom figure shows the average variable cost curve and the marginal cost curve—like those in Figure 9.7.

The figure highlights the links between the product and cost curves. At low levels of employment and output, as the firm hires more labor, marginal product and average product rise and output increases faster than costs. So marginal cost and average variable cost fall. Then, at the point of maximum marginal product, marginal cost is a minimum. As the firm hires more labor, marginal product decreases and marginal cost increases. But average product continues to rise, and average variable cost continues to fall. Then, at the point of maximum average product, average variable cost is a minimum. As the firm hires even more labor, average product decreases and average variable cost increases.

Shifts in the Cost Curves

The position of a firm's short-run cost curves in Figures 9.6 and 9.7 depend on two factors:

- Technology
- Prices of factors of production

Technology

A technological change that increases productivity shifts the total product curve upward. It also shifts the marginal product curve and the average product curve upward. With a better technology, the same inputs can produce more output, so an advance in technology lowers the average and marginal costs and shifts the short-run cost curves downward.

For example, advances in robotic technology have increased productivity in the automobile industry. As a result, the product curves of DaimlerChrysler, Ford, and GM have shifted upward, and their average and marginal cost curves have shifted downward. But the relationships between their product curves and cost curves have not changed. The curves are still linked, as in Figure 9.8.

Often a technological advance results in a firm using more capital, a fixed input, and less labor, a variable input. For example, today telephone companies use computers to connect long-distance calls instead of the human operators they used in the 1980s. When a telephone company makes this change, total variable cost decreases and total cost decreases, but total fixed cost increases. This change in the mix of fixed cost and variable cost means that at small output levels, average total cost might increase, but at large output levels, average total cost decreases.

Prices of Factors of Production

An increase in the price of a factor of production increases costs and shifts the cost curves. But how the curves shift depends on which resource price changes. An increase in rent or some other component of *fixed* cost shifts the fixed cost curves (*TFC* and *AFC*) upward and shifts the total cost curve (*TC*) upward but leaves the variable cost curves (*AVC* and *TVC*) and the marginal cost curve (*MC*) unchanged.

FIGURE 9.8

Product Curves and Cost Curves

Practice Online

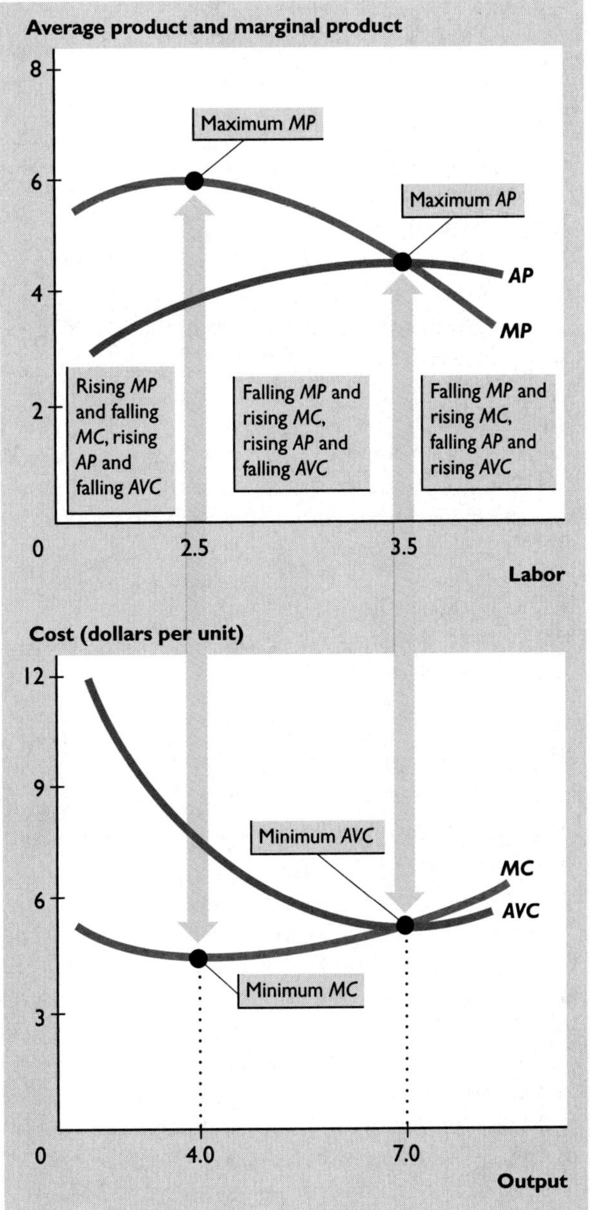

A firm's marginal cost curve is linked to its marginal product curve. If marginal product rises, marginal cost falls. If marginal product is a maximum, marginal cost is a minimum. If marginal product diminishes, marginal cost rises.

A firm's average variable cost curve is linked to its average product curve. If average product rises, average variable cost falls. If average product is a maximum, average variable cost is a minimum. If average product diminishes, average variable cost rises.

An increase in wage rates or some other component of *variable* cost shifts the variable cost curves (*TVC* and *AVC*) and the marginal cost curve (*MC*) upward but leaves the fixed cost curves (*AFC* and *TFC*) unchanged. So, for example, if the interest expense paid by a trucking company increases, the fixed cost of transportation services increases, but if the wage rate paid to truck drivers increases, the variable cost and marginal cost of transportation services increase.

CHECKPOINT 9.3

Study Guide pp. 137–140

Practice Online 9.3

3 Explain the relationship between a firm's output and costs in the short run.

Practice Problem 9.3

Tom leases a farmer's field for $120 a day and grows pineapples. Tom pays students $100 a day to pick and pack the pineapples. Tom leases capital at $80 a day. Table 1 gives the daily output.

a. Construct the total cost schedule.
b. Construct the average total cost schedule.
c. Construct the marginal cost schedule.
d. At what output is Tom's average total cost a minimum?

TABLE 1

Labor (students)	Output (pineapples per day)
0	0
1	100
2	220
3	300
4	360
5	400
6	420
7	430

Exercise 9.3

Lizzie hires students at $50 a day to paint houses. She leases equipment that costs her $100 a day. Table 2 shows her total product schedule.

a. Construct the total variable cost and total cost schedules.
b. Construct the average fixed cost, average variable cost, and average total cost schedules.
c. Construct the marginal cost schedule.
d. Check that the gap between total cost and total variable cost is the same at all outputs. Explain why.

TABLE 2

Labor (students)	Output (houses painted per week)
0	0
1	2
2	5
3	9
4	12
5	14
6	15

Solution to Practice Problem 9.3

a. Total cost is the sum of total fixed cost and total variable cost. Tom leases the farmer's field for $120 a day and leases capital for $80 a day, so Tom's total fixed cost is $200 a day. Total variable cost is the wages of the students. For example, when Tom hires 3 students, the total variable cost is $300 a day. So when Tom hires 3 students, total cost is $500 a day. The *TC* column of Table 3 shows the total cost schedule.

b. Average total cost is the total cost divided by total product. For example, when Tom hires 3 students, they pick and pack 300 pineapples a day, and Tom's total cost is $500 a day. Average total cost is $1.67 a pineapple. The *ATC* column of Table 3 shows the average total cost schedule.

c. Marginal cost is the increase in total cost that results from picking and packing one additional pineapple a day. The total cost (from Table 3) of picking and packing 100 pineapples a day is $300. The total cost of picking and packing 220 pineapples a day is $400. The increase in the number of pineapples is 120, and the increase in total cost is $100. So the marginal cost is the increase in total cost divided by the increase in the number of pineapples. Marginal cost equals $100 ÷ 120 pineapples, which is $0.83 a pineapple. The *MC* column of Table 3 shows the marginal cost schedule.

d. At the minimum of average total cost, average total cost and marginal cost are equal. Minimum average total cost is $1.67 a pineapple at 330 pineapples a day.

TABLE 3

Labor	*TP*	*TC*	*MC*	*ATC*
0	0	200		–
			1.00	
1	100	300		3.00
			0.83	
2	220	400		1.82
			1.25	
3	300	500		1.67
			1.67	
4	360	600		1.67
			2.50	
5	400	700		1.75
			5.00	
6	420	800		1.90
			10.00	
7	430	900		2.09

9.4 LONG-RUN COST

In the long run, a firm can vary both the quantity of labor and the quantity of capital. A small firm, such as Sam's Smoothies, can increase its plant size by moving into a larger building and installing more machines. A big firm such as General Motors can decrease its plant size by closing down some production lines.

We are now going to see how costs vary in the long run when a firm varies its plant—the quantity of capital it uses—along with the quantity of labor it uses.

The first thing that happens is that the distinction between fixed cost and variable cost disappears. All costs are variable in the long run.

Plant Size and Cost

When a firm changes its plant size, its cost of producing a given output changes. In Figure 9.7, the lowest average total cost that Sam can achieve is $4.25 a gallon, which occurs when she produces 8 gallons of smoothies an hour. Samantha wonders what would happen to her average total cost if she increased the size of her plant by renting a bigger building and installing a larger number of blenders and refrigerators. Will the average total cost of producing a gallon of smoothie fall, rise, or remain the same?

Each of these three outcomes is possible, and they arise because when a firm changes the size of its plant, it might experience

- Economies of scale
- Diseconomies of scale
- Constant returns to scale

Economies of Scale

If when a firm increases its plant size and labor employed by the same percentage, its output increases by a larger percentage, the firm's average total cost decreases. The firm experiences **economies of scale**. The main source of economies of scale is greater specialization of both labor and capital.

Economies of scale
A condition in which, when a firm increases its plant size and labor employed by the same percentage, its output increases by a larger percentage and its average total cost decreases.

Specialization of Labor If GM produced 100 cars a week, each production line worker would have to perform many different tasks. But if GM produces 10,000 cars a week, each worker can specialize in a small number of tasks and become highly proficient at them. The result is that the average product of labor increases and the average total cost of producing a car falls.

Specialization also occurs off the production line. For example, a small firm usually does not have a specialist sales manager, personnel manager, and production manager. One person covers all these activities. But when a firm is large enough, specialists perform these activities. Average product increases, and the average total cost falls.

Specialization of Capital At a small output rate, firms often must employ general-purpose machines and tools. For example, with an output of a few gallons an hour, Sam's Smoothies uses regular blenders like the one in your kitchen. But if Sam's produces hundreds of gallons an hour, it uses custom blenders that fill, empty, and clean themselves. The result is that the output rate is larger and the average total cost of producing a gallon of smoothie is lower.

Diseconomies of Scale

Diseconomies of scale
A condition in which, when a firm increases its plant size and labor employed by the same percentage, its output increases by a smaller percentage and its average total cost increases.

If when a firm increases its plant size and labor employed by the same percentage, output increases by a smaller percentage, the firm's average total cost increases. The firm experiences **diseconomies of scale**. Diseconomies of scale arise from the difficulty of coordinating and controlling a large enterprise. The larger the firm, the greater is the cost of communicating both up and down the management hierarchy and among managers. Eventually, management complexity brings rising average cost. Diseconomies of scale occur in all production processes but in some, perhaps, only at a very large output rate.

Constant Returns to Scale

Constant returns to scale
A condition in which, when a firm increases its plant size and labor employed by the same percentage, its output increases by the same percentage and its average total cost remains constant.

If when a firm increases its plant size and labor employed by the same percentage, output increases by that same percentage, the firm's average total cost remains constant. The firm experiences **constant returns to scale**. Constant returns to scale occur when a firm is able to replicate its existing production facility including its management system. For example, General Motors might double its production of Cavaliers by doubling its production facility for those cars. It can build an identical production line and hire an identical number of workers. With the two identical production lines, GM produces exactly twice as many cars. The average cost of producing a Cavalier is identical in the two plants. So when production increases, average total cost remains constant.

■ The Long-Run Average Cost Curve

Long-run average cost curve
A curve that shows the lowest average cost at which it is possible to produce each output when the firm has had sufficient time to change both its plant size and labor employed.

The **long-run average cost curve** shows the lowest average cost at which it is possible to produce each output when the firm has had sufficient time to change both its plant size and its labor force.

Figure 9.9 shows Sam's Smoothies' long-run average cost curve *LRAC*. This long-run average cost curve is derived from the short-run average total cost curves for different possible plant sizes.

With its current small plant, Sam's Smoothies operates on the average total cost curve ATC_1 in Figure 9.9. The other three average total cost curves are for successively bigger plants. In this example, for outputs up to 5 gallons an hour, the existing plant with average total cost curve ATC_1 produces smoothies at the lowest attainable average cost. For outputs between 5 and 10 gallons an hour, average total cost is lowest on ATC_2. For outputs between 10 and 15 gallons an hour, average total cost is lowest on ATC_3. And for outputs in excess of 15 gallons an hour, average total cost is lowest on ATC_4.

The segment of each of the four average total cost curves for which that plant has the lowest average total cost is highlighted in dark blue in Figure 9.9. The scallop-shaped curve made up of these four segments is Sam's Smoothies' long-run average cost curve.

Economies and Diseconomies of Scale

When economies of scale are present, the *LRAC* curve slopes downward. The *LRAC* curve in Figure 9.9 shows that Sam's Smoothies experiences economies of scale for output rates up to 9 gallons an hour. At output rates between 9 and 12 gallons an hour, the firm experiences constant returns to scale. And at output rates that exceed 12 gallons an hour, the firm experiences diseconomies of scale.

FIGURE 9.9
Long-run Average Cost Curve

Practice Online

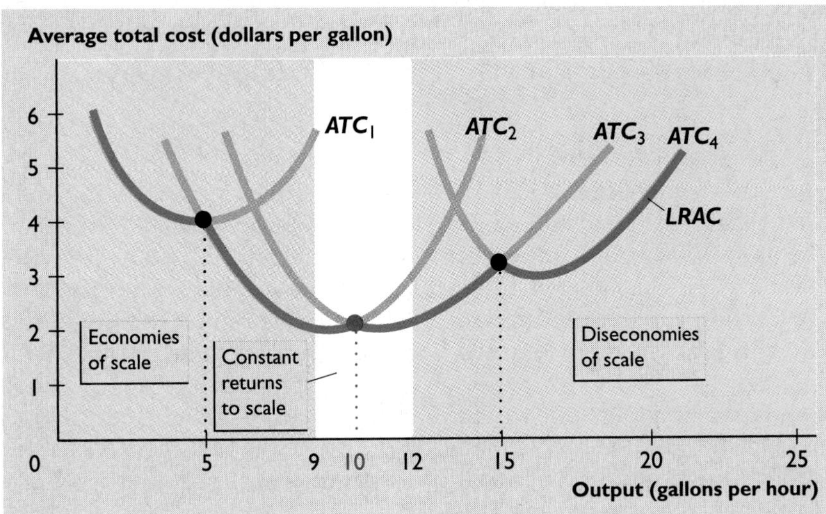

In the long run, Samantha can vary both capital and labor inputs. The long-run average cost curve traces the lowest attainable average total cost of producing each output.

Sam's experiences economies of scale as output increases to 9 gallons an hour, constant returns to scale for outputs between 9 gallons and 12 gallons an hour, and diseconomies of scale for outputs that exceed 12 gallons an hour.

Eye on the U.S. Economy

The ATM and the Cost of Getting Cash

Most banks use automated teller machines—ATMs—to dispense cash. But small credit unions don't have ATMs. Instead, they employ tellers.

Gemini Consulting of Morristown, New Jersey, estimates that the average total cost of a transaction is $1.07 for a teller and 27¢ for an ATM. Given these numbers, why don't small credit unions install ATMs and lay off their tellers?

The answer is scale. At a small number of transactions per month, it costs less to use a teller than an ATM. In the figure, the average total cost curve for transactions done with a teller is ATC_T. The average total cost curve for transactions done with an ATM is ATC_A. You can see that if the number of transactions is Q a month, the average total cost per transaction is the same for both methods. For a bank that does more than Q transactions per month, the least-cost method is the ATM. For a credit union that does fewer than Q transactions a month, its least-cost method is the teller. More technology is not always more efficient.

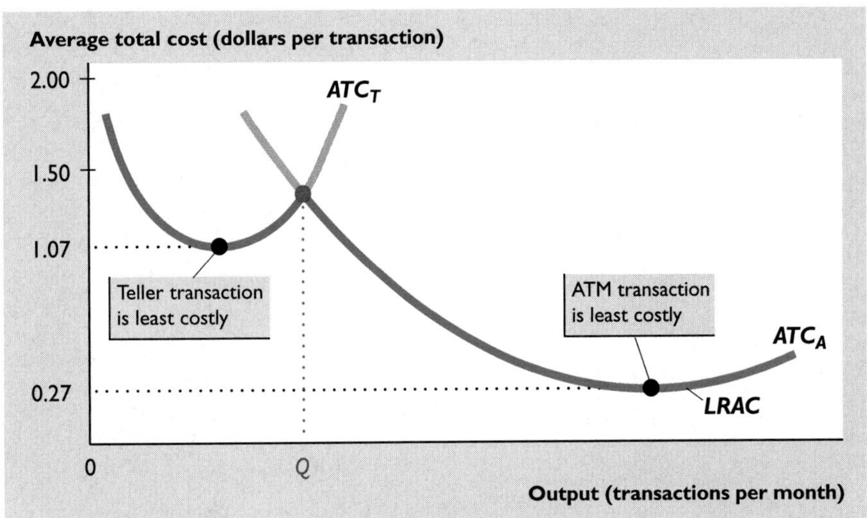

CHECKPOINT 9.4

Study Guide pp. 141–143

Practice Online 9.4

4 **Derive and explain a firm's long-run average cost curve.**

Practice Problem 9.4

Tom grows pineapples. He leases a farmer's field for $120 a day and capital for $80 a day. He hires students at $100 a day. Suppose that Tom now leases two fields for $240 a day and twice as much capital for $160 a day. Tom discovers that his output is the numbers in the third column of Table 1. The numbers in the second column are his output with 1 field and the original amount of capital.

a. Find Tom's average total cost curve schedule when he operates with two fields.

b. Make a graph of Tom's average total cost curves using 1 field and 2 fields, and show on the graph Tom's long-run average cost curve.

c. Over what output range will Tom operate with 1 field and at what output rate will he operate with 2 fields?

d. What happens to Tom's average total cost curve if he farms 2 fields and doubles his capital?

e. Does Tom experience economies of scale or diseconomies of scale?

TABLE 1

Labor (students per day)	Output with 1 field (pineapples per day)	Output with 2 fields (pineapples per day)
0	0	0
1	100	220
2	220	460
3	300	620
4	360	740
5	400	820
6	420	860
7	430	880

TABLE 2

TP (1 field)	*ATC* (1 field)	*TP* (2 fields)	*ATC* (2 fields)
100	3.00	220	2.27
220	1.82	460	1.30
300	1.67	620	1.13
360	1.67	740	1.08
400	1.75	820	1.10
420	1.90	860	1.16
430	2.09	880	1.25

Exercise 9.4

Lizzie hires students at $50 a day to paint houses. She leases equipment that costs her $100 a day. Suppose that Lizzie doubles the number of students she hires and doubles the amount of equipment that she leases. If Lizzie experiences diseconomies of scale, explain

a. What has happened to her average total cost curve.

b. What might be the source of those diseconomies of scale.

Solution to Practice Problem 9.4

a. Total cost is fixed cost of $400 a day plus $100 a day for each student hired. Average total cost is the total cost divided by output. The "*ATC* (2 fields)" column of Table 2 shows Tom's average total cost schedule.

b. Figure 1 shows Tom's average total cost curves using 1 field as ATC_1. This curve graphs the data on *ATC* and total product in Table 3 on p. 310. Using 2 fields, the average total cost curve is ATC_2. Tom's long-run average cost curve is the lower segments of these two *ATC* curves, highlighted in Figure 1.

c. If Tom produces up to 300 pineapples a day, he will operate with 1 field. If he produces more than 300 pineapples a day, he will operate with 2 fields.

d. When Tom farms 2 fields and doubles his capital, average total cost increases at low outputs (up to 300 a day) and decreases at high outputs (greater than 300 a day).

e. Tom experiences economies of scale up to an output of 740 pineapples a day, because as he increases his plant and produces up to 740 pineapples a day, the average total cost of picking and packing a pineapple decreases.

FIGURE 1

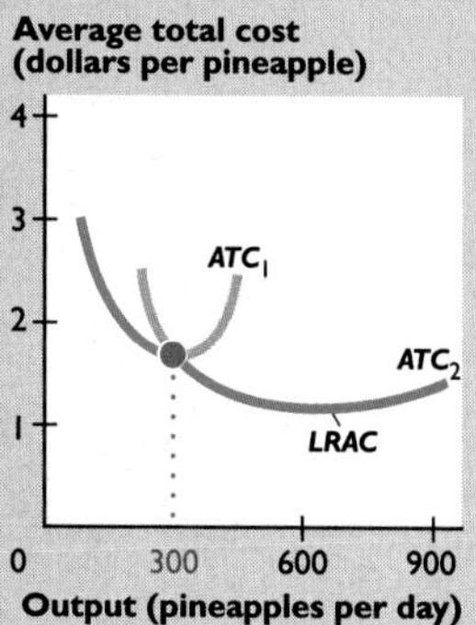

CHAPTER CHECKPOINT

Key Points

1 Explain how economists measure a firm's cost of production and profit.

- Firms seek to maximize economic profit, which is total revenue minus total cost.
- Total cost equals opportunity cost—the sum of explicit costs plus implicit costs and includes normal profit.

2 Explain the relationship between a firm's output and labor employed in the short run.

- In the short run, the firm can change the output it produces by changing labor only.
- A total product curve shows the limits to the output that the firm can produce with a given quantity of capital and different quantities of labor.
- As the quantity of labor increases, the marginal product of labor increases initially but eventually decreases—the law of decreasing returns.

3 Explain the relationship between a firm's output and costs in the short run.

- As total product increases, total fixed cost is constant, and total variable cost and total cost increase.
- As total product increases, average fixed cost decreases and average variable cost, average total cost, and marginal cost decrease at small outputs and increase at large outputs. Their curves are U-shaped.

4 Derive and explain a firm's long-run average cost curve.

- In the long run, the firm can change the size of its plant.
- Long-run cost is the cost of production when all inputs have been adjusted to produce at the lowest attainable cost.
- The long-run average cost curve traces out the lowest attainable average total cost at each output when both capital and labor inputs can be varied.
- The long-run average cost curve slopes downward with economies of scale and upward with diseconomies of scale.

Key Terms

Exercises

1. Joe runs a shoeshine stand at the airport. With no skills and no job experience, Joe has no alternative employment. The other shoeshine stand operators that Joe knows earn $10,000 a year. Joe pays the airport $2,000 a year for the space he uses, and his total revenue from shining shoes is $15,000 a year. He spent $1,000 on a chair, polish, and brushes and paid for these items using his credit card. The interest on his credit card balance is 20 percent a year. At the end of the year, Joe was offered $500 for his business and all its equipment. Calculate Joe's
   a. Explicit costs.
   b. Implicit costs.
   c. Economic profit.

2. Sonya used to sell real estate and earn $25,000 a year, but she now sells greeting cards. Normal profit for the retailers of greeting cards is $14,000. Over the past year, Sonya bought $10,000 worth of cards from manufacturers of cards. She sold these cards for $58,000. Sonya rents a shop for $5,000 a year and spends $1,000 on utilities and office expenses. Sonya owns a cash register, which she bought for $2,000 with her savings account. Her bank pays 3 percent a year on savings accounts. At the end of the year, Sonya was offered $1,600 for her cash register. Calculate Sonya's
   a. Explicit costs.
   b. Implicit costs.
   c. Economic profit.

TABLE 1

Labor (workers per day)	Total product (body boards per day)
0	0
1	20
2	44
3	60
4	72
5	80
6	84
7	86

3. Len's body board factory rents equipment for shaping boards and hires students. Table 1 sets out Len's total product schedule.
   a. Construct Len's marginal product and average product schedules.
   b. Over what range of workers do marginal returns increase?
   c. After how many workers employed do marginal returns decrease?

4. Yolanda runs a bullfrog farm in Yuma, Arizona. When Yolanda employed one person, she produced 1,000 bullfrogs a week. When she hired a second worker, her total product doubled. Her total product doubled again when she hired a third worker. When she hired a fourth worker, her total product increased, but by only 1,000 bullfrogs.
   a. Construct Yolanda's marginal product and average product schedules.
   b. Over what range of workers do marginal returns increase?
   c. After how many workers employed do marginal returns decrease?

5. Len, in exercise 3, pays $300 a week for equipment and $1,000 a week to each student he hires. Given his total product schedule in Table 1,
   a. Construct Len's total variable cost and total cost schedules.
   b. Calculate total cost minus total variable cost at each output rate. What does this quantity equal? Why?
   c. Construct the average fixed cost, average variable cost, and average total cost schedules.
   d. Construct the marginal cost schedule.
   e. Calculate the output at which Len's average total cost is a minimum.
   f. Calculate the output at which Len's average variable cost is a minimum.
   g. Explain why the output at which average variable cost is a minimum is smaller than the output at which average total cost is a minimum.

6. Yolanda, in exercise 4, pays $1,000 a week for equipment and $500 a week to each worker she hires. Given her description of how her total product changes as she hires more labor,
   a. Construct Yolanda's total variable cost and total cost schedules.
   b. Calculate total cost minus total variable cost at each output rate. What does this quantity equal? Why?
   c. Construct the average fixed cost, average variable cost, and average total cost schedules.
   d. Construct the marginal cost schedule.
   e. Calculate the output at which Yolanda's average total cost is a minimum.
   f. Calculate the output at which Yolanda's average variable cost is a minimum.
   g. Explain why the output at which average total cost is a minimum is larger than the output at which average variable cost is a minimum.

7. Table 2 shows the costs incurred at Pete's peanut farm. Complete the table.

TABLE 2

L	*TP*	*TVC*	*TC*	*AFC*	*AVC*	*ATC*	*MC*
0	0	0	100				
1	10	35					
2	24	70					
3	38	105					
4	44	140					
5	47	175					

8. Table 3 shows some of the costs incurred at Bill's Bakery. Calculate the values of *A*, *B*, *C*, *D*, and *E*. Show your work.

TABLE 3

L	*TP*	*TVC*	*TC*	*AFC*	*AVC*	*ATC*	*MC*
1	100	350	850	C	3.50	D	
2	240	700	B	2.08	2.92	5.00	2.50
3	380	A	1,550	1.32	2.76	4.08	E
4	440	1,400	1,900	1.14	3.18	4.32	5.83
5	470	1,750	2,250	1.06	3.72	4.79	11.67

9. Explain what the long-run average cost curve shows and how it is derived.

10. Can a firm that produces at the lowest possible average cost lower its average cost further by increasing production? Explain using the long-run average cost curve.

11. Explain the sources of economies of scale and diseconomies of scale and illustrate these two situations in a graph.

12. Provide examples of industries in which you think economies of scale exist and explain why you think they are present in these industries.

13. Provide examples of industries in which you think diseconomies of scale exist and explain why you think they are present in these industries.

Critical Thinking

14. MCI, a global communications company, spent billions of dollars laying fiber-optic cables under the oceans. Is the cost of this communications network a short-run cost or a long-run cost? Is it a sunk cost or an opportunity cost? Explain your answer.

15. Study *Eye on the U.S. Economy* on p. 313 and then answer the following questions:
    a. What is the main difference, from a cost point of view, between human tellers and ATMs?
    b. Why do you think ATMs have become so popular?
    c. Would it ever make sense for a bank in the United States not to use ATMs?
    d. Do you think that ATMs are as common in China as they are in the United States? Explain why or why not.

16. Suppose the government put a tax on banks for each ATM transaction but did not put a similar tax on human teller transactions.
    a. How would the tax affect a bank's costs and cost curves?
    b. Would the tax change the number of ATMs and the number of tellers that banks hire? If so, explain how. If not, why not?

Practice Online

Web Exercises

Use the links on your Foundations Web site to work the following exercises.

17. Visit the Bullfrogs and check out the prices of bullfrogs of various sizes. Assume that prices reflect the cost of production and answer the following questions:
    a. Does farming bullfrogs appear to display increasing marginal cost? Explain why or why not.
    b. Does farming bullfrogs appear to display decreasing marginal returns? Explain why or why not.
    c. Why might someone pay $20 for a large (6 inches plus) bullfrog when the price of a smaller (4 to 6 inch) bullfrog is only $12?

18. Visit the Federal Reserve Bank of St. Louis and read the article "Do Economies of Scale Exist in the Banking Industry?"
    a. What is the survivor technique for identifying whether the firms in an industry experience economies of scale?
    b. Why does the survivor technique work?
    c. What does the survivor technique imply about economies of scale in the banking industry?
    d. Sketch the long-run average cost curve of a bank that is consistent with what the survivor technique implies about economies of scale.

19. Obtain information about the cost of producing pumpkins.
    a. List all the costs referred to on the Web site.
    b. For each item, classify it as a fixed cost, a variable cost, or perhaps a combination of the two.
    c. Make some assumptions and sketch the average cost curves (*AFC*, *AVC*, and *ATC*) and the marginal cost curve.
    d. Identify the minimum points of the *AVC* and *ATC* curves in your graph.

CHAPTER 10

Perfect Competition

CHAPTER CHECKLIST

When you have completed your study of this chapter, you will be able to

1. **Explain a perfectly competitive firm's profit-maximizing choices and derive its supply curve.**
2. **Explain how output, price, and profit are determined in the short run.**
3. **Explain how output, price, and profit are determined in the long run.**

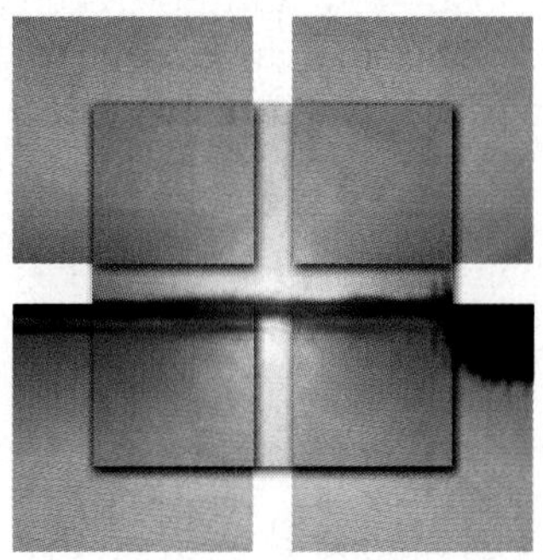

Some markets are highly competitive, and firms find it hard to earn profits. Other markets appear to be almost free from competition, and firms earn large profits. Some markets are dominated by fierce advertising campaigns in which each firm seeks to persuade buyers that it has the best products. And some markets display a warlike character. In this chapter, we study the first of the above market types, known as perfect competition.

What you learned in the previous chapter gets its first big workout in this chapter. If your understanding of a firm's cost curves is still a bit shaky, check back to Chapter 9 when you need to.

You're going to see how the principles of rational choice, balancing costs and benefits at the margin, and responding to incentives enable us to understand and predict the decisions that firms make in competitive markets.

MARKET TYPES

The four market types are

- Perfect competition
- Monopoly
- Monopolistic competition
- Oligopoly

Perfect Competition

Perfect competition
A market in which there are many firms, each selling an identical product; many buyers; no restrictions on the entry of new firms into the industry; no advantage to established firms; and buyers and sellers are well informed about prices.

Perfect competition exists when

- Many firms sell an identical product to many buyers.
- There are no restrictions on entry into (or exit from) the market.
- Established firms have no advantage over new firms.
- Sellers and buyers are well informed about prices.

These conditions that define perfect competition arise when the market demand for the product is large relative to the output of a single producer. And this situation arises when economies of scale are absent so the efficient scale of each firm is small. But a large market and the absence of economies of scale are not sufficient to create perfect competition. In addition, each firm must produce a good or service that has no characteristics that are unique to that firm so that consumers don't care from which firm they buy. Firms in perfect competition all look the same to the buyer.

Wheat farming, fishing, wood pulping and paper milling, the manufacture of paper cups and plastic shopping bags, lawn service, dry cleaning, and the provision of laundry services are all examples of highly competitive industries.

Other Market Types

Monopoly
A market for a good or service that has no close substitutes and in which there is one supplier that is protected from competition by a barrier preventing the entry of new firms.

Monopolistic competition
A market in which a large number of firms compete by making similar but slightly different products.

Oligopoly
A market in which a small number of firms compete.

Monopoly arises when one firm sells a good or service that has no close substitutes and a barrier blocks the entry of new firms. In some places, the phone, gas, electricity, and water suppliers are local monopolies—monopolies that are restricted to a given location. For many years, a global firm called DeBeers had a near international monopoly in diamonds.

Monopolistic competition arises when a large number of firms compete by making similar but slightly different products. Each firm is the sole producer of the particular version of the good in question. For example, in the market for running shoes, Nike, Reebok, Fila, Asics, New Balance, and many others make their own versions of the perfect shoe. The term "monopolistic competition" reminds us that each firm has a monopoly on a particular brand of shoe but the firms compete with each other.

Oligopoly arises when a small number of firms compete. Airplane manufacture is an example of oligopoly. Oligopolies might produce almost identical products, such as Kodak and Fuji film. Or they might produce differentiated products such as the colas produced by Coke and Pepsi.

We study perfect competition in this chapter, monopoly in Chapter 11, and monopolistic competition and oligopoly in Chapter 12.

10.1 A FIRM'S PROFIT-MAXIMIZING CHOICES

A firm's objective is to maximize *economic profit*, which is equal to *total revenue* minus the *total cost* of production. *Normal profit*, the return that the firm's entrepreneur can obtain in the best alternative business, is part of the firm's cost.

In the short run, a firm achieves its objective by deciding the quantity to produce. This quantity influences the firm's total revenue, total cost, and economic profit. In the long run, a firm achieves its objective by deciding whether to enter or exit a market.

These are the key decisions that a firm in perfect competition makes. Such a firm does *not* choose the price at which to sell its output. The firm in perfect competition is a **price taker**—it cannot influence the price of its product.

Price taker
A firm that cannot influence the price of the good or service that it produces.

Price Taker

To see why a firm in perfect competition is a price taker, imagine that you are a wheat farmer in Kansas. You have a thousand acres under cultivation—which sounds like a lot. But then you go on a drive through Colorado, Oklahoma, Texas, and back up to Nebraska and the Dakotas. You find unbroken stretches of wheat covering millions of acres. And you know that there are similar vistas in Canada, Argentina, Australia, and Ukraine. Your thousand acres are a drop in the ocean. Nothing makes your wheat any better than any other farmer's, and all the buyers of wheat know the price they must pay. If the going price of wheat is $4 a bushel, you are stuck with that price. You can't get a higher price than $4, and you have no incentive to offer it for less than $4 because you can sell your entire output at that price.

The producers of most agricultural products are price takers. We'll illustrate perfect competition with another agriculture example: the market for maple syrup. The next time you pour syrup on your pancakes, think about the competitive market that gets this product from the sap of the maple tree to your table!

Wheat farmers and maple syrup farmers are price takers.

Dave's Maple Syrup is one of the more than 10,000 similar firms in the maple syrup market of North America. Dave is a price taker. Like the Kansas wheat farmer, he can sell any quantity he chooses at the going price but none above that price. Dave faces a *perfectly elastic* demand. The demand for Dave's syrup is perfectly elastic because syrup from Casper Sugar Shack and all the other maple farms in the United States and Canada are *perfect substitutes* for Dave's syrup.

We'll explore Dave's decisions and their implications for the way a competitive market works. We begin by defining some revenue concepts.

Revenue Concepts

In perfect competition, market demand and market supply determine the price. A firm's *total revenue* equals this given price multiplied by the quantity sold. A firm's **marginal revenue** is the change in total revenue that results from a one-unit increase in the quantity sold. In perfect competition, marginal revenue equals price. The reason is that the firm can sell any quantity it chooses at the going market price. So if the firm sells one more unit, it sells it for the market price and total revenue increases by that amount. But this increase in total revenue is marginal revenue. So marginal revenue equals price.

Marginal revenue
The change in total revenue that results from a one-unit increase in the quantity sold.

The table in Figure 10.1 illustrates the equality of marginal revenue and price. The price of syrup is $8 a can. Total revenue is equal to the price multiplied by the quantity sold. So if Dave sells 10 cans, his total revenue is 10 × $8 = $80. If the quantity sold increases from 10 cans to 11 cans, total revenue increases from $80 to $88, so marginal revenue is $8 a can, the same as the price.

Figure 10.1 illustrates price determination and revenue in the perfectly competitive market. Market demand and market supply in part (a) determine the market price. Dave is a price taker, so he sells his syrup for the market price. The demand curve for Dave's syrup is the horizontal line at the market price in part (b). Because price equals marginal revenue, the demand curve for Dave's syrup is Dave's marginal revenue curve (*MR*). The total revenue curve (*TR*), in part (c), shows the total revenue at each quantity sold. Because he sells each can for the market price, the total revenue curve is an upward-sloping straight line.

Profit-Maximizing Output

As output increases, total revenue increases. But total cost also increases. And because of *decreasing marginal returns* (see pp. 298–300), total cost eventually increases faster than total revenue. There is one output level that maximizes economic profit, and a perfectly competitive firm chooses this output level.

FIGURE 10.1
Demand, Price, and Revenue in Perfect Competition

Practice Online

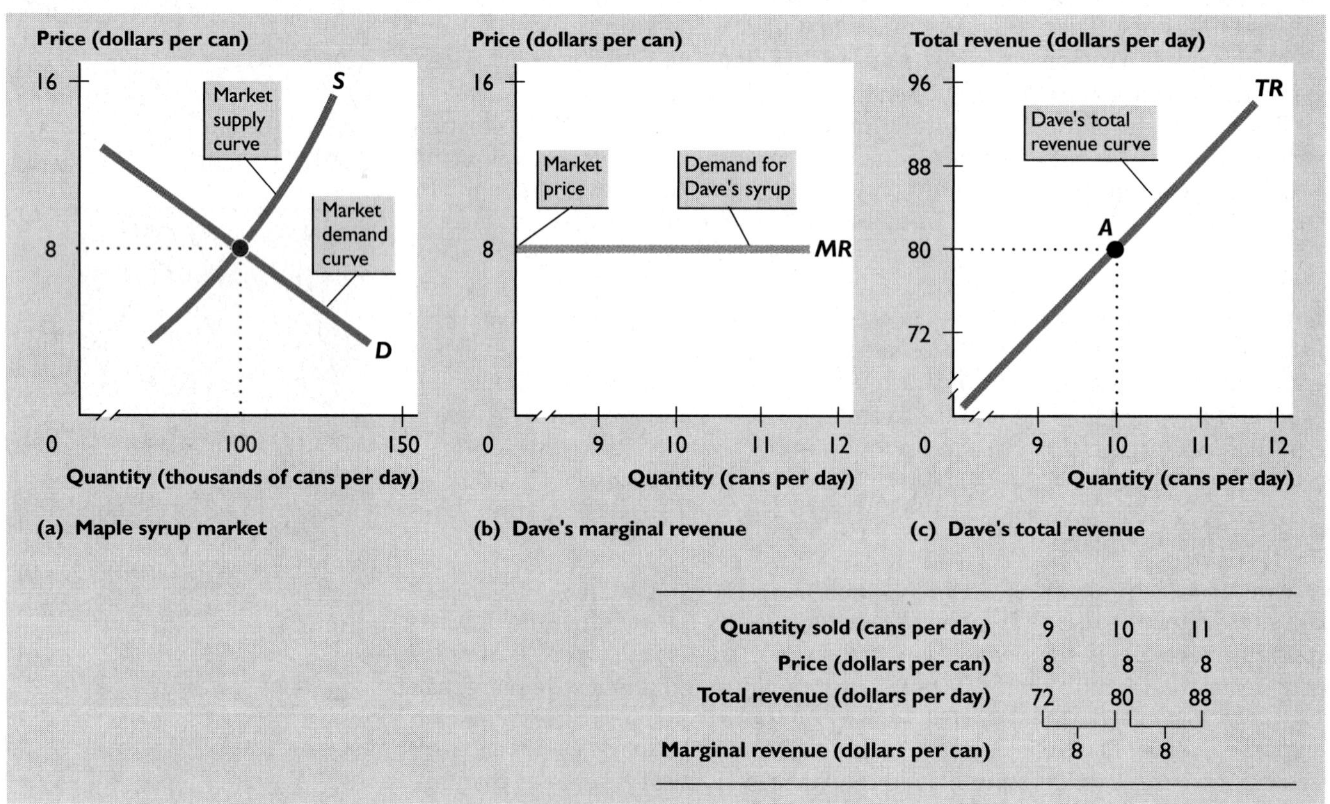

Quantity sold (cans per day)	9	10	11
Price (dollars per can)	8	8	8
Total revenue (dollars per day)	72	80	88
Marginal revenue (dollars per can)	8		8

Part (a) shows the market for maple syrup. The market price is $8 a can. The table calculates total revenue and marginal revenue.

Part (b) shows the demand curve for Dave's syrup, which is Dave's marginal revenue curve (*MR*).

Part (c) shows Dave's total revenue curve (*TR*). Point *A* corresponds to the second column of the table.

One way to find the profit-maximizing output is to use a firm's total revenue and total cost curves. Profit is maximized at the output level at which total revenue exceeds total cost by the largest amount. Figure 10.2 shows how to do this for Dave's Maple Syrup.

The table lists Dave's total revenue, total cost, and economic profit at different output levels. Figure 10.2(a) shows the total revenue and total cost curves. These curves are graphs of the numbers shown in the first three columns of the table. The total revenue curve (*TR*) is the same as that in Figure 10.1(c). The total cost curve (*TC*) is similar to the one that you met in Chapter 9 (p. 230). Figure 10.2(b) is an economic profit curve.

Dave makes an economic profit on outputs between 4 and 13 cans a day. At outputs of less than 4 cans a day and more than 13 cans a day, he incurs an economic loss. At outputs of 4 cans and 13 cans a day, total cost equals total revenue and Dave's economic profit is zero—Dave's *break-even points*.

The profit curve is at its highest when the vertical distance between the *TR* and *TC* curves is greatest. In this example, profit maximization occurs at an output of 10 cans a day. At this output, Dave's economic profit is $29 a day.

FIGURE 10.2

Total Revenue, Total Cost, and Economic Profit

Practice Online

(a) Revenue and cost

(b) Economic profit and loss

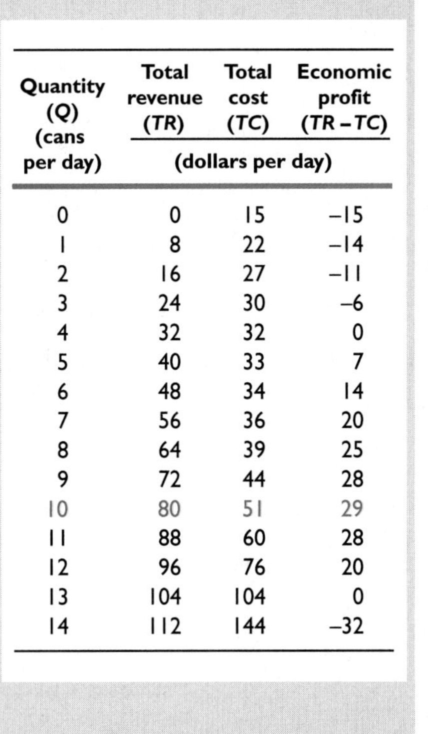

Quantity (Q) (cans per day)	Total revenue (TR)	Total cost (TC)	Economic profit (TR – TC)
	(dollars per day)		
0	0	15	–15
1	8	22	–14
2	16	27	–11
3	24	30	–6
4	32	32	0
5	40	33	7
6	48	34	14
7	56	36	20
8	64	39	25
9	72	44	28
10	80	51	29
11	88	60	28
12	96	76	20
13	104	104	0
14	112	144	–32

In part (a), economic profit is the vertical distance between the total cost and total revenue curves. Dave's maximum economic profit is $29 a day ($80 – $51) when output is 10 cans a day.

In part (b), economic profit is the height of the profit curve.

Marginal Analysis and the Supply Decision

Another way to find the profit-maximizing output is to use *marginal analysis*, which compares marginal revenue, *MR*, with marginal cost, *MC*. As output increases, marginal revenue is constant but marginal cost eventually increases.

If marginal revenue exceeds marginal cost (if $MR > MC$), then the extra revenue from selling one more unit exceeds the extra cost incurred to produce it. Economic profit increases if output *increases*. If marginal revenue is less than marginal cost (if $MR < MC$), then the extra revenue from selling one more unit is less than the extra cost incurred to produce it. Economic profit increases if output *decreases*. If marginal revenue equals marginal cost (if $MR = MC$), economic profit is maximized. The rule $MR = MC$ is a prime example of marginal analysis.

Figure 10.3 illustrates these propositions. The table records Dave's marginal revenue and marginal cost. If Dave increases output from 9 cans to 10 cans a day, marginal revenue is \$8 and marginal cost is \$7. Because marginal revenue exceeds marginal cost, economic profit increases. The last column of the table shows that economic profit increases from \$28 to \$29. The blue area in the figure shows this economic profit from the tenth can.

If Dave increases output from 10 cans to 11 cans a day, marginal revenue is still \$8 but marginal cost is \$9. Because marginal revenue is less than marginal cost, economic profit decreases. The last column of the table shows that economic profit decreases from \$29 to \$28. The red area in the figure shows this economic loss from the eleventh can.

Dave maximizes economic profit by producing 10 cans a day, the quantity at which marginal revenue equals marginal cost.

FIGURE 10.3
Profit-Maximizing Output

Practice Online

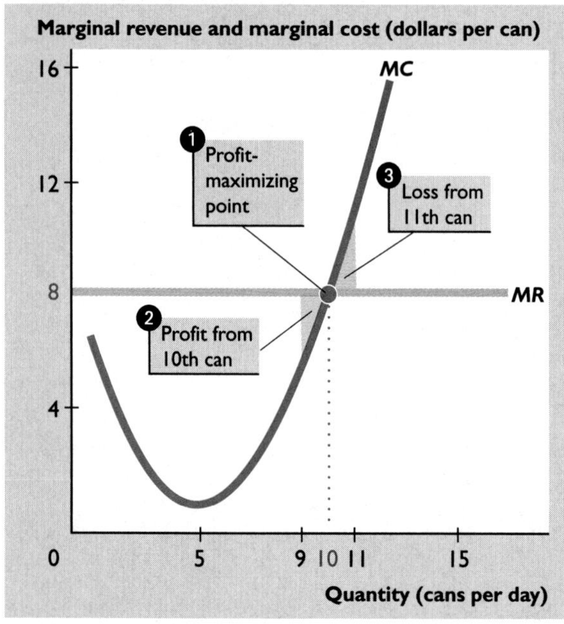

Quantity (*Q*) (cans per day)	Total revenue (*TR*) (dollars per day)	Marginal revenue (*MR*) (dollars per can)	Total cost (*TC*) (dollars per day)	Marginal cost (*MC*) (dollars per can)	Economic profit (*TR* – *TC*) (dollars per day)
8	64		39		25
		8		5	
9	72		44		28
		8		7	
10	80		51		29
		8		9	
11	88		60		28
		8		16	
12	96		76		20

1 Profit is maximized when marginal revenue equals marginal cost at 10 cans a day. 2 If output increases from 9 to 10 cans a day, marginal cost is \$7, which is less than the marginal revenue of \$8, and profit increases. 3 If output increases from 10 to 11 cans a day, marginal cost is \$9, which exceeds the marginal revenue of \$8, and profit decreases.

In the example that we've just worked through, Dave's profit-maximizing output is 10 cans a day. This quantity is Dave's *quantity supplied* at a price of $8 a can. If the price were higher than $8 a can, he would increase production. If the price were lower than $8 a can, he would decrease production. These profit-maximizing responses to different prices are the foundation of the law of supply: *Other things remaining the same, the higher the price of a good, the greater is the quantity supplied of that good.*

Exit and Temporary Shutdown Decisions

Sometimes, the price falls so low that a firm cannot cover its costs. What does the firm do in such a situation? The answer depends on whether the firm expects the low price to be permanent or temporary.

If a firm is incurring an economic loss that it believes is permanent and sees no prospect of ending, the firm exits the market. We'll study the consequences of this action later in this chapter where we look at the long run (pp. 260–261).

If a firm is incurring an economic loss that it believes is temporary, it will remain in the market, and it might produce some output or temporarily shut down. To decide whether to produce or to shut down, the firm compares the loss it would incur in the two situations.

If the firm shuts down, it incurs an economic loss equal to total fixed cost. If the firm produces some output, it incurs an economic loss equal to total fixed cost *plus* total variable cost *minus* total revenue. If total revenue exceeds total variable cost, the firm's economic loss is less than total fixed cost. So it pays the firm to produce. But if total revenue were less than total variable cost, the firm's economic loss would exceed total fixed cost. So the firm would shut down temporarily. Total fixed cost is the largest economic loss that the firm will incur.

The firm's economic loss equals total fixed cost when price equals average variable cost. So the firm produces if price exceeds average variable cost and shuts down if average variable cost exceeds price.

The Firm's Short-Run Supply Curve

A perfectly competitive firm's short-run supply curve shows how the firm's profit-maximizing output varies as the price varies, other things remaining the same. This supply curve is based on the marginal analysis and shutdown decision that we've just explored.

Figure 10.4 derives Dave's supply curve. Part (a) shows the marginal cost and average variable cost curves, and part (b) shows the supply curve. There is a direct link between the marginal cost and average variable cost curves and the supply curve. Let's see what that link is.

If the price is above minimum average variable cost, Dave maximizes profit by producing the output at which marginal cost equals price. We can determine the quantity produced at each price from the marginal cost curve. At a price of $8 a can, the marginal revenue curve is MR_1 and Dave maximizes profit by producing 10 cans a day. If the price rises to $12 a can, the marginal revenue curve is MR_2 and Dave increases production to 11 cans a day.

The firm shuts down if the price falls below minimum average variable cost. The **shutdown point** is the output and price at which the firm just covers its total variable cost. In Figure 10.4(a), if the price is $3 a can, the marginal revenue curve is MR_0, and the profit-maximizing output is 7 cans a day at the shutdown point.

Shutdown point
The output and price at which the firm just covers its total variable cost.

But both price and average variable cost equal $3 a can, so total revenue equals total variable cost and Dave incurs an economic loss equal to total fixed cost. At a price below $3 a can, if Dave produces any positive quantity, average *variable* cost exceeds price and the firm's loss exceeds total fixed cost. So at a price below $3 a can, Dave shuts down and produces nothing.

Dave's short-run supply curve, shown in Figure 10.4(b), has two separate parts: First, at prices that exceed minimum average variable cost, the supply curve is the same as the marginal cost curve above the shutdown point (*T*). Second, at prices below minimum average variable cost, Dave shuts down and produces nothing. His supply curve runs along the vertical axis. At a price of $3 a can, Dave is indifferent between shutting down and producing 7 cans a day. Either way, he incurs a loss of $15 a day, which equals his total fixed cost.

So far, we have studied one firm in isolation. We have seen that the firm's profit-maximizing actions depend on the price, which the firm takes as given. In the next section, you'll learn how market supply is determined.

FIGURE 10.4
Dave's Supply Curve

Practice Online

Part (a) shows that at $8 a can, Dave produces 10 cans a day; at $12 a can, he produces 11 cans a day; and at $3 a can, he produces either 7 cans a day or nothing. At any price below $3 a can, Dave produces nothing. The minimum average variable cost is the shutdown point.

Part (b) shows Dave's supply curve, which is made up of the marginal cost curve (part a) at all points *above* the shutdown point *T* (minimum average variable cost) and the vertical axis at all prices *below* the shutdown point.

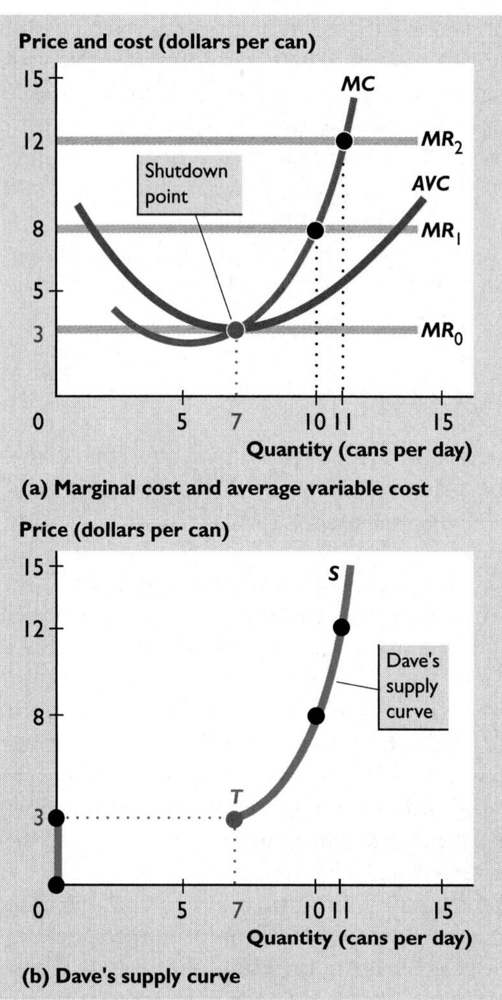

(a) Marginal cost and average variable cost

(b) Dave's supply curve

CHECKPOINT 10.1

1 Explain a perfectly competitive firm's profit-maximizing choices and derive its supply curve.

Study Guide pp. 150–154

Practice Online 10.1

Practice Problems 10.1

1. Sarah's Salmon Farm produces 1,000 fish a week. The marginal cost is $30 a fish, average variable cost is $20 a fish, and the market price is $25 a fish. Is Sarah maximizing profit? Explain why or why not. If Sarah is not maximizing profit, to do so, will she increase or decrease the number of fish she produces in a week?

2. Trout farming is a perfectly competitive industry, and all trout farms have the same cost curves. The market price is $25 a fish. To maximize profit, each farm produces 200 fish a week. Average total cost is $20 a fish, and average variable cost is $15 a fish. Minimum average variable cost is $12 a fish.
   a. If the price falls to $20 a fish, will trout farms continue to produce 200 fish a week? Explain why or why not.
   b. If the price falls to $12 a fish, what will the trout farmer do?
   c. What is one point on the trout farm's supply curve?

Exercise 10.1

Paula is an asparagus farmer, and the world asparagus market is perfectly competitive. The market price is $15 a box. Paula sells 800 boxes a week, and her marginal cost is $18 a box.

a. Calculate Paula's total revenue.
b. Calculate Paula's marginal revenue.
c. Is Paula maximizing profit? Explain your answer.
d. The price falls to $12 a box, and Paula cuts her output to 500 boxes a week. Her average variable cost and marginal cost fall to $12 a box. Is Paula maximizing profit? Is she earning an economic profit or incurring an economic loss?
e. What is one point on Paula's supply curve?

Solutions to Practice Problems 10.1

1. Profit is maximized when marginal cost equals marginal revenue. In perfect competition, marginal revenue equals the market price and is $25 a fish. Because marginal cost exceeds marginal revenue, Sarah is not maximizing profit. To maximize profit, she will decrease her output until marginal cost falls to $25 a fish (Figure 1).

FIGURE 1

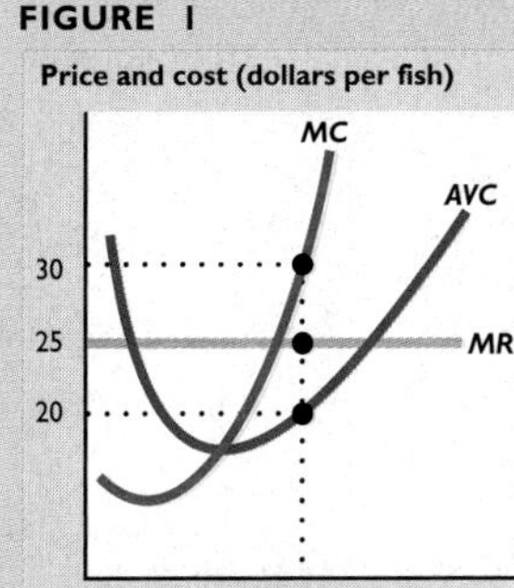

2a. The farm will produce fewer than 200 fish a week. The marginal cost increases as the farm produces more fish. So to reduce its marginal cost from $25 to $20, the farm cuts production.

2b. If the price falls to $12 a fish, farms cut production to the quantity where marginal cost equals $12. But because $12 is minimum average variable cost, this price puts farms at the shutdown point. Farms will be indifferent between producing the profit-maximizing output and producing nothing. Either way, they incur an economic loss equal to total fixed cost.

2c. At $25 a fish, the quantity supplied is 200 fish; at $12 a fish, the quantity supplied might be zero; at a price below $12 a fish, the quantity supplied is zero.

10.2 OUTPUT, PRICE, AND PROFIT IN THE SHORT RUN

To determine the price and quantity in a perfectly competitive market, we need to know how market demand and supply interact. We begin by studying a perfectly competitive market in the short run when the number of firms is fixed.

Market Supply in the Short Run

The market supply curve in the short run shows the quantity supplied at each price by a fixed number of firms. The quantity supplied at a given price is the sum of the quantities supplied by all firms at that price.

Figure 10.5 shows the supply curve for the competitive syrup market. In this example, the market consists of 10,000 firms exactly like Dave's Maple Syrup. The table shows how the market supply schedule is constructed. At prices below \$3, every firm in the market shuts down; the quantity supplied is zero. At a price of \$3, each firm is indifferent between shutting down and producing nothing or operating and producing 7 cans a day. The quantity supplied by each firm is *either* 0 or 7 cans, and the quantity supplied in the market is *between* 0 (all firms shut down) and 70,000 (all firms produce 7 cans a day each). At prices above \$3, we sum the quantities supplied by the 10,000 firms, so the quantity supplied in the market is 10,000 times the quantity supplied by one firm.

At prices below \$3, the market supply curve runs along the price axis. Supply is perfectly inelastic. At a price of \$3, the market supply curve is horizontal. Supply is perfectly elastic. At prices above \$3, the supply curve is upward sloping.

FIGURE 10.5
The Market Supply Curve

Practice Online

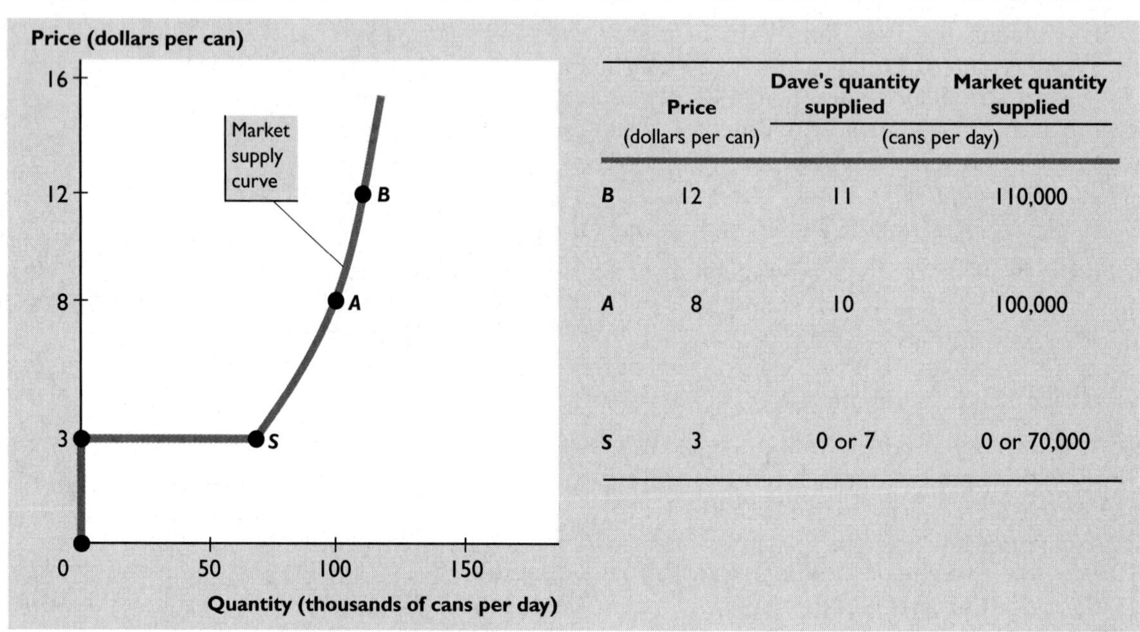

	Price (dollars per can)	Dave's quantity supplied (cans per day)	Market quantity supplied (cans per day)
B	12	11	110,000
A	8	10	100,000
S	3	0 or 7	0 or 70,000

A market with 10,000 identical firms has a supply schedule similar to that of the individual firm, but the quantity supplied is 10,000 times greater. At the shutdown price of \$3 a can, each firm produces either 0 or 7 cans a day, but the market supply curve is perfectly elastic at that price.

Short-Run Equilibrium in Good Times

Market demand and market supply determine the price and quantity bought and sold. Figure 10.6(a) shows a short-run equilibrium in the syrup market. The supply curve S is the same as that in Figure 10.5.

If the demand curve D_1 shows market demand, the equilibrium price is $8 a can. Although market demand and market supply determine this price, each firm takes the price as given and produces its profit-maximizing output, which is 10 cans a day. Because the market has 10,000 firms, market output is 100,000 cans a day.

Figure 10.6(b) shows the situation that Dave faces. The price is $8 a can, so Dave's marginal revenue is constant at $8 a can. Dave maximizes profit by producing 10 cans a day.

Figure 10.6(b) also shows Dave's average total cost curve (*ATC*). Recall that average total cost is the cost per unit produced. It equals total cost divided by the quantity of output produced.

Here, when Dave produces 10 cans a day, his average total cost is $5.10 a can. So the price of $8 a can exceeds average total cost by $2.90 a can. This amount is Dave's economic profit per can.

If we multiply the economic profit per can of $2.90 by the number of cans, 10 a day, we arrive at Dave's economic profit, which is $29 a day.

The blue rectangle shows this economic profit. The height of that rectangle is the profit per can, $2.90, and the length is the quantity of cans, 10 a day, so the area of the rectangle (height × length) measures Dave's economic profit of $29 a day.

FIGURE 10.6
Economic Profit in the Short Run

Practice Online

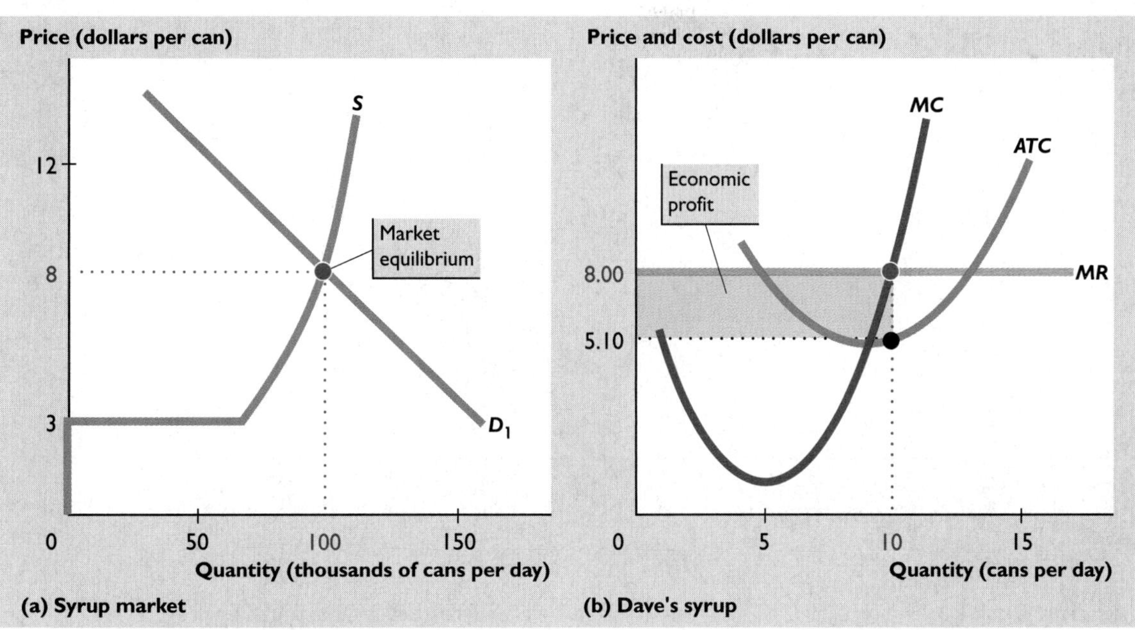

In part (a), with market demand curve D_1 and market supply curve S, the equilibrium market price is $8 a can.

In part (b), Dave's marginal revenue is $8 a can, so he produces 10 cans a day. At this quantity, price ($8) exceeds average total cost ($5.10), so Dave makes an economic profit shown by the blue rectangle.

Short-Run Equilibrium in Bad Times

In the short-run equilibrium that we've just examined, Dave is enjoying an economic profit. But such an outcome is not inevitable. Figure 10.7 shows the syrup market in a less happy state. The market demand curve is now D_2. The market still has 10,000 firms, and the costs of these firms are the same as before. So the market supply curve, S, is the same as before.

With the demand and supply curves shown in Figure 10.7(a), the equilibrium price of syrup is \$3 a can and the equilibrium quantity is 70,000 cans a day.

Figure 10.7(b) shows the situation that Dave faces. The price is \$3 a can, so Dave's marginal revenue is constant at \$3 a can. Dave maximizes profit by producing 7 cans a day.

Figure 10.7(b) also shows Dave's average total cost curve (*ATC*), and you can see that when Dave produces 7 cans a day, his average total cost is \$5.14 a can. So the price of \$3 a can is less than average total cost by \$2.14 a can. This amount is Dave's economic loss per can.

If we multiply the economic loss per can of \$2.14 by the number of cans, 7 a day, we arrive at Dave's economic loss, which is \$14.98 a day.

The red rectangle shows this economic loss. The height of that rectangle is the loss per can, \$2.14, and the length is the quantity of cans, 7 a day, so the area of the rectangle measures Dave's economic loss of \$14.98 a day.

FIGURE 10.7
Economic Loss in the Short Run

Practice Online

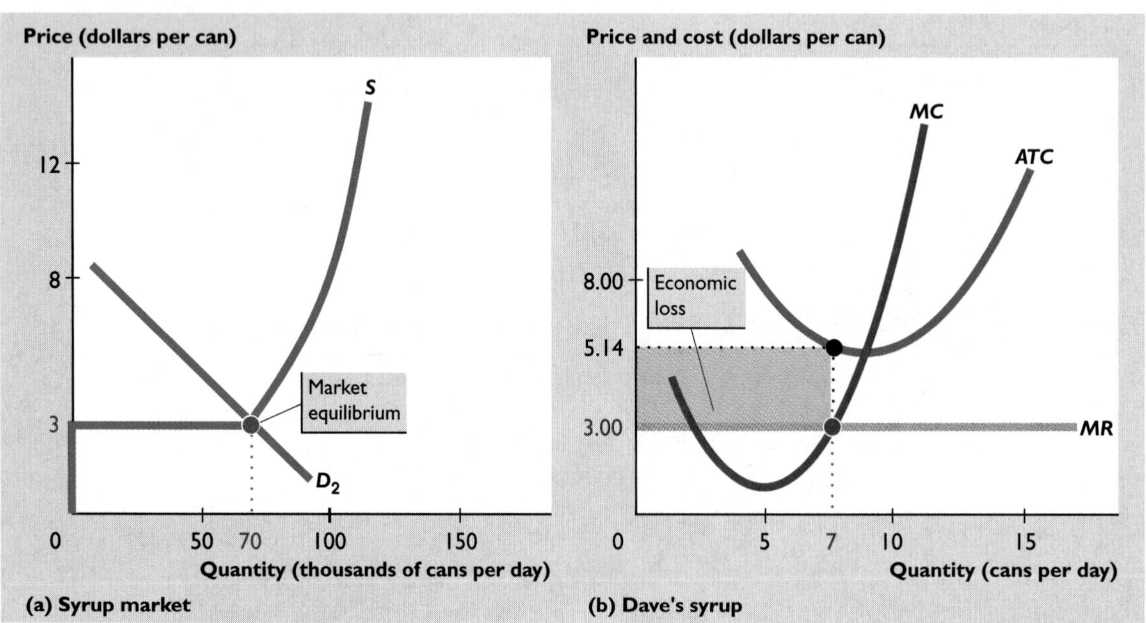

In part (a), with market demand curve D_2 and market supply curve S, the equilibrium market price is \$3 a can.

In part (b), Dave's marginal revenue is \$3 a can, so he produces 7 cans a day. At this quantity, price (\$3) is less than average total cost (\$5.14), so Dave incurs an economic loss shown by the red rectangle.

CHECKPOINT 10.2

2 **Explain how output, price, and profit are determined in the short run.**

Study Guide pp. 154–157

Practice Online 10.2

Practice Problem 10.2

Tulip growing is a perfectly competitive industry, and all tulip growers have the same cost curves. The market price of tulips is $25 a bunch, and each grower maximizes profit by producing 2,000 bunches a week. The average total cost of producing tulips is $20 a bunch, and the average variable cost is $15 a bunch. Minimum average variable cost is $12 a bunch.

a. What is the economic profit that each grower is making in the short run?
b. What is the price at the grower's shutdown point?
c. What is each grower's profit at the shutdown point?

Exercises 10.2

1. Tom's Tattoos is a tattooing business in a perfectly competitive market. The market price of a tattoo is $20. Table 1 shows Tom's total costs.
   a. How many tattoos an hour does Tom's Tattoos sell?
   b. What is Tom's Tattoos' economic profit in the short run?
2. In exercise 1, if the market price of a tattoo falls to $15,
   a. How many tattoos an hour does Tom's Tattoos sell?
   b. What is Tom's Tattoos' economic profit in the short run?
3. In exercise 1,
   a. At what market price will Tom's Tattoos shut down?
   b. At the shutdown point, what is Tom's Tattoos' economic loss?

TABLE 1

Quantity (tattoos per hour)	Total cost (dollars per hour)
0	30
1	50
2	65
3	75
4	90
5	110
6	140

Solution to Practice Problem 10.2

a. The market price ($25) exceeds the average total cost ($20), so tulip growers are making an economic profit of $5 a bunch. Each grower produces 2,000 bunches a week, so each grower makes an economic profit of $10,000 a week (Figure 1).

b. The price at which a grower will shut down is equal to minimum average variable cost—$12 a bunch (Figure 1).

c. At the shutdown point, the grower incurs an economic loss equal to total fixed cost. *ATC* = *AFC* + *AVC*. When 2,000 bunches a week are grown, *ATC* is $20 a bunch and *AVC* is $15 a bunch, so *AFC* is $5 a bunch. Total fixed cost equals $10,000 a week—$5 a bunch × 2,000 bunches a week. So at the shutdown point, the grower incurs an economic loss equal to $10,000 a week.

FIGURE 1

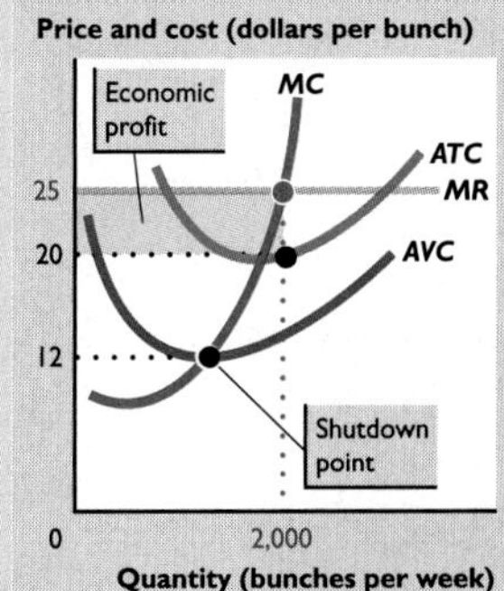

10.3 OUTPUT, PRICE, AND PROFIT IN THE LONG RUN

Neither good times nor bad times last forever in perfect competition. In the long run, a firm in perfect competition earns normal profit. It earns zero economic profit and incurs no economic loss.

Figure 10.8 shows the syrup market in a long-run equilibrium. The market demand curve is now D_3. The market still has 10,000 firms, and the costs of these firms are the same as before. So the market supply curve, *S*, is the same as before.

With the demand and supply curves shown in Figure 10.8(a), the equilibrium price of syrup is $5 a can and the equilibrium quantity is 90,000 cans a day.

Figure 10.8(b) shows the situation that Dave faces. The price is $5 a can, so Dave's marginal revenue is constant at $5 a can and Dave maximizes profit by producing 9 cans a day.

Figure 10.8(b) also shows Dave's average total cost curve (*ATC*), and you can see that when Dave produces 9 cans a day, his average total cost is $5 a can, which is also the minimum average total cost. That is, Dave can't produce syrup at an average total cost that is less than $5 a can no matter what his output is.

The price of $5 a can equals average total cost, so Dave has neither an economic profit nor an economic loss. He breaks even. But because his average total cost includes normal profit, Dave earns normal profit.

FIGURE 10.8

Long-run Equilibrium

Practice Online

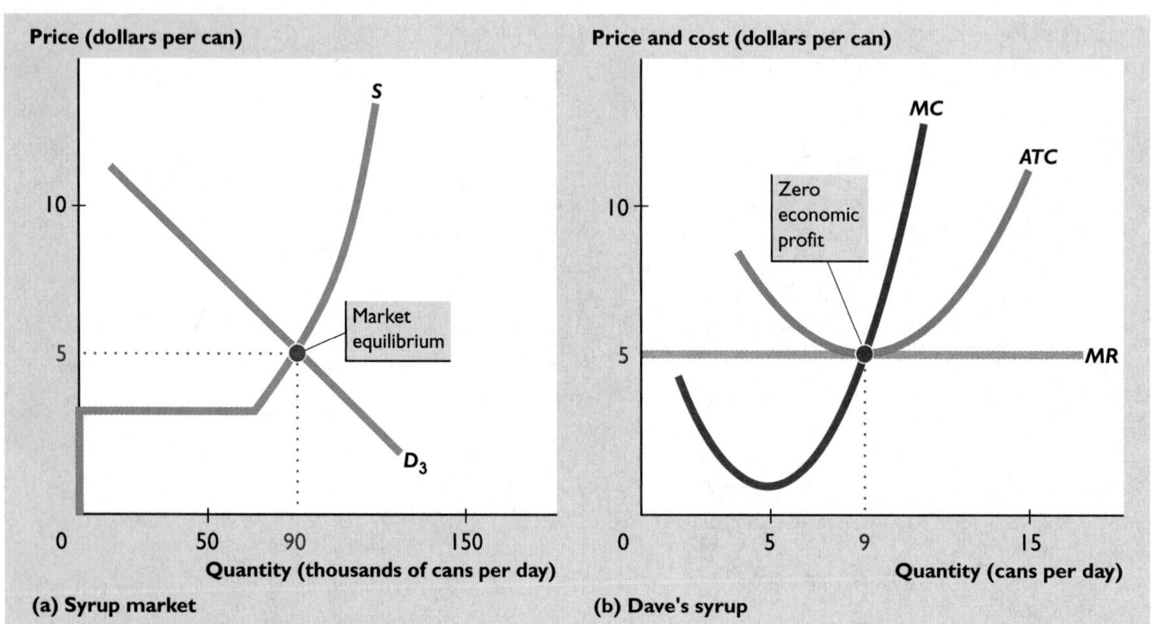

In part (a), with market demand curve D_3 and market supply curve S, the equilibrium market price is $5 a can.

In part (b), Dave's marginal revenue is $5 a can, so he produces 9 cans a day, where marginal cost equals marginal revenue. At this profit-maximizing quantity, price equals average total cost ($5), so Dave earns no economic profit. He earns normal profit.

Entry and Exit

In the short run, a perfectly competitive firm might make an economic profit (Figure 10.6) or incur an economic loss (Figure 10.7). But in the long run, a firm earns normal profit (Figure 10.8).

In the long run, firms respond to economic profit and economic loss by either entering or exiting a market. New firms enter a market in which the existing firms are making an economic profit. And existing firms exit a market in which they are incurring an economic loss. Temporary economic profit or temporary economic loss, like a win or loss at a casino, does not trigger entry and exit. But the prospect of persistent economic profit or loss does.

Entry and exit influence price, the quantity produced, and economic profit. The immediate effect of the decision to enter or exit is to shift the market supply curve. If more firms enter a market, supply increases and the market supply curve shifts rightward. If firms exit a market, supply decreases and the market supply curve shifts leftward.

Let's see what happens when new firms enter a market.

The Effects of Entry

Figure 10.9 shows the effects of entry. Initially, the market is in long-run equilibrium. Demand is D_0, supply is S_0, the price is $5 a can, and the quantity is 90,000 cans a day. A surge in the popularity of syrup increases demand, and the demand curve shifts to D_1. The price rises to $8 a can, and the firms in the syrup market increase output to 100,000 cans a day and make an economic profit.

Times are good for syrup producers like Dave, so other potential syrup producers want some of the action. New firms begin to enter the market. As they do so, supply increases and the market supply curve shifts rightward to S_1. With the

FIGURE 10.9
The Effects of Entry

Practice Online

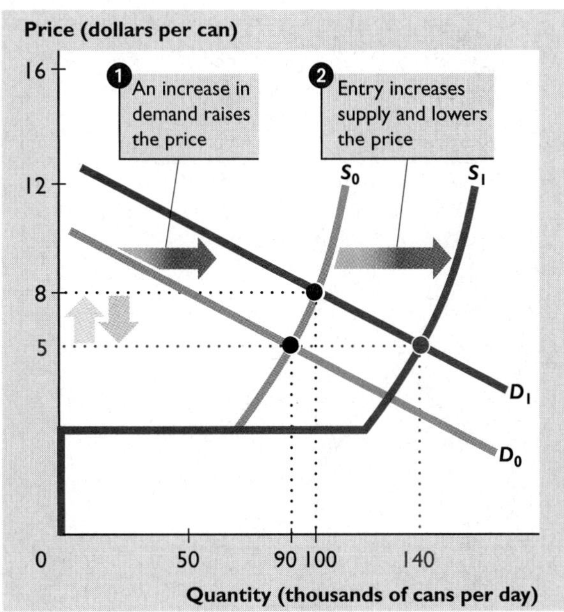

Starting in long-run equilibrium, ❶ demand increases and the demand curve shifts from D_0 to D_1. The price rises from $5 to $8 a can.

Economic profit brings entry. ❷ As firms enter the market, the supply curve shifts rightward, from S_0 to S_1. The equilibrium price falls from $8 to $5 a can, and the quantity produced increases from 100,000 to 140,000 cans a day.

greater supply and unchanged demand, the price falls from $8 to $5 a can and the quantity increases to 140,000 cans a day.

Market output increases, but because the price falls, Dave and the other producers decrease output, back to its original level. But because the number of firms in the market increases, the market as a whole produces more.

As the price falls, each firm's economic profit decreases. When the price falls to $5, economic profit disappears and each firm makes a normal profit. The entry process stops, and the market is again in long-run equilibrium.

You have just discovered a key proposition:

Economic profit is an incentive for new firms to enter a market, but as they do so, the price falls and the economic profit of each existing firm decreases.

The Effects of Exit

Figure 10.10 shows the effects of exit. Again we begin on demand curve D_0 and supply curve S_0 in long-run equilibrium. Now suppose that the development of a new high-nutrition, low-fat breakfast food decreases the demand for pancakes, and as a result, the demand for maple syrup decreases. The demand curve shifts from D_0 to D_2. Firms' costs are the same as before, so the market supply curve is S_0.

With demand at D_2 and supply at S_0, the price falls to $3 a can and 70,000 cans a day are produced. The firms in the syrup market incur economic losses.

Times are tough for syrup producers, and Dave must seriously think about leaving his dream business and finding some other way of making a living. But other producers are in the same situation as Dave. And some start to exit the market while Dave is still thinking through his options.

FIGURE 10.10
The Effects of Exit

Practice Online

Starting in long-run equilibrium, ❶ demand decreases and the demand curve shifts from D_0 to D_2. The price falls from $5 to $3 a can.

Economic loss brings exit. ❷ As firms exit the market, the supply curve shifts leftward, from S_0 to S_2. The equilibrium price rises from $3 to $5 a can, and the quantity produced decreases from 70,000 to 40,000 cans a day.

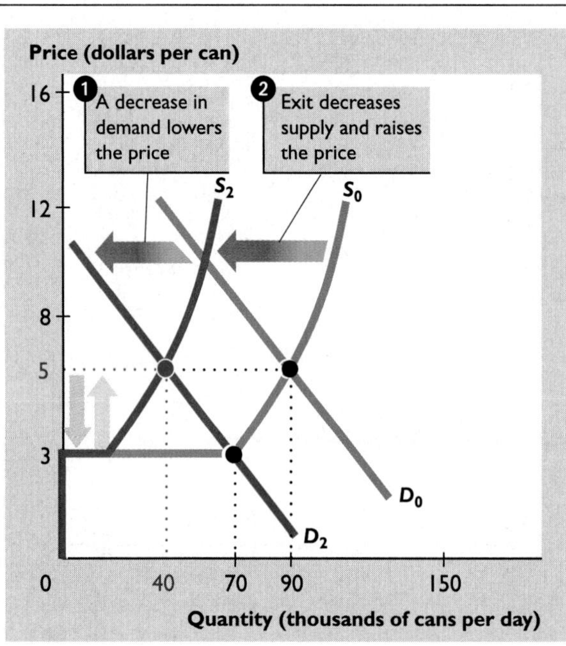

As firms exit, the market supply curve shifts leftward to S_2. With the decrease in supply, output decreases from 70,000 to 40,000 cans and the price rises from $3 to $5 a can.

As the price rises, Dave and each other firm that remains in the market move up along their supply curves and increase output. That is, for each firm that remains in the market, the profit-maximizing output *increases*. As the price rises and each firm sells more, economic loss decreases. When the price rises to $5, each firm makes a normal profit. Dave is happy that he can still make a living producing syrup.

You have just discovered a second key proposition:

Economic loss is an incentive for firms to exit a market, but as they do so, the price rises and the economic loss of each remaining firm decreases.

Eye on the U.S. Economy

Entry in Personal Computers, Exit in Farm Machines

An example of entry and falling prices occurred during the 1980s and 1990s in the personal computer market. When IBM introduced its first PC in 1981, there was little competition; the price was $7,000 (a bit more than $14,000 in today's money), and IBM earned a large economic profit on the new machine. But new firms such as Compaq, NEC, Dell, and a host of others entered the market with machines that were technologically identical to IBM's. In fact, they were so similar that they came to be called "clones." The massive wave of entry into the personal computer market shifted the supply curve rightward and lowered the price and the economic profit for all firms. Today, a $1,000 computer is much more powerful than its 1981 ancestor that cost 14 times as much.

An example of a firm leaving a market is International Harvester, a manufacturer of farm equipment. For decades, people associated the name "International Harvester" with tractors, combines, and other farm machines. But International Harvester wasn't the only maker of farm equipment. The market became intensely competitive, and the firm began to incur an economic loss. Now the company has a new name, Navistar International, and it doesn't make tractors any more. After years of economic losses and shrinking revenues, it got out of the farm-machine business in 1985 and started to make trucks.

International Harvester exited because it was incurring an economic loss. Its exit decreased supply and made it possible for the remaining firms in the market to earn a normal profit.

A Permanent Change in Demand

The long-run adjustments in the maple syrup market that we've just explored apply to all competitive markets. The market begins in long-run equilibrium. Price equals minimum average total cost, and firms are making normal profit. Then demand increases permanently. The increase in demand raises the price above average total cost, so firms make economic profits. To maximize profit, firms increase output to keep marginal cost equal to price.

The market is now in short-run equilibrium but not long-run equilibrium. It is in short-run equilibrium because the number of firms is fixed. But it is not in long-run equilibrium because each firm is making an economic profit.

The economic profit is an incentive for new firms to enter the market. As they do so, market supply starts to increase and the price starts to fall. At each lower price, a firm's profit-maximizing output is less, so each firm decreases its output. That is, as firms enter the market, market output increases but the output of each firm decreases. Eventually, enough firms enter for market supply to have increased by enough to return the price to its original level. At this price, the firms produce the same quantity that they produced before the increase in demand and they earn normal profit again. The market is again in long-run equilibrium.

The difference between the initial long-run equilibrium and the final long-run equilibrium is the number of firms in the market. A permanent increase in demand increases the number of firms. Each firm produces the same output in the new long-run equilibrium as initially and earns a normal profit. In the process of moving from the initial equilibrium to the new one, firms make economic profits.

The demand for airline travel in the world economy has increased permanently in recent years, and the deregulation of the airlines has freed up firms to seek profit opportunities in this market. The result was a massive rate of entry of new airlines. The process of competition and change in the airline market, although not a perfectly competitive market, is similar to what we have just studied.

A permanent decrease in demand triggers a similar response, except in the opposite direction. The decrease in demand brings a lower price, economic loss, and exit. Exit decreases market supply and eventually raises the price to its original level.

One feature of the predictions that we have just generated seems odd: In the long run, regardless of whether demand increases or decreases, the price returns to its original level. Is this outcome inevitable? In fact, it is not. It is possible for the long-run equilibrium price to remain the same, rise, or fall.

External Economies and Diseconomies

External economies
Factors beyond the control of an individual firm that lower its costs as the *market* output increases.

External diseconomies
Factors outside the control of a firm that raise the firm's costs as *market* output increases.

The change in the long-run equilibrium price depends on external economies and external diseconomies. **External economies** are factors beyond the control of an individual firm that lower its costs as the *market* output increases. **External diseconomies** are factors outside the control of a firm that raise the firm's costs as *market* output increases. With no external economies or external diseconomies, a firm's costs remain constant as the *market* output changes.

Figure 10.11 illustrates these three cases and introduces a new supply concept: the long-run market supply curve.

FIGURE 10.11
Long-run Changes in Price and Quantity

Practice Online

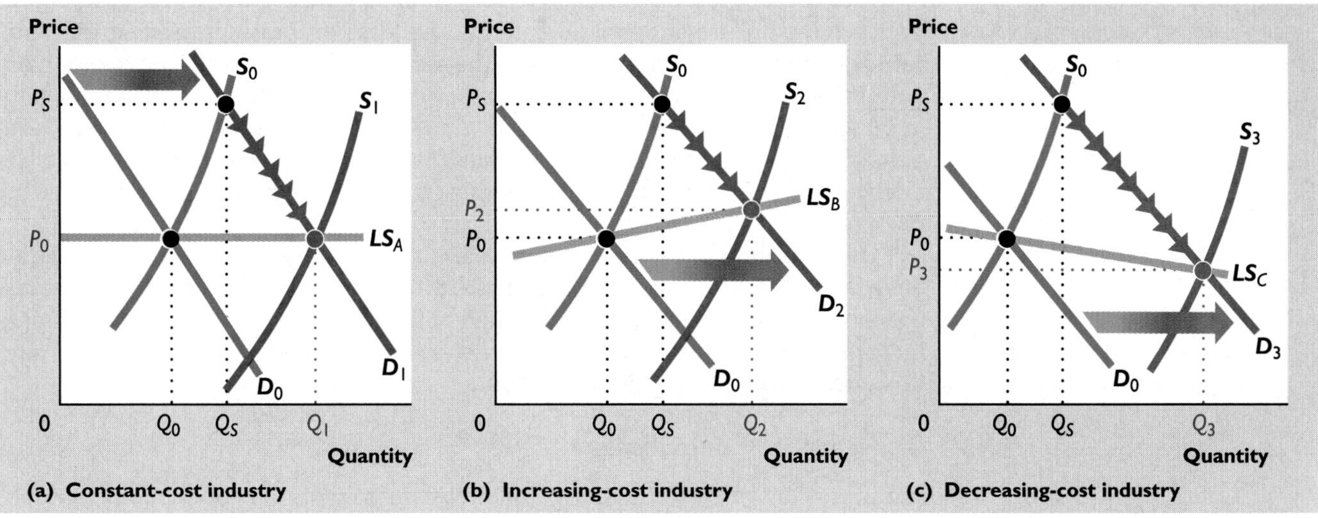

(a) Constant-cost industry

When demand increases from D_0 to D_1, entry occurs and the market supply curve shifts from S_0 to S_1. The long-run market supply curve, LS_A, is horizontal.

(b) Increasing-cost industry

The long-run market supply curve is LS_B; the price rises to P_2, and the quantity increases to Q_2. This case occurs in industries with external diseconomies.

(c) Decreasing-cost industry

The long-run market supply curve is LS_C; the price falls to P_3, and the quantity increases to Q_3. This case occurs in an industry with external economies.

A **long-run market supply curve** shows the relationship between the quantity supplied and the price when the number of firms changes so that each firm earns zero economic profit.

Long-run market supply curve
A curve that shows the relationship between the quantity supplied and the price when the number of firms changes so that each firm earns zero economic profit.

Figure 10.11(a) shows the case we have just studied: no external economies or diseconomies. The long-run market supply curve (LS_A) is perfectly elastic. In this case, a permanent increase in demand from D_0 to D_1 has no effect on the price in the long run. The increase in demand initially increases the price to P_S and increases the quantity to Q_S. Entry increases supply from S_0 to S_1, which lowers the price to its original level, P_0, and increases the quantity to Q_1.

Figure 10.11(b) shows the case of external diseconomies. The long-run market supply curve (LS_B) slopes upward. A permanent increase in demand from D_0 to D_2 increases the price in both the short run and the long run. As in the previous case, the increase in demand initially increases the price to P_S and increases the quantity to Q_S. Entry increases supply from S_0 to S_2, which lowers the price to P_2 and increases the quantity to Q_2.

One source of external diseconomies is congestion. The airline market provides a good example. With bigger airline market output, there is more congestion of airports and airspace, which results in longer delays and extra waiting time for passengers and airplanes. These external diseconomies mean that as the output of air transportation services increases (in the absence of technological advances), average cost increases. As a result, the long-run supply curve is upward sloping. So a permanent increase in demand brings an increase in quantity and a rise in the price.

Figure 10.11(c) shows the case of external economies. In this case, the long-run market supply curve (LS_C) slopes downward. A permanent increase in demand from D_0 to D_3 increases the price in the short run and lowers it in the long run.

Again, the increase in demand initially increases the price to P_S, and increases the quantity to Q_S. Entry increases supply from S_0 to S_3, which lowers the price to P_3 and increases the quantity to Q_3.

One of the best examples of external economies is the growth of specialist support services for a market as it expands. As farm output increased in the nineteenth and early twentieth centuries, the services available to farmers expanded and average farm costs fell. For example, new firms specialized in the development and marketing of farm machinery and fertilizers. As a result, average farm costs decreased. Farms enjoyed the benefits of external economies. As a consequence, as the demand for farm products increased, the output increased but the price fell.

Over the long term, the prices of many goods and services have fallen. Some have fallen because of external economies. But prices in markets with external diseconomies have also fallen. The reason in both cases is that technological advances increase supply and shift the long-run supply curve rightward. Let's now study this influence on a competitive market.

Technological Change

Firms are constantly discovering lower-cost techniques of production. For example, the cost of producing personal computers has tumbled. So have the costs of producing CD players, DVD players, and most other electronic products. Most cost-saving production techniques cannot be implemented without investing in new plants. Consequently, it takes time for a technological advance to spread through a market. Some firms whose plants are on the verge of being replaced will be quick to adopt the new technology, while other firms whose plants have recently been replaced will continue to operate with an old technology until they can no longer cover their average variable cost. Once average variable cost cannot be covered, a firm will scrap even a relatively new plant (embodying an old technology) in favor of a plant with a new technology.

New technology allows firms to produce at a lower cost. As a result, as firms adopt a new technology, their cost curves shift downward. With lower costs, firms are willing to supply a given quantity at a lower price or, equivalently, they are willing to supply a larger quantity at a given price. In other words, market supply increases, and the market supply curve shifts rightward. With a given demand, the quantity produced increases and the price falls.

Two forces are at work in a market undergoing technological change. Firms that adopt the new technology make an economic profit. So new-technology firms have an incentive to enter. Firms that stick with the old technology incur economic losses. They either exit the market or switch to the new technology.

As old-technology firms exit and new-technology firms enter, the price falls and the quantity produced increases. Eventually, the market arrives at a long-run equilibrium in which all the firms use the new technology and each firm makes zero economic profit (a normal profit). Because competition eliminates economic profit in the long run, technological change brings only temporary gains to firms. But the lower prices and better products that technological advances bring are permanent gains for consumers.

The process that we've just described is one in which some firms experience economic profits and others experience economic losses—a period of dynamic change for a market. Some firms do well, and others do badly. Often, the process has a geographical dimension: The expanding new-technology firms bring prosperity to what was once the boondocks, and with old-technology firms going out of business, traditional industrial regions decline. Sometimes, the new-technology firms are in a foreign country, while the old-technology firms are in the domestic economy. The information revolution of the 1990s has produced many examples of changes like these. Commercial banking (a competitive but less than perfectly competitive industry), which was traditionally concentrated in New York, San Francisco, and other large cities, now flourishes in Charlotte, North Carolina, which has become the nation's number three commercial banking city. Television shows and movies, traditionally made in Los Angeles and New York, are now made in large numbers in Orlando and Toronto.

Technological advances are not confined to the information and entertainment market. Food production is undergoing a major technological change because of genetic engineering.

Eye on the Global Economy

The North American Market in Maple Syrup

North American maple syrup production runs at about 8 million gallons a year. Most of this syrup is produced in Canada, but farms in Vermont, New York, Maine, Wisconsin, New Hampshire, Ohio, and Michigan together produce close to 20 percent of the total output.

The number of firms that produce maple syrup can only be estimated, because some are tiny and sell their output to a small local market. But there are around 9,500 producers in Canada and approaching 2,000 in the United States.

The syrup of each producer is not quite identical. And at the retail level, people have preferences about brands and sources of supply. But at the wholesale level, the market is highly competitive and a good example of perfect competition.

All of the events that can occur in a perfectly competitive market and that we've studied in this chapter have actually occurred in the maple syrup market over the past 20 years.

During the 1980s, the technology for extracting sap advanced as more taps were installed that use a plastic tube vacuum technology. During this period, farms exited the market and the average farm increased in scale. In 1980, the average farm had 1,400 taps; by 1990, this number was 2,000; and by 1996, the number of taps had increased to 2,400.

During the 1990s, with a steady growth in the demand for maple syrup, new farms entered the market.

Through the past 20 years, total production has increased and the price has held remarkably stable at around \$8 per half-gallon can. So increasing demand has brought economic profit, which in turn has brought entry and an increase in supply.

CHECKPOINT 10.3

Study Guide pp. 157–160

Practice Online 10.3

3 **Explain how output, price, and profit are determined in the long run.**

Practice Problem 10.3

Tulip growing is a perfectly competitive industry, and all tulip growers have the same cost curves. The market price of tulips is $15 a bunch, and each grower maximizes profit by producing 1,500 bunches a week. The average total cost of producing tulips is $21 a bunch. Minimum average variable cost is $12 a bunch, and the minimum average total cost is $18 a bunch. Tulip growing is a constant cost industry.

a. What is a tulip grower's economic profit in the short run?
b. How does the number of tulip growers change in the long run?
c. What is the price in the long run?
d. What is the economic profit in the long run?

Exercise 10.3

Tom's Tattoos is a tattooing business in a perfectly competitive market. Table 1 shows Tom's total costs.

a. If the market price is $20 per tattoo, what is Tom's economic profit?
b. If the market price is $20 per tattoo, do new firms enter or do existing firms exit the industry in the long run?
c. What is the price of a tattoo in the long run?
d. How many tattoos per hour does Tom sell in the long run?
e. What is Tom's economic profit in the long run?

TABLE 1

Quantity (tattoos per hour)	Total cost (dollars per hour)
0	30
1	50
2	65
3	75
4	90
5	110
6	140

FIGURE 1

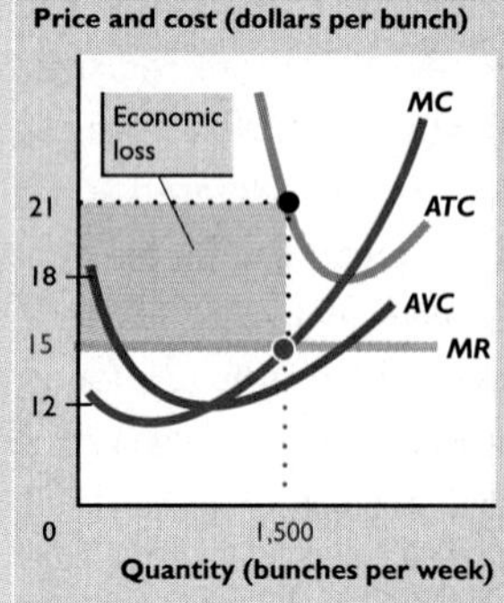

FIGURE 2

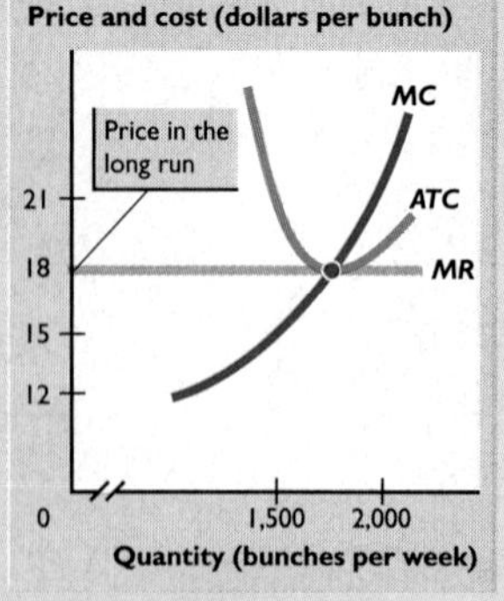

Solution to Practice Problem 10.3

a. The price is less than average total cost, so the tulip grower is incurring an economic loss in the short run. Because the price exceeds minimum average variable cost, the tulip grower continues to produce. The economic loss equals the loss per bunch ($21 minus $15) multiplied by the number of bunches (1,500), which equals $9,000 (Figure 1).

b. Because firms in the industry are incurring a loss, some firms will exit in the long run. So the number of tulip growers will decrease.

c. The price in the long run will be such that economic profit is zero. That is, as tulip growers exit, the price will rise until it equals minimum average total cost. Because tulip growing is a constant cost industry, the long-run price will be $18 a bunch (Figure 2).

d. Economic profit in the long run will be zero. Tulip growers will make normal profit (Figure 2).

CHAPTER CHECKPOINT

Key Points

1 Explain a perfectly competitive firm's profit-maximizing choices and derive its supply curve.

- A perfectly competitive firm is a price taker.
- Marginal revenue equals price.
- The firm produces the output at which price equals marginal cost.
- If price is less than minimum average variable cost, the firm temporarily shuts down.
- A firm's supply curve is the upward-sloping part of its marginal cost curve above minimum average variable cost and the vertical axis at all prices below minimum average variable cost.

2 Explain how output, price, and profit are determined in the short run.

- Market demand and market supply determine price.
- Firms choose the quantity to produce that maximizes profit, which is the quantity at which marginal cost equals price.
- In short-run equilibrium, a firm can make an economic profit or incur an economic loss.

3 Explain how output, price, and profit are determined in the long run.

- Economic profit induces entry, which increases supply and lowers price and profit. Economic loss induces exit, which decreases supply, raises price, and lowers the losses.
- In the long run, economic profit is zero and there is no entry or exit.
- The long-run effect of a permanent increase in demand on price depends on whether there are external economies (price falls) or external diseconomies (price rises) or neither (price remains constant).
- New technologies increase supply and in the long run lower the price and increase the quantity.

Key Terms

Exercises

1. In what type of market is each of the following goods and services sold? Explain your answers.
   a. Wheat
   b. Jeans
   c. Camera film
   d. Toothpaste
   e. Taxi rides in a town with one taxi company

2. Explain why in a perfectly competitive market, the firm is a price taker. Why can't the firm choose the price at which it sells its good?

TABLE 1

Price (dollars per batch)	Quantity demanded (batches of fortune cookies per day)
50	0
50	1
50	2
50	3
50	4
50	5
50	6

3. Table 1 shows the demand schedule for Lin's Fortune Cookies.
   a. In what type of market does Lin's Fortune Cookies operate? How can you tell?
   b. Calculate Lin's marginal revenue for each quantity demanded.
   c. Why does Lin's marginal revenue equal price?

4. Table 2 shows some cost data for Lin's Fortune Cookies, which operates in the market described in exercise 3. To answer these questions, draw Lin's short-run cost curves.

TABLE 2

Total product (batches of cookies per day)	Average fixed cost	Average variable cost	Average total cost	Marginal cost
	(dollars per batch)			
1	84.00	51.00	135	
				37
2	42.00	44.00	86	
				29
3	28.00	39.00	67	
				27
4	21.00	36.00	57	
				32
5	16.80	35.20	52	
				40
6	14.00	36.00	50	
				57
7	12.00	39.00	51	
				83
8	10.50	44.50	55	

   a. At a price of $50 per batch of cookies, what quantity does Lin produce and what is the firm's economic profit? Do firms enter or exit the industry?
   b. At a price of $35.20 per batch, what quantity does Lin produce and what is the firm's economic profit? Do firms enter or exit the industry?
   c. At a price of $83 per batch, what quantity does Lin produce and what is the firm's economic profit? Do firms enter or exit the industry?

5. Use the data in Table 2 to create Lin's short-run supply schedule and make a graph of Lin's short-run supply curve.

6. Explain why Lin's supply curve is only part of his marginal cost curve. Why will Lin never consider producing 2 batches of fortune cookies a day?

7. Suppose there are 1,000 fortune cookie producers that are exactly like Lin's Fortune Cookies. Table 3 shows the demand schedule for fortune cookies.
   a. What is the short-run equilibrium price of fortune cookies?
   b. What is the short-run equilibrium quantity of fortune cookies?
   c. What is the economic profit earned or loss incurred by each firm?
   d. Do firms enter or exit the industry? Why?
   e. What is the price in long-run equilibrium?
   f. Approximately how many firms are in the industry in long-run equilibrium?

TABLE 3

Price (dollars per batch)	Quantity demanded (batches per day)
92	4,000
85	4,500
78	5,000
71	5,500
64	6,000
57	6,500
50	7,000
43	7,500
36	8,000

8. Suppose that the restaurant industry is perfectly competitive. Joe's Diner is always packed in the evening but rarely has a customer at lunchtime. Why doesn't Joe's Diner close—temporarily shut down—at lunchtime?

9. 3M created the sticky note, which 3M called the Post-it note. Soon many other firms entered the sticky note market and started to produce sticky notes.
   a. What was the incentive for these firms to enter the sticky note market?
   b. As time goes by, do you expect more firms to enter this market? Explain why or why not.
   c. Can you think of any reason why any of these firms might exit the sticky note market?

10. In 1969, when Rod Laver completed his tennis grand slam, all tennis rackets were made of wood. Today, tennis players use graphite rackets.
    a. Draw two graphs of the market for wooden tennis rackets in 1969: one that shows the market as a whole and one that shows an individual producer of rackets.
    b. Show in the graphs the effect of a permanent decrease in the demand for wooden rackets.
    c. How did the economic profit from producing wooden rackets change and what effects did the change in profit have on the number of producers of wooden rackets?

11. During the 1980s and 1990s, the cost of producing a personal computer decreased.
    a. Draw two graphs of the market for personal computers: one that shows the market as a whole and one that shows an individual producer.
    b. Show in the graphs the effect of a decrease in the cost of producing a computer on the price of a computer, the quantity of computers bought, and the economic profit of producers in the short run and in the long run.

12. Small aluminum scooters became popular during 2000. Sketch the cost and revenue curves of a typical firm in the scooter industry when
    a. The scooter fashion began.
    b. The scooter fashion was two years old.
    c. The scooter fashion faded.

Critical Thinking

13. Airport security has been stepped up in the period since the attacks on September 11, 2001, and much of the additional security service is provided by private firms that operate in a competitive market. Use the perfect competition model to answer the following questions.
    a. Do you think that airport security providers earned an economic profit or incurred an economic loss during 2002? Explain your answer.
    b. Do you predict that the price of airport security services will increase or decrease in the near future? Why?
    c. Do you think that airport security services are subject to increasing cost or decreasing cost in the long run? Why?
14. Review *Eye on the Global Economy* on p. 265.
    a. List the features of the maple syrup market that make it an example of perfect competition.
    b. Draw a graph to describe the maple syrup market and the cost and revenue of an individual firm in 1980, assuming that the industry was in long-run equilibrium.
    c. Use your answer to part **b** to explain the effects of the technological changes in maple syrup farming during the 1980s.
    d. Suppose that Aunt Jemima invents a new maple-flavored syrup that no one can distinguish, in a blind test, from the real thing and can produce it for $5 a gallon. What effect would this invention have on the market for real maple syrup? Illustrate the effects graphically.
15. The combination of the DVD player, the flat plasma screen, and surround sound has revolutionized watching a movie at home. At the same time, advances in technology in the movie theater have raised the standard that the home entertainment alternative must achieve. Think about the effects of these technological changes on competitive markets for goods and services that are influenced by movie going and home movie watching. Identify the market for one related good or service that will expand and one that will contract. Describe in detail the sequence of events as the two markets you've identified respond to the new technologies.

Practice Online

Web Exercise

Use the links on your Foundations Web site to work the following exercise.

16. Open the spreadsheet that provides information about the world market for wheat and then answer the following questions:
    a. Is the world market for wheat perfectly competitive? Why or why not?
    b. What happened to the price of wheat during the 1990s?
    c. What happened to the quantity of wheat produced during the 1990s?
    d. What do you think were the main influences on the demand for wheat during the 1990s?
    e. What do you think were the main influences on the supply of wheat during the 1990s?
    f. Do you think farmers entered or exited the wheat market during the 1990s? Explain your answer.

CHAPTER 11

Monopoly

CHAPTER CHECKLIST

When you have completed your study of this chapter, you will be able to

1 **Explain how monopoly arises and distinguish between single-price monopoly and price-discriminating monopoly.**

2 **Explain how a single-price monopoly determines its output and price.**

3 **Compare the performance of a single-price monopoly with that of perfect competition.**

4 **Explain how price discrimination increases profit.**

5 **Explain how monopoly regulation influences output, price, economic profit, and efficiency.**

If you live in University City, Missouri, you buy your electricity from Union Electric or light your home with candles. If you live in Gainesville, Florida, and want cable TV service, you have only one option: buy from Cox Cable. These are examples of monopoly. Such firms can choose their own price. How do such firms choose the quantity to produce and the price at which to sell it? Do they charge too much?

Some firms—hairdressers, museums, and movie theaters are examples—give discounts to students. Are these firms run by generous folk to whom the model of profit-maximizing firms doesn't apply? Aren't these firms throwing profit away by cutting ticket prices and offering discounts?

In this chapter, we study monopoly. We learn how a monopoly behaves, and we discover whether monopoly is efficient and fair.

11.1 MONOPOLY AND HOW IT ARISES

The market for diamonds is close to being a monopoly.

A *monopoly* is a market with a single supplier of a good or service that has no close substitutes and in which natural or legal barriers to entry prevent competition.

Markets for local telephone service, gas, electricity, and water are examples of local monopoly. GlaxoSmithKline has a monopoly on AZT, a drug that is used to treat AIDS. DeBeers, a South African firm, controls 80 percent of the world's production of raw diamonds—close to being a monopoly but not quite one.

How Monopoly Arises

Monopoly arises when there are

- No close substitutes
- Barriers to entry

No Close Substitutes

If a good has a close substitute, even though only one firm produces it, that firm effectively faces competition from the producers of substitutes. Water supplied by a local public utility is an example of a good that does not have close substitutes. While it does have a close substitute for drinking—bottled spring water—it has no effective substitutes for doing the laundry, taking a shower, or washing a car.

Sometimes the arrival of a new product weakens a monopoly. For example, Federal Express, UPS, the fax machine, and e-mail have weakened the monopoly of the U.S. Postal Service; broadband fiber-optic phone lines and the satellite dish have weakened the monopoly of cable television companies.

The arrival of a new product can also create a monopoly. For example, the IBM PC of the early 1980s gave a monopoly in PC operating systems to Microsoft's DOS.

Barriers to Entry

Barrier to entry
A natural or legal constraint that protects a firm from competitors.

Anything that protects a firm from the arrival of new competitors is a **barrier to entry**. There are two types of barrier to entry:

- Natural
- Legal

Natural monopoly
A monopoly that arises because one firm can meet the entire market demand at a lower price than two or more firms could.

Natural Barriers to Entry A **natural monopoly** exists when the technology for producing a good or service enables one firm to meet the entire market demand at a lower price than two or more firms could. One electric power distributor can meet the market demand for electricity at a lower cost than two or more firms could. Imagine two or more sets of wires running to your home so that you could choose your electric power supplier.

Figure 11.1 illustrates a natural monopoly in the distribution of electric power. Here, the demand curve for electric power is D and the long-run average cost curve is $LRAC$. Economies of scale prevail over the entire length of this $LRAC$ curve, indicated by the fact that the curve slopes downward. One firm can produce 4 million kilowatt-hours at 5 cents a kilowatt-hour. At this price, the quantity demanded is 4 million kilowatt-hours. So if the price was 5 cents, one firm could supply the entire market. If two firms shared the market, it would cost each

FIGURE 11.1
Natural Monopoly

Practice Online

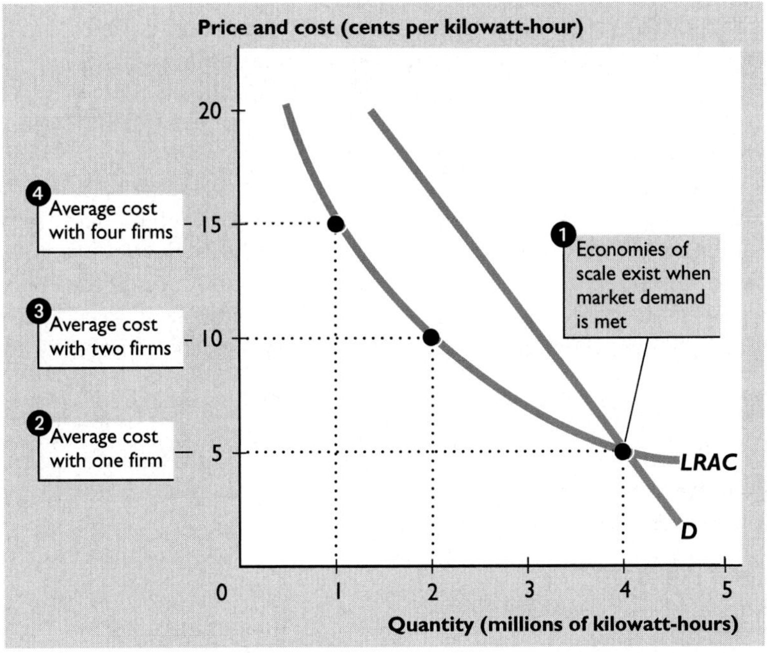

The demand curve for electric power is *D*, and the long-run average cost curve is *LRAC*.

❶ Economies of scale exist over the entire *LRAC* curve. One firm can distribute 4 million kilowatt-hours at a ❷ cost of 5 cents a kilowatt-hour. This same total output ❸ costs 10 cents a kilowatt-hour with two firms and ❹ 15 cents a kilowatt-hour with four firms. So one firm can meet the market demand at a lower cost than two or more firms can, and the market is a natural monopoly.

of them 10 cents a kilowatt-hour to produce a total of 4 million kilowatt-hours. If four firms shared the market, it would cost each of them 15 cents a kilowatt-hour to produce a total of 4 million kilowatt-hours. So in conditions like those shown in Figure 11.1, one firm can supply the entire market at a lower cost than two or more firms can.

The distribution of water and natural gas are two other examples of natural monopoly.

Legal Barriers to Entry Legal barriers to entry create a legal monopoly. A **legal monopoly** is a market in which competition and entry are restricted by the concentration of ownership of a natural resource or by the granting of a public franchise, government license, patent, or copyright.

Legal monopoly
A market in which competition and entry are restricted by the concentration of ownership of a natural resource or by the granting of a public franchise, government license, patent, or copyright.

A firm can create its own barrier to entry by buying up a significant portion of a natural resource. DeBeers, which controls more than 80 percent of the world's production of raw diamonds, is an example of this type of monopoly. There is no natural barrier to entry in diamonds. Even though the diamond is a relatively rare mineral, its sources of supply could have many owners who compete in a global competitive auction market. DeBeers was able to prevent such competition by being a dominant player and effectively controlling entry.

A *public franchise* is an exclusive right granted to a firm to supply a good or service, an example of which is the U.S. Postal Service's exclusive right to deliver first-class mail. A *government license* controls entry into particular occupations, professions, and industries. An example is Michael's Texaco in Charleston, Rhode Island, which is the only firm in the area licensed to test for vehicle emissions.

A *patent* is an exclusive right granted to the inventor of a product or service. A *copyright* is an exclusive right granted to the author or composer of a literary, musical, dramatic, or artistic work. Patents and copyrights are valid for a limited time period that varies from country to country. In the United States, a patent is valid for 20 years. Patents are designed to encourage the *invention* of new products and production methods. They also stimulate *innovation*—the use of new inventions—by encouraging inventors to publicize their discoveries and offer them for use under license. Patents have stimulated innovations in areas as diverse as soybean seeds, pharmaceuticals, memory chips, and video games.

Most monopolies are regulated by government agencies. We can better understand why governments regulate monopolies and what effects regulations have if we know how an unregulated monopoly behaves. So we'll first study an unregulated monopoly and then look at monopoly regulation at the end of this chapter.

A monopoly sets its own price, but in doing so, it faces a market constraint. Let's see how the market limits a monopoly's pricing choices.

Monopoly Price-Setting Strategies

A monopolist faces a tradeoff between price and the quantity sold. To sell a larger quantity, the monopolist must set a lower price. But there are two price-setting possibilities that create different tradeoffs:

- Single price
- Price discrimination

Single Price

Single-price monopoly
A monopoly that must sell each unit of its output for the same price to all its customers.

A **single-price monopoly** is a firm that must sell each unit of its output for the same price to all its customers. DeBeers sells diamonds (of a given size and quality) for the same price to all its customers. If it tried to sell at a higher price to some customers than to others, only the low-price customers would buy from DeBeers. Others would buy from DeBeers's low-price customers. So DeBeers is a *single-price* monopoly.

Price Discrimination

Price-discriminating monopoly
A monopoly that is able to sell different units of a good or service for different prices.

A **price-discriminating monopoly** is a firm that is able to sell different units of a good or service for different prices. Many firms price discriminate. Airlines offer a dizzying array of different prices for the same trip. Pizza producers charge one price for a single pizza and almost give away a second one. Different customers might pay different prices (like airfares), or one customer might pay different prices for different quantities bought (like the bargain price for a second pizza).

When a firm price discriminates, it appears to be doing its customers a favor. In fact, it is charging the highest possible price for each unit sold and making the largest possible profit.

Not all monopolies can price discriminate. The main obstacle to the practice of price discrimination is resale by the customers who buy for a low price. Because of resale possibilities, price discrimination is limited to monopolies that sell services that cannot be resold.

CHECKPOINT 11.1

1 Explain how monopoly arises and distinguish between single-price monopoly and price-discriminating monopoly.

Study Guide pp. 166–168

Practice Online 11.1

Practice Problems 11.1

1. Monopoly arises in which of the following situations?
   a. Coca-Cola cuts its price below that of Pepsi-Cola in an attempt to increase its market share.
   b. A single firm, protected by a barrier to entry, produces a personal service that has no close substitutes.
   c. A barrier to entry exists, but some close substitutes for the good exist.
   d. A firm offers discounts to students and seniors.
   e. A firm can sell any quantity it chooses at the going price.
   f. The government issues Tiger Woods, Inc. an exclusive license to produce golf balls.
   g. A firm experiences economies of scale even when it produces the quantity that meets the entire market demand.
2. Which of the cases **a** to **f** in problem 1 are natural monopolies and which are legal monopolies? Which can price discriminate, which cannot, and why?

Exercises 11.1

1. Which of the following are monopolies?
   a. A large shopping mall in downtown Houston
   b. Tiffany, the upscale jeweler
   c. Wal-Mart
   d. The Grand Canyon mule train
   e. The only shoe-shine stand licensed to operate in an airport
   f. The U.S. Postal Service
2. Which of the monopolies in exercise 1 are natural monopolies and which are legal monopolies? Which can price discriminate, which cannot, and why?

Solutions to Practice Problems 11.1

1. Monopoly arises when a single firm produces a good or service that has no close substitutes and a barrier to entry exists. Monopoly arises in **b**, **f**, and **g**. In **a**, there is more than one firm. In **c**, the good has some close substitutes. In **d**, a monopoly might be able to price discriminate, but other types of firms (for example, pizza producers and art museums) price discriminate and they are not monopolies. In **e**, the demand for the good that the firm produces is perfectly elastic and there is no limit to what the firm could sell if it wished. Such a firm is in perfect competition.
2. Natural monopoly exists when one firm can meet the entire market demand at a lower price than two or more firms could. So **g** is a natural monopoly, but **b** could be also. Legal monopoly exists when the granting of a right creates a barrier to entry. So **f** is a legal monopoly, but **b** could be also. Monopoly **b** could price discriminate because a personal service cannot be resold. Monopoly **f** could not price discriminate because golf balls can be resold.

11.2 SINGLE-PRICE MONOPOLY

To understand how a single-price monopoly makes its output and price decisions, we must first study the link between price and marginal revenue.

Price and Marginal Revenue

Because in a monopoly there is only one firm, the firm's demand curve is the market demand curve. Let's look at Bobbie's Barbershop, the sole supplier of haircuts in Cairo, Nebraska. The table in Figure 11.2 shows the demand schedule for Bobbie's haircuts. For example, at $12, consumers demand 4 haircuts an hour (row *E*).

Total revenue is the price multiplied by the quantity sold. For example, in row *D*, Bobbie sells 3 haircuts at $14 each, so total revenue is $42. *Marginal revenue* is the change in total revenue resulting from a one-unit increase in the quantity sold. For example, if the price falls from $16 (row *C*) to $14 (row *D*), the quantity sold increases from 2 to 3 haircuts. Total revenue rises from $32 to $42, so the change in total revenue is $10. Because the quantity sold increases by 1 haircut, marginal revenue equals the change in total revenue and is $10. Marginal revenue is placed between the two rows to emphasize that marginal revenue relates to the *change* in the quantity sold.

Figure 11.2 shows Bobbie's demand curve and marginal revenue curve (*MR*) and also illustrates the calculation that we've just made. Notice that at each output, marginal revenue is less than price—the marginal revenue curve lies below the demand curve. Why is marginal revenue less than price? It is because when the price is lowered to sell one more unit, two opposing forces affect total revenue.

FIGURE 11.2
Demand and Marginal Revenue

Practice Online

The table shows Bobbie's demand, total revenue, and marginal revenue schedules.

If the price falls from $16 to $14, the quantity sold increases from 2 to 3. ❶ Total revenue lost on 2 haircuts is $4; ❷ total revenue gained on 1 haircut is $14; and ❸ marginal revenue is $10.

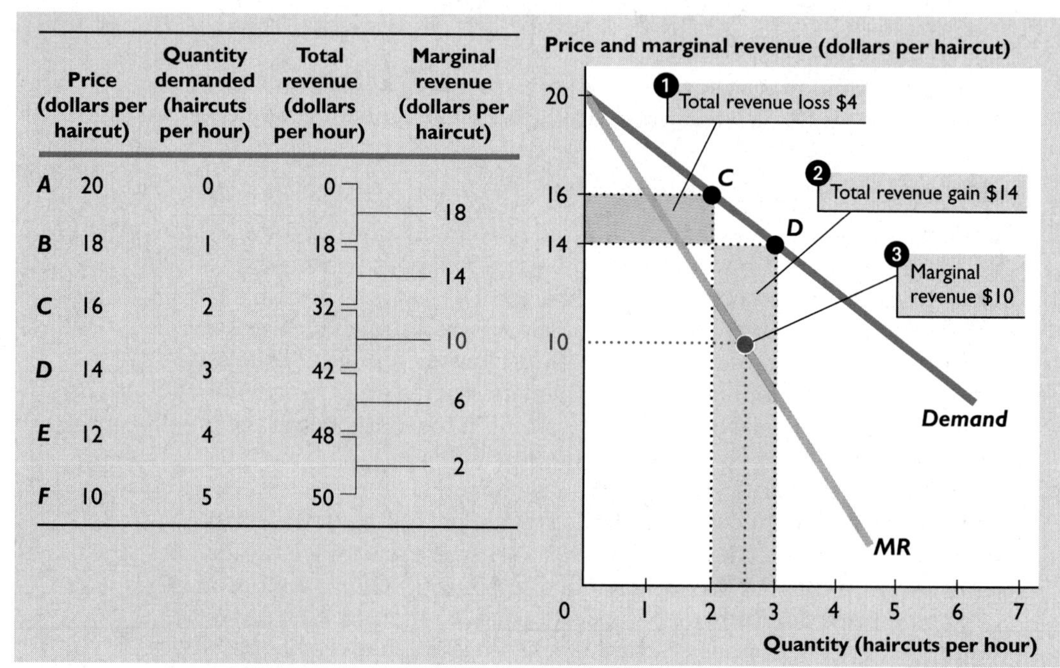

	Price (dollars per haircut)	Quantity demanded (haircuts per hour)	Total revenue (dollars per hour)	Marginal revenue (dollars per haircut)
A	20	0	0	
				18
B	18	1	18	
				14
C	16	2	32	
				10
D	14	3	42	
				6
E	12	4	48	
				2
F	10	5	50	

The lower price results in a revenue loss, and the increased quantity sold results in a revenue gain. For example, at a price of $16, Bobbie sells 2 haircuts (point C). If she lowers the price to $14 a haircut, she sells 3 haircuts and has a revenue gain of $14 on the third haircut. But she now receives only $14 a haircut on the first two—$2 less than before. As a result, she loses $4 of revenue on the first 2 haircuts. To calculate marginal revenue, she must deduct this amount from the revenue gain of $14. So her marginal revenue is $10, which is less than the price.

Marginal Revenue and Elasticity

In Chapter 5 (p. 126), you learned about the *total revenue test*, which determines whether demand is elastic or inelastic. Recall that if a price fall increases total revenue, demand is elastic, but if it decreases total revenue, demand is inelastic.

We can use the total revenue test to see the relationship between marginal revenue and elasticity. Figure 11.3 illustrates this relationship. As the price falls from $20 to $10, the quantity demanded increases from 0 to 5 an hour. Total revenue increases (part b), so demand is elastic and marginal revenue is positive (part a). As the price falls from $10 to $0, the quantity demanded increases from 5 to 10 an hour. Total revenue decreases (part b), so demand is inelastic and marginal revenue is

FIGURE 11.3
Marginal Revenue and Elasticity

Practice Online

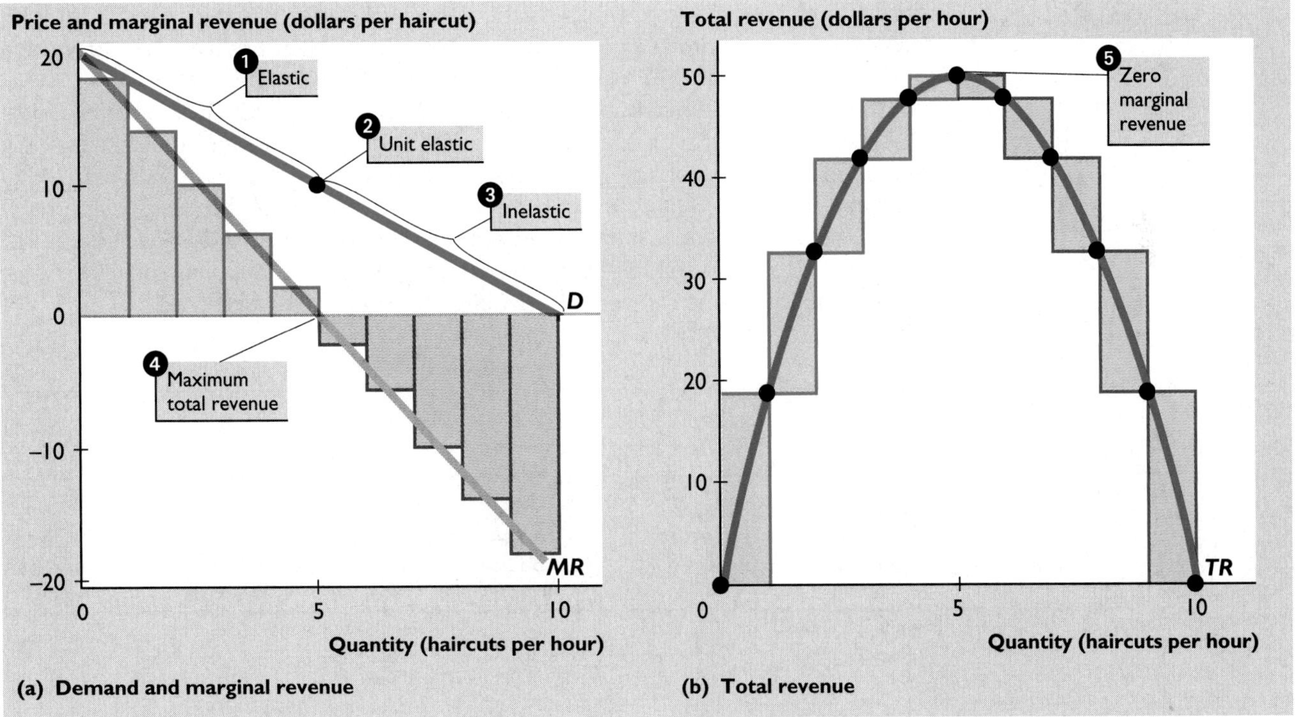

Over the range from 0 to 5 haircuts an hour, marginal revenue is positive and 1 demand is elastic. At 5 haircuts an hour, marginal revenue is zero and 2 demand is unit elastic. Over the range 5 to 10 haircuts an hour, marginal revenue is negative and 3 demand is inelastic. At zero marginal revenue in part (a), 4 total revenue is maximized. And at maximum total revenue in part (b), 5 marginal revenue is zero.

negative (part a). When the price is $10, total revenue is at a maximum, demand is unit elastic, and marginal revenue is zero.

The relationship between marginal revenue and elasticity implies that a monopoly never profitably produces an output in the inelastic range of its demand curve. It could charge a higher price, produce a smaller quantity, and increase its profit. Let's look at a monopoly's output and price decision.

Output and Price Decision

To determine the output level and price that maximize a monopoly's profit, we study the behavior of both revenue and costs as output varies.

Table 11.1 summarizes the information we need about Bobbie's revenue, costs, and economic profit. Economic profit, which equals total revenue minus total cost, is maximized at $12 an hour when Bobbie sells 3 haircuts an hour for $14 each. If she sold 2 haircuts for $16 each, her economic profit would be only $9. And if she sold 4 haircuts for $12 each, her economic profit would be only $8.

You can see why 3 haircuts is Bobbie's profit-maximizing output by looking at the marginal revenue and marginal cost. When Bobbie increases output from 2 to 3 haircuts, her marginal revenue is $10 and her marginal cost is $7. Profit increases by the difference, $3 an hour. If Bobbie increases output yet further, from 3 to 4 haircuts, her marginal revenue is $6 and her marginal cost is $10. In this case, marginal cost exceeds marginal revenue by $4, so profit decreases by $4 an hour.

Figure 11.4 shows the information contained in Table 11.1 graphically. Part (a) shows Bobbie's total revenue curve (*TR*) and her total cost curve (*TC*). It also shows Bobbie's economic profit as the vertical distance between the *TR* and *TC* curves. Bobbie maximizes her profit at 3 haircuts an hour and earns an economic profit of $12 an hour ($42 of total revenue minus $30 of total cost).

Figure 11.4(b) shows Bobbie's demand curve (*D*) and marginal revenue curve (*MR*) along with her marginal cost curve (*MC*) and average total cost curve (*ATC*). Bobbie maximizes profit by producing the output at which marginal cost equals marginal revenue—3 haircuts an hour. But what price does she charge for a haircut? To set the price, the monopoly uses the demand curve and finds the highest price at which it can sell the profit-maximizing output. In Bobbie's case, the highest price at which she can sell 3 haircuts an hour is $14 a haircut.

TABLE 11.1

A Monopoly's Output and Price Decision

Practice Online

	Price (dollars per haircut)	**Quantity demanded** (haircuts per hour)	**Total revenue** (dollars per hour)	**Marginal revenue** (dollars per haircut)	**Total cost** (dollars per hour)	**Marginal cost** (dollars per haircut)	**Profit** (dollars per hour)
A	20	0	0		12		−12
				18		5	
B	18	1	18		17		1
				14		6	
C	16	2	32		23		9
				10		7	
D	**14**	**3**	**42**		**30**		**12**
				6		10	
E	12	4	48		40		8
				2		15	
F	10	5	50		55		−5

When Bobbie produces 3 haircuts an hour, her average total cost is $10 (read from the *ATC* curve) and her price is $14 (read from the *D* curve). Her profit per haircut is $4 ($14 minus $10). Bobbie's economic profit is shown by the blue rectangle, which equals the profit per haircut ($4) multiplied by the number of haircuts (3 an hour), for a total of $12 an hour.

A positive economic profit is an incentive for firms to enter a market. But barriers to entry prevent that from happening in a monopoly. So in a monopoly, the firm can make a positive economic profit and continue to do so indefinitely.

A monopoly charges a price that exceeds marginal cost, but does it always make an economic profit? The answer is no! Bobbie makes a positive economic profit in Figure 11.4. But suppose that Bobbie's landlord increases the rent she pays for her barbershop. If Bobbie pays an additional $12 an hour in shop rent, her fixed cost increases by that amount. Her marginal cost and marginal revenue don't change, so her profit-maximizing output remains at 3 haircuts an hour. Her profit decreases by $12 an hour to zero. If Bobbie pays more than an additional $12 an hour for her shop rent, she incurs an economic loss. If this situation were permanent, Bobbie would go out of business. But monopoly entrepreneurs are creative, and Bobbie might find another shop at a lower rent.

FIGURE 11.4

A Monopoly's Profit-Maximizing Output and Price

Practice Online

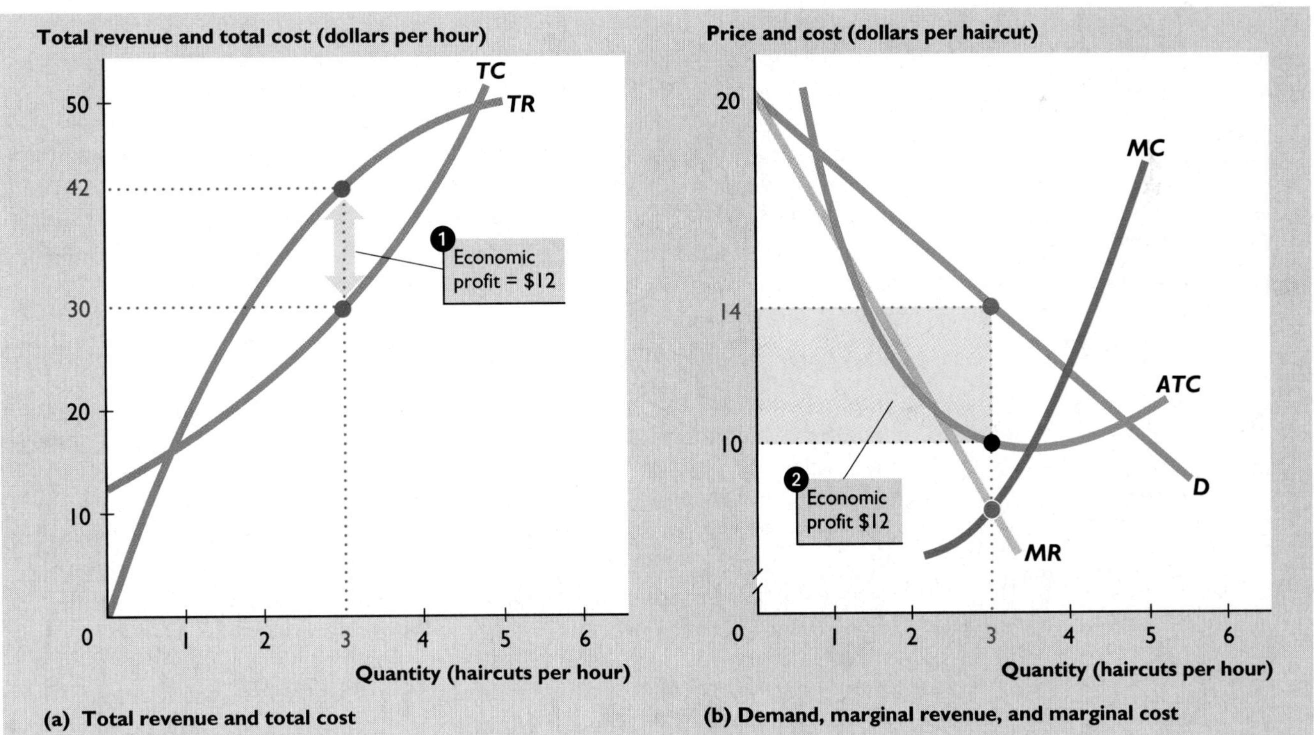

In part (a) economic profit is maximized when total revenue (*TR*) minus total cost (*TC*) is greatest. ❶ Economic profit, the vertical distance between *TR* and *TC*, is $12 an hour at 3 haircuts an hour.

In part (b), economic profit is maximized when marginal cost (*MC*) equals marginal revenue (*MR*). The price is determined by the demand curve (*D*) and is $14. ❷ Economic profit, the blue rectangle, is $12—the profit per haircut ($4) multiplied by 3 haircuts.

CHECKPOINT 11.2

Study Guide pp. 168–171

Practice Online 11.2

2 Explain how a single-price monopoly determines its output and price.

Practice Problem 11.2

Minnie's Mineral Springs is a single-price monopoly. The first two columns of Table 1 show the demand schedule for Minnie's spring water, and the middle and third columns show the firm's total cost schedule.

a. Calculate Minnie's total revenue schedule and marginal revenue schedule.
b. Sketch Minnie's demand curve and marginal revenue curve.
c. Calculate Minnie's profit-maximizing output, price, and economic profit.
d. If the owner of the water source that Minnie uses increases the fee that Minnie pays by $15.50 an hour, what are Minnie's new profit-maximizing output, price, and economic profit?
e. If instead of increasing the fee that Minnie pays by $15.50 an hour, the owner of the water source increases the fee that Minnie pays by $4 a bottle, what are Minnie's new profit-maximizing output, price, and economic profit?

TABLE 1

Price (dollars per bottle)	Quantity (bottles per hour)	Total cost (dollars per hour)
10	0	1.0
9	1	1.5
8	2	2.5
7	3	5.5
6	4	10.5
5	5	17.5

Exercise 11.2

Fossett's Round-the-World Balloon Rides is a single-price monopolist. The first two columns of Table 2 show the demand schedule for Fossett's rides, and the middle and third column show the firm's total cost schedule.

a. Calculate Fossett's total revenue schedule and marginal revenue schedule.
b. Sketch Fossett's demand curve and marginal revenue curve.
c. Calculate Fossett's profit-maximizing output, price, and economic profit.
d. If the government places a fixed tax on Fossett's of $60,000 a month, what are the new profit-maximizing output, price, and economic profit?
e. If instead of imposing a fixed tax on Fossett's, the government taxes Fossett's by $30,000 per ride, what are the new profit-maximizing output, price, and economic profit?

TABLE 2

Price (thousands of dollars per ride)	Quantity (rides per month)	Total cost (thousands of dollars per month)
220	0	80
200	1	160
180	2	260
160	3	380
140	4	520
120	5	680

Solution to Practice Problem 11.2

a. Total revenue equals price multiplied by quantity sold, and marginal revenue equals the change in total revenue when the quantity sold increases by one unit (Table 3).
b. Figure 1 shows Minnie's demand curve and marginal revenue curve.
c. The profit-maximizing output is 3 bottles an hour, where marginal revenue equals marginal cost. To calculate Minnie's marginal cost, find the change in total cost when the quantity produced increases by 1 bottle. Then plot marginal cost on Figure 1. Minnie's profit-maximizing price is $7 a bottle, and Minnie's economic profit is $15.50 an hour.
d. If the owner of the water source that Minnie uses increases the fee that Minnie pays by $15.50 an hour, Minnie's fixed cost increases but her marginal cost doesn't change. Her profit-maximizing output and price are unchanged, but she now earns no economic profit.
e. If Minnie pays an extra $4 a bottle, her marginal cost increases by this amount. Her new profit-maximizing output is 2 bottles an hour; the price is $8 a bottle; and economic profit is $5.50 an hour.

TABLE 3

Quantity (bottles per hour)	Total revenue (dollars per hour)	Marginal revenue (dollars per bottle)
0	0	
		9
1	9	
		7
2	16	
		5
3	21	
		3
4	24	
		1
5	25	

FIGURE 1

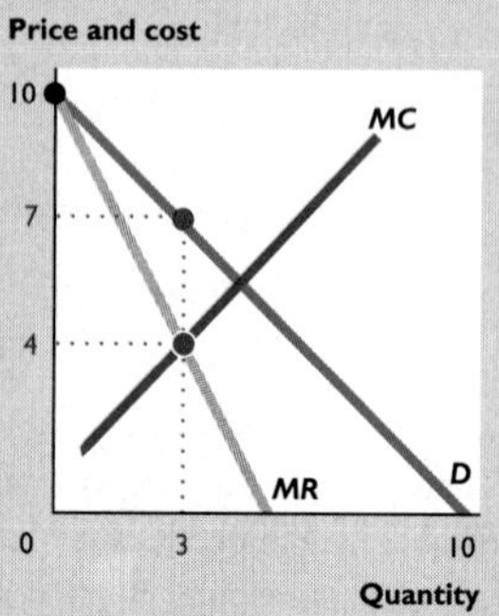

11.3 MONOPOLY AND COMPETITION COMPARED

Imagine a market in which many small firms operate in perfect competition. Then a single firm buys out all these small firms and creates a monopoly. What happens in this market to the quantity produced, the price, and efficiency?

Output and Price

Figure 11.5 shows the market that we'll study. The market demand curve is *D*. Initially, with many small firms in the market, the market supply curve is *S*, which is the sum of the supply curves—and marginal cost curves—of the individual firms. The equilibrium price is P_C, which makes the quantity demanded equal the quantity supplied. The equilibrium quantity is Q_C. Each firm takes the price P_C and maximizes its profit by producing the output at which its own marginal cost equals the price.

A single firm now buys all the firms in this market. Consumers don't change, so the demand curve doesn't change. But the monopoly recognizes this demand curve as a constraint on its sales and knows that its marginal revenue curve is *MR*.

The market supply curve in perfect competition is the sum of the marginal cost curves of the firms in the industry. So the monopoly's marginal cost curve is the market supply curve of perfect competition—labeled $S = MC$. The monopoly maximizes profit by producing the quantity at which marginal revenue equals marginal cost, which is Q_M. This output is smaller than the competitive output, Q_C. And the monopoly charges the price P_M, which is higher than P_C. So

Compared to perfect competition, a single-price monopoly produces a smaller output and charges a higher price.

FIGURE 11.5
Monopoly's Smaller Output and Higher Price

Practice Online

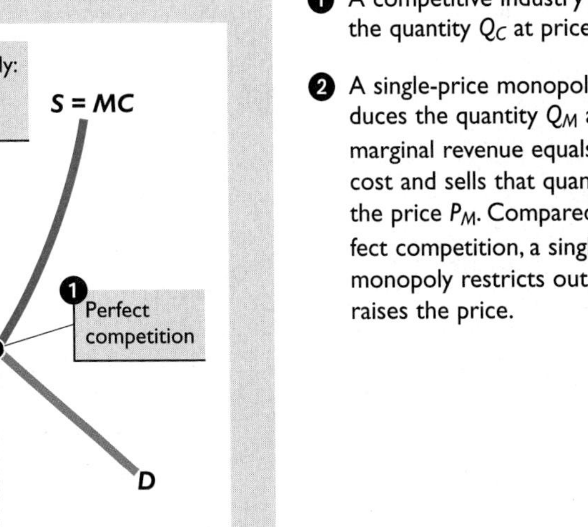

1. A competitive industry produces the quantity Q_C at price P_C.

2. A single-price monopoly produces the quantity Q_M at which marginal revenue equals marginal cost and sells that quantity for the price P_M. Compared to perfect competition, a single-price monopoly restricts output and raises the price.

Is Monopoly Efficient?

You learned in Chapter 6 that resources are used efficiently when marginal benefit equals marginal cost. Figure 11.6(a) shows that perfect competition achieves this efficient use of resources. The demand curve ($D = MB$) shows the marginal benefit to consumers. The supply curve ($S = MC$) shows the marginal cost (opportunity cost) to producers. At the competitive equilibrium, the price is P_C and the quantity is Q_C. Marginal benefit equals marginal cost and resource use is efficient. The sum of *consumer surplus* (Chapter 6, p. 145), the green triangle, and *producer surplus* (Chapter 6, p. 148), the blue area, is maximized.

Figure 11.6(b) shows that monopoly is inefficient. Monopoly output is Q_M and price is P_M. Price (marginal benefit) exceeds marginal cost and the underproduction creates a *deadweight loss* (Chapter 6, p. 154), shown by the gray area. Consumers lose partly by getting less of the good, shown by the gray triangle above P_C, and partly by paying more for the good. Consumer surplus shrinks to the smaller green triangle. Producers lose by selling less of the good, shown by the part of the gray area below P_C, but gain by selling their output for a higher price, shown by the dark blue rectangle. Producer surplus expands and is larger in monopoly than in perfect competition.

FIGURE 11.6
The Inefficiency of Monopoly

Practice Online

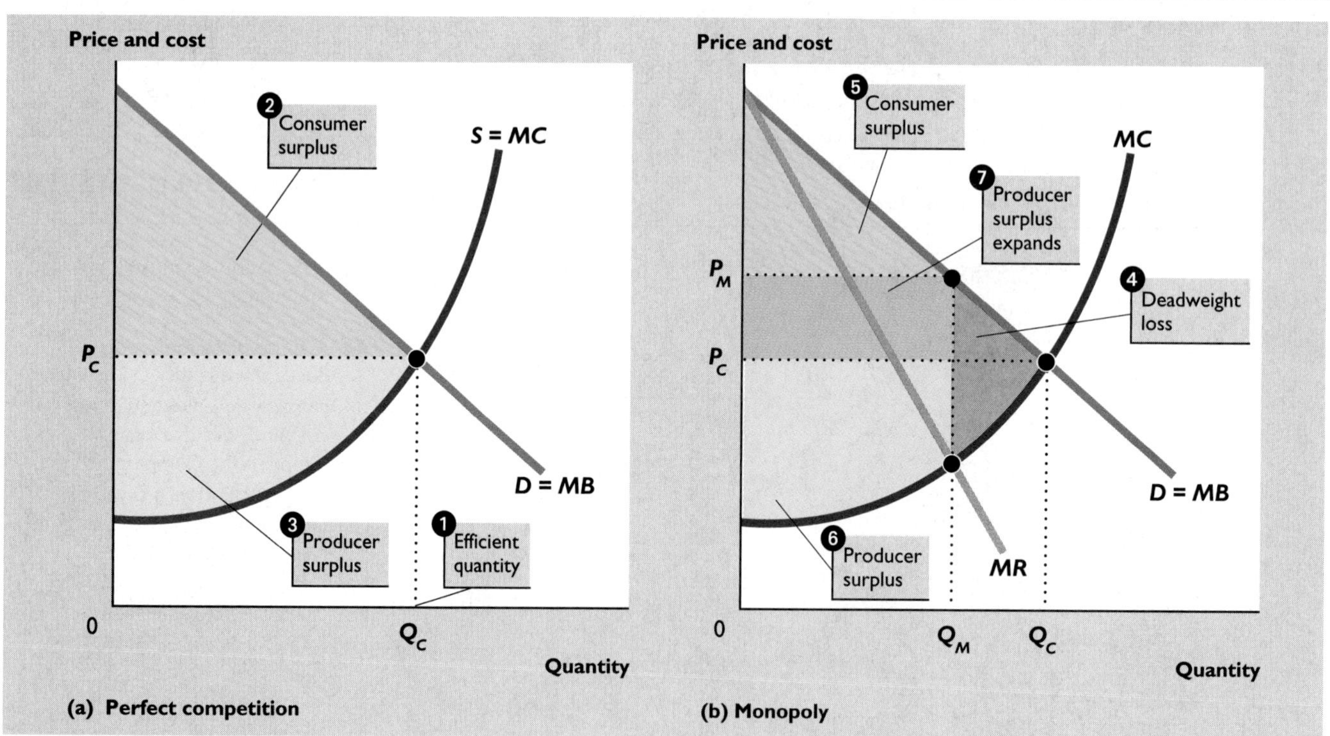

In perfect competition, (1) the equilibrium quantity is the efficient quantity, Q_C, because at that quantity, the price, P_C, equals marginal benefit and marginal cost. The sum of (2) consumer surplus and (3) producer surplus is maximized.

In a single-price monopoly, the equilibrium quantity, Q_M, is inefficient because the price, P_M, which equals marginal benefit, exceeds marginal cost. Underproduction creates a (4) deadweight loss. (5) Consumer surplus shrinks and (6) producer surplus (7) expands.

Is Monopoly Fair?

Monopoly is inefficient because it creates a deadweight loss. But monopoly also *redistributes* consumer surplus. The producer gains, and the consumers lose.

Figure 11.6 shows this redistribution. The monopoly gets the difference between the higher price, P_M, and the competitive price, P_C, on the quantity sold, Q_M. So the dark blue rectangle shows the part of the consumer surplus taken by the monopoly. This portion of the loss of consumer surplus is not a loss to society. It is redistribution from consumers to the monopoly producer.

Are the gain for the monopoly and loss for consumers fair? You learned about two standards of fairness in Chapter 6: fair *results* and fair *rules*. Redistribution from the rich to the poor is consistent with the fair results view. So on this view of fairness, whether monopoly redistribution is fair or unfair depends on who is richer: the monopolist or the consumers of its product. It might be either. Whether the *rules* are fair depends on whether the monopoly has benefited from a protected position that is not available to anyone else. If everyone is free to acquire the monopoly, then the rules are fair. So monopoly is inefficient and it might be, but is not always, unfair.

The pursuit of monopoly profit leads to an additional costly activity that we'll now describe: rent seeking.

Rent Seeking

Rent seeking is the act of obtaining special treatment by the government to create economic profit or to divert consumer surplus or producer surplus away from others. ("Rent" is a general term in economics that includes all forms of surplus such as consumer surplus, producer surplus, and economic profit.) Rent seeking does not always create a monopoly, but it always restricts competition and often creates a monopoly.

Rent seeking
The act of obtaining special treatment by the government to create economic profit or to divert consumer surplus or producer surplus away from others.

Scarce resources can be used to produce the goods and services that people value or they can be used in rent seeking. Rent seeking is potentially profitable for the rent seeker but costly to society because it uses scarce resources purely to transfer wealth from one person or group to another person or group rather than to produce the things that people value.

To see why rent seeking occurs, think about the two ways that a person might become the owner of a monopoly:

- Buy a monopoly
- Create a monopoly by rent seeking

Buy a Monopoly

A person might try to earn a monopoly profit by buying a firm (or a right) that is protected by a barrier to entry. Buying a taxicab medallion in New York is an example. The number of medallions is restricted, so their owners are protected from unlimited entry into the industry. A person who wants to operate a taxi must buy a medallion from someone who already has one. But anyone is free to enter the bidding for a medallion. So competition among buyers drives the price up to the point at which they earn only normal profit. For example, competition for the right to operate a taxi in New York City has led to a price of more than $165,000 for a taxi medallion, which is sufficiently high to eliminate economic profit for taxi operators and leave them with normal profit.

Create a Monopoly by Rent Seeking

Because buying a monopoly means paying a price that soaks up the economic profit, creating a monopoly by rent seeking is an attractive alternative to buying one. Rent seeking is a political activity. It takes the form of lobbying and trying to influence the political process to get laws that create legal barriers to entry. Such influence might be sought by making campaign contributions in exchange for legislative support or by indirectly seeking to influence political outcomes through publicity in the media or by direct contacts with politicians and bureaucrats. An example of a rent created in this way is the law that restricts the quantities of textiles that can be imported into the United States. Another is a law that limits the quantity of tomatoes that can be imported in the United States. These laws restrict competition, which decreases the quantity for sale and increases prices.

Rent Seeking Equilibrium

Rent seeking is a competitive activity. If an economic profit is available, a rent seeker will try to get some of it. Competition among rent seekers pushes up the cost of rent seeking until it leaves the monopoly earning only a normal profit after paying the rent-seeking costs.

Figure 11.7 shows a rent-seeking equilibrium. The cost of rent seeking is a fixed cost that must be added to a monopoly's other costs. The average total cost curve, which includes the fixed cost of rent seeking, shifts upward until it just touches the demand curve. Consumer surplus is unaffected. But the deadweight loss of monopoly now includes the original deadweight loss triangle plus the economic profit consumed by rent seeking, which the enlarged gray area shows.

FIGURE 11.7
Rent-Seeking Equilibrium

Practice Online

1. Rent seeking costs exhaust economic profit. The firm's rent-seeking costs are fixed costs. They add to total fixed cost and to average total cost. The *ATC* curve shifts upward until, at the profit-maximizing price, the firm breaks even.
2. Consumer surplus shrinks.
3. The deadweight loss increases.

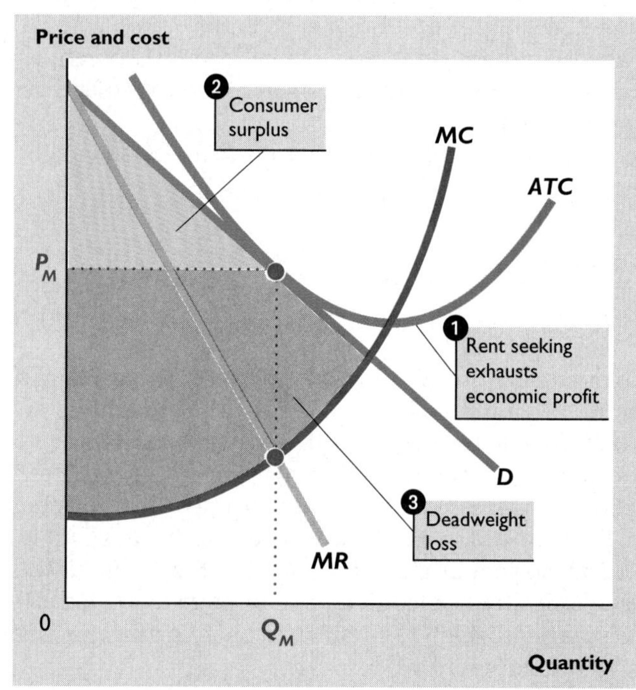

CHECKPOINT 11.3

3 Compare the performance of a single-price monopoly with that of perfect competition.

Study Guide pp. 172–174

Practice Online 11.3

Practice Problem 11.3

Township is a small isolated community served by one newspaper that can meet the market demand at a lower cost than two or more newspapers could. There is no local radio or TV station and no Internet access. The *Township Gazette* is the only source of news. Figure 1 shows the marginal cost of printing the *Township Gazette* and the demand for it. The *Township Gazette* is a profit-maximizing, single-price monopoly.

a. How many copies of the *Township Gazette* are printed each day?
b. What is the price of the *Township Gazette*?
c. What is the efficient number of copies of the *Township Gazette*?
d. What is the price at which the efficient number of copies could be sold?
e. Is the number of copies printed the efficient quantity? Explain why or why not.
f. On the graph, show the consumer surplus that is redistributed from consumers to the *Township Gazette*.
g. On the graph, show the deadweight loss that arises from the monopoly of the *Township Gazette*.

FIGURE 1

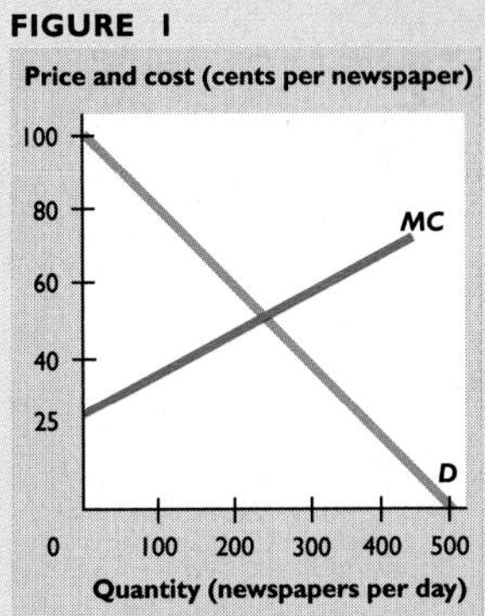

Exercise 11.3

Is Bobbie's Barbershop in Cairo, Nebraska, (on pp. 350–353) efficient? What is the consumer surplus that is transferred to Bobbie? What is the deadweight loss that she generates? How much would someone be willing to pay to buy Bobbie's monopoly?

Solution to Practice Problem 11.3

a. The profit-maximizing quantity of newspapers for the *Township Gazette* is 150 a day, where marginal revenue equals marginal cost (Figure 2).
b. The price is 70¢ a copy (Figure 2).
c. The efficient quantity of copies is 250, where demand (marginal benefit) equals marginal cost (Figure 2).
d. The efficient quantity would be bought at 50¢ a copy (Figure 2).
e. The number of copies printed is not efficient because the marginal benefit of the 150th copy exceeds its marginal cost (Figure 2).
f. The blue rectangle ❶ in Figure 2 shows the consumer surplus transferred from the consumers to the *Township Gazette*.
g. The gray triangle ❷ in Figure 2 shows the deadweight loss.

FIGURE 2

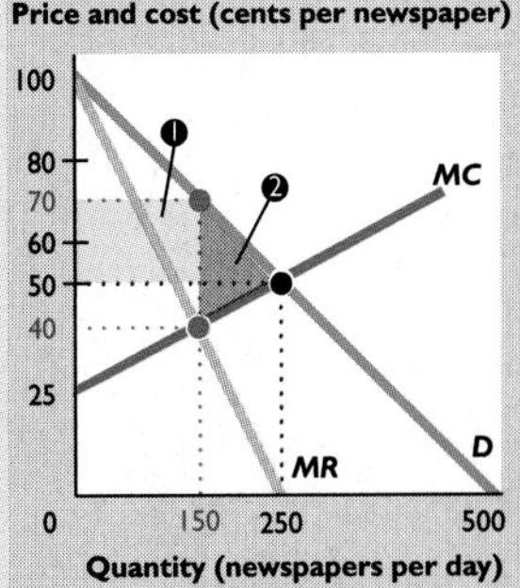

11.4 PRICE DISCRIMINATION

Price discrimination—selling a good or service at a number of different prices—is widespread. You encounter it when you travel, go to the movies, get your hair cut, buy pizza, or visit an art museum. At first sight, it appears that price discrimination contradicts the assumption of profit maximization. Why would a movie operator allow children to see movies at half price? Why would a hairdresser charge students and senior citizens less? Aren't these firms losing profit by being nice to their customers?

Deeper investigation shows that far from lowering profit, price discriminators make a bigger profit than they would otherwise. So a monopoly has an incentive to find ways of discriminating and charging each buyer the highest possible price. Some people pay less with price discrimination, but others pay more.

Most price discriminators are *not* monopolies, but monopolies do price discriminate when they can. To be able to price discriminate, a firm must

- Identify and separate different types of buyers.
- Sell a product that cannot be resold.

Price discrimination is charging different prices for a single good or service because the willingness to pay varies across buyers. Not all price *differences* are price *discrimination*. Some goods that are similar but not identical have different prices because they have different production costs. For example, the cost of producing electricity depends on time of day. If an electric power company charges a higher price for consumption between 7:00 and 9:00 in the morning and between 4:00 and 7:00 in the evening than it does at other times of the day, it is not price discriminating.

Price Discrimination and Consumer Surplus

The key idea behind price discrimination is to convert consumer surplus into economic profit. To extract every dollar of consumer surplus from every buyer, the monopoly would have to offer each individual customer a separate price schedule based on that customer's own willingness to pay. Such price discrimination cannot be carried out in practice because a firm does not have enough information about each consumer's demand curve. But firms try to extract as much consumer surplus as possible, and to do so, they discriminate in two broad ways:

- Among groups of buyers
- Among units of a good

Discriminating Among Groups of Buyers

To price discriminate among groups of buyers, the firm offers different prices to different types of buyers, based on things like age, employment status, or some other easily distinguished characteristic. This type of price discrimination works when each group has a different average willingness to pay for the good or service.

For example, a face-to-face sales meeting with a customer might bring a large and profitable order. For salespeople and other business travelers, the marginal benefit from an airplane trip is large and the price that such a traveler will pay for a trip is high. In contrast, for a vacation traveler, any of several different trips or even no vacation trip are options. So for vacation travelers, the marginal benefit of a trip is small and the price that such a traveler will pay for a trip is low. Because business travelers are willing to pay more than vacation travelers are, it is possible for an airline to profit by price discriminating between these two groups.

Discriminating Among Units of a Good

To price discriminate among units of a good, the firm charges the same prices to all its customers but offers a lower price per unit for a larger number of units bought. When Pizza Hut charges $10 for one home-delivered pizza and $14 for two, it is using this type of price discrimination. In this example, the price of the second pizza is only $4.

Let's see how an airline exploits the differences in demand by business and vacation travelers and increases its profit by price discriminating.

Profiting by Price Discriminating

Global Air has a monopoly on an exotic route. Figure 11.8 shows the demand curve (*D*) for travel on this route and Global Air's marginal revenue curve (*MR*). It also shows Global Air's marginal cost (*MC*) and average total cost (*ATC*) curves.

Initially, Global is a single-price monopoly and maximizes its profit by producing 8,000 trips a year (the quantity at which *MR* equals *MC*). The price is $1,200 a trip. The average total cost of a trip is $600, so economic profit is $600 a trip. On 8,000 trips, Global's economic profit is $4.8 million a year, shown by the blue rectangle. Global's customers enjoy a consumer surplus shown by the green triangle.

FIGURE 11.8
A Single Price of Air Travel

Practice Online

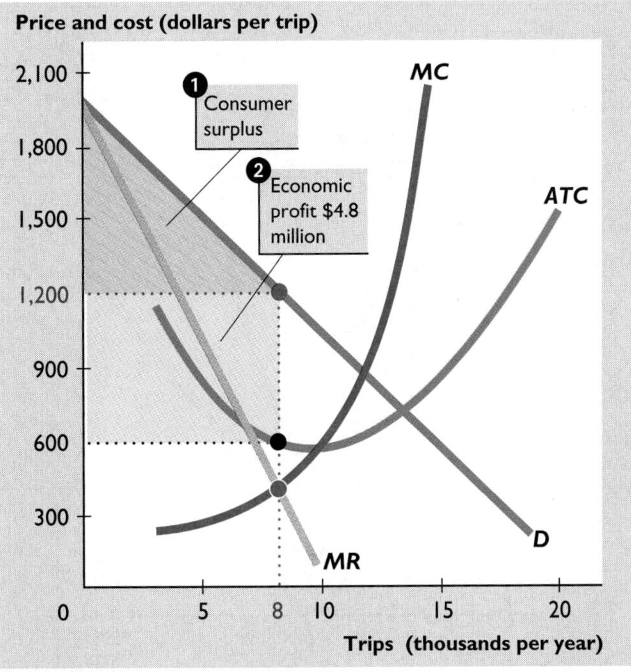

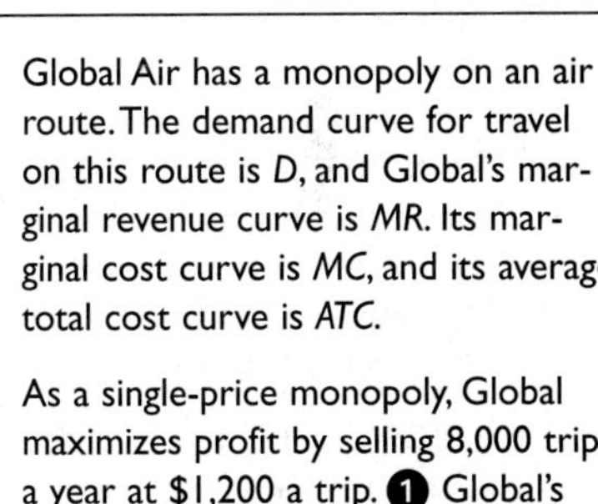
Global Air has a monopoly on an air route. The demand curve for travel on this route is *D*, and Global's marginal revenue curve is *MR*. Its marginal cost curve is *MC*, and its average total cost curve is *ATC*.

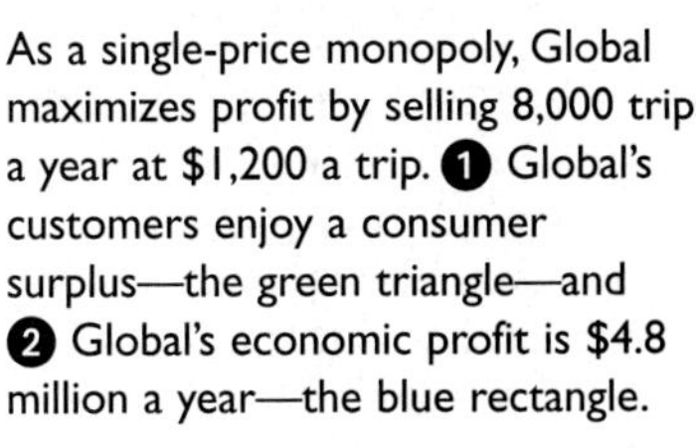
As a single-price monopoly, Global maximizes profit by selling 8,000 trips a year at $1,200 a trip. ❶ Global's customers enjoy a consumer surplus—the green triangle—and ❷ Global's economic profit is $4.8 million a year—the blue rectangle.

Global is struck by the fact that many of its customers are business travelers, and Global suspects that they are willing to pay more than $1,200 a trip. So Global does some market research, which tells Global that some business travelers are willing to pay as much as $1,800 a trip. Also, these customers almost always make their travel plans at the last moment. Another group of business travelers is willing to pay $1,600. These customers know a week ahead when they will travel and they never want to stay over a weekend. Yet another group is willing to pay up to $1,400. These travelers know two weeks ahead when they will travel and they don't want to stay away over a weekend.

So Global announces a new fare schedule. No restrictions, $1,800; 7-days advance purchase, no cancellation, $1,600; 14-days advance purchase, no cancellation, $1,400; 14-days advance purchase, must stay over weekend, $1,200.

Figure 11.9 shows the outcome with this new fare structure and also shows why Global is pleased with its new fares. It sells 2,000 trips at each of its four prices. Global's economic profit increases by the blue steps in the figure. Its economic profit is now its original $4.8 million a year plus an additional $2.4 million from its new higher fares. Consumer surplus has shrunk to the smaller green area.

Perfect Price Discrimination

Perfect price discrimination
Price discrimination that extracts the entire consumer surplus by charging the highest price that consumers are willing to pay for each unit.

But Global reckons that it can do even better. It plans to achieve **perfect price discrimination**, which extracts the entire consumer surplus. To do so, Global must get creative and come up with a host of additional business fares ranging between $2,000 and $1,200, each one of which appeals to a small segment of the business market and that together extract the entire consumer surplus from the business travelers.

FIGURE 11.9
Price Discrimination

Practice Online

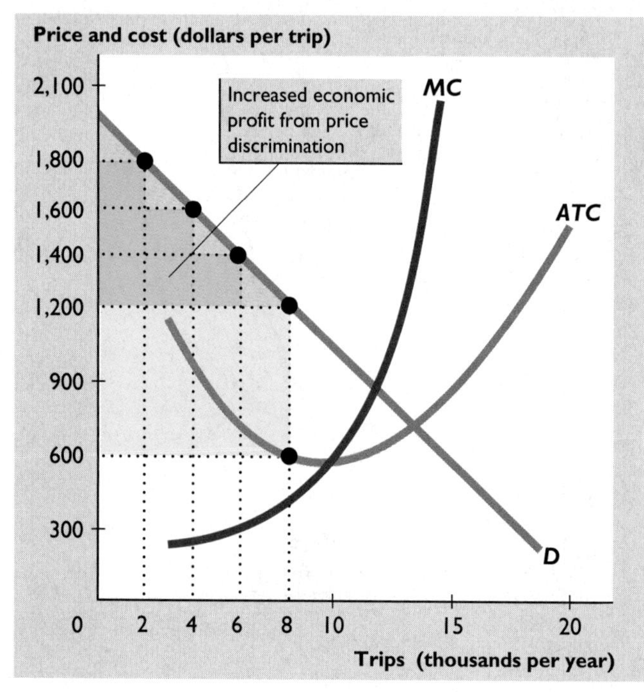

Global revises its fare structure. It now offers no restrictions at $1,800, 7-day advance purchase at $1,600, 14-day advance purchase at $1,400, and 14-day advance purchase, must stay over the weekend at $1,200.

Global sells 2,000 units at each of its four new fares. It economic profit increases by $2.4 million a year to $7.2 million a year, which is shown by the original blue rectangle plus the blue steps. Global's customers' consumer surplus shrinks.

Once Global is discriminating finely between different customers and getting from each the maximum they are willing to pay, something special happens to marginal revenue. Recall that for the single-price monopoly, marginal revenue is less than price. The reason is that when the price is cut to sell a larger quantity, the price is lower on all units sold. But with perfect price discrimination, Global sells only the marginal seat at the lower price. All the other customers continue to buy for the highest price they are willing to pay. So for the perfect price discriminator, marginal revenue equals price and the demand curve becomes the marginal revenue curve.

With marginal revenue equal to price, Global can obtain yet greater profit by increasing output up to the point at which price (and marginal revenue) is equal to marginal cost.

So Global now seeks additional travelers who will not pay as much as $1,200 a trip but who will pay more than marginal cost. More creative pricing comes up with vacation specials and other fares that have combinations of advance reservation, minimum stay, and other restrictions that make these fares unattractive to its existing customers but attractive to a further group of travelers. With all these fares and specials, Global extracts the entire consumer surplus and maximizes economic profit.

Figure 11.10 shows the outcome with perfect price discrimination. The dozens of fares paid by the original travelers who are willing to pay between $1,200 and $2,000 have extracted the entire consumer surplus from this group and converted it into economic profit for Global. The new fares between $900 and $1,200 have attracted 3,000 additional travelers but have taken their entire consumer surplus also. Global is earning an economic profit of more than $9 million a year.

FIGURE 11.10
Perfect Price Discrimination

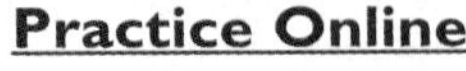

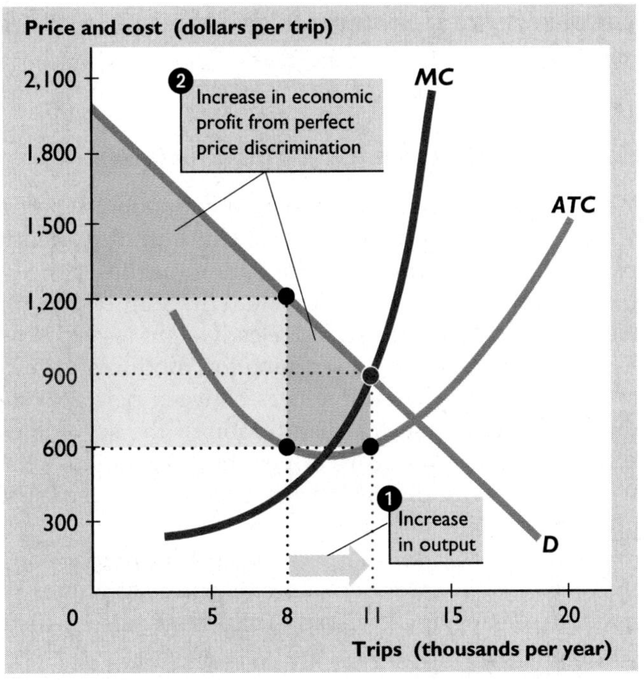

With perfect price discrimination, the demand curve becomes Global's marginal revenue curve. Economic profit is maximized when the lowest price equals marginal cost.

1 Output increases to 11,000 passengers a year, and 2 Global's economic profit increases to $9.35 million a year.

Eye on the U.S. Economy

Airline Price Discrimination

The normal coach fare from San Francisco to Washington, D.C., is $1,200. Book 14 days in advance, and this fare is $500. On a typical flight, United Airlines or American Airlines might have passengers paying as many as 20 different fares.

The airlines sort their customers according to their willingness to pay by offering a maze of advance-purchase and stayover restrictions that attract price-sensitive leisure travelers but don't get bought by business travelers.

Despite the sophistication of the airlines' pricing schemes, about 30 percent of seats fly empty. The marginal cost of filling an empty seat is close to zero, so a ticket sold at a few dollars would be profitable.

Extremely low prices are now feasible, thanks to Priceline.com. Shopping around airlines with bids from travelers, Priceline brokers about 1,000 tickets a day and gets the lowest possible fares.

Would it bother you to hear how little I paid for this flight?

From William Hamilton, "Voodoo Economics," © 1992 by the Chronicle Publishing Company, p. 3. Reprinted with permission of Chronicle Books.

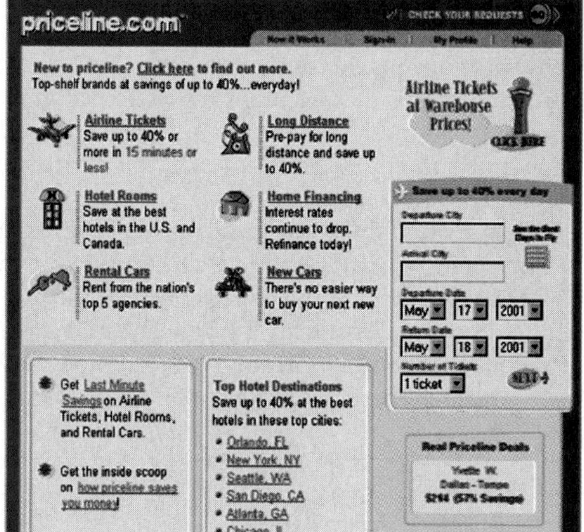

Price Discrimination and Efficiency

With perfect price discrimination, the monopoly increases output to the point at which price equals marginal cost. This output is identical to that of perfect competition. Perfect price discrimination pushes consumer surplus to zero but increases producer surplus to equal the sum of consumer surplus and producer surplus in perfect competition. Deadweight loss with perfect price discrimination is zero. So perfect price discrimination produces the efficient quantity.

But there are two differences between perfect competition and perfect price discrimination. First, the distribution of the surplus is different. It is shared by consumers and producers in perfect competition while the producer gets it all with perfect price discrimination. Second, because the producer grabs all the surplus, rent seeking becomes profitable.

Rent seekers use resources in pursuit of monopoly, and the bigger the rents, the greater is the incentive to use resources to pursue those rents. With free entry into rent seeking, the long-run equilibrium outcome is that rent seekers use up the entire producer surplus.

CHECKPOINT 11.4

4 Explain how price discrimination increases profit.

Study Guide pp. 174–176

Practice Online 11.4

Practice Problem 11.4

Village, a small isolated town, has one doctor. For a 30-minute consultation, the doctor charges a rich person twice as much as a poor person.

a. Does the doctor practice price discrimination?

b. Does the doctor's pricing system redistribute consumer surplus? If so, explain how.

c. Is the doctor using resources efficiently? Explain your answer.

d. If the doctor decided to charge everyone the maximum price that he or she would be willing to pay, what would be the consumer surplus?

e. In part **d**, is the market for medical service in Village efficient?

Exercises 11.4

1. Under what conditions is price discrimination possible?
2. Which of the following is *not* an example of price discrimination?
   a. A diner offers senior citizens a discount on Tuesday lunches.
   b. An airline offers stand-by fares at a 75 percent discount.
   c. An airline offers a 25 percent discount on a round-trip ticket for a week-end stay.
   d. A supermarket sells water for $2 a bottle or $18 for a box of 12 bottles.
   e. A bank charges a higher interest rate on a loan to buy a motorbike than the rate it charges the same person on a student loan.
   f. A California car wash pays a higher price for water than a California farmer pays.
   g. A cell phone company offers free calls on the weekend.
   h. A museum offers discounts to students and senior citizens.
   i. A power utility charges a steel smelter a higher price for electricity between 6:00 A.M. and 9:00 A.M. than it charges between midnight and 6:00 A.M.

Solution to Practice Problem 11.4

a. The doctor practices price discrimination because rich people and poor people pay a different price for the same service: a 30-minute consultation.

b. With price discrimination, the doctor takes some of the consumer surplus. So yes, consumer surplus is reduced and redistributed to the doctor as economic profit.

c. No, the doctor creates a deadweight loss and so is not using resources efficiently.

d. The doctor now practices perfect price discrimination. To maximize profit, the doctor increases the number of consultations to make the lowest price charged equal to marginal cost. The doctor takes the entire consumer surplus. So consumer surplus is zero.

e. The doctor no longer creates a deadweight loss, so resources are being used efficiently.

11.5 MONOPOLY POLICY ISSUES

The comparison of monopoly and competition makes monopoly look bad. Monopoly is inefficient, and it captures consumer surplus and converts it into economic profit or pure waste in the form of rent-seeking costs. If monopoly is so bad, why do we put up with it? Why don't we have laws that crack down on monopoly so hard that it never rears its head? We do indeed have laws that limit monopoly and regulate the prices that monopolies are permitted to charge. But monopoly also brings some benefits. We begin this review of monopoly policy issues by looking at the benefits of monopoly. We then look at the regulation of monopoly.

Gains from Monopoly

The main reason why monopoly exists is that it has potential advantages over a competitive alternative. These advantages arise from

- Economies of scale
- Incentives to innovate

Economies of Scale

Economies of scale can lead to *natural monopoly*—a situation in which a single firm can produce at a lower average total cost than a larger number of smaller firms can. Examples of industries in which economies of scale are so significant that they lead to a natural monopoly are becoming more rare. Public utilities such as gas, electric power, local telephone service, and garbage collection once were natural monopolies. But technological advances now enable us to separate the *production* of electric power and natural gas from their *distribution*. The provision of water though, remains a natural monopoly. Where significant economies of scale exist, it would be wasteful not to have a monopoly. So creating competition in a market that is a natural monopoly would be wasteful.

Incentives to Innovate

Invention leads to a wave of innovation as new knowledge is applied to the production process. Do large firms with monopoly power or small competitive firms lacking monopoly power innovate most? The evidence is mixed. Large firms do more research and development than do small firms, and they are usually the first to use a new technology. But their rate of productivity growth is no greater than that of small firms.

Regulating Natural Monopoly

Figure 11.11 shows the demand curve, *D*, the marginal revenue curve, *MR*, the long-run average cost curve, *LRAC*, and the marginal cost curve, *MC*, for a gas distribution company. The firm's marginal cost is constant at 10 cents a cubic foot. Average cost decreases as output increases. This firm is a natural monopoly.

If the firm is not regulated and maximizes profit, it produces only 2 million cubic feet a day, the quantity at which marginal cost equals marginal revenue. The firm prices gas at 20 cents a cubic foot and makes an economic profit of 2 cents a cubic foot, or $40,000 a day. This outcome is inefficient. Gas costs 20 cent a cubic

FIGURE 11.11
Regulating a Natural Monopoly

Practice Online

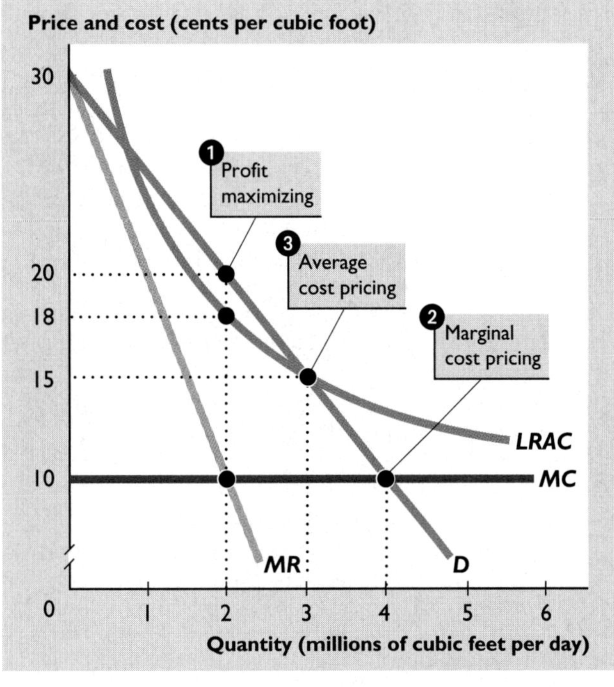

The demand curve for gas is the curve *D*. The natural monopoly's marginal cost, *MC*, is constant at 10 cents a cubic foot and its long-run average cost curve is *LRAC*.

1. The unregulated natural monopoly produces 2 million cubic feet and sets the price at 20 cents a cubic foot.
2. With a marginal cost pricing rule, the price is 10 cents a cubic foot and the quantity produced is 4 million cubic feet a day. The firm incurs an economic loss.
3. With an average cost pricing rule, the price is 15 cents a cubic foot and the quantity produced is 3 million cubic feet a day. The firm makes a normal profit.

foot when marginal cost is only 10 cents a cubic foot. Also, the gas company is making an economic profit. What can regulation do to change this outcome?

An efficient use of resources is achieved when marginal benefit equals marginal cost. You can see in Figure 11.11 that this outcome occurs if the price is regulated at 10 cents a cubic foot and if 4 million cubic feet a day are produced. A **marginal cost pricing rule** that sets price equal to marginal cost achieves this outcome.

Marginal cost pricing rule
A price rule for a natural monopoly that sets price equal to marginal cost.

The marginal cost pricing rule is efficient, but it leaves the natural monopoly incurring an economic loss. How can a firm cover its costs and, at the same time, obey a marginal cost pricing rule? One possibility is to use a two-part price (called a two-part tariff). For example, the gas company might charge a monthly fixed fee that covers its fixed cost and then charge for gas consumed at marginal cost. But a natural monopoly cannot always cover its costs in this way.

Regulators almost never use marginal cost pricing because of its consequences for the firm's profit. Instead, they use an **average cost pricing rule**, which sets the price equal to average cost and enables the firm to cover its costs and earn a normal profit.

Average cost pricing rule
A price rule for a natural monopoly that sets the price equal to average cost and enables the firm to cover its costs and earn a normal profit.

Figure 11.11 shows the average cost pricing outcome. The firm charges 15 cents a cubic foot and sells 3 million cubic feet a day. This outcome is better for consumers than the unregulated profit-maximizing outcome. The price is 5 cents a cubic foot lower, and the quantity consumed is 1 million cubic feet a day more. And the outcome is better for the producer than the marginal cost pricing rule outcome. The firm earns normal profit. The outcome is inefficient but less so than the unregulated profit-maximizing outcome.

CHECKPOINT 11.5

Study Guide pp. 176–178

Practice Online 11.5

5 **Explain how monopoly regulation influences output, price, economic profit, and efficiency.**

Practice Problem 11.5

The local water company is a natural monopoly. Figure 1 shows the demand for water and the water company's cost of providing water.

a. If the company is an unregulated profit-maximizer:
   i. What is the price of water?
   ii. What quantity of water would be supplied?
   iii. What would be the deadweight loss?

b. If the company is regulated to make normal profit:
   i. What is the price of water?
   ii. What quantity of water would be supplied?
   iii. What would be the deadweight loss?

c. If the company is regulated to be efficient:
   i. What is the price of water?
   ii. What quantity of water would be supplied?
   iii. What would be the deadweight loss?

FIGURE 1

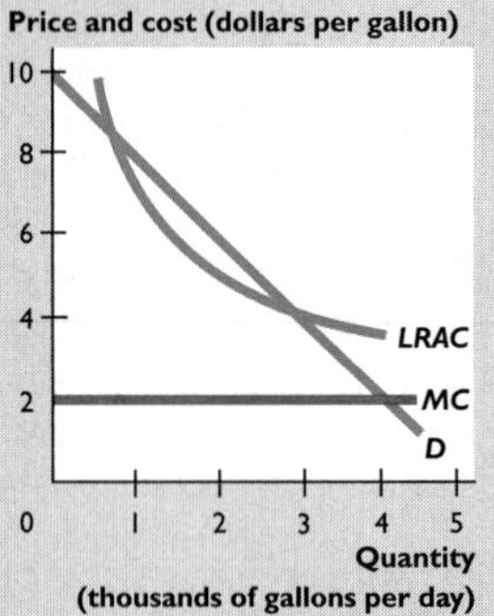

Exercise 11.5

Cox Cable has a monopoly in the provision of cable television service in many regions. If Cox Cable were regulated so that

a. Cable television service was efficient,
   i. Would the price of cable service change? If so, explain how and why.
   ii. Would Cox Cable make an economic profit, a normal profit, or an economic loss?
   iii. Would the consumer surplus change? If so, explain how and why.

b. Cox Cable made normal profit,
   i. Would the price of cable service change? If so, explain how and why.
   ii. Would the deadweight loss created by Cox Cable change? If so, explain how and why.
   iii. Would the consumer surplus change? If so, explain how and why.

FIGURE 2

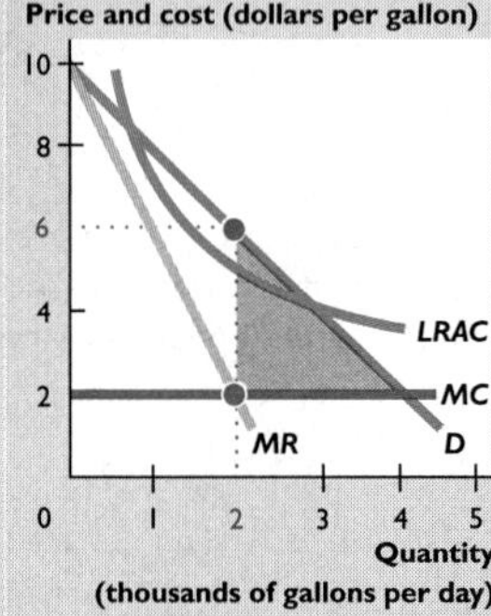

Solution to Practice Problem 11.5

a. The price of water is $6 a gallon, the quantity produced is 2,000 gallons a day, and the deadweight loss is $4,000 a day (the shaded triangle in Figure 2).

b. To make normal profit, the monopoly is regulated to set the price equal to average cost. Water is $4 a gallon, the quantity produced is 3,000 gallons a day, and the deadweight loss is $1,000 a day (the shaded triangle in Figure 3).

c. To be efficient, the monopoly is regulated to set the price (marginal benefit) equal to marginal cost. Water is $2 a gallon, the quantity produced is 4,000 gallons a day, and the deadweight loss is zero (Figure 4.)

FIGURE 3

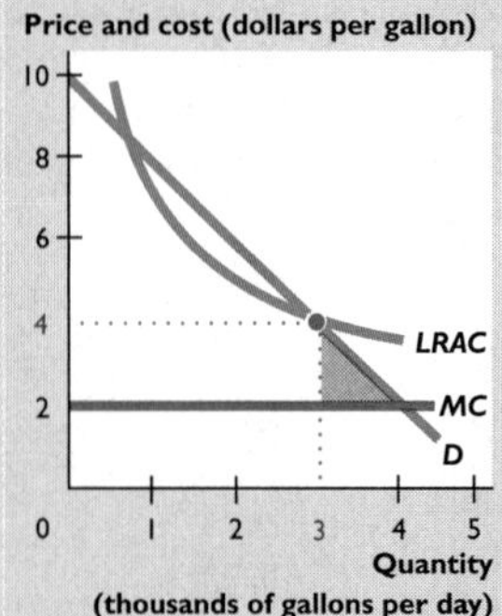

FIGURE 4

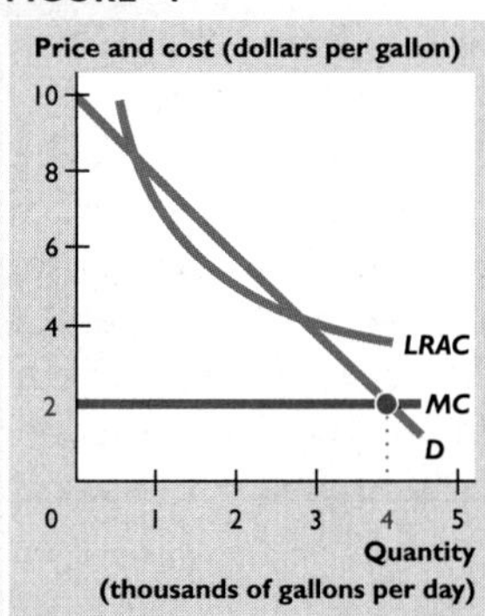

CHAPTER CHECKPOINT

Key Points

1 Explain how monopoly arises and distinguish between single-price monopoly and price-discriminating monopoly.

- A monopoly is a market with a single supplier of a good or service that has no close substitutes and in which legal or natural barriers to entry prevent competition.
- A monopoly can price discriminate when there is no resale possibility.
- Where resale is possible, a firm charges a single price.

2 Explain how a single-price monopoly determines its output and price.

- The demand for a monopoly's output is the market demand, and a single-price monopoly's marginal revenue is less than price.
- A monopoly maximizes profit by producing the output at which marginal revenue equals marginal cost and by charging the maximum price that consumers are willing to pay for that output.

3 Compare the performance of a single-price monopoly with that of perfect competition.

- A single-price monopoly charges a higher price and produces a smaller quantity than does a perfectly competitive market and creates a deadweight loss.
- Monopoly imposes a loss on society that equals its deadweight loss plus the cost of the resources devoted to rent seeking.

4 Explain how price discrimination increases profit.

- Perfect price discrimination charges a different price for each unit sold, obtains the maximum price that each consumer is willing to pay for each unit, and redistributes the entire consumer surplus to the monopoly.
- With perfect price discrimination, the monopoly produces the same output as would a perfectly competitive market, but rent seeking uses some of the surplus.

5 Explain how monopoly regulation influences output, price, economic profit, and efficiency.

- Natural monopolies can produce at a lower price than competitive firms can, and monopolies might be more innovative than competitive firms.
- Efficient regulation requires that price equal marginal cost, but for a natural monopoly, such a price is less than average cost.
- Average cost pricing is a rule that covers a firm's costs and provides a normal profit but is inefficient.

Key Terms

Average cost pricing rule, 293
Barrier to entry, 272
Legal monopoly, 273
Marginal cost pricing rule, 293
Natural monopoly, 272
Perfect price discrimination, 288
Price-discriminating monopoly, 274
Rent seeking, 283
Single-price monopoly, 274

Exercises

1. What are the two types of barrier to entry that can create a monopoly? Provide an example of each type. Why can't barriers to entry simply be torn down so that all markets become competitive?

2. Technological change is constantly creating and destroying barriers to entry and is changing the competitive and monopoly landscapes.
   a. Provide three examples of technological changes that have occurred during the past 20 years that have created a new barrier to entry and resulted in monopoly.
   b. Provide three examples of technological changes that have occurred during the past 20 years that have destroyed a barrier to entry and resulted in competition where previously monopoly was present.

3. Why isn't the demand for a monopoly's product perfectly elastic like that for the product of a firm in perfect competition?

4. Elixir Spring produces a unique and highly prized mineral water. The firm's total fixed cost is $5,000 a day, and its marginal cost is zero. Table 1 shows the demand schedule for Elixir water.
   a. Construct Elixir's total revenue schedule and marginal revenue schedule and make a graph of the demand and marginal revenue curves.
   b. Calculate and illustrate in a graph Elixir's profit-maximizing price, output, and economic profit.
   c. What is the elasticity of demand for Elixir water at the profit-maximizing quantity?

TABLE 1

Price (dollars per bottle)	Quantity (bottles per day)
10	0
9	1,000
8	2,000
7	3,000
6	4,000
5	5,000
4	6,000
3	7,000
2	8,000
1	9,000
0	10,000

5. The Blue Rose Company is the only flower grower to have cracked the secret of making a blue rose. The first two columns of Table 2 show the demand schedule for blue roses, and the middle and third column show the total cost schedule for producing them.
   a. Construct Blue Rose's total revenue and marginal revenue schedule and make a graph of the demand and marginal revenue curves.
   b. Calculate Blue Rose's marginal cost schedule and add it to your graph.
   c. Calculate Blue Rose's profit-maximizing price, output, and economic profit.

TABLE 2

Price (dollars per bunch)	Quantity (bunches per day)	Total cost (dollars per day)
80	0	80
72	1	82
64	2	88
56	3	100
48	4	124
40	5	160
32	6	208
24	7	268
16	8	340

6. Use the demand schedule for Elixir water in Table 1. Suppose that there are 1,000 springs, all able to produce this water at zero marginal cost. Suppose that for these firms, total fixed cost is also zero.
   a. What are the equilibrium price and quantity of Elixir water?
   b. Compare this equilibrium with the monopoly equilibrium in exercise 4.
   c. What is the consumer surplus if Elixir water is produced in perfect competition?
   d. What is the producer surplus if Elixir water is produced in perfect competition?
   e. What are the consumer surplus and producer surplus from Elixir water if a monopoly produces it?
   f. When the Elixir monopoly maximizes profit, what is the deadweight loss?

7. Suppose that 1,000 competitive firms produce Elixir water and that one of these firms begins quietly to buy the others.
   a. What is the most that a firm would be willing to pay to obtain a monopoly in Elixir water?
   b. Illustrate this maximum amount in a graph.
   c. If a firm pays the maximum amount it is willing to pay for a monopoly in Elixir water, what is the firm's economic profit? Explain.

8. Bobbie's Hair Care is a natural monopoly in a small isolated town. The first two columns of Table 3 show the demand schedule for Bobbie's haircuts, and the middle and third column show Bobbie's total cost. Bobbie has done a survey and discovered that she gets four types of customer each hour—one woman who is willing to pay $18, one senior citizen who is willing to pay $16, one student who is willing to pay $14, and one boy who is willing to pay $12.
   a. If Bobbie charges just a single price for haircuts, what is that price, how many haircuts per hour does she do, and what is her economic profit?
   b. If Bobbie price discriminates among the four types of customer she has identified, what is the price she charges to each type of customer?
   c. How many haircuts an hour does Bobbie sell?
   d. What is Bobbie's economic profit?
   e. Is the quantity of haircuts efficient? Explain why or why not.
   f. What are the consumer surplus and producer surplus?
   g. Who benefits from Bobbie's price discrimination?

TABLE 3

Price (dollars per haircut)	Quantity (haircuts per hour)	Total cost (dollars per hour)
20	0	20
18	1	21
16	2	24
14	3	30
12	4	40
10	5	54

9. A city art museum, which is a local monopoly, is worried that it is not generating enough revenue to cover its costs, and the city government is cutting its budget. The museum charges $1 admission and $5 for special exhibitions. The museum director asks you to help him solve his problem. Can you suggest a pricing scheme that will bring in more revenue? At the same time, can you help the museum get even more people to visit it?

10. A global telephone company has large fixed costs, but its marginal cost of a call, whether local, long-distance, or international, is almost zero.
   a. If this firm is a profit-maximizing monopoly, how does it determine the price of a call and the number of calls to carry?
   b. If this firm is a regulated monopoly that is required to produce the efficient number of calls, what is the price of a call?
   c. Can you suggest a scheme that enables the firm to earn an economic profit and at the same time produce the efficient quantity of calls?
   d. Why is average cost pricing not a way of achieving the efficient quantity of calls?

11. Someone suggests that the way to deal with a natural monopoly is to permit it to maximize profit and then tax its profit at a very high rate. If a monopoly faces a tax on its economic profit,
   a. What happens to the profit-maximizing price and quantity?
   b. What happens to the producer surplus, consumer surplus, and deadweight loss?
   c. Can you suggest an alternative tax that brings output closer to the efficient level?

Critical Thinking

12. The National Collegiate Athletic Association (NCAA) controls the market for college athletes. It sets the amounts paid to these athletes below what they would be in a competitive market and ensures that colleges do not violate the rules that it lays down.
    a. Is the NCAA a natural monopoly, a legal monopoly, or neither? Explain.
    b. Who benefits and who loses from the NCAA's control of the market for college athletes?
    c. Is the system operated by the NCAA efficient?

13. Major league baseball is exempt from laws designed to limit market power and operates as a monopoly.
    a. How might competition be introduced into the market for baseball?
    b. If the baseball market became competitive, what do you predict would happen to the number of teams and the economic profit of a team?
    c. If the baseball market became competitive, what do you predict would happen to the number of players and their average salaries?
    d. All things considered, would you favor or oppose the introduction of competition among leagues in baseball?

14. Before 1991, the eight Ivy League colleges (Brown, Columbia, Cornell, Dartmouth, Harvard, Princeton, the University of Pennsylvania, and Yale), along with MIT, shared information and agreed on rules for setting their prices of education (price equals tuition minus scholarship). Since 1991, these schools have set their prices in competition with each other. Compare the market for an Ivy League education before and after 1991. Predict what has happened to the efficiency of the market, to the distribution of producer and consumer surplus, and to deadweight loss.

Practice Online

Web Exercises

Use the links on your Foundations Web site to work the following exercises.

15. Visit the Web site of Robert Barro and read his article on competition and monopoly in the hi-tech sector.
    a. What is Robert Barro's central argument?
    b. Explain why you agree or disagree with Barro.
    c. What are the main implications of Barro's view for government policy toward monopoly?

16. Visit the Web site of the Department of Justice and review the information on the case of the United States versus Microsoft.
    a. Did the courts find Microsoft to be a monopoly?
    b. What are the main factors that the courts considered in reaching their conclusions about Microsoft?
    c. What remedies did the court propose?
    d. Compare the court's findings with the views of Robert Barro (in Web exercise 15).

17. Visit the Web site of United Airlines and get some prices for a trip from the major airport nearest you to anywhere in the world that interests you. Get the best fare possible and establish the restrictions on its use. Compare it with the normal fare. Explain how the restrictions increase United Airlines' total revenue.

Monopolistic Competition and Oligopoly

CHAPTER 12

CHAPTER CHECKLIST

When you have completed your study of this chapter, you will be able to

1. Explain how price and quantity are determined in monopolistic competition.
2. Explain why selling costs are high in monopolistic competition.
3. Explain the dilemma faced by firms in oligopoly.
4. Use game theory to explain how price and quantity are determined in oligopoly.

Every week, we receive newspapers stuffed with fliers and coupons to grab our attention and to persuade us that Albertsons, Kroger, Safeway, and Shop 'n' Save have the best deals in town. In perfect competition, there are no best deals or fliers. Each firm produces an identical product and is a price taker. How do firms that offer slightly different deals from other firms set their prices?

Until recently, only Intel Corporation made the chips that drive PCs. In 1994, the prices of PCs powered by Intel's fast Pentium chips collapsed. The reason: Intel faced competition from two new entrants, Advanced Micro Devices Inc. and Cyrix Corp. But with only three chip producers, we don't have much competition. How is the price of a computer chip determined?

To understand fliers, coupons, and the price of a computer chip, we need the richer models of monopolistic competition and oligopoly, which are explained in this chapter.

12.1 MONOPOLISTIC COMPETITION

You have studied two market structures: perfect competition and monopoly. In perfect competition, a large number of firms produce identical goods, there are no barriers to entry, and each firm is a price taker. In the long run, there is no economic profit. In monopoly, a single firm protected from competition by barriers to entry might earn an economic profit, even in the long run.

Many real-world markets are competitive, but not as fiercely so as perfect competition. Firms in these markets possess some power to set their prices as monopolies do. We call this type of market monopolistic competition.

Monopolistic competition is a market structure in which

- A large number of firms compete.
- Each firm produces a differentiated product.
- Firms compete on product quality, price, and marketing.
- Firms are free to enter and exit.

Large Number of Firms

In monopolistic competition, as in perfect competition, the industry consists of a large number of firms. The presence of a large number of firms has three implications for the firms in the industry.

Small Market Share

Each firm supplies a small part of the market. Consequently, although each firm can influence the price of its own product, it has little power to influence the market average price.

No Market Dominance

Each firm must be sensitive to the average market price of the product. But it does not pay attention to any one individual competitor. Because all the firms are relatively small, no single firm can dictate market conditions, so no one firm's actions directly affect the actions of the other firms.

Collusion Impossible

Firms sometimes try to profit from illegal agreements—collusion—with other firms to fix prices and not undercut each other. Collusion is impossible when the market has a large number of firms, as it does in monopolistic competition.

Product Differentiation

Product differentiation
Making a product that is slightly different from the products of competing firms.

Product differentiation is making a product that is slightly different from the products of competing firms. A differentiated product has close substitutes, but it does not have perfect substitutes. When the price of one firm's product rises, the quantity demanded of it decreases. For example, Adidas, Asics, Diadora, Etonic, Fila, New Balance, Nike, Puma, and Reebok all make differentiated running shoes. Other things remaining the same, if the price of Adidas running shoes rises and the prices of the other shoes remain constant, some people will switch from Adidas to another brand and Adidas will sell fewer shoes.

Competing on Quality, Price, and Marketing

Product differentiation enables a firm to compete with other firms in three areas: quality, price, and marketing.

Quality

The quality of a product is the physical attributes that make it different from the products of other firms. Quality includes design, reliability, the service provided to the buyer, and the buyer's ease of access to the product. Quality lies on a spectrum that runs from high to low. Go to the J. D. Power Consumer Center at jdpower.com, and you'll see the many dimensions on which this rating agency describes the quality of autos, financial services, travel and accommodation services, telecommunication services, and new homes—all examples of products that have a large range of quality.

Price

Because of product differentiation, a firm in monopolistic competition faces a downward-sloping demand curve. So, like a monopoly, the firm can set both its price and its output. But there is a tradeoff between the product's quality and price. A firm that makes a high-quality product can charge a higher price than a firm that makes a low-quality product can.

Marketing

Because of product differentiation, a firm in monopolistic competition must market its product. Marketing takes two main forms: advertising and packaging. A firm that produces a high-quality product wants to sell it for a suitably high price. To be able to do so, the firm must advertise and package its product in a way that convinces buyers that they are getting the higher quality for which they are paying. For example, drug companies advertise and package their brand-name drugs to persuade buyers that these items are superior to the lower-priced generic alternatives. Similarly, a firm that produces a low-quality product uses advertising and packaging to persuade buyers that although the quality is low, the low price more than compensates for this fact.

Entry and Exit

In monopolistic competition, there are no barriers to entry. Consequently, a firm cannot make an economic profit in the long run. When firms make economic profits, new firms enter the industry. This entry lowers prices and eventually eliminates economic profits. When economic losses are incurred, some firms leave the industry. Exit increases prices and profits and eventually eliminates the economic losses. In long-run equilibrium, firms neither enter nor leave the industry and the firms in the industry make zero economic profit.

Identifying Monopolistic Competition

To identify monopolistic competition, economists use two indexes of the extent to which a market is dominated by a small number of firms. These indexes are

- The four-firm concentration ratio
- The Herfindahl-Hirschman Index

Four-firm concentration ratio The percentage of the value of sales accounted for by the four largest firms in an industry.

The **four-firm concentration ratio** is the percentage of the value of sales accounted for by the four largest firms in an industry. The range of the concentration ratio is from almost zero for perfect competition to 100 percent for monopoly. The boundary between oligopoly and monopolistic competition is generally regarded as being around 40: A four-firm concentration ratio that exceeds 40 percent is regarded as an indication of oligopoly and a ratio of less than 40 percent is regarded as an indication of monopolistic competition.

Herfindahl-Hirschman Index The square of the percentage market share of each firm summed over the largest 50 firms (or summed over all the firms if there are fewer than 50) in a market.

The **Herfindahl-Hirschman Index**—also called the HHI—is the square of the percentage market share of each firm summed over the largest 50 firms (or summed over all the firms if there are fewer than 50) in a market. For example, if there are four firms in a market and the market shares of the firms are 50 percent, 25 percent, 15 percent, and 10 percent, the Herfindahl-Hirschman Index is

$$\text{HHI} = 50^2 + 25^2 + 15^2 + 10^2 = 3{,}450.$$

In perfect competition, the HHI is small. For example, if each of the largest 50 firms in an industry has a market share of 0.1 percent, the HHI is $0.1^2 \times 50 = 0.5$. In a monopoly, the HHI is 10,000—the firm has 100 percent of the market: $100^2 = 10{,}000$.

The HHI became a popular measure of the degree of competition during the 1980s, when the Justice Department used it to classify markets. A market in which the HHI is less than 1,000 is regarded as being competitive. A market in which the HHI lies between 1,000 and 1,800 is regarded as being moderately competitive. But a market in which the HHI exceeds 1,800 is regarded as being uncompetitive. The Justice Department scrutinizes any merger of firms in a market in which the HHI exceeds 1,000, and it is likely to challenge a merger if the HHI exceeds 1800.

A market with a high concentration ratio or HHI might nonetheless be competitive because the few firms in a market face competition from many firms that can easily enter the market and will do so if economic profits are available.

Eye on the U.S. Economy

Examples of Monopolistic Competition

These 10 industries are all examples of monopolistic competition. They have a large number of firms, shown in brackets after the name of the industry. The bars measure the percentage of industry total revenue received by the 20 largest firms. The number on the right is the Herfindahl-Hirschman Index.

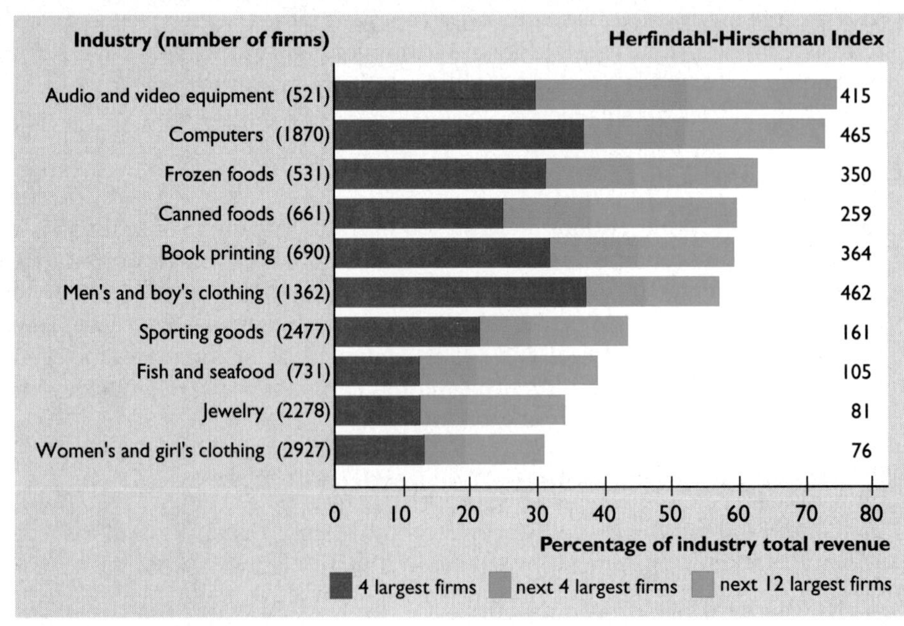

SOURCE: U.S. Census Bureau.

Output and Price in Monopolistic Competition

Think about the decisions that Tommy Hilfiger must make about Tommy jeans. First, the firm must decide on the design and quality of its jeans and on its marketing program. We'll suppose that Tommy Hilfiger has already made these decisions so that we can concentrate on the firm's output and pricing decision. But we'll study quality and marketing decisions in the next section.

For a given quality of jeans and a given amount of marketing activity, Tommy Hilfiger faces given costs and market conditions. How, given its costs and the demand for its jeans, does Tommy Hilfiger decide the quantity of jeans to produce and the price at which to sell them?

The Firm's Profit-Maximizing Decision

A firm in monopolistic competition makes its output and price decision just as a monopoly firm does. Figure 12.1 illustrates this decision for Tommy jeans. The demand curve for Tommy jeans is *D*. The *MR* curve shows the marginal revenue curve associated with this demand curve. It is derived just like the marginal revenue curve of a single-price monopoly that you studied in Chapter 11. The *ATC* curve shows the average total cost of producing Tommy jeans and *MC* is the marginal cost curve.

Tommy Hilfiger maximizes profit by producing the output at which marginal revenue equals marginal cost. In Figure 12.1, this output is 150 pairs of jeans a day. Tommy Hilfiger charges the price that buyers are willing to pay for this quantity, which is determined by the demand curve. This price is $70 a pair. When it produces 150 pairs of jeans a day, Tommy Hilfiger's average total cost is $20 a pair, and it makes an economic profit of $7,500 a day ($50 a pair multiplied by 150 pairs of jeans a day). The blue rectangle shows Tommy Hilfiger's economic profit.

FIGURE 12.1
Output and Price in Monopolistic Competition

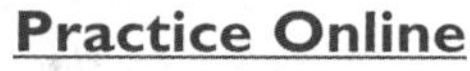

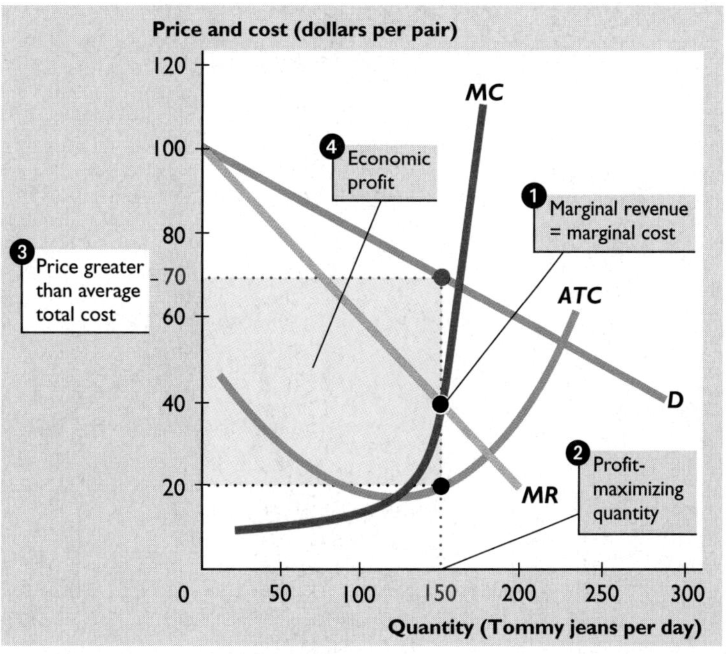

1 Profit is maximized where marginal revenue equals marginal cost. 2 The profit-maximizing quantity is 150 pairs of Tommy jeans a day. 3 The price of $70 a pair exceeds the average total cost of $20 a pair, so the firm makes an economic profit of $50 a pair. 4 The blue rectangle illustrates economic profit, which equals $7,500 a day ($50 a pair multiplied by 150 pairs).

So far, the firm in monopolistic competition looks just like a single-price monopoly. It produces the quantity at which marginal revenue equals marginal cost and then charges the price that buyers are willing to pay for that quantity, as determined by the demand curve. The key difference between monopoly and monopolistic competition lies in what happens next.

Long Run: Zero Economic Profit

There is no restriction on entry in monopolistic competition, so if firms in an industry are making an economic profit, other firms have an incentive to enter that industry.

As the Gap and Calvin Klein start to make jeans similar to Tommy jeans, some people will switch to these other brands and the demand for Tommy jeans will decrease. The demand curve for Tommy jeans and the marginal revenue curve start to shift leftward. At each point in time, the firm maximizes its profit by producing the quantity at which marginal revenue equals marginal cost and by charging the highest price that buyers are willing to pay for this quantity. As the demand curve shifts leftward, the profit-maximizing quantity and price fall.

Figure 12.2 shows the long-run equilibrium. The demand curve for Tommy jeans has shifted leftward to *D*', and the marginal revenue curve has shifted leftward to *MR*'. The firm produces 50 pairs of jeans a day and sells them for $30 each. At this output level, average total cost is also $30 a pair. So Tommy Hilfiger is making zero economic profit on its jeans. When all the firms in the industry are earning zero economic profit, there is no incentive for new firms to enter.

If demand is so low relative to costs that firms incur economic losses, exit will occur. As firms leave an industry, the demand for the products of the remaining firms increases and their demand curves shift rightward. The exit process ends when all the firms in the industry are making zero economic profit.

FIGURE 12.2
Output and Price in the Long Run

Practice Online

Economic profit encourages new entrants, and the entry of new firms decreases the demand for each firm's product. The demand curve and marginal revenue curve shift leftward.

When the demand curve has shifted to *D*', the marginal revenue curve is *MR*' and the firm is in long-run equilibrium.

1. The output that maximizes profit is 50 pairs of Tommy jeans a day, and
2. the price is $30 per pair. Average total cost is also $30 per pair, so
3. economic profit is zero.

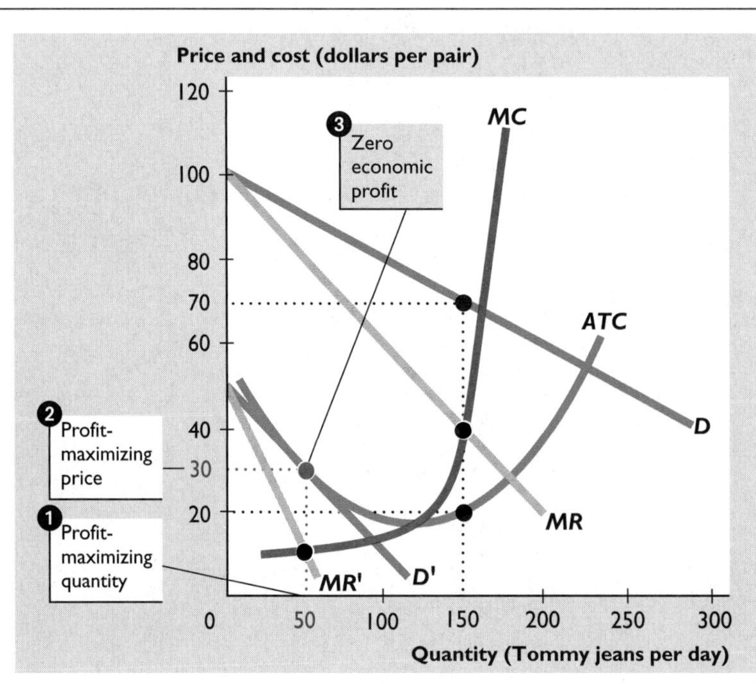

Monopolistic Competition and Efficiency

Efficiency requires that the marginal benefit of the consumer equal the marginal cost of the producer. Price measures marginal benefit, so efficiency requires price to equal marginal cost. In monopolistic competition, price exceeds marginal revenue and marginal revenue equals marginal cost, so price exceeds marginal cost—a sign of inefficiency.

But this inefficiency arises from product differentiation—variety—that consumers value and for which they are willing to pay. So the loss that arises because marginal benefit exceeds marginal cost must be weighed against the gain that arises from greater product variety. It is almost inconceivable that consumers would be better off with no variety and price equal to marginal cost. So in a broader view of efficiency, monopolistic competition brings gains for consumers.

Another interesting feature of firms in monopolistic competition is that they always have excess capacity in long-run equilibrium.

Excess Capacity

A firm's **capacity output** is the output at which average total cost is a minimum—the output at the bottom of the U-shaped *ATC* curve. This output is 125 pairs of jeans a day in Figure 12.3. Firms in monopolistic competition always have *excess capacity* in the long run. In Figure 12.3, Tommy Hilfiger produces 50 pairs of jeans a day and has excess capacity of 75 pairs of jeans a day. That is, Tommy Hilfiger produces a smaller output than that which minimizes average total cost. Consequently, the consumer pays a price that exceeds minimum average total cost. This result arises from the fact that the firm faces a downward-sloping demand curve. The demand curve slopes downward because of product differentiation, so product differentiation creates excess capacity.

Capacity output
The output at which average total cost is a minimum.

FIGURE 12.3
Excess Capacity

Practice Online

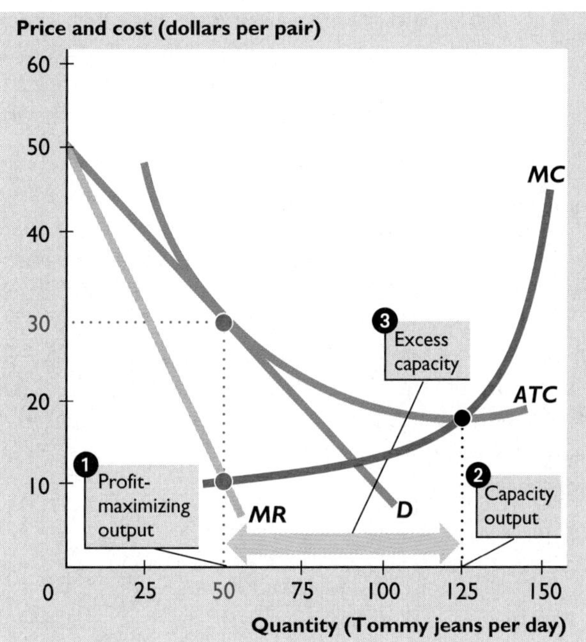

In long-run equilibrium, entry decreases the demand for one firm's output to the point at which the firm makes zero economic profit.

1. The firm produces 50 pairs of jeans a day.
2. The firm's capacity output is the output at which average total cost is a minimum—125 pairs a day.

Because the demand curve in monopolistic competition slopes downward, the output that maximizes profit is always less than capacity output in long-run equilibrium.

3. In long-run equilibrium, the firm operates with excess capacity.

CHECKPOINT 12.1

Study Guide pp. 184–187

Practice Online 12.1

1 **Explain how price and quantity are determined in monopolistic competition.**

Practice Problem 12.1

Natti is a dot.com entrepreneur who has established a Web site at which people can design and buy a pair of cool sunglasses. Natti pays $4,000 a month for her Web server and Internet connection. The glasses that her customers design are made to order by another firm, and Natti pays this firm $50 a pair. Natti has no other costs. Table 1 shows the demand schedule for Natti's sunglasses.

a. Calculate Natti's profit-maximizing output, price, and economic profit.
b. Do you expect other firms to enter the Web sunglasses business and compete with Natti?
c. What happens to the demand for Natti's sunglasses in the long run?
d. What happens to Natti's economic profit in the long run?

TABLE 1

Price (dollars per pair)	Quantity demanded (pairs per month)
250	0
200	50
150	100
100	150
50	200
0	250

Exercise 12.1

Lorie restrings tennis racquets. Her fixed costs are $1,000 a month, and it costs her $15 of labor time to restring one racquet. Table 2 shows the demand schedule for Lorie's restringing services.

a. Calculate Lorie's profit-maximizing output, price, and economic profit.
b. Do you expect other firms to enter the tennis racquet restringing business and compete with Lorie?
c. What happens to the demand for Lorie's restringing services in the long run?
d. What happens to Lorie's economic profit in the long run?

TABLE 2

Price (dollars per racquet)	Quantity demanded (racquets per month)
25	0
20	10
15	20
10	30
5	40
0	50

Solution to Practice Problem 12.1

a. Marginal cost, *MC*, is $50 a pair—the price that Natti pays her supplier of glasses. To find marginal revenue, plot the demand curve using the numbers in the demand schedule provided (see Figure 1). Note that the demand curve cuts to *x*-axis at 250 pairs a month. The marginal revenue, *MR*, curve has a slope twice that of the demand curve and cuts the *x*-axis at 125 pairs a month.

Profit is maximized when *MC* = *MR* and Natti sells 100 pairs a month. The price is $150, and average total cost, *ATC*, is $90—$50 marginal cost (and average variable cost) and $40 average fixed cost. Economic profit is $60 a pair on 100 pairs a month, which is $6,000 a month.

b. Because Natti is making an economic profit, other firms have an incentive to enter and will do so.
c. As firms enter Natti's market, the demand for Natti's sunglasses will decrease and the demand curve will shift leftward.
d. As the demand for Natti's sunglasses decreases, her economic profit also decreases. In the long run, she will earn zero economic profit.

FIGURE 1

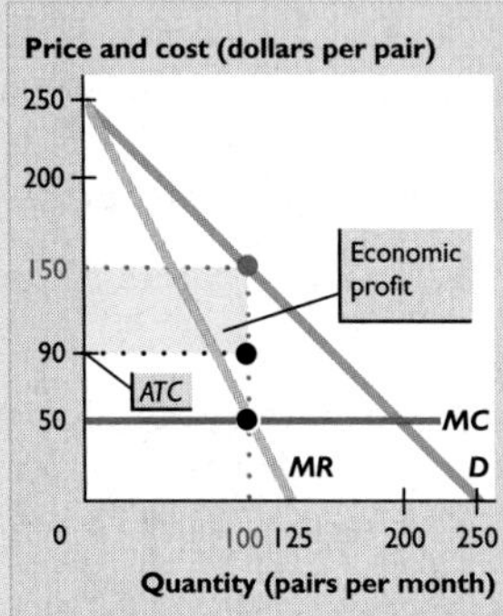

12.2 PRODUCT DEVELOPMENT AND MARKETING

When we studied a firm's output and price decision, we supposed that it had already made its product quality and marketing decisions. We're now going to study these decisions and the impact they have on the firm's output, price, and economic profit.

Innovation and Product Development

To enjoy economic profits, firms in monopolistic competition must be continuously developing new products. The reason is that wherever economic profits are earned, imitators emerge and set up business. So to maintain its economic profit, a firm must seek out new products that will provide it with a competitive edge, even if only temporarily. A firm that manages to introduce a new and differentiated product will temporarily have a less elastic demand for its product and will be able to increase its price temporarily. It will make an economic profit. Eventually, new firms that make close substitutes for the innovative product will enter and compete away the economic profit arising from this initial advantage. So to restore economic profit, the firm must again innovate.

Cost Versus Benefit of Product Innovation

The decision to innovate is based on the same type of profit-maximizing calculation that you've already studied. Innovation and product development are costly activities, but they bring in additional revenues. The firm must balance the cost and benefit at the margin. At a low level of product development, the marginal revenue from a better product exceeds the marginal cost. When the marginal dollar spent on product development (its marginal cost) brings in an additional dollar of revenue (its marginal benefit), the firm is spending the profit-maximizing amount on product development.

For example, when Eidos Interactive released Tomb Raider III, it was probably not the best game that Eidos could have created. Rather, it was the game that balanced the marginal benefit and willingness of the consumer to pay for further game enhancements against the marginal cost of these enhancements.

Efficiency and Product Innovation

Is product innovation an efficient activity? Does it benefit the consumer? There are two views about the answers to these questions. One view is that monopolistic competition brings to market many improved products that bring great benefits to the consumer. Clothing, kitchen and other household appliances, computers, computer programs, cars, and many other products keep getting better every year, and the consumer benefits from these improved products.

But many so-called improvements amount to little more than changing the appearance of a product or giving a different look to the packaging. In these cases, there is little objective benefit to the consumer.

But regardless of whether a product improvement is real or imagined, its value to the consumer is its marginal benefit, which equals the amount the consumer is willing to pay. In other words, the value of product improvements is the increase in price that the consumer is willing to pay. The marginal benefit to the producer is marginal revenue, which in equilibrium equals marginal cost. Because price exceeds marginal cost in monopolistic competition, product improvement is not pushed to its efficient level.

Marketing

Designing and developing products that are actually different from those of other firms are ways to achieve some product differentiation. But firms also attempt to create a consumer perception of product differentiation even when actual differences are small. Advertising and packaging are the principal means that firms use to achieve this end. An American Express card is a different product from a Visa card. But the actual differences are not the main ones that American Express emphasizes in its marketing. The deeper message is that if you use an American Express card, you can be like Tiger Woods (or another highly successful person).

Marketing Expenditures

Firms in monopolistic competition incur huge costs to ensure that buyers appreciate and value the differences between their own products and those of their competitors. So a large proportion of the prices that we pay cover the cost of selling a good. Advertising in newspapers and magazines and on radio, television, and the Internet is the main selling cost. But it is not the only one. Selling costs include the cost of shopping malls that look like movie sets; glossy catalogs and brochures; and the salaries, airfares, and hotel bills of salespeople.

The total scale of selling costs is hard to estimate, but some components can be measured. A survey conducted by a commercial agency suggests that for cleaning supplies and toys, around 15 percent of the price of an item is spent on advertising. Figure 12.4 shows some estimates for these and other industries.

FIGURE 12.4
Advertising Expenditures

Practice Online

Advertising expenditures are a large part of total revenue for producers of cleaning supplies, toys, confectionery, and cosmetics.

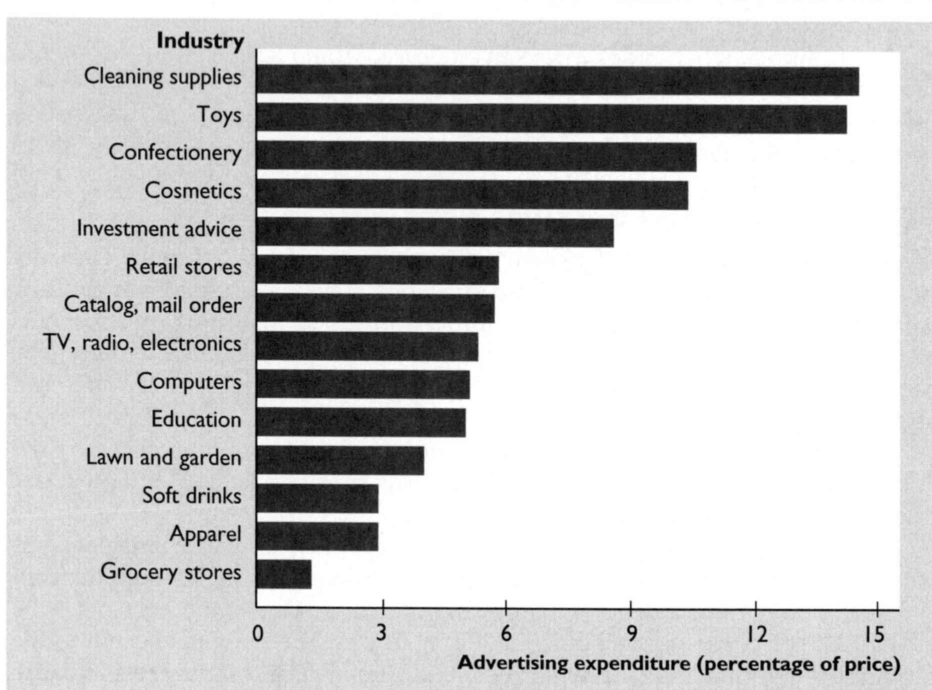

SOURCE: Schoenfeld & Associates, Lincolnwood, Illinois , reported at http://www.toolkit.cch.com/text/p03_7006.stm

For the U.S. economy as a whole, there are some 20,000 advertising agencies, which employ more than 200,000 people and have sales of $45 billion. But these numbers are only part of the total cost of advertising because firms have their own internal advertising departments, the costs of which we can only guess.

Advertising expenditures and other selling costs affect the profits of firms in two ways. They increase costs, and they change demand. Let's look at these effects.

Selling Costs and Total Costs

Selling costs such as advertising expenditures increase the costs of a monopolistically competitive firm above those of a perfectly competitive firm or a monopoly. Advertising costs and other selling costs are fixed costs. They do not vary as total output varies. So, just like fixed production costs, advertising costs per unit decrease as production increases.

Figure 12.5 shows how selling costs and advertising expenditures change a firm's average total cost. The blue curve shows the average total cost of production. The red curve shows the firm's average total cost of production plus advertising. The height of the red area between the two curves shows the average fixed cost of advertising. The *total* cost of advertising is fixed. But the *average* cost of advertising decreases as output increases.

The figure shows that if advertising increases the quantity sold by a large enough amount, it can lower average total cost. For example, if the quantity sold increases from 25 pairs of jeans a day with no advertising to 100 pairs of jeans a day with advertising, average total cost falls from $60 a pair to $40 a pair. The reason is that although the *total* fixed cost has increased, the greater fixed cost is spread over a greater output, so average total cost decreases.

FIGURE 12.5
Selling Costs and Total Costs

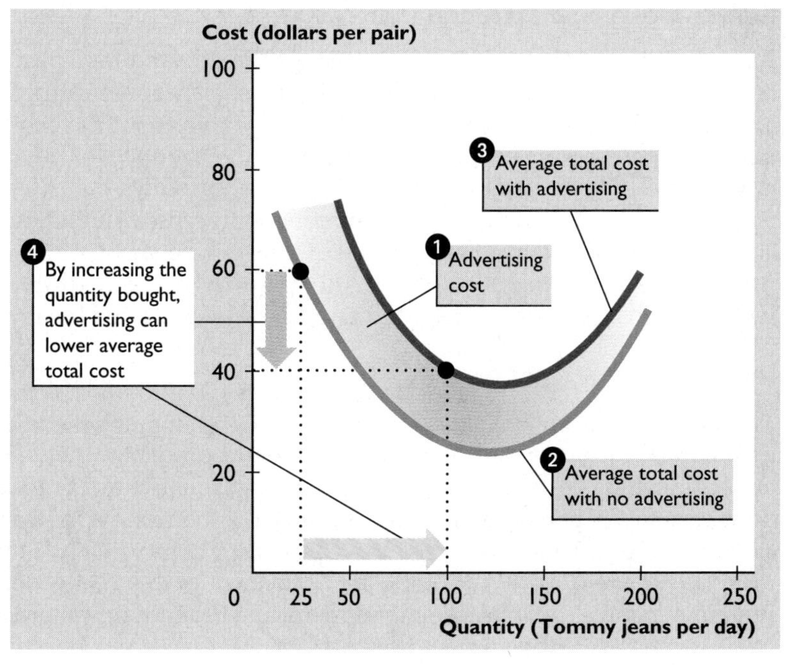

Selling costs such as the cost of advertising are fixed costs.

❶ When advertising costs are added to ❷ the average total cost of production, ❸ average total cost increases by more at small outputs than at large outputs.

❹ If advertising enables sales to increase from 25 pairs of jeans a day to 100 pairs a day, it *lowers* average total cost from $60 a pair to $40 a pair.

Eye on the U.S. Economy

The Selling Cost of a Pair of Running Shoes

Have you ever wondered what you're paying for when you buy a new pair of running shoes? Your new Nikes cost you $70. But who got that money?

The figure shows you the answer. The plastic and other materials from which the shoe is made cost $9. The producer, in Asia, paid $8 in wages and capital costs and normal profit. Nike pays $0.50 for shipping. The U.S. government collected $3 when the shoes were imported into the United States. These items total $20. The remaining $50 is selling cost. It is the cost (including normal profit) of Nike's marketing its shoes and of the retailer from whom you bought them. The table provides a more detailed breakdown of these costs.

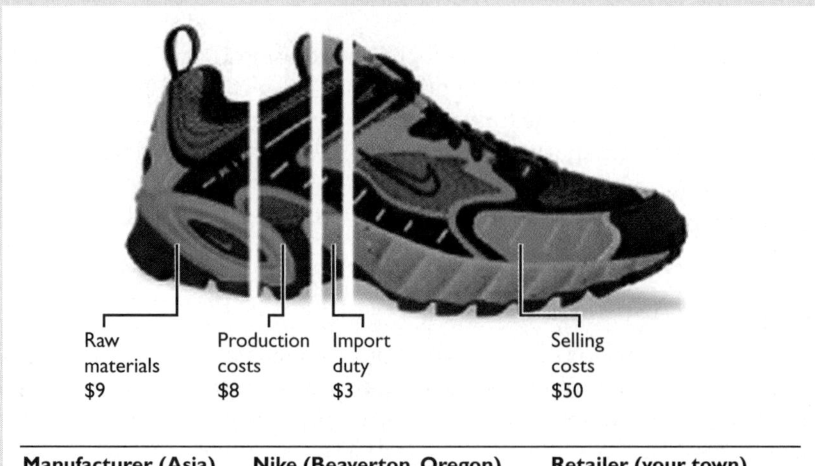

Manufacturer (Asia)		Nike (Beaverton, Oregon)		Retailer (your town)	
Materials	$9.00				
Cost of labor	$2.75	Cost of shoe to Nike	$20.00	Cost of shoe to retailer	$35.50
Cost of capital	$3.00	Sales, distribution, and administration	$5.00	Sales clerk's wages	$9.50
Profit	$1.75	Advertising	$4.00	Shop rent	$9.00
Shipping	$0.50	Research & development	$0.25	Retailer's other costs	$7.00
Import duty	$3.00	Nike's profit	$6.25	Retailer's profit	$9.00
Nike's cost	**$20.00**	**Retailer's cost**	**$35.50**	**Price paid by you**	**$70.00**

Selling Costs and Demand

Advertising and other selling efforts change the demand for a firm's product. But how? Does demand increase, or does it decrease? The most natural answer is that advertising increases demand. By informing people about the quality of its product or by persuading people to switch from the products of other firms, a firm might expect to increase the demand for its own product.

But all firms in monopolistic competition advertise. And all seek to persuade customers that they have the best deal. If advertising enables a firm to survive, it might increase the number of firms in the market. And to the extent that it increases the number of firms, it *decreases* the demand faced by any one firm.

Efficiency: The Bottom Line

The bottom line on the question of efficiency of monopolistic competition is ambiguous. In some cases, the gains from extra product variety unquestionably offset the selling costs and the extra cost arising from excess capacity. The tremendous varieties of books and magazines, clothing, food, and drinks are examples of such gains. It is less easy to see the gains from being able to buy brand-name drugs that have a chemical composition identical to that of a generic alternative. But many people do willingly pay more for the brand-name alternative.

CHECKPOINT 12.2

2 Explain why selling costs are high in monopolistic competition.

Study Guide pp. 187–189

Practice Online 12.2

Practice Problem 12.2

Bianca bakes delicious cookies. Her total fixed cost is $40 a day, and her average variable cost is $1 a bag. Few people know about Bianca's Cookies, and she is maximizing her profit by selling 10 bags a day for $5 a bag. Bianca thinks that if she spends $50 a day on advertising, she can increase her market and sell 25 bags a day for $5 a bag.

a. If Bianca's belief about the effect of advertising is correct, can she increase her economic profit by advertising?

b. If she advertised, would her average total cost increase or decrease at the quantity produced?

c. If Bianca's belief about the effect of advertising is correct, would she continue to sell her cookies for $5 a bag, or would she raise or lower her price?

Exercise 12.2

Bianca—the same Bianca as in the Practice Problem—changes the recipe that she uses and now bakes even more delicious cookies. Bianca's costs don't change, but people love her new cookies and think that they are much better than those of the other cookie producers.

a. How will the change described here affect Bianca's price, quantity produced, and economic profit?

b. Can she still increase her economic profit by advertising?

Solution to Practice Problem 12.2

a. With no advertising, Bianca's total revenue is $50 (10 bags at $5 a bag) and her total cost is $50 (total fixed cost $40 and total variable cost $10). So her economic profit is zero.

With $50 a day advertising expenditure, Bianca has a total revenue of $125 (25 bags at $5) and total cost of $115 (total fixed cost is now $90, and total variable cost is now $25). Her economic profit with no price change is $10. So Bianca can increase her economic profit by advertising.

b. If Bianca advertises, her average total cost decreases. With no advertising, her average total cost is $5 a bag ($50 ÷ 10). With advertising, her average total cost is $4.60 a bag ($115 ÷ 25 bags).

c. We can't say whether she would continue to sell her cookies for $5 a bag. It would depend on how her demand curve shifts. Advertising costs are fixed costs, so they don't change marginal cost, which remains at $1 a bag. She will sell the profit-maximizing quantity (the quantity at which marginal revenue equals marginal cost) for the highest price she can.

12.3 OLIGOPOLY

Another type of market that stands between the extremes of perfect competition and monopoly is oligopoly. *Oligopoly* is a market structure in which:

- A small number of firms compete.
- Natural or legal barriers prevent the entry of new firms.

Oligopoly is a market with a small number of firms, and each firm is large and can influence the market price. In any market, the price depends on the total quantity supplied. In monopoly, one firm controls this quantity and so also controls the price. In perfect competition, no firm is big enough to influence the total quantity supplied, so no firm can influence the price. Oligopoly is unlike both of these cases. More than one firm controls the quantity supplied, so no *one* firm controls the price. But each firm is large, and the quantity produced by each firm influences the price.

Like monopoly, the firms in an oligopoly operate behind a barrier to entry. And also like monopoly, the barriers to entry can arise for either natural reasons or legal reasons. A natural oligopoly is a market in which economies of scale exist but the output of a few firms is required to meet the market demand at the lowest possible cost. One firm could not meet the market demand at as low a price as a few firms could. But economies of scale are sufficiently large that more than a few firms could not survive and earn a normal profit.

A legal oligopoly arises when a legal barrier to entry protects the small number of firms in a market. A city might license two taxi firms, or two bus companies, for example.

Firms in an oligopoly might produce identical or differentiated products.

The problem for a firm in oligopoly is that its own profit-maximizing actions might decrease the profits of its competitors. But if each firm's actions decrease the profits of the other firms, all the firms end up with a lower profit.

Collusion

Cartel
A group of firms acting together to limit output, raise price, and increase economic profit.

One possible way of avoiding a self-defeating outcome is for the firms in an oligopoly to form a cartel. A **cartel** is a group of firms acting together—in collusion—to limit output, raise price, and increase economic profit. Cartels are illegal in the United States (and in most other countries) and are undertaken in secret. Firms in an oligopoly would like to be able to agree with each other to fix the price at a level that maximizes their joint profit.

Duopoly
A market in which there are only two producers.

It turns out that collusion usually breaks down. To understand why, and to learn how price and output are determined in an oligopoly, we're going to study a special case called duopoly. **Duopoly** is a market in which there are only two producers. You can probably see some examples of duopoly where you live. Many cities have only two local newspapers, two taxi companies, two copy centers, or two college bookstores. In the global economy, there are only two major producers of photographic film—Kodak and Fuji—and of commercial jet aircraft—Boeing in the United States and Airbus Industrie in Europe.

Although duopoly is common, the main reason for studying it is not its realism. We study it because it captures the essence of oligopoly and reveals the mutual interdependence of firms most effectively. Also, if collusion is difficult for a duopoly, it is even more difficult for an oligopoly with three or more firms.

Duopoly in Airplanes

Airbus and Boeing are the only makers of large commercial jet aircraft. Suppose that they have identical production costs. To keep things simple, we'll assume that the marginal cost of an airplane is $1 million and that total fixed cost is zero.

Figure 12.6 shows the market demand schedule and demand curve for airplanes. Airbus and Boeing must share this market. The total quantity of aircraft sold (and the quantities sold by each firm) depends on the price.

Competitive Outcome

If this industry had a large number of firms and was perfectly competitive, the marginal cost curve would be the industry supply curve. The equilibrium is where the industry supply curve (marginal cost curve) intersects the demand curve—12 airplanes a week would be sold for $1 million each. Total cost would be $12 million and total revenue would also be $12 million, so economic profit would be zero—a long-run equilibrium in perfect competition.

Monopoly Outcome

If this industry had only one firm, the firm would be a single-price monopoly because an airplane is a durable good that can be resold. The marginal revenue curve would be the one shown in Figure 12.6. Marginal revenue equals marginal cost when 6 airplanes a week are produced and the price is $13 million per airplane. Total cost would be $6 million and total revenue would be $78 million, so economic profit would be $72 million a week.

FIGURE 12.6
A Market for Airplanes

Practice Online

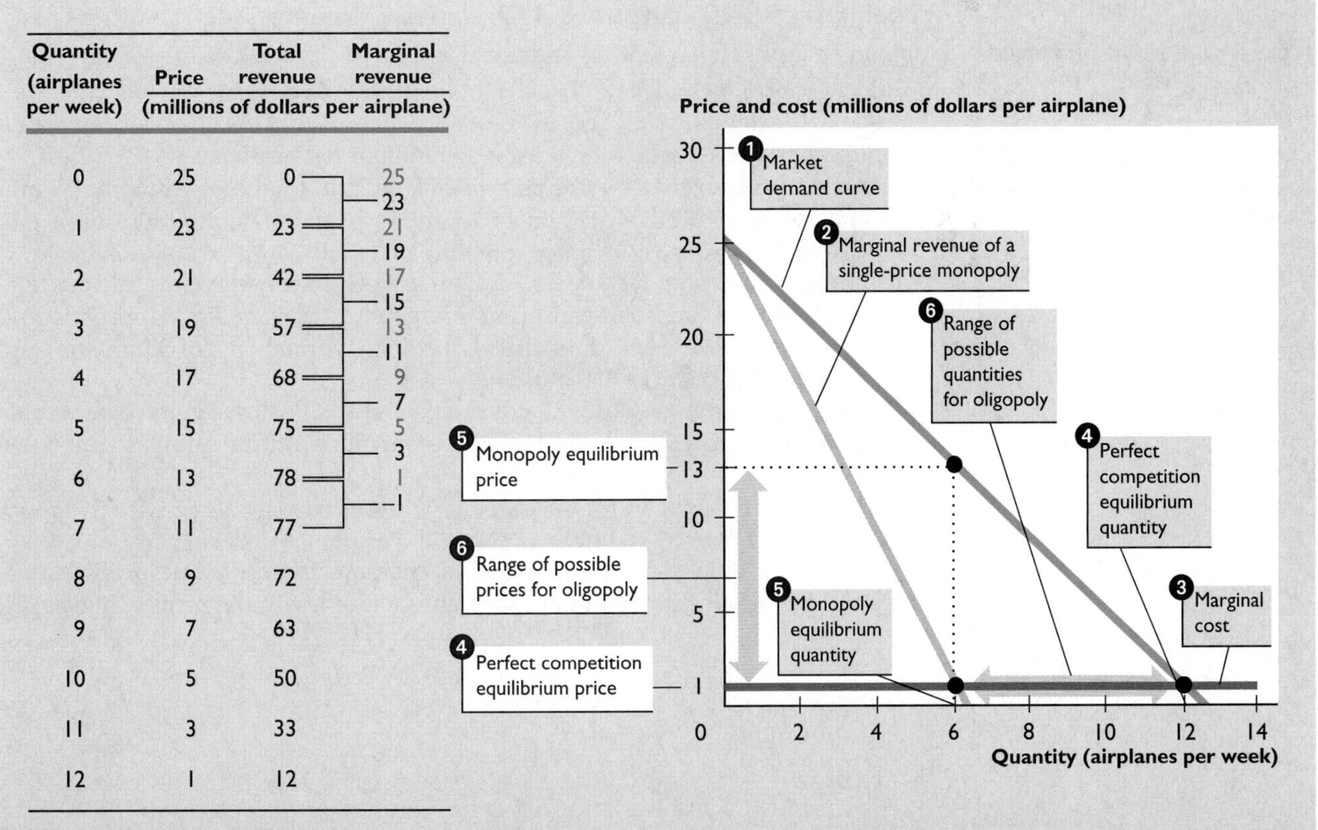

Quantity (airplanes per week)	Price (millions of dollars per airplane)	Total revenue (millions of dollars per airplane)	Marginal revenue (millions of dollars per airplane)
0	25	0	25
			23
1	23	23	21
			19
2	21	42	17
			15
3	19	57	13
			11
4	17	68	9
			7
5	15	75	5
			3
6	13	78	1
			–1
7	11	77	
8	9	72	
9	7	63	
10	5	50	
11	3	33	
12	1	12	

Range of Possible Oligopoly Outcomes

Because oligopoly is a market structure that lies between perfect competition and monopoly, these extremes that we've just found provide the maximum range within which the oligopoly outcome might lie. If Airbus and Boeing persistently cut their prices to increase their production and quantity sold, they might drive the price down all the way to the perfectly competitive price and end up with no economic profit. In contrast, if the two firms were able to collude and set the monopoly price, they could end up sharing the maximum available monopoly profit.

The Duopolists' Dilemma

TABLE 12.1 MONOPOLY OUTCOME

	Boeing	Airbus	Market total
Quantity (airplanes a week)	3	3	6
Price ($ million per airplane)	13	13	13
Total revenue ($ million)	39	39	78
Total cost ($ million)	3	3	6
Economic profit ($ million)	36	36	72

You've just seen that if this industry had only one firm, 6 airplanes a week would be produced and the price of an airplane would be $13 million. Economic profit would be $72 million a week. If this same outcome could be achieved with two firms in the industry, Airbus and Boeing might each produce 3 airplanes a week and make an economic profit of $36 million each (see Table 12.1).

Because this outcome is the one that maximizes monopoly profit, we know that there is no better outcome for the two firms in total. That is, their joint profits cannot be any higher than the $72 million a week that a monopoly can achieve.

But can one firm make a larger profit than $36 million a week at the expense of the other firm? To answer this question, we need to see what happens if one of the firms increases output by 1 airplane a week. Because the two firms in this example are identical, we can explore this question with either Boeing or Airbus increasing production by 1 airplane a week and the other holding output at 3 a week. We'll suppose that Boeing increases output to 4 airplanes a week and Airbus at first continues to produce 3 airplanes a week.

Boeing Increases Output to 4 Airplanes a Week

TABLE 12.2 BOEING INCREASES OUTPUT TO 4 AIRPLANES A WEEK

	Boeing	Airbus	Market total
Quantity (airplanes a week)	4	3	7
Price ($ million per airplane)	11	11	11
Total revenue ($ million)	44	33	77
Total cost ($ million)	4	3	7
Economic profit ($ million)	40	30	70

Table 12.2 shows what happens if Boeing produces 4 airplanes a week and Airbus produces 3 airplanes a week. To sell a total output of 7 airplanes a week, the price must fall. The demand schedule in Figure 12.6 tells us that the quantity demanded is 7 airplanes a week when the price is $11 million per airplane.

Market total revenue would now be $77 million, total cost would be $7 million, and economic profit would fall to $70 million. But the distribution of this economic profit is now unequal. Boeing would gain, and Airbus would lose.

Boeing would now receive $44 million a week in total revenue, have a total cost of $4 million, and earn an economic profit of $40 million. Airbus would receive $33 million a week in total revenue, incur a total cost of $3 million, and earn an economic profit of $30 million.

So by increasing its output by 1 airplane a week, Boeing can increase its economic profit by $4 million and cause the economic profit of Airbus to fall by $6 million.

This situation is better for Boeing, but would Airbus go along with it? Would it be in Airbus's interest to hold its output at 3 airplanes a week?

To answer this question, we need to compare the economic profit Airbus makes if it maintains its output at 3 airplanes a week with the profit it makes if it produces 4 airplanes a week. How much economic profit does Airbus make if it produces 4 airplanes a week with Boeing also producing 4 a week?

Airbus Increases Output to 4 Airplanes a Week

With both firms producing 4 airplanes a week, total output is 8 airplanes a week. To sell 8 airplanes a week, the price must fall further. The demand schedule in Figure 12.6 tells us that the quantity demanded is 8 airplanes a week when the price is $9 million per airplane.

Table 12.3 keeps track of the data. Market total revenue would now be $72 million, total cost would be $8 million, and economic profit would fall to $64 million. With both firms producing the same output, the distribution of this economic profit is now equal.

Both firms would now receive $36 million a week in total revenue, have a total cost of $4 million, and earn an economic profit of $32 million. For Airbus, this outcome is an improvement on the previous one by $2 million a week. For Boeing, this outcome is worse than the previous one by $8 million a week.

This situation is better for Airbus, but would Boeing go along with it? You know that Boeing would be worse off if it decreased its output to 3 airplanes a week because it would get the outcome that Airbus has in Table 12.2—an economic profit of only $30 million a week. But would Boeing be better off if it increased output to 5 airplanes a week?

TABLE 12.3 AIRBUS INCREASES OUTPUT TO 4 AIRPLANES A WEEK

	Boeing	Airbus	Market total
Quantity (airplanes a week)	4	4	8
Price ($ million per airplane)	9	9	9
Total revenue ($ million)	36	36	72
Total cost ($ million)	4	4	8
Economic profit ($ million)	32	32	64

Boeing Increases Output to 5 Airplanes a Week

To answer the question we've just posed, we need to calculate Boeing's economic profit if Airbus maintains its output at 4 airplanes a week and Boeing increases output to 5 a week.

Table 12.4 keeps track of the data. Total output is now 9 airplanes a week. To sell this quantity, the price must fall to $7 million per airplane. Market total revenue is $63 million and total cost is $9 million, so economic profit for the two firms is $54 million. The distribution of this economic profit is again unequal. But now both firms would lose.

Boeing would now receive $35 million a week in total revenue, have a total cost of $5 million, and earn an economic profit of $30 million—$2 million less than if it maintained its output at 4 airplanes a week (in Table 12.3). Airbus would receive $28 million a week in total revenue, incur a total cost of $4 million, and earn an economic profit of $24 million—$8 million less than before.

So neither firm can gain by increasing output beyond 4 airplanes a week. But there is a dilemma. If both firms stick to the monopoly output, they both produce 3 airplanes and make $36 million. If they both increase production to 4 airplanes a week, they both make $32 million. If only one of them increases production to 4 airplanes a week, that firm makes an economic profit of $40 million while the one that keeps production constant at 3 airplanes makes a lower economic profit of $30 million. So what will the firms do?

We can speculate about what they will do. But to work out the answer, we need to use some game theory. We'll leave the question that we've just asked dangling and return to it after we've learned the basic ideas about game theory that we need.

TABLE 12.4 BOEING INCREASES OUTPUT TO 5 AIRPLANES A WEEK

	Boeing	Airbus	Market total
Quantity (airplanes a week)	5	4	9
Price ($ million per airplane)	7	7	7
Total revenue ($ million)	35	28	63
Total cost ($ million)	5	4	9
Economic profit ($ million)	30	24	54

CHECKPOINT 12.3

Study Guide pp. 190–192

Practice Online 12.3

TABLE 1

Price (dollars per unit)	Quantity demanded (units per day)
12	0
11	1
10	2
9	3
8	4
7	5
6	6
5	7
4	8
3	9
2	10
1	11
0	12

TABLE 2

Quantity (units per day)	Total revenue (dollars per day)	Marginal revenue (dollars per unit)
0	0	
		11
1	11	
		9
2	20	
		7
3	27	
		5
4	32	
		3
5	35	
		1
6	36	
		–1
7	35	
		–3
8	32	
		–5
9	27	
		–7
10	20	
		–9
11	11	
		–11
12	0	

3 **Explain the dilemma faced by firms in oligopoly.**

Practice Problem 12.3

Isolated Island has two natural gas wells, one owned by Tom and the other owned by Jerry. Each well has a valve that controls the rate of flow of gas, and the marginal cost of producing gas is zero. Table 1 gives the demand schedule for gas on this island. What will the price of gas be on Isolated Island if Tom and Jerry:

a. Form a cartel and maximize their joint profit?
b. Are forced to sell at the perfectly competitive price?
c. Compete as duopolists?

Exercises 12.3

1. A third gas well is discovered on Isolated Island, and Joey owns it. There is no change in the demand for gas, and Joey's cost of production is zero, like Tom's and Jerry's costs. Now what is the price of gas on Isolated Island if Tom, Jerry, and Joey:
   a. Form a cartel and maximize their joint profit?
   b. Are forced to sell at the perfectly competitive price?
2. Kodak and Fuji are the only major producers of high-speed photo film. Each company has developed a fast-speed film and aggressively advertises it. The two firms are locked in a duopolists' dilemma.
   a. Describe the dilemma facing Kodak and Fuji.
   b. Suppose that Fuji and Kodak were to secretly from a cartel. What do you predict would:
      i. Happen to the price of film?
      ii. Be the change in the two firms' advertising and research and development budgets?

Solution to Practice Problem 12.3

a. If Tom and Jerry form a cartel and maximize their joint profit, they will charge the monopoly price. This price is the highest price that the market will bear when the quantity produced makes marginal revenue equal to marginal cost. Marginal cost is zero, so we need to find the quantity at which marginal revenue is zero. Marginal revenue is zero when total revenue is a maximum, which occurs when output is 6 units a day (see Table 2). The highest price at which 6 units a day can be sold is $6 a unit (see the demand schedule in Table 1).

b. The perfectly competitive price equals marginal cost, which is zero. In this case, output is 12 units a day.

c. If Tom and Jerry compete as duopolists, they will increase production above the monopoly level, but they will not drive the price down to zero.

12.4 GAME THEORY

Game theory is the main tool that economists use to analyze *strategic behavior*—behavior that recognizes mutual interdependence and takes account of the expected behavior of others. John von Neumann invented game theory in 1937, and today it is a major research field in economics.

Game theory
The tool that economists use to analyze *strategic behavior*—behavior that recognizes mutual interdependence and takes account of the expected behavior of others.

Game theory seeks to understand oligopoly and all other forms of economic, political, social, and even biological rivalries. Game theory uses a method of analysis specifically designed to understand games of all types, including the familiar games of everyday life. We will begin our study of game theory and its application to the behavior of firms by thinking about familiar games.

What Is a Game?

What is a game? At first thought, the question seems silly. After all, there are many different games. There are ball games and parlor games, games of chance and games of skill. But what is it about all these different activities that make them games? What do all these games have in common? All games share three features:

- Rules
- Strategies
- Payoffs

Let's see how these common features of games apply to a game called "the prisoners' dilemma." The **prisoners' dilemma** is a game between two prisoners that shows why it is hard to cooperate, even when it would be beneficial to both players to do so. This game captures the essential feature of the duopolists' dilemma that we've just been studying. The prisoners' dilemma also provides a good illustration of how game theory works and how it generates predictions.

Prisoners' dilemma
A game between two prisoners that shows why it is hard to cooperate, even when it would be beneficial to both players to do so.

The Prisoners' Dilemma

Art and Bob have been caught red-handed, stealing a car. Facing airtight cases, they will receive a sentence of 2 years for their crime. During his interviews with the two prisoners, the district attorney begins to suspect that he has stumbled on the two people who were responsible for a multimillion-dollar bank robbery some months earlier. But this is just a suspicion. The district attorney has no evidence on which he can convict them of the greater crime unless he can get them to confess. The district attorney decides to make the prisoners play a game with the following rules.

Rules

Each prisoner (player) is placed in a separate room and cannot communicate with the other player. Each is told that he is suspected of having carried out the bank robbery and that

- If both of them confess to the larger crime, each will receive a sentence of 3 years for both crimes.
- If he alone confesses and his accomplice does not, he will receive an even shorter sentence of 1 year, while his accomplice will receive a 10-year sentence.

Strategies

Strategies
All the possible actions of each player in a game.

In game theory, **strategies** are all the possible actions of each player. Art and Bob each have two possible actions:

- Confess to the bank robbery.
- Deny having committed the bank robbery.

Payoffs

Payoff matrix
A table that shows the payoffs for every possible action by each player given every possible action by the other player.

Because there are two players, each with two strategies, there are four possible outcomes:

- Both confess.
- Both deny.
- Art confesses and Bob denies.
- Bob confesses and Art denies.

Each prisoner can work out exactly what happens to him—his *payoff*—in each of these four situations. We can tabulate the four possible payoffs for each of the prisoners in what is called a payoff matrix for the game. A **payoff matrix** is a table that shows the payoffs for every possible action by each player given every possible action by the other player.

Table 12.5 shows a payoff matrix for Art and Bob. The squares show the payoffs for each prisoner: The red triangle in each square shows Art's, and the blue triangle shows Bob's. If both prisoners confess (top left), each gets a prison term of 3 years. If Bob confesses but Art denies (top right), Art gets a 10-year sentence and Bob gets a 1-year sentence. If Art confesses and Bob denies (bottom left), Art gets a 1-year sentence and Bob gets a 10-year sentence. Finally, if both of them deny (bottom right), neither can be convicted of the bank robbery charge but both are sentenced for the car theft—a 2-year sentence.

TABLE 12.5 PRISONERS' DILEMMA PAYOFF MATRIX

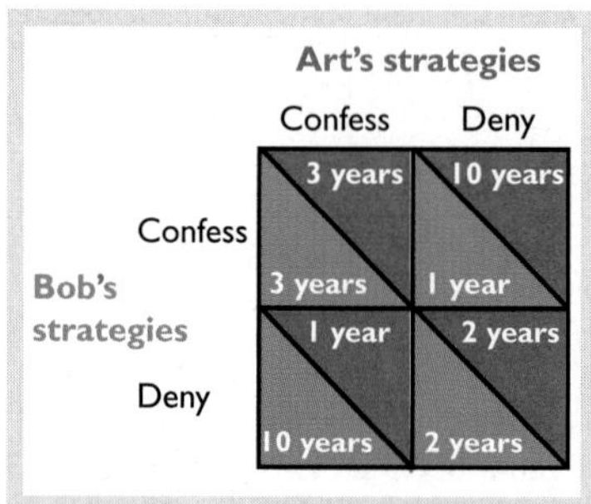

Each square shows the payoffs for the two players, Art and Bob, for each possible pair of actions. In each square, the red triangle shows Art's payoff and the blue triangle shows Bob's. For example, if both confess, the payoffs are in the top left square.

Equilibrium

Nash equilibrium
An equilibrium in which each player takes the best possible action given the action of the other player.

The equilibrium of a game occurs when each player takes the best possible action given the action of the other player. This equilibrium concept is called **Nash equilibrium**. It is so named because John Nash of Princeton University, who received the Nobel Prize for Economic Science in 1994, proposed it.

In the case of the prisoners' dilemma, equilibrium occurs when Art makes his best choice given Bob's choice and when Bob makes his best choice given Art's choice. Let's find the equilibrium.

First, look at the situation from Art's point of view. If Bob confesses, it pays Art to confess because in that case, he is sentenced to 3 years rather than 10 years. If Bob denies, it still pays Art to confess because in that case he receives 1 year rather than 2 years. So no matter what Bob does, Art's best action is to confess.

Second, look at the situation from Bob's point of view. If Art confesses, it pays Bob to confess because in that case, he is sentenced to 3 years rather than 10 years. If Art denies, it still pays Bob to confess because in that case he receives 1 year rather than 2 years. So no matter what Art does, Bob's best action is to confess.

Because each player's best action is to confess, each does confess, each gets a 3-year prison term, and the district attorney has solved the bank robbery. This is the equilibrium of the game.

Not the Best Outcome

The equilibrium of the prisoners' dilemma game is not the best outcome. Isn't there some way in which the prisoners can cooperate and get the smaller sentence? There is not, because they cannot communicate with each other. Each player can put himself in the other player's place and can figure out what the other will do. The prisoners are indeed in a dilemma. Each knows that he can serve only 2 years if he can trust the other to deny. But each also knows that it is not in the best interest of the other to deny. So each prisoner knows that he must confess, thereby delivering a bad outcome for both.

Let's now see how we can use the ideas we've just developed to understand the behavior of firms in oligopoly. We'll start by returning to the duopolists' dilemma.

The Duopolists' Dilemma as a Game

The dilemma of Airbus and Boeing is similar to that of Art and Bob. Each firm has two strategies. It can produce airplanes at the rate of

- 3 a week
- 4 a week

Because each firm has two strategies, there are four possible combinations of actions for the two firms:

- Both firms produce 3 a week (monopoly outcome).
- Both firms produce 4 a week.
- Airbus produces 3 a week and Boeing produces 4 a week.
- Boeing produces 3 a week and Airbus produces 4 a week.

TABLE 12.6 DUOPOLISTS' DILEMMA PAYOFF MATRIX

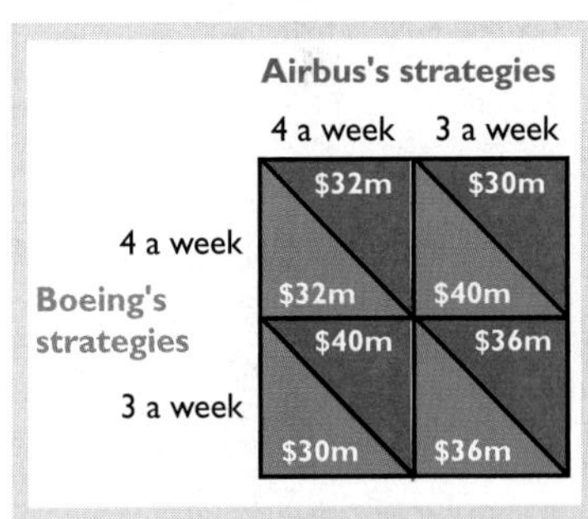

Each square shows the payoffs from a pair of actions. For example, if both firms produce 3 airplanes a week, the payoffs are recorded in the bottom right square. The red triangle shows Airbus's payoff, and the blue triangle shows Boeing's.

The Payoff Matrix

Table 12.6 sets out the payoff matrix for this game. It is constructed in exactly the same way as the payoff matrix for the prisoners' dilemma in Table 12.5. The squares show the payoffs for Airbus and Boeing. In this case, the payoffs are economic profits. (In the case of the prisoners' dilemma, the payoffs were losses.)

The table shows that if both firms produce 4 a week (top left), each makes an economic profit of $32 million. If both firms produce 3 a week (bottom right), they make the monopoly profit, and each firm earns an economic profit of $36 million. The top right and bottom left squares show what happens if one firm produces 4 a week while the other produces 3 a week. The firm that increases production makes an economic profit of $40 million, and the one that keeps production at the monopoly quantity makes an economic profit of $30 million.

Equilibrium of the Duopolists' Dilemma

What do the firms do? To answer this question, we must find the equilibrium of the duopoly game.

TABLE 12.7 DUOPOLISTS' DILEMMA'S EQUILIBRIUM

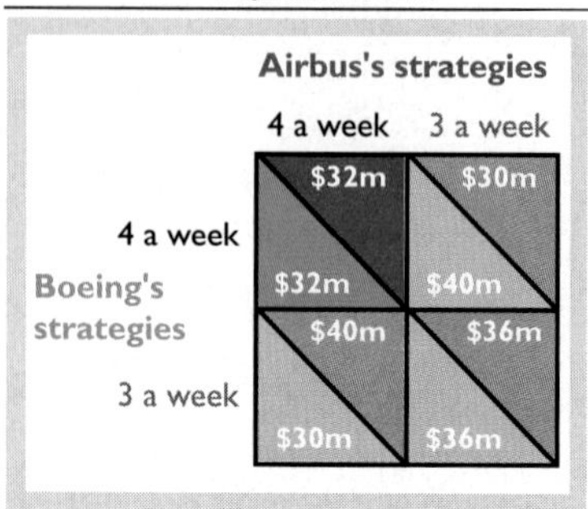

The equilibrium is a Nash equilibrium in which both firms produce 4 airplanes a week.

Using the information in Table 12.7, look at things from Airbus's point of view. Airbus reasons as follows: Suppose that Boeing produces 4 planes a week. If I produce 3 a week, I will make an economic profit of $30 million. If I also produce 4 a week, I will make an economic profit of $32 million. So I'm better off producing 4 a week. Airbus continues to reason: Now suppose Boeing produce 3 planes a week. If I produce 4 a week, I will make an economic profit of $40 million, and if I produce 3 a week, I will make an economic profit of $36 million. An economic profit of $40 million is better than an economic profit of $36 million, so I'm better off if I produce 4 a week. So regardless of whether Boeing produces 4 planes a week or 3 planes a week, it pays Airbus to produce 4 planes a week.

Because the two firms face identical situations, Boeing comes to the same conclusion as Airbus. So both firms produce 4 a week. The equilibrium of the duopoly game is that both firms produce 4 a week.

So, like the prisoners, the duopolists fail to cooperate and get a worse outcome than the one that cooperation would deliver.

Repeated Games

The games that we've studied are played just once. In contrast, most real-world games get played repeatedly. This fact suggests that real-world duopolists might find some way of learning to cooperate so that they can enjoy a monopoly profit.

If a game is played repeatedly, one player has the opportunity to penalize the other player for previous "bad" behavior. If Airbus produces 4 airplanes this week, perhaps Boeing will produce 4 next week. Before Airbus produces 4 this week, won't it take account of the possibility of Boeing producing 4 next week? What is the equilibrium of this more complicated dilemma game when it is repeated indefinitely?

The monopoly equilibrium may occur if each firm knows that the other will punish overproduction with overproduction—"tit for tat." Let's see why.

If both firms produce 3 airplanes in week 1, each makes an economic profit of $36 million. Suppose that Boeing contemplates producing 4 airplanes in week 2. This move will bring it an economic profit of $40 million and cut the economic profit of Airbus to $30 million. In week 3, Airbus punishes Boeing and produces 4 airplanes. But Boeing must go back to 3 airplanes to induce Airbus to cooperate again in week 4. Airbus now makes an economic profit of $40 million, and Boeing makes an economic profit of $30 million. Adding up the profits over three weeks of play, Boeing would have made $108 million by cooperating (3 × $36 million) compared with $106 million from producing 4 in week 2 and generating Airbus's tit-for-tat response.

What is true for Boeing is also true for Airbus. Because each firm makes a larger profit by sticking to the monopoly output, both firms do so, and the monopoly price, quantity, and profit prevail.

In reality, whether a duopoly (or more generally an oligopoly) works like a one-play game or a repeated game depends primarily on the number of players and the ease of detecting and punishing overproduction. The larger the number of players, the harder it is to maintain the monopoly outcome.

Eye on the Global Economy

Duopoly in Computer CPUs

The CPU in your computer is the central brainpower of the machine. Until 1995, one firm produced all the CPU chips in PCs—Intel Corporation. Intel made a large economic profit by producing the quantity of chips at which marginal cost equaled marginal revenue and pricing the chips to ensure that the quantity demanded equaled the profit-maximizing quantity produced.

Then, in 1995, a small number of new firms entered the industry. One of them, Advanced Micro Devices, Inc. (AMD), quickly established itself as a serious challenger to Intel.

But in terms of market share and profit share, Intel dominates this market, as the pie chart shows. In 2000, both firms had a global market, with 55 percent of Intel's total revenue and 60 percent of AMD's total revenue coming from outside the United States.

If, as new firms entered this industry, they had maintained Intel's price and shared the market, together they could have made economic profits equal to Intel's profit. But AMD and Intel were (and remain) in a duopolists' dilemma. Intel has no interest in sharing its market with another producer. And to break into the market and take revenue and profit away from Intel, AMD must either offer a clearly superior product at the same price at Intel's or offer a similar product at a lower price.

AMD opted mainly for the second approach (although some chip experts say that AMD offers both a superior product and a lower price).

Setting aside the question of whether an AMD chip performs better than an Intel chip, it is clear that AMD has brought the price of CPU chips down.

The graph shows the prices of some of the most popular CPU chips in October 2002. Notice that at comparable clock speeds, AMD chips are cheaper than Intel chips.

Athlon chips, AMD's main range of chips, cost less than Intel Pentium chips of comparable speed.

At the low end of the product range, AMD Duron chips are substantially cheaper than Intel Pentium chips of comparable speed.

Notice, though, that to compete at this low end of the product range, Intel has introduced the Celeron processor at a similar price to that of the cheapest AMD chips.

Competition between Intel and AMD is like the duopolists' dilemma that you've studied in this chapter. The game is played on both price and product design and quality and across a range of differentiated products.

In 2002, Intel remained vastly bigger than AMD, and AMD had a tough year. Its total revenue fell in 2002, and its profit almost vanished. Intel's total revenue was steady, but its profit also shrank. Before 2002, AMD was growing much faster than Intel.

This duopoly is going to be an interesting one to keep an eye on.

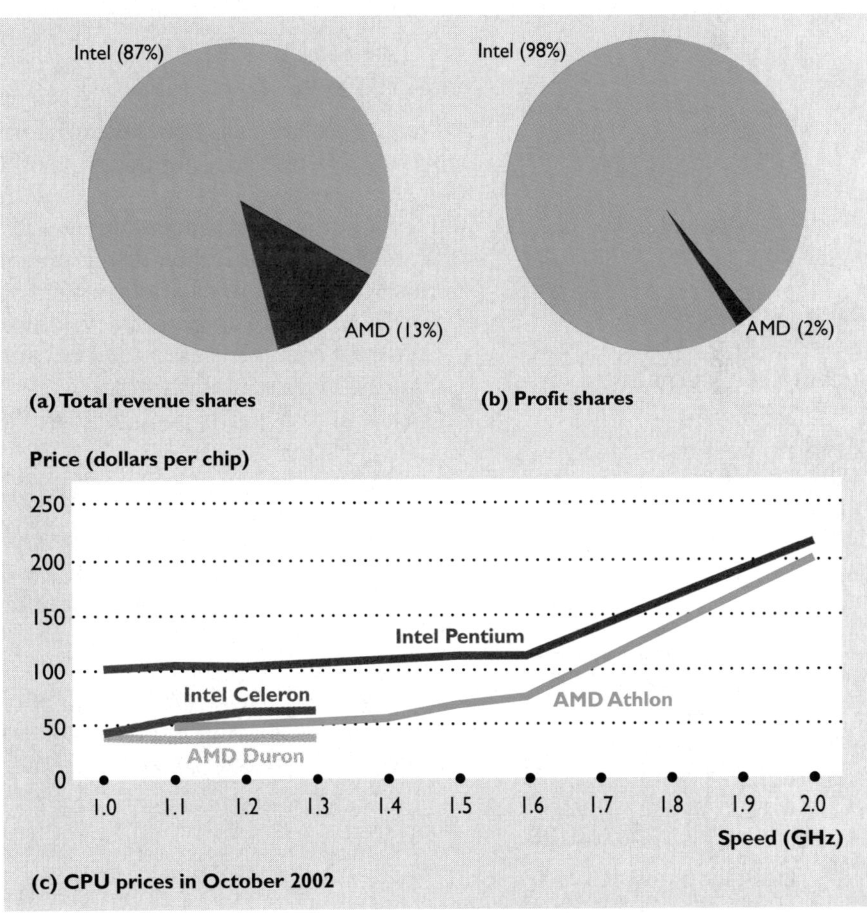

(a) Total revenue shares

(b) Profit shares

(c) CPU prices in October 2002

CHECKPOINT 12.4

Study Guide pp. 192–194

Practice Online 12.4

4 **Use game theory to explain how price and quantity are determined in oligopoly.**

Practice Problem 12.4

Bud and Wise are the only two makers of aniseed beer, a new-age product designed to displace root beer. Bud and Wise are trying to figure out how much of this new beer to produce. They each know that if they both limit production to 10,000 gallons a day, they will make the maximum attainable joint profit of $200,000 a day—$100,000 a day each. They also know that if either of them produces 20,000 gallons a day while the other produces 10,000 a day, economic profit will be $150,000 for the one that produces 20,000 gallons and an economic loss of $50,000 for the one that sticks with 10,000 gallons. And they also know that if they both increase production to 20,000 gallons a day, they will both earn zero economic profit.

a. Construct a payoff matrix for the game that Bud and Wise must play.
b. Find the Nash equilibrium.
c. What is the equilibrium if this game is played repeatedly?

Exercise 12.4

Bud and Wise are racing to develop a new brand of coconut milk that they both believe will be the next big thing in soft drinks. Bud and Wise each know that if they both spend $1 million a week on development, they will both develop the new milk at the same time and they will both earn zero economic profit from the milk and never recover their development cost. They also know that if one of them spends $1 million a week and the other spends nothing, the one that develops the new milk will make an economic profit of $2 million a week.

a. Construct a payoff matrix for this game.
b. Find the Nash equilibrium.
c. Is there any chance of cooperation in this research and development game?

Solution to Practice Problem 12.4

a. Table 1 is the payoff matrix for the game that Bud and Wise must play.
b. The Nash equilibrium is for both to produce 20,000 gallons. To see why, notice that regardless of the quantity that Bud produces, Wise makes more profit by producing 20,000 gallons. The same is true for Bud. So Bud and Wise each produce 20,000 gallons a day.
c. If this game is played repeatedly, both Bud and Wise produce the monopoly output of 10,000 gallons a day and earn maximum economic profit. They can achieve this outcome by playing a tit-for-tat strategy.

TABLE 1

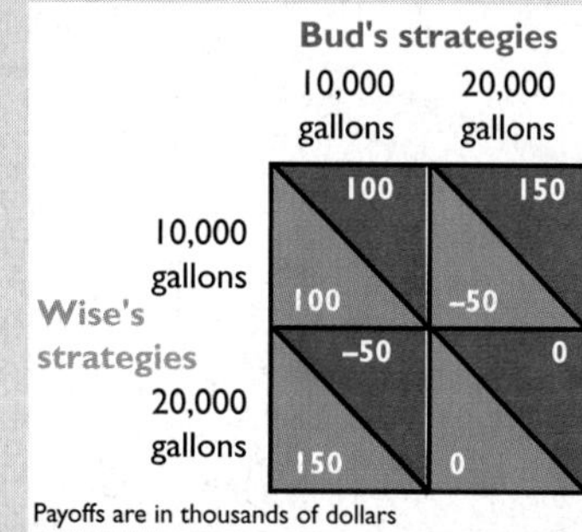

	Bud's strategies: 10,000 gallons	Bud's strategies: 20,000 gallons
Wise's strategies: 10,000 gallons	Bud 100, Wise 100	Bud 150, Wise −50
Wise's strategies: 20,000 gallons	Bud −50, Wise 150	Bud 0, Wise 0

Payoffs are in thousands of dollars

CHAPTER CHECKPOINT

Key Points

1 Explain how price and quantity are determined in monopolistic competition.

- Firms in monopolistic competition face downward-sloping demand curves and produce the quantity at which marginal revenue equals marginal cost.
- Entry and exit result in zero economic profit and excess capacity in long-run equilibrium.

2 Explain why selling costs are high in monopolistic competition.

- Firms in monopolistic competition innovate and develop new products to maintain economic profit.
- Advertising expenditures increase total cost, but they might lower average total cost if they increase the quantity sold by a large enough amount.
- Advertising expenditures might increase demand, but they might also decrease the demand facing a firm by increasing competition.
- Whether monopolistic competition is inefficient depends on the value people place on product variety.

3 Explain the dilemma faced by firms in oligopoly.

- Firms in oligopoly would make the same economic profit as a monopoly if they could act together to restrict output to the monopoly level.
- Each firm can make a larger profit by increasing production, but this action damages the economic profit of other firms.

4 Use game theory to explain how price and quantity are determined in oligopoly.

- Game theory is a method of analyzing strategic behavior.
- In a prisoners' dilemma, two prisoners acting in their own interest harm their joint interest.
- An oligopoly (duopoly) game is like the prisoners' dilemma.
- The firms might cooperate to produce the monopoly output or overproduce.
- In a one-play game, both firms overproduce, and the price and economic profit are less than they would be in monopoly.
- In a repeated game, a punishment strategy can produce a monopoly output, price, and economic profit.

Key Terms

Capacity output, 305
Cartel, 312
Duopoly, 312
Four-firm concentration ratio, 302
Game theory, 317
Herfindahl-Hirschman Index, 302
Nash equilibrium, 318
Payoff matrix, 318
Prisoners' dilemma, 317
Product differentiation, 300
Strategies, 318

Exercises

1. Which of the following goods and services are sold by firms in monopolistic competition?
   a. Cable television service
   b. Wheat
   c. Athletic shoes
   d. Soda
   e. Shaving cream
   f. Toothbrushes
   g. Ready-mix concrete
   Explain your selections.

2. The four-firm concentration ratio for audio equipment makers is 30 and for electric lamp makers is 89. The HHI for audio equipment makers is 415 and for electric lamp makers is 2,850. Which of these markets is an example of monopolistic competition?

FIGURE 1

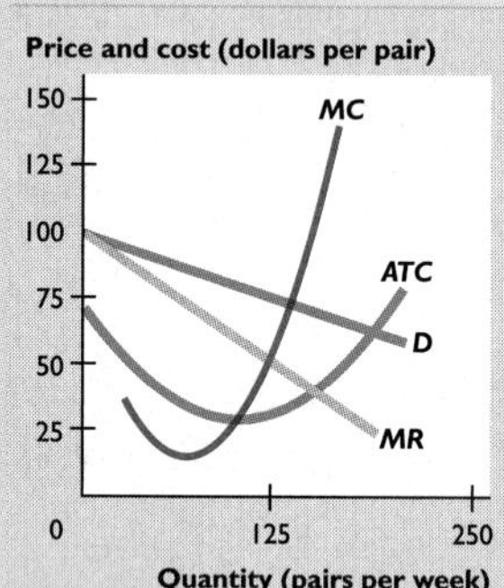

3. Figure 1 shows the demand, marginal revenue, and cost curves of Lite and Kool, Inc., a producer of running shoes in monopolistic competition.
   a. What quantity does Lite and Kool produce?
   b. What price does it charge?
   c. What is Lite and Kool's markup?
   d. How much profit does Lite and Kool make?
   e. Do firms in monopolistic competition always have excess capacity?
   f. Explain why Lite and Kool does or does not have excess capacity.
   g. Do you expect firms to enter the running shoes market or exit from that market in the long run? Explain your answer.

FIGURE 2

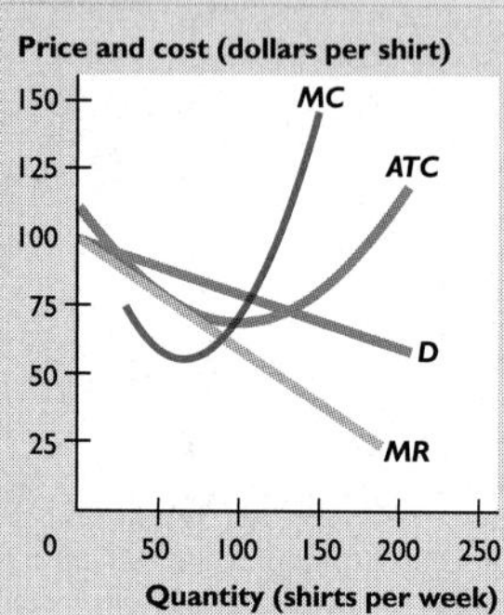

4. Figure 2 shows the demand curve, marginal revenue curve, and cost curves of Stiff Shirt, Inc., a producer of shirts in monopolistic competition.
   a. Show on the graph the quantity that Stiff Shirt produces.
   b. Show on the graph the price that Stiff Shirt charges.
   c. Show on the graph Stiff Shirt's markup.
   d. Show on the graph Stiff Shirt's profit.
   e. Does Stiff Shirt have excess capacity?
   f. If Stiff Shirt increased output, would its average total cost fall or rise?
   g. In light of your answer to part **f**, why doesn't Stiff Shirt increase its output?
   h. Do you expect firms to enter the shirt market or exit from that market in the long run? Explain your answer.
   i. Do you expect the price of a shirt to rise or fall in the long run? Explain your answer.

5. Jeb and George are discussing their respective businesses. Jeb says that there is no way he could lower his average total cost. He wouldn't be able to hold his costs to their current level if he either increased or decreased his production. George says that he is frustrated by the level of demand for his product and that he could cut his costs if only he could sell more. One of these people runs a diner, and the other is a wheat farmer.
   a. Who is which and why?
   b. What does this conversation imply about the efficiency of wheat farms and diners?
   c. What does this conversation imply about the economic profit earned by wheat farms and diners?

6. Mike's, a firm in monopolistic competition, produces running shoes. With no advertising, Mike's profit-maximizing output is 500 pairs a day and the price is $100 a pair. But the firms in this market begin to advertise, and so does Mike's. With advertising, Mike's profit-maximizing output increases to 1,000 pairs a day, but the price falls to $50 a pair.
   a. Sketch a demand, marginal revenue, average total cost, and marginal cost curves that are consistent with the no-advertising situation described.
   b. Sketch a demand, marginal revenue, average total cost, and marginal cost curves that are consistent with the advertising situation described.
   c. In which situation does Mike's have the larger markup?
   d. In which situation does Mike's have the larger excess capacity?

7. Isolated Island has two taxi companies, one owned by Ann and the other owned by Zack. Figure 3 shows the demand curve for taxi rides, *D*, and the average total cost curve of one of the firms, *ATC*.
   a. If Ann and Zack produce the same quantity of rides as would be produced in perfect competition, what are the quantity of rides, the price of a ride, and the economic profit of Ann and Zack?
   b. If Ann and Zack form a cartel and produce the same quantity of rides as would be produced in monopoly, what are the quantity of rides, the price of a ride, and the economic profit of Ann and Zack?
   c. Would Ann and Zack have an incentive to break the cartel agreement and cut their price to increase the number of rides? Explain why or why not.

FIGURE 3

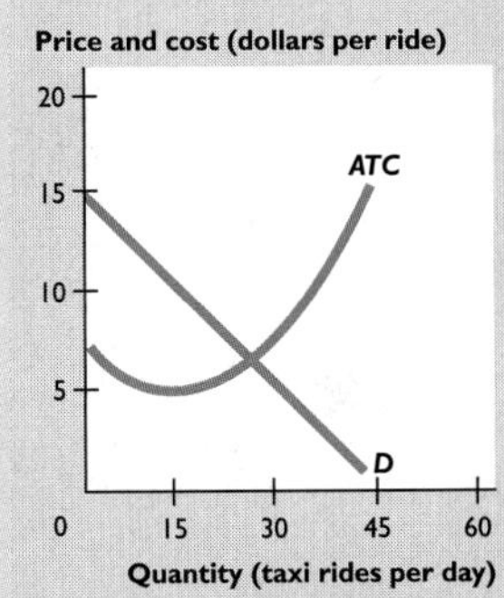

8. Use the information about Isolated Island in exercise 7. Suppose that Ann and Zack have two strategies: collude, fix the monopoly price, and limit the number of rides or break the collusion, cut the price, and produce more rides.
   a. Create a payoff matrix for the game that Ann and Zack play.
   b. Find the Nash equilibrium for this game if it is played just once.

9. Jenny loves the movies (payoff of +100) and hates the ball game (payoff of –100). Joe loves the ball game (payoff of +100) and hates the movies (payoff of –100). But both Jenny and Joe prefer to go out together (bonus payoff of +100 each in addition to the payoff from the activity they choose). If they go out on their own, they get no bonus payoff.
   a. Make a payoff matrix of the game that Jenny and Joe play.
   b. Is this game similar to the prisoners' dilemma or different in some way?
   c. What is the Nash equilibrium? What do Jenny and Joe do? Does it make a difference if the game is repeated many times?
   d. Do Jenny and Joe get the best outcome for each of them?

10. The United States claims that Canada subsidizes the production of softwood lumber and that imports of Canadian lumber damage the interests of U.S. producers. The United States has imposed a high tariff on Canadian imports to counter the subsidy. Canada is thinking of retaliating by refusing to export water to California. Table 1 shows a payoff matrix for the game that the United States and Canada are playing.
   a. What is the United States' best strategy?
   b. What is Canada's best strategy?
   c. What is the outcome of this game? Explain.
   d. Is this game like a prisoners' dilemma or different in some crucial way? Explain.
   e. Which country would benefit more from a free trade agreement?

TABLE 1

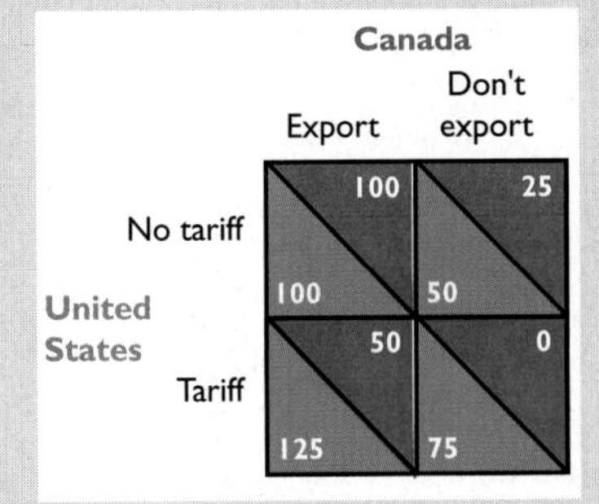

United States \ Canada	Export	Don't export
No tariff	Canada 100, US 100	Canada 25, US 50
Tariff	Canada 50, US 125	Canada 0, US 75

Critical Thinking

11. "Advertising and brand names are a social waste. We would be better off if brand names were not protected and if advertising were banned." Discuss these assertions, and in doing so, use the analysis of the effects of advertising and brand names presented in this chapter.

12. Do you think the market for word processing software such as Microsoft Word, Lotus WordPro, and WordPerfect is an example of oligopoly or monopolistic competition?
    a. Would consumers benefit from greater cooperation between software developers so that instead of having to choose among Microsoft Word, Lotus WordPro, and WordPerfect, they could buy just one word processor?
    b. What benefits do consumers enjoy with competition among software developers that would be lost from cooperation?
    c. Why (aside from the fact that it is illegal) is it impossible for software producers to collude and earn a larger economic profit?

13. Suppose that Netscape and Microsoft develop their own versions of a new Web browser that allows advertisers to target consumers with great precision. Advertisers pay Netscape or Microsoft a fee for providing this service. The new browser is easier and more fun to use than existing browsers. Each firm is trying to decide whether to sell the browser or to give it away.
    a. What are the possible benefits from each action?
    b. Sketch the payoff matrix for the game that Netscape and Microsoft must play.
    c. On the basis of your payoff matrix, what do Netscape and Microsoft do?

Practice Online

Web Exercises

Use the links on your Foundations Web site to work the following exercises.

14. Go to the U.S. Census Bureau and get the latest (1997) data on concentration ratios in manufacturing. Find, and explain your selections of,
    a. The four-firm concentration ratio and HHI for six consumer items that are examples of monopolistic competition.
    b. The four-firm concentration ratio and HHI for six consumer items that are too concentrated to be examples of monopolistic competition.
15. Visit the BBC and read the article on OPEC. Also visit OPEC and review the "About OPEC" pages.
    a. Is OPEC a cartel?
    b. What do you think OPEC's main objective is?
    c. What actions can OPEC take to achieve its main objective?
    d. What are the obstacles that OPEC must overcome?
    e. Use the ideas of the prisoners' dilemma to analyze the decisions of OPEC and its member countries.
    f. Use the ideas of the prisoners' dilemma to analyze the decisions of non-OPEC oil producers.
16. Visit EV World and read the article on ethanol price fixing by Archer Daniels Midland.
    a. Would you describe the market for ethanol as an oligopoly?
    b. What does the news article claim about the price of ethanol?
    c. Use the ideas of the prisoners' dilemma to analyze the decisions of Archer Daniels Midland and other producers of ethanol.

CHAPTER 13

GDP and the Standard of Living

CHAPTER CHECKLIST

When you have completed your study of this chapter, you will be able to

1. **Define GDP and explain why the value of production, income, and expenditure are the same for an economy.**
2. **Describe how economic statisticians measure GDP in the United States.**
3. **Distinguish between nominal GDP and real GDP and define the GDP deflator.**
4. **Explain and describe the limitations of real GDP as a measure of the standard of living.**

You've seen that equilibrium quantities and prices in the markets for goods, services, and factors of production determine *what, how,* and *for whom* goods and services are produced. What and for whom goods and services are produced influence the standard of living, a central concern of macroeconomics.

A focus on the standard of living directs our attention to the value of *total* production rather than the production of each individual good or service. You will discover that several different factors contribute to the standard of living, but one indicator dominates the others. It is called gross domestic product, or GDP. In this chapter, you will find out how economic statisticians measure GDP. You will also learn about other indicators of the standard of living as well as the scope and limitations of GDP as a measure of the standard of living.

13.1 GDP, INCOME, AND EXPENDITURE

How does your standard of living compare with that of your parents when they were your age? Who is better off: you or a college student in Beijing, China?

We defined the *standard of living* in Chapter 1 (p. 5) as the level of consumption of goods and services that people enjoy, *on the average*, measured by average income per person. So to answer the questions we've just posed, you might try to discover who has the higher income: you today or your parents in the 1970s, and you or a college student in China.

But it is the quantities of goods and services consumed that determine how well off people are. To consume goods and services, they must be produced. So another way to answer the questions posed is to discover who produces the greater total value of goods and services. Do we produce more per person today than our parents' generation did in the 1970s, and do we produce more per person than the people of China produce? To answer these questions, we need to measure total production.

GDP Defined

Gross domestic product (GDP)
The market value of all the final goods and services produced within a country in a given time period.

We measure total production as **gross domestic product**, or **GDP**, which is the market value of all the final goods and services produced within a country in a given time period. This definition has four parts that we'll examine in turn.

Value Produced

To measure total production, we must add together the production of apples and oranges, computers and popcorn. Just counting the items doesn't get us very far. Which is the greater total production: 100 apples and 50 oranges or 50 apples and 100 oranges?

GDP answers this question by valuing items at their *market value*—at the prices at which each item is traded in markets. If the price of an apple is 10 cents and the price of an orange is 20 cents, the market value of 100 apples plus 50 oranges is $20 and the market value of 50 apples and 100 oranges is $25. So by using market prices to value production, we can add the apples and oranges together.

What Produced

Final good or service
A good or service that is produced for its final user and not as a component of another good or service.

Intermediate good or service
A good or service that is produced by one firm, bought by another firm, and used as a component of a final good or service.

To calculate GDP, we value *all the final goods and services*. A **final good or service** is a good or service that is produced for its final user and not as a component of another good or service. It contrasts with an **intermediate good or service**, which is a good or service that is produced by one firm, bought by another firm, and used as a component of a final good or service. For example, a Ford SUV is a final good, but a Firestone tire on the SUV is an intermediate good.

GDP aims to be a full count of the value of everything that is produced. In practice, with one exception, GDP includes only those items that are traded in markets. It does not include the market value of goods and services that people produce for their own use. For example, GDP includes the value of a car wash that is bought but excludes the value of washing your own car. The exception is the market value of homes that people own. GDP puts a rental value on such homes and pretends that their owners rent them to themselves.

Where Produced

Only goods and services that are produced *within a country* count as part of that country's GDP. Nike Corporation, a U.S. firm, produces sneakers in Vietnam, and the market value of those shoes is part of Vietnam's GDP, not part of U.S. GDP. Toyota, a Japanese firm, produces automobiles in Georgetown, Kentucky, and the value of this production is part of U.S. GDP, not part of Japan's GDP.

When Produced

GDP measures the value of production *during a given time period*. This time period is either a quarter of a year—called the quarterly GDP data—or a year—called the annual GDP data. The Federal Reserve and others use the quarterly GDP data to keep track of the short-term evolution of the economy, and economists use the annual GDP data to examine long-term trends.

GDP measures not only the value of total production but also total income and total expenditure. The circular flow model that you studied in Chapter 2 explains why.

Circular Flows in the U.S. Economy

Four groups buy the final goods and services produced: households, firms, governments, and the rest of the world. Four types of expenditure correspond to these groups:

- Consumption expenditure
- Investment
- Government purchases of goods and services
- Net exports of goods and services

Consumption Expenditure

Consumption expenditure is the expenditure by households on consumption goods and services. It includes expenditures on popcorn and soda, candy and chocolate bars, and dental and dry cleaning services. Consumption expenditure also includes house and apartment rents, including the rental value of owner-occupied housing.

Consumption expenditure
The expenditure by households on consumption goods and services.

Investment

Investment is the purchase of new *capital goods* (tools, instruments, machines, buildings, and other constructions) and additions to inventories. Some firms produce capital goods, and other firms buy them. For example, IBM produces PCs and General Motors buys some of them; Boeing produces airplanes and United Airlines buys some of them.

Investment
The purchase of new *capital goods* (tools, instruments, machines, buildings, and other constructions) and additions to inventories.

Some of a firm's output might remain unsold at the end of a year. For example, if GM produces 4 million cars and sells 3.9 million of them, the other 0.1 million (100,000) cars remain unsold. In this case, GM's inventory of cars increases by 100,000. When a firm adds unsold output to inventory, we count those items as part of investment.

It is important to note that investment does *not* include the purchase of stocks and bonds. In macroeconomics, we reserve the term "investment" for the purchase of new capital goods and the additions to inventories.

Government Purchases of Goods and Services

Government purchases of goods and services
The purchases by all levels of government on goods and services.

Government purchases of goods and services are purchases by all levels of government of goods and services from firms. You saw in Chapter 2 (pp. 46–49) that governments buy a wide range of goods and services. For example, the U.S. Defense Department buys missiles and other weapons systems, the State Department buys travel services, the White House buys Internet services, and state and local governments buy cruisers for law-enforcement officers.

Net Exports of Goods and Services

Net exports of goods and services
The value of exports of goods and services minus the value of imports of goods and services.

Exports of goods and services
Items that firms in the United States produce and sell to the rest of the world.

Imports of goods and services
Items that households, firms, and governments in the United States buy from the rest of the world.

Net exports of goods and services is the value of exports of goods and services minus the value of imports of goods and services. **Exports of goods and services** are items that firms in the United States produce and sell to the rest of the world. **Imports of goods and services** are items that households, firms, and governments in the United States buy from the rest of the world. Imports are produced in other countries, so expenditure on imports is not included in expenditure on U.S-produced goods and services. If exports exceed imports, net exports are positive and increase expenditure on U.S.-produced goods and services. If imports exceed exports, net exports are negative and decrease expenditure on U.S.-produced goods and services.

Total Expenditure

Total expenditure on goods and services produced in the United States is the sum of consumption expenditure C, investment I, government purchases of goods and services G, and net exports of goods and services NX. That is,

$$\text{Total expenditure} = C + I + G + NX.$$

Total expenditure is the amount received by producers of final goods and services.

Income

Labor earns wages, capital earns interest, land earns rent, and entrepreneurship earns profits. Households receive these incomes. Some part of total income, called *undistributed profit,* is a combination of interest and profit that is not paid out to households. But from an economic viewpoint, undistributed profit is income paid to households and then loaned to firms. We call total income Y.

Benefits, Taxes, and Saving

Net taxes
Taxes paid minus benefits received.

Saving
The amount of income that remains after paying taxes and buying consumption goods and services.

Some households receive benefits from government and others pay taxes. **Net taxes** equal taxes paid minus benefits received. **Saving** is the amount of income that remains after paying taxes and buying consumption goods and services. Consumption expenditure, C, plus net taxes, NT, plus saving, S, equals income, Y.

Expenditure Equals Income

Figure 13.1 shows the circular flows of income and expenditure that we've just described. The figure is based on Figures 2.4 and 2.5 (on p. 45 and p. 47), but it includes some more details and additional flows.

The blue flow shows income and the red flows show consumption expenditure, investment, government purchases, and net exports. The green flows, net taxes, NT, and saving, S, are flows of money, not expenditures on goods and services. Investment flows from the financial markets, where firms borrow, to the firms that produce capital goods.

Because firms pay out everything they receive as incomes to the factors of production, total expenditure equals total income. That is,

$$Y = C + I + G + NX.$$

From the viewpoint of firms, the value of production is the cost of production, which equals income. From the viewpoint of purchasers of goods and services, the value of production is the cost of buying it, which equals expenditure. So

The value of production equals income equals expenditure.

The circular flow and the equality of income and expenditure provide two approaches to measuring GDP that we'll study in the next section.

FIGURE 13.1
The Circular Flow of Income and Expenditure

Practice Online

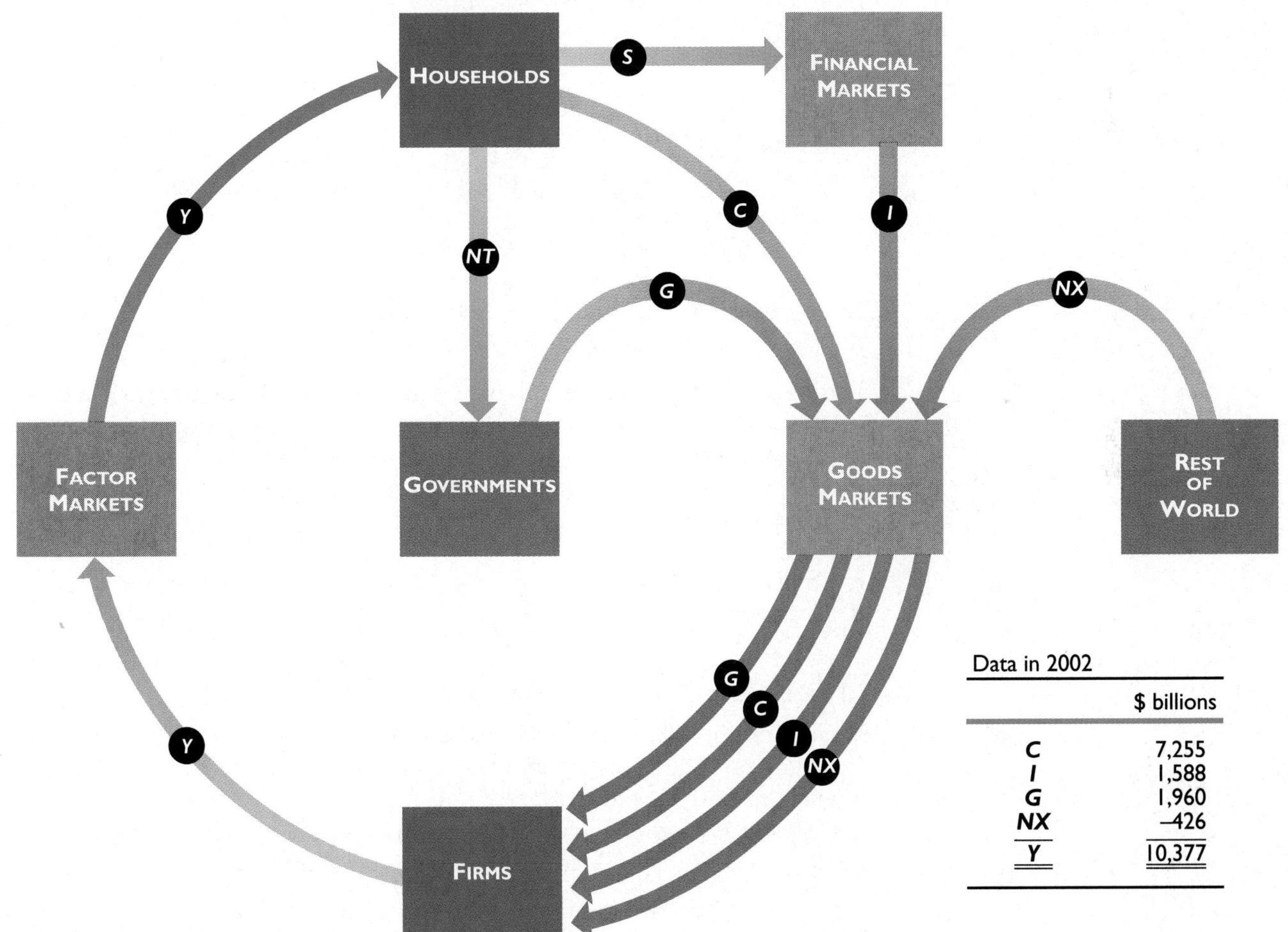

	\$ billions
C	7,255
I	1,588
G	1,960
NX	–426
Y	10,377

In the circular flow, the blue flow (*Y*) is income and the red flows (*C*, *I*, *G*, and *NX*) are expenditures on goods and services. The green flows are flows of money: Households pay net taxes (*NT*) to governments and save (*S*) some of their income. Firms borrow in financial markets to buy goods (*I*) from other firms. Expenditure equals income and equals the value of production.

CHECKPOINT 13.1

Study Guide pp. 200–202

Practice Online 13.1

1 Define GDP and explain why the value of production, income, and expenditure are the same for an economy.

Practice Problems 13.1

1. Classify each of the following items as a final good or service or an intermediate good or service:
   a. Banking services bought by a student.
   b. New cars bought by Hertz, the car rental firm.
   c. Newsprint bought by *USA Today* from International Paper.
   d. Ice cream bought by a diner and used to produce sundaes.

2. During 2001 on Lotus Island, net taxes were \$10 billion; consumption expenditure was \$30 billion; government purchases of goods and services were \$12 billion; investment was \$15 billion; and net exports were \$3 billion. Calculate
   a. Total expenditure.
   b. Total income.
   c. GDP.

Exercises 13.1

1. Classify each of the following items as a final good or service or an intermediate good or service:
   a. The fertilizer bought by a Florida tomato grower.
   b. The *Wall Street Journal* you bought today.
   c. The PlayStation 2 that you bought on eBay.
   d. The aircraft fuel bought by United Airlines.

2. During 2002 on Lotus Island, households spent \$60 million of their income on goods and services, saved \$20 million, and paid the rest of their income in net taxes; government purchases of goods and services were \$15 million; investment was \$25 million; and net exports were zero. Calculate
   a. GDP.
   b. Total income.
   c. Total expenditure.
   d. Net taxes.

Solutions to Practice Problems 13.1

1a. A final service—The student is the final user.
1b. Final goods—The new cars that Hertz buys are additions to its capital and as such they are investment.
1c. An intermediate good—Newsprint is a component of the newspaper.
1d. An intermediate good—Ice cream is a component of sundaes.

2a. Total expenditure is \$60 billion. Total expenditure = $C + I + G + NX$.
Inserting the values into the equation, we have:
Total expenditure = \$(30 + 15 +12 + 3) billion = \$60 billion.
2b. Total income = total expenditure = \$60 billion.
2c. GDP = total expenditure = \$60 billion.

13.2 MEASURING U.S. GDP

U.S. GDP is the market value of all the final goods and services produced within the United States during a year. In 2002, U.S. GDP almost reached the $10.4 trillion mark. The Bureau of Economic Analysis in the U.S. Department of Commerce measures GDP. To do so, it uses two approaches:

- Expenditure approach
- Income approach

The Expenditure Approach

The expenditure approach measures GDP by using data on consumption expenditure, investment, government purchases, and net exports. This approach is like attaching a meter to the circular flow diagram on all the flows running through the markets for goods and services to firms and measuring the magnitudes of those flows. Table 13.1 shows this approach. The first column gives the terms used in the National Income and Product Accounts of the United States. The next column gives the symbol we used in the previous section.

Using the expenditure approach, GDP is the sum of consumption expenditure on goods and services (*C*), investment (*I*), government purchases of goods and services (*G*), and net exports of goods and services (*NX*). The third column gives the expenditures in mid-2002. GDP measured by the expenditure approach was $10,377 billion (annual rate) in the second quarter of 2002.

Net exports were negative in 2002 because imports exceeded exports. Imports were $1,444 billion and exports were $1,018 billion, so net exports—exports minus imports—were –$426 billion as shown in the table.

The fourth column in Table 13.1 shows the relative magnitudes of the expenditures. Consumption expenditure makes up more than half of total expenditure; investment and government purchases are about the same percentage of total expenditure; and net exports is the smallest. In 2002, consumption expenditure was 69.9 percent, investment was 15.3 percent, government purchases were about 18.9 percent each, and net exports were a negative 4.1 percent of GDP.

TABLE 13.1
GDP: The Expenditure Approach

Practice Online

Item	Symbol	Amount in 2002 (billions of dollars)	Percentage of GDP
Consumption expenditure	*C*	7,255	69.9
Investment	*I*	1,588	15.3
Government purchases	*G*	1,960	18.9
Net exports	*NX*	–426	–4.1
GDP	*Y*	10,377	100.0

SOURCE: U.S. Department of Commerce, Bureau of Economic Analysis.

The expenditure approach measures GDP by adding together consumption expenditure (*C*), investment (*I*), government purchases (*G*), and net exports (*NX*). In 2002, GDP measured by the expenditure approach was $10,377 billion.

Expenditures Not in GDP

Total expenditure (and GDP) does not include all the things that people and businesses buy. GDP is the value of *final goods and services*, so spending that is *not* on final goods and services is not part of GDP. Spending on intermediate goods and services is not part of GDP, although it is not always obvious whether an item is an intermediate good or a final good; see Eye on the U.S. Economy. Also, we do not count as part of GDP spending on

- Used goods
- Financial assets

Used Goods

Expenditure on used goods is not part of GDP because these goods were part of GDP in the period in which they were produced and during which time they were new goods. For example, a 1999 automobile was part of GDP in 1999. If the car is traded on the used car market in 2002, the amount paid for the car is not part of GDP in 2002.

Financial Assets

When households buy financial assets such as bonds and stocks, they are making loans, not buying goods and services. The expenditure on newly produced capital goods is part of GDP, but the purchase of financial assets is not.

Eye on the U.S. Economy

Is a Computer Program an Intermediate Good or a Final Good?

When American Airlines buys a new reservations software package, is that like General Motors buying tires? If it is, then software is an *intermediate good* and it is not counted as part of GDP. Airline ticket sales, like GM cars, are part of GDP, but the intermediate goods that are used to produce air transportation or cars are *not* part of GDP.

Or when American Airlines buys new software, is that like General Motors buying a new assembly-line robot? If it is, then the software is a capital good and its purchase is the purchase of a final good. In this case, the software purchase is an *investment* and it *is* counted as part of GDP.

Brent Moulton is a government economist who works in the Bureau of Economic Analysis (BEA). Moulton's recent job was to oversee a periodic adjustment to the GDP estimates to incorporate new data and new ideas about the economy.

The biggest change was in how the purchase of computer software by firms is classified. Before 1999, it was regarded as an *intermediate good.* But since 1999, it has been treated as an *investment.*

How big a deal is this? When GDP in 1996 was recalculated, the change increased the estimate of the 1996 GDP by $115 billion. That is a lot of money. To put it in perspective, GDP in 1996 was $7,662 billion. So the adjustment was 1.5 percent of GDP.

This change is a nice example of the ongoing effort by the BEA to keep the GDP measure as accurate as possible.

The Income Approach

The Bureau of Economic Analysis measures GDP using the income approach by collecting data (from the Internal Revenue Service and other sources) on the incomes that firms pay households for the services of factors of production they hire—wages for labor, interest for the use of capital, rent for the use of land, and profits for entrepreneurship—and summing those incomes. This approach is like attaching a meter to the circular flow diagram on all the flows of factor incomes from firms to households and measuring the magnitudes of those flows. Let's see how the income approach works.

The National Income and Product Accounts divide incomes into five categories:

- Compensation of employees
- Net interest
- Rental income of persons
- Corporate profits
- Proprietors' income

Compensation of Employees

Compensation of employees is the payment for labor services. It includes net wages and salaries plus fringe benefits paid by employers such as health care insurance, social security contributions, and pension fund contributions.

Net Interest

Net interest is the interest households receive on loans they make minus the interest households pay on their own borrowing.

Rental Income of Persons

Rental income of persons is the payment for the use of land and other rented inputs. It includes payments for rented housing and imputed rent for owner-occupied housing. (Imputed rent is an estimate of what homeowners would pay to rent the housing they own and use themselves. By including this item in the national income accounts, we measure the total value of housing services, whether they are owned or rented.)

Corporate Profits

Corporate profits—the profits of corporations—are a combination of interest on capital and profit for entrepreneurship. Corporate profits paid out as dividends and undistributed profits are all counted as income.

Proprietors' Income

Proprietors are people who run their own businesses. Their income is a mixture of the previous four items. It is difficult to split the income earned by the owner-operator of a business into compensation for labor, payment for the use of capital, and profit, so the national income accounts lump all these items into a single category.

TABLE 13.2
GDP: The Income Approach

Practice Online

The sum of all incomes equals net domestic product at factor cost. GDP equals net domestic product at factor cost plus indirect taxes less subsidies plus capital consumption (depreciation). In 2002, GDP measured by the income approach was $10,377 billion. The compensation of employees—labor income—was by far the largest part of aggregate income.

Item	Amount in 2002 (billions of dollars)	Percentage of GDP
Compensation of employees	5,964	57.5
Net interest	678	6.5
Rental income of persons	153	1.5
Corporate profits	785	7.6
Proprietors' income	747	7.2
Net domestic product at factor cost	8,327	80.3
Indirect taxes less subsidies	660	6.4
Capital consumption	1,390	13.3
GDP	10,377	100.0

SOURCE: U.S. Department of Commerce, Bureau of Economic Analysis.

Net domestic product at factor cost
The sum of the five components of incomes—compensation of employees, net interest, rental income of persons, corporate profits, and proprietors' income.

Table 13.2 shows these five components of incomes and their relative magnitudes. These five components of incomes sum to **net domestic product at factor cost**. Net domestic product at factor cost is not GDP. We must make two further adjustments to get to GDP: one from factor cost to market prices and another from net product to gross product.

From Factor Cost to Market Price

The expenditure approach values goods and services at market prices, and the income approach values them at factor cost—the cost of the factors of production used to produce them. Indirect taxes (such as sales taxes) and subsidies (payments by government to firms) make these two values differ. Sales taxes make market prices exceed factor cost, and subsidies make factor cost exceed market prices. To convert the value at factor cost to the value at market prices, we must add indirect taxes and subtract subsidies.

From Gross to Net

Depreciation
The decrease in the value of capital that results from its use and from obsolescence—also called capital consumption.

The expenditure approach measures gross product, and the income approach measures net product. The difference is **depreciation**, the decrease in the value of capital that results from its use and from obsolescence—also called capital consumption. A firm's profit before subtracting the depreciation of capital is its gross profit. And its profit after subtracting the depreciation of capital is its net profit. Income includes net profit, so the income approach gives a *net* measure. Expenditure includes investment, which is the purchase of new capital. Because some new capital is purchased to replace depreciated capital, the expenditure approach gives a *gross* measure. So to get *gross* domestic product from the income approach, we must add depreciation to total income.

Table 13.2 summarizes these adjustments and shows that the income approach gives the same estimate of GDP as the expenditure approach.

Valuing the Output of Industries

The methods that are used to measure GDP can be used to measure the contribution that each industry makes to GDP. To measure the value of production of an industry, we count only the value added by that industry. **Value added** is the value of a firm's production minus the value of the intermediate goods it buys from other firms. Equivalently, a firm's value added equals the sum of the incomes (including profits) that the firm paid for the factors of production it used.

Value added
The value of a firm's production minus the value of the intermediate goods it buys from other firms.

Figure 13.2 illustrates value added by looking at the brief life of a loaf of bread. It starts with the farmer, who hires factors of production and grows wheat. We'll assume that the farmer uses no intermediate goods. The miller buys the wheat (for a loaf) from the farmer for 20¢. The value of the farmer's production is 20¢, and the farmer's value added is 20¢. The farmer's value added equals the incomes that the farmer paid for the factors of production plus the farmer's profit.

The miller hires factors of production to turn the wheat into flour. The baker buys the flour from the miller for 70¢. The miller's value added is 50¢—the value of the flour (70¢) minus the cost of the intermediate good (20¢ for wheat). The miller's value added equals the incomes that the miller paid for the factors of production plus the miller's profit.

The baker adds a further 80¢ of value by turning the flour into bread. The consumer buys the bread for its market price, $1.50. The market price equals the value added by the farmer (20¢), the miller (50¢), and the baker (80¢).

To value output, we count *only* value added because the total of the values added at all stages of production equals expenditure on the final good. By totaling values added, we avoid double counting. In Figure 13.2, the only final good is a loaf of bread. The red bar shows the value of the final good. The blue bars show the value added at each stage, and the sum of the blue bars equals the red bar. The transactions involving intermediate goods, shown by the green bars, are not part of value added and are *not* counted as part of the value of output or of GDP.

FIGURE 13.2
Value Added and Final Expenditure

Practice Online

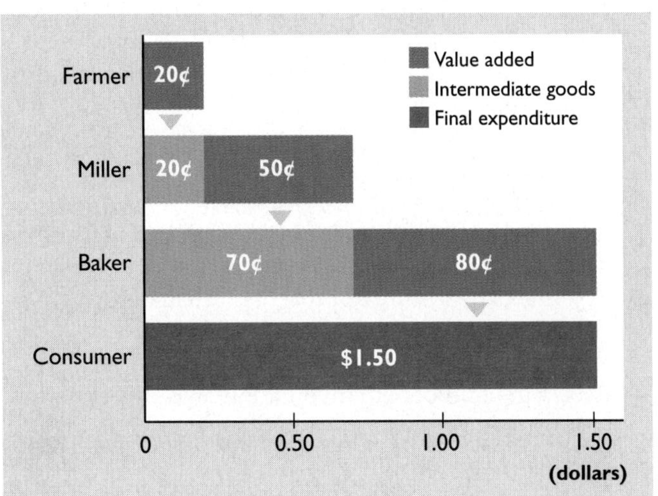

Value added is the value of a firm's production minus the value of the intermediate goods it buys from other firms. The baker's value added is the consumer's expenditure on bread minus the baker's intermediate expenditure on flour. The baker's value added equals the incomes paid, including profit, for the factors of production hired by the baker. The value of the bread (the final good) is equal to the sum of all values added.

CHECKPOINT 13.2

Study Guide pp. 203–205

Practice Online 13.2

2 Describe how economic statisticians measure GDP in the United States.

Practice Problem 13.2

Table 1 shows some of the items in the U.S. National Income and Product Accounts in 2001.

a. Calculate U.S. GDP in 2001.
b. Did you use the expenditure approach or the income approach to make this calculation?
c. How much did the U.S. government spend on goods and services in 2001?
d. By how much did capital in the United States depreciate in 2001?

TABLE 1

Item	Amount (billions of dollars)
Compensation of employees	5,875
Consumption expenditure	6,987
Indirect taxes less subsidies	630
Net interest	650
Corporate profits	732
Capital consumption	1,329
Rental income of persons	138
Investment	1,586
Net exports	–349
Proprietors' income	728

Exercises 13.2

1. Table 2 shows some of the items in the U.S. National Income and Product Accounts in 1997.
   a. Use the expenditure approach to calculate U.S. GDP in 1997.
   b. Use the income approach to calculate U.S. net domestic product at factor cost in 1997.
   c. Calculate GDP minus net domestic product at factor cost in 1997.
   d. Calculate indirect taxes less subsidies in 1997.
2. At the American Diner, the price of a mango smoothie is \$3.00. The diner buys the mango for 50¢, skim milk for 20¢, and flavoring for 1¢ from other firms and pays 25¢ for the labor and capital. Calculate the value added by the American Diner when it produces a mango smoothie.

TABLE 2

Item	Amount (billions of dollars)
Consumption expenditure	5,529
Government purchases	1,488
Net interest	424
Corporate profits	834
Rental income of persons	128
Investment	1,391
Net exports	–89
Compensation of employees	4,651
Proprietors' income	581
Capital consumption	1,013

Solution to Practice Problem 13.2

a. GDP = $C + I + G + NX$ (the expenditure approach) and GDP = Compensation of employees + Net interest + Rental income of persons + Corporate profits + Proprietors' incomes + Indirect taxes less subsidies + Capital consumption (the income approach). Inspect the data and notice that Government purchases (G) is missing. So you can't use the expenditure approach. But you can use the income approach. Insert the items in the equation and get

$$\text{GDP in billions} = \$5,875 + \$650 + \$138 + \$732 + \$728 + \$630 + \$1,329 = \$10,082 \text{ billion.}$$

b. You totaled the incomes for factors of production, so you used the income approach.

c. Use the expenditure approach to calculate G:

$$\text{GDP} = C + I + G + NX.$$

Insert the numbers that you know into this equation:

$$\text{GDP in billions} = \$10,082 = \$6,987 + \$1,586 + G - \$349.$$

$$G = \$10,082 \text{ billion} - \$8,224 \text{ billion} = \$1,858 \text{ billion.}$$

d. Depreciation equals capital consumption, which in 2001 was \$1,329 billion.

13.3 NOMINAL GDP VERSUS REAL GDP

You've seen that GDP measures total expenditure on final goods and services in a given period. In 2001, GDP was $10,082 billion. In 2002, GDP was $10,377 billion. Because GDP in 2002 was greater than in 2001, we know that one or two things must have happened during that period:

- We produced more goods and services.
- We paid higher prices for our goods and services.

Producing more goods and services contributes to an improvement in our standard of living. Paying higher prices means that our cost of living has increased but our standard of living has not. So it matters a great deal why GDP has increased.

You're going to learn how economists at the Bureau of Economic Analysis split the increase in GDP into two parts: one part that tells us the change in production and another that tells us the change in prices. The method they use has changed in recent years, and we will describe the new method.

We measure the increase in production by a number called real GDP. **Real GDP** is the value of the final goods and services produced in a given year when valued at constant prices. By comparing the value at constant prices of the goods and services produced, we can measure the increase in production.

Real GDP
The value of the final goods and services produced in a given year when valued at constant prices.

Calculating Real GDP

Table 13.3 shows the quantities produced and prices in 2002 for an economy that produces only apples and oranges. The first step toward calculating real GDP is to calculate **nominal GDP**, which is the value of the final goods and services produced in a given year valued at the prices that prevailed in that same year. Nominal GDP is just a more precise name for GDP that we use when we want to make it clear that we are not talking about real GDP.

Nominal GDP
The value of the final goods and services produced in a given year valued at the prices that prevailed in that same year.

Nominal GDP Calculation

To calculate nominal GDP in 2002, sum the expenditures on apples and oranges in 2002 as follows:

Expenditure on apples = 100 apples × $1 = $100.
Expenditure on oranges = 200 oranges × $0.50 = $100.
Nominal GDP in 2002 = $100 + $100 = $200.

Table 13.4 shows the quantities produced and prices in 2003. The quantity of apples produced increased to 160 and the quantity of oranges produced increased to 220. The price of an apple fell to 50¢, and the price of an orange increased to $2.25. To calculate nominal GDP in 2003, sum the expenditures on apples and oranges in 2003 as follows:

Expenditure on apples = 160 apples × $0.50 = $80.
Expenditure on oranges = 220 oranges × $2.25 = $495.
Nominal GDP in 2003 = $80 + $495 = $575.

To calculate real GDP, we choose one year, called the *base year*, against which to compare the other years. The choice of the base year is not important. It is just a common reference point. We'll use 2002 as the base year. By definition, real GDP equals nominal GDP in the base year. So real GDP in 2002 is $200.

TABLE 13.3 GDP DATA FOR 2002

Item	Quantity	Price
Apples	100	$1.00
Oranges	200	$0.50

TABLE 13.4 GDP DATA FOR 2003

Item	Quantity	Price
Apples	160	$0.50
Oranges	220	$2.25

Traditional Real GDP Calculation

The traditional method of calculating real GDP values the quantities produced in each year at the prices of the base year. Table 13.5 summarizes these prices and quantities for 2002 and 2003. The value of the 2003 quantities at the 2002 prices is calculated as follows:

TABLE 13.5 2003 QUANTITIES AND 2002 PRICES

Item	Quantity	Price
Apples	160	$1.00
Oranges	220	$0.50

Expenditure on apples = 160 apples × $1.00 = $160.
Expenditure on oranges = 220 oranges × $0.50 = $110.
Value of the 2003 quantities at 2002 prices = $270.

Using the traditional method, $270 would be recorded as real GDP in 2003.

New Method of Calculating Real GDP

The new method of calculating real GDP builds on the old method but takes a further step. The new method compares the quantities produced in 2002 and 2003 by using not only 2002 prices but also the 2003 prices. It then averages the two sets of numbers in a special way that we'll now describe.

To compare the quantities produced in 2002 and 2003 at 2003 prices, we need to calculate the value of 2002 quantities at 2003 prices. Table 13.6 summarizes these quantities and prices. The value of the 2002 quantities at the 2003 prices is calculated as follows:

TABLE 13.6 2002 QUANTITIES AND 2003 PRICES

Item	Quantity	Price
Apples	100	$0.50
Oranges	200	$2.25

Expenditure on apples = 100 apples × $0.50 = $50.
Expenditure on oranges = 200 oranges × $2.25 = $450.
Value of the 2002 quantities at 2003 prices = $500.

We now have two comparisons between 2002 and 2003. At the 2002 prices, the value of production increased from $200 in 2002 to $270 in 2003. The increase in value is $70, and the percentage increase is ($70 ÷ $200) × 100, which is 35 percent.

At the 2003 prices, the value of production increased from $500 in 2002 to $575 in 2003. The increase in value is $75, and the percentage increase is ($75 ÷ $500) × 100, which is 15 percent.

When we value production in 2002 prices, it increased by 35 percent in 2003. When we value production in 2003 prices, it increased by 15 percent in 2003. The new method of calculating real GDP uses the average of these two percentage increases. The average of 35 percent and 15 percent is (35 + 15) ÷ 2, which equals 25 percent. Real GDP is 25 percent greater in 2003 than in 2002. Real GDP in 2002 is $200, so real GDP in 2003 is $250.

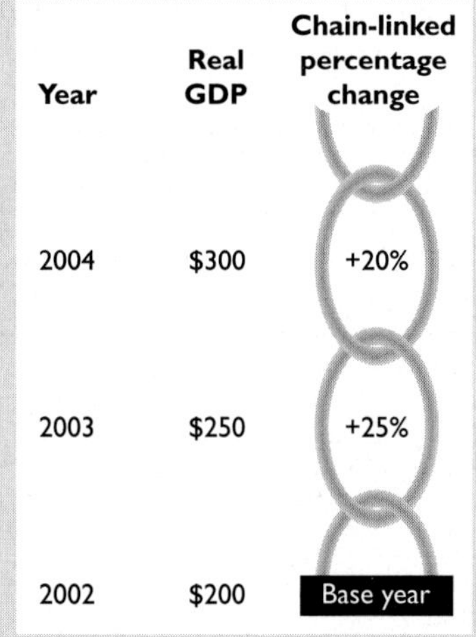

Chain Linking

The calculation that we've just described is repeated each year. Each year is compared with its preceding year. So, in 2004, the calculations are repeated but using the prices and quantities of 2003 and 2004. Real GDP in 2004 equals real GDP in 2003 increased by the calculated percentage change in real GDP for 2004. For example, suppose that real GDP for 2004 is calculated to be 20 percent greater than in 2003. You know that real GDP in 2003 is $250. So real GDP in 2004 is 20 percent greater than this value and is $300. In every year, real GDP is valued in base-year (2002) dollars.

By applying the calculated percentage change to the real GDP of the preceding real GDP, each year is linked back to the dollars of the base year like the links in a chain.

Eye on the U.S. Economy

Deflating the GDP Balloon

Nominal GDP increased every year between 1992 and 2002. Part of the increase reflects increased production, and part of it reflects rising prices.

You can think of GDP as a balloon that is blown up by growing production and rising prices. In the figure, the GDP deflator lets the inflation air—the contribution of rising prices—out of the nominal GDP balloon so that we can see what has happened to real GDP. The red balloon for 1992 shows real GDP in that year. The green balloon shows nominal GDP in 2002. The red balloon for 2002 shows real GDP for that year. To see real GDP in 2002, we use the GDP deflator to deflate nominal GDP.

With the inflation air removed, real GDP shows how the total value of production has changed. Production grew from 1992 through 2000, but in 2001, real GDP shrank. Over the 10 years, real GDP grew by 3.1 percent a year, and in 2002, it was 38 percent higher than it was in 1992.

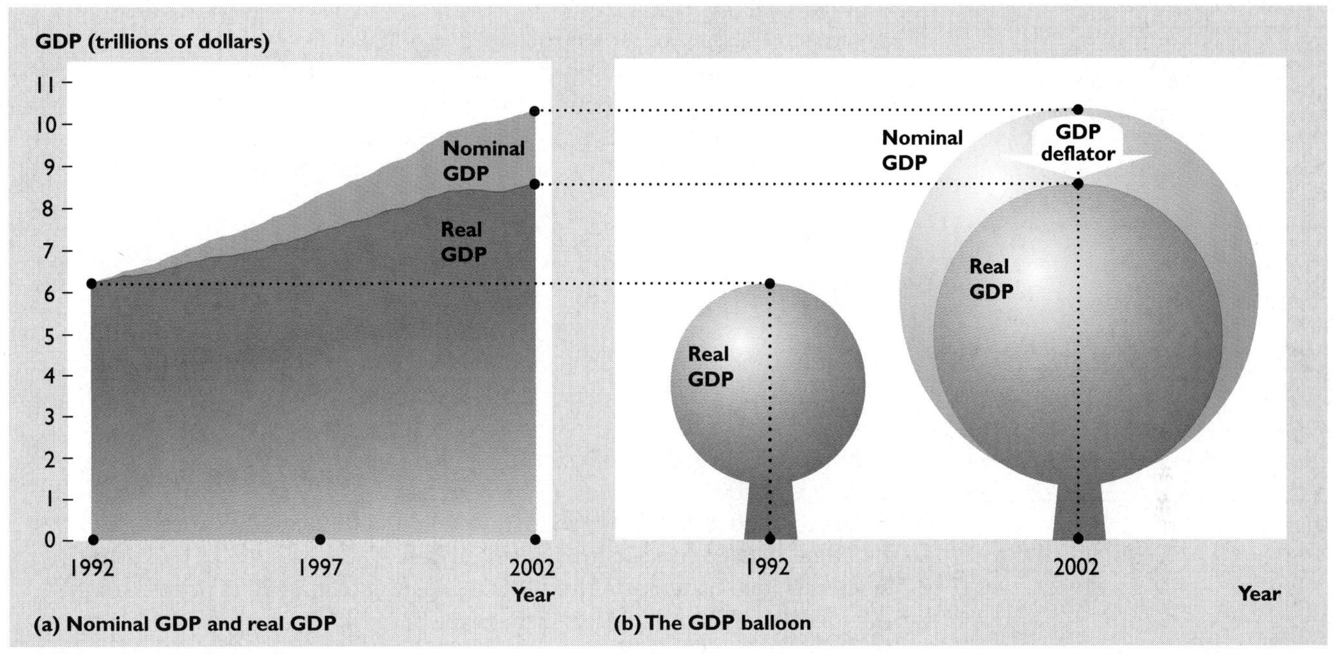

SOURCE: Bureau of Economic Analysis.

Calculating the GDP Deflator

The **GDP deflator** is an average of current prices expressed as a percentage of base-year prices. The GDP deflator measures the price level. We calculate the GDP deflator by using nominal GDP and real GDP in the following formula:

GDP deflator
An average of current prices expressed as a percentage of base-year prices.

$$\text{GDP deflator} = (\text{Nominal GDP} \div \text{Real GDP}) \times 100.$$

You can see why the GDP deflator is a measure of the price level. If nominal GDP rises but real GDP remains unchanged, it must be that prices have risen. The formula would deliver that result in the form of a higher GDP deflator. The larger the nominal GDP for a given real GDP, the higher are prices and the larger is the GDP deflator.

Table 13.7 shows how the GDP deflator is calculated. In 2002, the deflator is 100. In 2003, it is 230, which equals nominal GDP of $575 divided by real GDP of $250 and then multiplied by 100.

TABLE 13.7 CALCULATING THE GDP DEFLATOR

Year	Nominal GDP	Real GDP	GDP Deflator
2002	$200	$200	100
2003	$575	$250	230

CHECKPOINT 13.3

Study Guide pp. 205–207

Practice Online 13.3

3 Distinguish between nominal GDP and real GDP and define the GDP deflator.

Practice Problem 13.3

An island economy produces only bananas and coconuts. Table 1 gives the quantities produced and prices in 2001, and Table 2 gives the quantities produced and prices in 2002. The base year is 2001. Calculate

a. Nominal GDP in 2001.
b. Nominal GDP in 2002.
c. The value of 2002 production in 2001 prices.
d. The percentage increase in production when valued at 2001 prices.
e. The value of 2001 production in 2002 prices.
f. The percentage increase in production when valued at 2002 prices.
g. Real GDP in 2001 and 2002 by using the chain-linking method.
h. The GDP deflator in 2002.

TABLE 1

In 2001:

Item	Quantity	Price
Bananas	100	$10 a bunch
Coconuts	50	$12 a bag

TABLE 2

In 2002:

Item	Quantity	Price
Bananas	110	$15 a bunch
Coconuts	60	$10 a bag

Exercise 13.3

An island economy produces only lobsters and crabs. Table 3 gives the quantities produced and the prices in 2001, and Table 4 gives the quantities produced and the prices in 2002. The base year is 2001. Calculate

a. Nominal GDP in 2001.
b. Nominal GDP in 2002.
c. The value of 2002 production in 2001 prices.
d. The percentage increase in production when valued at 2001 prices.
e. The value of 2001 production in 2002 prices.
f. The percentage increase in production when valued at 2002 prices.
g. Real GDP in 2001 and 2002 by using the chain-linking method.
h. The GDP deflator in 2002.

TABLE 3

In 2001:

Item	Quantity	Price
Lobsters	90	$15 each
Crabs	20	$20 each

TABLE 4

In 2002:

Item	Quantity	Price
Lobsters	100	$20 each
Crabs	25	$25 each

Solution to Practice Problem 13.3

a. Nominal GDP in 2001 is $1,600—expenditure is $1,000 on bananas and $600 on coconuts (Table 1).
b. Nominal GDP in 2002 is $2,250—expenditure is $1,650 on bananas and $600 on coconuts (Table 2).
c. The value of 2002 production in 2001 prices is $1,820 (Table 5).
d. In 2001 prices, the value of production increased from $1,600 to $1,820, an increase of $220. The percentage increase is $(220 \div 1,600) \times 100$, or 13.75 percent.
e. The value of 2001 production in 2002 prices is $2,000 (Table 6).
f. In 2002 prices, the value of production increased from $2,000 to $2,250, an increase of $250. The percentage increase is $(250 \div 2,000) \times 100$, or 12.5 percent.
g. Real GDP in 2001 is $1,600. The average percentage increase in production is $(13.75 + 12.5) \div 2$, which is 13.125 percent. Real GDP in 2002 is 13.125 percent greater than $1,600, which is $1,810.
h. The GDP deflator in 2002 is (nominal GDP ÷ real GDP) × 100, which is 124.3.

TABLE 5

2002 quantities and 2001 prices

Item	Quantity	Price	Expenditure
Bananas	110	$10	$1,100
Coconuts	60	$12	$720
Value in 2001 prices			$1,820

TABLE 6

2001 quantities and 2002 prices

Item	Quantity	Price	Expenditure
Bananas	100	$15	$1,500
Coconuts	50	$10	$500
Value in 2002 prices			$2,000

13.4 REAL GDP AND THE STANDARD OF LIVING

We use estimates of real GDP to compare the standard of living across countries and over time. In 2002, real GDP per person in the United States was $36,000, which (at 2002 prices) is twice what it was in 1965. But are we twice as well off? Does this expansion of real GDP provide a full and accurate measure of the change in our standard of living?

It does not, for two reasons. First, the standard of living depends on *all* goods and services, not only on those included in GDP. Second, the standard of living depends on factors other than the goods and services produced.

Goods and Services Omitted from GDP

GDP measures the value of goods and services that are bought in markets. But it excludes

- Household production
- Underground production
- Leisure time
- Environment quality

Household Production

An enormous amount of production takes place every day in our homes. Preparing meals, cleaning the kitchen, changing a light bulb, cutting the grass, washing the car, and helping a student with homework are all examples of productive activities that do not involve market transactions and are not counted as part of GDP.

Because real GDP omits household production, it underestimates the value of the production of many people, most of them women. But market production is increasingly replacing household production. Two trends point in this direction. One is the number of people who have jobs outside the home, which has increased from 59 percent in 1965 to 67 percent in 2002. The other is the purchase of traditionally home-produced goods and services in the market. For example, more and more families now eat in fast-food restaurants—one of the fastest-growing industries in the United States—and use day-care services. These trends mean that an increasing proportion of food preparation and child care that were once part of household production are now measured as part of GDP. So real GDP grows more rapidly than does real GDP plus home production.

Underground Production

The underground economy is the part of the economy that is hidden from the view of the government either because people want to avoid taxes and regulations or because the goods and services being produced are illegal. Because underground economic activity is unreported, it is omitted from GDP.

The underground economy is easy to describe, even if it is hard to measure. It includes the production and distribution of illegal drugs, production that uses illegal workers who are paid less than the minimum wage, and jobs done for cash to avoid paying income taxes. This last category might be quite large and includes tips earned by cab drivers, hairdressers, and hotel and restaurant workers and a large range of other legal cash transactions.

Edgar L. Feige, an economist at the University of Wisconsin, estimates that the U.S. underground economy peaked at 20 percent of GDP in 1987 and decreased to about 16 percent of GDP during the early 1990s. The underground economy is larger than this in some Eastern European countries, which are making a transition from communist economic planning to a market economy.

Leisure Time

Leisure time is an economic good. Other things remaining the same, the more leisure we have, the better off we are. Our working time is valued as part of GDP, but our leisure time is not. Yet that leisure time must be at least as valuable to us as the wage we earn for working. If it were not, we would work instead. Over the years, leisure time has steadily increased. The workweek has become shorter, more people take early retirement, and the number of vacation days has increased. These improvements in our standard of living are not measured in real GDP.

Environment Quality

An industrial society produces more atmospheric pollution than an agricultural society does. For example, an industrial society burns more coal, oil, and gas. And it depletes resources, clears forests, and pollutes lakes and rivers.

But industrial activity increases wealth, and wealthy people value a clean environment and are better able to devote resources to protecting it. So pollution does not necessarily increase when production increases. Pollution in Germany provides an example. When East Germany, a relatively poor part of the country, opened its borders with West Germany in the late 1980s, it was discovered that East German rivers, lakes, and air were much more severely polluted than those of its richer West German neighbor.

Resources that are used to protect the environment are valued as part of GDP. For example, the production of catalytic converters that help to protect the atmosphere from automobile emissions is part of GDP. But pollution is not subtracted from GDP. If we didn't produce catalytic converters but instead polluted the atmosphere, we would not count the deteriorating atmosphere as a negative part of GDP. So if our standard of living is adversely affected by pollution, our GDP measure does not show this fact.

Other Influences on the Standard of Living

The quantity of goods and services consumed is a major influence on the standard of living. But other influences are

- Health and life expectancy
- Political freedom and social justice

Health and Life Expectancy

Good health and a long life—the hopes of everyone—do not show up directly in real GDP. A higher real GDP enables us to spend more on medical research, health care, a good diet, and exercise equipment. And as real GDP has increased, our life expectancy has lengthened—from 70 years at the end of World War II to nearly 80 years today. Infant deaths and death in childbirth, two scourges of the nineteenth century, have almost been eliminated.

But we face new health and life expectancy problems every year. Diseases such as AIDS and drug abuse are taking young lives at a rate that causes serious concern. When we take these negative influences into account, real GDP growth overstates the improvements in the standard of living.

Political Freedom and Social Justice

A country might have a very large real GDP per person but have limited political freedom and social justice. For example, a small elite might enjoy political liberty and extreme wealth while the majority of people have limited freedom and live in poverty. Such an economy would generally be regarded as having a lower standard of living than one that had the same amount of real GDP but in which everyone enjoyed political freedom. Today, China has rapid real GDP growth but limited political freedom, while Russia has slower real GDP growth and an emerging democratic political system.

Because of the limitations of real GDP, other measures such as the Human Development Index have been proposed (see Eye on the Global Economy).

Eye on the Global Economy

The Human Development Index

The limitations of real GDP that we've reviewed in this chapter affect the standard of living of every country. So to make international comparisons of the standard of living, we must look at real GDP and other indicators. Nonetheless, real GDP per person is a major component of international comparisons.

The United Nations has constructed a broader measure called the Human Development Index, or HDI, which combines real GDP, life expectancy and health, and education levels.

The figure shows the relationship between GDP and the HDI. Each dot represents a country. The United States, labeled in the figure, has the highest real GDP per person but the fourth highest HDI. The small African nation of Sierra Leone, also labeled, has the lowest HDI and the lowest real GDP per person.

Why is the United States not the highest-ranked nation on the HDI?

It's because life expectancy at birth in the United States is a bit shorter than it is in Norway, Sweden, and Canada—the three slightly more highly ranked nations.

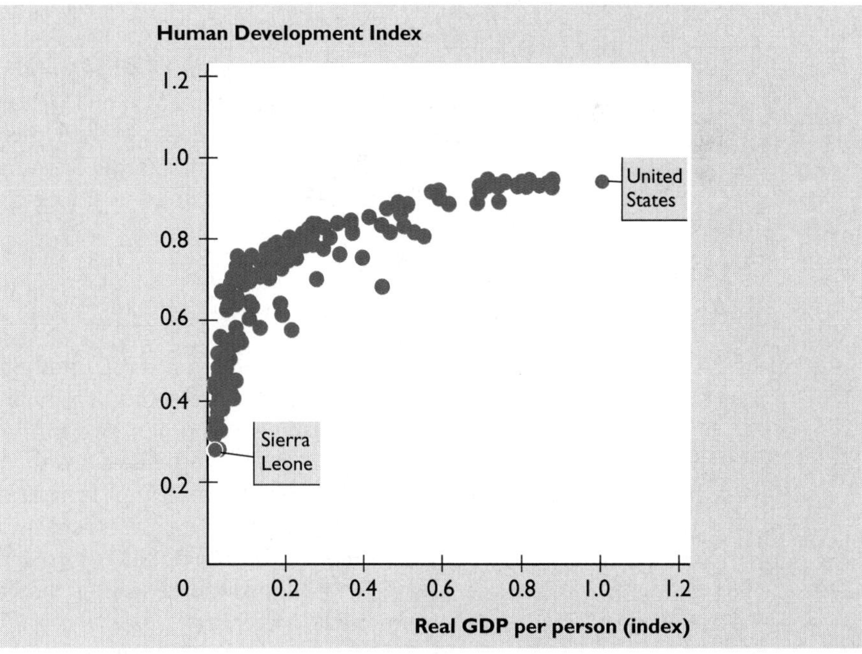

SOURCE: *United Nations Human Development Report*, 2002, http://www.undp.org/hdro/

CHECKPOINT 13.4

Study Guide pp. 207–210

Practice Online 13.4

4 **Explain and describe the limitations of real GDP as a measure of the standard of living.**

Practice Problem 13.4

The United Nations Human Development Report gives the following data for real GDP per person in 2000: China, $3,976; Russia, $8,377; Canada, $27,840; United States, $34,142. Other information suggests that household production is similar in Canada and the United States and smaller in these two countries than in the other two. The underground economy is largest in Russia and China and a similar proportion of the economy in these two cases. Canadians and Americans enjoy more leisure hours than do the Chinese and Russians. Canada and the United States spend significantly more to protect the environment, so air, water, and land pollution is less in those countries than in China and Russia. Given this information and ignoring any other influences on the standard of living

a. In which pair (or pairs) of these four countries is it easiest to compare the standard of living? Why?

b. In which pair (or pairs) of these four countries is it most difficult to compare the standard of living? Why?

c. What more detailed information would we need to be able to make an accurate assessment of the relative standard of living in these four countries?

d. Do you think that real-GDP-per-person differences correctly rank the standard of living in these four countries?

Exercise 13.4

Life expectancy at birth is 78.8 in Canada, 77.0 in the United States, 70.5 in China, and 66.1 in Russia. Freedom House rates political freedom each year, and its ratings are as follows: Canada and the United States, 1.1 (1.0 is the most free); Russia, 4.5; and China, 7.6 (ratings in the 7+ range are the least free). How do these facts change the relative rankings of living standards indicated by differences in real GDP per person?

Solution to Practice Problem 13.4

a. Two pairs—Canada and the United States, and China and Russia—are easy to compare because household production, the underground economy, leisure hours, and the environment are similar in the two countries in each pair.

b. Canada and the United States are the most difficult to compare with China and Russia because household production and the underground economy narrow the differences and leisure hours and the environment widen them.

c. We would need more detailed information on the value of household production, the underground economy, the value of leisure, and the value of environmental differences.

d. Differences in real GDP per person probably correctly rank the standard of living in these four countries because where the gap is small (Canada and the United States), other factors are similar, and where other factors differ, the gaps are huge.

CHAPTER CHECKPOINT

Key Points

1 Define GDP and explain why the value of production, income, and expenditure are the same for an economy.

- GDP is the market value of production of final goods and services in a given time period.
- We can value goods and services either by what it costs to produce (incomes) or by what people are willing to pay (expenditures).
- The value of production equals income equals expenditure.

2 Describe how economic statisticians measure GDP in the United States.

- We measure GDP by summing either expenditures on final goods and services (the expenditure approach) or incomes of all the factors of production (the income approach).
- GDP measures expenditure on final goods and services but excludes expenditure on intermediate goods, used goods, and financial assets.
- To value the output of a sector, we measure only the sector's value added.

3 Distinguish between nominal GDP and real GDP and define the GDP deflator.

- Nominal GDP is the value of production using the prices of the current year and the quantities produced in the current year.
- Real GDP is the value of production using the prices of a base year and the quantities in a current year.
- Changes in real GDP measure changes in production. Changes in nominal GDP combine changes in both production and prices.
- The GDP deflator is the ratio of nominal GDP to real GDP (multiplied by 100).

4 Explain and describe the limitations of real GDP as a measure of the standard of living.

- Real GDP per person is a major indicator of the standard of living.
- Real GDP omits household production, underground production, leisure time, environment quality, health and life expectancy, and political freedom and social justice.
- Broader indexes of the standard of living, such as the Human Development Index, take some of these omitted factors into account.

Key Terms

Consumption expenditure, 329
Depreciation, 336
Exports of goods and services, 330
Final good or service, 328
GDP deflator, 341
Government purchases of goods and services, 330
Gross domestic product (GDP), 328
Imports of goods and services, 330
Intermediate good or service, 328
Investment, 329
Net domestic product at factor cost, 336
Net exports of goods and services, 330
Net taxes, 330
Nominal GDP, 339
Real GDP, 339
Saving, 330
Value added, 337

Exercises

FIGURE 1

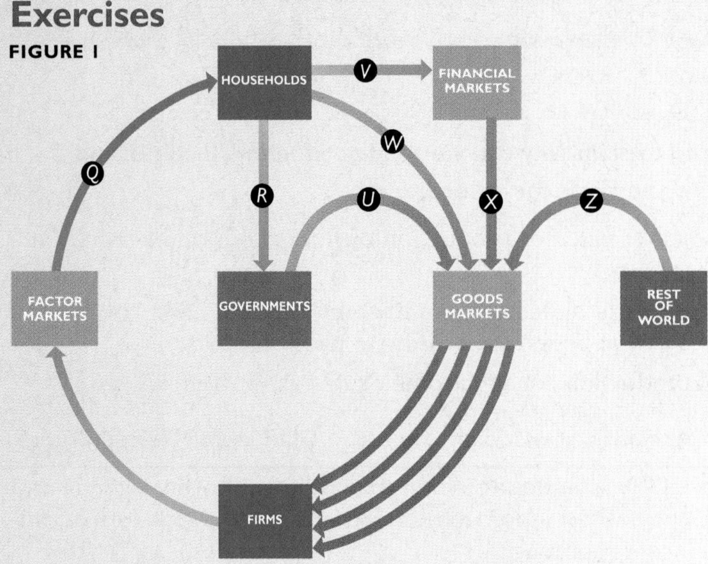

1. In Figure 1, name each of the flows labeled *Q*, *R*, *U*, *V*, *W*, *X*, and *Z*.

2. You are provided with the following data on the economy of Iberia: GDP was $100 billion, net taxes were $18 billion, government purchases of goods and services were $20 billion, household saving was $15 billion, consumption expenditure was $67 billion, investment was $21 billion, and exports of goods and services were $30 billion.
   a. Find the value of Iberia's import goods and services.
   b. Find Iberia's net exports.
   c. Label all the items in Figure 1 with their values in Iberia.

3. The values of some of the flows shown in Figure 1 in the U. S. economy in 1999 were U = $1.6 trillion, W = $6.2 trillion, X = $1.4 trillion, and Z = –$0.2 trillion. Calculate
   a. Q.
   b. $R + V$.
   c. GDP.

4. The values of some of the flows shown in Figure 1 in the Canadian economy in 2001 were Q = $1,092 billion, U = $204 billion, W = $621 billion, and Z = $57 billion. Calculate
   a. X.
   b. GDP.
   c. Compare Canada's GDP in 2001 with the U.S. GDP of 1999 and comment on the possible sources of the difference.

5. The national income accounts of Parchment Paradise are kept on (you guessed it) parchment. A fire destroyed the national statistics office, and the national income and product accounts are now incomplete. But they contain the following information for 2002: Net domestic product at factor cost was $2,900; consumption expenditure was $2,000; indirect taxes less subsidies

was $80; net interest was $200; rental income of persons was $100; investment was $800; government purchases of goods and services were $800; proprietors' income was $200; compensation of employees was $2,000; and net exports were –$200. You've been hired as an economist to reconstruct the missing numbers by calculating for 2002

a. GDP.
b. Corporate profits.
c. Capital consumption.

6. Nominal GDP in the United States in 2001 was $10,082.2 billion, and real GDP (in 1997 dollars) was $9,214.5 billion. Real GDP in 1997 (in 1997 dollars) was $7,813.2 billion.
   a. Calculate the GDP deflator in 2001.
   b. What was the GDP deflator in 1997?
   c. By what percentage did the price level rise between 1997 and 2001?
   d. By what percentage did real GDP rise between 1997 and 2001?
   e. By what percentage did nominal GDP rise between 1997 and 2001?

7. The GDP deflator in the United States in 1990 was 86.5, and real GDP in 1990 (in 1997 dollars) was $6,707.9 billion. The GDP deflator in the United States in 2000 was 106.9, and real GDP in 2000 (in 1997 dollars) was $9,191.4 billion.
   a. Calculate nominal GDP in 1990.
   b. Calculate nominal GDP in 2000.
   c. By what percentage did the price level rise between 1990 and 2000?
   d. By what percentage did real GDP rise between 1990 and 2000?
   e. By what percentage did nominal GDP rise between 1990 and 2000?

8. Use the information provided in Table 1 to calculate
   a. Nominal GDP in 2002.
   b. Nominal GDP in 2003.
   c. Real GDP in 2003 with base year 2002 using the traditional method.
   d. Real GDP in 2003 with base year 2002 using the chain method.
   e. The GDP deflator in 2003.
   f. Comment on the growth rate of real GDP in 2003.
   g. How does the growth rate of nominal GDP in 2003 divide between real GDP growth and inflation?

9. Use the information provided in Tables 1 and 2 to calculate
   a. Nominal GDP in 2004.
   b. Nominal GDP in 2005.
   c. Real GDP in 2004 with base year 2002 using the traditional method.
   d. Real GDP in 2005 with base year 2002 using the traditional method.
   e. Real GDP in 2004 with base year 2002 using the chain method.
   f. Real GDP in 2005 with base year 2002 using the chain method.
   g. The GDP deflator in 2004 and 2005.
   h. Comment on the growth rate of real GDP between 2003 and 2005.
   i. Comment on the changes in the price level between 2003 and 2005.
   j. How much of the growth of nominal GDP between 2002 and 2005 was the result of inflation and how much was the result of real GDP growth?

TABLE 1

(a) In 2002:

Item	Quantity	Price
Fun	40	$2
Food	60	$3

(b) In 2003:

Item	Quantity	Price
Fun	44	$3
Food	72	$2

TABLE 2

(a) In 2004:

Item	Quantity	Price
Fun	50	$3
Food	72	$3

(b) In 2005:

Item	Quantity	Price
Fun	51	$4
Food	80	$6

Critical Thinking

10. In 2002, the oil tanker *Prestige* sank in the Atlantic Ocean and the oil washed ashore on the beaches of Spain . Millions of dollars were spent cleaning up the mess, and much wildlife was killed.
    a. Describe how the effects of this oil spill appear in the national income accounts of Spain.
    b. Does the national accounts treatment of this event properly record the effects of the spill on the standard of living of the people who were affected? Explain why or why not.

11. How do underground economic activities affect the usefulness of the national income accounts for comparing the value of production over time and across countries? What underground economic activities do the national income accounts miss? Do these activities contribute to the standard of living? Do you think that it would be worth expanding the scope of the accounts to include estimates of the value of underground activities?

12. The United Nations Index of Human Development is based on the levels of GDP per person, life expectancy at birth, and indicators of the quality and quantity of education. Do you think the United Nations should expand its index to include items such as pollution, resource depletion, and political freedom? Are there any other factors that influence the standard of living that you think should be included in a comprehensive measure?

Practice Online

Web Exercises

Use the links on your Foundations Web site to work the following exercises.

13. Read the article on one of the great inventions of the twentieth century and the article in the Naples Daily News. Summarize the argument that the national income accounts are one of the great inventions and describe the improvement reported in the news article.

14. Visit the Bureau of Economic Analysis Web site and obtain the most recently released National Income and Product Account data for the United States. For the most recently available quarter,
    a. What are the values of consumption expenditure, investment, government purchases, and net exports?
    b. Check that when you sum the items in part **a**, the total equals GDP.
    c. Find the GDP deflator with the base year of 1997.
    d. Calculate real GDP.
    e. Was the cost of living higher in the most recent quarter than in 1997? Explain your answer.

15. Visit the International Monetary Fund World Economic Outlook Web site and obtain the most recently released real GDP data for the global economy.
    a. In which countries is real GDP growth the fastest?
    b. In which countries is real GDP shrinking?
    c. What is the GDP of the United States as a percentage of world GDP?
    d. On the basis of the growth rates over the past decade, in which regions does the standard of living appear to be improving fastest and in which does it appear to be improving the slowest?

CHAPTER 14

The CPI and the Cost of Living

CHAPTER CHECKLIST

When you have completed your study of this chapter, you will be able to

1 Explain what the Consumer Price Index (CPI) is and how it is calculated.

2 Explain the limitations of the CPI as a measure of the cost of living.

3 Adjust money values for inflation and calculate real wage rates and real interest rates.

You learned in Chapter 13 how the Bureau of Economic Analysis measures GDP, which provides information on the standard of living. In this chapter, we focus on measuring the cost of living.

The main measure of the cost of living is called the Consumer Price Index, or CPI. The Department of Labor publishes new CPI figures each month, and analysts in newspapers and on TV quickly leap to conclusions about the causes of recent changes in prices and the implications of the latest numbers for interest rate actions by the Federal Reserve.

How does the government determine the CPI? How well does it measure the cost of living and the inflation rate?

In this chapter, you will find out how economic statisticians measure the price level and the inflation rate and what the limitations of these measures are. You will also learn how we use price index numbers to strip away the veil of money and dollar values to see the real values that they represent.

14.1 THE CONSUMER PRICE INDEX

Consumer Price Index
A measure of the average of the prices paid by urban consumers for a fixed market basket of consumer goods and services.

The **Consumer Price Index** (CPI) is a measure of the average of the prices paid by urban consumers for a fixed market basket of consumer goods and services. The Bureau of Labor Statistics (BLS) calculates the CPI every month, and we can use these numbers to compare what the fixed market basket costs this month with what it cost in some previous month or other period.

Reading the CPI Numbers

Reference base period
A period for which the CPI is defined to equal 100. Currently, the reference base period is 1982–1984.

The CPI is defined to equal 100 for a period called the **reference base period**. Currently, the reference base period is 1982–1984. That is, the CPI equals 100 on the average, over the 36 months from January 1982 through December 1984.

In September 2002, the CPI was 181. This number tells us that the average of the prices paid by urban consumers for a fixed market basket of consumer goods and services was 81 percent higher in September 2002 than it was on the average during 1982–1984.

In August 2002, the CPI was 180.7. Comparing the September CPI with the August CPI tells us that the average of the prices paid by urban consumers for a fixed market basket of consumer goods and services increased by 0.3 of a percentage point in September 2002.

Constructing the CPI

Constructing the CPI is a huge operation that costs millions of dollars and involves three stages:

- Selecting the CPI basket
- Conducting the monthly price survey
- Calculating the CPI

The CPI Basket

The first stage in constructing the CPI is to select what is called the *CPI basket*. This "basket" contains the goods and services represented in the index and the relative importance attached to each of them. The idea is to make the relative importance of the items in the CPI basket the same as in the budget of an average urban household. For example, people spend more on housing than on bus rides, so the CPI places more weight on the price of housing than on the price of bus rides.

The BLS uses two baskets and calculates two CPIs. One, called CPI-U, measures the average price paid by *all* urban households. The other, called CPI-W, measures the average price paid by urban wage earners and clerical workers. Here, we will focus on CPI-U, the broader measure.

To determine the spending patterns of households and to select the CPI basket, the BLS conducts a Consumer Expenditure Survey. This survey is costly and therefore is undertaken infrequently. Today's CPI is based on data gathered in a survey of 1999–2000. Before 2002, the CPI was based on a 1993–1995 survey. The BLS plans more frequent updates of the CPI basket in the future.

Until recently, the time period covered by the Consumer Expenditure Survey was also the reference base period. But the BLS has now changed the basket on two occasions but retained 1982–1984 as the reference base period.

Figure 14.1 shows the CPI basket at the end of 2002. The basket contains around 80,000 goods and services arranged in the eight large groups shown in the figure. The most important item in a household's budget is housing, which accounts for 41 percent of total expenditure. Transportation comes next at 17 percent. Third in relative importance is food and beverages at 16 percent. These three groups account for almost three quarters of the average household budget. Medical care and recreation each take 6 percent, education and communication takes 6 percent, and apparel (clothing and footwear) takes 4 percent. Another 4 percent is spent on other goods and services.

The BLS breaks down each of these categories into smaller ones. For example, education and communication breaks down into textbooks and supplies, tuition, telephone services, and personal computer services.

As you look at these relatively important numbers, remember that they apply to the average household. Each individual household is spread around the average. Think about your own expenditure and compare it with the average.

The Monthly Price Survey

Each month, BLS employees check the prices of the 80,000 goods and services in the CPI basket in 30 metropolitan areas. Because the CPI aims to measure price changes, it is important that the prices recorded each month refer to exactly the same item. For example, suppose the price of a box of jelly beans has increased but a box now contains more beans. Has the price of a jelly bean increased? The BLS employee must record the details of changes in quality, size, weight, or packaging so that price changes can be isolated from other changes.

Once the raw price data are in hand, the next task is to calculate the CPI.

FIGURE 14.1
The CPI Basket

Practice Online

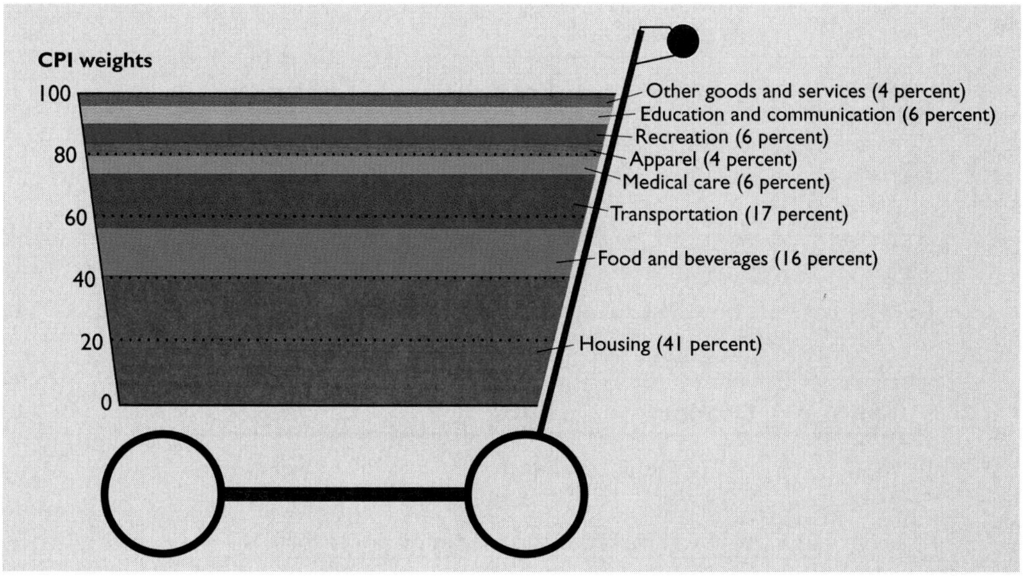

CPI weights
100
80
60
40
20
0
Other goods and services (4 percent)
Education and communication (6 percent)
Recreation (6 percent)
Apparel (4 percent)
Medical care (6 percent)
Transportation (17 percent)
Food and beverages (16 percent)
Housing (41 percent)

SOURCE: Bureau of Labor Statistics.

This shopping cart is filled with the items that an average household buys. Housing (41 percent), transportation (17 percent), and food and beverages (16 percent) take 74 percent of household income.

Calculating the CPI

The CPI calculation has three steps:

- Find the cost of the CPI basket at base period prices.
- Find the cost of the CPI basket at current period prices.
- Calculate the CPI for the base period and the current period.

We'll work through these three steps for a simple example. Suppose the CPI basket contains only two goods and services: oranges and haircuts. We'll construct an annual CPI rather than a monthly CPI with the reference base period 2000 and the current period 2003.

Table 14.1 shows the quantities in the CPI basket and the prices in the base period and the current period. Part (a) contains the data for the base period. In that period, consumers bought 10 oranges at $1 each and 5 haircuts at $8 each. To find the cost of the CPI basket in the base period prices, multiply the quantities in the CPI basket by the base period prices. The cost of oranges is $10 (10 at $1 each), and the cost of haircuts is $40 (5 at $8 each). So total expenditure in the base period on the CPI basket is $50 ($10 + $40).

Part (b) contains the price data for the current period. The price of an orange increased from $1 to $2, which is a 100 percent increase ($1 ÷ $1 × 100 = 100 percent). The price of a haircut increased from $8 to $10, which is a 25 percent increase ($2 ÷ $8 × 100 = 25 percent).

The CPI provides a way of averaging these price increases by comparing the cost of the basket rather than the price of each item. To find the cost of the CPI basket in the current period, 2003, multiply the quantities in the basket by their 2003 prices. The cost of oranges is $20 (10 at $2 each), and the cost of haircuts is $50 (5 at $10 each) So total expenditure on the fixed CPI basket at current period prices is $70 ($20 + $50).

TABLE 14.1
The Consumer Price Index: A Simplified CPI Calculation

Practice Online

(a) The cost of the CPI basket at base period prices: 2000

Item	CPI basket: Quantity	CPI basket: Price	Cost of CPI basket
Oranges	10	$1 each	$10
Haircuts	5	$8 each	$40
		Cost of CPI basket at base period prices	$50

(b) The cost of the CPI basket at current period prices: 2003

Item	CPI basket: Quantity	CPI basket: Price	Cost of CPI basket
Oranges	10	$2 each	$20
Haircuts	5	$10 each	$50
		Cost of CPI basket at current period prices	$70

You've now taken the first two steps toward calculating the CPI. The third step uses the numbers you've just calculated to find the CPI for 2000 and 2003. The formula for the CPI is

$$\text{CPI} = \frac{\text{Cost of CPI basket at current period prices}}{\text{Cost of CPI basket at base period prices}} \times 100.$$

In Table 14.1, you established that in 2000, the cost of the CPI basket was \$50 and in 2003, it was \$70. If we use these numbers in the CPI formula, we can find the CPI for 2000 and 2003. The base period is 2000, so for 2000, the CPI is

$$\text{CPI in 2000} = \frac{\$50}{\$50} \times 100 = 100.$$

For 2003, the CPI is

$$\text{CPI in 2003} = \frac{\$70}{\$50} \times 100 = 140.$$

The principles that you've applied in this simplified CPI calculation apply to the more complex calculations performed every month by the BLS.

Figure 14.2(a) shows the CPI in the United States during the 30 years between 1972 and 2002. The CPI increased every year during this period. During the late 1970s and in 1980, the CPI was increasing rapidly, but the rate of increase slowed during the 1980s and 1990s.

Measuring Inflation

A major purpose of the CPI is to measure *changes* in the cost of living and in the value of money. To measure these changes, we calculate the **inflation rate**, which is the percentage change in the price level from one year to the next. To calculate the inflation rate, we use the formula

Inflation rate
The percentage change in the price level from one year to the next.

$$\text{Inflation rate} = \frac{(\text{CPI in current year} - \text{CPI in previous year})}{\text{CPI in previous year}} \times 100.$$

Suppose that the current year is 2003 and the CPI for 2003 is 140. And suppose that in the previous year, 2002, the CPI was 120. Then the inflation rate in 2003 was

$$\text{Inflation rate} = \frac{(140 - 120)}{120} \times 100 = 16.7 \text{ percent}.$$

This inflation rate is very high—much higher than anything that we experience in the United States. You can check the latest inflation rate by visiting the BLS Web site. Let's calculate a recent U.S. inflation rate. In September 2002, the CPI was 181, and in September 2001, it was 178.3. So the inflation rate during the year to September 2002 was

$$\text{Inflation rate} = \frac{(181 - 178.3)}{178.3} \times 100 = 1.5 \text{ percent}.$$

Figure 14.2(b) shows the inflation rate between 1972 and 2002. The two parts of Figure 14.2 are related. When the price *level* in part (a) rises rapidly, the inflation rate in part (b) is high, and when the price level in part (a) rises slowly, the inflation rate in part (b) is low.

FIGURE 14.2
The CPI and the Inflation Rate: 1972–2002

Practice Online

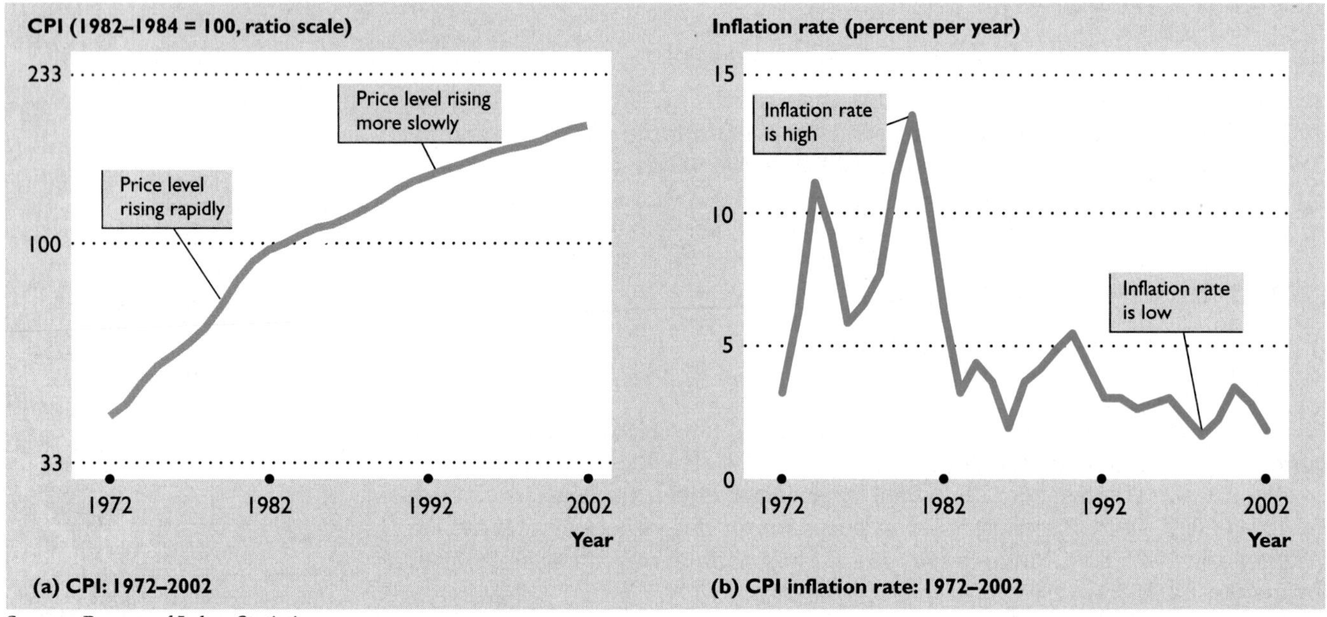

SOURCE: Bureau of Labor Statistics.

In part (a), the CPI (the price *level*) has increased every year. In part (b), the inflation rate has averaged 5 percent a year. During the 1970s and early 1980s, it exceeded 10 percent a year, but since the early 1980s, it has been around 3 percent a year.

700 Years of Inflation and Deflation

These extraordinary data show century averages of inflation in England since the 1300s. There was a burst of inflation during the sixteenth century after Europeans discovered America. But this inflation was less than 2 percent a year—less than we have today—and eventually subsided. During the Industrial Revolution, inflation was less than 1 percent a year. Only in the twentieth century did inflation become a serious problem.

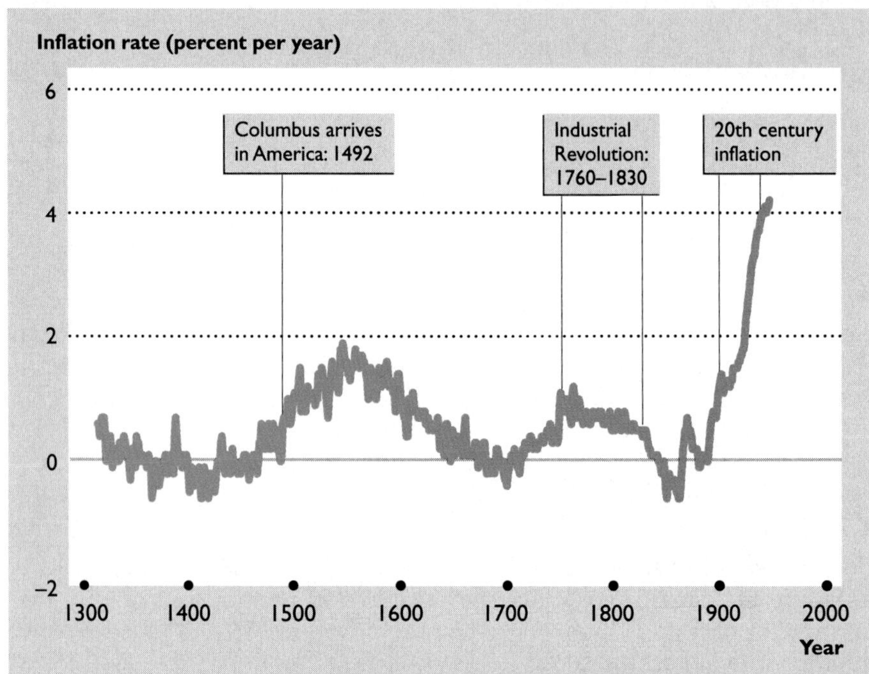

SOURCE: E.H. Phelps Brown and Sheila V. Hopkins, *Economica*, 1955.

CHECKPOINT 14.1

1 Explain what the Consumer Price Index (CPI) is and how it is calculated.

Study Guide pp. 216–219

Practice Online 14.1

Practice Problems 14.1

1. A Consumer Expenditure Survey in Sparta shows that people consume only juice and cloth. In 2003, the year of the Consumer Expenditure Survey and also the reference base year, the average household spent $40 on juice and $25 on cloth. The price of juice in 2003 was $4 a bottle, and the price of cloth was $5 a yard. In the current year, 2004, the price of juice is $4 a bottle and the price of cloth is $6 a yard. Calculate
   a. The CPI basket.
   b. The percentage of household budget spent on juice in the base year.
   c. The CPI in 2004.
2. Table 1 shows the CPI in Russia. Calculate Russia's inflation rate in 2001 and 2002. Did the price level rise or fall in 2002? Did the inflation rate increase or decrease in 2002?

TABLE 1

Year	CPI
2000	225
2001	274
2002	310

Exercise 14.1

A Consumer Expenditure Survey in the city of Firestorm shows that people consume only firecrackers and bandages. In 2002, the year of the Consumer Expenditure Survey and also the reference base year, the average household spent $150 on firecrackers and $15 on bandages. The price of a firecracker in 2002 was $2, and the price of bandages was $1 a pack. In the current year, 2003, the price of a firecracker is $3 and the price of bandages is $1.25 a pack. Calculate

a. The CPI basket.
b. The percentage of a household's budget spent on firecrackers in the base year.
c. The CPI in 2003.
d. The inflation rate in 2003.

Solutions to Practice Problems 14.1

1a. The CPI basket is the quantities bought during the Consumer Expenditure Survey year, 2003. Households spend $40 on juice at $4 a bottle, so the quantity of juice bought was 10 bottles. Households spend $25 on cloth at $5 a yard, so the quantity of cloth bought was 5 yards. The CPI basket is 10 bottles of juice and 5 yards of cloth.

1b. In the reference base year, expenditure on juice was $40 and expenditure on cloth was $25, so the household budget was $65. Expenditure on juice was 61.5 percent of the household budget: ($40 ÷ $65) × 100 = 61.5 percent.

1c. To calculate the CPI in 2004, find the cost of the CPI basket in 2003 and 2004. In 2003, the CPI basket costs $65 ($40 for juice and $25 for cloth). In 2004, the CPI basket costs $40 for juice (10 bottles at $4 a bottle) plus $30 for cloth (5 yards at $6 a yard), which sums to $70. The CPI in 2004 equals ($70/$65) × 100 = 107.7.

2. The inflation rate in 2001 is [(274 – 225) ÷ 225] × 100 = 21.8 percent. The inflation rate in 2002 is [(310 – 274) ÷ 274] × 100 = 13.1 percent. The price level increased and the inflation rate decreased in 2002.

14.2 THE CPI AND THE COST OF LIVING

Cost of living index
A measure of changes in the amount of money that people would need to spend to achieve a given standard of living.

The CPI is sometimes called a cost of living index. The purpose of a **cost of living index** is to measure changes in the amount of money that people would need to spend to achieve a given standard of living. The CPI does not measure the cost of living for two broad reasons.

First, the CPI does not try to measure all the components of the cost of living. For example, a severe winter might cause people to buy more natural gas and electricity to heat their homes. An increase in the prices of these items would increase the CPI, but the increased quantities bought would not change the CPI because the CPI basket is fixed. So part of this increase in spending, which is an increase in the cost of maintaining a given standard of living, would not show up as an increase in the CPI.

Second, even those components of the cost of living that are measured by the CPI are not always measured accurately. The result is that the CPI is possibly a biased measure of changes in the cost of living. Let's look at some of the problems faced by the BLS that might lead to bias in the CPI.

The Biased CPI

The main sources of bias in the CPI are

- New goods bias
- Quality change bias
- Commodity substitution bias
- Outlet substitution bias

New Goods Bias

New goods keep replacing old ones. For example, the PC has replaced the typewriter. The DVD is gradually replacing the videocassette player. The digital camera is replacing the film camera. These are just a few examples of a very long list of new goods to which you can easily add.

If you want to compare the price level in 2003 with that in 1993, you must somehow compare the price of a DVD today with that of a videocassette player in 1993. Because DVDs do a better job than videocassette players, you are better off with the new technology if the prices were the same. But DVDs are more expensive than videocassette players. How much of the higher price is a sign of the higher quality?

The BLS does its best to answer this type of question and employs many experts to help get the correct answer. But there is no sure way of making the necessary adjustment, and most likely, the arrival of new goods puts an upward bias into the CPI and its measure of the inflation rate.

Quality Change Bias

Cars, CD players, and many other items get better every year. For example, central locking, airbags, and antilock braking systems all add to the quality of a car. But they also add to the cost. Is the improvement in quality greater than the increase in cost? Or do car prices rise by more than can be accounted for by quality improvements? To the extent that a price rise is a payment for improved quality, it is not inflation. Again, the BLS does the best job it can to estimate the effects of quality improvements on price changes. But the CPI probably counts too much of any price rise as inflation and so overstates inflation.

Commodity Substitution Bias

Changes in relative prices lead consumers to change the items they buy. People cut back on items that become relatively more costly and increase their consumption of items that become relatively less costly. For example, suppose the price of beef rises while the price of chicken remains constant. Now that beef is more costly relative to chicken, you might decide to buy more chicken and less beef. Suppose that you switch from beef to chicken, spend the same amount on meat as before, and get the same enjoyment as before. Your cost of meat has not changed. But the CPI says that the price of meat has increased because it ignores your substitution between goods in the CPI basket.

Outlet Substitution Bias

When confronted with higher prices, people use discount stores more frequently and convenience stores less frequently. This phenomenon is called *outlet substitution*. Suppose, for example, that gas prices rise by 10 cents a gallon. Instead of buying from your nearby gas station for $1.50 a gallon, you now drive farther to a gas station that charges $1.40 a gallon. Your cost of gas has increased because you must factor in the cost of your time and the gas that you use driving several blocks down the road. But your cost has not increased by as much as the 10 cents a gallon increase in the pump price. However, the CPI says that the price of gas has increased by 10 cents a gallon because it does not measure outlet substitutions.

The growth of online shopping in recent years has provided an alternative to discount stores that makes outlet substitution even easier and potentially makes this source of bias more serious.

The Magnitude of the Bias

You've reviewed the sources of bias in the CPI. But how big is the bias? This question was tackled in 1996 by a Congressional Advisory Commission on the Consumer Price Index chaired by Michael Boskin, an economics professor at Stanford University. This commission said that the CPI overstates inflation by 1.1 percentage points a year. That is, if the CPI reports that inflation is 3.1 percent a year, most likely inflation is actually 2 percent a year. Some economists do not accept the Boskin Commission's conclusion, but most economists agree that there is some bias in the CPI.

To reduce the sources of bias that we've just reviewed, the BLS has decided to increase the frequency of its Consumer Expenditure Survey and to revise the CPI basket every two years.

Two Consequences of the CPI Bias

The bias in the CPI has two main consequences. It

- Distorts private contracts.
- Increases government outlays.

Distortion of Private Contracts

Many wage contracts contain a cost of living adjustment. Suppose that the UAW and General Motors Corporation agree on wage rate of $28 an hour initially that increases over three years at a rate of 2 percent a year plus the increase in the cost of living. Suppose that over the three years, the CPI increases by 3 percent each year but the true price increase is 1.9 percent a year (a 1.1 percentage point bias in the CPI). Table 14.2 shows the wage rates each year, the wage rates the UAW and GM intended, and the gap between the actual and intended wage rate—the wage bias. At the end of the first year, the wage rate rises by 5 percent to $29.40 an hour. The intention of the contract was for it to increase by 3.9 percent to $29.09. There is a 31¢ an hour bias. After the second year, the wage rate rises by a further 5 percent to $30.87 an hour instead of the intended $30.23. The bias is now 64¢ an hour. After three years, the workers are receiving $1.01 an hour more than they would have received if the CPI measured the true increase in prices.

Increases in Government Outlays

Because rising prices decrease the buying power of the dollar, the CPI is used to adjust the incomes of the 48 million Social Security beneficiaries, 22 million food stamp recipients, and 4 million retired former military personnel and federal civil servants (and their surviving spouses) and the budget for 27 million school lunches.

Close to a third of federal government outlays are linked directly to the CPI. If the CPI has a 1.1 percentage point bias, all of these expenditures increase by more than required to compensate for the fall in the buying power of the dollar and, although a bias of 1.1 percent a year seems small, accumulated over a decade, it adds up to almost a trillion dollars of additional government outlays.

The GDP Deflator: A Better Measure?

In Chapter 13, you learned about another measure of average prices: the *GDP deflator*. When we calculate the GDP deflator, we compare the current year's prices with the previous year's prices using the current year's and a previous year's baskets of goods and services. Because it uses current year quantities, the real GDP includes new goods and quality improvements and even allows for substitution effects of both commodities and retail outlets. So in principle, the GDP deflator is not subject to the biases of the CPI.

But in practice, the GDP deflator suffers from some of the CPI's problems. To arrive at its estimate of real GDP, the Commerce Department does not directly measure the physical quantities that are produced. Instead, it estimates quantities

TABLE 14.2
A Three-Year Wage Deal

Practice Online

	Fixed increase (percent)	CPI increase (percent)	Wage rate (dollars per hour)	True price increase (percent)	Intended wage rate (dollars per hour)	Wage bias (dollars per hour)
Initially			28.00		28.00	—
After 1 year	2	3	29.40	1.9	29.09	0.31
After 2 years	2	3	30.87	1.9	30.23	0.64
After 3 years	2	3	32.41	1.9	31.40	1.01

by dividing expenditures by price indexes. And one of these price indexes is the CPI. So the biased CPI injects a bias into the GDP deflator.

Also, the GDP deflator is broader than the CPI. GDP is the sum of expenditures on all final goods and services, not just consumption expenditures. So the GDP deflator reflects the prices of such items as paper mills bought by 3M to make Post-it Notes, nuclear submarines bought by the Defense Department, and Boeing 747s bought by British Airways. So the GDP deflator is not an alternative to the CPI as a measure of the cost of living.

Figure 14.3(a) shows the CPI and the GDP deflator measures of inflation. The two measures move up and down in similar ways, but the CPI measure exceeds the GDP deflator measure and in Figure 14.3(b) they gradually get farther apart.

FIGURE 14.3

Two Measures of Inflation and the Price Level

Practice Online

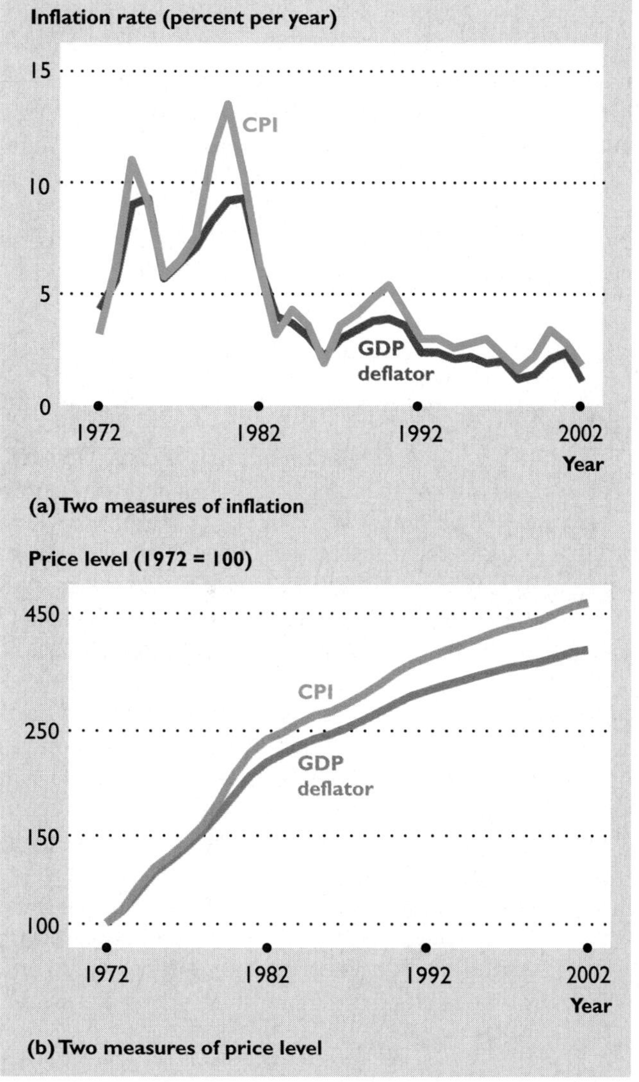

SOURCES: Bureau of Labor Statistics and Bureau of Economic Analysis.

The two measures of the inflation rate in part (a) fluctuate together, but the CPI rises more rapidly than the GDP deflator, and in part (b), the price levels get farther apart. Both measures probably overstate the inflation rate.

CHECKPOINT 14.2

Study Guide pp. 219–221

Practice Online 14.2

2 **Explain the limitations of the CPI as a measure of the cost of living.**

Practice Problem 14.2

Economists in the Statistics Bureau decide to check the substitution bias in the CPI. To do so, they conduct a Consumer Expenditure Survey in both 2001 and 2002. Table 1 shows the results of the survey. It shows the items that consumers buy and their prices. The Statistics Bureau fixes the reference base year as 2001 and asks you to

a. Calculate the CPI in 2002 using the 2001 CPI basket.
b. Calculate the CPI in 2002 using the 2002 CPI basket.
c. Explain whether there is any substitution bias in the CPI that uses the 2001 basket.

TABLE 1

	2001		2002	
Item	Quantity	Price	Quantity	Price
Broccoli	10	$3.00	15	$3.00
Carrots	15	$2.00	10	$4.00

Exercise 14.2

In Virtual Reality, time travel became possible only in 3002. Economists in the Statistics Bureau decided to conduct a Consumer Expenditure Survey in both 3001 and 3002 to check the substitution bias of the CPI. Table 2 shows the results of the survey. It shows the items that consumers buy and their prices. The Statistics Bureau fixes the reference base year as 3001 and asks you to

a. Calculate the CPI in 3002 using the 3001 CPI basket.
b. Calculate the CPI in 3002 using the 3002 CPI basket.
c. Explain whether there is any substitution bias in the CPI that uses the 3001 basket.

TABLE 2

	3001		3002	
Item	Quantity	Price	Quantity	Price
Games	20	$60	10	$70
Time travel	0	–	20	$8,000

Solution to Practice Problem 14.2

a. Table 3 shows the calculation of the CPI in 2002 using the 2001 basket. The cost of the 2001 basket at 2001 prices is $60, and the cost of the 2001 basket at 2002 prices is $90. So the CPI in 2002 using the 2001 basket is ($90 ÷ $60) × 100 = 150.

b. Table 4 shows the calculation of the CPI in 2002 using the 2002 basket. The cost of the 2002 basket at 2001 prices is $65, and the cost of the 2002 basket at 2002 prices is $85. So the CPI in 2002 using the 2002 basket is ($85 ÷ $65) × 100 = 131.

c. There is some substitution bias in the CPI that uses the 2001 basket. The price of broccoli remains constant, but the price of carrots rises by 100 percent. So consumers cut the quantity of carrots consumed and increase the quantity of broccoli consumed. They end up spending $85 on vegetables. But they would have spent $90 if they had not substituted the now relatively less costly broccoli. The cost of vegetables does not rise by 50 percent as shown by the CPI. Instead, because of substitution, the cost of vegetables increases by only 42 percent ($85 is 42 percent greater than $60). When we calculate the increase in the price of vegetables using the 2002 CPI basket, the increase is only 31 percent ($85 compared with $65). So the CPI is biased upward because it ignores the substitutions that people make in response to changes in the price of one item relative to the price of another.

TABLE 3

Item	2001 basket at 2001 prices	2001 basket at 2002 prices
Broccoli	$30	$30
Carrot	$30	$60
Totals	$60	$90

TABLE 4

Item	2002 basket at 2001 prices	2002 basket at 2002 prices
Broccoli	$45	$45
Carrot	$20	$40
Totals	$65	$85

14.3 NOMINAL AND REAL VALUES

In 2002, it cost 37 cents to mail a first-class letter. One hundred years earlier, in 1902, that same letter would have cost 2 cents to mail. Does it *really* cost you 18.5 times the amount that it cost your great-great-grandmother to mail a letter?

You know that it does not. You know that a dollar today buys less than what a dollar bought in 1902, so the cost of a stamp has not really increased to 18.5 times its 1902 level. But has it increased at all? Did it really cost you any more to mail a letter in 2002 than it cost your great-great-grandmother in 1902?

The CPI can be used to answer questions like these. In fact, that is one of the main reasons for constructing a price index. Let's see how we can compare the price of a stamp in 1902 and the price of a stamp in 2002.

Dollars and Cents at Different Dates

To compare dollar amounts at different dates, we need to know the CPI at those dates. Currently, the CPI has a base of 100 for 1982–1984. That is, the average of the CPI in 1982, 1983, and 1984 is 100. (The numbers for the three years are 96.4, 99.6, and 103.9, respectively. Calculate the average of these numbers and check that it is indeed 100.)

In 2002, the CPI was 180.3, and in 1902, it was 9. By using these two numbers, we can calculate the relative value of the dollar in 1902 and 2002. To do so, we divide the 2002 CPI by the 1902 CPI. That ratio is 180.3 ÷ 9 = 20. That is, prices on the average were 20 times higher in 2002 than in 1902.

We can use this ratio to convert the price of a 2-cent stamp in 1902 into its 2002 equivalent. The formula for this calculation is

$$\text{Price of stamp in 2002 dollars} = \text{Price of stamp in 1902 dollars} \times \frac{\text{CPI in 2002}}{\text{CPI in 1902}}$$

$$= 2 \text{ cents} \times \frac{180.3}{9} = 40 \text{ cents.}$$

So your great-great-grandmother had a raw deal! It *really* cost her more to mail that first-class letter than it cost you in 2002. She paid the equivalent of 40 cents, and you paid 37 cents.

The calculation that we've just done is an example of converting a *nominal* value into a *real* value. A nominal value is one that is expressed in current dollars. A real value is one that is expressed in the dollars of a given year.

Nominal and Real Values in Macroeconomics

Macroeconomics makes a big issue of the distinction between nominal and real values. You saw that distinction in Chapter 13, where you learned the difference between nominal GDP and real GDP. To calculate real GDP, we use the same idea that you've just used to calculate the real price of a postage stamp. But usually, in macroeconomics, we use the GDP deflator rather than the CPI as our measure of the price level. The reason is that we are dealing with economy totals, of which consumer spending is just one part. So real GDP is equal to nominal GDP divided by the GDP deflator and *not* nominal GDP divided by the CPI.

Eye on the Past

The Nominal and Real Price of a First-Class Letter

The figure shows the cost of a first-class letter since 1902. The green line is the nominal price—the actual price of a stamp in the dollars (cents) of the year in question. The red line is the real price—the price in terms of the 2002 dollar. You can see that the nominal price has gradually increased, but the real price has fluctuated, sometimes rising and sometimes falling. The highest real price, 44 cents, occurred in 1975, and the lowest real price, 18 cents, occurred in 1920.

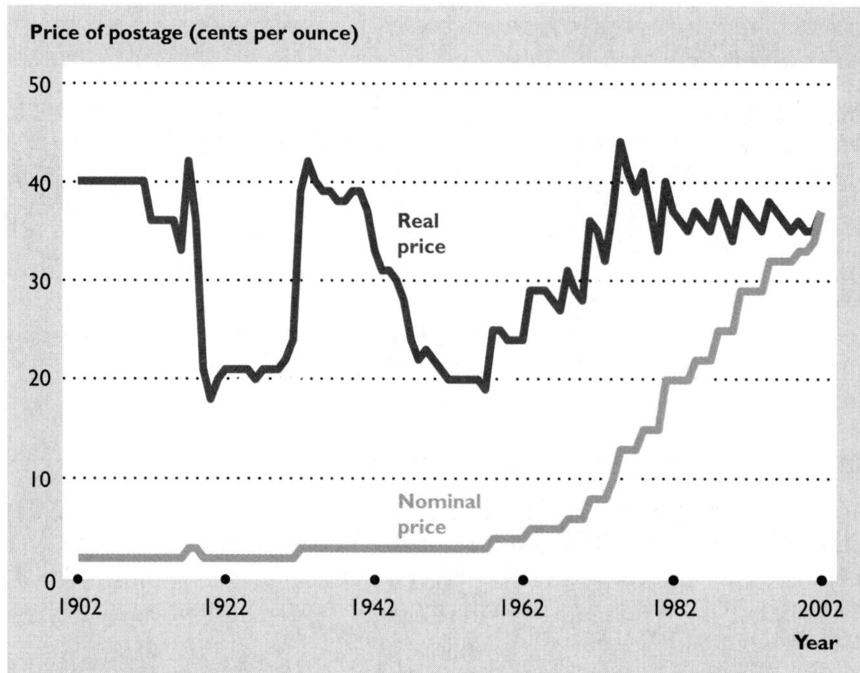

SOURCE: Robert Sahr, Oregon State University, http://www.orst.edu/dept/pol_sci/fac/sahr/stamp.htm.

Two other nominal–real distinctions play a big role in macroeconomics—and in your life. They are the distinctions between

- The nominal wage rate and the real wage rate
- The nominal interest rate and the real interest rate

Let's study these vital distinctions.

Nominal and Real Wage Rates

Nominal wage rate
The average hourly wage rate measured in *current* dollars.

Real wage rate
The average hourly wage rate measured in the dollars of a given reference base year.

The price of labor is the wage rate—the income that an hour of labor earns. In macroeconomics, we are interested in economy-wide performance, so we focus on the *average* hourly wage rate. The **nominal wage rate** is the average hourly wage rate measured in *current* dollars. The **real wage rate** is the average hourly wage rate measured in the dollars of a given reference base year.

To calculate the real wage rate, we divide the nominal wage rate by the CPI and multiply by 100. That is,

$$\text{Real wage rate in 2002} = \frac{\text{Nominal wage rate in 2002}}{\text{CPI in 2002}} \times 100.$$

In June 2002, the nominal wage rate (average hourly wage rate) of production workers was \$14.68 and the CPI was 179.9, so

$$\text{Real wage rate in June 2002} = \frac{\$14.68}{179.9} \times 100 = \$8.16.$$

Because we measure the real wage rate in constant base-year dollars, a change in the real wage rate measures the change in the quantity of goods and services that an hour's work can buy. In contrast, a change in the nominal wage rate measures a combination of a change in the quantity of goods and services that an hour's work can buy and a change in the price level. So the real wage rate takes the effects of inflation out of changes in the nominal wage rate.

The real wage rate is a significant economic variable because it measures the real reward for labor, which is a major determinant of the standard of living. The real wage rate is also significant because it measures the real cost of labor, which influences the quantity of labor that firms are willing to hire.

Figure 14.4 shows what has happened to the nominal wage rate and the real wage rate in the United States between 1972 and 2002. The nominal wage rate is the average hourly earning of production workers. This measure is just one of the several different measures of average hourly earnings that we might have used.

The nominal wage rate increased from $3.70 an hour in 1972 to $14.76 an hour in 2002. But the real wage rate decreased. In 1982–1984 dollars (the CPI base period dollars), the real wage rate was $8.85 in 1972 and $8.19 in 2002.

The real wage rate decreased as the nominal wage rate increased because the nominal wage rate didn't keep up with inflation. When the effects of inflation are removed from the nominal wage rate, we can see what is happening to the buying power of the average wage rate.

You can also see that the real wage rate has fluctuated. During the late 1970s, the real wage rate increased briefly. It then decreased until the mid-1990s, after which it increased slightly.

FIGURE 14.4
Nominal and Real Wage Rates: 1972–2002

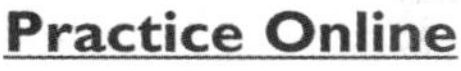

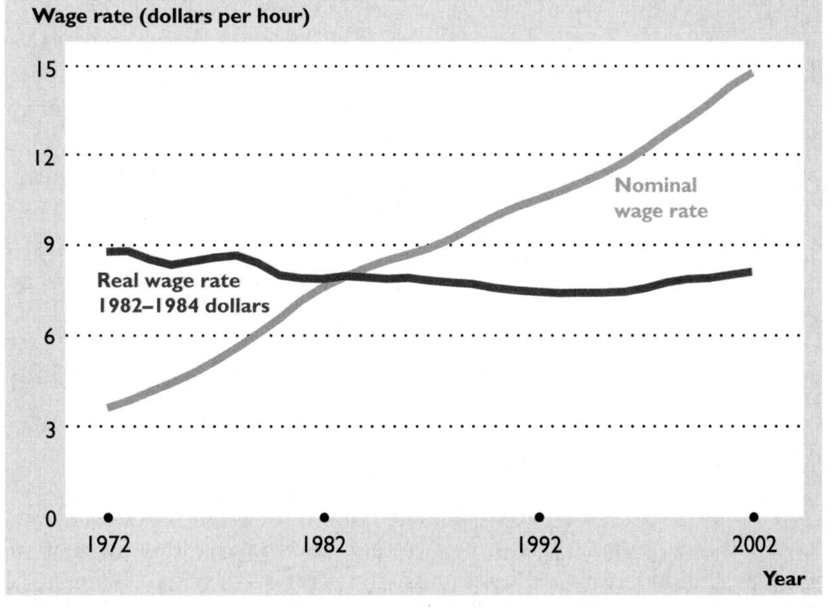

SOURCE: *Economic Report of the President*, 2002.

The nominal wage rate has increased every year since 1972. The real wage rate increased briefly during the late 1970s and then decreased through the mid-1990s, after which it increased slightly again. Over the entire 30-year period, the real wage rate decreased.

The Nominal and Real Wage Rates of Presidents of the United States

Does an airline pilot in 2003 earn a higher real wage rate than an airline pilot earned in 1963? Does a coal miner in 2003 earn more than a coal miner earned in 1963? We can use the formula that you've learned in this chapter to calculate the real wage rates of airline pilots and coal miners in 1963 and 2003 and compare them. But the comparison will be imprecise because these jobs have changed a great deal. In 1963, an airline pilot had to make many calculations that in 2003 are done by on-board computers. A 1963 coal miner used much more muscle power than his 2003 counterpart.

One job that has not changed much in more than 200 years is that of President of the United States. The job specification and the level of stress have remained similar over the decades. George Washington faced the challenge of creating a nation, Abraham Lincoln had to cope with civil war, Herbert Hoover with the Great Depression, Franklin Roosevelt with World War II, and George W. Bush with international terrorism.

It is tempting to calculate the real wage rates of U.S. Presidents to establish who was paid the most and who was paid the least.

The figure provides the data. The nominal wage rate (the green line) was set at $25,000 a year in 1789 and remained at that level until 1877, when it was doubled to $50,000 a year. It has increased in jumps to $400,000 in 2001.

The real wage rate (the red line) has followed a remarkable course. Expressed in 2000 dollars, George Washington earned $250,000 a year. The price level was falling during the first half of the nineteenth century, so the real wage rate climbed. It reached $500,000 a year, where it remained through the presidency of Abraham Lincoln. It dipped for Andrew Jackson because a burst of inflation during the Civil War lowered the buying power of his $25,000. The real wage rate then increased through the early 1900s and peaked at $1,500,000 for William Howard Taft.

Throughout the twentieth century, the President's real pay has been on a downward trend. Bill Clinton was the lowest-paid President in U.S. history!

Not counted in the President's salary are the perks that go with the job. The White House is more comfortable today, and presidential travel arrangements are a breeze compared to earlier times. So Bill Clinton probably didn't get such a raw deal.

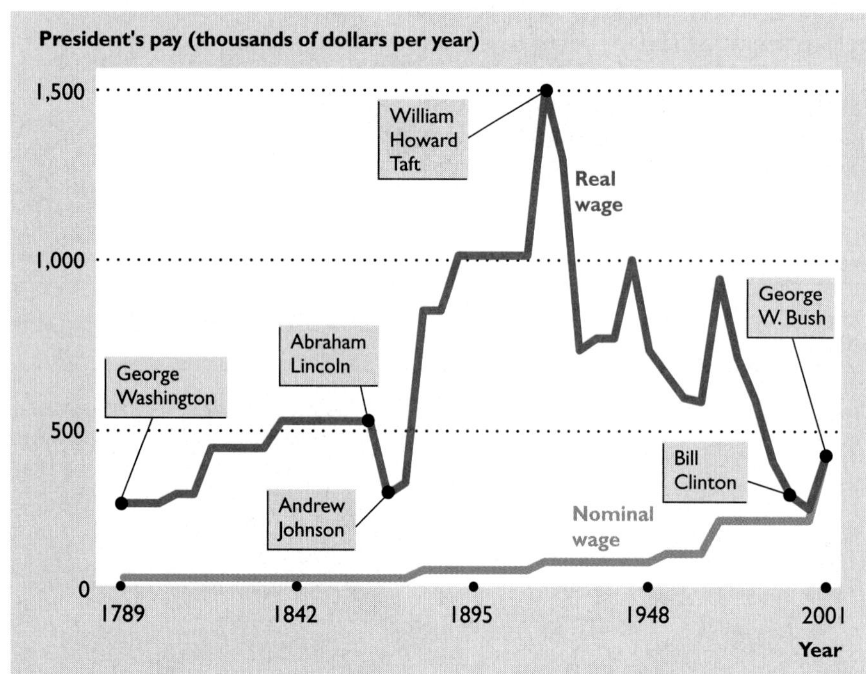

SOURCE: Robert Sahr, Oregon State University, http://www.orst.edu/dept/pol_sci/fac/sahr/sahr.htm.

Nominal and Real Interest Rates

You've just seen that we can calculate real values from nominal values by deflating them using the CPI. And you've seen that to make this calculation, we *divide* the nominal value by a price index. Converting a nominal interest rate to a real interest rate is a bit different. To see why, we'll start with their definitions.

A **nominal interest rate** is the percentage return on a loan, calculated by using dollars. For example, if you deposit $100 in a savings account on which the bank pays a nominal interest of 5 percent a year, you will receive $5 on your deposit.

A **real interest rate** is the percentage return on a loan, calculated by using purchasing power. That is, the real interest rate is the nominal interest rate adjusted for the effects of inflation.

Suppose that you have $100 in a bank account and that after one year, you take your money out of the bank. The bank pays you the $100 that you deposited plus the $5 interest that you've earned (at 5 percent a year). But suppose that during the year, prices have increased by 3 percent. You've now got $105, but you need $103 just to buy what $100 would have bought when you put your money in the bank. So how much interest have you really earned? You've earned $2, or a real interest rate of 2 percent a year.

To convert a nominal interest rate to a real interest rate, we *subtract* the *inflation rate*. That is,

Real interest rate = Nominal interest rate – Inflation rate.

Plug your numbers into this formula. Your nominal interest rate is 5 percent a year, the inflation rate is 3 percent a year, and your real interest rate is 5 percent minus 3 percent, which equals 2 percent a year.

Figure 14.5 shows the nominal interest rate and the real interest rate in the United States between 1972 and 2002. When the inflation rate was high, during the 1970s and 1980s, the gap between the real interest rate and the nominal interest rate was large. The real interest rate was even negative in the mid-1970s. When the real interest rate is negative, the lender pays the borrower!

Nominal interest rate
The percentage return on a loan, calculated by using dollars.

Real interest rate
The percentage return on a loan, calculated by using purchasing power—the nominal interest rate adjusted for the effects of inflation.

FIGURE 14.5
Nominal and Real Interest Rates: 1972–2002

Practice Online

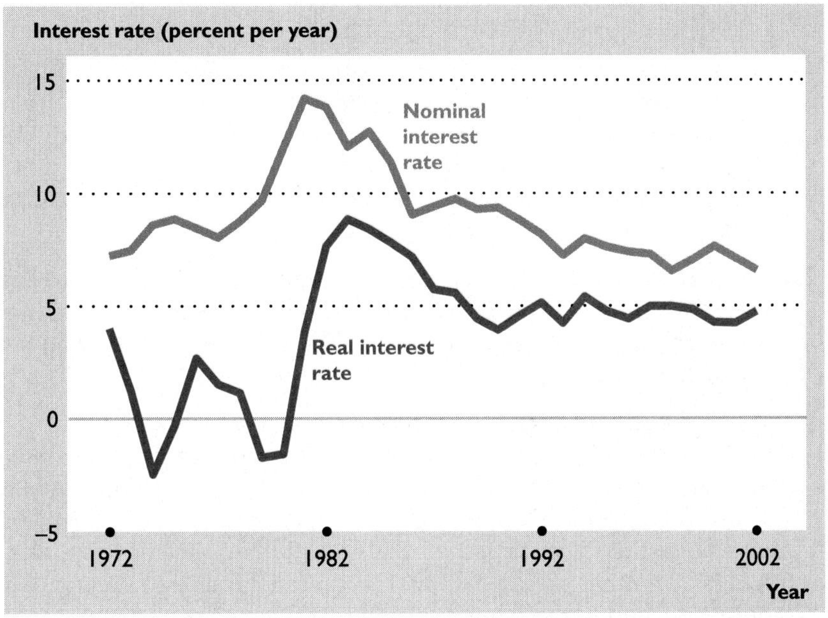

Interest rate (percent per year)
15
10
5
0
–5
Nominal interest rate
Real interest rate
1972
1982
1992
2002
Year

SOURCE: *Economic Report of the President*, 2002.

The real interest rate equals the nominal interest rate minus the inflation rate. During the 1970s, the real interest rate became negative.

CHECKPOINT 14.3

Study Guide pp. 221–224

Practice Online 14.3

3 **Adjust money values for inflation and calculate real wage rates and real interest rates.**

Practice Problems 14.3

1. Table 1 shows some gas prices and the CPI for three years. The reference base period is 1982–1984.
   a. Calculate the real price of gasoline in each year in 1982–1984 dollars.
   b. In which year was gasoline the most costly in real terms?
   c. In which year was gasoline the least costly in real terms?

2. Amazon.com agreed to pay its workers $20 an hour in 1999 and $22 an hour in 2001. The CPI for these years was 166 in 1999 and 180 in 2001.
   a. Calculate the real wage rate in each year.
   b. Did these workers really get a pay raise between 1999 and 2001?

3. Sally worked hard all year so that she could go to school full time the following year. She put her savings into a mutual fund that paid a nominal interest rate of 7 percent a year. The CPI was 165 at the beginning of the year and 177 at the end of the year. What was the real interest rate that Sally earned?

TABLE 1

Year	Price of gasoline (cents per gallon)	CPI
1971	36	40.5
1981	138	90.9
1991	112	136.2

TABLE 2

Year	Nominal interest rate	Inflation rate
	(percent per year)	
1992	4.6	1.7
1993	3.0	1.2
1994	2.1	0.7
1995	1.2	–0.1
1996	0.4	0.1
1997	0.4	1.7
1998	0.4	0.6
1999	0.1	–0.3
2000	0.1	–0.6
2001	0.1	–0.7
2002	0.1	–0.7

Exercise 14.3

Table 2 shows the nominal interest rate and inflation rate in Japan for several years.

a. Calculate the real interest rate for each year.
b. In which year was the real interest rate the highest?
c. In which year was the real interest rate the lowest?
d. Was the real interest rate in Japan negative in any year?

Solutions to Practice Problems 14.3

1a. To calculate the real price of gasoline in 1982–1984 dollars, multiply the nominal price by 100 and divide by the CPI. Table 3 shows the calculations.

1b. Gasoline was the most costly in real terms in 1981, when it was 152 cents (1982–1984 cents) per gallon.

1c. Gasoline was the least costly in real terms in 1991, when it was 82 cents (1982–1984 cents) per gallon.

2a. The real wage rate in 1999, expressed in dollars of the reference base year, was ($20 ÷ 166) × 100 = $12.05. The real wage rate in 2001, expressed in dollars of the reference base year, was ($22 ÷ 180) × 100 = $12.22 an hour.

2b. The real wage of these workers increased between 1999 and 2001.

3. The inflation rate during the year that Sally was working was (177 – 165) ÷ 165 × 100 = 7.3 percent. On the savings that Sally had in the mutual fund for the full year, she earned a real interest rate equal to the nominal interest rate minus the inflation rate, which is 7 – 7.3 = –0.3. Sally's real interest rate was negative. (Sally would have been even worse off if she had just kept her saving in cash. Her nominal interest rate would then have been zero, and her real interest rate would have been –7.3 percent.)

TABLE 3

Year	Price of gasoline (cents per gallon)	CPI	Price of gasoline (1982–1984 cents per gallon)
1971	36	40.5	89
1981	138	90.9	152
1991	112	136.2	82

CHAPTER CHECKPOINT

Key Points

1 Explain what the Consumer Price Index (CPI) is and how it is calculated.

- The Consumer Price Index (CPI) is a measure of the average prices of the goods and services that a typical urban household buys.
- The CPI is calculated by dividing the cost of the CPI basket in the current period by its cost in the base period and then multiplying by 100.

2 Explain the limitations of the CPI as a measure of the cost of living.

- The CPI does not include all the items that contribute to the cost of living.
- The CPI cannot provide an accurate measure of price changes because of new goods, quality improvements, and substitutions that consumers make when relative prices change.

3 Adjust money values for inflation and calculate real wage rates and real interest rates.

- To adjust a money value (also called a nominal value) for inflation, we express the value in terms of the dollar of a given year.
- To convert a dollar value of year *B* to the dollars of year *A*, multiply the value in year *B* by the price level in year *A* and divide by the price level in year *B*.
- The real wage rate equals the nominal wage rate divided by the CPI and multiplied by 100.
- The real interest rate equals the nominal interest rate minus the inflation rate.

Key Terms

Exercises

1. Looking at some travel magazines, you read that the CPI in Turkey in 2002 was 6,912 and in Russia, it was 670. You do some further investigating and discover that the reference base period in Turkey is 1994 and in Russia it is 1995. The CPI in Russia in 1994 was 34.
   a. By what percentage did prices rise in Turkey between 1994 and 2002?
   b. By what percentage did prices rise in Russia between 1995 and 2002?
   c. By what percentage did prices rise in Russia between 1994 and 1995?
   d. By what percentage did prices rise in Russia between 1994 and 2002?
   e. In which of these two countries did prices rise more between 1994 and 2002?

2. Two countries, Sahara and Arctica, conduct consumer surveys. In Sahara, consumers buy 70 units of bottled water, 20 units of food, and 10 units of housing. In Arctica, consumers buy no bottled water (they suck icicles, which are free), 80 units of housing, and 20 units of food. Both countries use dollars, and prices in these two countries are the same. In the reference base years, water costs $1 a unit, food costs $5 a unit, and housing costs $10 a unit. In the current year, water costs $2 a unit, food costs $6 a unit, and housing costs $11 a unit.
   a. What is the CPI in Sahara in the current year?
   b. What is the CPI in Arctica in the current year?
   c. In which of these two countries did the CPI rise faster?
   d. Why did the CPI rise faster in one country?

3. In Brazil, the reference base period for the CPI is December 1993. In September 2000, prices had risen by 1,565.93 percent since the base period. The inflation rate in Brazil during the year ending September 2001 was 6.46 percent, and during the year ending September 2002, the inflation rate was 7.93 percent.
   a. What is the CPI in Brazil for December 1993?
   b. Calculate Brazil's CPI in September 2000.
   c. Calculate Brazil's CPI in September 2001.
   d. Calculate Brazil's CPI in September 2002.
   e. Is the price level in Brazil rising or falling?
   f. Did Brazil's inflation rate increase or decrease in 2001 and in 2002?
   g. Was the inflation rate in Brazil between 2000 and 2002 greater or less than the inflation rate in the United States?

4. Keep a careful record of your own expenditures during a two-week period. Keep separate data for week 1 and week 2. In particular, record the items that you buy, their prices, and the quantities that you buy. Use these records to calculate
   a. Your own CPI basket based on your week 1 expenditures.
   b. The percentage of your expenditures on each item.
   c. The cost of your CPI basket in week 1.
   d. The cost of your CPI basket in week 2.
   e. Your personal CPI for week 2.
   f. Your personal inflation rate in week 2.

5. On the basis of your observations of your own expenditures in weeks 1 and 2 (recorded in your answer to exercise 4), explain and discuss the way in which your personal CPI is influenced by
   a. New goods
   b. Quality changes
   c. Commodity substitution
   d. Outlet substitution

6. Visit a local supermarket on two dates a month apart. Select 10 items of standard products that the shop always sells. Record the prices of these 10 items on the two dates. Assuming that a consumer buys one of each item in the basket you've chosen, calculate
   a. The cost of the basket in the first month.
   b. The cost of the basket in the second month.
   c. A price index for the second month.
   d. The inflation rate of these 10 prices over the month.

7. On the basis of the price observations recorded in your answer to exercise 6, explain and discuss the way in which commodity substitution and outlet substitution might occur and the effects that these substitutions might have on the inflation rate in your area during the month of observation.

8. In 2002, Annie, an 80-year-old, is telling her granddaughter Suzie about the good old days. She says that in 1932, when she was a child, you could buy a nice house for $15,000 and a jacket for $5. Suzie looks up some current prices and finds that a house that costs $200,000 and a jacket that costs $50 are today's equivalent of the ones that Annie says cost so little when she was a child. Suzie, an economics student, looks up the CPI for 1932 and discovers that it is 13.7. The reference base is 1982–1984. The CPI for 2002 is 180.3.
   a. What is the 2002 price that is equivalent to $15,000 in 1932?
   b. Which is the lower cost: $15,000 in 1932 or $200,000 in 2002?
   c. Which is the lower cost: $5 in 1932 or $50 in 2002?
   d. Is Annie correct about the good old days?

9. Annie and Suzie of exercise 8 continue their conversation. But the subject now changes to wages. Suzie points out that when houses and jackets were cheap, wages were low. Annie recalls that her mother earned 55¢ an hour in 1932, which was the average wage at that time. Suzie seizes on this number and says that the good old days don't sound so good compared to 2002, when the average hourly wage rate was $14.76. Use the information about the CPI provided in exercise 8.
   a. What is the 2002 wage rate that is equivalent to 55¢ in 1932?
   b. Which is the higher wage rate: 55¢ in 1932 or $14.76 in 2002?
   c. How do the calculations in parts **a** and **b** along with those in exercise 8 help to determine whether the good old days were better or worse than today?

10. In 2002, the interest rate was 19 percent a year in Argentina and 0.01 percent a year in Japan. The inflation rate was 39 percent a year in Argentina and –0.9 percent a year in Japan.
    a. What was the real interest rate in Argentina in 2002?
    b. What was the real interest rate in Japan in 2002?

Critical Thinking

11. Imagine that you are given $1,000 to spend and told that you must spend it all buying items from a Sears catalog. But you do have a choice of catalog. You may select from the 1903 catalog or from Sears.com today. You will pay the prices quoted in the catalog that you choose.
    a. Why might you lean toward choosing the 1903 catalog?
    b. Why might you lean toward choosing sears.com?
    c. The bottom line: What is your choice and why? Refer to any biases in the CPI that might be relevant to your choice.
12. "The CPI is too political to be left to governments to calculate. It should be calculated by an independent agency." Argue both sides of this proposition.

Practice Online

Web Exercises

Use the links on your Foundations Web site to work the following exercises.

13. Visit the Web site of the Bureau of Labor Statistics and find the CPI data for the U.S. city and for the region of the country or metropolitan area in which you live.
    a. Is your local CPI higher or lower than the national average?
    b. Explain the deviation of your regional CPI from the national average.
14. Visit the Web site of the Bureau of Labor Statistics and find data on the CPI-U and the CPI-W.
    a. How do these two versions of the CPI differ?
    b. Which version of the CPI showed the faster inflation rate during 2002?
    c. Which of the two CPI measures do you think more closely matches your personal inflation experience?
15. Visit the Web site of Professor Robert Sahr at Oregon State University and find data on the pay of members of Congress in 1900, 1950, and 2000. Also obtain the CPI for those years.
    a. Calculate the real pay of members of Congress in 1900 and 1950 in terms of 2000 dollars.
    b. In which of these years did Congress members receive the highest real earnings?
    c. In which of these years did Congress members receive the lowest real earnings?
16. Download the Excel spreadsheet that provides data on nominal interest rates and inflation rates for the United States and Italy during the 1990s.
    a. Calculate the real interest rate for each country and each year.
    b. In which year and country was the real interest rate higher on the average?
    c. Describe the similarities, if any, and the differences between the real and nominal interest rates for the two countries.

CHAPTER 15

Jobs and Unemployment

CHAPTER CHECKLIST

When you have completed your study of this chapter, you will be able to

1. **Define the unemployment rate and other labor market indicators.**
2. **Describe the trends and fluctuations in the indicators of labor market performance in the United States.**
3. **Describe the sources and types of unemployment, define full employment, and explain the link between unemployment and real GDP.**

Macroeconomics studies three big issues: The standard of living, the cost of living, and economic fluctuations. You learned in Chapter 13 how we measure real GDP, a main indicator of the standard of living. And you learned in Chapter 14 how we measure the CPI, a main indicator of the cost of living. In this chapter, you will learn how economists track economic fluctuations by monitoring the health of the labor market.

We become concerned when jobs are hard to find, and more relaxed when jobs are plentiful. We also care about the kinds of jobs that are available. We want well-paid and interesting jobs, so we spend time searching for the right job.

We'll describe a monthly survey that discovers the labor market status of the population and provides the raw material for job market statistics. We'll describe the trends and fluctuations in the indicators of labor market performance. And we'll look at the sources and types of unemployment and learn what we mean by "full employment."

15.1 LABOR MARKET INDICATORS

Every month, 1,600 field interviewers and supervisors working on a joint project between the Bureau of Labor Statistics (or BLS) and the Bureau of the Census survey 50,000 households and ask a series of questions about the age and labor market status of its members. This survey is called the Current Population Survey. Let's look at the types of data collected by this survey.

Current Population Survey

Working-age population
The total number of people aged 16 years and over who are not in jail, hospital, or some other form of institutional care.

Labor force
The number of people employed plus the number unemployed.

Figure 15.1 shows the categories into which the BLS divides the population. It also shows the relationships among the categories. The first category divides the population into two groups: the working-age population and others who are too young to work or who live in institutions and are unable to work. The **working-age population** is the total number of people aged 16 years and over who are not in jail, hospital, or some other form of institutional care. In June 2002, the estimated population of the United States was 287.5 million. In June 2002, the working-age population was 213.8 million and 73.7 million people were under 16 years of age or living in institutions.

The second category divides the working-age population into two groups: those in the labor force and those not in the labor force. The **labor force** is the number of people employed plus the number unemployed. In June 2002, the U.S. labor force was 143.7 million and 70.1 million were not in the labor force. Most of those not in the labor force were in school full time or had retired from work.

The third category divides the labor force into two groups: the employed and the unemployed. In June 2002 in the United States, 135 million were employed and 8.7 million were unemployed.

Population Survey Criteria

The survey counts as employed all persons who, during the week before the survey, either

1. Worked at least 1 hour as paid employees or worked 15 hours or more as unpaid workers in their family business or
2. Were not working but had jobs or businesses from which they were temporarily absent.

The survey counts as unemployed all persons who, during the week before the survey,

1. Had no employment,
2. Were available for work,

and either

1. Had made specific efforts to find employment some time during the previous four weeks or
2. Were waiting to be recalled to a job from which they had been laid off.

People in the working-age population who by the above criteria are neither employed nor unemployed are classified as not in the labor force.

FIGURE 15.1
Population Labor Force Categories

Practice Online

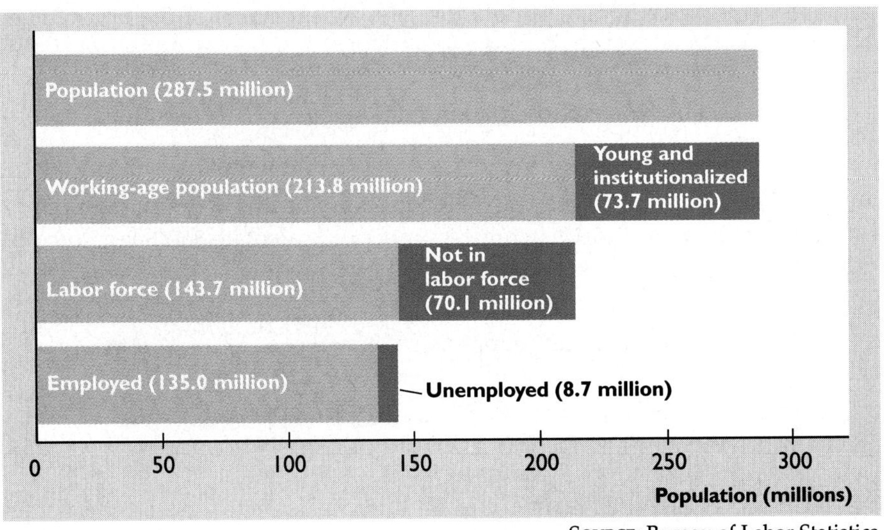

SOURCE: Bureau of Labor Statistics.

The U.S. population is divided into the working-age population and the young and institutionalized. The working-age population is divided into the labor force and those not in the labor force. The labor force is divided into the employed and the unemployed. The figure shows the data for June 2002.

Two Main Labor Market Indicators

Using the numbers from the Current Population Survey, the BLS calculates several indicators of the state of the labor market. The two main labor market indicators are

- The unemployment rate
- The labor force participation rate

The Unemployment Rate

The amount of unemployment is an indicator of the extent to which people who want jobs can't find them. It tells us the amount of slack in the labor market. The **unemployment rate** is the percentage of the people in the labor force who are unemployed. That is,

Unemployment rate
The percentage of the people in the labor force who are unemployed.

$$\text{Unemployment rate} = \frac{\text{Number of people unemployed}}{\text{Labor force}} \times 100.$$

In June 2002, the number of people unemployed was 8.7 million and the labor force was 143.7 million. We can use these numbers to calculate the unemployment rate in June 2002, which is

$$\text{Unemployment rate} = \frac{8.7 \text{ million}}{143.7 \text{ million}} \times 100$$
$$= 6.1 \text{ percent.}$$

The Labor Force Participation Rate

Labor force participation rate The percentage of the working-age population who are members of the labor force.

The number of people in the labor force is an indicator of the willingness of people of working age to take jobs. The **labor force participation rate** is the percentage of the working-age population who are members of the labor force. That is

$$\text{Labor force participation rate} = \frac{\text{Labor force}}{\text{Working-age population}} \times 100.$$

In June 2002, the labor force was 143.7 million and the working-age population was 213.8 million. We can use these numbers to calculate the labor force participation rate in June 2000, which is

$$\text{Labor force participation rate} = \frac{143.7 \text{ million}}{213.8 \text{ million}} \times 100$$
$$= 67.2 \text{ percent.}$$

Discouraged Workers

Discouraged worker A person who is available and willing to work but has not made specific efforts to find a job within the previous four weeks.

A **discouraged worker** is a person who does not have a job, is available and willing to work, but has not made specific efforts to find a job within the previous four weeks. Neither the unemployment rate nor the labor force participation rate includes discouraged workers. In June 2002, 5 million people not in the labor force wanted jobs. If we add this group to the labor force and the number unemployed, the unemployment rate becomes 9.2 percent—50 percent higher than the standard definition of the unemployment rate.

Part-Time Workers

Full-time workers People who usually work 35 hours or more a week.

Part-time workers People who usually work less than 35 hours a week.

Involuntary part-time workers People who work 1 to 34 hours per week but who are looking for full-time work.

The Current Population Survey measures the number of full-time workers and part-time workers. **Full-time workers** are those who usually work 35 hours or more a week. **Part-time workers** are those who usually work less than 35 hours a week. Part-time workers are divided into two groups: part time for economic reasons and part time for noneconomic reasons.

Part-time workers for economic reasons, also called **involuntary part-time workers**, are people who work 1 to 34 hours but who are looking for full-time work. These people are unable to find full-time work because of unfavorable business conditions or because of seasonal decreases in the availability of full-time work.

Part-time workers for noneconomic reasons do not want to work full time and are not available for such work. This group includes people with health problems, family or personal responsibilities, or education commitments that limit their availability for work.

The Bureau of Labor Statistics uses the data on full-time and part-time status to calculate the full-time labor force and the part-time labor force as well as the full-time unemployment rate and the part-time unemployment rate.

In June 2002, when the labor force was 143.7 million, the full-time labor force was 122.0 million and the part-time labor force was 21.7 million. An estimated 4.2 million involuntary part-time workers, or 19.4 percent of part-time workers, were looking for full-time work.

The Current Population Survey

The Bureau of Labor Statistics and the Bureau of the Census go to great lengths to collect accurate labor force data. They constantly train and retrain around 1,600 field interviewers and supervisors. Each month, each field interviewer contacts 37 households and asks basic demographic questions about all persons living at the address and detailed labor force questions about persons aged 15 or over.

Once a household has been selected for the survey, it is questioned for four consecutive months and then again for the same four months a year later. Each month, the addresses that have been in the panel eight times are removed and 6,250 new addresses are added. The rotation and overlap of households provide very reliable information about month-to-month and year-to-year changes in the labor market.

The first time that a household is in the panel, an interviewer, armed with a laptop computer, visits it. If the household has a telephone, most of the subsequent interviews are conducted by phone, many of them from one of the three telephone interviewing centers in Hagerstown, Maryland; Jeffersonville, Indiana; and Tucson, Arizona.

■ Aggregate Hours

The labor market indicators that we've just examined are useful signs of the health of the economy and directly measure what matters to most people: jobs and whether those jobs are full time or part time. But they don't tell us the *quantity of labor* employed.

The reason the number of people employed does not measure the quantity of labor employed is that jobs are not all the same. You've seen that people in part-time jobs work between 1 and 34 hours a week and people in full-time jobs work 35 or more hours a week. A Starbucks coffee shop might hire six students who work for three hours a day each. Another Starbucks might hire two full-time workers who work nine hours a day each. The total number of people employed is eight, but the total hours worked by six part-time workers is the same as the total hours worked by the two full-time workers.

To determine the total amount of labor employed, we measure labor in hours rather than in jobs. **Aggregate hours** are the total number of hours worked by all the people employed, both full time and part time, during a year and equal the number of people employed multiplied by the average work hours per person.

Aggregate hours
The total number of hours worked by all the people employed, both full time and part time, during a year.

In June 2002, 135 million people worked an average of 34.7 hours per week. With 50 workweeks per year, aggregate hours were

$$\text{Aggregate hours} = 135 \text{ million} \times 34.7 \times 50 = 234.2 \text{ billion.}$$

The measurement of aggregate hours is not very precise. But the estimation of the percentage change in aggregate hours from one month to another is more precise. For this reason, the Bureau of Labor Statistics publishes aggregate hours data as an index number rather than as a number of hours.

CHECKPOINT 15.1

Study Guide pp. 229–231

Practice Online 15.1

1 Define the unemployment rate and other labor market indicators.

Practice Problem 15.1

The Bureau of Labor Statistics reported that in January 2000, the labor force was 140.9 million, employment was 135.2 million, and the working-age population was 208.6 million. Average weekly hours were 34.5. Calculate for that month the

- **a.** Unemployment rate.
- **b.** Labor force participation rate.
- **c.** Aggregate hours worked in a week.

Exercises 15.1

1. The Bureau of Labor Statistics reported that in July 2002, the labor force was 143.9 million; employment was 135.3 million; and the working-age population was 214 million. Calculate for that month the
   - **a.** Unemployment rate.
   - **b.** Labor force participation rate.
2. Statistics Canada reported that in January 2002, the Canadian labor force was 16.2 million; Canadian employment was 14.8 million; and the Canadian working-age population was 24.8 million. Calculate for that month the Canadian
   - **a.** Unemployment rate.
   - **b.** Labor force participation rate.
3. Given the data in exercises 1 and 2, do you think jobs are harder to find in Canada or in the United States? Why?
4. Use the link on the Foundations Web site to obtain data on the labor force, employment, unemployment, and the working-age population for your own state in the most recent month for which data are available. For that month,
   - **a.** Calculate your state's unemployment rate.
   - **b.** Calculate your state's labor force participation rate.
   - **c.** Compare the labor market indicators in your state with the U.S. averages.

Solution to Practice Problem 15.1

- **a.** The unemployment rate is 4.0 percent. The labor force is the sum of the number employed plus the number unemployed. So the number unemployed equals the labor force minus the number employed, which equals 140.9 million – 135.2 million = 5.7 million. The unemployment rate is the number unemployed as a percentage of the labor force, which is (5.7 million ÷ 140.9 million) × 100 = 4.0 percent.
- **b.** The labor force participation rate is 67.5 percent. The labor force participation rate is the percentage of the working-age population who are in the labor force, which equals (140.9 million ÷ 208.6 million) × 100 = 67.5 percent.
- **c.** Aggregate hours worked in a week are 4,664.4 million. In January 2000, average weekly hours were 34.5 and employment was 135.2 million. So the aggregate hours worked in a week were 34.5 × 135.2 million = 4,664.4 million.

15.2 LABOR MARKET TRENDS AND FLUCTUATIONS

What do we learn about the U.S. labor market from changes in the unemployment rate, the labor force participation rate, part-time employment, and aggregate hours? Let's explore the trends and fluctuations in these indicators.

Unemployment

Figure 15.2 shows the U.S. unemployment rate over the 40 years from 1962 to 2002. Over these years, the average U.S. unemployment rate was 5.9 percent—about the same as the 2002 unemployment rate. The 1960s and the late 1990s were years of below-average unemployment, and the 1970s and 1980s were years of above-average unemployment.

During the 1960s, the unemployment rate fell to 3.5 percent. These years saw a rapid rate of job creation partly from the demands placed on the economy by the growth of defense production during the Vietnam War and partly from an expansion of consumer spending encouraged by an expansion of social programs. Another burst of rapid rate of job creation driven by the "new economy"—the high-technology sector driven by the expansion of the Internet—took the unemployment rate below average between 1995 and 2000.

In 2001 and 2002, the unemployment rate increased as the U.S. economy went into a recession. But the unemployment rate remained below or at its average level. In contrast to the 1960s and 1990s, the 1970s and 1980s were years of above average unemployment. The unemployment rate peaked at almost 10 percent during the 1982 recession. The unemployment rate was also high during a mid-1970s recession, which resulted from massive hikes in the world oil price, and in the 1990–1991 recession.

FIGURE 15.2
The U.S. Unemployment Rate: 1962–2002

Practice Online

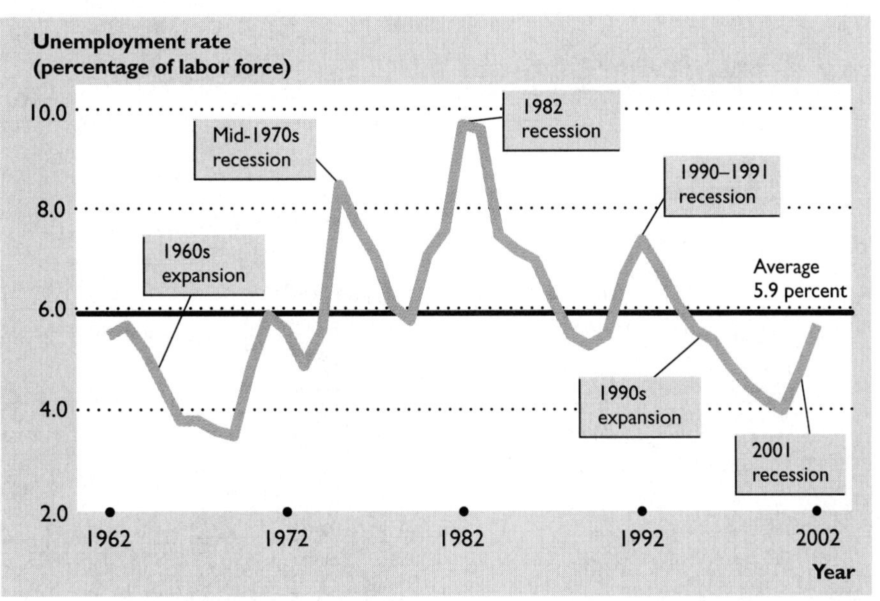

SOURCE: Bureau of Labor Statistics.

The average unemployment rate from 1962 to 2002 was 5.9 percent. The unemployment rate increases in recessions and decreases in expansions. Unemployment fell to an unusually low rate during the expansion of the 1990s and increased during the 2001 recession.

Eye on the U.S. Economy

The Labor Market in the Great Depression

The Great Depression was a period of prolonged and extreme economic hardship that lasted from 1929 until the end of the 1930s.

By 1933, the worst of the Depression years, real GDP had fallen by a huge 30 percent. And, as the figure shows, one in four of the people who wanted jobs couldn't find them.

The horrors of the Great Depression led to the New Deal and shaped political attitudes that persist today.

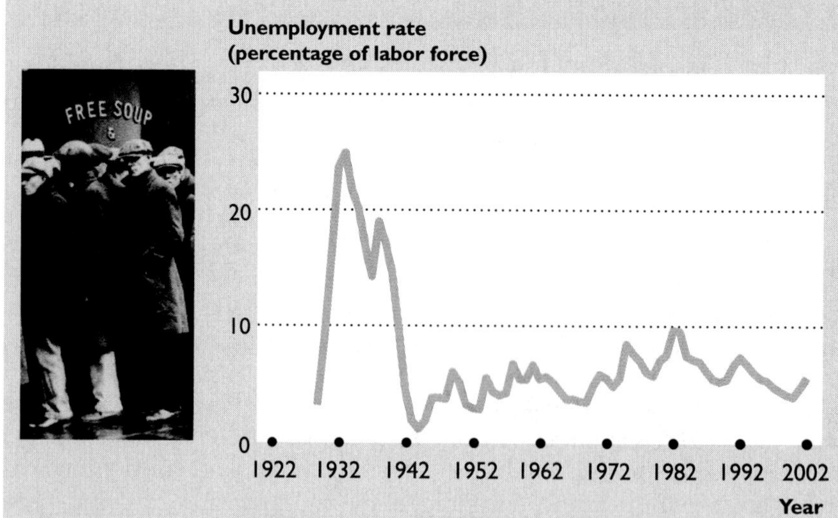

SOURCE: Bureau of Labor Statistics.

The Participation Rate

Figure 15.3 shows the labor force participation rate, which you can see has followed an upward trend. It increased from 59 percent during the 1960s to 67 percent during the 1990s. The cyclical fluctuations in the participation rate are mild

FIGURE 15.3

The Changing Face of the Labor Market: 1962–2002

Practice Online

During the past 40 years, the labor force participation rate has increased. The labor force participation rate of men has decreased, and that of women has increased.

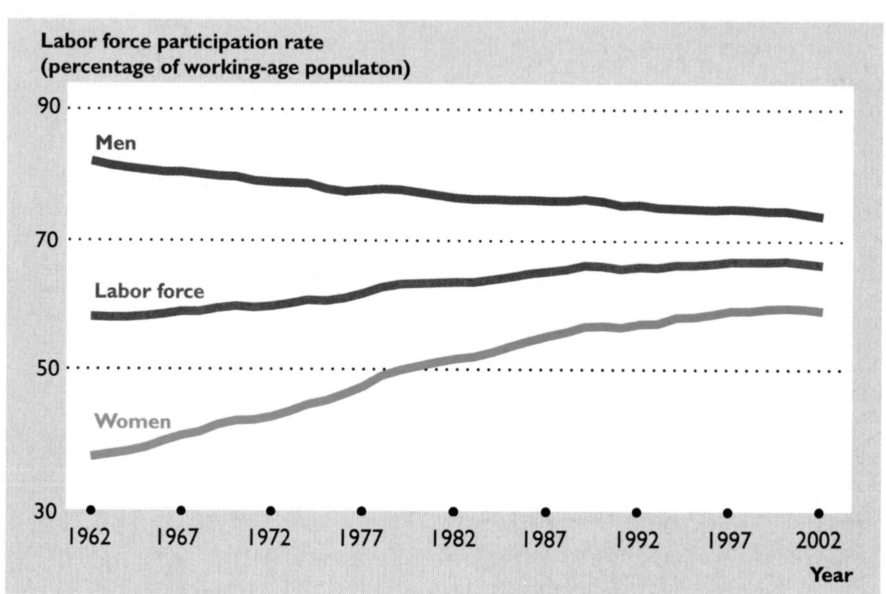

SOURCE: Bureau of Labor Statistics.

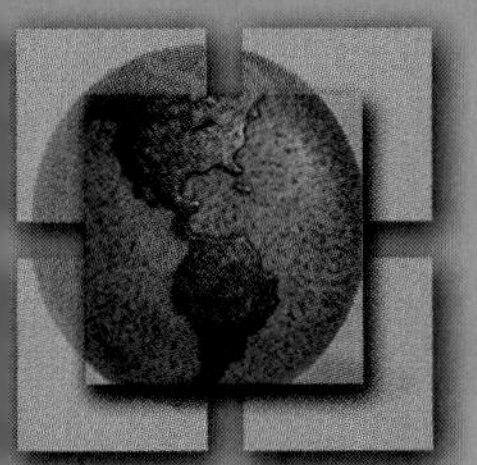

Eye on the Global Economy

Unemployment Around the World

In 1992, Canada and the United Kingdom had the highest unemployment rates and Japan the lowest. France, Germany, Italy, and the United States were in the middle of the pack.

Through the 1990s, unemployment rates fell in the United States, United Kingdom, and Canada but increased in Japan.

By 2002, the unemployment rates of the United States, United Kingdom and Japan had converged.

The average unemployment rate of France, Germany, and Italy increased through 1997 and then decreased but has remained the highest among the industrialized countries.

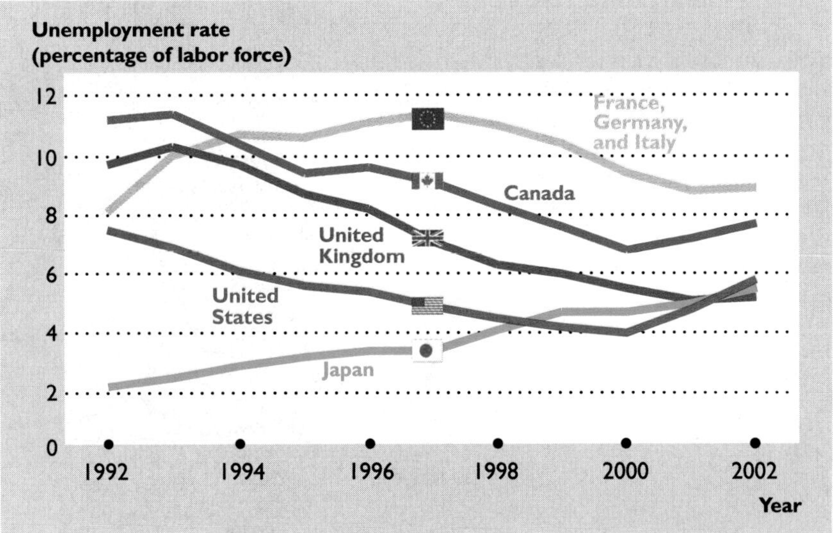

SOURCE: International Monetary Fund, *World Economic Outlook*, September 2002.

and result from unsuccessful job seekers becoming *discouraged workers*—people who leave the labor force in a recession and reenter in an expansion.

Why has the labor force participation rate increased? The main reason is an increase in the number of women who have entered the labor force. Figure 15.3 shows this increase. Between 1962 and 2002, the participation rate of women increased from 38 percent to 60 percent. This increase is spread across women of all age groups and occurred for four main reasons. First, more women pursued a college education and so increased their earning power. Second, technological change in the workplace created a large number of white-collar jobs with flexible work hours that many women found attractive. Third, technological change in the home increased the time available for paid employment. And fourth, families looked increasingly to a second income to balance tight budgets.

Figure 15.3 also shows another remarkable trend in the U.S. labor force: The participation rate of men *decreased* from 82 percent in 1962 to 74 percent in 2002. Decreased labor force participation by men occurred mostly among older men aged 55 and over. The participation rate of this group fell from 87 percent in 1962 to 67 percent in 2002. Most of this decrease occurred because many men retired at an earlier age. Some of this earlier retirement resulted from an increase in wealth. But some arose from job loss at an age at which finding a new job was difficult. For other men, decreased labor force participation occurred because more remained in full-time education.

■ Part-Time Workers

A part-time job is attractive to many workers because it enables them to balance family and other commitments with work. Part-time jobs are attractive to employers because they don't have to pay benefits to part-time workers and are less constrained by government regulations. Figure 15.4 shows some interesting facts about part-time workers. First, the percentage of workers who are part time has increased,

FIGURE 15.4
Part-time Workers: 1972–2002

Practice Online

Part-time workers are an increasing proportion of the labor force, up from 15 percent in 1972 to 17 percent in 2002. The percentage of workers who are part time and the percentage of part-time workers who would like full-time work increase in a recession and decrease in an expansion.

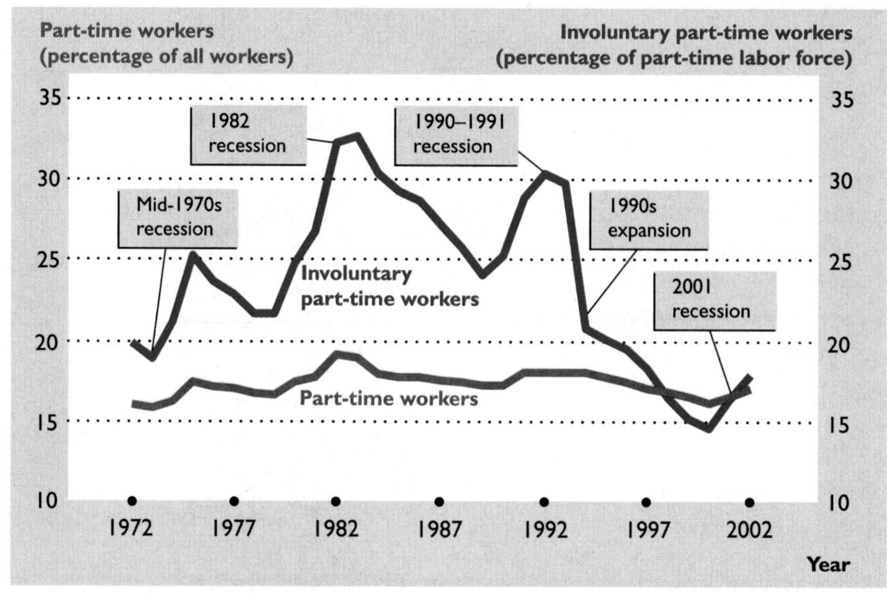

SOURCE: Bureau of Labor Statistics.

but not by much. In 1972, it was 16 percent and in 2002, it was 17 percent. Second, the part-time percentage fluctuates with the business cycle. In the 1982 recession, it reached 19.2 percent, and in the 1990–1991 recession, it reached 18.1 percent. During the expansion years after 1994, the part-time percentage declined.

The involuntary part-time rate—the percentage of part-time workers who want full-time work—has averaged 27 percent. But there are striking and large swings in the involuntary part-time rate. In the 1982 recession, the rate climbed to approach 33 percent. And in the 1990–1991 recession, the rate climbed to 30 percent. During the 1990s expansion, the involuntary part-time rate decreased rapidly, and even after rising again in the 2001 recession, it stood below its 1972 level.

Aggregate and Average Hours

Figure 15.5(a) shows aggregate hours in the U.S. economy from 1962 to 2002. Aggregate hours have an upward trend, but they have not grown as quickly as have the number of people employed. Between 1962 and 2002, the number of people employed in the U.S. economy doubled—an increase of 100 percent. During that same period, aggregate hours increased by 77 percent. Why the difference? Because average hours per worker decreased.

Figure 15.5(b) shows average hours per worker. After hovering at almost 39 hours a week during the early 1960s, average hours per worker decreased to about 34 hours a week during the 1990s. This shortening of the average workweek occurred partly because the average hours worked by full-time workers decreased and partly because the number of part-time jobs increased faster than the number of full-time jobs.

Fluctuations in aggregate hours and average hours per worker line up with the business cycle. Figure 15.5 identifies the four recessions, during which aggregate hours decreased and average hours per worker decreased faster than trend.

FIGURE 15.5
Aggregate Hours: 1962–2002

Practice Online

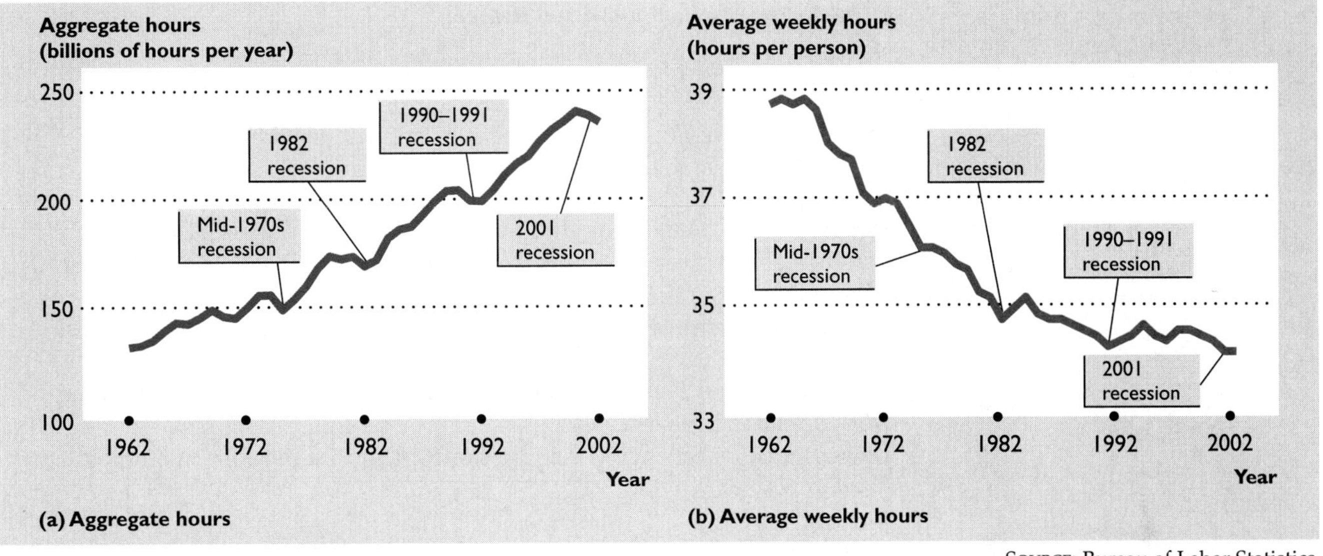

SOURCE: Bureau of Labor Statistics.

In part (a), between 1962 and 2002, aggregate hours increased by an average of 1.5 percent a year. Fluctuations in aggregate hours coincide with business cycle fluctuations.

In part (b), aggregate hours increased at a slower rate than the number of jobs because the average workweek has shortened.

Women in the Labor Force

The participation rate of women in the U.S. labor force has increased from 50 percent in 1980 to 60 percent in 2000. This upward trend is found in most of the world's rich advanced nations.

But the *level* of women's participation in the labor force varies a great deal around the world. Here, we compare seven other countries—Australia, Canada, France, Japan, Spain, Sweden, and the United Kingdom—with the United States.

Among these countries, Sweden's labor force has the largest participation rate of women and the United States comes second. Spain and Japan have the lowest rates.

Cultural factors play a role in determining national differences in women's work choices. But economic factors such as the percentage of women with a college degree will ultimately dominate cultural influences and bring a convergence of outcomes.

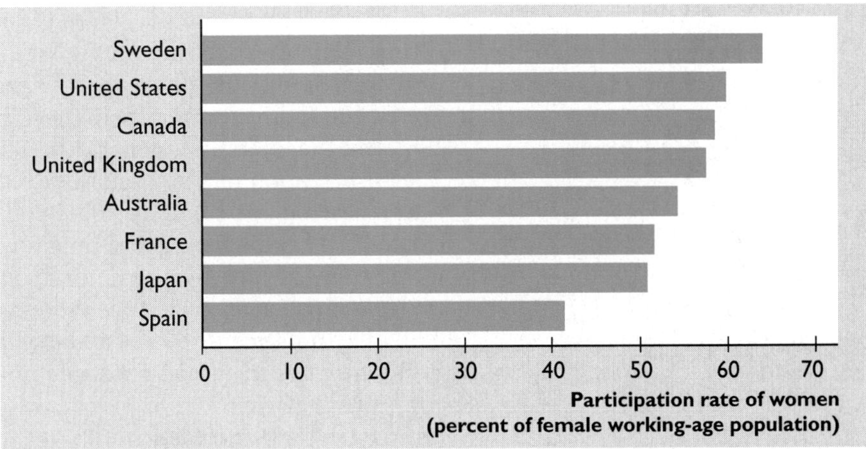

SOURCE: OECD.

CHECKPOINT 15.2

Study Guide pp. 231–234

Practice Online 15.2

2 Describe the trends and fluctuations in the indicators of labor market performance in the United States.

Practice Problem 15.2

Use the link on your Foundations Web site and view the data for Figures 15.2, 15.3, 15.4, and 15.5. Then answer the following questions:

a. In which decade—the 1960s, 1970s, 1980s, or 1990s—was the unemployment rate the lowest? What brought low unemployment in that decade?

b. In which decade was the unemployment rate the highest? What brought high unemployment in that decade?

c. Describe the trends in the participation rates of men and women and all workers. Why did these trends occur?

d. Describe the trends and fluctuations in part-time work. Why is part-time work on the increase?

e. Do aggregate hours increase at the same rate as the increase in employment? Explain why or why not.

Exercise 15.2

Use the link on your Foundations Web site and view the data for Figures 15.2, 15.3, 15.4, and 15.5. Then answer the following questions:

a. During which decade—the 1960s, 1970s, 1980s, or 1990s—did the labor force participation rate of women increase most? Suggest some reasons why this rapid increase occurred during that decade.

b. In which decade did the labor force participation rate of men decrease most? Suggest some reasons why this rapid decrease occurred during that decade.

c. Describe the trends in the unemployment rate; the labor force participation rates of men and women, part-time workers, and involuntary part-time workers; and aggregate hours since 1994. Why did these trends occur?

Solution to Practice Problem 15.2

a. The average unemployment rates in each decade were: 1960s, 4.8 percent; 1970s, 6.2 percent; 1980s, 7.3 percent; 1990s, 5.7 percent. The unemployment rate was lowest during the 1960s. Unemployment was low during the 1960s because defense spending on the Vietnam War and an expansion of social programs brought about a rapidly expanding economy.

b. The unemployment rate was highest during the 1980s. A deep recession in 1982 sent the unemployment rate to a peak of almost 10 percent.

c. The participation rate of women increased because (1) better-educated women earn more, (2) more white-collar jobs with flexible work hours were created, (3) people have more time for paid employment, and (4) families increasingly needed two incomes to balance their budgets. The participation rate of men decreased because more men remained in school and some men took early retirement. The overall participation rate increased.

d. Part-time work increased because it provides flexible hours for workers and cuts costs for firms.

e. Aggregate hours increase more slowly than employment because average hours per worker fall.

15.3 THE SOURCES AND TYPES OF UNEMPLOYMENT

How do people become unemployed, how long do they remain unemployed, and who is at greatest risk to become unemployed? Let's begin to answer these questions by looking at the events that move people into and out of the labor market and into and out of jobs.

Sources of Unemployment

The labor market is constantly churning. New jobs are created and old ones are destroyed. Some people move into the labor force, and some move out of it. The process of job creation and job destruction and the movement into and out of the labor force create unemployment.

People who become unemployed are

1. Job losers
2. Job leavers
3. Entrants or reentrants

Job Losers

People who are fired or laid off from their jobs, either permanently or temporarily, are called *job losers*. People lose their jobs for a variety of reasons. Some are just not a good match for the job they're doing, and they get fired. Firms fail, so their workers get laid off. And new technology destroys some jobs.

A job loser has two choices: Either look for another job or withdraw from the labor force. A job loser who decides to look for a new job remains in the labor force and becomes unemployed. A job loser who decides to withdraw from the labor force is not counted as being unemployed. Such a person is classified as "not in the labor force." Most job losers decide to look for a new job, and some of them take a long time to find one.

Job Leavers

People who voluntarily quit their jobs are called *job leavers*. Most people who leave their jobs do so for one of two reasons: Either they've gotten a better job or they've decided to withdraw from the labor force. Neither of these types of job leavers becomes unemployed. But a few people quit their jobs because they want to spend time looking for a better one. These job leavers become unemployed.

Entrants and Reentrants

People who have just left school and entered the job market are called *entrants*. Some entrants have a job lined up before leaving school and are never unemployed. But many entrants spend time searching for their first job, and during this period, they are unemployed.

People who have previously had jobs, then quit and left the labor force and have now decided to look for jobs are called *reentrants*. Some reentrants are people who have been out of the labor force rearing children, but most are discouraged workers—people who gave up searching for jobs because they were not able to find suitable ones and who have now decided to look again.

Figure 15.6 shows the magnitudes of the three sources of unemployment. Most of the people unemployed are job losers. Also, their number fluctuates most.

FIGURE 15.6
Unemployment by Reasons: 1982–2002

Practice Online

Everyone who is unemployed is a job loser, a job leaver, or an entrant or reentrant into the labor force. Job losers are the biggest group, and their number fluctuates most. Entrants and reentrants are the second biggest group. Their number also fluctuates. Job leavers are the smallest group.

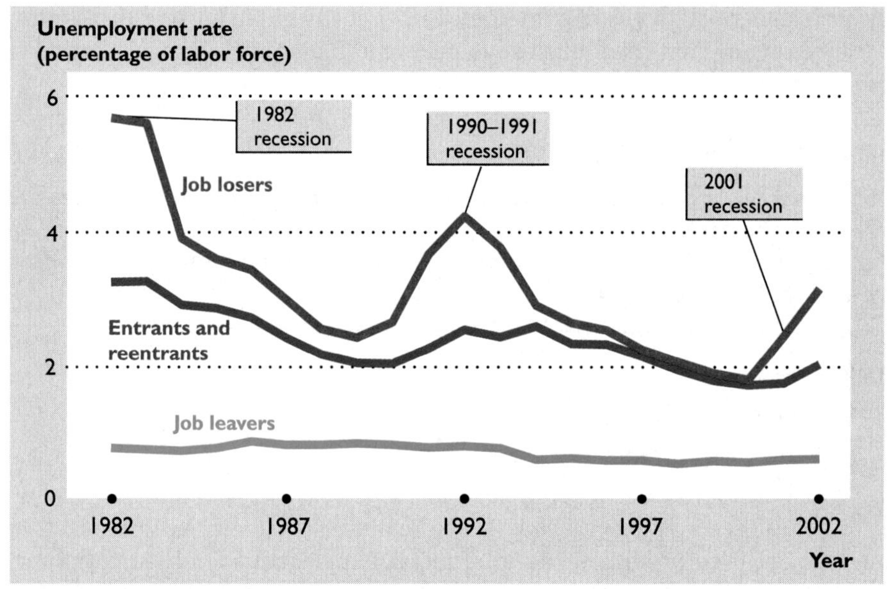

SOURCE: Bureau of Labor Statistics.

Entrants and reentrants are also a large component, and their number also fluctuates. Job leavers are the smallest and most stable source of unemployment.

How Unemployment Ends

People who end a period of unemployment are either

1. Hires and recalls or
2. Withdrawals

Hires and Recalls

People who have been unemployed but have been hired to start a new job are called *hires*. And people who have been temporarily laid off (they are classified as unemployed) and who start work again are called *recalls*. Firms are constantly hiring and recalling workers, so there are always people moving from unemployment to employment.

Withdrawals

People who have been unemployed and who decide to stop looking for jobs are called *withdrawals*. Most of these people are *discouraged workers*. They will most likely reenter the labor force later when they think that job prospects have improved.

Labor Market Flows: A Summary

Figure 15.7 provides a summary of the labor market flows that begin and end a period of unemployment.

FIGURE 15.7
Labor Market Flows

Practice Online

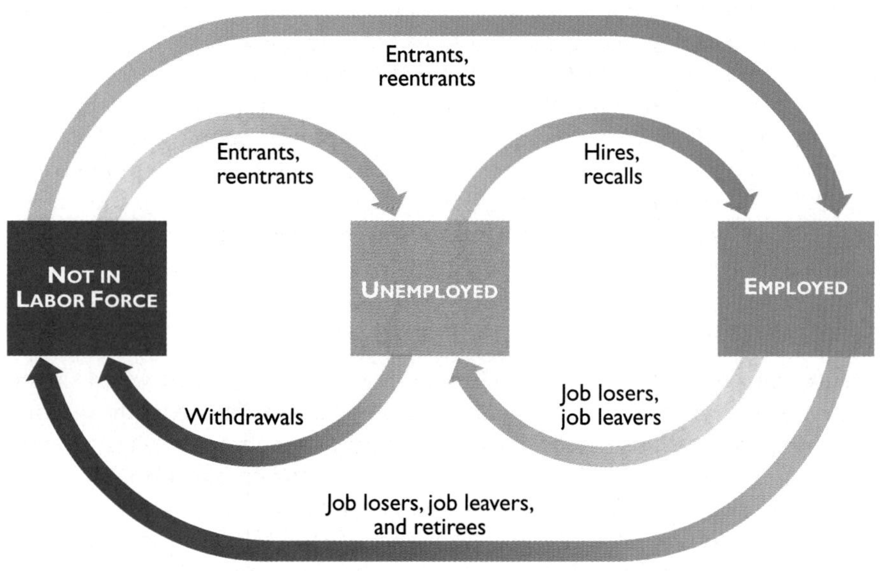

Unemployment results from employed people losing or leaving their jobs (job losers and job leavers) and from people entering the labor force (entrants and reentrants). Unemployment ends because people get hired or recalled or because they withdraw from the labor force.

Types of Unemployment

Unemployment is classified into four types:

- Frictional
- Structural
- Seasonal
- Cyclical

Frictional Unemployment

Frictional unemployment is the unemployment that arises from normal labor turnover—from people entering and leaving the labor force and from the ongoing creation and destruction of jobs. Frictional unemployment is a permanent and healthy phenomenon in a dynamic, growing economy.

Frictional unemployment
The unemployment that arises from normal labor turnover—from people entering and leaving the labor force and from the ongoing creation and destruction of jobs.

The unending flow of people into and out of the labor force and the processes of job creation and job destruction create the need for people to search for jobs and for businesses to search for workers. There are always some businesses with unfilled jobs and some people seeking jobs.

Look in your local newspaper, and you will see that there are always jobs being advertised. Businesses don't usually hire the first person who applies for a job, and unemployed people don't usually take the first job that comes their way. Instead, both firms and workers spend time searching out what they believe will be the best attainable match. By this search process, people can match their own skills and interests with the available jobs and find a satisfying job and income. While these unemployed people are searching, they are frictionally unemployed.

The amount of frictional unemployment depends on the rate at which people enter and reenter the labor force and on the rate at which jobs are created and destroyed. During the 1970s, the amount of frictional unemployment increased because of the postwar baby boom that began during the 1940s. By the late 1970s, the baby boom created a bulge in the number of people leaving school. As these people entered the labor force, the amount of frictional unemployment increased. Frictional unemployment remained high until the information-age expansion of the mid-1990s. Since 1994, frictional unemployment has decreased.

The amount of frictional unemployment is also influenced by unemployment compensation. The greater the number of unemployed people eligible for benefits and the more generous those benefits, the longer is the average time taken in job search and the greater is the amount of frictional unemployment. Unemployment benefits in Canada and Western Europe exceed those in the United States, and these economies have higher unemployment rates.

Structural Unemployment

Structural unemployment
The unemployment that arises when changes in technology or international competition change the skills needed to perform jobs or change the locations of jobs.

Structural unemployment is the unemployment that arises when changes in technology or international competition change the skills needed to perform jobs or change the locations of jobs. Structural unemployment usually lasts longer than frictional unemployment because workers must retrain and possibly relocate to find a job. For example, when a telephone exchange in Gary, Indiana, is automated, some jobs in that city are destroyed. Meanwhile, new jobs for life-insurance salespeople and retail clerks are created in Chicago, Indianapolis, and other cities. The former telephone operators remain unemployed for several months until they move, retrain, and get one of these jobs. Structural unemployment is painful, especially for older workers for whom the best available option might be to retire early but with a lower income than they had expected.

Sometimes, the amount of structural unemployment is modest. At other times, it is large, and at such times, structural unemployment can become a serious long-term problem. It was especially large during the late 1970s and early 1980s. During those years, oil price hikes and an increasingly competitive international environment destroyed jobs in traditional U.S. industries, such as auto and steel making, and created jobs in new industries, such as information processing, electronics, and bioengineering. Structural unemployment was also present during the early 1990s as many businesses and governments downsized.

Seasonal Unemployment

Seasonal unemployment
The unemployment that arises because of seasonal weather patterns.

Seasonal unemployment is the unemployment that arises because of seasonal weather patterns. Seasonal unemployment increases during the winter months and decreases during the spring and summer. A fruit picker who is laid off after the fall harvest and who gets rehired the following summer experiences seasonal unemployment. A construction worker who gets laid off during the winter and rehired in the spring also experiences seasonal unemployment.

Cyclical Unemployment

Cyclical unemployment
The fluctuating unemployment over the business cycle that increases during a recession and decreases during an expansion.

Cyclical unemployment is the fluctuating unemployment over the business cycle. Cyclical unemployment increases during a recession and decreases during an expansion. An autoworker who is laid off because the economy is in a recession and who gets rehired some months later when the expansion begins has experienced cyclical unemployment.

Duration and Demographics of Unemployment

Some people are unemployed for a week or two and others for a year or more. The longer the period of unemployment, the greater is the personal cost to the unemployed. The average duration of unemployment varies over the business cycle. In a recession, the average duration increases, and during an expansion, the average duration decreases.

Figure 15.8(a) compares the duration of unemployment in 2000 with that in 1983. In 2000, the economy was in a strong expansion and the unemployment rate was low. In 1983, the economy was recovering from a deep recession and the unemployment rate was high. You can see that in 2000, almost all of the unemployed found jobs in less than 14 weeks. But in 1983, almost a quarter of the unemployed took more than 26 weeks to find a job.

Unemployment does not affect all demographic groups in the same way. And the differences between the groups most and least affected by unemployment are large. Figure 15.8(b) shows that during the 1990s black teenagers had the highest unemployment rates, which averaged more than 30 percent. Whites aged 20 years and over had the lowest unemployment rates, which averaged a little more than 4 percent.

Why are teenage unemployment rates so high? There are two reasons. First, young people are still discovering what they are good at and trying different lines of work, so they leave their jobs more frequently than do older workers. Second, firms often hire teenagers on a short-term or trial basis, so the rate of job loss is higher for teenagers than for older workers.

FIGURE 15.8
Unemployment: Duration and Demographics

Practice Online

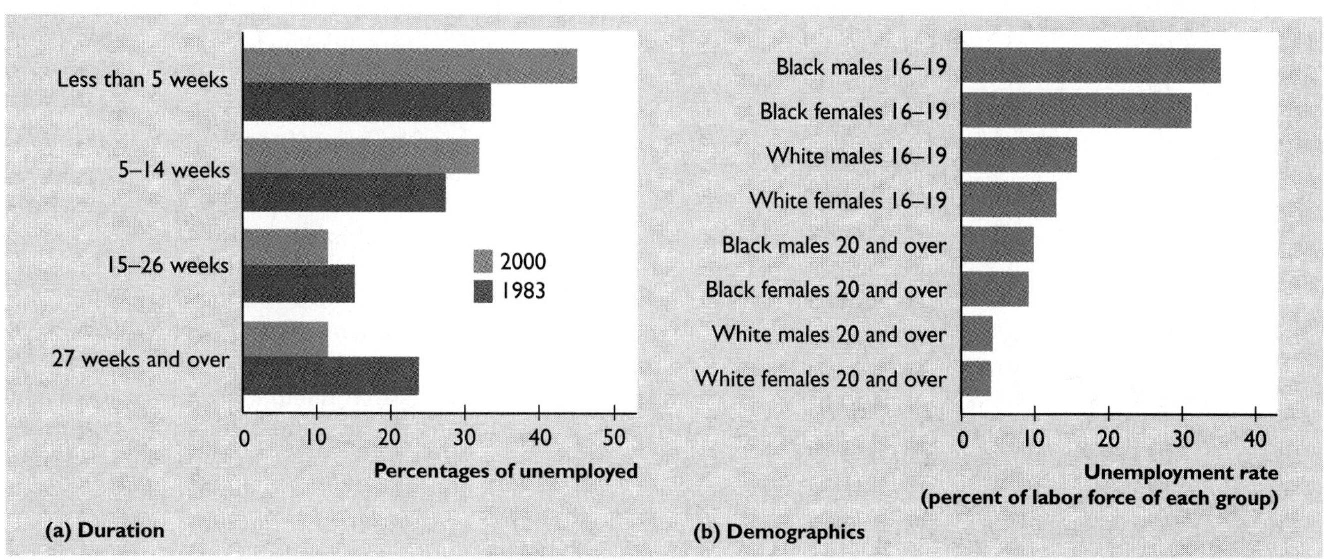

SOURCE: Bureau of Labor Statistics.

In part (a), the average unemployment rate was less in 2000 than in 1983. The lower the average unemployment rate, the shorter is the average duration of unemployment.

In part (b), on the average during the 1990s, blacks experienced more than twice the unemployment of whites, and teenagers experienced more than three times the unemployment of workers aged 20 and over.

You've seen that there is always *some* unemployment—someone looking for a job or laid off and waiting to be recalled. Yet one of the goals of economic policy is to achieve full employment. What do we mean by *full employment*?

Full Employment

Full employment
When there is no cyclical unemployment or, equivalently, when all the unemployment is frictional, structural, and seasonal.

Natural unemployment rate
The unemployment rate at full employment.

There can be a lot of unemployment at full employment, and the term "full employment" is an example of a technical economic term that does not correspond with everyday language. **Full employment** occurs when there is no cyclical unemployment or, equivalently, when all the unemployment is frictional, structural, and seasonal. The divergence of the unemployment rate from full employment is cyclical unemployment. The unemployment rate at full employment is called the **natural unemployment rate**. The term "natural unemployment rate" is another example of a technical economic term that does not correspond with everyday language.

Why do economists call a situation with a lot of unemployment one of full employment? And why is the unemployment rate at full employment called the "natural" unemployment rate? The reason is that the U.S. economy is a complex mechanism that undergoes constant change in its players, structure, and direction. For example, in 2002, around 3 million people retired and more than 3 million new workers entered the labor force. Thousands of businesses (including new start-ups) expanded and created jobs while thousands of others downsized or failed and destroyed jobs. This process of change creates frictions and dislocations that are unavoidable—that are natural. And they create unemployment.

Unemployment and Real GDP

Cyclical unemployment is the fluctuating unemployment over the business cycle—unemployment that increases during a recession and decreases during an expansion. At full employment, there is no cyclical unemployment. At a business cycle trough, cyclical unemployment is positive and at a business cycle peak, it is *negative*.

Figure 15.9(a) shows the unemployment rate in the United States between 1982 and 2002. It also shows the natural unemployment rate and cyclical unemployment. In this figure, the natural unemployment rate falls from 7 percent in 1982 to 6 percent in the late 1980s and early 1990s and to 5 percent in the late 1990s and 2000s. This path of the natural unemployment rate is an assumption.

There is not much controversy about the existence of a natural unemployment rate. But economists don't agree about its size or the extent to which it fluctuates. The majority view is that the natural rate changes slowly, and over the long term it averages around 6 percent.

An increasing number of economists think that fluctuations in frictional and structural unemployment bring fluctuations in the natural unemployment rate and that at times of rapid demographic change and rapid structural change, the natural unemployment rate can be high. But the true natural unemployment rate is unknown and is estimated with a large margin of uncertainty.

Cyclical unemployment was positive during most of the 1980s and the early 1990s (shaded red) and negative during the late 1980s and after 1997 (shaded blue).

Potential GDP
The level of real GDP that the economy would produce if it were at full employment.

Figure 15.9(b) shows real GDP in the United States from 1982 to 2002. The figure also shows **potential GDP**, which is the level of real GDP that the economy would produce if it were at full employment. Because the unemployment rate

FIGURE 15.9
The Relationship Between Unemployment and Real GDP

Practice Online

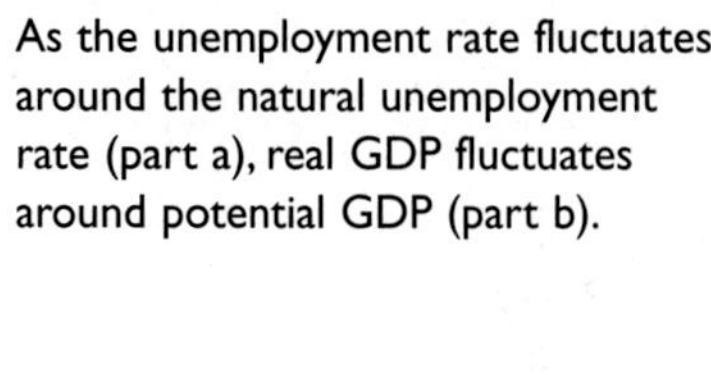

As the unemployment rate fluctuates around the natural unemployment rate (part a), real GDP fluctuates around potential GDP (part b).

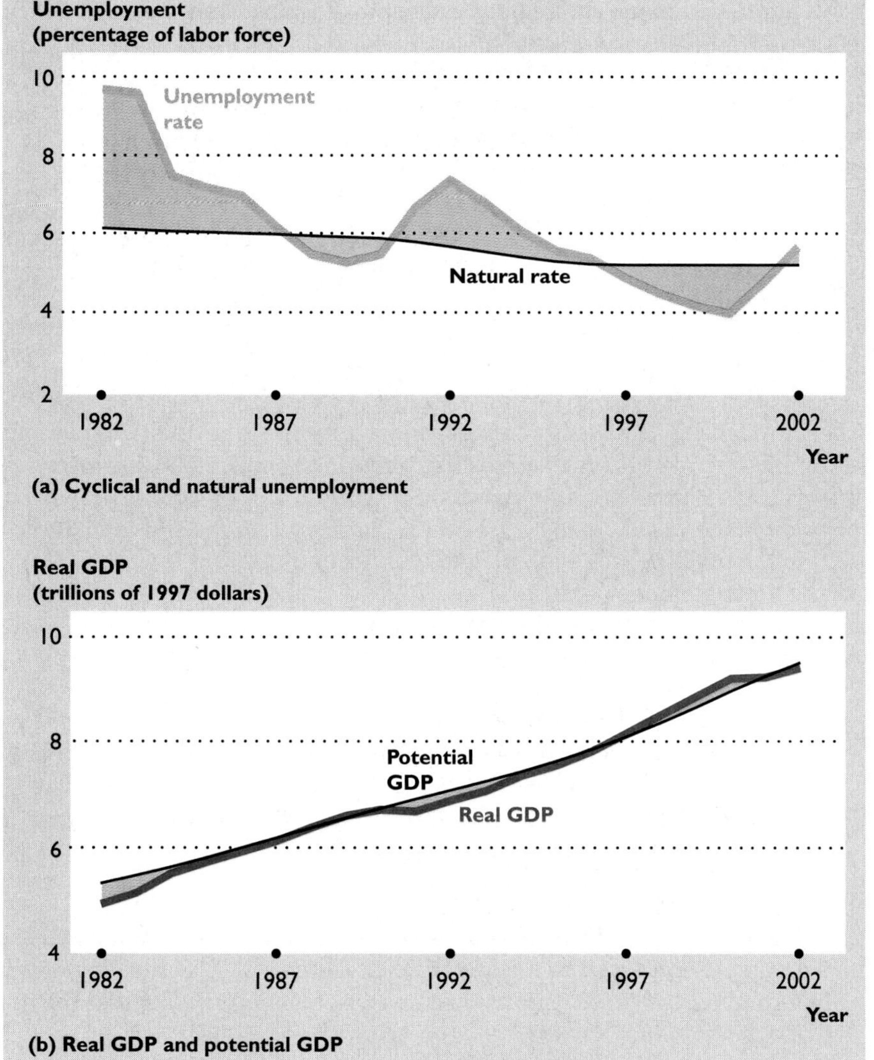

SOURCES: Bureau of Economic Analysis, Bureau of Labor Statistics, and Congressional Budget Office.

fluctuates around the natural unemployment rate, real GDP fluctuates around potential GDP. When the unemployment rate is above the natural unemployment rate (in part a), real GDP is below potential GDP (in part b); when the unemployment rate is below the natural unemployment rate, real GDP is above potential GDP; and when the unemployment rate equals the natural unemployment rate, real GDP equals potential GDP.

You will learn what determines the fluctuations around full employment and potential GDP in Chapter 20.

CHECKPOINT 15.3

Study Guide pp. 234–237

Practice Online 15.3

3 **Describe the sources and types of unemployment, define full employment, and explain the link between unemployment and real GDP.**

Practice Problem 15.3

A labor force survey in a Polynesian island records the following data for December 31, 2002: employed, 13,500; unemployed, 1,500; not in the labor force, 7,500. The survey also recorded during 2003: hires and recalls, 1,000; job losers, 750; job leavers 300; entrants, 150; reentrants, 450; withdrawals, 500. The working-age population increased during 2003 by 100. (All the job losers, entrants, and reentrants became unemployed.) Calculate for the end of 2003,

a. The unemployment rate.
b. The labor force participation rate.

Exercise 15.3

The Polynesian island labor force survey provides the following information about labor market flows during 2004: hires and recalls, 1,500; job losers, 550; job leavers, 300; entrants, 200; reentrants, 500; withdrawals, 450. The working-age population increased during 2004 by 150. Starting with the situation at the end of 2001 in the practice problem, calculate for the end of 2004:

a. The unemployment rate.
b. The labor force participation rate.
c. What do you predict happened to real GDP in 2004? Why?

Solution to Practice Problem 15.3

a. The number of people unemployed at the end of 2003 equals the number unemployed at the end of 2002, which is 1,500, plus the number of job losers (750), job leavers (300), entrants (150), and reentrants (450) minus the number of hires and recalls (1,000) and withdrawals (500). That is,

$$1,500 + 750 + 300 + 150 + 450 - 1,000 - 500 = 1,650.$$

Now calculate the number of people employed at the end of 2003. It equals the number employed at the end of 2002, which is 13,500, plus the number of hires and recalls (1,000) minus the number of job losers (750) and the number of job leavers (300). That is,

$$13,500 + 1,000 - 750 - 300 = 13,450.$$

Next calculate the labor force, which is the sum of the number unemployed and the number employed, which equals 1,650 + 13,450 = 15,100.

The unemployment rate is the percentage of the labor force who are unemployed, which is (1,650 ÷ 15,100) × 100 = 10.9 percent.

b. The labor force participation rate is the percentage of the working-age population who are in the labor force. The working-age population at the end of 2002 is the sum of number employed (13,500), number unemployed (1,500), and the number not in the labor force (7,500). That is,

$$13,500 + 1,500 + 7,500 = 22,500.$$

The working-age population increased during 2003 by 100 so, at the end of 2003, it equals 22,600.

The labor force participation rate is (15,100 ÷ 22,600) × 100 = 66.8 percent.

CHAPTER CHECKPOINT

Key Points

1 Define the unemployment rate and other labor market indicators.

- The unemployment rate is the number of people unemployed as a percentage of the labor force, and the labor force is the sum of the number of people employed and the number unemployed.
- The labor force participation rate is the labor force as a percentage of the working-age population.

2 Describe the trends and fluctuations in the indicators of labor market performance in the United States.

- The unemployment rate fluctuates with the business cycle.
- The female labor force participation rate has increased, and the male labor force participation rate has decreased.
- Aggregate hours trend upward more slowly than employment because average hours decrease. Aggregate hours and average hours fluctuate with the business cycle.

3 Describe the sources and types of unemployment, define full employment, and explain the link between unemployment and real GDP.

- Unemployment arises from the process of job creation and job destruction and from the movement of people into and out of the labor force.
- Unemployment can be frictional, structural, seasonal, or cyclical.
- The duration of unemployment fluctuates over the business cycle.
- Young people and minorities have the highest unemployment rates.
- Full employment occurs when there is no cyclical unemployment; the unemployment rate equals the natural unemployment rate.
- As the unemployment rate fluctuates around the natural unemployment rate, real GDP fluctuates around potential GDP.

Key Terms

Aggregate hours, 377
Cyclical unemployment, 388
Discouraged worker, 376
Frictional unemployment, 387
Full employment, 390
Full-time workers, 376
Involuntary part-time workers, 376
Labor force, 374
Labor force participation rate, 376
Natural unemployment rate, 390
Part-time workers, 376
Potential GDP, 390
Seasonal unemployment, 388
Structural unemployment, 388
Unemployment rate, 375
Working-age population, 374

Exercises

1. A BLS labor market survey interviewer visited four households.

   In the first household, Candy reported that she worked for 20 hours last week trying to get her Internet shopping business up and running. The rest of the week, she filled out application forms and attended two job interviews. Candy's husband Jerry worked for 40 hours at his job at General Motors. Candy and Jerry's 17-year-old daughter, who is still in high school, worked for 10 hours at her weekend convenience store job.

   In the second household, Joey, who works full time in a bank, reported that he was on his annual vacation. Joey's wife, Serena, who wants a full-time job, worked for 10 hours as a part-time checkout clerk.

   In the third household, Ari reported that he had no work last week but was going to be recalled to his regular farm job at the end of the month. Ari's housemate Kosta said that after months of search, he hasn't been able to find a job, so he has stopped looking and is now planning to go back to school.

   In the fourth household, Mimi and Henry reported that they are now senior citizens and are enjoying a well-earned retirement. Hank, their bachelor son who lives with them and is a professional artist, reported that he painted for 12 hours last week and sold one picture.

   a. Classify each of the ten people in these four households by the categories into which the BLS divides the population.
   b. Which of the people are part-time workers and which are full-time workers?
   c. Of the part-time workers, which are involuntary part-time workers?
   d. Calculate for these 10 people the
      i. Unemployment rate.
      ii. Labor force participation rate.
   e. Compare the unemployment rate and labor force participation rate of these four households with the U.S. data. How do these households differ from the average U.S. household?

2. The BLS survey found the following numbers in a small community:

   Total number of persons—320.

   Worked at least 1 hour as paid employees or worked 15 hours or more as unpaid workers in their family business—200.

   Were not working but had jobs or businesses from which they were temporarily absent—20.

   Had no employment—40.

   Were available for work and had made specific efforts to find employment some time during the previous 4 weeks—10.

   Were available for work and were waiting to be recalled to a job from which they had been laid off—6.

   a. Calculate for this community the
      i. Unemployment rate.
      ii. Labor force participation rate.

b. Compare the unemployment rate and labor force participation rate of this community with that for the households in exercise 1 and with the U.S. data. How does this community differ from the average U.S. household?

3. Describe the trends and fluctuations in the unemployment rate in the United States from 1962 through 2002. In which periods was the unemployment rate above average and in which periods was it below average?

4. Describe the trends and fluctuations in the labor force participation rate in the United States from 1962 through 2002, and contrast and explain the different trends for women and men.

5. What are the labor market flows that create and end a spell of unemployment? Of these flows, which fluctuate most and account for fluctuations in the unemployment rate?

6. Distinguish among the four types of unemployment: frictional, structural, seasonal, and cyclical. Provide an example of each type of unemployment in the United States today.

7. Describe the relationship between the unemployment rate and the natural unemployment rate as real GDP fluctuates around potential GDP. In which periods was real GDP below potential GDP?

Critical Thinking

8. The official measure of the unemployment rate omits many people who don't have a job but would like one. Do you think the omissions make the official unemployment rate an unhelpful indicator of the state of the economy? Or do you think that despite the omissions, the official measure provides useful information? Take a position on this issue and support your argument with examples.

9. If aggregate hours worked provides a more accurate measure of the quantity of labor employed than does the number of persons employed, why doesn't aggregate hours *not worked* provide a more accurate measure of the quantity of unemployment? (Hint: Think about the definition of unemployment.)

10. "Economics is supposed to be about scarcity. But if some labor is always unemployed, how can there be scarcity? All we need to do to produce more goods and services is employ the unemployed people."
    a. Do you agree or disagree with this statement? Why?
    b. Explain why scarcity and unemployment are not incompatible.

11. Most discussion and concern about unemployment arise from unemployed labor. Unemployed capital and land don't generate as much passion. But there is probably much more unemployment of capital and land than of labor.
    a. Provide some examples of unemployed capital and land.
    b. Explain why the unemployment of capital and land does not mean that scarcity isn't a problem.
    c. Can you think of benefits of unemployment that make some unemployment of all factors of production desirable?

Practice Online

Web Exercises

Use the links on your Foundations Web site to work the following exercises.

12. Visit the Bureau of Labor Statistics Web site and find the following labor market data for the United States in the most recent month and for the same month one year ago: the labor force, the number employed, the number unemployed, and the working-age population.
- **a.** Calculate for the two months the
  - **i.** Unemployment rate.
  - **ii.** Labor force participation rate.
- **b.** Describe the change in the labor market over the past year.

13. Visit the Bureau of Economic Analysis Web site and find the data on real GDP for the past year through the most recent quarter.
- **a.** Describe the change in real GDP over the past year.
- **b.** Explain how the change in real GDP relates to the changes in the labor market that you described in part **b** of exercise 1.

14. Visit the Bureau of Labor Statistics Web site and find labor market data for your own state.
- **a.** What have been the trends in employment, unemployment, and labor force participation in your own state during the past two years?
- **b.** On the basis of what you know about your own region, how would you set about explaining these trends?
- **c.** Try to identify the industries that have expanded most and those that have shrunk.
- **d.** What are the problems with your own regional labor market that you think need state government action to resolve?
- **e.** What actions do you think your state government must take to resolve them? Answer this question by using the demand and supply model of the labor market and predict the effects of the actions you prescribe.
- **f.** Compare the labor market performance of your own state with that of the nation as a whole.
- **g.** If your state is performing better than the national average, to what do you attribute the success? If your region is performing worse than the national average, to what do you attribute its problems?

15. Visit the Statistics Canada Web site and obtain labor market data for Canada.
- **a.** What have been the trends in employment, unemployment, and labor force participation in Canada during the past two years?
- **b.** Compare and contrast Canadian and U.S. labor market trends during these years.
- **c.** On the basis of what you've learned in this chapter about the types of unemployment, which types of unemployment do you think Canada has more of than the United States? Why?
- **d.** Is the natural unemployment rate in Canada higher or lower than that in the United States?
- **e.** To what do you attribute the difference in the natural unemployment rate in the two countries?

CHAPTER 16

Economic Growth

CHAPTER CHECKLIST

When you have completed your study of this chapter, you will be able to

1. **Define and calculate the economic growth rate, and explain the implications of sustained growth.**
2. **Identify the main sources of economic growth.**
3. **Review the theories of economic growth that explain why growth rates vary over time and across countries.**
4. **Describe policies that might speed economic growth.**

In the three previous chapters, you learned how we measure and monitor the standard of living, the cost of living, and economic fluctuations. In this chapter and those that follow, you will learn about the forces that determine macroeconomic performance. This chapter focuses on the standard of living and its pace of change.

Rich countries like the United States have become rich because they have enjoyed sustained growth of production and incomes. Poor countries like those of Africa are poor because they have not shared in the process of economic growth. What makes some countries and regions enjoy rising living standards, and others stagnate? Will our economy keep growing so that we have a higher standard of living than our parents did and our children have a higher standard of living than we do? These are among the questions that we'll answer in this chapter.

16.1 THE BASICS OF ECONOMIC GROWTH

Economic growth is a sustained expansion of production possibilities measured as the increase in real GDP over a given period. Rapid economic growth maintained over a number of years can transform a poor nation into a rich one. Such has been the experience of Hong Kong, South Korea, Taiwan, and some other Asian economies. Slow economic growth or the absence of growth can condemn a nation to devastating poverty. Such has been the fate of Sierra Leone, Somalia, Zambia, and much of the rest of Africa.

The main goal of this chapter is to help you to understand why some economies expand rapidly and others stagnate. We'll begin by learning how to calculate the economic growth rate and by discovering the magic of sustained growth.

Calculating Growth Rates

Economic growth rate
The annual percentage change of real GDP.

We express the **economic growth rate** as the annual percentage change of real GDP. To calculate this growth rate, we use the formula:

$$\text{Growth rate of real GDP} = \frac{\text{Real GDP in current year} - \text{Real GDP in previous year}}{\text{Real GDP in previous year}} \times 100.$$

For example, if real GDP in the current year is \$8.4 trillion and if real GDP in the previous year was \$8.0 trillion, then

$$\text{Growth rate of real GDP} = \frac{\$8.4\text{ trillion} - \$8.0\text{ trillion}}{\$8.0\text{ trillion}} \times 100 = 5\text{ percent}.$$

The growth rate of real GDP tells us how rapidly the total economy is expanding. This measure is useful for telling us about potential changes in the balance of economic power among nations. But it does not tell us about changes in the standard of living.

Real GDP per person
Real GDP divided by the population.

The standard of living depends on **real GDP per person**, which is real GDP divided by the population. So the contribution of real GDP growth to the change in the *standard of living* depends on the growth rate of real GDP per person. We use the above formula to calculate this growth rate, replacing real GDP with real GDP per person.

Suppose, for example, that in the current year, when real GDP is \$8.4 trillion, the population is 202 million. Then real GDP per person is \$8.4 trillion divided by 202 million, which equals \$41,584. And suppose that in the previous year, when real GDP was \$8.0 trillion, the population was 200 million. Then real GDP per person in that year was \$8.0 trillion divided by 200 million, which equals \$40,000.

Use these two real GDP per person values with the growth formula to calculate the growth rate of real GDP per person. That is,

$$\text{Growth rate of real GDP per person} = \frac{\$41{,}584 - \$40{,}000}{\$40{,}000} \times 100 = 4\text{ percent}.$$

The growth rate of real GDP per person can also be calculated by using the formula:

$$\text{Growth rate of real GDP per person} = \text{Growth rate of real GDP} - \text{Growth rate of population.}$$

In the example you've just worked through, the growth rate of real GDP is 5 percent. The population changes from 200 million to 202 million, so

$$\text{Growth rate of population} = \frac{202 \text{ million} - 200 \text{ million}}{200 \text{ million}} \times 100 = 1 \text{ percent,}$$

and

$$\text{Growth rate of real GDP per person} = 5 \text{ percent} - 1 \text{ percent} = 4 \text{ percent.}$$

This formula makes it clear that real GDP per person grows only if real GDP grows faster than the population grows. If the growth rate of the population exceeds the growth of real GDP, real GDP per person falls.

The Magic of Sustained Growth

Sustained growth of real GDP per person can transform a poor society into a wealthy one. The reason is that economic growth is like compound interest. Suppose that you put $100 in the bank and earn 5 percent a year interest on it. After one year, you have $105. If you leave that money in the bank for another year, you earn 5 percent interest on the original $100 and on the $5 interest that you earned last year. You are now earning interest on interest! The next year, things get even better. Then you earn 5 percent on the original $100 and on the interest earned in the first year and the second year. Your money in the bank is *growing* at a rate of 5 percent a year. Before too many years have passed, you'll have $200 in the bank. But after *how many* years?

The answer is provided by a powerful and general formula known as the **Rule of 70**, which states that the number of years it takes for the level of any variable to double is approximately 70 divided by the annual percentage growth rate of the variable. Using the Rule of 70, you can now calculate how many years it takes your $100 to become $200. It is 70 divided by 5, which is 14 years.

Rule of 70
The number of years it takes for the level of any variable to double is approximately 70 divided by the annual percentage growth rate of the variable.

The Rule of 70 applies to any variable, so it applies to real GDP per person. Table 16.1 shows the doubling time for a selection of other growth rates. You can see that real GDP per person doubles in 70 years (70 divided by 1)—an average human life span—if the growth rate is 1 percent a year. It doubles in 35 years if the growth rate is 2 percent a year and in just 10 years if the growth rate is 7 percent a year.

TABLE 16.1 GROWTH RATES

Growth rate (percent per year)	Years for level to double
1	70
2	35
3	23
4	18
5	14
6	12
7	10
8	9
9	8
10	7

We can use the Rule of 70 to answer other questions about economic growth. For example, in 2000, U.S. real GDP per person was approximately 8 times that of China. China's recent growth rate of real GDP per person was 7 percent a year. If this growth rate were maintained, how long would it take China's real GDP per person to reach that of the United States in 2000? The answer, provided by the Rule of 70, is 30 years. China's real GDP per person doubles in 10 (70 divided by 7) years. It doubles again to 4 times its current level in another 10 years. And it doubles yet again to 8 times its current level in another 10 years. So after 30 years of growth at 7 percent a year, China's real GDP per person is 8 times its current level and equals that of the United States in 2000.

Eye on the Past

How Fast Has Real GDP per Person Grown?

Professor Michael Kremer of Harvard University and Professor J. Bradford DeLong of the University of California, Berkeley, have constructed an extraordinary picture of real GDP in the global economy going back one million years. According to their numbers, human societies lived for a million years with no economic growth.

The top figure shows the numbers using the value of the dollar in 2000 as the measuring rod. Real GDP per person hovered around $100 per year from 1,000,000 BC until 1350! There were some wiggles and wobbles along the way. When Aristotle and Plato were teaching in Athens, around 500 BC, real GDP per person climbed to $175. But it slipped back over the next thousand years, and as the Roman Empire collapsed around 400 AD, it was $120. Even when the Pilgrim Fathers began to arrive in America in the 1620s, real GDP per person was similar to that of Ancient Greece!

Then, beginning around 1750, first in England and then in Europe and the United States, an astonishing change known as the Industrial Revolution occurred. Real GDP per person began to increase, apparently without limit. By 1850, real GDP per person was twice its 1650 level. By 1950, it was more than five times its 1850 level and by 2000, it was four times its 1950 level.

The bottom figure gives you a close-up view of U.S. real GDP per person over the past 100 years. In 1999, real GDP per person was almost six times its level in 1899. It has grown by 2 percent a year. But the growth rate has been uneven. The 1930s saw almost no growth, and the 1960s saw the fastest growth. Measured decade by decade, growth has been slowing since the 1960s.

But if we divide the 1990s into two periods, before and after the Internet (1994), we see a speedup in the growth rate after 1994. Some people think that in the current information age, we are at the beginning of a new increase in economic growth similar to that of the Industrial Revolution. No one knows yet whether this view is correct.

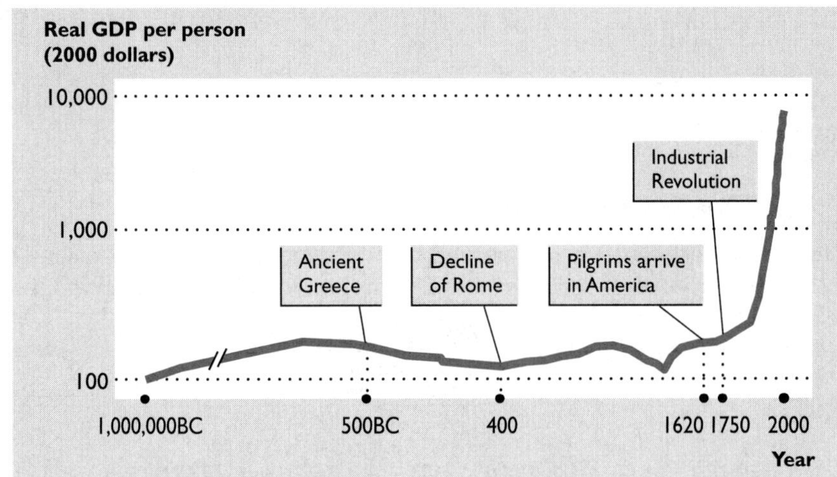

SOURCE: J. Bradford DeLong, *"Estimating World GDP, One Million B.C.–Present."*

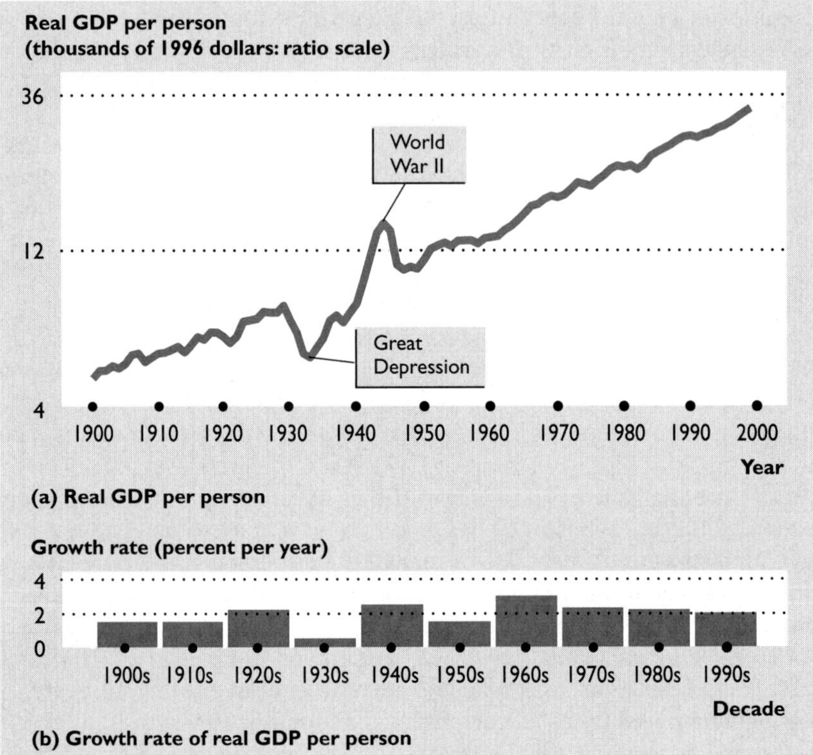

SOURCE: Bureau of Economic Analysis and Bureau of Labor Statistics.

CHECKPOINT 16.1

1 Define and calculate the economic growth rate, and explain the implications of sustained growth.

Study Guide pp. 242–245

Practice Online 16.1

Practice Problem 16.1

Mexico's real GDP was 1,448 billion pesos in 1998 and 1,501 billion pesos in 1999. Mexico's population growth rate in 1999 was 1.8 percent. Calculate

a. Mexico's economic growth rate in 1999.

b. The growth rate of real GDP per person in Mexico in 1999.

c. The approximate number of years it takes for real GDP per person in Mexico to double if the 1999 economic growth rate and population growth rate are maintained.

d. The approximate number of years it takes for real GDP per person in Mexico to double if the 1999 economic growth rate is maintained but the population growth rate slows to 1 percent a year.

Exercise 16.1

Canada's real GDP was $1,012 billion in 2000 and $1,028 billion in 2001. Canada's population was 30.8 million in 2000 and 31.1 million in 2001. Calculate

a. Canada's economic growth rate in 2001.

b. The growth rate of real GDP per person in Canada in 2001.

c. The approximate number of years it takes for real GDP per person in Canada to double if the 2001 economic growth rate and population growth rate are maintained.

d. The approximate number of years it takes for real GDP per person in Canada to double if the economic growth rate rises to 6 percent a year but the population growth rate remains the same as it was in 2001.

Solution to Practice Problem 16.1

a. Mexico's economic growth rate in 1999 was 3.7 percent. The economic growth rate equals the percentage change in real GDP:
[(Real GDP in 1999 – Real GDP in 1998)/Real GDP in 1998] × 100.
When we substitute the numbers, Mexico's economic growth rate equals [(1,501 billion – 1,448 billion)/1,448 billion] × 100, which is 3.7 percent.

b. The growth rate of real GDP per person in Mexico in 1999 was 1.9 percent. The growth rate of real GDP per person equals the growth rate of real GDP minus the population growth rate. When we substitute the numbers, the growth rate of real GDP per person equals 3.7 percent – 1.8 percent, or 1.9 percent.

c. It will take approximately 37 years for real GDP per person in Mexico to double. The Rule of 70 tells us that the level of a variable that grows at 1.9 percent a year will double in 70/1.9 years, which is approximately 37 years.

d. If Mexico's population growth rate falls to 1.0 percent a year, real GDP per person in Mexico will increase to 2.7 percent a year. The Rule of 70 tells us that real GDP in Mexico will double in 70/2.7 years, which is approximately 26 years.

16.2 THE SOURCES OF ECONOMIC GROWTH

Real GDP grows when the quantities of the factors of production grow or when persistent advances in technology make them increasingly productive. To understand what determines the growth rate of real GDP, we must understand what determines the growth rates of the factors of production and rate of increase in their productivity. We're going to see how the growth of physical capital and human capital and advances in technology interact to determine the economic growth rate.

We are interested in real GDP growth because it contributes to improvements in our standard of living. But our standard of living improves only if we produce more goods and services with each hour of labor. So our main concern is to understand the forces that make our labor more productive. For this reason, we begin by dividing all the influences on real GDP growth into those that increase

- Aggregate hours
- Labor productivity

Aggregate Hours

Over time, aggregate hours increase. This growth in aggregate hours comes from growth in the labor force rather than from growth in average hours per worker. As you saw in Chapter 15 (pp. 382–383), average hours per worker have *decreased* over the past decades. This decrease—and an associated *increase* in average leisure hours—is one of the benefits of economic growth.

The labor force depends on the population and the *labor force participation rate* (see Chapter 15, p. 376). While the participation rate has increased over the past few decades, it has an upper limit, and most of the growth of aggregate hours comes from population growth. So population growth is the only source of growth in aggregate labor hours that can be sustained over long periods.

Population growth brings economic growth, but it does not bring growth in real GDP per person unless labor hours become more productive.

Labor Productivity

Labor productivity
The quantity of real GDP produced by one hour of labor.

The quantity of real GDP produced by one hour of labor is called **labor productivity**. It is calculated by using the formula:

$$\text{Labor productivity} = \frac{\text{Real GDP}}{\text{Aggregate hours}}.$$

For example, if real GDP is $8,000 billion and if aggregate hours are 200 billion, then we can calculate labor productivity as

$$\text{Labor productivity} = \frac{\$8{,}000 \text{ billion}}{200 \text{ billion hours}} = \$40 \text{ an hour.}$$

You can turn this formula around and see that

$$\text{Real GDP} = \text{Aggregate hours} \times \text{Labor productivity}.$$

When labor productivity grows, real GDP per person grows. So the growth in labor productivity is the basis of rising living standards. The growth of labor productivity depends on three things:

- Saving and investment in physical capital
- Expansion of human capital
- Discovery of new technologies

These three sources of growth in labor productivity interact and are the primary sources of the extraordinary growth in productivity during the past 200 years. Let's look at each in turn.

Saving and Investment in Physical Capital

Saving and investment in physical capital increase the amount of capital per worker and increase labor productivity. Labor productivity took a dramatic upturn when the amount of capital per worker increased during the Industrial Revolution. Production processes that use hand tools can create beautiful objects, but production methods that use large amounts of capital per worker, such as auto plant assembly lines, enable workers to be much more productive. The accumulation of capital on farms, in textile factories, in iron foundries and steel mills, in coal mines, on building sites, in chemical plants, in auto plants, in banks, and in insurance companies has added incredibly to the productivity of our labor.

A strong and experienced farm worker of 1830, using a scythe, could harvest 3 acres of wheat in a day. A farm worker of 1831, using a mechanical reaper, could harvest 15 acres in a day. And a farm worker of today, using a combine harvester, can harvest and thresh 100 acres a day.

The next time you see a movie set in the old West, look carefully at the small amount of capital around. Try to imagine how productive you would be in such circumstances compared with your productivity today.

Expansion of Human Capital

Human capital—the accumulated skill and knowledge of people—comes from two sources:

- Education and training
- Job experience

A hundred years ago, most people attended school for around eight years. A hundred years before that, most people had no formal education at all. Today, 90 percent of Americans complete high school and more than 60 percent go to college or university. Our ability to read, write, and communicate effectively contributes enormously to our productivity.

While formal education is productive, school is not the only place where people acquire human capital. We also learn from on-the-job experience—from *learning by doing*. One carefully studied example illustrates the importance of learning by doing. Between 1941 and 1944 (during World War II), U.S. shipyards produced 2,500 Liberty Ships—a cargo ship built to a standardized design. In 1941, it took 1.2 million person-hours to build a ship. By 1942, it took 600,000, and by 1943, it took only 500,000. Not much change occurred in the physical capital employed during these years. But an enormous amount of human capital was accumulated. Thousands of workers and managers learned from experience and more than doubled their productivity in two years.

The expansion of human capital is the most fundamental source of economic growth because it directly increases labor productivity and is the source of the discovery of new technologies.

Discovery of New Technologies

The growth of physical capital and human capital has made a large contribution to economic growth. But the discovery and application of new technologies have made an even greater contribution.

The development of writing, one of the most basic human skills, was the source of some of the earliest productivity gains. The ability to keep written records made it possible to reap ever-larger gains from specialization and trade. Imagine how hard it would be to do any kind of business if all the accounts, invoices, and agreements existed only in people's memories.

Later, the development of mathematics laid the foundation for the eventual extension of knowledge in physics, chemistry, and biology. This base of scientific knowledge was the foundation for the technological advances of the Industrial Revolution 200 years ago and of today's Information Revolution.

Since the Industrial Revolution, technological change has become a part of everyday life. Firms routinely conduct research to develop technologies that are more productive, and partnerships between business and the universities are commonplace in fields such as biotechnology and electronics.

To reap the benefits of technological change, capital must increase. Some of the most powerful and far-reaching technologies are embodied in human capital—for example, language, writing, and mathematics. But most technologies are embodied in physical capital. For example, to reap the benefits of the internal combustion engine, millions of horse-drawn carriages had to be replaced by automobiles and trucks; more recently, to reap the benefits of computerized word processing, millions of typewriters had to be replaced by PCs and printers.

Sources of Growth: A Summary

Figure 16.1 summarizes the sources of economic growth. Your next task is to learn how these sources combine and how we identify the separate contributions of capital growth and the other influences on labor productivity.

FIGURE 16.1
The Sources of Economic Growth

Practice Online

Real GDP depends on aggregate labor hours and labor productivity. Labor productivity depends on the amount of physical capital and human capital and the state of technology. Growth in aggregate hours and growth in labor productivity bring real GDP growth.

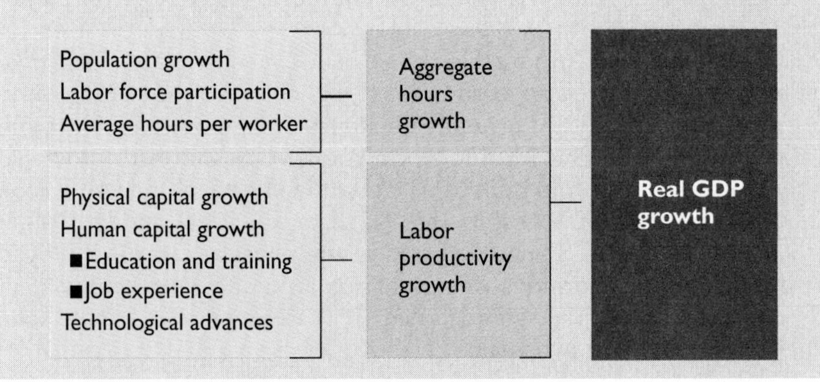

The Productivity Curve

The **productivity curve** is a relationship between real GDP per hour of labor and the quantity of capital per hour of labor with a given state of technology. Figure 16.2 illustrates the productivity curve. Capital per hour of labor, measured on the x-axis, is physical capital valued in 1996 dollars. (Remember that even though we use dollar values to measure capital, we are talking about *physical capital.*) Labor productivity (real GDP per hour of labor) is measured on the y-axis. The figure shows two productivity curves, one labeled PC_0 and the other labeled PC_1.

An increase in the quantity of capital per hour of labor increases labor productivity, which is shown by a movement along a productivity curve. For example, on PC_0, when capital per hour of labor is \$30, labor productivity is \$20 an hour. If capital per hour of labor increases to \$60, labor productivity increases to \$25 an hour.

At a given amount of capital per hour of labor, labor productivity increases if human capital increases or technology advances. An upward shift of the productivity curve illustrates these influences on labor productivity. For example, if capital per hour of labor is \$30 and a technological change increases labor productivity from \$20 to \$25, the productivity curve shifts upward from PC_0 to PC_1. Similarly, if capital per hour of labor is \$60, the same technological change increases labor productivity from \$25 to \$32 and shifts the productivity curve upward from PC_0 to PC_1.

Productivity curve
The relationship between real GDP per hour of labor and the quantity of capital per hour of labor with a given state of technology.

FIGURE 16.2
How Labor Productivity Grows

Practice Online

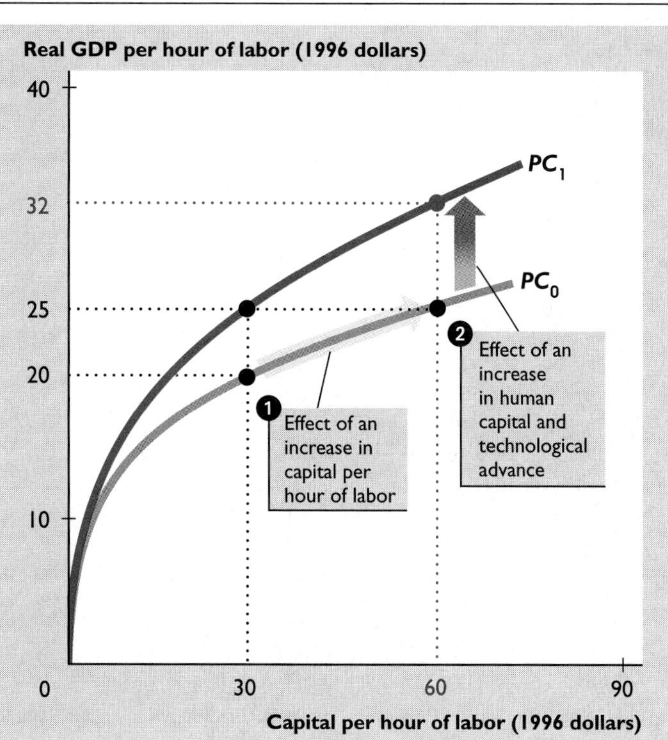

Labor productivity, which is measured by real GDP per hour of labor, can grow for two reasons:

1. An increase in capital per hour of labor brings a movement along the productivity curve PC_0. When capital per hour of labor increases from \$30 to \$60, real GDP per hour of labor increases from \$20 to \$25.
2. An increase in human capital and a technological advance shift the productivity curve upward from PC_0 to PC_1. With this increase in human capital and technological advance, real GDP per hour of labor increases from \$20 to \$25 when there is \$30 of capital per hour of labor and from \$25 to \$32 when there is \$60 of capital per hour of labor.

With constant average hours per worker and a constant labor force participation rate, aggregate hours grow at the same rate as the population. The capital stock grows at a rate determined by saving and investment. If the capital stock grows faster than the population, capital per hour of labor increases. If the capital stock grows slower than the population, capital per hour of labor decreases. And if the capital stock grows at the same rate as the population, capital per hour of labor is constant. The faster the growth rate of capital per hour of labor, the higher is the growth rate of real GDP per person.

But growth from capital alone is limited by decreasing returns.

Diminishing Returns

The shape of the productivity curve displays *decreasing returns*—each additional unit of capital per hour of labor produces a successively smaller additional amount of real GDP per hour of labor. For example, along productivity curve PC_0, if capital per hour of labor increases from zero to \$30, real GDP per hour of labor increases by \$20. But when capital per hour of labor increases by another \$30 to \$60, real GDP per hour of labor increases by only \$5 to \$25. Decreasing returns to capital are similar to decreasing returns to labor that you met in Chapter 9 (see pp. 224–226). You can see why decreasing returns apply to both capital and labor by thinking about Larry's Lawn Services, which owns one lawn mower and employs two workers. If Larry hires one more worker—a 50 percent increase in labor—he

Eye on the U.S. Economy

Labor Productivity and Economic Growth since 1962

The figure on this page shows that labor productivity growth was most rapid during the 1960s. It slowed after 1969 and slowed further after 1974. It speeded up again after 1995. But despite the spread of the personal computer and the expansion of the Internet, by the late 1990s labor productivity growth had not returned to that of the 1960s.

Why does labor productivity growth fluctuate? The figure on the next page provides a first look at the answer. The

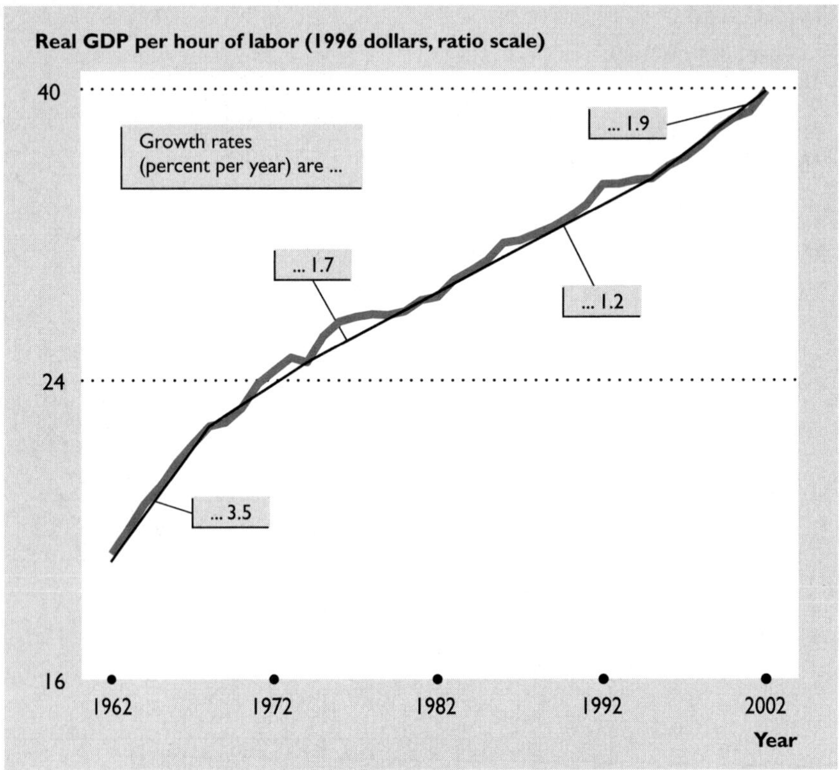

SOURCE: Bureau of Economic Analysis and Bureau of Labor Statistics.

gets more lawns mown, but not 50 percent more. Similarly, if Larry buys an extra lawn mower—a 100 percent increase in capital—he gets more lawns mown, but not 100 percent more.

More generally, one hour of labor working with $40 worth of capital produces less than twice the output of one hour of labor working with $20 worth of capital. But how much less? The answer is given by the one third rule.

The One Third Rule

To identify the contribution of capital growth to labor productivity growth, we use a feature of the productivity curve discovered by Robert Solow of MIT. By studying growth in the U.S. economy, Solow noticed a **one third rule**: On the average, with no change in human capital and technology, a *one percent* increase in capital per hour of labor brings a *one third percent* increase in labor productivity.

One third rule
The observation that on the average, with no change in human capital and technology, a *one percent* increase in capital per hour of labor brings a *one third percent* increase in labor productivity.

We can use the one third rule to identify the contribution of capital growth to labor productivity growth. Suppose, for example, that in a year, capital per hour of labor grows by 3 percent and labor productivity grows by 2.5 percent. The one third rule tells us that capital growth has contributed one third of 3 percent, which is 1 percent.

Labor productivity growth that is not attributed to capital growth arises from human capital growth and technological change. In the above example in which labor productivity grows by 2.5 percent and capital growth contributed 1 percent, the remaining 1.5 percent growth of labor productivity comes from human capital growth and technological change.

contribution of human capital growth and technological change fluctuated. But why did it fluctuate?

The 1960s enjoyed a period of rapid technological change based on spillovers from World War II and on the plastics revolution.

The contribution of human capital growth and technological change slowed during the 1970s because

(1) Its focus changed from increasing productivity to coping with energy price increases. Oil price hikes in 1973–1974 and 1979–1980 diverted research toward saving energy rather than increasing labor productivity. Airplanes became more fuel efficient, but they didn't operate with smaller crews. Real GDP per gallon of fuel increased faster but real GDP per hour of labor increased slower.

(2) More resources were devoted to protecting the environment and improving the quality of the workplace. The benefits of these activities—a cleaner environment and safer factories—are not counted as part of GDP. So the growth of these benefits was not counted as part of productivity growth.

(3) Taxes and government regulation expanded during the late 1960s and 1970s, so incentives were weakened and growth slowed.

(4) Rapid inflation distorted saving and investment decisions and shortened the horizon over which firms made their borrowing and lending plans.

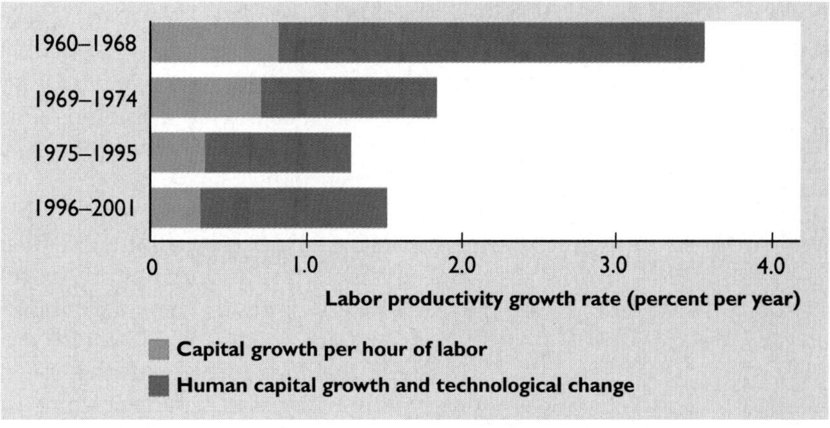

SOURCE: Bureau of Economic Analysis and Bureau of Labor Statistics.

CHECKPOINT 16.2

Study Guide pp. 245–248

Practice Online 16.2

2 **Identify the main sources of economic growth.**

Practice Problem 16.2

The table provides some data on the Canadian economy in 1998 and 1999.

Item	1998	1999
Aggregate hours (billions)	25.0	25.2
Real GDP (billions of 1992 dollars)	840	880
Capital per hour of labor (1992 dollars)	127	130

a. Calculate the growth rate of real GDP in 1999.
b. Calculate labor productivity in 1998 and 1999.
c. Calculate the growth rate of labor productivity in 1999.
d. If the one third rule applies in Canada, what were the sources of labor productivity growth in 1999? Explain your answer.

Exercise 16.2

The table provides some data on the U.S. economy in 2000 and 2001.

Item	2000	2001
Aggregate hours (billion)	240.6	238.8
Real GDP (billions of 1996 dollars)	9,191	9,215
Capital per hour of labor (1996 dollars)	98.91	102.13

a. Calculate the growth rate of real GDP in 2001.
b. Calculate labor productivity in 2000 and 2001.
c. Calculate the growth rate of labor productivity in 2001.
d. If the one third rule applies in the United States, what were the sources of labor productivity growth in 2001? Explain your answer.

Solution to Practice Problem 16.2

a. The growth rate of real GDP in 1999 was [($880 billion – $840 billion)/$840 billion] × 100, which equals 4.8 percent.
b. Labor productivity equals real GDP per hour of labor. In 1998, labor productivity was $840 billion/25 billion, which equals $33.60 per hour of labor. In 1999, labor productivity was $880 billion/25.2 billion hours, which equals $34.92 per hour of labor.
c. The growth rate of labor productivity in 1999 is [($34.92 – $33.60)/$33.60] × 100, which equals 3.93 percent.
d. The one third rule identifies the contribution of capital growth to labor productivity growth. Capital per hour of labor grew by [($130 – $127)/$127] × 100, which equals 2.36 percent.
So the one third rule tells us that 1/3 of the 2.36 percent of labor productivity growth, which is 0.79 percent, came from capital growth. The remainder of labor productivity growth, which is 3.14 percent, came from human capital growth and technological change.

16.3 THEORIES OF ECONOMIC GROWTH

We've seen that real GDP grows when the quantities of labor, capital, and human capital grow and when technology advances. Does this mean that all these factors *cause* economic growth? It might. But there are other possibilities. One of these factors might be the cause of real GDP growth and the others the effect. We must try to discover how the influences on economic growth interact with each other to make some economies grow quickly and others grow slowly. And we must probe the reasons why a country's long-term growth rate sometimes speeds up and sometimes slows down.

Growth theories are designed to study the interactions among the several factors that contribute to growth and to disentangle cause and effect. They are also designed to enable us to study how the various factors influence each other.

Growth theories are also designed to be universal. They are not theories about the growth of poor countries only or of rich countries only. They are theories about why and how poor countries become rich and rich countries become richer.

We're going to study three theories of economic growth, each of which gives some insights into the process of economic growth. But none provides a definite answer to the basic questions: What causes economic growth and why do growth rates vary? Economics has some way to go before it can provide a definite answer to these most important of questions.

We study three growth theories:

- Classical growth theory
- Neoclassical growth theory
- New growth theory

Classical Growth Theory

Classical growth theory predicts that the clash between an exploding population and limited resources will eventually bring economic growth to an end. According to classical growth theory, labor productivity growth is temporary. When labor productivity rises and lifts real GDP per person above the subsistence level, which is the minimum real income needed to maintain life, a population explosion occurs. Eventually, the population grows so large that labor productivity falls and returns real GDP per person back to the subsistence level.

Classical growth theory
The theory that the clash between an exploding population and limited resources will eventually bring economic growth to an end.

Adam Smith, Thomas Robert Malthus, and David Ricardo, the leading economists of the late eighteenth and early nineteenth centuries, proposed this theory, but the view is most closely associated with Malthus and is sometimes called the **Malthusian theory**. It is also sometimes called the Doomsday theory.

Malthusian theory
Another name for classical growth theory—named for Thomas Robert Malthus.

Many people today are Malthusians. They say that if today's global population of 6.3 billion explodes to 11 billion by 2200, we will run out of resources and return to a primitive standard of living. We must act, say the Malthusians, to contain the population growth.

The Basic Idea

To understand the basic idea of classical growth theory, let's transport ourselves back to the world of 1776. Adam Smith's *Wealth of Nations* has just been published, the Industrial Revolution is under way in Britain, and the United States of America is not yet born. Most of the 2.5 million people who live in the not yet independent United States of America work on farms or on their own land and perform their tasks using simple tools and animal power. They earn an average of 2 shillings (a bit less than $12 dollars in today's money) for working a ten-hour day.

Then advances in farming technology bring new types of plows and seeds that increase farm productivity. As farm productivity increases, farm production increases and some farm workers move from the land to the cities, where they get work producing and selling the expanding range of farm equipment. Real GDP per person rises, and people are prospering. But will the prosperity last? Classical growth theory says that it will not. The prosperity will induce a population explosion. And the population explosion will decrease real GDP per person.

Classical Theory of Population Growth

When the classical economists were developing their ideas about population growth, an unprecedented population explosion was under way. In Britain and other Western European countries, improvements in diet and hygiene had lowered the death rate while the birth rate remained unchanged. For several decades, population growth was extremely rapid.

For example, after being relatively stable for several centuries, the population of Britain increased by 40 percent between 1750 and 1800 and by another 50 percent between 1800 and 1830. At the same time, an estimated 1 million people (about 20 percent of the 1750 population) left Britain for America and Australia before 1800, and outward migration continued on a similar scale through the nineteenth century. This historical population explosion was the basis for the classical theory of population growth.

To explain the high rate of population growth, the classical economists used the idea of a subsistence real income. If the actual real income is less than the subsistence real income, some people cannot survive and the population decreases. In classical theory, when real income exceeds the subsistence real income, the population grows. But the increasing population decreases the amount of capital per hour of labor. So labor productivity and real GDP per person eventually decrease. And no matter how much technological change occurs, real GDP per person is always pushed back toward the subsistence level. This dismal implication led to economics being called the dismal science.

Productivity Curve Illustration

Figure 16.3 illustrates the classical growth theory, using the productivity curve. Initially, the productivity curve is PC_0. The economy is producing at point *A*, and real GDP per hour is just high enough for people to earn a subsistence real income.

Now capital per hour increases, which moves the economy along the productivity curve to point *B*. And technology advances, which shifts the productivity curve to PC_1 and moves the economy to point *C*. Real GDP per hour of labor is now above the level that provides a subsistence level of real income. So the population increases, and labor hours grow. Capital per hour of labor decreases and real GDP per hour of labor decreases as the economy moves down along the productivity curve PC_1. As long as real GDP per hour of labor exceeds the subsistence level, population growth brings a decrease in capital per hour of labor. Eventually, real GDP per hour of labor returns to the subsistence level at point *D*.

The economy has grown—real GDP has increased—but a larger population is earning only the subsistence real GDP per person.

FIGURE 16.3
Classical Growth Theory

Practice Online

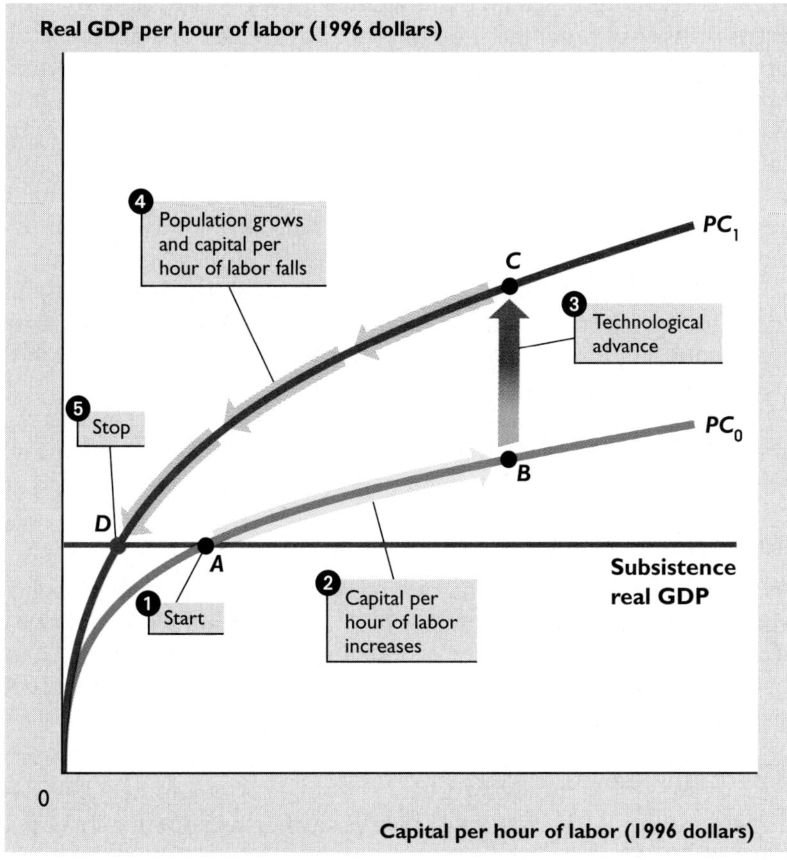

1. The economy starts out at point *A* on productivity curve PC_0 with real GDP per hour of labor at the subsistence level and the population constant.
2. The economy moves to point *B* as capital per hour of labor increases and real GDP per hour of labor increases above the subsistence level.
3. The economy moves to point *C* as technological advance (and the accumulation of human capital) increase productivity and the productivity curve shifts upward to PC_1.
4. With real GDP per hour of labor above the subsistence level, the economy moves toward point *D* as the population grows and capital per hour of labor decreases.
5. At point *D*, the economy is back at the subsistence level of real GDP per hour of labor.

Neoclassical Growth Theory

Neoclassical growth theory (developed by Robert Solow of MIT during the 1960s) predicts that real GDP per person will increase as long as technology keeps advancing. Real GDP will grow at a rate equal to the population growth rate plus the rate of productivity growth induced by technological change and the accumulation of human capital. So according to the neoclassical theory, growth will persist.

Neoclassical growth theory
The theory that real GDP per person will increase as long as technology keeps advancing.

Neoclassical growth theory asserts that population growth and the pace of technological change determine, but are not themselves influenced by, the growth rate of real GDP. Let's briefly examine the neoclassical view of population growth and technological change.

Population Growth

The population explosion of eighteenth century Europe that created the classical theory eventually ended. The birth rate fell, and the population growth rate slowed. This slowdown in population growth seemed to make the classical theory increasingly less relevant. And the slowdown in population growth eventually led to the development of a new economic theory of population growth.

Economists began to realize that although the population growth rate is influenced by economic factors, that influence is not the one identified by the classical economists. Key among the economic influences on population growth is the opportunity cost of a woman's time. As women's wage rates increase and their job opportunities expand, the opportunity cost of having children increases. Faced with a higher opportunity cost, families choose to have fewer children and the birth rate falls.

A second economic influence lowers the death rate. The technological advances that increase labor productivity also bring advances in health care that extend lives.

So two opposing economic forces influence population growth. As incomes increase, the birth rate decreases and the death rate decreases. It turns out that these opposing forces are offsetting, so the rate of population growth is independent of the rate of economic growth.

The historical population trends contradict the views of the classical economists and call into question the contemporary Doomsday conclusion that one day we will be swamped with too many people for the planet to feed.

Technological Change

In the neoclassical theory, the rate of technological change influences the rate of economic growth, but economic growth does not influence the pace of technological change. It is assumed that technological change results from chance. When we get lucky, we have rapid technological change; and when bad luck strikes, the pace of technological advance slows.

The Basic Idea

To understand the basic idea of neoclassical growth theory, imagine the world of the mid-1950s. Americans are enjoying post–World War II prosperity. Real GDP per person is around $12,000 a year in today's money. The population is growing at about 1 percent a year, and people are saving and investing enough to make capital grow at a similar rate. So real GDP per person is not growing much.

Then technology advances at a more rapid pace across a range of activities. The transistor revolutionizes an emerging electronics industry. New plastics revolutionize the manufacture of household appliances. Jet airliners start to replace piston engine airplanes and speed transportation. And Elvis and the Beatles change the face of popular music!

These technological advances bring new profit opportunities. Businesses expand and new businesses are created to exploit the new technologies. Investment and saving increase, so capital per hour of labor increases. The economy enjoys increased prosperity and growth. But will the prosperity last? And will the growth last? Neoclassical growth theory says that the prosperity will last but the growth will not unless technology keeps advancing.

The prosperity persists because no population explosion occurs to lower real GDP per person. But growth stops if technology stops advancing because capital accumulation brings diminishing returns, which slow the growth rate of real GDP and slow the level of saving and investment. Eventually, the growth rate of capital slows to that of the population and real GDP per person stops growing.

A Problem with Neoclassical Growth Theory

Neoclassical growth theory predicts that real GDP per person will grow at a rate that is determined by the pace of technological change. But the theory does not explain what determines technological change. In the neoclassical theory, technological change is like the weather—it rains down on us at a pace that we must simply accept. In reality, the pace of technological change results from choices. The new growth theory, which we'll now study, emphasizes the role of these choices.

New Growth Theory

New growth theory predicts that our unlimited wants will lead us to ever greater productivity and perpetual economic growth. According to new growth theory, real GDP per person grows because of the choices people make in the pursuit of profit. Paul Romer of the University of California at Berkeley developed this theory during the 1980s, but the new growth theory builds on ideas developed by Joseph Schumpeter during the 1930s and 1940s.

New growth theory
The theory that our unlimited wants will lead us to ever greater productivity and perpetual economic growth.

Choices and Innovation

The new growth theory emphasizes three facts about market economies:

- Human capital grows because of choices.
- Discoveries result from choices.
- Discoveries bring profit, and competition destroys profit.

Human Capital Growth and Choices People decide how long to remain in school, what to study, and how hard to study. And when they graduate from school, people make more choices about job training and on-the-job learning. All these choices govern the speed at which human capital grows.

Discoveries and Choices When people discover a new product or technique, they consider themselves lucky. They are right. But the pace at which new discoveries are made—and at which technology advances—is not determined by chance. It depends on how many people are looking for a new technology and how intensively they are looking.

Discoveries and Profits Profit is the spur to technological change. The forces of competition squeeze profits, so to increase profit, people constantly seek either lower-cost methods of production or new and better products for which people are willing to pay a higher price. Inventors can maintain a profit for several years by taking out a patent or copyright. But eventually, a new discovery is copied, and profits disappear.

Two other facts play a key role in the new growth theory:

- Many people can use discoveries at the same time.
- Physical activities can be replicated.

Discoveries Used by All Once a profitable new discovery has been made, everyone can use it. For example, when Marc Andreeson created Mosaic, the Web browser that led to the creation of Netscape Navigator and Microsoft's Internet Explorer, everyone who was interested in navigating the Internet had access to a new and more efficient tool. One person's use of a Web browser does not prevent others from using it. This fact means that as the benefits of a new discovery spread, socially free resources become available. These resources are free because nothing is given up when an additional person uses them. They have a zero opportunity cost.

Replicating Activities Production activities can be replicated. For example, there might be 2, 3, or 53 identical firms making fiber-optic cable by using an identical assembly line and production technique. If one firm increases its capital and output, that *firm* experiences diminishing returns. But the economy can increase its capital and output by adding another identical fiber cable factory, and the *economy* does not experience diminishing returns.

The assumption that capital does not experience diminishing returns is the central novel proposition of the new growth theory. And the implication of this simple and appealing idea is astonishing. As capital accumulates, labor productivity grows indefinitely as long as people devote resources to expanding human capital and introducing new technologies.

Perpetual Motion

Figure 16.4 illustrates new growth theory in terms of a perpetual motion machine. Economic growth is driven by insatiable wants that lead us to pursue profit and innovate. New and better products result from this process, which lead to new firms starting up and old firms going out of business. As firms start up and die, jobs are created and destroyed. New and better jobs lead to more leisure and more

FIGURE 16.4

A Perpetual Motion Machine

❶ People want a higher standard of living and are spurred by ❷ profit incentives to make the ❸ innovations that lead to ❹ new and better techniques and new and better products, which in turn lead to ❺ the birth of new firms and the death of some old firms, ❻ new and better jobs, and ❼ more leisure and more consumption goods and services. The result is ❽ a higher standard of living. But people want a yet higher standard of living, and the growth process continues.

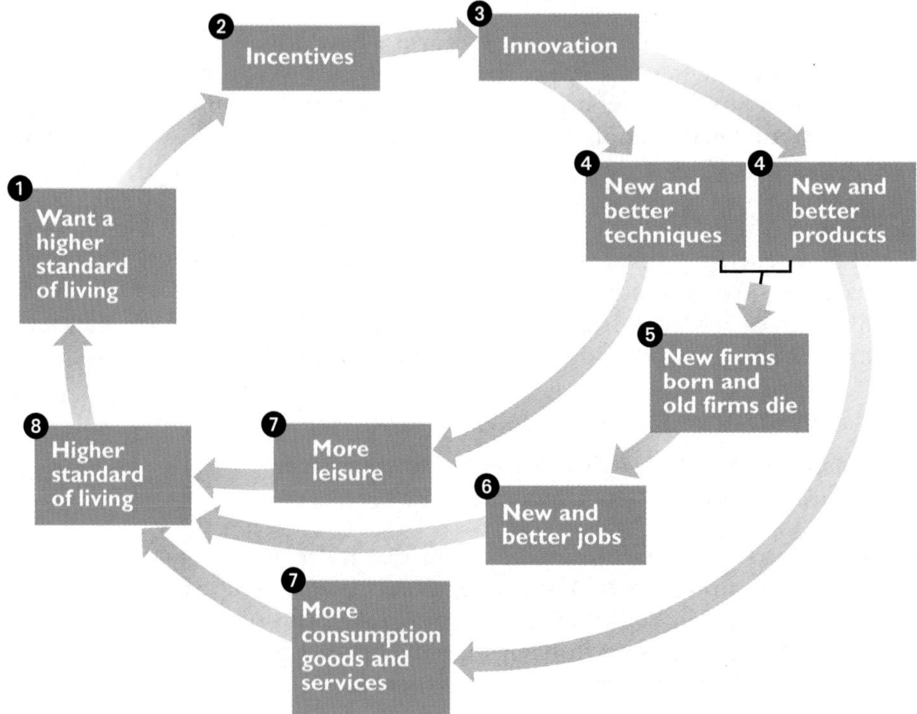

Based on a similar figure in *These Are the Good Old Days: A Report on U.S. Living Standards*, Federal Reserve Bank of Dallas 1993 Annual Report.

consumption. But our insatiable wants are still there, so the process continues, going round and round a circle of wants, profit incentives, innovation, and new products. The growth rate depends on people's ability to innovate and the incentives to do so. Over the years, the ability to innovate has changed. The invention of language and writing (the two most basic human capital tools), and later the development of the scientific method and the establishment of universities and research institutions, brought a huge increase in profit opportunities. Today, a deeper understanding of genes is bringing profit in a growing biotechnology industry. And astonishing advances in computer technology are creating an explosion of profit opportunities in a wide range of new information-age industries.

Productivity Curve and New Growth Theory

Figure 16.5 illustrates new growth theory by using the productivity curve. According to this theory, capital increases and technology advances together to bring unending growth. The economy starts out on the productivity curve PC_0 at point *A*. Capital per hour of labor increases, which brings a movement along the productivity curve and increases labor productivity. At the same time, technology advances and human capital grows, which shifts the productivity curve upward to PC_1. So, for a second reason, labor productivity increases. The economy moves to point *B*. This process repeats indefinitely and takes the economy next to point *C* and then beyond.

FIGURE 16.5
New Growth Theory

Practice Online

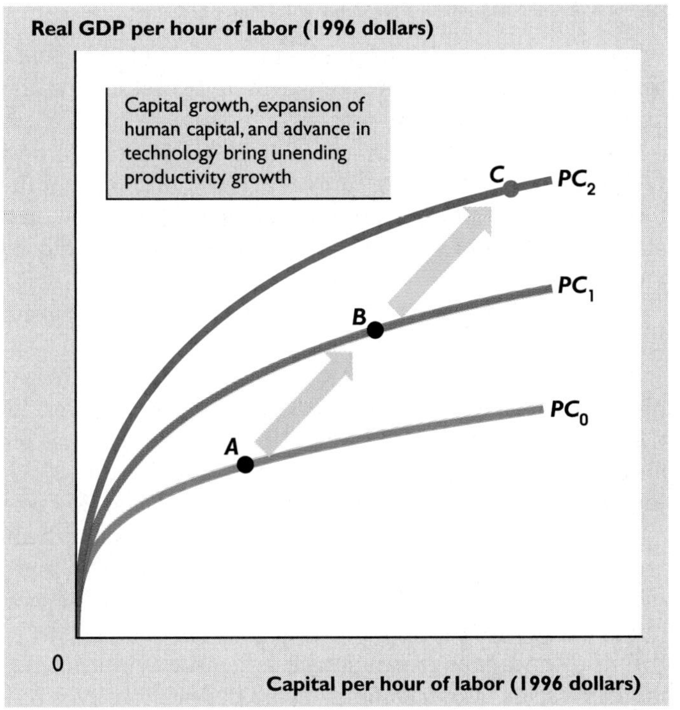

The economy starts out at point *A* on the productivity curve PC_0. An increase in capital per hour of labor brings a movement along the productivity curve PC_0 and the expansion of human capital and technological change increase labor productivity and shift the productivity curve upward to PC_1. The economy moves to point *B*.

The process repeats. The economy moves to point *C* and then to points of yet greater capital per hour of labor and labor productivity.

Eye on the U.S. Economy

Labor Productivity and Capital per Hour: 1960–2001

New growth theory is supported by the performance of the U.S. economy. In the figure, each dot represents a year from 1960 to 2001 and shows the U.S. data on labor productivity and capital per hour of labor. The two curves are the productivity curves of 1960 and 2001 based on the one third rule.

You can see that advances in technology and the expansion of human capital have shifted the productivity curve upward and overcome diminishing returns.

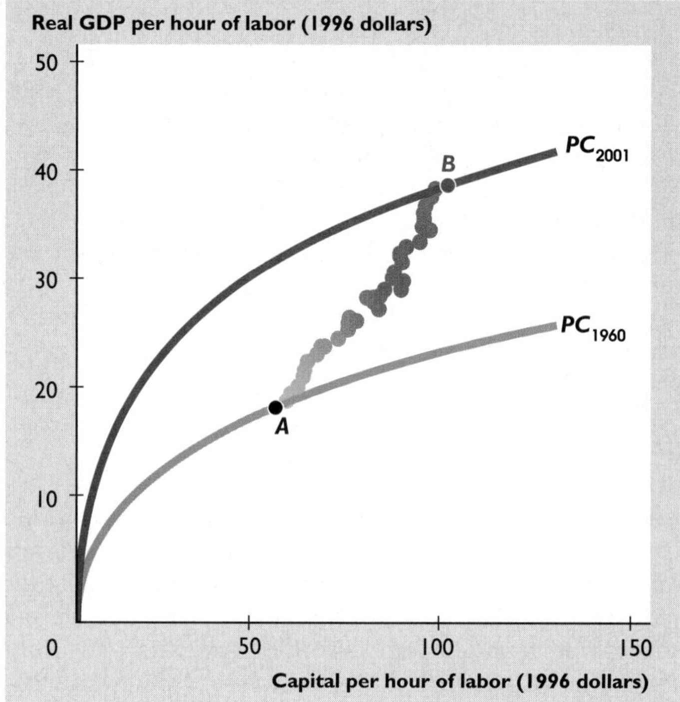

SOURCE: Bureau of Economic Analysis and Bureau of Labor Statistics.

Growth in the Global Economy

Economic growth is a global phenomenon, not just a national one. And the three growth theories make strikingly different predictions about the growth patterns that we should find in the global economy.

Classical growth theory predicts that the global economy will stagnate under the pressure of population growth. It also implies that the richest nations will be the ones with the fastest population growth and therefore they will be the first to stagnate. These predictions are resoundingly rejected by the experience of the world economy over the past few decades.

Neoclassical growth theory predicts that the global economy will grow and at a rate that is determined by the pace of technological change. All economies have access to the same technologies, and capital is free to roam the globe seeking the highest available profits. So neoclassical theory predicts that national levels of real GDP and national growth rates will converge. There is some sign of convergence among the rich countries. But convergence is slow, and it does not appear to be imminent for all countries (see Eye on the Global Economy).

New growth theory predicts that national growth rates depend on national incentives to save, invest, accumulate human capital, and innovate. Because these incentives depend on factors that are special to each country, national growth rates will not necessarily converge. Some real GDP per person gaps among rich countries and gaps between rich and poor countries might persist. Other gaps might close as poorer nations create better incentives to boost capital accumulation and technological change. New growth theory fits the facts more closely than do the other two theories.

Eye on the Global Economy

Persistent Gaps or Convergence?

The figure shows real GDP per person in the United States and in other countries and regions from 1962 to 2002.

Part (a) shows persistent gaps in real GDP per person. Growth rates in Canada and Europe's Big 4 (France, Germany, Italy, and the United Kingdom) have been similar to that of the United States, so the gaps between these countries haven't changed much.

Other Western European countries grew faster than the United States before 1975, slowed to the U.S. growth rate during the 1980s, and fell behind during the 1990s. After a brief period of catch-up, the former Communist countries of Central Europe fell increasingly behind the United States.

Africa and Central and South America persistently grew more slowly than the United States, so the gaps between the United States and these regions widened.

Part (b) of the figure tells a different story. It shows how the real GDP per person in East Asian economies has converged on that in the United States.

In 1962, Hong Kong, Singapore, Taiwan, and South Korea had levels of real GDP per person that ranged from 10 percent to 25 percent of that in the United States. By 2002, real GDP per person in Hong Kong equaled that in the United States. Singapore was close behind, and the two others were converging fast. These four small Asian countries are like fast trains running on the same track at similar speeds and with a roughly constant gap between them. Hong Kong is the lead train and runs about 10 years in front of South Korea, which is the last train. Real GDP per person in South Korea in 1992 was similar to that in Hong Kong in 1982, ten years earlier.

(a) Persistent gaps

(b) Convergence

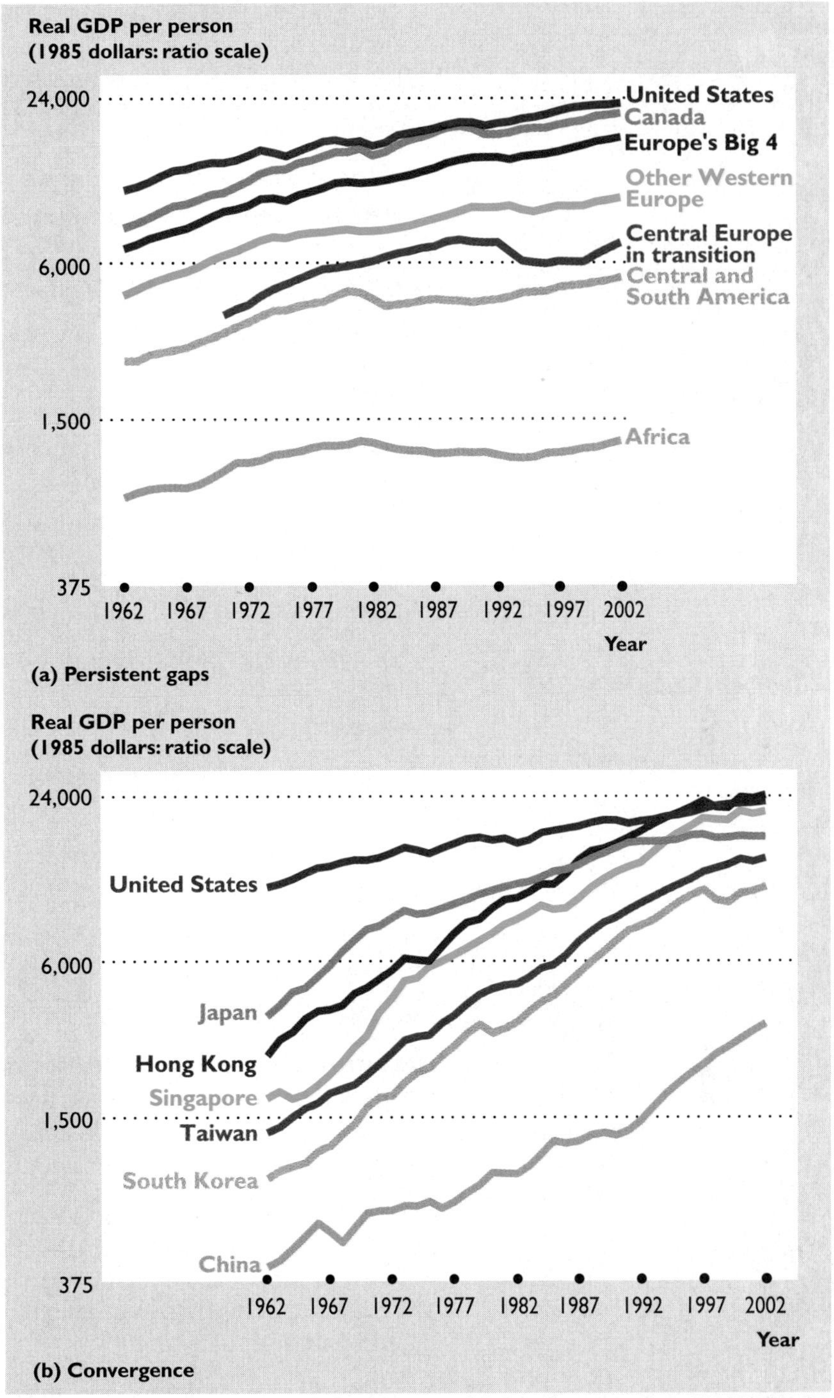

SOURCE: Alan Heston and Robert Summers, *Penn World Tables* 5.6 and *World Economic Outlook*.

Between 1962 and 2002, Hong Kong transformed itself from a poor developing country into one of the world's richest countries.

Part (b) of the figure also shows that China is catching up, but more slowly and from a very long way behind.

CHECKPOINT 16.3

Study Guide pp. 248–250

Practice Online 16.3

3 **Review the theories of economic growth that explain why growth rates vary over time and across countries.**

Practice Problems 16.3

1. What does classical growth theory say will eventually end economic growth? Does the evidence of history support the prediction of the classical growth theory?
2. What does neoclassical growth theory say about the source of persistent growth in real GDP per person?
3. Why does neoclassical growth theory predict that national levels of real GDP and national growth rates will converge?
4. What is the driving force of growth according to new growth theory?
5. What does new growth theory imply about growth in the global economy?

Exercises 16.3

1. Contrast the modern theory of population growth with the classical growth theory.
2. What is the main limitation of neoclassical growth theory?
3. What are the three facts about market economies that new growth theory emphasizes and how do those facts influence the economic growth rate? Provide examples of each.
4. Why don't diminishing returns limit growth in new growth theory?
5. Families in China are permitted to have only one child. Predict the effects of this policy according to classical, neoclassical, and new growth theories.

Solutions to Practice Problems 16.3

1. Classical growth theory predicts that real GDP per person will be persistently pulled toward the subsistence level. When real GDP per person exceeds the subsistence level, the population grows and real GDP per person decreases. The evidence of history does not support the prediction that economic growth will eventually end.
2. Neoclassical growth theory says that technological advance is the source of persistent growth in real GDP per person.
3. Neoclassical growth theory predicts convergence because all countries have access to the same technology and capital is free to roam the globe.
4. The driving force of growth according to new growth theory is a persistent incentive to innovate and an absence of diminishing returns.
5. New growth theory implies that national growth rates depend on national incentives to save, invest, and innovate so that gaps between rich and poor nations might persist.

16.4 ACHIEVING FASTER GROWTH

Why did it take more than a million years of human life before economic growth began? Why are some countries even today still barely growing? Why don't *all* societies save and invest in new capital, expand human capital, and discover and apply new technologies on a scale that brings rapid economic growth? What actions can governments take to encourage growth?

Preconditions for Economic Growth

The key reason why economic growth is either absent or slow is that some societies lack the incentive system that encourages growth-producing activities. And economic freedom is the fundamental precondition for creating the incentives that lead to economic growth.

Economic Freedom

Economic freedom is present when people are able to make personal choices, their private property is protected, and they are free to buy and sell in markets. The rule of law, an efficient legal system, and the ability to enforce contracts are essential foundations for creating economic freedom. Impediments to economic freedom are corruption in the courts and government bureaucracy; barriers to trade, such as import bans; high tax rates; stringent regulations on business, such as health, safety, and environmental regulation; restrictions on banks; labor market regulations that limit a firm's ability to hire and fire workers; and illegal markets, such as those that violate intellectual property rights.

Economic freedom
A condition in which people are able to make personal choices, their private property is protected, and they are free to buy and sell in markets.

No unique political system is necessary to deliver economic freedom. Democratic systems do a good job. But the rule of law, not democracy, is the key requirement for creating economic freedom. Nondemocratic political systems that respect the rule of law do a good job too. Hong Kong is the best example of a country with little democracy but a lot of economic freedom—and a lot of economic growth. No country with a high level of economic freedom is economically poor. But many countries with low levels of economic freedom stagnate.

Property Rights

Economic freedom requires the protection of private property—the factors of production and goods that people own. The social arrangements that govern the protection of private property are called **property rights**. They include the rights to physical property (land, buildings, and capital equipment), to financial property (claims by one person against another), and to intellectual property (such as inventions). Clearly established and enforced property rights provide people with the incentive to work and save. If someone attempts to steal their property, a legal system will protect them. Such property rights also assure people that government itself will not confiscate their income or savings.

Property rights
The social arrangements that govern the protection of private property.

Markets

Economic freedom also requires free markets. Buyers and sellers get information and do business with each other in *markets*. And market prices send signals to buyers and sellers that create incentives to increase or decrease the quantities demanded and supplied. Markets enable people to trade and to save and invest. But markets cannot operate without property rights.

Property rights and markets create incentives for people to specialize and trade, to save and invest, to expand their human capital, and to discover and apply new technologies. Early human societies based on hunting and gathering did not experience economic growth because they lacked property rights and markets. Economic growth began when societies evolved the institutions that create incentives. But the presence of an incentive system and the institutions that create it do not guarantee that economic growth will occur. They permit economic growth but do not make it inevitable.

Growth begins when the appropriate incentive system exists because people can specialize in the activities at which they have a comparative advantage and trade with each other. You saw in Chapter 3 how everyone gains from such activity. By specializing and trading, everyone can acquire goods and services at the lowest possible cost. Consequently, people can obtain a greater volume of goods and services from their labor.

As an economy moves from one with little specialization to one that reaps the gains from specialization and trade, its production and consumption grows. Real GDP per person increases, and the standard of living rises.

But for growth to be persistent, people must face incentives that encourage them to pursue the three activities that generate *ongoing* economic growth: saving and investment, expansion of human capital, and the discovery and application of new technologies.

Policies to Achieve Faster Growth

To achieve faster economic growth, we must either increase the growth rate of capital per hour of labor or increase the growth rate of human capital or the pace of technological advance. The main actions that governments can take to achieve these objectives are

- Create incentive mechanisms.
- Encourage saving.
- Encourage research and development.
- Encourage international trade.
- Improve the quality of education.

Create Incentive Mechanisms

Economic growth occurs when the incentive to save, invest, and innovate is strong enough. And these incentives require property rights enforced by a well-functioning legal system. Property rights and a legal system are key missing ingredients in many societies. For example, they are absent throughout much of Africa. The first priority for growth policy is to establish these institutions so that incentives to save, invest, and innovate exist. Russia is a leading example of a country that is striving to take this step toward establishing the conditions in which economic growth can occur.

Encourage Saving

Saving finances investment, which brings capital accumulation. So encouraging saving can increase the growth of capital and stimulate economic growth. The East Asian economies have the highest saving rates and highest growth rates. Some African economies have the lowest saving rates and the lowest growth rates.

Tax incentives can increase saving. Individual Retirement Accounts (IRAs) are an example of a tax incentive to save. Economists claim that a tax on consumption rather than on income provides the best incentive to save.

Encourage Research and Development

Everyone can use the fruits of basic research and development efforts. For example, all biotechnology firms can use advances in gene-splicing technology. Because basic inventions can be copied, the inventor's profit is limited and so the market allocates too few resources to this activity.

Governments can direct public funds toward financing basic research, but this solution is not foolproof. It requires a mechanism for allocating public funds to their highest-valued use. The National Science Foundation is one possibly efficient channel for allocating public funds to universities and public research facilities to finance and encourage basic research. Government programs such as national defense and space exploration also lead to innovations that have wide use. Laptop computers and Teflon coatings are two prominent examples of innovations that came from the U.S. space program.

Encourage International Trade

Free international trade stimulates economic growth by extracting all the available gains from specialization and trade. The fastest-growing nations today are those with the fastest-growing exports and imports. The creation of the North American Free Trade Agreement and the integration of the economies of Europe through the formation of the European Union are examples of successful actions that governments have taken to stimulate economic growth through trade.

Improve the Quality of Education

The free market would produce too little education because it brings social benefits beyond the benefits to the people who receive the education. By funding basic education and by ensuring high standards in skills such as language, mathematics, and science, governments can contribute enormously to a nation's growth potential. Education can also be expanded and improved by using tax incentives to encourage improved private provision. Singapore's Information Technology in Education program is one of the best examples of a successful attempt to stimulate growth through education.

How Much Difference Can Policy Make?

It is easy to make a list of policy actions that could increase a nation's economic growth rate. It is hard to convert that list into acceptable actions that make a big difference.

Societies are the way they are because they balance the interests of one group against the interests of another group. Change brings gains for some and losses for others. So change is slow. And even when change occurs, if the economic growth rate can be increased by even as much as half a percentage point, it takes many years for the full benefits to accrue.

A well-intentioned government cannot dial up a big increase in the economic growth rate. But it can pursue policies that will nudge the economic growth rate upward. And over time, the benefits from these policies will be large.

CHECKPOINT 16.4

Study Guide pp. 250–252

Practice Online 16.4

4 **Describe policies that might speed economic growth.**

Practice Problems 16.4

1. What are the preconditions for economic growth?
2. Why does much of Africa experience slow economic growth?
3. Why is economic freedom crucial for achieving economic growth?
4. What role do property rights play in encouraging economic growth?
5. Explain why, other things remaining the same, a country with a well-educated population has a faster economic growth rate than a country that has a poorly educated population.

Exercises 16.4

1. What is the key reason why economic growth is either absent or slow in some societies?
2. Why does Russia experience slow economic growth?
3. Is economic freedom the same as democracy? Can you think of a country that enjoys economic freedom and achieves rapid economic growth but does not have democracy?
4. Why are markets a necessary precondition for economic growth?
5. Explain why, other things remaining the same, a country that adopts free international trade (for example, Hong Kong) has a faster economic growth rate than a country that restricts international trade (for example, Myanmar).

Solutions to Practice Problems 16.4

1. The preconditions for economic growth are economic freedom, private property rights, and markets. Without these preconditions, people have little incentive to undertake the actions that lead to economic growth.
2. Some African countries experience slow economic growth because they lack economic freedom, private property rights are not enforced, and markets do not function well. People in these countries have little incentive to specialize and trade or to accumulate both physical and human capital.
3. Economic freedom is crucial for achieving economic growth because economic freedom allows people to make choices and gives them the incentives to pursue growth-producing activities.
4. Clearly defined private property rights and a legal system to enforce them give people the incentives to work, save, invest, and accumulate human capital.
5. A well-educated population has more skills and greater labor productivity than a poorly educated population. A well-educated population can contribute to the research and development that create new technology.

CHAPTER CHECKPOINT

Key Points

1 Define and calculate the economic growth rate, and explain the implications of sustained growth.

- Economic growth is the sustained expansion of production possibilities. The annual percentage change in real GDP measures the economic growth rate.
- Real GDP per person must grow if the standard of living is to rise.
- Sustained economic growth transforms poor nations into rich ones.
- The Rule of 70 tells us the number of years in which real GDP doubles—70 divided by the percentage growth rate of real GDP.

2 Identify the main sources of economic growth.

- Real GDP grows when aggregate hours and labor productivity grow.
- Real GDP per person grows when labor productivity grows.
- Saving, investment in physical capital and human capital, and technological advance bring labor productivity growth.
- The productivity curve shows how labor productivity changes when capital per hour of labor changes, other things remaining the same.
- The productivity curve shifts when human capital expands and technology advances.

3 Review the theories of economic growth that explain why growth rates vary over time and across countries.

- Classical growth theory predicts that economic growth will end because a population explosion will lower real GDP per person to its subsistence level.
- Neoclassical theory predicts that economic growth will persist at a rate that is determined by the pace of technological change.
- New growth theory predicts that capital accumulation, human capital growth, and technological change respond to incentives and can bring persistent growth in labor productivity.

4 Describe policies that might speed economic growth.

- Economic growth requires an incentive system created by economic freedom, property rights, and markets.
- It might be possible to achieve faster growth by encouraging saving, subsidizing research and education, and encouraging international trade.

Key Terms

Exercises

1. Explain why sustained growth of real GDP per person can transform a poor country into wealthy one.
2. In Ireland, the growth rate of real GDP per person averaged 10 percent a year during the 1990s. If this growth rate were to continue, in what year would real GDP per person be twice what it was in 2000?
3. Describe how U.S. real GDP per person has changed over the last 100 years.
4. Explain how the amount of capital increases, how human capital increases, and how technology advances.
5. What is the link between labor hours, labor productivity, and real GDP?
6. What is a productivity curve? Draw a graph of a productivity curve.
7. Explain how saving and investment in new capital, increases in human capital, and advances in technology change labor productivity. Use the productivity curve to illustrate your answer.
8. What is the one third rule? Who discovered the one third rule? How is the one third rule used?
9. If labor productivity grows by 5 percent when capital per hour of labor grows by 6 percent, what is capital's contribution to labor productivity growth? What else contributes to labor productivity growth and what is its contribution?
10. The following information has been discovered about the economy of Longland. The table provides data on the economy's productivity curve.

Capital per hour of labor (1996 dollars per hour)	Real GDP per hour of labor (1996 dollars per hour)
10	3.80
20	5.70
30	7.13
40	8.31
50	9.35
60	10.29
70	11.14
80	11.94

Does this economy conform to the one third rule? If so, explain why. If not, explain why not and explain what rule, if any, it does conform to. Explain how you would do the growth accounting for this economy.

11. In Longland, described in exercise 10, capital per hour of labor in 2001 was \$40 and real GDP per hour of labor was \$8.31. In 2003, capital per hour of labor had increased to \$50 and real GDP per hour of labor had increased to \$10.29 an hour.
   a. Does Longland experience diminishing returns? Explain why or why not.
   b. Use growth accounting to find the contribution of the growth of capital between 2001 and 2003 to the growth of labor productivity in Longland.
   c. Use growth accounting to find the contribution of technological change between 2001 and 2003 to the growth of labor productivity in Longland.

12. The following information has been discovered about the economy of Cape Despair. Subsistence real GDP is \$15 an hour. Whenever real GDP per hour of labor rises above this level, the population grows, and when real GDP per hour of labor falls below this level, the population falls. The table provides data on the productivity curve in Cape Despair.

Capital per hour of labor (1996 dollars per hour)	Real GDP per hour of labor (1996 dollars per hour)
20	8
40	15
60	21
80	26
100	30
120	33
140	35
160	36

   Initially, the population of Cape Despair is constant and real GDP per hour of labor is at its subsistence level. Then a technological advance shifts the productivity curve upward by \$7 at each level of capital per hour of labor.
   a. What are the initial capital per hour of labor and real GDP per hour of labor in Cape Despair?
   b. What happens to real GDP per hour of labor immediately following the technological advance?
   c. What happens to the population growth rate following the technological advance?
   d. What is the eventual quantity of capital per hour of labor in Cape Despair?

13. What do the classical, neoclassical, and new growth theories predict about growth in the global economy and which theory best fits the facts?

14. List five actions that governments can take to encourage economic growth, and provide an example of each.

Critical Thinking

15. What can governments in Africa do to encourage economic growth and raise their living standards?

16. Why do you think the standard of living in Asian economies has increased in the last decade by so much more than the standard of living in the United States?

17. What are the ingredients of economic freedom and how does each ingredient make economic growth more likely? Provide examples of nations that do not enjoy political freedom and that have a low economic growth rate and examples of nations that do enjoy political freedom and have a high economic growth rate. Are there any notable examples that contradict the view that economic freedom and economic growth go together?

18. Why might high taxes hold back economic growth? Would you recommend any changes in the U.S. tax laws to encourage faster growth? How would the changes that you recommend work?

19. Critically evaluate the two following contradictory statements.

    (1) Economic growth results from technological change, which results from creative people responding to incentives. A larger population has more creative people, so it brings faster technological advance. So population growth brings faster growth of real GDP per person.

    (2) Economic growth can be sustained only if we conserve natural resources. A larger population places strain on natural resources. So population growth brings slower growth of real GDP per person.

20. An increasing number of Chinese citizens who are educated in the United States are returning to China to work. How do you think this development might influence economic growth in China? Do you think the Chinese government would be wise to adopt policies that encourage more of its students attending foreign universities to return to China when they have completed their studies?

Practice Online

Web Exercises

Use the links on your Foundations Web site to work the following exercises.

21. Visit the IMF's World Economic Outlook database and obtain data on growth rates of real GDP per person for the United States, China, South Africa, and Mexico since 1990.
    - **a.** Draw a graph of the data.
    - **b.** Which country has the lowest real GDP per person and which has the highest?
    - **c.** Which country has experienced the fastest growth rate since 1990 and which has experienced the slowest?
    - **d.** Explain why the growth rates in these four countries are ranked in the order you have discovered.

22. Visit the Web site of the Penn World Tables and obtain data for any four countries (but not those of the previous exercise) that interest you. Describe and explain the patterns that you find for these countries.

Money and the Monetary System

CHAPTER 17

CHAPTER CHECKLIST

When you have completed your study of this chapter, you will be able to

1. **Define money and describe its functions.**
2. **Describe the monetary system and explain the functions of banks and other monetary institutions.**
3. **Describe the functions of the Federal Reserve System.**

You are now going to study the role of money in the economy. In this chapter and in Chapters 18 and 19, we address two main questions. First, what brings a persistent rise in the cost of living? Second, how does the Fed control the quantity of money and how do the Fed's actions influence interest rates and spending? This second question sets the scene for your study of economic fluctuations and stabilization policy.

The quick answer to the first question is that many factors cause changes in the cost of living. But one factor dominates in the long run. The cost of living rises when the *quantity* of money grows more quickly than real GDP. But what exactly is money? The present chapter answers this question and describes the institutions of the monetary system. How does money get "created" so that its quantity grows? And how is the quantity of money controlled? Chapter 18 answers these questions. What happens when the quantity of money increases? And how does the creation of too much money bring a rising cost of living? Chapter 19 answers these questions.

17.1 WHAT IS MONEY?

Money, like fire and the wheel, has been around for a very long time. An incredible array of items has served as money. North American Indians used wampum (beads made from shells), Fijians used whales' teeth, and early American colonists used tobacco. Cakes of salt served as money in Ethiopia and Tibet. What do wampum, whales' teeth, tobacco, and salt have in common? Why are they examples of money? Today, when we want to buy something, we use coins or notes (dollar bills), write a check, send an e-check, present a credit or debit card, or use a "smart card." Are all these things that we use today money? To answer these questions, we need a definition of money.

Definition of Money

Money
Any commodity or token that is generally accepted as a means of payment.

Money is any commodity or token that is generally accepted as a *means of payment*. This definition has three bits that we'll examine in turn.

A Commodity or Token

Money is always something that can be recognized and that can be divided up into small parts. So money might be an actual commodity, such as a bar of silver or gold. But it might also be a token, such as a quarter or a $10 bill. Money might also be a virtual token, such as an electronic record in a bank's database (more about this type of money later).

Generally Accepted

Money is *generally* accepted, which means that it can be used to buy anything and everything. Some tokens can be used to buy some things but not others. For example, a phone card is accepted as payment for a phone call. But you can't use your phone card to buy toothpaste. So a phone card is not money. In contrast, you can use a $5 bill to buy either a phone call or toothpaste—or anything else that costs $5 or less. So a $5 bill is money.

Means of Payment

Means of payment
A method of settling a debt.

A **means of payment** is a method of settling a debt. When a payment has been made, there is no remaining obligation between the parties to a transaction. The deal is complete. Suppose that Gus buys a car from his friend Ann. Gus doesn't have enough money to pay for the car right now, but he will have enough three months from now, when he gets paid. Ann agrees that Gus may pay for the car in three months' time. Gus buys the car with a loan from Ann and then pays off the loan. The loan that Ann made to Gus isn't money. Money is what Gus uses to pay off the loan.

So what wampum, whales' teeth, tobacco, and salt have in common is that they have served as a generally accepted means of payment, and that is why they are examples of money.

Money performs three vital functions. It serves as a

- Medium of exchange
- Unit of account
- Store of value

Medium of Exchange

A **medium of exchange** is an object that is generally accepted in return for goods and services. Money is a medium of exchange. Without money, you would have to exchange goods and services directly for other goods and services—an exchange called **barter**. Barter requires a *double coincidence of wants*. For example, if you want a soda and have only a paperback novel to offer in exchange for it, you must find someone who is selling soda and who also wants your paperback novel. Money guarantees that there is a double coincidence of wants because people with something to sell will always accept money in exchange for it. So money acts as a lubricant that smoothes the mechanism of exchange. It enables you to specialize in the activity at which you have a comparative advantage (see Chapter 3, pp. 79–81) instead of searching for a double coincidence.

Medium of exchange
An object that is generally accepted in return for goods and services.

Barter
The direct exchange of goods and services for other goods and services, which requires a double coincidence of wants.

Unit of Account

A **unit of account** is an agreed-upon measure for stating the prices of goods and services. To get the most out of your budget, you have to figure out whether going to a rock concert is worth its opportunity cost. But that cost is not dollars and cents. It is the number of movies, cappuccinos, ice-cream cones, or local phone calls that you must give up to attend the concert. It's easy to do such calculations when all these goods have prices in terms of dollars and cents (see Table 17.1). If a rock concert costs $32 and movie costs $8, you know right away that going to the concert costs you 4 movies. If a cappuccino costs $2, going to the concert costs 16 cappuccinos. You need only one calculation to figure out the opportunity cost of any pair of goods and services. For example, the opportunity cost of the rock concert is 128 local phone calls ($32.00 ÷ 25¢ = 128).

Now imagine how troublesome it would be if the rock concert ticket agent posted its price as 4 movies, and if the movie theater posted its price as 4 cappuccinos, and if the coffee shop posted the price of a cappuccino as 2 ice-cream cones, and if the ice-cream shop posted its price as 4 local phone calls! Now how much running around and calculating do you have to do to figure out how much that rock concert is going to cost you in terms of the movies, cappuccino, ice cream, or phone calls that you must give up to attend it? You get the answer for movies right away from the sign posted by the ticket agent. But for all the other goods, you're going to have to visit many different places to establish the price of each commodity in terms of another and then calculate prices in units that are relevant for your own decision. Cover up the column labeled "price in money units" in Table 17.1 and see how hard it is to figure out the number of local phone calls it costs to attend a rock concert. It's enough to make a person swear off rock! How much simpler it is using dollars and cents.

Unit of account
An agreed-upon measure for stating the prices of goods and services.

TABLE 17.1 A UNIT OF ACCOUNT SIMPLIFIES PRICE COMPARISONS

Good	Price in money units	Price in units of another good
Rock concert	$32.00	4 movies
Movie	$8.00	4 cappuccinos
Cappuccino	$2.00	2 ice-cream cones
Ice-cream cone	$1.00	4 local phone calls
Local phone call	$0.25	

Store of Value

Any commodity or token that can be held and exchanged later for goods and services is called a **store of value**. Money acts as a store of value. If it did not, it would not be accepted in exchange for goods and services. The more stable the value of a commodity or token, the better it can act as a store of value and the more useful it is as money. No store of value is completely stable. The value of a physical object, such as a house, a car, or a work of art, fluctuates over time. The value of the commodities and tokens that we use as money also fluctuates, and when there is inflation, money persistently falls in value.

Store of value
Any commodity or token that can be held and exchanged later for goods and services.

Money Today

Fiat money
Objects that are money because the law decrees or orders them to be money.

Money in the world today is called **fiat money**. *Fiat* is a Latin word that means "Let it be done." The modern word "fiat" means decree or order. So today's money is money because the law decrees or orders it to be money. The objects that we use as money today are

- Currency
- Deposits at banks and other financial institutions

Currency

Currency
Notes (dollar bills) and coins.

The notes (dollar bills) and coins that we use in the United States today are known as **currency**. Notes are money because the government declares them to be with the words printed on every dollar bill, "This note is legal tender for all debts, public and private."

Deposits

Deposits at banks, credit unions, savings banks, and savings and loan associations are also money. Deposits are money because they can be used directly to make payments.

Currency in a Bank Is Not Money

Bank deposits are one form of money, and currency *outside the banks* is another form. Currency *inside* the banks is not money. When you get some cash from the ATM, you convert your bank deposit into currency. You change the form of your money, but there is no change in the quantity of money. Deposits decrease, and currency increases. If we counted both bank deposits and currency inside the banks as money, when you get cash at the ATM, the quantity of money would *appear* to decrease—your currency would increase, but *both* deposits *and* currency inside the banks would decrease. You can see that counting deposits *and* currency inside the banks as money would be counting the same thing twice—called double counting.

Deposits Are Money but Checks Are Not

Checks are not money. To see why, think about what happens when Colleen buys some inline skates from Rocky's Rollers. Colleen has $500 in her deposit account, and Rocky has $3,000 in his deposit account. Both of them bank at the Laser Bank. The total bank deposits of Colleen and Rocky are $3,500.

To pay for her skates, Colleen writes a check for $200. Rocky takes the check to the bank and deposits it. The Laser Bank now credits Rocky's account and debits Colleen's account. Rocky's deposit increases from $3,000 to $3,200, and Colleen's deposit decreases from $500 to $300. The total deposits of Colleen and Rocky are still the same as before: $3,500. Rocky now has $200 more, and Colleen has $200 less than before.

This transaction has transferred money from Colleen to Rocky. The check itself was never money. There wasn't an extra $200 worth of money while the check was in circulation. The check only instructs the bank to transfer money from Colleen to Rocky. Figure 17.1 shows these transactions.

FIGURE 17.1
Paying by Check

Practice Online

LASER BANK 123 Dakota Street, Andover, MA 01810 (508) 555-3937

Date	Item	Debit	Credit	Balance
June 1 2001	Opening balance			$500.00
June 11 2001	Rocky's Rollers	$200.00		$300.00

(a) Colleen's account

LASER BANK 123 Dakota Street, Andover, MA 01810 (508) 555-3937

Date	Item	Debit	Credit	Balance
June 1 2001	Opening balance			$3,000.00
June 11 2001	Colleen's check		$200.00	$3,200.00

(b) Rocky's Rollers's account

When you pay by check, you tell your bank to take some money from your deposit and put it into someone else's deposit. The deposit is money, but the check is not money.

In the example, Colleen and Rocky use the same bank. The same story, but with additional steps, describes what happens if Colleen and Rocky use different banks. In that case, the check must be cleared and a payment made by Colleen's bank to Rocky's bank. We explain the details of the process of check clearing in Chapter 18, pp. 457–458. This process can take a few days, but the principles are the same as when two people use the same bank.

Credit Cards, Debit Cards, E-Checks, and E-Cash

We've seen that checks are not money, but what about credit cards, debit cards, e-checks, and e-cash? Are they money?

Credit Cards

A credit card is not money. It is a special type of ID card. To see why, suppose that Colleen uses her credit card to buy her inline skates. Colleen signs a credit card slip and leaves the store with her new skates. But she has not yet *paid* for the skates. She has taken a loan from the bank that issued her credit card. Rocky's bank credits his account with $200 (minus the bank's charge) and sends a charge to the bank that issued Colleen's credit card. Colleen eventually gets her credit card bill, which she pays, using money.

If you pay by check, you are often asked to show your driver's license. Your driver's license is obviously not money. It's just an ID card. A credit card is also an

ID card but one that enables you to get a loan at the instant you buy something. So when you use a credit card to buy something, the bank that issued your credit card pays for the goods and you pay later. The credit card is not the means of payment, and it is not money.

Debit Cards

A debit card is not money. To see why, think about what happens if Colleen uses her debit card to buy her inline skates. When the sales clerk swipes Colleen's card in Rocky's store, the Laser Bank's computer gets a message: Take $200 from Colleen's account and put it in the account of Rocky's Rollers. The transactions shown in Figure 17.1 are done in a flash. But again, the bank deposits are the money and the debit card is the tool that causes money to move from Colleen to Rocky.

E-Checks

Electronic check (or e-check)
An electronic equivalent of a paper check.

An **electronic check** (or **e-check**) is an electronic equivalent of a paper check. A group of more than 90 banks and other financial institutions have formed the Financial Services Technology Consortium to collaborate on developing the electronic check. First Virtual offers an Internet e-check system via email. Like a paper check, an e-check is not money. The deposit transferred is money.

E-Cash

Electronic cash (or e-cash)
An electronic equivalent of paper notes and coins.

Electronic cash (or **e-cash**) is an electronic equivalent of paper notes and coins. It is an electronic currency, and for people to be willing to use it, e-cash has to work like money. People use physical currency because it is portable, recognizable, transferable, untraceable, and anonymous and can be used to make change. The designers of e-cash aim to reproduce all of these features of notes and coins. Today's e-cash is portable, untraceable, and anonymous. But it has not yet reached the level of recognition that makes it universally accepted as a means of payment, so it doesn't meet the definition of money.

Like notes and coins, e-cash can be used in shops. It can also be used over the Internet. To use e-cash in a shop, the buyer uses a smart card that stores some e-cash and the shop uses a smart card reader. When a transaction is made, e-cash is transferred from the smart card directly to the shop's bank account. Users of smart cards receive their e-cash by withdrawing it from a bank account by using a special ATM or a special cell phone.

There are several versions of e-cash in U.S. dollars, euros, and many other currencies available from issuing banks on the Internet. Mondex, a firm owned by MasterCard International, is a prominent e-cash provider. But there are many others, one of which is the CYPHERMINT™ Pay Cash System, an e-cash system from Russia that is being marketed throughout the world.

A handy advantage of e-cash over paper notes arises when you lose your wallet. If it is stuffed with dollar bills, you're out of luck. If it contains e-cash recorded on your smart card, your bank can cancel the e-cash stored in the card and issue you replacement e-cash.

Although e-cash is not sufficiently widely accepted to serve as money today, it is likely that its use will grow and that it will gradually replace physical forms of currency.

Official Measures of Money: M1 and M2

Figure 17.2 shows the items that make up two official measures of money. **M1** consists of currency held outside banks and traveler's checks plus checkable deposits owned by individuals and businesses. M1 does not include currency inside the banks. **M2** consists of M1 plus savings deposits and small time deposits (less than $100,000), money market funds, and other deposits. Time deposits are deposits that can be withdrawn only after a fixed term. Money market funds are deposits that are invested in short-term securities that pay a higher interest rate than bank deposits.

M1
Currency held outside banks and traveler's checks plus checkable deposits owned by individuals and businesses.

M2
M1 plus savings deposits and small time deposits, money market funds, and other deposits.

Are M1 and M2 Really Money?

Money is a generally accepted means of payment. So the test of whether something is money is whether it serves this purpose. Currency passes the test. Checkable deposits also pass the test because they can be transferred from one person to another by writing a check. Because M1 consists of currency plus checkable deposits and each is a means of payment, M1 is money.

But what about M2? Some of the savings deposits in M2 are just as much a means of payment as the checkable deposits in M1. You can use the ATM at the grocery store checkout or gas station to transfer funds directly from your savings account to pay for your purchase. But other savings deposits, time deposits, and money market funds are *not* means of payment. Technically, they are not money. So all of M1 is money, but only part of M2 is money.

FIGURE 17.2
Two Measures of Money: September 2002

Practice Online

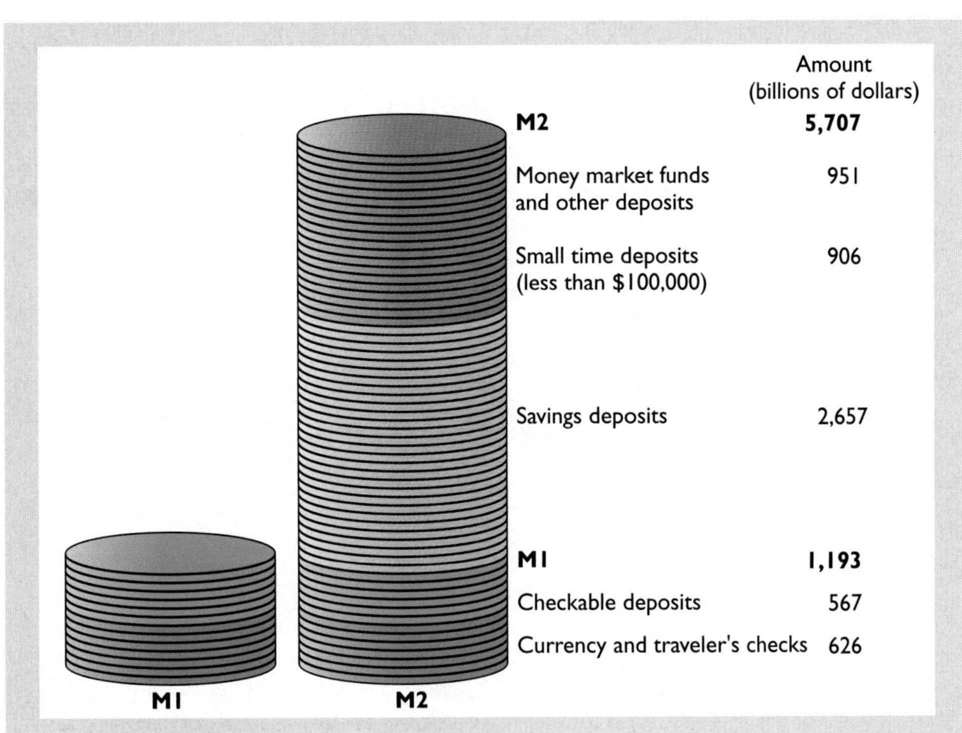

M1 Currency held outside banks and traveler's checks plus checkable deposits owned by individuals and businesses.

M2 M1 plus savings deposits plus small time deposits plus money market funds and other deposits.

SOURCE: Federal Reserve.

Eye on the Global Economy

The U.S. Dollar Abroad

At the end of 1999, there were around $500 billion worth of U.S. dollar bills in circulation. Of these, somewhere between $250 billion and $350 billion were circulating abroad.

The figure shows the growth of U.S. dollars held abroad. Russia is the biggest foreign user of U.S. dollars. Argentina is another big user. U.S. dollars are used extensively through the Middle East and Asia.

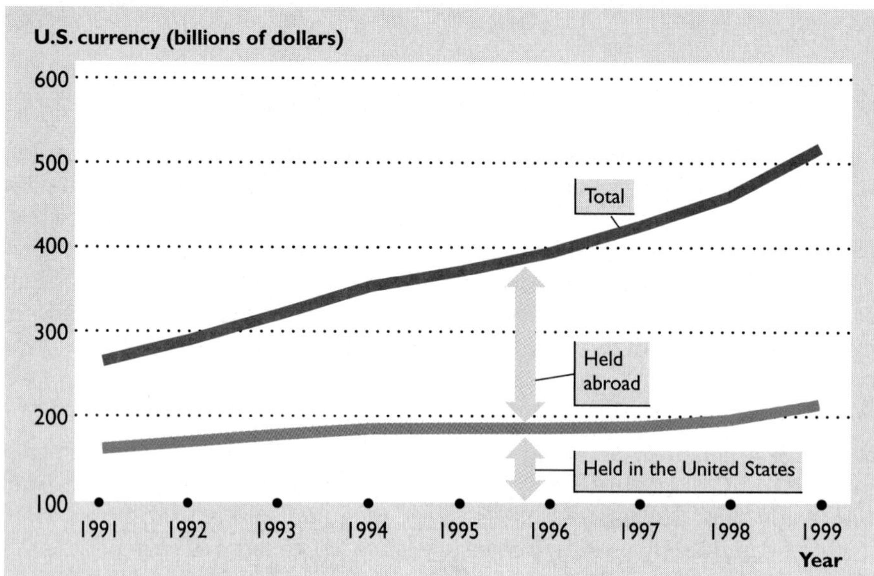

Source: U.S. Department of the Treasury, *The Use and Counterfeiting of United States Currency Abroad*, January 2000.

Figure 17.3 shows the changing composition of money in the United States. Currency decreased in relative importance between 1962 and 1986 but became increasingly important during the 1990s. Checkable deposits decreased in relative importance but made a temporary comeback during the mid-1990s.

FIGURE 17.3

The Changing Face of Money in the United States

Practice Online

The proportion of money held as checkable deposits has been falling. The proportion of money held as currency fell slightly from 1962 through 1986 but then increased, mainly because the amount of U.S. currency abroad increased.

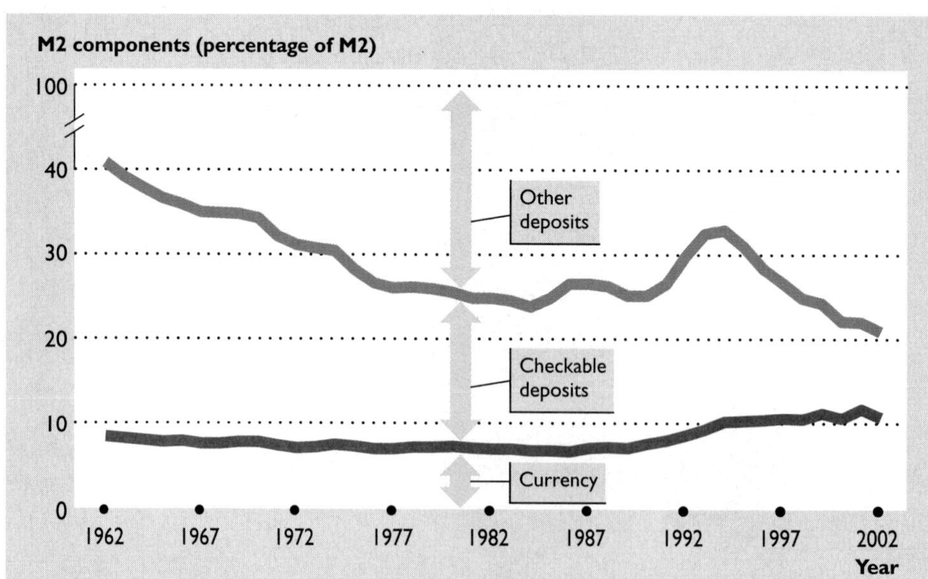

SOURCE: Federal Reserve.

CHECKPOINT 17.1

1 Define money and describe its functions.

Study Guide pp. 258–260

Practice Online 17.1

Practice Problems 17.1

1. In the United States today, money includes which of the following items?
   a. Your Visa card
   b. The quarters inside public phones
   c. U.S. dollar bills in your wallet
   d. The check that you have just written to pay for your rent
   e. The loan you took out last August to pay for your school fees

2. In January 2001, currency held by individuals and businesses was $534.9 billion; traveler's checks were $8.1 billion; checkable deposits owned by individuals and businesses were $559.3 billion; savings deposits were $1,889.7 billion; small time deposits were $1,052.6 billion; and money market funds and other deposits were $952 billion.
   a. What was M1 in January 2001?
   b. What was M2 in January 2001?

Exercises 17.1

1. Which of the following items are money?
   a. Checkable deposits at First Boston Bank
   b. General Motors stock held by individuals
   c. A Sacagawea dollar coin
   d. U.S. government securities
   e. Money market funds

2. Sara withdraws $2,000 from her time deposit account at Bank of America, keeps $100 in cash, and deposits the balance in her checking account at Citibank. What is the immediate change in M1 and M2?

3. In December 2001, currency held by individuals and businesses was $580.5 billion; traveler's checks in circulation were $7.7 billion; checkable deposits owned by individuals and businesses were $580.5 billion; savings deposits were $2,304.5 billion; time deposits were $970.1 billion; and money market funds and other deposits were $996.6 billion.
   a. What was M1 in December 2001?
   b. What was M2 in December 2001?

Solutions to Practice Problems 17.1

1. Money is defined as a means of payment. Only items **b** and **c** (the quarters inside public phones and U.S. dollar bills in your wallet) are money.

2a. M1 is the sum of currency held by individuals and businesses, $534.9 billion; traveler's checks, $8.1 billion; and checkable deposits owned by individuals and businesses, $559.3 billion. M1 is $1,102.3 billion.

2b. M2 is the sum of M1 ($1,102.3 billion), savings deposits ($1,889.7 billion), small time deposits ($1,052.6 billion), and money market funds and other deposits ($952 billion). M2 is $4,996.6 billion.

17.2 THE MONETARY SYSTEM

Monetary system
The Federal Reserve and the banks and other institutions that accept deposits and provide the services that enable people and businesses to make and receive payments.

The **monetary system** consists of the Federal Reserve and the banks and other institutions that accept deposits and that provide the services that enable people and businesses to make and receive payments. Figure 17.4 illustrates the institutions of the monetary system. Sitting at the top of the figure, the Federal Reserve (or Fed) sets the rules and regulates and influences the activities of the banks and other institutions. Three types of financial institutions accept the deposits that are part of the nation's money:

- Commercial banks
- Thrift institutions
- Money market funds

In this section, we describe the functions of these institutions, and in the final section of the chapter, we describe the structure and functions of the Fed.

Commercial Banks

Commercial bank
A firm that is chartered by the Comptroller of the Currency in the U.S. Treasury (or by a state agency) to accept deposits and make loans.

A **commercial bank** is a firm that is chartered by the Comptroller of the Currency in the U.S. Treasury (or by a state agency) to accept deposits and make loans. About 8,600 commercial banks operate in the United States today, down from 13,000 a few years ago. The number of banks has shrunk because in 1997, the rules under which banks operate were changed, permitting them to open branches in every state. A wave of mergers followed this change of rules.

Types of Deposit

A commercial bank accepts three broad types of deposit: checkable deposits, savings deposits, and time deposits. A bank pays a low interest rate (sometimes zero) on checkable deposits, and it pays the highest interest rate on time deposits.

FIGURE 17.4
The Institutions of the Monetary System

Practice Online

The Federal Reserve regulates and influences the activities of the commercial banks, thrift institutions, and money market funds, whose deposits make up the nation's money.

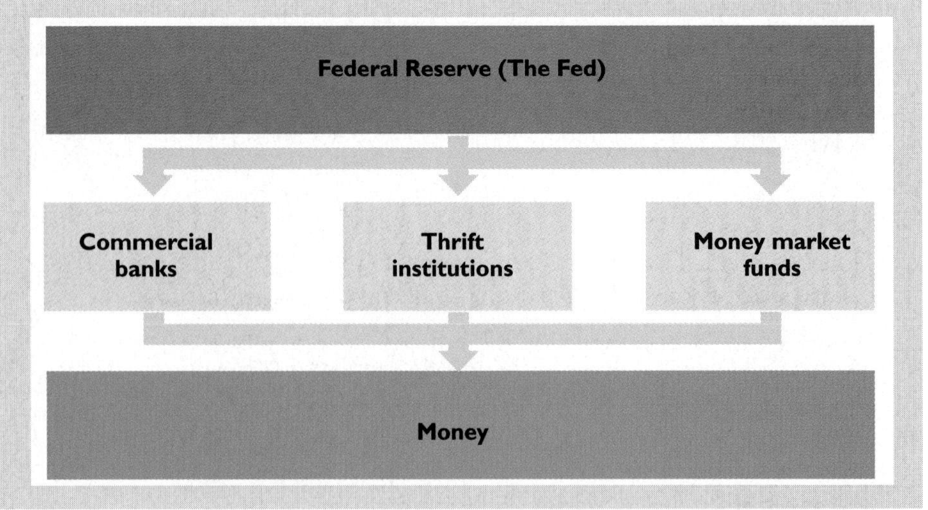

Profit and Prudence: A Balancing Act

The goal of a commercial bank is to maximize its stockholders' long-term wealth. To achieve this goal, a bank makes loans at a higher interest rate than the interest rate it pays on deposits. But lending is risky. The more a bank ties up its deposits in high-risk, high-interest rate loans, the bigger is the risk that it will not be able to pay its depositors when they want to withdraw funds. And if depositors perceive this risk, mass withdrawals might create a crisis for the bank. So a bank must perform a balancing act. It must be prudent in the way it uses the depositors' funds and balance security for the depositors against profit for its stockholders. To achieve security for its depositors, a bank divides its assets into four parts: cash assets, interbank loans, securities, and loans.

Cash Assets

A bank's *cash assets* consist of its reserves and funds that are due from other banks as payments for checks that are being cleared. A bank's **reserves** consist of currency in its vaults plus the balance on its reserve account at a Federal Reserve Bank. The currency in a bank's vaults is a reserve to meet its depositors' withdrawals. It replenishes the ATM every time you and your friends have raided it for cash for a midnight pizza. A commercial bank's deposit at a Federal Reserve Bank is similar to your own bank deposit. The bank uses its reserve account at the Fed to receive and make payments to other banks and to obtain currency. The Fed requires banks to hold a minimum percentage of deposits as reserves, called the **required reserve ratio** (Table 17.2 on p. 446). Reserves that exceed those needed to meet the required reserve ratio are called **excess reserves**.

Reserves
The currency in the bank's vaults plus the balance on its reserve account at a Federal Reserve Bank.

Required reserve ratio
The minimum percentage of deposits that banks and other financial institutions must hold in reserves.

Excess reserves
Bank reserves that exceed those needed to meet the required reserve ratio.

Interbank Loans

Banks that have excess reserves can lend them, and banks with a shortage of reserves can borrow them in an interbank loans market called the federal funds market. The interest rate in this market, called the **federal funds rate**, is the central target of the Fed's monetary policy actions.

Federal funds rate
The interest rate on interbank loans (loans made in the federal funds market).

Securities and Loans

Securities are bonds issued by the U.S. government and by other large, safe organizations. These bonds are traded every day on the bond market. A bank earns a moderate interest rate on securities, but it can sell them quickly if it needs cash. Loans are the provision of funds to businesses and individuals that earn the bank a high interest rate but that cannot be called in before the agreed date. A bank earns the highest interest rate on unpaid credit card balances, which are loans to its credit card holders.

Bank Deposits and Assets: The Relative Magnitudes

In the United States, checkable deposits at commercial banks (part of M1) are about 13 percent of total deposits. The other 87 percent of deposits are savings deposits and time deposits (part of M2). After performing their profit versus prudence balancing acts, the banks on the average keep about 6.5 percent of total deposits in cash assets and another 6.5 percent in interbank loans. The banks use 38 percent of total deposits to buy government bonds and 49 percent to make loans. Figure 17.5 summarizes the numbers in 2002.

FIGURE 17.5
Commercial Banks' Deposits and Assets

Practice Online

In 2002, commercial banks had $600 billion in checkable deposits and $3,900 in other deposits. They loaned $2,300 billion of these deposits, placed $1,600 billion in securities, and made $300 billion in interbank loans and kept $300 billion in cash assets.

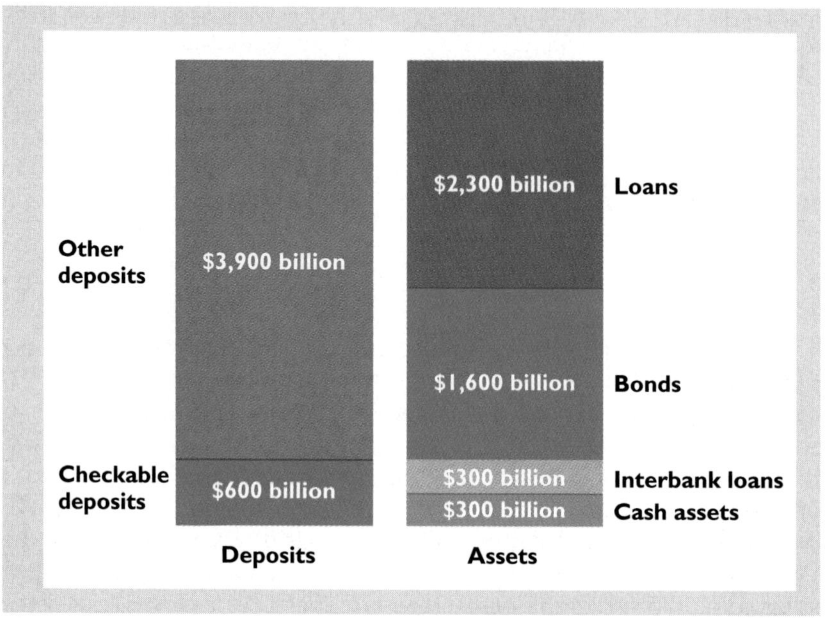

SOURCE: Federal Reserve.

Thrift Institutions

The three types of thrift institutions are savings and loan associations, savings banks, and credit unions. A **savings and loan association** (S&L) is a financial institution that accepts checkable deposits and savings deposits and that makes personal, commercial, and home-purchase loans. A **savings bank** is a financial institution that accepts savings deposits and makes mostly consumer and home-purchase loans. The depositors own some savings banks (called mutual savings banks). A **credit union** is a financial institution owned by a social or economic group, such as a firm's employees, that accepts savings deposits and makes mostly consumer loans.

Savings and loan association
A financial institution that accepts checkable deposits and savings deposits and that makes personal, commercial, and home-purchase loans.

Savings bank
A financial institution that accepts savings deposits and makes mostly consumer and home-purchase loans.

Credit union
A financial institution owned by a social or economic group such as a firm's employees, that accepts savings deposits and makes mostly consumer loans.

Like commercial banks, the thrift institutions hold reserves and must meet minimum reserve ratios set by the Fed.

The total deposits of thrift institutions in 2002 were $1,100 billion. Of these, $120 billion were checkable deposits included in M1 and $980 billion were savings deposits and time deposits included in M2.

Money Market Funds

A **money market fund** is a financial institution that obtains funds by selling shares and uses these funds to buy assets such as U.S. Treasury bills. Money market fund shares act like bank deposits. Shareholders can write checks on their money market fund accounts. But there are restrictions on most of these accounts.

Money market fund
A financial institution that obtains funds by selling shares and uses these funds to buy assets such as U.S. Treasury bills.

For example, the minimum deposit accepted might be $2,500 and the smallest check a depositor is permitted to write might be $500.

In 2002, the value of money market funds included in M2 was $950 billion.

Relative Size of Monetary Institutions

Commercial banks provide most of the nation's bank deposits. In Figure 17.6, we show the relative contributions of commercial banks, thrift institutions, and money market funds. Part (a) shows that checkable deposits at commercial banks are 41 percent of M1, in contrast to the 10 percent of the thrift institutions. Currency represents 49 percent (almost one half) of M1.

Part (b) shows that M1 is 21 percent of M2. The savings deposits and time deposits at commercial banks are another 44 percent of M2. Money market funds and other deposits provide 19 percent of M2, and deposits at thrift institutions provide 16 percent.

On the basis of these numbers, you can see that commercial banks are the dominant financial institutions in the monetary system.

FIGURE 17.6
The Deposits Behind M1 and M2

Practice Online

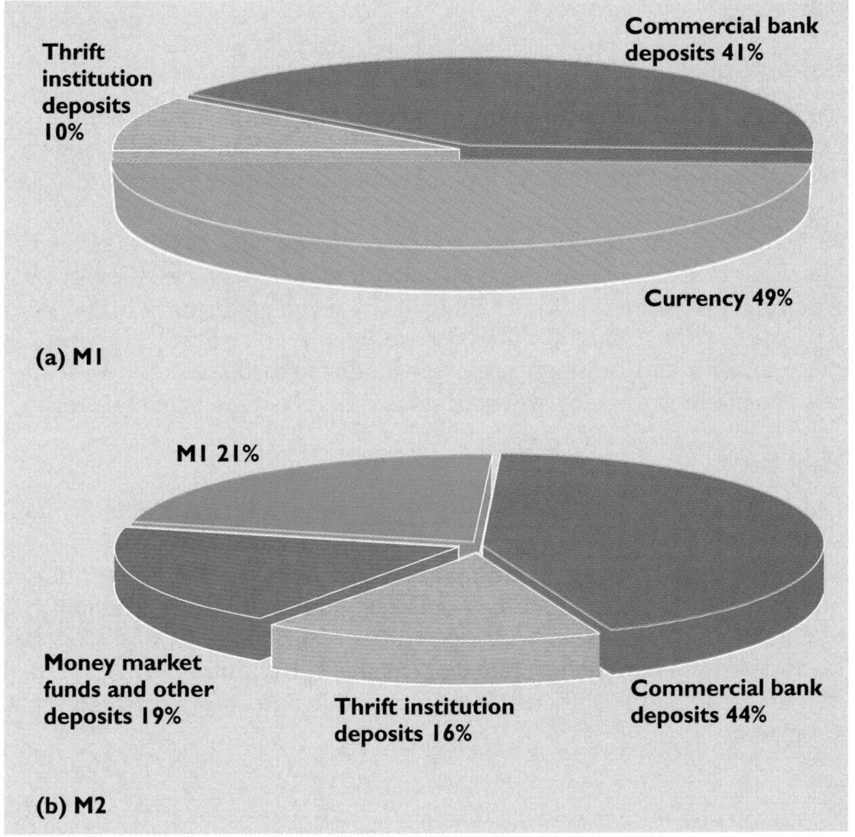

Deposits in commercial banks account for a much larger percentage of the nation's money than do the deposits in thrift institutions and money market funds.

Source: Federal Reserve.

The Economic Functions of Monetary Institutions

The institutions of the monetary system earn their incomes by performing four economic functions that people are willing to pay for. They are

- Create liquidity
- Lower the costs of lending and borrowing
- Pool risks
- Make payments

Create Liquidity

Liquid asset
An asset that can be easily, and with certainty, converted into money.

A **liquid asset** is an asset that can be easily and with certainty converted into money. Some bank* deposits *are* money. Other deposits are almost money and can be converted into money instantly and safely—they are liquid assets.

A bank creates liquid assets by borrowing short and lending long. Borrowing short means accepting deposits and standing ready to repay them whenever the depositor requests the funds. Lending long means making loan commitments for a long term.

For example, a bank might have accepted $1 million in checkable deposits that could be withdrawn at any time and loaned $1 million to a startup Coffee Shop business for an agreed-upon 5 years. The bank earns part of its income by being able to charge a higher interest rate on a 5-year loan than the interest rate it must pay on a checkable account.

Lower Costs

Banks lower the costs of lending and borrowing funds. People with funds to lend can easily find a bank and make a deposit. Because banks offer a range of types of deposit, it is easy to find the type of deposit that best matches the plans of the depositor.

People who want to borrow can do so by using the facilities offered by banks. Business and personal loans can be tailored to match the cash flows of borrowers. And consumers can obtain instant loans by using credit card facilities.

Again, banks make profits because people are willing to make deposits at much lower interest rates than those available to the banks on their loans. Interest rates on credit card loans are especially high and so are profitable for the banks.

Pool Risks

Lending funds, as banks do, is risky. Some loans don't get repaid. By lending to a large number of businesses and individuals, a bank lowers the average risk it faces. The bank knows the odds of a loan not being repaid like a lottery operator knows the odds of having to pay out on a winning number. The lottery operator offers odds that ensure it ends up with a profit. Similarly, the market for bank loans determines an interest rate that ensures that the amount earned on the loans that do get repaid is sufficiently high to pay for the losses on the ones that don't get repaid.

---

* We'll use the term "bank" to mean any institution that accepts deposits when there is no gain from distinguishing among these institutions.

Make Payments

Bank deposits are money because they can be transferred from one person or business to another at low cost. The banks provide the payments system that enables these transfers of ownership to occur.

The check-clearing system is the main mechanism provided by the banks. Think of this system as a giant delivery service like FedEx that, instead of moving packages overnight to anywhere in the nation, moves checks and calculates the amounts that each bank must pay or receive based on the totals of the checks paid by and received by their customers. The banks collect a fee for these check-clearing activities.

The credit card payments system is another major payments mechanism operated by the banks. When you buy a new pair of jeans and the checkout clerk swipes your Visa card, a signal goes to the bank that issued your card to get approval for and place a hold on the amount that you are about to spend. Later that day, when the jeans store has some spare time, it transmits the accumulated day's credit card information from its card reader to its own bank and gets its account credited for the day's takings. At that same moment, a message goes from the jeans store's bank to your card-issuing bank (and the banks of all its other customers) that places the charge for your purchase on your credit card account (and likewise for the other customers). All these electronic transactions are performed automatically. The banks collect fees for all these credit card payment activities.

Eye on the Global Economy

Big Banks

Before 1997, U.S. banks were not permitted to operate in more than one state. In 1997, that restriction was lifted, and since then, bank mergers and failures have decreased the number of banks from 13,000 to 8,600.

The largest U.S. banks are huge. But only two of the big U.S. banks, Citigroup and JP Morgan Chase, made the world's top 10 list in 2002.

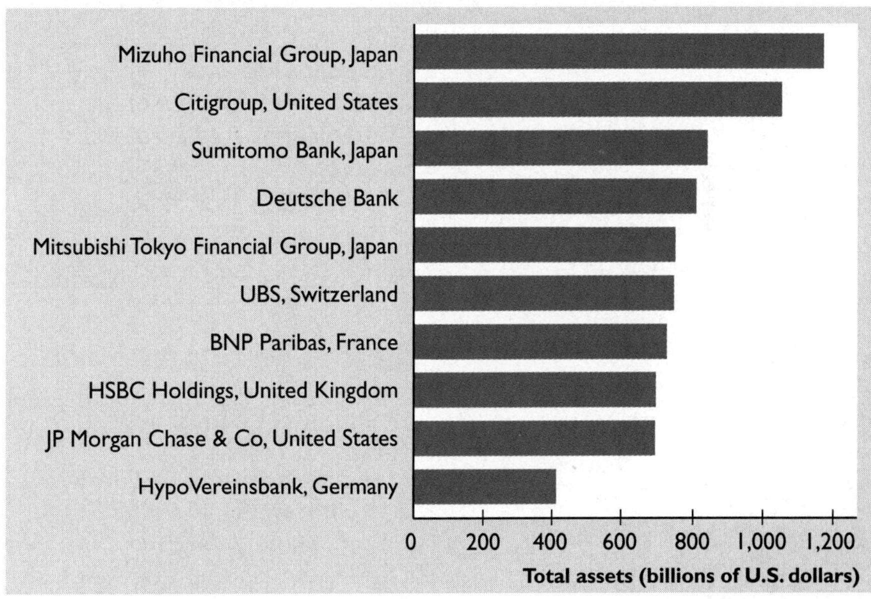

SOURCE: *The Banker*, July 2002.

CHECKPOINT 17.2

Study Guide pp. 261–263

Practice Online 17.2

2 Describe the monetary system and explain the functions of banks and other monetary institutions.

Practice Problems 17.2

1. What are the institutions that make up the monetary system?
2. What is a bank's "balancing act"?
3. A bank has the following deposits and assets: $320 in checkable deposits, $896 in savings deposits, $840 in small time deposits, $990 in loans to businesses, $400 in outstanding credit card balances, $634 in government securities, $2 in currency, and $30 in its reserve account at the Fed. Calculate the bank's
   - **a.** Total deposits
   - **b.** Deposits that are part of M1
   - **c.** Deposits that are part of M2
   - **d.** Loans
   - **e.** Securities
   - **f.** Reserves

Exercises 17.2

1. Explain how a bank makes a profit.
2. A savings and loan association has $550 in checkable deposits, $1,600 in home loans, $900 in savings deposits, $600 in government securities, $800 in time deposits, $50 in currency, and no deposit at the Fed. Calculate
   - **a.** Total deposits
   - **b.** Deposits that are part of M1
   - **c.** Deposits that are part of M2
   - **d.** Loans
   - **e.** Reserves
3. On which items does the S&L in exercise 2 pay interest (borrow short) and on which items does it receive interest (lend long)?

Solutions to Practice Problems 17.2

1. The institutions that make up the monetary system are the Fed, commercial banks, thrift institutions, and money market funds.
2. A bank makes a profit by borrowing from depositors at a low interest rate and lending at a higher interest rate. The bank earns no interest on reserves, but it must hold enough reserves to meet withdrawals. The bank's "balancing act" is to balance the risk of loans against the safety of reserves.

3a. Total deposits are $320 + $896 + $840 = $2,056.
3b. Deposits that are part of M1 are checkable deposits, $320.
3c. Deposits that are part of M2 include all deposits, $2,056.
3d. Loans are $990 + $400 = $1,390.
3e. Securities are $634.
3f. Reserves are $30 + $2 = $32.

17.3 THE FEDERAL RESERVE SYSTEM

The **Federal Reserve System**, which is organized into 12 Federal Reserve districts shown in Figure 17.7, is the central bank of the United States. A **central bank** is a public authority that provides banking services to banks and regulates financial institutions and markets. A central bank does not provide banking services to businesses and individual citizens. Its only customers are banks such as Bank of America and Citibank and the U.S. government.

The Fed conducts the nation's **monetary policy**, which means that it adjusts the quantity of money in the economy. The Fed's goals are to keep inflation in check, maintain full employment, moderate the business cycle, and contribute toward achieving economic growth. Complete success in the pursuit of these goals is impossible, and the Fed's more modest goal is to improve the performance of the economy and to move it closer to the goals than a hands-off approach would achieve. There is a range of opinion on whether the Fed succeeds in improving economic performance.

Federal Reserve System
The central bank of the United States.

Central bank
A public authority that provides banking services to banks and regulates financial institutions and markets.

Monetary policy
Adjusting the quantity of money in the economy.

The Structure of the Federal Reserve

The key elements in the structure of the Federal Reserve are

- The Board of Governors
- The Regional Federal Reserve Banks
- The Federal Open Market Committee

FIGURE 17.7
The Federal Reserve Districts

Practice Online

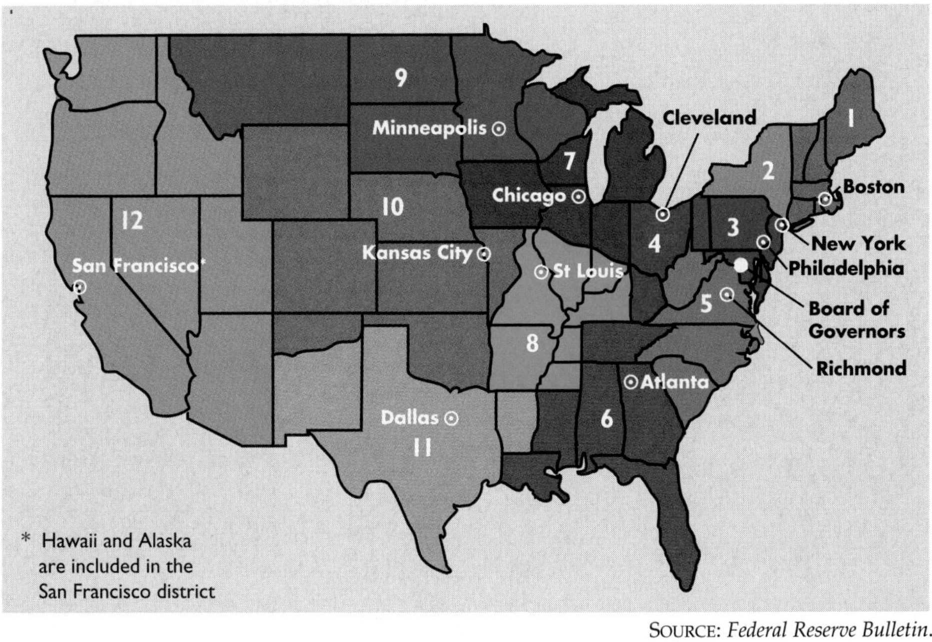

The nation is divided into 12 Federal Reserve districts, each having a Federal Reserve Bank. (Some of the larger districts also have branch banks.) The Board of Governors of the Federal Reserve System is located in Washington, D.C.

* Hawaii and Alaska are included in the San Francisco district

SOURCE: *Federal Reserve Bulletin*.

The Board of Governors

The Board of Governors has seven members, who are appointed by the President of the United States and confirmed by the Senate, each for a 14-year term. The terms are staggered so that one seat on the board becomes vacant every two years. The President appoints one of the board members as Chairman for a term of four years, which is renewable.

The Regional Federal Reserve Banks

There are 12 regional Federal Reserve Banks, one for each of 12 Federal Reserve districts shown in Figure 17.7. Each regional Federal Reserve Bank has nine directors, three of whom are appointed by the Board of Governors and six of whom are elected by the commercial banks in the Federal Reserve district. The directors of the regional Federal Reserve Banks appoint the bank's president, and the Board of Governors approves this appointment.

The Federal Reserve Bank of New York (known as the New York Fed) occupies a special place because it implements some of the Fed's most important policy decisions.

The Federal Open Market Committee

Federal Open Market Committee
The Fed's main policy-making committee.

The **Federal Open Market Committee** (FOMC) is the Fed's main policy-making committee (see Figure 17.8). The FOMC consists of the following twelve members:

- The chairman and the other six members of the Board of Governors
- The president of the Federal Reserve Bank of New York
- Four presidents of the other regional Federal Reserve Banks (on a yearly rotating basis)

The FOMC meets approximately every six weeks to review the state of the economy and to decide the actions to be carried out by the New York Fed.

FIGURE 17.8
The Structure of the FOMC

Practice Online

The Board of Governors sets required reserve ratios and, on the proposal of the regional Federal Reserve Banks, sets the discount rate. The Board of Governors and rotating presidents of the regional Federal Reserve Banks sit on the FOMC to determine open market operations.

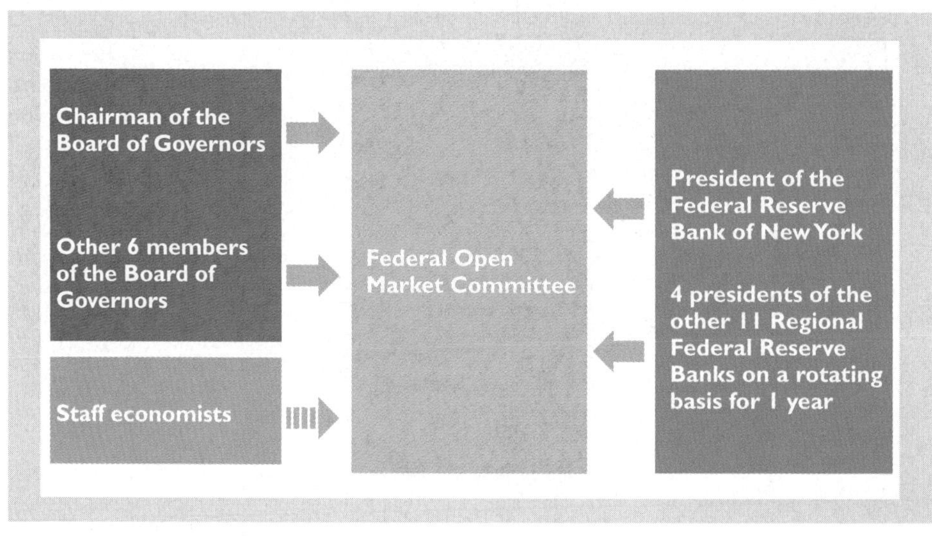

FOMC meeting

The Fed's Power Center

A description of the formal structure of the Fed gives the impression that power in the Fed resides with the Board of Governors. In practice, it is the chairman of the Board of Governors who has the largest influence on the Fed's monetary policy actions. Some remarkable people have been Fed chairmen.

The current chairman of the Board of Governors (in 2003) is Alan Greenspan, who was appointed by President Reagan in 1987 and reappointed by President Bush in 1992 and by President Clinton in 1996 and 2000. Alan Greenspan succeeded another influential chairman, Paul Volcker, who was appointed in 1979 by President Carter and reappointed in 1983 by President Reagan. Volcker ended the 1970s inflation but helped to create one of the most severe post–World War II recessions.

The chairman's power and influence stem from three sources. First, it is the chairman who controls the agenda and who dominates the meetings of the FOMC. Second, day-to-day contact with a large staff of economists and other technical experts provides the chairman with detailed background briefings on monetary policy issues. Third, the chairman is the spokesperson for the Fed and the main point of contact of the Fed with the President and government and with foreign central banks and governments.

The Fed's Policy Tools

The Federal Reserve has many responsibilities, but we'll examine its single most important one: regulating the amount of money floating around in the United States. How does the Fed control the quantity of money? It does so by adjusting the reserves of the banking system. Also, by adjusting the reserves of the banking system and standing ready to make loans to banks, the Fed is able to prevent bank failures. The Fed uses three main policy tools to achieve its objectives:

- Required reserve ratios
- Discount rate
- Open market operations

Required Reserve Ratios

TABLE 17.2 REQUIRED RESERVE RATIOS

Type of Deposit	Percent
Checkable deposits up to $41.3 million	3
Checkable deposits above $41.3 million	10
All other deposits	0

SOURCE: Federal Reserve.

Banks hold reserves. These reserves are currency in the institutions' vaults and ATMs plus deposits held with other banks or with the Fed itself. Banks and thrifts are required to hold a minimum percentage of deposits as reserves. This minimum percentage is known as a *required reserve ratio.* The Fed determines a required reserve ratio for each type of deposit. In 2002, banks were required to hold minimum reserves equal to 3 percent of checkable deposits up to $41.3 million and 10 percent of these deposits in excess of this amount. The required reserves on other types of deposits were zero—see Table 17.2.

Discount Rate

Discount rate
The interest rate at which the Fed stands ready to lend reserves to commercial banks.

The **discount rate** is the interest rate at which the Fed stands ready to lend reserves to commercial banks. A change in the discount rate begins with a proposal to the FOMC by at least one of the 12 Federal Reserve Banks. If the FOMC agrees that a change is required, it proposes the change to the Board of Governors for its approval.

Open Market Operations

Open market operation
The purchase or sale of government securities—U.S. Treasury bills and bonds—by the Federal Reserve in the open market.

An **open market operation** is the purchase or sale of government securities—U.S. Treasury bills and bonds—by the Federal Reserve in the open market. When the Fed conducts an open market operation, it makes a transaction with a bank or some other business but it does not transact with the federal government.

To understand how the Fed's policy tools work, you need to know about the monetary base.

The Monetary Base

Monetary base
The sum of coins, Federal Reserve notes, and banks' reserves at the Fed.

The **monetary base** is the sum of coins, Federal Reserve notes, and banks' reserves at the Fed. The monetary base is so called because it acts like a base that supports the nation's money. The larger the monetary base, the greater is the quantity of money that it can support. Chapter 18 explains how a change in the monetary base leads to a change in the quantity of money.

In September 2002, the monetary base was $670 billion. Figure 17.9 shows how this amount was distributed among its three components: Coins were $30 billion; banks' deposits at the Fed were $10 billion; and the bulk of the monetary base, $630 billion, was made up of Federal Reserve notes.

Federal reserve notes and banks' reserves at the Fed are *liabilities* of the Fed. The Fed's *assets* are

- Gold and deposits in other central banks
- U.S. government securities
- Loans to banks

The Fed holds gold that it could sell if it needed or wished to. It also has deposits in other central banks such as the Bank of Japan and the Bank of England that it can withdraw if it needs to. The Fed holds U.S. government securities that it can sell. Finally, the Fed makes loans to banks, which it can call in. (These loans are usually very small). The Fed charges the banks the discount rate on these loans.

FIGURE 17.9
The Monetary Base and Its Composition

Practice Online

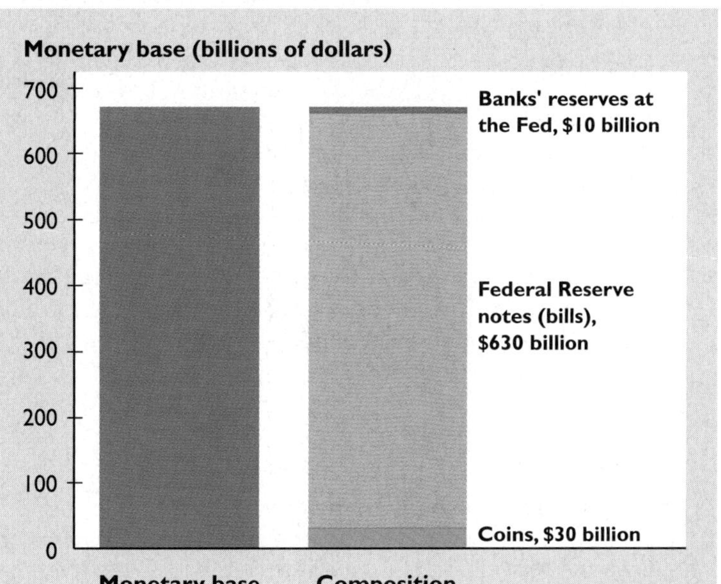

SOURCE: Federal Reserve.

The monetary base is the sum of banks' reserves at the Fed, coins, and Federal Reserve notes (bills). Most of the monetary base consists of Federal Reserve notes.

Why Are Dollar Notes a Liability of the Fed?

You might be wondering why Federal Reserve notes (dollar bills) are a liability of the Fed. When bank notes were invented, they gave their owner a claim on the gold reserves of the issuing bank. These notes were *convertible paper money* and their holders could convert them into gold. So when a bank issued a note, it held itself liable to convert it into gold. The notes were "backed" by gold.

Federal Reserve notes are nonconvertible. A *nonconvertible note* is a bank note that is not convertible into gold and that obtains its value by government fiat—hence the term *fiat money*. These notes are the legal liability of the Fed, and they are "backed" by the Fed's assets. If everyone turned in their dollar bills and banks withdrew their reserves, the Fed would pay out by selling its assets.

How the Fed's Policy Tools Work: A Quick First Look

The next chapter explains how the Fed's policy tools work and how they change the quantity of money. Here, we'll take a quick first look at the basic ideas.

By increasing the required reserve ratio, the Fed can force the banks to hold a larger quantity of monetary base. By raising the discount rate, the Fed can make it more costly for the banks to borrow reserves—borrow monetary base. And by selling securities in the open market, the Fed can decrease the monetary base. All of these actions decrease the quantity of money, other things remaining the same.

Similarly, by decreasing the required reserve ratio, the Fed can permit the banks to hold a smaller quantity of monetary base. By lowering the discount rate, the Fed can make it less costly for the banks to borrow monetary base. And by buying securities in the open market, the Fed can increase the monetary base. All of these actions increase the quantity of money, other things remaining the same.

CHECKPOINT 17.3

Study Guide pp. 263–265

Practice Online 17.3

3 **Describe the functions of the Federal Reserve System.**

Practice Problems 17.3

1. What is the Fed?
2. What is the FOMC?
3. What is the Fed's "power center"?
4. What are the Fed's main policy tools?
5. What is the monetary base?
6. Suppose that at the end of December 2005, the monetary base in the United States is $700 billion, Federal Reserve notes are $650 billion, and banks' reserves at the Fed are $20 billion. Calculate the quantity of coins.

Exercises 17.3

1. What is a central bank?
2. What is the central bank in the United States?
3. Suppose that at the end of December 2004, the monetary base in the United States is $750 billion, Federal Reserve bills are $700 billion, and currency in circulation is $40 billion. What are the commercial banks' deposits at the Fed?
4. Suppose that at the end of December 2005, the monetary base in Canada is $85 billion, Bank of Canada bills are $75 billion, and there is $3 billion of currency in circulation. What are the deposits of the Canadian banks at the Bank of Canada?

Solutions to Practice Problems 17.3

1. The Federal Reserve (Fed) is the central bank in the United States. The central bank in the United States is a public authority that provides banking services to banks and the U.S. government and that regulates the quantity of money and the monetary system.
2. The FOMC is the Federal Open Market Committee. The FOMC is the Fed's main policy-making committee.
3. The Fed's power center is the chairman of the Board of Governors. In 2003, that chairman is Alan Greenspan.
4. The Fed's main policy tools are required reserve ratios, the discount rate, and open market operations.
5. The monetary base is the sum of coins, Federal Reserve notes (dollar bills), and banks' reserves at the Fed.
6. To calculate the quantity of coins at the end of December 2005, we use the definition of the monetary base: coins plus Federal Reserve notes plus banks' reserves at the Fed. Coins equal the monetary base minus Federal Reserve notes minus banks' reserves at the Fed. If at the end of December 2005, the monetary base in the United States is $700 billion, Federal Reserve notes are $650 billion, and bank's reserves at the Fed are $20 billion, so the quantity of coins is $700 billion – $650 billion – $20 billion = $30 billion.

CHAPTER CHECKPOINT

Key Points

1 Define money and describe its functions.

- Money is anything that serves as a generally accepted means of payment.
- Money serves as a medium of exchange, a unit of account, and a store of value.
- M1 consists of currency, travelers' checks, and checkable deposits. M2 consists of M1 plus savings deposits, small time deposits, and money market funds.

2 Describe the monetary system and explain the functions of banks and other monetary institutions.

- Commercial banks, S&Ls, savings banks, credit unions, and money market funds are financial institutions whose deposits are money.
- Banks borrow short term and lend long term and make a profit on the spread between the interest rates that they pay and receive.
- Banks lend most of the funds they receive as deposits and hold only a small amount as reserves.
- Banks can borrow and lend reserves in the interbank federal funds market.

3 Describe the functions of the Federal Reserve System.

- The Federal Reserve is the central bank of the United States.
- The Fed influences the economy by setting the required reserve ratio for banks, by setting the discount rate, and by open market operations.

Key Terms

Barter, 429
Central bank, 443
Commercial bank, 436
Credit union, 438
Currency, 430
Discount rate, 446
Electronic cash (e-cash), 432
Electronic check (e-check), 432
Excess reserves, 437
Federal funds rate, 437
Federal Open Market Committee, 444
Federal Reserve System, 443
Fiat money, 430
Liquid asset, 440
M1, 433
M2, 433
Means of payment, 428
Medium of exchange, 429
Monetary base, 446
Monetary policy, 443
Monetary system, 436
Money, 428
Money market fund, 438
Open market operation, 446
Required reserve ratio, 437
Reserves, 437
Savings and loan association, 438
Savings bank, 438
Store of value, 429
Unit of account, 429

Exercises

1. What is money? Would you classify any of the following items as money?
   a. Store coupons for cat food
   b. A $100 Amazon.com gift certificate
   c. An S&L saving deposit
   d. Frequent Flier Miles
   e. Credit available on your Visa card
   f. The dollar coins that a coin collector owns
   g. Postage stamps issued to commemorate the 2002 Winter Olympic Games

2. What are the three vital functions that money performs? Which of the following items perform some but not all of these functions, and which perform all of these functions? Which of the items are money?
   a. A blank check
   b. A checkable deposit at the Bank of America
   c. A dime
   d. An antique clock
   e. Plastic sheets used to make Visa cards
   f. The coins in the Fed's museum
   g. Government bonds

3. Monica transfers $10,000 from her savings account at the Bank of Alaska to her money market fund. What is the immediate change in M1 and M2?

4. Naomi buys $1,000 worth of American Express travelers' checks and charges the purchase to her American Express card. What is the immediate change in M1 and M2?

5. Terry takes $100 from his checking account and deposits the $100 in his savings account. What is the immediate change in M1 and M2?

6. Vincenzo goes shopping. First, he visits an ATM, where he gets $200 from his savings account. Then he visits a clothing store, where he buys a shirt for $50 using his Visa card. At lunchtime, he meets Donna, his Italian girlfriend, who has just arrived from Rome and has only euros (the money of Italy) in her purse. Donna uses some of her euros to buy $100 from Vincenzo. Donna buys lunch and pays with the $100 that she got from Vincenzo. Did any of the transactions done by Vincenzo and Donna change the quantity of money?

7. In December 2002, banks in Australia had deposits of $500 billion, a required reserve ratio of 4 percent, and no excess reserves. The banks had $15 billion in currency. How much did the banks have in deposits at the Reserve Bank of Australia (the Australian central bank)?

8. In Canada in December 2005, the Bank of Canada (the central bank of Canada) had
   Gold and foreign exchange: $4 billion
   Banks' deposits: $3 billion
   Government securities: $10 billion
   Currency in circulation: $11 billion

The Canadian banks had
Checkable deposits: $400 billion
Savings deposits and time deposits: $600 billion
Currency inside the banks: $1 billion.
Calculate

a. The banks' reserves
b. The monetary base
c. M1
d. M2

9. In Mexico in January 2004, the Banco de México (the central bank of Mexico) reported that bills and coins outside the banks were 175 billion pesos. The Mexican banks had checkable deposits of 418 billion pesos and savings deposits and time deposits of 1782 billion pesos. Currency inside the banks was 28 billion pesos. The Mexican banks had deposits at the Banco de México of 186 billion pesos. Calculate
   a. The banks' reserves
   b. The monetary base
   c. M1
   d. M2

10. What are the main differences and similarities among commercial banks, thrift institutions, and money market funds? How do these institutions earn a profit? What are the main risks they face? How do they manage their exposure to risk?

11. List the policy tools of the Fed and sketch the way in which each tool works to change the quantity of money.

Critical Thinking

12. The President of the United States has no formal authority over the Federal Reserve. In contrast, in some countries, the government directs the central bank and decides what its interest rate policy shall be. Provide some reasons why the central bank should be independent of the government as it is in the United States.

13. Suppose that e-cash issued by private online banks becomes so popular that it completely replaces physical cash and no one has any use for notes issued by the Fed and coins issued by the U.S. mint. What role do you think the Fed could play in such a world?

14. If banks are required to hold reserves at the Fed, doesn't that mean that the required reserves are not really reserves at all and that the only true reserves the banks hold are their excess reserves?

Practice Online Web Exercises

Use the links on your Foundations Web site to work the following exercises.

15. Visit the Web site of the Federal Reserve. For the most recent week,
    a. What is M1?
    b. What is M2?
    c. What is the monetary base?
    d. What is the percentage increase in M1 over the past year?
    e. What is the percentage increase in M2 over the past year?
    f. What is the percentage increase in the monetary base over the past year?
16. Visit the page of the Federal Reserve Web site that provides data on the assets and liabilities of the commercial banks in the United States. For the most recent week and the same week a year earlier,
    a. What is the total amount of deposits?
    b. What is the total amount of cash assets?
    c. What is the total amount of loans?
    d. What is the percentage increase in deposits over the past year?
    e. What is the percentage increase in cash assets over the past year?
    f. What is the percentage increase in loans over the past year?
17. Visit the Web site of the Federal Reserve. For the most recent week,
    a. What is the total amount of reserves?
    b. What are the total borrowed reserves as a percentage of total reserves?
    c. What are excess reserves as a percentage of total reserves?
18. Visit the Open Market Operations page of the Federal Reserve Web site.
    a. What is the current target for the federal funds rate?
    b. How has the target for the federal funds rate changed over the past year?
    c. What do you think the Fed has been trying to do with the changes in the federal funds rate over the past year?

CHAPTER 18

Money Creation and Control

CHAPTER CHECKLIST

When you have completed your study of this chapter, you will be able to

1. **Explain how banks create money by making loans.**
2. **Explain how the Fed controls the quantity of money.**

Making imitation dollar bills is a serious crime. But creating billions of dollars' worth of money is a perfectly legal activity that banks perform every day. In this chapter, you're going to learn how banks create money by making loans.

This chapter builds on what you learned in Chapter 17. There, you saw that most of the money in the United States today is deposits in commercial banks and thrift institutions. You also learned about the structure of the Fed and the tools it uses to control the quantity of money that circulates in the United States.

You're now going to see exactly how money gets created and how the Fed controls its quantity. Understanding these processes is crucial to understanding how inflation occurs and how it can be kept under control. It is also crucial to understanding how the Fed tries to smooth the business cycle.

First, we'll study the links between the banks' reserves, the quantity of loans that banks make, and the quantity of deposits that they create. Then we'll learn how the Fed uses open market operations and other tools to influence the quantity of money.

18.1 HOW BANKS CREATE MONEY

Banks* create money out of thin air! But this doesn't mean that they have smoke-filled back rooms in which counterfeiters are busily working. Remember, most money is bank deposits, not currency. Banks create deposits, and they do so by making loans. But they cannot create any amount of money they wish. The amount of deposits they can create is limited by their reserves.

Creating a Bank

The easiest way to see how banks create money is to work through the process of creating a bank. Suppose that you and your friends decide to create the Virtual College Bank, an Internet bank that specializes in banking services for college students. You will need to go through the following eight steps:

- Obtain a charter to operate a commercial bank
- Raise some financial capital
- Buy some equipment and computer programs
- Accept deposits
- Establish a reserve account at a Federal Reserve Bank
- Clear checks
- Buy government securities
- Make loans

Obtaining a Charter

Your first task is to obtain a charter to operate a commercial bank. You apply to the Comptroller of the Currency for this charter and establish a federally chartered bank. (If you wanted to establish a state commercial bank, you would apply to your state treasurer's office.)

Raising Financial Capital

Your next task is to get some funds. You figure that you can open your bank with $200,000, so Virtual College Bank creates 2,000 shares, each worth $100, and sells these shares in your local community. Your bank now has a **balance sheet**—a statement that summarizes its assets and liabilities. The bank's assets are what it owns, and its liabilities are the claims against it, or what it owes, and its owners' equity. Table 18.1 shows your new bank's first balance sheet.

Balance sheet
A statement that summarizes assets (amounts owned) and liabilities (amounts owed).

TABLE 18.1
Virtual College Bank's Balance Sheet #1

Assets		Liabilities	
Cash	$200,000	Owners' equity	$200,000

You are now ready to take your third step.

*In this chapter, we'll use the term "bank" to include commercial banks and thrift institutions whose deposits are part of the money supply.

Eye on the Past

The "Invention" of Banking

Goldsmiths and their customers stumbled upon a brilliant idea that led to the creation of the first banks. You will gain useful insights into modern banks and the way they create money by looking at these early banks.

Because gold is valuable and easy to steal, the goldsmiths of sixteenth century Europe had well-guarded safes in which to keep their own gold. They also rented space in their safes to artisans and others who wanted to put their gold in safekeeping. The goldsmiths issued a receipt to the owners of the gold entitling them to reclaim their "deposits" on demand. These receipts were similar to the coat check token you get at a theater or museum.

Isabella has a gold receipt that shows that she has deposited 100 ounces of gold with Samuel Goldsmith. She is going to use her gold to buy some land from Henry. Isabella can make this transaction in one of two ways: She can visit Samuel, collect her gold, and hand the gold to Henry. Or she can give Henry her gold receipt, which will then enable Henry to claim the 100 ounces of gold from Samuel Goldsmith.

It is obviously much more convenient to pass the receipt to Henry. It is a simpler and safer transaction. When Henry wants to use the gold to buy something, he too can pass the receipt on to someone else.

So Samuel Goldsmith's gold receipt is circulating as a means of payment. It is money!

After some years, Samuel notices that the gold that people have placed in his safekeeping never leaves his vault. The receipts circulate, and the gold simply sits in the safe.

Samuel realizes that he can lend people gold receipts and charge them interest on the receipts. So he writes some receipts for gold that he doesn't have and lends these receipts.

After some further years, when many goldsmiths are doing what Samuel is doing, they begin to compete with each other for gold deposits, and instead of charging rent to gold owners, they start to pay interest on gold deposits.

Samuel and his fellow goldsmiths have made the transition from being goldsmiths to being bankers.

As long as they don't issue too many gold receipts, they will always be able to honor requests from depositors who wish to reclaim their gold.

Buying Equipment

You buy some office equipment, a server, banking database software, and a high-speed Internet connection. These items cost you $200,000. Table 18.2 shows your bank's new balance sheet.

TABLE 18.2
Virtual College Bank's Balance Sheet #2

Assets		Liabilities	
Cash	$0		
Equipment	$200,000	Owners' equity	$200,000

Accepting Deposits

You are now ready to start accepting deposits. You pass the word around that you are offering the best terms available and the lowest charges on checkable deposits. Deposits begin to roll in. After a hectic day of business, you have accepted $120,000 of deposits. Table 18.3 shows Virtual College Bank's new balance sheet.

TABLE 18.3
Virtual College Bank's Balance Sheet #3

Assets		Liabilities	
Cash	$120,000	Checkable deposits	$120,000
Equipment	$200,000	Owners' equity	$200,000

The deposits at Virtual College Bank are now part of the money supply. But the quantity of money in the economy has not increased. People have deposited either currency or checks drawn on other banks. To keep the story simple, we'll suppose that all these deposits are currency. So currency outside the banks has decreased by $120,000, and checkable deposits have increased by $120,000.

Establishing a Reserve Account

Now that Virtual College Bank has deposits, it must establish a reserve account at its local Federal Reserve Bank. We'll suppose that your virtual bank is in College Station, Texas, in the Dallas Federal Reserve District. Virtual College Bank now opens an account at the Dallas Fed and deposits in that account all its cash. Table 18.4 shows Virtual College Bank's new balance sheet.

TABLE 18.4
Virtual College Bank's Balance Sheet #4

Assets		Liabilities	
Cash	$0		
Reserves at the Dallas Fed	$120,000	Checkable deposits	$120,000
Equipment	$200,000	Owners' equity	$200,000

Reserves: Actual and Required You saw in Chapter 17 that banks don't keep $100 in bills for every $100 that people have deposited with them. In fact, a typical bank today has reserves of a bit less than $1 for every $100 of deposits. But there's no need for panic. These reserve levels are adequate for ordinary business needs.

The proportion of a bank's total deposits that are held in reserves is called the *reserve ratio*. Virtual College Bank's reserves are $120,000 and deposits are $120,000, so its reserve ratio is 100 percent.

The *required reserve ratio* is the ratio of reserves to deposits that banks are required, by regulation, to hold. We'll suppose that the required reserve ratio for virtual banks operated by college students is 25 percent, a much higher percentage than that for U.S. commercial banks (see Chapter 17, p. 446).

A bank's *required reserves* are equal to its deposits multiplied by the required reserve ratio. So Virtual College Bank's required reserves are

$$\text{Required reserves} = \$120{,}000 \times 25 \div 100 = \$30{,}000.$$

Actual reserves minus required reserves are *excess reserves*. Virtual College Bank's excess reserves are

$$\text{Excess reserves} = \$120{,}000 - \$30{,}000 = \$90{,}000.$$

Whenever banks have excess reserves, they are able to make loans. But before Virtual College Bank takes that step, it needs to learn how to clear checks.

Clearing Checks

Virtual College Bank's depositors want to be able to make and receive payments by check. So when Virtual College depositor Jay writes a check for $20,000 to buy some computers from Hal's PCs, which has a checkable deposit at the First American Bank, funds must move from Jay's account at your bank to Hal's account at First American. In the process, Virtual College loses reserves and First American gains reserves. Figure 18.1 tracks the balance sheet changes that occur.

When Hal's PCs banks Jay's check, First American sends the check to the Dallas Fed for collection. The Dallas Fed increases First American's reserves and decreases Virtual College's reserves by $20,000—see Figure 18.1(a). First American now has an extra $20,000 in its reserves at the Dallas Fed, and it increases Hal's PCs' checkable deposit by $20,000. First American's assets and liabilities have both increased by $20,000 in Figure 18.1(b). The Dallas Fed returns the cleared check to Virtual College. Virtual College now has $20,000 less in its reserve account, and it decreases Jay's checkable deposit by $20,000. Virtual College's assets and liabilities have both decreased by $20,000 in Figure 18.1(c).

FIGURE 18.1
Clearing a Check

Practice Online

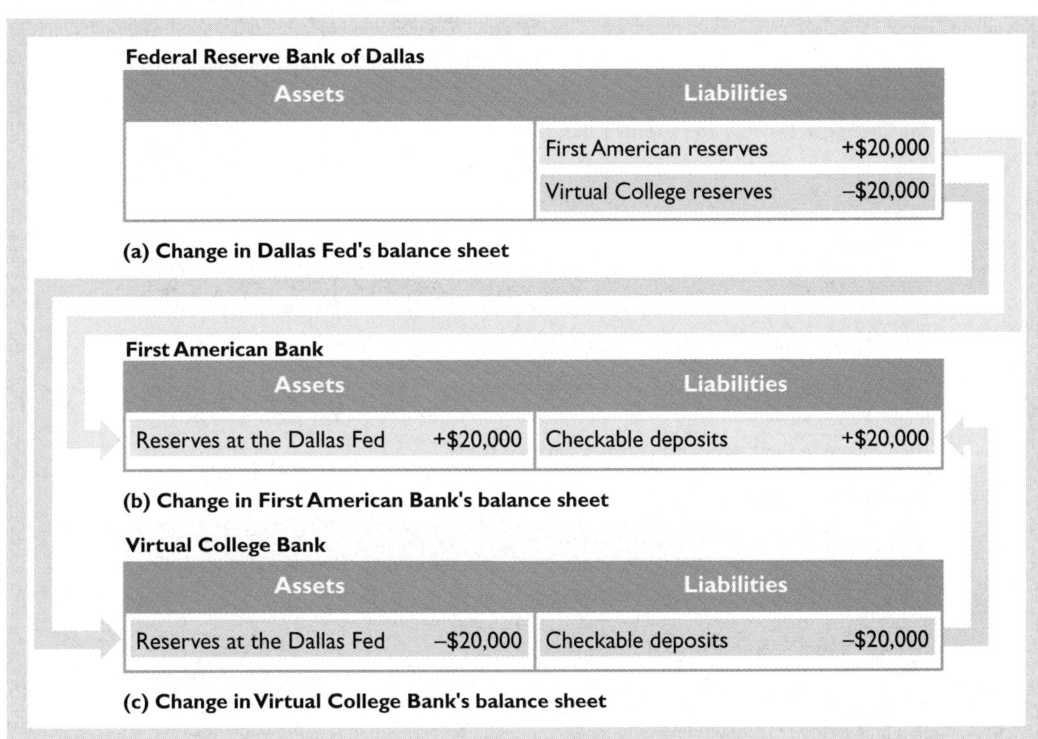

(a) First American sends a $20,000 check for collection to the Dallas Fed. The Dallas Fed increases First American's reserves by $20,000 and decreases Virtual College's reserves by $20,000.

(b) First American increases Hal's PCs' checkable deposit by $20,000. First American's assets and liabilities have both increased by $20,000.

(c) Virtual College decreases Jay's checkable deposit by $20,000. Virtual College's assets and liabilities have both decreased by $20,000.

The quantity of money is unaffected by these transactions. Checkable deposits have increased at First American and decreased at Virtual College, but total deposits are unchanged. Total bank reserves are also unaffected. First American's reserves have increased and Virtual College's reserves have decreased by the same amount.

Virtual College Bank is now ready to use some of its reserves to earn an income. It buys some government securities.

Buying Government Securities

Government securities provide Virtual College with an income and a safe asset that is easily converted back into reserves when necessary. Suppose that Virtual College decides to buy $60,000 worth of government securities. On the same day, First American decides to sell $60,000 of government securities to Virtual College. In reality, a bond broker will match the First American sale with Virtual College's purchase.

Figure 18.2 tracks the effects of this transaction on the balance sheets of the two banks and the Dallas Fed. Virtual College gives First American a check for $60,000, and First American transfers the government bonds to Virtual College. First American sends the check to the Dallas Fed for collection. The Dallas Fed

FIGURE 18.2
Making Interbank Loans and Buying Government Securities

Practice Online

(a) Virtual College buys $60,000 worth of government securities from First American and pays by check. The Dallas Fed increases First American's reserves by $60,000 and decreases Virtual College's reserves by the same amount.

(b) First American's reserves have increased and its government securities have decreased by $60,000.

(c) Virtual College's reserves have decreased and its government securities have increased by the $60,000.

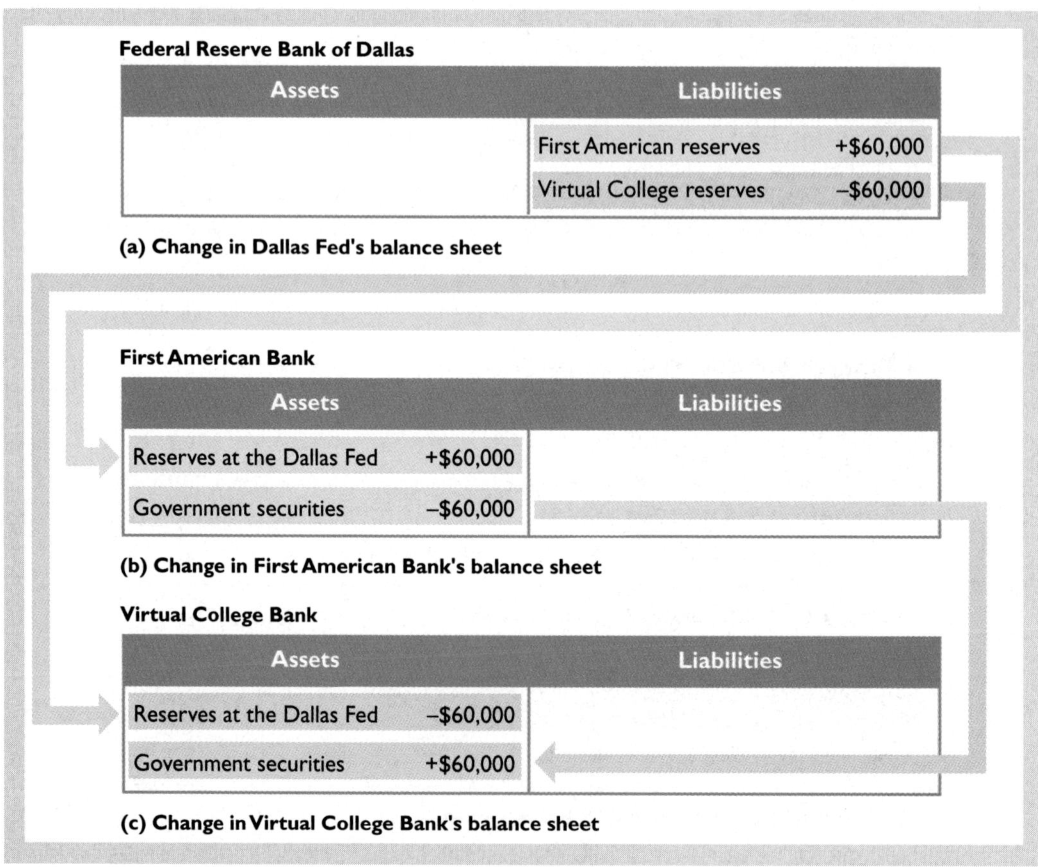

increases First American's reserves by $60,000 and decreases Virtual College's reserves by the same amount in Figure 18.2(a).

First American's reserves have increased and its government securities have decreased by the same $60,000 in Figure 18.2(b). Virtual College's reserves have decreased and its government securities have increased by the same $60,000 in Figure 18.2(c).

After all the transactions we've just followed in Figures 18.1 and 18.2, Virtual College's balance sheet looks like that in Table 18.5.

TABLE 18.5
Virtual College Bank's Balance Sheet #5

Assets		Liabilities	
Reserves at the Dallas Fed	$40,000	Checkable deposits	$100,000
Government securities	$60,000	Owners' equity	$200,000
Equipment	$200,000		
Total assets	$300,000	Total liabilities	$300,000

With deposits of $100,000 and a required reserve ratio of 25 percent, Virtual College must hold a minimum of $25,000 in reserves. Because it currently has $40,000 in reserves, Virtual College can make some loans.

Making Loans

With reserves of $40,000 and required reserves of $25,000, Virtual College has excess reserves of $15,000. So the bank decides to make loans of this amount. Table 18.6 shows the bank's balance sheet on the day the bank makes these loans. Loans of $15,000 are added to the bank's assets. Loans are an asset to the bank because the borrower is committed to repaying the loan on an agreed-upon schedule. The bank places the $15,000 loaned in the checkable deposit accounts of the borrowers. So the bank's checkable deposits increase by $15,000 to $115,000.

TABLE 18.6
Virtual College Bank's Balance Sheet #6

Assets		Liabilities	
Reserves at the Dallas Fed	$40,000	Checkable deposits	$115,000
Government securities	$60,000	Owners' equity	$200,000
Loans	$15,000		
Equipment	$200,000		
Total assets	$315,000	Total liabilities	$315,000

The bank has now created some money. Checkable deposits have increased by the amount of the loans, so the quantity of money has increased by $15,000. And although Virtual College has made loans equal to its excess reserves of $15,000, it still has those reserves! Because its deposits have increased, its required reserves have also increased. They are now 25 percent of $115,000, or $28,750. So the bank now has excess reserves of $11,250.

Before you get too excited and decide to lend another $11,250, let's see what happens when the borrowers of the $15,000 that you've just loaned start to spend their loans.

Spending a Loan To spend their loans, the borrowers write checks on their checkable deposits. Let's assume that they spend the entire $15,000. Most likely, the people to whom these checks are paid do not bank at Virtual College. That's what we'll assume. So when these checks are cleared, transactions like those that we described above take place. The receiving banks send the checks to the Dallas Fed for collection. The Fed increases the reserves of the receiving banks by $15,000 and decreases the reserves of Virtual College by $15,000. Virtual College's balance sheet now looks like that in Table 18.7.

TABLE 18.7
Virtual College Bank's Balance Sheet #7

Assets		Liabilities	
Reserves at the Dallas Fed	$25,000	Checkable deposits	$100,000
Government securities	$60,000	Owners' equity	$200,000
Loans	$15,000		
Equipment	$200,000		
Total assets	$300,000	Total liabilities	$300,000

Both reserves and deposits have decreased by $15,000 because this amount has been paid to people with accounts in other banks. If some of the checks drawn were paid to customers of Virtual College, deposits and reserves would have fallen by less than the full $15,000 and the bank would still have some excess reserves. But in the situation shown in Table 18.7, the bank is fully loaned—its reserves are just sufficient to meet the required reserve ratio.

But the banks that received the deposits that Virtual College has lost have also received reserves. These banks now have excess reserves, so they can make some loans. And these loans will create some more money. Also, when Virtual College bought government securities from First American, the reserves of First American increased by $60,000. So other banks now have reserves of $75,000 that they didn't have before that they could now lend. So yet more money can be created.

If you told the loan officer at your own bank that she creates money, she wouldn't believe you. People who work in banks see themselves as lending the money they receive from others, but (unless they've studied economics) they don't see the entire process, so they don't realize that they create money. But in fact, even though each bank lends only what it receives, the banking system creates money. To see how, let's see what happens in the entire banking system when one bank receives some new reserves.

The Limits to Money Creation

Figure 18.3 is going to keep track of what is happening in the process of money creation by a banking system in which each bank has a required reserve ratio of 25 percent. We'll start the process off with every bank holding exactly its required reserves. Then Al Capone, after years of shady dealing, decides to go to school. He takes $100,000 of notes from under his mattress and deposits them at Virtual College Bank. Virtual College now has $100,000 of new deposits and $100,000 of new reserves. With a required reserve ratio of 25 percent, the bank's required reserves are $25,000. So the bank makes a loan of $75,000 to Amy. Then Amy writes a check for $75,000 to buy a copy-shop franchise from Barb. At this point,

Virtual College has a new deposit of $100,000, a new loan of $75,000, and new reserves of $25,000. You can see this situation in Figure 18.3.

For Virtual College, that is the end of the story. But it's not the end of the story for the banking system. Barb deposits her check for $75,000 in First American, where deposits and reserves increase by $75,000. First American puts 25 percent of its increase in deposits ($18,750) into reserves and lends $56,250 to Bob. And Bob writes a check to Carl to pay off a business loan.

Figure 18.3 shows the state of play at the end of round 2. Total bank reserves have increased by $43,750 ($25,000 plus $18,750), total loans have increased by $131,250 ($75,000 plus $56,250), and total deposits have increased by $175,000 ($100,000 plus $75,000).

When Carl takes his check to Fleet PC, its deposits and reserves increase by $56,250. Fleet PC keeps $14,063 in reserves and lends $42,187. This process continues until there are no excess reserves in the banking system. But the process

FIGURE 18.3
The Multiple Creation of Bank Deposits

Practice Online

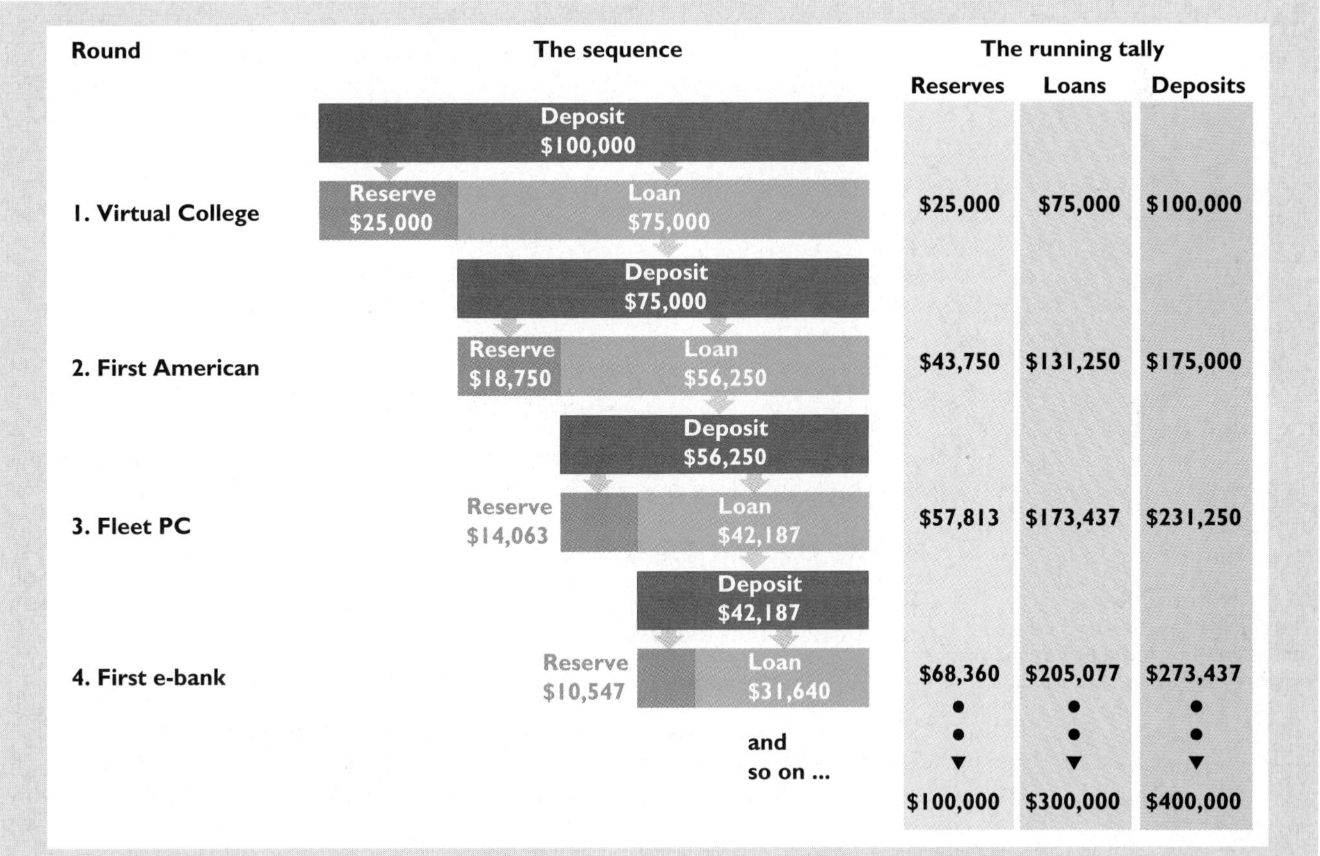

When a bank receives deposits, it keeps 25 percent in reserves and lends 75 percent. The amount loaned becomes a new deposit at another bank. The next bank in the sequence keeps 25 percent and lends 75 percent, and the process continues until the banking system has created enough deposits to eliminate its excess reserves. The running tally tells us the deposits and loans created at each stage. At the end of the process, an additional $100,000 of reserves creates an additional $400,000 of deposits.

takes a lot of further steps. Figure 18.3 shows one additional step. The figure also shows the final tallies: Reserves increase by \$100,000, loans increase by \$300,000, and deposits increase by \$400,000.

The sequence in Figure 18.3 is the first four rounds of the process. To work out the entire process, look closely at the numbers in the figure. At each stage, the loan is 75 percent (0.75) of the previous loan and the deposit is 0.75 of the previous deposit. Let's call that proportion L ($L = 0.75$). The complete sequence is

$$1 + L + L^2 + L^3 + L^4 + \ldots.$$

Remember, L is a fraction, so at each stage in this sequence, the amount of new loans and new deposits gets smaller. The total increase in deposits when the process ends is the sum of the above sequence multiplied by the initial increase in reserves, which is

$$\frac{1}{1 - L} \times \text{Initial increase in reserves.}$$

If we use the numbers from the example, the total increase in deposits is

$$\$100{,}000 + 75{,}000 + 56{,}250 + 42{,}187 + \ldots$$

$$= \$100{,}000 \times (1 + 0.75 + 0.5625 + 0.42187 + \ldots)$$

$$= \$100{,}000 \times (1 + 0.75 + 0.75^2 + 0.75^3 + \ldots)$$

$$= \$100{,}000 \times \frac{1}{(1 - 0.75)}$$

$$= \$100{,}000 \times \frac{1}{0.25}$$

$$= \$100{,}000 \times 4.$$

$$= \$400{,}000.$$

So even though each bank lends only the money it receives, the banking system as a whole does create money by making loans.

The Deposit Multiplier

Deposit multiplier
The number by which an increase in bank reserves is multiplied to find the resulting increase in bank deposits.

The **deposit multiplier** is the number by which an increase in bank reserves is multiplied to find the resulting increase in bank deposits. That is,

$$\text{Change in deposits} = \text{Deposit multiplier} \times \text{Change in reserves.}$$

In the example that we've just worked through, the deposit multiplier is 4. The \$100,000 increase in reserves brought a \$400,000 increase in deposits. The deposit multiplier is linked to the required reserve ratio by the following equation:

$$\text{Deposit multiplier} = \frac{1}{\text{Required reserve ratio}}.$$

In the example, the required reserve ratio is 25 percent, or 0.25. That is,

$$\text{Deposit multiplier} = \frac{1}{0.25} = 4.$$

CHECKPOINT 18.1

1 Explain how banks create money by making loans.

Study Guide pp. 270–273

Practice Online 18.1

Practice Problems 18.1

1. How do banks create new deposits by making loans, and what factors limit the amount of deposits and loans they can create?

2. The required reserve ratio is 0.1, and banks have no excess reserves. Jamie deposits $100 in his bank. Calculate
   a. The bank's excess reserves as soon as Jamie makes the deposit.
   b. The maximum amount of loans that the banking system can make.
   c. The maximum amount of new money that the banking system can create.

Exercises 18.1

1. Your bank manager tells you that he does not create money. He just lends the money that people deposit in the bank. Explain to him how he does create money.

2. If the banking system receives new deposits of $200 million, what determines the maximum amount of new money that the banks can create?

3. If a multibank system has a required reserve ratio of 0.05 and Erin deposits $50 in her bank, calculate
   a. The bank's excess reserves as soon as Erin makes her deposit.
   b. The maximum amount of loans that the banking system can make.
   c. The maximum amount of new money that the banking system can create.

Solutions to Practice Problems 18.1

1. Banks can make loans when they have excess reserves—reserves in excess of those required. When a bank makes a loan, it creates a new deposit for the person who receives the loan. The bank uses its excess reserves to create new deposits. The amount of loans that the bank can make, and therefore the amount of new deposits that it can create, is limited by two things: the amount of excess reserves and the required reserve ratio.

2a. The bank's excess reserves are $90. When deposits increase by $100, the bank is required to keep 10 percent of the deposit as reserves. That is, required reserves increase by $10 and the bank has $90 of excess reserves.

2b. The maximum amount of loans that the banking system can make is $900. When reserves increase by $100, the deposit multiplier determines the maximum increase in deposits that the banking system can have. Deposits increase to make the bank's required reserves increase by $100. The deposit multiplier equals 1/Required reserve ratio, which is 1/0.1 or 10. With the $100 increase in reserves, deposits can increase to $1,000. Jamie deposited $100, so the banking system can create an additional $900 of deposits. It does so by making loans of $900.

2c. The maximum amount of new money that can be created is $900. When a bank makes loans, it creates new money. The maximum amount of new money created by the banking system equals the maximum amount of loans that it can make.

18.2 INFLUENCING THE QUANTITY OF MONEY

The Fed constantly monitors and adjusts the quantity of money in the economy. To change the quantity of money, the Fed can use any of its three tools:

- Required reserve ratios
- Discount rate
- Open market operations

Let's see how these three tools work.

How Required Reserve Ratios Work

If the Fed increases the required reserve ratio, the banks must increase their reserves and decrease their lending, which decreases the quantity of money. If the Fed decreases the required reserve ratio, the banks can decrease their reserves and increase their lending, which increases the quantity of money. The Fed changes the required reserve ratio infrequently because a small change in the ratio would have a drastic effect on bank lending and the Fed has more refined tools at its disposal.

How the Discount Rate Works

If the Fed increases the discount rate, the banks must pay a higher price for any reserves that they borrow from the Fed. Faced with higher cost of reserves, the banks are less willing to borrow reserves and prefer to decrease their lending. So when the discount rate increases, the quantity of money decreases. Similarly, if the Fed decreases the discount rate, the banks pay a lower price for reserves that they borrow from the Fed. Faced with a lower cost of reserves, the banks are more willing to borrow reserves and increase their lending. So when the discount rate decreases, the quantity of money increases. The discount rate has limited effect because the banks rarely borrow from the Fed.

How an Open Market Operation Works

Open market operations are the Fed's major policy tool. When the Fed buys securities in an open market operation, it pays for them with newly created bank reserves and money. With more reserves in the banking system, the supply of interbank loans increases, the demand for interbank loans decreases, and the federal funds rate—the interest rate in the interbank loans market—falls. Similarly, when the Fed sells securities in an open market operation, buyers pay for the securities with bank reserves and money. With smaller reserves in the banking system, the supply of interbank loans decreases, the demand for interbank loans increases, and the federal funds rate rises. The Fed sets a target for the federal funds rate and conducts open market operations on the scale needed to hit its target.

A change in the federal funds rate is only the first stage in an adjustment process that follows an open market operation. If banks' reserves increase, the banks can increase their lending and create even more money. If banks' reserves decrease, the banks must decrease their lending, which decreases the quantity of money. We'll study the effects of open market operations in some detail, beginning with an open market purchase.

The Fed Buys Securities

Suppose the Fed buys $100 million of U.S. government securities in the open market. There are two cases to consider, depending on who sells the securities. A bank might sell some of its securities, or a person or business that is not a commercial bank—the general public—might sell. The outcome is essentially the same in the two cases, but you might need to be convinced of this fact. So we'll study the two cases, starting with the simpler case in which a commercial bank sells securities. (The seller will be someone who thinks the Fed is offering a good price for securities so that it is profitable to make the sale.)

A Commercial Bank Sells When the Fed buys $100 million of securities from the Manhattan Commercial Bank, two things happen:

1. The Manhattan Commercial Bank has $100 million less in securities, and the Fed has $100 million more in securities.
2. To pay for the securities, the Fed increases the Manhattan Commercial Bank's reserve account at the New York Fed by $100 million.

Figure 18.4 shows the effects of these actions on the balance sheets of the Fed and the Manhattan Commercial Bank. Ownership of the securities passes from the commercial bank to the Fed, so the bank's securities decrease by $100 million and the Fed's securities increase by $100 million, as shown by the red-to-blue arrow running from the Manhattan Commercial Bank to the Fed. The Fed increases the Manhattan Commercial Bank's reserves by $100 million, as shown by the green arrow running from the Fed to the Manhattan Commercial Bank. This action increases the monetary base and increases the reserves of the banking system.

The commercial bank's total assets remain constant, but their composition changes. Its holdings of government securities decrease by $100 million, and its reserves increase by $100 million. The bank can use these additional reserves to make loans. When the bank makes loans, the quantity of money increases by the process that we described in the previous section.

FIGURE 18.4
The Fed Buys Securities from a Commercial Bank

Practice Online

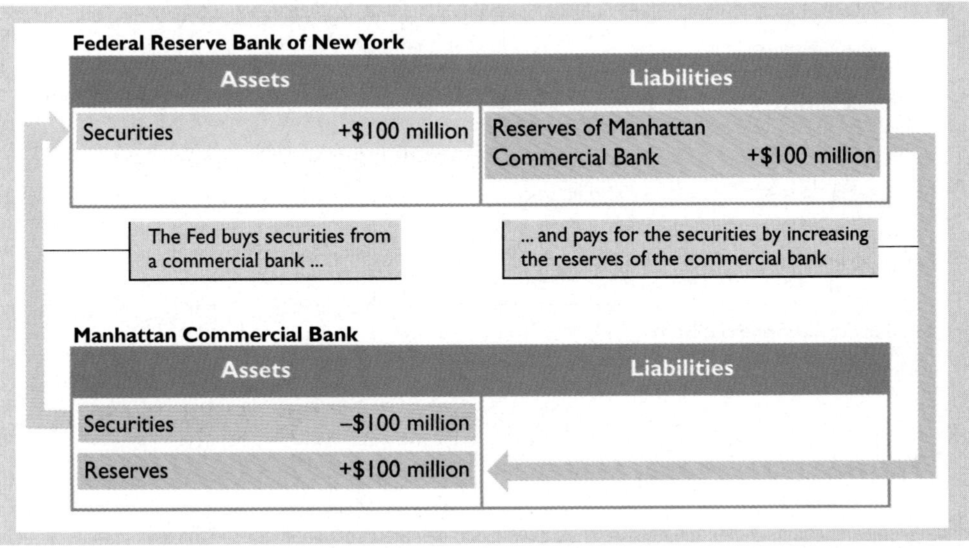

We've just seen that when the Fed buys government securities from a bank, the bank's reserves increase. What happens if the Fed buys government securities from the public—say, from Goldman Sachs, a financial services company?

The Nonbank Public Sells When the Fed buys $100 million of securities from Goldman Sachs, three things happen:

1. Goldman Sachs has $100 million less in securities, and the Fed has $100 million more in securities.
2. The Fed pays for the securities with a check for $100 million drawn on itself, which Goldman Sachs deposits in its account at the Manhattan Commercial Bank.
3. The Manhattan Commercial Bank collects payment of this check from the Fed, and the Manhattan Commercial Bank's reserves increase by $100 million.

Figure 18.5 shows the effects of these actions on the balance sheets of the Fed, Goldman Sachs, and the Manhattan Commercial Bank. Ownership of the securities passes from Goldman Sachs to the Fed, so Goldman Sachs's securities decrease by $100 million and the Fed's securities increase by $100 million (red-to-blue arrow). The Fed pays for the securities with a check payable to Goldman Sachs, which Goldman Sachs deposits in the Manhattan Commercial Bank. This payment increases Manhattan's reserves by $100 million (green arrow). It also

FIGURE 18.5
The Fed Buys Securities from the Public

Practice Online

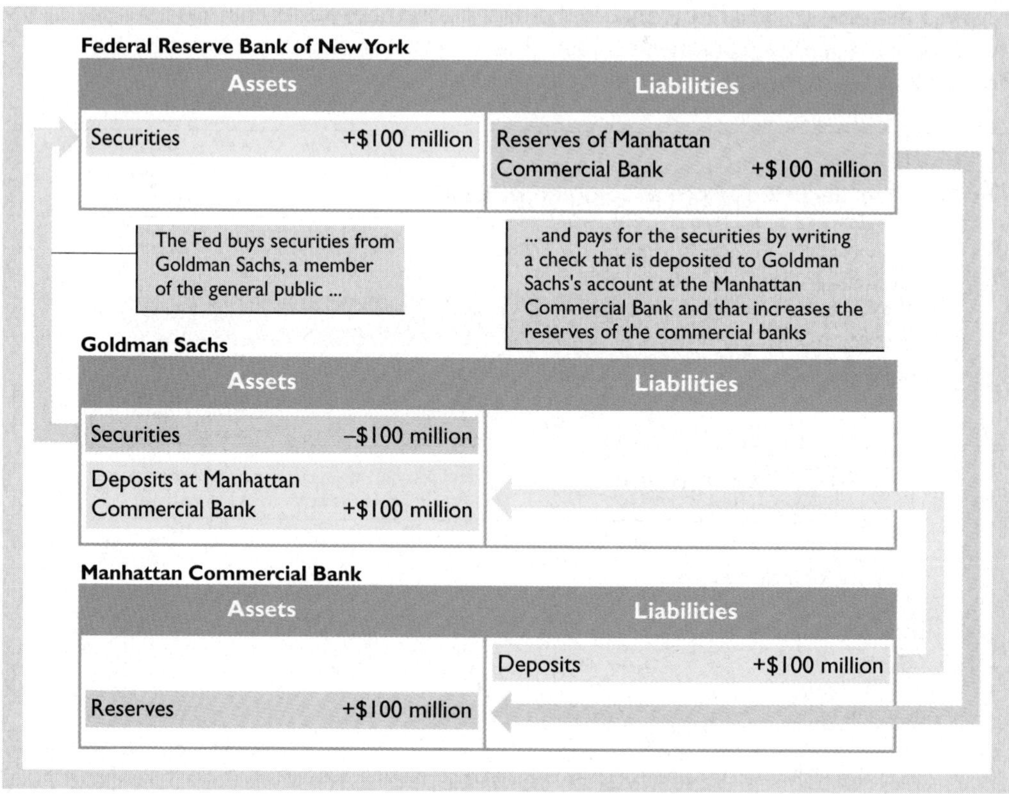

increases Goldman Sachs's deposit at the Manhattan Commercial Bank by $100 million (blue arrow). Just as when the Fed buys securities from a bank, this action increases the monetary base and increases the reserves of the banking system.

Goldman Sachs has the same total assets as before, but their composition has changed. It now has more money and fewer securities. The Manhattan Commercial Bank's reserves increase, and so do its deposits—both by $100 million. Because bank reserves and deposits have increased by the same amount, the bank has excess reserves, which it can use to make loans. When it makes loans, the quantity of money increases by the process that we described in the previous section.

We've worked through what happens when the Fed buys government securities from either a bank or the public. When the Fed sells securities, the transactions that we've just traced operate in reverse.

The Fed Sells Securities

If the Fed sells $100 million of U.S. government securities in the open market, most likely a person or business other than a bank buys them. (A bank would buy them only if it had excess reserves and it couldn't find a better use of its funds.)

When the Fed sells $100 million of securities to Goldman Sachs, three things happen:

1. Goldman Sachs has $100 million more in securities, and the Fed has $100 million less in securities.
2. Goldman Sachs pays for the securities with a check for $100 million drawn on its deposit account at the Manhattan Commercial Bank.
3. The Fed collects payment of this check from the Manhattan Commercial Bank by decreasing its reserves by $100 million.

These actions decrease the monetary base and decrease the reserves of the banking system. The Manhattan Commercial Bank is now short of reserves and must borrow in the federal funds market to meet its required reserve ratio.

The changes in the balance sheets of the Fed and the banks that we've just described are not the end of the story about the effects of an open market operation; they are just the beginning. A multiplier effect on the quantity of money now begins. To study this multiplier effect of an open market operation on the quantity of money, we build on the link between bank reserves and bank deposits that you studied in the previous section.

The Multiplier Effect of an Open Market Operation

An open market purchase that increases bank reserves also increases the *monetary base*. The increase in the monetary base equals the amount of the open market purchase, and initially, it equals the increase in bank reserves. To see why, recall that the *monetary base is the sum of Federal Reserve notes, coins, and banks' reserves at the Fed*. An open market purchase increases the banks' reserves at the Fed by the amount of the open market purchase. Nothing else changes, so the monetary base increases by the amount of the open market purchase.

If the Fed buys securities from the banks, the quantity of deposits (and quantity of money) does not change. If the Fed buys securities from the public, the quantity of deposits (and quantity of money) increases by the same amount as the increase in bank reserves. Either way, the banks have excess reserves that they now start to lend.

Figure 18.6 illustrates the multiplier effect of an open market purchase of securities from the banks. The following sequence of events takes place:

- An open market purchase creates excess reserves.
- Banks lend excess reserves.
- Bank deposits increase.
- The quantity of money increases.
- New money is used to make payments.
- Some of the new money is held as currency—a currency drain.
- Some of the new money remains in deposits in banks.
- Banks' required reserves increase.
- Excess reserves decrease but remain positive.

This sequence is similar to the one you studied in the previous section of this chapter but with one addition: the currency drain. When banks use excess reserves to make loans, bank deposits increase but currency held outside the banks also increases. An increase in currency held outside the banks is called the **currency drain**. The currency drain does not change the monetary base. Bank reserves decrease, currency increases, and the monetary base remains the same. But a currency drain decreases the amount of money that banks can create from a given increase in the monetary base because currency drains from their reserves and decreases the excess reserves available.

Currency drain
An increase in currency held outside the banks.

The sequence of rounds described in Figure 18.6 repeats, but each round begins with a smaller quantity of excess reserves than did the previous one. The process ends when excess reserves have been eliminated.

FIGURE 18.6

A Round in the Multiplier Process Following an Open Market Operation

Practice Online

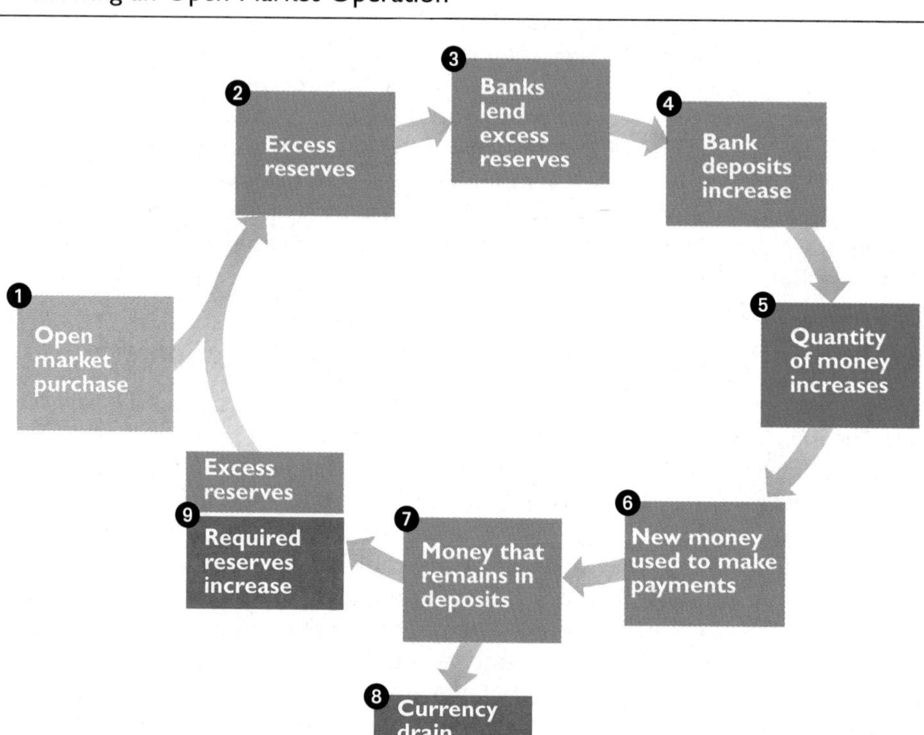

1 An open market purchase increases bank reserves and 2 creates excess reserves. 3 Banks lend the excess reserves, 4 new deposits are created, and 5 the quantity of money increases. 6 New money is used to make payments. 7 Households and firms receiving payments keep some on deposit in banks and some in the form of currency—8 a currency drain. The increase in bank deposits increases banks' reserves but also 9 increases banks' required reserves. Required reserves increase by less than actual reserves, so the banks still have some excess reserves, though less than before. The process repeats until excess reserves have been eliminated.

Figure 18.7 keeps track of the magnitudes of the increases in reserves, loans, deposits, currency, and money that result from an open market purchase of $100,000. In this figure, the currency drain is 33.33 percent of money and the required reserve ratio is 10 percent of deposits. These numbers are assumed to keep the arithmetic simple.

The Fed buys $100,000 of securities from the banks. The banks' reserves increase by this amount, but deposits do not change. The banks have excess reserves of $100,000, and they lend those reserves. When the banks lend $100,000 of excess reserves, $66,667 remains in the banks as deposits and $33,333 drains off and is held outside the banks as currency. The quantity of money has now increased by $100,000—the increase in deposits plus the increase in currency holdings.

The increased bank deposits of $66,667 generate an increase in required reserves of 10 percent of that amount, which is $6,667. Actual reserves have increased by the same amount as the increase in deposits—$66,667. So the banks now have excess reserves of $60,000. At this stage, we have gone around the circle shown in Figure 18.6 once. The process that we've just described repeats but begins with excess reserves of $60,000. Figure 18.7 shows the next two rounds. At the end of the process, the quantity of money has increased by a multiple of the increase in the monetary base. In this case, the increase is $250,000, which is 2.5 times the increase in the monetary base.

An open market *sale* works similarly to an open market *purchase*, but the sale *decreases* the quantity of money. (Trace the process again but with the Fed *selling* and the banks or public *buying* securities.)

FIGURE 18.7

The Multiplier Effect of an Open Market Operation

Practice Online

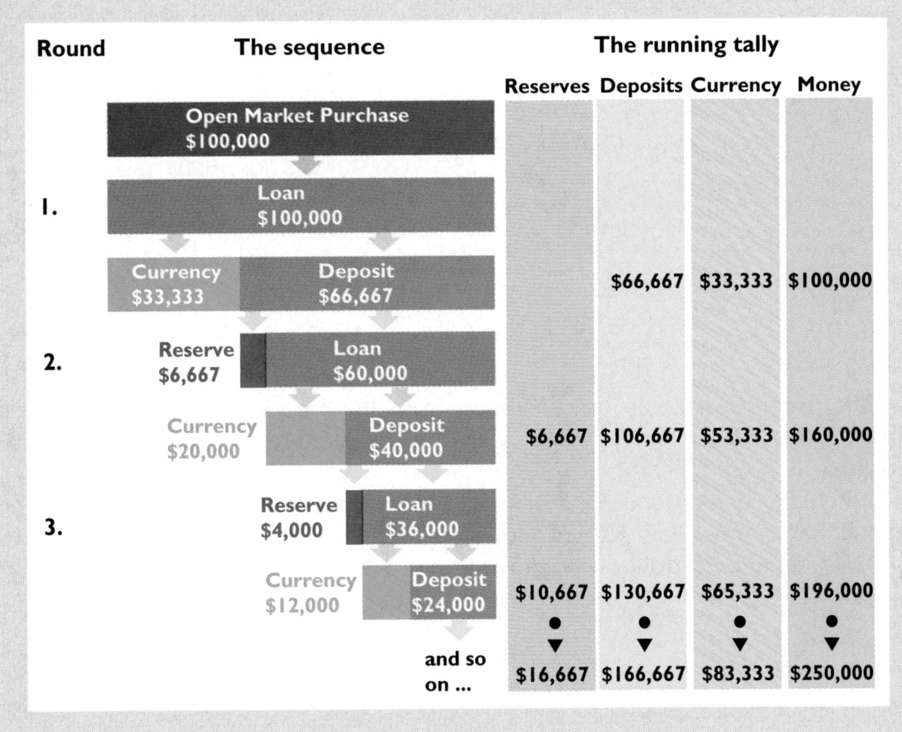

When the Fed provides the banks with $100,000 of additional reserves in an open market purchase, the banks lend those reserves. Of the amount loaned, $33,333 (33.33 percent) leaves the banks in a currency drain and $66,667 remains on deposit. With additional deposits, required reserves increase by $6,667 (10 percent required reserve ratio) and the banks lend $60,000. Of this amount, $20,000 leaves the banks in a currency drain and $40,000 remains on deposit. The process repeats until the banks have created enough deposits to eliminate their excess reserves. An additional $100,000 of reserves creates $250,000 of money.

The Money Multiplier

Money multiplier
The number by which a change in the monetary base is multiplied to find the resulting change in the quantity of money.

In the example we've just worked through, the quantity of money increases by 2.5 times the increase in the monetary base. The **money multiplier** is the number by which a change in the monetary base is multiplied to find the resulting change in the quantity of money. That is,

$$\text{Change in quantity of money} = \text{Money multiplier} \times \text{Change in monetary base.}$$

In the example, the change in monetary base is the size of the open market purchase, which is \$100,000, so

$$\text{Change in quantity of money} = 2.5 \times \$100{,}000 = \$250{,}000.$$

The money multiplier is determined by the banks' required reserve ratio and by the currency drain. In the above example, the required reserve ratio is 10 percent of deposits and the currency drain is 33.33 percent of money. So when the banks lend their initial \$100,000 of excess reserves, \$33,333 drains off as currency and \$66,667 remains in the banks as reserves and deposits.

With an additional \$66,667 of deposits and a 10 percent required reserve ratio, the banks' required reserves increase by \$6,667, so their excess reserves are \$60,000. Notice that \$60,000 is 0.6 of the original \$100,000 of excess reserves. That is, in the second round of lending, the banks lend 0.6 of the amount they loaned in the first round. Call this proportion L ($L = 0.6$). In the third round, the banks lend $0.6^2 = 0.36$ of the original amount (\$36,000 in Figure 18.7).

Because L is a fraction, at each stage in this sequence the amounts of new loans and new money created get smaller. The total amount of new money created at the end of the process is

$$\text{Quantity of money created} = \frac{1}{1 - L} \times \text{Open market purchase.}$$

If we use the numbers from the example, the total increase in the quantity of money is

$$\begin{aligned}\text{Quantity of money created} &= \$100{,}000 \times \frac{1}{(1 - 0.6)}\\ &= \$100{,}000 \times \frac{1}{0.4}\\ &= \$100{,}000 \times 2.5\\ &= \$250{,}000.\end{aligned}$$

The proportion L can be calculated from the currency drain and required reserve ratio. Call the currency drain C and the required reserve ratio R. So $C = 0.33$ and $R = 0.1$.

When the banks lend \$1, \$$C$ is held as currency and \$$(1 - C)$ remains on deposit. Banks must hold \$$R$ of reserves for each \$1 of deposits, so they are free to lend \$$(1 - R)$ of each dollar on deposit. When \$$(1 - C)$ remains on deposit, banks can lend \$$(1 - C) \times (1 - R)$. That is, the proportion L is

$$L = (1 - C) \times (1 - R).$$

Eye on the U.S. Economy

The Money Multiplier

We can measure the money multiplier in the United States by using the following formula:

Money multiplier = Quantity of money ÷ Monetary base.

Because there are two main definitions of money, M1 and M2, there are two money multipliers: the M1 multiplier and the M2 multiplier.

Also, there are two measures of the currency drain and bank reserve ratios. Part (a) shows the currency drain measures: the ratio of currency to M1 and the ratio of currency to M2.

Notice the increase in the ratio of currency to M1, which arises mainly from a surge in holdings of U.S. currency abroad.

In part (b), you can see that the reserve ratios have fallen as required reserve ratios have been decreased.

In part (c), you can see the two money multipliers. The M2 multiplier increased through the 1980s because required reserves decreased. This multiplier decreased during the 1990s because the currency drain increased. In 2002, this multiplier was about 8.

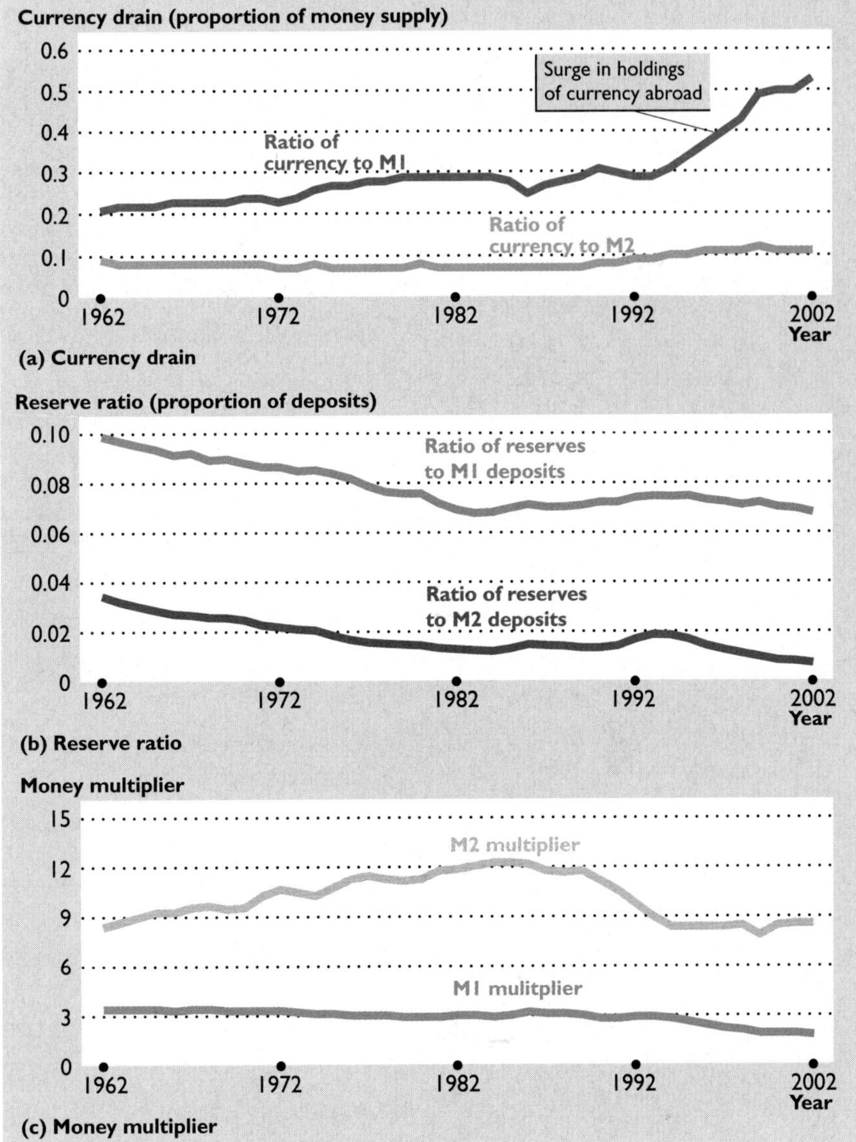

The M1 multiplier decreased from close to 4 in 1960 to about 2 in 2000.

The increasing currency drain is the main influence on this multiplier.

In terms of the numbers in our example,

$$L = (1 - 0.33) \times (1 - 0.1)$$

$$= (0.67) \times (0.9) = 0.6.$$

The larger the currency drain and the larger the required reserve ratio, the smaller is the money multiplier.

CHECKPOINT 18.2

Study Guide pp. 273–277

Practice Online 18.2

2 **Explain how the Fed controls the quantity of money.**

Practice Problems 18.2

1. Which of the Fed's tools does it use most often?
2. What is the money multiplier? What determines its magnitude?
3. If the Fed makes an open market purchase of $1 million of securities,
   a. Who can sell the securities to the Fed in an open market operation? Does it matter from whom the Fed buys the securities?
   b. What initial changes occur in the economy if the Fed buys from a bank?
   c. What is the process by which the quantity of money changes?
   d. What factors determine how much the quantity of money changes?

Exercises 18.2

1. What is an open market operation? How do open market operations influence the monetary base?
2. Explain how the banking system creates money when the Fed conducts an open market operation.
3. If the Fed makes an open market sale of $1 million of securities,
   a. What initial changes occur in the economy?
   b. What is the process by which the quantity of money in the economy changes?
   c. By how much does the quantity of money change?
   d. What is the magnitude of the money multiplier?

Solutions to Practice Problems 18.2

1. The Fed's most used tool is the open market operation.
2. The money multiplier is the number by which a change in the monetary base is multiplied to find the resulting change in the quantity of money. The currency drain and the banks' required reserve ratio determine its magnitude.

3a. The Fed buys securities from banks or the public. The Fed does not buy securities from the government. It does not matter from whom the Fed buys the securities. The change in the monetary base is the same.

3b. The monetary base increases by $1 million. Ownership of the securities passes from the bank to the Fed. As a result, the Fed's assets increase by $1 million. When the Fed pays for the securities, it increases the bank's deposit with the Fed by $1 million. The Fed's liabilities increase by $1 million. The bank's assets are the same, but their composition has changed. The bank has $1 million more in reserves and $1 million less in securities.

3c. The bank's reserves have increased by $1 million and its deposits have not changed, so it has excess reserves of $1 million. The bank makes loans and creates new deposits. The new deposits are new money.

3d. The required reserve ratio and the currency drain determine the increase in the quantity of money. The larger the required reserve ratio or the currency drain, the smaller is the increase in the quantity of money.

Key Points

1 Explain how banks create money by making loans.

- Banks create money by making loans.
- Banks hold a proportion of their deposits as reserves to meet the *required reserve ratio.*
- Reserves that exceed the required reserve ratio are *excess reserves*, which banks loan.
- The quantity of reserves and the required reserve ratio limit the total quantity of deposits that the banks can create.
- The deposit multiplier is the number by which an increase in bank reserves is multiplied to give the increase in bank deposits.
- The deposit multiplier equals one divided by the required reserve ratio.

2 Explain how the Fed controls the quantity of money.

- The Fed has three tools for controlling the quantity of money: required reserve ratios, the discount rate, and open market operations.
- An increase in the required reserve ratio forces the banks to hold more reserves and decreases the quantity of money that can be supported by a given amount of monetary base.
- An increase in the discount rate makes the banks pay a higher price for borrowed reserves, makes them less willing to borrow reserves, and decreases the quantity of money.
- When the Fed *buys* securities in an open market operation, it pays for them with newly created bank reserves. When the Fed *sells* securities in an open market operation, people pay for them with money and banks pay for them with reserves.
- An open market purchase increases the monetary base and creates the following sequence of events: banks lend excess reserves; the quantity of money increases; new money is used to make payments; some of the new money is held as currency—a currency drain; some of the new money remains on deposit in banks; banks' required reserves increase; excess reserves decrease. This sequence repeats until excess reserves are eliminated.
- The money multiplier determines the amount of money that banks can create from a given increase in the monetary base.
- The money multiplier is determined by the banks' required reserve ratio and by the currency drain.

Key Terms

Balance sheet, 454
Currency drain, 468
Deposit multiplier, 462
Money multiplier, 470

Exercises

1. If the banking system receives new deposits of $2 million, the required reserve ratio is 0.1, and there is no currency drain, calculate
   a. The bank's excess reserves as soon as the deposit is made.
   b. The maximum amount of loans that the banking system can make.
   c. The maximum amount of new money that the banking system can create.

2. If the banking system loses deposits of $3 million, the required reserve ratio is 0.1, and there is no currency drain, calculate
   a. The bank's excess reserves as soon as the deposit withdrawal occurs.
   b. The amount of loans that the banking system must call in.
   c. The amount of money that the banking system must destroy.

3. The required reserve ratio is 5 percent and the currency drain is 20 percent. If the Fed makes an open market purchase of $1 million of securities,
   a. What is the change in the monetary base?
   b. Which components of the monetary base change?
   c. By how much does the quantity of money change?
   d. How much of the new money is currency and how much is bank deposits?

4. Initially, the banking system has $2 trillion of deposits and no excess reserves. If the Fed lowers the required reserve ratio from 0.1 to 0.05, calculate the change in
   a. Reserves.
   b. Deposits.
   c. The quantity of money.

5. The First Student Bank has the following balance sheet (in millions of dollars).

Assets		Liabilities	
Reserves at the Fed	25	Demand deposits	90
Cash in ATMs	15	Savings deposits	110
Government securities	60		
Loans	100		

   The required reserve ratio on all deposits is 5 percent.
   a. What, if any, are the bank's excess reserves?
   b. What is the bank's deposit multiplier?
   c. How much will the bank loan?
   d. If there is no currency drain and if all the funds loaned are deposited in the First Student Bank, what are the bank's excess reserves, if any, after the loans made in part **c**?
   e. If there is no currency drain and if all the funds loaned remain deposited in the First Student Bank, what is the quantity of loans and total deposits when the bank has no excess reserves?
   f. If the required reserve ratio is decreased to 2 percent and if there is no currency drain and all the funds loaned remain deposited in the First Student Bank, what is the quantity of loans and total deposits when the bank has no excess reserves?

6. The Second Student Bank has the following balance sheet (in millions of dollars).

Assets		Liabilities	
Reserves at the Fed	3	Demand deposits	90
Cash in ATMs	2	Savings deposits	110
Government securities	85		
Loans	110		

The required reserve ratio on all deposits is 5 percent.
a. Does the bank have any excess reserves?
b. Does the bank have a shortage of reserves?
c. How much of the outstanding loans will the bank not renew?
d. If there is no currency drain and if all the loans that are repaid are paid out of deposits in the Second Student Bank, what is the bank's shortage of reserves, if any, after the loans are repaid in part **c**?
e. If there is no currency drain and if all the loans are repaid come from deposits in the Second Student Bank, what is the quantity of loans and total deposits when the bank has no excess reserves?

7. If the Fed wants to decrease quantity of money, what type of open market operation might it undertake? Explain the process by which the quantity of money decreases.

8. Suppose that the currency drain is 10 percent and the required reserve ratio is 1 percent. If the Fed sells $100,000 of securities on the open market, calculate the first round changes in
a. Excess reserves.
b. Deposits.
c. Currency in circulation.

9. What can the Fed do to increase the quantity of money and keep the monetary base constant? Explain why the Fed would or would not do each of the following:
a. Change the currency drain
b. Change the required reserve ratio
c. Change the discount rate
d. Conduct an open market operation

10. The commercial banks have the following balance sheet (in billions of dollars).

Assets		Liabilities	
Reserves	10	Deposits	210
Government securities	50		
Loans	150		

The required reserve ratio is 5 percent, there is no currency drain, and the Fed conducts an open market purchase of securities of $1 billion.
a. What is the initial change in the reserves of the banks?
b. By how much do loans increase?
c. By how much do deposits increase?

Critical Thinking

11. An early goldsmith banker earned a profit (and sometimes a large profit) simply by writing notes to certify that a person had deposited a certain amount of gold in his vault. By writing more notes than the amount of gold held, the goldsmith could lend the notes and charge interest on them.
    a. Did the goldsmith bankers make money out of thin air in a form of legal theft?
    b. Should the goldsmith bankers have been regulated to ensure that the amount of gold in their vaults equaled the value of the notes they created?
    c. What were the main benefits from the activities of the goldsmith bankers?
12. In the United States today, the Federal Reserve is the only bank that is permitted to create bank notes.
    a. Do you think that Citigroup and JP Morgan Chase should be permitted to issue their own private bank notes in competition with the Fed?
    b. Do you think the Fed should be the only bank that is permitted to issue e-cash?
13. Bank deposits are insured against the risk of bank failure. Can you think of any bad side effects of this arrangement?

Practice Online

Web Exercises

Use the links on your Foundations Web site to work the following exercises.

14. Visit the Web site of JP Morgan Chase and obtain the most recent balance sheet data for this bank.
    a. What is the total amount of deposits?
    b. What is the total amount of loans?
    c. What is the total amount of reserves held?
    d. What is the reserve ratio?
    e. Why can't you determine from the published balance sheet the deposits that are part of M1 and the deposits that are part of M2?
15. Visit the Web sites of JP Morgan Chase and Citigroup and obtain the most recent earnings data for these large banks.
    a. What are their profits during the most recent year?
    b. Explain how these banks earn such large profits.
16. Visit the Web site of the Federal Reserve and obtain the most recent data on the monetary base, M1, M2, and the composition of money and calculate for the most recent month
    a. The currency drain (using both M1 and M2).
    b. The banks' reserve ratio (using both the M1 deposits and the M2 deposits).
    c. The money multiplier (for both M1 and M2).
17. Visit the Web site of the Federal Reserve and obtain the most recent information on "Factors Affecting Reserve Balances of Depository Institutions."
    a. Have the reserves of depository institutions increased or decreased?
    b. Has the Fed increased or decreased the amount that it has loaned to depository institutions?

CHAPTER 19

Money, Interest, and Inflation

CHAPTER CHECKLIST

When you have completed your study of this chapter, you will be able to

1. **Explain what determines the demand for money and how the demand for money and the supply of money determine the *nominal* interest rate.**

2. **Explain how in the long run, the quantity of money determines the price level and money growth brings inflation.**

3. **Identify the costs of inflation and the benefits of a stable value of money.**

You know what money is, how banks create it, and how the Fed controls its quantity. In this chapter, you are going to learn about the effects of money on the economy.

First, you'll see how, on any given day, the quantity of money determines the interest rate. The effect of money on the interest rate is one of the channels through which the Fed influences expenditure plans and the business cycle. You'll learn more about these aspects of money in subsequent chapters.

Second, you'll see how, when we smooth out the influence of the business cycle and look at the long-term trends, the quantity of money determines the price level and money growth in excess of potential GDP growth brings inflation.

Finally, you'll see why inflation—ongoing *changes* in the price level—can have a big influence on people's lives.

WHERE WE ARE AND WHERE WE'RE HEADING

Before we explore the effects of money on the interest rate and the inflation rate, let's take stock of what we've learned and preview where we are heading.

The Real Economy and the Standard of Living

To understand why real GDP per person in the United States is almost 20 times that in Nigeria, or why real GDP per person in the United States in 2003 is twice what it was in 1963, we need to consider differences in the quantities of labor and capital and their productivity. These *real* factors are the source of differences in living standards across regions and countries and over time (Chapter 16). These real factors are independent of the price level. That is, to explain differences in real GDP across countries and over long time periods, we can ignore differences in the cost of living. In the long term, the forces that determine the standard of living are independent of those that determine the cost of living.

The Money Economy, the Cost of Living, and the Business Cycle

Money—the economy's means of payment—consists of currency and bank deposits (Chapter 17). Banks create deposits by making loans, and the Fed controls the quantity of money through its open market operations, which determine the monetary base and the federal funds—interbank loans—interest rate (Chapter 18).

The effects of money on the economy, which we explore in this chapter, are complex and to explain and understand them, we proceed in three steps. We take these steps in an order that might seem strange but that turns out to be the most effective.

Step one looks at the immediate effect of the Fed's actions. This effect is on the short-term nominal interest rate. The Fed raises and lowers the short-term nominal interest rate by changing the quantity of money.

Step two looks at the long-term effects of the Fed's actions. These effects are on the price level and the inflation rate—on the cost of living and its rate of change. The Fed lowers or raises the price level by decreasing or increasing the quantity of money. And the Fed lowers or raises the inflation rate by slowing down or speeding up the rate at which the quantity of money grows. We take these two steps in the current chapter.

Step three provides the blow-by-blow story of how the Fed's actions ripple through the economy and ultimately change the price level and the inflation rate. This story is a long one that needs to be broken down into manageable bites, and we explore it in Chapters 20 and 21 with the help of a model of the economy that enables us to understand the business cycle and the possibility of moderating the cycle by adjusting the quantity of money and the interest rate.

Some people approach a novel in this order: first, read the introduction, then the conclusion, and then the steps in between. Try it. It sometimes helps to keep track of where you are if you know where you are going to end up!

19.1 MONEY AND THE INTEREST RATE

To understand the Fed's short-run influence on the interest rate, we must understand what determines the demand for money, the supply of money, and the forces that bring equilibrium in the market for money. We'll begin by studying the demand for money.

The Demand for Money

The amount of money that households and firms choose to hold is the **quantity of money demanded**. What determines the quantity of money demanded? The answer is a benefit–opportunity cost calculation. The quantity of money that households and firms choose to hold is the quantity that balances the benefit of holding an additional dollar of money against the opportunity cost of doing so. But just what are the benefit and opportunity cost of holding money?

Quantity of money demanded
The amount of money that households and firms choose to hold.

Benefit of Holding Money

You've seen that money is the means of payment and that it serves as a medium of exchange, unit of account, and store of value (Chapter 17, pp. 428–429). You don't need any money to use it as a unit of account. You can keep financial records in dollars and cents even if you don't have any money. You don't need money to store your wealth. You can store it in the form of bonds, stocks, and mutual funds. Money and other financial assets are substitute stores of value. But you do need money to make payments and do transactions. These two features of money are the sources of benefit from holding money. The more money you hold, the easier it is for you to make payments and transactions.

The marginal benefit of holding money is the change in total benefit that results from holding one more dollar as money. The marginal benefit of holding money diminishes as the quantity of money held increases. If you hold only a few dollars in money, holding one more dollar brings large benefits—you can buy a cup of coffee, take a bus ride, or use a pay phone. If you hold enough money to make your normal weekly payments, holding one more dollar brings only a small benefit because you're not very likely to want to spend it. Holding even more money brings only a small additional benefit. You barely notice the difference in the benefit of having $1,000 versus $1,001 in your bank account.

To get the most out of your assets, you hold money only up to the point at which its marginal benefit equals its opportunity cost. But what is the opportunity cost of holding money?

Opportunity Cost of Holding Money

The opportunity cost of holding money is the interest rate forgone on an alternative asset. If you can earn 8 percent a year on a mutual fund account, then holding an additional $100 in money costs you $8 a year. Your opportunity cost of holding $100 in money is the goods and services worth $8 that you must forgo.

A fundamental principle of economics is that if the opportunity cost of something increases, people seek substitutes for it. Money is no exception. Other assets such as a mutual fund account are substitutes for money. And the higher the opportunity cost of holding money—the higher the interest income forgone by not holding other assets—the smaller is the quantity of money demanded.

Opportunity Cost: *Nominal* Interest Is a *Real* Cost

The opportunity cost of holding money is the nominal interest rate. In Chapter 14, (p. 367), you learned the distinction between the *nominal* interest rate and the *real* interest rate and that

Nominal interest rate = Real interest rate + Inflation rate.

We can use this equation to find the real interest rate for a given nominal interest rate and inflation rate. For example, if the nominal interest rate on a mutual fund account is 8 percent a year and the inflation rate is 2 percent a year, the real interest rate is 6 percent a year. Why isn't the real interest rate of 6 percent a year the opportunity cost of holding money? That is, why isn't the opportunity cost of holding $100 in money only $6 worth of goods and services forgone?

The answer is that if you hold $100 in money rather than in a mutual fund, your buying power decreases by $8, not by $6. With inflation running at 2 percent a year, on each $100 that you hold as money and that earns no interest, you lose $2 worth of buying power a year. On each $100 that you put into your mutual fund account, you gain $6 worth of buying power a year. So if you hold money rather than a mutual fund, you lose the buying power of $6 plus $2, or $8—equivalent to the nominal interest rate on the mutual fund, not the real interest rate.

Because the opportunity cost of holding money is the nominal interest rate on an alternative asset,

Other things remaining the same, the higher the nominal interest rate, the smaller is the quantity of money demanded.

This relationship describes the money holding decisions of individuals and firms. It also describes money holding decisions for the economy—the sum of the decisions of every individual and firm.

We summarize the influence of the nominal interest rate on money holding decisions in a demand for money schedule and curve.

The Demand for Money Schedule and Curve

Demand for money
The relationship between the quantity of money demanded and the nominal interest rate, when all other influences on the amount of money that people wish to hold remain the same.

The **demand for money** is the relationship between the quantity of money demanded and the nominal interest rate, when all other influences on the amount of money that people wish to hold remain the same. We illustrate the demand for money with a demand for money schedule and a demand for money curve, such as those in Figure 19.1. If the interest rate is 5 percent a year, the quantity of money demanded is $1 trillion. The quantity of money demanded decreases to $0.98 trillion if the interest rate rises to 6 percent a year and increases to $1.02 trillion if the interest rate falls to 4 percent a year.

The demand for money curve is *MD*. When the interest rate rises, everything else remaining the same, the opportunity cost of holding money rises and the quantity of money demanded decreases—there is a movement up along the demand for money curve. When the interest rate falls, the opportunity cost of holding money falls and the quantity of money demanded increases—there is a movement down along the demand for money curve.

FIGURE 19.1
The Demand for Money

Practice Online

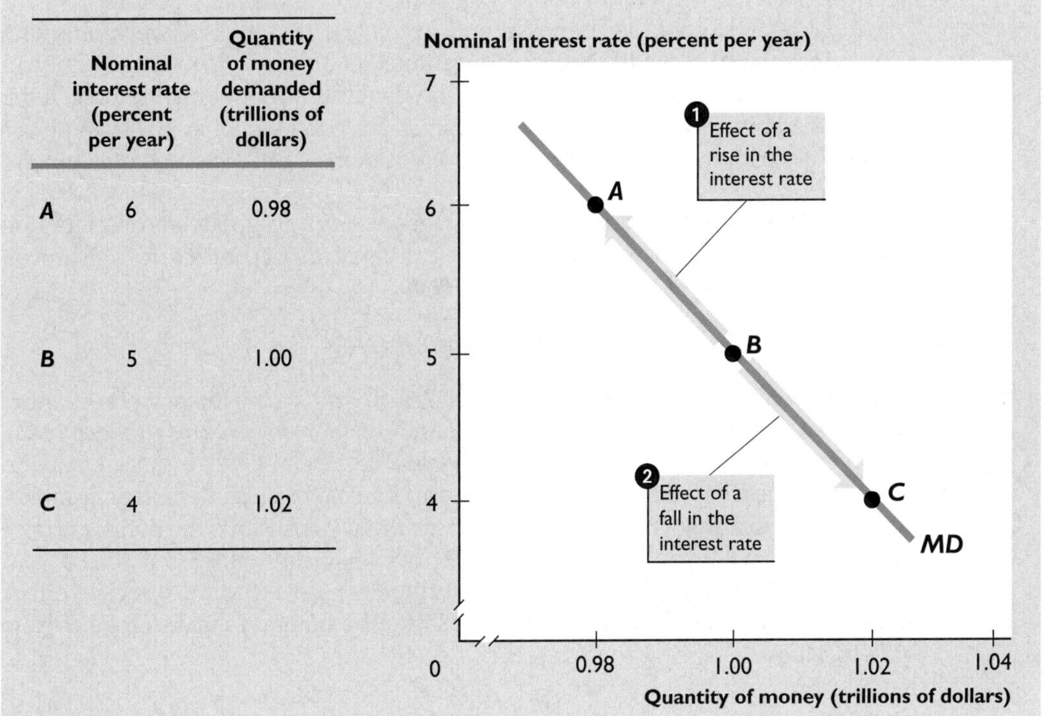

	Nominal interest rate (percent per year)	Quantity of money demanded (trillions of dollars)
A	6	0.98
B	5	1.00
C	4	1.02

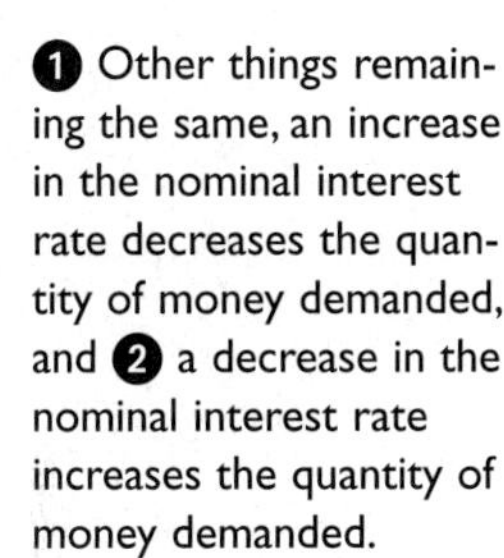

The demand for money schedule is graphed as the demand for money curve, *MD*. Rows *A*, *B*, and *C* in the table correspond to points *A*, *B*, and *C* on the curve. The nominal interest rate is the opportunity cost of holding money.

❶ Other things remaining the same, an increase in the nominal interest rate decreases the quantity of money demanded, and ❷ a decrease in the nominal interest rate increases the quantity of money demanded.

Changes in the Demand for Money

A change in the nominal interest rate brings a change in the quantity of money demanded and a movement along the demand for money curve. A change in any other influence on money holding changes the demand for money. The three main influences on the demand for money are

- The price level
- Real GDP
- Financial technology

The Price Level

The demand for money is proportional to the price level—an *x* percent rise in the price level brings an *x* percent increase in the quantity of money demanded at each nominal interest rate. The reason is that we hold money to make payments: If the price level changes, the quantity of dollars that we need to make payments changes in the same proportion.

Real GDP

The demand for money increases as real GDP increases. The reason is that expenditures and incomes increase when real GDP increases. So households and firms must hold larger average inventories of money to make the increased expenditures and income payments.

Financial Technology

Changes in financial technology change the demand for money. Most changes in financial technology come from advances in computing and record keeping. Some advances increase the quantity of money demanded, and some decrease it.

Daily interest checking deposits and automatic transfers between checking and savings deposits enable people to earn interest on money, lower the opportunity cost of holding money, and increase the demand for money. Automatic teller machines, debit cards, and smart cards, which have made money easier to obtain and use, have increased the marginal benefit of money and increased the demand for money.

Credit cards have made it easier for people to buy goods and services on credit and pay for them when their credit card account becomes due. This development has decreased the demand for money.

Shifts in the Demand for Money Curve

A change in any influence on money holdings other than the interest rate changes the demand for money and shifts the demand for money curve, as you can see in Figure 19.2. A rise in the price level, an increase in real GDP, or an advance in financial technology that lowers the opportunity cost of holding money or makes money more useful increases the demand for money and shifts the demand curve rightward from MD_0 to MD_1. A fall in the price level, a decrease in real GDP, or a technological advance that creates a substitute for money has the opposite effect. It decreases the demand for money and shifts the demand curve leftward from MD_0 to MD_2.

FIGURE 19.2
Changes in the Demand for Money

Practice Online

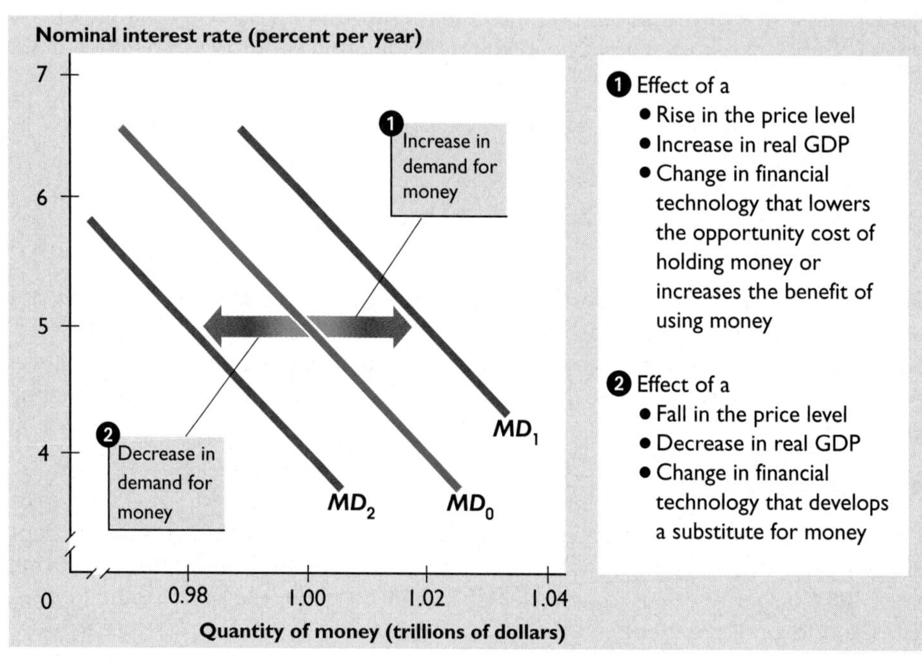

1. Effect of a
   - Rise in the price level
   - Increase in real GDP
   - Change in financial technology that lowers the opportunity cost of holding money or increases the benefit of using money

2. Effect of a
   - Fall in the price level
   - Decrease in real GDP
   - Change in financial technology that develops a substitute for money

The Nominal Interest Rate

People hold some of their financial wealth as money and some in the form of other financial assets. You have seen that the amount that people hold as money depends on the nominal interest rate that they can earn on other financial assets. Demand and supply determine the nominal interest rate. We can study the forces of demand and supply in either the market for financial assets or the market for money. Because the Fed influences the quantity of money, we focus on the market for money.

Figure 19.3 shows the market for money. The quantity of money supplied is determined by the actions of the banking system and the Fed. On any given day, there is a fixed quantity of money supplied. In Figure 19.3, that quantity is $1 trillion. The **supply of money**, which is the relationship between the quantity of money supplied and the nominal interest rate, is shown by the vertical line *MS*.

Supply of money
The relationship between the quantity of money supplied and the nominal interest rate.

Also, on any given day, the price level, real GDP, and the state of financial technology are fixed. Because these influences on the demand for money are fixed, the demand for money curve is given and is the curve *MD* in Figure 19.3.

The interest rate is the only influence on the quantity of money demanded that is free to fluctuate. And every day, the interest rate adjusts to make the quantity of money demanded equal the quantity of money supplied—to achieve money market equilibrium. In Figure 19.3, the equilibrium interest rate is 5 percent a year. At any interest rate above 5 percent a year, the quantity of money demanded is less than the quantity of money supplied. At any interest rate below 5 percent a year, the quantity of money demanded exceeds the quantity of money supplied.

FIGURE 19.3
Money Market Equilibrium

Practice Online

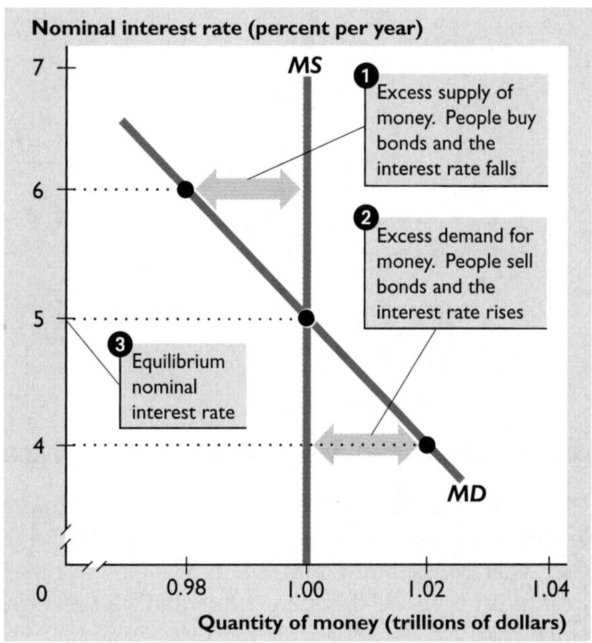

The supply of money curve is *MS*, and the demand for money curve is *MD*.

1. If the interest rate is 6 percent a year, the quantity of money held exceeds the quantity demanded. People buy bonds, the price of a bond rises, and the interest rate falls.
2. If the interest rate is 4 percent a year, the quantity of money held falls short of the quantity demanded. People sell bonds, the price of a bond falls, and the interest rate rises.
3. If the interest rate is 5 percent a year, the quantity of money held equals the quantity demanded. The money market is in equilibrium.

Eye on the U.S. Economy

Money and Credit Cards

The quantity of M1 money has decreased as a percentage of GDP. Part (a) of the figure shows that M1 fell from 20 percent of GDP in 1970 to less than 12 percent in 2002.

In sharp contrast to the use of M1 money, credit card ownership and use has expanded strongly. Part (b) of the figure shows the upward trend. In 1970, 16 percent (one in six) of families had a credit card. By 1999, 72 percent of families had a credit card. And by 2005, it is projected that 80 percent of families will use a credit card.

Most people use their credit card account as a substitute for money. When they buy goods or services, they use their credit card. And when the monthly bill arrives, many people pay off some of the outstanding balance, but not all of it. In 1998, 42 percent of credit card holders had an outstanding balance after making their most recent payment, and the average card balance was $4,000.

The changing financial technology has led to a steady decrease in the demand for money and a leftward shift of the demand for money curve. Part (c) of the figure shows the shifts in the demand curve for M1. Here, we're measuring the quantity of M1 as a percentage of GDP so that you can see the influence of the interest rate and financial technology on the demand for money.

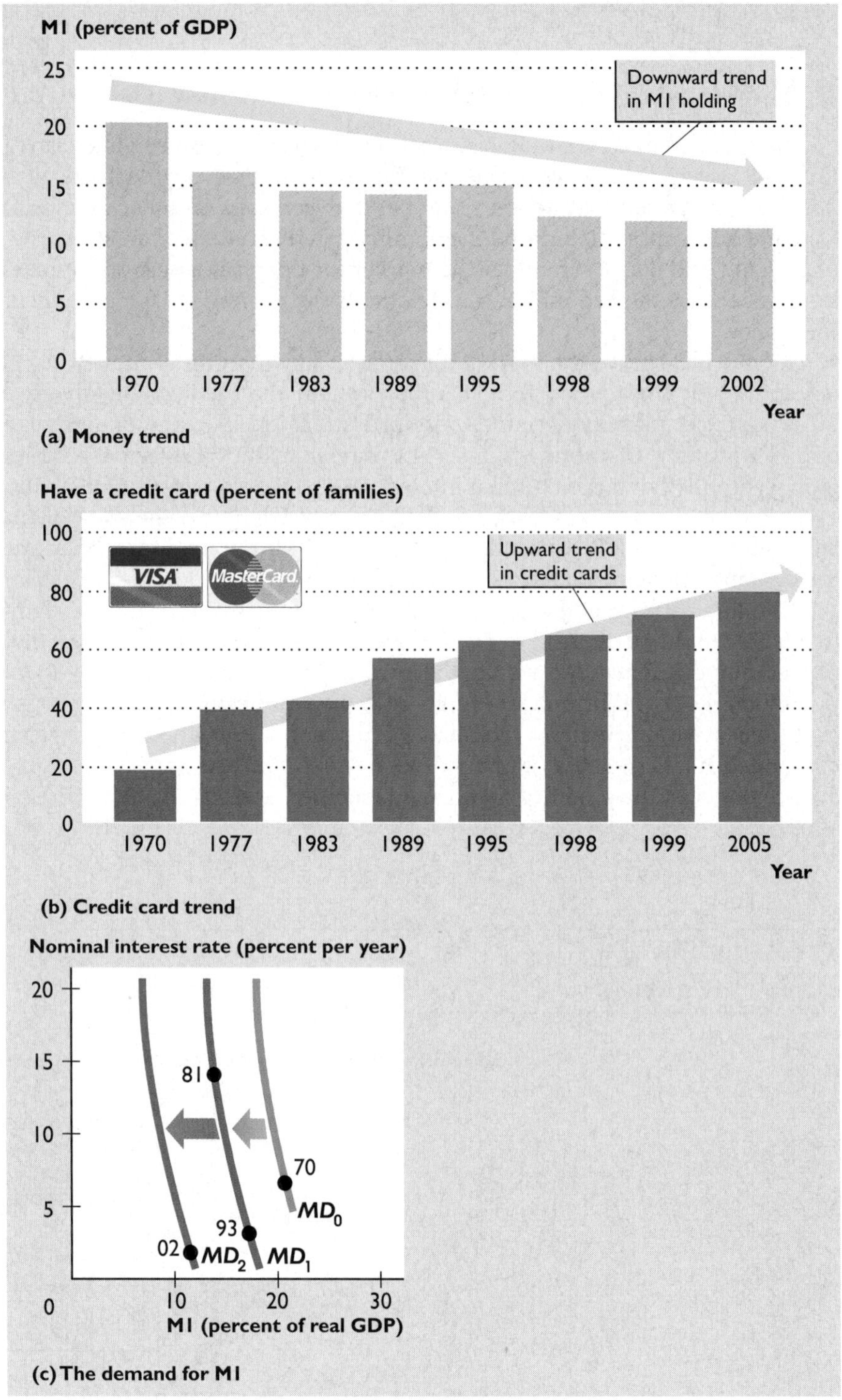

(a) Money trend

(b) Credit card trend

(c) The demand for M1

SOURCE: The Federal Reserve.

The Interest Rate and Bond Price Move in Opposite Directions When the government issues a bond, it specifies the dollar amount of interest that it will pay each year on the bond. Suppose that the government issues a bond that pays $100 of interest a year. The interest *rate* that you receive on this bond depends on the price that you pay for it. If the price is $1,000, the interest rate is 10 percent a year—$100 is 10 percent of $1,000.

If the price of the bond *falls* to \$500, the interest rate *rises* to 20 percent a year. The reason is that you still receive an interest payment of \$100, but this amount is 20 percent of the \$500 price of the bond. If the price of the bond *rises* to \$2,000, the interest rate *falls* to 5 percent a year. Again, you still receive an interest payment of \$100, but this amount is 5 percent of the \$2,000 price of the bond.

Interest Rate Adjustment If the interest rate is above its equilibrium level, people would like to hold less money than they are actually holding. So they try to get rid of money by buying other financial assets such as bonds. The demand for financial assets increases, the prices of these assets rise, and the interest rate falls. The interest rate keeps falling until the quantity of money that people want to hold increases to equal the quantity of money supplied.

Conversely, when the interest rate is below its equilibrium level, people are holding less money than they would like to hold. So they try to get more money by selling other financial assets. The demand for financial assets decreases, the prices of these assets fall, and the interest rate rises. The interest rate keeps rising until the quantity of money that people want to hold decreases to equal the quantity of money supplied.

Changing the Interest Rate

To change the interest rate, the Fed changes the quantity of money. Figure 19.4 illustrates two changes. The demand for money curve is *MD*. If the Fed increases the quantity of money to \$1.02 trillion, the supply of money curve shifts rightward from MS_0 to MS_1 and the interest rate falls to 4 percent a year. If the Fed decreases the quantity of money to \$0.98 trillion, the supply of money curve shifts leftward from MS_0 to MS_2 and the interest rate rises to 6 percent a year.

FIGURE 19.4
Interest Rate Changes

Practice Online

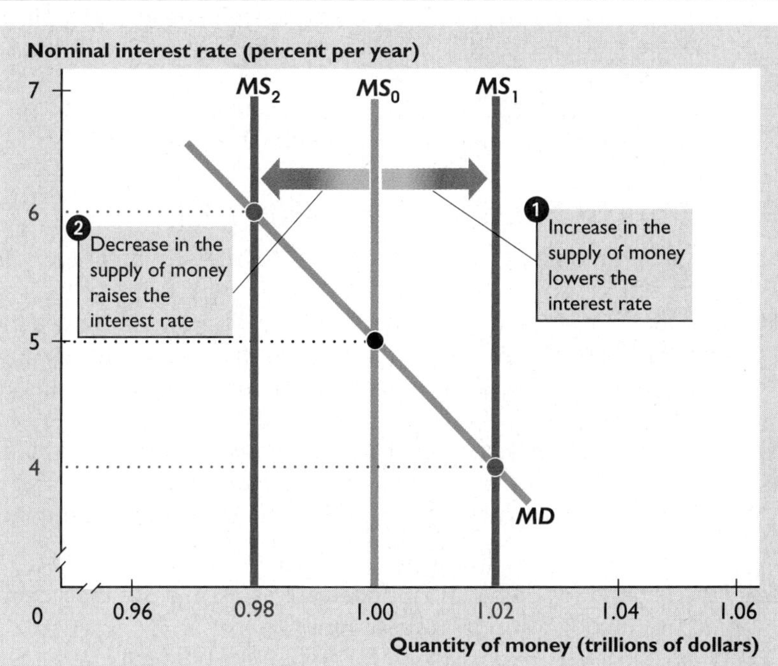

The demand for money is *MD*, and initially, the supply of money is MS_0. The interest rate is 5 percent a year.

1. The Fed increases the quantity of money and the supply of money curve shifts to MS_1. The interest rate falls to 4 percent a year.
2. The Fed decreases the quantity of money and the supply of money curve shifts to MS_2. The interest rate rises to 6 percent a year.

CHECKPOINT 19.1

Study Guide pp. 282–285

Practice Online 19.1

1 **Explain what determines the demand for money and how the demand for money and the supply of money determine the *nominal* interest rate.**

Practice Problems 19.1

1. Figure 1 shows the demand for money curve.
   a. If the quantity of money is \$4 trillion, what is the nominal interest rate?
   b. If real GDP increases, how will the interest rate change? Explain the process that brings about the change in the interest rate.
   c. In part **a**, the Fed decreases the quantity of money to \$3.9 trillion. Will bond prices rise or fall? Why? What happens to the nominal interest rate?

2. Suppose that the banks increase the fee they charge for credit cards, introduce a user fee on every credit card purchase, and increase the interest rate on outstanding credit card balances.
   a. How would the demand for money change?
   b. How would the nominal interest rate change?

FIGURE 1

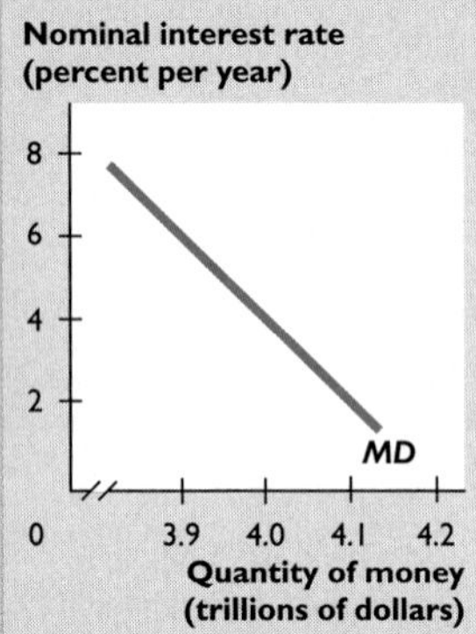

Exercises 19.1

1. Figure 1 shows the demand for money curve.
   a. If the quantity of money supplied is \$3.9 trillion, what is the nominal interest rate?
   b. If real GDP decreases, how will the interest rate change? Explain what happens in the market for bonds as the market returns to equilibrium.
   c. In part **a**, the Fed increases the quantity of money to \$4.0 trillion. What is the change in the nominal interest rate? What happens to the price of bonds?

2. Suppose that the banks launch an aggressive marketing campaign to get everyone to use credit cards for every conceivable transaction. They offer prizes to new cardholders and slash the interest rate on outstanding credit card balances.
   a. How would the demand for money change?
   b. How would the nominal interest rate change?

FIGURE 2

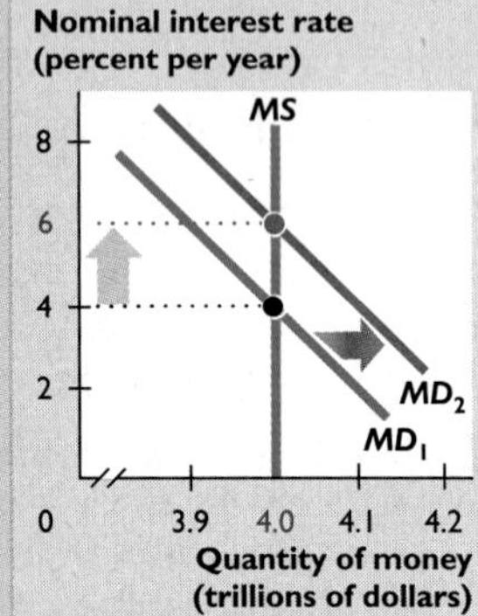

Solutions to Practice Problems 19.1

1a. The interest rate is 4 percent a year, at the intersection of MD_1 and MS (Figure 2).

1b. The demand for money increases and the demand for money curve shifts from MD_1 to MD_2. At an interest rate of 4 percent a year, people want to hold more money so they sell bonds. The price of a bond falls and the interest rate rises (Figure 2).

1c. At an interest rate at 4 percent a year, people would like to hold \$4 trillion. With only \$3.9 trillion of money available, they sell bonds. The price of a bond falls, and the interest rate rises. The new equilibrium nominal interest rate is 6 percent a year (Figure 3).

2a. The demand for money would increase as people use their credit cards less and use money for more transactions.

2b. With an increase in the demand for money, the nominal interest rate would rise.

FIGURE 3

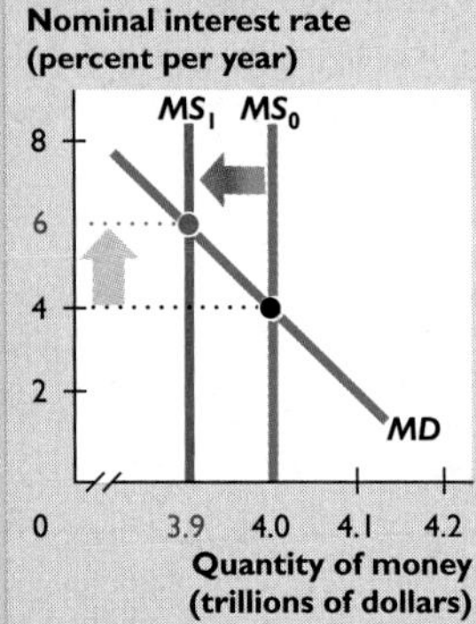

19.2 MONEY, THE PRICE LEVEL, AND INFLATION

Each day, the price level and real GDP are at levels that have resulted from previous decisions. When the Fed conducts an open market operation to change the quantity of money, the nominal interest rate is the only variable that is free to adjust to make the quantity of money demanded equal the quantity of money supplied. You've seen that if the Fed decreases the quantity of money, the interest rate rises, and if the Fed increases the quantity of money, the interest rate falls.

These changes in the nominal interest rate also change the real interest rate. The reason is that the inflation rate is slow to adjust. It does not change every time the Fed changes the quantity of money.

Changes in the real interest rate influence spending plans. If the real interest rate falls, firms borrow and invest more and households borrow and spend more on consumption goods, especially on big-ticket items such as homes and automobiles. Similarly, if the real interest rate rises, firms borrow and invest less and households borrow and spend less on consumption goods.

These changes in spending change production and prices. The details of the adjustment process are complex, and we explore them in the next two chapters. But the place where the adjustment process comes to rest is easier to describe. We're now going to explain the long-run outcome of a change in the quantity of money and a change in the growth rate of money.

■ The Money Market in the Long Run

The *long run* refers to the economy at full employment or when we smooth out the effects of the business cycle. Potential GDP, the current state of financial technology, the price level, and the nominal interest rate determine the quantity of money demanded at full employment. The actions of the Fed and the banking system determine the quantity of money supplied. In the short run, the nominal interest rate adjusts to bring equilibrium in the market for money, but in the long run, the price level does the adjusting. To see why, let's see what determines the other influences on the quantity of money demanded.

Potential GDP and Financial Technology

Potential GDP and the state of financial technology, two influences on the quantity of money demanded, are determined by real factors and are independent of the price level.

Potential GDP is the amount of real GDP when there is full employment. It depends on the quantities of labor and capital and on productivity. And potential GDP changes when the quantities of labor or capital or productivity change. But potential GDP does not change merely because the price level changes.

The Nominal Interest Rate in the Long Run

In 2001, businesses in the United States could borrow at a nominal interest rate of around 7 percent a year. Businesses in Russia paid a nominal interest rate of 60 percent a year, and businesses in Turkey paid 80 percent a year. Although the U.S. nominal interest rate has never been as high as these two cases, U.S. businesses faced a nominal interest rate of 16 percent a year during the 1980s.

Nominal interest rates vary across countries and over time for many reasons, but the dominant one is differences in inflation rates. The equilibrium nominal interest rate equals the equilibrium real interest rate plus the inflation rate. That is, the nominal interest rate exceeds the real interest rate by the inflation rate.

Investment and saving decisions in the global capital market determine the equilibrium real interest rate. The real interest rate, like potential GDP, is independent of the price level. It is also independent of the inflation rate in the long run.

But the nominal interest rate depends directly on the inflation rate. Borrowers are willing to pay a high nominal interest rate when there is inflation because the real value of loans decreases over time. And lenders insist on receiving a high nominal interest rate because the money with which they are repaid buys less than what the money they loaned would have bought.

An Example Suppose that when there is no inflation, investment equals saving at a real interest rate of 3 percent a year. Walt Disney Corporation is willing to pay an interest rate of 3 percent a year to get the funds it needs to pay for its new theme parks. Sue (along with millions of others) is willing to save and lend Disney the amount it needs for its theme parks at a real interest rate of 3 percent a year.

Now imagine that the inflation rate is steady at 2 percent a year. All dollar amounts, including theme park profits and car prices, are rising by 2 percent a year. If Disney was willing to pay 3 percent a year in interest when there was no inflation, it is now willing to pay 5 percent a year. Its profits are rising by 2 percent a year, so it is really paying only 3 percent a year. Similarly, if Sue was willing to lend at 3 percent a year when there was no inflation, she is now willing to lend only if the interest rate is 5 percent a year. The price of the car that Sue is planning to buy is rising by 2 percent a year, so she is really getting an interest rate of only 3 percent a year.

Because borrowers are willing to pay the higher rate and lenders are willing to lend only if they receive the higher rate when inflation is present, the nominal interest rate increases by an amount equal to the inflation rate.

We'll explain how the inflation rate is determined later in this chapter.

Money Market Equilibrium in the Long Run

You've seen how all of the influences on the quantity of money demanded except the price level are determined. Money market equilibrium determines the price level. Figure 19.5 illustrates how.

Part (a) emphasizes the idea that the demand for money depends on the price level and, for a given quantity of money, the equilibrium nominal interest rate depends on the price level. It looks at three *possible* short-run situations. Real GDP equals potential GDP in each of them. First, if the price level were 100, the demand for money would be MD_0. In this case, the equilibrium nominal interest rate would be 5 percent a year. Second, if the price level were 102, the demand for money would be MD_1 and the equilibrium nominal interest rate would be 6 percent a year. Finally, if the price level were 98, the demand for money would be MD_2 and the equilibrium nominal interest rate would be 4 percent a year.

Which of these three *possible* short-run situations describes the long run? Part (b) provides the answer. Saving and investment decisions determine the long-run equilibrium real interest rate, which we'll assume to be 3 percent a year. The nominal interest rate is the real interest rate plus the inflation rate. We'll assume that the inflation rate is 2 percent a year. So the long-run equilibrium nominal interest rate is 5 percent a year. Only one of the *possible* equilibrium situations shown in part (a) is consistent with the long-run equilibrium nominal interest rate. It is the

FIGURE 19.5
Long-Run Equilibrium

Practice Online

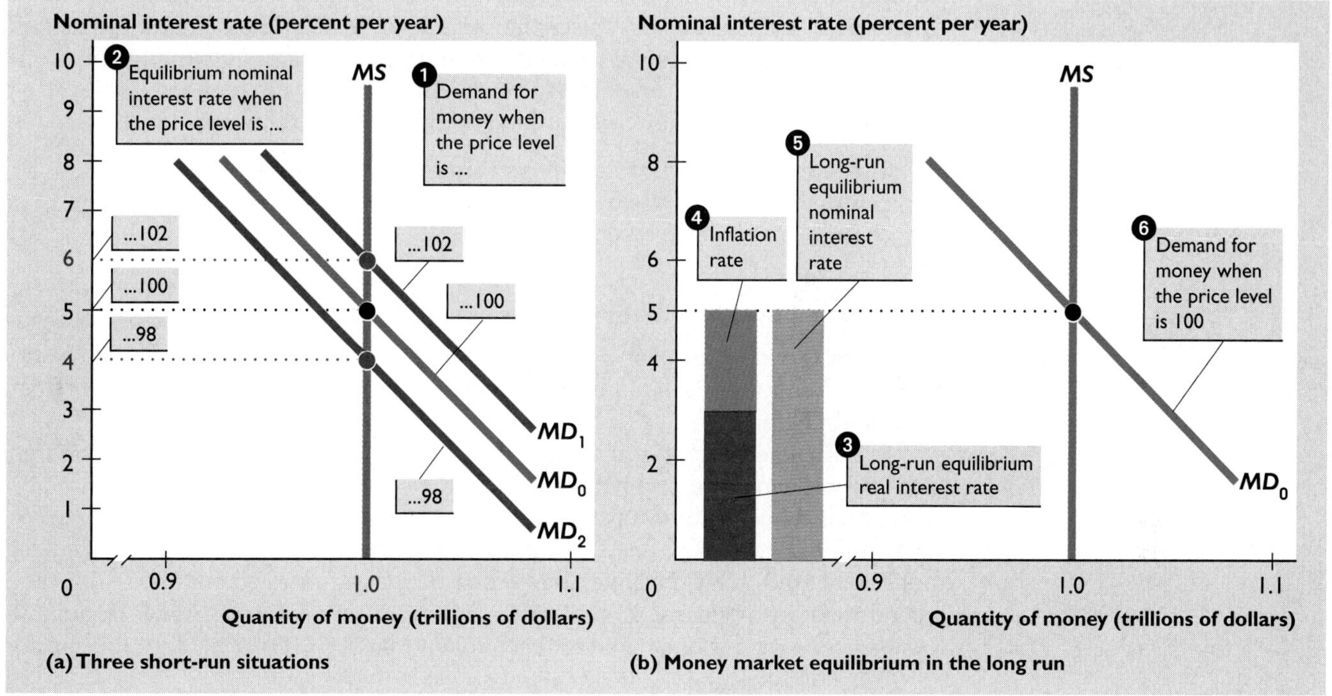

❶ The demand for money depends on the price level, so ❷ the equilibrium nominal interest rate also depends on the price level.

❸ The long-run equilibrium real interest rate (determined in the global financial market) plus ❹ the inflation rate determines the ❺ long-run equilibrium nominal interest rate.

❻ The price level adjusts to 100 to achieve money market equilibrium at the long-run equilibrium interest rate.

situation in which the price level is 100, the demand for money is MD_0, and the nominal interest rate is 5 percent a year.

You will see how this long-run equilibrium comes about by considering what happens if the Fed changes the quantity of money.

A Change in the Quantity of Money

Suppose that the quantity of money is initially \$1 trillion and the Fed then increases it by 2 percent to \$1.02 trillion. In the short run, the greater quantity of money lowers the nominal interest rate. With a lower interest rate, aggregate demand increases and the price level rises. Eventually, a new long-run equilibrium is reached at which the price level has increased in proportion to the increase in the quantity of money.

Because the quantity of money increased by 2 percent from \$1 trillion to \$1.02 trillion, the price level rises by 2 percent from 100 to 102.

Figure 19.6 illustrates these events. Initially, the supply of money curve is MS_0, the demand for money curve is MD_0, the nominal interest rate is at its long-run equilibrium level of 5 percent a year, and the price level that lies behind MD_0 is 100.

The quantity of money then increases and the supply of money curve shifts rightward to MS_1. Initially, the price level remains at 100, so the demand for money curve remains at MD_0. The nominal interest rate falls below its long-run equilibrium level to 4 percent a year. The lower interest rate brings increased spending, which eventually raises the price level to 102. The demand for money increases as the price level rises, and the interest rate rises. Eventually, the economy is back at its long-run equilibrium interest rate but at a higher price level.

You've just seen a key proposition about money and the price level:

In the long run and other things remaining the same, a given percentage change in the quantity of money brings an equal percentage change in the price level.

The Price Level in a Baby-Sitting Club

It is hard to visualize a long-run equilibrium and even harder to visualize and compare two long-run equilibrium situations. So an example of a simpler situation might help.

In an isolated neighborhood, there are no teenagers, but lots of young children and parents can't find any babysitters. So they form a club and sit for each other. The deal is that each time a parent sits for someone else, he or she receives a token that can be used to buy one sit from another member of the club. The organizer notices that the club is inactive. Every member has a few unspent tokens, but they spend them infrequently. To make the club more active, the organizer decides to issue every member one token for each token that is currently held, so the supply of tokens doubles.

FIGURE 19.6
A Change in the Price Level

Practice Online

1. The quantity of money increases by 2 percent from $1 trillion to $1.02 trillion and the supply of money curve shifts from MS_0 to MS_1.
2. In the short run, the interest rate falls to 4 percent a year.
3. In the long run, the price level rises by 2 percent from 100 to 102, the demand for money curve shifts from MD_0 to MD_1, and the nominal interest rate returns to its long-run equilibrium level.

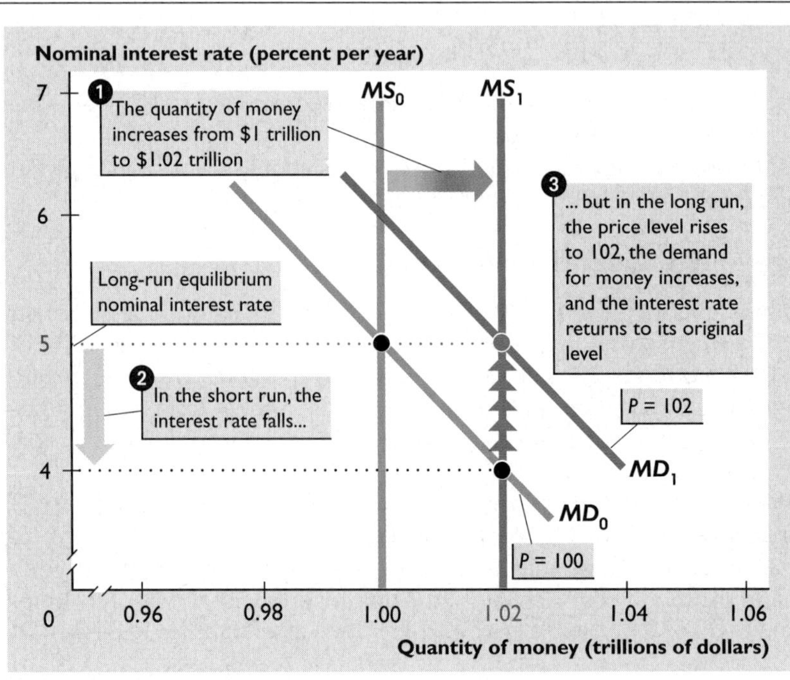

With more tokens to spend, parents start to plan more evenings out. Suddenly, the phones are ringing as parents seek babysitters. Every member of the club wants a sitter. But there are no more sitters than before. After making a few calls and finding no sitters available, anxious parents who really do need a sitter start to offer a higher price: two tokens per session. That does the trick. At the higher price, the quantity of baby-sitting services demanded decreases and the quantity supplied increases. Equilibrium is restored. Nothing real has changed, but the quantity of tokens and the price level have doubled.

Think of the equilibrium quantity of baby-sitting services as potential GDP, the quantity of tokens as the quantity of money, and the price of a baby-sitting session as the price level. You can then see how a given percentage change in the quantity of money at full employment brings an equal percentage change in the price level.

The Quantity Theory of Money

The proposition that when real GDP equals potential GDP, an increase in the quantity of money brings an equal percentage increase in the price level is called the **quantity theory of money**. We've derived this proposition by looking at equilibrium in the money market in the long run. Another way of seeing the relationship between the quantity of money and the price level uses the concepts of *the velocity of circulation* and *the equation of exchange*. We're now going to explore this alternative approach. We're then going to see how ongoing money growth brings inflation and see what determines the inflation rate in the long run.

Quantity theory of money
The proposition that when real GDP equals potential GDP, an increase in the quantity of money brings an equal percentage increase in the price level.

The Velocity of Circulation and Equation of Exchange

The **velocity of circulation** is the number of times in a year that the average dollar of money gets used to buy final goods and services. The value of final goods and services is nominal GDP, which is real GDP, Y, multiplied by the price level, P. If we call the quantity of money M, then the velocity of circulation is determined by the equation:

Velocity of circulation
The number of times in a year that the average dollar of money gets used to buy final goods and services.

$$V = (P \times Y) \div M.$$

In this equation, P is the GDP deflator divided by 100. For example, if the GDP deflator is 125, the price level is 1.25. If the price level is 1.25, real GDP, Y, is \$8 trillion, and the quantity of money, M, is \$2 trillion, then the velocity of circulation is calculated as

$$V = (1.25 \times \$8 \text{ trillion}) \div \$2 \text{ trillion, or}$$

$$V = 5.$$

That is, with \$2 trillion of money, the average dollar gets used 5 times so that \$2 trillion × 5 = \$10 trillion of goods and services are bought.

The **equation of exchange** states that the quantity of money, M, multiplied by the velocity of circulation, V, equals the price level P, multiplied by real GDP, Y. That is,

$$M \times V = P \times Y.$$

Equation of exchange
An equation that states that the quantity of money multiplied by the velocity of circulation equals the price level multiplied by real GDP.

The equation of exchange is *always* true because it is implied by the definition of the velocity of circulation. That is, if you multiply both sides of the equation that defines the velocity of circulation by M, you get the equation of exchange.

Using the above numbers—a price level of 1.25, real GDP, Y, of \$8 trillion, the quantity of money, M, of \$2 trillion, and the velocity of circulation of 5—you can see that

$$M \times V = \$2 \text{ trillion} \times 5 = \$10 \text{ trillion},$$

and

$$P \times Y = 1.25 \times \$8 \text{ trillion} = \$10 \text{ trillion}.$$

So,

$$M \times V = P \times Y = \$10 \text{ trillion}.$$

The Quantity Theory Prediction

We can rearrange the equation of exchange to isolate the price level on the left side. To do so, divide both sides of the equation of exchange by real GDP, Y, to obtain

$$P = M \times V \div Y.$$

On the left side is the price level. And on the right side are all the things that influence the price level. But this equation is still just an implication of the definition of the velocity of circulation. To turn the equation into a theory of what determines the price level, we use two other facts: (1) At full employment, real GDP equals potential GDP, which is determined only by real factors and not by the quantity of money; and (2) the velocity of circulation is relatively stable and does not change when the quantity of money changes.

So if M increases with V and Y constant, P must increase, and by the same percentage that M increased.

We can use the above numbers to illustrate this prediction. Real GDP, Y, is \$8 trillion, the quantity of money, M, is \$2 trillion, and the velocity of circulation, V, is 5. Put these values into the equation:

$$P = M \times V \div Y$$

to obtain

$$P = \$2 \text{ trillion} \times 5 \div \$8 \text{ trillion} = 1.25.$$

Now increase the quantity of money from \$2 trillion to \$2.4 trillion. The percentage increase in the quantity of money is

$$(\$2.4 \text{ trillion} - \$2 \text{ trillion}) \times 100 \div \$2 \text{ trillion} = 20 \text{ percent}.$$

Now find the new price level. It is

$$P = \$2.4 \text{ trillion} \times 5 \div \$8 \text{ trillion} = 1.50.$$

The price level rises from 1.25 to 1.50. The percentage increase in the price level is

$$(1.50 - 1.25) \times 100 \div 1.25 = 20 \text{ percent}.$$

The price level and the quantity of money increase by the same 20 percent.

Inflation and the Quantity Theory of Money

The equation of exchange tells us about the price *level,* the quantity of money, the level of real GDP and the level of the velocity of circulation. We can turn the equation into one that tells us about rates of change or growth rates. We do this because the inflation rate is the rate of change in the price level, and we want to know what determines the inflation rate.

In rates of change or growth rates,

Money growth + Velocity growth = Inflation + Real GDP growth.

For example, in Figure 19.7 in period 1, the quantity of money is growing at a rate of 4 percent a year and velocity is growing at a rate of 1 percent a year. So $M \times V$ is growing at a rate of 5 percent a year. But $M \times V = P \times Y$, so $P \times Y$ is growing at 5 percent a year. Real GDP is growing at 3 percent a year, so the inflation rate is 2 percent a year. That is,

4 percent a year + 1 percent a year = Inflation rate + 3 percent a year,

so,

Inflation rate = 4 percent a year + 1 percent a year – 3 percent a year,

or,

Inflation rate = 2 percent a year.

FIGURE 19.7
Money Growth and Inflation

Practice Online

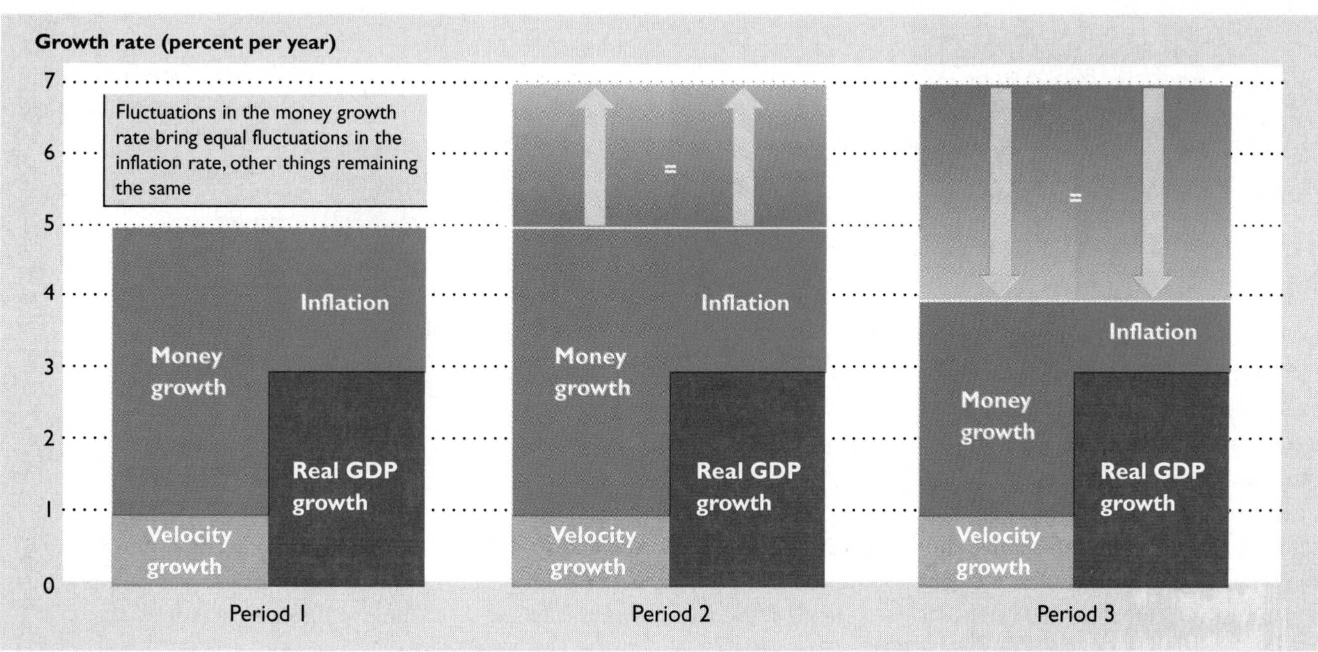

The velocity of circulation grows at 1 percent a year, and real GDP grows at 3 percent a year. In period 1, the quantity of money grows at 4 percent a year and the inflation rate is 2 percent a year. In period 2, money growth increases to 6 percent a year and the inflation rate rises to 4 percent a year. In period 3, money growth slows to 3 percent a year and the inflation rate slows to 1 percent a year.

Changes in the Inflation Rate

Recall two facts that turn the equation of exchange into a theory of what determines the price level: (1) At full employment, real GDP equals potential GDP, which is determined only by real factors and not by the quantity of money; and (2) the velocity of circulation is relatively stable and does not change when the quantity of money changes. In terms of growth rates, potential GDP growth and velocity growth are not influenced by the growth rate of the quantity of money. If the growth rate of the quantity of money changes, velocity growth and real GDP growth remain the same, the inflation rate changes by the same amount as the change in the money growth rate.

Figure 19.7 illustrates both an increase and a decrease in money growth and inflation. In each period, real GDP growth and velocity growth remain constant. In period 2, the money growth rate increases from 4 percent to 6 percent a year and the inflation rate increases from 2 percent to 4 percent a year. In period 3, the money growth rate decreases from 6 percent to 3 percent a year and the inflation rate decreases from 4 percent to 1 percent a year.

In reality, the inflation rate influences velocity and real GDP, so the link between money growth and inflation is not as precise as that shown in Figure 19.7. Velocity increases when the inflation rate speeds up. And faster inflation reduces potential GDP and slows real GDP growth. But these effects are small and are dominated by the main direct effect of money growth on the inflation rate.

Eye on the U.S. Economy

The Quantity Theory of Money in Action

During the 1960s, M2 velocity was constant, real GDP grew at 4.4 percent a year, the quantity of M2 grew at 6.7 percent a year, and the inflation rate was 2.3 percent a year.

During the 1970s, M2 growth climbed, real GDP growth shrank, and the inflation rate increased to 6.6 percent a year. During the 1980s and 1990s, M2 growth slowed and so did inflation. But during the 1990s, an increase in the velocity of circulation of M2 kept the inflation rate higher than it would otherwise have been by almost 2 percent a year.

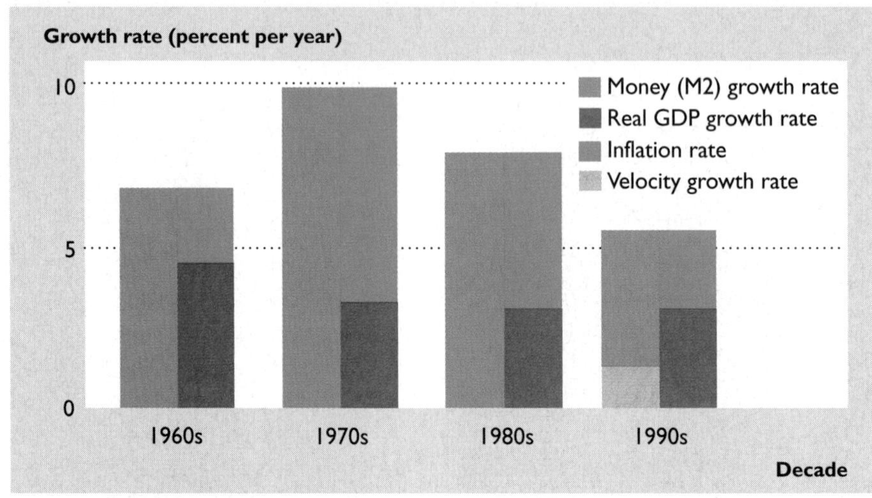

SOURCE: Federal Reserve.

Hyperinflation

When the inflation rate exceeds 50 percent *a month*, the inflation is called **hyperinflation**. Hyperinflation occurs when a government's expenditures exceed the sum of what it can collect in tax revenue and borrow. In such a situation, the government prints money and the quantity of money increases at an extraordinarily rapid rate. This phenomenon is rare but not unknown (see Eye on the Past below). The highest inflation rates in the world today, in the African nations of Angola and Zimbabwe, exceed 100 percent a year but are not considered hyperinflation.

Hyperinflation
Inflation at a rate that exceeds 50 percent *a month*.

Eye on the Past

Hyperinflation in Germany in the 1920s

An international treaty signed in 1919 required Germany to pay large amounts as compensation for war damage to other countries in Europe. To meet its obligations, Germany started to print money. The German money supply increased by 24 percent in 1921, by 220 percent in 1922, and by 43 *billion* percent in 1923!

Not surprisingly, the price level increased rapidly. The figure shows you how rapidly. In November 1923, when the hyperinflation reached its peak, the price level was more than doubling every day. Wages were paid twice a day, and people spent their morning's wages at lunchtime to avoid the loss in the value of money that the afternoon would bring.

In 1923, bank notes were more valuable as fire kindling than as money, and the sight of people burning Reichmarks (the name of Germany's money at that time) was a common one.

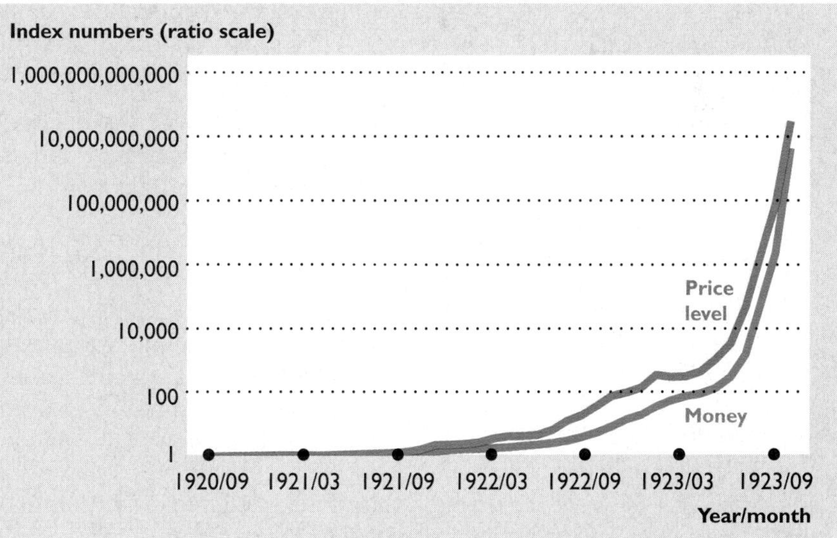

SOURCE: Phillip Cagan, "The Monetary Dynamics of Hyperinflation," in Milton Friedman (editor), *Studies in the Quantity Theory of Money*, University of Chicago Press, 1956.

CHECKPOINT 19.2

Study Guide pp. 285–287

Practice Online 19.2

2 Explain how in the long run, the quantity of money determines the price level and money growth brings inflation.

Practice Problems 19.2

1. In 1999, the Canadian economy was at full employment. Real GDP was $886 billion, the nominal interest rate was around 6 percent per year, the inflation rate was 2 percent a year, the price level was 110, and the velocity of circulation was constant at 10.
   a. Calculate the real interest rate.
   b. If the real interest rate remains unchanged when the inflation rate increases to 4 percent a year, explain how the nominal interest rate changes.
   c. What was the quantity of money in Canada?

2. If the quantity of money grows at a rate of 10 percent a year and potential GDP grows at 3 percent a year, what is the inflation rate in the long run?

Exercises 19.2

1. In 2002, the United Kingdom was at full employment. Nominal GDP was £850 billion, the real interest rate was 5 percent per year, the inflation rate was 6 percent a year, and the price level was 120.
   a. Calculate the nominal interest rate.
   b. If the real interest rate remains unchanged when the inflation rate in the long run decreases to 3 percent a year, explain how the nominal interest rate changes.

2. In 2003, the United Kingdom was at full employment. Nominal GDP was £900 billion, the nominal interest rate was 8 percent per year, the price level was 130, and the velocity of circulation was constant at 2. What was the quantity of money in the United Kingdom?

3. In exercise 2, if the velocity of circulation remains at 2, money grows at 8 percent a year, and real GDP grows at 5 percent a year in the long run, what is the inflation rate in the long run?

Solutions to Practice Problems 19.2

1a. The real interest rate equals the nominal interest rate minus the inflation rate. That is, the real interest rate equals 6 percent a year minus 2 percent a year, which equals 4 percent a year.

1b. The nominal interest rate rises from 6 percent a year to 8 percent a year.

1c. Velocity of circulation (V) = Nominal GDP ($P \times Y$) ÷ Quantity of money (M). Rewrite this equation as: Quantity of money (M) = Nominal GDP ($P \times Y$) ÷ Velocity of circulation (V). Nominal GDP is $886 billion × 110, or $975 billion. Quantity of money is $975 billion ÷ 10, which equals $97.5 billion.

2. With velocity constant, velocity growth is zero. So the inflation rate in the long run equals the money growth rate minus the real GDP growth rate, which is 10 percent a year minus 3 percent a year, or 7 percent a year.

19.3 THE COST OF INFLATION

Inflation decreases potential GDP, slows economic growth, and consumes leisure time. These outcomes occur for four reasons that we classify as the four costs of inflation. They are

- Tax costs
- Shoe-leather costs
- Confusion costs
- Uncertainty costs

Tax Costs

We've seen that inflation occurs when the quantity of money grows more rapidly than real GDP. But why would we ever want to make this happen? Why don't we keep the quantity of money growing at the same pace as real GDP grows? One part of the answer is that the government gets revenue from inflation.

Inflation Is a Tax

Inflation is a tax on holding money. To see how the inflation tax gets paid, suppose that the Coca-Cola Company keeps $100,000 in money on the average. With inflation at 10 percent a year, that money will buy only $90,000 of goods and services after one year. So Coca-Cola loses $10,000 a year—it pays $10,000 a year in inflation tax.

You've seen how Coca-Cola *pays* the inflation tax. But how does the government get *revenue* from it? The answer is by selling government securities that end up being held by the Federal Reserve. When the government issues securities, it must pay interest on them. But paying interest to the Fed costs the government nothing because it owns the Fed and gets the Fed's profits. So when the government issues securities that end up at the Fed, the government gets the value of those securities to spend. But when the Fed buys government securities, the quantity of money grows and money growth brings inflation.

So inflation is a tax. If this were the end of the story, the inflation tax would not be a problem. It would be just one more way for the government to collect revenue—an alternative to the income tax or the sales tax. Inflation would transfer resources from households and businesses to the government, but it would not be a cost to society. Some would pay and others would benefit, and the two actions would cancel each other out.

Inflation Tax, Saving, and Investment

The inflation tax is bigger than the tax on money holding, and it interacts with the income tax to lower saving and investment. The core of the problem is that inflation increases the nominal interest rate, and because income taxes are paid on nominal interest income, the true income tax rate rises with inflation. Let's consider an example.

Suppose that the real interest rate is 4 percent a year and the income tax rate is 50 percent. With no inflation, the nominal interest rate is also 4 percent a year and 50 percent of this rate is taxed. The real after-tax interest rate is 2 percent a year (50 percent of 4 percent). Now suppose the inflation rate is 4 percent a year, so the nominal interest rate is 8 percent a year. The after-tax nominal rate is 4 percent a year (50 percent of 8 percent). Now subtract the 4 percent inflation rate from this amount, and you see that the after-tax real interest rate is zero! The true income tax rate is 100 percent.

The higher the inflation rate, the higher is the true income tax rate on income from capital. And the higher the tax rate, the higher is the interest rate paid by borrowers and the lower is the after-tax interest rate received by lenders.

With a low after-tax real interest rate, the incentive to save is weakened and the supply of saving decreases. With a high cost of borrowing, the amount of investment decreases. And with a fall in saving and investment, the pace of capital accumulation slows and so does the long-term growth rate of real GDP.

Shoe-Leather Costs

The "shoe-leather costs" of inflation are costs that arise from an increase in the velocity of circulation of money and an increase in the amount of running around that people do to try to avoid incurring losses from the falling value of money.

When money loses value at a rapid anticipated rate, it does not function well as a store of value and people try to avoid holding it. They spend their incomes as soon as they receive them, and firms pay out incomes—wages and dividends—as soon as they receive revenue from their sales. The velocity of circulation increases.

During the 1990s, when inflation in Brazil was around 80 percent a year, people would end a taxi ride at the ATM closest to their destination, get some cash, pay the driver, and finish their journey on foot. The driver would deposit the cash in his bank account before looking for the next customer.

During the 1920s when inflation in Germany exceeded 50 percent a month—hyperinflation—wages were paid and spent twice in a single day!

Imagine the inconvenience of spending most of your time figuring out how to keep your money holdings close to zero.

One way of keeping money holdings low is to find other means of payment such as tokens, commodities, or even barter. All of these are less efficient than money as a means of payment. For example, in Israel during the 1980s, when inflation reached 1,000 percent a year, the U.S. dollar started to replace the increasingly worthless shekel. Consequently, people had to keep track of the exchange rate between the shekel and the dollar hour by hour and had to engage in many additional and costly transactions in the foreign exchange market.

Confusion Costs

We make economic decisions by comparing marginal cost and marginal benefit. Marginal cost is a real cost—an opportunity forgone. Marginal benefit is a real benefit—a willingness to forgo an opportunity. Although costs and benefits are real, we use money as our unit of account and standard of value to calculate them. Money is our measuring rod of value. Borrowers and lenders, workers and employers, all make agreements in terms of money. Inflation makes the value of money change, so it changes the units on our measuring rod.

Does it matter that our units of value keep changing? Some economists think it matters a lot. Others think it matters only a little.

Economists who think it matters a lot point to the obvious benefits of stable units of measurement in other areas of life. For example, suppose that we had not invented an accurate time-keeping technology and clocks and watches gained 5 to 15 minutes a day. Imagine the hassle you would have arriving at class on time or catching the start of the ball game. For another example, suppose that a tailor used an elastic tape measure. You would end up with a jacket that was either too tight or too sloppy, depending on how tightly the tape was stretched.

For a third example, recall the crash of the Mars Climate Orbiter.

> "Mars Climate Orbiter . . . failed to achieve Mars orbit because of a navigation error. . . . Spacecraft operating data needed for navigation were provided . . . in English units rather than the specified metric units. This was the direct cause of the failure." (Mars Program Independent Assessment Team Summary Report, March 14, 2000)

If rocket scientists can't make correct calculations that use just two units of measurement, what chance do ordinary people and business decision makers have of making correct calculations that involve money when its value keeps changing?

These examples of confusion and error that can arise from units of measurement don't automatically mean that a changing value of money is a big problem. But they raise the possibility that it might be.

Uncertainty Costs

A high inflation rate brings increased uncertainty about the long-term inflation rate. Will inflation remain high for a long time or will price stability be restored? This increased uncertainty makes long-term planning difficult and gives people a shorter-term focus. Investment falls, and so the growth rate slows.

But this increased uncertainty also misallocates resources. Instead of concentrating on the activities at which they have a comparative advantage, people find it more profitable to search for ways of avoiding the losses that inflation inflicts. As a result, inventive talent that might otherwise work on productive innovations works on finding ways of profiting from the inflation instead.

Uncertainty about inflation makes the economy behave a bit like a casino in which some people gain and some lose and no one can predict where the gains and losses will fall. Gains and losses occur because of unpredictable changes in the value of money. In a period of rapid, unpredictable inflation, resources get diverted from productive activities to forecasting inflation. It becomes more profitable to forecast the inflation rate correctly than to invent a new product. Doctors, lawyers, accountants, farmers—just about everyone—can make themselves better off, not by specializing in the profession for which they have been trained but by spending more of their time dabbling as amateur economists and inflation forecasters and managing their investment portfolios.

From a social perspective, this diversion of talent resulting from inflation is like throwing scarce resources onto the garbage heap. This waste of resources is a cost of inflation.

How Big Is the Cost of Inflation?

The cost of inflation depends on its rate and its predictability. The higher the rate, the greater is the cost. And the more unpredictable the rate, the greater is the cost. Peter Howitt of Brown University, building on work by Robert Barro of Harvard University, has estimated that if inflation is lowered from 3 percent a year to zero, the growth rate of real GDP will rise by between 0.06 and 0.09 percentage points a year. These numbers might seem small. But they are growth rates. After 30 years, real GDP would be 2.3 percent higher and the accumulated value of all the additional future output would be worth 85 percent of current GDP, or $8.5 trillion!

In hyperinflation, the costs are much greater. Hyperinflation is rare, but there have been some spectacular examples of it. Several European countries experienced hyperinflation during the 1920s after World War I and again during the 1940s after World War II. But hyperinflation is more than just a historical curiosity. It occurs in today's world. In 1994, the African nation of Zaire had a hyperinflation that peaked at a monthly inflation rate of 76 percent. Also in 1994, Brazil almost reached the hyperinflation stratosphere with a monthly inflation rate of 40 percent. A cup of coffee that cost 15 cruzeiros in 1980 cost 22 billion cruzeiros in 1994. And Russia has had a near hyperinflation experience in recent years.

CHECKPOINT 19.3

Study Guide pp. 288–290

Practice Online 19.3

Identify the costs of inflation and the benefits of a stable value of money.

Practice Problem 19.3

Suppose that you have $1,000 in your savings account and the bank pays an interest rate of 5 percent a year. The inflation rate is 3 percent a year. The government taxes the interest that you earn on your deposit at 20 percent.

a. Calculate the nominal after-tax interest rate that you earn.

b. Calculate the real after-tax interest rate that you earn.

Exercise 19.3

Sally has a credit card balance of $4,000. The credit card charges a nominal interest rate of 18 percent a year on unpaid balances. The inflation rate is 3 percent a year.

a. Calculate the real interest rate that Sally pays the credit card company.

b. If the inflation rate falls to 2 percent a year and the credit card company keeps the nominal interest rate at 18 percent a year, calculate the real interest rate that Sally pays.

Solution to Practice Problem 19.3

a. You earn $50 of interest and the government takes $10 of the interest in tax, so the interest income you earn after tax is $40. The nominal after-tax interest rate is 4 percent a year.

b. The real after-tax interest rate equals the nominal after-tax interest rate minus the inflation rate, which is 1 percent a year.

CHAPTER CHECKPOINT

Key Points

1 Explain what determines the demand for money and how the demand for money and the supply of money determine the *nominal* interest rate.

- The demand for money is the relationship between the quantity of money demanded and the nominal interest rate, other things remaining the same—the higher the nominal interest rate, other things remaining the same, the smaller is the quantity of money demanded.
- Increases in real GDP increase the demand for money. Some advances in financial technology increase the demand for money, and some advances decrease it.
- Each day, the price level, real GDP, and financial technology are given and money market equilibrium determines the nominal interest rate.
- To lower the interest rate, the Fed increases the supply of money. To raise the interest rate, the Fed decreases the supply of money.

2 Explain how in the long run, the quantity of money determines the price level and money growth brings inflation.

- In the long run, real GDP equals potential GDP and the real interest rate is the level that makes the quantity of investment demanded equal the quantity of saving supplied in the global financial market.
- The nominal interest rate in the long run equals the equilibrium real interest rate plus the inflation rate.
- Money market equilibrium in the long run determines the price level.
- An increase in the quantity of money, other things remaining the same, increases the price level by the same percentage.
- The inflation rate in the long run equals the growth rate of the quantity of money minus the growth rate of potential GDP.
- The equation of exchange and the velocity of circulation provide an alternative way of viewing the relationship between the quantity of money and the price level (and money growth and inflation).

3 Identify the costs of inflation and the benefits of a stable value of money.

- Inflation has four costs: tax costs, shoe-leather costs, confusion costs, and uncertainty costs.
- The higher the inflation rate, the greater are these four costs.

Key Terms

Demand for money, 480
Equation of exchange, 491
Hyperinflation, 495
Quantity of money demanded, 479
Quantity theory of money, 491
Supply of money, 483
Velocity of circulation, 491

Exercises

1. Review the factors that influence the quantity of money that people plan to hold and
   a. Draw a graph to illustrate the demand for money curve.
   b. Show the new demand for money curve that results from an increase in real GDP.
   c. Illustrate on your graph the effects of a change in the interest rate.
   d. Show the effects of an increase in the number of families that have a credit card.
   e. Explain how the spread of ATMs has influenced the demand for money.

2. The Fed decreases the quantity of money. Explain the effects of this action in the short run and the long run on
   a. The quantity of money demanded.
   b. The nominal interest rate.
   c. The real interest rate.
   d. Real GDP.
   e. The price level.

3. The Fed conducts an open market purchase of securities. [Hint: Check back with Chapter 18 if you need a reminder about the effects of an open market operation.] Explain the effects of this action in the short run and the long run on
   a. The quantity of money.
   b. The quantity of money demanded.
   c. The nominal interest rate.
   d. The real interest rate.
   e. Real GDP.
   f. The price level.

4. In 2000, the United States was at full employment. The quantity of money was growing at 8.3 percent a year, the nominal interest rate was 9.5 percent a year, real GDP grew at 5 percent a year, and the inflation rate was 3.1 percent a year.
   a. Calculate the real interest rate.
   b. Use the information given along with the quantity theory of money to see whether the velocity of circulation was constant. If it was not constant, how did it change? And if it changed, why might it have changed?

5. Suppose the government passes a new law that sets a limit on the interest rate that credit card companies can charge on overdue balances. As a result, the nominal interest rate charged by credit card companies falls from 15 percent a year to 7 percent a year. If the average income tax rate is 30 percent, explain how the real after-tax interest rate on overdue credit card balances changes.

6. Draw a graph of the money market to illustrate equilibrium in both the short run and the long run.
   a. Explain what happens to the real interest rate and the nominal interest rate in the short run.
   b. Explain what happens to the real interest rate and the nominal interest rate in the long run.
   c. Explain why the short-run effects are different from the long-run effects.

7. What is the quantity theory of money?

8. Define the velocity of circulation and explain how is it measured.

9. If the quantity of money is $3 trillion, real GDP is $10 trillion, the price level is 0.9, the real interest rate is 2 percent a year, and the nominal interest rate is 7 percent a year,
   a. What is the velocity of circulation?
   b. What is value of $M \times V$?
   c. What is the value of nominal GDP?

10. If the velocity of circulation is constant, real GDP is growing at 3 percent a year, the real interest rate is 2 percent a year, and the nominal interest rate is 7 percent a year,
    a. What is the inflation rate?
    b. What is the growth rate of money?
    c. What is the growth rate of nominal GDP?

11. If the velocity of circulation is growing at a rate of 1 percent a year, the real interest rate is 2 percent a year, the nominal interest rate is 7 percent a year, and the growth rate of real GDP is 3 percent a year,
    a. What is the inflation rate?
    b. What is the growth rate of money?
    c. What is the growth rate of nominal GDP?

12. List the costs of inflation and provide an example of each type of cost.

13. Explain what the costs of inflation were for Brazilians when inflation hit 40 percent a month in Brazil.

14. Explain why businesses paid workers twice a day during the hyperinflation in Germany after World War II and why workers spent their incomes as soon as they were paid.

Critical Thinking

15. With the spread of credit cards, debit cards, and e-cash, people will want to hold less and less money. Eventually, no one will want to hold any money and the Federal Reserve will have no role. Critically evaluate this view.

16. The Federal Reserve could easily eliminate inflation by making the quantity of money grow at a rate equal to the growth rate of real GDP minus the growth rate of the velocity of circulation. Do you think the Fed should pursue this objective? Explain why or why not.

17. The Federal Reserve could peg the interest rate by making the quantity of money adjust to match the quantity of money demanded at the chosen interest rate. Do you think the Fed should pursue this objective? Explain why or why not.

18. Do you think the Federal Reserve could simultaneously pursue a fixed interest rate and a money growth rate equal to the growth rate of real GDP minus the growth rate of the velocity of circulation? Explain why or why not.

Practice Online

Web Exercises

Use the links on your Foundations Web site to work the following exercises.

19. Visit the Web sites of the Federal Reserve and the Bureau of Economic Analysis and obtain the latest data on the quantity of M1 and M2, real GDP, and the price level.
    - **a.** Calculate the inflation rate, the growth rate of the two money aggregates, and the growth rate of real GDP.
    - **b.** Use the information you calculated in part **a** to determine whether the velocity of circulation was constant. If it was not constant, how did it change? If it changed, why might it have changed?
    - **c.** Given the information that you obtained in part **a**, do you think the Fed is trying to slow inflation, speed up inflation, or neither? If neither, what do you think the Fed is trying to do?

20. Visit the European Central Bank Web site.
    - **a.** Obtain data on money supply growth rates and inflation rates for the euro area.
    - **b.** Is the money supply in the euro area growing faster or slower than in the United States?
    - **c.** Would you expect inflation in the euro area to be higher, lower, or about the same as in the United States? Explain why.

21. Visit the International Monetary Fund's World Economic Outlook database Web site.
    - **a.** Obtain data on money supply growth rates and inflation rates for Advanced Economies and the Developing Economies.
    - **b.** Use a spreadsheet program (Excel or Lotus 1-2-3) to make a scatter diagram of the data placing money growth on the x-axis and inflation on the y-axis.
    - **c.** Do these data support or contradict the quantity theory of money?

CHAPTER 20

AS-AD and the Business Cycle

CHAPTER CHECKLIST

When you have completed your study of this chapter, you will be able to

1. **Provide a technical definition of recession and describe the history of the U.S. business cycle.**
2. **Explain the influences on aggregate supply.**
3. **Explain the influences on aggregate demand.**
4. **Explain how aggregate supply and aggregate demand determine real GDP and the price level.**
5. **Explain how fluctuations in aggregate supply and aggregate demand create the business cycle.**

From 1991 to 2001, our economy expanded. Then, in 2001, we had a recession. In 2002, a new expansion was under way, but people wondered whether it would persist or whether another "double-dip" recession was imminent.

In this chapter, we're going to study the aggregate supply–aggregate demand, or *AS-AD*, model which explains the business cycle—the recessions and expansions that alternate through our economic history.

The *AS-AD* model also provides a tool for studying policies to stabilize the business cycle. We study these policy actions in the next chapter. We begin with some definitions and a bit of business-cycle history.

20.1 BUSINESS-CYCLE DEFINITIONS AND FACTS

We defined the *business cycle* in Chapter 1 (p. 6) as a periodic but irregular up-and-down movement in production and jobs. A business cycle has two phases, expansion and recession, and two turning points, a peak and a trough. An expansion runs from a trough to a peak, and a recession runs from a peak to a trough.

Over the business cycle, real GDP fluctuates around trend. When real GDP is below trend, resources are *under*used—some labor is unemployed and capital is underemployed. When real GDP is above trend, resources are *over*used—people work longer hours than they are willing to put up with in the long run, capital is worked so intensively that it is not maintained in prime condition, delivery times lengthen, bottlenecks occur, and backorders increase.

Dating Business-Cycle Turning Points

The task of identifying and dating business-cycle phases and turning points is performed not by the U.S. government, but by a private research organization, the National Bureau of Economic Research (NBER). The NBER's Business Cycle Dating Committee meets after an obvious turning point and determines the exact month in which it occurred. The committee declared in November 2001 that a business-cycle peak occurred in March 2001. In November 2002, the committee reported that it was too early to say whether a trough had occurred.

To date the business-cycle turning points, the NBER needs a definition of recession. A standard definition of **recession** is a decrease in real GDP that lasts for at least two quarters (six months). The NBER uses a broader definition. It defines a recession as "a period of significant decline in total output, income, employment, and trade, usually lasting from six months to a year, and marked by widespread contractions in many sectors of the economy."

Recession
A decrease in real GDP that lasts for at least two quarters (six months) or a period of significant decline in total output, income, employment, and trade, usually lasting from six months to a year, and marked by widespread contractions in many sectors of the economy.

In this definition of recession, total output and income are the same thing as real GDP. You've seen that employment fluctuations closely match fluctuations in real GDP. Because real GDP measures production in all sectors of the economy, a decrease in real GDP means that many sectors of the economy are experiencing falling production. So although the NBER looks beyond real GDP to date the turning points precisely, a two-quarter decrease in real GDP is a good practical indicator of recession and gives almost the same dating as the more refined method of the NBER.

U.S. Business-Cycle History

The NBER has identified 32 complete cycles starting from a trough in December 1854. (In 2001, we entered the 33rd recession.) Over all 32 complete cycles, the average length of an expansion is 35 months (almost 3 years), the average length of a recession is 18 months, and the average time from trough to trough is 53 months (almost 4½ years). So over the 147 years since 1854, the U.S. economy has been in recession for about one third of the time and in expansion for about two thirds of the time.

The 147-year averages that we've just reviewed hide significant changes that have occurred in the length of a cycle and the relative length of the recession and expansion phases. Figure 20.1 shows these changes by dividing U.S. business-cycle history into three periods: 1854–1919 (before and during World War I);

FIGURE 20.1

Recession, Expansion, and Cycle Length: A Summary

Practice Online

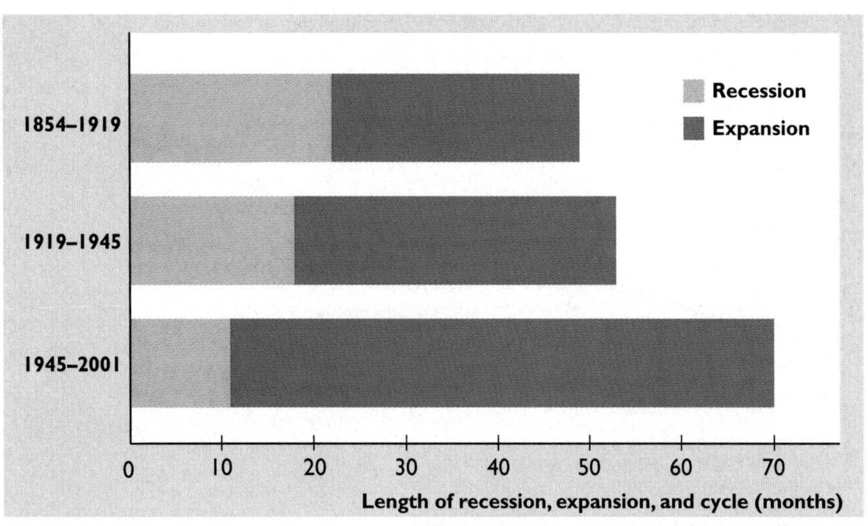

SOURCE: National Bureau of Economic Research.

During the nineteenth century and through World War I, recessions were almost as long as expansions. During the twentieth century, recessions have shortened, expansions have lengthened, and complete cycles have lengthened.

1919–1945 (between the two World Wars and through World War II); and 1945–2001 (the post–World War II years).

The figure shows that before 1919, recessions lasted for 22 months and expansions for 27 months on the average. So during this period, recession was almost as common an experience as expansion.

During the years between the wars and through World War II, the average recession shortened to 18 months and the average expansion lengthened to 35 months. (It is a coincidence that these durations are the same as the overall averages for the entire period since 1854.) One recession during this period, the Great Depression, was enormous and lasted for 43 months.

During the years since World War II, the average recession has shortened to 11 months and the average expansion has lengthened to 59 months (almost 5 years). The longest ever expansion is the one that began in March 1991 and ended in March 2001.

Recent Cycles

The current cycle began at a trough that followed a recession that ran from July 1990 to March 1991. The economy expanded from March 1991 until March 2001, an expansion that lasted for 120 months and was the longest in U.S. history. The previous record expansion was 106 months and ran from February 1961 to December 1969. The next longest expansion was 92 months and ran from November 1982 to July 1990.

Figure 20.2 shows three features of the recent cycles: real GDP fluctuations around potential GDP, the unemployment rate, and the inflation rate. The dates in the three parts of the figure are aligned above each other so that you can see the relationship between the three variables. The two most recent recessions are highlighted in all three parts.

FIGURE 20.2
The Current Cycle

Practice Online

The last two recessions (highlighted in all three parts) began in mid-1990 and the first quarter of 2001. The expansion that followed the 1990–1991 recession was the longest in U.S. history. When real GDP decreases in a recession (part a), the unemployment rate increases (part b), and a little later, the inflation rate decreases (part c). As real GDP increases toward potential GDP, the unemployment rate falls toward the natural rate and the inflation rate falls.

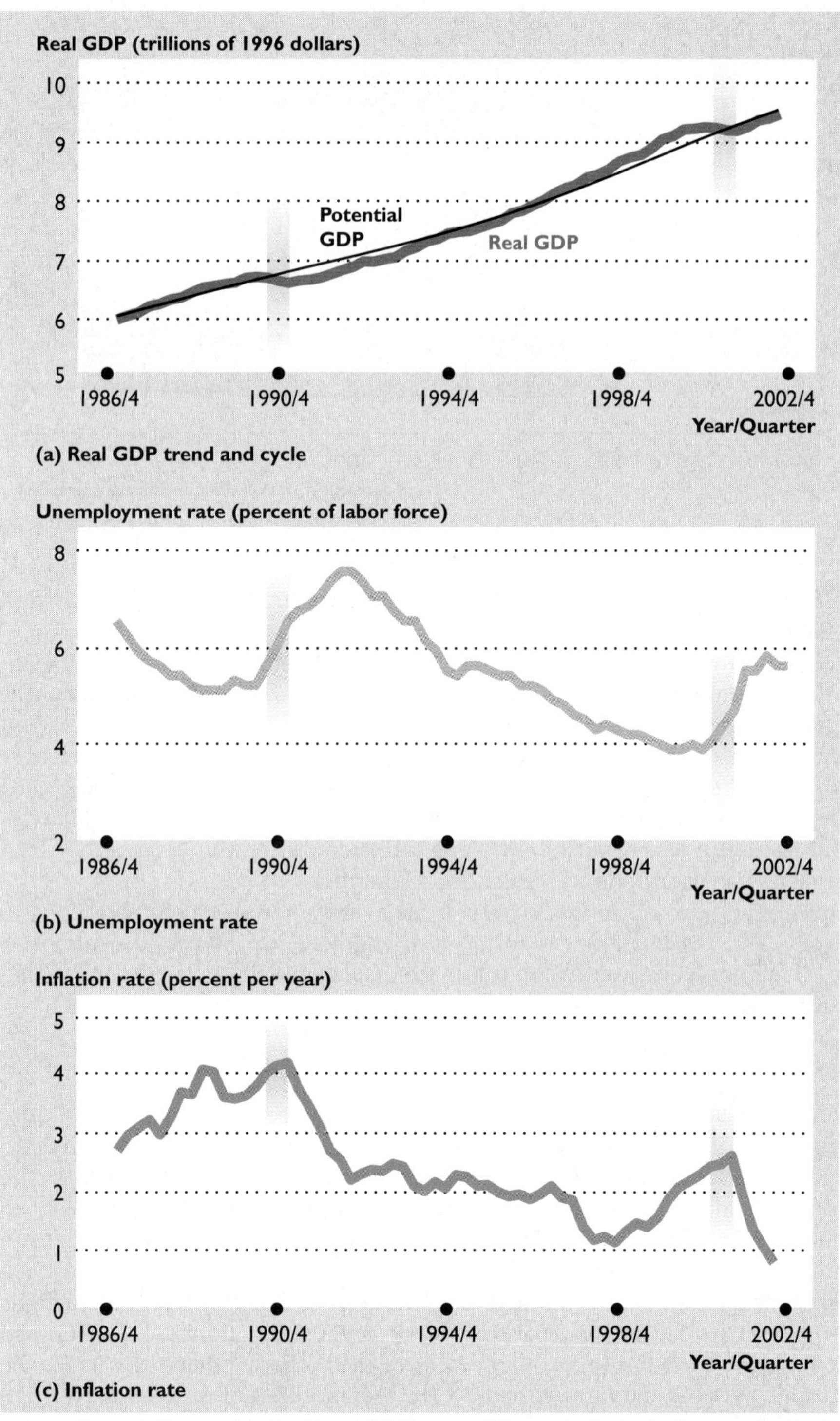

SOURCES: *Economic Report of the President*, 2001. Bureau of Economic Analysis, Congressional Budget Office, and Bureau of Labor Statistics.

In part (a), you can see that real GDP fell from a peak in mid-1990 to a trough in the first quarter of 1991, and it fell from a peak at the end of 2000 to a trough in the third quarter of 2001. In a recession, real GDP moves from above to below potential GDP. From the trough, real GDP begins its long expansion. In the expansion of the 1990s, real GDP reached potential GDP in 1998 and then moved above potential.

In part (b), you can see that the unemployment rate increased during the recession. It kept increasing after the recession was over but then began a long and steady decline. At its peak, the unemployment rate exceeded the natural rate. The natural unemployment rate decreased during the 1990s, but at its lowest level, in 2000, the unemployment rate was below the natural rate.

In part (c), the inflation rate reached a peak during the 1990 recession and then fell steadily until 1998. It then began to increase as real GDP moved above potential GDP. So the business cycle is not confined to the real economy. The money economy cycles alongside the real economy. The inflation rate decreases when real GDP is below potential GDP and increases when real GDP is above potential GDP.

CHECKPOINT 20.1

1 Provide a technical definition of recession and describe the history of the U.S. business cycle.

Study Guide pp. 296–298

Practice Online 20.1

Practice Problem 20.1

Table 1 shows real GDP in Canada from the first quarter of 1989 to the fourth quarter of 1993.

a. In which quarter was Canada at a business-cycle peak?
b. In which quarter was Canada at a business-cycle trough?
c. Did Canada experience a recession during these years?
d. In what periods did Canada experience an expansion?

TABLE 1

Billions of 1996 dollars

Year	Quarter 1	2	3	4
1989	700	703	705	706
1990	711	709	705	698
1991	689	691	694	696
1992	696	697	699	702
1993	708	712	716	722

Exercise 20.1

Table 2 shows real GDP in Mexico from the first quarter of 1994 to the last quarter of 1996.

a. In which quarters was Mexico at a business-cycle peak?
b. In which quarters was Mexico at a business-cycle trough?
c. Did Mexico experience a recession during these years?
d. In what years did Mexico experience an expansion?

TABLE 2

Trillions of 1993 pesos

Year	Quarter 1	2	3	4
1994	1.25	1.19	1.29	1.27
1995	1.21	1.16	1.28	1.27
1996	1.27	1.29	1.25	1.37

Solution to Practice Problem 20.1

a. Canada was at a business-cycle peak in the first quarter of 1990.
b. Canada was at a business-cycle trough in the first quarter of 1991.
c. The recession ran from the first quarter of 1990 to the first quarter of 1991.
d. Expansions ran from the first quarter of 1989 to the first quarter of 1990 and from the first quarter of 1991 to the fourth quarter of 1993.

20.2 AGGREGATE SUPPLY

Aggregate supply
The relationship between the quantity of real GDP supplied and the price level when all other influences on firms' production plans remain the same.

Aggregate supply is the relationship between the quantity of real GDP supplied and the price level when all other influences on firms' production plans remain the same. Other things remaining the same, the higher the price level, the greater is the quantity of real GDP supplied and the lower the price level, the smaller is the quantity of real GDP supplied.

To learn about aggregate supply, we'll begin by reviewing the fundamental real factors that determine the economy's capacity to produce goods and services. We'll go on to explore the link between aggregate supply and potential GDP and explain why a change in the price level induces a change in the quantity of real GDP supplied. Finally, we'll study the factors that make aggregate supply change.

Aggregate Supply Basics

The *quantity of real GDP supplied* (*Y*), depends on

- The quantity of labor employed
- The quantities of capital and human capital and the technologies they embody
- The quantities of land and natural resources used
- The amount of entrepreneurial talent available

At full employment, the real wage rate makes the quantity of labor demanded equal the quantity of labor supplied, and the quantity of real GDP supplied equals potential GDP. Over the business cycle, the quantity of real GDP supplied fluctuates around potential GDP and the quantity of labor employed fluctuates. The quantities of capital and human capital grow, technology advances, and the amount of entrepreneurial talent increases as the population increases. These changes are the sources of economic growth, but they occur gradually and do not fluctuate much over the business cycle.

Aggregate Supply and Potential GDP

Figure 20.3 shows an aggregate supply curve, *AS*, and a potential GDP line. Along the aggregate supply curve, the only influence on production plans that changes is the price level. A rise in the price level brings an increase in the quantity of real GDP supplied and a movement up along the aggregate supply curve; a fall in the price level brings a decrease in the quantity of real GDP supplied and a movement down along the aggregate supply curve. All the other influences on production plans remain constant. Among these other influences are

- The money wage rate
- The money prices of other resources

In contrast, along the potential GDP line, when the price level changes, the money wage rate and the money prices of other resources change by the same percentage as the change in the price level to keep the real wage rate (and other real prices) at the full-employment equilibrium level.

FIGURE 20.3
A Change in the Quantity of Real GDP Supplied

Practice Online

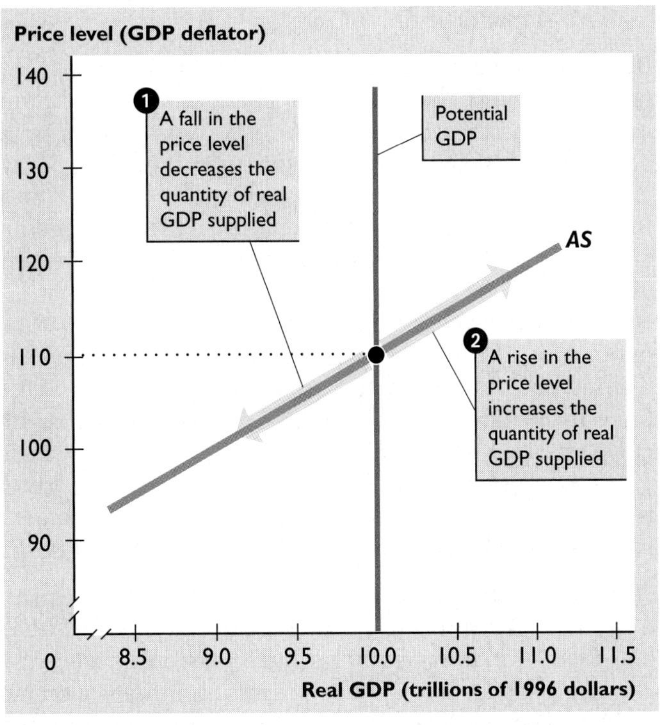

The aggregate supply (*AS*) curve shows the relationship between the quantity of real GDP supplied and the price level when the money wage rate, other resource prices, and potential output remain the same. The quantity of real GDP supplied ❶ decreases when the price level falls and ❷ increases when the price level rises.

Why the *AS* Curve Slopes Upward

Why does the quantity of real GDP supplied increase when the price level rises and decrease when the price level falls? The answer is that a movement along the *AS* curve brings a change in the real wage rate (and changes in the real cost of other resources whose money prices are fixed). If the price level rises, the real wage rate falls, and if the price level falls, the real wage rate rises.

Think about a concrete example. Suppose Microsoft has a contract with its programmers to pay them $200 an hour. Microsoft sells copies of Windows to computer makers (such as Dell Computer Corporation) for $100 a copy. The real wage rate of a programmer is 2 copies of Windows. That is, Microsoft must sell 2 copies of Windows to buy one hour of programming labor. Now suppose the price of a copy of Windows falls to $50. The real wage rate of a programmer has increased to 4 copies of Windows—Microsoft must now sell 4 copies of the program to buy one hour of programming labor.

If the price of a copy of Windows increased, the real wage rate of a programmer would fall. For example, if the price increased to $200 a copy, the real wage rate would be one copy of Windows—Microsoft would need to sell only one copy of the software to buy one hour of programmer time.

A change in the real wage rate means that the cost of labor changes relative to the revenue that an hour of labor can produce, and it changes a firm's profit. A rise in the real wage rate cuts into a firm's profit, and a fall in the real wage rate boosts a firm's profit. Firms respond to a change in the real wage rate and their profit in one of three possible ways:

- Go out of business or start up in business.
- Shut down temporarily or restart production.
- Change their output rate.

Business Failure and Startup New businesses are born and some existing businesses die every day. Real GDP changes when the number of firms in business changes. And the price level influences this number in the short run.

People create businesses in the hope of earning a profit. When profits are generally high, more firms start up and fewer existing firms fail. So the number of firms in business increases. When profits are squeezed or when losses arise, fewer new firms start up and more existing firms fail. So the number of firms in business decreases.

The price level relative to wage and other costs influences the number of firms in business. If the price level rises relative to costs, profits increase, the number of firms in business increases, and the quantity of real GDP supplied increases. If the price level falls relative to costs, profits fall, the number of firms in business decreases, and the quantity of real GDP supplied decreases.

In a severe recession, business failure can be contagious. The failure of one firm puts pressure on both its suppliers and its customers and can bring a flood of failures and a large decrease in the quantity of real GDP supplied.

Temporary Shutdowns and Restarts A firm that is incurring a loss might foresee a profit in the future. So rather than going out of business, such a firm might decide to shut down temporarily and lay off its workers.

The price level relative to costs is an influence on temporary shutdown decisions. If the price level rises relative to costs, fewer firms will decide to shut down temporarily; so more firms operate and the quantity of real GDP supplied increases. If the price level falls relative to costs, a larger number of firms find that they cannot earn enough to pay the wage bill and so temporarily shut down. The quantity of real GDP supplied decreases.

Changes in Output Rate The price level relative to costs influences even those firms that remain profitable and keep producing. You know that to produce more output, a firm must hire more labor. It is profitable to hire more labor if the additional labor brings in more revenue than it costs. If the price level rises and the money wage rate doesn't change, an extra hour of labor that was previously unprofitable becomes profitable. So when the price level rises and the money wage rate doesn't change, the quantity of labor demanded increases and production increases. For the economy as a whole, the quantity of real GDP supplied increases.

Production at a Pepsi Plant

A Pepsi bottling plant produces the quantity of Pepsi that maximizes profit. The production plant is fixed, but Pepsi can increase production by hiring more labor and working the plant harder. But each additional hour of labor hired produces fewer additional bottles of Pepsi than the previous hour produces. So Pepsi increases the quantity of labor hired and increases production only if the real wage rate falls. But if the price of Pepsi rises and wage rates and other costs don't change, the real wage rate *does* fall. Similarly, if the price of Pepsi falls and wage rates and other costs don't change, the real wage rate *rises*. In this situation, Pepsi decreases the quantity of labor demanded and decreases production.

What is true for Pepsi bottlers is true for the producers of all goods and services. So when the price level rises and the money wage rate and other resource prices remain constant, the quantity of labor demanded increases and the quantity of real GDP supplied increases.

Changes in Aggregate Supply

You saw in Figure 20.3 that a change in the price level changes the quantity of real GDP supplied and brings a movement along the aggregate supply curve. But it does not change aggregate supply.

Aggregate supply changes when any influence on production plans other than the price level changes. In particular, aggregate supply changes when

- Potential GDP changes.
- The money wage rate changes.
- The money prices of other resources change.

Changes in Potential GDP

Anything that changes potential GDP—real GDP at full employment—changes aggregate supply and shifts the aggregate supply curve. Figure 20.4 shows these changes. You can think of point *C* as an anchor point. The *AS* curve and potential GDP line are anchored at this point, and when potential GDP changes, *AS* changes along with it. Point *C* shifts to point *C'*, and the aggregate supply curve and potential GDP line shift rightward together. When potential GDP increases from $10 trillion to $11 trillion, the *AS* curve shifts from AS_0 to AS_1.

FIGURE 20.4
An Increase in Potential GDP

Practice Online

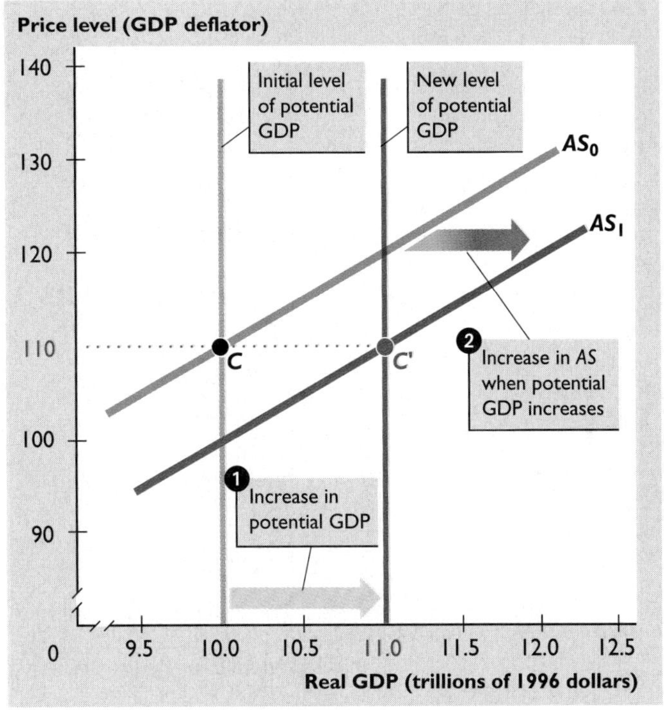

1 An increase in potential GDP increases aggregate supply. 2 The aggregate supply curve shifts rightward from AS_0 to AS_1.

Changes in Money Wage Rate and Other Resource Prices

A change in the money wage rate or in the money price of another resource changes aggregate supply because it changes firms' costs. The higher the money wage rate or the price of another resource, the higher are firms' costs and the smaller is the quantity that firms are willing to supply at each price level. So an increase in the money wage rate or the price of another resource decreases aggregate supply.

Suppose that the money wage rate is \$33 an hour and the price level is 110. Then the real wage rate is \$30 an hour (\$33 × 100 ÷ 110 = \$30). If the full-employment equilibrium real wage rate is \$30 an hour, the economy is at full employment and real GDP equals potential GDP. In Figure 20.5, the economy is at point *C* on the aggregate supply curve AS_0. The money wage rate is \$33 an hour at all points on AS_0.

Now suppose the money wage rate rises to \$36 an hour but the full-employment equilibrium real wage rate remains at \$30 an hour. Real GDP now equals potential GDP when the price level is 120, at point *D* on the aggregate supply curve AS_2. (If the money wage rate is \$36 an hour and the price level is 120, the real wage rate is \$36 × 100 ÷ 120 = \$30 an hour.) The money wage rate is \$36 an hour at all points on AS_2. The rise in the money wage rate *decreases* aggregate supply and shifts the aggregate supply curve leftward from AS_0 to AS_2.

A change in the money wage rate does not change potential GDP. The reason is that potential GDP depends only on the economy's real ability to produce and on the full-employment quantity of labor, which occurs at the equilibrium *real* wage rate. The equilibrium real wage rate can occur at any money wage rate.

FIGURE 20.5
A Change in the Money Wage Rate

Practice Online

A rise in the money wage rate decreases aggregate supply. The aggregate supply curve shifts leftward from AS_0 to AS_2. A rise in the money wage rate does not change potential GDP.

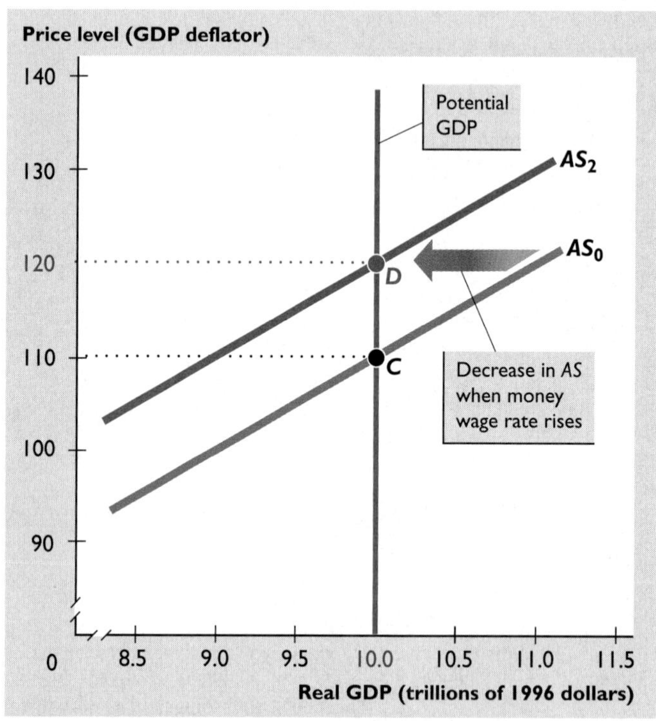

CHECKPOINT 20.2

2 Explain the influences on aggregate supply.

Study Guide pp. 298–301

Practice Online 20.2

Practice Problem 20.2

In May 2000, armed men took over the Parliament in Fiji and held the Prime Minister and other people as hostages. This action led to many other events. Explain the effect of each of the following events on Fiji's aggregate supply.

a. Downtown Suva (the capital of Fiji) was heavily looted and businesses were destroyed.
b. Dock workers in Australia refused to handle cargo to and from Fiji, including raw material going to Fiji's garment industry.
c. The number of tourists fell and many hotels closed.
d. As unemployment increased, the workweek was shortened.
e. The fresh tuna industry boomed with increased sales to Japan and the United States.
f. With widespread shortages, suppose that the unionized workers demanded higher wages and got them.

Exercise 20.2

Many events have followed the ending of apartheid in South Africa. Explain the effect of each of the following events on South Africa's aggregate supply.

a. Businesses around the world have established branches in South Africa.
b. More South Africans have access to education.
c. Trade sanctions ended.
d. Unemployment decreased.
e. Tourism increased and many new hotels were built.
f. AIDS became more prevalent.

Solution to Practice Problem 20.2

a. As businesses closed, real GDP supplied at the current price level decreased. The *AS* curve shifted leftward (Figure 1).
b. As Fiji's garment industry ran out of raw materials, production in the garment industry decreased and the quantity of real GDP supplied at the current price level decreased. The *AS* curve shifted leftward (Figure 1).
c. As many hotels closed, the quantity of tourist services supplied decreased and the quantity of real GDP supplied at the current price level decreased. The *AS* curve shifted leftward (Figure 1).
d. As employers cut the workweek and shared jobs among workers, production decreased and the *AS* curve shifted leftward (Figure 1).
e. As the tuna industry continued to expand, production increased. In isolation, its effect shifted the *AS* curve rightward (Figure 2).
f. As the wage rate increased, businesses that became unprofitable closed and real GDP produced at the current price level decreased. The *AS* curve shifted leftward (Figure 2).

FIGURE 1

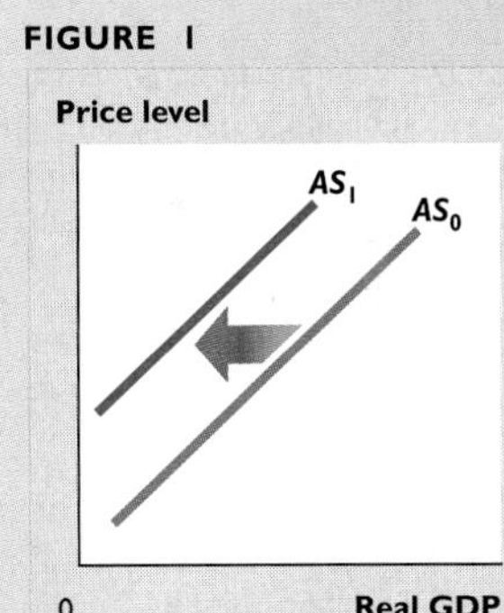

FIGURE 2

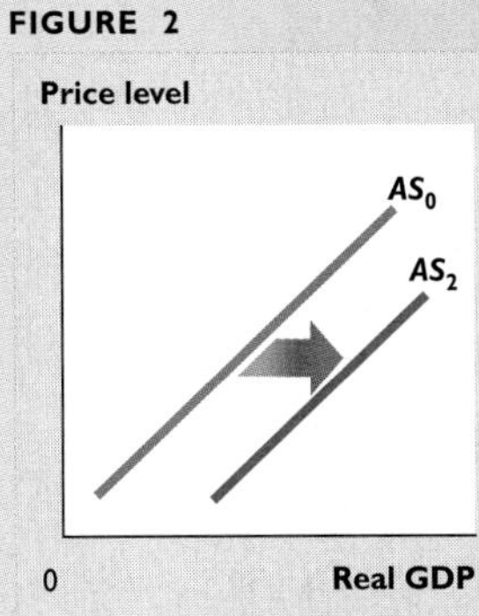

20.3 AGGREGATE DEMAND

Aggregate demand
The relationship between the quantity of real GDP demanded and the price level when all other influences on expenditure plans remain the same.

Aggregate demand is the relationship between the quantity of real GDP demanded and the price level when all other influences on expenditure plans remain the same: The higher the price level, the smaller is the quantity of real GDP demanded, and the lower the price level, the greater is the quantity of real GDP demanded.

To learn about aggregate demand, we'll first review the components of aggregate expenditure and the influences on them. We'll then explain why the price level influences spending plans. Finally, we'll study the factors that make aggregate demand change and explain why initial changes in expenditure have a multiplier effect that magnifies the ultimate change in aggregate demand.

Aggregate Demand Basics

The *quantity of real GDP demanded* is the total amount of final goods and services produced in the United States that people, businesses, governments, and foreigners plan to buy. This quantity is the sum of the real consumption expenditure (C), investment (I), government purchases (G), and exports (X) minus imports (M). That is,

$$Y = C + I + G + X - M.$$

Many factors influence expenditure plans; to study aggregate demand, we divide them into two groups: the price level and everything else. We'll first consider the influence of the price level on expenditure plans and then consider the other influences.

Aggregate Demand and the *AD* Curve

Figure 20.6 shows an aggregate demand curve, *AD*. Along the aggregate demand curve, the only influence on expenditure plans that changes is the price level. A rise in the price level decreases the quantity of real GDP demanded and brings a movement up along the aggregate demand curve; a fall in the price level increases the quantity of real GDP demanded and brings a movement down along the aggregate demand curve.

The price level influences the quantity of real GDP demanded because a change in the price level brings changes in

- The buying power of money
- The real interest rate
- The real prices of exports and imports

The Buying Power of Money

A rise in the price level lowers the buying power of money and decreases the quantity of real GDP demanded. To see why, think about the buying plans of Anna, who lives in Moscow, Russia. She has worked hard all summer and saved 20,000 rubles (the ruble is the currency of Russia), which she plans to spend attending graduate school when she has finished her economics degree. So Anna's money holding is 20,000 rubles. Anna has a part-time job, and her income from this job pays her expenses. The price level in Russia rises by 100 percent. Anna needs 40,000 rubles to buy what 20,000 rubles once bought. To make up some of

FIGURE 20.6
A Change in the Quantity of Real GDP Demanded

Practice Online

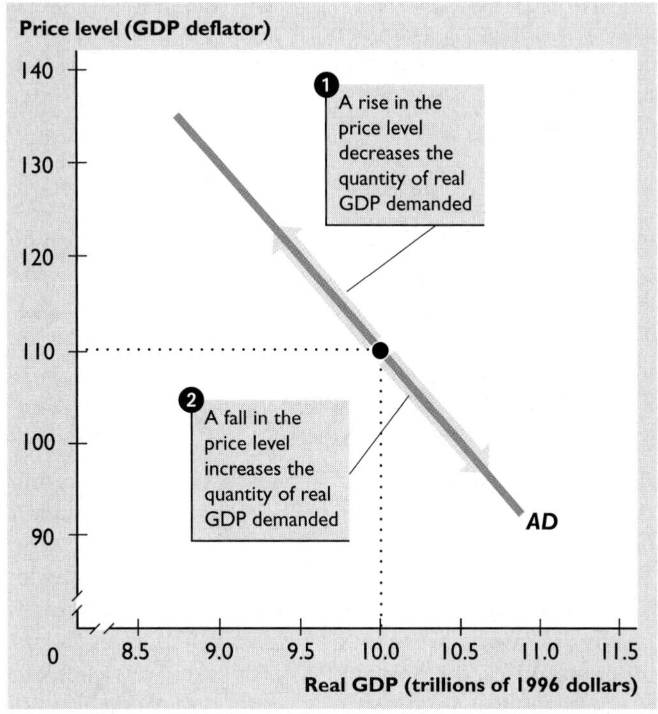

The aggregate demand curve (*AD*) shows the relationship between the quantity of real GDP demanded and the price level when all other influences on expenditure plans remain the same. The quantity of real GDP demanded ❶ decreases when the price level rises and ❷ increases when the price level falls.

the fall in the buying power of her money, Anna slashes her spending.

Similarly, a fall in the price level, other things remaining the same, brings an increase in the quantity of real GDP demanded. To see why, think about the buying plans of Mika, who lives in Tokyo, Japan. She too has worked hard all summer and saved 200,000 yen (the yen is the currency of Japan), which she plans to spend attending school next year. The price level in Japan falls by 10 percent; now Mika needs only 180,000 yen to buy what 200,000 yen once bought. With a rise in what her money buys, Mika decides to buy a DVD player.

The Real Interest Rate

When the price level rises, the real interest rate rises. You saw in Chapter 19 (p. 481) that an increase in the price level increases the amount of money that people want to hold—increases the demand for money. When the demand for money increases, the nominal interest rate rises. In the short run, the inflation rate doesn't change, so a rise in the nominal interest rate brings a rise in the real interest rate. Faced with a higher real interest rate, businesses and people delay plans to buy new capital and consumer durable goods and cut back on spending. So the quantity of real GDP demanded decreases.

Anna and Mika Again Think about Anna and Mika again. Both of them want to buy a computer. In Moscow, a rise in the price level increases the demand for money and raises the real interest rate. At a real interest rate of 5 percent a year,

Anna was willing to borrow to buy the new computer. But at a real interest rate of 10 percent a year, she decides that the payments would be too high, so she delays buying it. The rise in the price level decreases the quantity of real GDP demanded.

In Tokyo, a fall in the price level lowers the real interest rate. At a real interest rate of 5 percent a year, Mika was willing to borrow to buy a low-performance computer. But at a real interest rate of close to zero, she decides to buy a fancier computer that costs more: The fall in the price level increases the quantity of real GDP demanded.

The Real Prices of Exports and Imports

When the U.S. price level rises and other things remain the same, the prices in other countries do not change. So a rise in the U.S. price level makes U.S.-made goods and services more expensive relative to foreign-made goods and services. This change in real prices encourages people to spend less on U.S.-made items and more on foreign-made items. For example, if the U.S. price level rises relative to the foreign price level, foreigners buy fewer U.S.-made cars (U.S. exports decrease) and Americans buy more foreign-made cars (U.S. imports increase).

Anna's and Mika's Imports In Moscow, Anna is buying some new shoes. With a sharp rise in the Russian price level, the Russian-made shoes that she planned to buy are too expensive, so she buys a less expensive pair imported from Brazil. In Tokyo, Mika is buying a CD player. With the fall in the Japanese price level, a Sony CD player made in Japan looks like a better buy than one made in Taiwan.

In the long run, when the price level changes by more in one country than in other countries, the exchange rate changes. The exchange rate change neutralizes the price level change, so this international price effect on buying plans is a short-run effect only. But in the short run, it is a powerful effect.

■ Changes in Aggregate Demand

A change in any factor that influences expenditure plans other than the price level brings a change in aggregate demand. When aggregate demand increases, the aggregate demand curve shifts rightward, which Figure 20.7 illustrates as the rightward shift of the *AD* curve from AD_0 to AD_1. When aggregate demand decreases, the aggregate demand curve shifts leftward, which Figure 20.7 illustrates as the leftward shift of the *AD* curve from AD_0 to AD_2. The factors that change aggregate demand are

- Expectations about the future
- Fiscal policy and monetary policy
- The state of the world economy

Expectations

An increase in expected future income increases the amount of consumption goods (especially big-ticket items such as cars) that people plan to buy and increases aggregate demand.

An increase in expected future inflation increases aggregate demand because people decide to buy more goods and services before their prices rise.

An increase in expected future profit increases the investment that firms plan to undertake and increases aggregate demand.

FIGURE 20.7
Changes in Aggregate Demand

Practice Online

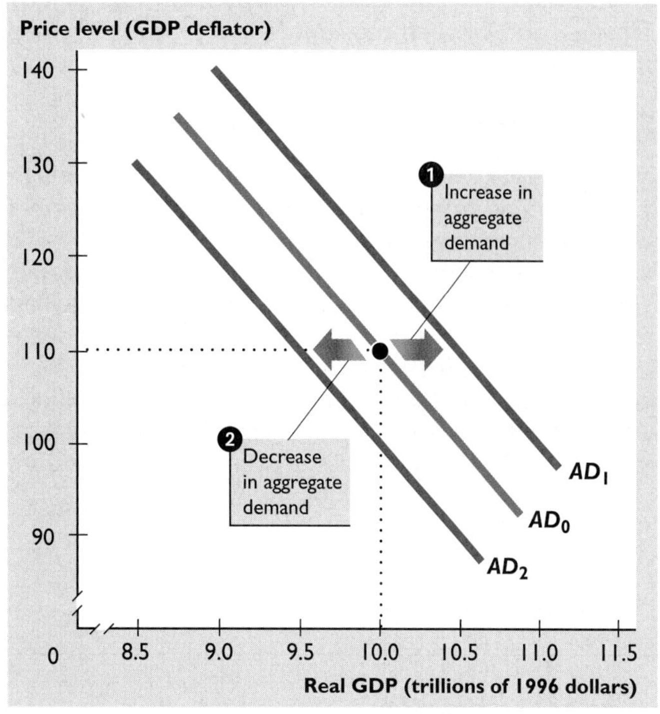

Aggregate demand:

❶ *Increases if*

- Expected future income, inflation, or profits increase.
- The government or the Federal Reserve takes steps that increase planned expenditure.
- The exchange rate falls or the global economy expands.

❷ *Decreases if*

- Expected future income, inflation, or profits decrease.
- The government or the Federal Reserve takes steps that decrease planned expenditure.
- The exchange rate rises or the global economy contracts.

Fiscal Policy and Monetary Policy

We study the effects of policy actions on aggregate demand in Chapter 31. Here, we'll just briefly note that the government can influence aggregate demand by setting and changing taxes, transfer payments, and government purchases of goods and services. And the Federal Reserve can influence aggregate demand by changing the quantity of money and the interest rate.

A tax cut or an increase in either transfer payments or government purchases increases aggregate demand. A cut in the interest rate or an increase in the quantity of money increases aggregate demand.

The World Economy

Two main influences that the world economy has on aggregate demand are the foreign exchange rate and foreign income. The foreign exchange rate is the amount of a foreign currency that you can buy with a U.S. dollar. Other things remaining the same, a rise in the foreign exchange rate decreases aggregate demand. To see how the foreign exchange rate influences aggregate demand, suppose that $1 exchanges for 100 Japanese yen. A Fujitsu phone made in Japan costs 12,500 yen, and an equivalent Motorola phone made in the United States costs $110. In U.S. dollars, the Fujitsu phone costs $125, so people around the world buy the cheaper U.S. phone. Now suppose the exchange rate rises to 125 yen per dollar. At 125 yen per dollar, the Fujitsu phone costs $100 and is now cheaper than the Motorola phone. People will switch from the U.S. phone to the Japanese phone.

U.S. exports will decrease and U.S. imports will increase, so U.S. aggregate demand will decrease.

An increase in foreign income increases U.S. exports and increases U.S. aggregate demand. For example, an increase in income in Japan and Germany increases Japanese and German consumers' and producers' planned expenditures on U.S.-made goods and services.

The Aggregate Demand Multiplier

The aggregate demand multiplier is an effect that magnifies changes in expenditure plans and brings potentially large fluctuations in aggregate demand. When any influence on aggregate demand changes expenditure plans, the change in expenditure changes income; and the change in income induces a change in consumption expenditure. The increase in aggregate demand is the initial increase in expenditure plus the induced increase in consumption expenditure.

Figure 20.8 illustrates this multiplier effect. Initially, the aggregate demand curve is AD_0. Investment then increases by \$0.4 trillion (ΔI) and the purple curve $AD_0 + \Delta I$ now describes aggregate spending plans at each price level. An increase in income induces an increase in consumption expenditure of \$0.6 trillion, and the aggregate demand curve shifts rightward to AD_1.

FIGURE 20.8
The Aggregate Demand Multiplier

Practice Online

❶ An increase in investment increases aggregate demand and increases income. ❷ The increase in income induces an increase in consumption expenditure, so ❸ aggregate demand increases by more than the initial increase in investment.

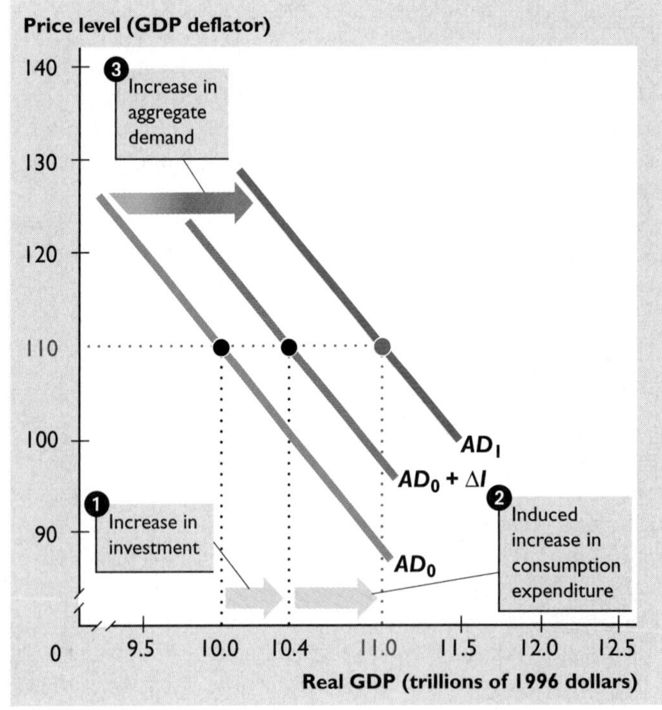

CHECKPOINT 20.3

3 Explain the influences on aggregate demand.

Study Guide pp. 301–303

Practice Online 20.3

Practice Problem 20.3

Mexico has signed free trade agreements with many countries, including the United States, Canada, and the European Union. Explain the effect of each of the following events on Mexico's aggregate demand in the short run.

a. The price level in Mexico increases faster than that in its trading partners.
b. The government of Mexico cuts taxes.
c. The United States and Canada experienced strong economic growth.
d. The European Union goes into a recession.
e. The Mexican government sets new environmental standards that require factories to upgrade their production facilities.
f. Mexico adopts an expansionary monetary policy and increases the quantity of money.

Exercise 20.3

Explain the effect on Japan's aggregate demand in the short run of each of the following events, one at a time.

a. The price level in Japan is constant, and the price level in its trading partners increases.
b. The price level in Japan rises.
c. The rest of Asia goes into recession.
d. The Asian economies experience very strong growth.
e. The yen strengthens against the U.S. dollar.
f. Japan adopts an expansionary fiscal policy and cuts taxes.

Solution to Practice Problem 20.3

a. As Mexico's price level increases faster than that of its trading partners, its exports become relatively more expensive. The quantity demanded of Mexican real GDP by its trading partners decreases. Mexico's aggregate demand does not change—there is a movement up along the *AD* curve (Figure 1).
b. A tax cut in Mexico increases Mexico's aggregate demand The *AD* curve shifts rightward (Figure 2).
c. Strong economic growth in Canada and the United States increases the demand for Mexican real GDP and increases aggregate demand in Mexico. The *AD* curve shifts rightward (Figure 2).
d. A recession in the European Union decreases European demand for goods and services from Mexico. So Mexico's exports decrease, and its aggregate demand decreases. The *AD* curve shifts leftward (Figure 3).
e. As factories upgrade their production facilities, investment increases. Aggregate demand in Mexico increases, and the *AD* curve shifts rightward (Figure 2).
f. An increase in the quantity of money increases aggregate demand, and the *AD* curve shifts rightward (Figure 2).

FIGURE 1

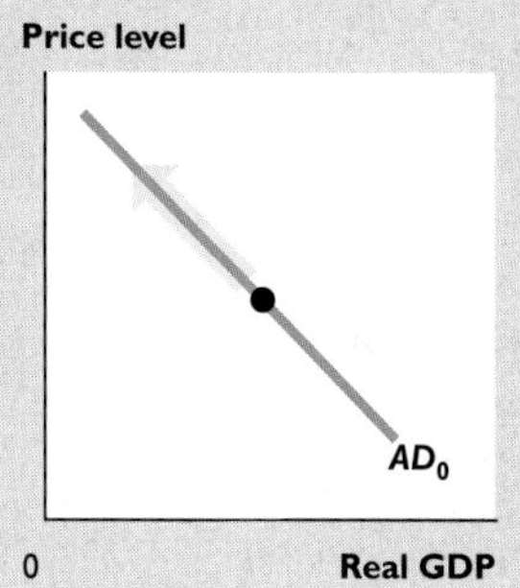

FIGURE 2

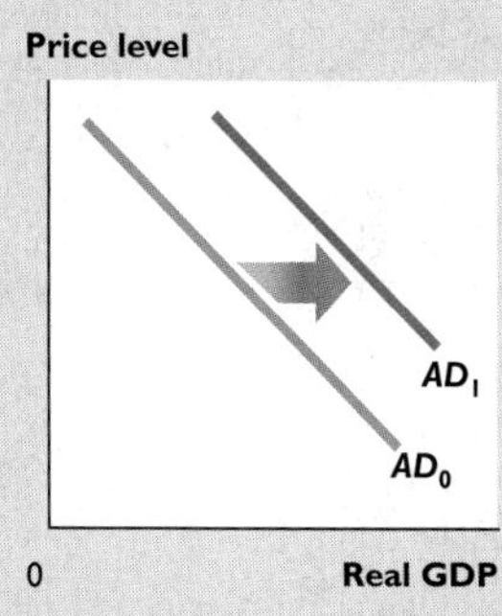

FIGURE 3

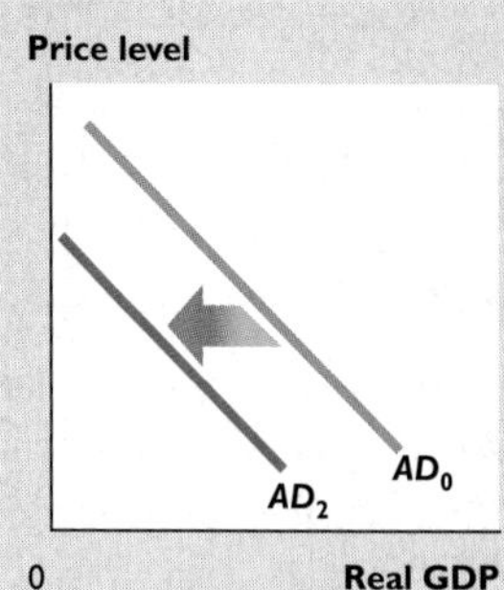

20.4 MACROECONOMIC EQUILIBRIUM

Macroeconomic equilibrium
When the quantity of real GDP demanded equals the quantity of real GDP supplied at the point of intersection of the *AD* curve and the *AS* curve.

Aggregate supply and aggregate demand determine real GDP and the price level. **Macroeconomic equilibrium** occurs when the quantity of real GDP demanded equals the quantity of real GDP supplied at the point of intersection of the *AD* curve and the *AS* curve. Figure 20.9(a) shows such an equilibrium at a price level of 110 and real GDP of $10 trillion.

To see why this position is the equilibrium, think about what happens if the price level is something other than 110. Suppose that the price level is 120 and that real GDP is $11 trillion (point *E* on the *AS* curve). The quantity of real GDP demanded is less than $11 trillion, so firms are unable to sell all their output. Unwanted inventories pile up, and firms cut production and prices until they can sell all their output, which occurs only when real GDP is $10 trillion and the price level is 110.

Now suppose the price level is 100 and real GDP is $9 trillion (point *A* on the *AS* curve). The quantity of real GDP demanded exceeds $9 trillion, so firms are unable to meet the demand for their output. Inventories decrease, and customers clamor for goods and services. So firms increase production and raise prices until firms can meet demand, which occurs only when real GDP is $10 trillion and the price level is 110.

FIGURE 20.9
Macroeconomic Equilibrium

Practice Online

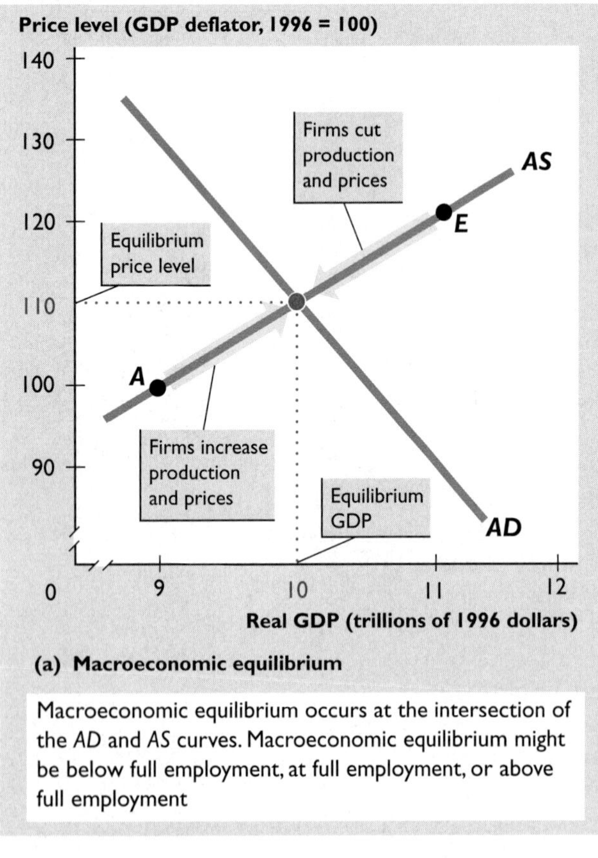

(a) Macroeconomic equilibrium

Macroeconomic equilibrium occurs at the intersection of the *AD* and *AS* curves. Macroeconomic equilibrium might be below full employment, at full employment, or above full employment

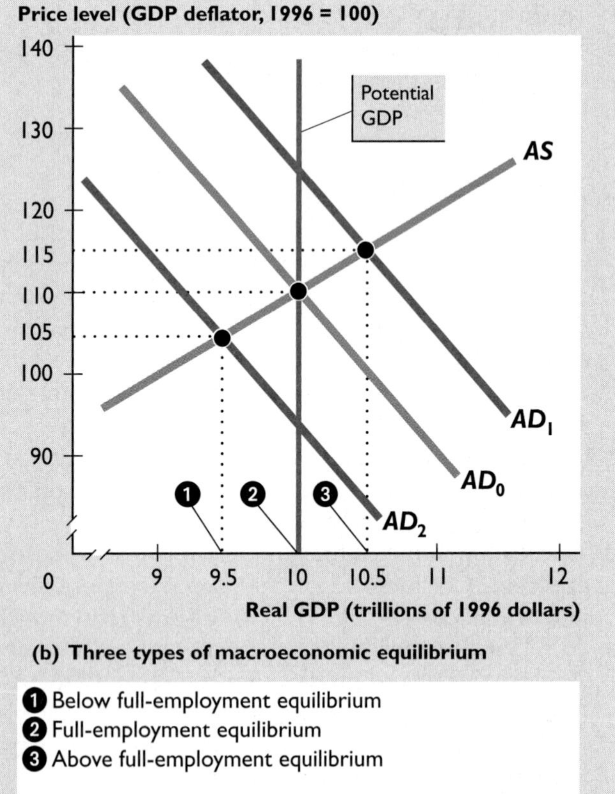

(b) Three types of macroeconomic equilibrium

1. Below full-employment equilibrium
2. Full-employment equilibrium
3. Above full-employment equilibrium

In macroeconomic equilibrium, the economy might be at full employment or above or below full employment, and Figure 20.9(b) shows these three possibilities. **Full-employment equilibrium**—equilibrium real GDP equals potential GDP—occurs where AD_0 intersects the aggregate supply curve AS. Fluctuations in aggregate demand bring fluctuations in real GDP around potential GDP. If aggregate demand increases to AD_1, firms increase production and raise prices until they can meet the higher demand. Real GDP increases to \$10.5 trillion and exceeds potential GDP in an **above full-employment equilibrium**. If aggregate demand decreases to AD_2, firms decrease production and cut prices until they can sell all their output. Real GDP decreases to \$9.5 trillion and is less than potential GDP in a **below full-employment equilibrium**.

Full-employment equilibrium
When equilibrium real GDP equals potential GDP.

Above full-employment equilibrium
When equilibrium real GDP exceeds potential GDP.

Below full-employment equilibrium
When potential GDP exceeds equilibrium real GDP.

CHECKPOINT 20.4

4 **Explain how aggregate supply and aggregate demand determine real GDP and the price level.**

Study Guide pp. 303–305

Practice Online 20.4

Practice Problem 20.4

Table 1 shows aggregate demand and aggregate supply schedules for the United Kingdom.

a. Plot the aggregate demand curve and the aggregate supply curve.
b. What is the macroeconomic equilibrium?
c. If potential GDP in the United Kingdom is £800 billon, what is the type of macroeconomic equilibrium?

TABLE 1

Price level (GDP deflator)	Real GDP demanded	Real GDP supplied
	(billions of 1995 pounds)	
90	800	650
100	775	700
110	750	750
120	725	800
130	700	850

Exercise 20.4

Table 2 shows aggregate demand and aggregate supply schedules for Australia.

a. Plot the aggregate demand curve and the aggregate supply curve.
b. What is the macroeconomic equilibrium?
c. If potential GDP in Australia is \$380 billion, what is the type of macroeconomic equilibrium?

TABLE 2

Price level (GDP deflator)	Real GDP demanded	Real GDP supplied
	(billions of 1996 dollars)	
95	430	370
105	420	390
115	410	410
125	400	430
135	390	450

Solution to Practice Problem 20.4

Figure 1 shows the *AD* and *AS* curves and potential GDP. Real GDP is less than potential GDP, so the economy is at a below full-employment equilibrium.

FIGURE 1

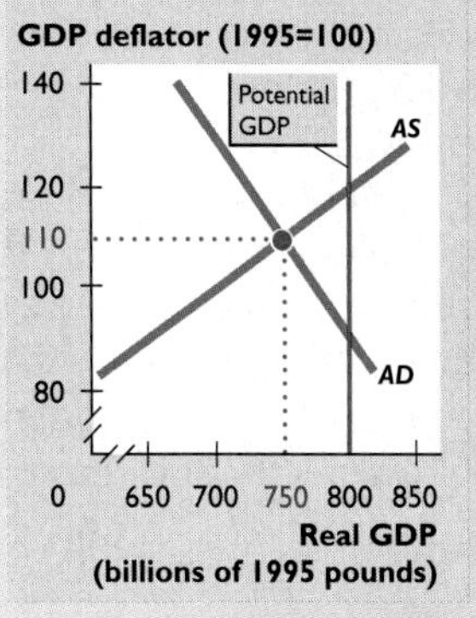

20.5 UNDERSTANDING THE BUSINESS CYCLE

Aggregate supply and aggregate demand determine real GDP and the price level. And changes in aggregate supply and aggregate demand bring changes in real GDP and the price level. These changes generate the business cycle.

The business cycle is an irregular cycle because the changes in aggregate supply and aggregate demand occur at irregular intervals and are of variable magnitude. And these changes initiate adjustments that are spread out over time.

To study the business cycle, we're first going to consider the effects of fluctuations in aggregate demand. Then we'll examine the effects of fluctuations in aggregate supply. Finally, we'll look at the adjustments that keep real GDP returning toward potential GDP when aggregate demand or aggregate supply shocks occur.

Aggregate Demand Fluctuations

We're going to describe a business cycle that results from fluctuations in aggregate demand with no changes in aggregate supply. In the U.S. economy, potential GDP grows and the full-employment price level rises over a business cycle. To focus on the cycle, we'll ignore economic growth and inflation. We'll suppose that potential GDP remains constant and that the full-employment price level is also constant.

Figure 20.10 illustrates the sequence of events. Throughout the cycle, potential GDP is $10 trillion and the full-employment price level is 110. Aggregate supply is shown by the *AS* curve, which does not change. Part (a) shows the changes in aggregate demand that bring an expansion, and part (c) tracks real GDP.

The economy starts out at a trough at point *A* at the intersection of AD_0 and *AS*. Real GDP is $9.5 trillion, and the price level is 105. Expecting high future profits, firms increase investment, and aggregate demand increases. The *AD* curve shifts rightward to AD_1, and the economy moves to point *B*. There is now full employment. The aggregate demand multiplier kicks in and increases in consumption expenditure keep *AD* increasing. The *AD* curve shifts further rightward to AD_2, and the economy moves to a cycle peak at point *C*. There is now above-full employment.

Figure 20.10(b) shows the changes in aggregate demand that bring a recession, and part (c) continues to track real GDP. The economy is at a peak at point *C* at the intersection of AD_2 and *AS*. Real GDP is $10.5 trillion, and the price level is 115. Now, expecting low future profits, firms decrease investment, and aggregate demand decreases. The *AD* curve shifts leftward to AD_3, and the economy moves to point *D*. There is full employment again. The aggregate demand multiplier decreases consumption expenditure and keeps *AD* decreasing. The *AD* curve shifts further leftward to AD_4, and the economy moves to a new cycle trough at point *E*.

Here, changes in profit expectations drive changes in investment and aggregate demand to create the business cycle. This factor is frequently the one at work. But sometimes other factors initiate a change in aggregate demand, and any of the factors that influence expenditure plans that we reviewed above (on pp. 518–520) could be at work. For smaller countries, a change in exports is frequently the initiating factor and the source of an international business cycle.

FIGURE 20.10
An Aggregate Demand Cycle

Practice Online

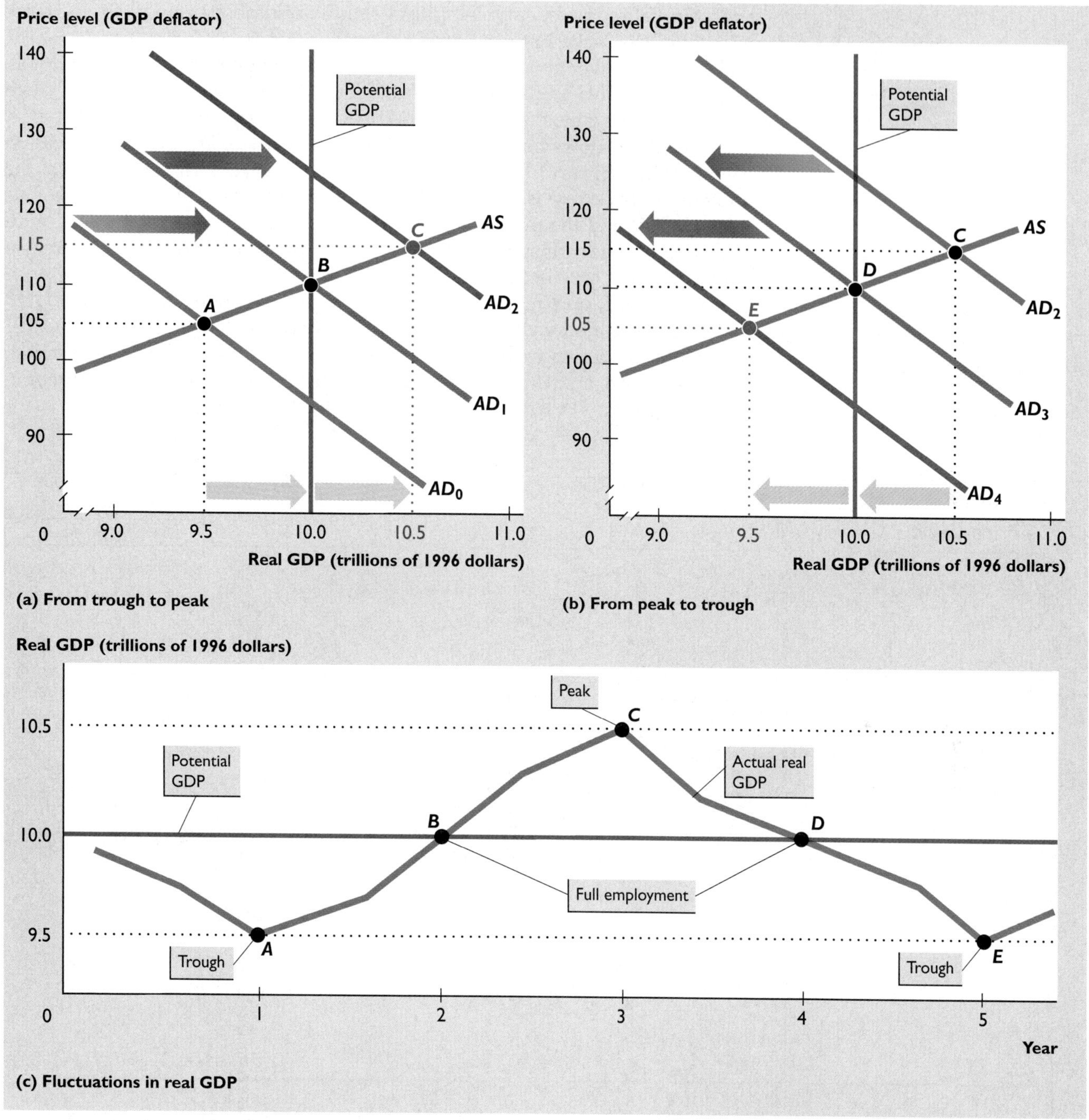

Real GDP is $9.5 trillion at the intersection of *AS* and AD_0 in part (a), and the economy is in a trough at point *A* in part (c). An increase in investment increases aggregate demand through AD_1 to AD_2. The economy moves from *A* through full employment at *B* to a cycle peak at *C*. A decrease in investment decreases aggregate demand through AD_3 to AD_4 in part (b). The economy moves from *C* through full employment at *D* to a new trough at *E*.

Aggregate Supply Fluctuations

Aggregate supply can fluctuate for two types of reasons. First, potential GDP grows at an uneven pace. During a period of rapid technological change and capital accumulation, potential GDP grows rapidly and above its long-term trend. The second half of the 1990s experienced this type of expansion.

Second, a change in the money price of a major resource, such as crude oil, might change. Oil is used so widely throughout the economy that a large change in its price affects almost every firm and impacts the aggregate economy.

Figure 20.11 shows how a large change in the price of oil can bring recession and expansion. In part (a), the aggregate demand curve is *AD* and initially, the aggregate supply curve is AS_0. Equilibrium real GDP is $10 trillion, which equals potential GDP, and the price level is 110. Then the price of oil rises. Faced with higher energy and transportation costs, firms decrease production. Aggregate supply decreases, and the aggregate supply curve shifts leftward to AS_1. The price level rises to 115, and real GDP decreases to $9.75 trillion. Because real GDP decreases, the economy experiences recession. Because the price level increases, the economy experiences inflation. A combination of recession and inflation, called **stagflation**, actually occurred in the United States and the global economy in the mid-1970s and early 1980s. But events like this are infrequent.

Stagflation
A combination of recession (falling real GDP) and inflation (rising price level).

FIGURE 20.11
An Oil Price Cycle

Practice Online

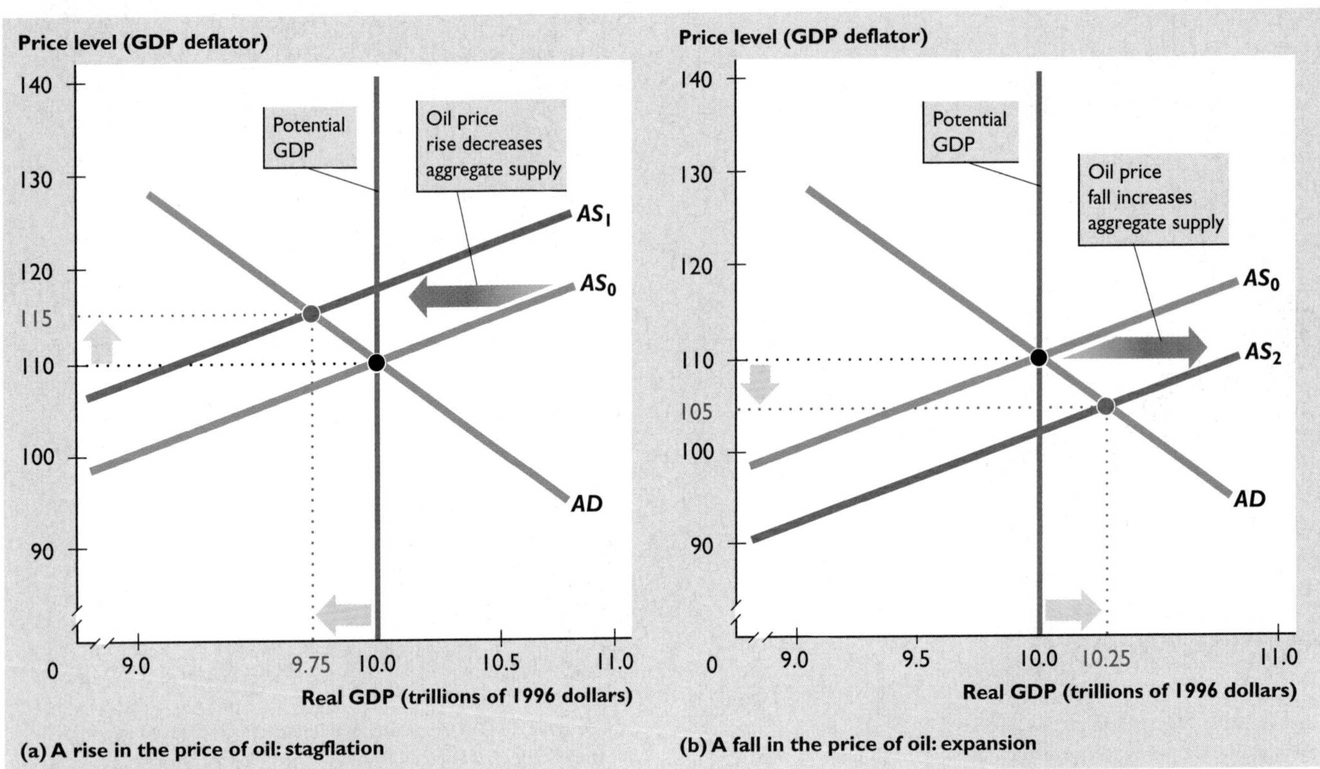

(a) A rise in the price of oil: stagflation

In part (a), a decrease in aggregate supply shifts the *AS* curve leftward to AS_1. Real GDP decreases, and the price level rises.

(b) A fall in the price of oil: expansion

In part (b), an increase in aggregate supply shifts the *AS* curve rightward to AS_2. Real GDP increases, and the price level falls.

In Figure 20.11(b), starting from the same full-employment equilibrium as before, the price of oil falls. With lower energy and transportation costs, firms increase production and the aggregate supply curve shifts rightward to AS_2. The price level falls to 105, and real GDP increases to $10.25 trillion. The economy experiences expansion and moves above full employment, but the price level falls. Similar events occurred in the United States and global economies during the mid-1980s, bringing strong economic expansion. The price level didn't fall, but inflation slowed, so the price level was lower than it otherwise would have been.

Eye on the Past

Oil Price Cycles in the U.S. and Global Economies

In 1973, a barrel of crude oil cost around $3.50—a bit more than $11.50 in 1996 dollars (see figure). Most of the world's crude oil came from a handful of nations mainly located in the Persian Gulf region, and the large producer nations were (and still are) members of an international cartel known as OPEC—the Organization of Petroleum Exporting Countries. (A cartel is an organization that seeks to control the supply and the price of a commodity and is illegal in the United States.)

In September 1973, OPEC cut the production of crude oil and raised its price to $10 a barrel—about $28 in 1996 dollars. This near tripling of the price of crude oil sent the United States, Europe, Japan, and the developing nations into recession.

Through the rest of the 1970s, the price of oil drifted upward slightly. Then, in 1980, OPEC delivered its second jolt to the global economy by again cutting production and then raising the price to $37 a barrel—$65 in 1996 dollars.

The global economy experienced another recession. But this recession was much more severe than that of the mid-1970s because the oil price shock was accompanied by a large decrease in aggregate demand that resulted from the Fed's monetary policy.

With the very high price of oil, it did not take long for OPEC to be joined by many other producers. Canada and the United States intensified exploration and increased North American oil production. Britain and Norway developed oil resources in the North Sea. And Mexico stepped up its production.

As these additional sources of supply came onstream, the price of oil tumbled. By 1998, it had fallen to $14 a barrel.

This gradual fall in the price of oil aided the expansion of the U.S. and global economies during the 1980s and 1990s.

During the late 1990s, the price of oil again increased and by 2001, it was back at its 1974 level in real terms.

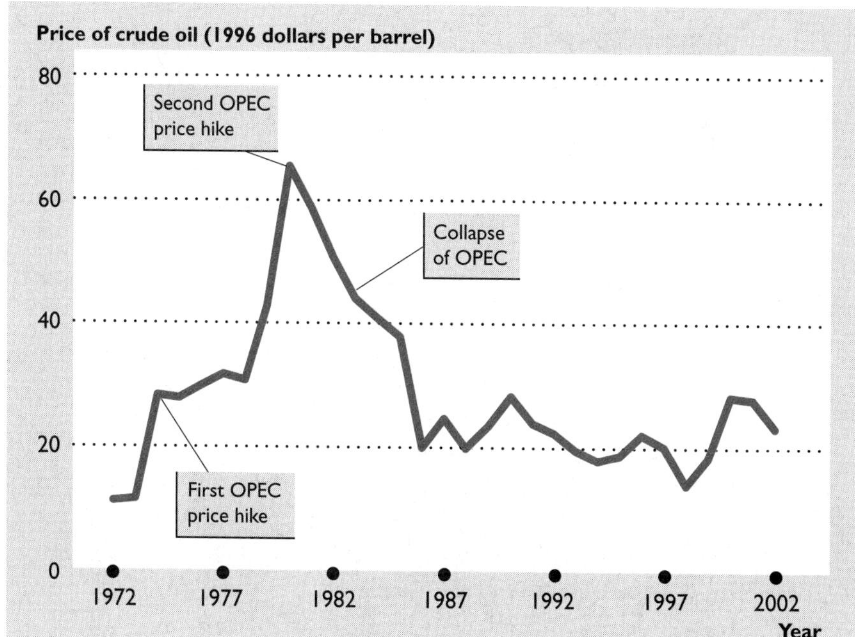

SOURCES: *International Financial Statistics*, International Monetary Fund and Bureau of Economic Analysis.

Adjustment Toward Full Employment

When the economy is away from full employment, forces begin to operate that move it back toward full employment. In Figure 20.12(a), aggregate supply is AS_0 and an increase in aggregate demand from AD_0 to AD_1 moves real GDP above full employment. There is now an **inflationary gap**—a gap that brings a rising price level. Workers have experienced a fall in the buying power of their wages, and firms' profits have increased. Workers demand higher wages, and firms, anxious to maintain their employment and output levels in the face of a labor shortage, meet those demands. As the money wage rate rises, aggregate supply decreases and the aggregate supply curve shifts leftward. Eventually, it will reach AS_1, where real GDP is back at potential GDP.

Inflationary gap
A gap that exists when real GDP exceeds potential GDP and that brings a rising price level.

In Figure 20.12(b), aggregate supply is AS_1 and a decrease in aggregate demand from AD_1 to AD_2 moves real GDP below full employment. There is a **deflationary gap**—a gap that brings a falling price level. The people who are lucky enough to have jobs see the buying power of their wages rise and firms' profits shrink. In these circumstances, and with a labor surplus, the money wage rate gradually falls and the aggregate supply curve shifts rightward. Eventually, it reaches AS_2, where real GDP is back at potential GDP.

Deflationary gap
A gap that exists when potential GDP exceeds real GDP and that brings a falling price level.

FIGURE 20.12
Adjustments Toward Full Employment

Practice Online

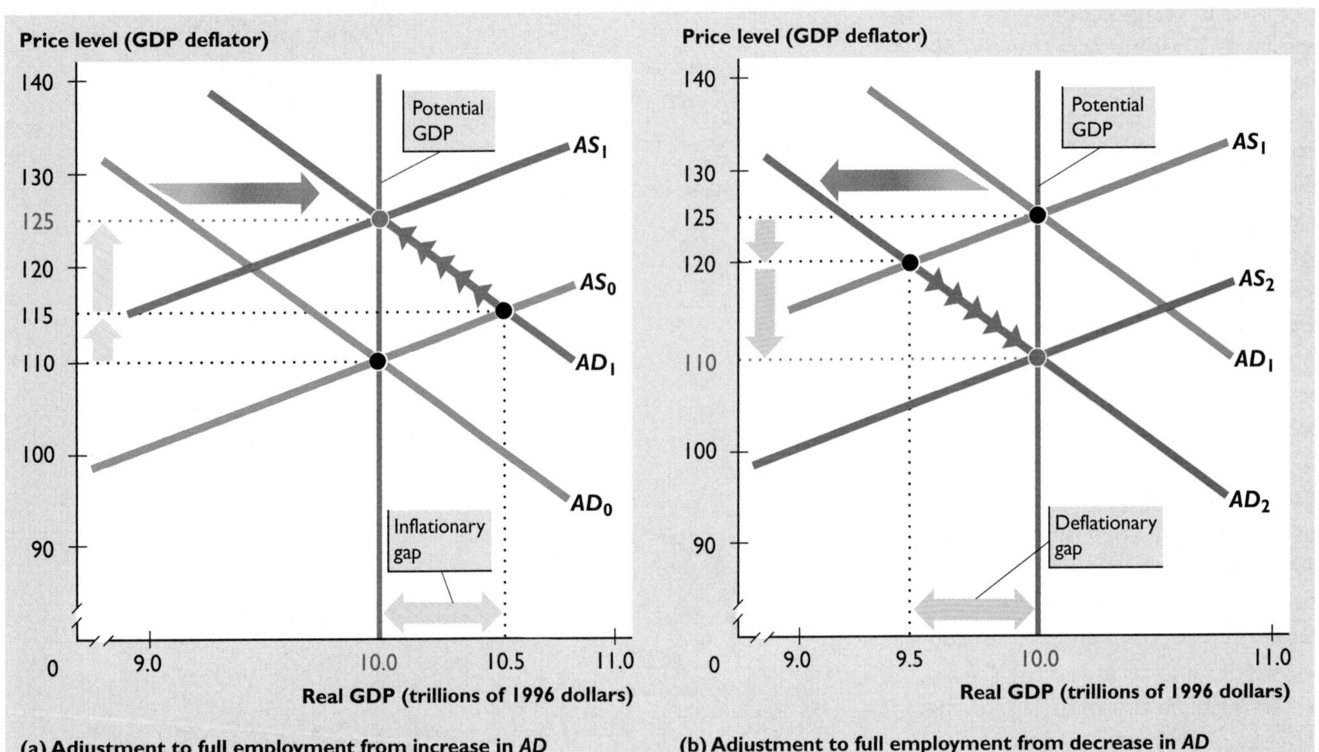

In part (a), real GDP exceeds potential GDP—an inflationary gap. The money wage rate rises, aggregate supply decreases, real GDP decreases, and the price level rises.

In part (b), potential GDP exceeds real GDP—a deflationary gap. The money wage rate falls, aggregate supply increases, real GDP increases, and the price level falls.

Eye on the U.S. Economy

The National Bureau Calls a Recession

The NBER's Business Cycle Dating Committee announced in November 2001 that a peak in business activity occurred in the U.S. economy in March 2001. So, according to the NBER committee, the expansion that began in March 1991 ended in March 2001 and a recession began. The expansion lasted exactly 10 years and was the longest that the NBER has observed.

To identify the date of the cycle peak, the NBER committee looked at industrial production, employment, real income, and wholesale and retail sales. But they paid most attention to employment.

You can see the employment cycle in part (a) of the figure, which shows that employment peaked in March 2001. The other factors considered by the NBER didn't peak in March but didn't contradict the employment numbers, so the committee was clear that March was the peak month.

Part (a) of the figure also shows that employment reached a trough in April 2002. But the trough was shallow, and in November 2002, the NBER reported that it was not yet ready to define the month of the business cycle trough.

The committee says that it gives relatively little weight to real GDP because it is measured only quarterly and is subject to ongoing and sometimes large revisions. Nonetheless, it is interesting to see what real GDP tells us. And long enough after the event, the revisions to real GDP are complete, so the numbers do provide a good indicator of the overall level of economic activity.

Part (b) of the figure shows the real GDP cycle. You can see that through 2000, real GDP exceeded potential GDP and there was an inflationary gap. Real GDP was shrinking during the first quarter of 2001, before the NBER says the recession began. In June 2001, real GDP was close to potential GDP, and after June, a deflationary gap opened up.

The real GDP trough occurred between the third and fourth quarters of 2001, after which the economy was expanding. But the expansion was not strong enough to eliminate the deflationary gap, which persisted through 2002.

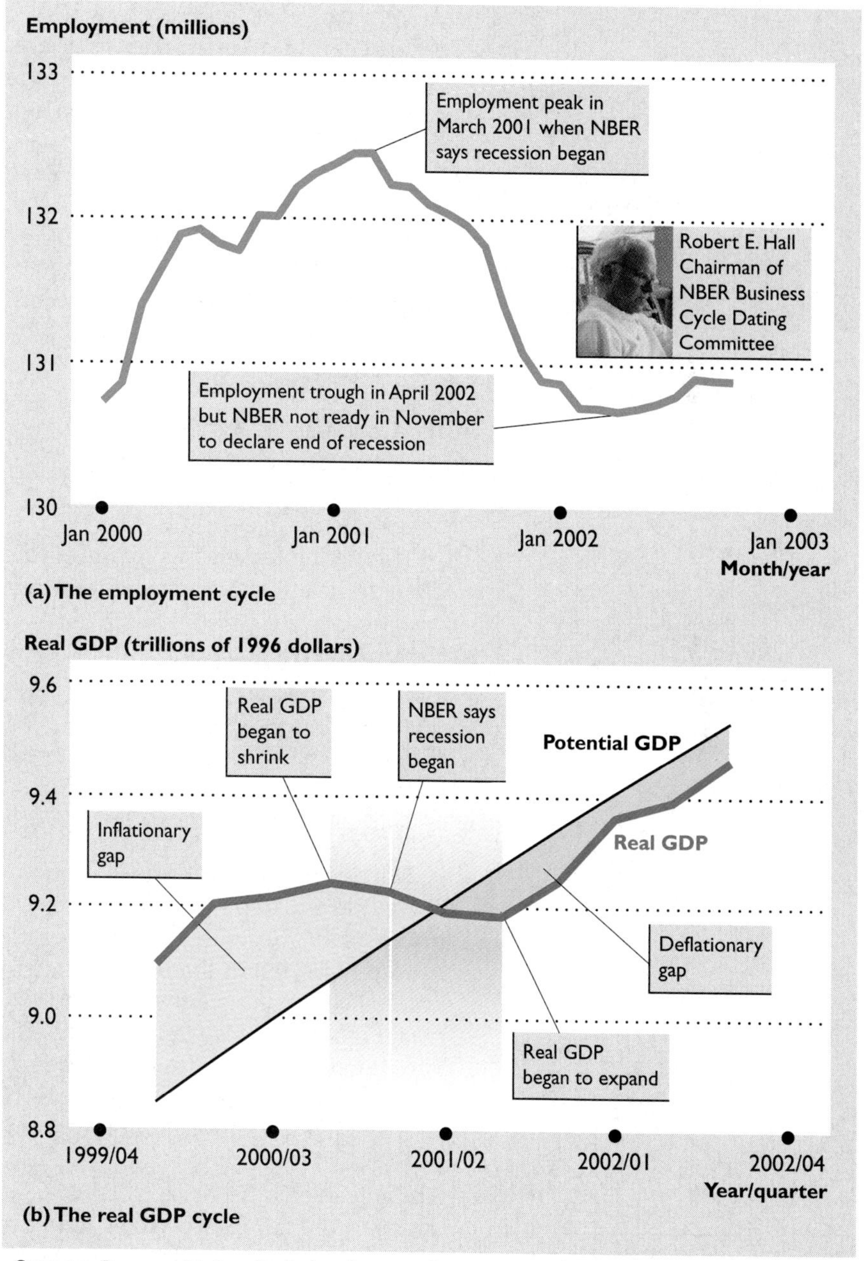

(a) The employment cycle

(b) The real GDP cycle

SOURCES: Bureau of Labor Statistics, Bureau of Economic Analysis, and Congressional Budget Office.

CHECKPOINT 20.5

Study Guide pp. 305–308

Practice Online 20.5

5 Explain how fluctuations in aggregate supply and aggregate demand create the business cycle.

Practice Problem 20.5

In the U.S economy, real GDP equals potential GDP. Then the following events occur one at a time:

- A deep recession hits the world economy.
- The world oil price rises by a large amount.
- U.S. businesses expect future profits to fall.

a. Explain the effect of each event on aggregate demand and aggregate supply in the United States.

b. Explain the effect of each event separately on the U.S. real GDP and price level.

c. Explain the combined effect of all the events together on the U.S. real GDP and price level.

d. Which event, if any, brings stagflation?

Exercise 20.5

In the Canadian economy, real GDP equals potential GDP. Then the following events occur one at a time:

- The world economy goes into a strong expansion.
- World oil price tumbles.
- Canadian businesses expect future profits to rise.

a. Explain the effect of each event on aggregate demand and aggregate supply in Canada.

b. Explain the effect of each event separately on Canadian real GDP and price level.

c. Explain the combined effect of all the events together on Canadian real GDP and price level.

FIGURE 1

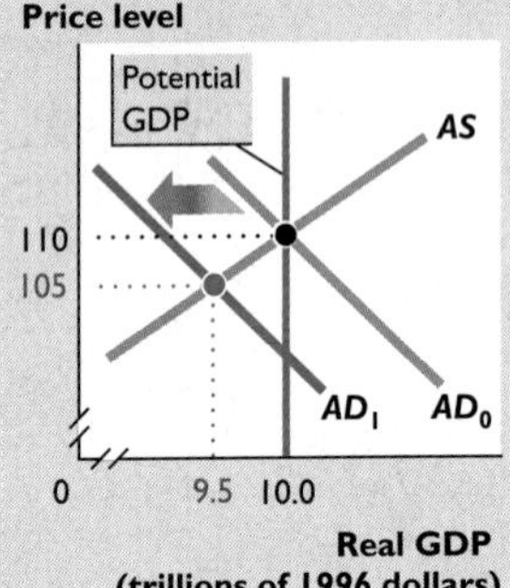

FIGURE 2

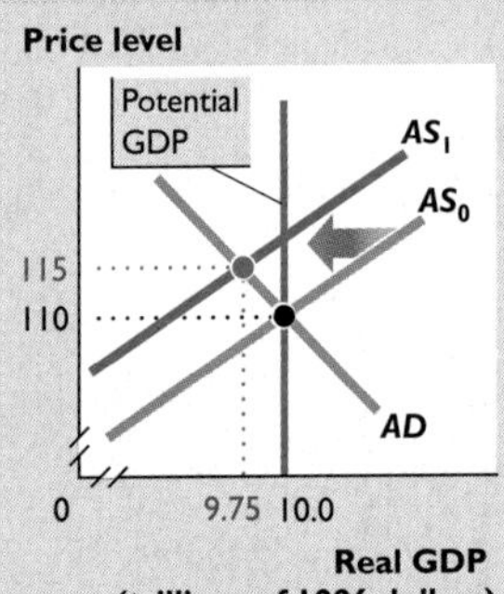

Solution to Practice Problem 20.5

a. A deep recession in the world economy decreases U.S. aggregate demand. A rise in the world oil price decreases U.S. aggregate supply. A fall in expected future profits decreases U.S. aggregate demand.

b. A deep recession in the world economy decreases U.S. aggregate demand. The *AD* curve shifts leftward. U.S. real GDP decreases, and the price level falls (Figure 1). A rise in the world oil price decreases U.S. aggregate supply. The *AS* curve shifts leftward. U.S. real GDP decreases, and the price level rises (Figure 2). A fall in expected future profits decreases U.S. aggregate demand. The *AD* curve shifts leftward. U.S. real GDP decreases, and the price level falls (Figure 1).

c. All three events decrease U.S. real GDP. The deep recession in the world economy and the fall in expected future profits decrease the price level. The rise in the world oil price increases the price level.

d. The oil price increase brings stagflation because it decreases aggregate supply, lowers equilibrium real GDP, and raises the price level.

CHAPTER CHECKPOINT

Key Points

1 Provide a technical definition of recession and describe the history of the U.S. business cycle.

- A recession is a decrease in real GDP that lasts for at least two quarters.
- U.S. recessions have been getting shorter, and expansions have been getting longer.

2 Explain the influences on aggregate supply.

- The aggregate supply curve slopes upward because with a given money wage rate, a rise in the price level lowers the real wage rate, increases the quantity of labor demanded, and increases the quantity of real GDP supplied.
- A change in potential GDP, a change in the money wage rate, or a change in the money price of other resources changes aggregate supply.

3 Explain the influences on aggregate demand.

- The aggregate demand curve slopes downward because a rise in the price decreases the buying power of money, raises the real interest rate, and raises the real price of domestic goods compared with foreign goods, and decreases the quantity of real GDP demanded.
- A change in expected future income, inflation, and profits, a change in fiscal policy and monetary policy, and a change in the foreign exchange rate and foreign real GDP change aggregate demand.

4 Explain how aggregate supply and aggregate demand determine real GDP and the price level.

- Aggregate supply and aggregate demand determine real GDP and the price level.
- Macroeconomic equilibrium occurs when the quantity of real GDP demanded equals the quantity of real GDP supplied and can be at full employment, above full employment, or below full employment.

5 Explain how fluctuations in aggregate supply and aggregate demand create the business cycle.

- Business cycles occur because aggregate supply and aggregate demand fluctuate.
- Away from full employment, gradual adjustment of the money wage rate moves real GDP toward potential GDP.

Key Terms

Above full-employment equilibrium, 523
Aggregate demand, 516
Aggregate supply, 510
Below full-employment equilibrium, 523
Deflationary gap, 528
Full-employment equilibrium, 523
Inflationary gap, 528
Macroeconomic equilibrium, 522
Recession, 506
Stagflation, 526

Exercises

FIGURE 1

1. Figure 1 shows real GDP in Germany from the first quarter of 1991 to the last quarter of 1994.
   a. In which quarter was Germany at a business-cycle peak?
   b. In which quarter was Germany at a business-cycle trough?
   c. Did Germany experience a recession during these years?
   d. In what years did Germany experience an expansion?

2. Over the course of the most recent U.S. business cycles, real GDP and the unemployment rate fluctuated in opposite directions. (See p. 508.)
   a. Did real GDP reach a peak at the same time that the unemployment rate reached its lowest level?
   b. Did real GDP reach a trough at the same time that the unemployment rate reached its highest level?
   c. Which of these two indicators begins to signal recession first?
   d. Which of these two indicators begins to signal expansion first?

3. Over the course of the most recent U.S. business cycles, real GDP and the inflation rate fluctuated together. (See p. 508.)
   a. Did real GDP reach a peak at the same time that the inflation rate reached its peak?
   b. Did real GDP reach a trough at the same time that the inflation rate reached its trough?
   c. Which of these two indicators begins to signal recession first?
   d. Which of these two indicators begins to signal expansion first?

4. At the beginning of 2001, the United States was at full employment.
   a. Suppose that in 2001, major union wage settlements pushed the money wage rate upward by 10 percent and that all other influences on aggregate supply remained the same. Explain the effect of the rise in the money wage rate on aggregate supply.
   b. Suppose that in 2001, the price level increased and all other influences on aggregate supply remained the same. Explain the effect of the rise in the price level on aggregate supply.
   c. Over time, potential GDP grows. Explain the effect of the increase in potential GDP on aggregate supply.

5. In 2004, the United States is at full employment. Then in 2005,
   a. The Fed cuts the quantity of money, and all other influences on aggregate demand remain the same. Explain the effect of the cut in the quantity of money on aggregate demand in the short run.
   b. The federal government cuts taxes, and all other influences on aggregate demand remain the same. Explain the effect of the tax cut on aggregate demand in the short run.
   c. The world economy goes into recession. Explain the effect of the world recession on U.S. aggregate demand in the short run.
   d. The U.S. price level rises faster than the price level in the world economy. Explain the effect of U.S. inflation on U.S. aggregate demand in the short run.

6. In 2003, the Japanese economy is at a below full-employment equilibrium.
   a. Compare the amount of unemployment in Japan with Japan's natural unemployment.
   b. Compare Japan's real GDP with its potential GDP.
   c. What policies could Japan adopt to restore full employment?
   d. In your answer to exercise 6c, would any of the policies create inflation? Explain.

7. Table 1 gives Canada's aggregate demand and aggregate supply schedules in 2004.
   a. Plot the aggregate demand curve.
   b. Plot the aggregate supply curve.
   c. What is the macroeconomic equilibrium?
   d. If potential GDP in Canada is $800 billion, what is the type of macroeconomic equilibrium?

TABLE 1

Price level (GDP deflator)	Real GDP demanded	Real GDP supplied
	(billions of 1992 dollars)	
90	900	600
100	850	700
110	800	800
120	750	900
130	700	1,000

8. Use the information provided in Table 1 together with the information that potential GDP is $800 billion to draw an *AS-AD* graph of the economy of Canada and then
   a. Show the effect of a rise in the world oil price on your *AS-AD* graph. Does it change aggregate supply or aggregate demand, and in what direction?
   b. Following the increase in the world price of oil, what is the new short-run equilibrium?
   c. What is the adjustment process that now begins to restore full employment? Do you expect that process to work slowly or rapidly? Why?

9. Use the information provided in Table 1 together with the information that potential GDP is $800 billion to draw an *AS-AD* graph of the economy of Canada and then
   a. Show the effect of a rise in the quantity of money in Canada on your *AS-AD* graph. Does it change aggregate supply or aggregate demand, and in what direction?
   b. Following the increase in the quantity of money, what is the new short-run equilibrium?
   c. What is the adjustment process that now begins to restore full employment? Do you expect that process to work slowly or rapidly? Why?

10. Use the information provided in Table 1 together with the information that potential GDP is $800 billion to draw an *AS-AD* graph of the economy of Canada and then
    a. Show the effect of a global recession on your *AS-AD* graph. Does the global recession change aggregate supply or aggregate demand, and in what direction?
    b. Following the onset of the global recession, what is the new short-run equilibrium?
    c. What is the adjustment process that now begins to restore full employment? Do you expect that process to work slowly or rapidly? Why?

11. For each of the events you analyzed in exercises 8 to 10, explain what happens to the unemployment rate and the real wage rate
    a. In the move to the initial short-run equilibrium.
    b. In the adjustment toward the new long-run equilibrium.

Critical Thinking

12. Review the NBER committee's task of identifying the correct date for the onset of recession in 2001.
    - **a.** Do you think the committee got the date of the onset of recession right?
    - **b.** Do you think the committee was correct in November 2002 to wait for more evidence before declaring the recession over?
    - **c.** Do you think the government rather than the NBER should determine the dates of recessions and expansions?

13. Because fluctuations in the world oil price make our economy fluctuate, someone suggests that we should vary the tax rate on oil, lowering the tax when the world oil price rises and increasing the tax when the world oil price falls, to stabilize the oil price in the U.S. market.
    - **a.** How do you think such an action would influence aggregate demand?
    - **b.** How do you think such an action would influence aggregate supply?
    - **c.** Lay out the arguments for and against such a policy.

14. Recessions have been getting shorter, and expansions have been getting longer.
    - **a.** When did the change in average length of recessions and expansions occur?
    - **b.** Can you think of some reasons why this change in the business cycle might have occurred?
    - **c.** What do you think of the view that policy actions designed to stabilize aggregate demand are responsible for this change in the business cycle?

Practice Online

Web Exercises

Use the links on your Foundations Web site to work the following exercises.

15. Visit the Web site of the National Bureau of Economic Research and read the announcements of November 2001 and November 2002 (and any later announcements made after this book was published).
    - **a.** What factors did the NBER committee consider to determine the onset of the 2001 recession?
    - **b.** Did the NBER committee look at real GDP? Why or why not?
    - **c.** Why did the NBER committee have a hard time determining when the 2001–2002 recession ended?
    - **d.** Where in the phases of the business cycle is the U.S. economy today (the day on which you are working this exercise).

16. Visit the Web site of the Economic Cycle Research Institute and obtain information on the dates of recessions and expansions in three countries other than the United States that interest you.
    - **a.** Compare the cycles dates in the countries you've chosen with those in the United States.
    - **b.** Compare the recessions in the three countries you've chosen and the United States.
    - **c.** In which country do you think aggregate demand fluctuates most?
    - **d.** The Economic Cycle Research Institute uses two definitions of the business cycle, one that is the same as the NBER definition and one called a "growth rate cycle." What is the difference between these two definitions? Which definition gives the higher frequency of recession?

Fiscal and Monetary Policy Effects

CHAPTER 21

CHAPTER CHECKLIST

When you have completed your study of this chapter, you will be able to

1. **Describe the federal budget process and explain the effects of fiscal policy.**
2. **Describe the Federal Reserve's monetary policy process and explain the effects of monetary policy.**

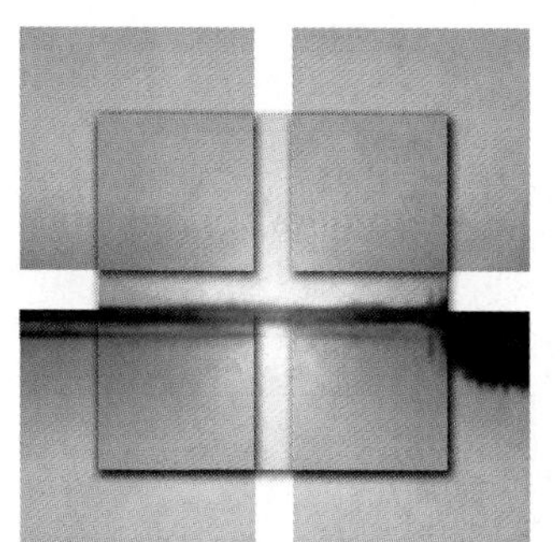

In 2002, the federal government spent $2 trillion, or 20 cents of every dollar that Americans earned. And the government spent more than it collected in taxes—the government had a deficit. What are the effects of government spending, taxes, and the government budget deficit (or surplus) on the economy?

Every six weeks or so, the Federal Open Market Committee (FOMC) meets at the Fed's Washington, D.C., headquarters. The eyes of Wall Street and the nation's financial managers focus on this event, looking for signs of changes in the interest rate. What are the effects of the Fed's actions on the economy?

In this chapter, we build on what you have learned about aggregate supply, aggregate demand, and money to explore the tools used by the federal government and the Federal Reserve to influence aggregate demand and counteract the forces that push the economy away from full employment.

21.1 THE FEDERAL BUDGET AND FISCAL POLICY

Fiscal policy
The use of the federal budget to smooth the business cycle and encourage economic growth.

Federal budget
An annual statement of the expenditures, tax receipts, and surplus or deficit of the government of the United States.

Budget surplus
The budget balance when tax receipts exceed expenditures.

Budget deficit
The budget balance when expenditures exceed tax receipts.

Balanced budget
The budget balance when tax receipts equal expenditures.

Fiscal policy is the use of the federal budget to smooth the business cycle and encourage economic growth. We begin our study of fiscal policy by describing the federal budget and the process that creates it.

The Federal Budget

The **federal budget** is an annual statement of the expenditures, tax receipts, and the surplus or deficit of the government of the United States. The government's surplus or deficit is equal to its tax receipts minus its expenditures. That is,

$$\text{Budget surplus } (+)/\text{deficit } (-) = \text{Tax receipts} - \text{Expenditures.}$$

The government has a **budget surplus** if tax receipts exceed expenditures, a **budget deficit** if expenditures exceed tax receipts, and a **balanced budget** if tax receipts equal expenditures. The government borrows to finance a budget deficit and repays its debt when it has a surplus. The amount of debt outstanding that arises from past budget deficits is called *national debt*.

A Personal Analogy The government's budget and the national debt are like a student's budget and debt—only bigger. If you take a student loan each year to go to school, you have a budget deficit and a growing debt. If after graduating and getting a job, you repay some of your loan each year, you have a budget surplus and a shrinking debt.

Budget Time Line

The President and Congress make the federal budget on the annual time line shown in Figure 21.1. Although the President proposes and ultimately approves

FIGURE 21.1
The Federal Budget Time Line for Fiscal 2004

Practice Online

The federal budget process begins with the President's proposals in February. Congress debates and amends these proposals and enacts a budget before the start of the fiscal year on October 1. The President signs the Budget Act into law. Throughout the fiscal year, Congress might pass supplementary budget laws. The budget outcome is calculated after the end of the fiscal year.

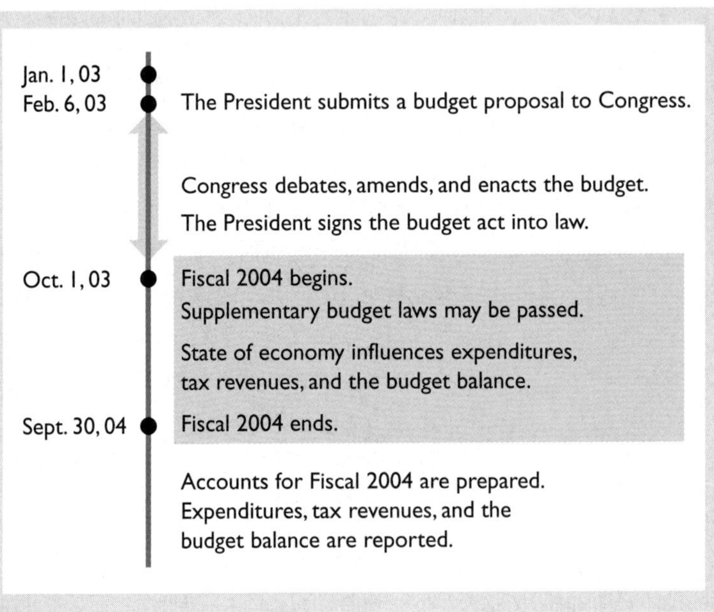

Eye on the Past

Federal Receipts and Expenditures

In 1902, the federal government collected $562 million in taxes, spent $485 million, and had a budget surplus of $77 million. In 2002, revenues were projected to be $1,950 billion, expenditures to be $2,050 billion, and the budget *deficit* to be $100 billion.

Expressed as percentages of GDP, tax revenues increased from 2.6 percent of GDP in 1902 to 18.6 percent of GDP in 2002. Expenditures grew from 2.3 percent of GDP in 1902 to 19.7 percent of GDP in 2002.

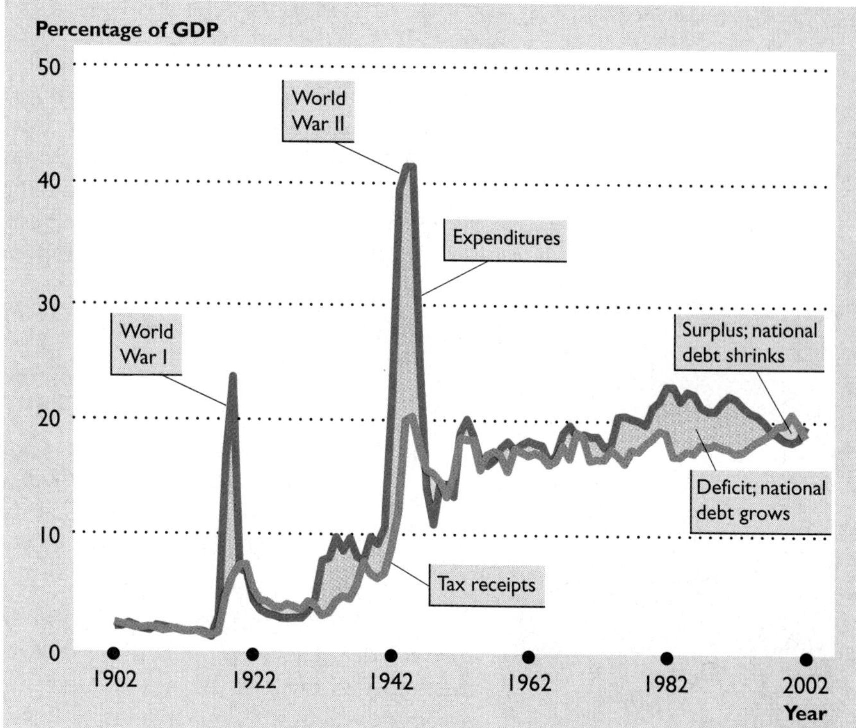

SOURCE: Office of Management and Budget, Historical Tables, Budget of the United States Government, Fiscal Year 2003.

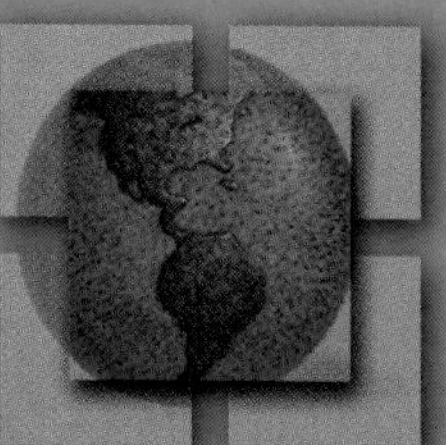

Eye on the Global Economy

The U.S. Budget in Global Perspective

Summing the budgets of all the governments in the world, the IMF estimates that budgets were in deficit by 3.4 percent of world GDP in 2002.

Japan had one of the biggest deficits at more than 7 percent of GDP. But the developing countries of Asia, which include China and India, had large deficits.

Canada was the only major advanced economy with a surplus in 2002.

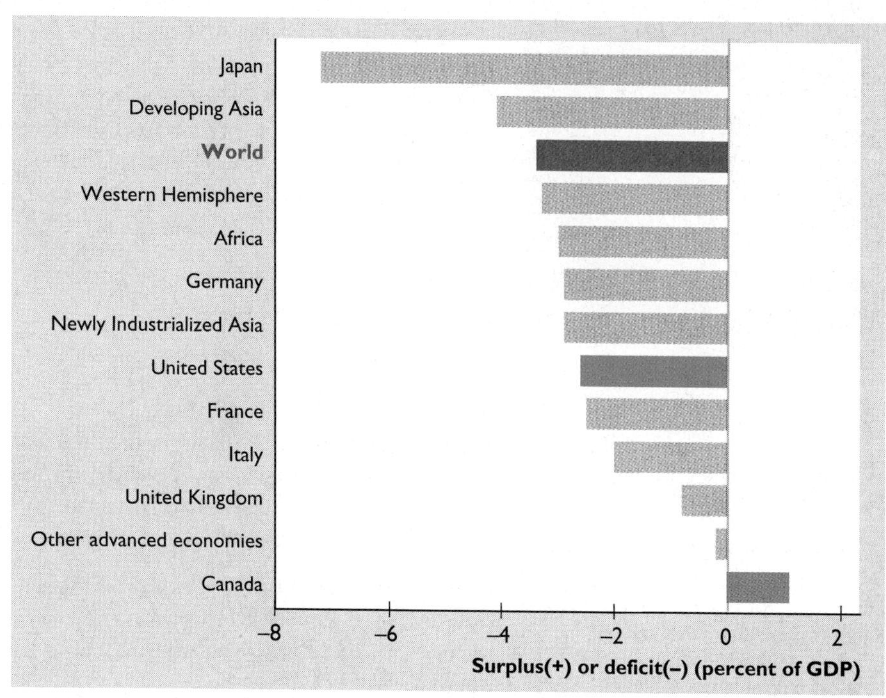

SOURCE: International Monetary Fund, *World Economic Outlook*, September 2002.

the budget, Congress makes the tough decisions on spending and taxes. The House of Representatives and the Senate develop their budget ideas in their respective Budget Committees, and conferences between the two houses resolve differences of view and draft the bills that become the Budget Act. The fiscal year is a year that runs from October 1 to September 30 of the next calendar year. Fiscal 2004 is the fiscal year that *ends* on September 30, 2004.

N. Gregory Mankiw

Stephen Friedman

The Employment Act of 1946

Fiscal policy operates within the framework of the landmark Employment Act of 1946, in which Congress declared that

> it is the continuing policy and responsibility of the Federal Government to use all practicable means . . . to coordinate and utilize all its plans, functions, and resources . . . to promote maximum employment, production, and purchasing power.

This act recognized a role for government actions to keep unemployment low, the economy expanding, and inflation in check. The *Full Employment and Balanced Growth Act of 1978*, more commonly known as the *Humphrey-Hawkins Act*, went further than the 1946 employment act and set a specific target of 4 percent for the unemployment rate, but this target has never been an unwavering policy goal.

Council of Economic Advisers and National Economic Council

The 1946 Employment Act established the President's Council of Economic Advisers, which writes an annual *Economic Report of the President*, a handy review of the current state of the economy. The Council consists of economists who are usually on leave from university jobs. N. Gregory Mankiw of Harvard University is the Chairman of President George W. Bush's Council of Economic Advisers.

The creation of the National Economic Council in 1993 has limited the role of the Council of Economic Advisers. The chairman of the National Economic Council, currently Stephen Friedman, formerly Chairman of Goldman Sachs, a leading global investment bank, is the President's chief economic adviser. The National Economic Council coordinates economic policy and attempts to ensure that the President's economic policy agenda is implemented.

Types of Fiscal Policy

Fiscal policy can be either

- Discretionary or
- Automatic

Discretionary fiscal policy
A fiscal policy action that is initiated by an act of Congress.

Automatic fiscal policy
A fiscal policy action that is triggered by the state of the economy such as an increase in payments to the unemployed and a decrease in tax receipts triggered by recession.

Discretionary Fiscal Policy A fiscal action that is initiated by an act of Congress is called **discretionary fiscal policy**. It requires a change in a spending program or in a tax law. For example, an increase in defense spending or a cut in the income tax rate is a discretionary fiscal policy.

Automatic Fiscal Policy A fiscal action that is triggered by the state of the economy is called **automatic fiscal policy**. For example, an increase in unemployment induces an increase in payments to the unemployed. A fall in incomes induces a decrease in tax receipts.

Discretionary Fiscal Policy: Demand-Side Effects

Discretionary fiscal policy influences both aggregate demand and aggregate supply. We'll look first at the demand-side effects. Changes in government purchases and changes in taxes have multiplier effects on aggregate demand because they include changes in consumption expenditure.

The Government Purchases Multiplier

Government purchases are a part of aggregate expenditure, so when government purchases change, aggregate demand changes. But the change in aggregate expenditure changes real GDP, which induces a change in consumption expenditure and a further change in aggregate demand. The **government purchases multiplier** is the magnification effect of a change in government purchases of goods and services on aggregate demand.

Government purchases multiplier
The magnification effect of a change in government purchases of goods and services on aggregate demand.

A Homeland Security Multiplier The terrorist attacks of September 11, 2001, brought a reappraisal of the nation's homeland security requirements and an increase in government purchases. This increase in purchases initially increased the incomes of producers of airport and border security equipment and security workers. Better-off security workers increased their consumption expenditures. With rising revenues, other businesses in all parts of the nation boomed and expanded their payrolls. A second round of increased consumption expenditures increased incomes yet further. The increase in security expenditures and its multiplier effect helped to end the 2001 recession.

The Tax Multiplier

The **tax multiplier** is the magnification effect of a change in taxes on aggregate demand. A *decrease* in taxes *increases* disposable income—income minus net taxes—which increases consumption expenditure. A decrease in taxes works like an increase in government purchases. But the magnitude of the tax multiplier is smaller than the government purchases multiplier. The reason is that a $1 tax cut generates *less than* $1 of additional expenditure. For example, suppose that a $1 increase in disposable income brings a 75 cents increase in consumption expenditure and a 25 cents increase in saving. In this case, the tax multiplier would be 0.75 times the magnitude of the government purchases multiplier.

Tax multiplier
The magnification effect of a change in taxes on aggregate demand.

A Bush Tax Cut Multiplier Congress enacted the Bush tax cut package that lowered taxes in 2002. These tax cuts had a multiplier effect. With more disposable income, people increased consumption expenditure. This spending increased other people's incomes, which spurred yet more consumption expenditure. Like the increase in security expenditures, the tax cut and its multiplier effect helped to end the 2001 recession.

The Balanced Budget Multiplier

The **balanced budget multiplier** is the magnification effect on aggregate demand of a *simultaneous* change in government purchases and taxes that leaves the budget balance unchanged. The balanced budget multiplier is positive because a $1 increase in government purchases increases aggregate demand by more than a $1 increase in taxes decreases aggregate demand. So when both government purchases and taxes increase by $1, aggregate demand increases.

Balanced budget multiplier
The magnification effect on aggregate demand of a *simultaneous* change in government purchases and taxes that leaves the budget balance unchanged.

Discretionary Fiscal Stabilization

If real GDP is below potential GDP, discretionary fiscal policy might be used in an attempt to restore full employment. The government might increase its purchases of goods and services, cut taxes, or do some of both. These actions would increase aggregate demand. If they were timed correctly and were of the correct magnitude, they could restore full employment. Figure 21.2 shows how.

In Figure 21.2(a), potential GDP is \$10 trillion. Real GDP is \$9 trillion and the price level is 105. There is a \$1 trillion *deflationary gap* (see Chapter 20, p. 528).

To eliminate the deflationary gap and restore full employment, the government takes a discretionary fiscal policy action. An increase in government purchases or a tax cut increases aggregate expenditure by ΔE. If this were the only change in spending plans, the *AD* curve would become $AD_0 + \Delta E$ in Figure 21.2(b). But the increase in government purchases or the tax cut sets off a multiplier process, which increases consumption expenditure. As the multiplier process plays out, aggregate demand increases and the *AD* curve shifts rightward to AD_1.

With no change in the price level, the economy would move from the initial equilibrium point *A* to point *B* on AD_1. But the increase in aggregate demand combined with the upward-sloping aggregate supply curve brings a rise in the price level. So the economy moves to a new equilibrium at point C. The price level rises to 110, and real GDP increases to \$10 trillion. Full employment is restored.

FIGURE 21.2
Expansionary Fiscal Policy

Practice Online

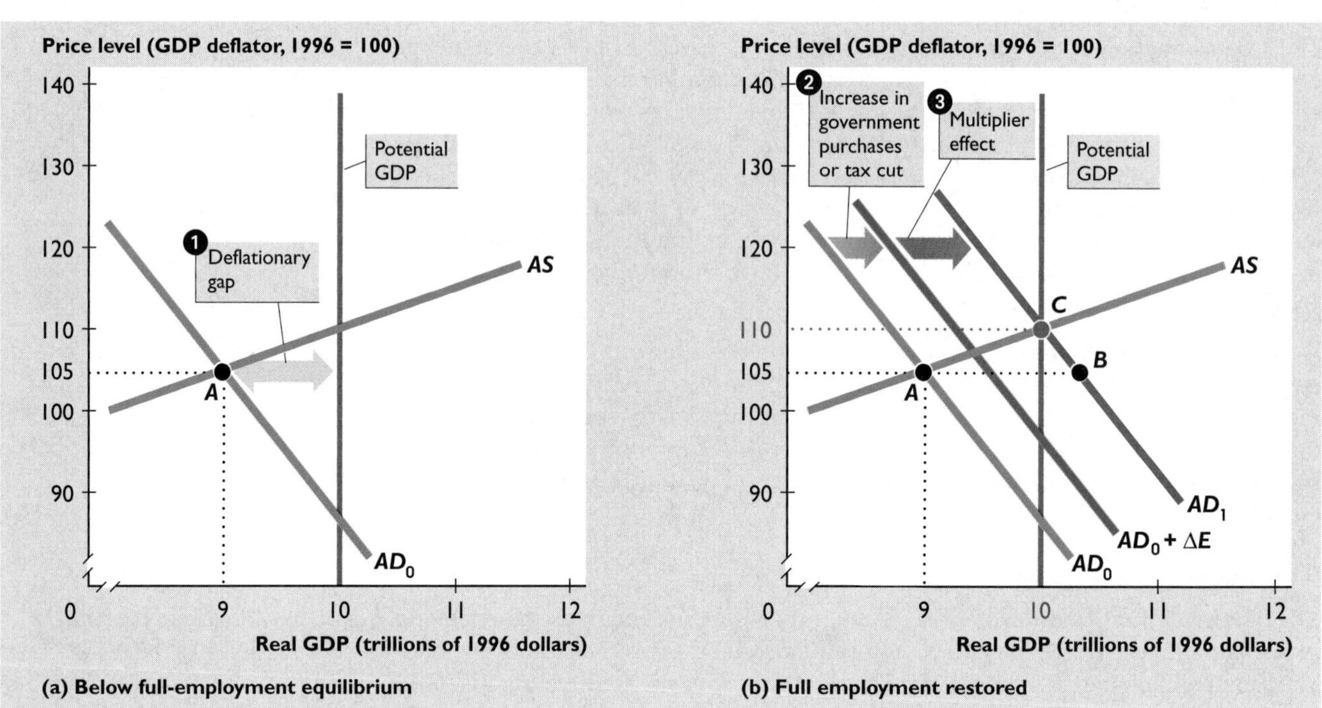

Potential GDP is \$10 trillion, real GDP is \$9 trillion, and ❶ there is a \$1 trillion deflationary gap. ❷ An increase in government purchases or a tax cut increases expenditure by ΔE. ❸ The multiplier increases induced expenditure. The *AD* curve shifts rightward to AD_1, the price level rises to 110, real GDP increases to \$10 trillion, and the deflationary gap is eliminated.

If an inflationary gap exists, discretionary fiscal policy can be used to decrease aggregate demand, restore full employment, and eliminate inflationary pressure. In this case, the government decreases its purchases of goods and services, raises taxes, or does some of both. These two actions decrease aggregate demand, decrease real GDP, and lower the price level. Figure 21.3 illustrates these effects.

In Figure 21.3(a), potential GDP is $10 trillion and equilibrium occurs at a real GDP of $11 trillion and a price level of 115. There is a $1 trillion *inflationary gap*.

To eliminate the inflationary gap and restore full employment, the government takes a discretionary fiscal policy action. A decrease in government purchases or a rise in taxes decreases aggregate expenditure by ΔE. If this were the only change in spending plans, the *AD* curve would become $AD_0 - \Delta E$. But the initial decrease in aggregate expenditure sets off a multiplier process, which decreases consumption expenditure. As the multiplier process plays out, aggregate demand decreases and the *AD* curve shifts leftward to AD_1.

With no change in the price level, the economy would move from the initial equilibrium point *A* to point *B* on AD_1 in Figure 21.3(b). But the decrease in aggregate demand combined with the upward-sloping *AS* curve brings a fall in the price level. So the economy moves to a new equilibrium at point *C*. The price level falls to 110, and real GDP decreases to $10 trillion. The inflationary gap has been eliminated, inflation has been avoided, and the economy is back at full employment.

FIGURE 21.3

Contractionary Fiscal Policy

Practice Online

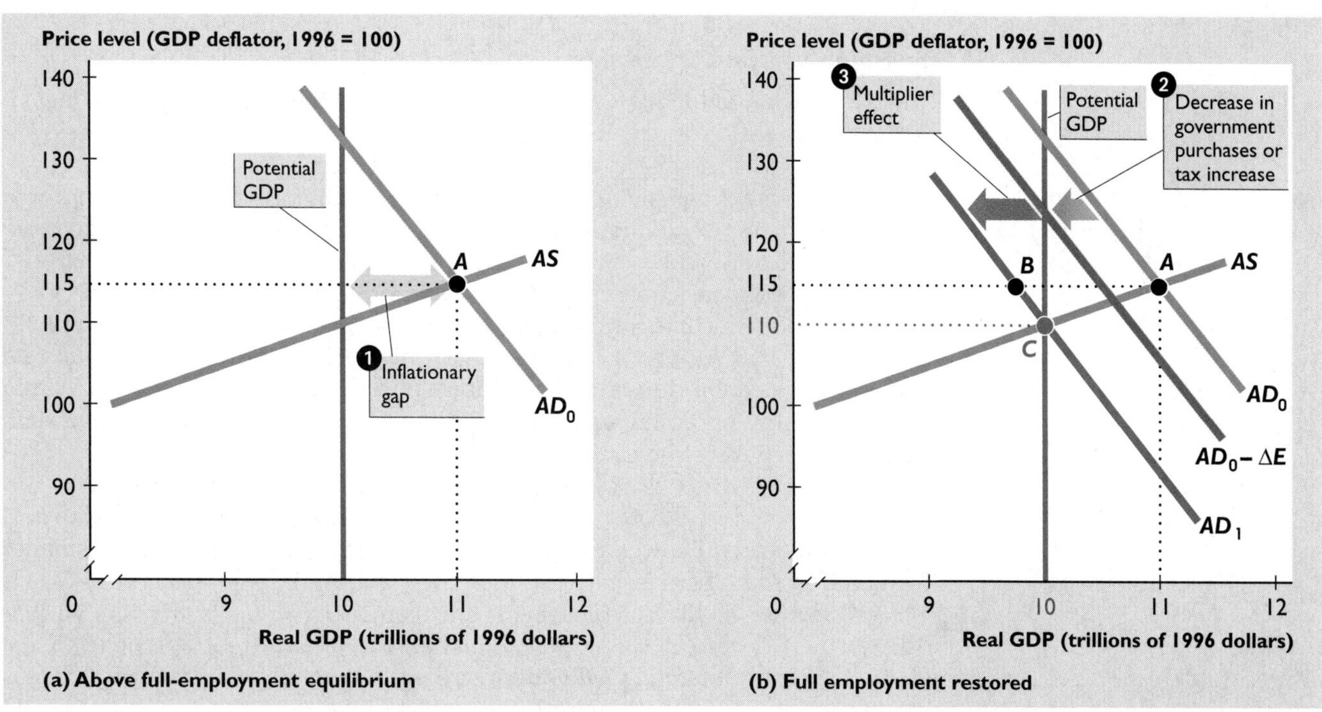

Potential GDP is $10 trillion, real GDP is $11 trillion, and ❶ there is a $1 trillion inflationary gap. ❷ A decrease in government purchases or a tax increase decreases expenditure by ΔE. ❸ The multiplier decreases induced expenditure. The *AD* curve shifts leftward to AD_1, the price level falls to 110, real GDP decreases to $10 trillion, and the inflationary gap is eliminated.

Discretionary Fiscal Policy: Supply-Side Effects

Both government purchases and taxes influence aggregate supply, and we now look at the supply-side effects of fiscal policy.

Supply-Side Effects of Government Purchases

Government provides services such as law and order, public education, and public health that increase production possibilities. For example, one of the reasons why we are more productive than the citizens of the poor developing countries is that we are better educated and healthier than they are. Government also provides social infrastructure capital such as highways, bridges, tunnels, and dams that increase our production possibilities. The interstate highway system that was begun during the 1950s is an example of the contribution that government purchases can make to the nation's production possibilities.

Government services and capital could be overprovided to the point at which they no longer increase production possibilities. But it is unlikely that we have reached such a point.

An *increase* in government purchases that increase the quantities of productive services and capital increases potential GDP and increases aggregate supply. A *decrease* in government purchases that decrease the quantities of productive services and capital decreases potential GDP and decreases aggregate supply.

Supply-Side Effects of Taxes

To pay for the productive services and capital that the government provides, it collects taxes. All taxes create disincentives to work, save, and provide entrepreneurial services. (The effects are like those in Chapter 7, pp. 168–174.)

Taxes on labor income decrease the supply of labor. And a smaller supply of labor means a higher equilibrium real wage rate and smaller equilibrium quantity of labor employed. With a smaller quantity of labor employed, potential GDP and aggregate supply are smaller than they would otherwise be.

Taxes on the income from capital decrease saving and decrease the supply of capital. A smaller supply of capital means a higher equilibrium real interest rate and a smaller equilibrium quantity of investment and capital employed. With a smaller quantity of capital, potential GDP and aggregate supply are smaller than they would otherwise be.

Taxes on the incomes of entrepreneurs weaken the incentive to take risks and create new businesses. With a smaller number of firms, the quantities of labor and capital employed are lower and potential GDP and aggregate supply are smaller than they would otherwise be.

An *increase* in taxes strengthens the disincentive effects that we've just described. It decreases the supply of labor, capital, and entrepreneurial services; decreases potential GDP; and decreases aggregate supply. And a tax cut has the opposite effects. It strengthens the incentives to work, save, and provide entrepreneurial services. So a tax cut increases potential GDP and aggregate supply.

Balanced Budget Supply-Side Effects

The supply-side effects of a balanced budget change in the scale of government are not clear. More productive spending increases potential GDP, but higher taxes to pay for the spending decreases potential GDP. So an increase in both taxes and government purchases might increase or decrease potential GDP and aggregate supply depending on which effect is stronger. Some economists (and politicians) believe that a larger scale of government increases potential GDP and aggregate supply despite the weakened incentives from higher tax rates. Others believe that the incentive effects are so powerful that smaller government is more productive and brings a greater potential GDP and aggregate supply.

Supply-Side Effects on the *AS* Curve

Figure 21.4 illustrates the effects of fiscal policy on aggregate supply. An increase in government purchases of productive services and capital or a tax cut increases potential GDP, and the aggregate supply curve shifts rightward from AS_0 to AS_1. A decrease in government purchases of productive services and capital or a tax rise decreases potential GDP, and the aggregate supply curve shifts leftward from AS_0 to AS_2.

Combined Demand and Supply Effects

When we combine the supply-side and demand-side effects, we see that an increase in government purchases or a tax cut increases equilibrium real GDP but might raise, lower, or have no effect on the price level. Figure 21.5 illustrates two cases for an expansionary fiscal policy.

FIGURE 21.4
The Effects of Fiscal Policy on Aggregate Supply

Practice Online

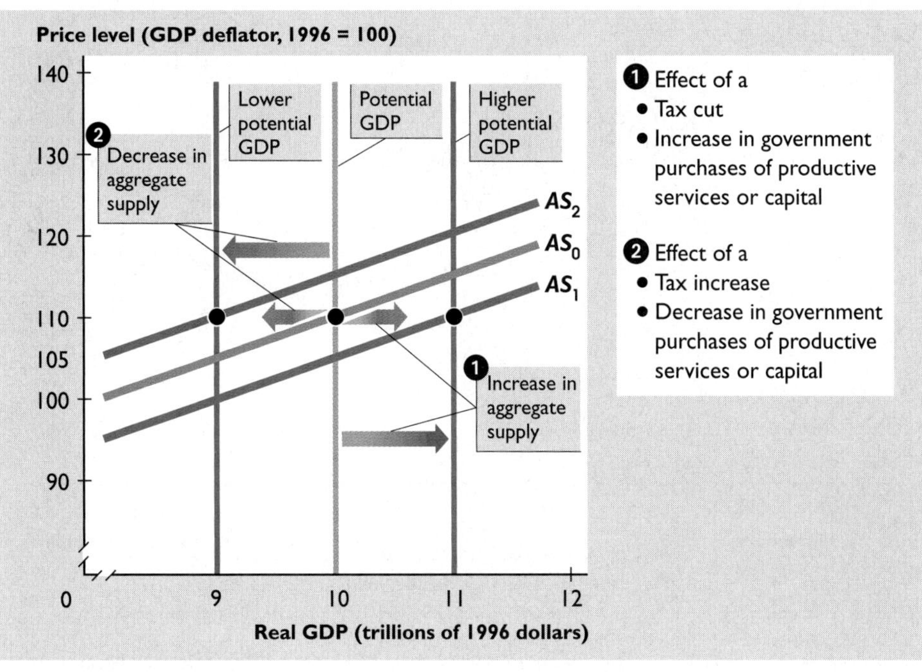

Figure 21.5(a) shows the case in which an expansionary fiscal policy increases aggregate demand by a large amount and shifts the *AD* curve from AD_0 to AD_1. The same fiscal actions also increase aggregate supply but this effect is small, so the *AS* curve shifts by a small amount, from AS_0 to AS_1. The combination of a large increase in aggregate demand and a small increase in aggregate supply increases real GDP and raises the price level.

Figure 21.5(b) shows the case in which an expansionary fiscal policy increases aggregate supply by a large amount, so the *AS* curve shifts from AS_0 to AS_1. The same fiscal actions increase aggregate demand but by a smaller amount and shift the *AD* curve from AD_0 to AD_1. The combination of a large increase in aggregate supply and a small increase in aggregate demand increases real GDP and *lowers* the price level. If the increase in aggregate demand and aggregate supply were equal, real GDP would increase and the price level would remain constant.

The outcome that actually occurs depends on the details of the fiscal policy. Some tax-cut packages would have larger supply-side effects than demand-side effects, and some would have larger demand-side effects than supply-side effects.

Some economists believe that the supply-side effects might be so powerful that a tax cut would end up *increasing* tax revenue. This outcome would occur if real GDP increased by a larger percentage than the percentage cut in tax rates so that when the lower tax rate is applied to the larger income, the total amount of tax revenue increases. There are no examples of this situation actually occurring.

FIGURE 21.5

The Combined Demand-Side and Supply-Side Effects of Fiscal Policy

Practice Online

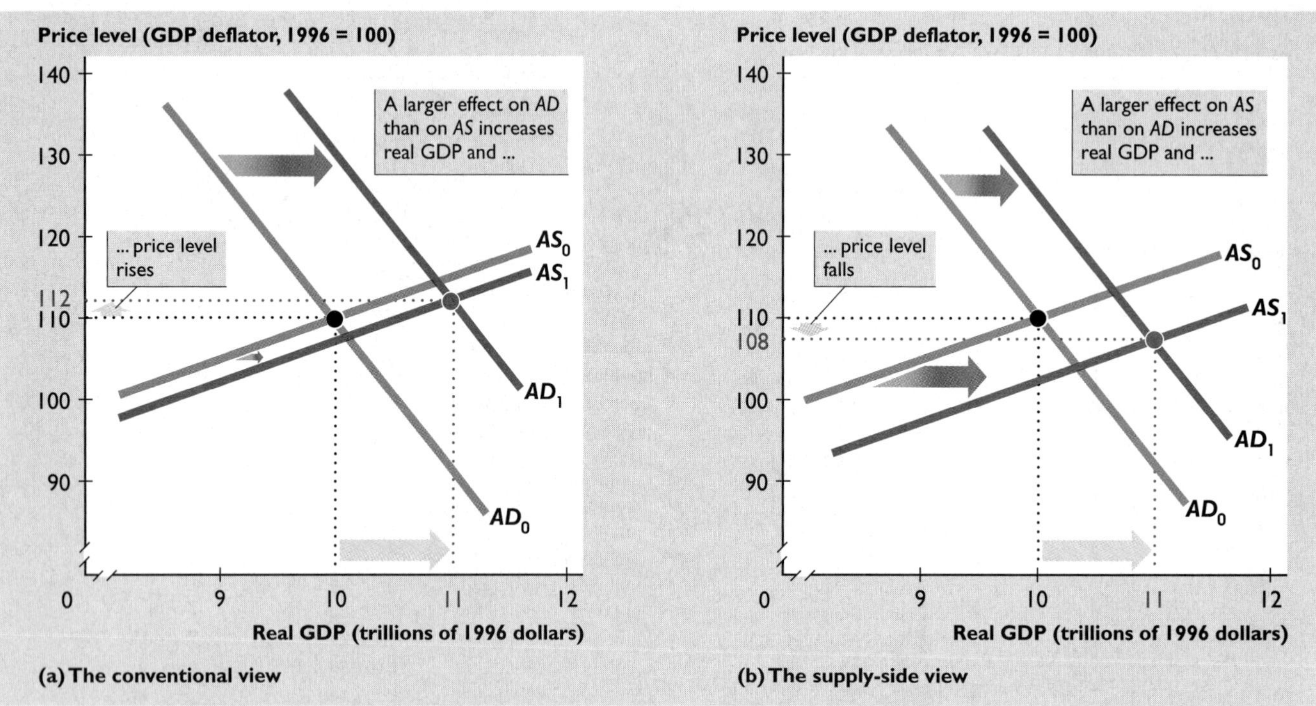

The conventional view (part a) is that an expansionary fiscal policy increases aggregate demand by more than it increases aggregate supply. Real GDP increases and the price level rises.

The supply-side view (part b) is that an expansionary fiscal policy increases aggregate supply by more than it increases aggregate demand. Real GDP increases and the price level falls.

Eye on the U.S. Economy

The 2003 Stimulus Package

At the beginning of 2003, it appeared that real GDP would be about $9,730 billion—some $130 billion below potential GDP—by the end of 2003. In the figure, aggregate demand curve AD_0 and aggregate supply curve AS_0 are consistent with this consensus view.

Concerned about the deflationary gap, President Bush proposed in January 2003 a tax cut of $100 billion in 2003 and $670 billion over the ten years through 2012.

The major tax change proposed was the abolition of personal income taxes on corporate profits paid to stockholders as dividends. This tax cut would lower the opportunity cost of funds to firms, increase investment in new capital, and increase both potential GDP and aggregate supply.

Aggregate demand curve AD_1 and aggregate supply curve AS_1 illustrate a good outcome for the President's plan.

For this outcome to occur the tax multiplier must be 1.3 and the supply-side effects of the tax cuts must equal the demand-side effects.

It is unlikely that these conditions will be met. The tax multiplier will probably be small because most of the lower taxes go to people with high incomes who will save a large part of their increased disposable income. So the increase in aggregate demand will be smaller than that shown in the figure. And the supply-side effects, which probably will be large, are not likely to occur quickly. So the increase in aggregate supply during 2003 will be smaller than that shown in the figure.

Most likely, real GDP will remain below potential GDP through 2003.

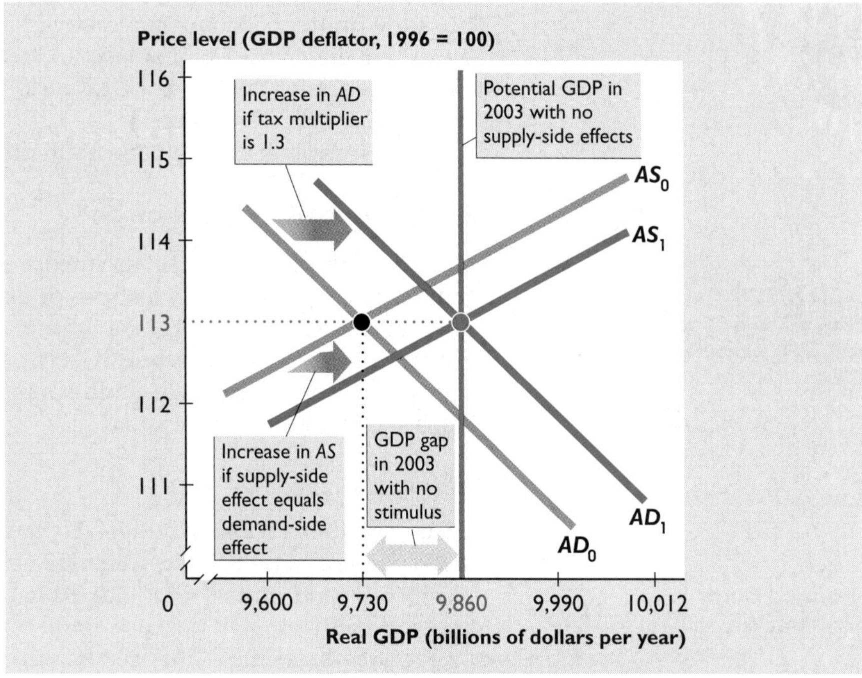

Limitations of Discretionary Fiscal Policy

Figures 21.2 and 21.3 make fiscal policy look easy. Calculate the deflationary gap or the inflationary gap, calculate the multiplier, and determine the magnitude of the change in government purchases or taxes that, with the multiplier effect, will eliminate the gap. In reality, things are not that easy. The use of discretionary fiscal policy is seriously hampered by three factors:

- Law-making time lag
- Estimating potential GDP
- Economic forecasting

Law-Making Time Lag

The law-making time lag is the amount of time it takes Congress to pass the laws needed to change taxes or spending. This process takes time because each member of Congress has a different idea about what is the best tax or spending program to change, so long debates and committee meetings are needed to reconcile conflicting views. The economy might benefit from fiscal stimulation today, but by the time Congress acts, a different fiscal medicine might be needed.

Estimating Potential GDP

It is not easy to tell whether real GDP is below, above, or at potential GDP. So a discretionary fiscal action might move real GDP *away* from potential GDP instead of toward it. This problem is a serious one because too much fiscal stimulation brings inflation and too little might bring recession.

Economic Forecasting

Fiscal policy changes take a long time to enact in Congress and yet more time to become effective. So fiscal policy must target forecasts of where the economy will be in the future. Economic forecasting has improved enormously in recent years, but it remains inexact and subject to error. So for a second reason, discretionary fiscal action might move real GDP *away* from potential GDP and create the very problems it seeks to correct.

Let's now look at automatic fiscal policy.

Automatic Fiscal Policy

Automatic stabilizers
Features of fiscal policy that stabilize real GDP without explicit action by the government.

Automatic fiscal policy is a consequence of tax receipts and expenditures that fluctuate with real GDP. These features of fiscal policy are called **automatic stabilizers** because they work to stabilize real GDP without explicit action by the government. Their name is borrowed from engineering and conjures up images of shock absorbers, thermostats, and sophisticated devices that keep airplanes and ships steady in turbulent air and seas.

Induced Taxes

Induced taxes
Taxes that vary with real GDP.

On the receipts side of the budget, tax laws define tax *rates*, not tax *dollars*. Tax dollars paid depend on tax rates and incomes. But incomes vary with real GDP, so tax receipts depend on real GDP. Taxes that vary with real GDP are called **induced taxes**. When real GDP increases in an expansion, wages and profits rise, so the taxes on these incomes—induced taxes—rise. When real GDP decreases in a recession, wages and profits fall, so the induced taxes on these incomes fall.

Needs-Tested Spending

Needs-tested spending
Spending on programs that entitle suitably qualified people and businesses to receive benefits—benefits that vary with need and with the state of the economy.

On the expenditure side of the budget, the government creates programs that pay benefits to suitably qualified people and businesses. The spending on such programs is called **needs-tested spending**, and it results in transfer payments that depend on the economic state of individual citizens and businesses. When the economy is in a recession, unemployment is high and the number of people experiencing economic hardship increases, but needs-tested spending on unemployment benefits and food stamps also increases. When the economy expands, unemployment falls, the number of people experiencing economic hardship decreases, and needs-tested spending decreases.

Induced taxes and needs-tested spending decrease the multiplier effects of changes in autonomous expenditure (such as investment and exports). So they moderate both expansions and recessions and make real GDP more stable. They achieve this outcome by weakening the link between real GDP and disposable income and so reduce the effect of a change in real GDP on consumption expenditure. When real GDP increases, induced taxes increase and needs-tested spending decreases, so disposable income does not increase by as much as the increase in real GDP. As a result, consumption expenditure does not increase by as much as it otherwise would have done and the multiplier effect is reduced.

CHECKPOINT 21.1

1 Describe the federal budget process and explain the effects of fiscal policy.

Study Guide pp. 314–318

Practice Online 21.1

Practice Problems 21.1

1. Classify each of the following as discretionary fiscal policy or automatic fiscal policy or neither.
   a. A decrease in tax receipts in a recession
   b. Additional expenditure to upgrade highways
   c. An increase in the public education budget
   d. A purchase of $1 billion of medicines to treat AIDS sufferers in Africa
   e. A cut in funding for NASA during an expansion
2. Explain the change in aggregate demand when
   a. Government purchases increase by $100 billion, which the government spends on national defense.
   b. Taxes are increased by $100 billion.
   c. Both parts **a** and **b** occur simultaneously.

Exercises 21.1

1. Classify each of the following as discretionary fiscal policy or automatic fiscal policy or neither.
   a. Huge fines are imposed on the tobacco companies
   b. A cut in the gas tax
   c. A cut in cross-border (custom) taxes
   d. The cost of refurnishing the White House basement
   e. An increase in payments to unemployed people
2. Illustrate, using an *AD-AS* graph, the effects of
   a. A $100 billion decrease in government purchases.
   b. A $100 billion decrease in taxes.
   c. Both parts **a** and **b** occurring simultaneously.

Solutions to Practice Problems 21.1

1a. A decrease in tax receipts in a recession is an automatic fiscal policy.
1b. Expenditure to upgrade highways is a discretionary fiscal policy.
1c. An increase in the public education budget is discretionary fiscal policy.
1d. A purchase of $1 billion of medicines is a discretionary fiscal policy.
1e. A cut in funding for NASA is a discretionary fiscal policy.

2a. Aggregate demand increases by more than $100 billion because the increase in government purchases has a multiplier effect that increases induced expenditure.
2b. Aggregate demand decreases by more than $100 billion because the tax increase has a multiplier effect that decreases induced expenditure.
2c. Aggregate demand increases because the increase in part **a** is larger than the decrease in part **b**.

21.2 THE FEDERAL RESERVE AND MONETARY POLICY

You learned about the structure of the Federal Reserve in Chapter 17, how the Fed controls the quantity of money in Chapter 18, and how the quantity of money influences interest rates in Chapter 19. Here, we're going to see how the Fed monitors the economy and examine the effects of its policy actions on aggregate demand and how the effects of those actions ripple through the economy to influence real GDP and the price level.

The Monetary Policy Process

The Fed makes monetary policy in a process that has three main elements:

- Monitoring economic conditions
- Meetings of the Federal Open Market Committee (FOMC)
- Monetary Policy Report to Congress

Monitoring Economic Conditions

Each Federal Reserve Bank constantly gathers information on its district by talking with business leaders, economists, market experts, and others. The Fed brings the results together in the **Beige Book**, which is published eight times a year. The Beige Book serves as a background document for the members of the Federal Open Market Committee.

Beige Book
A report that summarizes current economic conditions in each Federal Reserve district and each sector of the economy.

The Beige Book is a public document that is easily accessible on the Fed's Web site and is a good source of current information for businesses and anyone who wants to be well informed about the current state of the economy.

Meetings of the Federal Open Market Committee (FOMC)

The FOMC, which meets eight times a year, makes the monetary policy decisions. The FOMC's first and fourth meetings of the year run for two days (the other six meetings run for one day) and are opportunities for the committee to assess the longer-term outlook as well as the current period's open market operations.

After each meeting, the FOMC announces its decisions and describes its view of the likelihood that its goals of price stability and sustainable economic growth will be achieved. The FOMC publishes the minutes of its meetings after they have been confirmed as a correct record of the meeting at the next scheduled meeting. For example, the minutes of the first meeting of the year are published after the second meeting of the year.

Full transcripts of FOMC meetings are published with a five-year time lag. This delay enables the members of the FOMC to have a frank exchange of views without worrying about how their discussions might be interpreted by the traders in financial markets. The eventual publication of the transcripts permits a detailed public scrutiny of the FOMC's decision-making process.

Monetary Policy Report to Congress

Twice a year, in February and July, the Fed prepares a Monetary Policy Report to Congress, and the Fed chairman testifies before the House of Representatives Committee on Financial Services. The report and the chairman's testimony review the monetary policy and economic developments of the past year and the economic outlook for the coming year.

Influencing the Interest Rate

When the FOMC announces a policy change, its press release talks about the federal funds interest rate, the interest rate at which banks borrow reserves from each other, or the discount rate, the interest rate at which banks borrow reserves from the Fed. The press release does not talk about the quantity of money or the size of the open market operations it plans to conduct. This focus on interest rates makes it appear as though the Fed determines interest rates rather than the quantity of money. But this impression is misleading for two reasons: a long-run reason and a short-run reason.

In the Long Run

In the long run, saving supply and investment demand determine the real interest rate in global financial markets. The inflation rate, along with the real interest rate, determines the nominal interest rate (Chapter 19, p. 391). The inflation rate in the long run is determined by the growth rate of the quantity of money that results from the Fed's actions.

So in the long run, the Fed *influences* the nominal interest rate by the effects of its policies on the inflation rate. But it does not directly control the nominal interest rate, and it has no control over the real interest rate.

In the Short Run

In the short run, the Fed influences both the nominal interest rate and the real interest rate. To change the nominal interest rate, the Fed undertakes an open market operation that changes the quantity of money. It is by changing the quantity of money that the Fed achieves its target for the federal funds rate. The expected inflation rate doesn't change every time the Fed changes the nominal interest rate. So an open market operation changes the real interest rate in the short run.

The Fed Raises the Interest Rate

Suppose that the Fed fears inflation and decides it must to take action to decrease aggregate demand. The FOMC announces that it will raise the short-term interest rate. How does the Fed achieve this goal?

The FOMC instructs the New York Fed to sell securities in the open market. This action mops up bank reserves. Some banks are short of reserves and seek to borrow reserves from other banks. The federal funds interest rate rises. With fewer reserves, the banks make a smaller quantity of new loans each day until the quantity of loans outstanding has fallen to a level that is consistent with the new lower level of reserves. The quantity of money decreases.

The demand for money determines the quantity of money that will achieve the FOMC's interest rate target. The Fed could, if it chose, fix the quantity of money and let the interest rate adjust to its equilibrium level. Or the Fed can, and does, fix the interest rate and adjust the quantity of money to the level that makes the chosen interest rate the equilibrium rate.

Suppose, for example, that the short-term nominal interest rate is 5 percent a year and the FOMC decides that it needs to rise to 6 percent a year. Figure 21.6(a) illustrates what the Fed must do. The demand for money is *MD*, so when the interest rate is 5 percent a year, the quantity of money is $1 trillion. The Fed

FIGURE 21.6
Interest Rate Changes

Practice Online

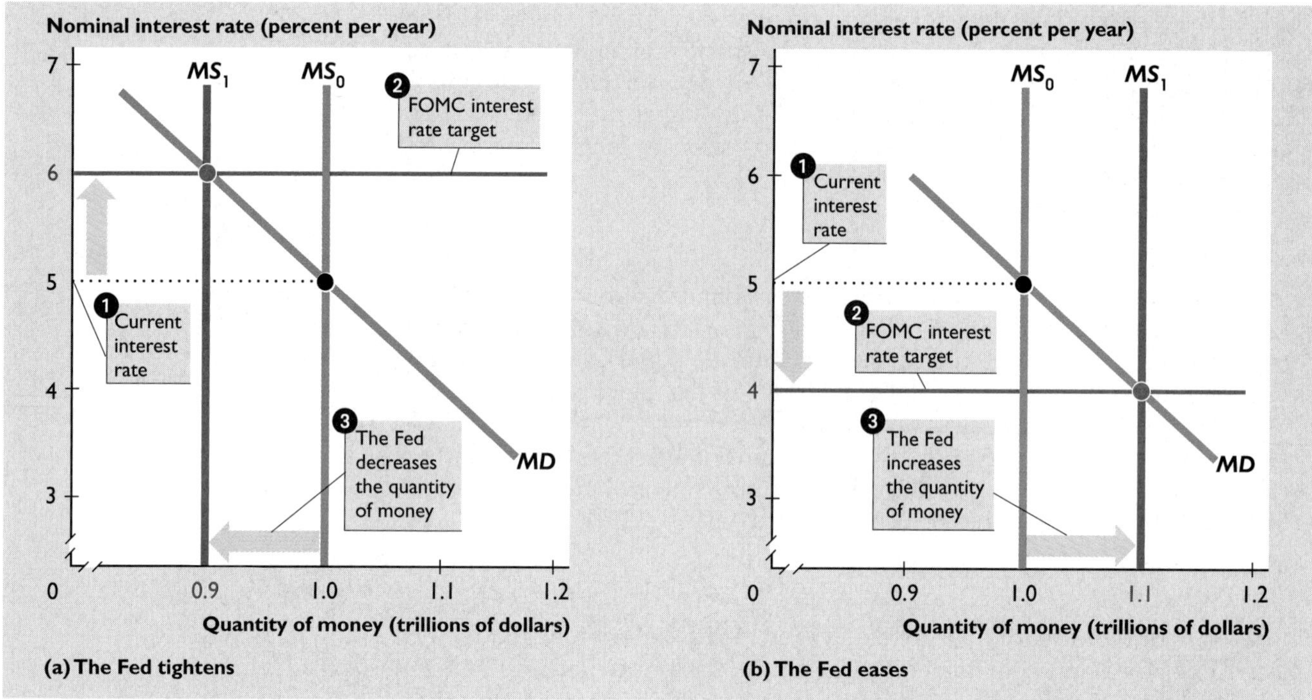

❶ The current interest rate is 5 percent a year, and ❷ the FOMC's target is 6 percent a year. To raise the interest rate to the target, the Fed must sell securities in the open market and ❸ decrease the quantity of money to $0.9 trillion.

❶ The current interest rate is 5 percent a year, and ❷ the FOMC's target is 4 percent a year. To lower the interest rate to the target, the Fed must buy securities in the open market and ❸ increase the quantity of money to $1.1 trillion.

conducts an open market sale on a sufficiently large scale to decrease the quantity of money from $1 trillion to $0.9 trillion. When the quantity of money is $0.9 trillion, the nominal interest rate is 6 percent a year, the FOMC's target level.

The Fed Lowers the Interest Rate

If the Fed fears recession, it acts to increase aggregate demand. The FOMC announces that it will lower the short-term interest rate. To achieve this goal, the FOMC instructs the New York Fed to buy securities in the open market. This action increases bank reserves. Flush with reserves, banks now seek to lend reserves to other banks. The federal funds rate falls. With more reserves, the banks increase their lending and the quantity of money increases.

Again, the demand for money determines the change in the quantity of money that achieves the Fed's interest rate target. Suppose the FOMC wants to lower the interest rate from 5 percent a year to 4 percent a year. Figure 21.6(b) shows what it must do. When the interest rate is 5 percent a year, the quantity of money is $1 trillion. The Fed conducts an open market purchase on a sufficiently large scale to increase the quantity of money from $1 trillion to $1.1 trillion. When the quantity of money is $1.1 trillion, the nominal interest rate is 4 percent a year, the FOMC's target level.

The Ripple Effects of the Fed's Actions

Suppose that the Fed increases the interest rate. What happens next?

Three main events follow:

- Investment and consumption expenditure decrease.
- The dollar rises, and net exports decrease.
- A multiplier process induces a further decrease in consumption expenditure and aggregate demand.

Investment and Consumption Expenditure

The interest rate influences investment and consumption expenditure. When the Fed increases the nominal interest rate, the real interest rate rises temporarily, and investment and expenditure on consumer durables decrease. The reason is that the interest rate is the *opportunity cost* of the funds used to finance investment and the purchase of big-ticket consumer items. So when the opportunity costs of buying capital and consumer goods rise, the quantities bought and expenditures on these items decrease.

The Dollar and Net Exports

A rise in the interest rate, other things remaining the same, means that the U.S. interest rate rises relative to the interest rates in other countries. Some people will want to move funds into the United States from other countries to take advantage of the higher interest rate they can now earn on their U.S. bank deposits and bonds. When money is moved into the United States, people buy dollars and sell other currencies, such as Japanese yen or British pounds. With more dollars demanded, the price of the dollar rises on the foreign exchange market.

The higher price of the dollar means that foreigners must now pay more for U.S.-made goods and services. So the quantity demanded and the expenditure on U.S.-made items decrease. U.S. exports decrease. Similarly, the higher price of the dollar means that Americans now pay less for foreign-made goods and services. So the quantity demanded and the expenditure on foreign-made items increase. U.S. imports increase.

The Multiplier Process

Because investment, consumption expenditure, and net exports are all interest-sensitive components of expenditure, a rise in the interest rate brings a decrease in aggregate expenditure.

You already know the rest of the story, because it is the same as that of the fiscal policy multipliers. The decrease in expenditure decreases incomes, and the decrease in income induces a decrease in consumption expenditure. The decreased consumption expenditure lowers aggregate expenditure. Real GDP and disposable income decrease further, and so does consumption expenditure. Real GDP growth slows, and the inflation rate slows.

If the Fed lowers the interest rate, the events that we've just described occur in the opposite directions, so real GDP growth and the inflation rate speed up.

Figure 21.7 summarizes the process that we've just described. It begins with the Fed's open market operations that change the quantity of money and interest rate and ends with the effects on real GDP and the price level.

FIGURE 21.7
Ripple Effects of the Fed's Actions

Practice Online

The Fed's open market operations change the quantity of money and the interest rate. Expenditure plans eventually change, and so does aggregate demand. Eventually, the Fed's open market operation has ripple effects that change real GDP and the price level.

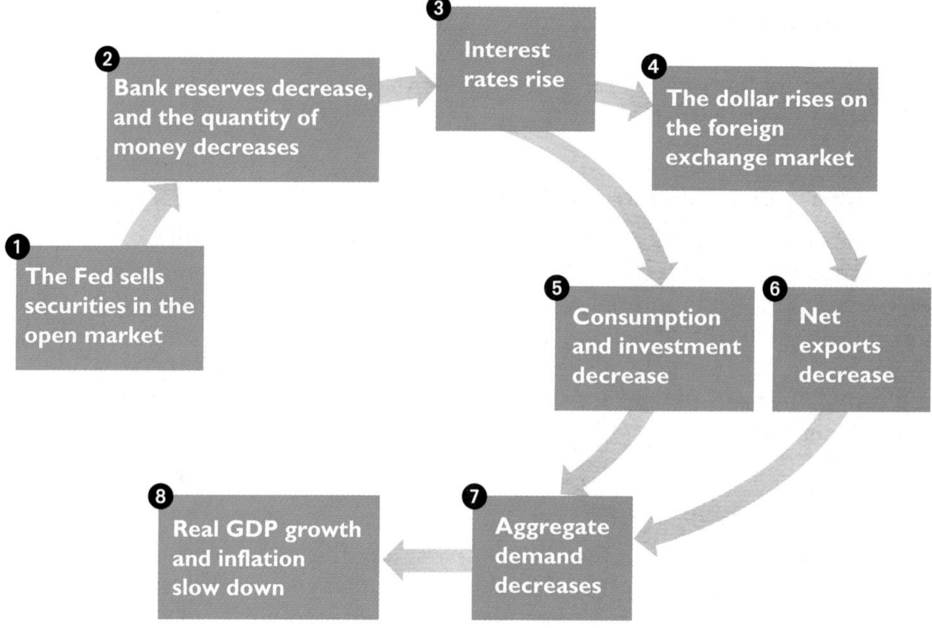

(a) The Fed tightens

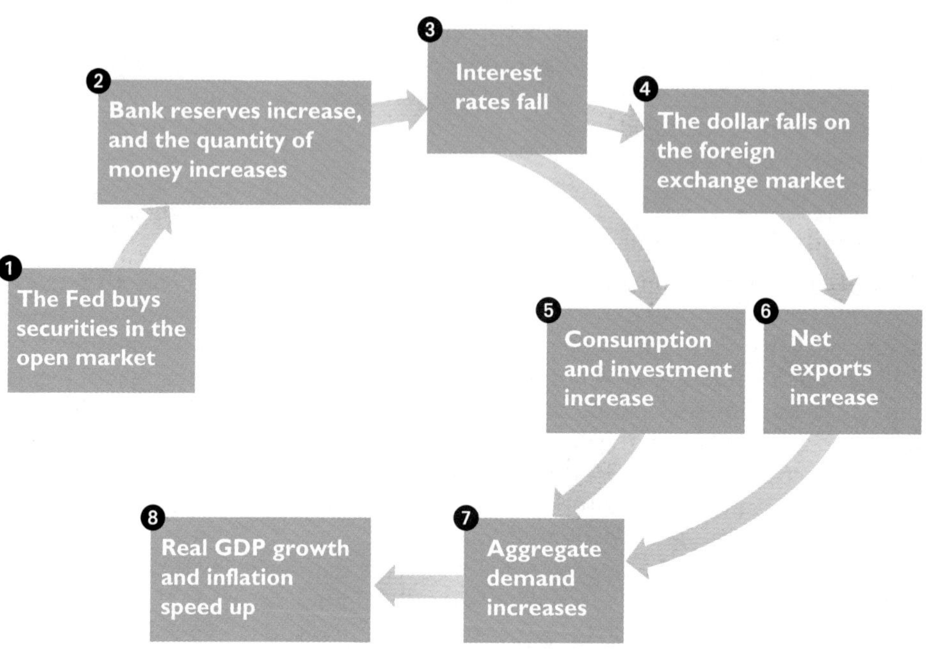

(b) The Fed eases

Monetary Stabilization in the *AS-AD* Model

We've described the broad outline of how the Fed's actions influence the economy. Let's now see how monetary policy might be used to stabilize real GDP.

The Fed Tightens to Fight Inflation

In Figure 21.8, part (a) shows investment demand and part (b) shows aggregate demand and aggregate supply. Initially, the interest rate is 5 percent a year and the quantity of investment is $2 trillion. At this level of investment (think of investment demand as representing all the interest-sensitive components of aggregate expenditure), aggregate demand is AD_0 in part (b). The aggregate supply curve is *AS*, so equilibrium real GDP is $11 trillion, which exceeds potential GDP.

The Fed now conducts an open market sale that increases the interest rate to 6 percent a year. The quantity of investment demand decreases to $1.5 trillion. If this were the only change in aggregate expenditure, aggregate demand would be $AD_0 - \Delta I$. But the multiplier decreases aggregate demand and the aggregate demand curve shifts leftward to AD_1.

The Fed's actions have eliminated an inflation threat, brought real GDP to equal potential GDP, and lowered the price level. In reality, real GDP is growing and the price level is rising, so the Fed's actions would slow real GDP growth and slow inflation rather than decrease real GDP and the price level.

FIGURE 21.8

Monetary Stabilization: Avoiding Inflation

Practice Online

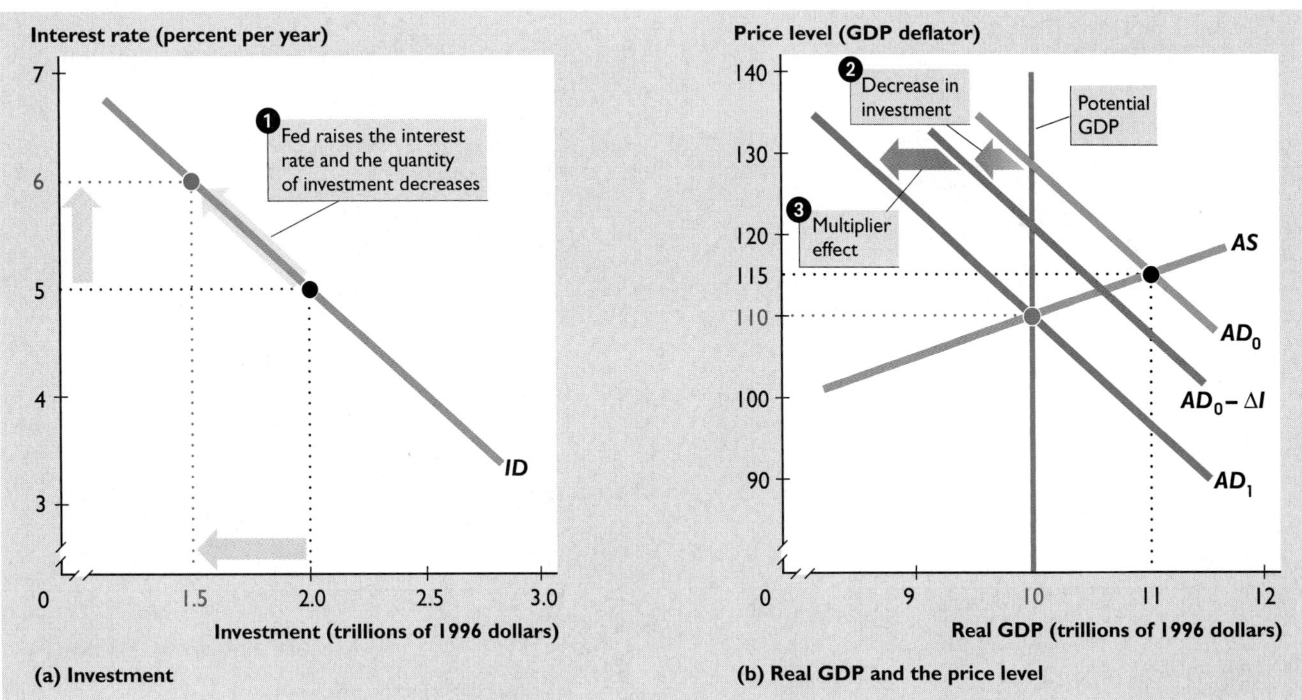

Real GDP exceeds potential GDP (part b). To avoid inflation, ❶ the Fed raises the interest rate (part a). ❷ Expenditure decreases by ΔI, and ❸ the multiplier induces additional expenditure cuts. The aggregate demand curve shifts to AD_1, real GDP decreases to potential GDP, and inflation is avoided.

The Fed Eases to Fight Recession

Figure 21.9 is similar to Figure 21.8, which you've just examined. The starting point in part (a) is the same. The interest rate is 5 percent a year, and the quantity of investment demanded is $2 trillion. But the starting point in part (b) is different. Now, at the equilibrium level of investment (and other components of aggregate expenditure), aggregate demand is AD_0 in part (b). The aggregate supply curve is *AS*, so equilibrium real GDP is $9 trillion, which is less than potential GDP.

The Fed now conducts an open market purchase that lowers the interest rate to 4 percent a year. The quantity of investment increases to $2.5 trillion. Other interest-sensitive expenditure items (not shown in the figure) also increase. If this were the only change, aggregate demand would increase to $AD_0 + \Delta I$.

With an increase in aggregate expenditure, the multiplier increases aggregate demand. The aggregate demand curve shifts to AD_1. The Fed's actions have eliminated a recession and brought real GDP to equal potential GDP at $10 trillion and the price level to 110.

The Size of the Multiplier Effect

The size of the multiplier effect of monetary policy depends on the sensitivity of expenditure plans to the interest rate The larger the effect of a change in the interest rate on aggregate expenditure, the greater is the multiplier effect and the smaller is the change in the interest rate that achieves the Fed's objective.

FIGURE 21.9

Monetary Stabilization: Avoiding Recession

Practice Online

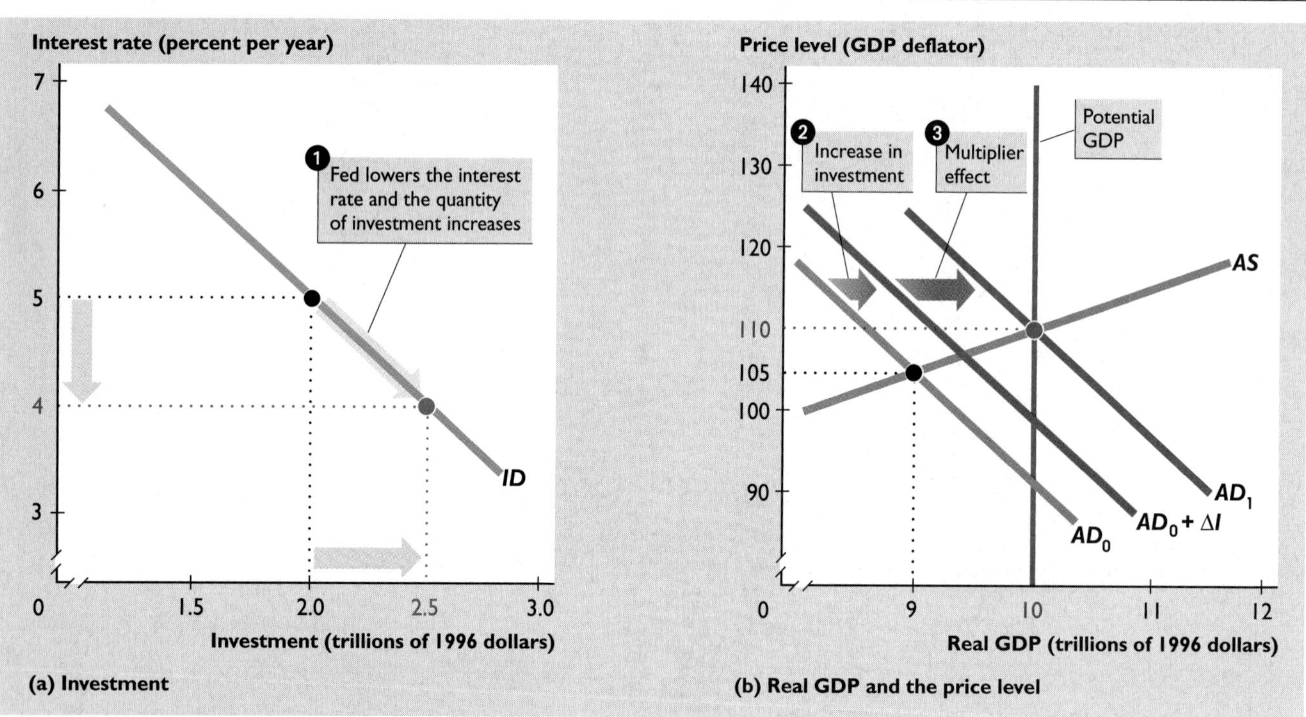

Real GDP is less than potential GDP (part b). To avoid recession, ❶ the Fed lowers the interest rate (part a). ❷ Expenditure increases by ΔI, and ❸ the multiplier induces additional expenditure. The aggregate demand curve shifts to AD_1, real GDP increases to potential GDP, and recession is avoided.

Limitations of Monetary Stabilization Policy

Monetary policy has an advantage over fiscal policy because it cuts out the lawmaking time lags. The FOMC meets eight times a year and can conduct telephone meetings between its scheduled meetings if the need arises. And the actual actions that change the quantity of money are daily actions taken by the New York Fed operating under the guidelines decided by the FOMC. So monetary policy is a continuous policy process and is not subject to the long decision lag and the need to create a broad political consensus that confronts fiscal policy.

But monetary policy shares the other two limitations of fiscal policy: Estimating potential GDP is hard, and economic forecasting is error-prone. Monetary policy suffers an additional limitation: Its effects are indirect and depend on how private decisions respond to a change in the interest rate. These responses are themselves hard to forecast and vary from one situation to another in unpredictable ways. A related problem is that the time lags in the operation of monetary policy are longer than those for fiscal policy. So the forecasting horizon must be longer.

In this chapter, we've described the fiscal and monetary policy processes and explained the effects of stabilization policies on real GDP and the price level.

Eye on the U.S. Economy

The Fed in Action

The figure shows the federal funds rate and the 3-month Treasury bill rate between 1972 and 2002. The 3-month Treasury bill rate is a good general indicator of the cost of short-term loans to the federal government and large firms.

Notice how closely these interest rates move together. The federal funds rate, which the Fed directly targets, is the main influence on the short-term interest rate at which the government and businesses borrow.

Interest rate hikes brought three recessions: in the mid-1970s, early 1980s, and early 1990s. Through most of the 1990s, the Fed tried to keep the economy expanding while avoiding inflation. So interest rates and money growth were kept steady.

In 2000, the Fed raised short-term interest rates. But fearing recession, the Fed lowered rates aggressively during 2001 and 2002 to an unusually low 1.7 percent a year.

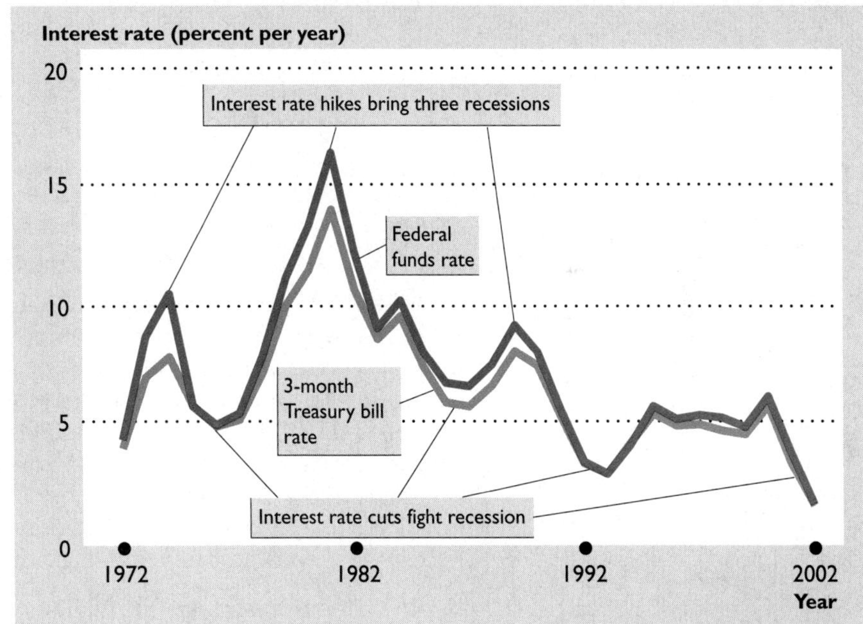

SOURCE: Federal Reserve Board.

CHECKPOINT 21.2

Study Guide **pp. 318–321**

Practice Online 21.2

2 **Describe the Federal Reserve's monetary policy process and explain the effects of monetary policy.**

Practice Problems 21.2

1. If the Fed cuts the quantity of money, explain how each of the following items changes.
   a. Businesses' purchases of new capital equipment
   b. Households' purchases of new cars and houses
   c. Foreigners' purchases of U.S.-made goods and services
   d. Americans' purchases of Canadian-made goods and services
2. What is the multiplier effect of monetary policy? How does it work? How does the size of the expenditure multiplier influence the size of the multiplier effect of monetary policy?

Exercises 21.2

1. If the Fed lowers the interest rate, explain how each of the following items changes.
   a. U.S exports
   b. U.S. imports
   c. Investment
   d. The value of the dollar on the foreign exchange market
2. Explain the process by which the Fed's monetary policy influences aggregate demand in the United States.
3. Compare the effectiveness of monetary policy and fiscal policy for stabilizing U.S real GDP and employment.

Solutions to Practice Problems 21.2

1a. When the Fed cuts the quantity of money, the interest rate rises and businesses delay their purchases of new capital equipment.

1b. Households will delay their purchases of new cars and houses.

1c. As the U.S. interest rate rises and foreign interest rates remain the same, the dollar strengthens. U.S.-made goods and services become relatively more expensive for foreigners to buy. Foreigners' purchases of U.S.-made goods and services decrease.

1d. As the dollar strengthens, Canadian-made goods become cheaper for Americans to buy. Americans' purchases of Canadian-produced goods increase.

2. When the Fed increases the quantity of money, interest rates fall and the foreign exchange value of the dollar falls. As interest rates fall, aggregate expenditure increases because investment, consumption expenditure, and net exports increase. The multiplier effect of monetary policy is the increase in aggregate expenditure divided by the increase in the quantity of money.
When the interest rate changes, part of autonomous expenditure changes and the expenditure multiplier determines the change in aggregate demand. The larger the expenditure multiplier, the larger is the multiplier effect of monetary policy.

CHAPTER CHECKPOINT

Key Points

1 Describe the federal budget process and explain the effects of fiscal policy.

- The federal budget is an annual statement of the expenditures, tax receipts, and surplus or deficit of the government of the United States.
- Fiscal policy is the use of the federal budget to finance the federal government and to stabilize the economy.
- Fiscal policy can be either discretionary or automatic.
- Changes in government purchases and changes in taxes have multiplier effects on aggregate demand and can be used to try to keep real GDP at potential GDP.
- In practice, law-making time lags, the difficulty of estimating potential GDP, and the limitations of economic forecasting seriously hamper discretionary fiscal policy.
- Automatic stabilizers arise because tax receipts and expenditures fluctuate with real GDP.

2 Describe the Federal Reserve's monetary policy process and explain the effects of monetary policy.

- The Fed makes monetary policy in an open and transparent process that involves three main elements: the Beige Book, meetings of the Federal Open Market Committee, and the Monetary Policy Report to Congress.
- When the FOMC announces a policy change, it is in terms of the interest rate, not the quantity of money.
- In the long run, the Fed influences the nominal interest rate by the effects of its policies on the inflation rate. But it does not directly control the nominal interest rate, and it has no control over the real interest rate.
- In the short run, the Fed can determine the nominal interest rate, but to do so, it must undertake open market operations that change the quantity of money.
- When the Fed changes the interest rate, the effects ripple through the economy by changing aggregate demand.
- The size of the multiplier effect of monetary policy depends on the sensitivity of expenditure plans to the interest rate.
- Monetary policy has no law-making time lag, but its effects are indirect and depend on how the interest rate influences private decisions.

Key Terms

Automatic fiscal policy, 538
Automatic stabilizers, 546
Balanced budget, 536
Balanced budget multiplier, 539
Beige Book, 548
Budget deficit, 536
Budget surplus, 536
Discretionary fiscal policy, 538
Federal budget, 536
Fiscal policy, 536
Government purchases multiplier, 539
Induced taxes, 546
Needs-tested spending, 546
Tax multiplier, 539

Exercises

1. How did the role of fiscal policy change in 1946? What are the main provisions of the landmark act that changed it? What further change occurred in 1978?

2. Sort the following items into those that are discretionary fiscal policy actions, those that are automatic fiscal policy actions, and those that are not fiscal policy.
   - **a.** An increase in expenditure on homeland security
   - **b.** An increase in unemployment benefits paid during the 2001 recession
   - **c.** The Bush tax cuts
   - **d.** An open market operation
   - **e.** The fall in taxes paid by corporations because their profits fell in 2001
   - **f.** Increased expenditures on national defense arising from the war against terrorism
   - **g.** A rise in the federal funds rate
   - **h.** An increase in Medicaid expenditure brought about by a flu epidemic
   - **i.** The changes in farm subsidies arising from the 2002 Farm Bill
   - **j.** A fall in customs revenue that resulted from a decrease in U.S. imports

3. Suppose that the U.S. government increases its expenditure on highways and bridges by $100 billion in 2003. Explain the effect that this expenditure would have on
   - **a.** Autonomous expenditure.
   - **b.** Aggregate demand.
   - **c.** Real GDP.
   - **d.** Needs-tested spending.
   - **e.** The government's budget surplus.

4. Suppose that Congress passes additional tax cuts that total $100 billion in 2004. Explain the effect that this tax cut would have on
   - **a.** Consumption expenditure before any change in real GDP occurs.
   - **b.** Consumption expenditure induced by a change in real GDP.
   - **c.** Aggregate demand.
   - **d.** Real GDP.
   - **e.** The government's budget surplus.

5. The income tax rate is higher in Sweden than it is in the United States. Also, Sweden has more generous payments to the unemployed and others who fall on hard economic times. And the percentage of expenditure on imported goods and services is much larger in Sweden than in the United States. Which country, Sweden or the United States, do you think is likely to have
   - **a.** The larger government purchases multiplier?
   - **b.** The larger tax multiplier?
   - **c.** The more effective automatic stabilizers?
   - **d.** The greater fluctuations in real GDP over the business cycle?
   - **e.** The greater fluctuations in the government budget balance over the business cycle?
   - **f.** The larger supply-side effects of fiscal policy?

6. Describe the supply-side effects of fiscal policy and explain how a tax cut or an increase in government purchases might influence
   a. Potential GDP.
   b. Aggregate supply.
   c. Equilibrium real GDP and the price level.
   Use an aggregate supply–aggregate demand graph to illustrate the effects you've described.
7. Suppose that the Fed sees an expansion slowing and forecasts a recession in the near future. What change in its monetary policy would lessen the effect of the recession? Use appropriate graphs to explain and illustrate the effect of the Fed's actions on
   a. Interest rates.
   b. The quantity of money.
   c. Investment.
   d. The foreign exchange value of the dollar.
   e. Net exports.
   f. Aggregate demand.
   g. Real GDP and the price level.
8. Suppose that the Fed sees the current expansion gaining too much steam and forecasts an increase in inflation in the near future. What change in its monetary policy would lessen the likelihood of inflation? Use appropriate graphs to explain and illustrate the effect of the Fed's actions on
   a. Interest rates.
   b. The quantity of money.
   c. Investment.
   d. The foreign exchange value of the dollar.
   e. Net exports.
   f. Aggregate demand.
   g. Real GDP and the price level.
9. Explain why monetary policy is used more often than fiscal policy to stabilize the economy.
10. Explain the effect of a decrease in the quantity of money on aggregate demand. What determines how big the change in aggregate demand will be?
11. If the U.S. government wanted to increase investment, would it encourage the Fed to change its monetary policy or would the government change its fiscal policy? Explain why. What effect would the policy change have on the price level?
12. If the U.S. government wanted to increase exports, would it encourage the Fed to change its monetary policy or would the government change its fiscal policy? Explain why. What effect would the policy change have on the composition of aggregate expenditure?

Critical Thinking

13. Suppose that Bill Frist (Republican) and Tom Daschle (Democrat) are debating the effects of fiscal policy on real GDP and the price level. Bill Frist says that a tax cut will increase real GDP and keep the price level stable. Tom Daschle says that the tax cut will only line the pockets of the rich and have no effects on output or the price level.
    a. Using the aggregate supply–aggregate demand model, provide an explanation of what Bill Frist says will happen.
    b. Using the aggregate supply–aggregate demand model, provide an explanation of what Tom Daschle says will happen.
    c. Highlight the differences in assumptions about how the economy works and sketch a research project that could settle the debate.
14. Review the main limitations of discretionary fiscal policy and contrast those limitations with the benefits of automatic fiscal policy.
15. In the U.S. recession of 2001, government purchases increased and taxes were cut. Explain how the government's actions
    a. Changed aggregate demand.
    b. Changed the budget surplus and outstanding government debt.
16. Describe and critically evaluate the effects of the actions taken by the Federal Reserve and the federal government during 2002 to stimulate the U.S. economy and lift it from recession.

Practice Online

Web Exercises

Use the links on your Foundations Web site to work the following exercises.

17. Visit the Office of Management and Budget Web site and review the history of the budget surplus/deficit and the national debt. What events have led to the greatest increases in the national debt? In which periods has the debt been paid down? Looking at the history of the U.S. federal budget, do you think the current plan to pay off the national debt will be carried out? Why or why not?
18. Visit the Federal Reserve's Web site and review the current state of the U.S. economy using the latest issue of the Beige Book. In light of what you discover about real GDP, inflation, and the unemployment rate, set out your policy recommendations to
    a. The FOMC.
    b. Congress.
19. Visit the IMF World Economic Outlook Web site to review the current state of the global economy. [Change the 2002 in this URL to the current year and change 02 to 01 before October.] In light of what you discover about real GDP growth and inflation, set out your policy advice to the governments of the major countries.

CHAPTER 22

International Trade

CHAPTER CHECKLIST

When you have completed your study of this chapter, you will be able to

1. **Describe the patterns and trends in international trade.**
2. **Explain why nations engage in international trade and why trade benefits all nations.**
3. **Explain how trade barriers reduce international trade.**
4. **Explain the arguments used to justify trade barriers and show why they are incorrect but also why some barriers are hard to remove.**

We live in a global economy, and macroeconomic disturbances in one part of the world quickly transmit to other parts. Also, wages in most nations are lower than wages in the United States. How can we compete with countries that pay their workers a fraction of U.S. wages?

Would it be better if we isolated our economy from the rest of the world? Or are there some gains from trading with other nations that are worth the macroeconomic disturbances and international competition they bring?

In this chapter, you are going to learn about international trade. You will discover how all nations can gain by specializing in producing the goods and services in which they have a comparative advantage and trading with other countries. You will discover that all countries can compete, no matter how high their wages. And you'll learn why, despite the fact that international trade brings benefits to all countries, they nevertheless restrict trade.

22.1 TRADE PATTERNS AND TRENDS

The goods and services that we buy from people in other countries are called *imports*. The goods and services that we sell to people in other countries are called *exports*. What are the most important things that we import and export? Most people would probably guess that a rich nation such as the United States imports raw materials and exports manufactured goods. Although that is one feature of U.S. international trade, it is not its most important feature. The vast bulk of U.S. exports and imports are manufactured goods. We sell foreigners earth-moving equipment, airplanes, supercomputers, scientific equipment, movies, and magazines, and we buy televisions, VCRs, blue jeans, and T-shirts from them. Also, we are a major exporter of agricultural products and raw materials. We also import and export a huge volume of services.

Trade in Goods

In 2002, manufactured goods accounted for 47 percent of U.S. exports and for 58 percent of U.S. imports. Raw materials and semimanufactured items accounted for 16 percent of U.S. exports and for 20 percent of U.S. imports, and agricultural products accounted for only 5 percent of U.S. exports and 3 percent of U.S. imports. The largest U.S. export and import item in 2002 was autos and auto parts.

But goods accounted for only 72 percent of U.S. exports and 84 percent of U.S. imports in 2002. The rest of U.S. international trade in 2002 was in services.

Trade in Services

You might be wondering how a country can export and import services. Here are some examples.

If you take a vacation in France and travel there on an Air France flight from New York, the United States imports transportation services from France. The money you spend in France on hotel bills and restaurant meals is also classified as a U.S. import of services. Similarly, the vacation taken by a French student in the United States counts as a U.S. export of services to France.

When we import TV sets from South Korea, the owner of the ship that transports them might be Greek and the company that insures them might be British. The payments that we make for the transportation and insurance are U.S. imports of services. Similarly, when a U.S. shipping company transports California wine to Tokyo, the transportation cost is a U.S. export of a service to Japan. U.S. international trade in these types of services is large and growing.

Trends in the Volume of Trade

In 1960, we exported 5 percent of total output and imported 4 percent of the goods and services that we bought. In 2002, we exported 10 percent of total output and imported 14 percent of the goods and services that we bought.

On the export side, automobiles, aircraft, food, and raw materials have remained large items and have held a roughly constant share of total exports. But the composition of imports has changed. Food and raw material imports have fallen steadily. Imports of fuel increased dramatically during the 1970s, fell during the 1980s, and increased again during the 1990s. Imports of machinery have grown and today approach 50 percent of total imports.

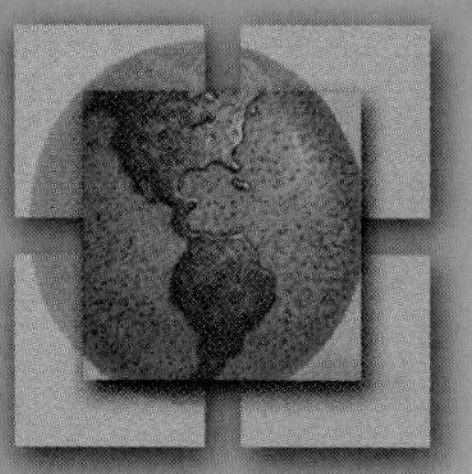

Eye on the Global Economy

The Major Items That We Trade with Other Nations

The figure shows the U.S. volume of trade and balance of trade for the 20 largest items traded in 2002. If a bar has more red (imports) than blue (exports), the United States has a trade deficit in that item.

Automobiles and parts is the largest item traded. Fuels, travel, computers, and aircraft and parts are also large items. Notice that travel is a larger item than most goods.

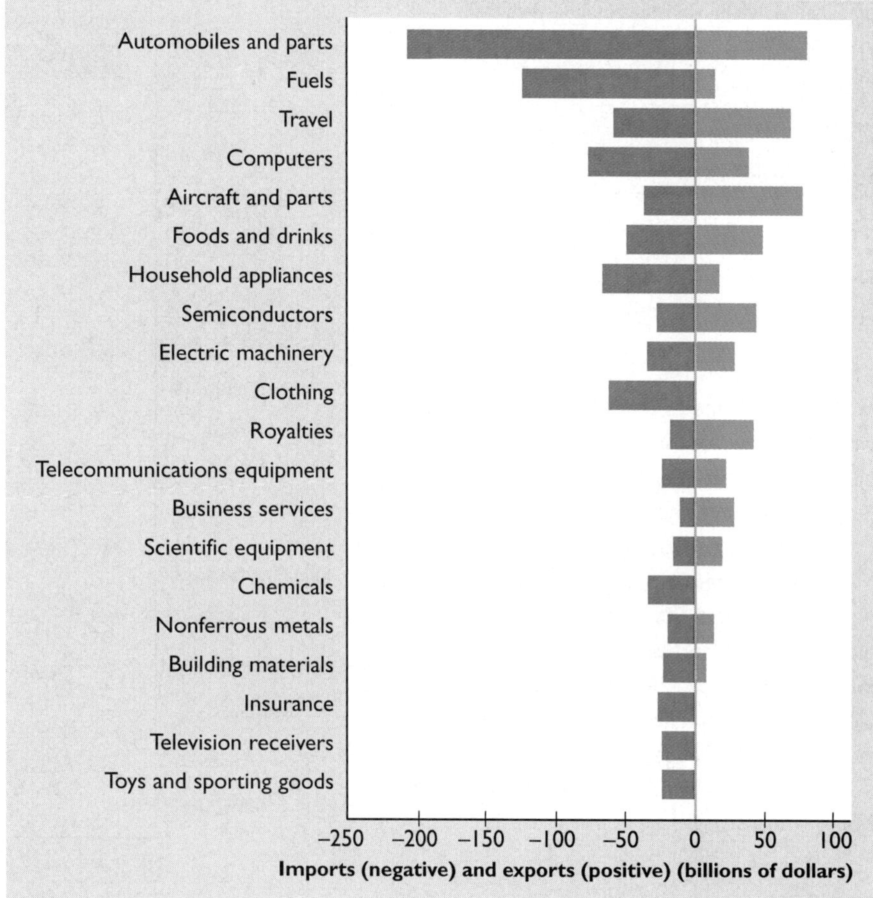

SOURCE: Bureau of Economic Analysis.

Trading Partners and Trading Blocs

The United States has trading links with every part of the world and is a member of several international organizations that seek to promote international trade and regional trade.

U.S. Trading Partners

Canada is the United States' biggest trading partner. Mexico and Japan are the second biggest and almost equal. Our other large trading partners are China, Germany, and the United Kingdom. But we also have significant volumes of trade with the other rapidly expanding Asian economies such as South Korea, Taiwan, Singapore, and Hong Kong. Eye on the Global Economy on p. 858 shows the data for our 17 largest trading partners.

Trading Blocs

Trading blocs are groupings of nations in an international organization. The world today divides into three major geographical blocs, and the United States is a member of two of them. The two blocs of which the United States is a member are the North American Free Trade Agreement and the Asia-Pacific Economic Cooperation. The other large bloc is the European Union. We'll provide a brief description of each of these groupings.

The Major U.S. Trading Partners and Volumes of Trade

The figure shows the U.S. volume of trade and balance of trade with its 17 largest trading partners in 2002. If a bar has more red (imports) than blue (exports), the United States has a trade deficit with that country.

Canada is the major trading partner of the United States by a big margin. Mexico and Japan come next, followed by China, Germany, and the United Kingdom. Trade with the newly industrialized countries of Asia (South Korea, Taiwan, Singapore, and Hong Kong) is also large.

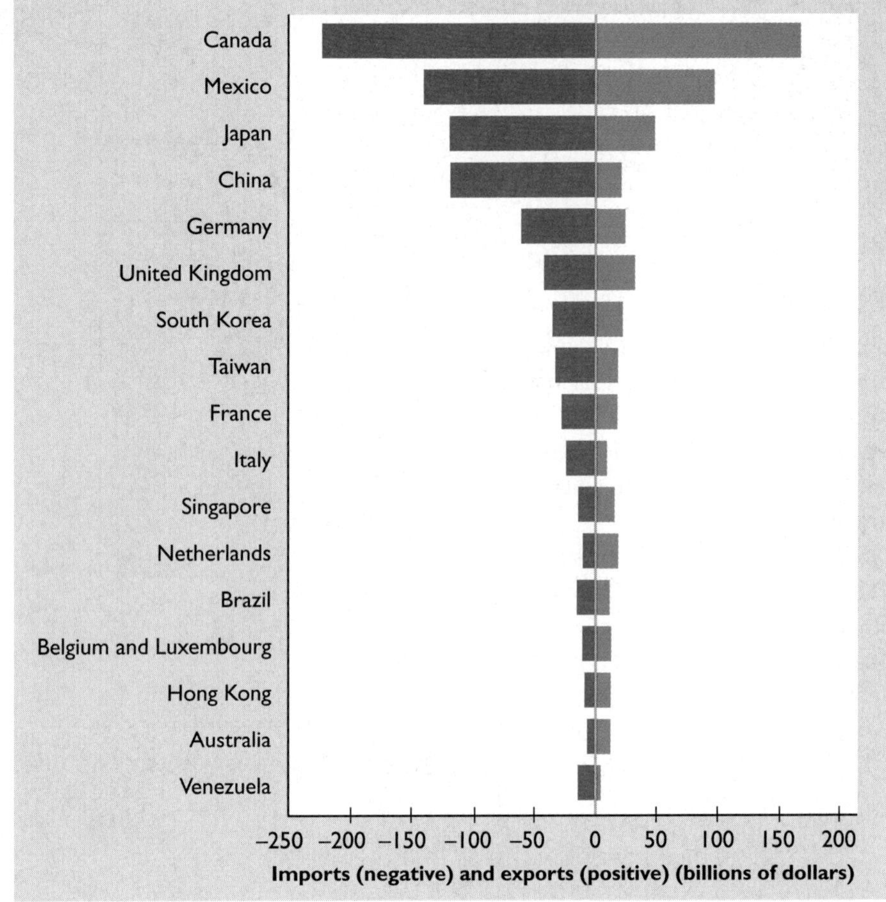

SOURCE: Bureau of Economic Analysis.

North American Free Trade Agreement The North American Free Trade Agreement, or NAFTA, is an agreement among the United States, Canada, and Mexico, to make trade among the three countries easier and freer. The Agreement came into effect in 1994. During the years since then, trade among the three nations has expanded rapidly.

The American continents consist of 35 nations and the governments of the 34 democracies (which excludes Cuba) have entered into a Free Trade of the Americas process. The objective of this process is to achieve free international trade among all the nations of the Americas by 2005.

Asia-Pacific Economic Cooperation Asia-Pacific Economic Cooperation, or APEC, is a group of 21 nations that border the Pacific Ocean. The largest of these are the United States, China, Japan, and Canada, but other significant members are Australia, Indonesia, and the dynamic new industrial Asian economies. In 2002, APEC nations conducted 47 percent of the world's international trade.

APEC was established in 1989 as an informal discussion group, but it has developed into an organization that promotes freer trade and cooperation among its member nations.

European Union The European Union, or EU, is a group of 15 nations of Western Europe. The EU began as the European Common Market when six countries (Belgium, Germany, France, Italy, Luxembourg, and the Netherlands) embarked on a process of economic integration in 1951. The EU has developed its own money, the euro, and institutions of government that are more like those of a federal state than a group of independent states.

Balance of Trade and International Borrowing

The value of exports minus the value of imports is called the **balance of trade**. In 2002, the United States imported more than it exported. When a country imports more than it exports, it has a trade deficit and pays by borrowing from foreigners or selling some of its assets. When a country exports more than it imports, it has a trade surplus and lends to other countries or buys more foreign assets to enable the rest of the world to pay its deficit.

Balance of trade
The value of exports minus the value of imports.

CHECKPOINT 22.1

1 Describe the patterns and trends in international trade.

Study Guide pp. 326–328

Practice Online 22.1

Practice Problem 22.1

Use the link on your Foundations Web site to answer the following questions:

a. In 1990, what percentage of Canadian production was exported to the United States and what percentage of total goods and services bought by Canadians was imported from the United States?

b. In 2000, what percentage of Canadian production was exported to the United States and what percentage of total goods and services bought by Canadians was imported from the United States?

Exercise 22.1

Use the link on your Foundations Web site to answer the following questions:

a. In 1990, what percentage of Mexican production was exported to the United States and what percentage of total goods and services bought by Mexicans was imported from the United States?

b. In 1998, what percentage of Mexican production was exported to the United States and what percentage of total goods and services bought by Mexicans was imported from the United States?

Solution to Practice Problem 22.1

a. In 1990, Canada exported 16.5 percent of total production to the United States and imported 14.4 percent of total goods and services purchased from the United States.

b. In 2000, Canada exported 22.6 percent of total production to the United States and imported 27 percent of goods and services purchased from the United States.

22.2 THE GAINS FROM INTERNATIONAL TRADE

Comparative advantage is the fundamental force that generates international trade. And comparative advantage arises from differences in opportunity costs. You met this idea in Chapter 3 (pp. 79–81), but we're now going to put some flesh on the bones of the basic idea. We'll begin by looking at an item that we export.

Why the United States Exports Airplanes

Boeing produces many more airplanes each year than airlines in the United States buy. Most of Boeing's production goes to airlines in other parts of the world. The United States is an exporter of airplanes. Why?

The answer is that the United States has a comparative advantage in the production of airplanes. The opportunity cost of producing an airplane is lower in the United States than in most other countries. So buyers can obtain airplanes from Boeing for a lower price than the price at which they could buy them from other potential suppliers. And Boeing can sell airplanes to foreigners for a higher price than it could obtain from an additional U.S. buyer.

So both countries gain. The foreign buyer gains from lower-priced airplanes. And Boeing's stockholders, managers, and workers gain from higher-priced airplanes. A win-win situation!

Figure 22.1 illustrates the effects of international trade in airplanes. The demand curve *D* shows the demand for airplanes in the United States. This curve tells us the quantity of airplanes that U.S. airlines are willing to buy at various prices. The demand curve also tells us the most that an additional airplane is worth to a U.S. airline at each quantity.

The supply curve *S* shows the supply of airplanes in the United States. This curve tells us the quantity of airplanes that U.S. aircraft makers are willing to sell at various prices. The supply curve also tells us the opportunity cost of producing an additional airplane at each quantity.

No Trade

First, let's see what happens in the market for airplanes if there is no international trade. Figure 22.1(a) shows the situation. The airplane market is in equilibrium when 400 airplanes are produced by U.S. aircraft makers and bought by U.S. airlines. The price is $80 million an airplane.

Trade

Second, let's see what happens in the market for airplanes if international trade takes place. Figure 22.1(b) shows the situation. The price of an airplane is determined in the world market, not the U.S. domestic market. Suppose that world demand and world supply determine a world equilibrium price of $100 million per airplane. In Figure 22.1(b), the world price line shows this price.

The U.S. demand curve, *D*, tells us that at $100 million an airplane, U.S. airlines buy 300 airplanes a year. The U.S. supply curve, *S*, tells us that at $100 million per airplane, U.S. aircraft makers produce 800 airplanes a year. So domestic production at 800 a year exceeds domestic purchases of 300 a year.

The quantity produced in the United States minus the quantity purchased by U.S. airlines is the quantity of U.S. exports, which is 500 airplanes a year.

FIGURE 22.1
An Export

Practice Online

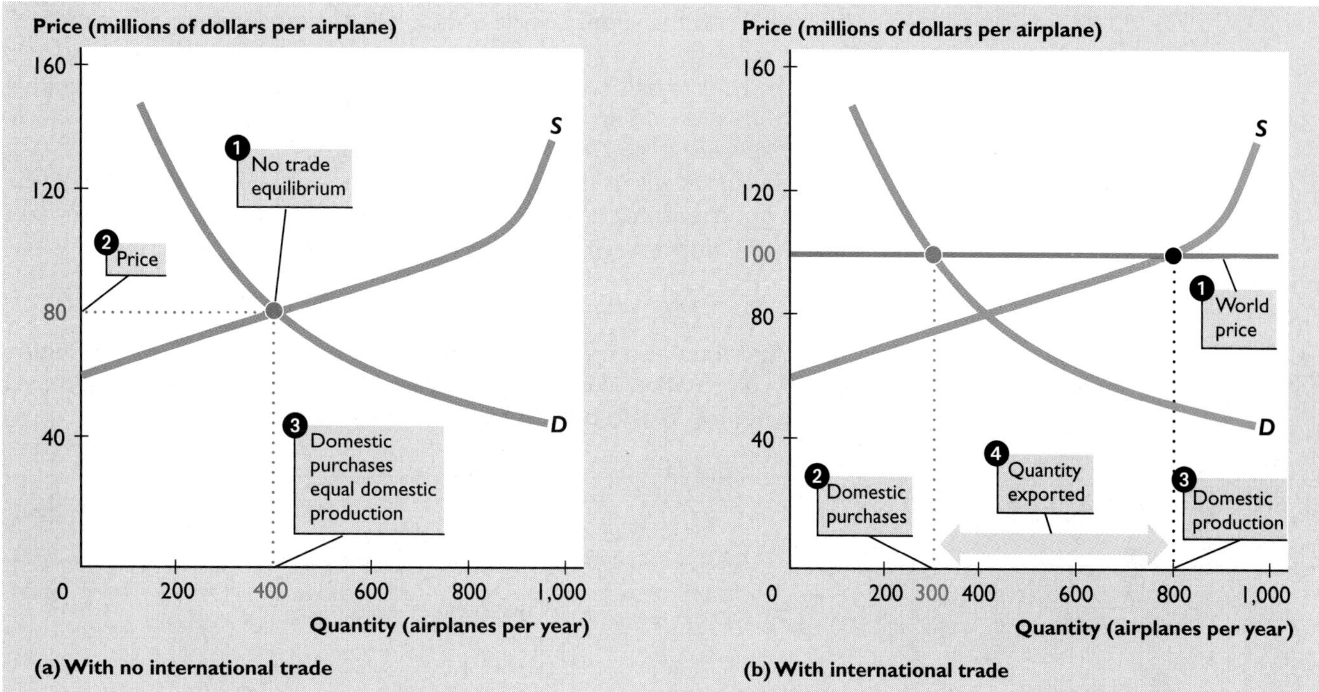

With no international trade in airplanes, ❶ equilibrium at the intersection of the domestic demand and supply curves determines ❷ the price at $80 million an airplane and ❸ the quantity at 400 airplanes a year.

With international trade, world demand and supply determine ❶ the world price, which is $100 million an airplane. ❷ Domestic purchases decrease to 300 a year, and ❸ domestic production increases to 800 a year; ❹ 500 airplanes a year are exported.

Comparative Advantage

You can see that U.S. aircraft makers have a comparative advantage in producing airplanes by comparing the U.S. supply curve and the world price line. At the equilibrium quantity of 800 airplanes a year, the world opportunity cost of producing an airplane is $100 million. But the U.S. supply curve tells us that only the 800th airplane has an opportunity cost of $100 million. Each of the other 799 airplanes has an opportunity cost of less than $100 million.

Why the United States Imports T-Shirts

Americans spend more than twice as much on clothing as the value of U.S. apparel production. That is, more than half of the clothing that we buy is manufactured in other countries and imported into the United States. Why?

The answer is that the rest of the world (mainly Asia) has a comparative advantage in the production of clothes. The opportunity cost of producing a T-shirt is lower in Asia than in the United States. So buyers can obtain T-shirts from Asia for a lower price than the price at which they could buy them from U.S. garment makers. And Asian garment makers can sell T-shirts to Americans for a higher price than they could obtain from an additional Asian buyer.

So again, both countries gain. The U.S. buyer gains from lower-priced T-shirts, and Asian garment makers gain from higher-priced T-shirts. Another win-win situation!

Figure 22.2 illustrates the effects of international trade in T-shirts. Again, the demand curve *D* and the supply curve *S* show the demand and supply in the U.S. domestic market only.

The demand curve tells us the quantity of T-shirts that Americans are willing to buy at various prices. The demand curve also tells us the most that an additional T-shirt is worth to an American at each quantity.

The supply curve tells us the quantity of T-shirts that U.S. garment makers are willing to sell at various prices. The supply curve also tells us the opportunity cost of producing an additional T-shirt in the United States at each quantity.

No Trade

Again, we'll first look at a market with no international trade, shown in Figure 22.2(a). The T-shirt market is in equilibrium when 20 million shirts are produced by U.S. garment makers and bought by Americans. The price is $8 a shirt.

FIGURE 22.2
An Import

Practice Online

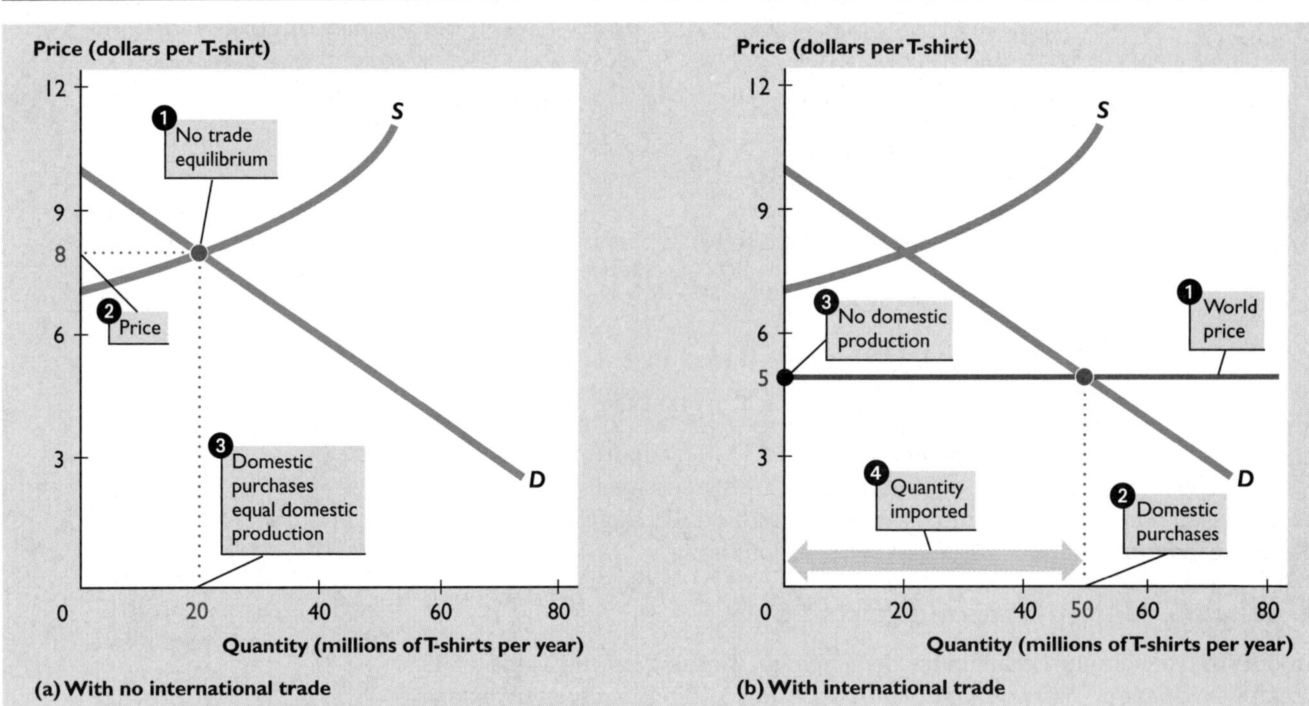

With no international trade in T-shirts, ❶ equilibrium at the intersection of the domestic demand and supply curves determines ❷ the price at $8 a shirt and ❸ the quantity at 20 million shirts a year.

With international trade, world demand and supply determine the ❶ world price, which is $5 a shirt. ❷ Domestic purchases increase to 50 million shirts a year, and ❸ domestic production decreases to zero. ❹ The entire 50 million shirts a year are imported.

Trade

Figure 22.2(b) shows what happens in the market for T-shirts if international trade takes place. Now the price of a T-shirt is determined in the world market, not the U.S. domestic market. Suppose that world demand and world supply determine a world equilibrium price of $5 a shirt. In Figure 22.2(b), the world price line shows this price.

The U.S demand curve, *D*, tells us that at $5 a shirt, Americans buy 50 million shirts a year. The U.S. supply curve, *S*, tells us that at $5 a shirt, U.S. garment makers produce no T-shirts. So there is no domestic production, and domestic purchases are 50 million T-shirts a year. The entire quantity of T-shirts purchased in the United States is the quantity imported.

Comparative Advantage

Now you can see that Asian garment makers have a comparative advantage in producing T-shirts by comparing the U.S. supply curve and the world price line. At the equilibrium quantity of 50 million T-shirts a year, the world opportunity cost of producing a T-shirt is $5. But the U.S. supply curve tells us that no U.S. garment maker has such a low opportunity cost, not even at smaller outputs. So Asian garment makers have a comparative advantage in producing T-shirts.

Gains from Trade and the *PPF*

The demand and supply model that you've just studied makes it clear why we export some goods and import others. But it doesn't show directly the gains from international trade. Another way of looking at comparative advantage uses the production possibilities frontier (*PPF*) that you learned about in Chapter 3. This approach shows the gains from trade in a powerful way, as you're about to discover.

Let's explore comparative advantage by looking at production possibilities in the United States and China.

Production Possibilities in the United States and China

To focus on the essential idea, suppose that the United States can produce only two goods: communications satellites and sports shoes. China can also produce only these same two goods. But production possibilities are different in the two countries.

If the United States uses all of its resources to produce satellites, its output is 10 satellites per year and no sports shoes. If it uses all of its resources to produce sports shoes, its output is 100 million pairs of shoes a year and no satellites. We'll assume that the U.S. opportunity cost of producing a satellite is constant. To produce 10 satellites, the United States must forgo 100 million pairs of shoes, which means that to produce 1 satellite, the United States must forgo 10 million pairs of shoes. That is,

The U.S. opportunity cost of producing 1 satellite is 10 million pairs of shoes.

In contrast, if China uses all of its resources to make satellites, it can produce 2 satellites a year and no sports shoes. And if it uses all of its resources to make sports shoes, it can produce 100 million pairs of shoes a year and no satellites. We'll assume that China's opportunity cost of producing a satellite is constant. To produce 2 satellites, China must forgo 100 million pairs of shoes, which means that to produce 1 satellite, China must forgo 50 million pairs of shoes. That is,

China's opportunity cost of producing 1 satellite is 50 million pairs of shoes.

The assumption that the opportunity costs of producing a satellite in the United States and in China are constant makes the point that we're illustrating in the simplest and cleanest way. We could assume increasing opportunity cost. We would reach the same conclusion that we'll reach here, but the story would be a bit more complicated and the point wouldn't jump out as clearly as it does by making the assumption of constant opportunity costs.

Figure 22.3(a) shows the production possibilities for the United States, and Figure 22.3(b) shows the production possibilities for China. The assumption that the opportunity costs are constant means that the two *PPF*s are linear. Along the U.S. *PPF*, 1 satellite costs 10 million pairs of shoes. And along China's *PPF*, 1 satellite costs 50 million pairs of shoes.

FIGURE 22.3
Production Possibilities in the United States and China

Practice Online

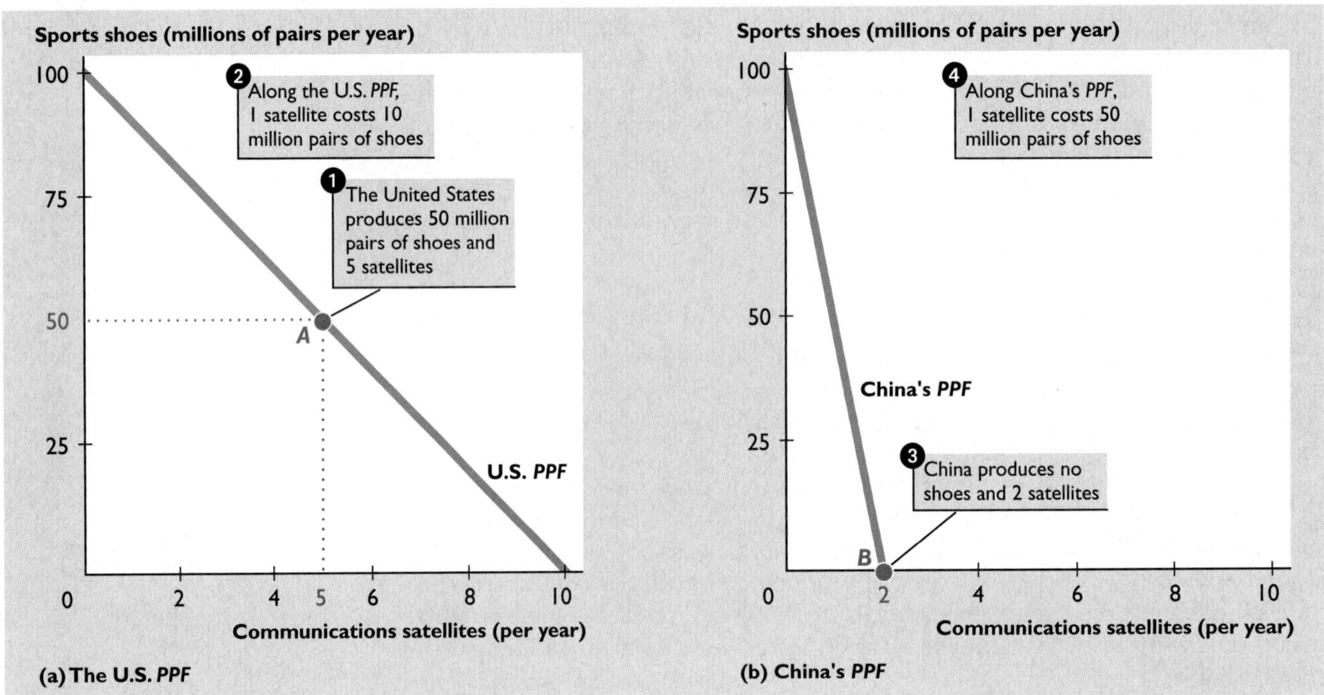

❶ The United States produces at point *A* on its *PPF* (part a). ❷ The opportunity cost of a satellite is 10 million pairs of shoes. ❸ China produces at point *B* on its *PPF* (part b). ❹ The opportunity cost of a satellite is 50 million pairs of shoes.

The opportunity cost of a satellite is lower in the United States than in China, so the United States has a comparative advantage in producing satellites. The opportunity cost of a pair of shoes is lower in China than in the United States, so China has a comparative advantage in producing shoes.

No Trade

With no international trade, we'll suppose that the United States produces 5 satellites and 50 million pairs of shoes at point *A* on its *PPF*. And we'll suppose that China produces 2 satellites and no shoes at point *B* on its *PPF.*

Comparative Advantage

In which of the two goods does China have a comparative advantage? Recall that comparative advantage is a situation in which one nation's opportunity cost of producing a good is lower than another nation's opportunity cost of producing that same good. China has a comparative advantage in producing shoes. The opportunity cost of a pair of shoes is 1/50,000,000 of a satellite in China and 1/10,000,000 of a satellite in the United States.

You can see China's comparative advantage by looking at the *PPF*s for China and the United States in Figure 22.3. China's *PPF* is steeper than the U.S. *PPF*. To produce an additional 1 million pairs of shoes, China must give up fewer satellites than does the United States. So China's opportunity cost of shoes is less than the U.S. opportunity cost of shoes. This means that China has a comparative advantage in producing shoes.

The United States has a comparative advantage in producing satellites. In Figure 22.3, the U.S. *PPF* is less steep than China's *PPF*. This means that the United States must give up fewer shoes to produce an additional satellite than does China. The U.S. opportunity cost of producing a satellite is 10 million pairs of shoes, which is less than China's 50 million pairs. So the United States has a comparative advantage in producing satellites.

Because China has a comparative advantage in producing shoes and the United States has a comparative advantage in producing satellites, both China and the United States can gain from specialization and trade. China specializes in shoes, and the United States specializes in satellites.

Achieving the Gains from Trade

If the United States, which has a comparative advantage in producing satellites, allocates all of its resources to that activity, it can produce 10 satellites a year. If China, which has a comparative advantage in producing shoes, allocates all of its resources to that activity, it can produce 100 million pairs a year. By specializing, the United States and China together can produce 100 million pairs of shoes and 10 satellites. With no trade, their total production had been 7 satellites (5 from the United States and 2 from China) and 50 million pairs of shoes (all produced by the United States).

So with specialization and trade, the United States and China can consume outside their production possibilities frontiers.

To achieve the gains from specialization, the United States and China must trade with each other. Suppose they agree to the following deal: China agrees to pay the United States 30 million pairs of shoes per satellite; the United States agrees to sell China 3 satellites a year at this price.

With this deal in place, the United States has 90 million pairs of shoes and 7 satellites—a gain of 40 million pairs of shoes and 2 satellites. China now has 10 million pairs of shoes and 3 satellites—a gain of 10 million pairs of shoes and one satellite.

Figure 22.4 shows these gains from trade. The United States originally produced and consumed at point *A*. It now produces at point *P* and consumes at point *A*'. China originally produced and consumed at point *B*. It now produces at point *Q* and consumes at point *B*'. As a result of specialization and trade, both countries can consume outside their production possibilities frontiers. Both countries gain from trade.

In this example, the United States can out-produce China and has an *absolute advantage* (see Chapter 3, p. 72), but it can get shoes at a lower cost by trading satellites for shoes with China. Gains from specialization and trade are always available when opportunity costs diverge.

Dynamic Comparative Advantage

Resources and technology determine comparative advantage. But just by repeatedly producing a particular good or service, people become more productive in that activity, a phenomenon called **learning-by-doing**. **Dynamic comparative advantage**, a comparative advantage that a person (or country) obtains by specializing in an activity, results from learning-by-doing.

Hong Kong, South Korea, and Taiwan are examples of economies that have pursued dynamic comparative advantage vigorously. They have developed electronics and biotechnology industries in which initially they did not have a comparative advantage, but through learning-by-doing, they have become low opportunity cost producers in those industries.

Learning-by-doing
Repeatedly performing the same task and becoming more productive at producing a particular good or service.

Dynamic comparative advantage
A comparative advantage that a person (or country) obtains by specializing in an activity, resulting from learning-by-doing.

FIGURE 22.4
The Gains from Trade

Practice Online

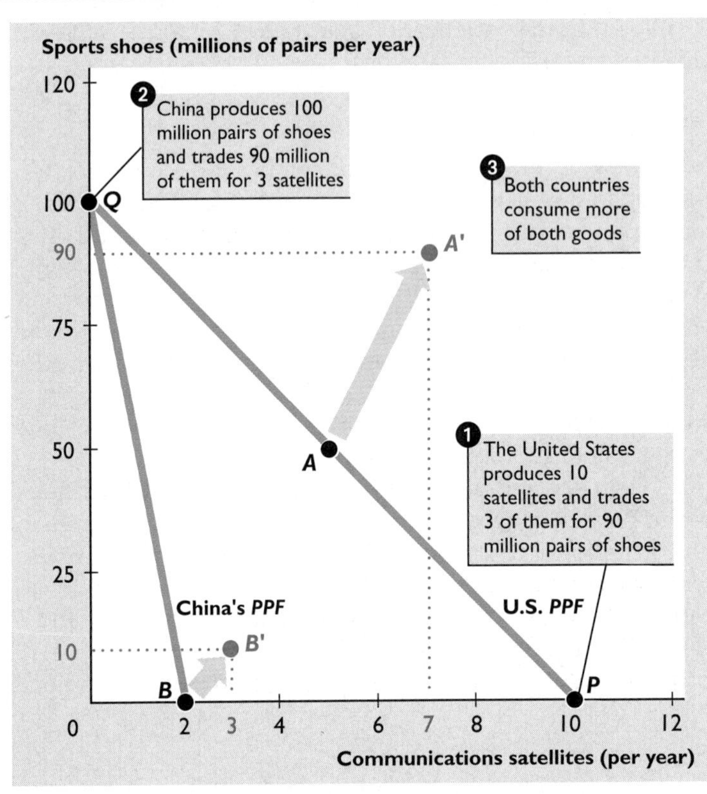

1. If the United States specializes in satellites, it produces 10 a year at point *P*.
2. If China specializes in shoes, it produces 100 million pairs a year at point *Q*.
3. If shoes and satellites are traded at 30 million pairs of shoes per satellite, both countries can increase their consumption of both goods and consume at points *A*' and *B*'. The gains from trade are the increases in consumption of the two countries.

CHECKPOINT 22.2

2 Explain why nations engage in international trade and why trade benefits all nations.

Study Guide pp. 328–331

Practice Online 22.2

Practice Problem 22.2

During most of the Cold War, the United States and Russia did not trade with each other. The United States produced manufactured goods and farm produce. Russia produced manufactured goods and farm produce. Suppose that in the last year of the Cold War, the United States could produce 100 million units of manufactured goods or 50 million units of farm produce and Russia could produce 30 million units of manufactured goods or 10 million units of farm produce.

a. What was the opportunity cost of 1 unit of farm produce in the United States?
b. What was the opportunity cost of 1 unit of farm produce in Russia?
c. Which country had a comparative advantage in producing farm produce?
d. With the end of the Cold War and the opening up of trade between Russia and the United States, which good did the United States import from Russia?
e. Did the United States gain from this trade? Explain why or why not.
f. Did Russia gain from this trade? Explain why or why not.

Exercise 22.2

In 2003, the United States does not trade with Cuba. Suppose that the United States can produce 1,000 million units of manufactured goods or 500 million units of food. Suppose that Cuba can produce 2 million units of manufactured goods or 5 million units of food.

a. What was the opportunity cost of 1 unit of food in the United States?
b. What was the opportunity cost of 1 unit of food in Cuba?
c. Which country had a comparative advantage in producing food?
d. Suppose that the United States opens up trade with Cuba. Which good will the United States import from Cuba?
e. Will the United States gain from this trade? Explain why or why not.
f. Will Cuba gain from this trade? Explain why or why not.

Solution to Practice Problem 22.2

a. The U.S. opportunity cost of 1 unit of farm produce was 2 units of manufactured goods.
b. The Russian opportunity cost of 1 unit of farm produce was 3 units of manufactured goods.
c. The United States had a comparative advantage in producing farm produce because the U.S. opportunity cost of a unit of farm produce was less than the Russian opportunity cost of a unit of farm produce.
d. The United States imported from Russia the good in which Russia had a comparative advantage. The United States imported manufactured goods.
e. and f. Both the United States and Russia gained because each country ended up with more of both goods. When countries specialize in producing the good in which they have a comparative advantage and then trade with each other, both countries gain.

22.3 INTERNATIONAL TRADE RESTRICTIONS

Governments use two main tools to restrict international trade and protect domestic industries from foreign competition. They are

- Tariffs
- Nontariff barriers

Tariff
A tax on a good that is imposed by the importing country when an imported good crosses its international boundary.

Nontariff barrier
Any action other than a tariff that restricts international trade.

A **tariff** is a tax on a good that is imposed by the importing country when an imported good crosses its international boundary. A **nontariff barrier** is any action other than a tariff that restricts international trade. Examples of nontariff barriers are quantitative restrictions and health and safety standards.

Tariffs

The temptation for governments to impose tariffs is a strong one. First, tariffs provide revenue to the government. Second, they enable the government to satisfy special interest groups in import-competing industries. But as we will see, free international trade brings enormous benefits that are reduced when tariffs are imposed. Let's see how.

Eye on the Past

The History of the U.S. Tariff

U.S. tariffs today are modest in comparison with their historical levels. The figure shows the average tariff rate—total tariffs as a percentage of total imports. Tariffs peaked during the 1930s when Congress passed a law known as the Smoot-Hawley Act. The General Agreement on Tariffs and Trade (GATT), an international agreement to eliminate trade restrictions that was signed in 1947, resulted in a series of rounds of negotiations that have brought widespread tariff cuts. Today, the World Trade Organization (WTO) continues the work of GATT.

The United States is a party to the North American Free Trade Agreement (NAFTA), which became effective on January 1, 1994, and under which barriers to international trade between the United States, Canada, and Mexico will be virtually eliminated after a 15-year phasing-in period.

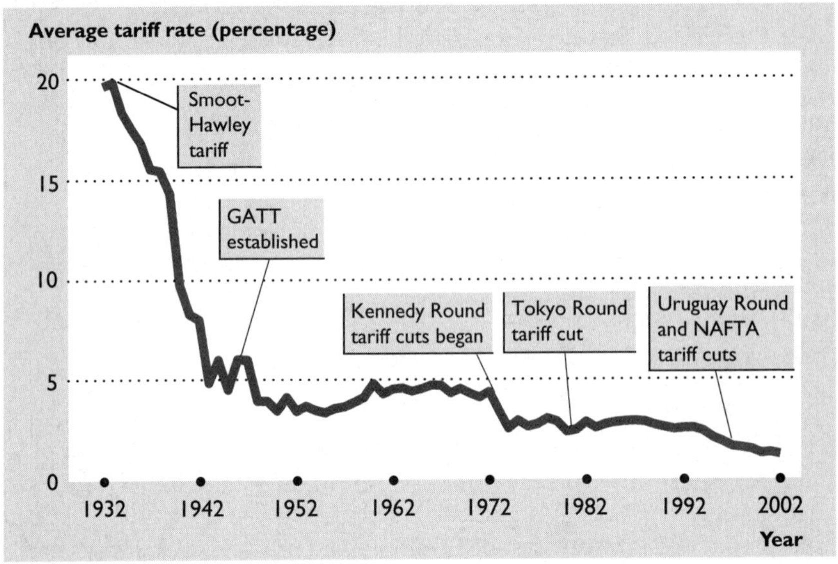

SOURCES: The Budget for Fiscal Year 2003, Historical Tables, Table 2.5 and Bureau of Economic Analysis, National Income and Product Accounts

To analyze how tariffs work, let's return to the example of U.S. T-shirt imports. Figure 22.5 shows the market for T-shirts in the United States. Part (a) is the same as Figure 22.2(b) and shows the situation with free international trade. The United States produces no T-shirts and imports 50 million shirts a year at the world market price of $5 a shirt.

Now suppose that under pressure from U.S. garment makers, the U.S. government imposes a tariff on imported T-shirts. In particular, suppose that a tariff of 50 percent is imposed. What happens?

- The price of a T-shirt in the United States rises.
- The quantity of T-shirts bought in the United States decreases.
- The quantity of T-shirts produced in the United States increases.
- The quantity of T-shirts imported by the United States decreases.
- The U.S. government collects the tariff revenue.
- U.S. consumers lose.

FIGURE 22.5
The Effects of a Tariff

Practice Online

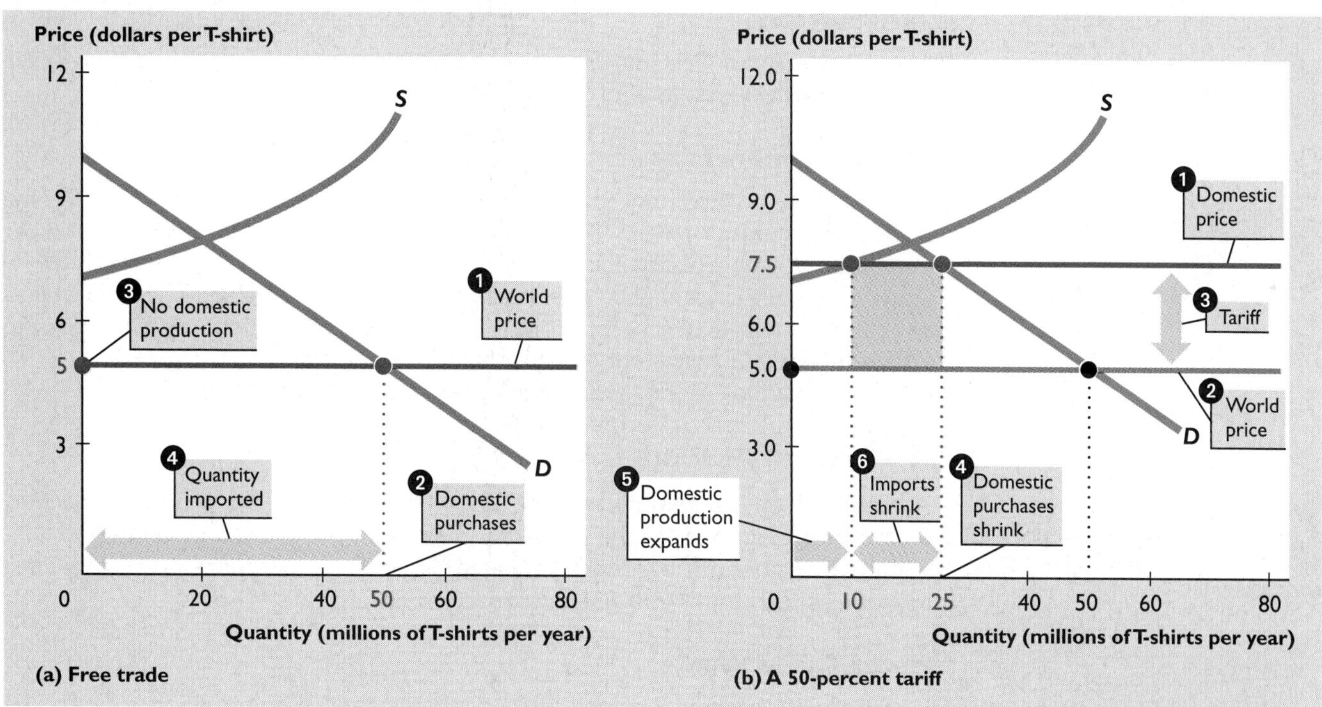

With free trade (part a), ❶ the world price is $5 a T-shirt and ❷ the United States buys 50 million T-shirts. ❸ The United States produces no T-shirts and ❹ imports 50 million T-shirts.

In part (b), the United States imposes a tariff on imports of T-shirts. ❶ The domestic price equals ❷ the world price plus ❸ the tariff, so the tariff raises the price that Americans pay for a T-shirt.

❹ The quantity of T-shirts purchased decreases, ❺ the quantity produced in the United States increases, and ❻ the quantity imported decreases. The U.S. government collects tariff revenue shown by the purple rectangle.

Rise in Price of a T-Shirt

To buy a T-shirt, Americans must pay the world market price plus the tariff. So the price of a T-shirt rises by 50 percent to $7.50. Figure 22.5(b) shows the domestic price line, which lies 50 percent (or $2.50) above the world price line.

Decrease in Purchases

The higher price of a T-shirt brings a decrease in the quantity demanded, which Figure 22.5(b) shows as a movement along the demand curve for T-shirts from 50 million a year at $5 a shirt to 25 million a year at $7.50 a shirt.

Increase in Domestic Production

The higher price of a T-shirt stimulates domestic production, which increases from zero to 10 million shirts a year—a movement along the supply curve in Figure 22.5(b).

Decrease in Imports

T-shirt imports decrease by 35 million from 50 million to 15 million a year. Both the decrease in purchases and the increase in domestic production contribute to this decrease in imports.

Tariff Revenue

The government collects tariff revenue of $2.50 per shirt on the 15 million shirts imported each year, a total of $37.5 million, as shown by the purple rectangle.

U.S. Consumers Lose

A T-shirt costs only $5 to produce—the opportunity cost of that shirt is $5. But the American consumer pays $7.50 for a T-shirt. So the consumer pays $2.50 a shirt more than its opportunity cost. Consumers are willing to buy up to 50 million T-shirts a year at a price that equals the opportunity cost of a shirt. The tariff makes people pay more than the opportunity cost and deprives them of items they are willing to buy at a price that exceeds the opportunity cost.

Let's now look at the other tools for restricting trade: nontariff barriers.

Nontariff Barriers

Quota
A specified maximum amount of a good that may be imported in a given period of time.

A **quota**, which is a quantitative restriction on the import of a good that specifies the maximum amount of the good that may be imported in a given period, is a widely used nontariff barrier. The United States imposes quotas on many items, including sugar, tomatoes, bananas, and textiles.

How a Quota Works

Figure 22.6 shows how a quota works. Begin by identifying the situation with free international trade. The United States produces no T-shirts and imports 50 million shirts a year at the world market price of $5 a shirt.

Now suppose that the United States imposes a quota that restricts imports to 15 million T-shirts a year. The imports permitted under the quota plus the quantity produced in the United States is the market supply in the United States. This market supply curve is the one labeled S + *quota* in Figure 22.6.

FIGURE 22.6
The Effects of a Quota

Practice Online

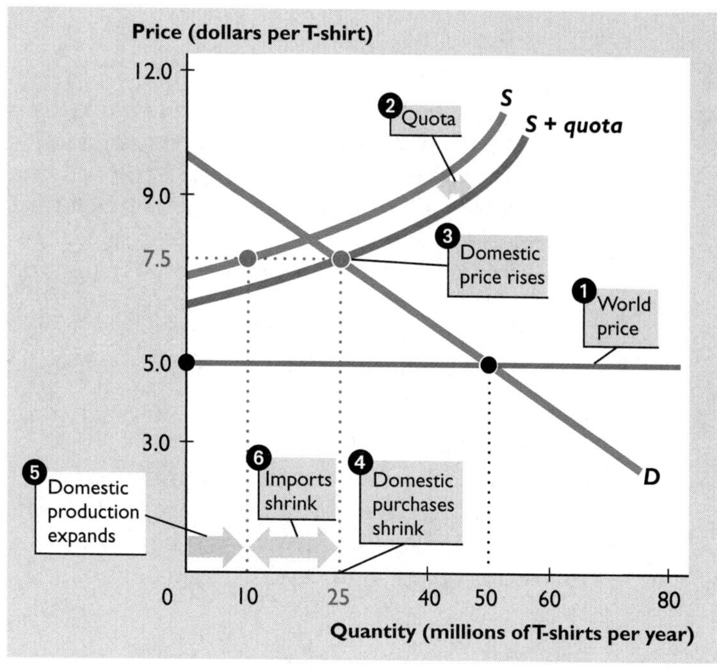

❶ The world price is $5 a T-shirt. ❷ A quota of 15 million shirts a year is added to the U.S. supply to give the market supply curve, *S + quota*. ❸ The equilibrium domestic price rises to $7.50 a shirt, and ❹ domestic purchases decrease. ❺ The United States produces 10 million shirts a year, and ❻ U.S. imports equal the quota of 15 million a year.

With this new supply curve, the U.S. price of a T-shirt is $7.50, the price that makes the quantity demanded by Americans equal the quantity supplied by U.S. producers plus imports. This quantity is 25 million shirts a year.

At a price of $7.50, U.S. garment makers produce 10 million shirts a year and U.S. imports equal the quota of 15 million a year.

We've made the outcome with a quota in Figure 22.6 the same as that with a tariff in Figure 22.5(b). But there is a difference between a tariff and a quota. In the case of a tariff, the U.S. government collects tariff revenue. In the case of a quota, there is no tariff revenue and the difference between the world price and the U.S. price goes to the person who has the right to import T-shirts under the import quota regulations.

Health, Safety, and Other Nontariff Barriers

Thousands of detailed health, safety, and other regulations restrict international trade. Here are just a few examples. All U.S. imports of food products are examined by the Food and Drug Administration to determine if the imported food is "pure, wholesome, safe to eat, and produced under sanitary conditions." In 2001, the scare of foot and mouth disease virtually closed down international trade in live cattle and beef. The European Union has banned imports of most genetically modified foods, such as U.S.-produced soybeans and Canadian granola. Australia has banned the import of U.S. grapes to protect its domestic grapes from a virus that is present in California. Restrictions also apply to many nonfood items. Although regulations of the type we've just described are not designed to limit international trade, they have that effect.

CHECKPOINT 22.3

Study Guide pp. 331–334

Practice Online 22.3

3 Explain how trade barriers reduce international trade.

Practice Problems 22.3

1. Before 1995, the United States imposed tariffs on goods imported from Mexico and Mexico imposed tariffs on goods imported from the United States. In 1995, Mexico joined NAFTA. U.S. tariffs on imports from Mexico and Mexican tariffs on imports from the United States are gradually being removed. Explain how the removal of tariffs will change
   - **a.** The price that U.S. consumers pay for goods imported from Mexico.
   - **b.** The quantity of U.S. imports from Mexico.
   - **c.** The quantity of U.S. exports to Mexico.
   - **d.** The U.S. government's tariff revenue from trade with Mexico.
2. In 2000, the U.S. government placed a ban on potato imports from Canada. Explain how this ban influences
   - **a.** The price that U.S. consumers pay for potatoes.
   - **b.** The quantity of potatoes consumed in the United States.
   - **c.** The price received by Canadian potato growers.
   - **d.** The U.S. and Canadian gains from trade.

Exercises 22.3

1. In 2000, the U.S. Congress and Senate extended an arrangement that limits the tariffs on imports from China. If the United States imposed higher tariffs on imports from China, explain how a higher tariff on toys will change
   - **a.** The price that U.S. consumers pay for toys imported from China.
   - **b.** The quantity of U.S. imports of toys from China.
   - **c.** The quantity of toys produced in the United States.
   - **d.** The U.S. government's tariff revenue from trade in toys with China.
   - **e.** The U.S. and Chinese gains from trade.
2. Australia has a comparative advantage in producing beef, but the United States sets a quota on beef imports from Australia. Explain how the quota influences
   - **a.** The price that U.S. consumers pay for beef.
   - **b.** The quantity of beef produced in the United States.
   - **c.** The U.S. and Australian gains from trade.

Solutions to Practice Problems 22.3

1a. The price that U.S. consumers pay for goods imported from Mexico will fall.
1b. The quantity of U.S. imports from Mexico will increase.
1c. The quantity of U.S. exports to Mexico will increase.
1d. The U.S. government's tariff revenue from trade with Mexico will fall to zero.

2a. The price that U.S. consumers pay for potatoes will rise.
2b. The quantity of potatoes consumed in the United States will fall.
2c. The price received by Canadian potato growers will fall.
2d. Both the U.S. and Canadian gains from trade will decrease.

22.4 THE CASE AGAINST PROTECTION

For as long as nations and international trade have existed, people have debated whether a country is better off with free international trade or with protection from foreign competition. The debate continues, but for most economists, a verdict has been delivered and it is the one you have just seen. Free trade promotes prosperity for all countries: Protection reduces the potential gains from trade. We've seen the most powerful case for free trade: All countries benefit from their comparative advantage. But there is a broader range of issues in the free trade versus protection debate. Let's review these issues.

Three Arguments for Protection

The three main arguments for protection and restricting international trade are

- The national security argument
- The infant-industry argument
- The dumping argument

Let's look at each in turn.

The National Security Argument

The national security argument for protection is that a country must protect industries that produce defense equipment and armaments and those on which the defense industries rely for their raw materials and other intermediate inputs. This argument for protection does not withstand close scrutiny.

First, it is an argument for international isolation, for in a time of war, there is no industry that does not contribute to national defense. Second, if the case is made for boosting the output of a strategic industry, it is more efficient to achieve this outcome with a subsidy to the firms in the industry, which is financed out of taxes, than with a tariff or quota. A subsidy would keep the industry operating at the scale judged appropriate, and free international trade would keep the prices faced by consumers at their world market levels.

The Infant-Industry Argument

The **infant-industry argument** for protection is that it is necessary to protect a new industry to enable it to grow into a mature industry that can compete in world markets. The argument is based on the idea of dynamic comparative advantage, which can arise from learning-by-doing.

Infant-industry argument
The argument that it is necessary to protect a new industry to enable it to grow into a mature industry that can compete in world markets.

Learning-by-doing is a powerful engine of productivity growth, and comparative advantage evolves and changes because of on-the-job experience. But these facts do not justify protection.

The infant-industry argument is valid only if the benefits of learning-by-doing not only accrue to the owners and workers of the firms in the infant industry, but also spill over to other industries and parts of the economy. For example, there are huge productivity gains from learning-by-doing in the manufacture of aircraft. But almost all of these gains benefit the stockholders and workers of aircraft producers such as Boeing. Because the people making the decisions, bearing the risk, and doing the work are the ones who benefit, they take the dynamic gains into account when they decide on the scale of their activities. In this case, almost no benefits spill over to other parts of the economy, so there is no need for government assistance to achieve an efficient outcome.

The Dumping Argument

Dumping
When a foreign firm sells its exports at a lower price than its cost of production.

Dumping occurs when a foreign firm sells its exports at a lower price than its cost of production. A firm that wants to gain a global monopoly might use dumping. In this case, the foreign firm sells its output at a price below its cost to drive domestic firms out of business. When the domestic firms have gone, the foreign firm takes advantage of its monopoly position and charges a higher price for its product. Dumping is usually regarded as a justification for temporary countervailing tariffs.

But there are powerful reasons to resist the dumping argument for protection. First, it is virtually impossible to detect dumping because it is hard to determine a firm's costs. As a result, the test for dumping is whether a firm's export price is below its domestic price. But this test is a weak one because it can be rational for a firm to charge a lower price in markets in which the quantity demanded is highly sensitive to price and a higher price in a market in which demand is less price-sensitive.

Second, it is hard to think of a good that is produced by a natural global monopoly. So even if all the domestic firms were driven out of business in some industry, it would always be possible to find several and usually many alternative foreign sources of supply and to buy at prices determined in competitive markets.

Third, if a good or service were a truly global natural monopoly, the best way to deal with it would be by regulation—just as in the case of domestic monopolies. Such regulation would require international cooperation.

The three arguments for protection that we've just examined have an element of credibility. The counterarguments are in general stronger, so these arguments do not make the case for protection. But they are not the only arguments that you might encounter. The many other arguments that are commonly heard are quite simply wrong. They are fatally flawed.

Fatally Flawed Arguments for Protection

Six commonly made but flawed arguments for restricting international trade are that protection

- Saves jobs
- Allows us to compete with cheap foreign labor
- Brings diversity and stability
- Penalizes lax environmental standards
- Protects national culture
- Prevents rich countries from exploiting developing countries

Saves Jobs

The argument is: When we buy shoes from Brazil or shirts from Taiwan, U.S. workers lose their jobs. With no earnings and poor prospects, these workers become a drain on welfare and spend less, causing a ripple effect of further job losses. The proposed solution to this problem is to ban imports of cheap foreign goods and to protect U.S. jobs. The proposal is flawed for the following reasons.

First, free trade does cost some jobs, but it also creates other jobs. It brings about a global rationalization of labor and allocates labor resources to their highest-valued activities. Because of international trade in textiles, tens of thousands of workers in the United States have lost jobs because textile mills and other factories have closed. But tens of thousands of workers in other countries now have jobs because textile mills have opened there. And tens of thousands of U.S. workers now have better-paying jobs than textile workers because other export industries have expanded and created more jobs than have been destroyed.

Second, imports create jobs. They create jobs for retailers that sell imported goods and for firms that service those goods. They also create jobs by creating incomes in the rest of the world, some of which are spent on imports of U.S.-made goods and services.

Although protection does save some particular jobs, it does so at an inordinate cost. For example, textile jobs are protected in the United States by quotas imposed under an international agreement called the Multifiber Arrangement. The U.S. International Trade Commission (ITC) has estimated that because of quotas, 72,000 jobs exist in textiles that would otherwise disappear and annual clothing expenditure in the United States is $15.9 billion, or $160 per family, higher than it would be with free trade. In other words, the ITC estimates that each textile job saved costs consumers $221,000 a year.

Allows Us to Compete with Cheap Foreign Labor

With the removal of protective tariffs in U.S. trade with Mexico, prominent Texan Ross Perot said that jobs rushing to Mexico would make a "giant sucking sound" (see the cartoon). Let's see what's wrong with this view.

The labor cost of a unit of output equals the wage rate divided by labor productivity. For example, if a U.S. autoworker earns $30 an hour and produces 15 units of output an hour, the average labor cost of a unit of output is $2. If a Mexican auto assembly worker earns $3 an hour and produces 1 unit of output an hour, the average labor cost of a unit of output is $3. Other things remaining the same, the higher a worker's productivity, the higher is the worker's wage rate. High-wage workers have high productivity. Low-wage workers have low productivity.

"I don't know what the hell happened—one minute I'm at work in Flint, Michigan, then there's a giant sucking sound and suddenly here I am in Mexico."

SOURCE: © The New Yorker Collection 1993 Mick Stevens from cartoonbank.com. All rights reserved.

Although high-wage U.S. workers are more productive, on the average, than lower-wage Mexican workers, there are differences across industries. U.S. labor is relatively more productive in some activities than in others. For example, the productivity of U.S. workers in producing movies, financial services, and customized computer chips is relatively higher than their productivity in the production of metals and some standardized machine parts. The activities in which U.S. workers are relatively more productive than their Mexican counterparts are those in which the United States has a comparative advantage. By engaging in free trade, increasing our production and exports of the goods and services in which we have a comparative advantage, and decreasing our production and increasing our imports of the goods and services in which our trading partners have a comparative advantage, we can make ourselves and the citizens of other countries better off.

Brings Diversity and Stability

A diversified investment portfolio is less risky than one that has all of its eggs in one basket. The same is true for an economy's production. A diversified economy fluctuates less than an economy that produces only one or two goods.

But big, rich, diversified economies like those of the United States, Japan, and Europe do not have this type of stability problem. Even a country such as Saudi Arabia that produces almost only one good (in this case, oil) can benefit from specializing in the activity at which it has a comparative advantage and then investing in a wide range of other countries to bring greater stability to its income and consumption.

Penalizes Lax Environmental Standards

A new argument for protection is that many poorer countries, such as Mexico, do not have the same environmental standards that we have, and because they are willing to pollute and we are not, we cannot compete with them without tariffs. So if they want free trade with the richer and "greener" countries, they must clean up their environments to our standards.

This argument for trade restrictions is weak. While everyone wants a clean environment, a poor country is less able than a rich one to devote resources to achieving this goal. The best hope for a better environment in the developing countries is rapid income growth through free trade. As their incomes grow, developing countries will have the means to match their desires to improve their environment. Also, because poor countries are willing to accept "dirty" activities (such as iron ore smelting and chemical production), it is easier for rich countries to achieve the high environmental standards that they seek.

Protects National Culture

The national culture argument for protection is not heard much in the United States, but it is a commonly heard argument in Canada and Europe.

The expressed fear is that free trade in books, magazines, movies, and television programs means U.S. domination and the end of local culture. So, the reasoning continues, it is necessary to protect domestic "culture" industries from free international trade to ensure the survival of a national cultural identity.

Protection of these industries is common and takes the form of nontariff barriers. For example, regulations often require local content on radio and television broadcasting and in magazines.

The cultural identity argument for protection has no merit. Writers, publishers, and broadcasters want to limit foreign competition so that they can earn larger economic profits. There is no actual danger to national culture. In fact, many of the creators of so-called American cultural products are not Americans, but the talented citizens of other countries, ensuring the survival of their national cultural identities in Hollywood! Also, if national culture is in danger, there is no surer way of helping it on its way out than by impoverishing the nation whose culture it is. And protection is an effective way of doing just that.

Prevents Rich Countries from Exploiting Developing Countries

Another new argument for protection is that international trade must be restricted to prevent the people of the rich industrial world from exploiting the poorer people of the developing countries, forcing them to work for slave wages.

Wage rates in some developing countries are indeed very low. But by trading with developing countries, we increase the demand for the goods that these countries produce, and, more significantly, we increase the demand for their labor. When the demand for labor in developing countries increases, the wage rate also increases. So, far from exploiting people in developing countries, trade improves their opportunities and increases their incomes.

We have reviewed the arguments that are commonly heard in favor of protection and the counterarguments against them. There is one counterargument to protection that is general and quite overwhelming. Protection invites retaliation and can trigger a trade war. The best example of a trade war occurred during the Great Depression of the 1930s when the Smoot-Hawley Tariff was introduced. Country after country retaliated with its own tariff, and in a short period, world trade had almost disappeared. The costs to all countries were large and led to a renewed international resolve to avoid such self-defeating moves in the future. They also led to the creation of GATT and are the impetus behind NAFTA, APEC, and the European Union.

Why Is International Trade Restricted?

Why, despite all the arguments against protection, is trade restricted? There are two key reasons:

- Tariff revenue
- Rent seeking

Tariff Revenue

Government revenue is costly to collect. In developed countries, such as the United States, well-organized tax collection systems exist that can generate billions of dollars of income tax and sales tax revenues. These tax collection systems are made possible by the fact that firms that must keep properly audited financial records do most economic transactions. Without such records, the revenue collection agencies (such as the Internal Revenue Service in the United States) would be severely hampered in their work. Even with audited financial accounts, some proportion of potential tax revenue is lost. Nonetheless, for industrialized countries, the income tax and sales taxes are the major sources of revenue and the tariff plays a very small role.

But governments in developing countries have a difficult time collecting taxes from their citizens. Much economic activity takes place in an informal economy with few financial records. So these countries collect only a small amount of revenue from income taxes and sales taxes. The one area in which economic transactions are well recorded and audited is international trade. So this activity is an attractive base for tax collection in these countries and is used much more extensively than in the developed countries.

Rent Seeking

The major reason why international trade is restricted is because of rent seeking. *Rent seeking* is lobbying and other political activity that seeks to capture the gains from trade. Free trade increases consumption possibilities on the average, but not everyone shares in the gain and some people even lose. Free trade brings benefits to some and imposes costs on others, with total benefits exceeding total costs. It is the uneven distribution of costs and benefits that is the principal source of impediment to achieving more liberal international trade.

Suppose that we had a tariff on T-shirts, as in the example that you studied earlier in this chapter. A few thousand (perhaps a few hundred) garment makers and their employees who must switch to some other activity would bear the cost of the United States moving to free trade. The millions of T-shirt buyers would reap the benefits of moving to free trade. The number of people who gain will, in general, be enormous in comparison with the number who lose. The gain per person will therefore be small. The loss per person to those who bear the loss will be large. Because the loss that falls on those who bear it is large, it will pay those people to incur considerable expense to lobby against free trade. On the other hand, it will not pay those who gain to organize to achieve free trade. The gain from trade for any one individual is too small for that individual to spend much time or money on a political organization to lobby for free trade. The loss from free trade will be seen as being so great by those bearing that loss that they will find it profitable to join a political organization to prevent free trade. Each group is weighing benefits against costs and choosing the best action for themselves. But the anti-free-trade group will undertake a larger quantity of political lobbying than the pro-free-trade group.

Compensating Losers

If, in total, the gains from free international trade exceed the losses, why don't those who gain compensate those who lose so that everyone is in favor of free trade? To some degree, such compensation does take place. When Congress approved the NAFTA deal with Canada and Mexico, it set up a $56 million fund to support and retrain workers who lost their jobs because of the new trade agreement. During the first six months of the operation of NAFTA, only 5,000 workers applied for benefits under this scheme.

The losers from freer international trade are also compensated indirectly through the normal unemployment compensation arrangements. But only limited attempts are made to compensate those who lose from free international trade. The main reason why full compensation is not attempted is that the costs of identifying all the losers and estimating the value of their losses would be enormous. Also, it would never be clear whether a person who has fallen on hard times is suffering because of free trade or for other reasons, perhaps reasons that are largely under the control of the individual. Furthermore, some people who look like losers at one point in time may, in fact, end up gaining. The young autoworker who loses his job in Michigan and becomes a computer assembly worker in Minneapolis resents the loss of work and the need to move. But a year or two later, looking back on events, he counts himself fortunate. He has made a move that has increased his income and given him greater job security.

It is because we do not, in general, compensate the losers from free international trade that protectionism is such a popular and permanent feature of our national economic and political life.

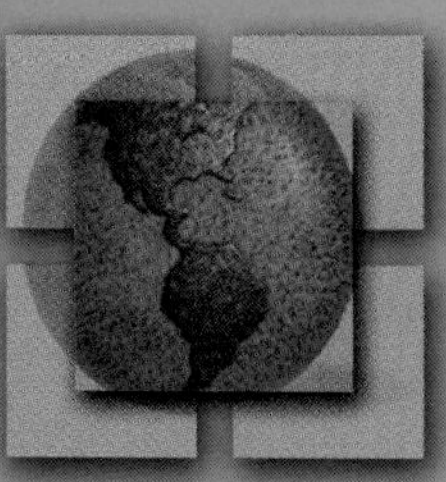

Eye on the Global Economy

Competing with Low-Wage Nations

New Balance athletic shoes are made in two ways:

At a New Balance factory in Norridgewock, Maine, skilled workers who earn $14 an hour operate "see-and-sew" machines—$100,000 automated sewing machines guided by cameras. It costs $4 to make a pair of shoes in Maine.

At a subcontractor's factory in China, low-skilled women in their teens and early twenties who earn 40 cents an hour operate ordinary sewing machines. It costs $1.30 to make a pair of shoes in China.

New Balance is willing to pay the additional $2.70, which is about 4 percent of the retail price of a shoe, to produce shoes in the United States.

New Balance produces 25 percent of its output in the United States and the rest in Asia.

Nike, Reebok, and all the other makers of athletic shoes produce their entire output in Asia.

The Asian economies have a comparative advantage in making athletic shoes. Even when New Balance has invested heavily in equipment to make its U.S. work force much more productive than the Chinese work force, the labor cost alone of a pair of shoes is more than three times the cost in China. Add the capital cost to the equation, and New Balance pays much more for its shoes than do its competitors.

You would predict, and you'd be correct, that New Balance is not the most profitable shoemaker.

CHECKPOINT 22.4

Study Guide pp. 334–336

Practice Online 22.4

4 Explain the arguments used to justify trade barriers and show why they are incorrect but also why some barriers are hard to remove.

Practice Problems 22.4

1. Japan sets quotas on imports of rice. California rice growers would like to export more rice to Japan. What are Japan's arguments for restricting imports of Californian rice? Are these arguments correct? Who loses from this restriction in trade?
2. The United States has, from time to time, limited imports of steel from Europe. What is the argument that the United States has used to justify this quota? Who wins from this restriction? Who loses?
3. The United States maintains a quota on imports of textiles. What is the argument for this quota? Is this argument flawed? If so, explain why.

Exercises 22.4

1. Texan Ross Perot has argued against NAFTA. What is his argument against a free trade zone in North America? What was wrong with Perot's argument? Whom did Perot see as the loser from NAFTA?
2. The Summit of the Americas in April 2001 decided to extend NAFTA to cover all of the Americas. What was President George W. Bush's argument for this extension? Who will be the winners? Who will be the losers?
3. Hong Kong has never restricted trade. What gains has Hong Kong reaped by unilaterally adopting free trade with all nations? Is there any argument for restricted trade that might have benefited Hong Kong?

Solutions to Practice Problems 22.4

1. Japan has used a number of arguments for low quotas on rice imports. Some of these are that Japanese consumers can get a better quality of rice from Japanese producers and that the quota limits competition faced by Japanese producers. The arguments are not correct. If Japanese consumers do not like the quality of Californian rice, they will not buy it. The quota does limit competition, but the Japanese quota allows Japanese farmers to use their land less efficiently. The big losers are the Japanese consumers because the price of rice in Japan is about three times the price paid by U.S. consumers.
2. The U.S. argument for a quota on imports of European steel is that European producers dump steel on the U.S. market. With a quota, U.S. producers will face less competition in the market for steel and U.S. jobs will be saved. Workers in the steel industry and owners of steel companies will win at the expense of U.S. buyers of steel.
3. The argument for a quota on U.S. imports of textiles is that textiles are produced in developing countries where labor is cheap. That is, the quota protects the jobs of U.S. workers. The argument is flawed because the United States does not have a comparative advantage in the manufacture of textiles and so a quota allows the U.S. textile industry to be inefficient. With free trade in textiles, the U.S. textile industry would exit but it would be smaller and more efficient.

CHAPTER CHECKPOINT

Key Points

1 Describe the patterns and trends in international trade.

- Large flows of trade take place between countries; most trade is in manufactured goods exchanged among rich industrialized countries.
- Since 1960, the volume of U.S. trade has more than doubled.

2 Explain why nations engage in international trade and why trade benefits all nations.

- When opportunity costs between countries diverge, comparative advantage enables countries to gain from international trade.
- By increasing production of goods in which it has a comparative advantage and then trading some of the increased output, a country can consume at points outside its production possibilities frontier.

3 Explain how trade barriers reduce international trade.

- Countries restrict international trade by imposing tariffs and quotas.
- Trade restrictions raise the domestic price of imported goods, lower the volume of imports, and reduce the total value of imports.

4 Explain the arguments used to justify trade barriers and show why they are incorrect but also why some barriers are hard to remove.

- The arguments that protection is necessary for national security, for infant industries, and to prevent dumping are weak.
- Arguments that protection saves jobs, allows us to compete with cheap foreign labor, makes the economy diversified and stable, protects national culture, prevents rich countries from exploiting developing countries, and is needed to offset the costs of environmental policies are fatally flawed.
- Trade is restricted because tariffs raise government revenue and because protection brings a small loss to a large number of people and a large gain per person to a small number of people.

Key Terms

Balance of trade, 565
Dumping, 580
Dynamic comparative advantage, 572
Infant-industry argument, 579
Learning-by-doing, 572
Nontariff barrier, 574
Quota, 576
Tariff, 574

Exercises

FIGURE 1

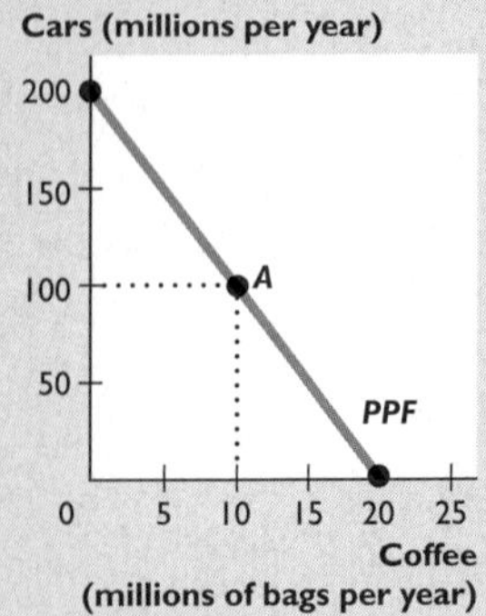

FIGURE 2

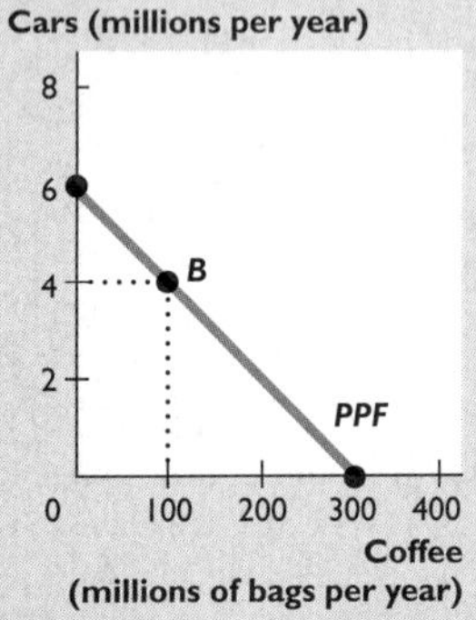

1. Suppose that with no international trade between the United States and Brazil, Figure 1 shows the U.S. production possibilities and the quantities of coffee and cars produced (point *A*). Figure 2 shows Brazil's production possibilities and the quantities of coffee and cars produced (point *B*).
   a. What is the opportunity cost of a bag of coffee in the United States?
   b. What is the opportunity cost of a bag of coffee in Brazil?
   c. Which country has a comparative advantage in producing coffee?
   d. Which country has a comparative advantage in producing cars?
   e. With free trade between Brazil and the United States, what does the United States import from Brazil and what does it export to Brazil? Explain your answer.
   f. Does Brazil gain from trade with the United States? Why or why not?

2. When free trade occurs in exercise 1, the world price of a bag of coffee is 1/25th of a car. If Brazil completely specializes in coffee and exports half of it to the United States,
   a. Show on Figure 2 the quantities of the two goods that Brazil consumes.
   b. Show on Figure 1 the quantities of the two goods that the United States consumes.

3. The table provides information about production possibilities in Kenya and Morocco.

Item	Kenya's production possibilities			
	A	*B*	*C*	*D*
Coffee (millions of bags per year)	0	2	4	6
Oranges (millions per year)	3	2	1	0

Item	Morocco's production possibilities			
	A	*B*	*C*	*D*
Coffee (millions of bags per year)	0	1	2	3
Oranges (millions per year)	6	4	2	0

   a. What is the opportunity cost of producing a bag of coffee in Kenya?
   b. What is the opportunity cost of producing a bag of coffee in Morocco?
   c. What is the opportunity cost of producing an orange in Kenya?
   d. What is the opportunity cost of producing an orange in Morocco?
   e. Suppose that there is no trade between Kenya and Morocco and that in each country, production and consumption are 2 million bags of coffee and 2 million oranges. Make a graph of the two *PPF*s and mark on them the point at which each country produces and consumes.
   f. Now suppose that trade opens up between the two countries and that each specializes in producing the item at which it has a comparative advantage. What now is the total quantity produced of coffee and oranges?

g. If one bag of coffee exchanges for one orange on the world market, what are the volumes of exports and imports of Kenya and Morocco?
h. What are the consumption levels of coffee and oranges in Kenya and Morocco?

4. Look at the information provided in the figure in Eye on the Global Economy on p. 475.
   a. Select an item from the figure in which the United States has a comparative advantage.
   b. Select an item from the figure in which the rest of the world has a comparative advantage.
   c. Make some assumptions about prices and quantities and draw your own figures similar to Figure 22.1 and 22.2 to illustrate the situation in the markets for the two items you chose in parts **a** and **b**.
   d. Make some assumptions about opportunity costs and draw your own figures similar to the two parts of Figure 22.3 to illustrate the U.S. *PPF* and the rest-of-the-world *PPF* for the two items you chose in parts **a** and **b**.

5. Figure 3 shows the car market in Brazil when Brazil places no restriction on imports of cars. The world price of a car is $10,000. If the government of Brazil introduces a 20 percent tariff on car imports, what will be
   a. The price of a car in Brazil?
   b. The quantity of cars imported into Brazil?
   c. The quantity of cars produced in Brazil?
   d. The government's tariff revenue?

FIGURE 3

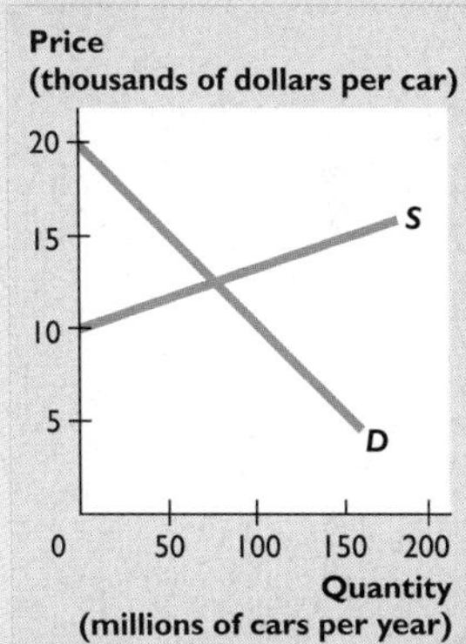

6. Suppose that in exercise 5, the Brazilian government introduces a quota of 50 million cars a year. Show on the figure
   a. The price of a car in Brazil.
   b. The quantity of cars imported into Brazil.
   c. The quantity of cars produced in Brazil.

7. If the tariff described in exercise 5 was imposed,
   a. Who would gain and who would lose?
   b. Why might a tariff be imposed?

8. If the quota described in exercise 6 was imposed,
   a. Who would gain and who would lose?
   b. Why might a quota be imposed?

Critical Thinking

9. In the 1950s, Ford and General Motors established a small car-producing industry in Australia and argued for a high tariff on car imports. The tariff has remained through the years. In 2000, the tariff was cut from 22.5 percent to 15 percent. What might have been the argument for the high tariff? Is the tariff the best way to achieve the goals of the argument?

10. The Canadian government argues against free trade in magazines and movies. Why is the Canadian government concerned about the quantity of U.S. magazines and movies that Canadians see? What is wrong with the Canadian government's argument? Who in Canada gains from the government's argument?

11. The U.S. government imposes a quota on lamb imports from New Zealand and Australia. New Zealand and Australia have lobbied the U.S. government for an increase in the quota. What is the argument put forward by the New Zealand and Australian governments? What is the counterargument put forward by the U.S. government? Which argument is really an example of rent seeking?
12. In 1845, French economist Frédéric Bastiat wrote a satirical "petition of the candlemakers" in which he argued that competition from the sun was unfair to the makers of artificial lighting. He suggested that to level the playing field, boost the production of artificial light, and create much employment and economic activity, the government should pass a law ordering the shutting up of all windows, openings, and chinks through which sunlight may enter buildings.
    - **a.** Explain why passing the law called for in Bastiat's petition would create inefficiency.
    - **b.** Explain why the argument presented in Bastiat's petition is similar to that of people who argue for protection from foreign competition.

Practice Online

Web Exercises

Use the links on your Foundations Web site to work the following exercises.

13. Visit the Web site of the World Trade Organization (WTO).
    - **a.** What is the WTO?
    - **b.** Review the ten benefits of the WTO trading system listed on the Web site. Do you agree that these are benefits? Who benefits?
    - **c.** Review the ten common misunderstandings about the WTO listed on the Web site. Do you agree that these are misunderstandings? Explain why or why not.
14. Visit the Agriculture Negotiations page of the WTO Web site.
    - **a.** What are the problems facing international trade in agricultural products?
    - **b.** What is the WTO plan for dealing with these problems?
    - **c.** If international trade in agricultural products becomes freer, do you expect U.S. farms to expand or contract? Why?
15. Visit the Global Trade Watch page on the Web site of the Public Citizen.
    - **a.** What are the views expressed by Global Trade Watch?
    - **b.** Are these views among the ten common misunderstandings about the WTO?
    - **c.** Are the views of Global Trade Watch consistent with the ideas about the gains from international trade that you've studied in this chapter?
    - **d.** Explain why you agree or disagree with the views of Global Trade Watch.
16. Visit the Web site of the U.S. International Trade Commission (USITC).
    - **a.** What are the main functions and responsibilities of the USITC?
    - **b.** How does the role of the USITC differ from that of the WTO?
    - **c.** Review the page on effects of the proposed Free Trade Agreement between the United States and the Southern Africa Customs Union. Whom do you think would gain from such an agreement and why?

Glossary

Above full-employment equilibrium When equilibrium real GDP exceeds potential GDP. (p. 523)

Absolute advantage When one person is more productive than another person in several or even all activities. (p. 81)

Aggregate demand The relationship between the quantity of real GDP demanded and the price level when all other influences on expenditure plans remain the same. (p. 516)

Aggregate hours The total number of hours worked by all the people employed, both full time and part time, during a year. (p. 377)

Aggregate supply The relationship between the quantity of real GDP supplied and the price level when all other influences on production plans remain the same. (p. 510)

Allocative efficiency The combination of goods and services on the PPF that we value most highly. (p. 73)

Automatic fiscal policy A fiscal policy action that is triggered by the state of the economy such as an increase in payments to the unemployed and a decrease in tax receipts triggered by recession. (p. 538)

Automatic stabilizers Features of fiscal policy that stabilize real GDP without explicit action by the government. (p. 546)

Average cost pricing rule A price rule for a natural monopoly that sets the price equal to average cost and enables the firm to cover its costs and earn a normal profit. (p. 293)

Average fixed cost Total fixed cost per unit of output. (p. 231)

Average product Total product divided by the quantity of an input. The average product of labor is total product divided by the quantity of labor employed. (p. 226)

Average total cost Total cost per unit of output, which equals average fixed cost plus average variable cost. (p. 231)

Average variable cost Total variable cost per unit of output. (p. 231)

Balance of trade The value of exports minus the value of imports. (p. 565)

Balance sheet A statement that summarizes assets (amounts owned) and liabilities (amounts owed). (p. 454)

Balanced budget The budget balance when tax receipts equal expenditures. (p. 536)

Balanced budget multiplier The magnification effect on aggregate demand of a *simultaneous* change in government purchases and taxes that leaves the budget balance unchanged. (p. 539)

Barrier to entry A natural or legal constraint that protects a firm from competitors. (p. 272)

Barter The direct exchange of goods and services for other goods and services, which requires a double coincidence of wants. (p. 429)

Beige Book A report that summarizes current economic conditions in each Federal Reserve district and each sector of the economy. (p. 548)

Below full-employment equilibrium When potential GDP exceeds equilibrium real GDP. (p. 523)

Benefit The benefit of something is the gain or pleasure that it brings. (p. 14)

Big tradeoff A tradeoff between efficiency and fairness that recognizes the cost of making income transfers. (p. 158)

Black market An illegal market that operates alongside a government-regulated market. (p. 177)

Budget deficit The budget balance when expenditures exceed tax receipts. (p. 536)

Budget surplus The budget balance when tax receipts exceed expenditures. (p. 536)

Business cycle A periodic but irregular up-and-down movement in production and jobs. (p. 6)

Capacity output The output at which average total cost is a minimum. (p. 305)

Capital Tools, instruments, machines, buildings, and other constructions that have been produced in the past and that businesses now use to produce goods and services. (p. 40)

Cartel A group of firms acting together to limit output, raise price, and increase economic profit. (p. 312)

Central bank A public authority that provides banking services to banks and regulates financial institutions and markets. (p. 443)

Ceteris paribus Other things remaining the same (often abbreviated as *cet. par.*). (p. 10)

Change in demand A change in the quantity that people plan to buy when any influence on buying plans other than the price of the good changes. (p. 94)

Change in supply A change in the quantity that suppliers plan to sell when any influence on selling plans other than the price of the good changes. (p. 101)

Change in the quantity demanded A change in the quantity of a good that people plan to buy that results from a change in the price of the good. (p. 94)

Change in the quantity supplied A change in the quantity of a good that suppliers plan to sell that results from a change in the price of the good. (p. 101)

Circular flow model A model of the economy that shows the circular flow of expenditures and incomes that result from decision makers' choices and the way those choices interact to determine what, how, and for whom goods and services are produced. (p. 44)

Classical growth theory The theory that the clash between an exploding population and limited resources will eventually bring economic growth to an end. (p. 409)

Coase theorem The proposition that if property rights exist, only a small number of parties are involved, and transactions costs are low, then private transactions are efficient and the outcome is not affected by who is assigned the property right. (p. 200)

Commercial bank A firm that is chartered by the Comptroller of the Currency in the U.S. Treasury (or by a state agency) to accept deposits and make loans. (p. 436)

Comparative advantage The ability of a person to perform an activity or produce a good or service at a lower opportunity cost than someone else. (p. 79)

Complement A good that is consumed with another good. (p. 95)

Complement in production A good that is produced along with another good. (p. 102)

Constant returns to scale A condition in which, when a firm increases its plant size and labor employed by the same percentage, its output increases by the same percentage and its average total cost remains constant. (p. 238)

Consumer Price Index A measure of the average of the prices paid by urban consumers for a fixed market basket of consumer goods and services. (p. 352)

Consumer surplus The marginal benefit from a good or service minus the price paid for it, summed over the quantity consumed. (p. 145)

Consumption expenditure The expenditure by households on consumption goods and services. (p. 329)

Consumption goods and services Goods and services that are bought by individuals and used to provide personal enjoyment and contribute to a person's standard of living. (p. 36)

Copyright A government-sanctioned exclusive right granted to the inventor of a good, service, or productive process to produce, use, and sell the invention for a given number of years. (p. 211)

Correlation The tendency for the values of two variables to move in a predictable and related way. (p. 11)

Cost of living The number of dollars it takes to buy the goods and services that achieve a given standard of living. (p. 5)

Cost of living index A measure of changes in the amount of money that people would need to spend to achieve a given standard of living. (p. 358)

Credit union A financial institution owned by a social or economic group such as a firm's employees, that accepts savings deposits and makes mostly consumer loans. (p. 438)

Cross elasticity of demand A measure of the extent to which the demand for a good changes when the price of a substitute or complement changes, other things remaining the same. (p. 135)

Cross-section graph A graph that shows the values of an economic variable for different groups in a population at a point in time. (p. 26)

Currency Notes (dollar bills) and coins. (p. 430)

Currency drain An increase in currency held outside the banks. (p. 468)

Cyclical unemployment The fluctuating unemployment over the business cycle that increases during a recession and decreases during an expansion. (p. 388)

Deadweight loss The decrease in consumer surplus and producer surplus that results from an inefficient level of production. (p. 154)

Decreasing marginal returns When the marginal product of an additional worker is less than the marginal product of the previous worker. (p. 224)

Deflation A situation in which the cost of living is falling and the value of money is rising. (p. 5)

Deflationary gap A gap that exists when potential GDP exceeds real GDP and that brings a falling price level. (p. 528)

Demand The relationship between the quantity demanded and the price of a good when all other influences on buying plans remain the same. (p. 91)

Demand curve A graph of the relationship between the quantity demanded of a good and its price when all the other influences on buying plans remain the same. (p. 92)

Demand for money The relationship between the quantity of money demanded and the nominal interest rate, when all other influences on the amount of money that people wish to hold remain the same. (p. 480)

Demand schedule A list of the quantities demanded at each different price when all the other influences on buying plans remain the same. (p. 92)

Deposit multiplier The number by which an increase in bank reserves is multiplied to find the resulting increase in bank deposits. (p. 462)

Depreciation The decrease in the value of capital that results from its use and from obsolescence—also called capital consumption. (p. 336)

Direct relationship A relationship between two variables that move in the same direction. (p. 28)

Discount rate The interest rate at which the Fed stands ready to lend reserves to commercial banks. (p. 446)

Discouraged worker A person who is available and willing to work but has not made specific efforts to find a job within the previous four weeks. (p. 376)

Discretionary fiscal policy A fiscal policy action that is initiated by an act of Congress. (p. 538)

Diseconomies of scale A condition in which, when a firm increases its plant size and labor employed by the same percentage, its output increases by a smaller percentage and its average total cost increases. (p. 238)

Dumping When a foreign firm sells its exports at a lower price than its cost of production. (p. 580)

Duopoly A market with only two firms. (p. 312)

Dynamic comparative advantage A comparative advantage that a person (or country) obtains by specializing in an activity, resulting from learning-by-doing. (p. 572)

Economic depreciation An opportunity cost of a firm using capital that it owns—measured as the change in the *market value* of capital over a given period. (p. 219)

Economic freedom A condition in which people are able to make personal choices, their private property is protected, and they are free to buy and sell in markets. (p. 419)

Economic growth The sustained expansion of production possibilities. (p. 83)

Economic growth rate The annual percentage change of real GDP. (p. 398)

Economic model A description of some aspect of the economic world that includes only those features of the world that are needed for the purpose at hand. (p. 9)

Economic profit A firm's total revenue minus total cost. (p. 219)

Economic theory A generalization that summarizes what we understand about the economic choices that people make and the economic performance of industries and nations based on models that have repeatedly passed the test of corresponding well with real-world data. (p. 9)

Economics The social science that studies the choices that we make as we cope with *scarcity* and the *incentives* that influence and reconcile our choices. (p. 3)

Economies of scale A condition in which, when a firm increases its plant size and labor employed by the same percentage, its output increases by a larger percentage and its average total cost decreases. (p. 237)

Efficiency A situation in which the quantities of goods and services produced are those that people value most highly—in which we cannot produce more of a good or service without giving up some of another good or service that people value more highly. (p. 72)

Elastic demand When the percentage change in the quantity demanded exceeds the percentage change in price. (p. 120)

Elastic supply When the percentage change in the quantity supplied exceeds the percentage change in price. (p. 130)

Electronic cash (or **e-cash**) An electronic equivalent of paper notes and coins. (p. 432)

Electronic check (or **e-check**) An electronic equivalent of a paper check. (p. 432)

Entrepreneurship The human resource that organizes labor, land, and capital. (p. 41)

Equation of exchange An equation that states that the quantity of money multiplied by the velocity of circulation equals the price level multiplied by real GDP. (p. 491)

Equilibrium price The price at which the quantity demanded equals the quantity supplied. (p. 105)

Equilibrium quantity The quantity bought and sold at the equilibrium price. (p. 105)

Excess burden The amount by which the burden of a tax exceeds the tax revenue received by the government—the deadweight loss from a tax. (p. 174)

Excess demand A situation in which the quantity demanded exceeds the quantity supplied. (p. 106)

Excess reserves Bank reserves that exceed those needed to meet the required reserve ratio. (p. 437)

Excess supply A situation in which the quantity supplied exceeds the quantity demanded. (p. 106)

Explicit cost A cost paid in money. (p. 219)

Export goods and services Goods and services produced in one country and sold in other countries. (p. 36) Items that firms in the United States produce and sell to the rest of the world. (p. 330)

External diseconomies Factors outside the control of a firm that raise the firm's costs as *market* output increases. (p. 262)

External economies Factors beyond the control of an individual firm that lower its costs as the *market* output increases. (p. 262)

Externality A cost or a benefit that arises from production that falls on someone other than the producer; or a cost or benefit that arises from consumption that falls on someone other than the consumer. (p. 194)

Factor markets Markets in which factors of production are bought and sold. (p. 44)

Factors of production The productive resources used to produce goods and services—land, labor, capital, and entrepreneurship. (p. 38)

Federal budget An annual statement of the expenditures, tax receipts, and surplus or deficit of the government of the United States. (p. 536)

Federal funds rate The interest rate on interbank loans (loans made in the federal funds market). (p. 437)

Federal Open Market Committee The Fed's main policy-making committee. (p. 444)

Federal Reserve System The central bank of the United States. (p. 443)

Fiat money Objects that are money because the law decrees or orders them to be money. (p. 430)

Final good or service A good or service that is produced for its final user and not as a component of another good or service. (p. 328)

Firms The institutions that organize the production of goods and services. (p. 44)

Fiscal policy The use of the federal budget to smooth the business cycle and encourage economic growth. (p. 536)

Four-firm concentration ratio The percentage of the value of sales accounted for by the four largest firms in an industry. (p. 302)

Frictional unemployment The unemployment that arises from normal labor turnover—from people entering and leaving the labor force and from the ongoing creation and destruction of jobs. (p. 387)

Full employment When there is no cyclical unemployment or, equivalently, when all the unemployment is frictional, structural, and seasonal. (p. 390)

Full-employment equilibrium When equilibrium real GDP equals potential GDP. (p. 523)

Full-time workers People who usually work 35 hours or more a week. (p. 376)

Functional distribution of income The distribution of income among the factors of production. (p. 42)

Game theory The tool that economists use to analyze *strategic behavior*—behavior that recognizes mutual interdependence and takes account of the expected behavior of others. (p. 317)

GDP deflator An average of current prices expressed as a percentage of base-year prices. (p. 341)

Goods and services The objects that people value and produce to satisfy human wants. Goods are physical objects, and services are tasks performed for people. (p. 4)

Goods markets Markets in which goods and services are bought and sold. (p. 44)

Government goods and services Goods and services that are bought by governments. (p. 36)

Government purchases multiplier The magnification effect of a change in government purchases of goods and services on aggregate demand. (p. 539)

Government purchases of goods and services The purchases by all levels of government of goods and services. (p. 330)

Great Depression A period during the 1930s in which the economy experienced its worst-ever recession. (p. 6)

Gross domestic product (GDP) The market value of all the final goods and services produced within a country in a given time period. (p. 328)

Herfindahl-Hirschman Index— The square of the percentage market share of each firm summed over the largest 50 firms (or summed over all the firms if there are fewer than 50) in a market. (p. 302)

Households Individuals or groups of people living together. (p. 44)

Human capital The knowledge and skill that people obtain from education, on-the-job training, and work experience. (p. 39)

Hyperinflation Inflation at a rate that exceeds 50 percent a month. (p. 495)

Implicit cost An opportunity cost incurred by a firm when it uses a factor of production for which it does not make a direct money payment. (p. 219)

Imports of goods and services Items that households, firms, and governments in the United States buy from the rest of the world. (p. 330)

Incentive A reward or a penalty—a "carrot" or a "stick"—that encourages or discourages an action. (p. 2)

Income elasticity of demand A measure of the extent to which the demand for a good changes when income changes, other things remaining the same. (p. 136)

Increasing marginal returns When the marginal product of an additional worker exceeds the marginal product of the previous worker. (p. 224)

Induced taxes Taxes that vary with real GDP. (p. 546)

Inelastic demand When the percentage change in the quantity demanded is less than the percentage change in price. (p. 120)

Inelastic supply When the percentage change in the quantity supplied is less than the percentage change in price. (p. 130)

Infant-industry argument The argument that it is necessary to protect a new industry to enable it to grow into a mature industry that can compete in world markets. (p. 579)

Inferior good A good for which demand decreases when income increases. (p. 95)

Inflation A situation in which the cost of living is rising and the value of money is shrinking. (p. 5)

Inflation rate The percentage change in the price level from one year to the next. (p. 355)

Inflationary gap A gap that exists when real GDP exceeds potential GDP and that brings a rising price level. (p. 528)

Intellectual property rights The property rights of the creators of knowledge and other discoveries. (p. 211)

Interest Income paid for the use of capital. (p. 41)

Intermediate good or service A good or service that is produced by one firm, bought by another firm, and used as a component of a final good or service. (p. 328)

Inverse relationship A relationship between two variables that move in opposite directions. (p. 29)

Investment The purchase of new *capital goods* (tools, instruments, machines, buildings, and other constructions) and additions to inventories. (p. 329)

Investment goods Goods that are bought by businesses to increase their productive resources. (p. 36)

Involuntary part-time workers People who work 1 to 34 hours a week but who are looking for full-time work. (p. 376)

Labor The work time and work effort that people devote to producing goods and services. (p. 39)

Labor force The number of people employed plus the number unemployed. (p. 374)

Labor force participation rate The percentage of the working-age population who are members of the labor force. (p. 376)

Labor productivity The quantity of real GDP produced by one hour of labor. (p. 402)

Land The "gifts of nature," or natural resources, that we use to produce goods and services. (p. 38)

Law of decreasing returns As a firm uses more of a variable input, with a given quantity of fixed inputs, the marginal product of the variable input eventually decreases. (p. 226)

Law of demand Other things remaining the same, if the price of a good rises, the quantity demanded of that good decreases; and if the price of a good falls, the quantity demanded of that good increases. (p. 91)

Law of market forces When there is a shortage, the price rises; when there is a surplus, the price falls. (p. 106)

Law of supply Other things remaining the same, if the price of a good rises, the quantity supplied of that good increases; and if the price of a good falls, the quantity supplied of that good decreases. (p. 98)

Learning-by-doing Repeatedly performing the same task and becoming more productive at producing a particular good or service. (p. 572)

Legal monopoly A market in which competition and entry are restricted by the concentration of ownership of a natural resource or by the granting of a public franchise, government license, patent, or copyright. (p. 273)

Linear relationship A relationship that graphs as a straight line. (p. 28)

Liquid asset An asset that can be easily, and with certainty, converted into money. (p. 440)

Long run The time frame in which the quantities of *all* resources can be varied. (p. 222)

Long-run average cost curve A curve that shows the lowest average cost at which it is possible to produce each output when the firm has had sufficient time to change both its plant size and labor employed. (p. 238)

Long-run market supply curve A curve that shows the relationship between the quantity supplied and the price when the number of firms changes so that each firm earns zero economic profit. (p. 263)

Loss Income earned by an entrepreneur for running a business when that income is negative. (p. 41)

M1 Currency held outside banks and traveler's checks plus checkable deposits owned by individuals and businesses. (p. 433)

M2 M1 plus savings deposits and small time deposits, money market funds, and other deposits. (p. 433)

Macroeconomic equilibrium When the quantity of real GDP demanded equals the quantity of real GDP supplied at the point of intersection of the *AD* curve and the *AS* curve. (p. 522)

Macroeconomics The study of the aggregate (or total) effects on the national economy and the global economy of the choices that individuals, businesses, and governments make. (p. 3)

Malthusian theory Another name for classical growth theory—named for Thomas Robert Malthus. (p. 409)

Margin A choice on the margin is a choice that is made by comparing *all* the relevant alternatives systematically and incrementally. (p. 15)

Marginal benefit The benefit that arises from a one-unit increase in an activity. The marginal benefit of something is measured by what you *are willing* to give up to get one more unit of it. (p. 15)

Marginal cost The cost that arises from a one-unit increase in an activity. The marginal cost of something is what you *must* give up to get one more unit of it. (p. 15) The marginal cost of producing a good is the change in total cost that results from a one-unit increase in output. (p. 230)

Marginal cost pricing rule A price rule for a natural monopoly that sets price equal to marginal cost. (p. 293)

Marginal external benefit The benefit from an additional unit of a good or service that people other than the consumer of the good or service enjoy. (p. 206)

Marginal external cost The cost of producing an additional unit of a good or service that falls on people other than the producer. (p. 196)

Marginal private benefit The benefit from an additional unit of a good or service that the consumer of that good or service receives. (p. 206)

Marginal private cost The cost of producing an additional unit of a good or service that is borne by the producer of that good or service. (p. 196)

Marginal product The change in total product that results from a one-unit increase in the quantity of labor employed. (p. 224)

Marginal revenue The change in total revenue that results from a one-unit increase in the quantity sold. (p. 247)

Marginal social benefit The marginal benefit enjoyed by society—by the consumers of a good or service and by everyone else who benefits from it. It is the sum of marginal private benefit and marginal external benefit. (p. 206)

Marginal social cost The marginal cost incurred by the entire society—by the producer and by everyone else on whom the cost falls. It is the sum of marginal private cost and marginal external cost. (p. 196)

Market Any arrangement that brings buyers and sellers together and enables them to get information and do business with each other. (p. 44)

Market demand The sum of the demands of all the buyers in a market. (p. 93)

Market equilibrium When the quantity demanded equals the quantity supplied—when buyers' and sellers' plans are consistent. (p. 105)

Market supply The sum of the supplies of all the sellers in the market. (p. 100)

Means of payment A method of settling a debt. (p. 428)

Medium of exchange An object that is generally accepted in return for goods and services. (p. 429)

Microeconomics The study of the choices that individuals and businesses make and the way these choices respond to incentives, interact, and are influenced by governments. (p. 3)

Minimum wage law A government regulation that makes hiring labor for less than a specified wage illegal. (p. 184)

Monetary base The sum of coins, Federal Reserve notes, and banks' reserves at the Fed. (p. 446)

Monetary policy Adjusting the quantity of money in the economy. (p. 443)

Monetary system The Federal Reserve and the banks and other institutions that accept deposits and provide the services that enable people and businesses to make and receive payments. (p. 436)

Money Any commodity or token that is generally accepted as a means of payment. (p. 428)

Money market fund A financial institution that obtains funds by selling shares and uses these funds to buy assets such as U.S. Treasury bills. (p. 438)

Money multiplier The number by which a change in the monetary base is multiplied to find the resulting change in the quantity of money. (p. 470)

Monopolistic competition A market in which a large number of firms compete by making similar but slightly different products. (p. 246)

Monopoly A market for a good or service that has no close substitutes and in which there is one supplier that is protected from competition by a barrier preventing the entry of new firms. (p. 246)

Nash equilibrium An equilibrium in which each player takes the best possible action given the action of the other player. (p. 318)

National debt The total amount that the federal government has borrowed to make expenditures that exceed tax revenue—to run a government budget deficit. (p. 48)

Natural monopoly A monopoly that arises because one firm can meet the entire market demand at a lower price than two or more firms could. (p. 272)

Natural unemployment rate The unemployment rate at full employment. (p. 390)

Needs-tested spending Spending on programs that entitle suitably qualified people and businesses to receive benefits—benefits that vary with need and with the state of the economy. (p. 546)

Negative externality A production or consumption activity that creates an external cost. (p. 194)

Negative relationship A relationship between two variables that move in opposite directions. (p. 29)

Neoclassical growth theory The theory that real GDP per person will increase as long as technology keeps advancing. (p. 411)

Net domestic product at factor cost The sum of the five components of incomes—compensation of employees, net interest, rental income of persons, corporate profits, and proprietors' income. (p. 336)

Net exports of goods and services The value of exports of goods and services minus the value of imports of goods and services. (p. 330)

Net taxes Taxes paid minus benefits received. (p. 330)

New growth theory The theory that our unlimited productivity will lead us to ever greater productivity and perpetual economic growth. (p. 413)

Nominal GDP The value of the final goods and services produced in a given year valued at the prices that prevailed in that same year. (p. 339)

Nominal interest rate The percentage return on a loan expressed in dollars. (p. 367)

Nominal wage rate The average hourly wage rate measured in *current* dollars. (p. 364)

Nontariff barrier Any action other than a tariff that restricts international trade. (p. 574)

Normal good A good for which demand increases when income increases. (p. 95)

Normal profit The return to entrepreneurship. Normal profit is part of a firm's opportunity cost because it is the cost of not running another firm. (p. 219)

Oligopoly A market in which a small number of firms compete. (p. 246)

One third rule The observation that on the average, with no change in human capital and technology, a *one percent* increase in capital per hour of labor brings a *one third percent* increase in labor productivity. (p. 407)

Open market operation The purchase or sale of government securities—U.S. Treasury bills and bonds—by the Federal Reserve in the open market. (p. 446)

Opportunity cost The opportunity cost of something is the best thing you *must* give up to get it. (p. 13)

Part-time workers People who usually work less than 35 hours a week. (p. 376)

Patent A government-sanctioned exclusive right granted to the inventor of a good, service, or productive process to produce, use, and sell the invention for a given number of years. (p. 211)

Payoff matrix A table that shows the payoffs for each player for every possible combination of actions by the players. (p. 318)

Payroll tax A tax on employers based on the wages they pay their workers. (p. 173)

Perfect competition A market in which there are many firms, each selling an identical product; many buyers; no restrictions on the entry of new firms into the industry; no advantage to established firms; and buyers and sellers are well informed about prices. (p. 246)

Perfect price discrimination Price discrimination that extracts the entire consumer surplus by charging the highest price that consumers are willing to pay for each unit. (p. 288)

Perfectly elastic demand When the quantity demanded changes by a very large percentage in response to an almost zero percentage change in price. (p. 120)

Perfectly elastic supply When the quantity supplied changes by a very large percentage in response to an almost zero percentage change in price. (p. 130)

Perfectly inelastic demand When the quantity demanded remains constant as the price changes. (p. 120)

Perfectly inelastic supply When the quantity supplied remains the same as the price changes. (p. 130)

Personal distribution of income The distribution of income among households. (p. 42)

Positive externality A production or consumption activity that creates an external benefit. (p. 194)

Positive relationship A relationship between two variables that move in the same direction. (p. 28)

***Post hoc* fallacy** The error of reasoning that a first event *causes* a second event because the first occurred *before* the second. (p. 11)

Potential GDP The level of real GDP that the economy would produce if it were at full employment. (p. 390)

Price ceiling The highest price at which it is legal to trade a particular good, service, or factor of production. A rent ceiling is an example of a price ceiling. (p. 176)

Price-discriminating monopoly A monopoly that is able to sell different units of a good or service for different prices. (p. 274)

Price elasticity of demand A measure of the extent to which the quantity demanded of a good changes when the price of the good changes and all other influences on buyers' plans remain the same. (p. 118)

Price elasticity of supply A measure of the extent to which the quantity supplied of a good changes when the price of the good changes and all other influences on sellers' plans remain the same. (p. 130)

Price floor The lowest price at which it is legal to trade a particular good, service, or factor of production. The minimum wage is an example of a price floor. (p. 184)

Price taker A firm that cannot influence the price of the good or service that it produces. (p. 247)

Prisoners' dilemma A game between two prisoners that shows why it is hard to cooperate, even when it would be beneficial to both players to do so. (p. 317)

Producer surplus The price of a good minus the marginal cost of producing it, summed over the quantity produced. (p. 148)

Product differentiation Making a product that is slightly different from the products of competing firms. (p. 300)

Production efficiency A situation in which we cannot produce more of one good or service without producing less of some other good or service—production is at a point *on* the *PPF*. (p. 72)

Production possibilities frontier The boundary between the combinations of goods and services that can be produced and the combinations that cannot be produced, given the available factors of production and the state of technology. (p. 62)

Productivity curve The relationship between real GDP per hour of labor and the quantity of capital per hour of labor with a given state of technology. (p. 405)

Profit Income earned by an entrepreneur for running a business. (p. 41)

Property rights Legally established titles to the ownership, use, and disposal of factors of production and goods and services that are enforceable in the courts. (pp. 199, 419)

Public provision The production of a good or service by a public authority that receives the bulk of its revenue from the government. (p. 208)

Quantity demanded The amount of any good, service, or resource that people are willing and able to buy during a specified period at a specified price. (p. 91)

Quantity of money demanded The amount of money that households and firms choose to hold. (p. 479)

Quantity supplied The amount of any good, service, or resource that people are willing and able to sell during a specified period at a specified price. (p. 98)

Quantity theory of money The proposition that when real GDP equals potential GDP, an increase in the quantity of money brings an equal percentage increase in the price level. (p. 491)

Quota A specified maximum amount of a good that may be imported in a given period of time. (p. 576)

Rational choice A choice that uses the available resources to most effectively satisfy the wants of the person making the choice. (p. 13)

Real GDP The value of the final goods and services produced in a given year when valued at constant prices. (p. 339)

Real GDP per person Real GDP divided by the population. (p. 398)

Real interest rate The percentage return on a loan expressed in purchasing power—the nominal interest rate adjusted for the effects of inflation. (p. 367)

Real wage rate The average hourly wage rate measured in the dollars of a given reference base year. (p. 364)

Recession A decrease in real GDP that lasts for at least two quarters (six months) or a period of significant decline in total output, income, employment, and trade, usually lasting from six months to a year, and marked by widespread contractions in many sectors of the economy. (p. 506)

Reference base period A period for which the CPI is defined to equal 100. Currently, the reference base period is 1982-1984. (p. 352)

Rent Income paid for the use of land (p. 41)

Rent ceiling A government regulation that makes it illegal to charge more than a specified rent for housing. (p. 176)

Rent seeking The act of obtaining special treatment by the government to create economic profit or to divert consumer surplus or producer surplus away from others. (p. 283)

Required reserve ratio The minimum percentage of deposits that banks and other financial institutions must hold in reserves. (p. 437)

Reserves The currency in the bank's vaults plus the balance on its reserve account at a Federal Reserve Bank. (p. 437)

Rule of 70 The number of years it takes for the level of any variable to double is approximately 70 divided by the annual percentage growth rate of the variable. (p. 399)

Saving The amount of income that remains after paying taxes and buying consumption goods and services. (p. 330)

Savings and loan association A financial institution that accepts checkable deposits and savings deposits and that makes personal, commercial, and home-purchase loans. (p. 438)

Savings bank A financial institution that accepts savings deposits and makes mostly consumer and home-purchase loans. (p. 438)

Scarcity The condition that arises because the available resources are insufficient to satisfy wants. (p. 2)

Scatter diagram A graph of the value of one variable against the value of another variable. (p. 26)

Search activity The time spent looking for someone with whom to do business. (p. 178)

Seasonal unemployment The unemployment that arises because of seasonal weather patterns. (p. 388)

Shortage A situation in which the quantity demanded exceeds the quantity supplied. (p. 106)

Short run The time frame in which the quantities of some resources are fixed. In the short run, a firm can usually change the quantity of labor it uses but not its technology and quantity of capital. (p. 222)

Shutdown point The output and price at which price the firm just covers its total variable cost. (p. 251)

Single-price monopoly A monopoly that must sell each unit of its output for the same price to all its customers. (p. 274)

Slope The change in the value of the variable measured on the y-axis divided by the change in the value of the variable measured on the x-axis. (p. 31)

Stagflation A combination of recession (falling real GDP) and inflation (rising price level). (p. 526)

Standard of living The level of consumption of goods and services that people enjoy, on the average; it is measured by average income per person. (p. 5)

Store of value Any commodity or token that can be held and exchanged later for goods and services. (p. 429)

Strategies All the possible actions of each player in a game. (p. 318)

Structural unemployment The unemployment that arises when changes in technology or international competition change the skills needed to perform jobs or change the locations of jobs. (p. 388)

Subsidy A payment that the government makes to private producers that depends on the level of output. (p. 209)

Substitute A good that can be consumed in place of another good. (p. 94)

Substitute in production A good that can be produced in place of another good. (p. 101)

Sunk cost A previously incurred and irreversible cost. (p. 14)

Supply The relationship between the quantity supplied and the price of a good when all other influences on selling plans remain the same. (p. 98)

Supply curve A graph of the relationship between the quantity supplied of a good and its price when all the other influences on selling plans remain the same. (p. 99)

Supply of money The relationship between the quantity of money supplied and the nominal interest rate. (p. 483)

Supply schedule A list of the quantities supplied at each different price when all the other influences on selling plans remain the same. (p. 99)

Surplus A situation in which the quantity supplied exceeds the quantity demanded. (p. 106)

Symmetry principle The requirement that people in similar situations be treated similarly. (p. 157)

Tariff A tax on a good that is imposed by the importing country when an imported good crosses its international boundary. (p. 574)

Tax incidence The division of the burden of the tax between the buyer and the seller. (p. 168)

Tax multiplier The magnification effect of a change in taxes on aggregate demand. (p. 539)

Time-series graph A graph that measures time on the x-axis and the variable or variables in which we are interested on the y-axis. (p. 26)

Total cost The cost of all the factors of production used by a firm. (p. 229)

Total fixed cost The cost of the fixed factors of production used by a firm—the cost of land, capital, and entrepreneurship. (p. 229)

Total product The total quantity of a good produced in a given period. (p. 223)

Total revenue The total revenue from the sale of a good equals the price of the good multiplied by the quantity sold. (p. 126)

Total revenue test A method of estimating the price elasticity of demand by observing the change in total revenue that results from a price change (with all other influences on the quantity sold remaining unchanged). (p. 126)

Total variable cost The cost of the variable factor of production used by a firm—the cost of labor. (p. 229)

Tradeoff A constraint or limit to what is possible that forces an exchange or a substitution of one thing for something else. (p. 65)

Transactions costs The opportunity costs of conducting a transaction. (p. 200)

Trend A general tendency for the value of a variable to rise or fall. (p. 26)

Unemployment The state of being available and willing to work but unable to find an acceptable job. (p. 5)

Unemployment rate The percentage of the people in the labor force who are unemployed. (p. 375)

Unit elastic demand When the percentage change in the quantity demanded equals the percentage change in price. (p. 120)

Unit elastic supply When the percentage change in the quantity supplied equals the percentage change in price. (p. 130)

Unit of account An agreed-upon measure for stating the prices of goods and services. (p. 429)

Utilitarianism A principle that states that we should strive to achieve "the greatest happiness for the greatest number." (p. 158)

Value added The value of a firm's production minus the value of the intermediate goods it buys from other firms. (p. 337)

Velocity of circulation The number of times in a year that the average dollar of money gets used to buy final goods and services. (p. 491)

Voucher A token that the government provides to households that can be used to buy specified goods or services. (p. 210)

Wages Income paid for the services of labor. (p. 41)

Working-age population The total number of people aged 16 years and over who are not in jail, hospital, or some other form of institutional care. (p. 374)

Index

Key terms and pages where they are defined appear in **boldface**.

Credits

(continuation from page iv)

Cover Image © 2003, D. Wiggett/First Light/Panoramic Images.

Chapter 1: p. 3 left and right: Scott Foresman/Addison Wesley Longman, Focus on Sports; p. 4 top: Owen Franken/Stone; p. 4 center: George Rose/Getty Images; p. 4 bottom: Digital Image © 2001/ PhotoDisc, Inc.; p. 5 top: © CORBIS; p. 5 bottom: Digital Image © 2001/PhotoDisc, Inc.; p. 6 top: AP/Wide World Photos; p. 6 bottom: © Bettmann/CORBIS; p. 9: Science & Society Picture Library/Science Museum; p. 10: © Bettmann/CORBIS; p. 14 left: Digital Image © 2001/PhotoDisc, Inc.; p. 14 right: Copyright © David Young-Wolff/PhotoEdit; p. 16 left: Copyright © David Young-Wolff/PhotoEdit; p. 16 right: Copyright © CORBIS.

Chapter 2: p. 37 (all) PhotoDisc, Inc.; p. 40 top and bottom: Digital Image © 2001/ PhotoDisc, Inc.

Chapter 4: p. 90 left: Superstock; p. 90 center: AP/Wide World Photos; p. 90 right: © Steven Rubin/The Image Works; p. 109 top: Digital Image © 2001/PhotoDisc, Inc.; p. 109 bottom: Photo courtesy of Washington State University.

Chapter 5: p. 125 left: © Bennett Dean; Eye Ubiquitous/CORBIS; p. 125 right: Darama/Corbis Stock Market.

Chapter 7: p. 179: AP/Wide World Photos; p. 181: Digital Image © 2001/PhotoDisc, Inc.; p. 187: Digital Image © 2001/PhotoDisc, Inc.

Chapter 8: p. 194 left: © CORBIS; p. 194 right: © George Lepp/ CORBIS; p. 195 left: © Peter Turnley/CORBIS; p. 195 right: © CORBIS; p. 203 left: © Roy Corral/CORBIS; p. 203 right: © Doug Wilson/CORBIS.

Chapter 10: p. 247 top: Digital Image © 2001/PhotoDisc, Inc.; p. 247 bottom: © Jonathan Blair/CORBIS; p. 261 left: ©Jeff Zaruba Studio/CORBIS; p. 261 right: ©2000 Richard Day/MID-WESTOCK; p. 265: © James Marshall/CORBIS.

Chapter 11: p. 272: Superstock; p. 290: Courtesy of priceline.com.

Chapter 12: p. 300: ©Vincent DeWitt/Stock, Boston, Inc./Picture Quest; p. 310: Courtesy of Nike, Inc. p. 312: AP/Wide World Photos.

Chapter 13: p. 334: © Reuters NewMedia Inc./CORBIS.

Chaper 15: p. 377: Courtesy of U.S. Census Bureau; p. 380: © CORBIS; p. 387: Copyright © David Young-Wolff/PhotoEdit; p. 388: © Jim Sugar Photography/ CORBIS.

Chapter 16: p. 404 top: © Minnesota Historical Society/CORBIS; p. 404 bottom: © Bob Rowan; Progressive Image/CORBIS.

Chapter 17: p. 445: Copyright © John Neubauer/PhotoEdit.

Chapter 18: p. 455: Scala/Art Resource, NY.

Chapter 19: p. 495: © Bettmann/CORBIS.

Chapter 20: p. 529: Photo courtesy of Stanford University.

Chapter 21: p. 538 top: Photo by Ingrid Kannel; p. 538 bottom: AP/Wide World Photos.

Chapter 32: p. 810: © MIT Museum.

The Addison-Wesley Series in Economics

Abel/Bernanke
Macroeconomics

Bade/Parkin
Foundations of Economics

Bierman/Fernandez
Game Theory with Economic Applications

Binger/Hoffman
Microeconomics with Calculus

Boyer
Principles of Transportation Economics

Branson
Macroeconomic Theory and Policy

Bruce
Public Finance and the American Economy

Byrns/Stone
Economics

Carlton/Perloff
Modern Industrial Organization

Caves/Frankel/Jones
World Trade and Payments

Chapman
Environmental Economics: Theory, Application, and Policy

Cooter/Ulen
Law and Economics

Downs
An Economic Theory of Democracy

Ehrenberg/Smith
Modern Labor Economics

Ekelund/Tollison
Economics

Fusfeld
The Age of the Economist

Gerber
International Economics

Ghiara
Learning Economics

Gordon
Macroeconomics

Gregory
Essentials of Economics

Gregory/Stuart
Russian and Soviet Economic Performance and Structure

Hartwick/Olewiler
The Economics of Natural Resource Use

Hubbard
Money, the Financial System, and the Economy

Hughes/Cain
American Economic History

Husted/Melvin
International Economics

Jehle/Reny
Advanced Microeconomic Theory

Klein
Mathematical Methods for Economics

Krugman/Obstfeld
International Economics

Laidler
The Demand for Money

Leeds/von Allmen
The Economics of Sports

Lipsey/Courant/Ragan
Economics

Melvin
International Money and Finance

Miller
Economics Today

Miller/Benjamin/North
The Economics of Public Issues

Miller/Benjamin
The Economics of Macro Issues

Mills/Hamilton
Urban Economics

Mishkin
The Economics of Money, Banking, and Financial Markets

Parkin
Economics

Perloff
Microeconomics

Phelps
Health Economics

Riddell/Shackelford/Stamos/Schneider
Economics: A Tool for Critically Understanding Society

Ritter/Silber/Udell
Principles of Money, Banking, and Financial Markets

Rohlf
Introduction to Economic Reasoning

Ruffin/Gregory
Principles of Economics

Sargent
Rational Expectations and Inflation

Scherer
Industry Structure, Strategy, and Public Policy

Schotter
Microeconomics

Stock/Watson
Introduction to Econometrics

Studenmund
Using Econometrics

Tietenberg
Environmental and Natural Resource Economics

Tietenberg
Environmental Economics and Policy

Todaro/Smith
Economic Development

Waldman
Microeconomics

Waldman/Jensen
Industrial Organization

Williamson
Macroeconomics

Macroeconomic Data

These macroeconomic data series show some of the trends in GDP and its components, the price level, and other variables that provide information about changes in the standard of living and the cost of living—the central questions of macroeconomics. You will find these data in a spreadsheet that you can download from your Foundations Web site.

	NATIONAL INCOME AND PRODUCT ACCOUNTS	1978	1979	1980	1981	1982	1983	1984	1985	1986	1987
	EXPENDITURES APPROACH										
the sum of	1 Personal consumption expenditures	1,430.4	1,596.3	1,762.9	1,944.2	2,079.3	2,286.4	2,498.4	2,712.6	2,895.2	3,105.3
	2 Gross private domestic investment	436.0	490.6	477.9	570.8	516.1	564.2	735.5	736.3	747.2	781.5
	3 Government purchases	455.6	503.5	569.7	631.4	684.4	735.9	800.8	878.3	942.3	997.9
	4 Exports	186.1	228.7	278.9	302.8	282.6	277.0	303.1	303.0	320.3	365.6
less	5 Imports	212.3	252.7	293.8	317.8	303.2	328.6	405.1	417.2	452.2	507.9
equals	6 Gross domestic product	2,295.9	2,566.4	2,795.6	3,131.3	3,259.2	3,534.9	3,932.7	4,213.0	4,452.9	4,742.5
	INCOMES APPROACH										
the sum of	7 Compensation of employees	1,336.0	1,500.8	1,651.7	1,825.7	1,926.0	2,042.7	2,255.9	2,425.2	2,570.7	2,755.6
	8 Proprietors' income	170.1	183.7	177.6	186.2	179.9	195.5	247.5	267.0	278.6	303.9
	9 Rental income of persons	22.4	24.5	31.3	39.6	39.6	36.9	39.5	39.1	32.2	35.8
	10 Corporate profits	217.2	222.5	198.5	219.0	201.2	254.1	309.8	322.4	300.7	346.6
	11 Net interest	114.5	144.2	183.9	226.5	256.3	267.2	309.6	326.7	343.6	361.5
equals	12 National income	1,860.2	2,075.6	2,243.0	2,497.1	2,603.0	2,796.5	3,162.3	3,380.4	3,525.8	3,803.4
plus	13 Indirect business tax minus subsidies	152.1	157.5	172.1	204.7	183.2	245.4	252.7	290.8	360.0	339.3
	14 Consumption of fixed capital	261.5	300.4	345.2	394.8	436.5	456.1	482.4	516.5	551.6	586.1
	15 Net factor incomes from rest of world	22.1	32.9	35.3	34.7	36.5	36.9	35.3	25.3	15.5	13.7
equals	16 Gross domestic product	2,295.9	2,566.4	2,795.6	3,131.3	3,259.2	3,534.9	3,932.7	4,213.0	4,452.9	4,742.5
	17 Real GDP (billions of 1996 dollars)	4,760.6	4,912.1	4,900.9	5,021.0	4,919.3	5,132.3	5,505.2	5,717.1	5,912.4	6,113.3
	18 Real GDP growth (percent per year)	5.5	3.2	–0.2	2.5	–2.0	4.3	7.3	3.8	3.4	3.4
	OTHER DATA										
	19 Population (millions)	222.6	225.1	227.7	230.0	232.2	234.3	236.3	238.5	240.7	242.8
	20 Labor force (millions)	102.3	105.0	106.9	108.7	110.2	111.6	113.5	115.5	117.8	119.9
	21 Employment (millions)	96.0	98.8	99.3	100.4	99.5	100.8	105.0	107.2	109.6	112.4
	22 Unemployment (millions)	6.2	6.1	7.6	8.3	10.7	10.7	8.5	8.3	8.2	7.4
	23 Labor force participation rate (percent)	63.2	63.7	63.8	63.9	64.0	64.0	64.4	64.8	65.3	65.6
	24 Unemployment rate (percent of labor force)	6.1	5.8	7.1	7.6	9.7	9.6	7.5	7.2	7.0	6.2
	25 Real GDP per person (1996 dollars per year)	21,388	21,826	21,521	21,834	21,187	21,904	23,293	23,974	24,568	25,178
	26 Growth rate of real GDP per person (percent per year)	4.4	2.0	–1.4	1.5	–3.0	3.4	6.3	2.9	2.5	2.5
	27 "Quantity of money (M2, billions of dollars)"	1,365.5	1,473.1	1,599.1	1,754.6	1,909.5	2,126.0	2,309.7	2,495.4	2,732.1	2,831.1
	28 GDP deflator (1996 = 100)	48.2	52.2	57.0	62.4	66.3	68.9	71.4	73.7	75.3	77.6
	29 GDP deflator inflation rate (percent per year)	7.1	8.3	9.2	9.3	6.2	4.0	3.7	3.2	2.2	3.0
	30 Consumer price index (1982-1984 = 100)	65.2	72.6	82.4	90.9	96.5	99.6	103.9	107.6	109.6	113.6
	31 CPI inflation rate (percent per year)	7.6	11.3	13.5	10.3	6.1	3.2	4.3	3.5	1.9	3.7
	32 Current account balance (billions of dollars)	–15.1	–0.3	2.3	5.0	–5.5	–38.7	–94.3	–118.2	–147.2	–160.7